PSYCHOLOGY IN FOCUS

A Level

Edited by
Mike Haralambos
and David Rice

Written by
Mike Haralambos, David Rice,
Nigel Foreman, Steve Jones, Paul Stenner,
Steve Brown, Peter Kinderman, Keith Sharp

with Wendy Askam and Tracey Holland

CPL

Causeway Press

Dedication

To Kate, Jane and James
To Kathleen

Acknowledgements

Cover and page design	Caroline Waring-Collins (Waring-Collins Design Consultancy)
Graphic origination	John A. Collins, Anneli Jameson, Caroline Waring-Collins (Waring-Collins Design Consultancy)
Graphics	Tim Button, Chris Collins, Elaine M. Sumner (Waring-Collins Design Consultancy)
Author index and typing	Ingrid Hamer
Reader	Mike Kidson
Advisers	David Alcorn, Olwyn Hamer, Martyn Wigfield, Linda Montague, Kathleen O'Leary, Rod Paterson, Merseyside Police

Picture credits

Advertising Archives 111, 544 (m), 728 (m and r), 766 (t); Alexandra Milgram (from the film Obedience by Stanley Milgram ©1965, distributed by Pennsylvania State University, Audio Visual Services) 179, 195 (l and r); Allen Lane, Penguin Books Ltd 74, 75; bfi Collections 552 (tr), 555 (l), 672 (tl and ml); Boddingtons 766 (m); Brick 142, 148, 193, 231 (r), 291, 329 (l), 351, 498, 539, 544 (t), 613, 645, 689 (b), 714 (b), 723, 787, 791, 795, 798; Bruce Coleman Collection 211 (l and r), 601 (bl), 603, 604, 607, 609 (t), 616 (l and r), 618 (l), 623, 624, 625 (l), 630; Camera Press 29 (tl), 46, 66, 83 (ml and r), 99 (ml), 102 (l), 168 (tr), 206, 207; Colin M. Turbull 461 (b); David Hoffman 125, 150 (b); Elaine Frearson 557; Ethnological Museum, Berlin/World of Leather 585; Format (and Maggie Murray) 592 (b); Harlow Primate Laboratory, University of Wisconsin 59 (l and r), 60 (l and r), 745; Hulton Deutsch 49, 117 (m), 301 (bl), 581, 592 (t); Imperial War Museum 70 (l); J.F. Batellier/Free Association Books 756; Manchester Studies Unit 570 (bl); Mary Evans Picture Library 132 (r), 139, 552 (tl); Mattel UK Ltd 561; Mike Haralambos 236 (br); Museum of the American Indian 303; Network 25 (br), 53, 61, 89, 98, 138; Oxford Scientific Films 601 (br), 608, 609 (b), 622, 626, 628 (l and r), 632 (t), 635, 636, 642 (l), 647 (t), 647 (m), 700; PA Photos 676; Peter Newark's Pictures 276; Peter Newark's Military Pictures 99 (tr); Peter Newark's Western Americana 128 (l); P.G. Zimbardo, Inc., Stanford, CA. 170 (l and r), 199 (t and b); Photodisc 508 (l), 715 (l); Popperfoto 28, 70 (br), 164, 178 (m), 184 (b), 315 (t), 320 (tr), 321 (r), 325 (t), 377, 431 (t), 464, 465, 566 (b), 580, 643, 784 (r), 801 (t); Rex Features 29 (tr and bl), 36, 41 (l and r), 78 (t), 83 (bl), 102 (r), 122, 129, 156 (m and br), 159, 168 (br), 184 (mr), 185 (br), 212, 259, 279 (br), 315 (m), 320 (bl), 321 (l), 325 (m), 340, 347, 364 (l and r), 399 (l), 518, 540, 552 (br), 559, 566 (m), 667 (t), 697, 715 (ml); Royal Geographical Society 161, 162 (l, tr and br); Sally and Richard Greenhill 329 (r), 568; Science Photo Library 92, 112, 376, 601 (t), 618 (r), 625 (r), 627, 633, 709, 710; Smithsonian Institution 737; Times Newspapers Ltd 301 (br); Topham Picturepoint 29 (mr), 48, 78 (b), 97, 101 (l and r), 117 (b), 128 (r), 132 (l), 175, 178 (br), 188, 216, 257, 320 (bl), 325 (b), 375, 392, 395, 508, 555 (mr), 593, 605, 642 (r), 690, 801 (ml and mr); Tropix Photo Library 318 (r); United Nations (and Ray Witlin) 570 (br); US Department of Agriculture 314; Waring-Collins Design Consultancy 9, 25 (bl), 236 (ml), 297, 305

Cover picture

DALI, Salvador.
The Persistence of Memory (Persistance de la mémoire). 1931.
Oil on canvas, 9 1/2 x 13" (24.1 x 33 cm).
The Museum of Modern Art, New York, Given anonymously.
Photograph © 2000 The Museum of Modern Art, New York.

British Library Cataloguing in Publication Data
A catalogue record for this book is available from the British Library.

ISBN 1 902796 05 5

Causeway Press Limited
PO Box 13, Ormskirk, Lancs L39 5HP

© Mike Haralambos, David Rice, Paul Stenner, Steve Brown, Nigel Foreman, Steve Jones, Peter Kinderman, Keith Sharp, Wendy Askam

First impression 2002
Printed and bound by The Bath Press, Bath.

Mike Haralambos co-authored some of the chapters
in the A2 and contributed to others.

1 Short-term and long-term memory

Memory is essential to all our lives. Without a memory of the past, we cannot operate in the present or think about the future. We would not be able to remember what we did yesterday, what we have to do today or have planned to do tomorrow. Without memory we could not learn anything. We would not even know who we are without a memory of ourselves.

Memory is involved in processing vast amounts of information. This information takes many different forms. It may be images – for example, the faces of people we know; it may be sounds – for example, the sound of spoken words in a conversation; it may be meanings – for example, the meanings of words printed on a page. Memory involves not only taking in this vast range of information, but also storing it, and retrieving it when it is needed.

Chapter summary

- Unit 1 examines the two main types of memory store – short-term memory and long-term memory.
- Unit 2 outlines and assesses some of the main models of memory – the multistore model, the

- levels of processing model, the working memory model, and models of long-term memory.
- Unit 3 looks at the methods used in memory research.

Unit 1 Types of memory

KEY ISSUES

1. What are the three stages of the memory process?
2. What are the two main types of memory store?

1.1 The three stages of the memory process

Psychologists believe that the process of memory involves three stages: *encoding*, *storage* and *retrieval*. For anything to be remembered, it must go through all of these stages. First, it must be encoded or put into some form that can be stored. Information may be encoded visually (as images), acoustically (as sounds), or semantically (as meanings). Second, the encoded information must be stored or held in memory until it is needed. Third, the stored information must be available to be retrieved or recovered from memory when required. Figure 1 provides a diagram of the three stages of the memory process.

For remembering to take place, information must be successfully encoded, stored and retrieved. If failure occurs at any of these stages, the information will not be retrieved – it will be forgotten. Some forgotten material was never encoded properly in the first place and, as a result, was lost. Some was encoded, but for some reason not stored. Some was encoded

and stored, but, for various reasons, cannot be retrieved. Forgetting is examined in the following chapter.

Key terms

Encoding *Transforming incoming information into a form that can be stored in memory.*

Storage *Holding information in memory until it is needed.*

Retrieval *Locating information in memory and 'getting it out' so it can be used.*

1.2 Short-term memory

Over a century ago, the American philosopher and psychologist William James (1890) suggested that there are two main types of memory store. The first holds information for a few seconds until you have used it – for example, remembering a phone number you have looked up just long enough to dial it. The second holds information for longer periods – from a few minutes to the rest of your life. James called these memory stores primary and secondary memory. Nowadays, psychologists usually call them short-term memory (STM) and long-term memory (LTM).

Short-term memory and long-term memory differ from each other in three main ways.

- Capacity: the amount of information the memory store holds.
- Duration: the length of time the memory store holds information.
- Coding: the way information is encoded in the memory store.

Figure 1 The three stages of memory

Encoding	→	Storage	→	Retrieval
Put in memory		Maintain in memory		Recover from memory

The capacity of STM

The digit span technique This is a simple but effective way of measuring the capacity of STM. The experimenter reads out lists of digits (numbers) and asks people to repeat them in the same order as they were presented. By making the lists longer and longer, you can find the point at which STM is 'full' and no longer able to take in any more information. You can test your own short-term memory storage capacity by using the lists in Table 1. Read each horizontal line of numbers out loud to yourself, then cover up the numbers immediately. Repeat the numbers and check your answer. What is the longest sequence of digits you can remember?

Table 1	Digit span technique								
1	9	2	6						
3	6	7	1	4					
9	7	3	4	5	8				
7	2	4	0	8	6	1			
9	0	6	7	4	3	2	5		
9	7	3	4	1	5	2	0	6	
5	6	7	4	8	5	8	7	8	1
3	6	4	1	9	8	7	2	3	2	4

Most people can remember about 7 numbers. George Miller (1956) described the capacity of STM as 'the magical number seven, plus or minus two'. In a series of experiments, Miller found that the short-term memory store could hold, on average, between 5 and 9 items of information. How does that compare with your score on the digit span test?

Chunking Miller found, however, that the actual amount of information STM can hold can be greatly increased by a process known as *chunking*. This refers to the grouping of items into larger units or chunks. So instead of struggling to remember a string of letters like H P T P M P S U I O A O, we find it easy to remember the same letters rearranged into a word – HIPPOPOTAMUS. The string of letters is made up of 12 items of information, which overloads STM; the word is one chunk, which takes up only one space in STM leaving room to spare.

Miller suggested that no matter how large a chunk is, it takes up only one space in STM, so we can store up to 'seven plus or minus two' chunks, regardless of their size. However, later research does not confirm this. Simon (1974) found that STM was quite capable of holding 7 or so chunks of information if each chunk was a single word, but if the chunks were larger, then capacity drops. For example, capacity drops to 4 for two-word phrases and 3 for eight-word phrases. In the world of chunks, size does matter.

Chunking works if a list is simply divided into segments. So, for example, a list of 12 digits:

1 4 9 1 6 2 5 3 6 4 9 6

is easier to store in STM as 4 chunks:

1 4 9 - 1 6 2 - 5 3 6 - 4 9 6.

Chunking is even more effective if the chunks have meaning. For example, try and remember these pairs of letters: BB-CA-BC-IT-VC-DR-OM. As these letters are presented in pairs, they are already chunked, and should fit within short-term memory. However, you might still find it difficult to remember the letters. If they are chunked differently, then they become much easier to remember: BBC-ABC-ITV-CDROM. These are the same letters

Companies often provide freephone numbers which can be easily chunked to aid memory, eg 0900 45 46 47.

presented in the same order, yet they suddenly become much easier to remember. This illustrates an important point: simply breaking a sequence up into fewer segments is not as helpful to memory as breaking the sequence up into fewer *meaningful* segments.

Key terms

Digit span technique *A method of measuring the capacity of short-term memory by asking people to remember and repeat ever-longer lists of digits.*

The 'magical number seven plus or minus two' *Miller proposed that short-term memory could hold between five and nine items.*

Chunking *Organising items of information into groups (or chunks) to make the most efficient use of short-term memory's limited capacity.*

The duration of STM

Short-term memory is so called for a good reason – information is held there for a short time. This time can be extended by *rehearsal* – the repeating of information. For example, if you keep repeating a phone number to yourself, it will stay longer in STM.

Brown (1958) and Peterson and Peterson (1959) claimed that information held in STM disappears within about 20 seconds if it is not rehearsed. In one experiment, participants were asked to learn sets of three consonants, for example VGT and FCN. Before being asked to recall the letters, they were asked to count backwards in threes from a three-digit number (eg, 997, 994, 991 and so on). The point of doing this was to prevent rehearsal of the letters. After 6 seconds of counting backwards, 50% of the letters were correctly recalled. After 18 seconds of counting, recall dropped to under 10%. This suggests that information held in STM is quickly lost if rehearsal is

Figure 2 The duration of STM

Recall of information from STM when rehearsal is prevented (adapted from Peterson & Peterson, 1959).

prevented. The results of this experiment are shown in Figure 2.

However, the graph in Figure 2 is misleading. Recall of the first set of letters is nearly 100%. Recall of the second set of letters drops slightly, and there is a steady drop in recall for each subsequent set of letters. It appears that participants were confusing later sets of letters with earlier ones. Figure 2 shows what happens when participants are tested repeatedly with different sets of letters. This suggests that measuring the duration of STM is more complicated than Peterson and Peterson's experiment suggests (see Chapter 2, Activity 1, p 24). However, despite this, researchers generally agree that STM has a limited duration – that information rapidly disappears from STM if it is not rehearsed.

The method of measuring the duration of STM by preventing rehearsal is known as the *Brown-Peterson technique* after the researchers who first used it. The rapid loss of information in STM when rehearsal is prevented is known as the *Brown-Peterson effect*.

Encoding in STM

There is evidence that information can be coded in STM semantically (in terms of meaning), acoustically (in terms of sound) or visually (in terms of images). However, the main coding system used in STM appears to be acoustic.

Semantic coding Evidence from chunking suggests that information can be coded in STM semantically – that is, on the basis of meaning. If we can give meaning to numbers, letters and groups of words, we can chunk them, and so increase the amount of information we can hold in STM. Thus, a meaningful set of numbers – such as 2 4 6 8 10; a meaningful set of letters – such as A B C D E; and a meaningful set of words – such as 'I picked up the pen' are coded to some extent in terms of their meaning.

Acoustic coding Evidence suggests that the principal coding system used in STM is acoustic – that is, information is stored largely as sound. When a person is presented with a list of numbers or letters, they will try to hold them in STM by rehearsing them. Rehearsal involves saying the items over and over to themselves. Rehearsal is a verbal process, regardless of whether the list of items is presented acoustically (someone

reads them out), or visually (on a sheet of paper).

Conrad (1964) demonstrated this. He showed lists of printed letters to participants and asked them to write down as many as they could remember. He found that the mistakes they made tended to be a result of mixing up the *sounds* of the letters rather than their appearance. For example, participants typically mixed up B and V, because they sound similar. They didn't confuse F and E, even though they look similar. Conrad suggested that this happened because people *said* the letters to themselves rather than just looked at them. When the letters were sounded out in this way, similar sounding letters were confused.

You may have experienced this yourself. When you are rehearsing a phone number as you pick up the receiver to dial for a pizza, you will not be put off by the sight of other numbers written on a pad by the phone. But, if anyone starts to say numbers to you, your rehearsal is interrupted and you forget the number you were trying to dial.

Hinztmann (1967) suggested that information is usually coded in STM in an articulatory way. Articulatory means 'in the form of speech' or 'in words'. This implies that we have an 'inner voice' rehearsing items in STM.

Key terms

Rehearsal *Repeating information in order to retain it in STM.*

Brown-Peterson technique *A method of measuring the duration of STM by preventing rehearsal of information.*

Brown-Peterson effect *The rapid loss of information from STM when rehearsal is prevented.*

Semantic coding *The coding of information in terms of meaning.*

Acoustic coding *The coding of information in terms of sound.*

Articulatory coding *The coding of information in the form of speech.*

1.3 Long-term memory

Name three different vegetables. What was the date of the Battle of Hastings? Think of an event from your childhood. What did you have for breakfast yesterday? Assuming you know the answers, all this information has been retrieved from long-term memory (LTM). Stored in LTM is each person's knowledge of the world, their past life and their plans for the future. And much of this information can be recalled in an instant.

The capacity of LTM

As noted earlier, for most people the capacity of short-term memory is limited to between 5 and 9 items of information – 'the magical number seven, plus or minus two'. There is no magical number for long-term memory. Its capacity appears to be unlimited. LTM holds vast amounts of information – so vast it is not possible to measure its extent.

The duration of LTM

Compared with the 20 seconds or so duration of STM, the duration of LTM seems limited only by the length of human life.

Activity 1 Coding in STM

Item A Remembering words

Read List A once. Cover the list. After a short interval (about 15 seconds) write the list down in the same order as it is printed. Now do the same with List B.

List A	**List B**
MAD	PEN
CAP	COW
CAT	BAR
MAP	DAY
CAD	SUP

The words in List A are similar in sound.

The words in List B have distinct sounds.

Questions

1 Which list in Item A did you remember best?

2 Look at Item B. Which category was remembered best by the participants in this experiment?

3 What does Item B indicate about the type of coding that is used in short-term memory?

Item B Experimental results

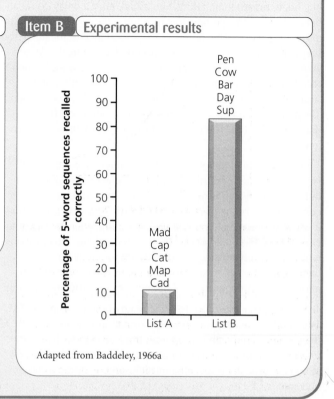

Adapted from Baddeley, 1966a

Many people in their old age can readily recall events from their childhood. In STM, information that is not rehearsed disappears quickly. The same is not true of LTM – which is probably just as well. If LTM was dependent on rehearsal, we would spend our entire lives repeating our names so as not to forget them.

Encoding in LTM

As noted earlier, the coding of information in short-term memory appears to be mainly acoustic. Support for this view is provided by the experiment in Activity 1. It indicates that words with distinct sounds are easier to recall from STM than words with similar sounds. It is easier to discriminate words with distinct sounds – they stand out from each other. The results of this experiment point to the importance of sound and suggest that information in STM is mainly coded acoustically (Baddeley, 1966a).

Researchers generally agree that coding in long-term memory is largely semantic – information is coded in terms of meaning. If this is the case, then words with distinct meanings should be easier to learn and recall than words with similar meanings. Words with distinct meanings will be easier to discriminate because they will stand out from each other. This was

---

Figure 3 Sound and meaning in LTM

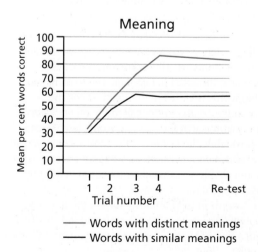

Participants were given 4 attempts (trials) to recall the words then re-tested after a delay (adapted from Baddeley, 1966b).

demonstrated in an experiment. Participants were asked to learn 10 words with distinct meanings – for example, old, late, thin, wet, hot – and 10 words with similar meanings – for example, big, huge, broad, long, tall. When asked, after a delay, to recall both sets of words, participants recalled more of the words with distinct meanings. This points to the importance of meaning and suggests that information in LTM is coded semantically. When groups of words with distinct and similar *sounds* were learned, recall from LTM was more or less the same for both groups. Sound apparently makes little difference, meaning does. Again, this points to the importance of semantic coding in LTM (Baddeley, 1966b). The results of these experiments are shown in Figure 3.

In everyday life, people rarely learn things 'word for word'. However, studies of retrieval from LTM in everyday situations indicate that coding is mainly semantic. Try and remember a conversation you had in the last two days. You won't remember it word for word, but you will probably remember the gist of the conversation, in other words, its overall meaning. This explains why simply 'memorising' word for word for an exam is so ineffective. The key to successful revision is meaning, which allows you to understand and remember what you are learning.

Although semantic coding is the main coding system in LTM, other codes are also used. Some information is stored visually as images (try to remember what your front door looks like – an image drawn from LTM will probably come to mind); some is stored acoustically (especially music); some is stored as tastes and smells.

1.4   Evidence for two memory stores

There is considerable evidence to support the idea that STM and LTM really are two distinct memory stores. As this unit has shown, they differ in terms of capacity, duration and the main coding system used by each. The following evidence provides further support for the idea of two memory stores.

Awareness We are conscious or aware of information in STM at any given moment. Often this is because we are busy rehearsing the information so as not to lose it before we have a chance to use it. LTM, by contrast, is a vast memory bank of material which is available to consciousness when needed, but which otherwise lies quietly outside our conscious awareness.

Serial position effect Experiments show that when participants are presented with a list of words, they tend to remember the first few and the last few words and are more likely to forget those in the middle of the list. This is known as the *serial position effect* – it is illustrated in Figure 4. The tendency to recall the earlier words is called the *primacy effect*; the tendency to recall the later words is called the *recency effect*. The usual explanation is that the first few words have been transferred to LTM while the last few – the most recent – are still in STM. This explanation is supported by experiments using the Brown-Peterson technique – preventing rehearsal in STM by asking participants to count backwards. This cuts out the recency effect – words in STM are lost, but not the primacy effect – the first few words have been transferred to LTM. This supports the idea that STM and LTM are separate memory stores (Glanzer & Cunitz, 1966).

Brain damage Studies of patients with brain damage also indicate the existence of two separate memory stores. For

Figure 4 The serial position effect

Adapted from Glanzer & Cunitz, 1966

example, chronic alcoholics sometimes develop Korsakoff's syndrome which causes damage to parts of the brain. This has little effect on STM but severely impairs LTM (Butters & Cermak, 1980). Some patients experience the opposite effect. For example, a patient known as KF suffered brain damage as a result of a motorcycle accident. This had no effect on LTM but led to poor performance on many STM tasks (Shallice & Warrington, 1970). It is difficult to explain the evidence from

Summary

1 Memory consists of three processes – encoding, storage and retrieval.

2 There are two main memory stores – short-term memory and long-term memory.

3 STM has a limited capacity – Miller measured it as between 5 and 9 items of information. The actual amount of information in STM can be expanded by chunking.

4 The duration of STM is around 20 seconds if information is not rehearsed. Rehearsal can increase duration.

5 The main method of encoding information in STM is acoustic – by sound. Other forms of encoding are also used.

6 LTM appears to have unlimited capacity.

7 The duration of LTM can be a lifetime. Rehearsal is not needed to retain information in LTM.

8 The main method of encoding information in LTM is semantic – by meaning. Other forms of encoding are also used.

9 There is considerable evidence to support the view that STM and LTM are two distinct memory stores. This includes differences in capacity, duration, encoding and awareness; the serial position effect; evidence from brain damaged patients, and differences in brain activity.

brain-damaged patients without assuming there are two distinct memory systems (Eysenck & Keane, 1995).

Brain activity Various techniques, such as brain scans, have been developed for investigating activity in the brain. These techniques indicate different kinds of brain activity when STM is in use and when LTM is in use (Baddeley, 1997).

Forgetting The process of forgetting appears to be different in STM and LTM. This is examined in the following chapter.

Unit 2 Models of memory

KEY ISSUES

1. **What are the main models of memory?**
2. **What are their strengths and weaknesses?**

2.1 Multistore models of memory

Models of memory seek to provide a picture of how the whole memory system works. They attempt to identify the various parts which make up the system, indicate what each part does, and to show how the parts work together.

A number of multistore models of memory have been developed, so called because they suggest that memory consists of several stores. The most influential multistore model was developed by Richard Atkinson and Richard Shiffrin (1968). It consists of three main stores – the sensory memory store, the short-term memory store and the long-term memory store. This section outlines Atkinson and Shiffrin's model.

Sensory store

The sensory store transfers information to short-term memory. It is made up of five stores, one for each of the senses – sight, hearing, touch, taste and smell. Research has focused on the visual or *iconic* store and the auditory or *echoic* store.

The iconic store Iconic memory was investigated in a series of experiments conducted by George Sperling (1960). He presented participants with 3 rows of 4 letters on a card for 50 milliseconds. They recalled only 4 or 5 of the 12 letters, though they claimed to have seen more. To test this claim, Sperling devised a procedure to 'jog their memory'. He sounded a tone immediately after the presentation to signal which row of letters participants were to recall – each row was signalled by a different tone. Participants now recalled 3 items from whichever row they were asked to remember. This indicated that, for a split second, most of the information (9 out of 12 letters) was being held in iconic memory. When the tone was sounded 0.3 seconds after the letters were presented, recall dropped from 9 to 6 letters. It dropped to an average of 4.5 letters when the tone was sounded 1 second after the presentation. This indicates that information disappears rapidly from iconic memory.

Iconic memory does not appear to use a coding system – it simply holds a brief image of what was in front of us. This brief image held in iconic memory is the cause of 'after-images' – as, for example, when a child 'writes' her name in the air with a sparkler on bonfire night.

The echoic store This store holds sounds for up to 4 seconds. This enables a sentence to be held in echoic memory. As a result, when we are listening to someone talking, we hear them saying whole sentences rather than separate words (Baddeley, 1997).

Transferring sensory information We are flooded with sensory information and pay no attention to most of it. As you are reading this book, you are probably paying no attention to the sounds and smells around you, or to other images within your range of vision. Information which is attended to passes into STM. Information which is not attended to is rapidly lost as new information enters the sensory memory store and pushes the old information out.

STM and LTM

Atkinson and Shiffrin's multistore model sees STM as a crucial part of the memory system. Without it, information cannot get into or out of LTM. Information can only be retrieved from LTM by entering STM. Information can only be stored in LTM by passing through STM.

In terms of the multistore model, rehearsal has an important part to play. It increases the time information can be held in STM and it is vital for transferring information to LTM. Atkinson and Shiffrin suggest that the longer information is held in STM, the more likely it is to be transferred into LTM. There is some experimental evidence to support this view. Participants were asked to rehearse a list of items out loud. In general, the more frequently an item was rehearsed, the more likely it was to be recalled from LTM (Rundus, 1971).

Figure 5 The multistore model of memory

Evaluation of the multistore model

The three stores The multistore model is based on evidence from a wide range of sources – from the findings of experiments, to studies of brain-damaged patients. As outlined in Section 1.4, there is considerable evidence for the existence of STM and LTM as separate memory stores. And, as this section has indicated, there is evidence for the existence of a sensory store. Most researchers still accept the idea of three different memory stores (Eysenck & Keane, 1995).

Are the three stores unitary? Atkinson and Shiffrin do not see the sensory store as a single, unitary (one part) store. Instead, they suggest there are five sensory stores – one for each sense. But they see no such divisions within STM and LTM – they see them as unitary stores. However, both STM and LTM may well have different memory systems operating within them.

Take the case of KF discussed earlier. He suffered brain damage from a motorcycle accident which severely impaired his STM but left his LTM intact. In terms of the multistore model, this cannot happen since all information in LTM passes through STM. However, further investigation revealed that KF's STM impairment was mainly for verbal material such as spoken letters, words and numbers. His short-term memory for visual material and meaningful sounds, such as telephones ringing and cats mewing, was largely unaffected (Shallice & Warrington, 1974). This suggests the possibility of more than one short-term memory store.

A similar point can be made about LTM. LTM contains an enormous range of diverse material. It contains knowledge about the world, personal experiences, and skills such as how to play a guitar and how to ride a bicycle. Most researchers now reject the view that this vast range of diverse information is contained in a simple, unitary long-term memory store. Instead, they suggest there are different types of LTM, different subsystems within LTM. Again, the multistore model presents an oversimplified picture.

A linear model For the most part, the multistore model is a linear model. Information travels in a straight line from the sensory store to STM to LTM. It is then retrieved from LTM when required. The model leaves little room for the possibility that LTM influences, or even directs, other parts of the memory system. Yet there is evidence that LTM does just this. For example, expert chess players have a much better short-term memory for the arrangement of pieces on a chessboard. They can remember the positions of around 24 pieces compared to about 10 pieces for novice players. However, this only applies if the pieces are arranged according to the rules of chess. If they are arranged randomly, then the experts do no better than anyone else (de Groot, 1966). This suggests that the STM of expert chess players is informed by their knowledge of the game – which is held in LTM. In this case, LTM is directly influencing STM.

Similarly, chunking into meaningful units is only possible if STM 'knows' what a meaningful unit is – and that requires STM to be able to draw on LTM in order to chunk information in the first place.

This kind of evidence questions whether STM and LTM are as separate and distinct as the multistore model suggests. It also questions the idea that information just sits in LTM until it is retrieved by STM. It suggests that LTM plays an active role in memory, influencing, and maybe even directing, STM.

How important is rehearsal? The multistore model suggests that the longer information is in STM and the more it is rehearsed, the more likely it is to be transferred to LTM. A number of studies have questioned this view. For example, in one experiment, participants were asked to read a list of words over and over again. These words were then included in a longer list which they were asked

to recall. The 'old' words, which had been well rehearsed, were not recalled any more frequently than the 'new' words included in the longer list (Tulving, 1967). Judging from this experiment, rehearsing words does not increase the probability of their recall.

Evidence from everyday situations suggests that rehearsal is a lot less important than the multistore model suggests. People rarely rehearse information in their everyday lives yet information is constantly entering LTM (Eysenck & Keane, 1995).

A passive and mechanical model. The multistore model has been criticised as a rather passive model of memory. For example, it tends to picture LTM as a passive storage dump. Information just sits there until it is needed. However, there is evidence to suggest that LTM is actively involved in the memory system as a whole. The multistore model has also been criticised for providing a rather mechanical model of memory. For example, it tends to picture information being mechanically shunted from one store to another.

Key terms

Multistore model *A model that pictures memory as a series of memory stores.*

Sensory memory store *A number of memory stores which hold incoming sensory information for very short periods of time.*

Iconic store *A sensory memory store for visual information.*

Echoic store *A sensory memory store for auditory information.*

2.2 Levels of processing model

The levels of processing model was introduced by Fergus Craik and Robert Lockhart in 1972. It provided an alternative to the multistore model. Craik and Lockhart did not reject the idea of memory stores – for example they accepted the existence of STM and LTM. However, rather than focusing on stores and how information is transferred from one store to another, they focused on how information is encoded and processed.

Levels of processing

According to Craik and Lockhart (1972), information can be encoded and processed at different *levels*. They argued that the level at which information is processed accounts for the likelihood of it being learned and remembered. They identified various levels of processing from the shallowest to the deepest. The following examples, based on processing words, are taken from one of their experiments in which participants were presented with questions on printed cards.

- At the shallowest level, words are processed visually in terms of their physical appearance. For example, is the following word in capital or lower case letters? FISH.
- At a deeper level, words are processed acoustically, in terms of their sound. For example, does the following word rhyme with 'pin'? STYLE. This is a deeper level of processing since it involves an analysis of both the appearance of the word and its sound.
- At the deepest level, words are processed semantically, in terms of their meaning. For example, is a PANCAKE a form of transport? To answer this, participants must focus on the meaning of the words.

Craik and Lockhart claimed that the deeper the level of processing, the stronger, more durable and longer lasting the memory.

The results of one of Craik and Lockhart's experiments are shown in Figure 6. Participants were asked a series of questions similar to those in the above paragraph. Later, they were asked to recall the words they had been questioned about. Figure 6 suggests that 'deep' processing in terms of meaning is a more effective way of remembering information than visual or acoustic processing.

Rehearsal

According to Atkinson and Shiffrin (1968), the more times information is rehearsed, the more likely it is to be remembered. According to Craik and Lockhart, it is the level of processing rather than the frequency of rehearsal that affects the durability of the memory. They distinguished between two types of rehearsal.

- **Simple maintenance rehearsal** This simply holds information. It prevents information from being forgotten during the holding process but does not lead to long-term memories.
- **Elaborative rehearsal** This increases the depth at which information is processed. It involves some kind of analysis or evaluation of the information. Only elaborative rehearsal leads to long-term memories.

Elaboration

Craik and Tulving (1975) developed the levels of processing model with the idea of *elaboration*. They suggested that how well information is remembered depends not only on the level of processing, but also on how complex or elaborate the processing is within each level. Thus, semantic processing produces better memory, but more complex semantic processing produces even better memory.

The following experiment illustrates the kind of evidence on which the idea of elaboration is based. Participants were presented with sentences containing a blank space followed by a word. They were asked whether the word fitted the space. Some of the sentences were very simple and others were more complex. Craik and Tulving assumed that the more complex the sentence, the more elaborate the processing would be. Here is an example of a simple sentence and a more complex sentence.

Simple sentence	Word
She read the	newspaper

Complex sentence	
The great bird swooped down and carried off the struggling	chicken

Later, the participants were shown the sentences without the additional words. This time they were asked to remember the word that had accompanied each sentence. Recall was twice as high for words accompanying complex sentences, suggesting that elaboration improves long-term memory. Craik and Tulving argued that the words had to be more thoroughly processed to fit into a complex sentence and, as a result, they became easier to remember. It was not just whether semantic encoding took place that was important, but also the amount of elaboration of that semantic encoding.

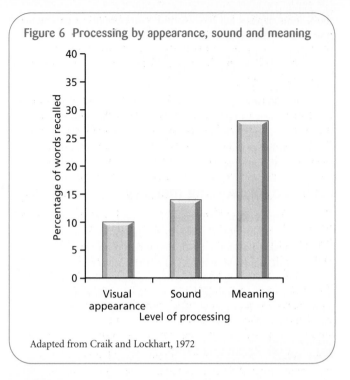

Figure 6 Processing by appearance, sound and meaning

Adapted from Craik and Lockhart, 1972

Evaluation

Change of direction The levels of processing model changed the direction of memory research. It showed that encoding was not a simple, straightforward process. This widened the focus from seeing long-term memory as a simple storage unit to seeing it as a complex processing system.

Supporting evidence Craik and Lockhart's ideas led to hundreds of experiments, most of which confirmed the superiority of 'deep' semantic processing for remembering information.

Measurement The ideas of 'depth' and 'elaboration' are vague and ill-defined. As a result, they are difficult to measure. This can lead to a circular argument – it is predicted that deeply processed information will be remembered better, but the measure of depth of processing is how well the information is remembered.

Distinctiveness Later research indicated that processing is more complex and varied than the levels of processing model suggests. In other words, there is more to processing than depth and elaboration. For example, research by Bransford et al. (1979) indicated that a sentence such as, 'A mosquito is like a doctor because both draw blood' is more likely to be recalled than the more elaborated sentence, ' A mosquito is like a racoon because they both have head, legs and jaws'. It appears that it is the distinctiveness of the first sentence which makes it easier to remember – it's unusual to compare a doctor to a mosquito. As a result, the sentence stands out and is more easily recalled.

2.3 Working memory model

The working memory model was introduced by Alan Baddeley and Graham Hitch in 1974. It is a model of short-term memory. Baddeley and Hitch argue that the picture of STM provided by the multistore model is far too simple. According to the multistore model, STM holds limited amounts of information for short periods of time with relatively little processing. It is a unitary system. This means it is a single system without any subsystems. It does not have various components or parts which specialise in different tasks.

Baddeley and Hitch's working memory presents a more complex picture of STM. Working memory is not a unitary system. It has a number of components or subsystems, each of which specialise in particular tasks – learning, reasoning, comprehension and problem solving. The traditional view saw information being held and rehearsed in STM and little more. From the point of view of working memory, information is analysed, evaluated and 'worked on'.

Evidence for working memory

What evidence is there that working memory exists, that it is made up of a number of parts, that it performs a number of different tasks? Baddeley (1986) conducted an experiment in which participants were asked to perform two tasks at the same time – a digit span task which required them to remember a list of numbers (see p 9) and a reasoning task which required them to answer true or false to the type of questions shown in Table 2.

Table 2	Reasoning tasks	
BA	A follows B (true or false)	
AB	B is not preceded by A (true or false)	

Adapted from Baddeley, 1986

According to the traditional view of STM, once participants reach around 7 digits in their digit span task, there would be no room left to do anything else. STM has a limited capacity – it would be full. As a result, there would be no room left in STM to perform the reasoning task. This did not happen in Baddeley's experiment. As the number of digits increased in the digit span tasks, participants took longer to answer the reasoning questions, but not much longer – only fractions of a second. And, they didn't make any more errors in the reasoning tasks as the number of digits increased. The results of this experiment are shown in Figure 7.

Figure 7 Reasoning and digit span tasks

— Time taken to perform reasoning tasks
— Percentage of errors

Adapted from Baddeley, 1986

Baddeley and Hitch (1974) conducted similar 'two-task' experiments on digit span and learning tasks, and digit span and comprehension tasks. The results were similar to those shown in Figure 7.

These results cannot be explained in terms of the traditional unitary model of STM. A new model – working memory – was needed to provide an explanation. A multicomponent or multipart system makes sense of these results. One component of working memory can be working on the digit span task while another component can be working on the reasoning task. Just because the component working on the digit span task reaches the limit of its capacity (with around 7 digits) does not mean that other components cannot operate successfully on other tasks.

The parts of working memory

Baddeley and Hitch's model sees working memory as having a controlling system, called the *central executive*, which supervises and coordinates a number of subsidiary systems or 'slave systems'. They studied two of these systems – the *articulatory* or *phonological loop* which deals with information in the form of speech, and the *sketchpad* or *visuo-spatial sketchpad* which deals with visual images. A simplified diagram of working memory is shown in Figure 8. It does not show other possible subsidiary systems which may be contained in working memory.

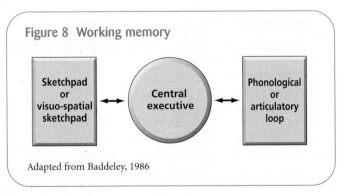

Figure 8 Working memory

Adapted from Baddeley, 1986

The phonological loop

The phonological or articulatory loop consists of two parts (see Figure 9).

The phonological store This store holds spoken words for 1½ - 2

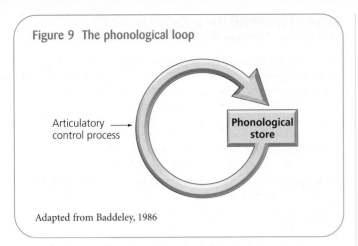

Figure 9 The phonological loop

Articulatory control process ⟶ Phonological store

Adapted from Baddeley, 1986

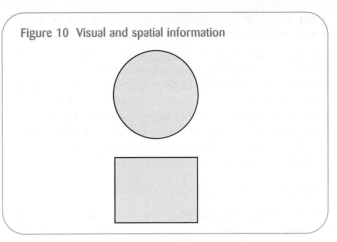

Figure 10 Visual and spatial information

seconds. Spoken words enter the store directly. Written words must first be converted into an articulatory (spoken) code before they can enter the phonological store.

The articulatory control process This process acts like an inner voice rehearsing information from the phonological store. It circulates information round and round like a tape loop. This is how we remember a telephone number we have just heard. As long as we keep repeating it, we can retain the information in working memory.

The articulatory control process also converts written material into an articulatory code and transfers it to the phonological store (Baddeley, 1997).

The capacity of the phonological loop was demonstrated by the following experiment (Baddeley et al., 1975). Participants were given lists of short words and long words to recall. They recalled more of the short words than the long words. The researchers found that the phonological loop can hold the number of items that can be said in about 2 seconds. Since short words can be said in a shorter time than long words, more short words were recalled. This is known as the *word-length effect*. Try it yourself in Activity 2.

The sketchpad

The sketchpad or visuo-spatial sketchpad deals with visual and spatial information. Visual information refers to what things look like – there is a circle and a square in Figure 10. Spatial information refers to the layout of items relative to each other – the circle is above the square in Figure 10.

The sketchpad does not simply store visual and spatial information, it also analyses and manipulates this information. There is evidence that images are constructed and displayed on the sketchpad and 'looked at'. In one experiment, participants were asked to memorise a drawing of a boat like the one in Figure 11 (Kosslyn & Shwartz, 1981). They were then asked questions about different aspects of the boat. They appeared to answer the questions by 'looking' at an image in their head. Participants who had just answered a question about the motor at the back of the boat took longer to answer a question about the front of the boat than those who had been asked a question about the porthole in the middle of the boat. It was as if they were taking time to move their eyes along the image of the boat in their memory, and the further they had to move their eyes, the longer it took.

The sketchpad also displays and manipulates visual and spatial information held in long-term memory. For example, the spatial layout of your house is held in LTM. Try answering this question: How many windows are there in the front of your house? You probably find yourself picturing the front of your

Figure 11 Drawing of a boat

Activity 2   The word-length effect

Item A Short words	Item B Long words	Questions
Some Harm Bear Love Snack	Interrogation Satisfactory Simultaneous Configuration Opportunity	1 Read the list of words in Item A once. Close your eyes and try and repeat the words in order 4 times. 2 Do the same with the words in Item B. 3 Assuming you had difficulty with Item B, what does this suggest about the capacity of the phonological loop?

house and counting the windows. An image has been retrieved from LTM and pictured on the sketchpad.

Evidence suggests that working memory uses two different systems for dealing with visual and verbal information. A visual processing task and a verbal processing task can be performed at the same time. It is more difficult to perform two visual tasks at the same time because they interfere with each other and performance is reduced. The same applies to performing two verbal tasks at the same time. This supports the view that the phonological loop and the sketchpad are separate systems within working memory.

The central executive

The central executive controls the phonological loop and the sketchpad. It decides which system is required and coordinates the retrieval of information from LTM. In the example given earlier, the central executive decided that the sketchpad was the best way of working out the number of windows in the front of your house, and retrieved an image of your house from LTM.

The central executive decides what working memory pays attention to. For example, two activities sometimes come into conflict such as driving a car and talking. Rather than hitting a cyclist who is wobbling all over the road, it is preferable to stop talking and concentrate on driving. The central executive directs attention and gives priority to particular activities (Baddeley, 1997).

Evaluation of working memory

Multipart system Researchers today generally agree that short-term memory is made up of a number of components or subsystems. The working memory model has replaced the idea of a unitary (one part) STM as suggested by the multistore model.

Explanations The working memory model explains a lot more than the multistore model. It makes sense of a range of tasks – verbal reasoning, comprehension, reading, problem solving and

Key terms

Working memory *A model which sees short-term memory as made up of a number of parts, each specialising in particular tasks.*

Phonological or articulatory loop *The part of working memory that deals with spoken and written material.*

Phonological store *A short-term store which forms part of the phonological loop.*

Articulatory control process *Rehearses information from the phonological store. Also converts written material into an articulatory code and transfers it to the phonological store.*

Word-length effect *The retention of information in STM depends not so much on the number of words, but on how long it takes to articulate those words. STM appears to hold as many words as a person can speak in about 2 seconds.*

Sketchpad or visual-spatial sketchpad *The part of working memory that deals with visual and spatial information.*

Central executive *Activates, coordinates and controls the various parts of working memory.*

visual and spatial processing. And the model is supported by considerable experimental evidence.

Brain damage As noted earlier (see p13), the multistore model could not explain memory impairment in certain brain-damaged people. For example, KF suffered brain damage from a motorcycle accident which impaired his short-term memory. KF's impairment was mainly for verbal information – his memory for visual information was largely unaffected (Shallice & Warrington, 1974). This cannot be explained in terms of a unitary STM. However, it can be explained in terms of the multicomponent working memory model – only one component of STM was damaged.

Rehearsal This plays a central part in the multistore model of memory – it is the only way information can pass from STM into LTM. However, evidence from everyday situations suggests that people rarely rehearse information. Rehearsal plays a relatively small part in the working memory model. It takes place in only one component – the phonological loop. In this respect, the working memory model reflects the operation of memory in everyday life.

The central executive There is little direct evidence for how the central executive works and what it does. However, the idea of a central executive 'makes sense' in terms of the working memory model. In any system made up of different parts, something must activate, coordinate and control the parts. More research is needed in order to discover how the central executive does this (Eysenck & Keane, 1995).

2.4   Models of long-term memory

Atkinson and Shiffrin's multistore model presented a unitary model of long-term memory. Most researchers now reject this view. They see LTM as a multipart system made up of two or more components or subsystems.

Procedural and declarative memory

A number of researchers make a distinction between *procedural* and *declarative* long-term memory (Cohen & Squire, 1980; Tulving, 1983).

Procedural memory This is a memory for skills – knowing how to do things. It includes memories for brushing your teeth, playing a guitar, riding a bicycle, tying your shoelaces and using a computer keyboard. These memories are only consciously recalled during the early stages of learning. For example, once the procedure has been learned, you brush your teeth with little or no awareness of the skills involved.

Declarative memory This is a memory for specific information. It includes, for example, knowledge that London is the capital of the United Kingdom, zebras are animals with striped coats and the Mississippi is a river in the USA. It also includes personal information such as the date of your birthday, the make of your car and what you had for lunch yesterday. Recalling information from declarative memory involves some degree of conscious effort – information is consciously brought to mind and 'declared'.

Evidence Studies of amnesia – memory loss due to brain damage – provide support for the distinction between procedural memory and declarative memory. Amnesiacs often have severely impaired declarative memory – they cannot

Figure 12 Models of LTM

Key terms

Procedural memory *Memory for skills – knowing how to do things.*

Declarative memory *Memory for specific information.*

Episodic memory *Memory for personal experiences, often linked to particular times and places.*

Semantic memory *Memory for information about the world, including knowledge of words and their meanings.*

remember specific information they have learned in the past, or form memories for new information they encounter. However, their procedural memory remains largely unaffected – they can recall skills they have already learned and are able to learn and retain new skills (Cohen, 1984).

Further support for the view that procedural and declarative memory are separate parts of LTM, is provided by people with Huntington's disease. There is evidence that their declarative memory is largely unaffected – they can learn and recall new information – but their procedural memory is impaired – they have difficulty learning new skills (Heindel et al., 1988).

Episodic and semantic memory

Endel Tulving (1972) suggested that declarative memory is made up of two components – *episodic memory* and *semantic memory*.

Episodic memory This part of LTM stores personal experiences which are often associated with a particular time and place – your first date, your driving test and what you did and where you were on the eve of the millennium.

Semantic memory Whereas episodic memory is like an autobiography, semantic memory is more like an encyclopaedia. It contains information about the world. Tulving (1972) described semantic memory as a 'mental thesaurus' since it contains knowledge of words and their meanings.

Evidence To what extent are episodic and semantic memories different memory systems? Clearly, they work together. Knowing what you had for breakfast yesterday – an episodic memory – requires a knowledge of cereals, toast and coffee drawn from semantic memory. However, there is evidence for a distinction between these types of memory.

There is an increase in blood flow to parts of the brain which are active. Participants in an experiment were asked to think about personal events – episodic memories. This resulted in increased blood flow to the frontal region of the brain, suggesting a high level of activity there. They were then asked to think about general knowledge, such as the capital cities of various countries – semantic memories. This resulted in increased blood flow to areas at the back of the brain (Tulving, 1989). This suggests that episodic and semantic memory are located in different parts of the brain and may, to some extent, be different memory systems.

Summary

1. The multistore model of memory consists of three memory stores – the sensory store, STM and LTM.

2. Rehearsal increases the time information can be held in STM. It also transfers information from STM to LTM.

3. The multistore model has been criticised for presenting an oversimplified picture of memory.

4. The levels of processing model states that the level at which information is processed affects the likelihood of it being learned and remembered.

5. The deeper the level, the more thorough the processing and the greater the likelihood of retrieval. Information encoded semantically appears to be more deeply processed than information encoded visually or acoustically.

6. Elaboration of processing states that the likelihood of retrieval is affected not only by the level of processing but also by further processing – elaboration – within a level.

7. Although there are problems with measuring depth and elaboration, the levels of processing model has provided important insights into the working of memory.

8. Working memory is a model of short-term memory. It sees STM as a multipart system. The various parts specialise in different tasks.

9. The parts or components of working memory include the phonological loop which deals with spoken and written material, the sketchpad which deals with visual and spatial material, and the central executive which coordinates and controls the various parts.

10. There is considerable evidence to support the working memory model. However, there is little direct evidence for the functions of the central executive.

11. Most researchers now see LTM as a multipart system made up of two or more parts or subsystems.

Unit 3 Experiments

KEY ISSUES

1. How true-to-life are memory experiments?
2. Can the findings of experiments be applied to everyday life?
3. What are the advantages of laboratory experiments?

A large part of the research on memory is based on experiments conducted in laboratories. Those who take part in the experiments – the participants – are asked to perform tasks such as recalling lists of words and numbers. Both the setting – the laboratory – and the tasks are a long way from everyday life. In many cases, the setting is artificial and the tasks fairly meaningless. Does this matter?

3.1 Ecological validity

Psychologists use the term *ecological validity* to refer to the extent to which the findings of research studies can be generalised to other settings. An experiment has high ecological validity if its findings can be generalised, that is applied or extended, to settings outside the laboratory.

It is often assumed that if an experiment is realistic or true-to-life, then there is a greater likelihood that its findings can be generalised. If it is not realistic – if the laboratory setting and the tasks are artificial – then there is less likelihood that the findings can be generalised. In this case, the experiment will have low ecological validity.

Many experiments designed to investigate memory have been criticised for having low ecological validity. First, the laboratory is an artificial situation. People are removed from their normal social settings and asked to take part in a psychological experiment. They are directed by an 'experimenter' and may be placed in the company of complete strangers. For many people, this is a brand new experience, far removed from their everyday lives. Will this setting affect their actions, will they behave normally?

Often, the tasks participants are asked to perform can appear artificial and meaningless. Few, if any, people would attempt to memorise and recall a list of unconnected words in their daily lives. And it is not clear how tasks such as this relate to the use of memory in everyday life. The artificiality of many experiments has led some researchers to question whether their findings can be generalised to real life. As a result, many memory experiments have been criticised for having low ecological validity.

3.2 The case for experiments

Consider the following example. A researcher wishes to find out the importance of light on the growth of plants. She conducts the following experiment. Every factor or variable, except one, which is known to affect the growth of plants is held constant – kept the same. Plants of the same species and size are kept at the same temperature and humidity, grown in the same type and amount of soil and given the same volume of water at the same time. Only the light changes – one group of plants is exposed to more of the same light than the other group. A single variable – light – has been isolated from all other variables in order to discover the effect it has on plant growth. Experiments allow researchers to *control* variables and to discover the effect of one variable (eg light) on another variable (eg plant growth).

Researchers who study human memory in the laboratory adopt a similar approach. They claim that only by controlling variables can reliable findings about memory be produced. They argue that the world outside the laboratory contains a vast number of variables that cannot be controlled by the researcher. As a result, it is not possible to say what affects what.

Take the following example. How do people remember faces in the 'real world'? The researcher has no control over the range of factors that affect people's memory for faces in everyday life. For example, the researcher cannot control the amount of attention people give to the face in the first place, the length or number of times they see the face, their relationship to the person concerned, the similarity of other faces they have seen, and so on   (Cohen, 1996).

In the laboratory, participants can be shown the same faces, for the same length of time, in the same setting. In this way, at least some of the variables which may affect memory for faces can be controlled.

Conclusion Many researchers believe that an understanding of human memory requires both experimental and naturalistic studies, that is research in the laboratory and studies of people in their 'natural' everyday settings. Alan Baddeley (1997) states, 'We need to blend the control of the laboratory with the richness of the everyday world if we are to understand the whole of human memory'. The value of combining experimental and naturalistic research is examined in Chapter 3 which looks at eyewitness testimony.

Key terms

Ecological validity *The extent to which the findings of research studies can be generalised to other settings.*

Control of variables *Control by the researcher over the factors which are assumed to affect behaviour.*

Naturalistic studies *Studies of people in their natural, everyday settings.*

Summary

1. Many laboratory experiments on memory have been criticised for being artificial and unrealistic.

2. Researchers have questioned whether the findings from experiments can be applied to the use of memory in everyday life. As a result, memory experiments have been criticised for having low ecological validity.

3 Laboratory experiments allow researchers to control many of the variables which may affect memory.

 4 Many researchers argue that the findings of both experimental and naturalistic research must be combined for a full understanding of human memory.

References

Atkinson, R.C. & Shiffrin, R.M. (1968). Human memory: A proposed system and its control processes. In K.W. Spence (Ed.), *The psychology of learning and motivation: Advances in research and theory*, Vol.2. New York: Academic Press.

Baddeley, A.D. (1966a). Short-term memory for word sequences as a function of acoustic, semantic and formal similarity. *Quarterly Journal of Experimental Psychology, 18*, 362-365.

Baddeley, A.D. (1966b). The influence of acoustic and semantic similarity on long-term memory for word sequences. *Quarterly Journal of Experimental Psychology, 18*, 302-309.

Baddeley, A.D. (1976). *The psychology of memory*. London: Harper & Row.

Baddeley, A.D. (1986). *Working memory*. Oxford: OUP.

Baddeley, A.D. (1997). *Human memory: Theory and practice* (2nd ed.). Hove: Psychology Press.

Baddeley, A.D. & Hitch, G. (1974). Working memory. In G.A. Bower (Ed.), *Recent advances in learning and motivation, Vol. 8*. New York: Academic Press.

Baddeley, A.D., Thomson, M. & Buchanan, M. (1975). Word length and the structure of short-term memory. *Journal of Verbal Learning and Verbal Behavior, 14*, 575-589.

Bransford, J.D., Franks, J.J., Morris, C.D. & Stein, B.S. (1979). Some general constraints on learning and memory research. In L.S. Cermak & F.I.M. Craik (Eds.), *Levels of processing in human memory*. Hillsdale, NJ: Lawrence Erlbaum Associates.

Brown, J. (1958). Some tests of the decay theory of immediate memory. *Quarterly Journal of Experimental Psychology, 10*, 12-21.

Butters, N. & Cermak, L.S. (1980). *Alcoholic Korsakoff's syndrome: An information-processing approach*. London: Academic Press.

Cohen, G. (1996). *Memory in the real world* (2nd ed.). Hove: Psychology Press.

Cohen, N.J. (1984). Preserved learning capacity in amnesia: Evidence for multiple memory systems. In L.R. Squire & N. Butters (Eds.), *The neuro-psychology of memory*. New York: Guilford.

Cohen, N.J. & Squire, L.R. (1980). Preserved learning and retention of pattern analysing skill in amnesia: Dissociation of knowing how and knowing that. *Science, 210*, 207-210.

Conrad, R. (1964). Acoustic confusions in immediate memory. *British Journal of Psychology, 55*, 429-432.

Craik, F.I.M. & Lockhart, R.S. (1972). Levels of processing: A framework for memory research. *Journal of Verbal Learning and Verbal Behaviour, 11*, 671-684.

Craik, F.I.M. & Tulving, E. (1975). Depth of processing and the retention of words in episodic memory. *Journal of Experimental Psychology: General, 1*, 268-294.

de Groot, A.D. (1965). *Thought and choice in chess*. The Hague: Mouton.

Eysenck, M.W. & Keane, M.T. (1995). *Cognitive psychology: A student's handbook* (3rd ed.). Hove: Lawrence Erlbaum Associates.

Glanzer, M. & Cunitz, A.R. (1966). Two storage mechanisms in free recall. *Journal of Verbal Learning and Verbal Behavior, 5*, 351-360.

Heindel, W.C., Butters, N. & Salmon, D.P. (1988). Impaired learning of a motor skill in patients with Huntingdon's disease. *Behavioural Neuroscience, 102*, 141-147.

Hintzmann, D.L. (1967). Articulatory coding in short-term memory. *Psychonomic Science, 3*, 161-162.

James, W. (1890). *Principles of psychology, Vol. 1*. New York: Holt.

Kosslyn, S.M. & Shwartz, S.P. (1981). Empirical constraints of theories of visual mental imagery. In J. Long & A.D. Baddeley (Eds.), *Attention and Performance IX*. Hillsdale, NJ: Lawrence Erlbaum Associates.

Miller, G.A. (1956). The magical number seven plus or minus two: Some limits on our capacity for processing information. *Psychological Review, 63*, 81-97.

Peterson, L.R. & Peterson, M.J. (1959). Short-term retention of individual verbal items. *Journal of Experimental Psychology, 58*, 193-198.

Rundus, D. (1971). Analysis of rehearsal processes in free recall. *Journal of Experimental Psychology, 89*, 63-77.

Shallice, T. & Warrington, E.K. (1970). Independent functioning of verbal memory stores: A neuropsychological study. *Quarterly Journal of Experimental Psychology, 22*, 261-273.

Shallice, T. & Warrington, E.K. (1974). The dissociation between long-term retention of meaningful sounds and verbal material. *Neuropsychologia, 12*, 553-555.

Sperling, G. (1960). The information available in brief visual presentations. *Psychological Monographs: General and Applied, 74*, 1-29.

Tulving, E. (1967). The effects of presentation and recall of material in free-recall learning. *Journal of Verbal Learning and Verbal Behaviour, 6*, 175-184.

Tulving, E. (1972). Episodic and semantic memory. In E. Tulving & W. Donaldson (Eds.), *Organisation of memory*. London: Academic Press.

Tulving, E. (1983). *Elements of episodic memory*. Oxford: OUP.

Tulving, E. (1985). How many memory systems are there? *American Psychologist, 40*, 385-398.

Tulving, E. (1989). Memory: Performance, knowledge and experience. *European Journal of Cognitive Psychology, 1*, 3-26.

2 Forgetting

Introduction

Why do we forget? There are two simple answers to this question. First, the memory has disappeared – it is no longer there. Second, the memory is still stored in the memory system but, for some reason, it cannot be retrieved. These two answers summarise the main theories of forgetting developed by psychologists. The first answer is more likely to be applied to forgetting in short-term memory, the second to forgetting in long-term memory.

Chapter summary

- Unit 1 outlines theories of forgetting in short-term memory.
- Unit 2 examines theories of forgetting in long-term memory.
- Unit 3 looks at the relationship between forgetting and emotion.

Unit 1 Forgetting in short-term memory

KEY ISSUES

1. What are the main theories of forgetting in STM?
2. What are their strengths and weaknesses?

As outlined in the previous chapter, STM has a limited duration and a limited capacity. It can only hold information for a short period of time. It can only hold small amounts of information. These observations form the basis for the first two theories of forgetting discussed below. Both theories assume that forgetting occurs because information is lost from STM.

1.1 Trace decay

This explanation of forgetting in short-term memory assumes that memories leave a *trace* in the brain. A trace is some form of physical and/or chemical change in the nervous system. *Trace decay theory* states that forgetting occurs as a result of the automatic decay or fading of the memory trace.

Trace decay appears to occur rapidly. As the previous chapter indicated, STM has a limited duration – information is held there for only a short period of time. The Brown-Peterson effect states that information disappears from STM within about 20 seconds if it is not rehearsed (see pp 9-10). Peterson and Peterson (1959) explained this rapid loss in terms of trace decay. The memory trace fades over time until it disappears completely. At this point, information is forgotten.

Evaluation Evidence from experiments questions the idea of trace decay. In one experiment (Waugh & Norman, 1965), participants were presented with a series of 16 numbers, for example 4, 9, 7, 3, 6 etc. They were then given a number from the series – this number was known as the probe – and asked which number followed it. For example, if the probe is 7, the correct answer is 3. This procedure is known as the *serial probe technique*.

The numbers were presented at different speeds. If information

fades away due to the passage of time, then numbers presented at a faster rate have less time in which to decay than numbers presented at a slower rate. If trace decay is occurring, then memory should be better – more correct answers should be given – when the numbers are presented quickly. Presentation rate appeared to make little difference. There was no significant relationship between the speed of presentation and recall of the correct numbers. This finding throws doubt on the trace decay theory of forgetting.

Key term

Trace decay theory *Forgetting in STM occurs as a result of the automatic decay of the memory trace.*

1.2 Displacement

Trace decay theory focuses on time – the limited duration of STM. *Displacement theory* focuses on capacity – the limited amount of space in STM. In George Miller's famous phrase, the capacity of STM is 'the magical number seven, plus or minus two'. In other words, STM can hold between 5 and 9 items – numbers, words or chunks.

Displacement theory provides a very simple explanation of forgetting. Because of its limited capacity, STM can only hold small amounts of information. When STM is 'full', new information displaces or 'pushes out' old information. The old information which is displaced is forgotten in STM.

Evaluation There is some evidence to support the idea of displacement. In one experiment, participants were presented with a list of numbers. The more numbers that followed a particular probe number, the less likely that probe number was to be remembered (Shallice, 1967). It can be argued that the later numbers tended to displace the earlier numbers. As a result, the earlier numbers became more difficult to remember. However, it can also be argued that because the earlier numbers were presented earlier in time, they were forgotten as a result of trace decay. Shallice investigated this possibility and claimed that although time appeared to have some effect on recall, the number of items following a probe number seemed to have a greater effect. This experiment suggests that displacement provides a better explanation of forgetting in STM than trace decay.

1.3 Interference

Interference theory states that forgetting occurs because memories interfere with and disrupt one another. Old memories can disrupt new memories – this is known as *proactive interference*, meaning forward interference. Alternatively, new memories can disrupt old memories – this is known as *retroactive interference*, meaning backward interference.

Interference is more likely when memories are similar. For example, if you change your telephone number, the old number can interfere with the new number. This may result in you forgetting the new number. This is an example of proactive interference – the old memory disrupts the new one. And, the similarity of the memories – two telephone numbers – makes interference more likely.

The following experiment on forgetting in STM supports the idea of interference (Loess, 1968). Participants were presented with lists of three words from a particular category, for example animals. They were asked to count backwards for 15 seconds to prevent rehearsal, then asked to recall the three animals. This was done six times with six different lists of animals. The first list of words was well recalled, the second list less well recalled and by the third or fourth list, recall was reduced to an even lower level. In terms of interference theory, this is an example of proactive interference – the earlier lists of words interfered with the later lists resulting in an increase in forgetting. Since all the words belong to the same semantic or meaning category – animals – they are similar. As a result, interference is likely.

The category was then changed, for example to vegetables, and the same procedure was followed. Recall improved immediately. In terms of interference theory, the old category did not interfere with the new category because the categories were different. Proactive interference ceased because vegetables are distinct from animals. This is known as *release from proactive interference*. However, after the first list of vegetables, proactive interference began again because the following lists of vegetables belonged to the same category.

Evaluation Support for interference theory is based mainly on the findings of laboratory experiments. However, these experiments may have little relationship to what happens in everyday life. As a result, it may not be possible to generalise from the findings. In other words, these experiments may have low ecological validity. The following experiment provides a more realistic test of interference theory (Slamecka, 1966).

Participants were given a word, for example, 'animal' and asked for a word they associated with it, for example 'dog'. They gave the first word which came to mind which probably reflects what would happen in an everyday situation. They were then asked to learn a new set of words which were linked to 'animal' such as 'cow', 'bear', 'cat', and so on. They were then asked to recall these words including the first word they associated with 'animal' – in this example 'dog'. In terms of

interference theory, this should result in retroactive interference because the words belonged to the same semantic category. New learning should disrupt older memories and participants would probably forget the first word – 'dog' – they associated with 'animal'. They didn't. There was no evidence of interference. They remembered the word they were most likely to associate with the category 'animal'. This experiment suggests that when participants behave 'normally' and select their usual associations, interference may not occur.

Key terms

Displacement theory *Forgetting occurs when information is displaced or 'pushed out' of STM when its capacity is exceeded.*

Interference theory *Forgetting occurs as a result of similar memories interfering with and disrupting each other.*

Proactive interference *Older memories interfering with newer memories.*

Retroactive interference *Newer memories interfering with older memories.*

Release from proactive interference *Proactive interference ceases to affect recall.*

Conclusion

This unit has looked at three theories of forgetting in short-term memory. There is experimental evidence both to support and question each theory. It is possible that, at various times, forgetting in STM may be a combination of two or all of these processes – trace decay, displacement and interference. The answer is far from clear. One of the foremost experts on memory, Alan Baddeley (1997), concludes that, 'The explanation of forgetting … remains an open question'.

Many ingenious experiments have been devised to examine forgetting in STM. However, as noted earlier, they may have low ecological validity. As a result, the findings of laboratory research may not be applicable to forgetting in everyday situations.

Summary

1. Trace decay theory explains forgetting in terms of the limited duration of STM. It states that forgetting occurs as a result of the progressive decay of the memory trace over time.

2. Displacement theory explains forgetting in terms of the limited capacity of STM. It states that forgetting occurs when information is displaced from STM when its capacity is exceeded.

3. Interference theory states that forgetting occurs as a result of similar memories interfering with and disrupting each other.

4. The findings on forgetting in STM are inconclusive – no firm conclusions can be reached.

Activity 1   Forgetting in STM

Item A   The Brown-Peterson effect

This graph shows the recall of information from STM when rehearsal is prevented (see p 8 for a fuller description of this experiment).

Adapted from Peterson & Peterson, 1959

Questions

1   Explain the results shown in Item A in terms of trace decay theory.

2   Explain the results shown in Item B in terms of interference theory.

3   How can Item C be used to criticise trace decay theory?

Item B   Experimental results

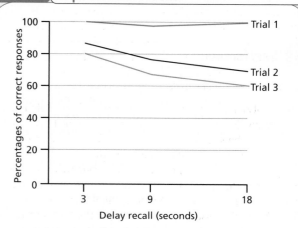

This graph shows the findings of an experiment in which participants were asked to learn sets of consonants, for example, FNC. They were then asked to recall the letters after various intervals of time. They were given a different set of letters for each trial.

Adapted from Keppel & Underwood, 1962

Item C   The Brown-Peterson effect

The results shown in Item A are an average of the results of repeated trials, each using a different set of three letters. The first few trials produced similar results to those shown in Item B.

Unit 2 Forgetting in long-term memory

KEY ISSUES

1. **What are the main theories of forgetting in LTM?**
2. **What are their strengths and weaknesses?**

Most psychologists assume that long-term memory has an unlimited capacity. If this is correct, then forgetting from LTM cannot be due to displacement. LTM cannot 'fill up' and 'overflow' as new information pushes out old information.

Many psychologists believe that once information enters LTM, it stays there permanently. If this is the case, then forgetting is not due to a loss of information from LTM, but a failure to access and retrieve information. However, not all researchers accept this point of view as the following section indicates.

2.1 Trace decay

Trace decay theory has also been used to explain forgetting in

long-term memory. It states that memories automatically decay over time. There is little evidence to support this explanation. If the memory trace decays steadily over time, then older memories will always be forgotten before more recent ones. If you remember your first day at school or work but cannot remember your second day, this suggests that memories do not necessarily fade with time. Older people often recall events and friends from their youth more readily than recent events and friends. Again, this suggests that memories do not automatically decay over time.

The importance of time is questioned by the following experiment (Jenkins & Dallenbach, 1924). Participants were asked to learn lists of nonsense syllables. Their recall was better if they slept after learning the lists rather than stayed awake for the same period of time. This suggests it is not the passage of time itself that causes information to be forgotten – memories do not appear to progressively fade over time. Instead, it seems to be what happens during that time that is important.

2.2 Interference

Hundreds of experiments have indicated that interference plays a part in forgetting in long-term memory. As noted in Unit 1, interference can be proactive – earlier memories disrupt later memories, or retroactive – later memories disrupt earlier memories. Experimental evidence indicates that the more similar the information, the more likely that interference will occur. The following example illustrates the type of experiment designed to examine the role of interference in forgetting (McGeoch & McDonald, 1931).

Participants learned a list of adjectives until they could recall them perfectly. Some of the participants then spent 10 minutes resting while others learned new material. The new material varied in similarity to the original list – from very different (3-digit numbers such as 268), to very similar (synonyms – adjectives with the same meaning to those in the first list). The more similar the new material to the original, the more the recall of the original list declined. Participants who spent 10 minutes resting without any new material to learn had the highest recall, those who had to learn the synonyms had the lowest recall. This suggests that retroactive interference affected recall. It indicates that the more similar the later material, the greater the interference and the higher the level of forgetting. The results of this experiment are shown in Table 1.

Evaluation Laboratory experiments are carefully designed to produce interference. The above study indicates this. Participants were asked to learn a list of adjectives with the same meanings as those on the original list. Situations like this are unlikely to occur in everyday life. As a result, generalisations from the laboratory to the wider world must be treated with caution. Such experiments might have low ecological validity.

Table 1	Retroactive interference

Activity	Average (mean) recall of ten adjectives
Rest	4.50
Learn 3-digit numbers	3.68
Learn nonsense syllables	2.58
Learn unrelated adjectives	2.17
Learn antonyms (adjectives with opposite meanings)	1.83
Learn synonyms (adjectives with the same meanings)	1.25

Adapted from McGeoch & McDonald, 1931

Many researchers believe that interference is unlikely to be a major factor in forgetting in everyday life (Eysenck & Keane, 1995). However, it can occur as an oft-quoted example from Loftus (1980) indicates. A young woman in moments of passion with her present boyfriend tended to cry out the name of her previous boyfriend. This is a rather unfortunate example of proactive interference.

Experiments on interference are compressed into a relatively short period of time and information is encoded in the same setting – the laboratory. Again this indicates low ecological validity. In everyday life, the encoding of information which might interfere with existing information, is usually spread out over a longer period of time and often takes place in different settings. This may well reduce the effects of interference. For example, the new information may be associated with a particular time, place or person which will make it different from existing information. The importance of such factors can be seen from the following section.

Activity 2   Interference in LTM

Item A   Finding your car

You park your car in a different place every day. You often have problems finding it.

Item B   Remembering names

Teachers sometimes have difficulty remembering the names of their students, especially when they teach different groups every day.

Questions

1   Use the idea of interference to explain why you often have problems finding your car.

2   How does the idea of interference explain why teachers sometimes have difficulty remembering their students' names?

2.3 Retrieval failure

If information is stored in long-term memory, then it is available. However, it may or may not be accessible. If it is accessible, then it is retrieved when required. If it is not accessible, it is not retrieved when required and, at that point in time, it is forgotten. This is known as *retrieval failure.*

Tip-of-the-tongue effect The distinction between availability and accessibility is illustrated by the tip-of-the-tongue (TOT) effect. This occurs when people know they know something but are unable to recall it. Brown and McNeill (1966) devised an experiment to create TOT effects. Participants were presented with definitions of uncommon words and asked to identify the words that fitted the definitions. Often they produced words that were similar in sound or meaning to the correct words. For example, when the correct word was 'sampan' (a small Chinese boat), participants' answers included 'sarong', 'Cheyenne', 'barge' and 'junk'. The first two words sound like the correct answer, the last two words have similar meanings.

The TOT effect illustrates the distinction between availability and accessibility. The words are available in LTM – participants recognised them immediately they were told. However, they were not accessible and so could not be retrieved.

Key terms

Retrieval failure *The failure to retrieve information from memory.*

Availability *Whether or not information is stored in memory.*

Accessibility *Whether or not information which is available can be retrieved.*

Tip-of-the-tongue effect *Knowing that information is available in memory but being unable to retrieve it.*

Retrieval cues

There is considerable evidence that information is more likely to be retrieved from long-term memory if appropriate *retrieval cues* are present. This evidence comes from both laboratory experiments and everyday experience. A retrieval cue is a hint or clue that can help retrieval. Tulving (1974) argued that information will be more readily retrieved if the cues present when the information was encoded are also present when its retrieval is required. For example, if you proposed to your partner when a certain song was playing on the radio, you will be more likely to remember the details of the proposal when you hear the same song again. The song is a retrieval cue – it was present when the information was encoded and retrieved.

Context Retrieval cues may be based on *context* – the setting or situation in which information is encoded and retrieved. Examples include a particular room, driving along a motorway, a certain group of people, a rainy day and so on. Context also refers to the way information is presented. For example, words may be printed, spoken or sung, they may be presented in meaningful groups – in categories such as lists of animals or furniture – or as a random collection without any link between them. Evidence indicates that retrieval is more likely when the context at encoding matches the context at retrieval.

State Retrieval clues may also be based on *state* – the physical or psychological state of the person when information is encoded and retrieved. For example, a person may be alert, tired, happy, sad, drunk or sober when the information was encoded. They will be more likely to retrieve the information when they are in a similar state.

Cue-dependent forgetting This occurs when information in LTM cannot be retrieved because appropriate retrieval cues are absent. The information is available but not accessible because of a lack of retrieval cues.

Context-dependent retrieval

A number of experiments have indicated the importance of context-based cues for retrieval. An experiment conducted by Tulving and Pearlstone (1966) asked participants to learn lists of words belonging to different categories, for example names of animals, clothing and sports. Participants were then asked to recall the words. Those who were given the category names recalled substantially more words than those who were not. The categories provided a context, and naming the categories provided retrieval cues. Tulving and Pearlstone argued that cue-dependent forgetting explains the difference between the two groups of participants. Those who recalled fewer words lacked appropriate retrieval cues. (See Activity 3 for further details of this experiment).

An interesting experiment conducted by Godden and Baddeley (1975) indicates the importance of setting for retrieval. Participants learned lists of words either on land or 15 feet underwater. They were then asked to recall the words either in the same setting (for example, learning on land and recalling on land), or in the opposite setting (for example, learning on land and recalling underwater). The results, shown in Figure 1, indicate that when the settings for learning and recall are the same, participants retrieved significantly more words. The similarity of the contexts provided retrieval cues. Forgetting was due, in part, to an absence of context-dependent retrieval cues.

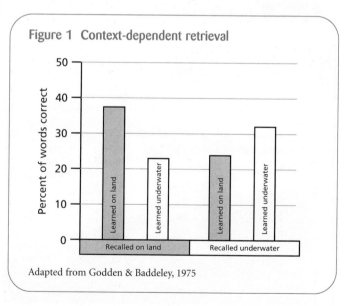

Figure 1 Context-dependent retrieval

Adapted from Godden & Baddeley, 1975

State-dependent retrieval

The basic idea behind state-dependent retrieval is that memory will be best when a person's physical or psychological state is similar at encoding and retrieval. For example, if someone tells you a joke on Saturday night after a few drinks, you'll be more likely to remember it when you're in a similar state – at a later date after a few more drinks. Stone cold sober on Monday morning, you'll be more likely to forget the joke.

A study by Goodwin et al. (1969) investigated the effect of alcohol on state-dependent retrieval. They found that when people encoded information when drunk, they were more likely to recall it in the same state. For example, when they hid money and alcohol when drunk, they were unlikely to find them when sober. However, when they were drunk again, they often discovered the hiding place. Other studies found similar state-dependent effects when participants were given drugs such as marijuana or barbiturates.

Evidence for state-dependent retrieval in terms of mood is less convincing. From this point of view, recall should be better when a person's mood state, for example, happy or sad, at encoding is the same as their mood at retrieval (Bower, 1981). A review of 40 studies indicates a tendency, but not a particularly strong one, for people to recall information when their mood at encoding matches their mood at retrieval (Ucros, 1989). However, mood effects are usually greater when participants are asked to recall personal experiences rather than the lists of words often used in experiments. This suggests that mood effects may be stronger in real life than in laboratory settings. This calls into question the ecological validity of laboratory experiments.

Forgetting and retrieval-failure theory – evaluation

According to retrieval-failure theory, forgetting occurs when information is available in LTM but is not accessible. Accessibility depends in large part on retrieval cues. Forgetting is greatest when context and state are very different at encoding and retrieval. In this situation, retrieval cues are absent and the likely result is cue-dependent forgetting.

There is considerable evidence to support this theory of forgetting from laboratory experiments. The ecological validity of these experiments can be questioned, but their findings are supported by evidence from outside the laboratory. For example, many people say they can't remember much about their childhood or their schooldays. But returning to the house in which they spent their childhood or attending a school reunion often provides retrieval cues which trigger a flood of memories.

How does cue-dependent forgetting compare to the other theories of forgetting in LTM? According to Michael Eysenck (1998), a leading researcher, 'It has proved easy to demonstrate powerful effects of cue-dependent forgetting inside and outside the laboratory. It seems probable that this is the main reason for forgetting in long-term memory.'

Key terms

Retrieval cue *A clue or hint which helps retrieval.*

Context *The setting or situation in which information is encoded and retrieved.*

State *The physical or psychological state of a person when information is encoded and retrieved.*

Cue-dependent forgetting *Forgetting due to the absence of appropriate retrieval cues.*

Summary

1. There is little evidence for trace decay in LTM.

2. There is considerable evidence from laboratory experiments for interference in LTM. However, interference does not appear to be a major factor in forgetting in everyday life.

3. Evidence from both laboratory experiments and everyday experience supports the idea of cue-dependent forgetting. Forgetting appears to be greatest when context and state are very different at encoding and retrieval.

Activity 3 Retrieval cues – part 1

Word list

dog	grenade	knife	doctor
cat	gun	spoon	lawyer
horse	rifle	fork	teacher
cow	bomb	pan	dentist
apple	cotton	hammer	football
orange	silk	saw	cricket
pear	wool	spanner	basketball
banana	rayon	screwdriver	tennis
chair	blue	oil	shirt
table	red	gas	socks
bed	green	coal	skirt
sofa	yellow	wood	shoes

Adapted from Tulving & Pearlstone, 1966

Questions

1 Read the list three times.

2 Cover the list and write down as many of the words as you can remember.

3 Ask a friend to do the same. Show them the retrieval cues on page 32 before and during the time when they write the words down.

4 Have they recalled more words than you? If so, suggest why.

Unit 3 Emotional factors in forgetting

KEY ISSUES

1. **What are flashbulb memories and repressed memories?**
2. **How is emotion related to the recall of these memories?**

This unit examines the part played by emotion in the retrieval of information from long-term memory. It looks at two types of emotionally-charged memories. The first, flashbulb memories, are readily recalled, often in vivid detail. The second, repressed memories, are extremely difficult to recall. Emotion appears to have a significant, but very different, effect on the retrieval of these two types of memories.

3.1 Flashbulb memories

People sometimes have very vivid and detailed memories of where they were and what they were doing when a major event occurred. These memories are known as *flashbulb memories*. They are shaped by events which are experienced as emotionally charged, dramatic, surprising and important.

Brown and Kulik (1977) asked people a series of questions about ten major events, for example the assassination of President John F. Kennedy in 1963. They found that memories for such events were particularly vivid, detailed and long lasting. People usually remembered where they were when they heard the news, how they heard the news, what they and others were doing at the time, and the emotional impact of the news on themselves and those around them.

According to Brown and Kulik (1982), flashbulb memories are special – they are quite different from other memories. They suggest that there is a special mechanism in the brain which is activated by events which produce high levels of emotion and surprise, and which are seen as particularly significant. As a result, the entire scene is 'printed' in memory in a 'flash'. This is why flashbulb memories are so accurate and long lasting.

The Challenger explosion

Other researchers have questioned this view. First, they argue that flashbulb memories are no different from ordinary memories which are long lasting and important to the person concerned. A study by Rubin and Kozin (1984) found that significant and distinctive personal events such as graduating from high school and a first romance were recalled in much the same way as flashbulb memories.

Second, researchers have questioned the accuracy of flashbulb memories. In 1986, the American space shuttle *Challenger* exploded shortly after lift-off, killing all the astronauts on board. One study tested participants' memories for the *Challenger* disaster a few days after it happened and again nine months later. There was evidence of forgetting during the nine-month interval and some participants gave different, and sometimes inaccurate, details on the two occasions. Despite this, 92% of the participants retained complete and accurate memories of the event over the nine-month period (McCloskey et al., 1988). Somewhat different results were obtained from a similar study which tested memory for the *Challenger* explosion at two weeks and again at eight months after the event. Accuracy fell from 77% to 55% over the eight months, suggesting that so-called flashbulb memories are prone to forgetting just like ordinary memories. Memory for the event was best when it produced a strong emotional reaction (Bohannon, 1988). This suggests that participants who tended to forget did not find the *Challenger* explosion emotionally and personally significant. If this is the case, then a flashbulb memory would not have been formed (Conway, 1995).

A study of the resignation of the British prime minister Margaret Thatcher in 1990 helps to distinguish flashbulb memories from ordinary memories (Conway et al., 1994). Participants from a number of countries were tested a few days after the news of her resignation, and again after eleven months. Eighty-six per cent of the British participants had flashbulb memories of the event 11 months later, compared to only 29% of non-British participants. For most of the British participants, the event produced a strong emotional response and it was seen as very important. Most of the non-British participants were not emotionally involved, not particularly interested and, as a result, did not form flashbulb memories. They forgot many aspects of the event – it was just an 'ordinary memory'.

Evaluation Researchers disagree about the existence of flashbulb memories. Some argue they are a distinctive type of memory characterised by the emotional response an event produces and the importance attached to the event (Conway, 1995). Others see nothing special about so-called flashbulb memories. They see them as subject to the normal processes of forgetting just like any other memories. There is some evidence to support both points of view.

Key term

Flashbulb memory *A long-lasting, and vivid memory of a person's circumstances and feelings when they heard the news of a major event which affected them emotionally and which they saw as important. The memory also includes specific details of the event.*

Activity 4   Flashbulb memories

Item A | Death of Princess Diana

People often remember what they felt and where they were when they of heard the news of Diana's death in 1997.

Item B | Turkish earthquake, 1999

People who survive earthquakes often have flashbulb memories of the event.

Questions

1 Suggest why the events pictured in Items A and B might produce flashbulb memories.

2 Why are African Americans more likely than white Americans to have flashbulb memories of the events in Item C?

Item C | Assassinations

Malcolm X

Martin Luther King (centre) on the balcony of the Memphis motel where he was shot the next day.

African Americans had more flashbulb memories than white Americans for the assassinations of Malcolm X in 1965 and Martin Luther King in 1968 (Brown & Kulik, 1982).

3.2   Motivated forgetting

Sometimes we do not want to remember something. Forgetting information because we do not want to remember it is known as *motivated forgetting*. We may or may not be aware of this process.

Suppression

Deliberate and conscious motivated forgetting is known as *suppression*. Suppression has been demonstrated in laboratory experiments. For example, Weiner and Reed (1969) showed that participants are able to forget information they have just been given when instructed to do so. People can 'forget on demand'. This may work in real-life situations, too. As a motor-racing driver begins a race, he might deliberately try to forget the start

of the last race when he stalled the car, or the race before that when he crashed at the start.

Repression

Repression is motivated forgetting without conscious awareness. It makes memories very difficult to retrieve. The idea of repression was introduced by Sigmund Freud in the nineteenth century. According to Freud, most forgetting is simply the discarding of information that is no longer needed (Freud & Breuer, 1895). However, certain memories are repressed – pushed out of consciousness and into the unconscious. These are traumatic memories – extremely distressing memories – which threaten an individual's wellbeing. Consider the following case.

Irene, a young 20-year-old woman, lived with her mother in an attic. Her mother had reached the final stages of tubercu

Irene watched her slowly dying for 60 days and nights. When her mother finally died, Irene was highly distraught. She tried repeatedly to revive the corpse. Soon after, Irene apparently had no memory of the events surrounding her mother's death. She would ask: 'When did she die? What did she die from? Was I not there to take care of her?'

Some time later, Irene began to have fits during which she would act out events from her life in great detail, including the period leading up to her mother's death and the death itself. She remembered none of this and still had no conscious memory that her mother had died. Clearly the event had not disappeared from memory – Irene's behaviour during her fits would not have been possible if she had no memory for her mother's death. The event remained in long-term memory but had been repressed (Hunter, 1957).

Repressed childhood memories

There is increasing evidence of repressed memories from cases of sexual abuse in childhood. One study examined hospital records of young girls who had been treated for sexual abuse (Williams, 1994). Seventeen years later, the women were tracked down. Thirty-eight per cent had no conscious memory of the events for which they were treated, though many reported later incidents of sexual abuse.

Repressed memories are difficult but not impossible to retrieve. Take the following case. In 1969, Eileen's eight-year-old friend Susan disappeared. Twenty years later Eileen suddenly remembered what had happened to her friend. Eileen's daughter reminded her of Susan. One day she was looking into her daughter's eyes and the long-repressed memory returned. Eileen had seen her own father sexually abuse Susan and then beat her to death with a rock. He threatened to kill Eileen if she told anyone. Twenty years after the event, her father was found guilty of murder and sentenced to life imprisonment (Zimbardo et al., 1995).

Evaluation of repression

It is difficult to evaluate the evidence on repressed memories for the following reasons.

- They are not easy to retrieve.
- Creating the kind of traumatic experiences described above would be extremely difficult in the laboratory.
- Even if this could be done, it would be unethical. The British Psychological Society's ethical guidelines for research state that participants should be protected from physical and psychological harm (BPS, 1998).
- Researchers have tried to create repressed memories in the laboratory by making participants feel anxious. But the mild anxiety that results is hardly the basis for repression. These experiments have provided little or no evidence for repressed memories (Holmes, 1990).

Most of the evidence for repressed memories comes from clinical studies in which psychiatrists ask their clients detailed and probing questions about past events. This approach has its own problems as the next section indicates.

False memory syndrome

To the person retrieving repressed memories, the events they recall are real. Often, however, there is no independent evidence to support or refute their stories. This has led to the idea of *false memory syndrome* – the possibility that so-called repressed memories are false, that they refer to events that never happened.

There is evidence that memories for traumatic events can be false. For example, Pynoos and Nader (1989) studied children's memories of a sniper attack in a school playground. One of the children recalled hearing shots and seeing someone lying on the ground. This seemed a plausible memory, until Pynoos and Nader discovered that the child had been on holiday at the time and so could not possibly have witnessed the event. Where did the memory come from?

The possibility that false information can be 'planted' in people's memories was investigated by Loftus (1993). She asked the older brother of a 14-year-old boy to tell him that he had been lost in a shopping centre when he was five years old. The younger brother was convinced that the memory was true and, within two weeks, began to 'remember' details of this non-existent event, including the names of shops, details of the person who found him, and how he felt at the time. When he was told that the memory was false, the boy found this very difficult to believe and said he definitely remembered being lost and looking for his family.

False memories do exist. However, this does not necessarily mean that repressed memories are false. What it does mean is that when repressed memories are retrieved, they should be treated with caution. Wherever possible, independent evidence of their accuracy should be obtained. (For further discussion of false memory syndrome, see p 40).

3.3 Emotion and everyday forgetting

Clearly, most everyday events are very different from the traumatic experiences that lead to repressed memories or the emotionally-charged events that produce flashbulb memories. Does emotion affect the recall of everyday events?

Diary studies Marigold Linton (1975), a psychologist, kept a diary of events in her life over a six-year period. She rated the events in terms of their importance and her emotional response to them. She found little relationship between importance, emotional involvement and recall. However, she found she was more likely to forget unpleasant events and to remember pleasant ones.

A similar study was conducted by Willem Wagenaar (1968), a Dutch psychologist. He recorded 2400 events in his daily life over a six-year period. He found, unlike Linton, that he was more likely to remember events in which he was emotionally

Key terms

Motivated forgetting *Forgetting information because of a desire not to remember it.*

Suppression *Deliberate and conscious motivated forgetting.*

Repression *Motivated forgetting without conscious awareness.*

False memory syndrome *A memory of an event that never happened.*

Response bias *A tendency to respond in a particular way.*

involved. Like Linton, he was more likely to forget unpleasant events. However, this applied only to recall over shorter intervals of time.

These two studies fail to show a clear-cut relationship between everyday forgetting and emotion. However, they are studies of particular individuals. Because of this, it is not possible to make generalisations from them.

Depression Studies of people with depression indicate a *response bias* in recall – a tendency to remember certain things and to forget others. Laboratory experiments indicate that depressed people are more likely to recall negative items (for example, negative adjectives) and to forget positive items (Zuroff et al., 1983). Similarly, when people with depression look back over their lives, they are more likely to forget happy events and to remember unhappy events. In this respect, their response bias colours their recall (Eysenck & Keane, 1995).

In terms of state-dependent retrieval, events are more likely to be recalled if a person's psychological state at encoding, matches their state at retrieval. This may explain why people with depression are more likely to forget happy events from their past life.

Summary

1. Emotion plays an important part in the formation of flashbulb memories. Usually, they are easily retrieved and remarkably accurate.

2. Some researchers argue that flashbulb memories are little different from many other significant and emotionally-charged memories.

3. Emotion also plays an important part in the formation of repressed memories. They are extremely difficult to retrieve.

4. It is difficult to distinguish repressed memories from false memories.

5. The relationship between emotion and the recall of everyday events is not clear-cut.

Activity 3   Retrieval cues - pt 2

Retrieval cues

animals fruit furniture	weapons cloth colours	cutlery tools fuels	professions sports clothing

Adapted from Tulving & Pearlstone, 1966

References

Baddeley, A.D. (1997). *Human memory: Theory and practice* (2nd ed.). Hove: Psychology Press.

Bohannon, J.N. (1988). Flashbulb memories for the Space Shuttle disaster: A tale of two theories. *Cognition, 29,* 179-196.

Bower, G.H. (1981). Mood and memory. *American Psychologist, 32,* 129-148.

BPS (British Psychological Society). (1998). *Code of conduct, ethical principles and guidelines.* Leicester: BPS.

Brown, R. & Kulik, J. (1977). Flashbulb memories. *Cognition, 5,* 73-99.

Brown, R. & Kulik, J. (1982). Flashbulb memory. In U. Neisser (Ed.), *Memory observed: Remembering in natural contexts.* San Francisco: W.H. Freeman.

Brown, R. & McNeill, D. (1966). The 'tip of the tongue' phenomenon. *Journal of Verbal Learning and Verbal Behavior, 5,* 325-337.

Cohen, G. (1996). *Memory in the real world* (2nd ed.). Hove: Psychology Press.

Conway, M.A. (1995). *Flashbulb memories.* Hove: Lawrence Erlbaum Associates.

Conway, M.A., Anderson, S.J., Larsen, S.F., Donnelly, C.M., McDaniel, M.A., McClelland, A.G.R. & Rawles, R.E. (1994). The formation of flashbulb memories. *Memory and Cognition, 22,* 326-343.

Eysenck, M. (1998). Memory. In M. Eysenck (Ed.), *Psychology: An integrated approach.* Harlow: Longman.

Eysenck, M.W. & Keane, M.T. (1995). *Cognitive psychology: A student's handbook* (3rd ed.). Hove: Lawrence Erlbaum Associates.

Freud S. & Breuer, J. (1895). *Studies on hysteria.* Penguin Freud Library Vol. 3 (published 1991). London: Penguin.

Godden, D. & Baddeley, A.D. (1975). Context-dependent memory in two natural environments: On land and under water. *British Journal of Psychology, 66,* 325-331.

Goodwin, D.W., Powell, B., Bremer, D., Hoine, H. & Stern, J. (1969). Alcohol and recall: State dependent effects in man. *Science, 163,* 1358.

Holmes, D.S. (1990). The evidence for repression: An examination of sixty years of research. In J. Singer (Ed.), *Repression and dissociation: Implications for personality theory, psychopathology, and health.* Chicago: University of Chicago Press.

Hunter, I.M.L. (1957). *Memory: Facts and fallacies.* Baltimore: Penguin.

Jenkins, J.G. & Dallenbach, K.M. (1924). Obliviscence during sleep and waking. *American Journal of Psychology, 35,* 605-612.

Keppel, G. & Underwood, B.J. (1962). Proactive inhibition in short-term retention of single items. *Journal of Verbal Learning and Verbal Behavior, 1,* 153-161.

Linton, M. (1975). Memory for real-world events. In D.A. Norman & D.E. Rumelhart (Eds.), *Explorations in cognition.* San Francisco: Freeman.

Loftus, E.F. (1980). *Memory.* Reading MA: Addison-Wesley.

Loftus, E.F. (1993). The reality of repressed memories. *American Psychologist, 48,* 518-537.

Loess, H. (1968). Short-term memory and item similarity. *Journal of Verbal Learning and Verbal Behavior, 7,* 87-92.

McCloskey, M., Wilbe, C.G. & Cohen, N.J. (1988). Is there a special flashbulb-memory mechanism? *Journal of Experimental Psychology: General, 117,* 171-181.

McGeoch, J.A. & McDonald, W.T. (1931). Meaningful relation and retroactive inhibition. *American Journal of Psychology, 43,* 579-588.

Peterson, L.R. & Peterson, M.J. (1959). Short-term retention of individual verbal items. *Journal of Experimental Psychology, 58,* 193-198.

Pynoos, R.S. & Nader, K. (1989). Children's memory and proximity to violence. *Journal of the American Academy of Child and Adolescent Psychiatry, 28,* 236-241.

Rubin, D.C. & Kozin, M. (1984). Vivid memories. *Cognition, 16,* 81-95.

Shallice, T. (1967). Paper presented at NATO symposium on short-term memory. Cambridge, England. Cited in A.D. Baddeley (1976). *The psychology of memory.* New York: Harper & Row.

Slamecka, N.J. (1966). Differentiation versus unlearning of verbal associations. *Journal of Experimental Psychology, 71,* 822-828.

Tulving, E. (1974). Cue-dependent forgetting. *American Scientist, 62,* 74-82.

Tulving, E. & Pearlstone, Z. (1966). Availability versus accessibility of information in memory for words. *Journal of Verbal Learning and Verbal Behavior, 5,* 381-391.

Ucros, C.G. (1989). Mood state-dependent memory. A meta-analysis. *Cognition and Emotion, 3,* 139-167.

Wagenaar, W.A. (1986). My memory: A study of autobiographical memory over six years. *Cognitive Psychology, 18,* 225-252.

Waugh, N.C. & Norman, D.A. (1965). Primary memory. *Psychological Review, 72,* 89-104.

Weiner, B. & Reed, H. (1969). Effects of the instructional sets to remember and to forget on short-term retention: Studies of rehearsal control and retrieval inhibition (repression). *Journal of Experimental Psychology, 79,* 226-232.

Williams, L.M. (1994). Recall of childhood trauma: A prospective study of women's memories of child sexual abuse. *Journal of Consulting and Clinical Psychology, 62,* 1167-1176.

Zimbardo, P.G., McDermott, M., Jansz, J. & Metaal, M. (1995). *Psychology: A European text.* London: Harper Collins.

Zuroff, D.C., Colussy, S.A. & Wielgus, M.S. (1983). Selective memory and depression: A cautionary note concerning response bias. *Cognitive Therapy and Research, 7,* 223-232.

3 Eyewitness testimony

▶ Introduction

Eyewitness testimony is a legal term. It refers to an account given by people of an event they have witnessed. For example, they may be required to give a description at a trial of a robbery or a road accident they have seen.

Clearly, memory is very important for eyewitness testimony. An accurate memory for an event can lead to the conviction of a guilty person or the release of an innocent person. Alternatively, an inaccurate memory can lead to the conviction of an innocent person or a failure to convict a guilty person.

This chapter looks at the various factors which affect eyewitness testimony.

Chapter summary

- Unit 1 outlines different perspectives on the study of memory.
- Unit 2 looks at eyewitness memory for faces and people.

- Unit 3 examines eyewitness memory for events.
- Unit 4 looks at ways of improving eyewitness memory.

Unit 1 Perspectives on memory

KEY ISSUES

1. How does the study of everyday memory differ from traditional laboratory research?
2. What is constructive memory?

1.1 Introduction

Eyewitness testimony is an example of everyday memory – the use of memory in the world outside the laboratory. The study of everyday memory differs in important respects from the more traditional laboratory-based research described in the previous two chapters. They represent two different research traditions. Each has tended to use different methods and adopt different perspectives. Before looking at eyewitness testimony, it will be useful to look at these two traditions.

1.2 Two research traditions

Chapter 1 closed with a brief look at some of the methods used in memory research. This section returns to the question of methods.

Traditional laboratory research Over the last 100 years, memory research has been dominated by traditional laboratory experiments. These experiments have attempted to isolate some of the variables which are believed to affect memory. This means separating them from the vast range of factors which may influence memory. Once they have been isolated in the laboratory, these variables can be controlled and their effects measured. For example, a variable such as word length can be controlled – the length of words can be systematically varied by the experimenter. In this way, the effect of word length, for example on the capacity of short-term memory, can be measured.

However, as noted in previous chapters, laboratory experiments have been criticised for a lack of ecological validity. They have been seen as unrealistic and artificial. The tasks performed in experiments often bear little relationship to everyday life. For example, learning nonsense syllables, then counting backwards in threes, then attempting to recall these syllables, is hardly an everyday activity. Nor is it a particularly meaningful activity. As a result, critics have argued it is not possible to generalise from the findings of laboratory experiments – to apply the results of experiments to the wider world outside the laboratory (Neisser, 1978).

Naturalistic research Naturalistic research focuses on behaviour in terms of 'natural', normal, everyday situations. In this respect, its methods generally have higher ecological validity than traditional laboratory experiments. Experiments are still used, but the focus is on recreating or simulating events and experiences from outside the laboratory, and on the performance of tasks which are meaningful and relevant to the participants.

This can be seen from research on eyewitness testimony. Participants have been asked to recall events from films, pictures or reports of a robbery or a car crash. Researchers do their best to make such material realistic and to ensure it reflects the 'real thing' – real events in the real world.

1.3 Two perspectives

The traditional perspective The first two chapters have been mainly concerned with what can be called traditional questions on memory. Examples of such questions are: 'What is the capacity and duration of STM?' and 'Is STM a single or multipart memory system?' Researchers have tended to assume that the best way to answer these questions is the controlled laboratory experiment. According to their critics, both the questions and the methods are inappropriate. The questions and the experiments designed to answer them ignore many of the factors which affect memory in everyday life.

The everyday memory perspective From this point of view, what matters is how memory operates in everyday settings. This results in different methods and different questions. Consider the following quotations from Gillian Cohen, one of the leading researchers on everyday memory. Memory is 'influenced by a lifetime of past experiences, by history and culture, by current motives and emotions, by intelligence and personality traits, by future goals and plans'. In addition, 'remembering usually occurs in a social context and one of its main functions is to serve interpersonal communication. Memory is not just a private data bank: it is shared, exchanged, constructed, revised and elaborated in all our social interactions' (Cohen, 1996).

In many respects, this is a very different view of memory from that presented in the previous chapters. And, it results in different questions, for example: How is recall affected by the social context? As we shall see, eyewitness testimony occurs in social contexts such as police stations and courtrooms. And, the questions asked by police and lawyers can substantially affect the information 'remembered' by eyewitnesses.

1.4 Constructive memory

Previous chapters have presented a fairly simple picture of the basic memory process. It involves putting information in, storing it, and then getting that same information out again. Problems can arise – such as forgetting – but the overall process is not that complicated.

A rather different picture is presented by studies of everyday memory. They indicate that people's beliefs about the world influence how they see the world and how they remember events. And they indicate that memories are partly shaped by the social situations in which they are formed and retrieved. The following experiment illustrates these points. It was conducted

Figure 1 Argument on a subway train

Adapted from Allport & Postman, 1947

in the USA in the 1940s.

All the participants were white Americans. They were divided into groups of seven. One participant from each group was shown the picture in Figure 1, described it to a second participant, who described it to a third, and so on. Over half the participants who received the final description reported that the black man, not the white man was holding the razor. Some even had him waving the razor in a threatening manner.

Some of the questions raised by this experiment and probable answers to them are outlined below.

- Does it matter that the participants were white? Yes.
- Did they hold stereotypes that pictured blacks as hot-tempered and violent? Yes.
- Did these factors colour what they saw and what they heard? Yes.
- Does this mean that both the original memories and the memories as they were recalled were influenced by these factors? Yes.

The authors of this research concluded, 'When an actual perceptual fact is in conflict with expectations, expectation may prove a stronger determinant of perception and memory than the situation itself' (Allport & Postman, 1947). In other words, we see what we expect to see and this forms the basis of memory for an event.

People are constantly trying to make sense of the world around them, and in doing so, they strive to make everything meaningful. They apply existing knowledge, beliefs and expectations about the world – which they draw from long-term memory – in order to understand what's going on.

The terms *constructive memory* and *reconstructive memory* are used to describe this process of shaping, interpreting and making sense of information. These terms are used because they emphasise the view that people do not just passively absorb information and regurgitate it at a later date. Instead they actively shape information and build their own memories. As a result, they are constantly constructing and reconstructing their memories.

Reconstruction The view of memory outlined above was first put forward by Sir Frederick Bartlett (1932) in his book *Remembering*. He argued that people are constantly searching for meaning. As a result, they 'reconstruct' memories in ways which make sense to them. In a famous experiment, Bartlett asked British participants to read a story entitled *The war of the ghosts* – a folktale told by Native Americans from British Columbia in western Canada (see Activity 1). They were then asked to recall the story. Bartlett found that his participants reconstructed *The war of the ghosts* in terms of their experience, knowledge, expectations and beliefs, which at times were very different from those of the Native Americans. Their memory of the story was shaped by British *culture* – the learned, shared beliefs, attitudes and values of members of British society. For example, references to ghosts were played down by the participants since ghosts are not a major aspect of British culture. And the more often the participants recounted the story, the more 'British' it became.

Schemas Bartlett used the idea of *schemas* to explain the process of reconstructing memories. Schemas are mental representations of situations, events, people and objects. For instance, the stereotype of African Americans which participants used to interpret the picture of an argument on the subway train is an example of a schema. Stereotypes represent classes of people – nationalities, women, gays, ethnic minorities, the elderly and so on.

The importance of schemas to everyday life and to the construction of memory can be seen from the following example. If you hear the words, 'Mike ate in a restaurant', you would probably assume that Mike was eating food he had purchased in that restaurant. Why do you assume that? It doesn't say that at all. Your assumption is based on a 'restaurant schema' which contains information about what a restaurant is and what normally happens in one. By using a 'restaurant schema' you could probably give a fairly accurate description of Mike's behaviour from entering to leaving the restaurant. And if you recalled an actual meal you had eaten in a restaurant, you would probably add details from your 'restaurant schema' rather than recalling exactly what happened during your meal.

Schemas make sense of situations. They make life predictable, they provide people with guides for action. Think of the following events – a wedding, a birthday party, a funeral, bonfire night, Christmas Day. Each has a schema which gives meaning to the event, and which tells people how to behave and what to expect.

Bartlett's view of reconstructive memory focuses on the retrieval of memories. The process of recalling a memory involves a reconstruction of that memory in terms of schemas. The idea of constructive memory focuses more on the formation of the original memory. It suggests that this memory is constructed in terms of schemas (Eysenck, 1993).

Key terms

Constructive and reconstructive memory *The idea that memories are constructed and reconstructed in terms of existing knowledge, beliefs and expectations.*

Schemas *Mental representation of classes or categories of people, objects, events and situations.*

Culture *The learned, shared behaviour of members of a particular society. It includes shared beliefs, attitudes and values.*

Summary

1. Traditional laboratory research has been criticised as unrealistic and artificial.

2. Naturalistic research focuses on the use of memory in everyday situations. When experiments are used, they are often fairly realistic.

3. The idea of constructive and reconstructive memory assumes that people's beliefs and social contexts shape memories, both when they are encoded and retrieved.

4. Schemas are a major factor in the construction of memories.

Activity 1   Constructing memories

Item A   The war of the ghosts

One night two young men from Egulac went down to the river to hunt seals, and while they were there it became foggy and calm. Then they heard war-cries, and they thought: 'Maybe this is a war-party'. They escaped to the shore, and hid behind a log. Now canoes came up, and they heard the noise of paddles, and saw one canoe coming up to them. There were five men in the canoe, and they said:

'What do you think? We wish to take you along. We are going up the river to make war on the people.'

One of the young men said, 'I have no arrows'.

'Arrows are in the canoe,' they said.

'I will not go along. I might be killed. My relatives do not know where I have gone. But you,' he said turning to the other, 'may go with them'.

So one of the young men went, but the other returned home.

And the warriors went on up the river to a town on the other side of Kalama. The people came down to the water, and they began to fight, and many were killed. But presently the young man heard one of the warriors say: 'Quick, let us go home: that Indian has been hit'. Now he thought: 'Oh, they are ghosts'. He did not feel sick, but they said he had been shot.

So the canoes went back to Egulac, and the young man went ashore to his house, and made a fire. And he told everybody and said: 'Behold I accompanied the ghosts, and we went to fight. Many of our fellows were killed, and many of those who attacked us were killed. They said I was hit, and I did not feel sick.'

He told it all, and then he became quiet. When the sun rose he fell down. Something black came out of his mouth. His face became contorted. The people jumped up and cried.
He was dead.

From Bartlett, 1932

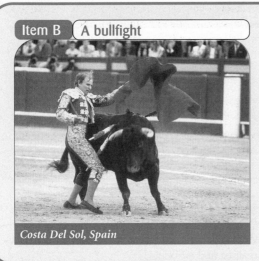

Item B   **A bullfight**

Costa Del Sol, Spain

Questions

1 a) Read *The war of the ghosts*.

   b) After a 15 minute interval, rewrite the story staying as closely as possible to the original.

   c) How does your version differ from the original?

   d) Suggest reasons for the difference.

2   Imagine you have made your first visit to a bullfight.

   a) How might your memory of the bullfight differ from the memory of a regular fan?

   b) Why might the memories differ?

Unit 2 Eyewitness memory for faces and people

KEY ISSUES

1. **How reliable is eyewitness memory for faces and people?**

2. **What factors affect the selection of suspects from identity parades?**

2.1 The importance of eyewitness testimony

In 1976, a committee headed by Lord Devlin issued a report on eyewitness testimony and identity parades. All the identity parades in England and Wales in 1973 – over 2000 – were examined. Forty-five per cent resulted in a suspect being identified, and 82% of these suspects were later convicted. In over 300 cases, eyewitness identification was the only evidence of the suspect's guilt. Seventy-four per cent of these suspects were later convicted (Baddeley, 1997). This gives some indication of the importance given to eyewitness testimony, particularly by jurors. The following experiment illustrates this.

Participants acted as jurors in a case of armed robbery and murder. When they were presented with circumstantial evidence, such as the defendant being seen entering the building where the victim lived, only 18% thought he was guilty. Then eyewitness testimony was added to the evidence. An eyewitness claimed to have seen the defendant committing the crime. Now, 72% of the participants thought he was guilty. Even when the participants were told that the eyewitness had very bad eyesight and was not wearing his glasses at the time, 68% still thought the defendant was guilty (Loftus, 1974). This indicates the power of eyewitness testimony.

Mistaken identity

Eyewitnesses can be mistaken – from time to time, innocent people are fined or imprisoned purely on the basis of eyewitness testimony. It has been estimated that even a fairly low rate of mistaken identity might result in hundreds, or even thousands of people being wrongly convicted (Fruzetti et al., 1992).

The unreliability of eyewitness identification is indicated by the following study. A 13-second film of a mugging was shown on prime-time television. Following this, an identity parade of six suspects was shown, and viewers were asked to telephone and pick the mugger out of the parade. More than 2000 viewers responded, but only 14% chose the right person. As there were six suspects, it would be expected that 17% of viewers would choose correctly if they were choosing at random. In all probability, people who had *not* witnessed the crime would be more likely to choose the correct suspect than the actual eyewitnesses (Buckhout, 1980).

2.2 Face recognition

In an identification parade, eyewitnesses are asked to recognise people they have usually seen only once before. In other words, they are asked to recognise strangers. The television experiment described above suggests they are not very good at this.

Laboratory studies Face recognition studies conducted in laboratories typically involve showing participants a set of photographs to be remembered. They are then shown a second set, which includes some of the first set and asked to identify the faces from the first set. Face recognition from this type of experiment is usually better than face recognition from eyewitness experiments. These experiments usually simulate an incident, such as a robbery, then ask participants to identify the suspect in an identity parade.

In the experiments using photographs, participants are given exactly the same picture to recognise – usually a full-face head and shoulders. In the eyewitness experiments, participants see the person to be recognised in very different contexts (in the incident and in the line-up) and often from different angles (for example, a side view in the incident and a full face in the line-up). These differences make recognition more difficult. However, such experiments provide greater insights into the problems of eyewitness identification in real life since they reflect the 'real thing'. As a result, they probably have greater ecological validity.

Everyday face recognition In everyday life, faces are not often seen in isolation from other aspects of a person. We usually recognise people rather than faces – by their clothes, voices, build and context, as well as by their faces. Context is an important factor. In Gillian Cohen's words, 'It is hard to recognise your bank manager at the disco or your dentist in evening dress' (Cohen, 1996). It is even harder when you may only have seen a person for a few seconds and then try to recognise them in a different context. In terms of identity parades, this suggests it is difficult to recognise someone seen robbing a bank when they are placed in a line-up. The contexts are very different so one of the main cues which can aid memory is missing.

In everyday life, the less familiar people are – the less well we know them – the more likely we are to wrongly identify them. In one study, 22 people recorded the errors they made in recognising people during an eight-week period. There were 314 cases of mistaking an unfamiliar person for a person they knew, often because of similarities in clothing, build and hair (Young et al., 1985). In such cases, the cues which often aid memory gave the wrong impression and resulted in mistaken identity. Again, this indicates the kind of error that can occur in eyewitness identification. Usually the suspect is unfamiliar to the eyewitness.

Cross-race identification bias Research indicates that people find it easier to recognise and identify people from their own race then people from a different race (see Item C in Activity 2). This is known as *cross-race identification bias*. It is reflected in the phrase 'they all look the same to me' which is sometimes used by people to describe members of a different race than themselves. In terms of eyewitness testimony, this suggests that if an eyewitness and a suspect belong to a different racial group, then the identification must be treated with considerable caution.

2.3 Identity parades

In view of the points outlined so far, selecting the correct suspect from an identity parade is problematic. The composition of identity parades and the way they are conducted can magnify the problem.

Functional size The number of people in the line-up who are similar to the eyewitness's description of the suspect can affect the chances of a correct identification. The more people who match the eyewitness's description, the greater the *functional size* of the parade. Doob and Kirshenbaum (1973) report the unfortunate case of Ron Shatford. Following the robbery of a shop, an eyewitness described the robber as 'very neatly dressed and rather good-looking'. Shatford was arrested as a suspect. He was good-looking and was placed in an identity parade alongside eleven unattractive men. The witness immediately identified Shatford as the robber. In this case, the functional size of the parade was one, because the witness described the robber as being attractive, and only one attractive man was present. After Shatford had served 15 months of a prison sentence, another man confessed to the robbery. Shatford had been wrongly imprisoned because the identity parade had a small functional size.

Assuming the suspect is present It is also important for the witness to be told that the suspect might not actually be in the parade. Wells (1993) points out that if the police fail to do this, then it is natural for the witness to assume that the suspect is present. Why else would the police have gone to the trouble of setting up the identity parade? This leads to the witness feeling that they must make a positive identification. Based on the assumption that the suspect is present, eyewitnesses may compare the people in the parade and choose the person who is closest to their memory of the suspect.

Type of parade Lindsay et al. (1991) found that the problems of functional size and witnesses mistakenly choosing the person most like the suspect could be reduced by presenting the people in the parade one at a time. This reduces the opportunity for the witness to compare people and so reduces the likelihood of mistakenly identifying one of them as the suspect. Witnesses are also more likely to say that the suspect is not there than when a traditional identity parade is used.

Key terms

Cross-race identification bias *The likelihood that people will correctly recognise and identify members of their own race rather than members of other races.*

Functional size of an identity parade *The number of people in the parade who are similar to they eyewitness's description of the suspect.*

Summary

1. Eyewitness identification of a suspect can strongly influence the decisions of juries.

2. Eyewitness identification is often unreliable.

3. Face recognition is affected by a range of factors. These include context and familiarity with the person concerned.

4. A number of factors influence eyewitness identification from an identity parade. They include:
   - The functional size of the parade
   - Whether the eyewitness is informed that the suspect may not be present in the parade
   - Whether members of the parade are presented singly or together.

Activity 2   Identifying people

Item A   That daft hat!

That's him! He's the culprit! I'd recognise that daft hat anywhere....

Item B   Instructing witnesses

After witnessing a crime, participants were told either that the suspect was in the identity parade (biased instructions) or that he might or might not be present (unbiased instructions). Participants then viewed a parade in which the suspect was either present or absent.

	Percentage of false identifications	
	Unbiased instructions	Biased instructions
Suspect present	0	25
Suspect absent	33	78

Adapted from Malpass & Devine, 1981

Item C   Cross-race identification bias

Eighty-six shopworkers in Texas were asked to identify three customers – one white, one African American and one Mexican American – who had purchased something from the shop earlier that day. One third of the shop-workers were white, one third African American, and one third Mexican American.

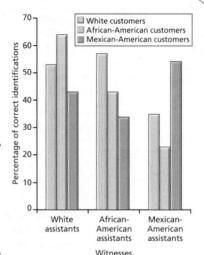

Adapted from Platz & Hosch, 1988

Questions

1   What problem with identity parades does Item A illustrate?

2   Summarise and explain the results of the experiment shown in Item B.

3   Explain the results shown in Item C in terms of cross-race identification bias.

Unit 3 Eyewitness memory for events

KEY ISSUES

1. **What factors affect the accuracy of eyewitness memory for events?**

2. **What are the limitations of experimental research in this area?**

Research has indicated that eyewitness memory for events can be changed by various factors. These include the addition of new information after the event has occurred and the way eyewitnesses are questioned about the event. This has been shown by a series of experiments conducted by Elizabeth Loftus and her colleagues.

3.1   The effects of leading questions

If a case reaches court, an eyewitness might be asked to give evidence and will be questioned by lawyers for the prosecution and the defence. Their memory of an event can be changed by this questioning. For example, they may be asked *leading questions* which direct them to give a particular interpretation of the event. This interpretation may be incorrect. The following experiment shows how this can happen.

Loftus and Palmer (1974) showed participants a film of a road accident involving a number of cars. After seeing the film, participants described what had happened, as if they were eyewitnesses giving evidence. Following this, they were asked a series of specific questions about the incident. Some of the

Figure 2 Two memories

Original memory

Memory after the 'smashed' question

participants were asked, 'About how fast were the cars going when they *smashed* into each other?' Others were asked, 'About how fast were the cars going when the *bumped* into each other?' Those who were asked the 'smashed' question thought the cars were going faster than those who were asked the 'bumped' question. The information presented in the question systematically affected the way in which the participants remembered the accident.

One week later, the same participants were asked if they had seen any broken glass at the scene of the accident. Thirty-two per cent of the participants who had previously been asked the 'smashed' question said that they had seen broken glass, compared with just 14% of the participants asked the 'bumped' question. In fact, there had been no broken glass in the accident. The addition of false detail to the memory of an event is called *confabulation*.

Key terms

Leading question *A question which leads a person to give a particular answer.*

Confabulation *The addition of inaccurate information which changes a memory.*

3.2 What happens to original memory?

What happened to the participants' original memory of the car crash? There are a number of possibilities.

- The original memory has been lost and replaced by a new one.
- The original memory remains intact but participants give the answer they believe the researcher wants to hear.
- The original memory has been reconstructed.

The original memory has been lost

The road accident experiment indicated that memory can be changed by asking leading questions and supplying misleading information. Does this mean that the original memory has been lost and replaced with a false one? Loftus argues that this is the case. In one experiment she offered participants $25 if they recalled an event accurately (Loftus, 1979). She found that this incentive did not prevent their testimony from being affected by leading questions. Loftus claims that if their original memory had been intact, then the offer of money would prevent the influence of leading questions. She believes the original memory has been permanently changed.

Some support for this view is provided by the following experiment (Lindsay, 1990). Participants were shown a series of slides in which a man stole money and a calculator from an office. Following this, they were presented with an account of the crime that included misleading information. They were then questioned about the crime and told *not* to rely on this account or they would get the answers wrong. This instruction should have ensured that participants relied on their original memory rather than the inaccurate information presented after the event. However, they were affected by the misleading information – they added false details to the series of slides they had been shown. One interpretation of this is that the original memory has been lost and replaced by a new memory.

The original memory is intact

Other researchers disagree with Loftus. They argue that the original memory remains intact (McCloskey & Zaragoza, 1985). The apparent change in memory occurs because participants are responding to *demand characteristics*. These are characteristics of an experiment which direct and encourage participants to behave in a particular way. For example, the 'bumped' and 'smashed' questions in the Loftus experiment encouraged participants to give different answers. Participants may respond to demand characteristics by giving answers they feel are desired or expected by the experimenter. As a result, they are responding to the situation rather than changing their original memory.

Evidence from the Lindsay experiment described above, questions this view. Participants were explicitly told to ignore the misleading account which followed the slide presentation. This should have more effect on their recall than the less obvious and more subtle demand characteristics of the original Loftus experiment. Yet despite the instructions to ignore the misleading account, participants added some of the false information it contained. This suggests that demand characteristics alone cannot explain changes in the original memory.

The original memory is reconstructed

Unit 1 outlined the idea of constructive and reconstructive memory. From this point of view, memories are constructed and reconstructed in terms of existing knowledge, beliefs and expectations. People are constantly trying to make sense of available information. If new information is introduced which appears relevant to an existing memory, then it can form the basis for a reconstruction of that memory. Thus, additional information suggested by a leading question can be built into a reconstructed memory. In this way, incorrect details may be 'remembered' or confabulated.

This may have happened in the car crash experiment described earlier when participants were asked if they'd seen broken glass. A number of the participants built this new and inaccurate information into their reconstruction. It may be that many of the distortions of memory that occur are brought about by the reconstructive processes described in Unit 1.

3.3 Resisting misleading information

So far, this unit has given the impression that eyewitnesses are easily misled. It has presented evidence of errors and distortions of memory resulting from leading questions and false information. However, eyewitnesses are unlikely to be misled when false information is obviously and 'blatantly' incorrect. Also, they are less likely to be misled when false information refers to a central rather than a peripheral aspect of an event they have witnessed. False information is most likely to change a memory if it is plausible – if it seems probable and reasonable. The following experiment conducted by Elizabeth Loftus (1979) illustrates these points.

Participants were shown a series of slides which pictured a man stealing a large red wallet from a woman's bag. When questioned later, 98% of participants correctly identified the colour of the wallet. They were then read an account of the crime in which the colour of the stolen wallet was given as brown and the colours of other items, which were peripheral to the scene, were changed. The participants were given a further test. All but two maintained that the wallet was red. Many more were misled by the inaccurate description of the colour of unimportant items. It appears that memory for important items is not easily distorted by misleading information.

An experiment conducted by Loftus and Greene (1980) indicated that to be effective, misleading information must be plausible and not too obvious. Participants were more likely to be misled into 'remembering' a man's moustache, when he did not have one, if the misleading information was stated in passing ('Did the intruder, who was tall and had a moustache, say anything to the professor?') rather than being the main focus of a sentence ('Was the moustache worn by the intruder light or dark brown?').

3.4 False memory syndrome

One of the most controversial areas of eyewitness testimony is *false memory syndrome*. This was introduced in Chapter 2 – see p30. If parts of memory for an event can be altered through the use of leading questions and inaccurate information, there is also the possibility that entirely false memories can be constructed. Can a completely new 'fictional memory', which has nothing to do with what a person actually witnessed, be constructed?

In the real world, it is extremely difficult to provide firm evidence to prove that false memories exist. However, experimental evidence indicates that completely false memories can be created, especially in young children. The following experiment illustrates this.

Children in a nursery school were told about a man called Sam Stone who was very clumsy and broke things. A month later, a man visited the school and spent some time in the classroom. Next day, the children were shown a ripped book and a grubby teddy bear. None of the children made connections between Sam Stone, the man who visited the school, and the damaged book and grubby toy. For the next ten weeks they were asked leading questions which suggested these connections – for example, 'I wonder if Sam Stone was wearing long pants or short pants when he ripped the book?' At the end of ten weeks, 72% of the children blamed Sam Stone for the damage and 45% said they actually saw him do it. One child 'saw' Sam Stone paint melted chocolate on the bear, another 'saw' him rip the book in a temper, and another 'saw' him soak the book in warm water until it fell apart (Leichtman & Ceci, 1995). These 'eyewitness accounts' were, of course, based on completely false memories.

This type of evidence raises the possibility of false accusations, particularly in cases of alleged child abuse. The child's memory may be affected by repeated and suggestive questioning. False memories – which seem completely real to the child – may be created (Ceci & Bruck, 1993).

3.5 Effects of expectation

Sometimes memories of an event reflect the observer's expectations rather than what actually happened. This is known as *confirmation bias*. It is illustrated by the following experiment. Students from two universities in the United States were shown a film of a violent football game between their two teams. They reported afterwards that their opponents had committed many more fouls than their own team. This confirmed each group's bias in favour of their own team. Their memories were influenced by seeing their own team as the 'good guys' and the opposition as the 'bad guys'. The opposition were also seen as an inferior team who needed to commit fouls in order to have any chance of winning (Hastorf & Cantrill, 1954). Similar confirmation bias is seen regularly in Britain when people discuss a football match – the number of fouls committed by the opposition is often exaggerated and those committed by their own team minimised.

3.6 Violence and weapon focus

Another factor influencing memory for events is the degree of violence contained in the event. Loftus and Burns (1982) showed participants two filmed versions of a crime. In one version, the robbers made a clean getaway without any violence. In the other version, a small boy was shot in the face as the robbers escaped. Loftus and Burns found that the inclusion of violence in the film impaired participants' memory for other details occurring up to two minutes before the shooting happened. If violent events lead to poorer memory, this has major implications for the use of eyewitness testimony in cases of violent crime.

A related factor influencing eyewitness memory is *weapon focus*. This refers to an eyewitness's concentration on a weapon to the exclusion of other details of a crime. In crimes where a weapon is involved, it is not unusual for witnesses to be able to describe the weapon much more clearly than the person holding it! Loftus et al. (1987) showed participants a series of slides of a customer in a restaurant. There were two versions. In one version the customer was holding a gun, in the other version the same customer held a chequebook. Participants who saw the gun version tended to focus on the gun. As a result, they were less likely to identify the customer in an identity parade than those who had seen the chequebook version.

3.7 Limitations of experimental evidence

The experiments conducted on eyewitness testimony are usually more realistic than the more traditional laboratory experiments described in the first two chapters. They attempt to recreate and simulate actual events, they aim to be true-to-life. But, despite these efforts, they are not 'real'. Participants know they are experiments and this knowledge will, to some extent, affect their behaviour. And, because of this, generalisations from laboratory experiments must be treated with caution. This can be seen from comparing the findings of experiments with real-life eyewitness testimony.

A number of experiments have indicated that high levels of stress impair eyewitness memory. This is suggested by the Loftus experiments on violent crime and the weapon focus. However, the following evidence from an actual crime contradicts this view. A robber stole guns and money from a gunshop. There was a shootout on the street which resulted in the death of the robber and serious injury to the owner. Eyewitnesses who reported most stress provided the most accurate accounts of this event. Despite suffering nightmares as a result of their experience, these witnesses produced remarkably accurate and detailed accounts.

The eyewitnesses were interviewed by researchers 4-5 months after the incident. The researchers asked misleading questions in an attempt to distort their memories of the event. These questions had no effect – none of the eyewitnesses were misled. Again, this finding appears to contradict the results of a number of laboratory studies (Yuille & Cutshall, 1986).

This study does not necessarily undermine the findings of laboratory experiments. What it does do is suggest that these findings be treated with caution. And, it indicates the need for naturalistic observations – observation of behaviour in 'natural', real-life settings (Stephenson, 1996).

Key terms

Confirmation bias *The idea that people tend to seek out evidence that confirms their own beliefs and expectations. This can result in a biased and distorted memory of an event.*

Weapon focus *The tendency of an eyewitness to focus on a weapon to the exclusion of other aspects of an event.*

Summary

1. Eyewitness memory for an event can be distorted by leading questions and misleading information.

2. Some researchers argue that this means the original memory has been lost and replaced by a false one.

3. Others disagree. They argue that the original memory remains intact. The apparent change in memory is due to demand characteristics.

4. Memory involves a process of reconstruction. The addition of new information can form the basis for a reconstructed memory. This may result in confabulation.

5. Eyewitnesses are less likely to be misled if false information is obviously incorrect and refers to a central rather than peripheral aspect of the event.

6. There is evidence for the construction of completely false memories – memories of events that never happened.

7. The way in which an event is perceived and remembered is affected by the eyewitness's expectations.

8. Violent events can be more difficult to recall accurately, especially if a weapon is involved. Eyewitnesses tend to focus on the weapon to the exclusion of other aspects of the event.

9. Evidence from real-life eyewitness testimony appears to contradict some of the findings of laboratory experiments.

Activity 3   Memory for events

Item A   Crowd trouble

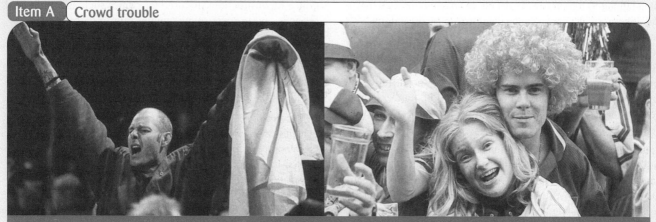

There has been trouble at a football match. Eyewitnesses have been asked to identify the troublemaker from a series of photographs. Most chose the man on the left.

Item B   Sexual abuse

In 1988, Margaret Michaels, a 26-year-old nursery school teacher from New Jersey was sentenced to 47 years in prison for sexually abusing children in her care. Apart from the children, there were no other witnesses and no physical evidence of abuse. However, the testimonies of 19 child witnesses were remarkably consistent. For example, they all stated that Ms Michaels danced naked round the classroom and forced them to strip. The social workers who conducted the interviews often asked leading and suggestive questions. They told the children that Ms Michaels was a bad person, urged them to describe acts which they had previously said didn't happen, and offered them bribes for information. After 5 years, the appeals court overturned the verdict on the grounds that the children's testimony could not be trusted.

Adapted from Brehm et al., 1999

Item C   Bank robbery

One hundred and ten eyewitnesses to bank robberies were interviewed. Some had been bystanders, others were bank workers who had been directly threatened by the robbers. The bankworkers recalled more than the bystanders. Even after 15 months, they still recalled a wide range of detail from the event, including not only the weapons of the bank robbers but their clothing and their behaviour.

Adapted from Christianson & Hubinette, 1993

Questions

1   Use the idea of confirmation bias to explain why most people chose the man on the left in Item A.

2   What light can studies of false memory syndrome throw on the case in Item B?

3   Why does the study in Item C suggest that experimental evidence should be treated with caution?

Unit 4 Improving eyewitness memory

KEY ISSUES

1. **Can hypnosis improve eyewitness memory?**

2. **Do police reconstructions improve eyewitness testimony?**

3. **Are there ways of questioning witnesses which increase the accuracy of their testimony?**

So far, this chapter has focused on the factors that contribute to the low reliability of eyewitness testimony. This unit looks at ways in which eyewitness testimony might be improved.

4.1   Hypnosis

Occasionally there are newspaper reports of an eyewitness being helped to remember the details of an event through the use of hypnosis. Hypnosis helps witnesses to relax, and, in theory, allows the hypnotist to reconstruct the known details of the event in the mind of the witness. The use of hypnosis has met with mixed results. In 1977, a bus driver, whose bus containing 26 children had been hijacked, was successfully hypnotised to recall all but one of the letters and numbers on the registration plate of the hijackers' van. The three suspects were tracked down.

However, an analysis of the results of the large number of studies on hypnosis and eyewitness testimony found that there was no evidence that hypnosis reliably aided recall (Orne et al., 1984). If anything, hypnosis results in more confabulation as the suggestible witness 'remembers' false details. Hypnosis makes people less cautious. This can lead to 'memories' of events that never happened.

Putnam (1979) showed how suggestible hypnotised witnesses

could be. Participants were shown a videotape of an accident involving a car and a bicycle. After a delay, they answered a series of questions about the accident. Some of the participants were later hypnotised. They were told that under hypnosis it would be possible for them to see the entire accident again, only this time they would be able to slow it down and zoom in on details if they chose to. Putnam found that more errors were made by the participants who had been hypnotised, especially when leading questions were asked. Participants who were hypnotised were more open to suggestion than those who were not hypnotised.

Given these considerations, it is not surprising that British courts are very unlikely to accept testimony based on hypnosis.

4.2   Police reconstructions

Police reconstructions are used for crimes such as murder and robbery, and in cases of missing persons. In cases of robbery, reconstructions are filmed for television programmes such as *Crimewatch*. In murder cases, a person dressed in similar clothes to the victim retraces the victim's last known movements. This usually takes place a week later, in the same place and at the same time.

The aim of reconstructions is twofold. First, to obtain eyewitnesses who have not yet come forward. Second, to 'jog the memory' of eyewitnesses who have come forward – they are invited to attend the reconstruction. The hope is that they will remember further details of the victim's movements, and, in particular, any other persons who were in the vicinity. The person representing the victim is accompanied by police officers who question people along the route.

Reconstructions are based on the idea of cue-dependent recall. In the above example, the cues are similar clothes, time and place. As the previous chapter indicated, recall is more likely when the context at encoding matches the context at retrieval (see p26).

Reconstructions sometime produce useful information. However, a word of warning is necessary. As this chapter has shown, testimony is often inaccurate when eyewitnesses are reporting on actual events. A reconstruction, which does not exactly mirror the real thing, may lead to further inaccuracies. In particular, it may lead to confabulation – the adding of false detail to the memory of an event.

4.3 Cognitive interviewing

The *cognitive interview* aims to help eyewitnesses recall events accurately. It is based on four general principles.

* It aims to reinstate the environmental and personal context of the crime in the mind of the witness. This includes sights, sounds, smells, feelings and emotions.
* It asks witnesses to report every detail, even if they think that the detail is trivial.
* It encourages witnesses to recount the details of the event in different orders.
* It asks witnesses to report the incident from a range of perspectives, including those of other bystanders, or even those of the criminals themselves (Geiselman et al., 1985).

A laboratory experiment compared the cognitive interview with a standard police interview and hypnosis. A standard police interview asks witnesses to recall the event and then answer detailed questions about the aspects of the event that the police think are important. Participants watched a short film of a violent crime. Two days later, they were divided into three groups and interviewed by a police officer. Participants interviewed using the standard police interview made an average of 29.4 correct statements. Participants interviewed using the cognitive interview made an average of 41.1 correct statements. Those interviewed using hypnosis produced an average of 38.0 correct statements (Geiselman et al., 1985).

Leading questions A further experiment investigated whether the cognitive interview could reduce the influence of leading questions. Participants watched a film of an incident in which

an intruder carrying a blue backpack entered a classroom. They were asked the leading question, 'Was the guy with the green backpack nervous?' Later on, they were questioned about the event using either the cognitive interview or the standard police interview. Those questioned using the cognitive interview were less likely to be influenced by the leading question. They were more likely to correctly recall that the intruder was carrying a blue backpack (Geiselman et al., 1985).

The enhanced cognitive interview

A revised version of the cognitive interview – the *enhanced cognitive interview* – was developed by Fisher et al., (1987). It encouraged interviewers to use open-ended questions (eg, 'What did the suspect do next?') rather than fixed-choice questions which often result in very short answers (eg, 'Did the suspect walk or run?' Answer – 'He ran.'). Interviewers were also encouraged to follow the witness's train of thought. For example, if a witness remembered a detail 'out of sequence', they should be questioned about that detail there and then rather than waiting for its 'proper place' in the sequence of events to come round.

The enhanced cognitive interview was tested in a laboratory experiment. Participants were questioned about a violent crime. Those interviewed with the enhanced cognitive interview correctly recalled 45% more details than those interviewed with the basic cognitive interview. However, this improvement was accompanied by a 28% increase in the number of incorrect statements (Fisher et al., 1987).

Evidence from outside the laboratory indicates the benefits of the enhanced cognitive interview. Police in Miami were trained in this technique. It resulted in a 46% increase in the number of details reported by eyewitnesses. Where additional evidence was available to assess their statements, it appeared that 90% of the reported details were correct (Fisher et al., 1990).

These studies make an obvious but important point – the way eyewitnesses are questioned can make a significant difference to what they remember and report.

Summary

1. The use of hypnosis to improve eyewitness memory has produced mixed results.

2. Police reconstructions may improve eyewitness testimony, but they may lead to confabulation.

3. Techniques such as the cognitive interview can improve the detail and accuracy of eyewitness testimony.

Key terms

Cognitive interview *An interviewing technique which aims to improve the detail and accuracy of eyewitness testimony.*

Enhanced cognitive interview *A revised version of the cognitive interview.*

References

Allport, G.W. & Postman, L.J. (1947). *The psychology of rumour.* New York: Holt.

Baddeley, A.D. (1997). *Human memory: Theory and practice* (2nd ed.). Hove: Psychology Press.

Bartlett, F.C. (1932). *Remembering: A study in experimental and social psychology.* New York: Macmillan.

Brehm, S.S., Kassin, S.M. & Fein, S. (1999). *Social psychology* (4th ed.). Boston MA: Houghton Mifflin.

Buckhout, R. (1980). Nearly 2,000 witnesses can be wrong. *Bulletin of*

the Psychonomic Society, 16, 307-310.

Ceci, S.J. & Bruck, M. (1993). Suggestibility of the child witness: A historical review and synthesis. *Psychological Bulletin, 113,* 403-439.

Christianson, S.A. & Hubinette, B. (1993). Hands up! A study of witnesses' emotional reactions and memories associated with bank robberies. *Applied Cognitive Psychology, 7,* 365-379.

Cohen, G. (1996). *Memory in the real world* (2nd ed.). Hove: Psychology Press.

Doob, A.N. & Kirshenbaum, H.M. (1973). Bias in police lineups –

partial remembering. *Journal of Police Science and Administration, 1,* 287-293.

Eysenck, M.W. (1993). *Principles of cognitive psychology.* Hove: Erlbaum.

Fisher, R.P., Geiselman, R.E. & Amador, M. (1990). A field test of the cognitive interview: Enhancing the recollections of actual victims and witnesses of crime. *Journal of Applied Psychology, 74,* 722-727.

Fisher, R.P., Geiselman, R.E., Raymond, D.S., Jurkevich, L.M. & Warhaftig, M.L. (1987). Enhancing enhanced eyewitness memory: Refining the cognitive interview. *Journal of Police Science and Administration, 15,* 291-297.

Fruzetti, A.E., Toland, K., Teller, S.A. & Loftus, E.F. (1992). Memory and eyewitness testimony. In M. Gruneberg & P. Morris (Eds.), *Aspects of memory: The practical aspects.* London: Routledge.

Geiselman, R.E., Fisher, R.P., MacKinnon, D.P. & Holland, H.L. (1985). Eyewitness memory enhancement in police interview: Cognitive retrieval mnemonics versus hypnosis. *Journal of Applied Psychology, 70,* 401-412.

Hastorf, A.H. & Cantrill, H. (1954). They saw a game: A case study. *Journal of Abnormal and Social Psychology, 97,* 399-401.

Leichtman, M.D. & Ceci, S.J. (1995). The effects of stereotypes and suggestions on preschoolers' reports. *Developmental Psychology, 31,* 568-578.

Lindsay, D.S. (1990). Misleading suggestions can impair eyewitnesses' ability to remember event details. *Journal of Experimental Psychology: Learning, Memory and Cognition, 16,* 1077-1083.

Lindsay, R.C.L., Lea, J.A., Nosworthy, G.J., Fulford, J.A., Hector, J., Le Van, V. & Seabrook, C. (1991). Biased lineups: Sequential presentation reduces the problem. *Journal of Applied Psychology, 76,* 741-745.

Loftus, E.F. (1974). Reconstructing memory: The incredible eyewitness. *Psychology Today, 8,* 116-119.

Loftus, E.F. & Burns, T.E. (1982). Mental shock can produce retrograde amnesia. *Memory and Cognition, 10,* 318-323.

Loftus, E.F. & Greene, E. (1980). Warning: Even memory for faces may be contagious. *Law and Human Behaviour, 4,* 323-334.

Loftus, E.F., Loftus, G.R. & Messo, J. (1987). Some facts about 'weapon focus'. *Law and Human Behaviour, 11,* 55-62.

Loftus, E.F. & Palmer, J.C. (1974). Reconstruction of automobile destruction: An example of the interaction between language and memory. *Journal of Verbal Learning and Verbal Behavior, 13,* 585-589.

Malpass, R.S. & Devine, P.G. (1981). Eyewitness identification: Lineup instructions and the absence of the offender. *Journal of Applied Psychology, 66,* 482-489.

McCloskey, M. & Zaragoza, M.S. (1985). Misleading postevent information and memory for events: Arguments and evidence against memory impairment hypotheses. *Journal of Experimental Psychology: General, 114,* 1-16.

Neisser, U. (1978). Memory: What are the important questions? In M.M. Gruneberg, P.E. Morris & R.N. Sykes (Eds.), *Practical aspects of memory.* London: Academic Press.

Orne, M.T., Soskis, D.A., Dinges, D.F. & Orne, E.C. (1984). Hypnotically-induced testimony. In G.L. Wells & E.F. Loftus (eds.), *Eyewitness testimony: Psychological perspectives.* New York: Cambridge University Press.

Platz, S.J. & Hosch, H.M. (1988). Cross-racial/ethnic eyewitness identification: A field study. *Journal of Applied Social Psychology, 18,* 972-984.

Putnam, B. (1979). Hypnosis and distortions in eyewitness memory. *International Journal of Clinical and Experimental Hypnosis, 27,* 437-448.

Stephenson, G.M. (1996). Applied social psychology. In M. Hewstone, W. Stroebe & G.M. Stephenson (Eds.), *Introduction to social psychology* (2nd ed.). Oxford: Blackwell.

Wells, G.L. (1993). What do we know about eyewitness identification? *American Psychologist, 48,* 553-571.

Young, A.W., Hay, D.C. & Ellis, A.W. (1985). The faces that launched a thousand slips: Everyday difficulties and errors in recognising people. *British Journal of Psychology, 76,* 495-523.

Yuille, J.C. & Cutshall, J.L. (1986). A case study of eyewitness memory of a crime. *Journal of Applied Psychology, 71,* 291-301.

Introduction

Think of a mother duck swimming along with her ducklings following her in single file. It is as if there is some kind of tie between them.

Think of a mother sitting on a park bench on a warm spring day. Her two-year-old son toddles around on the grass. Every now and again he returns to his mother just to touch her knee or smile at her. He never wanders far. Again, it is as if there is a tie between them.

This invisible tie joins the young to their caregivers. Psychologists believe that it is important for the young of many species, both human and non-human, to form a close relationship with their caregivers – their survival may depend on it. For example, young animals who have a tendency to wander off may be unable to find food, they may injure themselves, they may be killed. Clearly, a strong tie to a caregiver is a valuable asset – it promotes survival.

For the relationship to be effective it needs to work both ways – the young must be tied to caregivers *and* caregivers need to be tied to the young. For example, if parents don't establish a close relationship with their children, they may neglect them – they may not feed them properly or they may not protect them.

In humans, the tie between infant and caregiver is known as attachment. This chapter looks at attachment.

Chapter summary

- **Unit 1 looks at the development of attachments.**
- **Unit 2 outlines the main types of attachment.**
- **Unit 3 looks at explanations for different types of attachment.**
- **Unit 4 examines the relationship between** culture and attachment types.
- **Unit 5 looks at the relationship between attachment types and later life.**
- **Unit 6 outlines and assesses various theories of attachment.**

Unit 1 The development of attachments

KEY ISSUES

1 What are the stages of development of attachments?
2 How is attachment related to other aspects of the infant's development?

1.1 Attachment

Attachment is a strong, long-lasting emotional tie or bond to a particular individual. Psychologists believe that it is both normal and healthy for infants to form an attachment to one or more of their caregivers, and that this attachment is important for later development.

One of the most influential child psychologists, John Bowlby, suggested that a single, primary attachment relationship is essential for the healthy psychological development of the child. In his view, this first and most important attachment is ideally with the mother or a 'mother figure'. He believed that, 'mother love in infancy and childhood is as important for mental health as are vitamins and proteins for physical health' (Bowlby, 1951).

Attachments in infancy usually have the following characteristics.

- They are selective – they are formed with specific individuals.
- They involve proximity seeking – efforts are made to be physically close or near to the attachment figure.
- They provide comfort and security.
- They lead to distress on separation from the attachment figure (Schaffer, 1996).

This unit looks at the development of attachment between infants and caregivers. Most psychologists see it as a gradual process. Attachments are not created in an instant – they develop over a period of months.

1.2 Stages of attachment

Most researchers believe that attachment develops through a series of stages. Two of the most influential accounts of the development of attachment are by Rudolph Schaffer and Peggy Emerson (1964) and John Bowlby (1969). Both accounts suggest three main stages to the attachment process.

Stage 1 Birth to 6 weeks

Schaffer and Emerson called this the *asocial stage*. Asocial means non-social. According to Schaffer and Emerson, babies during this period do not act in a social manner. They respon

Table 1	Stages of attachment

Stage 1   Birth to around 6 weeks – asocial or pre-attachment stage

Stage 2   6 weeks to 7 months – indiscriminate attachments or attachment-in-the-making

Stage 3   From 7 months – specific attachments or clear-cut attachment

Key terms

Attachment *A strong, long-lasting emotional tie to a particular individual.*

Proximity seeking *Seeking to remain physically close to an attachment figure.*

to people in much the same way as they do to balloons, puppets and anything else that comes their way. Nor do they show any recognition of individual people. Everyone is much the same as everyone else, and everything else, at this stage.

Bowlby did not entirely agree. Whilst he accepted that infants at this stage make little or no distinction between different people, he did believe that they are equipped with a range of behaviours (including crying, babbling, smiling, clinging and reaching) that form the basis for *sociability* – for behaving in social ways towards people. These behaviours are designed to create and maintain proximity (physical closeness) with the primary caregiver – ordinarily the mother. For example, crying brings the mother to the infant, clinging keeps her close. Bowlby's version of this stage is usually called the *pre-attachment phase* (Schaffer, 1966).

Later research suggests that human infants are not as asocial as Schaffer and Emerson claim. Infants appear more settled

Mother and baby

when held by their caregiver, and smile more broadly when they hear her (or his) voice. There is evidence that one-week-old babies are able to recognise their mother's face (Bushnell et al., 1989), and that two-week-old babies who have been breast-fed can identify their mother's smell (Cernoch & Porter, 1985). Stern (1977) claims that infants are innately prepared – they have an inborn *predisposition* – to look into their caregiver's eyes, look away and look back again in a kind of rhythmic social dance. Meltzoff and Moore (1977) showed that infants can imitate facial expressions, and Wolff (1969) sees crying as a sophisticated form of communication, with different types of cry meaning different things.

This evidence suggests that very young babies do respond in a special way to human beings, and that they are able to recognise specific individuals, in particular their main caregiver. However, researchers generally agree that actual attachment has not yet occurred.

Stage 2   From 6 weeks to 7 months

Schaffer and Emerson called this the *indiscriminate attachment* stage. Indiscriminate means making no distinctions, seeing no difference. According to Schaffer and Emerson, infants can now distinguish between people and things, and show a general sociability towards people. This claim is supported by Ahrens

(1954) who suggested that young children begin to smile 'socially' at around 6 weeks. Infants can now distinguish between familiar and unfamiliar people, but pay little attention to differences between individuals. They show no fear of strangers, will cry for attention from anyone and can be comforted by anyone.

Again, Bowlby did not entirely agree. He accepted that infants at this stage are not yet fully attached to a specific person. However, he suggested that they are beginning to distinguish between people, and are already showing a preference for one particular person – usually the mother. The infant is more likely to smile at the mother and be comforted by her when distressed. Bowlby's version of this stage is usually called the *attachment-in-the-making phase*.

Sociability is more developed and more clearly expressed at this stage. Infants show a clear preference for, and pleasure from, the company of other human beings. This can be seen from infants responding to and seeking responses from others, and from the pleasure they derive from this. Some researchers see sociability as an inborn tendency or predisposition (Buss & Plomin, 1984). They see it as the basis for the development of attachment.

Schaffer later divided Stage 2 into two parts: a) 6 weeks to 3 months when the infant shows a preference for human company and develops a general sociability towards people, and b) 3 to 7 months when the infant begins to distinguish between people and recognises familiar and unfamiliar people (Schaffer, 1977).

Stage 3   From 7 months

At around 7 months, Schaffer and Emerson suggest the infant enters the *specific attachment stage*, and forms a strong emotional bond with a particular individual. This individual is usually the mother, but not necessarily. Specific attachment is indicated by the infant showing distress when they are separated from the attachment figure or preferred adult. This is known as *separation protest* and is taken as evidence for *separation anxiety*. From around 7 months infants protest if separated from their attachment figure, and show special joy when they are reunited with them. The attachment figure can comfort them more effectively than anyone else. Schaffer and Emerson used separation protest as an indicator that attachment has occurred, as a way of identifying the main attachment figure, and as a way of measuring the strength of the attachment.

Around the same time that infants develop specific attachments and separation anxiety, they are also likely to develop *stranger anxiety* – a fear of strangers. It is no longer possible to leave an infant with just anyone without them showing distress. Infants are likely to withdraw from strangers, turn to the caregiver for support when a stranger is near, or whimper, cry or bawl in the presence of strangers.

Bowlby also sees this third stage as the time when the infant forms a strong emotional bond with an attachment figure. Like Schaffer and Emerson, he sees separation anxiety and stranger anxiety appearing at this stage. Bowlby notes how infants often become visibly upset and make strenuous efforts to maintain proximity when separated from their attachment figure. For example, they crawl after her or cry for her attention. Bowlby's version of this stage is usually called the *clear-cut attachment phase*.

Who is the primary attachment figure? For Bowlby, the first and most important attachment figure is nearly always the mother. In most cases, she is also the main caregiver – the main provider of emotional and physical care for the infant.

Schaffer and Emerson's (1964) research questions this view. They studied 60 infants in Scotland, observing them once a month from birth to 12 months, then again at 18 months. 60% of the infants formed their *primary attachment*, their first and most important attachment, with their mother. However, 40% formed their primary attachment with someone other than their mother – with their father, older sister or brother, or grandparent. Schaffer and Emerson found that caregiving, as such, was not the main basis for attachment. Infants did not necessarily form their primary attachment with the person who provided them with physical care – the person who fed, washed and dressed them and changed their nappies. Nor does the amount of time spent with the infant appear to be the basis for the primary attachment. Instead, infants were likely to form a primary attachment with the most responsive and stimulating person around them.

One or more attachments? Bowlby believed that infants form their main attachment with their mother. He accepted that they form other attachments but saw these as secondary – less important and less strong – compared to the primary attachment relationship. Schaffer and Emerson's research questions this 'special relationship'. Although most infants have only one attachment at 7 months, most have *multiple attachments* by 18 months – 29% had more than one attachment at 7 months; 60% more than one at 10 months; 87% more than one at 18 months.

Many of the infants who formed multiple attachments did not appear to have a primary attachment. In other words, their attachments with various people were equally strong – there was no special relationship with one particular attachment figure.

Evaluation

This section has focused on the development of attachment and the *stages* this development goes through. Many researchers believe that most children in all societies go through these stages in much the same way. If this is so, then the idea of stages is a useful model for the first part of a child's development.

However, there are a number of problems with this view.

- First, the idea of stages suggests that early development is 'fixed' – that children automatically go through particular stages at particular ages. In fact, development is more fluid than this. Although most children do appear to follow this general path of development, the age at which they do so varies more than the model suggests.
- Second, there are important differences between infants in

terms of their attachment behaviour. Some may become more securely attached than others. This point will be examined in the following unit.
- Third, before reaching any firm conclusions about stages of development, the idea needs to be examined in different societies with different patterns of childrearing. The stage model was first developed from observations of children raised in Western societies. It may not apply to other societies. This point will be examined in Unit 4.

1.3   Attachment and development

Social development As noted earlier, psychologists see the formation of attachments as a normal and healthy part of the child's development. In particular, it is a major part of the child's *social development* – the development of social skills and the ability to form relationships with others. This aspect of the child's development is linked to other aspects of development such as cognitive and physical development.

Cognitive development This refers to the development of thinking, reasoning and problem-solving skills. An important aspect of cognitive development is the ability to form *schemas* (see pp 34-35). A schema is an organised framework of information which represents things in the world. In order to form specific attachments, the infant will need to develop basic schemas of their attachment figures which will include what they look like, what they do, and the infant's relationship with them.

In order to form these schemas, infants need to develop the concept of *object permanence* – an awareness that when an object is no longer visible, it still exists (Piaget, 1957). Very young infants lose interest in an object which moves out of sight. If you shake a rattle in front of them and then hide it, they turn their attention elsewhere. Some researchers believe that object permanence develops around the age of 7 months, when specific attachments and separation anxiety appear. Object permanence means that the infant realises that when their attachment figure is out of sight, they are still somewhere but

Key terms

Asocial Non-social. Responding in similar ways to inanimate objects and people.

Sociability A preference for, and pleasure from, the company of other human beings. Behaviour which fosters the development of attachment and social relationships in general.

Indiscriminate attachments Having equal preference for various people.

Specific attachment Forming an attachment to a particular person who is preferred to others.

Multiple attachments Forming attachments with two or more people.

Primary attachment The first and most important attachment relationship.

Separation protest Protest at separation from an attachment figure.

Separation anxiety The anxiety felt when separated from an attachment figure.

Stranger anxiety The anxiety felt in the presence of a stranger.

not with them. This awareness is important for the formation of attachments and for the development of separation anxiety. As Schaffer and Emerson (1964) noted, separation anxiety and separation protest appear around 7 months, the time at which object permanence develops.

Visual perception Research indicates that the newborn infant's vision is more fuzzy and blurred than an adult's (Atkinson & Braddick, 1981). As infants' visual perception develops, they are increasingly capable of making fine distinctions which are necessary to recognise things, particularly individual faces. This development is important – it allows the infant to distinguish between people and helps them to recognise their attachment figures.

As infants grow older, their interest in human faces increases as does their ability to distinguish between different faces and respond to different facial expressions. In one experiment infants were shown a picture of a human face and two other pictures in which the facial features were scrambled (see Item A, Activity 1). At one month, infants showed no preference between the three 'faces', at two months they showed a marked preference for the realistic face (Maurer & Berrera, 1981). By the age of four months, it appears that infants not only distinguish between different facial expressions, but respond appropriately to them, for example by smiling at a picture of a happy face (Serrano et al., 1995). These developments, indicated by evidence from experiments, mirror the development of sociability at Stage 2.

Physical development This also plays a role in attachment. Separation anxiety begins around the time the child starts to crawl. This is when proximity seeking – the attempt to stay close to the attachment figure – becomes especially important. In Bowlby's view, from around 7 months infants use their attachment figure as a *secure base*. The infant is starting to crawl and is becoming increasingly mobile. They use their attachment figure as a base from which to explore the world around them. Every so often they come back and 'touch base' before returning to their explorations. In this way, the attachment figure provides a safe and secure base from which

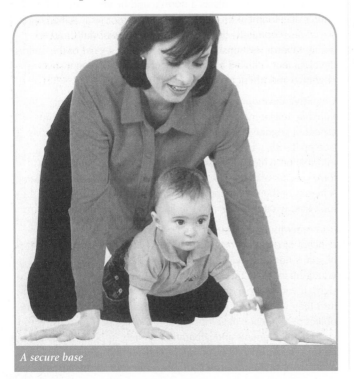

A secure base

Key terms

Social development *The development of social skills and the ability to form relationships with others.*

Cognitive development *The development of thinking, reasoning and problem-solving skills.*

Object permanence *An awareness that when an object is no longer visible it still exists.*

Schema *An organised framework of information which represents things in the world.*

Secure base *The base provided by an attachment figure from which the infant can explore, and return to for security.*

infants investigate the world. This can be seen as the beginnings of independence.

Summary

1 Some researchers believe that attachment develops through a number of stages.

2 Three main stages have been identified.
   - The asocial or pre-attachment stage
   - Indiscriminate attachments or attachment-in-the-making
   - Specific attachments or clear-cut attachment.

3 Separation anxiety and stranger anxiety appear when infants have formed one or more specific attachments.

4 Bowlby believed that infants form a strong emotional bond with a primary attachment figure – usually the mother. All other attachments are secondary – less important and less strong.

5 Research evidence indicates that infants are likely to form primary attachments with the most responsive and stimulating person around them who may or may not be the mother and/or main caregiver.

6 Evidence suggests that most infants have formed multiple attachments by the age of 18 months.

7 The idea of stages for the development of attachment has been criticised. In particular, the process appears more fluid than fixed stages suggest.

8 The development of attachment is related to other aspects of the infant's development – for example, their cognitive and physical development.

Activity 1   Attachment

Item A   Looking at 'faces'

This bar graph shows the average length of time babies aged 1 month and 2 months spent looking at the 3 'faces'.

Average time spent looking (seconds)

Legend: 1 month / 2 months

Adapted from Maurer & Barrera, 1981

Item B   Object permanence

A five-month-old infant sees a toy placed under a cloth and learns to find it there. When it is placed under a second cloth, he looks again under the first cloth.

Adapted from Piaget, 1957

Item C   Collective childrearing

Children and metapelets on a kibbutz

In Israel about 3% of the population live in about 270 kibbutzim. These settlements vary in size from 100 – 2,000 members. Most are based on agriculture with some light industry.

Many kibbutzim had a system of collective childrearing, though today it has all but disappeared. Married couples shared a single bedroom/living room. Children spent most of the day and all of the night away from their parents in children's houses. They were cared for by metapelets – caregivers and educators.

Mothers visited their infants in the communal nursery four or five times a day. These visits continued for six months until breastfeeding stopped. Then parents spent about two hours a day, after work, with their children. This was seen as 'fun time'. It was the only time when parents and brothers and sisters came together as a group. As they grew up, children moved through a series of children's houses, the same age group staying together until adulthood. The peer group was an important source of security and companionship. Children of the same age group tended to see each other as brothers and sisters.

A study by Fox (1977) found that one and two-year-old children were equally attached to their mother and the metapelet who cared for them. Both provided a secure base for exploration and both could reassure the infant when they felt insecure. In some cases, although the children protested equally when left by either their mother or their metapelet, they appeared to be more comforted by their mother at reunion and more likely to seek her out. This may have been due to the fact that some metapelets came and went as often as every four months. Attachment appeared stronger when the metapelet was a more permanent figure.

Adapted from Bettelheim, 1969; Fox, 1977

Questions

1   a) What does the bar chart in Item A show?
    b) How might the findings of this research relate to the development of attachment?

2   What does the experiment in Item B suggest about the infant's ability to form specific attachments?

3   What support does Item C provide for the idea of multiple attachments?

Unit 2   Types of attachment

KEY ISSUES

1 How is attachment measured and classified?
2 What are the main types of attachment?

Like all relationships, attachment relationships vary – they are not all the same. This unit is concerned with differences between types of attachments. It looks at ways of assessing and classifying attachment relationships. In particular, it compares secure and insecure attachments between infants and caregivers.

2.1 Classifying attachment types: the Strange Situation

Mary Ainsworth and her colleagues designed an experiment to describe and assess the attachment relationship between caregiver and infant (Ainsworth et al., 1978). It is known as the Strange Situation because it takes place in an environment which is strange to the participants – a room with toys scattered around which can be observed by the researchers. The experiment contains a number of episodes which provide various measures of the attachment relationship. The procedure is outlined in Table 2.

The experiment is designed to become increasingly stressful for the infant. For example, in later episodes the infant is left alone, and in the company of a stranger. There are three main sources of possible distress.

- A strange or unfamiliar environment
- Separation from the caregiver
- The presence of a stranger.

Table 2   The Strange Situation

No. of episode	Persons	Time present	Activity
1	Caregiver, infant and and observer	30 secs	Observer shows caregiver and infant the experimental room then leaves.
2	Caregiver and infant	3 mins	Caregiver sits and watches, infant explores and plays with toys.
3	Stranger, caregiver and infant	3 mins	Stranger enters, silent at first, then talks to caregiver, then interacts with infant. Caregiver leaves room quietly.
4	Stranger and infant	3 mins	First separation from caregiver. Stranger interacts (talks and plays) with infant.
5	Caregiver and infant	3 mins	First reunion. Caregiver returns, stranger leaves. Caregiver greets, comforts and tries to settle infant. Caregiver leaves and says goodbye.
6	Infant alone	3 mins	Second separation. Infant left alone in room.
7	Stranger and infant	3 mins	Continuation of second separation. Stranger enters and interacts with infant.
8	Caregiver and infant	3 mins	Second reunion. Caregiver enters, greets infant and picks infant up. Stranger leaves quietly.

Adapted from Ainsworth et al., 1978

The experiment provides various measures of the attachment relationship. They include the following.

- The infant's reaction to separation from their caregiver.
- The infant's reaction to reunion with their caregiver.
- The infant's reaction to the presence of a stranger.
- The infant's willingness to explore a strange environment with their caregiver, with a stranger, or alone.

The experiment lasts around 21 minutes and is normally used with infants from 12 to 18 months old. If the infant becomes very upset, or the caregiver wants to return, then episodes 4, 6 or 7 are cut short (ie, when the infant is left either alone, or with the stranger). The caregiver in most experiments is the mother.

2.2 Types of attachment

Ainsworth identified three types of attachments from observations of a large sample of infants in the Strange Situation (Ainsworth et al., 1978).

Securely attached When the caregiver is present, the infant explores the strange environment, plays happily with the toys, and uses the caregiver as a secure base. The infant shows moderate distress when separated from the caregiver, goes to her for comfort when she returns, and is easily soothed. The infant clearly prefers the caregiver to the stranger.

Insecurely attached – avoidant The infant pays little attention to the caregiver and shows little concern when she leaves. For her part, the caregiver tends to ignore the infant. The infant shows little stranger anxiety and, if distressed, is as likely to be comforted and calmed down by the stranger as by the caregiver. On reunion with the caregiver, the infant makes little effort to renew contact and sometimes actively avoids contact by looking or turning away. Shows no real preference for caregiver or stranger.

Insecurely attached – resistant The infant is very distressed when separated from the caregiver and is difficult to comfort on reunion. The infant rushes to her but may show anger, and struggle to be put down. The caregiver's behaviour is similarly inconsistent – sometimes rejecting and angry toward the infant, sometimes overly sensitive and responsive. The infant tends to ignore the stranger and resists the stranger's attempts to interact and provide comfort. Exploration of the environment is limited as the infant has difficulty moving away from the caregiver.

A fourth attachment type, insecure attachment – disorganised, was later suggested by Main and Solomon (1986)

Insecure attachment – disorganised The infant shows no set pattern of behaviour at separation or reunion, hence the term 'disorganised'. They may appear wary of the caregiver rather than the stranger, and may move towards the caregiver yet not look at her. This kind of behaviour is associated with abused infants or those whose mothers are severely depressed.

The above classification was based on studies of infants in the USA, where most of the experiments using the Strange Situation have been conducted. Most researchers use the first three classifications. A survey of 18 studies from the USA reveals the following percentages of infants in each of these three classifications – secure 65%; avoidant 21%; resistant 14% (van IJzendoorn & Kroonenberg, 1988).

Most researchers see a secure attachment as 'normal' and 'best'. This is based on the view that a secure attachment is the most beneficial for the child's later development. Some research indicates that children with secure attachments in infancy are more likely to be popular with their peers, friendly and cooperative; independent and confident with strangers; curious, ready to investigate and eager to learn; positive in their outlook and emotionally mature (Carlson & Stroufe, 1995). Other research suggests that insecurely attached children are more likely to be hostile and socially inadequate (Bretherton, 1985). The relationship between attachment types and later development is examined in Unit 5.

Key term

Strange Situation *An experimental procedure designed to measure and classify attachment relationships between infants and caregivers.*

2.3 Stability of attachment

Various questions arise concerning attachment. How stable is the attachment relationship over time? For example, if an infant has a secure attachment at 12 months, is it likely to remain secure at 18 months? How stable is the attachment relationship with different attachment figures at the same time period? For example, if an infant has a secure relationship with their mother at 12 months, is a secure relationship with their father at 12 months also likely?

Research indicates that if family circumstances do not change and are fairly stress-free, then the type of attachment relationship is likely to remain the same from 12 to 18 months. In other words, a stable family environment leads to a stable attachment, both with the same attachment figure over time, and with different attachment figures at the same time. For example, one study using the Strange Situation found that only 2 out of 50 infants (4%) changed their type of attachment between 12 and 18 months (Waters, 1978).

The type of attachment is more likely to be unstable, ie to change, when the infant's family situation is unstable. The change is usually from a secure to an insecure attachment. This tends to occur when there is conflict between the parents, unemployment, or illness in the family. Unstable attachments are also linked to poverty. All these situations place pressure on the family.

2.4 The Strange Situation – evaluation

The Strange Situation has been described as 'the most powerful and useful procedure' for the study of infant development (Lamb et al., 1985). It is widely used and has generated a massive amount of research. The following reasons have been given for this positive evaluation.

- The Strange Situation is easily replicated – its systematic procedures allow the experiment to be repeated under the same conditions. This means that all the infants are responding to a similar situation. As a result, differences in their behaviour are not due to differences in the experiment.
- The Strange Situation provides a variety of measures for assessing the attachment relationship. This is important as a single measure can give a false impression. For example, the

attachment may appear secure if an infant is moderately distressed when *separated* from their caregiver. However, when *reunited* with their caregiver, the infant might do their best to escape from her arms. Only when this further measure – reunion – is used, does it become possible to classify the attachment as insecure-avoidant.

- Research evidence indicates the possibility that different types of attachment, as measured by the Strange Situation, may have different effects on the child's development. If this is so, then it gives a real point to studying and classifying attachment patterns from 12 to 18 months. The relationship between attachment types and later development is examined in Unit 5.

Not all evaluations of the Strange Situation have been so positive. There are three main criticisms of the procedure.

- First, it has been criticised for being unrealistic. This means the setting for the experiment is not true to life, it does not reflect everyday situations. As a result, it may not be possible to generalise the findings to real-life settings. If this is so, the Strange Situation lacks ecological validity. As its name suggests, the Strange Situation provides a strange and unfamiliar environment for the caregiver and infant. Does their attachment classification reflect the Strange Situation rather than their actual attachment? Research indicates that attachment appears much stronger in the Strange Situation than when caregiver and infant are observed at home (Bronfenbrenner, 1979). Clearly, in this setting, the situation is less strange.
- Second, the Strange Situation was created in the USA and the classification of attachment types was based on studies of American infants. Can the same procedures and the same classifications be applied to other societies with different cultures? If the answer is no, as some researchers argue, then the use of the Strange Situation is limited to the USA or, at

Summary

1. The Strange Situation is normally used with infants from age 12 to 18 months. It measures and classifies the attachment relationship between the infant and their main caregiver – usually the mother.

2. Four main types of attachment relationship have been identified. Most researchers use the first three. The four types are:
   - Secure
   - Insecure-avoidant
   - Insecure-resistant
   - Insecure-disorganised.

3. Attachment relationships are usually stable from 12 to 18 months if family circumstances remain the same during that time. They are more likely to change if family circumstances change.

4. The Strange Situation is easily replicated. It provides a variety of measures for assessing the attachment relationship.

5. The Strange Situation has been criticised
   - for lacking ecological validity – it may not be possible to generalise its findings to other settings;
   - as ethically unsound – it may result in stress for infants and caregivers.

best, to Western societies. Again, this questions the ecological validity of the Strange Situation. This point will be examined in Unit 4.

- Third, the ethics of the Strange Situation have been questioned. Is it acceptable to place infants and caregivers in situations which can produce mild and, in some cases, extreme anxiety? As noted earlier, certain episodes in the experiment are cut short if the infant appears extremely distressed. And, the caregiver can return if she feels the infant really needs her. Even so, should these situations be allowed to arise in the first place? Many researchers would argue that any distress has only short-term effects and that these are outweighed by the benefits of the research.

Unit 3 Explaining attachment types

KEY ISSUES

1 What effect does the caregiver's behaviour have on the attachment relationship?

2 What effect does the infant's temperament have on the attachment relationship?

3 What effect do the circumstances of the family have on the attachment relationship?

3.1 Attachment and the caregiver

A number of researchers believe that the behaviour of the primary caregiver, usually the mother, shapes the attachment relationship. Different types of behaviour from the mother will therefore lead to different types of attachment. For example, the *sensitivity hypothesis* states that the more responsive mothers are to infants during their early months, the more secure the attachment will be at 12 months (Ainsworth & Bell, 1969).

Mary Ainsworth and her colleagues studied infants throughout their first 12 months (Ainsworth et al., 1978). They found the following relationships between attachment type and the mother's behaviour.

Secure attachment Mothers are sensitive to the infant's needs. They respond appropriately and readily to the infant's signals and communicate positively. They provide warmth and close physical contact, especially when the infant is distressed. They are accepting, cooperative and accessible to the child. This is likely to result in a secure attachment at 12 months.

Insecure-avoidant Mothers are not sensitive and responsive to the infant's signals. They tend to be impatient and neglect the infant.

Insecure-resistant The mother's behaviour is inconsistent. She sometimes responds positively and sensitively, at other times she ignores the infant's attempts to gain her attention.

Evaluation These suggested links between the mother's behaviour and the type of attachment are neat and tidy and appear to make sense. For example, the behaviour of the infant in an insecure-resistant attachment is inconsistent and this reflects their mother's inconsistent behaviour.

A survey of research from the USA provides support for the view that sensitive and responsive mothering leads to secure attachment (Lamb et al., 1985). However, the link between the mother's behaviour and other types of attachment is not as clear-cut as Ainsworth's research indicates. Research from outside the USA raises further questions. For example, research in Germany found no difference in sensitivity between mothers with securely attached children and mothers with insecure-

avoidant children (Grossmann et al., 1985). This research will be examined in more detail in Unit 4.

The sensitivity hypothesis places the major responsibility for the type of attachment on the mother's shoulders. And, if different types of attachment have different effects on the child's development, then the mother can be praised or blamed. However, as the following section suggests, this may be uncalled for.

3.2 Attachment and infant temperament

There are two sides to a relationship. In terms of the attachment relationship, the two sides are caregiver and infant. The previous section looked at the mother's contribution to the attachment relationship. This section looks at the infant's contribution. It examines the argument that differences in infants' *temperament* can result in different types of attachment. This is known as the *temperament hypothesis* (Kagan, 1984). It states that infants rather than caregivers shape the attachment relationship.

Temperament refers to personality, to an individual's characteristics. For example, infants can be even-tempered or irritable, responsive or withdrawn, active or inactive, soothed easily or with difficulty. A longitudinal study – a study of the same group over time – of 138 infants in New York by Thomas and Chess (1977) classified 40% of the infants as having 'easy' temperaments, 10% 'difficult' temperaments, 15% as 'slow to warm up' and 35% as 'mixed'. Since many aspects of temperament are evident during the first weeks of life and continue into adulthood, some researchers, including Thomas and Chess, assume they are largely inborn or innate.

What effect does infant temperament have on the attachment relationship? There is some evidence to support the temperament hypothesis. For example, one study found that newborn babies who became upset when their feeding was interrupted were more likely to be classified as insecurely attached at 12 months (Miyake et al., 1985). However, other studies have found no relationship between temperament and type of attachment (Vaughn et al., 1989).

Evaluation The evidence relating to the temperament hypothesis is inconclusive – no firm conclusion can be reached. Some researchers argue that the attachment relationship is probably shaped by a combination of the infant's temperament and the mother's behaviour (Belsky & Rovine, 1987).

One study indicated that the mother's responsiveness was influenced by her perception of the infant's temperament. Mothers who saw their children as 'difficult' became less responsive to them by 24 months (Spangler, 1990). Research such as this suggests that a combination of the sensitivity hypothesis and the temperament hypothesis explains attachment type.

Some researchers argue that many aspects of the infant's temperament are inborn. They imply that these characteristics are fixed at birth and largely unchangeable. However, temperament is also shaped by a child's experiences. For example, a child who cries easily but is effectively comforted by their mother may learn to cry less. Again, this suggests that what matters is a combination of infant temperament and caregiver response.

3.3 Attachment and family circumstances

As Section 2.3 indicated, changes in family circumstances can lead to changes in the type of attachment relationship. This suggests that factors other than the sensitivity of the main caregiver and the temperament of the child will affect attachment relationships.

In general, research indicates that attachment types in middle-class families are stable between 12 and 18 months. However, major changes in family life, such as the mother taking a job

Key terms

Sensitivity hypothesis *The idea that the more responsive and sensitive mothers are to infants during their early months, the more secure the attachment relationship will be at 12 months.*

Temperament *An individual's personality, their characteristics.*

Temperament hypothesis *The idea that differences in infants' temperament can result in different types of attachment.*

Summary

1. Research from the USA provides support for the sensitivity hypothesis in terms of secure attachment. However, the link between sensitivity and other types of attachment is not particularly strong.

2. Evidence relating to the temperament hypothesis is inconclusive – no firm conclusion can be reached.

3. Some researchers argue that a combination of the mother's sensitivity and the infant's temperament shape the attachment relationship.

4. Family circumstances and social class can affect attachment relationships.

outside the home, can lead to a change in attachment. In one study of middle-class families, 47% of infants and mothers changed their type of attachment relationship from 12 to 19 months in response to a change in family circumstances (Thompson et al., 1982).

Such changes are more common in low-income families. For example, unemployment, illness and marital breakup are more common in families living in poverty (Haralambos & Holborn, 2000). A study of low-income families indicated that a third of mothers and infants changed their type of attachment – usually from secure to insecure – from 12 to 18 months (Vaughn et al., 1979).

Conclusion The evidence presented in this unit suggests that no one factor can explain attachment types. A multitude of factors can affect family life, which in turn can affect the attachment relationship.

Activity 2   Explaining attachment types

Item A   Responsiveness training

100 low-income mothers in Holland, whose children were assessed as extremely irritable shortly after birth, were selected to take part in an experiment. Half the mothers were chosen at random to take part in three short training sessions to improve their sensitivity and responsiveness to their child. The other mothers received no training. At 12 months all the mothers and babies were observed at home and in the Strange Situation. Those who had participated in the training sessions were more likely to be responsive to their children who, in turn, were more likely to be securely attached to the mother.

Attachment and responsiveness training

| | Attachment classification | |
	Number secure	Number insecure
Training	31	19
No training	11	39

Adapted from van den Boom, 1994

Item B   Irritable infants

A study of mothers with highly irritable infants found no link between the infant's temperament and the type of attachment formed. However, when the researcher looked at the mother's social situation, a link was found. Irritable infants were likely to form secure attachments if their mother had social support from relatives and friends. Irritable infants whose mothers had little social support were more likely to form insecure attachments.

Adapted from Crockenberg (1981)

Questions

1. What support, if any, does Item A provide for
   a) the sensitivity hypothesis
   b) the temperament hypothesis?
2. No one factor alone can explain attachment types. What evidence does Item B provide for this statement?

Unit 4 Culture and attachment types

KEY ISSUES

1 **What is the relationship between culture and attachment?**
2 **Is the Strange Situation an appropriate method for studying attachment in different cultures?**

Culture is the learned shared behaviour of members of society. It includes norms – accepted and expected ways of behaving, and values – beliefs about what is good and worthwhile. To some extent, different cultures have different norms about childrearing and different values about the way children and parents ought to behave. What effect does culture have on attachment?

Table 3 is a survey of various studies which have used the Strange Situation to investigate attachment in different countries. It indicates that, in all countries, secure attachment is the most common type of attachment. However, there are significant differences between countries. For example, Germany has a relatively high proportion of insecure-avoidant attachments. What accounts for these differences?

Table 3 Culture and attachment

Country	Number of studies	Secure	Insecure-avoidant	Insecure-resistant
Germany	3	56.6	35.3	8.1
Great Britain	1	75.0	22.2	2.8
Netherlands	4	67.3	26.3	6.4
Sweden	1	74.5	21.6	3.9
Israel	2	64.4	6.8	28.8
Japan	2	67.7	5.2	25.0
China	1	50.0	25.0	25.0
United States	18	64.8	21.1	14.1
Overall average		65.0	21.3	13.7

Adapted from van IJzendoorn & Kroonenberg, 1988

Japan Studies of Japanese infants and mothers using the Strange Situation show a relatively high proportion of insecure-resistant attachments. One of the main characteristics of this type of attachment is extreme distress on separation from the caregiver. Researchers have explained this in terms of traditional Japanese childrearing norms. Under normal circumstances, children are never left alone at 12 months, and their mothers rarely leave them in the care of anyone else. As a result, they are more likely to be distressed when left with a stranger or left alone in the Strange Situation.

Researchers argue that the relatively high proportion of attachments classified as insecure-resistant is due to traditional Japanese childrearing practices. Some of the procedures used in the Strange Situation place considerable stress on Japanese children (Takahashi, 1990).

Israel Studies of infants raised in Israeli kibbutzim show a similarly high proportion of insecure-resistant attachments. The traditional system of communal childrearing in kibbutzim is described in Activity 1 on page 49. One study using the Strange Situation classified over half the attachments as insecure-resistant and only 37% as secure (Sagi et al., 1985). This has been explained as follows. Infants have little contact with strangers. The kibbutz is a largely self-contained community, which, in some respects, is like a large extended family – children are seen as 'children of the kibbutz'. As a result, being left alone or with a stranger in the Strange Situation can be particularly distressing and lead to a high proportion of attachments being classified as insecure-resistant (Lamb et al., 1985).

Germany A study of German infants and mothers using the Strange Situation classified 49% of attachments as insecure-avoidant and only 33% as secure (Grossmann et al., 1985). Insecure-avoidant relationships are characterised by the infant paying little attention to the caregiver and showing little concern when she leaves. For her part, the caregiver tends to ignore the infant. The researchers observed the German mothers at home and found no evidence that they were insensitive, unresponsive or indifferent to their children. The parents valued independence – they wanted their children to be self-reliant, to 'stand on their own two feet' and not make demands on them. Some of the behaviour in the Strange Situation which is supposed to indicate secure attachment was seen by German parents as evidence of 'clinging' and 'spoilt' children. As a result of the norms and values which directed childrearing, a high proportion of attachments were classified as insecure-avoidant.

Conclusion

What does the research evidence from different cultures mean? How can it be interpreted? There are no simple answers to these questions.

Culture and the Strange Situation A number of researchers have questioned the use of the Strange Situation across cultures. It may not be suitable for measuring and classifying attachment in different cultures. The Strange Situation was developed in the USA; the classifications were based on observations of American infants and mothers. Certain types of behaviour were seen as indicating a secure attachment. And a secure attachment was seen as the best form of attachment, as the type most likely to benefit the child's development.

Does the Strange Situation, the way it is designed, and the way its findings are interpreted reflect, at least to some extent, the norms and values of one particular culture? Evidence from the studies outlined above suggests the answer may be yes. Behaviour seen as normal and beneficial in the USA may be seen differently in other societies. As noted earlier, infant behaviour seen as indicating a secure attachment in the USA was seen by many German parents as reflecting a 'spoilt' and 'clinging' child. And, in terms of an American designed experiment, a large proportion of German infants were labelled as insecure-avoidant. But was their attachment *really* insecure? Just because the German infants were encouraged to be independent doesn't necessarily mean their attachment was insecure. If this is the case, then the Strange Situation may be flawed – it was unable to measure the true nature of their attachment. The Strange Situation assumes that the behaviour of all children in all cultures means the same thing. This is a highly questionable assumption.

Culture and childrearing Whatever the strengths and weaknesses of the Strange Situation, the evidence indicates that childrearing practices vary from culture to culture and, as a result, so do attachment relationships. Thus in some cultures the attachment relationship emphasises independence (eg Germany), and in other cultures dependence (eg Japan).

But, to go on to say that one type of attachment is better than another is highly questionable. Who is to say that American infants are better prepared for later life than German or Japanese infants? Making this kind of judgement can be seen as *ethnocentrism* – seeing the world and judging other cultures in terms of the norms and values of your own culture. Bearing this in mind, Gavin Bremner (1994) concludes that 'at least when considering attachment across cultures we should probably abandon the notion that there is a single correct style of parenting or even that an insecure attachment is inevitably poorer than a secure attachment'.

Key term

Ethnocentrism *Seeing and evaluating other cultures in terms of the norms and values of your own culture.*

Summary

1. To some extent childrearing practices vary from culture to culture.

2. Most studies suggest that secure attachment is the most common form of attachment in all societies.

3. There are marked differences between societies in terms of the proportion of attachment types.

4. These differences may be due to differences in culture – in particular, differences in the norms and values associated with childrearing.

5. The Strange Situation may not produce valid (true) measures and classifications of attachment across cultures.

6. The view that one type of attachment is better than another may be unjustified. It may simply be a reflection of ethnocentrism.

7. Evidence from different cultures can be used to support the view that there is a universal tendency to form a secure attachment. It can also be used to argue that there is not such a tendency.

Unit 5 The effects of attachment types

KEY ISSUES

1 What effects might attachment relationships have on a child's early development?

2 What effects might they have on later life?

The significance of attachment Do attachment relationships matter? One answer is yes they do if they affect children's development. Bowlby (1973) argued that a secure attachment between an infant and mother figure is essential for later life. He believed that the primary attachment relationship provides a child with a model or template for all their future relationships. He called this model the *internal working model*. For example, if an infant experiences a warm and close relationship with a mother figure, this will form the basis for their future relationships. They will tend to expect and develop similar relationships in later life. Mary Ainsworth (1978) took a similar position arguing that different attachment types will have different effects on the child's later development and behaviour.

Most of the research has looked at possible relationships between attachment types measured between 12 and 18 months and the child's development up to age 6 or 7 years. Researchers typically begin with the hypothesis that secure attachments are more beneficial for development than insecure attachments. In general, their findings appear to support this view. In terms of cognitive, social and emotional development, a secure attachment seems to be advantageous. Research indicates that children with secure attachments in infancy are more likely to be popular with their peers, friendly and cooperative; independent and confident with strangers; curious, ready to investigate and eager to learn; positive in their outlook and

emotionally mature (Carlson & Sroufe, 1995). Children with insecure attachments in infancy tend to be hostile and to have problems with social relationships (Bretherton, 1985).

Evaluation

At first sight, the above evidence is very impressive. The links between early attachment and later development seem strong. And the links appear to make sense. For example, a securely attached child will develop an internal working model which leads to positive relationships. This explains why they are more likely to make friends and be popular with their peers. In addition, a securely attached child uses their main caregiver as a secure base from which to explore and investigate. This will encourage cognitive development and therefore explains their readiness to investigate and eagerness to learn in later years.

Family stability The relationship between early attachment and later development is not as neat and tidy as it appears. Some studies find little evidence to support a direct link. The strongest evidence for a link comes from families in which child care and family circumstances remain stable over the period when the child is assessed. It may well be this stability, rather than the attachment relationship itself, which accounts for the child's development. For example, the child might be receiving the same quality of parenting at 6 years as they did at 12 months. Maybe it is the quality of parenting at 6 years which affects the child's behaviour rather than their attachment relationship at 12 months. If this is the case, then the apparent link between attachment and development simply reflects a third factor – stability. In other words, it is the stability of child care and the circumstances of the family which shapes both the attachment relationship and the child's development (Lamb et al., 1985). This is an important point. It suggests that the child's development is not fixed by attachment relationships formed between 12 and 18 months. It suggests that these relationships are not as crucial and formative as many researchers believe.

Family instability Research indicates that the link between attachment and development is weakest when major changes occur in family life. As noted earlier, such changes include divorce, remarriage, unemployment and serious illness. They tend to produce instability and can result in changes to the type and quality of parenting. When a child's development is assessed at 6 or 7 years, the assessment may reflect these factors rather than attachment at 12 months.

Conclusion Early attachments may be significant, they may have important influences on development. But we can't be sure – the link is not definitely established. Parents may not be as crucial to the child's development as attachment theorists claim. Researchers such as Judith Harris (1999) argue that the peer group has a greater influence than parents on the child's social development. In other words, the child's friends may have more effect on their social development than their attachment relationship. As Schaffer (1996) concludes, the relationship between attachment and later development is 'nowhere near as straightforward as has been suggested by many attachment theorists'.

Key terms

Internal working model *A model or template for relationships. It develops from the primary attachment relationship and forms the basis for all future relationships.*

Peer group *A group made up of people with similar social characteristics, for example age and status.*

5.2 Effects on later life

Does the type of attachment in infancy affect behaviour in adulthood? Research by Hazen and Shaver (1987) indicated that romantic relationships in adult life often reflect the three attachment types identified by Ainsworth. People who had secure attachments as infants tended to form similar relationships in adult life. They were likely to have close and trusting relationships with their partner. Those who experienced insecure-avoidant attachments during infancy tended to feel uncomfortable about becoming close to their partner and fearful about making a commitment. And those who had insecure-resistant attachments as infants tended to feel they weren't receiving enough love from their partner and to worry that their partner might leave them. Research also indicates a similar link between the type of friendships people develop as adults and their attachment type in

infancy (Bartholomew & Horowitz, 1991).

Evaluation

Although there is evidence to support a link between types of infant attachment and relationships in adult life, there are problems with the research.

Identifying attachment types The identification of the type of attachment in infancy is based on participants' descriptions of their relationships with their parents. There are three main problems with this approach.

- First, it relies on participants' memories which may be unreliable.
- Second, participants may try to present themselves in the best possible light to researchers. They may claim to have had secure attachments when, in fact, their attachments were less desirable.
- Third, participants' present romantic relationship may colour their views of their early attachments. For example, in one study, 80% of the participants in secure, long-term romantic relationships rated their infant attachments as secure. However, when their interviews were analysed, only 50% were judged to have had secure attachments (Bartholomew, 1993).

The intervening years A lot of things happen between infancy and adult life. These include a variety of relationships, some romantic, some not, all of which will have some effect on present relationships.

Some researchers argue that the suggested link between attachment types in infancy and adult relationships tends to ignore experiences during the intervening years (Levitt, 1991). While early attachment may have some influence on adult life, it is far from being the only influence.

Summary

1	Many researchers start from the assumption that secure attachments are more beneficial for development than insecure attachments. There is considerable evidence to support this view.
2	However, both the type of attachment and the child's development may be shaped by the stability of parenting and family circumstances. This suggests that attachment relationships may not be as formative and significant for development as many researchers believe.
3	Research indicates that relationships in adult life reflect attachment types in infancy. However, the evidence is not conclusive.

Unit 6 Theories of attachment

KEY ISSUES

1 **What are the main theories of attachment?**

2 **What contribution has animal research made to understanding attachment in humans?**

6.1 Early theories of attachment

Up until the 1950s, there was broad agreement in psychology that the human infant forms an attachment to the mother because she provides the baby with milk and comfort.

Psychoanalysis

Sigmund Freud (1856-1939), the founder of psychoanalysis, believed that both infants and adults possess a *libido*, an inborn drive or appetite for physical pleasure. This libido provides our main motivation or driving force from the moment of birth. Many of our physical pleasures are supplied by other people, and Freud believed we form emotional attachments to those people who gratify our libidinal desires.

In new-born infants, the libido expresses itself primarily as a desire to be fed and kept warm and secure, and the child forms an attachment to the person who satisfies these desires. In most cases, this person is the mother. Freud claimed 'by her care of the child's body' the mother establishes a relationship to the child which is 'unique, without parallel, established unalterably for a whole lifetime as the first and strongest love-object and as the prototype of all later love relations' (Freud 1940, cited in Young-Breuhl, 1990).

In psychoanalytic theory then, the child forms an attachment to the mother because she satisfies the child's need for feeding and comfort. Forming a secure attachment to a caring mother is crucial to the future wellbeing of the child, as the success of later relationships is determined by the security of this first attachment. Infants who fail to form a secure attachment to the mother are unlikely to form successful relations with anyone else in childhood or adulthood.

Psychoanalytic theory also provides an explanation for the mother's attachment to the child. It states that physical contact with the child, especially breastfeeding, provides satisfaction for the mother's own libidinal desires for physical stimulation.

Evaluation Psychoanalytic theory has always been open to the criticism that it uses abstract ideas (like libido) that are not open to direct observation or measurement, and are therefore difficult to study scientifically. However, while some condemn psychoanalysis as unscientific (eg Eysenck, 1985), others praise it as rich and insightful (eg Mitchell, 1975).

Learning theory

The main alternative to psychoanalysis in explaining the social development of the child is *learning theory*. There are two main strands to learning theory: the first, *behaviourism*, was launched in the USA by John Watson in 1913, and was enormously influential in psychology up until the 1960s; the second, *social learning theory*, grew out of behaviourism in the 1940s and largely replaced it in influence from the 1960s. It is still very significant in child psychology today.

Behaviourism explained all animal and human behaviour in terms of learning by *conditioning*. One important feature of conditioning is that rewards have a major effect on learning. Behaviours or responses that are rewarded are more likely to be learned than those that are ignored or punished. The behaviourists call rewards *positive reinforcers*.

B.F. Skinner (1904-1990), one of the most important behaviourists, showed that a rat could be conditioned to press a lever by rewarding (or *reinforcing*) it for approaching, touching and pressing the lever. The rat was rewarded with food pellets automatically released from a food dispenser when the lever was pressed. Every time a food pellet was released, the food dispenser clicked. Interestingly, Skinner found that a rat would continue to press the lever even when the food dispenser was empty, provided it could hear the food dispenser click. Skinner explained that the rat had learned an association between the food pellets and the clicking of the food dispenser, until in the end the click became a kind of reward in itself. In Skinner's terminology, the food pellets were the *primary reinforcer*, while the clicking of the food dispenser had become a *secondary reinforcer*.

Social learning theory In the 1950s, social learning theorists like Dollard and Miller (1950) tried to link behaviourist ideas with those of psychoanalysis. They suggested that the human infant, when hungry, feels uncomfortable, and enters a *drive state* – that is, the baby is motivated to find some way to alleviate or lessen the discomfort of being hungry. Of course, in early infancy the baby can do little more than howl, and it is up to other people, usually the mother, to feed it. Being fed satisfies the infant's hunger and makes it feel comfortable again. In social learning theory terminology, *drive reduction* (that is, alleviating the infant's hunger and releasing it from the drive state of being hungry) is rewarding, and the child learns that food is a reward or primary reinforcer. The person who supplies the food, the mother, is associated with the food and becomes a secondary reinforcer (just as the click of the food dispenser became a secondary reinforcer to Skinner's rat). After a while, the mere presence of the mother is a source of comfort and security to the child, and the child develops an attachment to her. Social learning theory suggests that hunger is a *primary drive* – an innate or inborn drive state that emerges naturally when the infant needs to be fed. Attachment is a *secondary drive* that the child learns through the mother being so strongly associated with feeding.

Social learning theory also provides an explanation for the mother's attachment to the child. It suggests that the infant's behaviour like smiling and cooing (or at the very least stopping crying!) provides reinforcement to the mother to repeat her feeding behaviour.

Later versions of social learning theory placed less emphasis on reinforcement and drives. Albert Bandura (1965), for example, argued that learning can occur without any reward or positive reinforcement. People can learn simply by observing the behaviour of others. This is known as *imitation* or *modelling*. People simply watch, listen to and learn from others, and model their own behaviour accordingly.

Caregivers can provide models for infants to copy. If they are loving, attentive and responsive, then infants may imitate this behaviour. This can contribute to the formation of attachments to their caregivers (Hay & Vespo, 1988).

Evaluation of early theories

Behaviourism has been widely criticised for being *reductionist*. This means it 'reduces' the complexities of human behaviour to over-simple ideas such as learned responses and reinforcement. It then uses these ideas as building blocks to explain complex human behaviours such as attachment. Much of the time, behaviourism seemed to be trying to explain human psychology in terms of the behaviour of rats pressing levers.

Social learning theory goes beyond behaviourism, recognising that human behaviour is complex, as is the social environment in which infants are raised. As a result, behaviour cannot be reduced to a few basic processes. For example, social learning theory recognises there is more than one way of learning with its addition of the idea of imitation or modelling.

Psychoanalysis and learning theory have both been referred to by John Bowlby as 'cupboard theories' of love and attachment. Both see infants as forming an attachment with the person who feeds them (much as a cat loves you when you go to the cupboard to get its food). However, research into attachments does not bear out the claim that infants necessarily form attachments with those who feed them. Schaffer and Emerson (1964) conducted a study of 60 infants in Glasgow, observing them every four weeks from birth until 12 months and then again at 18 months (see p 47). For many of the children, their primary attachment figure – the individual they were most strongly attached to – was the person who usually fed, bathed and changed them. However, for a large minority (40%), their primary attachment figure was not responsible for any of these caregiving activities. In general, infants formed primary attachments with people who were responsive to their behaviour and provided them with stimulation, for example, by talking, singing, laughing, touching and playing. Infants tend to attach to the most stimulating adult, not necessarily the most nurturing one. Feeding, as such, did not appear to be a major factor in the formation of attachments. These findings provide some support for later social learning theories which suggest that responsive behaviour by caregivers may be imitated by infants and this contributes to the formation of attachments.

Key terms

Libido *An important drive in motivating people to seek physical, sensual and sexual pleasure.*

Drive *An appetite or desire that motivates people. Examples include hunger, thirst and sexual desire.*

Conditioning *A form of learning in which a person or animal is trained to give a response to a stimulus.*

Positive reinforcer *A reward. Rewarding behaviour leads to that behaviour being learned and repeated.*

Association *A connection or link made between two things that are often presented together, for example, milk and mother.*

Primary reinforcer *A positive reinforcer that is rewarding in itself, for example, food.*

Secondary reinforcer *A neutral stimulus that is associated with a primary reinforcer often enough that it becomes a reward itself.*

Drive state *A state of motivation arising from being in a state of need. For example, hunger is a drive state arising from lack of food.*

Drive reduction *The reduction of a drive state. For example, food reduces the drive state of hunger.*

Primary drive *An innate drive arising from a biological need such as hunger or thirst.*

Secondary drive *An acquired or learned drive. For example, a desire for mother's company because her presence has become associated with the satisfaction of the primary drive for food.*

Imitation or modelling *Leaning by observing and copying the behaviour of others. Can occur without positive reinforcement.*

Reductionist *An approach which attempts to explain something in terms of its basic components.*

6.2 Evidence from animal research

Psychoanalytic theory and some social learning theories argue that infants become attached to their caregivers because the caregivers provide them with food. They see the desire for food as a primary drive and attachment as a secondary drive. Attachment is therefore seen as a by-product of feeding. This view was challenged by evidence from animal research.

Ethology and imprinting

Ethology is the study of animals in their natural environment. It assumes that animal behaviour is in part innate or genetically based. Innate behaviours are seen to have evolved because they are adaptive – they increase the likelihood that the individual will survive and reproduce.

Although ethology is primarily concerned with animal behaviour, ideas from ethology have provided insights into human behaviour. In particular, they influenced John Bowlby's theory of attachment which is examined in Section 6.3.

One of the most famous experiments in ethology was conducted by Konrad Lorenz (1935). He divided a large clutch of greylag goose eggs into two groups. One group was hatched by the mother goose and the goslings followed her around. The second group was placed in an incubator. On hatching, the first thing the goslings saw was Lorenz – they promptly followed him around as if he were their mother. Lorenz then marked each group to distinguish it from the other and placed all the goslings under an upturned box. They were then released in the presence of the mother goose and Lorenz. Each group went straight to their 'mother figures'. Lorenz's goslings followed him everywhere and became distressed if they lost sight of him.

Lorenz called this form of tie *imprinting*. In the case of the goslings, imprinting directs them to attach themselves to the first moving object they see after hatching. In a very short space of time they learn what the object looks like and how it differs from other objects. Lorenz believed that imprinting only occurs during a *critical period* – a short period of time when the individual is particularly sensitive and impressionable. In the case of the goslings, the critical period was the first few hours after hatching.

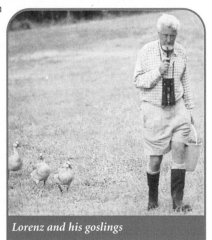
Lorenz and his goslings

Lorenz saw imprinting as *adaptive behaviour*. It protected the young by keeping them close to their mother so promoting their chances of survival and reproduction.

In summary, Lorenz argued that imprinting is:

- An innate predisposition to establish a bond
- A rapid process which occurs during a fairly short critical period
- An adaptive behaviour which has evolved over millions of years as a means of protecting the young.

The two 'mothers'

Contact comfort

Evaluation Lorenz applied his idea of imprinting to certain species of birds. Since then, ethologists have modified his views and applied them to a wider range of species. Imprinting is now seen to occur in many *precocial* animals – animals that can feed themselves and move around freely shortly after birth.

The idea of a critical period has been replaced with the idea of a *sensitive period*. A critical period suggests that if imprinting does not occur during this period, it won't occur at all. Later research indicates that this is not so – imprinting can occur outside the so-called critical period. Because of this, the term sensitive period is now used. Imprinting is more likely to occur and occurs more easily during sensitive periods. For example, a duck imprints more readily during the first 24 hours after hatching but it can imprint outside this period (Hess, 1958).

Lorenz's research had an important influence on theories of attachment in humans. Imprinting occurs without any food being involved. For example, goslings and ducklings feed themselves – they are *not* fed by their mothers. This suggests that imprinting is itself a primary drive, that it is not a by-product of feeding by the

Key terms

Adaptive behaviour *Behaviour which helps organisms adapt to their environment. In terms of ethology, adaptation often refers to genetically based behaviour patterns which have evolved because they increase the likelihood that the individual will survive and reproduce.*

Imprinting *A partly innate, partly learned process during which an infant rapidly forms a strong tie with a mother figure.*

Innate *Inborn, genetically based, inherited through the genes.*

Critical period *A period of time when imprinting must take place if it is to occur at all.*

Sensitive period *A period of time when infants are particularly sensitive to imprinting.*

Precocial animals *Animals that are born late in their development, and can feed themselves and move around freely shortly after birth.*

Contact comfort *Direct physical contact which provides comfort and security.*

mother. This raises the possibility that attachment in humans might be a primary drive. If this is the case, then it calls into question the 'cupboard love' theories of psychoanalysis and early social learning theory which see attachment as a by-product of feeding.

Harlow's research with rhesus monkeys

The significance of feeding in forming attachments was also challenged by Harry Harlow's research with rhesus monkeys (Harlow, 1959). He believed that comfort and security rather than food were the crucial factors involved in attachment. To test this hypothesis, he designed the following experiment.

Eight newborn monkeys were separated from their mothers and isolated in individual cages. Each was provided with two *surrogate mothers* made of wire cylinders (surrogate means substitute). One of the 'mothers' was wrapped in soft towelling cloth which, in Harlow's words, provided 'contact comfort'. Four of the monkeys received milk from a bottle attached to the wire 'mother', four from a bottle attached to the cloth 'mother'. The two groups drank the same amount of milk and gained weight at the same rate. However, those who were fed by the wire 'mother' visited her *only* to feed. Babies in both groups spent most of their time nestled close to the cloth 'mother'. When they were frightened they always ran to the cloth 'mother' – regardless of whether or not 'she' was the one who provided food.

Harlow concluded that comfort and security rather than food formed the basis for attachment. The babies who were fed by a wire 'mother' failed to form an attachment to her. Instead, they spent much of the time clinging to the soft, cuddly 'mother' who provided them with contact comfort.

However, this attachment was not sufficient for healthy social development. In later life the monkeys were either indifferent or abusive to other monkeys and had difficulty with mating and parenting. For example, the first monkey to have a baby ignored the infant and pushed it away when it tried to make contact.

Evaluation Harlow's research was very influential. His single most important claim was that comfort and security rather than feeding formed the basis for attachment. As with ethology, this challenged the view of psychoanalysis and early social learning theory that attachment was a by-product of feeding.

Harlow saw the cloth 'mother' as ideal for contact comfort. In his words, 'She is available 24 hours a day to satisfy her infant's overwhelming compulsion to seek bodily contact' (1959). In the short term, the cloth 'mother' may have provided for the baby's needs. However, in the long term she failed to do so – the babies had problems with social relationships in later years. In another experiment, babies with cloth 'mothers' were allowed to play with three other young monkeys for an hour a day. When they grew up they were no different from monkeys who had been raised with their natural mothers. This suggests that for healthy psychological development, social contact may be more important than contact comfort or even 'mothering' (Harlow & Suomi, 1970).

Harlow's research was based on rhesus monkeys. It may not be appropriate to generalise from non-human animals to humans. Findings which apply to non-human animals may not apply to humans. One reason for this is that non-human animal behaviour is based less on learning and more on innate, genetically-based behaviour patterns. Despite these cautions, findings from animal behaviour can provide insights into human behaviour.

Harlow's research has been criticised on ethical grounds. In terms of today's morality, it is wrong to manipulate animals in this way. In addition, the consequences were very damaging – both for the monkeys involved in the experiment and their young. This breaks the British Psychological Society's code of ethics for the use of animals in research (BPS, 1998).

6.3 Bowlby's theory of attachment

In a series of publications from the 1940s to the 1980s, John Bowlby developed what many consider the most comprehensive and influential theory of attachment.

Proximity Bowlby was strongly influenced by ethology. He saw attachment behaviour in all species as innate. He believed it had evolved as a means of protecting the young. As such it was adaptive behaviour – it promoted their survival. Bowlby saw the key to attachment as *proximity* – it served to keep the infant and caregiver near to each other. This provided protection from predators who might injure or kill the infant.

Bowlby saw attachment as a two-way process. Both infant and caregiver are genetically 'programmed' to maintain proximity – each has developed behaviours which keep them physically close. For example, human infants coo and smile and their caregivers respond with warmth and affection; infants cry and their caregivers respond with attention and concern. Separation leads to feelings of anxiety in both infant and caregiver, which also serves to maintain proximity. In many species infants are wary of strangers. Bowlby suggests that this is an innate survival mechanism. It may alert the infant to danger. And a cry at the sight of someone strange or unfamiliar usually brings a caregiver running.

From proximity – a *physical* attachment – grows a strong *emotional* bond between infant and caregiver. Proximity, and the behaviours which have developed to maintain it, lead to emotional closeness. In humans, we use the word 'love' to

Activity 3   Comfort and security

Item A   Fear

A mechanical teddy bear beating a drum is brought into the cage. The terrified baby clings to its cloth 'mother'.

Item B   Curiosity

After a while, the baby 'would turn to look at the previously terrifying bear without the slightest sign of alarm. Indeed, the infant would sometimes even leave the protection of the "mother" and approach the object that a few minutes before had reduced it to abject terror' (Harlow, 1959).

Question

Look at Items A and B. What support does this experiment provide for Harlow's view that attachment is based on comfort and security rather than feeding?

describe this closeness between infant and caregiver. Bowlby argues that this emotional bond is essential for the child's development.

Monotropy Bowlby believed that human infants have an innate tendency to become attached to one particular person. He called this idea of one special relationship *monotropy*. Bowlby recognised that infants eventually form many attachments – to parents, siblings (brothers and sisters), grandparents, aunts and uncles and family friends. However, he believed that a single primary attachment relationship was essential for the healthy psychological development of the child. Ideally, this attachment is with the mother. In his words the child needs, 'a warm, intimate, and continuous relationship with his mother (or permanent mother-substitute – one person who steadily "mothers" him) in which both find satisfaction and enjoyment' (Bowlby, 1953). Bowlby believed there was a sensitive period for the establishment of this special relationship. For most children it must take place during their first 12 months.

Internal working model Bowlby believed that a child's relationship with their mother figure provides a model or template for all their future relationships. He called this model the *internal working model*. It develops from the primary attachment relationship. For example, if a child experiences a warm, close relationship with their mother, they will tend to expect and develop similar relationships in later life. The primary attachment relationship also provides a model for the child's self-image. For example, if the mother is cold and rejecting, the child will tend to develop a negative self-image and experience low self-esteem and a lack of worth. This may well lead to unsatisfactory relationships in later life.

Cognitive development Bowlby believed that a strong attachment with a mother figure was essential for the child's cognitive development – the development of thinking, reasoning and problem-solving skills. Exploration of the environment is critical for cognitive development. Bowlby argued that attachment provides a base from which the infant can explore new environments, secure in the knowledge that the mother figure provides a safe haven to which it can return.

Evaluation

Is attachment innate? Bowlby's theory of attachment suffers from the same problems as all theories which claim that behaviour is directed or influenced by genes – it is difficult, if not impossible to verify. Despite rapid advances in genetics, there is no direct evidence of a gene or genes for attachment. They may exist but they have yet to be discovered. In view of this, Bowlby's claim that attachment is innate is, at best, a possibility.

Is attachment adaptive? How can we be sure that attachment is adaptive, that it serves to promote the chances of infants surviving and reproducing? Bowlby argued that it evolved to protect the young from predators. This may apply to the early stages of human evolution, but predators – in the sense of wild animals – are hardly a problem in modern human societies. If we accept Bowlby's argument, attachment appears little more than a 'hangover' from a previous era.

And why did Bowlby single out protection from predators as basis for attachment? As Rudolph Schaffer notes, 'attachment serves so many useful functions that to single this one out as the

biological basis seems somewhat far-fetched' (1989).

Multiple attachments To what extent does monotropy exist in practice? In other words, to what extent do infants have a single primary attachment figure? Schaffer and Emerson's (1964) study of 60 infants from Glasgow showed that most formed their first attachment with one particular person. But nearly one third formed multiple attachments – to two or more persons – in which there appeared to be no preferred attachment figure. This became increasingly common as the infants grew older – by 18 months most had developed multiple attachments with no preferred attachment figure. Schaffer (1971) claims that Bowlby's idea of monotropy is 'not borne out by the facts'. And Thomas (1995) suggests that multiple attachments may be more desirable than a single primary attachment. The child's social, emotional and cognitive development may well benefit more from a network of attachments.

The role of the father For Bowlby the mother-infant relationship was central to the attachment process. The mother was the primary caregiver and the primary attachment figure. Bowlby saw the main role of the father as supporting the mother. He supports her financially, allowing her to devote herself to caring for the child. He supports her emotionally, providing her with love and companionship. This helps the mother to 'maintain that harmonious and contented mood' which creates an atmosphere in which the infant thrives (Bowlby, 1953).

However, a number of studies have shown that fathers are often a lot more than supporting actors. Research evidence indicates that infants usually show no preference for mothers or fathers in unstressful situations. However, in stressful situations, they tend to favour the mother (Lamb, 1976). As the infant grows older, this preference for the mother tends to disappear. One study indicated that boys between the ages of 15 and 24 months showed a preference for their fathers (Lamb, 1977). This type of evidence suggests that fathers are not the marginal figures pictured by Bowlby. Instead, it suggests they play an important part in the attachment process.

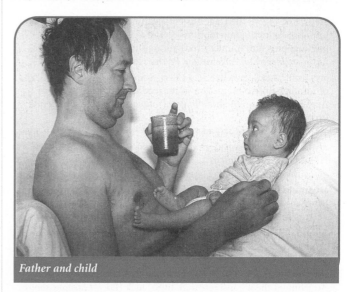

Father and child

A sensitive period Bowlby was clearly influenced by the ideas of imprinting and sensitive periods derived from ethology. He suggested that powerful and lasting attachments are made to a mother figure during a sensitive period. And, if they are not made during this period, they are unlikely to be made later. However, as Durkin (1995) points out, attachments in humans are not all-or-nothing relationships with one person 'getting stuck' to another. Relationships develop and change over time. Infants do not 'blindly' and mechanically imprint on a mother figure during a sensitive period. They have some degree of choice when making their attachments. In this respect, attachment relationships in infancy are similar to social relationships in later life.

Cognitive development There is evidence to support Bowlby's claim that secure attachment is important for cognitive development. For example, Hazen and Durrett (1982) found that securely attached young children were more independent explorers of their environment and were also more innovative in their approach to problem solving.

Conclusion It is generally recognised that forming attachments to a few people is part of the normal process of child development. The evidence suggests that Bowlby overestimated the importance of a single attachment to a mother figure. And, as this evaluation has noted, there are other aspects of Bowlby's theory which are questionable. However, in some respects, it was an advance on earlier theories which saw attachment as a by-product of feeding and pictured the infant as a passive individual who was fed and, as a result, became attached. Bowlby saw both caregivers and infants actively involved in attachment behaviour and the formation of attachments.

Key term

Monotropy *The idea of one special relationship. In terms of attachment, the view that infants have an innate tendency to form a single primary attachment to their mother or a mother figure.*

Summary

1 Psychoanalytic theory states that the infant forms an attachment to the mother because she satisfies their need for feeding and comfort.

2 Early versions of social learning theory state that the infant becomes attached to the person who feeds it.

3 Animal research suggests that infants do not necessarily form attachments to the person who feeds them.

4 Lorenz saw imprinting as a largely instinctive process which occurs during a fairly short critical period. It keeps infants in close proximity to their mothers and evolved as a means of protecting the young.

5 From his research with rhesus monkeys, Harlow claimed that contact comfort – direct physical contact which provides comfort and security – was the basis for attachment.

6 Bowlby saw attachment behaviour as innate. It had evolved as a means of protecting infants by maintaining proximity with their mothers. From this physical closeness develops a strong emotional bond.

7 Bowlby believed that a single primary attachment to a mother figure was essential for the child's healthy psychological development.

8 The following criticisms have been made of Bowlby's theory.
- It is not possible to prove that attachment is innate and adaptive.
- Research evidence indicates that he overestimated the significance of a primary attachment to a mother figure.
- His idea of a sensitive period for attachment is questionable.

References

Ahrens, S.R. (1954). Beitrage zur entwicklung des physiognomie und mimiker-kennes (Contributions on the development of physiognomy and mimicry recognition). *Zeitschrift fur Experimentelle und Angewandte Psychologie, 2*, 412-454.

Ainsworth, M.D.S. & Bell, S.M. (1969). Some contemporary patterns of mother-infant interaction in the feeding situation. In A. Ambrose (Ed.), *Stimulation in early infancy.* New York: Academic Press.

Ainsworth, M.D.S., Blehar, M.C., Waters, E. & Wall, S. (1978). *Patterns of attachment: A psychological study of the strange situation.* Hillsdale, NJ: Erlbaum.

Atkinson, J. & Braddick, O.J. (1981). Acuity, contrast sensitivity and accommodation in infancy. In R.N. Aslin, J.R. Roberts & M.R. Petersen (Eds.), *The development of perception: Psychobiological perspectives, vol. 2: the visual system.* New York: Academic Press.

Bandura, A. (1965). Influence of model's reinforcement contingencies on the acquisition of imitative responses. *Journal of Personality and Social Psychology, 1*, 589-595.

Bartholomew, K. (1993). From childhood to adult relationships: Attachment theory and research. In S. Duck (Ed.), *Learning about relationships.* Newbury Park, CA: Sage.

Bartholomew, K. & Horowitz, L.M. (1991). Attachment styles among young adults: A test of a four-category model. *Journal of Personality and Social Psychology, 61*, 226-244.

Belsky, J. & Rovine, M. (1987). Temperament and attachment security in the Strange Situation: a rapprochement. *Child Development, 58*, 787-795.

Bettelheim, B. (1969). *The children of the dream.* London: Thames & Hudson.

Bowlby, J. (1953). *Childcare and the growth of love.* Harmondsworth: Penguin.

Bowlby, J. (1969). *Attachment and loss, vol. 1: Attachment.* London: Hogarth.

Bowlby, J. (1973). *Attachment and loss, vol. 2: Separation.* London: Hogarth.

BPS (British Psychological Society). (1998). *Code of conduct, ethical principles and guidelines.* Leicester: BPS.

Bremner, J.G. (1994). *Infancy* (2nd ed.). Oxford: Blackwell.

Bretherton, I. (1985). Attachment theory: Retrospect and prospect. In I. Bretherton & E. Walters (Eds.), Growing points of attachment theory and research. *Child Development Monographs, 50*, nos. 1-2.

Bronfenbrenner, U. (1979). *The ecology of human development: Experiments by nature and design.* Cambridge, Mass: Harvard University Press.

Bushnell, I.W.R., Sai, F. & Mullin, J.T. (1989). Neonatal recognition of the mother's face. *British Journal of Developmental Psychology, 7*, 3-15.

Buss A.H. & Plomin, R. (1984). *Temperament: Early developing personality traits.* Hillsdale, NJ: Erlbaum.

Carlson, E.A. & Sroufe, L.A. (1995). Contribution of attachment theory to developmental psychopathology. In D. Cicchetti & D.J. Conen (Eds.), *Developmental psychopathology: Vol 1. Theory and methods.* New York: Wiley.

Cernoch, J.M. & Porter, R.H. (1985). Recognition of maternal axillary odours by infants. *Child Development, 56,* 1593-1598.

Crockenberg, S.B. (1981). Infant irritability, mother responsiveness, and social support influences on the security of infant-mother attachment. *Child Development, 52,* 857-865.

Dollard, J. & Miller, N.E. (1950). *Personality and psychotherapy.* New York: McGraw-Hill.

Durkin, K. (1995). *Developmental social psychology.* Oxford: Blackwell.

Eysenck, H. (1985). *The decline and fall of the Freudian Empire.* Harmondsworth: Penguin.

Fox, N. (1977). Attachment of Kibbutz infants to mother and metapelet. *Child Development, 48,* 1228-1239.

Grossmann, K., Grossmann, K.E., Spangler, S., Suess, G. & Unzner, L. (1985). Maternal sensitivity and newborn orientation responses as related to quality of attachment in Northern Germany. *Monographs of the Society for Research in Child Development, 50,* (1-2 Serial No. 209).

Haralambos, M. & Holborn, M. (2000). *Sociology: Themes and perspectives* (5th ed.). London: Collins Educational.

Harlow, H.F. (1959). Love in infant monkeys. *Scientific American, 200,* 68-74.

Harlow, H.F. & Suomi, S.J. (1970). The nature of love – simplified. *American Psychologist, 25,* 161-168.

Harris, J.R. (1999). *The nurture assumption.* London: Bloomsbury.

Hay, D.F. & Vespo, J.E. (1988). Social learning perspectives on the development of the mother-child relationship. In B. Birns & D.F. Hay (Eds.), *The different faces of motherhood.* New York: Plenum Press.

Hazen, N.L. & Durrett, M.E. (1982). Relationship of security of attachment to exploration and cognitive mapping abilities in 2-year olds. *Developmental Psychology, 18,* 751-759.

Hazen, C. & Shaver, P.R. (1987). Conceptualizing romantic love as an attachment process. *Journal of Personality and Social Psychology, 52,* 511-524.

Hess, E.H. (1958). Imprinting in animals. *Scientific American,* March, 71-80.

Kagan, J. (1984). *The nature of the child.* New York: Basic Books.

Lamb, M.E. (1976). Effects of stress and cohort on mother- and father-infant interaction. *Developmental Psychology, 12,* 435-443.

Lamb, M.E. (1977). The development of mother-infant and father-infant attachments in the second year of life. *Developmental Psychology, 13,* 637-648.

Lamb, M.E., Thompson, R.A., Gardner, W. and Charnov, E.L. (1985). *Infant-mother attachment: The origins and significance of individual differences in Strange Situation behaviour.* Hillsdale, NJ: Erlbaum.

Levitt, M.J. (1991). Attachment and close relationships: A life-span perspective. In J. L. Gewirtz & W.M. Kurtines (Eds.), *Intersections with attachment.* Hillsdale, NJ: Erlbaum.

Lorenz, K.Z. (1935). The companion in the bird's world. *Auk, 54,* 245-273.

Main, M. & Soloman, J. (1986). Discovery of a disorganised disoriented attachment pattern. In T.B. Brazelton & M.W. Yogman (Eds.), *Affective development in infancy.* Norwood, NJ: Ablex.

Maurer, D. & Barrera, M. (1981). Infants perception of natural and distorted arrangements of a schematic face. *Child Development, 52,* 196-202.

Meltzoff, A.N. & Moore, M.K. (1977). Imitation of facial and manual gestures by human neonates. *Science, 198,* 75-78.

Mitchell, J. (1975). *Psychoanalysis and feminism.* Harmondsworth: Penguin.

Miyake, K., Chen, S.J. & Campos, J.J. (1985). Infant temperament, mother's mode of interaction and attachment in Japan: An interim report. In I. Bretherton & E. Waters (Eds.), Growing points of attachment theory and research. *Monographs of the Society for Research in Child Development, 50,* 276-297.

Piaget, J. (1957). The child's view of reality. *Scientific American,* March.

Sagi, A., Lamb, M.E., Lewkowicz, K.S., Shoham, R., Dvir, R. & Estes, D. (1985). Security of infant-mother, -father, and -metapelet attachments among kibbutz reared Israeli children. *Monographs of the Society for Research in Child Development, 50,* (1-2 Serial No. 209).

Schaffer, H.R. (1977). *Mothering.* London: Fontana.

Schaffer, H.R. (1989). Early social development. In A. Slater & G. Bremner (Eds.), *Infant development.* Hove: Lawrence Erlbaum Associates.

Schaffer, H.R. (1996). *Social development.* Oxford: Blackwell.

Schaffer, H.R. & Emerson, P.E. (1964). The development of social attachments in infancy. *Monographs of the Society for Research on Child Development, 29.*

Serrano, J.M., Iglesias, J. & Loeches, A. (1995). Infants' responses to adult static facial expressions. *Infant Behaviour and Development, 18,* 477-482.

Spangler, G. (1990). Mother, child, and situational correlates of toddlers' social competence. *Infant Behaviour and Development, 13,* 405-419.

Stern, D. (1977). *The first relationship: Infant and mother.* Cambridge, MA: Harvard University Press.

Takahashi, K. (1990). Are the key assumptions of the 'strange situation' procedure universal? *Human Development, 33,* 23-30.

Thomas, A. & Chess, S. (1977). *Temperament and development.* New York: Brunner/Mazel.

Thomas, L.K. (1998). Multicultural aspects of attachment. http://bereavement.demon.co.uk/lbn/attachment/lennox/htlm.

Thompson, R.A., Lamb, M.E. & Estes, D. (1982). Stability of infant-mother attachment and its relationship to changing life circumstances in an unselected middle-class sample. *Child Development, 53,* 144-148.

van den Boom, D.C. (1994). The influence of temperament and mothering on attachment and exploration: An experimental manipulation of sensitive responsiveness among lower-class mothers with irritable infants. *Child Development, 65,* 1457-1477.

van IJzendoorn, M.H. & Kroonenberg, P.M. (1988). Cross-cultural patterns of attachment: A meta-analysis of the Strange Situation. *Child Development, 59,* 147-156.

Vaughn, B.E., Lefever, G.B., Seifer, R. & Barglow, P. (1989). Attachment behaviour, attachment security, and temperament during infancy. *Child Development, 60,* 728-737.

Waters, E. (1978). The reliability and stability of individual differences in infant-mother attachment. *Child Development, 49,* 483-494.

Wolff, P.H. (1969). The natural history of crying and other vocalisations in early infancy. In B. Foss (Ed.), *Determinants of infant behaviour, vol. 4.* London: Methuen.

Young-Breuhl, E. (1990). *Freud on women.* London: Hogarth.

5 Deprivation and privation

Introduction

Chapter 4 looked at attachment between the child and its caregiver – usually the mother or a 'mother figure' – during the child's early years. A number of researchers have argued that this attachment is essential for the child's wellbeing during infancy and in later life. In particular, it is seen as important for the child's emotional development, social development, cognitive development, and physical development.

If the child fails to form an attachment during infancy, or if an attachment is formed but is then disrupted or broken, this may have harmful effects throughout life. First, it may result in psychological problems. Second, it may affect social development – the ability to form close and lasting relationships with others and to follow social norms (the accepted and expected ways of behaving in society). Third, it may impair cognitive development – for example, it may retard intelligence. Fourth, it may affect physical development leading to ill-health and stunted growth.

This chapter looks at research which investigates the possible effects of a failure to form an attachment and the disruption or loss of an existing attachment.

Chapter summary

- **Unit 1 examines early research into the possible effects of a lack of attachment or a disruption or loss of attachment.**
- **Unit 2 looks at the possible effects of a disruption or loss of attachment.**
- **Unit 3 looks at the possible effects of a failure to form an attachment.**

Unit 1 Early research

KEY ISSUES

1. **What is maternal deprivation?**
2. **How might it harm children's development?**
3. **What other factors might harm children's development?**

1.1 Bowlby's maternal deprivation hypothesis

John Bowlby (1951) claimed that a strong attachment to a mother figure was essential for a child's psychological health, both in infancy and in later life. Bowlby used the term *maternal deprivation* to refer to either 1) a failure to form this attachment during the early months or 2) a disruption or loss of an existing attachment. In both cases the child is deprived of the love of a mother figure. In Bowlby's words, 'The young child's hunger for his mother's love and presence is as great as his hunger for food'. This love and presence are as essential for healthy psychological development as 'vitamins and minerals are for physical development' (Bowlby, 1973).

In short, if attachment to a mother figure is absent or broken, then the effects on the child could be serious. However, Bowlby believed that these effects could be reduced by the return of an absent mother or the provision of a mother substitute.

According to Bowlby, fostering or adoption may provide adequate care since they involve a single mother figure with whom a primary attachment can be made. Institutional care, for

example local authority care homes and orphanages, is unlikely to provide a replacement mother figure.

Internal working model Bowlby believed that the importance of the mother figure lies in the model she provides for all future relationships. This model or template develops out of the primary attachment relationship. Bowlby called it the internal working model. He argued that there is a link between early and later relationships. In particular, if the child has experienced maternal deprivation, then this may well lead to unsatisfactory relationships in later life – for example, the inability to form close and long-lasting relationships.

1.2 Deprivation and psychopathy

Bowlby's maternal deprivation hypothesis was based in part on his own research. Bowlby worked as a psychiatrist at the London Child Guidance Clinic during the 1930s. He recorded case histories of some of the boys he saw which formed the basis for his research, published in 1946 and titled *Forty-four juvenile thieves: Their characters and their home lives*. Bowlby selected a sample of 44 'thieves' and compared them to 44 boys with no criminal record who had attended the clinic. He classed 14 of the thieves as *affectionless psychopaths*.

According to Bowlby, affectionless psychopaths act impulsively with little regard for the consequences of their actions. They show no shame or remorse and have little or no concern for others. They are unable to form close, meaningful and long-lasting relationships. Bowlby believed that affectionless psychopathy often results from maternal deprivation. 12 out of the 14 'affectionless thieves' had 'early and prolonged separations from their mothers'. They had spent most of their early years in residential homes or hospitals. Of the remaining 74 children in the sample, only 7 had experienced early separations. This evidence appears to support Bowlby's claim that maternal deprivation in early life results in psychological and behavioural problems in later life.

However, there are problems with Bowlby's research. First, his sample was not representative. The vast majority of juvenile thieves are not referred to children's clinics for treatment. Second, much of the data was retrospective – based on looking back and recalling past events. It relied on the memories of the juveniles and their mothers. As a result, it may be inaccurate. Third, the diagnosis of affectionless psychopathy was made by Bowlby himself. He may have been biased, looking hard for what he hoped and expected to find. Fourth, a correlation between two things doesn't necessarily mean that one causes the other. We cannot be sure that the separations themselves caused the maladjustment. For example, both the separations and the maladjustment may have been caused by discord and conflict within the family. This possibility is examined in the next section.

Key term

Maternal deprivation *According to Bowlby, the absence of the love and care of a mother or mother figure due to either a failure to form an attachment or the loss of an existing attachment.*

Affectionless psychopathy *A lack of affection and concern for others. An inability to form close and lasting relationships. A lack of guilt or remorse for antisocial behaviour.*

1.3 Deprivation or discord?

Michael Rutter (1981) questioned Bowlby's view that separation, in and of itself, produced harmful effects for the child. He argued that the events and experiences that preceded the separation may be more important than the separation itself. Consider the following.

First, a child is separated from its mother because of the mother's longstanding illness or death. Second, a child is separated from its mother because of the mother's divorce, psychological disorder, or addiction to alcohol or heroin. Rutter suggests that the second examples are more likely to produce harmful effects. And, in his words, these effects are '*not* because of the separation involved but rather because of the discord and disharmony which led to the break'.

Evidence to support this view was provided by Rutter's study of over 2000 boys between the ages of 9 and 12 living on the Isle of Wight and in London (Rutter et al., 1976). He looked at the relationship between separation and delinquency. If the separation was due to the physical illness or death of the mother, there was no correlation with delinquency. However, if the separation was due to the psychological disorder of one or both parents, or to discord within the family, then the boys were four times more likely to become delinquent. Rutter concluded that it is the conflict and stress which precedes separation rather than the separation itself which is likely to be the underlying cause of antisocial behaviour.

However, two critical points should be made about Rutter et al's study. Like Bowlby's *Forty-four juvenile thieves*, the data was collected retrospectively (after the event) and may,

therefore, be unreliable; and the evidence is correlational, therefore no cause and effect can be established.

1.4 The effects of institutions

Apart from his own research, Bowlby based his maternal deprivation hypothesis on a number of other studies. During the 1930s and 40s, there was a growing body of research which seemed to indicate that psychological health, cognitive development and social development were linked to early attachment experience. For example, Goldfarb (1943) looked at the effects on children of being raised in an institution. He compared two groups of 15 children. The first group went directly from their 'natural' mothers to foster parents before the age of one. The second group were raised in a residential nursery then fostered between the ages of 6 months and $3^{1}/_{2}$ years.

The two groups were assessed between the ages of 10 and 14. The institutional group lagged behind on every measure of development. They had lower IQs, poorer language skills, they were less able to form relationships and less likely to follow rules and social norms.

What accounts for these differences? The physical care – food, clothing, hygiene – in the residential and foster homes was similar. The quality of care provided by the two groups of foster parents was similar. The main difference seemed to be the presence or absence of attachment during the early months. This, Goldfarb suggested, explains the differences between the two groups. In his words, 'strong anchors to specific adults were not established' in the case of the children who spent their early years in the institution.

Evaluation Although it appeared to provide strong support for Bowlby's maternal deprivation hypothesis, there are problems with Goldfarb's research. His sample was not random. Infants in the first group had been selected for immediate fostering. Those in the second group had been kept in the nursery before being fostered. This might mean there were differences between the two groups. Maybe members of the institutional group were more prone to illness, more socially withdrawn, less attractive, and therefore less likely to appeal to foster parents. Differences such as these, rather than attachment, may account for the differences between the two groups in later life.

Goldfarb argued that the problems of the children raised in the nursery were due to a failure to form attachments during infancy. But, these problems may be due, at least in part, to the conditions within the nursery. Babies under 9 months were kept in single cubicles and their only human contact was when they were fed and changed. In view of this, it is not surprising that they had poor language and social skills. Later research has shown that babies raised in a stimulating environment in institutions have far fewer problems than those in Goldfarb's study (Smith et al., 1998). Thus the lack of stimulation resulting from social isolation, rather than a failure to form attachments, may have caused the developmental problems experienced by the children in Goldfarb's research.

1.5 Deprivation and privation

In *Maternal deprivation reassessed* (1981), Michael Rutter argues that Bowlby's use of the term deprivation was vague and imprecise. Rutter felt there was an important distinction to be made between *privation* and *deprivation*. He defined privation as a lack or absence of attachment due to a failure to form an attachment between infant and caregiver. A newborn baby who is placed in an orphanage and fails to make an attachment is an example of privation. Deprivation refers to the loss of an attachment that has already been made, in other words, the loss of something that was previously there. The separation of mother and child due to the mother's illness or death is an example of deprivation.

Rutter argues that the distinction between privation and deprivation is important because each may have different effects. He believes that harmful, long-term effects are due more to privation than deprivation. For example, an inability to form lasting relationships in later life is more likely to result from a *lack* of attachment (privation) than a *loss* of attachment (deprivation).

Despite this criticism, Rutter accepted Bowlby's main argument, that attachment is important for healthy psychological development.

Key terms

Social norms *The accepted and expected ways of behaving in society.*

Stimulation *Something outside the individual to which they respond. In the case of infants and children, stimulation includes attention and affection from others and physical contact and social interaction with others.*

Privation *A lack of attachment due to the failure to form an attachment.*

Deprivation *A loss of an existing attachment due to the separation of an infant and its attachment figure.*

Summary

1. Bowlby believed that a single primary attachment to a mother figure was essential for the child's healthy psychological development.

2. Early research often failed to consider factors other than privation and deprivation which may contribute to developmental problems. These include:
   - Lack of stimulation during infancy
   - The conflict and stress which may precede separation.

3. According to Rutter, Bowlby failed to distinguish between privation and deprivation. This distinction is important because each may have different effects.

Activity 1   Deprivation and privation

Item A   Separation and antisocial behaviour

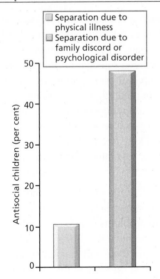

Separation due to physical illness
Separation due to family discord or psychological disorder

Antisocial children (per cent)

This bar chart shows the reasons for parent-child separation in relation to antisocial behaviour.

Adapted from Rutter et al., 1976

Item B   The 'non-recoverables'

After the overthrow of the dictator Nicolae Ceaucescu in 1990, the appalling conditions in Romanian orphanages were revealed to the world. Many of the 40,000 infants and children in these institutions were referred to as 'non-recoverables'. They were found tied to their beds, starving and filthy. Often, they had never been held. No one had talked to them. They rock back and forth, staring blankly.

Adapted from Sachs, 1990, quoted in Zimbardo et al., 1995

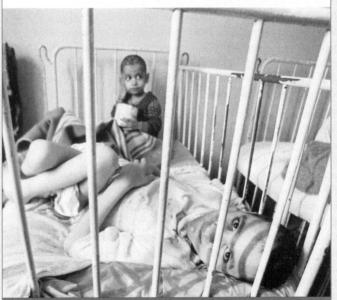

Children in a Romanian orphanage

Questions

1. Use Item A to argue that Bowlby overestimated the importance of maternal deprivation.

2. Suggest reasons for the behaviour of the children in Item B.

Unit 2 The effects of deprivation/separation

KEY ISSUES

1. What are the short-term effects of separation?
2. What are the long-term effects of separation?

Separation is an alternative term for deprivation. It is a more neutral term and sounds less problematic. The word separation does not necessarily imply that the experience is harmful.

Children may be separated from their caregivers in a number of ways. They may experience separation for a few hours every day if their caregiver goes out to work. They may be placed in day care – with a childminder or in a nursery school. They may experience temporary separations for days or weeks due to hospitalisation – when they or their caregiver stays in hospital. Or they may experience long-term separation due to the death or divorce of their parents.

This unit looks at the possible short-term and long-term effects of separation on the child's development. The possible effects of day care are examined in the following chapter.

2.1 Short-term effects

In an early study, Spitz and Wolf (1946) looked at 123 babies whose mothers were in prison. While in prison, the women cared for their babies from birth to around nine months. Then, for a three month period, the babies were taken away from their mothers and placed in a nursery. Although the standard of physical care provided was high, the babies showed signs of distress – frequent crying, a loss of appetite and a failure to gain weight. Spitz and Wolf believed that this distress was due to the absence of the mothers and the loss of the love they provided. The babies resumed their normal behaviour and gained weight when they were returned to their mothers.

Bowlby used this research to support his maternal deprivation hypothesis. However, as with Goldfarb's (1943) research on infants raised in institutions (see p 65), it is not clear whether the effects were due to an absence of maternal love or to a lack of stimulation in the institution.

Hospitalisation Evidence of the significance of short-term separation was provided by James and Joyce Robertson who worked closely with Bowlby and were involved in developing the maternal deprivation hypothesis. The Robertsons and Bowlby made a series of films about short-term separation, for example *A two-year-old goes to hospital* (1952). At the time, many psychologists believed that children experience anxiety when deprived of the care of their primary caregiver, but most felt that this anxiety could be easily overcome by good physical care. The Robertsons and Bowlby disagreed. They suggested that this anxiety might lead to an extreme and pathological reaction. (Pathological means diseased. They used this term to suggest that the consequences were similar to a physical illness.)

One of their films was about a two-year-old boy going into hospital. Another film showed a boy, also two years old, being admitted to a residential nursery. Despite good *physical* care, the emotional support wasn't there. Both boys displayed acute distress. This was the central point of the films. The boys experienced *bond disruption* – a temporary break in the attachment to their primary caregiver. The boy in residential care was only there for nine days. But he changed rapidly from a cheerful and affectionate to a withdrawn and despairing child. On his return home, he was sullen, rejecting towards his mother, and there were severe behaviour problems throughout his childhood including repeatedly running away from home.

This was in contrast to two young girls, also filmed by the Robertsons. Aged around two, the girls stayed with the Robertsons while their mother was in hospital. They had visited the Robertsons beforehand, and when they came to stay they brought personal items, such as toys, and maintained contact with their father. They also followed their normal daily routine and the Robertsons made a point of being mother substitutes. The girls showed some signs of distress but generally adapted well. The Robertsons claimed that the key was continued maternal care during separation – the stress of bond disruption was reduced because there was substitute emotional care.

Evaluation The films were based on very small samples so it is not possible to make generalisations. However, the separation distress they reveal reflected what staff in hospitals and residential nurseries had regularly observed. The films were extremely influential. In particular, they changed hospital visiting policies and raised awareness about the importance of emotional as well as physical care.

The protest-despair-detachment model

When a child is separated from its main caregiver, the first response is likely to be crying. Some children stop crying quite quickly and turn their attention elsewhere. If separation continues then the child is likely to respond in a recognisable sequence of stages. Bowlby and the Robertsons were the first to outline this *protest-despair-detachment model* which may occur over a period of days or weeks. In response to separation, a child may go through the following stages.

1 **Protest** The child cries but can be comforted. The child is agitated, fearful and angry and tries to regain the attention of their attachment figure.

2 **Despair** The child becomes outwardly calmer and appears apathetic – showing little emotion or interest in their surroundings. Inwardly, the fear and anger remain. The child no longer looks for the attachment figure, shows little interest in comfort offered by others, and may seek self-comfort through thumb-sucking or rocking.

3 **Detachment** This stage may occur after prolonged separation. The child appears to be coping well and responds to other people. However, the child seems emotionally detached – not really involved in relationships with others. Little interest is shown when the attachment figure eventually reappears.

It is important to note that a) this is only one possible response to separation and b) if a child goes through the first stage, they do not necessarily go on to the second and third.

Factors affecting the separation response

Infants and young children respond to temporary separation in a variety of ways. Some find it extremely distressing, other do not. Some go through the three stages of protest, despair and detachment, others do not. This section looks at some of the factors which may affect the way young children experience and respond to separation.

Age Distress from temporary separation seems less evident in infants below the age of 6 months or so, as firm attachments have yet to be formed. It appears most frequently between the ages of 7 months and three years, particularly during the period 12-18 months (Maccoby, 1980). Older children cope better, probably because they have learned that separation is followed by reunion. Also their language skills have developed, so parents can explain that the separation will be short – a few hours or a few days – and so children can look forward to the reunion. Younger children may feel abandoned and may even blame themselves for the separation.

Strange environment Distress appears greater when separation takes place in a strange environment rather than a familiar one (Ross et al., 1975). However, young children admitted to hospital with their mother show less distress than those admitted alone (Fagin, 1966). This suggests that both separation and the strangeness of the environment affect the level of distress.

Multiple attachments As noted in Chapter 4, most children form multiple attachments – with their mother, father, siblings (brothers and sisters) and grandparents. Distress resulting from separation from their primary caregiver can be reduced by the presence of other attachment figures. For example, distress on entry to a residential nursery can be reduced if the child is accompanied by a sibling (Heinicke & Westheimer, 1965).

Multiple attachments mean that the child is not dependent on a single caregiver. When both parents are regularly involved with caregiving, children show less distress when left alone with strangers (Kotelchuk, 1976).

Continuity In general, the more the child's everyday routines can be maintained, the less serious the distress. The Robertsons' film about the young girls whose mother was in hospital illustrated this point. Although living with the Robertsons, the girls continued their daily routines. This provided some continuity with their lives before the separation.

Experience of separations If children have regular experience of short-term separations (and reunions), they are less likely to experience distress. A study of four-year-old children who spent four days in hospital having their tonsils removed showed that those who had experienced regular separations were less likely to find their stay distressing. They were used to being away from home having stayed overnight, without their parents, at grandparents and friends (Stacey et al., 1970).

Individual differences No two people are the same. Children differ in terms of their characteristics and personalities. For example, some are confident and outgoing, others are shy and lacking in confidence. Such differences will affect their experience of and response to separation.

Family circumstances Research indicates that children from low-income, so-called 'disadvantaged' families, may experience separation as more stressful than children from higher-income families. It has been suggested that conflict and insecurity are more likely in low-income families due to the pressures of poverty. This magnifies the negative effects of separation (Quinton & Rutter, 1976).

Key terms

Bond disruption *A temporary break in the attachment relationship due to separation.*

The protest-despair-detachment model *The stages a child may go through in response to separation from their main caregiver.*

Conclusion There is general agreement that the effects of temporary separation can be distressing for many young children. However, in most cases, the effects are likely to be short-term – most children soon resume their normal behaviour when reunited with their caregiver. As a result, temporary separation is unlikely to have long-term effects on the child's development.

This section has shown that the separation experience is affected by a range of factors. These factors must be taken into account in any explanation of children's response to separation. However, researchers generally agree that in times of distress children are in greatest need of their caregivers. Therefore, even if distress is caused by something other than separation, then separation will probably make it worse.

Working mothers

So far, this unit has looked at irregular and infrequent separations, such as stays in hospital. What about regular and frequent separations, for example when both parents go out to work?

Bowlby (1953) issued the following warning to mothers – 'If you don't do your five years' hard labour when the child is young, you do it later'. This implied that the mother should stay at home and look after her children, at least until they start full-time education. This reflected the general view of the role of mothers during the 1950s. From the 1950s, there has been a steady growth in the employment of mothers with young children. How might the resulting separations affect the child?

Most researchers now agree that early fears about the effects of working mothers on their children were greatly exaggerated. In fact some research indicates that the effects can be beneficial – children of working mothers tend to be more independent and self-sufficient then children who receive full-time mothering. However, the main finding from research is that there is no simple answer to the question of how working mothers affect children's development. There are a wide range of factors which need to be taken into account. These include:

- The child's age – some researchers believe that full-time mothering is essential during the first year though others disagree
- The child's sex – there is some evidence that boys tend to experience more ill effects than girls
- The child's temperament
- The number of hours the mother works
- The quality of childcare when she is at work
- The amount of support provided by the father.

These are some of the many factors which contribute to the atmosphere in which the child is raised and the relationship between children and their mothers. As a result, there is no simple, straightforward cause and effect relationship between working mothers and child development (Schaffer, 1996).

2.2 Long-term effects

So far, this unit has focused on the short-term effects of separation, effects that tend to last for days and weeks rather than years. Are there longer-term effects?

Separation and disadvantage A longitudinal study (a study of the same group over time) looked at 5000 children born in 1946 (Douglas, 1975). The study indicated a link between prolonged or repeated hospital admissions, especially under the age of four, and behaviour disturbance and antisocial behaviour in adolescence.

However, this correlation does not necessarily mean that separation caused antisocial behaviour in adolescence. Both the separation and the behaviour may have been caused by other factors. Clarke and Clarke (1976) re-analysed the data and concluded that, in many cases, both the hospital admissions, which led to the separations, and the antisocial behaviour were due to poverty and disadvantage. Children raised in poverty are more likely to suffer from ill-health as a result of inadequate housing and poor nutrition. They are also more likely to be arrested for alleged crimes and to behave in ways seen as disruptive and antisocial, particularly by teachers. This behaviour may result, in part, from discord and conflict within the family which stems from the stress of living in poverty. It may result from failure at school which again might be due, in part, to poverty. Or it can be seen, more generally, as a reaction to their disadvantaged situation. Behaviour in adolescence may therefore be a response to disadvantage rather than a response to separation at an early age.

Reasons for separation There are all sorts of reasons for temporary separations. Some may be joyful, such as the child going on holiday with a friend's family. Others may be distressing, such as a serious illness which results in the mother's admission to hospital. Do the reasons for separation make a significant difference to the long-term effects?

Rutter's study of over 2000 boys between the ages of 9 and 12 suggests a possible answer to this question. As outlined in Unit 1, Rutter looked at the relationship between separation and delinquency. If the separation was due to the physical illness or death of the mother, or to holidays or housing difficulties, there was no correlation between delinquency and separation. However, if the separation was due to the psychological disorder of one or both parents, or to discord and conflict within the family, then the boys were four times more likely to become delinquent. Rutter suggests it is the reasons for the separation, not simply the separation itself, which produce long-term effects.

Conclusion As with short-term effects, there is no simple, straightforward relationship between separation and long-term effects. A child experiences a whole range of significant events between their early years and later life. Any of these can affect future behaviour. It is extremely difficult to separate the effects of these events from the effects of separation during the early years.

Parental death

The death of a parent results in a permanent separation from an attachment figure. Bifulco et al. (1992) studied a group of 249 women who were separated from their mothers before they were 17, either through separation for more than a year, or through the mother's death. The group as a whole had twice the normal rate of depression and anxiety disorders in adulthood. However, the women who were under the age of 6 when their mothers had *died* had a particularly high rate of depression. This was not true where *separation* occurred before the age of 6. This suggests two things. First, there is a sensitive period before the age of 6 when children are particularly attached to their main caregiver. Second, there is a difference between permanent separation (even where there is substitute maternal care from a father, grandparent or step-parent) and temporary separation.

There are some similarities between the response to death and the response to other forms of separation. Bowlby (1953) notes the similarity between adult mourning and the despair stage of response to separation in a young child.

A number of factors will modify the effect of parental death. They include the amount and quality of substitute care which is subsequently provided and the effect the death has on the rest of the family, particularly the remaining parent. Recovery may depend to some extent on how well children are helped to cope with their mourning. For example, Bowlby (1953) believes that adults should encourage children to grieve 'naturally' rather than trying to divert their attention from the bereavement.

Divorce

The divorce rate rose rapidly in all Western societies during the 20th century. It is estimated that if present trends continue, around 40% of marriages in the UK will end in divorce. During the 1990s, about 65% of divorces involved couples with children under the age of 16. In 1997, around 30% of the children affected were under 5, and over 70% under 10 (*Social Trends*, 1999).

It is difficult to separate the long-term effects of divorce from the many other factors which affect children's development. Findings from a range of studies suggest the following long-term effects of divorce.

- A lower level of self control. Children of divorced parents tend to be more disruptive and disobedient both at home and at school. This applies particularly to boys who tend to be aggressive, while girls are more likely to withdraw into themselves.

- A lower level of academic attainment – progress at school suffers.

- A tendency to leave school early and to take low-paid, low-skill jobs. Children of divorced parents are more likely to start a family before the age of 20 and more likely to get divorced themselves. The combination of low qualifications, low pay and dependent children often leads to financial difficulties.

- A high level of emotional and psychological problems – young men in particular are more likely to suffer from depression.
(Richards, 1994; Schaffer, 1996).

These findings are generalisations. They do not apply to all children of divorced couples. As with all types of separation, the effects of divorce are influenced by a wide range of factors. These include the age of the child when the parents divorce, the financial circumstances of the family unit after the parents divorce, the relationship of the divorced couple, their relationship with the children, whether the parents re-marry and the relationship between step-parent and children.

The pre-divorce family A number of researchers have suggested that relationships within the family before the divorce may be as important, if not more important, than the divorce itself. Using data from two large-scale longitudinal studies – the British National Child Development Study and the US National Survey of Children – Cherlin et al., (1991) found that the apparent effects of divorce were often present well before the divorce took place. For example, if children's progress at school was poor and their conduct disruptive, this often occurred before as well as after the divorce.

According to Schaffer (1996), many of the effects attributed to divorce may be due to parental conflict which was present before, during and after the divorce. Research indicates that children from divorced families in which there is little conflict are better adjusted than children from two-parent families where there is regular conflict between the parents (Amato & Keith, 1991).

How might parental conflict harm children's development? Young children are often frightened by parental conflict. Most, if not all, children are unsettled, distressed and hurt. Children don't get used to parental conflict and learn to live with it. Things get worse rather than better. Parents are short-tempered and often take out their frustration on the children. They tend to be preoccupied with their own conflict and neglect the child's emotional development. Faced with this daily conflict, children have difficulty controlling their own emotions. Like their parents, who provide a model for their behaviour, children often have difficulty regulating emotions such as aggression. This suggests that the actual separation produced by divorce is only part of a wider pattern of behaviour which affects the child's development (Cummings, 1994; Schaffer, 1996).

Conclusion

This unit has examined the short-term and long-term effects of separation on children's development. The evidence suggests there is no simple, straightforward relationship between separation and development. Separation affects children in all sorts of ways for all sorts of reasons. A multitude of factors modify the effects of separation. Many of the supposed effects of separation are, at least in part, due to factors which precede the separation. In view of this, generalisations about the effects of separation must be treated with caution.

Summary

1 Studies of hospitalisation indicate that infants and young children may find separation distressing. However, the effects are usually short-term.

2 A number of factors may affect the separation response. These include:
   - The age of the child
   - The familiarity of the environment
   - The presence of other attachment figures
   - Whether or not daily routines are maintained
   - Previous experience of separations
   - Individual differences
   - Family circumstances
   - The reasons for the separation

3 There is no simple cause and effect relationship between working mothers and children's development.

4 Research indicates that divorce may have long-term, harmful effects on children's development.

5 Some researchers argue that these effects are due to a history of parental conflict rather than divorce itself.

6 The separation experience is influenced by a range of factors. As a result, generalisations about the effects of separation must be treated with caution.

Activity 2   Evacuation

Item A   The evacuation

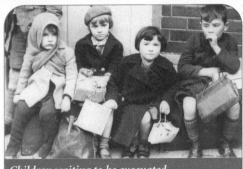

Children waiting to be evacuated.

In September 1939, 1.5 million children were evacuated from major British cities that were likely to be bombed by the Germans. Most of them returned home within a year. They were sent to live with families in the countryside. Children under 5 were accompanied by their mothers. Many of the children were distressed as they left home – they didn't know where they were going or how long they were going to be there. Others were apprehensive but excited at the prospect of life in the countryside.

Many were lucky. Often from low-income, inner-city slums, this was their first experience of the countryside, of fresh air, good food and a decent home. With kind foster parents they flourished. Others were not so lucky. They felt unloved and uncared for. Some missed their mums and could think of little else. There were sometimes problems when the behaviour of working-class children clashed with the expectations of their middle-class foster parents. A minority of evacuees had dreadful experiences. They were overworked and, in some cases, physically and sexually abused.

Adapted from Lynn, 1989; Lancaster & Lancaster, 1993

Returning home

Item B **Contrasting reactions**

After nearly 50 years, two women look back on their lives as evacuees. Margaret wouldn't have missed it 'for anything'. Freda, despite being cared for by a kind woman, wished it had never happened.

Margaret I learned to appreciate so many things in life and even today I much prefer the country to the town.

For years and years after I came home I kept in touch with my foster parents and I still visit Ulverston, my second home. I am sorry to say that my foster parents are now no longer with us, but they will always have a special place in my heart.

The first family I stayed with, and mostly my second, they did a wonderful job of looking after me and it must have been from love, it certainly can't have been for the $37\frac{1}{2}$p the government gave them.

Freda The whole experience marked me for life. Until fairly recent years I suffered bad bouts of homesickness if I was away from home for any time; I find it exceptionally difficult to trust anyone other than my husband; for a large part of my young adult life I suffered badly from depression and feelings of rejection. I am angry that the whole scheme was so ill thought out and put into operation – they were messing about with children's lives, for God's sake, how dare they give it so little thought.

Adapted from Wicks, 1988

Question

Generalisations about the experience and effects of separation should be treated with caution. Discuss, with some reference to the evacuation during World War II.

Unit 3 The effects of privation

KEY ISSUES

1. **What effect does privation during the early years have on later life?**
2. **To what extent can these effects be reversed?**

Privation refers to a failure to form an attachment to a main caregiver. Early researchers, such as Bowlby and Goldfarb, believed that privation in infancy resulted in harmful effects in later life. These effects were seen as largely irreversible and permanent. The child was therefore pictured as a prisoner of their early experience.

Privation has generally been seen as more harmful than separation. For example, Rutter (1981) argued that long-term, harmful effects were more likely to be due to privation.

This unit looks at two types of privation – children raised in institutions during their early years, and 'isolated' children who have been locked away by their parents and isolated from the wider society.

3.1 Institutional childcare

This section looks at children who have spent their early years in institutions – orphanages or residential nurseries. The first part looks at institutions in which the quality of care is low, the second part at institutions where the quality of care is high. This comparison provides some indication of the importance of different types of care.

Low quality care

A longitudinal study of children brought up in a Lebanese orphanage was conducted by Wayne Dennis (1973). The children were placed in the orphanage shortly after birth. They were looked after by caregivers who had themselves been raised in the orphanage until the age of 6. The caregivers provided the children with basic physical care – they bathed, dressed, changed and fed them. However, they rarely spoke to or played with them – babies were left to lie in their cribs all day. Once they could walk they were left in playpens with only a ball to play with.

Dennis assessed the infants at 2 months and they appeared normal for their age. However, at the end of a year their cognitive development had slumped to only half the normal level. At age 6, the boys and girls were sent to separate institutions. The girls continued to receive little attention and stimulation. At 16, they had an average IQ of 50 (100 is the average for the general population). They could hardly read, they could not tell the time or dial a telephone number.

The boys were luckier. They were trained for jobs outside the institution by workers who came from the surrounding area. They were also taken on trips. Compared to the girls, their experiences were more varied and their environment was more stimulating. By age 15, the boys' average IQ was 80, a substantial improvement on their early years and within the range that would allow them to function normally in the wider society.

Some of the children from the orphanage were adopted. Those who were adopted before they were 2 (when their IQ averaged 50) had normal IQs (around 100) when they were tested 2-3 years later. Those who were adopted between the ages of 2 and 6 were only slightly below normal in terms of IQ when tested later.

This study indicates that, at least to some extent, the effects of privation depend on the environment. The more stimulating the environment, the more normal the child's intellectual development. It also suggests that to some degree children can catch up when their development has fallen behind. However, it appears that the amount of catching up depends partly on the age of the child. There may be a critical period of intellectual development between the ages of 2 and 6. Children adopted before the age of 2 developed normally, those adopted between 2 and 6 improved considerably but their IQ remained below normal. However, there is another possibility – children selected for early adoption may have been more intelligent than those adopted later.

High quality care

Barbara Tizard and her colleagues studied 65 English working-class children who had been raised in a residential nursery from just after birth until 2 or more years of age (Hodges & Tizard, 1989). The children were assessed at age 4^1/$_2$, 8 and 16 and compared with a similar group of working-class children who had been raised at home.

The nursery had well-trained staff who provided high standards of care. The children were given plenty of attention and there was no shortage of books and toys. This was reflected in the children's cognitive development. By age 4^1/$_2$, they had an average IQ score of 105 and their language development was normal for children of their age.

The children had little opportunity to form close attachments to their caregivers. There was a high turnover of staff and by age 2, an average of 24 caregivers had looked after each child for at least a week; by age 4 the average was 50. In addition, the nursery discouraged strong attachments between staff and children.

Most of the children in the nursery were adopted or restored to their biological families between the ages of 2 and 7. Tizard assessed their development at age 4^1/$_2$, 8 and 16. By age 8, most of the adopted and some of the restored children had formed close attachments to their parents. The adoptive parents really wanted a child and put considerable effort into building a relationship. The biological parents were less sure about their child's return – often they had financial problems and other children to care for. As a result, fewer of the restored children formed close attachments. According to their teachers, some of the children from both groups (adopted and restored) showed problems. They described them as attention-seeking, particularly from adults, restless, disobedient, quarrelsome and unpopular with their peers.

At 16, this picture was largely repeated. Adopted children in general had close and affectionate relationships with their parents. Restored children were more likely to have poor family relationships. But some members of *both* groups were still rated by teachers as attention seeking, unpopular with their peers and quarrelsome. They were less likely to have a 'special friend' but more likely to be friendly to any of their classmates. However, this assessment applied to only *half* the children raised in the nursery. And the researchers point out that their behaviour characteristics are *differences* and not necessarily *difficulties*.

Conclusion

What does this study show?

- First, 'early institutional care and the lack of close attachments had not had the drastically damaging effects predicted by Bowlby' (Hodges & Tizard, 1989).
- Second, the quality of care and the stimulation received by children raised in an institution can have real effects on their cognitive development. This is indicated by a comparison of the studies of Lebanese and English children.
- Third, attachments to parents can be made *after* the age of 2, though the strength of the attachment depends, to some extent, on the amount of love and care provided by the parents.
- Fourth, despite these attachments, there do appear to be lasting effects of privation in the case of some children which continue at least to the age of 16
- Fifth, these lasting effects applied to only half the institutionalised children. This suggests the effects of privation are *not* inevitable.
- Sixth, these effects are *differences* and not necessarily difficulties or problems.

Reversing the effects of privation

The studies examined so far in this unit indicate that the effects of privation are not inevitable, that they are not necessarily permanent, that they can be reversed. This section looks at two studies which suggest that the effects of privation are reversible.

A longitudinal study examined 13 children classified as 'mentally retarded' (Skodak & Skeels, 1945). Their average IQ was 64. They had been raised in an understaffed, overcrowded orphanage where they received little attention. Aged between 11 and 21 months, they were moved to a woman's ward in an institution for the mentally retarded. There, both staff and inmates lavished them with love and attention, played with them and took them on outings.

The transformation was dramatic. Within 19 months they changed from apathetic, withdrawn infants to lively, alert young children. Their average IQ rose from 64 to 92. Over the same period, the average IQ of a control group of 12 children who remained in the orphanage dropped from 87 to 61. By the age of 3 or 4, most of the children in the experimental group (those who had been moved to the woman's ward) had been adopted by families and went on to standard schools.

Over 20 years later, a follow-up study showed that the gains made by these children were lasting. Their grades at school were significantly higher than those of the control group, four went to college and one achieved a PhD. They had a wide range of jobs including teacher, sales manager and airline stewardess. Only one member of the control group had a skilled job. The rest either had unskilled jobs, were unemployed, or still lived in the orphanage (Skeels, 1966).

This study suggests that the effects of early privation can be reversed given the right environment. It indicates that the effects of early childhood experience need not be permanent.

The following investigation is not a study of privation as such, but again it suggests that the effects of early childhood experience can be reversed. Kagan (1976) studied Native American children in an isolated village in Guatemala in Central America. During their first year, the children spent most of their time in dark, windowless huts – it was assumed that sunlight and fresh air were harmful to babies. They slept a lot, they had no toys, and their parents rarely played with or talked to them. They appeared passive, withdrawn and unresponsive. In terms of their development at age one, they were 3 to 4 months behind infants of the same age in the United States.

Once they could walk, at around 13-16 months, the infants

were allowed out and soon learned to play and interact like 'normal' infants. In a follow-up study in late childhood, they achieved normal scores for their age on a range of cognitive and social tests (Kagan, 1976).

This was not a study of privation – the children had formed relationships with their mothers from an early age. However, it does indicate that being deprived of stimulation during the first year of life does not necessarily have permanent effects on children's development. They can catch up – the effects are reversible.

Methodological problems

There have been a number of criticisms of the methods used in studies of institutional privation. They include the following.

Samples This unit has looked at three studies of children raised in institutions. Unit 1 looked at a further study conducted by Goldfarb (1943). In each case, the sample size was different and, in terms of their social background and nationality, the members of each sample were different. In addition, the numbers in each sample were small – for example, 13 in Skeels' study, 15 in Goldfarb's, and 65 in Tizard's. Because of the differences between the samples it is difficult to compare the studies. Because of the small samples it is difficult to generalise from the results.

Dropout All four studies were longitudinal – they studied members of the same group over time. All longitudinal studies face the problem of 'dropout' – some of the children or their parents may refuse to take part or cannot be contacted at later stages of the research. Tizard's original sample of 65 was reduced to 51 at age 8 and to 42 at age 16 – a 35% reduction. This can affect the results, especially if those who drop out are different in important respects from those who remain.

Validity of data Tizard's study was based largely on questionnaires and interviews with nursery staff, parents and teachers. They were asked to make assessments of the children. How valid (true) were these assessments? For example, the assessments made by teachers were probably influenced by the fact that they knew which of their pupils had been raised in the nursery. This knowledge may well have led them to see these children differently.

Time scale Longitudinal studies of children raised in institutions usually stop when the children are teenagers. To fully gauge the effects of privation, the children should be studied throughout their lives. This raises at least two problems. First, the original researchers will be dead before the study ends. Second, in view of the dropout rate in Tizard's study (35% between ages 4$\frac{1}{2}$ and 16), how many will be left in the sample when they approach old age?

3.2 Isolated children

Isolated children provide examples of extreme privation. During their early years they have usually been locked away by their parents and isolated from the wider society.

The Czech twins Identical twin boys were born in Czechoslovakia in 1960. Their mother died shortly after their birth. They spent their first 18 months in an institution then went to live with their father and his new wife. She took an instant dislike to them. The twins were shut away in a small, unheated room and kept apart from the rest of the family. The only time they left the room was when they were locked in the cellar as a punishment. They were deprived of proper food, exercise, sunshine and, apart from each other, human companionship.

When they were rescued at the age of 7, they looked like 3-year-olds. They were abnormally small, they could hardly walk because of rickets, they relied mainly on gestures to communicate and could barely talk. At first, they were terrified of the new sights and sounds around them – traffic, television, mechanical toys.

The twins were placed in a residential nursery for preschool children. At age 8, they were placed in the care of two sisters who provided a loving and secure family environment. The twins soon put on weight and learned to walk and talk. At first, they were sent to a school for retarded children. They then went on to primary and secondary schools. By age 14, they were in a class of children who were only 18 months younger than themselves. Their language development was now normal for their age and their IQ, estimated to be 40 when they were discovered, was now around 100. The twins later married and had children and are reported to be enjoying warm and stable relationships (Koluchová, 1972, 1991).

Isabelle Apart from her mother, who was a deaf mute, Isabelle hardly saw anybody until she was 6$\frac{1}{2}$. She spent her early years in a darkened room. When she was discovered, she was thought to be deaf and mentally retarded. After considerable loving care and expert help, she developed in leaps and bounds. She learned more quickly than children of her own age and went through several stages of development at an accelerated rate. By the time she finished high school at 16, Isabelle had caught up with her classmates (Davis, 1949).

Genie Some time before she was 2, Genie was locked in a darkened room by her father who thought she was retarded. During the day she was tied to a chair, at night she was tied up in a sleeping bag. Other members of the family were forbidden to speak to her and she was beaten by her father if she made a sound. When she was 13, her mother escaped with her – at which point her father committed suicide. On admission to hospital, Genie weighed 59 lbs, she was unable to walk and the only sounds she made were a few whimpers.

Despite being placed with a family and receiving expert help, Genie's development was limited. She remained in schools for mentally retarded students and though her IQ increased, it was well below normal at age 20. Her use of language was restricted to short phrases such as, 'Father hit arm. Big wood. Genie cry'. Her social behaviour never developed to the point where she could function in the wider society (Curtiss, 1977).

Conclusion It is difficult to draw any firm conclusions from studies of isolated children for the following reasons.

- The cases are few in number, and even fewer are well-documented and researched.
- The experiences of the children, both during their early and later years, vary considerably. For example, the Czech children had each other, Isabelle had her mother – albeit a deaf mute, and Genie had nobody.
- There is no way of knowing whether they were retarded at birth. For example, Genie's backwardness may have been innate (inborn).

However, researchers have drawn the following tentative conclusions from studies of isolated children.

- Extreme isolation, a lack of caregiving and normal social relationships during the early years can severely limit a child's development.
- However, this setback is not always irreversible. Children are not necessarily prisoners of their early childhood experience. In developmental terms, they can catch up as the cases of the Czech twins and Isabelle suggest.
- This indicates that some researchers may have placed too much emphasis on the early years with ideas such as critical and sensitive periods. Studies of isolated children suggest that these periods are not as crucial as was once thought. Effective learning and normal development can occur even if they have not occurred during the early years.

3.3 The outcomes of privation

As with separation, there is no simple, straightforward relationship between privation during the early years and behaviour in later life. Even when children have similar experiences of privation, as in the Tizard study, some are apparently affected by this experience as teenagers, others are not.

Clarke & Clarke (1998) point out that early experience represents 'no more than an initial step on the ongoing path of life'. This means that privation is only a first step. Its effects may be modified or changed by later 'steps' in the path of life. This point is illustrated by the studies examined in this unit. They

have shown that early experience matters but is not irreversible. Many of the children raised in institutions and even some of those who experienced extreme isolation develop normally, despite their early years of privation.

Summary

1. Studies of children raised in institutions indicate that privation does not necessarily have harmful effects.

2. The quality of care provided by the institutions has important effects on the child's development.

3. Strong attachment to foster parents can be made after the child leaves the institution. These attachments can be formed after the age of 2.

4. For *some* children raised in institutions, privation does appear to have lasting effects, at least until the age of 16.

5. Extreme isolation can severely restrict a child's development. However, some children can recover from this experience and develop normally.

6. It is difficult to reach firm conclusions from studies of isolated children.

7. The effects of privation can be reversed, modified and changed by a child's experience after the early years.

Activity 3   Isolated children

Item A   Changes in IQ scores

The Czech twins

[Graph: IQ vs Age (years). Y-axis IQ from 40 to 100. X-axis Age from 7 to 14. Two lines labelled Twin P and Twin J rising from about 40 at age 7 to near 95–98 at age 14.]

Genie

[Graph: IQ vs Age (years). Y-axis IQ from 40 to 100. X-axis Age from 14 to 20. One line rising from 40 at age 14 to about 74 at age 20.]

Adapted from Smith et al., 1998

Item B   Kamala and Amala

In 1920 two girls were reportedly discovered in a wolf den in Bengal, India. Aged about two and eight years, they were taken to an orphanage where they were looked after by the Reverend J.A.L. Singh and his wife. The young child, Amala, died soon after she arrived at the orphanage, the elder girl, Kamala, remained in the orphanage until 1929 when she too died. Despite the fact that Amala and Kamala were called 'wolf-children' and found in a wolf's den, there is no evidence that they were actually raised by wolves. The Reverend Singh wrote the following description of their behaviour in 1926.

'At the present time Kamala can utter about forty words. She is able to form a few sentences, each sentence containing two, or at the most, three words. She never talks unless spoken to, and when

Kamala and Amala soon after they were brought to the orphanage.

spoken to she may or may not reply. She is obedient to Mrs Singh and myself only. Kamala is possessed of very acute hearing and evidences an exceedingly acute animal-like sense of smell. She can smell meat at a great distance. Never weeps or smiles but has a 'smiling appearance'. Shed a single tear when Amala died and would not leave the place where she lay dead. She is learning very slowly to imitate. Does not now play at all and does not mingle with other children. Once both Amala and Kamala somewhat liked the company of an infant by the name of Benjamin while he was crawling and learning to talk. But one day they gave him such a biting and scratching that the infant was frightened and would never approach the wolf-children again.

Amala and Kamala liked the company of Mrs Singh, and Kamala, the surviving one of the pair, is much attached to her. The eyes of the children possessed a peculiar glare, such as that observed in the eyes of dogs or cats in the dark. Up to the present time Kamala sees better at night than during the daytime and seldom sleeps after midnight. The children used to cry or howl in a peculiar voice neither animal nor human. Kamala still makes these

Kamala receiving a biscuit from Mrs Singh.

noises at times. She is averse to all cleanliness, and serves the calls of nature anywhere, wherever she may happen to be at the time. Used to tear her clothes off. Hence a loin cloth was stitched to her in such a fashion that she could not open or tear it. Kamala used to eat and drink like a dog, lowering her mouth down to the plate, and never used her hands for the purpose of eating or drinking. She would gnaw a big bone on the ground and would rub it at times in order to separate the meat from the bone. At the present time she uses her hands for eating and walks straight on two legs but cannot run at all.'

Adapted from Hurd, 1973

Questions

1 a) Briefly summarise the changes in IQ scores shown on the graphs in Item A.

   b) Suggest reasons for the differences between the scores of the Czech twins and Genie.

2 Read Item B. Assuming Kamala had not died, do you think she would ever have been ready to enter the wider society? Give reasons for your answer.

References

Amato, P.R. & Keith, B. (1991). Parental divorce and the well-being of children: A meta-analysis. *Psychological Bulletin, 110,* 26-46.

Bilfulco, A., Harris, T. & Brown, G.W. (1992). Mourning or early inadequate care? Re-examining the relationship of maternal loss in childhood with adult depression and anxiety. *Development and Psychopathology, 4,* 433-449.

Bowlby, J. (1946). *Forty-four juvenile thieves.* London: Balliere, Tindall and Cox.

Bowlby, J. (1951). *Maternal care and mental health.* Geneva, Switzerland: World Health Organisation.

Bowlby, J. (1965). *Child care and the growth of love* (2nd ed.). Harmondsworth: Penguin.

Bowlby, J. (1973). *Attachment and loss, vol. 2: Separation.* London: Hogarth.

Cherlin, A.J., Furstenberg, F.F. Jr., Chase-Lonsdale, P.L., Kiernan, K.E., Robins, P.K., Morrison, D.R. & Teitler, J.O. (1991). Longitudinal studies of effects of divorce on children in Great Britain and the United States. *Science, 252,* 1386-1389.

Clarke, A.M. & Clarke, A.D.B. (1976). *Early experience: Myth and evidence.* London: Open Books.

Clarke, A.M. & Clarke, A.D.B. (1998). Early experience and the life path. *The Psychologist, 11,* 433-436.

Cummings, E.M. (1994). Marital conflict and children's functioning. *Social Development, 3,* 16-36.

Curtiss, S. (1977). *Genie: A psycholinguistic study of modern-day 'wild child'.* New York: Academic Press.

Davis, K. (1949). *Human society.* New York: Macmillan.

Dennis, W. (1973). *Children of the crèche.* New York: Appleton-Century-Crofts.

Douglas, J.W.B. (1975). Early hospital admissions and later disturbances of behaviour and learning. *Developmental Medicine and Child Neurology, 17,* 456-480.

Fagin, C.M.R.N. (1966). *The effects of maternal attendance during hospitalisation on the post-hospital behaviour of young children: A comparative study.* Philadelphia: Davis.

Goldfarb, W. (1943). The effects of early institutional care on adolescent personality. *Journal of Experimental Education, 12,* 106-129.

Heinicke, C.M. & Westheimer, I.J. (1965). *Brief separations.* London: Longman.

Hodges, J & Tizard, B. (1989). Social and family relationships of ex-institutional adolescents. *Journal of Child Psychology and Psychiatry, 30,* 77-97.

Hurd, G. (Ed.). (1973). *Human societies: An introduction to sociology.* London: Routledge & Kegan Paul.

Kagan, J. (1976). Resilience and continuity in psychological development. In A.M. Clarke and A.D.B. Clarke (Eds.), *Early experience: Myth and evidence.* New York: Free Press.

Koluchová, J. (1972). Severe deprivation in twins: A case study. *Journal of Child Psychology and Psychiatry, 13,* 107-114.

Koluchová, J. (1991). Severely deprived twins after twenty-two years' observation. *Studia Psychologica, 33*, 23-28.

Kotelchuk, M. (1976). The infant's relationship to the father: Experimental evidence. In M.E. Lamb (Ed.), *The role of the father in child development*. New York: Wiley.

Lancaster, T. & Lancaster, S. (1993). *The era of the Second World War*. Ormskirk: Causeway.

Lynn, V. (1989). *We'll meet again*. London: Sidgwick & Jackson.

Maccoby, E.E. (1980). *Social development : Psychological growth and the parent child relationship*. New York: Harcourt Brace Jovanovich.

Quinton, D. & Rutter, M. (1976). Early hospital admissions and later disturbances of behaviour. *Developmental Medicine and Child Neurology, 18*, 447-459.

Richards, M.P.M. (1994). The international year of the family: Family research. *The Psychologist, 8*, 17-24.

Ross, G., Kagan, J., Zelazo, P. & Kotelchuk, M. (1975). Separation protest in infants in home and laboratory. *Developmental Psychology, 11*, 256-7.

Rutter, M. (1981). *Maternal deprivation reassessed*. (2nd ed.). Harmondsworth: Penguin.

Rutter, M., Graham, P., Chadwick, D.F.D. & Yule, W. (1976). Adolescent turmoil: Fact or fiction. *Journal of Child Psychology and Psychiatry, 17*, 35-56.

Schaffer, H.R. (1996). *Social development*. Oxford: Blackwell.

Skeels, H.M. (1966). Adult status of children with contrasting early life experiences: A follow-up study. *Monographs of the Society for Research in Child Development, 31*, no. 3.

Skodak, M. & Skeels, H.M. (1945). A follow-up study of children in adoptive homes. *Journal of Genetic Psychology, 66*, 21-58.

Smith, P.K., Cowie, H. & Blades, M. (1998). *Understanding children's development* (3rd ed.). Oxford: Blackwell.

Spitz, R.A. & Wolf, K.M. (1946). Anaclitic depression. *Psychoanalytic Study of the Child, 2*, 313-342.

Stacey, M., Dearden, R., Pill, R. & Robinson, D. (1970). *Hospitals, children and their families: The report of a pilot study*. London: Routledge & Kegan Paul.

Wicks, B. *No time to wave goodbye*. London: Bloomsbury.

Zimbardo, P.G., McDermott, M., Jansz, J. & Metaal, N. (1995). *Psychology: A European text*. London: Harper Collins.

6 Day care

▶ Introduction

The demand for day care – nurseries, play groups and childminders – is growing rapidly in Western societies. This is due mainly to changing attitudes – in particular views of the role of mothers – and the increasing numbers of women entering the labour force. In the United Kingdom in 1971, just over 50% of women in the 25 to 44 age group were economically active – either in work or seeking work. By 1997, this figure had risen to over 75%. In 1998, 60% of married or cohabiting women (living with a partner but not married) with preschool children were economically active compared to 36% of lone mothers with preschool children. A survey by the Department of Education revealed that 4 out of 5 non-working mothers would take up paid employment if they could find and afford adequate day care (*Social Trends*, 1999).

Day care is now at the forefront of British government policy. The Labour government's National Childcare Strategy aims to provide good quality, affordable day care for children up to 14 years of age.

This chapter looks at the possible effects of day care on children.

Chapter summary

- **Unit 1 looks at the variation in children's day care experience.**
- **Unit 2 examines research into the possible** effects of day care on attachment, cognitive development and social development.

Unit 1 Variation in day care

KEY ISSUES

1. **How might variations in day care affect children?**
2. **Why does this make it difficult to generalise about the effects of day care?**

Varieties of day care The type of day care available for children varies considerably. It ranges from playgroups, usually organised by parents, to childminders, to day nurseries. There is also variation within each type. Playgroups may, as their name suggests, focus on play. However, they may also involve an educational component. Stories may be read to the children, educational toys provided, and children may be taught the alphabet and how to write the letters.

Similar variation exists in nurseries. Some are organised along the lines of reception classes in primary schools with an emphasis on preparation for full-time education. Others may be little different from playschools.

Similarly, childminders vary in terms of what they do with the children in their care and how many children they look after.

Quality of day care The quality of day varies enormously. For example, in day nurseries the number of staff to children varies as does their commitment to and involvement with the children. The quality of the buildings, equipment and toys also varies.

Researchers suggest that the following factors are found in high quality day care.

- A rich, varied and stimulating environment
- Small groups, particularly for infants
- A variety of activities, some structured, some unstructured

- Qualified staff who are responsive to children.

Many day nurseries fall short of these standards. For example, one survey in the USA described 86% of day nurseries as 'poor or mediocre', with only 14% described as 'good' (Cost, Quality and Outcomes Study Team, 1995).

Studies of childminding indicate similar variations in quality. A study of 66 childminders in London found that many were highly competent, but some provided little love, attention or stimulation for the children in their care (Mayall & Petrie, 1983).

Age and time in day care Children's experience of day care is affected by the age at which they enter day care – for example, before the age of one or later – and how long they spend in day care – how many hours a day, how many days a week, how many months or years. Their experience may also be affected by how often their day care is changed – for example from childminder to nursery, or from one childminder to another.

Numbers in childcare As Table 1 shows, the number of children in day care has grown rapidly. In England and Wales, the number of day care places for children under 8 rose from 648,000 in 1987 to 998,000 in 1997. This does not include unregistered childminders – those who are not registered with (and regularly inspected by) the local authority (*Social Trends*, 1999).

Problems with the evidence

As the previous section indicates, there are wide variations in the type of day care, the quality of day care, the age at which children enter day care, the length of time they spend there and the number of times their day care provision changes. All these factors will have an effect on the child's day care experience.

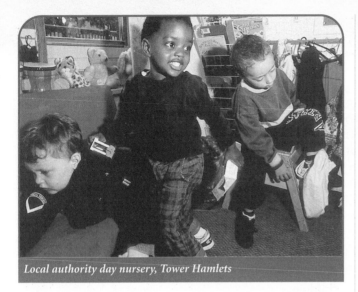

Local authority day nursery, Tower Hamlets

Because of these variations, any conclusions about the effects of day care on children must be regarded with caution. Researchers must take great care about generalising from particular studies.

In addition, a number of other factors must be taken into account. They include:

- **The social background of the children** – for example, their social class and ethnicity. Parents from low-income families may be able to afford only the least expensive day care which may be the lowest quality care. As a result, the effects of day care on children may vary from rich to poor.
- **Relationships within the family** – children's response to day care may reflect relationships within the family rather than day care itself. For example, if relationships between their parents are strained, then this may result in a negative experience of day care.
- **Individual differences** – children are different, their personalities vary. Some may benefit more from day care than others. For example, children who are shy and unsociable may find day nurseries threatening.

Most of the research on day care has been conducted in the

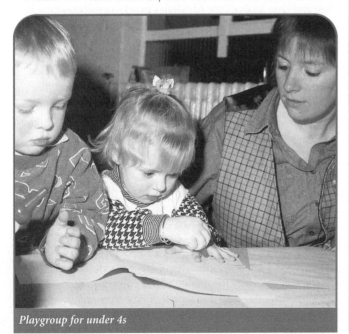

Playgroup for under 4s

Table 1	Day care places for children	

England & Wales	*Thousands*	
	1987	1997
Day nurseries		
Local authority provided	29	20
Registered	32	180
Non-registered	1	2
All day nursery places	62	202
Childminders		
Local authority provided	2	4
Other registered	152	379
All childminder places	154	383
Playgroups		
Local authority provided	3	2
Registered	423	408
Non-registered	7	3
All playgroup places	433	413

Adapted from Social Trends, 1999

USA. And much of this research has been conducted in day care centres attached to universities. These centres are not typical. They are usually of high quality and those who use them – the university staff – have high status, well-paid jobs. As a result, their children are hardly representative of the day care population as a whole. Again, these findings and, in particular, any generalisations from them, must be treated with caution (Howes & Olenick, 1986).

Key terms

Day care *The care of children during the day outside the family unit.*

Day nurseries *Organisations set up to care for preschool children during the day. They usually employ qualified staff.*

Childminders *Individuals who take care of one or more preschool children.*

Playgroups *Voluntary groups organised and run by parents to take care of children.*

Individual differences *Differences in personality and characteristics between people.*

Summary

1. There are wide variations in the type and quality of day care, the age at which children enter day care, the length of time they spend there, and the number of times their day care provision changes.

2. In addition to these factors, the children's social background, relationships within the family, and individual differences will affect their experience of day care.

3. In view of the above factors, it is difficult to generalise about the effect of day care on children. Any conclusions must be treated with caution.

Unit 2 The effects of day care

KEY ISSUES

1. **What effect might day care have on attachment?**
2. **What effect might day care have on cognitive development?**
3. **What effect might day care have on social development?**

2.1 Day care and attachment

What effect does day care have on the children's attachment to their parents?

As outlined in Chapter 4, there was concern, particularly during the 1950s and 1960s, that temporary separations from the main caregiver during infancy could lead to insecure attachments. And this insecurity may lead to long-term psychological harm. However, by the 1980s most researchers believed that good quality day care had no negative effects on attachment.

In the late 1980s, some researchers had a change of mind. In the USA, Belsky and Rovine (1988) analysed the results of five studies which had measured attachment security using the Strange Situation (see pp 49-51). They claimed that for children under the age of one, day care for over 20 hours a week increased the risk of insecure attachments. Data from the five studies indicated there was a 43% chance of insecure attachment when infants were in day care for over 20 hours a week compared with 26% for those with no day care or less than 20 hours. After the age of one, day care appeared to have no negative effects on the security of the child's attachment.

Other researchers have questioned these findings. Clarke-Stewart (1989) makes the following points.

- First, the higher levels of insecure attachment may have more to do with the mothers than day care as such. Mothers who place their children in day care as infants may find child care particularly difficult and frustrating. This, rather than the day care experience, may result in less secure attachment.
- Second, it is questionable whether insecure attachments lead to more general emotional insecurity in the child as Belsky and Rovine (1988) suggested.
- Third, is the Strange Situation a valid measure of attachment security? The method was developed mainly using infants who had been raised without regular separation from their mothers. It may not be a true measure of attachment for children with working mothers since those children experience regular, everyday separations.

Some researchers argue that day care does not pose a serious threat to attachment. Others argue that there are so many factors involved, there is insufficient evidence to blame day care. In their view, further research is needed before reaching any firm conclusions.

2.2 Day care and cognitive development

Cognitive development refers to intellectual growth from infancy to adulthood. It refers to thinking, reasoning, problem solving, language skills and mathematical skills.

The traditional view is that good quality day care, particularly if it has an educational component, benefits the cognitive development of working-class children, but has little effect on middle-class children. According to this view, middle-class parents are more likely to read to their children, provide them with educational toys, play with them, talk to them at greater length, and teach them to perform a wider variety of tasks. As a result, day care has little to add.

However, a number of studies suggest that the cognitive development of children from all social classes may benefit from day care. For example, a study of 146 Swedish children compared children in day nurseries with those looked after by a childminder and those who remained at home. When these children were assessed at the age of 8, those who had been in day nurseries were consistently better than the other groups on tests of verbal and mathematical ability. Moreover, the longer the children had been in day care, the higher their scores. Childminding came out worst (Broberg et al., 1997).

Similar findings come from an American study based on 150 children, aged 2-4 years. Those who attended day nurseries had better intellectual development then those placed with childminders or those remaining at home (Clarke-Stewart, 1991).

The results of other studies are not so straightforward. An American study, based on a sample of 1000 3-4 year olds, found that white (but *not* black) children who began day care before the age of one had the lowest vocabulary scores whatever their social class. Starting day care after the age of one appeared to have no effect (Baydar & Brooks-Gunn, 1991). Rather different results came from another American study. Children from low-income families who started day care before the age of one had higher reading and maths scores when they started school than similar children who stayed with their mothers. However, middle-class children who started day care before the age of one had lower scores than middle-class children who spent their preschool years at home (Caughy et al., 1994).

Interpreting the results The above findings are not straightforward. At times they appear contradictory. This may result from a number of factors.

- The type of day care provision varies both between countries and within countries.
- Children enter day care at different ages.
- They are assessed at different ages, using different tests.
- Samples vary in size and composition – for example in the social background of the children in each sample.
- The quality of day care can vary considerably.

Helen Bee (1997) suggests that this last point may explain many of the differences between research findings. In her words, 'When the day-care setting for a child provides *more* enrichment that the child would normally receive at home, we see some beneficial cognitive effects. When day care is less stimulating that the child's home care would have been, it has negative effects.' However, Bee admits that there is insufficient evidence to support this explanation – it therefore remains a suggestion.

Head Start

This section looks briefly at preschool day centres specifically designed to improve cognitive development. It focuses on the Head Start programmes in the USA where much of the research on preschool education has been conducted.

Operation Head Start was launched in the USA in the 1960s. It was a massive programme of preschool education designed for children from low-income families. These children were failing in droves in the school system. Their failure was seen to result from a lack of stimulation and 'richness' in their family lives. They were labelled as 'culturally deprived' – deprived of many of the things middle-class children received in their preschool years such as a wide vocabulary. Preschool education was seen as a way of compensating for this so-called 'deficiency' in their home background. It would provide additional stimulation, it would enrich their lives, boost their cognitive development and give them a 'head start' when they began elementary (primary) school. Similar thinking lay behind British programmes of preschool compensatory education which began in the late 1960s in low-income areas.

Children usually entered the Head Start programme at the age of 3 or 4. A large amount of research was conducted to examine the effectiveness of Head Start. A summary of the research findings indicates the following (Zigler & Styfco, 1993).

Children typically gain around 10 IQ points after a year of Head Start. This gain usually disappears within a few years of starting elementary school. But there are some advantages. Children who went through the programme were less likely to be placed in special education classes, they appeared to adjust better to the school environment and were more likely to obtain a high school certificate. As adults, they were less likely to be unemployed, to have a criminal record and to depend on welfare (Barnett, 1993).

In terms of cognitive development, as measured by IQ tests, reading and maths tests, it appears that unless preschool programmes are followed on by further special programmes throughout the child's educational career, then the initial gains provided by Head Start largely disappear (Cole & Cole, 1996).

2.3 Day care and social development

Social development refers to the development of the child's relationships with other people. It is concerned with the process by which the child becomes a part of the wider society while, at the same time, becomes a separate and distinct individual. This involves learning and acting in terms of the norms – the accepted ways of behaving – which operate in the wider society, and also learning to become a relatively independent person. Psychologists tend to have the following picture of the socially well-adjusted child. This child gets on with other people and stands on their own two feet. In other words, they have developed relationship skills and a certain level of independence.

A large body of research, mainly from the USA, has been concerned with how day care affects children's social development. To some extent the findings are contradictory. Some studies indicate that day care has positive effects on social development. Children who attend day centres appear to be more independent and self-sufficient, they cope better with new situations, they are more popular with their peers (children of

the same age), they are more cooperative and helpful both with other children and their parents. In general, their social skills and their knowledge of the wider social world are more developed than children who do not attend day care centres.

Other studies point to the negative effects of day care on social development. These studies suggest that children who attend day care centres are more aggressive and less likely to comply with the requests and follow the instructions of their parents and teachers. It is important not to overstate this level of aggression – it is well within the range found in children in general (Cole & Cole, 1996).

Interpreting the results Why are the findings apparently contradictory? A number of reasons have been suggested.

- The effect of day care on social development may depend on the quality of day care. A number of researchers have argued that if day care is well organised, with stimulating and clearly structured tasks, then this will contribute to the child's social development. Children will tend to be aggressive in an unstimulating and unstructured environment (Clarke-Stewart et al., 1994).
- Assessing children's aggression involves a difficult judgement. Behaviour seen as aggressive by one person may be seen as indicating independence by another. Children who want to do things their way may be seen as either aggressive or independent (Clarke-Stewart, 1989).
- Even if some children in day care are more aggressive, this may have nothing to do with day care as such. Children who are aggressive may be more likely to be placed in day care because their parents find them difficult to handle. Alternatively, their aggression may stem from their family relationships. If both parents are in full-time employment, they may well be under stress, especially with one or more preschool children. In some cases, it may be stress within the family unit, rather than day care, that results in aggressive children (Clarke-Stewart, 1989).

Conclusion Most researchers believe that high quality day care is beneficial for children's social development. The child is exposed to a wider social world and most children learn to get along with larger groups of people. In doing so, they develop a wider range of social skills and greater independence from the family unit.

Culture and day care

The material on day care presented in this chapter is based on research conducted in Western Europe and, particularly, in the USA. To what extent do these findings apply to all cultures?

Culture refers to the learned, shared behaviour of members of a society. It is the 'way of life' of people in society. It includes the norms (accepted and expected ways of behaving), the values (what people consider important and worthwhile), the attitudes (the opinions and ways of thinking), and the beliefs (what people hold to be true), which are generally shared by members of society.

Culture varies from society to society. To what extent will this affect day care?

The USA and Japan A comparison of nursery schools in the USA and Japan indicates the importance of culture (Tobin et al., 1989). The American teachers were shown a video of a Japanese school and the Japanese teachers a video of an

American school. In the Japanese classrooms there were 30 children and one teacher, in the American classrooms 18 children with two teachers. Both the Americans and the Japanese were surprised by the size of the other's classes. The Japanese felt that the small class sizes would be harmful to the children's social development. In the words of one teacher, children 'need to have the experience of being in a large group in order to learn to relate to lots of children in lots of kinds of situations'.

The American teachers emphasised the importance of independence, self-reliance and self-sufficiency. This reflected the importance placed on individualism in American culture. The Japanese teachers disapproved of this emphasis. In the words of one Japanese teacher, 'a child's humanity is realised most fully not so much on his ability to be independent from the group as his ability to cooperate and feel part of the group'.

When children misbehaved and when there were arguments and fights, American teachers tended to intervene, taking the children on one side and discussing the problem. To the Japanese, 'that is a bit too heavy, too adult-like, too severe and controlled for young children'. They preferred to let the children settle disputes and solve problems amongst themselves without what they saw as adult interference.

This is an important study. It shows that the way day care is organised reflects, to some extent, the culture of society. It shows that social development means different things in different cultures. The Japanese and American teachers encouraged behaviour which was valued in their particular cultures. It is important to realise that many aspects of day care in our society reflect the norms and values of our culture. It follows that what we consider high quality day care cannot automatically be applied across the board to all cultures.

Key terms

Cognitive development *Intellectual growth from infancy to adulthood. The development of reasoning and problem-solving skills.*

Operation Head Start *A programme of preschool education for children from low-income families, begun in the 1960s in the USA.*

Compensatory education *Education designed to make up or compensate for what is seen as lacking in low-income children's social background.*

Social development *The development of the child's relationship with other people. The growth of social skills and, in Western Europe and particularly in the USA, independence and self-reliance.*

Culture *The learned, shared behaviour of members of society. It includes shared norms, values, attitudes and beliefs.*

Summary

1. In the 1950s and 1960s, there was concern that temporary separations from the main caregiver during infancy could lead to insecure attachments.

2. By the 1980s, most researchers believed that high quality day care had no negative effects on attachment.

3. In the late 1980s, some researchers argued that day care for over 20 hours a week before the age of one could lead to insecure attachments. Other researchers questioned this view.

4. Research findings on the effect of day care on cognitive development vary.

   - Some research indicates that high quality day care benefits cognitive development in all children.
   - Other research suggests that only certain children benefit from day care. For some, day care may hold back their cognitive development.

5. A number of factors may account for the different findings. They include the quality of day care, the age at which children enter day care, and the social background of the children.

6. Research suggests that day care can have positive effects – for example, the development of social skills – and negative effects – for example, aggressiveness – on children's social development.

7. The organisation of day care and the behaviour encouraged by the staff reflects the culture of society.

References

Barnett, W.S. (1993). Benefit-cost analysis of preschool education: Findings from a 25-year follow-up. *American Journal of Orthopsychiatry, 63,* 500-508.

Baydar, N. & Brooks-Gunn, J. (1991). Effects of maternal employment and child-care arrangements on preschoolers' cognitive and behavioural outcomes: Evidence from the children of the National Longitudinal Survey of Youth. *Developmental Psychology, 27,* 932-945.

Bee, H. (1997). *The developing child* (8th ed.). New York: Longman.

Belsky, J. & Rovine, M. (1988). Nonmaternal care in the first year of life and the security of infant-parent attachment. *Child Development, 59,* 157-167.

Caughy, M.O., DiPietro, J.A. & Strobino, D.M. (1994). Day-care participation as a protective factor in the cognitive development of low-income children. *Child Development, 65,* 457-471.

Clarke-Stewart, K.A. (1989). Infant day care: Maligned or malignant? *American Psychologist, 44,* 266-273.

Clarke-Stewart, K.A. (1991). A home is not a school. *Journal of Social Issues, 47,* 105-123.

Clarke-Stewart, K.A., Gruber, C.P. & Fitzgerald, L.M. (1994). *Children at home and in day care.* Hillsdale, NJ: Erlbaum.

Cole, M. & Cole, S.R. (1996). *The development of children* (3rd ed.). New York: W.H. Freeman.

Cost, Quality, & Child Outcomes Study Team (1995). *Cost, quality, and child outcomes in child care centres, executive summary* (2nd ed.). Denver: Economics Department, University of Colorado at Denver.

Howes, C. & Olenick, M. (1986). Family and childcare influences on toddlers' compliance. *Child Development, 57,* 202-216.

Mayall B. & Petrie, P. (1983). *Childminding and day nurseries: What kind of care?* London: Heinemann Educational Books.

Social Trends (1999). London: The Stationery Office.

Tobin, J.J., Wu, D.Y.H. & Davison, D.H. (1989). *Preschool in three cultures: Japan, China, and the United States.* New Haven: Yale University Press.

Zigler, E. & Styfco, S.J. (1993). Using research and theory to justify and inform Head Start expansion. *Social Policy Report, Society for Research in Child Development, 7,* 1-21.

▶ Introduction

A headteacher sits at her desk. The day had started badly. Her new car had broken down and she was forced to walk the last two miles of her journey to work, arriving hot and flustered. She is working through the school accounts – they don't balance. Constant interruptions make matters worse. The Head of Psychology walks in demanding money for textbooks which the school can't afford. A parent phones worried about his son's progress in mathematics. Just as she returns to the school accounts, her secretary walks in with a pile of urgent papers to sign. By this time, the headteacher is under stress. Her pulse is racing, she is sweating and her stomach feels as though it is in a tight knot.

This example illustrates several aspects of stress. First, stress is often caused by external events, largely outside a person's control. Second, stress affects a person's internal state, for example it can lead to an increase in heart rate. Third, stress is usually seen as a negative experience.

This chapter is mainly concerned with the physiological aspects of stress, with stress as a bodily response.

Chapter summary

- Unit 1 outlines different views of stress.
- Unit 2 looks at the relationship between the brain and the nervous system and stress.
- Unit 3 looks at the effects of short-term and long-term stress on the body.
- Unit 4 discusses the relationship between stress and the immune system.
- Unit 5 examines the relationship between stress and coronary heart disease.

Unit 1 Defining stress

KEY ISSUES

1. What are the different views of stress?
2. Can stress have both negative and positive effects?
3. What is the relationship between arousal and stress?

1.1 Views of stress

Stress as an external stimulus

The term stress was first used in physics. In this sense, it refers to the application of an outside or external force which places strain on an object. For example, a large weight is hung on a metal rod. The rod is placed under stress by the weight, bends, and may eventually break. The weight acted as a *stressor*.

Similar definitions of stress are used in psychology. For example, stress can be seen as an external stimulus which places a strain on the individual (a stimulus is anything that affects an individual's behaviour). Examples of stressful external stimuli or stressors include taking an exam, moving house, divorce and a new job. In each case, these examples can be seen as external forces which place strain on the individual and which might, like the force on the metal rod, cause them to 'snap'.

Stress as an internal response

Other approaches see stress as an internal response to external stressors. In this sense, stress is something happening *inside* the person rather than an *outside* force acting on the person. It is the psychological and physiological changes produced by a stressor. These changes are known as the *stress response*.

Psychological aspects of the stress response may include a state of tension involving emotions such as fear, anxiety and anger. Examples of physiological aspects of the stress response include an increase in heart rate and the release of sugar into the bloodstream. These changes increase alertness and energy. If the stressor is prolonged, as in the case of long-term unemployment, or if there are repeated stressors, one after the other, then the stress response can be long lasting and harmful. It may lead to illness or even death.

Stress as a transaction

The first approach to stress focuses on the stressor, the external stimulus which places a strain on the individual. The second approach focuses on the stress response, the individual's internal reaction to a stressor. A third view sees stress as a *transaction* between the individual and their environment. From this point of view, stress is seen in terms of the meanings people give to both their environment and their ability to cope with it. In this respect, an event only becomes a stressor when a person perceives or interprets it as such. For example, one person may see a divorce as a calamity, another person may see it as a welcome release and an opportunity for a fresh start. In the first case divorce will probably be experienced as a stressor, in the second case, as a relief.

As well as giving meanings to events, people also assess their ability to cope with those events. Faced with redundancy, one person may feel they cannot cope and this may lead to a stress response. Another person may feel they can cope quite adequately and, as a result, take things in their stride.

Stress as a transaction sees stressors and the stress response resulting from the meanings and interpretations people give both to events and their ability to cope with those events. If they feel they cannot cope, then they experience the psychological and physiological aspects of the stress response (Cox, 1978).

1.2 Negative and positive aspects of stress

Approaches which focus on the stress response tend to see stress as a negative and harmful state. Stress can threaten psychological and physical wellbeing, it can result in illness and even death. For example, Lazurus and Folkman (1984) define stress as 'the negative emotional and physiological process that occurs as individuals try to adjust to or deal with environmental circumstances that disrupt, or threaten to disrupt, their daily functioning'.

This view of stress as harmful is particularly appropriate for severe and prolonged stress. However, in the short term, moderate levels of stress 'can be stimulating, motivating and desirable' (Bernstein et al., 1997). Without stress life would have no challenges – there would be no progress, no striving to achieve higher standards. Overcoming challenges is essential for a species' adaptation and survival and this involves the positive use of stress.

1.3 Arousal and the fight-or-fight response

Arousal The idea of arousal is central to many definitions of stress. Stress is seen to involve mental and physical arousal. This means the brain and the body are in a state of heightened alertness. There is a readiness for action, a readiness to respond mentally and physically to a stressor. High levels of arousal usually accompany highly emotional states – fear, anger, excitement, apprehension. They also involve physiological changes such as a rise in the heart rate which increases energy and alertness.

The fight-or-flight response Walter Cannon's (1932) idea of the fight-or-flight response provides an understanding of the relationship between arousal and stress. Cannon saw the fight-or-flight response as a reaction to stressors. He argued that it is a biologically-based survival mechanism which evolved in humans

Activity 1   Stress and stressors

Item A   Stressors

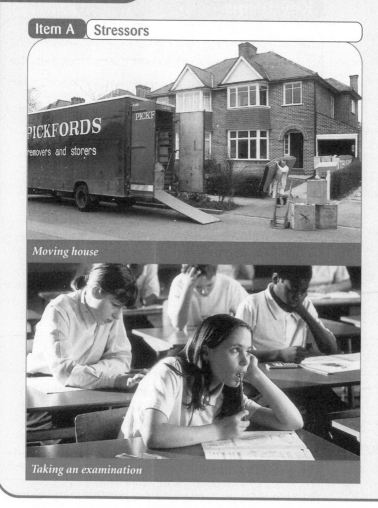

Moving house

Taking an examination

Item B   Positive stress

Mountain climbing

Item C   Homo erectus

Homo erectus, an ancestor of homo sapiens, appeared around 1.3 million years ago and, judging from the fossil remains, evolved in Africa and spread across Europe and Asia. Homo erectus was a hunter. At one site in southwestern Kenya archaeologists found the bones of over 50 adult baboons, apparently ambushed and clubbed or stoned to death by homo erectus hunters. Baboons are big-boned, formidable creatures with long, sharp canine teeth. The males are about the size of a man. At a site 100 miles northeast of Madrid in Spain, archaeologists have managed to reconstruct an elephant hunt which took place about 400,000 years ago. The hunters set fire to dry summer grass and stampeded the herd into a bog. They rushed in jabbing the elephants with spears and beating them with rocks while attempting to avoid flailing trunks and sharp tusks. At times the hunters could become the hunted. The bones of predators, such as sabre-toothed big cats, have been found at a number of homo erectus sites.

Adapted from E. White and D. Brown, 1973

Questions

1   Re-read the description of the headteacher in the introduction. Which parts illustrate a) the idea of stress as an external stimulus; b) the idea of stress as an internal response?

2   Use the pictures in Item A to illustrate the view of stress as a transaction.

3   With reference to Item B, suggest how the stress response can have a positive effect.

4   Hunting has been a major source of food for humans for 99% of their existence. Using information from Item C, suggest how and why the fight-or-flight response may have evolved.

and other animals. The basis of his idea is summed up in the following example. Faced with a predator which threatened their life, human beings had two main options – fight or flight. They could either stand their ground, defend themselves and kill or ward off the predator or they could escape by flight – running away or climbing to safety. Their chances of survival would be improved if their minds and bodies changed in ways which increased their ability to fight or flee. The short-term physiological aspects of the stress response do just this.

In response to a stressor, chemicals are released in the brain and the body producing the following physiological changes.

The heart rate accelerates increasing the blood pumped round the body and brain. Sugar is released from the liver for extra energy and muscle strength. Saliva and mucus dry up increasing the size of air passages to the lungs. Breathing deepens which increases the oxygen in the blood. These and other physiological changes increase energy and alertness in preparation for a rapid response to a threat.

Key terms

Stress *There are three main ways of looking at stress. As:*

1   An external stimulus which places a strain on the individual.

2   An internal state of psychological and physiological change in response to a stressor.

3   A transaction between the individual and their environment. This transaction results in a stress response if the individual believes they cannot cope with the demands they see placed upon them.

Stressor *Something which causes stress.*

Stress response *The psychological and/or physiological response to a stressor.*

Arousal *A heightened state of mental and physical alertness. A readiness to respond.*

Fight-or-flight response *A response to a situation seen as a threat or an emergency. It involves physiological changes which prepare the body for rapid activity.*

Summary

1   Approaches to stress tend to focus on a) the stressor and the strain it places on the individual, b) the response to that stressor, in other words the stress response, c) the way the individual perceives both a possible stressor and their ability to cope with it.

2   The effects of stress can be positive or negative. Stress can be used positively to overcome a challenge. It can also have negative effects leading to illness and even death.

3   Arousal is a major part of the stress response.

4   The fight-or-flight response sees stress as a biologically-based survival mechanism which evolved to prepare the body for rapid activity.

Unit 2 The nervous system

KEY ISSUES

1. **What is the nervous system?**

2. **How does the nervous system respond to stressors?**

3. **What effects does this response have on bodily functions?**

This unit introduces the idea of the *nervous system* as the biological control system that organises behaviour. The way people see, hear, dream, remember, plan, think and act is controlled by the nervous system, especially by the brain.

2.1   Stress and the nervous system

Brain processes are involved in every aspect of stress behaviour from interpreting an event as a stressor to organising and directing stress responses. The following summarises some of the brain processes that are involved.

- The brain receives information from the outside world through the senses – sight, hearing, smell, touch and taste.
- This information is processed – organised, interpreted and given meaning.
- Processing draws on memory – past experience and knowledge.
- Decisions are made about how to respond to incoming information.
- On the basis of these decisions, the brain sends output signals to muscles and organs to bring about responses.
- Responses include bodily movements such as running, reaching, gesturing and speaking, and physiological changes within the body, such as speeding or slowing the heart rate.

The following examples indicate the importance of the brain in stress behaviour. On a visit to the zoo, you see a lion pacing up and down its cage. On a safari holiday in Africa, a lion comes charging towards you. All the above brain processes are involved in interpreting and directing responses to these events. In the first example, you would be unlikely to see the situation as dangerous and simply walk on by. In the second example, you would, in all likelihood, interpret the event as a stressor and make an appropriate stress response which would involve physiological changes and activity – in all probability, flight.

Both the interpretation of an event as a stressor and the activation of the stress response are directed by the nervous system. An understanding of stress therefore requires an understanding of how the nervous system works.

2.2 Neurons

The nervous system is composed of a huge number of nerve cells, known as *neurons*. Neurons are the basic building blocks of the nervous system. They operate together, processing information and transferring information from one neuron to another, thereby organising our behaviour. Neurons carry information from the eyes, ears, skin and other senses to the brain. They form the connections within the brain that transfer information to memory, access information from memory, and produce output signals to control responses.

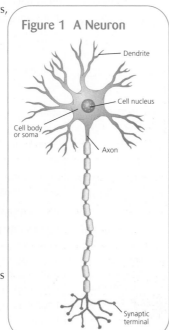

Figure 1 A Neuron

Dendrite

Cell nucleus

Cell body or soma

Axon

Synaptic terminal

There are 10,000,000,000 neurons in the brain – more than the number of stars in our universe. In one region of the brain, a group of neurons may process visual information from the eyes, in another, auditory information from the ears. In other regions, groups of neurons are involved in such things as memory, planning behaviour, organising movements and gestures, and speaking.

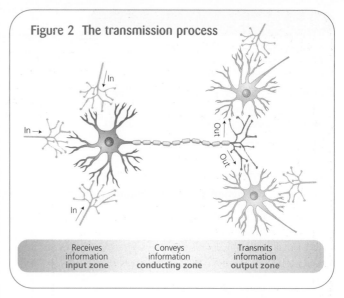

Figure 2 The transmission process

| Receives information **input zone** | Conveys information **conducting zone** | Transmits information **output zone** |

Neurons are extremely small, but they can be seen under a microscope. They vary in appearance. A typical neuron is shown in Figure 1. It consists of:

- a *cell body* or *soma*, which has *dendrites* extending from it – this is the receiving and information processing part of the neuron
- an *axon* which carries information in the form of small electrical signals
- *synaptic terminals* which are the points at which these electrical signals can be transferred to other neurons.

Neurotransmitters

Communication between neurons is achieved by the release of chemicals known as *neurotransmitters*. Neurotransmitters are released from the synaptic terminals of the sending neuron and picked up by the surface of the receiving neuron (see Figure 2). The receiving neuron has special receptors on the dendrites and the cell body to which the neurotransmitter molecules attach. The neurotransmitter molecules, by locking on to the receptors, influence the electrical activity of the receiving neuron, making it more (or sometimes, less) likely to send signals itself. As we shall see, certain neurotransmitters are directly involved in the stress response.

2.3 The brain

The brain is the centre of all intelligent processing in the nervous system. It is a large, complex organ in which pathways of neurons transport information from one region to another. The surface of the human brain is called the *cerebral cortex* (see Figure 3). This is where a lot of higher processing takes place –

Figure 3 The surface of the human brain

Cerebral cortex

where we think and process information. It is within the cortex that information from the senses is interpreted as stressors.

Key terms

Nervous system *The biological control system that organises behaviour.*

Neuron *The main processing unit within the nervous system. It passes information from one place to another, communicating with other neurons via chemical transmission.*

Neurotransmitter *A chemical used to communicate between neurons.*

Cerebral cortex *The cortex is the surface of the brain where higher processing – thinking and problem solving – takes place.*

Figure 4   The hypothalamus and pituitary gland

Hypothalamus

Pituitary gland

Figure 6   Branches of the autonomic nervous system

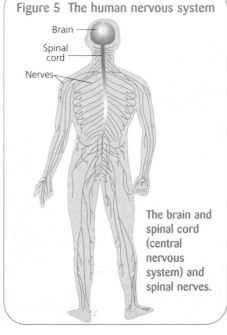

Sympathetic   Parasympathetic

Eyes
Dilates pupil   Contracts pupil

Lungs
Relaxes bronchi   Constricts bronchi

Heart
Accelerates, strengthens heart beat   Slows heart beat

Stomach, intestines
Inhibits activity   Stimulates activity

Blood vessels of internal organs
Contracts vessels   Dilates vessels

Beneath the cortex, there are many hidden structures which can only be seen directly by opening the brain. These are referred to as *subcortical*, meaning under the cortex. Many perform vital tasks, in conjunction with the cortex, in relation to memory, emotion and motor control – movement of muscles. Two of these structures – the *hypothalamus* and the *pituitary gland* – play an important part in the stress response (see Figure 4). Their role will be examined shortly.

2.4   The central and peripheral nervous systems

Together the brain and spinal cord form the *central nervous system* (CNS), where information processing takes place. The other main division of the nervous system is the *peripheral nervous system* (PNS). It is divided into two parts, the *somatic nervous system* and the *autonomic nervous system*. The somatic nervous system (soma means body), connects the CNS with the rest of the body, by means of pathways which conduct information to and from the brain and the muscles and glands (see Figure 5).

The autonomic nervous system

The autonomic nervous system (ANS) is responsible for a variety of functions that keep the body in a stable state. These include control of heart rate, perspiration, eye sensitivity and digestion. These functions are involved in the stress response. For example, heart rate increases in response to a stressor.

Figure 5   The human nervous system

Brain

Spinal cord

Nerves

The brain and spinal cord (central nervous system) and spinal nerves.

The ANS is divided into two parts, the *sympathetic branch* and the *parasympathetic branch*. These act in parallel, but they often have opposing effects. For example, the sympathetic branch increases heart rate and the parasympathetic branch decreases heart rate (see Figure 6).

The autonomic nervous system is so called because it is relatively 'autonomous'. Many of its functions are 'automatic' – they require little or no conscious thought. The ANS is somewhat independent of the central nervous system, though the two work together, since the hypothalamus has an important controlling influence on activity within the ANS.

The sympathetic branch This branch comes into play and dominates the ANS when we are alerted or aroused. In response to a stressor, the hypothalamus releases the neurotransmitter chemical noradrenaline which is the main neurotransmitter activating the sympathetic branch. This directs the sympathetic branch to produce many of the changes

Figure 7 The nervous system

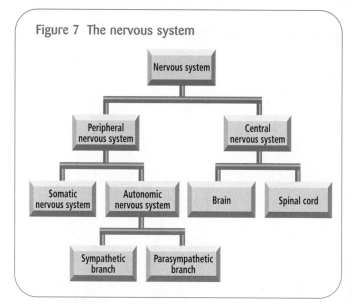

associated with the stress response. These include releasing sugar from the liver (for use by the muscles in fighting or in rapid escape), increasing heart rate and the strength of heart contractions (so that the body has plenty of blood pumped to it, again for sudden action), increasing lung function to oxygenate the blood, and diverting blood supply from the stomach and skin to the muscles of the limbs for vigorous action. The pupils of the eye dilate (widen) to increase the sensitivity of the eye by allowing more light to enter. The sympathetic branch comes into action swiftly to release and use energy when we need to be active. It produces many of the changes which Cannon described as the fight-or-flight response.

Many of the functions associated with activity in the sympathetic branch are arousing or activating. Arousal is not easily defined and measured, but it is taken to mean the general level of activation within the nervous system. High levels of arousal are associated with stressful states.

The parasympathetic branch In many ways, the parasympathetic branch of the ANS has opposite effects to the sympathetic branch. The parasympathetic branch works alongside the sympathetic branch to ensure a balance in the ANS. Whether the heart is beating quickly (speeded by the sympathetic branch) or slowly (slowed by the parasympathetic branch) is determined by

Key terms

Central nervous system (CNS) *Consists of the brain and the spinal cord. The part of the nervous system where information processing takes place.*

Peripheral nervous system (PNS) *Consists of two parts – the somatic nervous system and the autonomic nervous system.*

Somatic nervous system *Connects the CNS with the organs and muscles of the body.*

Autonomic nervous system (ANS) *Keeps the body in a stable state by controlling basic functions such as heart rate. The ANS is divided into two branches.*

Sympathetic branch *The part of the ANS which is concerned with the release and use of energy when activity is required.*

Parasympathetic branch *The part of the ANS which is concerned with the storage of energy.*

the balance of activity in these two systems.

Activity in the parasympathetic branch results in the storage of energy and the building up of energy for future use. For example, when an emergency is over, it is necessary to conserve energy and build up resources again. Here the parasympathetic branch takes over and slows the heart, stores sugars and stimulates stomach secretions and digestion. This builds up energy in preparation for future emergencies.

So far, this unit has provided a brief description of the various parts which make up the nervous system. Although each part has separate functions, they are all interconnected. This can be seen from Figure 7 which provides a diagrammatic representation of the nervous system.

2.5 The endocrine system

The *endocrine system* consists of glands – collections of cells that secrete (release) hormones into the bloodstream. Hormones are chemicals that circulate in the blood and act as messengers, affecting particular target cells or organs. In some ways, hormones are similar to neurotransmitters. Both are chemicals, both transmit messages, and in some cases, both involve the same chemicals. The messages sent from neuron to neuron by neurotransmitters are almost instantaneous – they take a few thousandths of a second. Hormones are slower-acting, taking seconds, or even minutes, to travel through the bloodstream and produce an effect. The initial physiological response to a stressful situation would die down rapidly without hormones – they are responsible for prolonging the stress response.

The stress response in the endocrine system operates in the following way. The adrenal gland, (see Figure 9), is stimulated by the sympathetic branch of the ANS. Directed by the

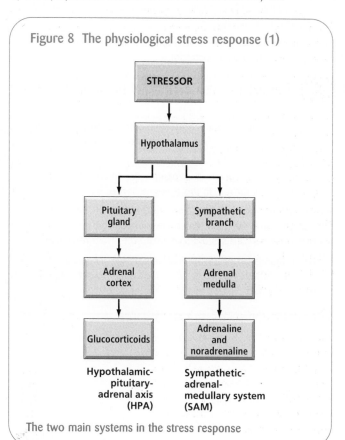

Figure 8 The physiological stress response (1)

The two main systems in the stress response

hypothalamus, the sympathetic branch sends messages, via neurotransmitters, to the inner core of the adrenal gland – the adrenal medulla. This results in the secretion of adrenaline, which constricts the blood vessels and increases the heart rate, and noradrenaline which stimulates the secretion of a hormone which directs the liver to increase the blood sugar level. The stress response described in this paragraph is sometimes called the *sympathetic-adrenal-medullary system* (SAM).

The adrenal gland is also stimulated by the pituitary gland. The pituitary gland is situated just below the hypothalamus and is sometimes known as the 'master gland' as it controls the other glands in the endocrine system. In response to a stressor, the pituitary gland is directed by the hypothalamus to release adrenocorticotropic hormone (ACTH), the body's major 'stress hormone'. ACTH stimulates the outer layer of the adrenal gland – the adrenal cortex – to secrete a group of hormones known as glucocorticoids which help to increase the body's energy level. The system described in this paragraph is sometimes known as the *hypothalamic-pituitary-adrenal axis* (HPA). It is illustrated simply in Figure 8 and in more detail in Figure 9.

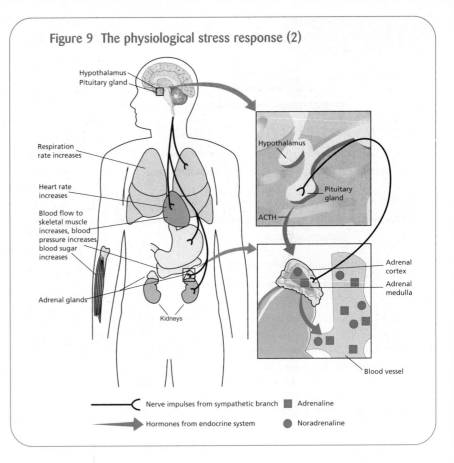

Figure 9 The physiological stress response (2)

Hypothalamus
Pituitary gland

Respiration rate increases

Heart rate increases

Blood flow to skeletal muscle increases, blood pressure increases, blood sugar increases

Adrenal glands

Kidneys

Hypothalamus

Pituitary gland

ACTH

Adrenal cortex

Adrenal medulla

Blood vessel

—— Nerve impulses from sympathetic branch   ■ Adrenaline

⟶ Hormones from endocrine system   ● Noradrenaline

Key terms

Hypothalamus *A small structure at the base of the brain which is involved in controlling the autonomic nervous system and the endocrine system.*

Endocrine system *The system of glands which secretes hormones into the bloodstream.*

Hormones *Chemicals released by glands which circulate in the bloodstream and act as messengers affecting particular cells and organs.*

Pituitary gland *The main endocrine gland. Sometimes known as the 'master gland' because it regulates the other glands in the endocrine system.*

Adrenal glands *The main 'stress glands', so called because they play a major role in the stress response.*

Sympathetic-adrenal-medullary system (SAM) *The route through which the brain directs the sympathetic branch of the autonomic nervous system to activate the stress response.*

Hypothalamic-pituitary-adrenal axis (HPA) *The route through which the brain directs the endocrine system to activate the stress response.*

Summary

1 To some extent, all parts of the nervous system, the endocrine system, and the body, are involved in the stress response.

2 The brain is involved in perceiving and interpreting an event as a stressor and organising and initiating the stress response. It directs the autonomic nervous system and the endocrine system to respond to a stressor. It also directs motor responses such as running.

3 The hypothalamus activates the sympathetic branch of the autonomic nervous system. The sympathetic branch produces many of the physiological changes involved in the stress response, for example, accelerating the heart rate and dilating the pupils.

4 In response to a stressor, the hypothalamus stimulates the pituitary gland to secrete ACTH, the body's major 'stress hormone'.

5 The adrenal gland is stimulated by both the sympathetic branch of the ANS and the pituitary gland to secrete hormones which activate the stress response.

Activity 2   The stress response

Item A   Train journeys

A crowded London commuter train

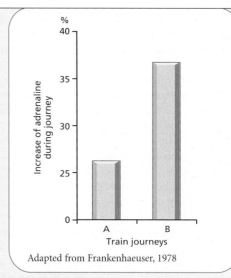

Adapted from Frankenhaeuser, 1978

The bar chart shows the percentage increase in adrenaline secretion during two commuter train journeys.
Journey A is a normal commuter trip, journey B has a 10% increase in passengers.

Item B   Taking exams

These graphs show the levels of adrenaline and noradrenaline in a student before,
during and after an exam.

Adapted from Frankenhaeuser, 1978

Questions

1 Briefly describe the changes in levels of adrenaline and noradrenaline shown in Items A and B.

2 Outline the physiological stress response which has produced these changes.

3 Suggest reasons for the activation of the stress response.

Unit 3 The effects of stress

KEY ISSUES

1. **What are short-term and long-term stress?**

2. **What are the main stages in the physiological response to short-term and long-term stress?**

3. **What is the relationship between long-term stress and physical illness?**

3.1 Short-term and long-term stress

Short-term stress refers to a sudden burst of energy and emotional feelings in response to situations which are seen as emergencies. Short-term stress is sometimes known as acute stress. It may result in a spurt of activity in order to deal with the emergency. Usually people describe their experience of short-term stress in terms of their feelings – fear, anger, excitement – rather than in terms of their physiological responses. However, they may say their heart was racing or they were dripping with sweat. Short-term stress is quite different from, and generally considered far less dangerous than, long-term stress. However, the sudden shock produced by severe short-term stress can result in physical harm, for example a heart attack.

Long-term stress can occur either when a stressor is prolonged, for example long-term exposure to cold, or because several stressful events occur one after the other. Long-term stress is sometimes known as chronic stress. People sometimes describe their experience of long-term stress with phrases like, 'I always feel tense', 'I'm constantly under pressure', 'I feel like I'm going to pieces'. Long-term stress might involve months or years of coping with bullying, a serious illness, the gradual collapse of a business, or long-term unemployment. It may result in poor concentration, poor memory and a lack of clear thinking.

3.2 The General Adaptation Syndrome (GAS)

The term stress was introduced into psychology in the 1950s by Hans Selye (pronounced 'selyay'). He was the first researcher to make detailed studies of the physiological changes that take place under conditions of short-term and long-term stress. Much of his research was based on experiments with laboratory animals. He exposed them to a variety of stressors including bacterial infections, toxins (poisons), physical restraint and extreme heat and cold. Based on the results of his experiments, Selye argued that all stressors, no matter how different they are, produce much the same reaction, the same *general* bodily response. He therefore defined stress as 'the nonspecific response of the body to any demand made upon it' (Selye, 1956). This means that the body does not have a specific response to a particular stressor, it has the same response to all stressors.

Selye's model of the stress response is known as the *General Adaptation Syndrome (GAS)*. 'General' refers to his belief that there is the same general bodily response to all stressors. 'Adaptation' refers to his view that the stress response enables organisms to adapt to stressors. 'Syndrome' means a typical or characteristic combination of factors – in this case the typical combination of factors that make up the stress response.

Selye identified three main stages in the stress response – alarm, resistance and exhaustion (see Figure 10).

Alarm reaction The first stage, the alarm reaction, mobilises the body for swift action such as Cannon's fight-or-flight response. It occurs over seconds or minutes in the face of a sudden stressor. An abrupt increase in arousal of the autonomic nervous system is produced by a release of adrenaline and noradrenaline. The rate and strength of heart beat increase, raising blood pressure, and stored red blood cells are released from the spleen, increasing oxygen carriage in the blood. Stored sugar is released from the liver, for extra energy (particularly for the muscles), and blood supply is shifted away from the skin and viscera (stomach and intestines) toward the muscles and brain. There is increased tone (tension) in the muscles, respiration deepens, and the pupils dilate (widen) to allow more light into the eye for improved visual function. The blood increases its ability to

coagulate (to clot in order to form scar tissue) and there is enhancement of the body's systems for repairing damaged tissue. All of these changes improve survival chances in a fight-or-flight situation – they increase the body's level of resistance to a stressor. A very severe stress response, however, can be life threatening – the shock produced by sudden physiological changes can lead to a heart attack. But, if the stressor disappears or subsides, the body can return to its resting level. This is the typical response to short-term stress. The body has successfully adapted to a stressor and the stress response ends.

Resistance stage The resistance stage occurs when a stressor persists. The release of hormones from the pituitary gland and the adrenal cortex increases, but the alarm symptoms of the first stage disappear, giving an appearance of a return to normal physiological functioning. However, at this stage, arousal is still high as the body's resistance to the stressor is raised. But resistance is lowered if new stressors appear.

The resistance stage can harm health. For example, it can reduce the effectiveness of the immune system, so lowering the body's resistance to disease.

Exhaustion stage The exhaustion stage is reached when a stressor persists still longer, and the body's defences can no longer cope. The adrenal glands cease to function normally. There is a drastic fall in blood sugar levels. At this stage the individual has few if any reserve resources – even a mild additional stressor has an exaggerated effect. The symptoms associated with the alarm stage such as raised blood pressure can reappear irreversibly – that is, blood pressure remains permanently high and does not return to normal even when the stressor has passed. At this stage, although there is a massive decline in resistance to all forms of stress, there is still a readiness for immediate activity and energy expenditure.

The exhaustion stage is associated with the development of *psychosomatic illness* – disorders of the body which are caused in part by psychological (mental and emotional) factors. These include stomach ulcers and other digestive problems, heart disease and hypertension (permanently raised blood pressure). Selye called these the *diseases of adaptation*. They occur when the energy needed for the body's defence mechanisms in the adaptation stage has been exhausted. Illness is the cost of an unsuccessful defence against long-term stress. In extreme cases, it can result in death.

Evaluation of the GAS

Strengths The General Adaptation Syndrome has been extremely influential. It is based on a great deal of careful observation and has led to a large amount of research. In particular, it has identified a link between psychological factors and physical illness. Many common stressors such as unemployment, marital conflict, preparing for an examination and the death of a close relative are associated with the stress response outlined by the General Adaptation Syndrome. These stressors are often accompanied by the physiological changes described by Selye and sometimes result in the psychosomatic illnesses he identified. (The relationship between stress and illness is examined in the following unit.)

Weaknesses As the transaction approach states, people do not always respond in the same way to stressors and the experience of stress. Selye largely ignored the importance of individual differences. People differ in their interpretation of a possible

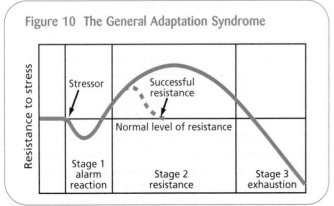

Figure 10 The General Adaptation Syndrome

Resistance to stress

Stressor

Successful resistance

Normal level of resistance

Stage 1 alarm reaction

Stage 2 resistance

Stage 3 exhaustion

stressor. They may see it as having little or no effect on them, as mildly stressful or extremely stressful. They also differ in their assessment of their ability to cope with a stressor. Some feel they can cope quite adequately, others feel they are unable to cope. All these interpretations and assessments will affect every stage of the General Adaptation Syndrome. In this respect, Selye ignored the psychological aspects of stressors and stress response.

Key terms

Short-term stress *A sudden burst of energy in response to a stressor. It dies down rapidly once the stressor has passed.*

Long-term stress *Longer-lasting stress in response to a prolonged stressor or a number of stressors.*

General Adaptation Syndrome *A model which identifies the main physiological changes in the stress response. These are the alarm stage, the resistance stage and the exhaustion stage.*

Diseases of adaptation *Physical illnesses caused by stress when the body's energy levels are considerably reduced.*

Psychosomatic illness *A physical illness caused in part by psychological factors ('psycho' means psychological, 'soma' means body).*

Selye claimed that all stressors produce the same physiological response. In other words, the response is general and non-specific. However, there is evidence to suggest that there are specific physiological responses to specific stressors. For example, stressors which lead to anxiety appear to result in the release of more adrenaline than noradrenaline, and stressors which lead to aggression appear to result in the release of more noradrenaline (Cox, 1978). This suggests that Selye overstated his case. Although stressors may often produce the same physiological response, they may not always do so.

Summary

1   The General Adaptation Syndrome states that
  - All stressors produce the same physiological response
  - This response can continue through three stages
  - It can result in physical illness.

2   The General Adaptation Syndrome has been criticised
  - For failing to recognise individual differences in the stress response
  - On the basis of evidence which suggests that there may be specific physiological responses to specific stressors.

Unit 4 Stress and the immune system

KEY ISSUES

1. **What is the immune system?**
2. **How might stress affect the immune system?**
3. **How might this increase the risk of illness?**

Traditionally, the medical profession assumed that physical illness had little or nothing to do with the mind. Thoughts, perceptions and emotions were seen to have little or no effect on physical health. This view has been increasingly challenged over the past fifty years, partly as a result of the large body of research which indicates a link between stress and illness.

Today, health psychologists recognise that many factors may contribute to the onset and development of illness. These include genetic factors, diet, exercise, age, gender and ethnicity. Because of this it makes little sense to ask: Does stress cause illness? Given the many factors involved, the question becomes: Does stress increase the likelihood of illness? Health psychologists are therefore concerned with the *contribution* stress makes to the onset and development of illness.

4.1 Stress and the common cold

Many studies of the link between stress and illness are vague and imprecise. They point to stressors in the individual's environment and link them to past, present or future illness. Often there is little indication of the strength of the stressor, people's perception of the stressor, or the level of stress they are experiencing. Other factors which may contribute to the onset of illness are often left out of the equation. In other words, they are not controlled for. The following study makes good many of

these shortcomings. It looks at the relationship between stress and the common cold (Cohen et al., 1991).

Three hundred and ninety-four healthy participants completed a questionnaire designed to measure their stress level. They listed the stressful events they had experienced over the last year, assessed their ability to cope with these events and noted how often they felt negative emotions such as hostility, anger and depression. On the basis of this information, each participant was given a 'psychological stress index' from 3 (lowest stress) to 12 (highest stress).

The participants were then given nasal drops which exposed them to one of five common cold viruses. Most showed signs of infection, but only around a third were judged by a doctor to

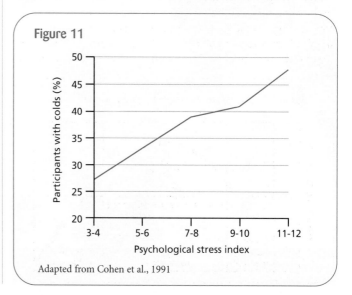

Figure 11

Participants with colds (%) — Psychological stress index

Adapted from Cohen et al., 1991

have an actual cold. Comparing these results with participants' stress index indicated a direct relationship between stress and illness. The higher the stress index, the more likely participants were to catch a cold. This is shown graphically in Figure 11. Figure 12 shows the percentage of participants who developed a cold from each of the five viruses. In each case there is a direct relationship between stress levels and catching a cold.

The researchers attempted to control for other variables which may have affected these results. In other words, they tried to control for factors other than stress which may have contributed to the onset of a cold. They controlled for age, gender, education, allergies, weight, smoking, alcohol consumption, diet, sleep, exercise, and a range of personality factors. None of these variables appeared to make a difference. In addition, the participants were carefully monitored in special housing for a few days before and after their exposure to the viruses. In view of all these checks and controls, the researchers concluded that there was a direct relationship between stress and illness.

But how exactly did stress contribute to the onset of colds? What was the actual mechanism involved? It appeared that in some way stress lowered the body's resistance to cold viruses. In other words, stress may have affected the body's *immune system*.

4.2 The immune system

The immune system protects the body from harmful viruses and bacteria. To take a simple case: a virus attacks the body. It gets into the bloodstream and circulates around the body. The immune system is designed to identify the virus as a harmful 'foreign' agent, to seek it out, and to destroy it.

The immune system contains cells known as *lymphocytes* which recognise and destroy harmful viruses and bacteria which invade the body. They lock on to the invaders, multiply rapidly, and destroy them. There are two types of lymphocytes – B cells and T cells. B cells produce *antibodies* which are released into the fluid surrounding the body's cells to destroy the invading viruses and bacteria. If the invader gets inside a cell, T cells lock on to the infected cell, multiply, and destroy it.

If there is a link between stress and illness, then one possibility is that stress reduces the efficiency of the immune

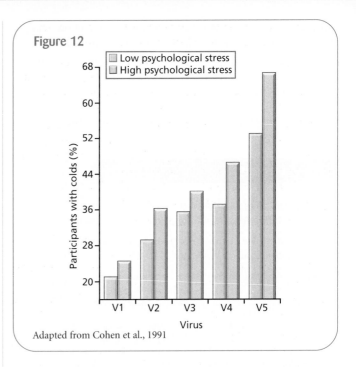

Figure 12

Adapted from Cohen et al., 1991

system. This will lower the body's resistance to disease-causing viruses and bacteria. If there is a link between stress and the immune system, then this suggests there is also a link between the immune system and the brain. As noted earlier, the brain is directly involved in the perception of stressors and the stress response.

The immune system and the brain Numerous direct neural connections appear to exist between the brain and the immune system. For example, many nerve fibres connect the brain to the sympathetic branch of the autonomic nervous system. And, many of the nerve fibres from the sympathetic branch end among lymphocytes in the thymus gland – a gland in the neck which produces lymphocytes. Lymphocytes have receptors – specially designed receivers – for a number of different neurotransmitters. In view of these connections, it is possible that the brain can communicate directly with the immune system and affect its functioning. For example, messages from the brain may affect the production and the effectiveness of B cells and T cells.

The brain may also influence the immune system via the endocrine system. As outlined earlier, in response to a stressor the hypothalamus directs the pituitary gland to release ACTH hormone which travels to the adrenal cortex and causes further hormones to be released. Some of these hormones are known to suppress the immune system, so reducing its effectiveness.

Measuring the efficiency of the immune system Does stress reduce the effectiveness of the immune system? Before this question can be answered, some measure of the efficiency of the immune system is required. Two main measures have been used. First, counting the number of T cells and B cells and assessing the antibody levels in the blood. Second, assessing how well the immune cells are functioning. For example, are they able to reproduce effectively? This can be done by artificially stimulating them with a chemical.

4.3 Stress, illness and the immune system

A large number of studies have indicated a link between stress, the immune system and illness. They suggest that stress reduces

A cell in the immune system attacking bacteria (the cylinder-shaped cells)

the efficiency of the immune system which lowers the body's resistance to disease. First, a look at some of the evidence.

A number of studies have looked at the relationship between taking examinations – a well-known stressor – and the functioning of the immune system. Various measurements indicating the efficiency of the immune system have been taken. In general, these studies indicate that the stress of examinations reduces the effectiveness of the immune system. For example, one study examined 40 medical students six weeks before their exams and again during their exams. The students revealed higher levels of stress during their exams and the percentage of T cells showed significant reductions at exam time (Glaser et al., 1986).

Studies of men and women who have recently divorced or separated – often an extremely stressful experience – indicate poorer functioning of the immune system compared with married couples of similar age and social position. For example, immune cells from divorced and separated people did not reproduce as effectively as those from their married counterparts (Kiecolt-Glaser et al., 1987).

A whole range of stressors appear to reduce the effectiveness of the immune system. They include events such as the death of a husband or wife, everyday events which people find annoying and frustrating, and living in an environment which is perceived as threatening – for example in the vicinity of a nuclear accident (Taylor, 1995).

Evaluation The description of the immune system outlined above is far from complete. The system is extremely complex

Summary

1 A reduction in the efficiency of the immune system will reduce the body's resistance to disease.

2 There is evidence which indicates that stress can reduce the efficiency of the immune system.

3 The brain directs the perception of stressors and the stress response.

4 There are connections between the brain and the immune system. This raises the possibility that the brain may affect the immune system as part of the stress response.

5 In view of the complexity of the immune system, these findings are suggestive rather than conclusive. In other words, we cannot be certain that stress suppresses the immune system.

and includes many components. Far more research is needed to unravel its complexities, to discover how its parts work together to defend the body, and to pinpoint its relationship to the nervous system and the endocrine system.

A number of studies have indicated that while a stressor may suppress one or more parts of the immune system, it appears to leave other parts unaffected. Again, more research is needed to discover why this is so.

In addition, the immune system may be affected by a whole range of factors in people's lives. These include drugs such as alcohol, caffeine and nicotine, a person's general health, their diet, physical activity, sleep patterns, age and medication. Although many studies attempt to control for such factors in order to isolate the effect of stress, complete control is unlikely (Kiecolt-Glaser & Glaser, 1988)

Despite this, the weight of evidence suggests that apart from short-term acute stress, the experience of stress does suppress the immune system. This provides an important explanation for the relationship between stress and illness. Suppression of the immune system makes the body more vulnerable to illness.

Key terms

Immune system *Protects the body from disease-causing viruses and bacteria.*

Lymphocytes *Specialised cells – B cells and T cells – which recognise and destroy harmful viruses and bacteria.*

Antibodies *Proteins released by B cells which destroy harmful viruses and bacteria.*

Activity 3   Control, stress and the immune system

In this experiment, two rats experience the same stressors – a series of electric shocks. Each rat has a lever which it can press. The rat on the left can end each shock by pressing its lever. The rat on the right has no control over the shocks – its lever does nothing. However, it receives exactly the same series of shocks as the first rat.

The researchers then investigated the effect of this procedure on one aspect of the rats' immune system – the reproduction of T cells. T cells from the rat that could end the shock multiplied in the same way as those of rats who were not exposed to the shocks. However, the reproduction of T cells from the rat who received uncontrollable shocks was significantly reduced. Similar experiments have supported these findings.

Adapted from Laudenslager et al., 1983

Question

Using the above data, provide an explanation for the relationship between control, stress and the immune system.

Unit 5 Stress and coronary heart disease (CHD)

KEY ISSUES

1. What is coronary heart disease?
2. How might stress contribute to coronary heart disease?

Coronary heart disease (CHD) refers to illnesses caused by the narrowing of the arteries which supply the heart with blood. This process is known as *atherosclerosis*. It is caused by fatty material being deposited on the walls of the arteries. A narrowing of the arteries reduces the flow of oxygen carried in the blood to the heart.

There are two main types of CHD – *angina pectoris*, commonly known as angina and *myocardial infarction*, commonly known as a heart attack. Angina is less serious. It results in chest pains, usually after physical exertion, because the blood flow to the heart muscle is insufficient to provide the additional oxygen required. A heart attack results from a blockage of an artery supplying the heart with blood. A narrowed artery is more easily blocked by a deposit or a blood clot. This can reduce oxygen supply to the point where part of the heart dies. The result is a heart attack which can prove fatal. CHD is one of the main causes of death in Western industrial societies.

5.1 Risk factors and CHD

Before looking at possible relationships between CHD and stress, other factors, which have been linked to CHD, will be briefly outlined. The following risk factors have been identified:

- Gender – men are more likely than women to suffer from CHD
- Age – the elderly are most at risk
- High levels of cholesterol in the blood
- High blood pressure
- Cigarette smoking
- Diabetes
- Low levels of physical activity
- Obesity – being seriously overweight
- Diet – particularly diets high in saturated fat
- Family history of CHD which suggests genetic factors may be involved.

None of these risk factors is particularly good at predicting who will get CHD. And, there is some evidence which does not appear to support them. For example, people living in the midwestern states of the USA have high smoking rates and their diets are extremely high in saturated fats. Despite this, their level of CHD is significantly below the more industrialised parts of the USA (Davison & Neale, 1998).

On their own, each of the risk factors listed above explains only a tiny proportion of CHD. Even taken together, or in various combinations, they leave most of CHD unexplained (Evans, 1998). Because of this, some researchers have turned to psychological factors. In particular, they have looked at stress as a possible risk factor for CHD.

5.2 Stress and CHD

This section outlines a number of studies which indicate a relationship between stress and CHD.

Life events A number of studies indicate that the physiological stress response to life events may increase the risk of CHD. Life events are significant events in people's lives which they usually experience as stressful. One study looked at negative life events over a period of one year – events such as divorce and the death of a close friend or relative. These events were accompanied by rises in blood pressure and in the production of fatty acids which leads to an increase in blood cholesterol. This can lead to atherosclerosis – a narrowing of the arteries by deposits of fatty material (Theorell & Emlund, 1993).

Stress at work A number of studies have looked at stress at work in relation to CHD. The following factors appear to increase the level of stress and the risk of CHD: lack of control over work, few opportunities to make decisions, low job satisfaction, monotonous and repetitive tasks, and a lack of job security, all of which are associated with low status occupations. A number of these factors have been linked to high blood pressure and high blood cholesterol, both of which increase the risk of CHD (Evans, 1998).

Type A behaviour pattern

A large amount of research has indicated that individuals with particular behaviour patterns are more likely to experience stress and to suffer from CHD. Two heart specialists, Friedman and Rosenman (1974), identified the *Type A behaviour pattern* which they claimed made people more vulnerable to CHD. The Type A individual is driven to achieve, highly competitive, aggressive, hostile, impatient, fast talking and fast thinking, and often involved in two or more activities at the same time. The first major study to examine the relationship between Type A behaviour and CHD was based on a sample of 3524 Californian men between the ages of 39 and 59. All were free from CHD at the start of the research. They were studied over an 8½ year period.

At the end of that time, 7% of the sample had developed at least some signs of CHD. Of this 7%, two-thirds were Type A individuals. The research showed that Type A individuals generally had higher blood cholesterol levels and higher levels of adrenaline and noradrenaline than Type Bs. The secretion of adrenaline and noradrenaline is part of the physiological stress response. They increase the level of fatty acids in the blood which may lead to atherosclerosis.

More recent studies have not supported the link between Type A behaviour and CHD. This may be because different methods were used to identify the Type A behaviour pattern. It may also be due to the possibility that the behaviours included in Type A are too broad.

A number of researchers have focused on particular aspects of the Type A pattern. One study divided the Type A behaviour into 12 distinct parts. Only two parts predicted atherosclerosis – 'potential for hostility' and 'anger-in' (feeling uncomfortable about expressing anger openly). Atherosclerosis was marked in individuals who scored highly on measurements of hostility and suppressed anger (Dembroski et al., 1985).

Cynical hostility Some researchers claim that *cynical hostility* is a better predictor of CHD than the broader Type A pattern. Cynical means having little faith in human sincerity or goodness. Those with a cynically hostile attitude assume that people are basically selfish and will use unfair means for their own gain. This attitude encourages a hostile and oppositional approach to others marked by suspicion, distrust, resentment, aggression and anger.

There is evidence that individuals who score highly on measures of cynical hostility react more readily to stressors and their stress response lasts longer. In particular, their heart rate and blood pressure are particularly high, as are their secretions of adrenaline and noradrenaline. A number of studies have indicated a link between cynical hostility and CHD (Taylor, 1995). However, not all studies support these findings. Again, one of the problems is measurement. It is not easy to measure vague and imprecise things like cynicism and hostility. Different measuring scales often produce different results.

The stress response and CHD

What are the mechanisms which link the stress response to CHD? First, stress activates the sympathetic branch of the autonomic nervous system. This leads to a constriction of the blood vessels and a rise in blood pressure and the heart rate. As a result, more and more blood is pushed through shrinking arteries. Long-term stress may lead to wear and tear on, and damage to, the arteries. Activation of the sympathetic branch also leads to an increase in the release of fatty acids into the bloodstream which can increase the chance of atherosclerosis.

Second, stress also activates parts of the endocrine system via the hypothalamic-pituitary-adrenal axis (see pp 87-88). This leads to the secretion of 'stress hormones' including adrenaline and noradrenaline which again leads to an increase in the release of fatty acids into the bloodstream. This increases blood cholesterol levels which, in turn, increase the risk of atherosclerosis and CHD.

Evaluation

The evidence for a link between stress and CHD is not simple and clear-cut. Some of the results of research are contradictory. This may be partly due to the difficulty of measuring vague concepts such as stress, hostility and cynicism. In addition, the physiological stress response is extremely complex and only partially understood. Despite these problems, the weight of evidence does suggest a link between stress and CHD. This is not to say that stress causes CHD, only that in many cases, it might be one of the causes. In other words, stress is probably a contributory factor to CHD.

Key terms

Coronary heart disease *Illnesses caused by the narrowing of the arteries which supply the heart with blood.*

Atherosclerosis *A narrowing of the arteries caused by a build up of fatty material on the artery walls.*

Angina pectoris *Commonly known as angina. An illness caused by insufficient blood flow to the heart. Results in chest pains, usually after physical exertion.*

Myocardial infarction *Commonly known as a heart attack. Results from a blockage of an artery supplying the heart with blood. Can reduce oxygen supply to the point where part of the heart dies.*

Type A behaviour pattern *A pattern of behaviour characterised by competitiveness, impatience, hostility and aggression.*

Cynical hostility *A behaviour pattern characterised by cynicism and hostility. It assumes that others are basically selfish and insincere and regards them with distrust and hostility.*

Summary

1   Apart from stress, a number of risk factors for CHD have been identified. On their own, or in various combinations, these risk factors leave most of CHD unexplained. Partly because of this, some researchers have looked at stress as a possible risk factor for CHD.

2   Research has indicated that a range of stressors are accompanied by rises in blood pressure and blood cholesterol levels. An increase in fatty acids in the bloodstream can lead to atherosclerosis.

3   Some research has indicated that people with Type A behaviour patterns are more vulnerable to CHD. Not all research supports this finding.

4   More recent research points to cynical hostility as a risk factor for CHD.

5   The stress response produces physiological changes which may contribute to CHD.

References

Bernstein, D.A., Clarke-Stewart, A., Roy, E.J. & Wickens, C.D. (1997). *Psychology* (4th ed.). Boston: Houghton Mifflin.

Cannon, W.B. (1932). *The wisdom of the body.* New York: Norton.

Cohen, S., Tyrrell, D.A.J. & Smith, A.P. (1991). Psychological stress and susceptibility to the common cold. *New England Journal of Medicine, 325,* 606-612.

Cox, T. (1978). *Stress.* London: Macmillan.

Davison, G.C. & Neale, J.M. (1998). *Abnormal psychology* (7th ed.). New York: John Wiley.

Dembroski, T.M., MacDougall, J.M., Williams, R.B., Haney, T.L. & Blumenthal, J.A. (1985). Components of type A, hostility, and anger-in: Relationships to angiographic findings. *Psychosomatic Medicine, 47,* 219-233.

Evans, P. (1998). Stress and coping. In M. Pitts & K. Phillips, (Eds.), *The psychology of health: An introduction.* London: Routledge.

Frankenhaeuser, M. (1978). Psychoneuroendocrine approaches to the study of emotion as related to stress and coping. *Nebraska Symposium on Motivation, 26,* 123-162.

Friedman, M. & Rosenman, R.H. (1974). *Type A behaviour and your heart.* New York: Knopf.

Glaser, R., Rice, J., Speicher, C.E., Stout, J.C. & Keicolt-Glaser, J.K.

(1986). Stress depresses interferon production by leukocytes concomitant with a decrease in natural killer cell activity. *Behavioural Neuroscience, 100,* 675-678.

Kiecolt-Glaser, J.K., Fisher, L., Ogrocki, P., Stout, J.C., Speicher, C.E. & Glaser, R. (1987). Marital quality, marital disruption and immune function. *Psychosomatic Medicine, 49,* 13-34.

Kiecolt-Glaser, J.K. & Glaser, R. (1988). Methodological issues in behavioural immunology research with humans. *Brain, Behaviour, and Immunity, 2,* 67-78.

Laudenslager, M.L., Ryan, S.M., Drugan, R.C., Hyson, R.L. & Maier, S.F. (1983). Coping and immunosuppression: Inescapable but not escapable shock suppresses lymphocyte proliferation. *Science, 211,* 68-570.

Lazarus, R.S. & Folkman, S. (1984). *Stress, appraisal, and coping.* New York: Springer.

Selye, H. (1956). *The stress of life.* New York: McGraw-Hill.

Taylor, S.E. (1995). *Health psychology* (3rd ed.). New York: McGraw-Hill.

Theorell, T. & Emlund, N. (1993). On physiological effects of positive and negative life changes: A longitudinal study. *Journal of Psychosomatic Research, 37,* 653-659.

White, E. & Brown, D. (1973). *The first men.* New York: Time-Life.

8 Sources of stress

Introduction

A list of the events, situations and experiences that people perceive as stressors is practically endless. Psychologists have therefore looked at this multitude of stressors and tried to discover whether they have anything in common. It appears they have. For example, events which are perceived as unpredictable and uncontrollable are often experienced as stressful. The first part of this chapter classifies stressors in terms of the characteristics they share.

Different people perceive different events as stressors and respond to them in different ways. Why? The short answer is individual differences – people differ in terms of their personality, behaviour patterns, gender, social class, ethnicity and culture. The second part of this chapter looks at the relationship between individual differences and the experience of stress.

Chapter summary

- Unit 1 identifies and classifies sources of stress.
- Unit 2 examines the effect of individual differences on the perception of stressors and the experience of stress.
- Unit 3 considers the question of measurement in stress research. It assesses the strengths and weaknesses of various methods of measuring the stress response.

Unit 1 Sources of stress

KEY ISSUES
1 What is a transactional model of stress?
2 What are the main sources of stress?

1.1 The transactional model of stress

The previous chapter provided a brief outline of the transactional model of stress. This model states that stress results from a transaction between the individual and their environment. Environment includes all the events and relationships the individual experiences. Events may include marriage and divorce, moving house, changing jobs and going on holiday. Relationships include relationships with friends, family, and colleagues at work.

Whether or not the individual experiences stress depends on the way they perceive both their environment and their ability to cope with it. This is where the idea of transaction come in – the individual interacts with their environment, perceives it in a certain way and gives meaning to it. Stress arises from an individual's perception that the demands of the environment place a strain on, or are greater than, their resources. Resources include their time, energy, money, strength of will, and level of support from family and friends.

Stress occurs when a person feels they will have difficulty coping or cannot cope. This is an important point. It means that a stressor is not simply out there in the environment – it only becomes a stressor when people define it as such and feel it will strain or overcome their resources for dealing with it.

Take the following examples of redundancy. A teacher in his

mid-50s is made redundant. He welcomes this event as it includes a generous package – a large lump sum and an enhanced pension. It's the opportunity he's been waiting for to take early retirement, to travel and to improve his golf. A second teacher in his mid-40s is made redundant. He has a family to support and is worried about his prospects of finding another job. To him, redundancy is a disaster and he is concerned about his ability to cope with the situation. Redundancy is perceived very differently by these two teachers. And, because of this difference in perception, it will probably be experienced as far more stressful by the second teacher than by the first.

Cognitive appraisal

Richard Lazarus (1976) developed one of the first transactional models of stress. He argued that *cognitive appraisal* is the key to understanding stress. Cognitive means thinking; appraisal means making a judgement or evaluating.

Primary appraisal is the first appraisal people make. They decide whether an event is positive, neutral or negative. If they decide the event is negative, they then make a further appraisal in terms of its possible *harm, threat,* or *challenge*. If a person has been fired from their job they may see present harm as shame and embarrassment, threat as possible future damage such as problems due to lack of income, or they may see the situation as a positive challenge – an opportunity to train for the job they always wanted.

Secondary appraisal involves an evaluation of coping abilities and resources for dealing with the situation. The experience of stress will depend on both the primary and secondary appraisal. If harm and threat are seen as high and coping abilities and resources perceived as low, then a high level of stress is

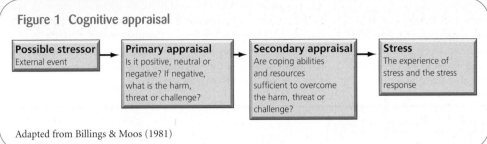

Figure 1 Cognitive appraisal

Possible stressor	→	Primary appraisal	→	Secondary appraisal	→	Stress
External event		Is it positive, neutral or negative? If negative, what is the harm, threat or challenge?		Are coping abilities and resources sufficient to overcome the harm, threat or challenge?		The experience of stress and the stress response

Adapted from Billings & Moos (1981)

probable. If coping abilities and resources are seen as high, then the experience of stress may well be minimal.

The transactional model has the advantage of accounting for *individual differences* in the stress response – the differences between people, which lead them to respond in different ways to a possible stressor. Individual differences are examined in Unit 2.

Many recent views of stress adopt a transactional model. In terms of this model, the source of stress is the cognitive appraisal of events. Only when an event is perceived as stressful does it become a stressor. However, research has indicated that some events are more likely than others to be perceived as stressors. The rest of this unit looks at these events and asks what it is about them which makes them likely to be appraised as stressful.

1.2 Lack of control

Research evidence indicates that people often experience stress when they believe they have little or no control over a situation.

Lack of control at work A study of Swedish sawmill workers indicated a relationship between lack of control and high levels of stress (Frankenhaeuser, 1975). The workers did little more than feed timber into cutting and planing machines. The work was repetitive and monotonous and the workers felt there was nothing they could do about it. Machines controlled the speed of their work and their work operations. Since the machines had to be constantly 'fed' and tended, workers were prevented from moving round the factory floor, so having little opportunity for social contact. Their control over their work was minimal.

Compared to other workers in the mill, these workers had high blood pressure, a high rate of stomach and intestinal disorders, including ulcers, and they were more likely to suffer from headaches. Urine analysis showed they had high levels of adrenaline and noradrenaline. These findings suggest they were experiencing stress. The study concludes that this was primarily due to a lack of control over their work environment.

Key terms

Transactional model *Stress is the result of a transaction between the individual and their environment.*

Cognitive appraisal *An evaluation or judgement of an event (primary appraisal) and of the resources available to cope with it (secondary appraisal).*

Individual differences *The difference between individuals, for example differences in personality, age, gender and social class.*

Activity 1 Primary appraisal

Item A   A study of primary appraisal

Four groups of American college students were shown a film of an initiation ceremony. The ceremony involved genital surgery which formed part of the young people's initiation into adulthood. The soundtrack for the first group provided an anthropological description which discussed the ceremony in terms of the young people's culture and described it as a normal part of growing up. The soundtrack for the second group focused on the young people's excitement in participating in the initiation rite and their pride in the transition from adolescence to adulthood. The soundtrack for the third group emphasised the apprehension and fear felt by the initiates and the pain they suffered. The fourth group watched the film without any soundtrack.

The stress levels of the four groups of students were measured. The highest level of stress was experienced by the group who listened to the soundtrack which emphasised the pain the initiates were going through. The lowest levels of stress were experienced by the first two groups.

Stress was measured by self-reports – reports by group members of the stress levels they thought they experienced. It was also measured by their heart rate and the electrical resistance of their skin, both of which indicate the level of arousal of the autonomic nervous system.

Adapted from Speisman et al., 1964

Azande boys from Sudan in Africa during their initiation ceremony. They are pictured here in the circumcision camp.

Question

How does this study indicate the importance of primary appraisal?

Experimental evidence Two groups were shown colour transparencies of victims of violent deaths. Participants in the first group were told they could stop the 'slide show' by pressing a button. Those in the second group were not given this option. As it happened, both groups saw the same pictures for the same length of time. However, the results indicated that the second group – those *without* the stop button – found the viewing more stressful. Stress was measured by the electrical resistance of the skin which indicates the level of arousal in the autonomic nervous system. This experiment suggests that the perception of having control over the situation will affect the level of stress experienced (Geer & Maisel, 1973).

Activity 2   Lack of control

Item A   Choosing seats

A study of male passengers on a commuter train indicated that, in general, stress levels increased the more crowded the train became, even though all the passengers managed to get a seat. Stress was measured by the amount of adrenaline in urine samples. Interestingly, those who joined the train at the first stop, and had a longer journey to the city, had lower levels of adrenaline than those who joined the train later. Apparently, what made the difference was the wider choice of seats available to the first passengers. Though they still found a seat, choice was limited for the passengers who joined the train later in the journey.

Adapted from Lundberg, 1976

Item B   Stuck in traffic

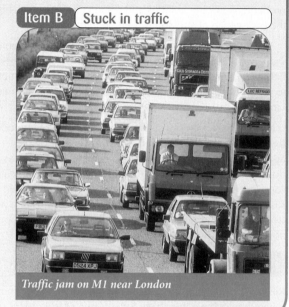

Traffic jam on M1 near London

Questions

1   How can lack of control help to explain the different levels of stress experienced by the passengers in Item A?

2   Look at Item B. People often experience stress when they are stuck in a traffic jam. Use the idea of lack of control to explain this.

1.3   Unpredictability

Events which are unpredictable often produce higher levels of stress than events which are predictable. If an event is predictable, people expect it and can prepare for it. As a result, it comes as less of a shock than something unexpected which comes 'out of the blue'. In addition, they have time to develop coping strategies which may reduce the stress. For example, research indicates that the sudden and unexpected death of a child is often more stressful for the parents than the death of a child after a long-term illness (Hazzard et al., 1992).

Unpredictability is linked with high levels of stress in many areas of life. The stress associated with life-threatening illnesses is magnified by unpredictability. A study of people with AIDS reveals many areas of uncertainty. Was the diagnosis correct – have I really got AIDS? Will I be able to function normally tomorrow? Symptoms of AIDS often flare up and die down rapidly which means people can't make even short-term plans. Is there a cure around the corner? How long have I got to live? (Weitz, 1989)

Unpredictability is a feature of many jobs associated with high stress levels. These include firefighters, ambulance drivers and paramedics, and doctors and nurses in accident and emergency departments. Workers in these occupations are often unable to predict what they will be doing, what demands will be placed on them, and where they will be from one hour to the next.

Experimental evidence Laboratory experiments with both

humans and animals indicate that unpredictable stressors produce more stress than predictable stressors. In one experiment, rats were given a series of shocks. They were unable to predict when the shocks would occur. They were then given the opportunity to press a bar at the start of a series of shocks. This provided a warning tone before each shock. The rats soon learned to press the bar indicating they preferred predictable to unpredictable shocks (Abbott et al., 1984). Experiments with humans produced similar results. Participants show less arousal and report lower levels of stress when shocks are predictable, even when the shocks were of exactly the same intensity (Katz & Wykes, 1982).

These results have been explained in the following ways. First, if a stressor is predictable, people can prepare for it. Second, if there are a number of predictable stressors, this gives people the opportunity to relax until the next warning signal.

Disasters are often unpredictable. They include natural disasters such as earthquakes, volcanic eruptions, floods, avalanches and mud slides, and human-made disasters such as terrorist bombs in peacetime and missile attacks and bombing raids in wartime. Even when a warning is available or given, people are usually unable to predict the scale of the disaster and exactly when it will occur. Consider the following example.

At 5.04 pm on Saturday, October 17, 1989, an earthquake hit San Francisco. Within minutes, 63 people were dead, nearly 3,800 injured and more than 28,000 homes and businesses damaged or destroyed. The city was blacked out apart from fires fed by broken gas mains, roads were fractured, and bridges collapsed (Canby, 1990). After the earthquake a team of psychologists interviewed nearly 800 people from the area. They found the stress response tended to follow a typical pattern. The *emergency phase* lasted 3-4 weeks during which people were extremely anxious and distressed, preoccupied with the quake, and keen to talk about it. The *inhibition phase* (3-8 weeks) followed. There was a sudden decline in talking about the quake, but an increase in stress-related behaviour such as arguments and irritability. By the *adaptation phase*, from 8 weeks onwards, most people seemed to have got back to normal. However, one year later, around 20% still felt distressed about the earthquake (Pennebaker & Harber, 1991).

Activity 3   Unpredictability

Item A   Missing in action

The USA became involved in the Vietnam War during the early 1960s. By the end of the war in 1975, over 57,000 American servicemen had died. Many others had been in prison camps or were 'missing in action'. A study showed that the wives of those missing in action suffered more emotional stress and physical illness than wives whose husbands were in prison camps or killed in action.

Adapted from Hunter, 1979

US troops in Vietnam move forward in a rice field under helicopter gunship cover.

Mt St Helens erupting in 1980

Crisis calls

Appointments at mental health clinic

Item B   Mt St Helens

On May 18, 1980, Mount St Helens in northwestern USA erupted. It was the most powerful volcanic eruption the world had known for 60 years. Although there were warnings, and most people were evacuated from the area, the exact time of the eruption could not be predicted, nor was the scale and power of the blast anticipated. Sixty people were killed and the blast of hot gas, ash and rock destroyed an area of 150 square miles.

Psychologists studied the behaviour of people in the small agricultural town of Othello near the disaster area. After the eruption they found a 198% increase in stress-related illness, a 235% increase in the diagnosis of mental health problems, and an 18.6% increase in the death rate. Crisis calls to the emergency services increased dramatically, as did appointments at the local mental health clinic.

Adapted from Adams & Adams, 1984

Questions

1   Look at Item A. Suggest an explanation for the high levels of stress experienced by the wives of servicemen missing in action.

2   Read Item B. Use the ideas of unpredictability and lack of control to provide an explanation for the behaviour of the residents of Othello after the eruption.

1.4   Conflict and frustration

Conflict is used here to refer to internal conflict. People often experience conflict when they have two incompatible goals or courses of action. They can only attain one goal or follow one course of action at the expense of the other. For example, a couple are forced to choose between the following – 1) a family holiday which they really need because they haven't been away for four years; 2) a new car because the old one is only fit for the scrap heap. However, they can only afford one of these options. Internal conflict can result from this incompatibility, especially if there is little to choose between the goals.

Conflict can produce frustration. In fact, frustration is often defined as a negative feeling that results from delaying or preventing the attainment of a goal or a course of action. Examples of situations which typically produce frustration are:

missing an important appointment because the train was late; being overlooked for promotion which you feel is long overdue.

Internal conflict and frustration can be sources of stress.

Role conflict This occurs when a person feels that, to some extent, their roles are incompatible – the performance of one social role is impaired by other, equally important, roles. For example, women often find difficulty combining their roles as wife, mother, employee and housewife. Each role is demanding in terms of time, emotion and energy and the effective performance of one role can impair the performance of others. The result can be stressful, especially in emergency situations – for example, if a child is ill and requires nursing and taking time off work is out of the question. Increasing numbers of women are entering the labour force in Western societies. However, they still have the main responsibility for domestic tasks – housework and childcare (Haralambos, 1996). This suggests that, for many women, role conflict and the stress it produces may be increasing.

Key terms

Incompatible goals *The presence of two or more goals where the attainment of one goal prevents the attainment of another goal.*

Frustration *A negative feeling that results from the delay or prevention of a course of action or the attainment of a goal.*

Role conflict *A situation in which the requirements for the successful performance of two or more social roles conflict.*

1.5 Life events

Life events are significant changes in a person's life which disrupt their normal routines. They include marriage and divorce, a new job or the loss of an existing job, moving house, the death of a close relative or the birth of a new member of the family. They include both positive and negative events, events which are seen as desirable and undesirable. A number of researchers argue that life events are a major source of stress.

The most famous application of this idea is the Social Readjustment Rating Scale (SRRS) devised by Holmes and Rahe (1967). They argued that whenever an individual had to make 'a substantial adjustment to the environment, the likelihood of stress is high'. Holmes and Rahe began their research by examining the medical records of around 5000 people. They found that, in many cases, significant life changes occurred in the months preceding the onset of illness. They selected 43 of these life events and asked a sample of 394 people to rate the degree of 'social readjustment' required for each event. Based on the results, they constructed the SRRS – see Table 1. Each life event was ranked and assigned a number of *life change units* (LCUs) from 100 (death of spouse – husband or wife) to 11 (minor violations of the law such as a speeding ticket). A person's *stress score* is the sum of all the life change units for events they have experienced within a period of 12 months.

Evaluation of the SRRS

Advantages

Ease of measurement and use The SRRS offers a simple, straightforward measure of stress. It is quick and easy to

Table 1	Social Readjustment Rating Scale	
Rank	**Life event**	**Value**
1	Death of spouse	100
2	Divorce	73
3	Marital separation	65
4	Jail term	63
5	Death of close family member	63
6	Personal injury or illness	53
7	Marriage	50
8	Fired at work	47
9	Marital reconciliation	45
10	Retirement	45
11	Change in health of family member	44
12	Pregnancy	40
13	Sex difficulties	39
14	Gain of new family member	39
15	Business readjustment	39
16	Change in financial state	38
17	Death of a close friend	37
18	Change to different line of work	36
19	Change in number of arguments with spouse	35
20	Mortgage or loan over $10,000	31
21	Foreclosure of mortgage or loan	30
22	Change in responsibilities at work	29
23	Son or daughter leaving home	29
24	Trouble with in-laws	29
25	Outstanding personal achievement	28
26	Wife begins or stops work	26
27	Begin or end school	26
28	Change in living conditions	25
29	Revision of personal habits	24
30	Trouble with boss	23
31	Change in work hours or conditions	20
32	Change in residence	20
33	Change in schools	20
34	Change in recreation	19
35	Change in church activities	19
36	Change in social activities	18
37	Mortgage or loan less than $10,000	17
38	Change in sleeping habits	16
39	Change in number of family get-togethers	15
40	Change in eating habits	15
41	Vacation	13
42	Christmas	12
43	Minor violations of the law	11

Holmes and Rahe (1967)

administer – people just tick off the events that have happened to them over a period of 12 months. It is easy to score – the researcher simply adds up the total of life change units. Partly as a result of this, the SRRS was used in thousands of studies.

Stress and illness (1) If the SRRS is an effective instrument for measuring stress, then the higher the individual's stress score, the greater their risk of subsequent illness. Many studies have claimed to have found this relationship. For example, people with heart disease have been shown to have higher life change unit scores than healthy people. However, as we shall see, the relationship between high LCU scores and the onset of illness is not particularly strong.

Disadvantages

Stress and illness (2) Although there is a correlation between high LCU scores and later illness, it is not a particularly strong one. A survey of studies using the SRRS indicates a correlation of around 0.3 (Sarafino, 1994). If a high LCU score is always associated with illness, the correlation would be 1.0. If it is never associated with illness, the correlation would be 0. A correlation of 0.3 indicates a fairly weak relationship.

Correlation vs causation Just because two things are correlated does not necessarily mean that one causes the other. Some illnesses can develop undetected over long periods of time. Some of the life events included in the SRRS may result from the early stages of an illness rather than causing that illness. Possible examples are changes in eating and sleeping habits, trouble with in-laws and the boss, and sex difficulties, all of which may be a response to a developing illness (Brown, 1986).

Cognitive appraisal and individual differences Those who complete the SRRS questionnaire simply tick off the life events they have experienced. This says nothing about the meaning they give to these events, nothing about their cognitive appraisal of these life changes. In terms of the transactional model, the only valid (true) measurement of stress is of perceived stress. The 43 life events on the SRRS may be perceived very differently by different people. For example, a son or daughter leaving home may be experienced as a loss by one set of parents, as a blessed relief by another set. The SRRS does not take individual differences in response to possible stressors into account.

More recent measuring instruments have tried to correct these shortcomings. For example, the Life Experiences Survey takes cognitive appraisal into account by asking participants for their assessments of the life events they have experienced (Sarason et al., 1978).

Retrospective data Information about life events is usually collected at least 6 months and often up to 18 months after the events have happened. Asking people to recall events may produce invalid data. They may simply forget. And, there is evidence to suggest that people who are ill when they are filling in the questionnaire are more likely to remember negative events.

To overcome the problems of retrospective data, researchers have used a prospective approach which follows healthy individuals over a number of years, noting their life events and illnesses. This method has produced stronger correlations (Brown & Harris, 1989).

Do change and readjustment lead to stress? The basic idea behind the SRRS is that the change and readjustment produced by life events leads to stress. A number of researchers have questioned this view, arguing that factors other than change and readjustment may account for many of the SRRS life events being perceived as stressful. There is evidence that changes seen as negative, eg divorce, produce more stress than changes seen as positive, eg marriage. The top 6 events in the SRRS would probably be perceived as negative. This, rather than the readjustment they require, may result in stress. In the same way, many of the events on the SRRS may be perceived as uncontrollable and/or unpredictable. Again this perception, rather than change and readjustment, may lead to stress (Brown, 1986).

Conclusion Because of the above criticisms, the SRRS is rarely used today. Despite this, it was a landmark in the measurement of stress. Without it, the more recent scales, which represent refinements of and improvements on the SRRS, would not have been developed.

Key term

Life events *Significant changes in a person's life which require a substantial readjustment in their normal routines.*

Activity 4   Life events and stress

Marriage, number 7 on the SRRS

Death of a close friend, number 17 on the SRRS

Change in eating habits to a vegetarian diet, number 40 on the SRRS

Christmas, number 42 on the SRRS

Questions

1   Briefly suggest how the life events pictured above might lead to stress.

2   Suggest reasons for their ranking on the Social Readjustment Rating Scale. For example, why is marriage rated as more stressful than Christmas?

Daily hassles and uplifts

Major life events don't occur every day. As their name suggests, *daily hassles* often do. Daily hassles are 'the irritating, frustrating, distressing demands that to some degree characterise everyday transactions with the environment' (Kanner et al., 1981). Table 2 lists the ten most common daily hassles experienced by 100 middle-aged adults.

A number of researchers argue that daily hassles lead to more stress and have a greater impact on physical and mental health than life events. In one study, using a hassles scale of 117 items, 100 middle-aged adults completed the scale each month for nine consecutive months. They also completed the SRRS life events scale. Hassles scores were a better predictor of psychological problems, such as depression and anxiety, than life events scores (Kanner et al., 1981).

The opposite of daily hassles – which get people down – are *daily uplifts* which, as their name suggests, give people a boost which makes them feel better. Table 3 lists the 10 most common daily uplifts experienced by 100 middle-aged adults.

Some studies combine the hassles and uplifts scales. For example, one study showed that people are likely to experience an increase in daily hassles and a decrease in daily uplifts a few days before the onset of a respiratory infection, eg a cold (Stone et al., 1987). The results of this study are shown in Figure 2.

How might daily hassles lead to stress and illness? First, their effect may be cumulative – the minor stresses produced by daily hassles may build up and wear people down, so making them more vulnerable to psychological and physical disorders. Second, the effects of daily hassles may combine with the effects of life events to produce higher levels of stress.

Evaluation The daily hassles scale has some of the same problems as the SRRS. The link between hassles and psychological and physical disorders is correlational. It is therefore difficult to separate cause from effect – to say what causes what. For example, the increase in hassles preceding a cold may be due to feeling rundown as a result of the early

Table 2	Daily hassles
1	Concerns about weight
2	Health of a family member
3	Rising prices of common goods
4	Home maintenance
5	Too many things to do
6	Misplacing or losing things
7	Outside home maintenance
8	Property, investment or taxes
9	Crime
10	Physical appearance

Kanner et al., 1981

Table 3	Daily uplifts
1	Relating well to spouse or lover
2	Relating well to friends
3	Completing a task
4	Feeling healthy
5	Getting enough sleep
6	Eating out
7	Meeting your responsibilities
8	Visiting, phoning or writing to someone
9	Spending time with the family
10	Finding your home a pleasant environment

Kanner et al., 1981

Figure 2 Hassles, uplifts and respiratory infection

—— Days preceding symptom onset
—— Control days

Number of undesirable events (hassles) in the 10 days before the onset of respiratory infection. Control days refer to a 10 day period which was not followed by a respiratory infection.

Number of desirable events (uplifts) in the 10 days before the onset of respiratory infection.

Adapted from Stone et al. 1987

stages of the illness. Because of this, situations which people would normally take in their stride are interpreted and experienced as hassles. However, in the research outlined above (Stone et al., 1987), this criticism may not apply – two days before the onset of a cold the rates of hassles and uplifts had returned to average levels.

1.6 Workplace stressors

In recent years the workplace has been seen as the major source of stress. A Trades Union Congress survey claimed that two out of three workers experienced occupational stress. According to one report, stress has overtaken the common cold as the main cause of absence from work (Furedi, 1999). This section looks at some of the findings of research concerned with stress in the workplace.

Work overload One way of identifying work overload is in terms of the number of hours worked per week. This assumes that long hours result in work overload. A number of studies suggest a relationship between long hours, stress and ill-health. For example, a study of workers under the age of 45 in light industry found that those who worked over 48 hours a week were twice as likely to develop coronary heart disease than those who worked 40 hours or less (Breslow & Buell, 1960).

However, research indicates that it is the *perception* of work overload that is the important factor rather than the number of hours and the actual amount of work. In this sense, work overload is a perception held by a worker that they are required to work too long and/or too hard.

Repetitive work Jobs which require frequent repetition of a simple task have often been linked to indicators of stress. As noted earlier, a study of Swedish sawmill workers, who did little more than 'feed' machines with timber, indicated that they suffered from a high rate of stress-related illnesses – stomach and intestinal disorders, hypertension (high blood pressure) and frequent headaches. Urine analysis revealed high levels of

adrenaline and noradrenaline which suggests they were experiencing stress (Frankenhaeuser, 1975; see also p97).

Workers find repetitive jobs boring and monotonous. There is little opportunity to take pride in the job or feel a sense of achievement. Here's how one worker described the task he performed, day in and day out, at an engineering factory.

'I make these washers on this press. If I work fast I can take home good money. It's the same thing over and over again though. Put the blank on, drop the guard, that presses out the washer. I put it in that box and get the next blank. It's the same all day, over and over again. Sometimes it gets on top of you' (Cox, 1978).

Social isolation In some work situations, workers are isolated from each other. This often happens when machines control work operations, as in the case of the sawmill workers described above. Workers are tied to machines with little opportunity to move around the shop floor and talk to each other. Social isolation is related to various indicators of stress, for example high levels of adrenaline and noradrenaline (Cooper & Marshall, 1976).

Lack of control As noted earlier, people often experience stress when they believe they have little or no control over a situation. Lack of control is often associated with the sources of workplace stress outlined so far in this section. Many workers feel they have to accept work overload to keep their jobs, improve their chances of promotion or, in the case of overtime, to pay the bills. Lack of control is often a characteristic of repetitive work, especially when machines control the speed of work and the way the task is performed. And workers can do little about social isolation if they are tied to a machine.

Self-report studies indicate that workers experiencing stress often complain of a lack of control in the workplace. In particular, they feel excluded from decision-making processes. For example, a survey conducted by the Manufacturing, Science and Finance Union indicated that one of the main causes of stress according to their members was 'little or no involvement in decision making' (*Labour Research*, July, 1995).

Environmental factors A variety of environmental or physical aspects of the workplace have been linked with stress. These include temperature, humidity, noise, vibration, lighting and ventilation. For example, a number of studies have found that high noise levels in factories appear to be linked with hypertension, headaches and stomach and intestinal disorders (Bell et al., 1990).

Role ambiguity A role is a set of directives about how to behave when occupying a particular social position or status. Role ambiguity occurs when the guidelines for a role are unclear and ill-defined. It is regularly reported as one of the main factors contributing to stress in the workplace. For example, a survey in the USA based on a sample of 1500 respondents found that 35% were unclear about their job responsibilities and felt they had no clear guidelines for task performance. Role ambiguity appeared to be linked with low job satisfaction and low self-confidence (Kahn et al., 1964).

Role conflict As noted earlier, role conflict can be a source of stress. Role conflict occurs when the requirements of two or more roles conflict or when aspects of one particular role conflict. An example of the first instance is when a work role conflicts with a non-work role, such as the role of parent. A full-time job can conflict with the responsibilities of looking after young children. An example of the second instance – when aspects of a role conflict – is provided by middle management who have responsibilities to shop-floor workers and to higher management. Demands from higher management for greater output may conflict with demands from the shop floor for better working conditions (Arnold et al., 1991).

Evaluation Despite the large amount of research on stress in the workplace, it is difficult to pinpoint specific sources of stress and separate them from other factors which may contribute to stress. Take the example of noise in the workplace. It has been linked to stress and stress-related illness. But people who work in noisy environments often have low-income, low-skill, low-status jobs, they often work long hours and have little control over their work. Outside the workplace, low income and poor housing may add further pressures to their lives. It is difficult to separate the effect of noise at work from all the other factors which may affect stress levels and health (Banyard, 1996).

Key term

Role ambiguity *A situation in which the guidelines for a role are unclear and ill-defined.*

Many employers now take stress in the workplace very seriously. Stress is bad for business – it is seen to cause ill-health, absenteeism, high staff turnover and low job performance, all of which cost companies money. And in 1999, for the first time, workers in the UK successfully sued employers for stress and stress-related illness caused by work. Around a third of employers now offer stress counselling to their employees.

Some researchers believe that this emphasis on stress has got out of hand. They suggest that practically every emotional problem at work is now translated into the fashionable jargon of stress. According to the sociologist Frank Furedi (1999), 'After a while propaganda about stress will have the effect of convincing people that the everyday difficulties are indeed ruining their health. Worse still, we are in danger of creating a world where we lose confidence in people's ability to cope with the normal challenges associated with the world of work.' But this does not mean that stress is absent from the workplace. Nor does it remove responsibility from employers for reducing stress.

Summary

1. The transactional model of stress states that stress is a transaction between the individual and their environment. From this point of view, an event only becomes a stressor when the individual interprets and perceives it as such.

2. Research has indicated that situations with the following characteristics are likely to be perceived as stressors and experienced as stressful.

   - Lack of control – when people feel they have little or no control over a situation.
   - Unpredictability – when events cannot be predicted and, as a result, cannot be prepared for.
   - Conflict and frustration which result from incompatible goals or courses of action.
   - Life events – significant changes in a person's life which require a major readjustment to their normal routines.
   - Daily hassles – everyday events which people find annoying, irritating, frustrating and distressing.

3. A number of workplace stressors have been identified. They include work overload, repetitive work, social isolation, lack of control, environmental factors, role ambiguity and role conflict.

Unit 2 Individual differences and stress

KEY ISSUES

1 What are individual differences?

2 How might they affect the perception of stressors and the experience of stress?

2.1 Individual differences

Unit 1 looked at the types of situations which are likely to be 1) perceived as stressors and 2) experienced as stressful. Some people are more likely than others to perceive situations as stressors and experience them as stressful. This unit asks why this is so. The short answer is because of individual differences.

Some of the more important factors which differentiate individuals are:

- **Culture** – the learned, shared behaviour of members of a society. To some extent people from different cultures see the world differently and behave in different ways.
- **Subculture** – the learned, shared behaviour of particular groups within a society, for example ethnic minority groups. While they share much of the mainstream culture, they may have distinctive norms, values and beliefs, for example, religious beliefs. In other words, they may have their own subculture.
- **Social class** – all modern industrial societies have a class system, a system of social inequality which divides people in terms of wealth and income, power and status.
- **Ethnicity** – to some extent members of ethnic minority groups have their own identity, lifestyle and subculture.
- **Gender** – there are important differences in identity and experience between men and women.
- **Age** – age differences can affect people's outlook, concerns and priorities, their interests and behaviour.
- **Individual experiences** – every individual has a unique life-history with experiences which are unique to themselves.
- **Personality** – people can be differentiated in terms of their personality characteristics.
- **Outlook on life** – the way individuals see the world. For example, some people see life in optimistic terms whilst others have a pessimistic view of the world.

- **Resources** – individuals differ in terms of the resources they have available for dealing with situations. Resources include time, energy, health, money and social support, (that is the amount of support available from others).
- **Biology** – to some extent every individual differs in terms of their biological makeup.

All the above factors contribute to individual differences. They can make a difference to the perception of possible stressors and the experience of stress. These factors are sometimes known as *stress moderators* because they modify the experience of stress.

Only some of the individual differences in the above list have been systematically researched in relation to stress. Those that have will form the basis of the rest of this unit.

2.2 Personality and behaviour patterns

Most of the research on individual differences and stress has focused on individual differences in *personality* and *behaviour patterns*. Personality is difficult to define and the term has been used in many different ways. A typical definition sees an individual's personality as their characteristic ways of behaving, thinking, feeling, reacting and perceiving the world. Behaviour patterns refer to a set of activities and reactions which are patterned in a certain way – they have certain common characteristics. At times, the terms personality and behaviour patterns are used interchangeably. For example, some researchers use the term Type A personality, others use Type A behaviour patterns. They are effectively referring to the same thing.

Activity 5   Individual differences

Item A   Culture and divorce

In traditional Apache culture, divorce was simple, straightforward and frequent. To divorce his wife, a man simply took his few possessions and returned to his parents' wickiup (wicker hut). To divorce her husband, a woman removed his belongings and placed them outside his parents' wickiup.

Apache women

Item B   Daily hassles

Daily hassles	Students (n=161)	Mothers (n=120)	Elderly (n=150)
Time pressure	1	2	4
Future security	2	4	3
Finances	3	1	4
Household	3	1	4
Neighbourhood	4	3	1
Health	4	3	1

Participants in this New Zealand survey were asked to rank the daily hassles on a scale of 1 to 4 with 1 being the most severe, 4 being the least severe. The mothers had one or more young children at home. (n = the number of participants in each group in the survey.)

Adapted from Zimbardo et al., 1995

Questions

1 Divorce is number 2 on the Social Readjustment Rating Scale. What does Item A suggest about cultural differences in the perception of stressors and the experience of stress?

2 Look at Item B.

a) What does it indicate about the importance of individual differences and stress?

b) Suggest reasons for the main differences in ranking by the three groups.

Type A personality and behaviour

During the 1950s, two heart specialists Friedman and Rosenman noticed that heart attack victims tended to have certain ways of behaving. They called these the Type A pattern (Friedman & Rosenman, 1974; see also pp 94-95). Type A people are highly competitive, they are impatient, hostile, aggressive, impulsive, and they find it difficult to relax. Table 4 is a measure of Type A personality devised by Friedman and Rosenman. It gives a picture of how they see the Type A pattern.

The Type B pattern is the opposite of Type A. Type B individuals are not driven to succeed and impress, they can relax and do nothing without feeling guilty, they are not competitive and hostile, they are easy-going rather than impatient.

In a study entitled *Type A behaviour and your heart*, Friedman and Rosenman (1974) examined over 3500 healthy middle-aged men during an $8^{1}/2$ year period. They found that those with Type A patterns were twice as likely to have heart diseases than those with Type B patterns. Although some studies provided support for these findings, others did not. Later studies indicated that the crucial factor which predicted heart disease, was hostility rather than the broad range of behaviour patterns included in Type A. For example, 118 male law students were given a personality test designed to measure hostility. Those with high scores were five times more likely than those with low scores to die before the age of 50 (Barefoot et al., 1989).

Cynical hostility A pattern of behaviour known as *cynical hostility* has recently been identified (Woodall & Matthews, 1993). It appears that people with this behaviour pattern are particularly prone to stress and stress-related illness. They are suspicious, resentful and distrustful of others, they frequently get angry and antagonistic and they rapidly become hostile when challenged.

Behaviour patterns, stress and illness What is the relationship between particular behaviour patterns, stress and illness? There are a number of possibilities. People with Type A and cynical hostility patterns may be more likely to perceive events as stressors and to react to them more strongly. The repetition of this response over a period of time may lead to stress-related illnesses and particularly to heart disease.

If an individual often reacts excessively to stressors, they are placing strain on several body systems: they experience raised blood pressure, increased heart rate and other symptoms produced by the arousal of the sympathetic nervous system. This may create wear and tear within the circulation system, perhaps damaging blood vessels and forcing the heart to pump blood at high pressure through narrowed blood vessels. In addition, the release of stress-related hormones, such as cortisol, from the adrenal glands tends to raise the fat content in the blood. The deposit of fats in arteries is an important factor leading to the narrowing of the arteries and heart disease.

On the other hand, these relationships are hard to prove. Certainly people who exhibit a great deal of hostility and aggression do appear to have higher levels of fats in their blood. But, they may just have a general tendency to overactivity within the autonomic nervous system (perhaps genetically inherited) so that both the hostility and the heart disease might be caused by this third factor. In other words, we cannot say that cynical hostility causes the heart illnesses (Bernstein et al., 1997).

Table 4   A measure of the Type A personality

Are you a Type A? Take this short test. If you check a majority of the items, you probably fit the Type A pattern.

----- 1   Do you find it difficult to restrain yourself from hurrying others' speech (finishing their sentences for them)?

----- 2   Do you often try to do more than one thing at a time (such as eat and read simultaneously)?

----- 3   Do you often feel guilty if you use extra time to relax?

----- 4   Do you tend to get involved in a great number of projects at once?

----- 5   Do you find yourself racing through yellow lights when you drive?

----- 6   Do you need to win in order to derive enjoyment from games and sport?

----- 7   Do you generally move, walk, and eat rapidly?

----- 8   Do you agree to take on too many responsibilities?

----- 9   Do you detest waiting in lines?

----- 10 Do you have an intense desire to better your position in life and impress others?

Friedman & Rosenman, 1974

Hardiness

Suzanne Kobasa (1979), claimed that people with a certain personality type – which she termed *hardiness* – are less likely to perceive events as stressors. And, if they do perceive them as stressors, they are likely to experience lower levels of stress.

Kobasa studied managers who worked for a public service company in a large American city. Using the Social Readjustment Rating Scale, she selected those who had experienced a relatively high number of life event stressors over the previous three years. She then compared those who were frequently ill with those who had few illnesses to see if she could discover any differences between the two groups. She found that those who were rarely ill had a personality type and outlook on life which she called hardiness.

Hardiness has three dimensions.

- **Challenge** – seeing change as a challenge rather than a threat.
- **Commitment** – getting directly involved in situations and focusing on solving problems.
- **Control** – believing that the individual has control over their own actions and can influence their environment.

Why were the hardy managers more healthy? First, they were less likely to perceive life events as stressors. Second, if they did see them as stressors, they tended to see them as a challenge rather than a threat. As a result, they were more likely to face the problem and take steps to solve it. They were therefore likely to experience the situation as less stressful.

Later evidence provides some support for the benefits of hardiness. For example, in one experiment, two groups of students were given a task, told they were being videotaped and that their performance would be evaluated. The first group had high scores on a measure of hardiness, the second group had low scores. The hardy group perceived the task as less threatening and showed fewer signs of frustration (Wiebe, 1991).

Evaluation Despite some support for Kobasa's findings, her concept of hardiness and her view of its relationship to stress and illness have been criticised. Some researchers have argued that hardiness, as such, makes little difference to the experience of stress and its relationship to illness. People who score highly on measures of hardiness may simply take better care of themselves and this accounts for their better health (Allred & Smith, 1989). Other researchers have argued that people who score low on measures of hardiness may simply interpret their experiences in a negative way. This, rather than low hardiness, may explain their experience of stress and their susceptibility to illness. And the tests designed to assess hardiness may be measuring *negative affectivity* (see below) rather than hardiness (Funk, 1992).

Negative affectivity

This term refers to a general tendency to experience dissatisfaction, distress and a range of negative emotions. People with high negative affectivity are more likely to perceive events as stressors and to experience a high level of stress. A review of research findings found a consistent, but fairly weak link between high negative affectivity and stress-related illnesses such as ulcers and heart disease (Friedman & Booth-Kewley, 1987).

Pessimistic explanatory style

Some people have a tendency to explain negative experiences in pessimistic terms. They tend to blame themselves for what's happened and see stressful events as outside their control. For example, a pessimistic explanatory style for divorce may state, 'It's my fault', 'I have problems with all my relationships', 'I can't see the situation changing'. They tend to see stressors in a very negative light and because of their pessimism about the past, present and future, often experience high levels of stress. They are likely to perceive stressors as long term and are pessimistic about their ability to deal with them. A study of 99 Harvard University graduates found that those with a pessimistic explanatory style at age 25 were more likely to be in poor health or dead at ages 45-50 (Peterson et al., 1988).

Dispositional optimism

This refers to people with an optimistic disposition and outlook on life. They tend to see things in a positive light and believe that everything will work out in the end. They are more likely to see stressors as short term and less likely to blame themselves for the situation. As a result they usually perceive fewer events as stressors and experience lower levels of stress. In one study, heart bypass patients with high scores on a questionnaire designed to measure dispositional optimism, recovered more rapidly in hospital and returned to normal life more quickly after their discharge (Scheier et al., 1989).

Conclusion Negative affectivity and pessimistic explanatory style appear to predispose people to stress and reduce their ability to deal effectively with stressful situations. On the other hand, dispositional optimism presents a picture of the stress-resistant individual who is much better able to cope with stressful situations.

2.3 Gender

There is some evidence of gender differences in the perception of stressors and the experience of stress. In one experiment, males and females were placed in a routine, non-stressful

Key terms

Personality *Characteristic ways of behaving, thinking, feeling, reacting and perceiving the world.*

Behaviour patterns *A set of activities and reactions which have certain common characteristics.*

Type A pattern *A type of personality and/or a set of behaviour patterns characterised by competitiveness, impatience, hostility and aggression.*

Cynical hostility *A type of personality and/or a set of behaviour patterns characterised by suspicion, resentment and hostility.*

Hardiness *A personality type which sees change as a challenge, which has a strong commitment to get involved and a belief that the individual can control their own actions and influence their environment.*

Negative affectivity *A general tendency to experience dissatisfaction, distress and a range of negative emotions.*

Pessimistic explanatory style *A tendency to explain negative events in pessimistic terms, often involving self-blame.*

Dispositional optimism *An optimistic disposition and outlook on life.*

situation and then in a stressful situation – they were given an intelligence test. Females showed little increase in the secretion of adrenaline from one situation to the next. However, males showed a marked increase, which suggests that they perceived the test as a stressor and were experiencing stress (Johansson & Post, 1972). In general, research indicates that, compared to men, women show smaller increases in the standard physiological measures of stress – heart rate, blood pressure and secretion of 'stress-hormones' (Matthews et al., 1991).

A number of reasons have been suggested for these differences. First, biological differences between males and females may affect their physiological reaction to stress. Second, women are less likely to have Type A personalities and hostile behaviour patterns (Weidner & Collins, 1993). Third, the way women have traditionally been socialised for a female role, with an emphasis on caring, might make them less aggressive and competitive.

However, things might be changing. Type A behaviour patterns are linked to the male occupational role in Western society. The male work role often involves competition, aggression and striving for advancement. As women enter the labour force in increasing numbers and, in particular, increasingly enter traditional male occupations, their behaviour patterns may well become similar to those of men. There is evidence to support this view. One study found that in response to stressors, the levels of adrenaline in female engineering students and bus drivers were similar to those of men (Frankenhaeuser et al., 1983).

As noted in the previous unit, women often have the dual burden of paid employment and domestic tasks – housework and childcare. This not only involves more work, it can also result in role conflicts if the demands of being a wage earner and a mother conflict. This may increase the number of stressors in women's lives and their experience of stress. Evidence from a study of male and female white collar workers at the Volvo plant in Gothenburg, Sweden, suggests that this may be the case. At work, noradrenaline levels for both sexes were similar. But, after work, levels for men declined while those of women rose (Frankenhaeuser et al., 1989).

2.4 Class and ethnicity

Social class In general, research indicates that people in the lower levels of the class system live more stressful lives than people in higher levels. This appears particularly so for people living in poverty, at the bottom of the class system. One of the main reasons suggested for this, is the multitude of stressors in their environment – low income, substandard and overcrowded housing, high levels of unemployment, low social status and high levels of street crime and burglary (Pitts & Phillips, 1998).

Ethnicity Research into ethnicity and stress is limited. However, studies in the USA suggest there may be differences between African Americans and the white majority. The rate of hypertension – high blood pressure – is particularly high among lower class African Americans. Hypertension is generally regarded as a stress-related illness. Part of the explanation for this is to do with class rather than ethnicity. In general, lower-class African Americans have more severe stressors in their environment than lower-class whites. For example, their rate of unemployment is over twice that of their white counterparts and their income significantly lower.

However, this forms only part of the explanation. A study which carefully matched black and white women in terms of

Summary

1 Individual differences affect the perception of possible stressors and the experience of stress.

2 A number of personality types and behaviour patterns appear to predispose people to perceive events as stressors and to experience high levels of stress. These include:

- Type A personality and behaviour patterns
- Cynical hostility
- Negative affectivity
- Pessimistic explanatory styles.

3 Other individual differences appear to have the opposite effect. They include:

- Type B personality and behaviour patterns
- Hardiness
- Dispositional optimism.

4 Differences in terms of gender, social class and ethnicity appear to affect the amount of stress people experience in their daily lives.

their income and class position found that black women were twice as likely to have hypertension (Adams-Campbell et al., 1993). One suggestion for this difference is the widespread racism in American society – in housing, occupation, leisure and day-to-day interaction. A major source of stress may be African-Americans' perception that, to some extent, their route to self-improvement is blocked by racism (Anderson, 1991).

Unit 3 Measuring stress

KEY ISSUES

1 How is stress identified and measured?

2 How accurate are measurements of stress?

Research on stress stands and falls on the identification and measurement of stress. How do we know that stress is present? How can we measure the level of stress? This unit looks at these questions.

3.1 Physiological measures

The physiological stress response provides one way of identifying and measuring stress. Since stress involves physiological changes, measurements can be made from samples of blood, urine or saliva. The presence or level of certain hormones and neurotransmitter chemicals indicates the level of activity in particular nervous systems.

There are a number of problems with this approach. Simply measuring the level of a hormone does not tell us how stressed an individual is feeling. In addition, there are daily cycles in the production of hormones so levels will be affected by the time of day when samples are taken.

3.2 Laboratory experiments

Laboratory experiments provide an opportunity to control and

measure certain stressors. For example, extremes of heat and cold are sometimes used as stressors in experiments. Temperature can be easily measured and controlled. Animal experiments provide examples of the control and measurement of stressors. Sleep deprivation experiments are conducted by placing the animal on an upturned flower pot in a pool of water. Every time it falls asleep, its nose drops into the water and it promptly wakes up. The length of sleep deprivation can be timed accurately. Animals are stressed by overcrowding and isolation. Again, these conditions can be timed and, in the case of overcrowding, the density of animals in a fixed area can be measured.

Laboratory experiments with humans have used all sorts of unpleasant experiences to induce stress. They include electric shocks, overcrowding and exposure to high and low temperatures. Again, there is ample opportunity for measurement. In the case of electric shocks, their number, duration and intensity can be measured accurately.

There are, however, a number of problems with laboratory experiments.

- Although they can measure certain aspects of a stressor, for example, temperature, this does not necessarily say anything about its impact on the individual. For example, a comfortable temperature for one person may be uncomfortably hot for another.

- An event or experience only becomes a stressor when it is perceived as such. Despite the accuracy of measurement in the laboratory, this does not tell us how the individual perceives the intended stressor.

- The laboratory is an artificial situation and participants tend to see it as such. For example, one experimental procedure involves participants submerging their arm in a bucket of ice cold water. This hardly reflects their experience of stress in life outside the laboratory.

- Laboratory experiments don't last long. At best they can only measure the strength of short-term stressors and the effect of short-term stress.

- Laboratory experiments raise ethical issues about the treatment of participants, both animal and human. For example, the British Psychological Society's guidelines for the use of animals in research state, 'If the animals are confined, constrained, harmed or stressed in any way the investigator must consider whether the knowledge to be gained justifies the procedure' (BPS, 1998).

3.3 Self-reports

Self-report studies ask people to report their perceptions of stressors and their experience of stress. These studies have the advantage of looking at stress from the point of view of those who experience it. Participants are often asked to keep diaries and, for example, report on daily hassles over a period of days, weeks or months. This overcomes one of the problems with many stress measures which provide only a one-off measure of stress, a snapshot of stress levels at a particular point in time. A diary report can note stress levels at various times during the day or week. The advantage of this can be seen from a study of stress in British drivers (Gulian et al., 1990). Drivers were asked to keep a diary of their feelings when driving, over a five day period. They reported feeling more stress in the evening and midweek. Their stress levels also appeared to be related to driving conditions, how well they'd slept, their age, health and driving experience, and whether or not they perceived driving as a stressful activity.

At best, however, self-report studies can only give a rough and ready guide to stress levels. Asking people to report on their feelings of stress cannot provide an objective and accurate measure of stress levels. Subjective feelings cannot be measured in the same way as temperature. In addition, people may exaggerate or minimise their experience of stress. For example, people with a pessimistic outlook may have a tendency to report higher stress levels than people with an optimistic outlook, even when their experience of stress is similar.

A variation on self-report studies asks participants to assess events which are then used as the basis for a questionnaire designed to measure stress. This method was used to construct the Social Readjustment Rating Scale (SRRS). A sample of 394 people were asked to rate life events in terms of the amount of social readjustment they required. There are a number of problems with this approach. First, many members of the sample may not have experienced some of the 43 life events they were asked to assess, for example death of a spouse and

divorce, the top two items on the SRRS. Second, they were asked to make 'snap judgements' about social readjustment, something they had probably not considered before. Despite this, there was considerable agreement on the ranking from a sample composed of different age groups, men and women, Protestants and Catholics. However, the level of agreement was lower between African Americans and whites.

Triangulation

Often researchers combine various methods, a procedure known as *triangulation*. This can provide a means of checking on the accuracy of the data produced by different methods. For example, if physiological data contradicted data from self-report studies, then this leads the researcher to question the methods and the data they have produced.

Triangulation also produces a fuller picture as different methods produce different types of data. For example, a study of fire-fighters combined self-report and physiological measures. The heart rate of each fire-fighter was recorded when they were at work using a portable electrocardiogram. They also kept a diary recording events they perceived as stressful (Douglas et al., 1988).

Summary

1. There are various ways of measuring stress. Each has strengths and weaknesses.

2. Physiological measures provide evidence about the body's response to stress but this does not tell us how the individual is feeling – that is their experience of stress.

3. Laboratory studies can provide accurate measures of certain stressors. However, the laboratory situation is artificial, and limited to the study of short-term stress.

4. Self-report studies provide an opportunity to obtain people's perceptions of stressors and their experience of stress. However, they cannot provide objective and accurate measures of stress levels.

5. Triangulation provides a means of checking on the accuracy of data produced by different research methods.

Key terms

Physiological measures *The measurement of physiological or bodily processes such as the levels of hormones and neurotransmitters, and heart rate.*

Self-report method *A method which asks people who are being studied to provide information about themselves.*

Triangulation *Using and comparing data produced from two or more research methods.*

References

Abbott, B.B., Schoen, L.S. & Badia, P. (1984). Predictable and unpredictable shock: Behavioural measures of aversion and physiological measures of stress. *Psychological Bulletin, 96*, 45-71.

Adams, P.R. & Adams, G.R. (1984). Mount Saint Helen's ashfall:

Evidence for a disaster stress reaction. *American Psychologist, 39*, 252-260.

Adams-Campbell, L.L., Brambilla, D.J. & McKinley, S.M. (1993). Correlates of prevalence of self-reported hypertension among

African-American and white women. *Ethnic Diseases, 3*, 119-125.

Allred, K.D. & Smith, T.W. (1989). The hardy personality: Cognitive and physiological responses to evaluative threat. *Journal of Personality and Social Psychology, 56*, 257-266.

Anderson, L.P. (1991). Acculturative stress: A theory of relevance to black Americans. *Clinical Psychology Review, 11*, 685-702.

Arnold, J., Robertson, I.T. & Cooper, C.L. (1991). *Work psychology*. London: Pitman.

Banyard, P. (1996). *Applying psychology to health*. London: Hodder & Stoughton.

Barefoot, J.C., Dodge, K.A., Peterson, B.L., Dahlstrom, W.G. & Williams, R.B., Jr. (1989). The Cook-Medley hostility scale: Item content and ability to predict survival. *Psychosomatic Medicine, 51*, 46-57.

Bell, P.A., Fisher, J.D., Baum, A. & Greene, T.C. (1990). *Environmental psychology*, (3rd ed.). Fort Worth: Holt, Rinehart and Winston.

Bernstein, D.A., Clarke-Stewart, A., Roy, E.J. & Wickens, C.D. (1997). *Psychology* (4th ed.). Boston: Houghton Mifflin.

Billings, A.G. & Moos, R.H. (1981). The role of coping responses and social resources in attenuating the stress of life events. *Journal of Behavioral Medicine, 4*, 139-157.

BPS (British Psychological Society). (1998). *Code of conduct, ethical principles and guidelines*, Leicester: BPA

Breslow, L. & Buell, P. (1960). Mortality from coronary heart disease and physical activity of work in California. *Journal of Chronic Disability,11*.

Brown, G.W. & Harris, T.O. (1978). *Social origins of depression: A study of psychiatric disorder in women*. London: Tavistock.

Brown, R. (1986). *Social psychology: The second edition*. New York: Free Press.

Canby, T.Y. (1990). Earthquake: prelude to the big one. *National Geographic, 177*, no 5, 76-105.

Cooper, C.J. & Marshall, J. (1976). Occupational sources of stress: A review of the literature relating to coronary heart disease and mental ill health. *Journal of Occupational Psychology, 49*, 11-28.

Cox, T. (1978). *Stress*. London: Macmillan.

Douglas, R.B., Blanks, R., Crowther, A. & Scott, G. (1988). A study of stress in West Midlands firemen, using ambulatory electrocardiograms. *Work and Stress, 2*, 309-318.

Frankenhaeuser, M. (1975). Sympathetic-adrenomedullary activity behaviour and the psychosocial environment. In P.H. Venables & M.J. Christie (Eds.), *Research in psychophysiology*. New York: Wiley.

Frankenhaeuser, M. (1983). The sympathetic-adrenal and pituitary-adrenal response to challenge; Comparison between the sexes. In T.M. Dembroski, T.H. Schmidt & G. Blumchen (Eds), *Biobehavioural bases of coronary heart disease*. Basel: Karger.

Frankenhaeuser, M., Lundberg, M., Fredriksson, B., Melin, M. & Thomisto, A., (1989). Stress on and off the job as related to sex and occupational status in whitecollar workers. *Journal of Organisational Behaviour, 10*, 321-346.

Friedman, H.S. & Booth-Kewley, S. (1987). The 'disease-prone' personality; A meta-analytic view of the construct. *American Psychologist, 42*, 539-555.

Friedman, M. & Rosenman, R.H. (1974). *Type A behaviour and your heart*. New York: Knopf.

Funk, S.C. (1992). Hardiness: A review of theory and research. *Health Psychology, 11*, 335-345.

Furedi, F. (1999). Time to put up or shut up. *Independent on Sunday*, 10th October.

Geer, J. & Maisel, E. (1973). Evaluating the effects of the prediction-control confound. *Journal of Personality and Social Psychology, 23*, 314-319.

Gulian, E., Glendon, A.I., Matthews, G. & Davies, D. (1990). The stress of driving: A diary study. *Work and Stress, 4*, 7-16.

Haralambos, M. (Ed.) (1996). *Sociology: A new approach* (3rd ed.). Ormskirk: Causeway.

Hazzard, A., Weston, J. & Gutterres, C. (1992). After a child's death: Factors related to parental bereavement. *Journal of Developmental & Behavioural Paediatrics, 13*, 24-30.

Holmes, T.H. & Rahe, R.H. (1967). The social readjustment rating scale. *Journal of Psychosomatic Research, 11*, 213-218.

Hunter, E.J. (1979, May). Combat casualities who remain at home. Paper presented at Western Regional Conference of the Interuniversity Seminar, 'Technology in Combat'. Navy Postgraduate School, Monterey, CA.

Johansson, G. and Post, B. (1972). Catecholamine output of males and females over a one-year period. *Rep. Psychol. Lab.*, University of Stockholm (379).

Kahn, R.L., Wolfe, D.M., Quinn, R.P., Snoek, J.D & Rosenthal, R.A. (1964). *Organisational stress: Studies in role conflict and ambiguity*. New York: John Wiley.

Kanner, A.D., Coyne, J.C., Schaeffer, C. & Lazarus, R.S. (1981). Comparison of two modes of stress measurement: Daily hassles and uplifts versus major life events. *Journal of Behavioural Medicine, 4*, 1-39.

Katz, R. & Wykes, T. (1985). The psychological difference between temporally predictable and unpredictable stressful events: evidence for information control theories. *Journal of Personality and Social Psychology, 48*, 781-790.

Kobasa, S.C. (1979). Stressful life events and health: An inquiry into hardiness. *Journal of Personality and Social Psychology, 37*, 1-11.

Lazarus, R.S. (1976). *Patterns of adjustment*. New York: McGraw-Hill.

Lundberg, U.(1976). Urban commuting: Crowdedness and catacholamine excretion. *Journal of Human Stress, 2*, 26-32.

Matthews, K.A., Davis, M.C., Stoney, C.M., Owens, J.F. & Caggiula, A.R. (1991). Does the gender relevance of the stressor influence sex differences in psychophysiological responses? *Health Psychology, 10*, 112-120.

Pennebaker, J.W. & Harber, K.D. (1991, April). *Coping after the Loma Prieta earthquake: A preliminary report*. Paper presented at the Western Psychological Association Convention, San Francisco, CA.

Peterson, C., Seligman, M.E.P. & Vaillant, G.E. (1988). Pessimistic explanatory style is a risk factor for physical illness: A thirty-five-year longitudinal study. *Journal of Personality and Social Psychology, 55*, 23-27.

Pitts, M. & Phillips, K. (Eds.) (1998). *The psychology of health: An introduction*. London: Routledge.

Sarafino, E.P. (1994). *Health psychology: Biopsychosocial interactions* (2nd ed.). New York: John Wiley.

Sarason, I.G., Johnson, J.H. & Siegel, J.M. (1978). Assessing the impact of life changes: Development of the Life Experiences Survey. *Journal of Consulting and Clinical Psychology, 46*, 932-946.

Scheier, M.F., Matthews, K.A., Owens, J., Magovern, G.J., Sr., Lefebvre, R.C., Abbott, R.A. & Carver, C.S. (1989). Dispositional optimism and recovery from coronary artery bypass surgery: The beneficial effects on physical and psychological well-being. *Journal of Personality and Social Psychology, 57*, 1024-1040.

Speisman, J., Lazarus, R.S., Mordkoff, A. & Davidson, L. (1964). Experimental reduction of stress based on ego defence theory. *Journal of Abnormal and Social Psychology, 68*, 367-380.

Stone, A.A., Reed, B.R. & Neale, J.M. (1987). Changes in daily event frequency precede episodes of physical symptoms. *Journal of Human Stress, 13*, 70-74.

Weidner, G. & Collins, R.L. (1993). Gender, coping, and health. In H.W. Krohne (Ed.), *Attention and avoidance*. New York: Springer-Verlag.

Weitz, R. (1989). Uncertainty and the lives of persons with AIDS. *Journal of Health and Social Behaviour, 30*, 270-81.

Wiebe, D.J. (1991). Hardiness and stress modification: A test of proposed mechanisms. *Journal of Personality and Social Psychology, 60*, 89-90.

Woodall, K.L. & Matthews, K.A. (1993). Changes in and stability of hostile characteristics: Results from a 4-year longitudinal study of children. *Journal of Personality and Social Psychology, 64*, 491-499.

Zimbardo, P.G., McDermott, M., Jansz. J. & Metaal, N. (1995). *Psychology: A European text*. London: Harper Collins.

9 Stress management

Introduction

Stress has become one of the major concerns of the new millennium. In the 'Popular Psychology' sections of American bookshops, book after book provides advice on coping with stress. The UK is following suit, with *The little book of calm* topping two million sales in 2000. Stress has become the focus of a cartoon series starring Stressed Eric, a harassed executive. And stress made British legal history in 1999 when Birmingham City Council was ordered by the courts to pay £67,000 to a former employee for personal injury caused by work-related stress. Unison, the trade union which backed her claim, has over 7000 more cases on its books.

Individuals and organisations are increasingly aware of the problems caused by stress. They are increasingly concerned about how to treat stress. This chapter looks at various methods of dealing with the negative effects of stress.

Chapter summary

- **Unit 1 looks at the use of drugs in stress management.**
- **Unit 2 examines biofeedback as a technique for reducing stress.**
- **Unit 3 considers cognitive-behavioural strategies which attempt to reduce stress by**

changing the way people think and behave.
- **Unit 4 assesses the contribution of social support to stress reduction.**
- **Unit 5 presents a critical discussion of stress management.**

Unit 1 Drug treatment

KEY ISSUES

1. Can drugs provide effective treatment for stress?

2. What are the disadvantages of drug treatment?

Units 1 and 2 look at physiological approaches to stress management. These approaches are designed to reduce stress by altering bodily processes.

Stress is sometimes accompanied by anxiety and depression. Drugs can be used to treat these disorders.

Antianxiety drugs The most commonly prescribed antianxiety drugs, or anxiolytics, belong to a family of drugs known as *benzodiazepines*. These are also known as minor tranquillisers, and produced under trade names such as Librium and Valium.

Antianxiety drugs decrease arousal and relax the body by reducing tension in the muscles. Since the stress response involves high arousal, tranquillisers may, in some cases, reduce stress. But drugs have no direct effect on the stressor – for example, they do not mend a broken marriage or solve financial problems. However, they may put a person in a better frame of mind so they can cope more effectively with stressors.

There are a number of possible problems with benzodiazepines.

1 In many cases, when the medication is stopped, anxiety returns.

2 If taken in large doses over a long period of time, people can become psychologically and/or physically dependent on them.

3 There can be undesirable side effects such as drowsiness, impaired memory and depression.

4 They may reduce concentration which can be dangerous in situations such as driving (Comer, 1998).

Antidepressant drugs There are a number of antidepressant drugs which are manufactured under various trade names such as Prozac and Tofranil. Antidepressant drugs can reduce

An advert for Prozac

depression and so help the individual to cope more effectively with stressors. However, they can have many of the same problems as benzodiazepines. Antidepressants sometimes have undesirable side effects – in the case of Prozac, nausea, diarrhoea and dizziness. After the medication stops, depression can recur. Drugs may do little or nothing to solve the problem which led to stress in the first place. They may simply provide temporary relief rather than encouraging the individual to face up to and take steps to deal with the problem which led to their depression. In addition, these drugs may produce physical and/or psychological dependence where people feel they need drugs to cope with their problems. Again, this can be counterproductive.

Beta-blockers Long-term stress is often accompanied by high

blood pressure which can lead to strokes and hypertension. Beta-blockers are drugs which slow the heart and reduce the strength of its contraction, so reducing blood pressure. They block receptors on the heart which are stimulated by noradrenaline. In this way, they decrease sympathetic nervous system activity. This probably has psychological as well as physiological effects. The individual may feel calm and relaxed as a result of suppression of the sympathetic nervous system.

As with all drug treatments, there is the possibility of side effects. Large doses of beta-blockers can lead to depression and impotence (Taylor, 1995).

Key terms

Antianxiety drugs or anxiolytics *Drugs prescribed to reduce anxiety.*

Benzodiazepines *Antianxiety drugs commonly known as minor tranquillisers. They decrease arousal and reduce tension in the muscles.*

Antidepressant drugs *Drugs prescribed to reduce depression.*

Beta-blockers *Drugs which slow the heart and reduce the strength of its contraction, so reducing blood pressure.*

Summary

1   Stress is often accompanied by anxiety and depression. Drugs are sometimes used to treat these disorders. They may reduce stress.

2   The stress response is often accompanied by high blood pressure. Beta-blockers can reduce blood pressure.

3   There are a number of problems with drug treatment.

- The possibility of physical and psychological dependence
- Undesirable side effects
- After usage stops, the problem (eg depression) often returns
- Drugs have no direct effect on the stressor.

Unit 2 Biofeedback

KEY ISSUES

1. **What is biofeedback?**
2. **What are the advantages and disadvantages of this technique?**

Biofeedback is a method which provides people with information about bodily processes such as their heart rate and blood pressure. Often people are unaware of these processes. Biofeedback allows them to 'see' or 'hear' them. For example, heart rate can be monitored and displayed visually on a computer screen. Alternatively, it can be converted into sound, with the tone increasing in pitch the higher the heart rate.

Biofeedback gives people both an awareness of their bodily processes and a means of measuring them. The aim is to help people to control them. Laboratory studies indicate that, with the help of biofeedback, participants can make significant short-term changes in their biological processes, for example raising their heart rate or lowering their blood pressure (Shapiro et al., 1970).

Biofeedback has been used to treat various stress-related illnesses such as migraine headache and hypertension. For example, migraine headache may result from the physiological stress response which involves a redistribution of blood from the skin and the gut to the brain. If a person is able to reverse this process, then the severity of their migraine might be reduced. An increase in body temperature indicates that they have achieved this. A thermometer on a finger provides temperature

feedback and the aim is to increase the temperature.

Evaluation

Does biofeedback work? In particular, does it reduce stress, does it effectively treat stress-related illnesses such as hypertension? The short answer to these questions is we don't really know.

Biofeedback and relaxation Even when biofeedback appears to work, it may be relaxation, rather than biofeedback itself, which produces positive results. Relaxation training, which involves steadily relaxing the muscles, is often used alongside biofeedback. Some researchers argue that in the treatment of hypertension, relaxation techniques do more than biofeedback to reduce blood pressure. And, given that relaxation training is

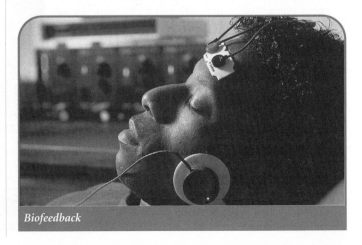

Biofeedback

usually far less expensive than biofeedback, there is a case for simply learning to relax (Blanchard et al., 1979).

Biofeedback and control Biofeedback gives people a feeling of control. This sense of control, rather than biofeedback itself, may produce beneficial effects. Tension headaches are believed to result from tension in the muscles of the forehead. By attaching electrodes to a person's forehead, the amount of tension can be monitored and fed back as sound – a high pitch when the muscles contract, a low pitch when they are relaxed. Biofeedback has been effective in relaxing the muscles and reducing headaches. However, some studies have indicated that simply believing that muscle tension was being relaxed – even if it wasn't – can lead to a reduction in tension headaches (Holroyd et al., 1984).

This suggests that the key factor might be a sense of control. As noted in the previous chapter, a sense of control can play a major part in reducing stress.

Most of the time people can't be wired up to a heart monitor or walk round with a thermometer on the end of their finger. Can the supposed benefits of biofeedback be carried over into everyday situations to deal with the hassles of daily life? Some supporters of biofeedback believe that people can eventually learn to control their bodily processes without the use of monitoring devices (Turk et al., 1979). Other researchers disagree. However, in the case of tension headaches, there is evidence that people learn to recognise the beginning of tension and are able to reduce it without the help of monitoring devices (Tarler-Benlolo, 1978).

Short-term benefits Biofeedback may well have short-term benefits, for example, short-term reductions in heartrate and blood pressure. But will this solve anything? In particular, does it deal with the real problems in people's lives? The answer is probably not. However, it may put people in a better frame of mind to deal with those problems.

Conclusion It is too early to celebrate the benefits of biofeedback. As one researcher said, 'Don't hold the party yet' (Melzack, 1975). From a survey of available evidence, Davison and Neale (1998) conclude, 'There is only limited evidence that biofeedback has any specific effects other than distraction, relaxation, and instilling a beneficial sense of control'.

Key terms

Biofeedback *A technique which allows people to monitor their bodily processes. This can give them some control over those processes.*

Summary

1. Laboratory studies indicate that people can exercise some control over their bodily processes with the help of biofeedback.

2. There is some evidence that biofeedback can bring improvements for hypertension and migraine sufferers. However, its effects are probably short term rather than long term.

3. Biofeedback is often used alongside relaxation techniques. Learning to relax may be more beneficial than biofeedback.

4. Biofeedback can give people a sense of control. It may be this, rather than biofeedback itself, which helps to reduce stress.

Unit 3 Psychological approaches

KEY ISSUES

1. **What are the main psychological approaches to stress management?**
2. **What are their strengths and weaknesses?**

Psychological approaches to stress reduction focus on changing the way people think and behave. They are usually known as cognitive-behavioural approaches because they involve cognitive changes – changes in the way people perceive stressors and think about stress – and behavioural changes – actual changes in their behaviour when they respond to and deal with stressful situations. Psychological approaches aim to provide the individual with control over their perception of stressors and their strategies for dealing with stress.

Type A behaviour

As outlined in Chapters 7 and 8, there is evidence which suggests that Type A behaviour patterns increase the risk of stress and coronary heart disease. If this is the case, then a change in these behaviour patterns should lead to a reduction in stress and heart disease. There is some evidence to support this. In one study, over 1000 men who had suffered a heart attack were divided into two groups. The first group were given standard cardiac counselling about reducing risk factors such as smoking and overactivity. In addition to this, the second group took part in a programme designed to reduce Type A behaviour. For example, they were discouraged from seeing stressors as direct personal challenges and from responding to them with aggression and hostility. After three years of counselling, the risk of a further heart attack for men on the Type A reduction programme was 7.2% annually compared to 13.2% for the men who received only standard cardiac counselling (Friedman et al., 1984).

Evaluation This research suggests three possibilities.

1. That a reduction in Type A behaviour reduces stress and, therefore, the risk of coronary heart disease.

2. The key factor was reducing the hostility component rather than the whole range of Type A behaviours (Haaga, 1987).

3. Since the group who took part in the Type A reduction programme received more attention, it was this, rather than a reduction in Type A behaviour, that accounted for their lower rate of heart attacks.

Stress management programmes

Stress management programmes are designed to reduce stress and improve coping skills. Many of these programmes have been developed by health psychologists. People who participate in such programmes either see psychologists on a one-to-one basis, or attend workshops where they are taught stress management techniques and given 'stress counselling'. In addition, there are numerous books and videos on stress management which allow you to 'do it yourself'.

Stress management is big business. Many large organisations employ 'stress consultants' to advise on work practices with the aim of reducing stress in the workplace. They are also employed to give stress management courses to workers.

Stress management programmes are also used to treat people with stress-related illnesses from migraine headaches to hypertension and coronary heart disease.

Stress as a transaction The transactional model of stress forms the basis of many stress management programmes. The transactional model argues that cognitive appraisal is the key to understanding stress. First, a possible stressor is appraised. It becomes a stressor if it is perceived as such. Second, coping abilities and resources for dealing with the situation are appraised. If, for example, abilities and resources are perceived as inadequate, then a high level of stress is likely (see pp 96-97 for a more detailed outline of the transactional model).

It follows from the transactional model that stress can be reduced by cognitive means – by changing the way stressors, coping abilities and resources are appraised. For example, many people worry about giving a speech to a large audience. A standard stress management technique for reducing this concern is to imagine those who might criticise you sitting naked in the audience. The key idea in many stress management programmes is *control* over the perception of stressors and coping strategies.

Increasing hardiness

The previous chapter outlined Kobasa's (1979) research on *hardiness* (see pp 106-107). She claimed that people with a certain personality type, which she called hardiness, were more resistant to stress. People with this type of personality have the following characteristics.

- They see change as a challenge rather than a threat. As a result, they are less likely to perceive change as a stressor.
- They are more likely to face problems and take steps to solve them.
- They believe that people have control over their own actions and can influence their environment.

Hardiness training Kobasa's colleague, Salvator Maddi, founder of the Hardiness Institute in California, has designed a stress management programme based on the idea of hardiness (Maddi, 2000). The programme begins with a Hardi Survey Assessment which assesses people's level of hardiness. It then offers a series of programmes designed to increase hardiness – the HardiTraining Course, HardiWorkshops and HardiCoaching.

The HardiTraining Course is designed to build 'hardy attitudes'. It aims to help people to 'strengthen their beliefs about their effectiveness and coping strategies'. By doing this they will increase their ability to 'view disruptive changes in a more balanced, optimistic light, and to meet them head-on with constructive actions'. The following recipe is provided for increasing hardiness and reducing stress.

- Rather than focusing directly on 'stressful circumstances', they should be viewed in a broader perspective. By doing

this, 'they won't seem so terrible after all'.
- Analysing stressful circumstances in order to understand and control them.
- Developing and carrying out an action plan in order to eliminate the stressful aspects of the situation.
- Accepting that some things cannot be changed, without becoming bitter or self-pitying about the situation.

The Hardiness Institute claims that by following these guidelines, individuals will become increasingly hardy and stress-resistant. They will gain 'stress mastery and personal power'.

Stress inoculation

This term was coined by the psychologist Donald Meichenbaum (1977). He argued that just as a person can be inoculated against a flu virus and become resistant to it, so they can be 'inoculated' against stress and become 'stress-resistant'. He developed a stress management programme which aimed to do just this.

Phase 1 First a person must identify the sources of stress in their life, examine how they cope with stressful situations, and consider alternative ways of coping. According to Meichenbaum, going through this process gives people a sense of control.

Phase 2 The next step is to learn a series of skills for dealing with stressful situations. This involves learning a list of coping self-statements, all of which are positive, reassuring and encouraging. At the same time negative self-statements which are self-critical and defeatist, must be identified and rejected. For example, before giving a speech, negative statements such as, 'I'll panic', 'I'll forget my lines', and 'I'll sound boring', must be replaced by positive statements such as 'I'm well prepared', 'I'm nervous but that means I'll give of my best'. Table 1 gives examples of coping self-statements to prepare, confront and cope with stressful situations.

Phase 3 The final step is to appraise the performance. People must give themselves full credit for successful coping. Again the emphasis is on positive statements. If the speech referred to

Table 1 Coping self-statements	
Preparation	I can develop a plan to deal with it.
	No negative self-statements, just think rationally.
Confrontation	One step at a time; I can handle this situation.
	Relax; I'm in control. Take a slow deep breath.
Coping	Don't try to eliminate fear totally; just keep it manageable.
	It's not the worst thing that can happen.
Self-reinforcement	I was able to do it because I was well prepared.
	I'm really pleased with the progress I'm making.

Adapted from Zimbardo et al., 1995

above went well, rather than saying 'I was lucky' or giving credit to 'a sympathetic audience', a statement like 'I put the work in so I deserved the applause' is far more appropriate. This can be self-reinforcing, increasing self-confidence and improving self-image. Examples of self-reinforcing statements are given in Table 1.

To become 'stress-resistant' a person must first practice with a therapist – the psychologist who is helping them to deal with stress. Then they must practice the approach in real life stress situations until it becomes 'second nature'. In addition, they must prepare their own list of coping self-statements – one that works best for them.

Stress management programmes offer a wide, and sometimes bewildering, range of cognitive-behavioural strategies. They often combine biofeedback and relaxation training with a variety of cognitive techniques designed to discourage negative and encourage positive thoughts and perceptions.

At times stress management programmes read like an instruction manual as the following examples indicate.

- Slow down – try to do things at a slower pace.
- Organise your life – disorganisation produces stress.
- Strike a balance – don't let one aspect of your life, for example work, get blown out of proportion.
- Write about your feelings – it will help you cope.
- Seek social support – support from family and friends can cushion the impact of stress.
  (Above examples taken from Coon, 1998).

Many stress management programmes operate rather like a cafeteria. They offer a broad range of skills and techniques from which the individual chooses those that work best for them (Taylor, 1995).

Evaluation

How effective are stress management programmes? This is a difficult question to answer as there are many different programmes.

Aspects of stress management programmes have been built into treatment programmes for a variety of stress-related illnesses from migraine, to hypertension and coronary heart disease. They have met with some success. For example, stress management has been shown to reduce the risk of CHD (Carver & Humphries, 1982).

One advantage of stress management programmes is that they avoid the undesirable side effects of drug treatment. And, unlike drugs, some programmes deal directly with the stressor. They train people to identify stressors, to develop plans for dealing with them, and to take action to solve their problems.

Some of the benefits of stress management programmes may result from a perception of control rather than the detailed strategies they provide. Trained by an expert and armed with a list of instructions, the individual may feel in control of the situation. And this may lead to stress reduction.

Some stress management programmes have been criticised for failing to deal with the actual sources of stress. They may change perceptions and give a feeling of control but do they actually change the situation which gave rise to stress in the first place? In many cases the answer is no. For example, workplace stressors such as work overload, repetitive jobs and social isolation are not directly addressed by many stress management programmes. Such programmes may:

- Make it easier for people to live with stressors
- Give an illusion of control
- Cover up the real sources of stress so discouraging attempts to remove stressors
- Or, put people in a better frame of mind to deal with the actual causes of stress.

Stress management programmes can be seen as a smokescreen used by employers to exploit their workers. Rather than doing something about the actual causes of stress, for example work overload, apparently caring employers provide their workers with stress management programmes. This implies that the problem to be solved is stressed workers rather than stress-producing work situations.

Stress management programmes focus on the individual rather than the wider society. The individual follows their programme and practices their stress management techniques. But the real problem may be society as a whole. Rather than changing the individual, it might be society that needs changing. Western society emphasises achievement and competition. These emphases may be major stressors as people strive incessantly to achieve, and compete constantly for income and material possessions. As the market place becomes increasingly global,

Key terms

Cognitive-behavioural approaches *Approaches to stress management based on cognitive and behavioural changes.*

Stress management programmes *A set of techniques and strategies designed to reduce stress and improve coping skills.*

Hardiness training *A training programme which aims to increase people's hardiness.*

Stress inoculation *A training programme which aims to make people resistant to stress.*

Coping self-statements *Positive statements about the self which aim to increase self-confidence, improve coping skills, and make the individual more resistant to stress.*

Summary

1. Cognitive-behavioural approaches argue that stress can be reduced by a) changing the way people perceive stressors and think about stress and b) changing the way they behave when responding to stressful situations.

2. There is some evidence that reducing Type A behaviour can reduce stress and stress-related illness.

3. Many stress management programmes are based on cognitive-behavioural approaches.

4. Stress management programmes have met with some success. They have the advantage of avoiding the undesirable side effects of drug treatment and of dealing directly with the stressor.

5. Stress management programmes have been criticised for failing to deal with the real causes of stress.

6. Stress management programmes deal with the individual rather than society. If major stressors are built into the structure of society, stress management programmes may divert attention from the real problem.

competition intensifies with calls to raise productivity, increase efficiency, reduce costs, meet deadlines and sell aggressively.

In this respect, stressors may be built into the very structure of society. It can be argued that by focusing on the individual, stress management programmes divert attention from the real problem – the wider society.

Unit 5 continues the evaluation of stress management programmes.

Unit 4 Social support

KEY ISSUES

1. What is social support?
2. How might it reduce stress?
3. Are its effects always beneficial?

Stress management programmes often advise people to seek social support. In general, research indicates that people with a wide network of family and friends experience less stress in response to a stressor and cope with it more successfully. Social support refers to the support available to the individual from others. Cohen and Wills (1985) identify four main aspects of social support.

Esteem support The experience of stress can lead to self-doubt and low self-esteem, especially when a person is having difficulty in coping. Love, care and attention from family and friends can reassure a person that they are valued and worthwhile. This can raise their sense of self-worth which, in turn, can help them to cope more effectively.

Informational support This refers to useful information provided by others. It can help a person to reappraise both a stressor and their coping strategy. It may involve advice from people who have experienced a similar situation, for example bereavement, divorce or unemployment. This advice may lead to more effective coping strategies.

Instrumental support This involves a range of activities which provide practical assistance. For example, it refers to a loan or gift of money to help a friend in financial difficulties. It includes services such as babysitting, gardening, home decorating, shopping, and caring for somebody when they are ill. Instrumental support, by making life easier, can help a person cope more effectively with a stressful situation.

Social companionship refers to spending time with other people – talking over a cup of coffee, going to the pub or cinema, going on holiday with friends. Social companionship can prevent people from dwelling on their problems, provide an opportunity for enjoyment, and put them in a better frame of mind to cope.

However, simply being surrounded by family and friends does not necessarily mean that a person experiences positive support. They may see the attention of others as an intrusion, and their attempts to help as interference. Many researchers argue that *perceived social support* – the amount of support a person feels they are receiving – is the key to understanding the relationship between social support and stress.

Benefits of social support

What evidence is there for the beneficial effects of social support? A large body of research indicates that people with a high level of social support are less prone to stress and more likely to cope with stress. For example, after an accident in 1979 at the Three Mile Island nuclear plant in the USA, people living nearby with high levels of social support experienced less stress than those with low levels of support (Fleming et al., 1982). A number of laboratory studies indicate the importance of social support. In one study women were placed in a stressful situation either alone or with a close friend. Blood pressure was used as a measure of stress. The women who were alone had significantly higher blood pressure than those accompanied by a friend (Kamarck et al., 1995).

Social support and health Research indicates that high levels of social support:

- Reduce the likelihood of illness
- Speed recovery from illness
- Reduce the risk of death from illness.

A large scale study in California looked at nearly 7000 people over a nine year period. It found that people with a large number of social contacts were less likely to die during this period than those with few social contacts (Berkman & Syme, 1979). A study of 133 women with breast cancer indicated that those who had more friendships and those who had jobs outside the home tended to live longer (Waxler-Morrison et al., 1991).

Evaluation

Social support can have a negative side. For example, people suffering from asthma may find their condition is made worse if they see their family as over-protective and over-concerned (Banyard, 1996).

The *matching hypothesis* suggests that social support is only effective when there is a match between an individual's needs and the type of support provided by those in their social network. For example, a person with financial difficulties may find it embarrassing to talk about their problem with family members, but may welcome a loan from a friend. A study of cancer patients indicated that different

Summary

1   Research indicates that people with a wide social network experience less stress and cope with stress more effectively.

2   Research evidence indicates that high levels of social support:
- Reduce the likelihood of illness
- Speed recovery from illness
- Reduce the risk of death from illness.

3   Social support can have negative effects. For example, it may be seen as an intrusion into a person's private life.

kinds of support are required from different members of the social network. Emotional support was required from family and close friends; informational support and advice from doctors and nurses. Receiving informational support from a family member can be seen as inappropriate and make matters worse. In general, being overly cheerful or trying to minimise the seriousness of the illness was seen as unhelpful, whether it came from family, friends, or doctors (Dakof & Taylor, 1990).

Overall, the evidence suggests that the effects of social support are beneficial – they usually reduce stress and help people to cope with stress. However, the relationship between stress and social support is not simple and clear-cut. At times, people may feel overwhelmed by well-intentioned comfort, advice and offers of help. They may interpret 'support' as an intrusion into their private lives. In such cases, social support may add to the stress they are already experiencing.

Key terms

Social support *The support available to the individual from members of their social network. It includes esteem support, informational support, instrumental support and social companionship.*

Perceived social support *The amount of social support a person feels they are receiving.*

Matching hypothesis *Suggests that social support is only effective when there is a match between a person's needs and the type of support they receive.*

Activity 1   Social support

Item A   A close-knit community

From early morning to late at night little groups formed and faded, trading with goodwill, candour or cattishness the detailed gossip of a closed society. Over a period the health, honesty, conduct, history and connections of everyone in the neighbourhood would be examined. Each would be criticised, praised, censured openly or by hint and finally allocated by tacit consent a position on the social scale.

Adapted from Roberts, 1973

Item B   Pets

Research suggests that people live longer, and recover more quickly from an illness, if they have a pet. One study showed that pet owners were more likely to be alive one year after admission to hospital with a heart attack than similar people without pets. Another study found that when people stroked their own dog, their blood pressure fell. This did not happen when they stroked a strange dog.

Adapted from Baun et al., 1984

Questions

1 In a close-knit social network, social support can have both positive and negative effects. Discuss with some reference to Item A.

2 Read Item B. Suggest reasons for the apparent beneficial effects of pet ownership.

Unit 5 Stress management – a critical approach

KEY ISSUES

1. **Should the stress response be seen in a positive light?**
2. **How effective are stress management interventions in organisations?**

The 1990s could well be described as the decade of stress. The phrase 'I'm stressed' entered everyday conversation. The term stress was expanded to cover a multitude of negative emotions and experiences from anxiety and depression to feeling tired, worn out and fed up. Doctors are now diagnosing and treating stress and a rapidly growing stress management industry provides advice and treatment for individuals and organisations.

Stress is blamed for a whole range of physical illnesses and psychological disorders. It is said to be costing industry vast sums of money in absence from work and poor performance at work. Stress is now pictured almost exclusively in negative terms. It is sometimes seen as a new strain of disease, which, in the late 1990s, is reaching epidemic proportions.

5.1 Re-evaluating the stress response

In a paper entitled *Killing the messenger: The pathologising of the stress response*, Angela Patmore (1997) rejects the idea of stress as a disease which requires diagnosis and treatment. Stress itself is not the problem. The real problem is the causes of stress – the stressors. These are the things which require treatment. Patmore rejects many of the 'treatments' for stress proposed by the stress management industry. In her view, they do little or nothing to deal with the actual causes of stress. This section outlines some of her arguments.

The stress response should be seen as a positive response rather than a threat to individual wellbeing. It is a valuable survival mechanism which galvanises people 'into mental and physical activity, enhances awareness and prompts adaptation to change and challenge'. The stress response can be compared to a burglar alarm. It warns of a threat in the environment and galvanises the individual to take action and deal with the situation. But, many of the techniques of stress management are designed to calm people down and subdue the stress response. As a result, 'instead of looking for the burglar, we are taking the alarm down off the wall and throwing it in the dustbin'. In other words, the stress response – the alarm – should not be subdued. Instead, it should be used to identify the problem and to deal with it.

According to Patmore, many stress management techniques start from the assumption that the stress response is harmful. Since the stress response is activating and arousing, it follows that 'treatment' should be de-activating and de-arousing. This can be seen from a range of 'calming down' techniques such as biofeedback, muscle relaxation and deep breathing. Counselling and psychotherapy are often designed to reduce stress by damping down the stress response. And the same applies to drug treatments as the term tranquilliser suggests.

If the stress response is viewed as a valuable adaptive mechanism, then many stress management techniques are 'at best useless and at worst disabling'. By suppressing or closing down the stress response, they can prevent people from identifying the threat or challenge and prevent them from dealing with the threat or rising to the challenge. As a result, 'people are not being activated to help themselves'.

Patmore's ideas provide an important alternative to many of the arguments outlined in this chapter. She is one of the few researchers to challenge the accepted wisdom of stress management.

5.2 Stress management in organisations

Stress management is big business. Organisations are increasingly employing 'stress consultants' in an attempt to reduce or eliminate stress in the workplace. According to Rob Briner (1999), stress management intervention in organisations is based on the following assumptions. First, the way the organisation is structured and the way work is organised creates organisational stressors. These stressors cause undesirable states in employees such as psychological distress, ill-health and low job satisfaction. They also cause undesirable behaviours such as poor work performance, frequent absence from work and high turnover – a high level of resigning from work. Second, the way to deal with these problems is stress management intervention. This will reduce or remove organisational stressors which will lead to a reduction in undesirable employee states and behaviour.

Stress management intervention sometimes starts with a 'stress audit' or 'stress diagnosis' based on a questionnaire which asks employees to identify aspects of their jobs which they find 'stressful'. Partly on the basis of questionnaire results, the 'stress consultants' attempt to redesign jobs and working practices in order to eliminate stressors. For example, they may attempt to 'enrich' jobs by giving employees more responsibility and cutting out boring and tedious tasks with the aim of increasing job satisfaction. This, the argument goes, will reduce stress and improve both the wellbeing and performance of employees.

So far, so good, but Briner (1999) found little evidence to support either the assumptions or the practice of stress management intervention. He examined research evidence on the effects of stress on employee performance, absence and illness. He found the evidence was either weak – stress appears to explain only 2-3% of the variation in these factors – or non-existent. Briner then looked at a number of stress management interventions in organisations. At best, he found their

Summary

1. Many researchers and most people in the wider society see stress in a negative light.

2. Some researchers argue that the stress response should be seen as a valuable adaptive mechanism.

3. From this point of view, stress management techniques which aim to suppress the stress response may be harmful.

4. Despite their widespread use, stress management interventions in organisation may have, at best, limited benefits.

effectiveness was limited and short term. Often the results were mixed. For example, one study found increases in job satisfaction and job commitment but also increases in absenteeism and job turnover (Cordery et al., 1991).

Briner concludes that at least part of the demand by organisations for stress management intervention is due to the current preoccupation in society with the idea of stress. As a result, the stress consultants, or 'stress busters' as they are sometimes called, are riding high on a wave of popular concerns and anxieties.

Activity 2   The culture of stress

Item A   Stress and the media

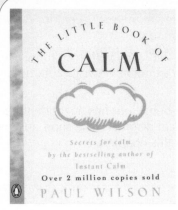

One of the bestselling books of the new millennium.

Stressed Eric is an adult cartoon series starring a forty-something executive. His high stress levels are graphically portrayed by a swollen blood vessel in his temple which throbs alarmingly.

Item B   Stress management

The stress response is a signal that something is wrong in the environment, and that the real threat, whether at work or at home, should be urgently addressed. In so far as stress management prevents this from happening, it may be said to be harmful.

Adapted from Patmore, 1997

Questions

1   What does Item A indicate about current attitudes towards stress?

2   Which aspects of stress management might produce the 'harmful' effects referred to in Item B?

References

Banyard, P. (1996). *Applying psychology to health.* London: Hodder & Stoughton.

Baun, M.M., Bergstrum, N., Langston, M.F. & Thoma, L. (1984). Physiological effects of human animal bonding. *Nursing Research, 33,* 126-129.

Berkman, L.F. & Syme, S.L. (1979). Social networks, host resistance, and mortality: A nine-year followup study of Alameda County residents. *American Journal of Epidemiology, 109,* 186-204.

Blanchard, E.B., Miller, S.T., Abel, G.G., Haynes, M.R. & Wicker, R. (1979). Evaluation of biofeedback in the treatment of borderline essential hypertension. *Journal of Applied Behaviour Analysis, 12,* 99-109.

Briner, R. B. & Reynolds, S. (1999). The costs, benefits and limitations of organizational level stress interventions. *Journal of Organizational Behavior, 20,* 647-664.

Carver, C.S. & Humphries, C. (1982). Social psychology of the Type A coronary-prone behaviour pattern. In G.S. Saunders & J. Suls (Eds.), *Social psychology of health and illness.* Hillsdale, NJ: Erlbaum.

Cohen, S. & Wills, T.A. (1985). Stress, social support, and the buffering process. *Psychology Bulletin, 98,* 310-357.

Comer, R.J. (1998). *Abnormal psychology* (3rd ed.). New York: W.H. Freeman.

Coon, D. (1998). *Introduction to psychology: Exploration and application* (8th ed.). Pacific Grove, CA: Brooks/Cole.

Cordery, J.L., Mueller, W.S. & Smith, L.M. (1991). Attitudinal and behavioural effects of autonomous group working: A longitudinal field study. *Academy of Management Journal, 34,* 464-476.

Dakof, G.A. & Taylor, S.E. (1990). Victims' perceptions of social support: What is helpful from whom? *Journal of Personality and Social Psychology, 58,* 80-89.

Davison, G.C. & Neale, J.M. (1998). *Abnormal psychology* (7th ed.). New York: John Wiley & Sons.

Fleming, R., Baum, A., Gisriel, M.M. & Gatchel, R.J. (1982). Mediating influences of social support on stress at Three Mile Island. *Journal of Human Stress,* September, 14-23.

Friedman, M., Thoresen, C.E., Gill, J.J., Powell, L.H., Ulmer, D., Thompson, L., Price, V.A., Rabin, D.D., Breall, W.S., Dixon, T., Levy, R. &

Bourg, E. (1984). Alteration of Type A behaviour and reduction in cardiac recurrences in post-myocardial infarction patients. *American Heart Journal, 108,* 237-248.

Haaga, D.A. (1987). Treatment of the Type A behaviour pattern. *Clinical Psychology Review, 7,* 557-574.

Holroyd, K., Penzien, D., Hursey, K., Tobin, D., Rogen, L., Holm, J., Marcille, P., Hall, J. & Chila, A. (1984). Change mechanisms in EMG biofeedback training: Cognitive changes underlying improvements in tension headache. *Journal of Consulting and Clinical Psychology, 52,* 1039-1053.

Kamarck, T.W., Annunziato, B. & Amateau, L.M. (1995). Affiliations moderate the effects of social threat on stress-related cardiovascular responses: Boundary conditions for a laboratory model of social support. *Psychosomatic Medicine, 57,* 183-194.

Kobasa, S.C. (1979). Stressful life events and health: An inquiry into hardiness. *Journal of Personality and Social Psychology, 37,* 1-11.

Maddi, S. (2000). www.hardinessinstitute.com

Meichenbaum, D.H. (1977). *Cognitive-behaviour modification.* New York: Plenum.

Melzack, R. (1975). The McGill Pain Questionnaire: Major properties and scoring methods. *Pain, 1,* 277-299.

Patmore, A. (1997). *Killing the messenger: The pathologising of the stress response.* Gosfield: Patmore.

Roberts, R. (1973). *The classic slum.* Harmondsworth: Penguin.

Shapiro, D., Tursky, B. & Schwartz, G.E. (1970). Control of blood pressure in man by operant conditioning. *Circulation Research, 26,* 127-132.

Tarler-Benlolo, L. (1978). The role of relaxation in biofeedback training. *Psychological Bulletin, 85,* 727-755.

Taylor, S.E. (1995). *Health psychology* (3rd ed.). New York: McGraw-Hill.

Turk, D.C., Meichenbaum, D.H. & Burman, W.H. (1979). Application of biofeedback for the regulation of pain: A critical review. *Psychological Bulletin, 86,* 1322-1338.

Waxler-Morrison, N., Hislop, T.G., Mears, B. & Can, L. (1991). The facts on social relationships on survival with women with breast cancer: A prospective study. *Social Science and Medicine, 3,* 177-183.

Zimbardo, P., McDermott, M., Jansz, J. & Metaal, N. (1995). *Psychology: A European text.* London: Harper Collins.

▶ Introduction

Darla Shaw refuses to throw anything away. In addition to what most people would regard as rubbish, she owns a large stock of theatrical costumes, a life-size Santa on skis, a papier-mâché mermaid and an assortment of stuffed alligators. Her collection grew to such an extent that she was forced to buy an abandoned opera house in order to store it. She finds time to play in a kazoo band and wears a fireman's coat in the winter (Weeks & James, 1995).

Does Darla's behaviour indicate some form of psychological abnormality? Or, is she merely eccentric? Before attempting to answer these questions, it is necessary to explore the idea of abnormality.

Abnormality is difficult to define. Views of abnormality change across cultures, they vary within cultures over time, and they vary from group to group within the same society. It is essential to examine views of abnormality since they form the basis for defining and identifying psychological disorders.

How do psychologists decide what is normal and what is abnormal? And once behaviour has been identified as abnormal, how do they then decide whether or not it constitutes a psychological disorder? The short answer is with great difficulty. Their attempts to answer these questions form the basis of this chapter.

Chapter summary

- Unit 1 looks at abnormality in terms of deviation from statistical norms of behaviour and deviation from social norms.
- Unit 2 asks how failure to function adequately might provide indicators of psychological abnormality.
- Unit 3 looks at psychological abnormality as deviation from ideal mental health.
- Unit 4 examines the relationship between culture and ideas of abnormality.
- Unit 5 questions whether psychological disorders are really 'mental illnesses'.

Unit 1 Statistical norms and social norms

Ⓚ KEY ISSUES

1. Does behaviour which deviates from statistical norms indicate psychological abnormality?
2. Does behaviour which deviates from social norms indicate psychological abnormality?

1.1 Deviation from statistical norms

In statistical terms, human behaviour is abnormal if it falls outside the range which is typical for most people. In other words, it is abnormal if it deviates from statistical norms.

This can be illustrated by the distribution of IQ (intelligence quotient) scores shown in Figure 1. The average score is 100 and most people fall around the middle. Those with very low or very high scores fall at the extremes. They are relatively few in number. In statistical terms they are abnormal – the word abnormal literally means away from the norm.

Statistical infrequency forms the basis for diagnosing mental retardation which is classified as a psychological disorder. DSM-IV, the fourth edition of the American Psychiatric Association's *Diagnostic and statistical manual of mental disorders* (1994) defines mental retardation as an IQ of 70 and below. Around

2% to 3% of the population fall into this category (Barlow & Durand, 1999).

However, just because certain behaviours or characteristics are statistically infrequent does not necessarily mean they are *seen* as abnormal or as indicating a psychological disorder. They

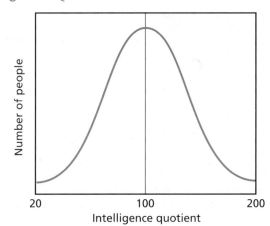

Figure 1 IQ distribution

IQ distribution among adults. It forms a normal distribution curve.

are more likely to be defined as such if they are considered undesirable. For example, being a genius is very rare, is usually regarded as highly desirable, and few, if any, would see it as a psychological disorder. On the other hand, being 'severely mentally retarded' is just as rare but is generally considered as undesirable, abnormal, and as requiring psychological treatment.

There are many examples of statistically infrequent behaviours which are not considered abnormal, either in general or in psychological terms. Olympic athletes, bestselling authors, famous painters, Oscar winning film stars, and singers with number one hits all deviate from statistical norms of human behaviour. Clearly, a definition of psychological abnormality cannot be based on statistical infrequency alone.

1.2 Deviation from social norms

Social norms are approved and expected ways of behaving in a particular society. For example, in all societies there are social norms governing dress. Members of society generally share norms that define acceptable male and female clothes and that specify appropriate dress for different age groups. For example, in British society a 70-year-old grandmother dressed as a male teenager would contravene the norms for both her gender and her age group. Norms of dress also specify appropriate and expected behaviour for particular occasions. A funeral, a day out on the beach, a working day in the office or on the building site – all these situations are governed by norms which specify appropriate dress.

In terms of social norms, abnormal behaviour can be seen as behaviour which deviates from or violates social norms. But does this type of 'abnormal behaviour' indicate psychological abnormality, does it indicate the presence of a psychological disorder? In certain cases, the answer may be yes.

The self-starvation of an anorexic is abnormal both in terms of social norms and psychological functioning. It deviates from social norms of eating behaviour and is classified by psychologists as a psychological disorder. The same applies to people with phobias – an extreme fear of something which leads them to avoid it at all costs. A phobia is classified as a psychological disorder. The behaviour that results from phobias often contravenes social norms. People with phobias for enclosed spaces, spiders, eating in public, or crossing a bridge sometimes behave in ways that are generally seen as strange, peculiar and bizarre. In other words, they deviate from accepted social norms.

But does *all* deviance from social norms indicate psychological abnormality. Quite clearly, the answer is no! Think about successive generations of young people from the 1950s to the present day. Their preferences in terms of music, hairstyles and clothes have often deviated from society's norms and been met with general disapproval. However, few would see their behaviour as an indication of psychological disorder. Think about those who violate not only social norms but also legal norms. Does the behaviour of burglars, bank robbers, joy riders, prostitutes and bigamists result from psychological disorders? Occasionally it might, but few psychologists would see this as the main reason for these activities.

Most people, most of the time, conform to social norms. In view of this, deviance from social norms can be seen as abnormal behaviour. In certain cases this may be due to psychological abnormality. In most instances, this is probably not the case. Because of this, deviance from social norms does not provide a sound basis for indicating psychological abnormality.

Key terms

Statistically infrequent behaviour *Behaviour which is uncommon. Statistically infrequent behaviour falls outside the range which is typical for most people.*

Social norms *Approved and expected ways of behaving in a particular society.*

Summary

1   Many behaviours which are statistically infrequent do not result from psychological abnormality. A definition of psychological abnormality cannot be based on statistical infrequency alone.

2   The behaviour of people with psychological disorders often deviates from social norms. However, in most instances, deviance from social norms does not indicate psychological abnormality.

Activity 1   Eccentricity

Item A   John Slater

An eccentric is a person who deviates from established patterns of behaviour, in other words from social norms. Their behaviour strikes many people as odd. John Slater is an eccentric. He once walked from Land's End to John o'Groats in his bare feet, wearing only striped pyjamas and accompanied by his pet labrador, Guinness. Slater has been a Royal Marine bandsman, a truck driver, steward on a luxury yacht, social worker, salesman, insurance broker, waiter, driftwood artist, painter and decorator and fund-raiser. For most of the past ten years, he has lived in a cave, which is flooded with seawater at high tide. He says that he enjoys the 'cathedral-like silence in caves, which helps me to think and work things out'.

Adapted from Weeks & James, 1995

Item B Perfectly normal

John Slater's behaviour is very unusual, but does it indicate a psychological disorder? According to a study of 1000 eccentrics, the answer is quite definitely no. The study was based on in-depth interviews, personality questionnaires and a range of tests which reveal psychological disorders. The results showed that eccentrics had fewer disorders than the general population. Most eccentrics were happy and well-adjusted, they 'know they're different and glory in it'.

Adapted from Weeks & James, 1995

Item C Punks

Questions

1 What do Items A and B suggest about the problems of using deviance from social norms as an indicator of psychological disorders?

2 a) Judging from Item C, what social norms do punks break?

b) Is this a reason for seeing them as psychologically abnormal?

Explain your answer.

Unit 2 Failure to function adequately

KEY ISSUES

1. **How might failure to function adequately provide indicators of psychological abnormality?**

2. **What are the strengths and limitations of these indicators?**

A failure to function adequately means that a person is unable to live a normal life, unable to experience the normal range of emotions, or engage in the normal range of behaviour. For example, they may be unable to hold down a job, they may be unable to take part in everyday activities like shopping, walking down the street or travelling by bus or train. They may see the world in ways which prevent them from normal participation in social life – for example, they may have 'visions' and hear 'voices' which others cannot see or hear. They may live in the depths of depression, unable to experience the normal range of emotions.

A failure to function adequately is sometimes seen as indicating both abnormal behaviour and psychological abnormality. This unit looks at various indicators of psychological abnormality which can be grouped under the heading of failure to function adequately. It has been argued that the more of these indicators that are present, and the more extreme they are, then the greater the likelihood of psychological disorder (Zimbardo et al., 1995).

2.1 Dysfunctional behaviour

In this case psychological abnormality is indicated by

dysfunctional or maladaptive behaviour – behaviour which interferes with a person's ability to lead a normal, everyday life. For example, alcoholism is dysfunctional if it prevents a person from holding down a job; fear of crowds is dysfunctional if it prevents a person from shopping at the weekend.

Consider the case of Billy, a 13-year-old. He had no friends at school. Unlike most of the other children, he refused to attend any of the sports or social events connected with school. He dreaded being called on to speak in class, feeling physically sick at the prospect. Teachers were lucky to get a 'yes' or a 'no' out of him. Instead of eating at lunchtime, he locked himself in a cubicle in the boys' toilet. Billy was painfully shy. He was afraid of being embarrassed and humiliated in the presence of everybody except his parents. He was diagnosed as having a social phobia (Barlow & Durand, 1998). Billy's disorder is dysfunctional in the sense that it prevents him from leading a normal life.

Most people would probably agree that Billy's behaviour is dysfunctional. But there are plenty of examples which are not so clear-cut. What about the tramp who turns his back on conventional society, sleeps rough, doesn't eat properly and dies an early death as a result of his lifestyle? Who's to say that his behaviour is dysfunctional? He may be happy and fulfilled, he may see conventional lifestyles as dysfunctional and, psychologically, he may be perfectly normal.

In one sense behaviour that many people admire can be seen as dysfunctional in that it interferes with normal life, may harm physical health and even lead to death. For example, people have gone on hunger strike in support of causes such as animal rights and social justice. In 1924, Gandhi, one of the leaders of the movement for Indian independence, went on a 21 day fast to focus attention on and hopefully end the hostility between Hindus and Muslims in India. He had been ill for several months and knew the fast might be fatal. Although it could be seen as dysfunctional, few, if any, would see his behaviour as indicating psychological abnormality.

2.2 Personal distress

A failure to function adequately may be due to personal distress. And this distress may indicate psychological abnormality. Obviously personal distress is not limited to people with psychological disorders. For example, distress caused by the death of a close relative is seen as a normal and expected response. Sometimes, however, distress is a sign of psychological disorder. For example, distress is the main symptom of depression. People suffering from depression may experience disturbed sleep, constipation, headaches and constant tiredness. They are likely to feel intensely unhappy, to see themselves as undesirable and inadequate and their future as bleak and hopeless.

However, some psychological disorders do not involve personal distress. People with mania experience intense joy and elation – they are 'over the moon'. Psychopaths – people with antisocial personality disorder – show a complete disregard for the rights and feelings of others. They may lie, cheat and steal, verbally abuse and physically assault others, yet show no sign of shame, guilt or remorse. Their actions don't appear to cause them personal distress.

There is a further problem – how do we measure personal distress? Distress is a subjective experience – it refers to emotions and feelings which are very difficult to measure. And people's views about what counts as distress vary. One person may say they are very distressed whereas another person with similar feelings may say that they are a bit 'fed up'. This makes if difficult to measure and compare levels of distress.

Clearly there are problems with using personal distress as an indicator for psychological abnormality. However, combined with other indicators, it may help to identify certain psychological disorders.

2.3 Observer discomfort

People who frequently cause upset or discomfort to others are sometimes seen as unable to function adequately. Their behaviour can disrupt social interaction and damage social relationships. Others may find them embarrassing, threatening or upsetting. This is known as *observer discomfort*. It is sometimes seen as an indicator for psychological abnormality. From this point of view, alcoholics may be seen as abnormal if they bring distress to their friends and families. However, this indicator relies heavily on people's judgement and this will vary from person to person. For example, a streaker may cause acute embarrassment to some, but the reaction of others may range from annoyance, to amusement, to indifference. Indeed, observer discomfort may well say more about the observer than the observed.

2.4 Unpredictable behaviour

Unpredictable or unexpected behaviour is sometimes seen as evidence of a failure to function adequately. And this type of

behaviour may indicate psychological abnormality. Consider the following case of mania – an emotional state of extreme joy and elation, usually accompanied by hyperactivity and flights of fancy.

One morning, Mr W. told his wife he was quitting his job as a postman. He hardly slept that night, writing furiously at his desk. Next morning he withdrew the family savings and spent the lot on aquariums and a range of equipment for tropical fish. In a state of high excitement, he informed his wife that he had discovered a way to modify this equipment so that fish would live forever. 'We'll be millionaires,' he proclaimed (Davison & Neale, 1998). Mr W. was diagnosed as having mania. His behaviour was certainly unpredictable and unexpected – his wife got the shock of her life.

Behaviour is unpredictable and unexpected if it does not seem to fit the situation. For example, if people appear to over-react – if they appear over-enthusiastic, over-concerned, or over-anxious. But, who is to say whether someone is over-reacting, whether their response is out of proportion to the situation? Archimedes (287-212 BC), one of the greatest mathematicians of all time, is said to have jumped out the bath and run down the street shouting 'Eureka' ('I have found it') after coming up with the idea of displacement of volume in water. His behaviour was unpredictable and unexpected but hardly indicative of psychological disorder. And, if Mr W's fish *had* lived forever, maybe he would not have been diagnosed as manic.

2.5 Irrational behaviour

If a person's behaviour does not make sense to others, if others cannot communicate with them in a reasonable way, then the person's actions are often seen as irrational. This is sometimes taken as a indication of a failure to function adequately, and of psychological abnormality. Consider the following statement by a man hospitalised for schizophrenia.

'The inmates, here, hate me extremely because I am sane. They talk to me telepathically, continuously and daily almost without cessation, day and night. By the power of their imagination, they create extreme pain in my head, brain, eyes, heart, stomach and in every part of my body. By telepathy and imagination, they force me to say orally whatever they desire, whenever they desire and as long as they desire. I never said a word of my own. I never created a thought or image of my own' (Arieti, 1974). Most people would probably consider this statement to be irrational and, as a result, have difficulty communicating with the man. And they, like the psychiatrist who diagnosed his disorder, would probably see him as psychologically abnormal.

However, behaviour seen as irrational, may have nothing to do with psychological abnormality. The ideas of many of the world's greatest thinkers were often seen as irrational at the time – for example, Galileo who challenged the 17th century view that the earth was the centre of the universe and Darwin whose theory of natural selection challenged accepted views of the creation of humanity in the 19th century. From today's perspective, such thinkers were ahead of their time rather than irrational.

2.6 Conclusion

This unit has looked at five aspects of failure to function

adequately. Each provides a possible indicator of psychological abnormality. Neither on their own nor together do these indicators provide a clear-cut and indisputable dividing line between psychological normality and abnormality. For example, personal distress *may* or *may not* indicate a psychological disorder. And a psychological disorder *may* or *may not* result in personal distress.

Where do we go from here? It has been argued that the more of these indicators that are present, and the more extreme they are, then the more likely they are to indicate psychological abnormality (Zimbardo et al., 1995). The problem is that this relies heavily on judgement. First, a judgement must be made on the presence or absence of these indicators – for example, is personal distress present? Second, a judgement must be made on the level of these indicators – for example, how extreme is the personal distress?

Judgements, by their very nature, are not hard and fast, they are interpretations and evaluations and to some degree will vary from person to person. And they will be influenced by the background of the person making the judgements. Most psychiatrists and psychologists are white, middle-class, university-educated males. To some extent, these factors will influence their judgements. Dougal Mackay puts it this way.

'In the final analysis, therefore, clinical intuition is used to determine whether the individual is to be regarded as normal or abnormal. The subjective nature of this criterion would suggest that there is a greater likelihood of the patient being described as "sick" if his experiences and behaviour do not closely resemble those of the psychiatrist who is assessing him' (1975).

All the indicators of psychological abnormality in this unit must be seen in the context of social norms. What counts as personal distress, observer discomfort, dysfunctional behaviour, unpredictable behaviour and irrational behaviour depend in large part on social norms. What would you make of the following behaviour? A man refused to speak to his mother-in-law and father-in-law. If he found himself alone in the house with his mother-in-law, he would cover himself with a blanket until she left. You may find this behaviour dysfunctional, unpredictable and irrational. However, in terms of traditional Cheyenne Indian norms, it is normal and expected (Stands In Timber & Liberty, 1967). As Robert Comer puts it, 'Efforts to

define psychological abnormality typically raise as many questions as they do answers. The major difficulty is that the very concept of abnormality is relative: it depends on the norms and values of the society in question' (1998).

Despite all the problems of defining psychological abnormality, most researchers argue that it is real, it exists. People do have psychological disorders, in many cases these disorders cause them considerable pain and suffering, and they want an end to this pain and suffering. Activity 2 illustrates this point.

Key terms

Dysfunctional behaviour *Behaviour which interferes with a person's ability to lead a normal life.*

Personal distress *The distress and discomfort caused to a person by their own thoughts and actions.*

Observer discomfort *The unease and discomfort caused to a person by observing another's behaviour.*

Unpredictable behaviour *Behaviour which is unexpected, which cannot be predicted.*

Irrational behaviour *Behaviour which does not appear to be based on reason and logic – it does not seem to make sense.*

Summary

1   Failure to function adequately provides various indicators of psychological abnormality.

2   Indicators of psychological abnormality include dysfunctional behaviour, personal distress, observer discomfort, unpredictable behaviour and irrational behaviour.

3   It has been argued that the more of these indicators that are present, and the more extreme they are, then the more likely they are to indicate psychological abnormality.

4   Whether or not these indicators are present and how extreme they are relies heavily on the judgements of psychiatrists and psychologists.

Activity 2   Psychological disorders

Item A   Depression

Katie was an attractive but very shy 16-year-old. She suffered from severe depression. This is how she described her situation in later years.

'The experience of depression is like falling into a deep, dark hole that you cannot climb out of. You scream as you fall, but it seems like no one hears you. Depression affects the way you interpret events. It influences the way you see yourself and the way you see other people. I remember looking in the mirror and thinking that I was the ugliest creature in the world. Soon I found myself trying to sever the few interpersonal connections that I did have, with my closest friends, with my mother, and my oldest brother. I was almost impossible to talk to. I was angry and frustrated all the time. One day I went over the edge. My mother and I had a disagreement about some unimportant little thing. I went to my bedroom where I kept a bottle of whiskey or vodka or whatever I was drinking at the time. I drank as much as I could until I could pinch myself as hard as I could and feel nothing. Then I got out a very sharp knife that I had been saving and slashed my wrist deeply. I did not feel anything but the warmth of the blood running from my wrist.'

Adapted from Barlow & Durand, 1998

Summary

1 The medical model sees psychological disorder as an illness which shares many similarities with physical illness.

2 Szasz rejects the whole idea of mental illness which he regards as a myth. He sees psychological disorders as problems in living, as social rather than medical problems.

3 The idea of psychological abnormality can be seen as a mechanism of social control which punishes people who deviate from social norms and who threaten the interests of the powerful.

4 Most psychologists and psychiatrists reject the view that psychological abnormality is simply a cultural construct. They argue that many psychological disorders are found and recognised in all cultures, that they often have 'real' organic causes and often cause 'real' suffering.

References

American Psychiatric Association (1994). *Diagnostic and statistical manual of mental disorders* (4th ed.). Washington, DC: Author.

Arieti, S. (1974). *Interpretation of schizophrenia*. New York: Basic Books.

Barlow, D.H. & Durand, V.M. (1999). *Abnormal psychology: An integrative approach* (2nd ed.). Pacific Grove, CA: Brooks/Cole.

Benedict, R. (1934). *Patterns of culture*. New York: Mentor.

Bentall, R.P. (1990). The illusion of reality: A review and integration of psychological research on hallucinations. *Psychological Bulletin, 107*, 82-95.

Berry, J.W., Poortinga, Y.H., Segall, M.H. & Dasen, P.R. (1992). *Cross-cultural psychology: Research and applications*. Cambridge: Cambridge University Press.

Comer, R.J. (1998). *Abnormal psychology* (3rd ed.). New York: W.H. Freeman.

Copsey, N. (1997). *Keeping faith: The provision of community health services within a multifaith context*. London: Sainsbury Centre for Mental Health.

D'Silva, B. (1996). *When gay meant mad. Independent on Sunday*, 4 August.

Davison, G.C. & Neale, J.M. (1998). *Abnormal psychology* (7th ed.). New York: John Wiley & Sons.

Hall, E.T. (1973). *The hidden dimension*. New York: Doubleday.

Heather, N. (1976). *Radical perspectives in psychology*. London: Methuen.

Houghton, J. (1980). One personal experience: Before and after mental illness. In I.G. Rabkin, L. Gelb & J.B. Lazar (Eds.), *Attitudes toward the mentally ill: Research perspectives*. Rockville, MD: National Institute of Mental Health.

Johnstone, L. (1989). *Users and abusers of psychology: A critical look at traditional psychiatric practice*. London: Routledge.

Jahoda, M. (1958). *Current concepts of positive mental health*. New York: Basic Books.

Kleinman, A. & Good, B. (1985). *Culture and depression: Studies in the anthropology and cross-cultural psychiatry of affective disorder*. Berkeley: University of California Press.

Klineberg, I. (1971). Race and IQ. *Courier*, November.

Lowie, R.H. (1954). *Indians of the plains*. New York: McGraw Hill.

Mackay, D. (1975). *Clinical psychology – theory and therapy*. London: Methuen.

Moynahan, B. (1994). *The Russian century*. London: BCA.

Nazroo, J.Y. (1997). *Ethnicity and mental health: Findings from a national community study*. London: Policy Studies Institute.

Rack, P. (1984). *Race, culture and mental disorder*. London: Tavistock.

Stands in Timber, J. & Liberty, M. (1967). *Cheyenne memories*. New Haven: Yale University Press.

Szasz, T. (1961). *The myth of mental illness: Foundations of a theory of personal conduct*. New York: Harper & Row.

Szasz, T. (1989). *Law, liberty, and psychiatry: An inquiry into the social uses of mental health practices*. Syracuse, NY: Syracuse University Press.

Tannahill, R. (1989). *Sex in history*. London: Sphere Books.

Weeks, D. & James, J. (1995). *Eccentrics: A study of sanity and strangeness*. New York: Villard.

Westen, D. (1996). *Psychology: Mind, brain and culture*. New York: John Wiley.

World Health Organisation. (1979). *Schizophrenia: An international follow-up study*. New York: John Wiley.

Yap, P.M. (1974). *Comparative psychiatry*. Toronto: University of Toronto Press.

Zimbardo, P., McDermott, M., Jansz, J. & Metall, N. (1995). *Psychology: A European text*. London: Harper Collins.

11 Models of abnormality

▶ Introduction

The last chapter looked at definitions of abnormality. This chapter looks at models of abnormality. A model is a framework for understanding and explaining something. A model of abnormality provides an explanation for psychological disorders – an account of their origins and causes. It also provides suggestions for the treatment of those disorders.

Models of abnormality fall into two main groups. First, the biological or medical model which sees abnormality as the result of some underlying physical or organic problem, such as a dysfunction of the brain or the nervous system. Second, psychological models which see abnormality arising from psychological problems, caused by a person's thoughts, needs and experiences.

Chapter summary

- Unit 1 traces the history of views of abnormality in the West to the early years of the 20th century.
- Unit 2 looks at the biological or medical model of abnormality.

- Units 3 to 6 look at psychological models of abnormality.
- Unit 7 outlines the sociocultural model of abnormality.

Unit 1 A brief history of abnormality

KEY ISSUES

1. How have views of psychological abnormality in the Western world changed over time?
2. To what degree have these views alternated between biological and psychological models?

1.1 Before the 18th century

Both biological and psychological models of abnormality have been around for a long time.

Many ancient cultures held a kind of early psychological model. They believed that abnormality was due to possession by spirits. In these cultures, priests and shamans (religious curers) practised exorcism – chants, dances, prayers and laying on of hands – to expel the spirits. Some cultures practised trepanning – boring a hole in the skull to release the spirits – a treatment that a surprising number of patients seem to have survived.

The Greeks and Romans of classical times tended to favour a more biological model – the theory of humours, proposed by the 'father of medicine' Hippocrates (c.460-377 BC), and developed by Galen (c.130-200 AD). This theory suggested that both psychological abnormality and physical illness were caused by imbalances in four vital fluids, or humours, of the body. These fluids were blood, yellow bile, black bile, and phlegm. Galen believed that too much blood led to emotional instability; excess of yellow bile led to anger; excess of black bile led to melancholy or depression; and excess of phlegm led to lethargy. Under the influence of Galenic theory, exorcism was largely replaced by medical physicians prescribing diets, exercise and drugs.

In medieval times, the biological model declined and the idea of spirit possession was revived. The Christian church was suspicious of classical Greek and Roman ideas, including Galenic medicine, seeing them as 'pagan'. Wave after wave of plague and other contagious diseases hit Europe during this period. Galenic medicine failed to explain how people caught diseases from each other, or to cure the victims of these epidemics (Porter, 1997). Many people felt that disease was more likely to be the work of the Devil than the result of imbalances in bodily humours. Psychological disorders were often seen to result from possession by the Devil. By late medieval times, anyone deviating from the norms of society risked being accused of witchcraft and Devil-worship and of being tortured, hanged or burned at the stake.

Despite this, Galenic medicine did not entirely disappear. A

Execution of witches in 1655

few voices, like Paracelsus (1493-1541) and Johannes Weyer (1515-1588), insisted that abnormal people were sick rather than evil. 'Hospitals' were built, although many of these were little better than zoos or prisons. St Mary's of Bethlehem in London (better known as Bedlam) was converted into a hospital for the 'insane' in 1547, and put its collection of chained up 'lunatics' on show to the paying public.

1.2   The 18th century

The first modern psychological model emerged in Paris in the 1790s. Philippe Pinel (1745-1826) suggested that psychological disorder was the result of stressful events in life, and that the abnormal needed sympathy and time to recuperate, not torture or chaining up. Under his guidance, Parisian hospitals like the Sâlpetrière became refuges (or asylums) for the psychologically disordered, designed to help the inmates recover – not to imprison them or put them on show. Pinel's humane treatment of his patients, involving such modern practices as occupational therapy and talking through problems, became known as 'moral treatment'. Similar developments took place in England (where Quakers opened the York Retreat in 1796) and later in America. Bedlam was finally closed and possession by the Devil, exorcism, and witchcraft were increasingly rejected as superstitious nonsense.

The biological model of abnormality developed slowly during this period. Physicians continued to use bleeding (a leftover from Galen) for all manner of physical and mental disorders, and there was a flurry of interest in the healing powers of magnets, inspired by the claims of the notorious con-man Franz Anton Mesmer (1734-1815). In the meantime, governments were incarcerating every kind of 'deviant' (the sick, the 'mad', beggars, orphans, prostitutes, unmarried mothers and so on) in institutions – just in case crime, immorality or psychological disorder were as contagious as plague (Foucault, 1977).

1.3   The 19th century

In the 19th century, biology and medicine developed much more rapidly. Charles Darwin's theory of evolution (1859) drew attention to the importance of biological inheritance, and Louis Pasteur's discovery of germs in the 1860s at last explained how

Summary

1   In ancient times, an early psychological model of spirit possession was widespread. This was treated by exorcism and trepanning.

2   In classical Greece and Rome, a biological model of imbalance of humours was favoured. This became known as the Galenic theory. Abnormality was treated with diets, exercise and drugs.

3   During the medieval period, spirit possession and exorcism revived, and the Galenic biological model declined.

4   In the 18th century, new psychological models emerged. Pinel's approach was influential, seeing abnormality as the result of stress, and treating it with 'moral treatment'.

5   Advances in biology and medicine led to the rise of psychiatry in the 19th century. By 1900, the biological model was dominant.

contagious diseases spread. Soon after, the idea that psychological disorders could have biological causes was strengthened by the discovery that 'general pariesis' (a form of insanity) was caused by syphilis – a sexually transmitted disease. From the 1840s, professional associations of 'mad-doctors' or 'alienists' (later called psychiatrists) were established in Europe and America, and by the 1860s, the German scientist Wilhelm Griesinger could confidently assert that all 'mental diseases are brain diseases'. Some of these diseases he thought were inherited, some due to infection.

Between 1883 and 1913, Griesinger's pupil Emil Kraepelin (1855-1926) developed his classification system of psychological disorders. He distinguished between psychoses (true 'insanity' where the patient has lost touch with reality), neuroses (anxiety disorders), personality disorders, and retardation. All the classification systems used by psychiatry up to the present day are based on Kraepelin's original system (Stone, 1998). By the end of the 19th century, the biological or medical model of abnormality was dominant. Psychiatrists took control of the asylums and turned them into 'mental hospitals'

Two women visitors to Bedlam in the 18th century. They have bought tickets to view the antics of the patients.

Pinel freeing patients from chains and shackles in Paris

housing large numbers of patients. 'Moral treatment' was seen as too time-consuming in terms of the attention it paid to the individual needs of patients. It was largely replaced by more economical treatments like physical restraint, cold baths, bleeding and purging – clearing out the stomach and the bowels.

Despite its triumph, however, 19th century psychiatry was not very optimistic about its chances of curing psychological disorders (Porter, 1997). The success rate of medical treatments was poor – psychiatrists claimed this was because many disorders were inherited and therefore incurable. The only solution many psychiatrists could see lay in eugenic programmes of selective breeding and sterilisation. In the first half of the 20th century, laws were passed in many Western countries, including the USA and Scandinavia, permitting the compulsory sterilisation of the mentally 'unfit' (Dowbiggin, 1998). In Nazi Germany in the 1930s, mental patients were gassed. Since then, eugenic programmes have been much less popular in psychiatric circles.

Unit 2 The biological (medical) model of abnormality

KEY ISSUES

1. **What are the main features of the biological model?**
2. **What are the implications for treatment of this model?**

2.1 Main features of the biological model

The biological model is favoured by medicine and psychiatry – the branch of medicine that specialises in mental disorders. The biological model was the dominant view of abnormality at the beginning of the 20th century. Despite serious challenges from various psychological models, it remains dominant today. The biological model uses the medical language of patient, symptoms, diagnosis, illness, disease, treatment and cure (Maher, 1966). Psychiatry tends to see abnormality as mental illness, although many psychiatrists now prefer the term disorder to illness.

The biological model classifies mental disorders. The main classification systems in use today are the ICD-10 (the World Health Organisation's *International Classification of Diseases*, 10th edition) published in 1992, and the American DSM-IV (*Diagnostic and Statistical Manual of Mental Disorders*, 4th edition) published in 1994. Psychiatric systems classify disorders according to their symptoms. For example, both the ICD-10 and DSM-IV place depression in a category of mood disorders. The symptoms of depression include low mood, fatigue, loss of concentration, reduced sex drive, change in weight, disruption of normal patterns of sleep, slowed (or, in some cases, agitated) mental and physical activity, feelings of worthlessness or guilt, and preoccupation with death.

The biological model regards psychological disorders as a sign or symptom of an underlying physical or organic disorder – usually some dysfunction of the brain or nervous system. Different psychological disorders are believed to be caused by different organic disorders. Brain scanning techniques, such as PET or CAT scans, are often used to find evidence for the physical basis for psychological abnormality. In the case of depression, PET scans suggest that depressives have a lower uptake of glucose in the brain, which may explain the slower mental functioning and loss of concentration (Lingjaerde, 1983).

The brain dysfunctions and organic disorders that are believed to cause abnormality can arise in a number of ways. Some may be genetically inherited and run in families. Some may be caused by infection. Some may arise from damage to the nervous system, as a result of exposure to environmental pollution, alcohol or drug abuse, or the impact of life experiences like overwork or child abuse. Some people may be genetically more vulnerable to being harmed by certain experiences.

In the case of depression, the disorder has been linked to biological factors such as genetic inheritance and imbalances in neurotransmitter chemicals and hormones.

Genetic inheritance

According to the biological model, the presence of certain genes can predispose people to psychological disorders. In other words, certain genes can make people more vulnerable to disorders. Three types of studies – family studies, adoption studies and twin studies – have provided evidence to support this view.

Family studies In this type of study, the family tree of a person with a psychological disorder is traced to see if the disorder 'runs in the family'. Family study evidence suggests that a person is ten times more likely to suffer from a mood disorder such as depression if a parent or sibling (brother or sister) has a similar disorder (Weissman, 1987). The problem with these studies is that families tend to share home environments and this, rather than genetic inheritance, may cause disorders to run in the family.

Adoption studies These studies compare people who have been adopted with their biological and adoptive parents. Since they were raised apart from their biological relatives, similarities with their biological relatives would indicate genetic influences. In terms of depression, most studies show a higher rate of depression in their biological relatives – up to 20% of those relatives suffered from the disorder compared with 5-10% of their adoptive relatives, which is the rate for the general population (Harrington et al., 1993). The problem with evidence from adoptive studies is that unless the children have been adopted at or near birth, they have shared part of their life with their biological families. As a result, they may have learned abnormal behaviour from their biological parents. Again, it is difficult to separate genetic and environmental factors.

Twin studies These studies investigate how likely it is that pairs of twins share the same disorder. They compare identical (monozygotic) twins who have the same genes and fraternal (dizygotic twins) who share around 50% of their genes. If genes are a factor in psychological disorder, then we would expect a higher proportion of identical twins to share a disorder. A number of studies have confirmed this. For example, a study based on nearly 200 pairs of twins found that when an identical twin had depression, there was a 46% chance that the other twin would also have the disorder. The figure for fraternal twins was 20% (McGuffin et al., 1996).

However, twins not only share all or many of their genes, they also share much of their environment. Even when raised apart, they often live in the same neighbourhood, go to the same school, and spend time together. Again, it is difficult to separate genetic and environmental influences. In addition, samples of identical twins raised apart are small, so making it difficult to draw firm conclusions.

Biochemistry

The biological model suggests that psychological disorders may be due to an imbalance of chemicals in the nervous system and the endocrine system. In other words, there may be too much or too little of certain neurotransmitter chemicals and hormones. These biochemicals affect mood and behaviour. (See Chapter 7, pp 85-88, for a discussion of neurotransmitters and hormones.)

Neurotransmitters One theory links depression to low levels of the neurotransmitters serotonin and noradrenaline. However, the relationship between neurotransmitters and depression is complex – more research is needed to discover the exact biochemical mechanism of the disorder (Barlow & Durand, 1999).

Hormones People suffering from depression often have high levels of the hormone cortisol. Cortisol is sometimes referred to as a 'stress hormone' because it is produced in times of stress. The high levels of cortisol are not surprising as many depressive episodes are preceded by stressful events. Given this, the high levels of cortisol may be a result rather than a cause of depression – they may be produced as a response to stress rather than causing the disorder (Ladd et al., 1996).

2.2   Treatment and the biological model

The biological model states that psychological disorders are caused, at least in part, by biological factors. This suggests that treatment should address those factors. Many of the suggested treatments aim to change bodily functioning and alter biochemical levels.

Drug treatment A range of drug treatments have been developed which alter the body's biochemistry. For example, Prozac, an antidepressant drug, increases the level of the neurotransmitter serotonin. Antidepressants such as Prozac appear to be effective in 65-75% of cases. This suggests that depression is, at least in part, due to chemical imbalances.

However, drugs can have negative side effects. For example, Prozac, can cause insomnia, headaches and gastrointestinal disorders. And drugs can lead to physical addiction, especially if taken in high doses over long periods of time (Comer, 1998).

Gene therapy The Human Genome Project, which aims to map the complete genetic makeup of human beings, has been underway since 1990. However, gene therapy for genetically based disorders has hardly begun. One day, individually tailored genetic engineering may liberate those at risk from inherited disorders.

However, the evidence suggests that genes alone do not cause psychological disorders. They simply increase the probability that individuals will develop disorders. The *diathesis-stress model* states that psychological disorders result from an interaction between genes and the environment. Diathesis means a condition which makes an individual more susceptible to a disorder. When the diathesis – in this case a genetic predisposition – combines with certain life events such as stressors, the disorder is more likely to develop. The diathesis-stress model suggests that gene therapy, on its own, will not provide a 'magical cure' for psychological disorders.

Electroconvulsive therapy (ECT) ECT involves passing an electric current through the brain which causes a brain seizure or convulsions. It is sometimes used in cases of severe depression, though less so nowadays, partly because of side effects such as memory loss. Although it appears to reduce symptoms of depression in around 60-70% of cases, it is not clear how ECT works. However, it is known to release a variety of neurotransmitters in the brain (Comer, 1998).

Brain surgery This is the most extreme biological treatment for psychological disorders. It has a long history starting with trepanning in prehistoric times, though today it is only used as a last resort.

2.3   Evaluation of the biological model

Greater understanding In recent years, rapid advances in biochemistry and genetics have increased our understanding of the biological aspects of psychological disorders. However, this understanding is far from complete. The complexities of brain chemistry and human genetics have yet to be unravelled.

Inconclusive evidence The evidence is inconclusive. To what extent does neurotransmitter activity cause psychological disorders? What contribution do genes make to the onset of psychological disorders? The short answer is we don't really know. As yet, no specific genes have been identified that make major contributions to psychological disorders. Available evidence suggests that many genes may contribute to psychological disorders, each having a relatively small effect. However, the picture is far from clear (Barlow & Durand, 1999).

Reductionism This is the reduction of something to its most basic elements or parts. Can psychological disorders be reduced to biological factors, as extreme versions of the biological model suggest? The answer is probably no. Complex mental and emotional processes are unlikely to be caused solely by genes and neurotransmitters. At most, biological factors probably predispose people to psychological disorders as the diathesis-stress model suggests. In terms of this model, psychological disorders result from an interplay between biology and the environment.

Cause and effect As noted in the case of the role of hormones in depression, some biological changes may result from, rather than cause, psychological disorders. For example, if someone jumps out at you in the dark, it is fear that causes the adrenaline rush, not the adrenaline that causes the fear. In certain cases, biochemical imbalances may be caused by (rather than causing) psychological disorders.

The classification system Classification systems of psychological disorders are largely based on the biological or medical model. Critics question their claim to be objective and scientific for the following reasons. There are frequent and sudden changes in classifications including the appearance of new disorders, the re-classification of existing disorders, and the removal of other disorders – as in the case of homosexuality. At times these changes appear to reflect changes in attitudes in the wider society rather than the application of scientific knowledge.

Treatment Many of the treatments suggested by the biological model have been criticised as unethical and ineffective. Drug treatment can have negative side effects. It can lead to physical and psychological dependence. In addition, it may only treat the symptoms of a disorder rather than its cause. For example, drugs may simply readjust neurotransmitter levels and do nothing about the situation which caused the disorder in the first place. Many researchers would agree with Ronald Comer that 'drugs alone do not provide a long-term solution' to most cases of psychological disorders (Comer, 1998).

However, many psychiatrists and patients argue that drugs can relieve extremely distressing symptoms and place people in a better frame of mind to overcome their disorder (see Activity 1, Item B).

A humane approach? Supporters of the biological model claim that it is more humane than other models. It portrays psychological disorder as illness – something that just happens to a person. No blame is attached to the individual for suffering from the disorder. This is in contrast to some psychological models which imply that people cannot cope with life or have brought their disorders upon themselves. However, critics are doubtful that it really helps to see disorders as illness, since this encourages the 'patient' to depend on the 'doctor' and not to take any personal responsibility for their own recovery.

Key terms

Biological or medical model *A model which states that psychological disorders are caused, at least in part, by biological factors such as neurotransmitter imbalance and genetic inheritance.*

Diathesis-stress model *A model which states that psychological disorders are caused by an interaction between the environment and a condition – the diathesis – which makes people more susceptible to disorders.*

Summary

1. The biological model classifies psychological disorders in terms of their symptoms.

2. It assumes that psychological disorders have a biological basis.

3. It states that the presence of certain genes can predispose individuals to psychological disorders.

4. An imbalance of chemicals in the nervous system and endocrine system is seen as a major cause of psychological disorders.

5. Drug treatments which alter the body's biochemistry are seen as one of the main treatments for psychological disorders.

6. Evidence to support the biological model is inconclusive. The complexities of brain chemistry and human genetics are only partially understood.

7. Many researchers argue that biological factors are only part of the picture. They must be seen in a wider context, as the diathesis-stress model suggests.

Activity 1   The biological model

Item A   Twins and psychological disorders

The bar chart shows the likelihood of twins having the same psychological disorder. Identical or monozygotic twins have the same genes. Fraternal or dizygotic twins share around 50% of their genes. The concordance level refers to the extent to which twins share a particular characteristic – in this case a psychological disorder. If the concordance level is 1, then each pair of twins in the study share a particular characteristic.

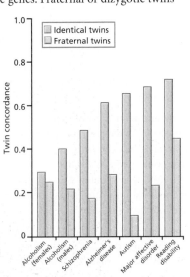

Bar chart legend: Identical twins, Fraternal twins. Y-axis: Twin concordance (0 to 1.0). X-axis categories: Alcoholism (females), Alcoholism (males), Schizophrenia, Alzheimer's disease, Autism, Major affective disorder, Reading disability.

Adapted from Sarason & Sarason, 1996

Item B   'Magic bullets'

Sometimes known as 'magic bullets' because of their shape and the belief in their curative powers, Prozac has been prescribed to millions of people worldwide.

Prozac is extremely popular with many psychiatrists and people suffering from depression. In a book entitled *Listening to Prozac* (1993), Peter Kramer, an American psychiatrist, claims that Prozac not only reduced some of his patients' symptoms of depression, it also transformed their personalities and behaviour. He describes the case of Tess.

'Within weeks of starting Prozac, Tess settled into a satisfying dating routine. I'd never seen a patient's social life reshaped so rapidly and dramatically. Low self-worth and poor interpersonal skills – the usual causes of social awkwardness – are so deeply ingrained and difficult to influence that ordinarily change comes gradually, if ever. But Tess blossomed all at once.'

Despite this glowing report, there is evidence that Prozac may have harmful effects in certain cases. This evidence indicates possible links with violence and suicidal tendencies. For example, a 63-year-old man from Cornwall suffocated his wife and threw himself off a cliff in 1996. He had been taking Prozac for eleven days. His family blames the drug and has issued court proceedings against the manufacturers.

Adapted from Kramer, 1993 and Boseley, 1999

Unit 3 The psychodynamic model of abnormality

KEY ISSUES

1. **What are the main features of the psychodynamic model?**
2. **How does the psychodynamic model approach the treatment of psychological disorders?**

3.1 Main features of the psychodynamic model

The psychodynamic model of abnormality was the first major challenge to the dominance of the biological model since the days of Pinel and 'moral treatment'. Early contributions to the psychodynamic approach were made in France in the late 19th century by hypnotists like Jean Martin Charcot who worked at the Sâlpetrière in Paris, Pinel's old hospital.

In the 1880s, a Viennese doctor named Sigmund Freud (1856-1939) studied in Paris under Charcot. Drawing initially on the ideas of the French hypnotists, Freud went on to launch his own approach, *psychoanalysis,* in the 1890s.

Over the years, Freud attracted followers, many of whom eventually broke away and developed their own approaches. The term *psychodynamic* refers to psychoanalysis and its various offshoots. Despite their differences, the psychodynamic theories have certain things in common.

- They see the mind as active and complex, with some important mental processes operating unconsciously.
- They see psychological disorders as arising from some kind of mental conflict.
- The preferred form of treatment is the 'talking cure', encouraging the patient to talk through their problems, fantasies and fears to uncover the underlying mental conflicts.

3.2 Sigmund Freud and psychoanalysis

Freud's psychoanalysis is the most important of the psychodynamic theories. Freud's ideas developed and changed over time, becoming more complex as they progressed. The main ideas are as follows.

The psyche In Freudian psychoanalysis, the mind, or *psyche*, is seen as being governed by three main mental processes – innate drives, reason and morality. Freud (1923) divided the psyche into three parts.

- The unconscious mind or Id (Latin for 'it'). This is the largest part of the psyche. It is innate and is the source of our desires and impulses. It is entirely selfish and operates on the *pleasure principle,* concerned only with the gratification of its desires.

- The conscious mind or Ego (Latin for 'I'). This develops from the Id and is fully formed round about the age of 2 years. It works on the *reality principle* and is concerned with keeping our thoughts and actions in step with the real world and society.
- The Superego (Latin for 'above-I'), which contains our moral values – the ego ideal (what we would like to be) and the conscience (what we feel we ought to be). The Superego is formed around the age of 5 or 6 and regulates our thoughts and actions morally.

If the Id's cry is 'I want', the Superego says 'Thou shalt not', and the job of the Ego is to try to cope with their conflicting demands, as well as all the awkward restrictions imposed by reality and society.

Innate drives Freud saw human beings as motivated by innate or inborn drives. These drives take the form of impulses and desires and are rooted in the Id.

Much of their activity remains on an unconscious level. Freud (1920; 1923) identified two main drives. The first is Eros, the life drive (named after the Greek god of love), the active ingredient of which is the libido (Latin for 'lust'), the appetite for sensual and sexual pleasure. The second is Thanatos, the aggressive drive (named after the Greek god of death), which gives rise to our feelings of aggression towards others and towards the self.

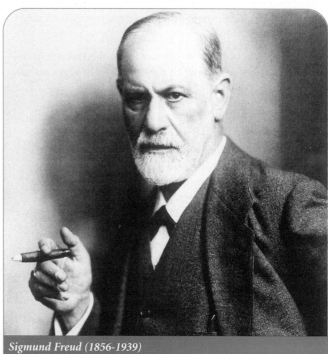

Sigmund Freud (1856-1939)

Psychic conflict

In psychoanalytic theory, every individual experiences conflict between the different parts of the psyche. The root cause of this is that society can only exist if our unconscious sexual and aggressive impulses are kept in check. As a result, we are torn between our desires to gratify our impulses, and our wish to live in a peaceful, ordered society (Freud, 1930). This creates conflict between the pleasure principle and the reality principle within the individual psyche. The Id demands instant gratification for its erotic and aggressive desires, regardless of whether they are socially acceptable or even possible; the Ego tries to police these desires into acceptable and realistic channels; and the Superego seeks to impose moralistic rules to block many of the Id's desires altogether.

Ego defences In its struggle to referee the psychological civil war going on in our heads, the Ego uses a number of defence mechanisms. Among these defences are:

*   **Displacement** Redirecting repressed desires and impulses on to a relatively safe target. For example, if we are angry with the boss, we take it out on the dog.
*   **Sublimation** Transforming aggressive and sexual desires into some socially acceptable expression – for example, artists and musicians expressing these desires in their work.
*   **Projection** Attributing your own unacceptable impulses to someone else. For example, a person who cannot acknowledge hating their brother accuses their brother of hating them.
*   **Denial** An extreme form of self-protection which denies what has happened – for example, a terminal cancer patient refusing to accept they are dying.
*   **Repression** This is the most important defence mechanism in Freud's theory. The Ego censors Id impulses and refuses to allow them access to conscious awareness. The Ego also uses repression to protect itself from threatening or traumatic experiences from the outside world. Traumas (from the Greek trauma meaning wound) may include experiences we all share, like the first realisation in childhood that we are not the centre of our mother's life. For some people, they may also include extremely painful experiences such as child abuse.

Without defences the Id would run amok, the Ego would be destroyed and society would be ripped apart. However, we pay a price for our defences.

Psychological disorder

It is repression in particular that leads to a range of psychological disorders which Freud called *neuroses* – anxiety disorders, panic attacks, hysteria, phobias and obsessive and compulsive behaviour. Repression pushes things out of conscious awareness – it does not make them go away. Repressed memories of traumatic experiences continue to haunt us, producing neurotic symptoms (Freud & Breuer, 1895). Repression of sexual and aggressive impulses can result in similar symptoms. These traumas and impulses often originate in childhood. Repression keeps them frozen in their childish state so we cannot grow out of them. We remain haunted and threatened by these childish anxieties and fears.

Struggles between the Ego and the Id cause neurosis, and struggles between the Ego and Superego cause moral anxiety. Psychoanalytic therapy can deal with these (see below).

However, if Id impulses prove too strong for the Ego, the Id may invade the Ego and take control of it. This wrecks the reality principle, and insanity results (Freud, 1923). Freud did not think that insanity was treatable – certainly not by psychoanalytic techniques.

Depression Freud explained depression as arising from a sense of loss. Typically, when a person is bereaved, the process of mourning involves taking the character of the lost loved one into their own psyche, so 'keeping them alive'. If your feelings towards the lost loved one were positive, then the preserved loved one in your psyche will be loving and comforting.

However, if your feelings towards the loved one contained repressed hatred or resentment, then the preserved loved one in your psyche will turn malevolent and be punishing and hostile. Your hatred is directed back at your own Ego, leading to feelings of being unloved and worthless, and the Ego is destroyed by what it tried to preserve (Freud, 1917). Later losses reactivate this earlier bereavement, leading to depression. Depression can also arise if there is conflict between the Superego and Ego, where the Superego harasses the Ego as immoral and unworthy (Freud, 1923).

Later developments

Freud's followers developed psychodynamic thinking in a number of different ways. Some put more emphasis on the role of the Ego. Alfred Adler (1870-1937) focused on the Ego struggling for mastery over the self and seeking to adjust to society. Adler had a major influence on American psychodynamic theory and on the beginnings of humanistic psychology. In Britain, Freud's daughter Anna (1895-1982) did important work on the Ego and its defences. Others put more emphasis on the unconscious, like Carl Gustav Jung (1887-1961) whose interest in the religious and spiritual side of human nature has made him popular with more mystically inclined therapists and New Age groups.

British psychodynamic theory was greatly influenced by Melanie Klein (1882-1960) and *object relations theory*. This focuses on the importance of emotional bonds, especially with the mother, in the development of the child. Disruption of these bonds is seen as a source of psychological disorder. John Bowlby's work on attachment (see Chapters 4 and 5) was influenced by object relations theory.

3.3 Treatment and the psychodynamic model

Psychoanalytic treatment is designed to uncover repressed impulses and traumatic memories and bring them to conscious awareness. Freud's favoured method was to focus on the patient's dreams. He believed that dreams contain repressed material in a disguised form (Freud, 1900).

Psychoanalysis invites patients to *free associate* on dreams, neurotic symptoms or childhood memories. Free association involves the patient letting their mind wander freely and saying whatever comes into their head. This in itself often uncovers repressed events and exposes uncomfortable desires. The psychoanalyst interprets the patient's words, dreams and behaviour, identifying and challenging their defence mechanisms.

Bringing repressed material to consciousness is a painful process and leads to the release of pent-up emotion. This process is known as *catharsis*. Neurotic symptoms should now disappear, leaving the patient with conscious awareness of what they had tried to repress. The patient is now able to grow out of their childish fears and anxieties, working through the repressed material, making sense of their experience, and coming to terms with it.

An important sign that therapy is actually taking place is when the patient engages in *transference*. This involves transferring repressed feeling towards others – for example, parents and siblings – in the patient's life, and 'taking them out' on the analyst. The patient loves, hates, fears or provokes the analyst, displacing pent-up feelings on to the analyst. When transference is over, psychoanalytic therapy is complete. The ultimate aim of psychoanalysis is to make the unconscious conscious, to cure neurotic symptoms, and to help the patient gain greater insight and self understanding.

3.4 Evaluation of the psychodynamic model

The psychodynamic model differs from the biological model in several important ways.

- It rejects the biological model's view that abnormality is sharply distinct from normality. Everybody suffers from mental conflicts, but some are more extreme than others.
- It does not try to explain psychological disorder in terms of brain dysfunction or inherited predispositions.
- It considers drug treatments, shocks and brain surgery as unhelpful in getting to grips with the underlying causes of psychological disorders.
- The psychodynamic model was more optimistic than early 20th century psychiatry, and held out the promise that some disorders at least could be cured.
- Although it accepted the broad outlines of psychiatric classification, the psychodynamic model has always focused on the individual case. Two people may be depressed, but their depression may have very different origins and meanings, and simply to label both as having 'mood disorder' does not get us very far.

In one important respect the psychodynamic model resembled the biological model. It retained a doctor-patient relationship, with the psychoanalyst taking the role of the professional and the patient seeking expert guidance.

The psychodynamic model is very controversial. It has been supported for producing powerful insights into the human mind and dismissed as little more than fantasy. First the criticisms.

It is unscientific Evidence supporting the psychodynamic model comes from clinical case studies of individual patients. These studies rely heavily on the therapist's interpretations and are open to bias. They are largely based on information acquired retrospectively – adults recalling their early years. The accuracy of childhood memories is open to question. In addition, concepts like Id, Ego and Superego and processes such as repression cannot be directly observed and measured. According to the philosopher Karl Popper (1959), psychodynamic theory fails to produce testable hypotheses and is simply not scientific.

Freud was quite prepared to go beyond empirical evidence – 'hard facts' and observable and measurable data – if his theories produced greater meaning and insight. If his findings could not be confirmed in the laboratory, then that was just too bad. For Freud, supporting evidence from Shakespeare's plays was of much greater significance than evidence from experimental psychology. Kline (1988; 1989) claims that there is strong evidence to support Freud's theory from real life, and that experimental psychology has yet to find a way of evaluating psychodynamic theory.

It does not work Eysenck (1952) published figures which suggested that psychodynamic therapy was worse than useless in the treatment of psychological disorders. However, this claim has been questioned. Psychoanalysis in the USA has been attacked as little more than a money spinner with some people spending their entire adult lives in analysis – which costs them a fortune. However, Freud's own cases usually lasted only a few weeks. And some recent studies suggest that short-term psychodynamic therapy can be beneficial to some patients (Messer et al., 1992).

It is deterministic and pessimistic Freud's theory has been criticised for suggesting that people's lives are dominated by unconscious drives and childhood experiences. Critics argue his theory is pessimistic because it offers little escape from these determining influences – people are pictured as prisoners of their drives and early experiences. However, Freud argued that this only happens if these factors are repressed. The whole point of psychoanalysis is to give people greater insight and the freedom to take control of their lives. Freud does claim that people have antisocial sexual and aggressive desires. But, in a more optimistic vein, he also claims that the Ego produces desires for social harmony (Freud, 1930).

It blames parents Critics argue that psychodynamic theory blames parents for all our ills. It does tend to see the individual as a product of their parenting. And there is evidence to support this view – for example the effects of child abuse on adult life. However, this evidence is controversial. The psychodynamic model has been accused of fuelling the recent panic over false memory syndrome and 'recovered memories' of child abuse which may not have actually occurred (see pp 30 and 40). But, by the late 1890s, Freud was convinced that many adult claims of sexual abuse during childhood were fantasies.

It is culture specific Critics have argued that psychodynamic

Key terms

Id *The unconscious mind which is the source of desires and impulses which spring from innate drives.*

Ego *The conscious part of the mind which keeps thoughts and actions in line with the demands of the wider society.*

Superego *The part of the mind which contains moral values – what people would like to be and think they ought to be.*

Ego defences *The various strategies used by the Ego to defend itself against Id impulses and traumatic experiences.*

Repression *The most important Ego defence. It prevents Id impulses and traumatic memories from entering conscious awareness.*

Free association *A technique used in psychoanalytic therapy in which the patient lets their mind wander freely.*

Catharsis *The release of pent-up emotion when the patient brings repressed material into conscious awareness.*

Transference *In therapy, where the patient directs their repressed feelings towards others on to the analyst.*

theory only applies to the sexually repressed Victorian period and has little relevance to the relatively open and free sexual expression of more recent times. Others, for example feminists like Lynne Segal (2000), argue that it remains relevant and continues to provide important insights.

Positive views The psychodynamic model flourished between the 1920s and the 1960s, and is still influential today. Many psychiatrists were attracted by psychodynamic ideas and adopted them into their own practice.

Psychoanalysis has been the most influential psychological theory of the 20th century, having a significant effect on a whole range of disciplines from anthropology, women's studies and theology, to literary criticism and cinema studies.

By rejecting the sharp distinction between normality and abnormality, the psychodynamic model created greater sympathy for people with psychological disorders. In addition, psychoanalysis with its focus on talking as opposed to drugs, shocks and brain surgery, offered more humane treatment than the biological model. Finally, its supporters see the value of the model in its power to enhance our understanding of ourselves and from the number of people who testify how it has helped them in their own lives.

Summary

1   The psychodynamic model sees the mind as active and complex, with some mental processes operating unconsciously.

2   Psychological disorders arise from mental conflict – in particular conflict between the Id, Ego and Superego.

3   Repression is a major cause of psychological disorders. It pushes impulses and traumatic experiences out of conscious awareness, but they continue to threaten the individual.

4   Psychoanalytic treatment is designed to bring repressed material into conscious awareness. Once there, the patient can make sense of their experience and come to terms with it.

5   The psychodynamic model has been criticised as unscientific, deterministic, pessimistic, culture specific, and, in terms of the treatment it offers, as ineffective. However, its influence has been widespread and many individuals have nothing but praise for the way it has helped their lives.

Activity 2   The psychodynamic model

Item A   The psyche

Questions

1   a) Identify the Id, Ego and Superego in Item A.

    b) Suggest how they may come into conflict.

2   Use the psychodynamic model to explain the client's behaviour in Item B.

Item B   Psychoanalysis

By the fourth therapy session, I realised that he had never mentioned his father. It seemed as if there wasn't and never had been a father. I asked myself: How could it be that this man who is so unhappy and has so many problems fails to even mention his father? I guessed that he was either so ashamed of his father that he couldn't talk about him or he harboured so much anger toward him that consciously or unconsciously he couldn't deal with it. I decided to wait and see what would happen rather than push the client in the direction of talking about something that was very sensitive for him.

During the ninth session he told me about a dream he had had the night before. A large dark man sat at a table and a small child watched from a corner as the man ate great quantities of food and ordered a small, frightened woman to bring him more and more. After he ate each helping, he would raise a gun and shoot down a few people who were standing in a row against the wall.

The client reported how frightened he had felt during the dream. As we discussed his associations to the dream, it became clear to me that the man in the dream represented his father. After several more sessions, he told me he felt very angry with me because I constantly told him what to do and verbally cut him down. After pointing out that in reality I had said almost nothing, I asked him if I seemed like the man in the dream. Finally the dike burst. For the rest of the session and the next one, all of his seething hatred toward his father came out. He blurted out that when he was a child he had seen his father strike his mother several times. When he saw this happen, he had wanted to kill his father.

Adapted from Sarason & Sarason, 1996

Unit 4 The behavioural model of abnormality

KEY ISSUES

1. **What are the main features of the behavioural model?**

2. **What is behavioural therapy?**

4.1 Main features of the behavioural model

Learned behaviour

The behavioural model can be seen as a reaction to the psychodynamic model – it changes the focus from the mind to behaviour. *Behaviourism* was launched in the USA in 1913 by John Watson (1878-1958). Behaviourists insist that psychology should be the study of behaviour rather than the inner workings of the mind. Unlike mental processes, behaviour can be directly observed. This provides the foundation for a scientific psychology based on empirical evidence – 'hard facts' which can be observed and measured in the laboratory.

According to the behavioural model, all behaviour – both normal and abnormal – is learned. Many of these learned behaviours are useful – they help people to live normal and constructive lives. However, abnormal and maladaptive behaviours are also learned.

Behaviour is learned by a process known as *conditioning*. There are two main processes of conditioning – *classical conditioning* and *operant conditioning*.

B.F. Skinner in the laboratory. Much of the evidence for operant conditioning was based on experiments with rats.

Classical conditioning The idea of classical conditioning is illustrated by the following experiment conducted by John Watson and Rosalie Rayner (1920). A boy aged 11 months, known as Little Albert, was allowed to play with a white rat for several weeks. He showed no fear of the rat and appeared to enjoy playing with it. One day, when Albert reached for the rat, a steel bar was struck with a hammer behind his head. The loud noise frightened him. This was repeated five times, after which Albert became extremely frightened of the rat and did his best to avoid it. The experimenters had conditioned Albert to fear white rats (see p 194).

Classical conditioning involves learning an association between two stimuli – in the above example, the stimuli are the rat and the loud noise. The two are associated because the noise occurs in the presence of the rat. The learned response to one stimulus – in this case fright and avoidance – is extended to the other stimulus. Little Albert learned to fear and avoid white rats without the loud noise being present – he has learned a conditioned response.

Operant conditioning This view of learning was developed by the American psychologist B.F. Skinner (1904-1990). In operant conditioning, behaviour is learned by *reinforcement*. Positive reinforcement encourages certain behaviours by means of rewards – for example giving a child praise or sweets for 'good behaviour'. Negative reinforcement encourages behaviours by removing unpleasant events when those behaviours occur – for example, ceasing to scold children when they tidy their room. Behaviour which is ignored, that is given no reinforcement, becomes extinct or fades away. The use of punishment to suppress a behaviour is not always reliable.

Abnormal behaviour

According to the behavioural model, abnormal behaviour is learned in the same way as normal behaviour. The example of Little Albert showed how a phobia – an extreme and irrational fear – can be learned by a process of classical conditioning.

In terms of operant conditioning, abnormal behaviour can result from reinforcement. For example, the early stages of drug abuse can be encouraged by positive reinforcement – the pleasure or comfort associated with drug use (Carey & Carey, 1995). From a behavioural perspective, depression results from a lack of positive reinforcement (rewards) and/or an excess of unpleasant experiences (punishments). This often involves a life change. For example, unemployment and retirement can lead to a loss of positive reinforcement – a loss of rewarding social relationships and reduced status and income. Life changes can also lead to unpleasant experiences such as the shame and stigma of unemployment or, in the case of retirement, being treated in terms of the negative stereotypes of old age.

Research by Lewinsohn et al. (1979) showed that depressed people received fewer positive reinforcements and are likely to have more unpleasant experiences than nondepressed people. The researchers found that a lack of positive social reinforcement – the approval and companionship of others – was particularly important.

4.2   Treatment and the behavioural model

According to the behavioural model, the problem is the behaviour and treatment – *behaviour therapy* – involves modifying or changing that behaviour. The idea of 'mental' or 'psychological disorder' is replaced by the idea of inappropriate or maladaptive behaviour. A behavioural therapist is more like a teacher than a doctor – their role is to teach new behaviours rather than to cure mental illnesses.

Classical conditioning Behaviour therapies based on classical conditioning include *systematic desensitisation* and *aversion therapy*. Systematic desensitisation (Wolpe, 1958) is used for deconditioning phobic fears. A phobia arises when something harmless has become associated with something frightening. In the Little Albert study, a white rat became associated with a frightening noise until the rat itself became an object of fear. In systematic desensitisation, the client is taught to relax and confront the feared object or situation in a calm and peaceful setting. The idea is that the object of fear will become associated with a pleasant feeling of relaxation and calm, and lose its frightening associations.

Aversion therapy is often used for treating addictions. It aims to change maladaptive behaviour by associating it with something unpleasant. For example, a client may be given an electric shock or a nausea (sickness) inducing drug whenever they reach for a cigarette. In this case, the idea is that they will associate unpleasant feelings with cigarettes and stop smoking.

Operant conditioning In behaviour modification programmes based on operant conditioning, the therapist rewards adaptive behaviour and withholds rewards from maladaptive behaviour. The idea is to change behaviour by applying reinforcement. An approach known as a *token economy* is based on this idea. It is sometimes used in schools, prisons and mental hospitals to change behaviour. Behaviour seen as appropriate is rewarded with tokens which can be exchanged for privileges such as longer breaks, sweets, or a movie. Tokens are withheld when behaviour is seen as inappropriate.

4.3   Evaluation of the behavioural model

Like the psychodynamic model, the behavioural approach is critical of the biological model. It rejects the view that normality and abnormality are sharply distinct. All behaviours are acquired in the same way. It rejects the idea that psychological disorders arise from underlying brain dysfunctions and biochemical imbalances. All disorders are maladaptive behaviours, arising from conditioning. It firmly rejects any role for inheritance in abnormality.

However, the behavioural approach is also very critical of the psychodynamic model, with its emphasis on concepts like the Id, Ego and Superego, and processes like repression. According to the behaviourists, all of these are unobservable and unmeasurable.

A scientific approach? Behaviourists claim that their approach is scientific – they focus exclusively on behaviour that can be directly observed and measured. Behaviourists claim support from a vast range of evidence from laboratory experiments.

Reductionist, determinist and demeaning? Behaviourists have been criticised for what many see as a simplistic and narrow view of human behaviour. Can all human behaviour be reduced to learning by association and reinforcement? Behaviourism is an entirely deterministic account of human behaviour. But are we really the prisoners of our conditioning? Much of the laboratory evidence for behaviourism comes from studies of non-human animals. How far can experiments on rats apply to human beings? Critics argue that a model which leaves out thoughts, feelings and mental processes cannot capture the complexity of human nature and behaviour. Some see the behavioural model as reducing us to the status of rats (Heather, 1976).

Understanding causes Is abnormal behaviour caused by learning? Just because abnormal behaviour can be changed by behaviour therapy based on conditioning, this does not necessarily mean that the behaviour was learned this way in the first place. For example, if depression is lifted by positive reinforcement, this does not necessarily mean that it was caused by an absence of positive reinforcement. For behaviourism, changing maladaptive behaviour solves all psychological problems because the behaviour *is* the problem. Critics say that this is like treating measles by painting out the spots – it ignores the underlying causes. Many believe that the behavioural model fails to provide an adequate explanation for psychological disorders (Davison & Neale, 1998).

Treatment Behaviour therapy appears to be effective for certain disorders – for example, phobias – but not for others. Some forms of treatment have only limited, short-term benefits. For example, the effects of aversion therapy are often limited to the therapist's office and do not extend to the client's everyday life (Comer, 1998).

Ethical issues In some cases, treatment is imposed on people without their consent – for example, token economies in schools, prisons and mental hospitals. Aversion therapy can cause clients pain, or at least discomfort. By today's standards, some instances of aversion therapy are unethical – for example, the 'treatment' sometimes applied to homosexuals in the 1960s – see pp 127 and 129. And some of the early experiments, for example Little Albert, would be completely out of bounds in terms of today's ethical guidelines.

Key terms

Classical conditioning *A form of learning based on an association between two stimuli.*

Operant conditioning *A form of learning based on the use of reinforcement.*

Positive reinforcement *The encouragement of behaviours by means of rewards.*

Negative reinforcement *The encouragement of behaviours by removing unpleasant events when those behaviours occur.*

Systematic desensitisation *Confronting feared objects or situations in a calm and relaxed setting and associating these feelings with them.*

Aversion therapy *A technique which aims to change maladaptive behaviour by associating it with something unpleasant.*

Token economy *A technique which reinforces appropriate behaviour by giving or withholding tokens which can be exchanged for privileges.*

Summary

1 The behavioural model argues that all behaviour – normal and abnormal – is learned in the same way.

2 There are two main processes of learning – classical conditioning and operant conditioning.

3 The behavioural model focuses on behaviour rather than the mind.

4 Behaviour therapy is concerned with changing abnormal behaviour. It uses techniques such as systematic desensitisation, aversion therapy and the token economy.

5 Behaviourists claim their approach is scientific – it is based on observable behaviour and supported by evidence from laboratory experiments. Critics claim it is too narrow and simplistic – in particular, it largely omits thoughts and feelings.

Activity 3   The behavioural model

Item A   Obscene phone calls

A 32-year-old married man made up to twenty obscene phone calls a week to young women. His therapy involved making obscene calls to young women in a nearby office. They then met him in the presence of the therapist. The client found these meetings extremely unpleasant – he felt ashamed and embarrassed. He felt no strong urge to make further obscene calls, and over the next nine months no such calls were reported by people in the neighbourhood.

Adapted from Boudewyns et al., 1975

Item B   Fear of criticism

A 35-year-old postman lived in fear of being criticised. The therapist created a list of anxiety-producing scenes. For example:

* Mrs Smith complains you are late delivering her mail.
* Your wife criticises you for forgetting to do the shopping on your way home.

The client was taught to relax deeply and imagine these scenes while remaining calm. Eventually, he learned to confront these imaginary situations without becoming anxious and agitated. Gradually, his fear of criticism in real life reduced.

Adapted from Davison & Neale, 1998

Questions

1 What types of behaviour therapy are being used in Items A and B?

2 With reference to Items A and B, suggest how they work.

Unit 5 The humanistic model of abnormality

KEY ISSUES

1. **What are the main features of the humanistic model?**

2. **What type of therapy does it recommend?**

5.1   The main features of the humanistic model

The humanistic model emerged during the 1950s and 1960s as a reaction against the psychodynamic and behavioural models. It accused both of being deterministic. It called itself 'the third force' in clinical psychology.

The humanistic model presents an optimistic picture of human beings. It emphasises the essential goodness and dignity of human nature. Every human being has the potential for *self-actualisation* – to find fulfilment, to achieve happiness, to discover meaning in life, and to develop self-understanding and a sense of self-worth. Problems arise when the road to self-actualisation is blocked.

Carl Rogers (1902-1987), one of the founders of humanistic psychology, argued that the potential for self-actualisation can be blocked in infancy (Rogers, 1951; 1959). Children need

positive regard, particularly from their parents. They need to feel loved and accepted, needed and valued. From this, they develop a positive self-image and a feeling of self-worth. Positive regard needs to be unconditional and non-judgemental. If parents constantly place conditions on their love, for example, 'We'll only love you if you behave, if you do well at school …', then children will tend to judge themselves and behave in terms of standards imposed by others, rather than becoming a person in their own right. If they are constantly criticised by their parents, then children will tend to develop a negative self-image and question their worth. This will tend to block the path to self-actualisation – they will be unlikely to develop self-acceptance and a positive view of self. Rogers does not suggest that parents should uncritically accept everything a child does. Instead, he states that the act rather than the child be criticised – for example, 'That was a bad thing to do' rather than, 'You are a bad girl'.

Unconditional positive regard during infancy and childhood opens the door to self-actualisation. It allows people to accept themselves, to recognise both their strengths and weaknesses; it encourages a sense of self-worth, and provides a route to self-fulfilment.

5.2 Humanistic therapy

Humanistic therapy aims to provide people with an opportunity to be honest with themselves. This is seen as a starting point for self-actualisation. Rogers' *client-centred therapy* focuses on people as individuals who can shape their own lives.

The therapist must not give advice, tell clients what to do, or interpret their behaviour. Instead, the therapist must create a warm, supporting and accepting environment which allows clients to discover themselves and search for their own, individual meanings. Therapists must show unconditional positive regard – they must be accepting and uncritical, sincere and genuine. This will encourage clients to be honest and accepting about themselves and to realise their potential for self-fulfilment and personal growth. This is the route by which they will recognise and become their true selves.

5.3 Evaluation of the humanistic model

The humanistic model rejects many aspects of the psychodynamic, behavioural and biological models. It rejects the psychodynamic view as too pessimistic and the behavioural view as demeaning. It refuses to accept the classification system of psychological disorders which is based on the biological model. It rejects the view that disorders have a biological basis. And it is opposed to treatments, such as drug therapy, recommended by the biological model.

The humanistic model was popular during the 1960s and early 70s, particularly in the USA. It reflected many of the ideas current at the time. The hippies' slogan 'love and peace', and their belief that if people could discover their true selves then the world would be a better place, mirrored aspects of the humanistic model. Today, the model has largely gone out of fashion with psychotherapists, but is extremely popular in the counselling industry.

In its favour, the humanistic model takes an optimistic view of human nature, seeing people as essentially good. It avoids the stigma – the shame – of mental illness with its reluctance to diagnose and label psychological disorders. Instead, its starting point is the road to psychological health and wellbeing. Critics often see this focus as counterproductive, arguing that many psychological disorders require specific types of treatment and, in some cases, medical treatment. They point to research which indicates that client-centred therapy is not particularly successful in providing 'cures' for disorders (Greenberg et al., 1994).

Some critics question the apparent optimism of the humanistic model. They suggest it implies that disorders result from personal failure – in particular, the failure to achieve self-actualisation.

Key terms

Self-actualisation *Realising the human potential for self-awareness, self-worth and self-fulfilment.*

Unconditional positive regard *Seeing others in a positive light and recognising their worth without any conditions.*

Client-centred therapy *A therapy which allows clients to discover and accept themselves without advice, judgement or criticism from the therapist.*

The humanistic model *A model which sees psychological well-being resulting from self-actualisation.*

Summary

1. The humanistic model sees human beings as essentially good.

2. Children need unconditional positive regard in order to develop self-acceptance and self-worth.

3. Problems arise when the route to self-actualisation is blocked.

Activity 4   Client-centred therapy

Item A   Listening to the client

Client Yes, I know I shouldn't worry about it, but I do. Lots of things – money, people, clothes. I can't stand people laughing at me. I can't stand ridicule. That's why I'm afraid of kids. When I meet somebody I wonder what he's actually thinking of me. Then later on I wonder how I match up to what he's come to think of me.

Therapist You feel that you're pretty responsive to the opinions of other people.

Client Yes, but it's things that shouldn't worry me.

Therapist You feel that it's the sort of things that shouldn't be upsetting, but they do get you pretty much worried anyway.

Client Things just seem to be piling up, piling up inside of me. At home, I used to wear it off by socking the doors. It's a feeling that things were crowding up and they were going to burst.

Therapist You feel that it's a sort of oppression with some frustration and that things are just unmanageable.

Client In a way, but some things just seem illogical. I'm afraid I'm not very clear here but that's the way it comes.

Therapist That's all right. You say just what you think.

Adapted from Snyder, 1947

Question

What aspects of client-centred therapy are illustrated by Item A?

Unit 6 The cognitive model of abnormality

KEY ISSUES

1. **What are the main features of the cognitive model?**
2. **What is cognitive therapy?**

6.1 The main features of the cognitive model

The cognitive model developed in the 1960s and 70s and is very influential today. It draws ideas from all the psychological models discussed so far.

The cognitive model starts from the idea that to understand human behaviour, we must understand human thought. This involves understanding how people see themselves and the world around them, how they interpret and make sense of their own behaviour and the behaviour of others.

The cognitive model assumes that people's thoughts direct their emotions and behaviour. Psychological disorders are seen to result from 'errors in thinking', 'irrational assumptions' and 'negative perceptions' which are harmful to the individual.

Consider the following 'irrational beliefs'.

- I must always please others.
- I must always be perfect in what I do.

Anyone holding these beliefs is doomed to failure and disappointment. It is impossible to please all of the people all of the time. And no matter how hard a person strives, a life of perfection is beyond their reach.

Cognition and depression

Aaron Beck's (1967; 1997) theory of depression illustrates the cognitive approach to psychological disorders. According to Beck, negative thinking produces negative moods which can lead to depression. Beck uses the term *cognitive triad* to refer to the three main forms of negative thinking – negative views of 1) the self ('I am worthless'), 2) the world ('Everything is against me'), and 3) the future ('Nothing is ever going to change').

Negative thoughts can produce errors in thinking. These errors include:

- **Arbitrary inference** A conclusion based on insufficient evidence or no evidence at all. For example, my car broke down because I am a worthless person.
- **Selective abstraction** A conclusion based on one of many aspects of a situation. I forgot to put salt in the potatoes which ruined the entire dinner party and showed what a useless host I am.
- **Overgeneralisation** A generalisation based on a single, often trivial event. A teacher assumes that he is no good at his job because a student falls asleep in his class.

Beck argues that negative thoughts lead to negative emotions which can lead to depression.

There is plenty of evidence to support Beck's theory. Research indicates that compared to nondepressed people, depressed individuals are more negative in terms of themselves, the world, and the future. In addition, they are more likely to make the kind of errors in thinking that Beck identifies. The key question,

however, is whether negative thinking precedes and contributes to the onset of depression or whether it results from depression and contributes to its maintenance. According to Davison and Neale (1998), 'the relationship in all likelihood works both ways; depression can make thinking more negative, and negative thinking can probably cause and certainly worsen depression'.

Longitudinal studies – studies of a group of people over time – are needed to investigate this question. The ongoing Temple-Wisconsin study of cognitive vulnerability to depression provides some preliminary answers. A sample of first year university students, none of whom was suffering from depression at the time, were assessed every few months. Results for the first $2^1/2$ years suggest that those students who were prone to negative thinking were more likely to become depressed. Seventeen per cent of high-risk participants (those with high scores for negative thinking) compared to 1% of low-risk participants (those with low scores) went on to experience a period of severe depression (discussed in Barlow and Durand, 1999).

6.2 Cognitive therapy

As the model implies, cognitive therapy for psychological disorders involves changing thoughts in order to change emotions and behaviour. Albert Ellis (1962), developed *rational-emotive therapy* which, as its name suggests, encourages rational thinking in order to change emotions. The therapist's job is to help their clients to recognise the irrational assumptions which govern their lives and to change them into rational and positive views of themselves and the world.

Beck's *cognitive therapy*, which is often used in cases of depression, encourages clients to challenge negative thoughts, and change them into more constructive ones. Clients are helped to recognise errors in thinking and encouraged to correct them. Beck claims that this will change their emotions and behaviour and, in many cases, lift their depression.

6.3 The cognitive model – evaluation

Successful treatment Research indicates that Beck's cognitive therapy is as successful as antidepressant drugs in treating depression (Hollon & Beck, 1994). This, in itself, provides support for the cognitive model.

Cause and effect The cognitive model has been criticised for seeing thoughts as the cause of psychological disorders. Critics argue that because people with depression tend to see the world in negative terms, then negative thinking is a consequence of their depression rather than its cause. However, as the provisional results of the Temple-Wisconsin study indicate, negative thinking, in and of itself, appears to make people more vulnerable to depression.

Origins of cognitive errors The cognitive model has been criticised for failing to explain where negative thoughts come from in the first place. However, Beck argues that experiences in childhood and adolescence, such as loss of a parent, rejection by friends or criticism from teachers, can produce a negative outlook. He believes that, in later life, negative beliefs and cognitive errors are triggered in situations which resemble the context in which they first develop. These situations may reflect, for example, a childhood loss or an adolescent failure.

Key terms

Cognitive model of abnormality *A model which states that psychological disorders are caused by errors in thinking, irrational assumptions and negative views of self, the world and the future.*

Cognitive therapy *A therapy which encourages people to identify, challenge and change cognitive errors and negative thoughts.*

Summary

1. The cognitive model assumes that people's thoughts direct their emotions and behaviour.

2. Cognitive errors and negative thoughts can affect mood and behaviour, and can lead to psychological disorders.

3. Therapy involves the correction of cognitive errors and the translation of negative thoughts into positive thoughts.

Activity 5 — Negative thoughts

Item A — Thinking the worst

During an episode of depression

I remember an incident when I took the subway with my wife. She went through the turnstile before me and I was positive that she was going to desert me. She had probably had enough of me and was fed up with my behaviour.

After the depression had passed

Of course, nothing could have been further from the truth. Her kindness and devotion, compassion, concern and, more than anything else, her love, sustained me during my depression. She, more than anyone, helped me to get better.

Adapted from Endler, 1990

Item B — Never satisfied!

Questions

1 a) Identify the cognitive error in Item A.
   b) How might negative thoughts cause and reinforce depression?

2 How might a cognitive therapist encourage the people in Item B to challenge and change their negative thoughts?

Unit 7 The sociocultural model

KEY ISSUES

1. **What are the main features of the sociocultural model?**

2. **How does it differ from biological and psychological models of abnormality?**

7.1 The main features of the sociocultural model

The sociocultural model starts from the view that people are social and cultural beings. They are members of various social groups – families, communities and society as a whole – and they share a culture with other members of their society. From this perspective, their behaviour is shaped by their position in society, by their family relationships and occupational roles, and by the norms, values and beliefs of their culture. All these

factors make them more or less vulnerable to psychological disorders.

Culture As the following chapter indicates, there is evidence of a rapid rise in eating disorders – anorexia and bulimia – in Western societies. One explanation for this is a change in the cultural ideal for the female figure. Reflected in models such as Kate Moss and Jodi Kidd, the 'ideal figure' is becoming thinner and thinner. Some researchers see this as one of the factors explaining the obsession to lose weight of young women with eating disorders.

The previous chapter outlined a number of culture-bound syndromes – psychological disorders which are only found in particular cultures. The norms, values and beliefs of these cultures may be a factor in producing culture-bound disorders.

As Unit 1 indicates, ideas about what count as psychological disorders, what causes them and how they should be treated are partly shaped by culture. And, we don't have to go back hundreds of years to make this point. As noted in the previous chapter, homosexuality was classified as a psychological disorder until 1973. As culture changes, attitudes change, and in some cases, so do psychological disorders.

Family relationships A number of researchers argue that family relationships can make people more or less prone to psychological disorders. For example, conflict between parents may place a considerable strain on children which may make them more vulnerable to disorders. One explanation of eating disorders sees them as resulting from relationships within the family (see pp 157-158).

The class system This system of social division is found in all Western societies. In general, the lower a person's position in the class system, the lower their income, social status and power. And, the lower their position, the more likely they are to suffer from certain psychological disorders – for example, depression. One explanation of this finding states that the pressures and stress of life at the bottom of the class system makes people more vulnerable to a range of disorders (Zima et al., 1996).

Gender Women in Western societies are over twice as likely as men to be diagnosed as suffering from anxiety disorders and depression. One explanation for this is the cultural definition of women's roles and their position in society – in particular, their lack of power and control over their own lives. Compared to men, women are more likely to have low-status, low-skill and low-paid jobs. They are more likely to be dependent on state benefits and more likely to live in poverty (Haralambos & Holborn, 2000). And research suggests that marriage is no solution. Compared with unmarried women, wives are more likely to suffer from depression, other psychological disorders, and physical ill-health. In the words of the American sociologist Jessie Bernard (1976) 'In truth, being a housewife makes women sick'.

7.2 Evaluating the sociocultural model

The models of psychological abnormality outlined in this chapter have tended to focus on the individual. As a result, they have largely ignored the wider social and cultural influences on behaviour. There is growing evidence that part of the explanation for psychological disorders lies in culture and society.

Critics have argued that the sociocultural model fails to explain why particular *individuals* develop psychological disorders. However, this is not the point of the model. What it

Key term

Sociocultural model of abnormality *A model that sees certain groups of people as more or less vulnerable to psychological disorders as a result of their culture, their position in society, and their social relationships.*

does explain is why certain *groups* of people are more vulnerable than others to certain psychological disorders.

The sociocultural model does not offer the kind of treatments or therapies suggested by the other models. In general, these models offer treatment on an individual level. The sociocultural model implies that changes in culture, society and social relationships are required to improve people's chances of recovering from psychological disorders. And just as, if not more importantly, these changes may actually reduce the extent of disorders.

However, changing culture and society is easier said than done. In most Western societies the gap between rich and poor has increased over the past thirty years. The rich and the powerful will not give up their privileges easily. Groups such as gays, women and ethnic minorities have had to organise, demonstrate and protest to improve their position in society and change the stereotypes and prejudices of the mainstream culture. The changes implied by the sociocultural model are far more difficult to put into practice than a course of treatment with a therapist.

The sociocultural model is an addition rather than an alternative to biological and psychological models of abnormality. It answers questions they cannot answer and provides a broader explanation of psychological disorders. Only in the last thirty years have psychologists recognised the importance of culture and society, a recognition that is long overdue (Comer, 1998).

Summary

1 To some extent, people's behaviour is shaped by their culture, their position in society and their social relationships. These factors can make them more or less prone to psychological disorders.

2 The sociocultural model implies that changes in culture and society are required to improve people's chances of recovering from psychological disorders, and to prevent those disorders from occurring in the first place.

Activity 6   Culture and society

Item A   St Vitus dance

St Vitus dance

The engraving shows peasant women overcome by a psychological disorder known as St Vitus dance. This disorder is unique to medieval Europe. It began in Germany in the late 14th century and spread rapidly to Holland, Belgium, France and Italy. The dancers held hands and formed circles, dancing manically and deliriously for hours. They called out the names of spirits and seemed oblivious to bystanders, appearing neither to see nor hear them.

Adapted from Hayden, 1981

Item B   The Jerusalem syndrome

Standing at the Wailing Wall, a 50-year-old Californian man, dressed in white robes made out of sheets, preaches the word of God. He claims he is the prophet Elijah and that God speaks to him on a daily basis. At any one time in Jerusalem there are several Jesus Christs and Virgin Marys, plus an assortment of prophets. All are convinced they are Biblical figures. They have what is known locally as 'Jerusalem syndrome'. They are foreign visitors who have been so enthralled with the Biblical sites, they have taken on new identities. Most get over Jerusalem syndrome in 4 or 5 days, when it's time to go home.

Adapted from Today, BBC Radio 4, 27.7.99

Item C   Poor and powerless

Linda Jenkins is an unemployed single mother with three children living in Liverpool. She is 33, pale and careworn. She looks older. The only holiday she has had in years was a trip to a local seaside resort organised by Gingerbread, the single parent support group. Even then, she had to go collecting round the pubs to raise her contribution.

Life is a demeaning juggling act with the £103 a week she gets in benefit. Heating, hot water and electricity are turned on just before her children get back from school. Linda walks to the city centre markets to save a few pence on fruit and vegetables, and cuts off the ends of toothpaste tubes to squeeze out a little extra. Even her shoes are secondhand.

Linda describes her situation, 'It's horrible. I just don't see any future round here. I'm pushing my kids hard at school so they'll have a chance. I pray to God that they have itchy feet and just get out of here. I want to work. I want to go to college. But the kind of work someone unqualified like me can get won't cover the child-minding fees and I won't be a latchkey mother. There've been times when I've wanted to kill myself. I try to keep how hard it is from the kids. But Lawrence, the oldest, said to me when he was seven: "We're poor, aren't we?"'

Adapted from the Observer, 3.10.1993

Single mother in church crypt shelter for the homeless

Questions

1   How does the sociocultural model help to explain the behaviour in Items A and B?

2   Women's lack of power in society and control over their lives has been seen as a major reason for their higher rates of depression. Discuss with reference to Item C.

References

American Psychiatric Association (1994). *Diagnostic and statistical manual of mental disorders* (4th ed.). Washington, DC: Author.

Barlow, D.H. & Durand, V.M. (1999). *Abnormal psychology: An integrative approach* (2nd ed.). Pacific Grove, CA: Brooks/Cole.

Beck, A.T. (1967). *Depression: Clinical, experimental and theoretical aspects.* New York: Harper & Row.

Beck, A.T. (1997). Cognitive therapy: Reflections. In J.K. Zeig (Ed.), *The evolution of psychotherapy: The third conference.* New York: Brunner/Mazel.

Bernard, J. (1976). *The future of marriage.* Harmondsworth: Penguin.

Boseley, S. (1999). Revealed: The danger of taking Prozac. *The Guardian,* 4.9.1999.

Boudewyns, P.A., Tanna, V.L. & Fleischman, D.J.A. (1975). A modified shame aversion therapy for compulsive obscene telepone calling. *Behavior Therapy, 6*, 704-707.

Carey, K.B. & Carey, M.P. (1995). Reasons for drinking among psychiatric outpatients: Relationship to drinking patterns. *Psychology of Addictive Behavior, 9*, 251-257.

Comer, R.J. (1998). *Abnormal psychology* (3rd ed.). New York: W.H. Freeman.

Davison, G.C. & Neale, J.M. (1998). *Abnormal psychology* (7th ed.). New York: John Wiley & Sons.

Dowbiggin, I.R. (1998). *Keeping America sane: Psychiatry and eugenics in the United States and Canada* 1880-1940. Ithaca, NY: Cornell University Press.

Ellis, A. (1962). *Reason and emotion in psychotherapy*. Secaucus, NJ: Lyle Stuart.

Endler, N.S. (1990). *Holiday of darkness*. New York: Wiley-Interscience.

Eysenck, H. (1952). The effects of psychotherapy: An evaluation. *Journal of Consulting Psychology, 16*, 319-324.

Foucault, M. (1977). *Madness and civilisation*. London: Tavistock.

Freud, S. (1900). The interpretation of dreams. In A. Richards (Ed.) (1976). *The interpretation of dreams*. London: Pelican.

Freud, S. (1917). Mourning and melancholia. In A. Richards (Ed.) (1991). *On metapsychology*. London: Penguin.

Freud, S. (1920). Beyond the pleasure principle. In A. Richards (Ed.) (1991). *On metapsychology*. London: Penguin.

Freud, S. (1923). The ego and the id. In A. Richards (Ed.) (1991). *On metapsychology*. London: Penguin.

Freud, S. (1930). Civilisation and its discontents. In A. Dickson (Ed.) (1991). *Civilisation, society and religion*. London: Penguin.

Freud, S. & Breuer, J. (1895). Studies on hysteria. In A. Richards (Ed.) (1991). *Studies on hysteria*. London: Penguin.

Greenberg, L., Elliott, R. & Lietaer, G. (1994). Research on experiential psychotherapies. In A.E. Bergin & S.L. Garfield (Eds.), *Handbook of psychotherapy and behavior change*. New York: Wiley.

Haralambos, M. & Holborn, M. (2000). *Sociology: Themes and perspectives* (5th ed.). London: Harper Collins.

Harrington, R.C., Fudge, H., Rutter, M.L., Bredenkamp, D., Groothues, C. & Pridham, J. (1993). Child and adult depression: A test of continuities with data from a family study. *British Journal of Psychiatry, 162*, 627-633.

Hayden, M.R. (1981). *Huntington's corea*. New York: Springer-Verlag.

Heather, N. (1976). *Radical perspectives in psychology*. London: Methuen.

Hollon, S.D. & Beck, A.T. (1994). Cognitive and cognitive-behavioral therapies. In A.E. Bergin and S.L. Garfield (Eds.), *Handbook of psychotherapy and behavior change* (4th ed.). New York: John Wiley.

Kline, P. (1988). *Psychology exposed*. London: Routledge.

Kline, P. (1989). Objective tests of Freud's theories. In A.M. Colman & J.G. Beaumont (Eds.), *Psychology Survey No.7*, Leicester: British Psychological Society.

Kramer, P. (1993). *Listening to Prozac: A psychiatrist explores mood-altering drugs and the meaning of the self*. New York: Viking.

Ladd, C.O., Owens, M.J. & Nemeroff, C.B. (1996). Persistent changes in corticotropin-releasing factor neuronal systems induced by maternal deprivation. *Endocrinology, 137*, 1212-1218.

Lewinsohn, P.M., Youngren, M.A. & Grosscup, S.J. (1979). Reinforcement and depression. In R.A. Depue (Ed.), *The psychobiology of the depressive disorders*. New York: Academic Press.

Lingjaerde, O. (1983). The biochemistry of depression. A survey of monoaminergic, neuroendocrinological, and bio-rhythmic disturbances in endogenous depression. *Acta Psychiatrica Scandinavica Supplementum, 302*, 36-51.

Maher, B.A. (1966). *Principles of psychopathology: An experimental approach*. New York: McGraw-Hill.

McGuffin, P., Katz, R., Watkins, S. & Rutherford, J. (1996). A hospital-based twin register of the heritability of DSM-IV unipolar depression. *Archives of General Psychiatry, 53*, 129-136.

Messer, A.A. (1985). Narcissistic people. *Medical Aspects of Human Sexuality, 19*, 169-184.

Popper, K. (1959). *The logic of scientific discovery*. London: Hutchinson.

Porter, R. (1997). *The greatest benefit: A medical history of humanity from antiquity to the present*. London: Harper Collins.

Prochaska, J.O. & Norcross, J.C. (1994). *Systems of psychotherapy: A transtheoretical analysis* (3rd ed.). Pacific Grove, CA: Brooks/Cole.

Rogers, C.R. (1951). *Client-centered therapy*. Boston: Houghton-Mifflin.

Rogers, C.R. (1959). A theory of therapy, personality, and inter-personal relationships as developed in the client-centered framework. In S. Koch (Ed.), *Psychology: A study of a science Vol.3*. New York: McGraw-Hill.

Sarason, I.G. & Sarason, B.R. (1996). *Abnormal psychology* (8th ed.). Upper Saddle River, NJ: Prentice-Hall.

Segal, L. (2000). *Why feminism? Gender, psychology, politics*. Oxford: Polity.

Snyder, W.V. (1947). *Casebook of non-directive counseling*. Boston: Houghton Mifflin.

Stone, M. (1998). *Healing the mind*. London: Pimlico.

Watson, J.B. (1913). Psychology as the behaviourist sees it. *Psychology Review, 20*, 158-177.

Watson, J.B. & Rayner, R. (1920). Conditioned emotional reactions. *Journal of Experimental Psychology, 3*, 1-14.

Weissman, M. (1987). Advances in psychiatric epidemiology: Rates and risks for major depression. *American Journal of Public Health, 77*, 445-451.

Wolpe, J. (1958). *Psychotherapy by reciprocal inhibition*. Stanford, CA: Stanford University Press.

World Health Organization (1992). *The ICD-10 Classification of mental and behavioural disorders: Clinical descriptions and diagnostic guidelines*. Geneva: Author.

Zima, B.T., Wells, K.B., Benjamin, B. & Duan, N. (1996). Mental health problems among homeless mothers. *Archives of General Psychiatry, 53*, 332-338.

12 Eating disorders

▶ **Introduction**

Food and thinness have been described as national obsessions. Judging by the sales of cookery books, the number of food and drink programmes on TV and the rapid growth of gourmet restaurants, the nation has never been so interested in food. And, judging from the number of slimming magazines, slimming products and slimming programmes, people have never been so preoccupied with thinness.

In recent years a new concern has entered the public consciousness – eating disorders. Hardly a week goes by without a tabloid newspaper accusing a pop star, actress or model of suffering from anorexia or bulimia. Recent victims of tabloid journalism include Victoria Beckham (Posh Spice), and Calista Flockhart who plays Ally McBeal.

Eating disorders first appeared in DSM, the American Psychiatric Association's *Diagnostic and statistical manual of mental disorders*, in the third edition published in 1980. This chapter examines the characteristics and explanations of the two main eating disorders – anorexia nervosa and bulimia nervosa.

Chapter summary

- Unit 1 outlines the clinical characteristics of anorexia nervosa and bulimia nervosa.

- Unit 2 examines the main explanations of these disorders and the evidence on which these explanations are based.

Unit 1 The characteristics and extent of eating disorders

KEY ISSUES

1. What are the clinical characteristics of anorexia and bulimia?
2. How widespread are these eating disorders?
3. Are they modern disorders?

1.1 Anorexia nervosa

Anorexia nervosa literally means 'loss of appetite for emotional reasons'. However, people with anorexia neither lose their appetite nor their interest in food – they usually have strong feelings of hunger and are preoccupied with food. Anorexics typically restrict their calorie intake to 600-800 calories a day. Their primary concern, often described as an obsession, is to lose weight. This drive for thinness is accompanied by an intense fear of being overweight. Failure to lose weight – or worse putting weight on – often leads to depression, anxiety and even panic. Anorexics usually take great pride in their ability to lose weight and to control their desire to eat. Many, however, are never satisfied with their weight loss, and this drives them deeper into the disorder.

Anorexics tend to have a distorted view of their body. They overestimate their body size and proportions. Where others see them as thin or even emaciated, they often see themselves as grossly overweight. Some accept they are thin but see certain parts of their body, for example their stomach, thighs or buttocks, as 'too fat'. This distorted image is maintained despite frequent measurements of body parts, weighing themselves and checking their body in a mirror.

Anorexia typically begins with a diet when a person is slightly overweight. It develops into a disorder when the pursuit of thinness is relentless, when food intake is severely restricted, when weight loss is rapid and the person becomes extremely thin. By the time anorexics are treated, they average 25% to 30% below normal weight for their height and age (Hsu, 1990).

For anorexics, their self-esteem and their estimation of themselves in the eyes of others depends on the appearance of their bodies. But they are in a no-win situation since, however much weight they lose, they remain dissatisfied and set themselves ever more stringent goals for weight loss. A possible consolation is the pride many take in their self-control, discipline and self-denial.

Food is never far from anorexics' thoughts. Some dream about it, some read cookbooks from cover to cover, others prepare gourmet meals for their families without taking a bite themselves. When they do eat, it is often in secret, sometimes accompanied by rituals such as cutting the food into tiny pieces.

Some anorexics are obsessed with exercise, often pushing themselves to the point of exhaustion in order to lose even more weight.

DSM IV gives the following criteria for anorexia nervosa.

- Refusal to keep body weight at or above 85% of what is normal for height and age.
- Intense fear of gaining weight or becoming fat.
- Distorted body image.
- In females, absence of at least three consecutive menstrual periods.

DSM IV identifies two subtypes of anorexia – the restricting type which involves restricting food intake, and the binge-eating/purging type which involves bingeing on small amounts of food and then attempting to get rid of the food, usually by self-induced vomiting.

It is estimated that around 95% of anorexics are female, with more than 90% of the severe cases starting between the ages of 14 and 19 (Killian, 1994)

Anorexia can have very serious consequences. Estimates vary between 2% and 20% of anorexics dying from the disorder – as a result of medical problems brought about by starvation, or from suicide (Slade, 1995; Sullivan, 1995).

1.2 Bulimia nervosa

It was once thought the bulimia nervosa was merely a symptom of anorexia nervosa, but in 1978 the American Psychiatric Association recognised it as an eating disorder in its own right. The symptoms include:

- Recurrent episodes of binge eating.
- Recurrent inappropriate compensatory behaviour to prevent weight gain – eg vomiting, using laxatives (which cause emptying of the bowels), diuretics (which increase the output of urine), fasting, or excessive exercise.
- A minimum average of 2 binges per week for at least 3 months.
- An obsession with body shape and weight.

There are important similarities and differences between anorexia nervosa and bulimia nervosa. Bulimia nervosa means 'as hungry as an ox for emotional reasons'. The bulimic individual typically binges on a huge amount of calorie rich food, feels incredibly guilty, and then takes steps to remove the food from their body, either through vomiting, taking laxatives, or taking diuretics. For this reason it is often referred to as the 'binge-purge syndrome' even though there are some non-purging bulimics who rely on excessive exercise or fasting to remove the unwanted calories. Unlike the anorexic, however, the bulimic doesn't usually have an abnormally low weight because purging doesn't remove all the unwanted calories.

Like anorexia, bulimia usually starts with dieting. Once it gets underway, the bulimic consumes between 2000 and 5000 calories a day – up to twice as much as most people. The typical bulimic has one or two daily binges, gobbling high calorie food such as ice cream, sweets, cakes, crisps and biscuits until they feel uncomfortably full. A binge is preceded by a feeling of extreme tension which is relieved by eating. It is followed by guilt, disgust and self-reproach. To compensate for this, most bulimics follow a binge with a purge – they attempt to get rid of the unwanted food, usually by making themselves vomit, in an attempt to undo its effects.

Where the anorexic often feels in control of their food intake and takes pride in their self-discipline, the bulimic usually feels out of control and is ashamed of their lack of discipline. As the binge-purge cycle develops, bulimics are likely to feel useless and powerless and disgusted with their behaviour. As a result, they go to great lengths to conceal their activities from family and friends.

Like anorexics, bulimics are preoccupied with their body. Most feel that their self-esteem and popularity depend on their body shape and weight (Garfinkel, 1992). Despite their efforts, most have normal weight for their height and age. Purging is not particularly efficient. Even shortly after eating, vomiting removes only half the calories consumed and laxatives have little effect on calorie reduction.

It is estimated that 90% to 95% of bulimics are female. The disorder usually begins between the ages of 15 and 21. Over half recover within 5 years (Comer, 1998).

1.3 The extent of eating disorders

Anorexia and bulimia are usually presented in the media and by some researchers as modern disorders. If this is the case, then it suggests that eating disorders are related in some way to recent changes in society. However, as this section indicates, the evidence is not conclusive.

Statistics from Europe and the USA reveal a steady increase in reported cases of eating disorders from the 1950s onwards. Figures for the 1970s show a four-fold increase in cases of anorexia compared to the 1950s. This increase continued in the 1980s then appeared to level off in the 1990s (Barlow & Durand, 1999).

The increase in reported cases of bulimia has been even more dramatic. It has now overtaken anorexia as the main eating disorder. A joint five-year study conducted by the Institute of Psychiatry in London and Boston University in the USA reveals a rise from 15 out of 100,000 women suffering from bulimia in 1988 to just over 50 per 100,000 in 1993. The figure for anorexia remained steady at just over 20 per 100,000 (*Independent on Sunday, 1.12.1996*).

However, these figures must be treated with caution. Awareness of eating disorders, both by the public and professionals, has grown steadily. The American Psychiatric Association did not recognise bulimia as a separate disorder until 1978. Increasing awareness leads to increasing referral and diagnosis. Many of the statistics come from treatment centres and may not be representative of eating disorders in the wider society. As anorexia is a rare disorder, very large populations must be surveyed to reliably estimate its prevalence. Even if this was done, it is doubtful whether many anorexics would agree to participate in such a survey (Szmukler & Patton, 1995). One important study casts doubt on the reported rise in cases of anorexia. It was based on a detailed examination of clinical records from 1935 to 1979 for the town of Rochester in Minnesota (Lucas et al., 1991). It found no significant changes in the prevalence of anorexia during these years.

Available data indicates that bulimia was rare before the 1970s and has increased rapidly since then (Kendler et al.,

Summary

1. Anorexia nervosa is an obsession with body weight and shape. It is an intense fear of gaining weight which results in a refusal to keep body weight at or above 85% of what is normal for height and age. Food intake is severely restricted.

2. Bulimia nervosa is also characterised by an extreme concern with body weight and shape. Bulimics typically have recurrent episodes of binge eating followed by purges aimed at removing food from their bodies.

3. Most anorexics and bulimics are female. The disorders usually begin between the ages of 14 and 21. Available evidence suggests that the extent of eating disorders grew rapidly during the last quarter of the 20th century.

1991). And despite the problems with measurement, most researchers believe that anorexia has increased in the last half of the 20th century, though they would be cautious about labelling it as a modern disorder (Szmukler & Patton, 1995). Evidence about the   extent of eating disorders in earlier centuries is examined in Section 2.3.

Anorexia and bulimia are predominantly female disorders.

However, there is some evidence from the 1990s that the proportion of young men suffering from eating disorders is increasing. The picture is not clear since this evidence is based on small samples, usually drawn from treatment centres. Some researchers now estimate that 10% of those suffering from eating disorders are male (Dobson, 1997).

Unit 2 Explanations of eating disorders

KEY ISSUES

1. **What are the main explanations of eating disorders?**
2. **What evidence are these explanations based on?**

2.1 Biological explanations

Biological explanations argue that the onset and/or development of eating disorders are, at least in part, due to genetic factors or to some biological abnormality or malfunction which may or may not be genetically based.

Genetic factors There is some evidence which suggests that eating disorders may have a genetic basis. Research indicates that female relatives of young women with eating disorders are between 5 and 10 times more likely than the general population to develop eating disorders themselves (Strober & Humphrey, 1987; Strober et al., 1990). However, this does not necessarily indicate genetic influence. Since relatives are likely to live together, the influence may be environmental rather than genetic.

Twin studies provide stronger evidence for the contribution of genetic factors to eating disorders. Holland et al. (1984) studied 30 pairs of female twins, with at least one twin in each pair having anorexia. They found that if an identical or monozygotic twin suffered from anorexia, there was a 55% chance that their twin would also suffer from the disorder. This compared to a 7% chance that fraternal or dizygotic twins would both suffer from anorexia. Since identical twins share the same genes and fraternal twins share about half of their genes, this suggests that genetic factors may contribute to anorexia. Similar studies for bulimia show less marked differences between identical and fraternal twins though they still indicate the possibility of some genetic influence.

Twin studies have two main problems – the samples are very small and they are not representative of twins in the wider society. Treasure and Holland (1995) estimate that a sample of 10,000-20,000 twin pairs would be needed to discover the importance of genetic factors for eating disorders.

Neurotransmitters and hormones There is considerable evidence of abnormalities in the regulation and levels of neurotransmitters and hormones in people suffering from eating disorders. In a series of studies Fichter and Pirke (1995) aimed to discover whether these abnormalities were a cause or a consequence of eating disorders. Their evidence provides 'overwhelming' support for the *starvation hypothesis*, that these abnormalities result from severely reduced food intake rather than cause it. Starvation experiments with healthy participants

produced changes in hormone and neurotransmitter levels which were similar to those found in people suffering from eating disorders.

Once eating disorders are underway, what effects do the changes in neurotransmitters and hormones have? People with eating disorders often have high levels of anxiety. This may, in part, result from abnormally high levels of the neurotransmitter serotonin. Serotonin is made from tryptophan, an animo acid which comes from food. Reducing food intake reduces the amount of tryptophan, causing serotonin levels to drop, so reducing anxiety. This may make sense of the claim often made by people with eating disorders that if they don't eat, they feel better. If this argument is correct, neurotransmitter abnormality helps to maintain the disorder by discouraging the intake of food.

Gastric emptying Anorexics often complain that they are 'blocked' or excessively full after eating relatively small amounts of food. Research indicates that this may be related to their pattern of *gastric emptying* – the movement of food through the digestive system. Gastric emptying is delayed in anorexics. This produces a feeling of fullness which discourages eating. Caloric intake is reduced which results in weight loss. Delayed gastric emptying follows rather than precedes a severe reduction in food intake. It therefore serves to maintain or worsen the disorder rather than cause it. Quite why delayed gastric emptying results from extreme food reduction is an open question. It may be a mechanism that has evolved because of its survival value during periods of 'natural' starvation. It may, for example, increase the efficiency of nutrient absorption (Robinson & McHugh, 1995).

Biological explanations - evaluation Twin studies indicate a possible genetic basis which may predispose people – make them more vulnerable – to eating disorders. However, as noted earlier, these studies are based on very small and unrepresentative samples. Available evidence indicates that biological factors such as hormone and neurotransmitter levels and gastric emptying rates only become significant after the onset of eating disorders. In other words, they are a consequence rather than a cause of the disorders. To date, research into biological factors does not provide a convincing explanation for the cause of eating disorders, nor does it explain changes in their incidence over time – why their extent apparently increased rapidly over the past 25 years.

2.2 Psychodynamic explanations

Many of the early explanations for anorexia were based on psychodynamic theory. This suggests that some adolescents are frightened by the approach of adulthood because it involves moving towards sexual and social maturity and moving away from their parents. Anorexics are unable to face the growing separation from their parents and become fixated – excessively attached – to the oral stage of their development. This is the first stage of psychological development when infants are completely dependent on their caregivers, usually their mother. Anorexic behaviour is an unconscious attempt to return to the security of the oral stage of infancy. The disorder draws mother and adolescent closer together – the adolescent remains dependent and the mother retains her caring role.

Anorexia can be seen as a 'solution' to the daunting prospect of becoming a sexually mature adult. In Freudian theory, eating and sex are seen as related, and a refusal to eat can therefore be interpreted as a refusal of sexuality. Bruch (1978) argues that adolescent anorexics are unconsciously trying to prevent the onset of sexual maturity. A severe restriction of food can stop the development of secondary sex characteristics such as breasts, halt menstruation and give the body the appearance of a prepubescent girl. As a result, the girl appears sexually immature.

Pregnancy is associated with an adult role. Bruch suggests that pregnancy and 'fatness' are linked in the anorexic's mind. Restricting food intake can therefore be seen as an unconscious attempt to avoid pregnancy and the adult role that pregnancy implies.

Evaluation Psychodynamic theory has been criticised because it is based on ideas such as the unconscious which cannot be directly observed and measured. Despite this, there is evidence to support its views on anorexia. Anorexic adolescents look 'immature' and this could be one way to avoid the demands of 'maturity'.

2.3 Cultural explanations

Anorexia and bulimia are often described as Western disorders. They are usually seen as developing from cultural ideals for the female form that are common in Western societies. If this is so, then the apparent rise of eating disorders over the past 50 years will be paralleled by a slimmer and slimmer ideal female figure. What evidence is there for these claims?

The past Evidence from the past is meagre. One of the earliest cases of self-starvation is Saint Catherine of Sienna in the 14th century. In Europe, from the Middle Ages to the 18th century there are reports of 'starving girls' denying themselves food for religious reasons. How widespread this behaviour was or whether it was actually anorexia nervosa, is difficult to determine. The term was first mentioned in the medical literature by Sir William Gull in 1874. Historical records provide little evidence of behaviour that could be described as bulimia. It appears to be a fairly recent development.

Although the evidence is sketchy, it suggests a number of conclusions. First, eating disorders were less common in past centuries in Europe. Second, self-starvation, which may indicate anorexia, had a somewhat different meaning – a concern with purity and spirituality. According to Szmukler and Patton (1995) it was not until the 1960s that fear of fatness became a major *identifying* characteristic of eating disorders and the main motive given by those who suffered from them. The evidence suggests that the meanings given to eating disorders and their prevalence (extent) are strongly influenced by culture.

Non-Western societies Available evidence indicates that eating disorders are extremely rare in non-Western societies. Reports

Key terms

Monozygotic twins *Twins who share the same genes – identical twins.*

Dizygotic twins *Twins who share approximately half their genes – fraternal twins.*

Neurotransmitter *A chemical used to communicate between neurons or nerve cells.*

Hormone *A chemical that circulates in the blood and activates particular cells or organs.*

Starvation hypothesis *The idea that abnormalities in the levels of neurotransmitters and hormones result from rather than cause severely reduced food intake.*

Gastric emptying *The movement of food through the digestive system.*

Oral stage *In Freudian theory, the first stage of psychological development. During this stage the mouth is the focus of satisfaction.*

from India, Africa, Malaysia, China and New Guinea indicate that when eating disorders are found, they occur in Westernised groups in the population – those most exposed to Western culture and, in particular, Western ideals of the female figure (DiNicola, 1990). Support for these findings is provided by a comparison of 50 Arab female undergraduates at universities in London and 60 similar undergraduates in Cairo, Egypt. There were 6 cases of bulimia in London, none in Cairo (Nasser, 1986).

For many researchers, the evidence suggests that eating disorders are strongly influenced by Western culture. However, one study questions this view. Dr Hans Hoek spent three years looking for cases of eating disorders in Curacao, a Caribbean island where being 'fat' is considered beautiful. None of the doctors he questioned had come across cases of eating disorders. However, after a painstaking search through 144,000 medical records, Hoek claimed to have found 8 cases of anorexia. This led Hoek to question the view that Western culture with its ideals of female slimness is a major influence on eating disorders (*Horizon*, 22.1. 1999).

Western culture Evidence from Western societies, particularly from the 1960s onwards, indicates the ideal female figure is slim and that this ideal is becoming increasingly slimmer. In the 1960s, fashion models such as Twiggy and Jean Shrimpton were often described as 'skinny'; by the 1990s, models such as Kate Moss and Jodie Kidd were sometimes described as 'emaciated'. A study by Garner et al. (1980) showed a 20 year trend to thinner ideals for young women. This trend was accompanied by the rise of the 'diet culture' – organisations such as Weight Watchers, books and magazines devoted to slimming diets, and supermarkets stacked with low-fat and no-fat food. In most cases, eating disorders in the West today appear to be motivated by a desire to be thin and are preceded by dieting.

Available evidence from the 1990s suggests that the proportion of young men with eating disorders is increasing. This may indicate a growing concern with slimness amongst young men. The 1990s have seen a rapid increase in the numbers and sales of magazines aimed at the teenage to thirty-something male market. Examples include *FHM*, *Loaded* and *Men's Health*. Judging by the often semi-naked images of young men portrayed in these magazines, particularly in the adverts, the ideal male figure is thin, sometimes 'super-thin'. Such images may reflect, reinforce and even create perceptions of the ideal male figure.

Evaluation The evidence suggests that the meanings, motivation and extent of eating disorders in the West are influenced by Western culture. However, evidence from the past and from non-Western societies is sparse and sketchy. Even evidence from the West on the extent of eating disorders over the past 50 years must be treated with caution as Section 1.3 indicated. However, even if we accept the influence of Western culture, it doesn't explain why some individuals succumb to eating disorders and others do not.

Activity 1   Culture and eating disorders

Item A   Shape and culture

Researchers showed pictures of thin, normal and plump women to men of the Matsigenka, an isolated tribe in Peru. They preferred the plump 'apple-shaped' women, saying that the slender, 'wasp-shaped' women were skinny and probably recovering from diarrhoea. However, members of the tribe who had moved into towns and cities preferred the 'wasp-shaped' women.

Adapted from the Guardian, 26.11.1998

Item B   Standards of beauty

'Seated Bather' by Renoir (1841-1919)

'Supermodel' Jodie Kidd

Item C   Getting lighter

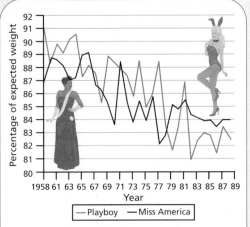

This graph shows the average body weight of Miss America contestants and *Playboy* centrefold models from 1959 to 1989 as a percentage of their expected weight in terms of age and height. Over 60% weighed 15% or more below expected weight which is one of the criteria for anorexia.

Adapted from Wiseman et al., 1992

Item E   Male models

Male models are getting thinner.

Item D   Slimming

4 page slimming special
If you feel more slobby than slim, don't despair. There's time to shed a few pounds before Christmas, and our brilliant tips will give you all the inspiration you need. Just look at our successful slimmers!

6 SHOPPING TIPS TO HELP YOU STAY SLIM

★ Always write a shopping list before going to the supermarket – and stick to it. And pay cash, too, so that you can't overspend.

★ Never go shopping when you're feeling hungry.

★ Try not to go to the supermarket on your own – if you're with someone else who knows you're on a diet, they won't let you sneak fattening things into your trolley.

★ Look out for low-calorie alternatives to your favourite treats.

★ Remind yourself how much weight you've already lost when you walk past the cake counter.

★ Make an effort with your appearance when you go shopping. If you look and feel good, you'll be positive about sticking to your diet.

Adapted from *Woman* magazine, 18.11.1996

Questions

1   The spread of Western culture is related to the rise in eating disorders. Briefly discuss with reference to Item A.

2   Use Item B to suggest why eating disorders may have become more widespread in the 20th century.

3   a) Outline the trends shown in Item C.

    b) How might this help to explain the apparent increase in eating disorders?

4   a) What does the introduction to the 4 page slimming special in Item D imply about overweight people?

    b) What do the slimming tips imply about 'successful' and 'unsuccessful' slimmers?

5   How might Item E help to explain the apparent rise in eating disorders among young men?

2.4   Behavioural explanations

From a behavioural view, eating disorders can be seen as learned behaviour which is maintained by positive reinforcement. Since slimness is so highly prized in Western culture, a young person who starts a diet, sticks to it and loses weight is likely to receive positive reinforcement or rewards – praise, approval, admiration – from others. At the same time, there is the pressure of punishment – being overweight can bring disapproval and even ridicule.

Giving positive reinforcement to a behaviour encourages repetition and even exaggeration of that behaviour. This may lead a person from extreme dieting to anorexia. A number of researchers have noted the pleasure and pride which many anorexics feel from not eating or eating very little (Gilbert, 1986). These feelings may develop into the main reinforcement for the disorder. Restricted eating may begin as a means to achieving a slim figure, but it may develop into an end in itself as the anorexic derives satisfaction from successfully controlling their intake of food (Wyrwicka, 1984).

Evaluation Behavioural views provide a fairly strong case for the maintenance or persistence of anorexia, but are weaker when attempting to explain its origin. Why, for example, doesn't every dieter travel the anorexic route from dieting to disorder given the positive reinforcements available along the way? The behavioural model is not particularly useful for explaining bulimia. It may help to explain purging – to reduce the anxiety produced by a binge. However, it fails to explain why bulimics binge in the first place (de Silva, 1995).

2.5   Cognitive explanations

Behavioural models tend to ignore cognitions – in particular they have little to say about what anorexics and bulimics think about their bodies. One of the main features of anorexia is distorted or faulty ideas about body weight and shape and about eating. For example, in the advanced stages of anorexia, many anorexics still see themselves as fat whereas others see them as pitifully emaciated – little more than skin and bone.

Garner and Bemis (1982) identify a number of *cognitive errors* or errors in thinking which underlie and influence the behaviour of anorexics. They include:

- **Selective abstraction** Selecting small parts of a situation and coming to conclusions on this basis, while ignoring other evidence. For example, 'I am very special if I am thin'.
- **Dichotomous reasoning** Thinking in terms of extremes. For example, 'If I am not in complete control, then I will lose all control'.

- **Magnification** Exaggerating the importance of events. For example, 'Gaining a pound will push me over the brink'.

The conclusions drawn from this type of thinking are never questioned or critically examined. As a result, they help to maintain the disorder. Wrapped up in faulty cognitions, the anorexic becomes increasingly isolated in their own little world, which from their point of view makes perfect sense.

Cognitive errors about body shape and weight are also found in bulimics. Many have normal weight for their age and height, yet regard themselves as grossly overweight. The key cognition in terms of bulimia appears to be, 'I have failed, so I might as well go on eating' (de Silva, 1995).

Evaluation Cognitive models help to explain the maintenance of eating disorders. They have the advantage of looking at the disorder from the point of view of the sufferer and showing how it makes sense in their eyes. However, as with behavioural models, cognitive perspectives largely fail to explain why some dieters develop an eating disorder and others do not. In other words, they are not very good at explaining the origins of eating disorders.

2.6   Family systems approaches

This is a general term used to describe approaches which explain behaviour in terms of interaction within the family unit. They see eating disorders as a response to things 'going wrong' within the family. Such families are sometimes described as *dysfunctional*. Family systems approaches draw on many of the approaches described so far. The following studies illustrate how these approaches may be combined to explain anorexia.

Hilde Bruch Bruch sees anorexia resulting from dysfunctional relationships between parents and their children. She claims that parents of anorexics tend to dominate their children, allowing them little control over their own lives. They decide when the child needs attention. They decide when the child is hungry, tired or upset and what to do about it. And often, they get it wrong. For example, they may feed the children when they are anxious rather than hungry. As a result, children may grow up confused, unable to rely on their own judgement. They fail to develop self-reliance, they look to others for guidance, are very sensitive to the wishes and opinions of others and vulnerable to criticism. In Bruch's words, such children 'experience themselves as not being in control of their behaviour, needs and impulses, as not knowing their own bodies' (Bruch, 1973).

Bruch (1973) interviewed the parents of 51 anorexic girls. They tended to be financially well-off and achievement oriented, placing considerable pressure on their daughter to succeed. However, this is not for their daughter's benefit. They saw her not as a person in her own right but as a person who can make *their* lives more satisfying and complete. Most of the girls were high achievers, but they excelled to please others and not to please themselves. This results in a lack of autonomy and a sense of who they are. Again the girls had little control over their own lives.

Adolescence brings increasing pressure for autonomy and independence. Added to this are the bodily changes resulting from the onset of puberty which are outside the young person's control. At this stage in their development, anorexics tend to feel particularly helpless and out of control. To overcome these feelings they seek extreme control over their own body. By controlling their diet, they can alter their body shape. As one anorexic told Bruch, 'You want to prove that you have control, that you can do it' (Bruch, 1978).

A number of studies have supported Bruch's findings. They indicate that anorexics feel they have little control over their lives, that they tend to seek approval and are extemely concerned about how others see them (Comer, 1998).

Salvador Minuchin According to Minuchin et al. (1978), anorexia is a response to relationships within dysfunctional families. Such families have the following characteristics.

- **Enmeshment** Family members are bound together in a tight and constricting network. This insistence on 'togetherness' swamps the young person who loses their sense of identity and self-control.
- **Overprotectiveness** Family members show extreme concern for each other's wellbeing.
- **Rigidity** There is pressure to keep things the way they are rather than changing to adapt to new situations such as adolescence.
- **Conflict** Family relationships tend to be in a state of constant conflict. This conflict is usually denied, covered up and unresolved.

Adolescence threatens the fragile stability of such families. It is a time when young people move towards independence and freedom from family ties. In the face of this threat, parents place pressure on the young person to adopt a 'sick role' in order to return them to the 'bosom of the family'. Anorexia provides a solution. The young person is drawn back into the family –

parents protect her, worry about her, show concern for her. In this way the pattern of family relationships is maintained. In addition, the young person's illness deflects attention from the conflicts underlying family relationships.

There are two main criticisms of this study. First, some of the family characteristics identified by Minuchin et al. may, at least in part, be a result of anorexia rather than the cause. Parents of an anorexic child have good reason to be protective and concerned. Second, some studies have failed to confirm Minuchin et al's findings. For example, one study found wide variation in terms of enmeshment for families of anorexics (Dare et al., 1994).

Evaluation In their favour, family systems approaches do provide explanations for the origins of eating disorders. They do suggest why some people and not others develop eating disorders.

However, there are a number of problems with family studies. First, they are largely based on accounts by clinicians of their patients and their patients' families. This may produce biased samples – their patients may not be representative of those with eating disorders in the wider society. Many of the differences identified by clinicians between the families of those with eating disorders and 'normal' families disappear in community-based studies (Eisler, 1995). Second, many of the studies are retrospective – they look back on family interaction well after the disorder has started. As a result, much of the family behaviour reported may be a response to the disorder rather than a cause. Third, the evidence to support particular family studies is often sparse, based on very small samples and contradicted by evidence from other studies. From a survey of family studies, Eisler (1995) reaches the following conclusion: 'Families of both anorexics and bulimics vary considerably and do not conform to a single pattern'.

Key terms

Positive reinforcement Rewards. Rewarding behaviour is likely to lead to that behaviour being learned and repeated.

Cognitive errors Faulty perceptions, mistaken ideas, errors in thinking.

Dysfunctional families Families in which relationships are harmful to their members.

Summary

1. Genetic factors may predispose some people to eating disorders.

2. Biological factors such as abnormalities in neuro-transmitter and hormone levels are seen to result from and maintain eating disorders rather than cause them.

3. Psychodynamic explanations see eating disorders as an unconscious attempt to return to the oral stage of infancy.

4. Cultural explanations see them as a reflection of pressures to be slim.

5. Behavioural approaches see eating disorders as an extreme example of reinforcement for an ideal figure.

6. Cognitive explanations argue that faulty cognition contributes to the maintenance of eating disorders.

7. Family systems approaches see eating disorders as a response to dysfunctional family life.

Activity 2   Case studies

At age 15, Julie was 5'1" and weighed 10 stone. Her mother, a well-meaning but overbearing and demanding woman, constantly criticised Julie about her weight. Her friends were kinder, but their comments were similar. Julie's confidence was not helped by the fact she'd never had a date. Her friends told her she was attractive and would have no trouble getting dates if she lost some weight.

Many unsuccessful diets followed, but this time Julie was determined to succeed. The pounds began dropping off. She experienced a new sense of control and mastery. Her new-found figure brought praise from her friends, even from her mother. At last, Julie began to feel good about herself. But, now she was in control, nothing could stop her dieting. By the time she received professional help, at age 17, Julie weighed 5 stone 5 pounds yet still thought she looked fine.

Adapted from Durand & Barlow, 1997

Phoebe was a popular, attractive, intelligent all-American girl. She excelled at everything she did. At high school she achieved top grades and was considered a model student. She was elected home-coming queen and prom queen and appeared to have the world at her feet. She played for several of the school teams and was a poised and confident ballet dancer. She was headed for a leading university.

Yet Phoebe was haunted by a secret thought. She was convinced she was fat and ugly and saw this as a threat to her popularity and success. She began to restrict her eating at age 11. Later she began the occasional binge. One day, sat alone in front of the TV, she ate two big boxes of candy. Depressed, guilty and desperate, she forced herself to vomit. It was the perfect solution – she felt an overwhelming sense of relief. From then on her life became a secretive binge-purge cycle. This continued until her second year at university when, realising things had got totally out of control, Phoebe sought professional help.

Adapted from Durand & Barlow, 1997

Question

Using some of the preceding theories of eating disorders, explain the behaviour of Julie and Phoebe.

References

Barlow, D.H. & Durand, V.M. (1999). *Abnormal psychology: An integrative approach* (2nd ed.). Pacific Grove, CA: Brooks/Cole.

Bruch, H. (1973). *Eating disorders: Obesity, anorexia nervosa, and the person within.* New York: Basic Books.

Bruch, H. (1978). *The golden cage: The enigma of anorexia nervosa.* Cambridge, MA: Harvard University Press.

Comer, R.J. (1998). *Abnormal psychology* (3rd ed.). New York: W.H. Freeman.

Dare, C., LeGrange, D., Eisler, I. & Rutherford, J. (1994). Redefining the psychosomatic family: Family process of 26 eating disordered families. *International Journal of Eating Disorders, 16,* 211-226.

de Silva, P. (1995). Cognitive-behavioural models of eating disorders. In G. Szmukler, C. Dare & J. Treasure (Eds.), *Handbook of eating disorders: Theory, treatment and research.* Chichester: Wiley.

DiNicola, V.F. (1990). Anorexia multiforme: Self-starvation in historical and cultural context. II: Anorexia nervosa as a culture reactive syndrome. *Transcultural Psychiatric Research Review, 27,* 245-286.

Dobson, R. (1997). Anorexia – now it's Nineties man who suffers. *Independent on Sunday,* 8.6.1997.

Durand, V.M. & Barlow, D.H. (1997). *Abnormal psychology: An introduction.* Pacific Grove, CA: Brooks/Cole.

Eisler, I. (1995). Family models of eating disorders. In G. Szmukler, C. Dare & J. Treasure (Eds.), *Handbook of eating disorders: Theory,*

treatment and research. Chichester: Wiley.

Fichter, M.M. & Pirke, K.M. (1995). Starvation models and eating disorders. In G. Szmukler, C. Dare & J. Treasure (Eds.), *Handbook of eating disorders: Theory, treatment and research.* Chichester: Wiley.

Garfinkel, P.E. (1992). Evidence in support of attitudes to shape and weight as a diagnostic criterion of bulimia nervosa. Special section: Eating disorders in DSM-IV. *International Journal of Eating Disorders, 11,* 321-325.

Garner, D.M. & Bemis, K.M. (1982). A cognitive-behavioural approach to anorexia nervosa. *Cognitive Therapy and Research, 6,* 123-150.

Gilbert, S. (1986). *Pathology of Eating.* London: Routledge & Kegan Paul.

Hoek, H.W. (1999). Interview in *Horizon.* BBC TV, 22.1.1999.

Holland, A.J., Murray, R., Russell, G.F.M. & Crisp, A.H. (1984). Anorexia nervosa: A study of 34 pairs of twins and one set of triplets. *British Journal of Psychiatry, 145,* 414-419.

Hsu, L.K.G. (1990). *Eating disorders.* New York: Guilford Press.

Kendler, K.S., Maclean, C., Neale, M., Kessler, R., Heath, A. & Eaves, L. (1991). The genetic epidemiology of bulimia nervosa. *American Journal of Psychiatry, 148,* 1627-1637.

Killian, K.D. (1994). Fearing fat: A literature review of family systems understandings and treatments of anorexia and bulimia. *Family Relations, 43,* 311-318.

Lucas, A.R., Beard, C.M., O'Fallon, W.M. & Kurlan, L.T. (1991). 50-year trends in the incidence of anorexia nervosa in Rochester, Minn.: A population-based study. *American Journal of Psychiatry, 148*, 917-922.

Minuchin, S., Rosman, B.L. & Baker, L. (1978). *Psychosomatic families.* Cambridge, MA: Harvard University Press.

Nassar, M. (1986). Comparative study of the prevalence of abnormal eating attitudes among Arab female students of both London and Cairo universities. *Psychological Medicine, 16*, 621-625.

Robinson, P.H. & McHugh, P.R. (1995). A physiology of starvation that sustains eating disorders. In G. Szmukler, C. Dare & J. Treasure (Eds.), *Handbook of eating disorders: Theory, treatment and research.* Chichester: Wiley.

Slade, P. (1995). Prospects for prevention. In G. Szmukler, C. Dare & J. Treasure (Eds.), *Handbook of eating disorders: Theory, treatment and research.* Chichester: Wiley.

Strober, M. & Humphrey, L.L. (1987). Familial contributions to the etiology and course of anorexia nervosa and bulimia. Special Issue: Eating disorders. *Journal of Consulting and Clinical Psychology, 55*, 654-659.

Strober, M., Lampert, C., Morrell, W., Burroughs, J. & Jacobs, C. (1990). A controlled family study of anorexia nervosa: Evidence of familial aggregation and lack of shared transmission with affective disorders. *International Journal of Eating Disorders, 9*, 239-253.

Sullivan, P.F. (1995). Mortality in anorexia nervosa. *American Journal of Psychiatry, 152*, 1073-1075.

Szmukler, G.I. & Patton, G. (1995). Sociocultural models of eating disorders. In G. Szmukler, C. Dare & J. Treasure (Eds.), *Handbook of eating disorders: Theory, treatment and research.* Chichester: Wiley.

Treasure, J. & Holland, A. (1995). Genetic factors in eating disorders. In G. Szmukler, C. Dare & J. Treasure (Eds.), *Handbook of eating disorders: Theory, treatment and research.* Chichester: Wiley.

Wiseman, C.V., Gray, J.J., Mosimann, J.E. & Ahrens, A.H. (1992). Cultural expectations of thinness in women: An update. *International Journal of Eating Disorders, 11*, 85-89.

Wyrwicka, W. (1984). Anorexia nervosa as a case of complex instrumental conditioning. *Experimental Neurology, 84*, 579-589.

▶ Introduction

Very few people live in isolation from other human beings. Apart from the occasional hermit who chooses to live alone, or unfortunates such as Robinson Crusoe forced by circumstances to live a solitary existence, human beings live in social groups. As members of society, they interact on a regular basis with other human beings. Their behaviour is influenced by others and they, in turn, influence the behaviour of others. As such, people are social beings. These fairly obvious observations form the basis of social psychology. Put simply, social psychology is the study of people as members of social groups – it is the study of the social side of human behaviour.

This is the first of three chapters on social psychology. It looks at conformity. It examines why most people, most of the time, conform to the accepted standards of behaviour of the groups to which they belong. In this respect, it looks at how the majority influence the behaviour of the minority. The chapter also looks at the other side of the coin – how minorities can sometimes influence the behaviour of the majority of people in a social group.

Chapter summary

- **Unit 1 looks at conformity or majority influence. It outlines some of the experiments conducted to investigate conformity and examines various explanations for conformity.**

- **Unit 2 looks at minority influence. It examines ways in which a minority can influence the behaviour of a majority.**

Unit 1 Conformity – majority influence

KEY ISSUES

1 What are social norms?
2 Why do most people conform to social norms?
3 What are social roles?
4 What encourages conformity to social roles?

Social influence is the influence of social factors on behaviour. It refers to the effect that the presence of others has on the way people think, feel and behave. *Conformity* is a major aspect of social influence. The term conformity is used in two main ways. First, it refers generally to following the accepted ways of behaving of particular groups within society, or of society as a whole. Second, it refers to a change in the behaviour of a minority which results from the influence of the majority. The minority changes its behaviour so that it matches the behaviour of the majority. In this sense, conformity is also known as *majority influence*.

1.1 Social norms

The idea of social norms provides a key to understanding social influence in general and conformity in particular. Social norms are the accepted standards of behaviour of social groups. These groups range from friendship and work groups to nation states. Thus in British society norms of acceptable behaviour include queuing for public transport, waiting in line at a post office counter or a fastfood takeout and taking your turn in a doctor's waiting room.

There are norms defining appropriate behaviour for every

social group. For example, students, workers, partygoers, friends, neighbours, patients in a hospital and drinkers in a pub are all usually aware of the norms governing their behaviour. And, as the individual moves from group to group, their behaviour changes accordingly.

Social norms vary from society to society. This can be seen clearly from norms concerning food. In traditional Bedouin society of North Africa, sheep's eyes are regarded as a delicacy whereas in the West they are not even considered fit to eat. The Bedouin eat with their fingers and a loud and prolonged burp at the end of a meal is a compliment to the host. In the West such behaviour would be considered the height of bad manners. Or, as a social psychologist might say, it would not conform to Western norms of eating behaviour.

Norms provide order in society. Imagine a situation in which 'anything goes'. The result is likely to be confusion and disorder. This can sometimes be seen in the classroom if

Bedouin eating, Syria 1923

teacher and students fail to establish a set of norms for conducting a lesson. Norms help to make social life predictable and comprehensible. If there were no norms stating how people should express pleasure or irritation, warmth or hostility, it would be difficult to understand how others felt, to predict their behaviour and respond to them in appropriate ways.

It is difficult to see how human society could operate without social norms. Human beings need social norms to guide and direct their behaviour, to provide order and predictability in social relationships and to make sense of and understand each others' actions. These are some of the reasons why most people, most of the time, conform to social norms.

1.2 Why do people conform?

Social psychologists have identified two main factors which encourage conformity. First, people conform when they are unsure about what to do in a particular situation. They seek guidance from others, whom, they see as better informed than themselves, and conform to their behaviour and opinions. This is called *informational social influence*. Second, people conform because they want to be liked. They conform to the behaviour of others in order to gain their approval. This is called *normative social influence* (Deutsch & Gerard, 1955).

Informational social influence When people are uncertain about

Key terms

Social influence *The influence of others on the attitudes, beliefs and behaviour of the individual.*

Conformity *1) Acting in terms of the accepted behaviour of a social group. 2) A change in the behaviour of a minority to fit the behaviour of the majority.*

Social norms *The accepted and expected ways of behaving of a social group.*

what to do, they often look to others for guidance. This can happen when they find themselves in a novel situation – their first day at work, college or university, their first dinner party or visit to the opera. They want to do the right thing but may lack the appropriate information. Observing others can provide this information. For example, at your first formal dinner party you may be presented with a bewildering array of cutlery. Watching more experienced guests will guide your selection – they know the norms which fit the situation. This is known as informational social influence – people conform because the behaviour of others provides information and guidance for appropriate action.

Sometimes situations are ambiguous and ill-defined. Consider the following example. A fire alarm goes off. Has it gone off

Activity 1   Social norms

Item A   Kikuyu women, Kenya

Item B   Tibetan nuns in 1904

Item C   Russian women in 1890

Questions

Use the pictures to discuss the following statements.
1. Most people conform to social norms.
2. Social norms vary from society to society.
3. Social norms are learned rather than innate or inborn.

accidentally, is it an unannounced fire drill, or is there a fire? Again, people look to others for guidance. They may ask what others think and observe what they do. And, if they appear to know the answer, people may well conform to their behaviour.

Informational social influence is based on the need to be right. When people are unsure of their own judgement, they often accept the judgement of others. When they are uncertain about what to do, they often accept the actions of others as a guide.

Normative social influence All social groups have norms which define appropriate behaviour for their members. In general, conforming to group norms brings acceptance and approval, while nonconformity can bring disapproval and even rejection. People are social beings, they have a need to belong, to feel part of a social group. Because of this, social groups can place considerable pressure on individuals to conform to group norms. Conformity is rewarded with approval and praise. Nonconformity is punished with disapproval, ridicule and even ostracism – the individual is shunned by group members.

Normative social influence involves altering behaviour to fit the expectations of others. People yield to group pressure and behave in a way that others consider appropriate, reasonable and desirable in order to gain social acceptance and approval.

So far, this section has examined the two main forms of social influence which encourage conformity. It now considers two types of conformity – *public compliance* and *private acceptance*.

Public compliance How many times have you agreed with what your friends say, while privately rejecting their opinions? How often have you 'gone along' with the behaviour of others and acted in a similar manner despite disapproving of this course of action? These are examples of public compliance. People often conform in public to the norms of others even though these norms contradict their privately held beliefs.

Public compliance often occurs in response to normative social influence. In the presence of others people often act in terms of social norms and give the impression they approve of those norms in order to gain acceptance and approval.

Private acceptance In this case people conform to the norms of others because they believe those norms are right. This can result in a change to their private beliefs and attitudes. They *internalise* the norms of others – make them their own and act in terms of them. Private acceptance is a more powerful and longlasting influence than public compliance. It can result in a genuine change in beliefs and attitudes. For this reason, private acceptance is also known as *conversion* – the individual is 'converted' to the beliefs of others.

Key terms

Informational social influence *Being influenced by others to conform to their behaviour because of uncertainty about how to behave.*

Normative social influence *Being influenced by others to conform to their behaviour because of a desire to gain their approval.*

Public compliance *Conforming to the behaviour of others despite privately disagreeing with their behaviour.*

Private acceptance *Conforming to the behaviour of others because their behaviour is seen to be right.*

1.3 Experimental studies of conformity

This section examines a number of experiments designed to investigate conformity. They were conducted in laboratory situations.

Sherif – the autokinetic effect

Muzafer Sherif (1935) devised an experiment to investigate the development of group norms and conformity to those norms. He used the *autokinetic effect* – an optical illusion in which a stationary spot of light in a darkened environment appears to move around. Sherif divided his participants into two groups. The first group was tested individually. Each participant sat alone in a darkened room, looking at a stationary point of light. They were told the light was actually moving and asked to estimate how far it moved. Each participant made one hundred estimates. At first the estimates varied widely before settling down to a fairly standard pattern – a *personal norm*. However, there were considerable differences between the estimates which each participant produced. For example, some thought the light was moving an inch or so, others believed it moved as far as ten inches.

The participants were then placed in small groups of two or three. At first, the estimates of group members varied widely – each member based their estimate on their personal norm. Then their estimates steadily converged, becoming more and more similar. Finally, the group reached a consensus – an agreement. A group norm had developed to which the participants conformed. This can be seen from Figure 1 which shows the results of one group's estimates.

Sherif reversed the procedure with the second set of participants. They began in small groups and each group rapidly developed a group estimate to which each member conformed. Finally, these participants were tested individually. Each was placed alone in the darkened room and asked again to estimate the movement of light. Their answers, as individuals, mirrored those of their group. In other words, they continued to follow the group norm despite the fact that nobody else was there.

Sherif's experiment demonstrates a number of things. First, it shows how group norms develop. Second, it shows how individuals conform to group norms. Third, it shows the effect of informational social influence. The situation was ambiguous. In fact there was no correct answer (other than the answer 'no

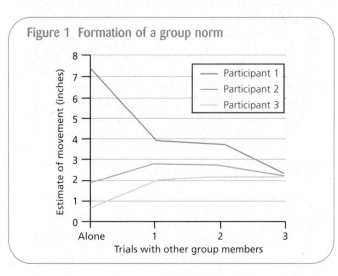

Figure 1 Formation of a group norm

Activity 2 — Normative and informational influence

Item A — At the golf club

Elaine, Ingrid, Pauline and Mary-Anne were enjoying a drink in the clubhouse after a round of golf. Elaine was telling the others a story. She had been asked by a neighbour if she could arrange a game of golf for a 15-year-old boy from Finland who was in England on holiday. She asked John, the young assistant professional, to play with him. 'Do you know,' Elaine said, 'I got the shock of my life. The boy from Finland was black and my neighbour hadn't even told me. So I went to John and apologised. Not that I've got anything against blacks,' she added. The other women nodded and murmured agreement.

However, Mary-Anne, who recounted this story later, was taken aback. 'I was disgusted with Elaine's attitude,' she said. 'But I was even more disgusted with myself. I had given Elaine every indication that I was in complete agreement with her.'

Story told to author 15.2.1998

Questions

1   Read Item A.
   a) Is Mary-Anne's behaviour an example of normative social influence or informational social influence?
   b) Is it an example of public compliance or private acceptance?
   Give reasons for your answers to both questions.

2   How can the idea of informational social influence help to explain the behaviour described in Item B?

Item B — The Martians are coming

'The girls huddled around their radios trembling and weeping in each other's arms. They separated themselves from their friends only to take their turn at the telephone to make long distance calls to their parents, saying goodbye for what they thought might be the last time. Terror-stricken girls, hoping to escape from the Mars invaders, rushed to the basement of the dormitory.'

With these words, an American college student recalls the reaction of herself and her friends to a radio broadcast in 1938. The broadcast was a radio play by Orson Welles based on H.G. Wells' *War of the Worlds*, a novel about an invasion from Mars. It was so realistic that hundreds of thousands of people, who missed the announcement that it was only a play, were convinced the Martians had invaded. There was widespread panic at the news that millions had been killed by Martian death rays.

Many people just didn't know how to respond. They turned to family and friends to see whether they should believe what they'd heard. They interpreted what they saw in terms of the radio programme. One person looked out of his window and saw that Wyoming Avenue was 'black with cars. People were rushing away, I figured'. Another recounted, 'No cars came down my street. Traffic is jammed on account of the roads being destroyed, I thought.'

Thousands fled towns and cities and took to the hills.

Adapted from Cantril, 1940

Orson Welles broadcasting War of the Worlds

New York Times

Copyright, 1938, by The New York Times Company

Radio Listeners in Panic, Taking War Drama as Fact

Many Flee Homes to Escape 'Gas Raid From Mars'—Phone Calls Swamp Police at Broadcast of Wells Fantasy

A wave of mass hysteria seized thousands of radio listeners throughout the nation between 8:15 and 9:30 o'clock last night when a broadcast of a dramatization of H. G. Wells's fantasy, "The War of the Worlds," led thousands to believe that an interplanetary conflict had started with invading Martians spreading wide death and destruction ... ... in New Jersey ... New York ...

and radio stations here and in other cities of the United States and Canada seeking advice on protective measures against the raids.

The program was produced by Mr. Welles and the Mercury Theatre on the Air over station WABC and the Columbia Broadcasting System's coast-to-coast network, from 8 to 9 o'clock.

"The radio ... AS INTERPLANETARY...

---

movement') since the light was not moving. In this situation, participants were happy to adjust their own judgements to fit those of others. Finally, the experiment provides an example of private acceptance. Participants internalised the group norm and made it their own. Even when they sat alone in the darkened room, they continued to base their individual estimates on the group norm.

Majority influence Strictly speaking, Sherif's experiment is not an example of conformity in terms of majority influence. Majority influence means a majority influences a minority who then conform to the majority view. There was no majority or minority in Sherif's experiment, simply a number of people who had different views. They then came together and formed a collective view (van Avermaet, 1996).

Jacobs and Campbell (1961) conducted a variation of Sherif's experiment to assess the importance of majority influence. They used groups of four, made up of three confederates or stooges (accomplices who worked with the researchers) and one 'real' participant. The three confederates gave either very large or very

small estimates of how far the light had moved. In almost every case the participant conformed to their estimate. One by one the confederates were replaced by participants. As each new participant entered the group, they accepted the group norm. Finally, all the confederates were removed and the four participants continued to agree on the group norm. This study shows that a majority can have a significant influence on the judgements of a minority.

Solomon Asch

The task given to the participants in Sherif's study was ambiguous since there was no correct answer other than 'no movement'. In this situation conformity is to be expected as people look to others for guidance. But what about a situation where people are sure that the judgements of the majority are wrong? Will they conform then? This was the question asked by Solomon Asch (1951, 1956) in a series of experiments conducted in the early 1950s.

Asch designed a simple, straightforward and unambiguous

task. Participants were presented with two cards. On one card was a single 'standard' line, on the other were three 'comparison' lines. Participants were asked to judge which of the comparison lines was equal in length to the standard line. Various pairs of cards were used. Figure 2 shows one example.

Figure 2   Line judgement task

Standard line   Comparison lines

First, a control group of 37 participants were given the task. A control group is used for comparison with the experimental group. The factors expected to influence the experimental group's behaviour – in this case pressure to conform – are removed. The participants were simply asked to judge the comparison lines without any social pressure to conform to the judgements made by other people. Thirty-five members of the control group made no errors, one made a single error and one made two errors. This indicates that the task was straightforward and unambiguous.

In the experimental situation, there was only one participant, the rest were confederates working with Asch. The participant was seated at a table along with 6 to 8 confederates. He thought they were participants like himself and did not realise that the entire experiment was about his behaviour. The comparison lines were presented and each person was asked to state their judgements aloud. The participant was seated near the end of the table and was next to last to state his judgements. To begin with, the confederates gave accurate judgements and the participant readily agreed – after all, the answers were obvious. Then, on one comparison task, *all* the confederates gave the same wrong answer. They continued to do this on 12 of the 18 trials, that is for 12 out of the 18 pairs of cards. Asch repeated the experiment with a number of different participants. The question is, would the participants fall into line and conform to judgements which were obviously wrong?

There was a surprising amount of conformity. In the control group only 0.7% of the judgements were incorrect. In the experimental groups, 37% of the judgements made by the participants were incorrect. Of the 125 participants in the experimental groups, only 25% gave the correct answer in every

Asch's conformity experiment. The participant is seated second from the right at the table.

case compared with 95% in the control group.

Why did so many participants conform to what was clearly an incorrect judgement? A small minority stated that they actually saw the lines in the same way as the rest of the group. Some participants recognised that they saw things differently from the group but concluded that their own perceptions must be inaccurate. They thought they must be suffering from eye strain or they had been seated in an awkward position from which it was difficult to see the cards. Other participants remained convinced that they were right yet, despite this, they still conformed. According to one such participant, 'Here was a group; they had a definite idea; my idea disagreed; this might arouse anger. I was standing out as a sore thumb. I didn't want particularly to make a fool of myself. I felt I was definitely right but they might think I was peculiar' (Asch, 1955). This quotation is typical of the reasons given by participants who were convinced they were right yet still conformed. It is clearly a case of normative social influence. These participants didn't want to 'rock the boat', 'stand out like a sore thumb' and risk the disapproval of other group members. It was a case of public compliance rather than private acceptance. They knew they were right but went along with the majority and gave the wrong answer. The power of majority influence can be seen from their behaviour. They were tense, they sweated, squirmed, mumbled and giggled – sure signs of the pressure they were under to conform to the majority view.

'Faceless' conformity

The participants in Asch's experiment were presented with a group of people who all gave answers that were clearly incorrect. In a face-to-face situation, the pressure to conform was considerable. Was it the actual presence of others which generated this pressure?

Crutchfield (1955) devised a version of the Asch experiment which did not involve face-to-face communication. Each participant was placed in a separate booth, facing a screen which displayed questions and what they believed were the answers of the other participants. The questions were simple and the correct answers obvious. In around half the cases, the answers displayed on the screen were incorrect. Each participant believed they were the last to answer, after having seen everybody else's answers. In fact, the answers on the screen were placed there by the experimenter – they were not those of the other participants.

Crutchfield's results were similar to those of Asch. For example, on an Asch-type perceptual task the conformity level was 30% – in other words, 30% of the responses conformed to the wrong answer. These participants had clearly been influenced by what they believed to be the answers of their fellow participants. This experiment indicates that pressure to conform can operate without face-to-face communication. Even an awareness of the presence of unknown and unseen others is sufficient to generate this pressure.

Evaluation

Laboratory experiments The findings of Sherif, Asch and Crutchfield are drawn from experiments in laboratories. Laboratory settings and the tasks involved in experiments are a long way from normal, everyday life. After all, how many people sit in a darkened room staring at a light or match lines on cards when the answer is obvious? If participants define the situation as artificial and the tasks as unreal, can the results of experiments be generalised to life outside the laboratory? These are standard criticisms of laboratory experiments in psychology. They refer to the issue of ecological validity – the extent to which research findings can be generalised to other settings. Some researchers argue that if the experiment bears little relationship to the outside world, if the tasks are artificial and 'unreal', then the experiment has low ecological validity. As a result, its findings may be limited to the laboratory; it may not be possible to generalise the results to other settings.

However, the experimental method can be defended. In fact, it can be argued it has certain advantages over normal, everyday social settings. Asch's line-matching experiments illustrate this. Why create an artificial situation in which people – the confederates – behave in such an unreal manner? Why confront participants with complete strangers? The answer is that if participants conform in this setting it will show the power of *pure* group pressure. The confederates' judgements are clearly wrong. They are complete strangers – the participants will never see them again so in this respect their disapproval won't mean that much. The experiment has therefore created a situation to indicate the power of group pressure. Everything else that might encourage conformity has been stripped away. We would be unlikely to find a similar situation to study outside the laboratory.

Time Asch's experiments were conducted in the early 1950s in the USA. Can the results be generalised to other times and other places? The relatively high level of conformity in Asch's research was seen by some as a reflection of American society in the 1950s. This was a time when non-conformity was discouraged. The McCarthy 'witch hunts' – investigations into so-called unAmerican activities – hounded anybody suspected of communist sympathies, accusing them of treason. Thousands lost their jobs and hundreds were imprisoned for failing to conform to the 'American Way'. So-called 'subversives', such as the playwright Arthur Miller, were punished for their non-conformist attitudes by having to face the House of unAmerican Activities to defend their actions.

There is some evidence to suggest that Asch's results may, in part, reflect the society of his day. For example, Nicholson et al. (1985) replicated Asch's experiment (repeated it under the same conditions) and found lower conformity levels. This may be due to changes in American society, but it could also be due to other factors such as differences in the samples. Despite these differences, most social psychologists agree with Elliot Aronson that, 'decades of research indicate that conformity for normative reasons can occur simply because we do not want to risk social disapproval even from complete strangers we will never see again' (Aronson et al., 1997).

Culture Can Asch's findings be generalised to other places, in particular other cultures? Different societies have different cultures. Culture is the learned, shared behaviour of members of a society. It includes norms, values, attitudes and beliefs. To some extent, people from different cultures see the world in different ways. Culture can affect the results of experiments in two main ways. First, people from different cultures may see experiments in different ways. They may give different meanings to the tasks they are asked to perform. They may, therefore, respond differently to the same stimulus. If so, the results of experiments may reflect cultural differences. Second, the

Key terms

Autokinetic effect *An optical illusion in which a stationary spot of light in a darkened environment appears to move.*

Personal norm *A standardised belief or behaviour of a particular person.*

Individualist cultures *Cultures which emphasise the individual – individual freedom and personal responsibility.*

Collectivist cultures *Cultures which emphasise the group – group responsibility and collective effort.*

importance placed on conformity may differ from culture to culture. If so, we need to understand the culture in order to understand the results of experiments.

Asch's experiments have been replicated in 13 countries outside the USA. In the original experiments 37% of the judgements were incorrect. However, in the experiments conducted in other societies the percentage of errors varied considerably – from 14% in Belgium to 51% in Zimbabwe (Smith & Bond, 1993). As with the Asch experiments, the participants in Belgium and Zimbabwe were students, in the case of Zimbabwe, Bantu students. Many reasons have been suggested for these variations, including minor changes in experimental design. However, the main reason put forward to explain these variations is cultural differences.

Social psychologists have made a distinction between *individualist* and *collectivist* cultures. In individualist cultures, a high value is placed on individual freedom, self-help, self-reliance and individual responsibility. By comparison, collectivist cultures place more emphasis on collective responsibility, group cooperation, collective effort and dependence on social groups. As a result, group pressure to conform – majority influence – is greater in collectivist cultures. Results from the Asch experiments conducted in different societies show that the percentage of errors is higher in collectivist cultures. This suggests that the pressure to conform is higher in collectivist cultures (such as the Bantu of Zimbabwe) than in individualist cultures (such as the USA). This indicates that culture is an important variable affecting human behaviour. It must, therefore, be taken into account in order to understand and assess the results of psychological research (Moghaddam et al., 1993; Smith & Bond, 1993).

1.4 Factors affecting conformity

The previous section has indicated a number of factors which affect levels of conformity. These include the ambiguity of the situation as in the Sherif experiments, the unanimity of the group as in the Asch experiments, and the cultural background of the participants. This section briefly reviews some of the other factors that can affect levels of conformity.

Group identification Research has indicated that normative social influence is stronger in groups to which people feel they belong. Within such groups the costs of non-conformity are higher than in groups of strangers. People have more to lose if they offend or upset their family, friends and workmates. To what extent do feelings of belonging to and identifying with groups influence conformity?

Abrams et al. (1990) attempted to answer this question using experiments based on those of Sherif and Asch. The participants were psychology students. They were placed in two groups, one containing people they believed were fellow psychology students, the other containing people they were told were students of ancient history. In Abrams' version of Sherif's autokinetic experiment, the convergence of estimates, which Sherif found in all groups, only occurred in the 'psychology group'. In Abrams' version of Asch's line judgement experiment, the level of conformity in the 'psychology group' was even higher than in the original Asch experiment. However, the level of conformity in the 'ancient history' group was considerably lower.

These experiments added a new dimension to studies of conformity. It appears that social influence to conform is stronger when people identify with a group. In this case the participants saw the 'psychology group' as people like themselves, as peers. As a result, they expected to share their attitudes and beliefs, they expected to agree with them and wanted to fit in with them. Approval from those they saw as their peers meant more to them than approval from the 'ancient history' group. There is less pressure to conform when people are seen as different from ourselves.

Group size Experiments have indicated that group size has an important effect on conformity. Asch (1951) found that in a one-to-one situation – one participant and one confederate – the confederate's incorrect answers make little difference. After all, it is only one person's judgement against another. However, if there are two confederates, the participant's error rate, and therefore conformity, rises to 13%. With three confederates, conformity rises still further to 33%. Asch found that conformity does not rise much beyond this level, no matter how big the group gets. The results from one of his experiments are shown in Figure 3.

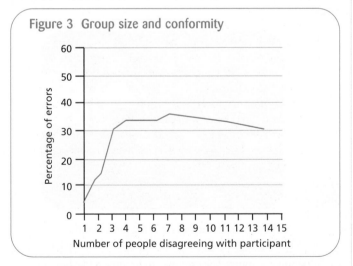

Figure 3 Group size and conformity

y-axis: Percentage of errors
x-axis: Number of people disagreeing with participant

Social support In another version of his conformity experiment, Asch (1955) gave the participants a 'supporter' or 'ally'. This confederate gave the correct answer in every case, while other confederates continued to give wrong answers. No longer was the participant alone; social support had been provided. In this situation, the conformity rate reduced dramatically to an average of 5.5%. A number of other studies have produced similar results. It appears that having someone to 'back us up' gives people the confidence to resist normative social influence.

Personality Research has indicated that there are wide differences in conformity between individuals. This has led

some researchers to argue that this reflects differences in personality. They claim that some people have personality characteristics which predispose them to conform. For example, Asch (1956) suggested that people with low self-esteem – a low opinion of themselves – tend to conform because they are more likely to fear disapproval and rejection from the group. Research has indicated that the following characteristics are associated with conformity: low self-esteem, a high need for social approval, feelings of inferiority and insecurity, high levels of anxiety and low IQ (Hogg & Vaughan, 1995).

However, the relationship between personality and conformity is not as clear-cut as this research suggests. Some studies have found little or no relationship between them. One of the main findings is that there is little consistency in people's behaviour. In one situation they conform, in another situation they don't. If their personality was the main factor affecting their behaviour, then this inconsistency would be unlikely. It appears that the social situation is more important in accounting for conformity than differences in personality (Aronson et al., 1997).

Gender For many years it was assumed that women were more conforming than men. Research indicated that though gender differences in conformity were small, they did exist. The methodology of these studies, and therefore their findings, have been criticised. Eagly and Carli (1981) found that male researchers were more likely to find higher levels of conformity in women than female researchers. This may, in part, be due to male researchers using tasks in their experiments which were more familiar to male participants.

Support for this view comes from a conformity experiment conducted by Sistrunk and McDavid (1971). Male and female participants were asked to identify various things while being subjected to group pressure to give the wrong answer – and so conform. Some participants were given traditionally male items (eg, a wrench), others were given traditionally female items (eg, different types of needlework), while others were given 'neutral' items (eg, identifying rock stars). Conformity for women was highest on male items, conformity for men was highest on female items, and for 'neutral' items, conformity levels were similar for both sexes – see Figure 4.

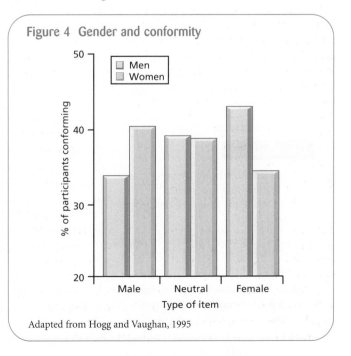

Figure 4 Gender and conformity

Legend: Men, Women
y-axis: % of participants conforming
x-axis: Type of item (Male, Neutral, Female)

Adapted from Hogg and Vaughan, 1995

This study indicates that there are no significant differences in conformity behaviour between women and men. It also suggests that gender differences revealed by other studies may be due to the nature of the experiments rather than any real differences between men and women.

1.5   Conformity and social roles

This unit began with an introduction to social norms, one of the major organising principles of human society. It closes with an introduction to social roles. Like norms, roles guide and direct human behaviour.

Activity 3   Factors affecting conformity

Item A   Culture and conformity

Inuit hunter

According to J.W. Berry (1967) societies whose economy is based on hunting and fishing will have different values than those based on agriculture. The successful hunter needs to be adventurous, assertive and independent. By comparison, the successful farmer needs to cooperate with others and recognise his or her dependence on the social group. This can be seen during planting and harvest seasons. In view of these differences, we should expect farming societies to place a higher value on conformity than hunting societies.

Berry tested this proposition by comparing a hunting and fishing society, the Inuit (Eskimos) of Baffin Island in Canada, with a farming society, the Temne of Sierra Leone in West Africa. Participants from each society were given an Asch-type conformity task. As predicted, the Temne had a significantly higher conformity rate than the Inuit. In the words of one Temne, 'When the Temne people choose a thing, we must all agree with the decision – this is what we call cooperation'. By comparison, the Inuit usually disregarded the incorrect answers of the group. When they did conform, and agreed to the incorrect answer, they did so with 'a quiet, knowing smile'.

Adapted from Berry, 1967

Item B   Where do I belong?

I was born and raised in England. I was a student at the University of Minnesota in the USA for four years. During that time, I got to know about twenty students from England at the university. Around half of them decided to stay in America. It was noticeable that these students developed American accents. Those students, like myself, who returned home retained their English accents.

Story told to author, 15.10.1997

Questions

1 Read Item A. Why do we need to take culture into account when interpreting the results of conformity experiments?

2 Use the idea of group identification to explain the behaviour of the two groups of students in Item B.

3 Read Item C. Suggest reasons for the high level of conformity in Latino gangs.

Item C   Latino gangs

Los Angeles has 570 Latino gangs. They are split into two groups. The Chicanos, Mexican-Americans born in the US, who often don't speak any Spanish. Their rivals are those Latino gangs whose members are recent immigrants from Mexico and other Spanish speaking countries and who have evolved a language of their own called *calo*. Older members

(*veteranos*) are held in great respect by their 'home boys', having defended the honour of the *barrio* (territory) for over a decade or more of fierce urban warfare.

Each gang has its own initiation ceremony. For example, to become a Playboy, a prospective member has to get 'jumped in' – beaten up – by a minimum of three gang members and has only limited means to defend him or herself. While the beating takes place, others look on and count up to 13 slowly. Once initiated, members take on nicknames and adopt the dress codes of their comrades.

Hand signals and tattoos are important signifiers of gang loyalties. Tattoos are usually done by *carnals* (fellow gang members) often using home-made instruments. They cannot be removed by the authorities and are thus a symbol of defiance.

Adapted from *The Observer*, 6.2.1994

In the words of William Shakespeare:

> All the world's a stage,
> And all the men and women merely players:
> They have their exits, and their entrances;
> And one man in his time plays many parts.
> (*As You Like It*, Act 2, Scene 7)

These lines capture the essence of social roles. They are parts people play as members of social groups. Think of the roles you play in a single day. Before leaving home you may perform the role of son or daughter, brother or sister, husband or wife. At school or college you are a student in class, a friend at breaktime, and maybe a team member if you play a sport. On the way home you may be a customer in a shop and in the evening you probably return to your roles as a family member or a friend.

Attached to each role is a 'script' which states how the role should be played. For example, solicitors are expected to have a detailed knowledge of certain aspects of the law, to support their clients' interests and respect the confidentiality of their business. Solicitors' attire is expected to be sober, their manner restrained and their standing in the community beyond reproach.

Roles are social. They involve social relationships in the sense that an individual plays a role in relation to other roles. Thus the role of doctor is played in relation to the role of patient, the role of husband in relation to the role of wife.

Roles organise and regulate social life. They provide guidelines for action and give social life order and predictability. Interacting in terms of their respective roles, teacher and student, for example, know what to expect, what to do and how to do it.

With each social role you adopt, your behaviour changes to fit the expectations both you and others have of that role. If these expectations are not met, you may fail in your role. Imagine your teacher arriving in a bathing costume, playing a guitar and singing the psychology lecture to the class. This may well disrupt the lesson and students may have difficulty knowing how to respond.

There is considerable pressure to conform to social roles. Consider the so-called 'breaching experiments' conducted by the American sociologist Harold Garfinkel (1967). He asked his students to go into familiar situations and behave in unexpected ways, in other words, to dispense with normal role play. Some went into department stores and haggled over the price of goods, others went home to their families and behaved as if they were lodgers. The students had stepped out of their roles. They were not playing the parts of customers, sons, or daughters, as they should. The response to their actions was confusion, incomprehension, and even anger and hostility.

Social roles provide an example of social influence in general and conformity in particular. Most of us, most of the time, conform to the guidelines provided by the roles we perform. We conform to the expectations of others, we respond to their approval when we play our roles well, and to their disapproval when we play our roles badly. But how far will this conformity go? Would you follow your role to the letter even if this conflicted with deeply held beliefs? Could you lose yourself so completely in your role that your behaviour was totally out of character? These are some of the questions examined in the following section.

The Stanford Prison experiment

Philip Zimbardo and his colleagues (Haney, Banks & Zimbardo, 1973) recruited students from Stanford University in California, to play the roles of prisoners and guards in a mock prison. On the basis of interviews, psychological tests and physical examinations, those chosen to participate were judged to be mentally and physically healthy.

With the cooperation of the local police department, the 'prisoners' were arrested and handcuffed at their homes, taken to a police station and placed in a detention cell. They were then blindfolded and taken to the 'prison' in the basement of the psychology department at the university. There, they were locked in their cells 24 hours a day, while the 'guards' were rotated on 8 hour shifts.

On arrival, the prisoners were stripped, sprayed with a delousing solution (a deodorant spray) and forced to stand naked in the prison yard. They were then dressed in a loose-fitting smock stamped with an ID number, rubber sandals, a cap made from a nylon stocking and a lock chain attached to one ankle. From then on they were referred to only by number, not by name, and in reply to the guards, they had to say 'Mr Correctional Officer, Sir'. The guards were supplied with khaki shirts and trousers, reflecting sunglasses, whistles, police nightsticks and handcuffs.

The guards appeared to relish their new roles, performing them with vigour and authority. Any misbehaviour from the prisoners resulted in loss of privileges such as reading books or writing letters. But, as time went on, the guards became increasingly brutal and ground the prisoners down. At the first hint of protest or rebellion, loss of privileges now became loss of food, sleep, blankets and washing facilities. The guards kept inventing new forms of punishment such as solitary confinement (in a cupboard) and cleaning toilets with bare hands. Prisoners were routinely woken in the middle of the night and marched out to the cell yard to be counted. The guards verbally abused the prisoners, taunting and humiliating them.

For most of the time, the prisoners obeyed. Most shuffled round their cells, helpless and apathetic. Although one began a hunger strike, the rest did exactly as they were told. But the strain was telling. On the third day, one prisoner was released from the experiment because of 'acute emotional disturbance'. Another was released after developing a psychosomatic rash over most of his body. The experiment had been designed to last for two weeks; the researchers decided to end it after six days.

The participants had assumed their roles rapidly. As the days went by, they developed their roles. A 'good' guard was tough, aggressive and arrogant. Even the less aggressive guards publicly conformed to this role model.

As for the prisoners, their role was soon established. They stuck to the rules so that the guards would have no reason to punish them. They even sided with the guards against the prisoner on hunger strike. Rather than becoming a hero, he was simply a nuisance who drew attention to the prisoners and caused trouble. The other prisoners rejected him.

Evaluation According to the researchers, the Stanford Prison experiment shows the power and potency of social influence. In many respects the participants became the roles they were playing. Normal, well-adjusted university students became either brutal overseers or pathetic subordinates. Clearly their

A guard and prisoners in the Stanford prison

roles had a powerful influence on their behaviour. Or did they?

For a start, the prison, built in the basement of the psychology department of Stanford University, was hardly realistic. The participants were given little indication of how to behave. For example, the guards were told simply to 'maintain the reasonable degree of order within the prison necessary for its effective functioning'. In a real prison, new guards and prisoners are subject to detailed rules, and are trained and guided by more experienced officers and 'old lags'. Critics have argued that without such rules and guidance, Zimbardo's experiment is unlikely to tell us much about how people really behave in prisons.

Moreover, the experiment was just that, an experiment. The prison was a mock prison, the participants were in 'fancy dress' acting out parts they had been told to play. They had probably seen movies like *Cool Hand Luke* (1967), which portrays stereotypes of brutal prison guards, with the most vicious guards wearing reflecting sunglasses. This suggests that when Zimbardo issued the guards with similar sunglasses (which are very impractical indoors!), he was providing them with a cue to 'play' the guards in films like *Cool Hand Luke*. Were the participants then simply behaving like actors in a movie? Most of the guards in the experiment later claimed this was exactly what they were doing. Critics have argued that the Stanford Prison experiment shows little more than play-acting on a film set, and tells us virtually nothing about the effect of roles on people's behaviour in real life.

The following points can be made to counter this criticism. First, if the prisoners were simply play-acting, why did they show symptoms of stress, symptoms that were so severe that the experiment had to be stopped after only six days. Second, why did the guards' aggression towards the prisoners steadily

intensify? Doesn't this indicate that the guards became increasingly involved in their roles, that they were identifying with their roles?

From this point of view, the experiment shows how readily people adopt social roles and conform to them. It shows the power of social influence.

The Stanford Prison experiment has also been criticised on ethical grounds. This criticism is examined on pp 198-200.

Key term

Social roles *The parts people play as members of a society, for example mother, son, teacher, student. Each role has a 'script' which states how the role should be performed.*

Summary

1. Informational social influence encourages conformity when people are unsure of the correct response. It is based on the desire to be right. It can lead to private acceptance – conforming to the norms of others because they are seen to be right.

2. Normative social influence encourages conformity because people seek the approval of others. It is based on the desire to be liked and accepted. It can lead to public compliance – conforming to group norms in public – but it does not necessarily lead to private acceptance.

3. Sherif's experiment, based on the autokinetic effect, indicates that the presence of others leads to the formation of group norms and conformity to those norms. It is an example of informational social influence.

4. Asch's line-matching experiments show that people are sometimes prepared to deny what they know to be true in order to gain the approval of the group. This is an example of normative social influence.

5. A number of factors influence levels of conformity. They include culture, whether or not people identify with the group, the size of the group and the level of social support for nonconformity.

6. According to Zimbardo et al., the Stanford Prison experiment shows how readily people conform to social roles.

Unit 2 Minority influence

KEY ISSUES

1 What is minority influence?

2 What factors affect minority influence?

3 How have psychologists seen conformity – as a 'good' or a 'bad' thing?

Unit 1 has been primarily concerned with majority influence – the pressures on the minority to conform to the views and behaviour of the majority. This unit looks at the possibility of reversing the direction of social influence – the minority influencing the majority. This is known as *minority influence* or *innovation*. Minority influence occurs when a minority 'rejects the established norm of the majority of group members and induces the majority to move to the position of the minority' (Turner, 1991).

2.1   Consistency

The French social psychologist Serge Moscovici argued that minorities are most likely to influence majorities if they are consistent in their views. They must be consistent over time, in other words, they must not change their views. And, they must be consistent among themselves, that is they must all hold the same views.

Moscovici designed a series of experiments to examine minority influence. One of these experiments will now be described (Moscovici et al., 1969).

The participants were first given eye tests to ensure they were not colour-blind. They were then placed in a group consisting of four participants and two confederates. They were shown 36 slides which were clearly different shades of blue and asked to state the colour of each slide out loud. In the first part of the experiment the two confederates answered green for each of the slides. They were totally consistent in their responses. In the second part of the experiment they answered green 24 times

and blue 12 times. In this case they were inconsistent in their answers. Would the responses of the two confederates influence those of the four participants? In other words, would there be minority influence?

Here are the results. First, those of a control group. A control group is used for comparison with an experimental group. The factors expected to influence the experimental group's behaviour are removed. So, in this case, the control group did not include confederates. Only 0.25% of the control group's answers were green, the rest were blue. For the experimental group, 1.25% of the participants' answers were green when the confederates gave inconsistent answers (ie, 24 green, 12 blue). This rose to 8.42% green when the confederates answers were consistent (ie, 36 green). These results are shown in Figure 5.

Moscovici's experiment suggests that minorities can influence majorities. However, it indicates that this influence is much more effective when the minority are consistent in their responses. When the minority gave inconsistent answers, they were largely ignored by the majority. Later research has largely confirmed these findings.

Moscovici (1985) sees consistency as the key to minority influence for the following reasons.

- The minority speaks with a single voice. There are no ifs, buts and maybes; no contradictions. Consistency leaves the majority in no doubt about the alternative views being expressed.
- This gives the impression that the minority are convinced they are right and are committed to their viewpoint.
- As a result, the minority appear confident and assured. This can lead to the majority taking the minority view seriously. The majority will therefore be more likely to question their own views.
- A consistent minority disrupts established norms and creates uncertainty, doubt and conflict.
- One way to resolve this conflict and to remove the uncertainty is for the majority to accept the minority view.

Moscovici argues that majority influence tends to be based on public compliance. It is likely to be a case of normative social influence. In this respect, power of numbers is important – the majority have the power to reward and punish with approval and disapproval. And because of this, there is pressure on minorities to conform. Since majorities are often unconcerned about what minorities think about them, minority influence is rarely based on normative social influence. Instead, it is usually based on informational social influence – providing the majority with new ideas, new information which leads them to re-examine their views. In this respect, minority influence involves private acceptance – converting the majority by convincing them that the minority's views are right.

Flexibility and compromise A number of researchers have questioned whether consistency alone is sufficient for a minority to influence a majority. They argue that the key is how consistency is interpreted by the majority. If the consistent minority are seen as inflexible, rigid, uncompromising and dogmatic, they will be unlikely to change the views of the

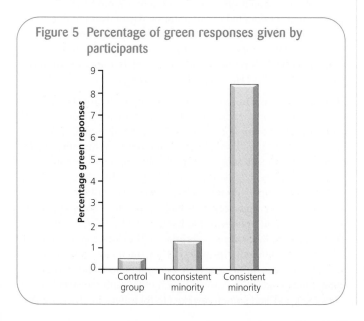

Figure 5   Percentage of green responses given by participants

(y-axis: Percentage green reponses, 0 to 9; x-axis: Control group, Inconsistent minority, Consistent minority) majority. However, if they appear flexible and compromising, they are likely to be seen as less extreme, as more moderate, cooperative and reasonable. As a result, they will have a better chance of changing majority views (Mugny & Papastamou, 1980).

Some researchers have gone further and suggested that it is not just the *appearance* of flexibility and compromise which is important but *actual* flexibility and compromise. This possibility was investigated by Nemeth and Brilmayer (1987). Their experiment was based on a mock jury in which groups of three participants and one confederate had to decide on the amount of compensation to be given to the victim of a ski-lift accident. When the consistent minority (the confederate) argued for a very low amount and refused to change his position, he had no effect on the majority. However, when he compromised and moved some way towards the majority position, the majority also compromised and changed their view. This experiment questions the importance of consistency. The minority position changed, it was not consistent, and it was this change that apparently resulted in minority influence.

Key term

Minority influence *When a minority changes the beliefs and/or behaviour of a majority.*

2.2 Other factors affecting minority influence

Group identification

People tend to identify with people they see as similar to themselves. For example, men tend to identify with men, African Caribbeans with African Caribbeans, psychology students with psychology students, and so on. Research indicates that if the majority identify with the minority, then they are more likely to take the views of the minority seriously and change their own views in line with those of the minority. For example, one study showed that a gay minority arguing for gay rights had less influence on a straight majority than a straight minority arguing for gay rights (Maass et al., 1982). The non-gay majority identified with the non-gay minority. They tended to see the gay minority as different from themselves, as self-interested and concerned with promoting their own particular cause.

Zeitgeist

Zeitgeist is a German word meaning 'spirit of the times' or 'mood of the times'. Zeitgeist refers to the prevailing attitudes and values in society at a particular time. Research indicates that if the minority viewpoint is in line with the prevailing zeitgeist, then the majority will be more likely to accept it. For example, in Western societies today, the zeitgeist is more likely to support equality for women than it was fifty years ago. One study conducted in the 1970s indicated that minorities were more likely to influence majorities if they argued in favour of women's rights rather than against them (Paicheler, 1976).

The problem with this argument is that, in one sense, the minority is not really a minority because their views are in line with the current zeitgeist, with the attitudes and values of the majority in society. The argument doesn't tell us how the zeitgeist changed in the first place. For example, how did views

supporting equality for women – once a minority view – become accepted by the majority in society?

Social cryptoamnesia One answer to this question is provided by the idea of *social cryptoamnesia* – a kind of social forgetting (Perez et al., 1995). Minority ideas are often rejected because people find it difficult to identify with those who put them forward. Women's rights provides an example. Many men *and* women found it difficult to identify with the suffragettes in the early 20th century and the feminists of the mid-20th century. Social cryptoamnesia states that people tend to forget those who put forward the new ideas but remember the ideas themselves. This allows them to take on minority ideas without identifying with the minority. For example, equal rights for women ceases to be associated with 'crazy' suffragettes or 'pushy', 'strident' feminists. Equality for women now makes sense and appears reasonable. Minority influence is therefore indirect and delayed. It becomes detached and removed from the minority who first promoted it and takes effect some time after it first appeared. In this way the idea of social cryptoamnesia provides an explanation for how the zeitgeist changes (Perez et al., 1995).

Argument refutation and desertion

An interesting experiment conducted by Russell D. Clark III (1990) indicates two possible factors that can increase minority influence. First, if the minority can refute the majority's arguments, that is, show them to be incorrect. Second, if one or more members of the majority desert the majority and support the minority position.

Clark based his experiment on the play *Twelve Angry Men* in which a son is accused of murdering his father and a jury discusses the trial and reaches a verdict. Clark's findings indicated that the more of the majority's arguments that the minority could refute, the more influence they had. It also showed that desertion by majority members to the minority increased minority influence. The minority was most effective when these factors were combined – refuting majority arguments and desertion by majority members.

2.3 Evaluation

Most of the research on minority influence is based on experiments conducted in laboratories. This raises the question of ecological validity. Is it possible to generalise from the findings of laboratory research to other settings? Edward Sampson (1991) is particularly critical of laboratory research on minority influence. He makes the following points.

Real groups The participants in laboratory experiments are rarely 'real groups'. More often than not they are a collection of students who do not know each other and will probably never meet again. As such they are very different from minority groups in the wider society who seek to change majority opinion. For example, members of women's rights, gay rights and animal rights organisations, people in black power and black consciousness groups, and members of pressure groups such as Greenpeace and Friends of the Earth are very different from participants in laboratory experiments. They operate in different settings with different constraints. They often face much more determined opposition. They are committed to a cause, they often know each other, provide each other with considerable social support and sometimes devote their lives to changing the views of the majority.

Power and status Laboratory experiments are largely unable to represent and simulate the wide differences in power and status that often separate minorities and majorities. As Sampson (1991) notes, history is littered with examples of how majorities can crush minorities who attempt to express divergent views. Student pro-democracy demonstrators in Tiananmen Square in Beijing were powerless in the face of government forces. In 1989 they were brutally swept aside by troops and tanks and many were later executed (see p188).

A lack of power is often linked to a lack of social status. Ethnic minorities, women, gays, the poor and the underprivileged tend to have low status in society. As a result, their views are often ignored.

Protest Minorities do influence majorities. Western societies now have laws protecting the rights of groups such as ethnic minorities, gays, women and the disabled. But minority influence does not triumph simply because of the consistency of their arguments or their willingness to be flexible or to compromise. Often it results from massive protests such as the civil rights demonstrations by African Americans in the 1950s and 60s and the uprisings in Eastern Europe which overthrew the communist regimes in 1989.

Conclusion Edward Sampson does not suggest we ignore the laboratory findings on minority influence – they provide important insights. But neither should we ignore 'the harsh realities of life'. In his words, 'we need to see the broader social contexts in which minorities are able to wield influence and the conditions under which they are ruthlessly put down or even benignly pacified' (Sampson, 1991).

Key terms

Zeitgeist *The spirit of the times. The prevailing attitudes and values in society at a particular time.*

Social cryptoamnesia *A tendency to forget the people who put forward new ideas but to remember the ideas themselves. Minority ideas become part of the ideas of the majority, but the majority forget where they came from.*

2.4   Conformity – the case for and against

Most of the research on conformity has been North American and has focused on the way majority pressure can control and distort the judgement of the individual. American researchers have tended to see conformity in a negative light, as a threat to individual liberty. This view has been seen as a reflection of American culture which emphasises (at least after the McCarthy era of the early 1950s) individual freedom and self-reliance (Moghaddam et al., 1993; Smith & Bond, 1993). Starting from the assumption that independence is good and conformity is bad can influence both research design and the way that the results of research are interpreted.

It can be argued that conformity studies are often designed to highlight the dangers of conformity. The Stanford Prison experiment can be seen in this light. Looking back on the experiment, Zimbardo et al. (1995) see it as a valuable warning to us all. However, it would have been equally possible to set up an experiment to show the positive effects of conformity, eg to

ask participants to play caring roles in a hospital situation. Asch's line-matching experiment is presented in hundreds of psychology textbooks as an example of majority influence. Yet only 37% of the judgements made by the participants were incorrect. In other words, in 63% of their judgements they were not swayed by the influence of the majority. This emphasis can be interpreted as a reflection of the values Americans place on individuality and independence. By focusing on the minority of incorrect judgements, they portray the Asch experiment as a warning of the threat of majority influence to individual freedom.

This preoccupation with majority influence may help to explain why it was European psychologists, particularly the Frenchman Moscovici, who developed the study of minority influence. It has been argued that conformity is viewed in a more positive light in Europe where it is more likely to be seen as the outcome of negotiation rather than the imposition of majority views.

Whether conformity is seen as a good or a bad thing depends in part on culture. Different cultures view conformity in different ways. In non-Western societies, particularly traditional, small-scale societies, researchers have noted a greater emphasis on group solidarity and a more positive view of conformity. For example, the traditional culture of Australian aborigines states that problems should be solved by groups rather than individuals and decisions should be unanimous. When approached by psychologists to take IQ tests, aborigines were reluctant to take the tests as individuals and found it difficult to understand the request to do so (Haralambos & Holborn, 2000).

The above paragraphs raise a number of important points. First, we should guard against ethnocentrism, ie seeing things solely from the point of view of our own culture and assuming that view is correct. There are different ways of seeing conformity and we should not assume that our view is the only one and that everybody shares it. Second, everybody – psychologists included – sees the world through the lens of their own culture. Thus, to some degree, psychologists' views of conformity will reflect their cultural backgrounds. This will influence the research they conduct and their interpretation of the results.

In general, it makes little sense to talk about conformity as 'good' or 'bad'. Such judgements depend in a large part on the circumstances. All societies require a certain level of conformity in order to function. Imagine a situation where social norms were constantly violated – people refusing to pay for groceries at the supermarket or to stop at a red light, or ignoring greetings from friends. The result would be confusion, disorder, even chaos. As Zimbardo and Leippe (1991) put it, conformity 'lubricates the wheels of social interaction'. On the other hand, conformity can be seen as harmful, producing 'blind' obedience and herd-like behaviour.

Similarly, non conformity can be seen as 'good ' or 'bad' depending on the situation. A certain level of nonconformity can be seen as beneficial to society. If conformity were total, society would stagnate – there would be no change, no improvement, no new ideas, no creativity. There would be no inventions which 'break the rules', there would be no advances in science or in society. In the words of Moghaddam et al., 'Almost all great intellectual and social movements began as minority movements. Think, for example, of the opposition faced by Galileo and other scientists who argued that the earth is not the centre of the universe, and of the ridicule and resentment confronting the suffragettes in their struggle for women's rights'. Nonconformity has also been seen as positive in order to resist behaviour which is cruel or evil, as, for example, opposing dictatorships such as Hitler's in Germany.

But nonconformity can also have its downside. Breaking social norms can be obstructive and even dangerous. For example, disobeying the Highway Code can endanger life and limb. Nonconformity is not necessarily a sign of independent-mindedness or creative thinking. It can be a result of personal inadequacy, obstinacy or sheer bloody-mindedness.

Summary

1. Minority influence occurs when a minority rejects the norms of the majority and the majority accepts the position of the minority.

2. According to Moscovici, consistency is the key to minority influence – consistency of views within the minority and over time. Minority influence is usually based on informational social influence and on private acceptance.

3. Later research indicates that minority influence will be more effective if the minority appear flexible and ready to compromise.

4. Majorities are more ready to accept the minority view if they can identify with the minority.

5. Minority views are more likely to be accepted if they are in line with the prevailing zeitgeist in society.

6. The zeitgeist may be changed by social cryptoamnesia – the majority accepts minority views but forgets where they came from.

7. Minority influence is more likely to be effective if majority ideas can be refuted and if majority members desert to the minority.

8. Much of the research on conformity has been based on the assumption that conformity is a bad thing. This can influence both research design and how the results of the research are interpreted.

9. Without a certain degree of conformity, it is difficult to see how social life could operate. However, without minority influence, there would be no social change and society would stagnate.

Activity 4   Minority influence

Item A   Trial by jury

In October 1997, a jury in Boston, Massachusetts found 19-year-old English nanny Louise Woodward guilty of the murder of the baby she was caring for. The nine women and three men considered the evidence for three days. Immediately after the trial, when asked for their first impressions, the jury were split evenly down the middle. Next morning, four members thought Louise was guilty, four thought she was innocent and the others were unsure. By day three, it was ten guilty, two innocent until finally all agreed to a guilty verdict.

According to Tracey Mannix, aged 24, the youngest member of the jury, four jurors were convinced of Louise's guilt from the start. They didn't waver in their conviction and refused to give an inch. They wore down the other members and forced a guilty verdict through. Tracey said 'I held out as long as I could. It was the toughest decision of my life. I just believed, given the evidence, she did not kill that baby.'

Adapted from *The Mirror*, 3.11.1997

COUNTDOWN TO JURY'S GUILTY VERDICT

1 Six guilty...six innocent

SPLIT: Minutes after the case ends the jurors are evenly divided.

2 Four guilty...four innocent... four don't know

SHIFTING: The vote next morning shows the doubts setting in.

3 Ten guilty...two innocent

PRESSURE: By Day 3, just Tracey and one other juror hold out.

4 Twelve guilty

VERDICT: They agree to say they are all certain Louise is guilty.

Item B   The White House cat

US President Calvin Coolidge shocked the fashionable guests at the White House breakfast by pouring his heavily creamed coffee into a saucer. Taken aback but unfailingly polite, Coolidge's guests did the same. They waited wide-eyed for the President to take the first sip. At which point Coolidge picked up the saucer, leaned over, and presented it to the White House cat.

Item C   Protest and demonstration

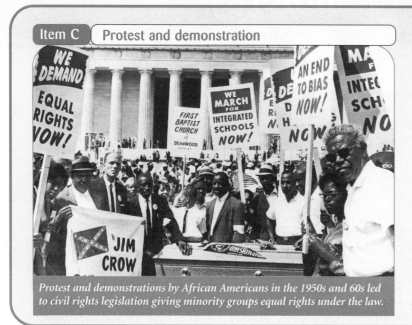

Protest and demonstrations by African Americans in the 1950s and 60s led to civil rights legislation giving minority groups equal rights under the law.

Questions

1. Explain the behaviour of the jury in Item A.

2. Explain the behaviour of the guests in Item B.

3. What support does Item C provide for Sampson's (1991) statement that 'we need to see the broader social contexts in which minorities are able to wield influence'?

References

Abrams, D., Wetherell, M., Cochrane, S., Hogg, M.A. & Turner, J.C. (1990). Knowing what to think by knowing who you are: Self-categorisation and the nature of norm formation, conformity and group polarisation. *British Journal of Social Psychology, 29* (part 2), 97-119.

Aronson, E., Wilson, T.D. & Akert, R.M. (1997). *Social psychology* (2nd ed.). New York: Addison Wesley Longman.

Asch, S.E. (1951). Effects of group pressure on the modification and distortion of judgements. In H. Guetzkow (Ed.), *Groups, leadership and men.* Pittsburgh: Carnegie

Asch, S.E. (1955). Opinions and social pressure. *Scientific American, 193,* 31-35.

Asch, S.E. (1956). Studies of independence and conformity: A minority of one against a unanimous majority. *Psychological Monographs, 70* (9, Whole No. 416).

Berry, J.W. (1967). Independence and conformity in subsistence-level societies. *Journal of Personality and Social Psychology, 7,* 415-418.

Cantril, H. (1940). *The invasion from Mars: A study in the psychology of panic.* New York: Harper & Row.

Clark, R.D., III. (1990). Minority influence: The role of argument refutation of the majority position and social support for the minority position. *European Journal of Social Psychology, 20,* 487-497.

Crutchfield, R.A. (1955). Conformity and character. *American Psychologist, 10,* 191-198.

Deutsch, M. & Gerard, H.B. (1955). A study of normative and informational social influences upon individual judgement. *Journal of Abnormal and Social Psychology, 51,* 629-636.

Eagly, A.H. & Carli, L.L. (1981). Sex of researchers and sex-typed communications as determinants of sex differences in influenceability: A meta-analysis of social influence studies. *Psychological Bulletin, 90,* 1-20.

Garfinkil, H. (1967). *Studies in ethnomethodology.* Englewood Cliffs, NJ: Prentice Hall.

Haney, C., Banks, C. & Zimbardo, P.G. (1973). Interpersonal dynamics in a simulated prison. *International Journal of Criminology and Penology, 1,* 69-97.

Haralambos, M. & Holborn, M. (2000). *Sociology: Themes and perspectives* (5th ed.). London: Collins Educational.

Hogg, M.A. & Vaughan, G.M. (1995). *Social psychology: An introduction.* Hemel Hempstead: Prentice Hall/Harvester Wheatsheaf.

Jacobs, K.C. & Campbell, D.T. (1961). The perpetuation of an arbitrary tradition through several generations of a laboratory microculture. *Journal of Abnormal and Social Psychology, 62,* 649-658.

Maass, A., Clark, R.D., III & Haberkorn, G. (1982). The effects of differential ascribed category membership and norms on minority influence. *European Journal of Social Psychology, 12,* 89-104.

Moghaddam, F.M., Taylor, D.M. & Wright, S.C. (1993). *Social psychology in cross-cultural perspective.* New York: W.H. Freeman.

Moscovici, S. (1985). Social influence and conformity. In G. Lindzey & E. Aronson (Eds.), *Handbook of social psychology* (3rd ed., vol. 2). New York: Random House.

Moscovici, S., Lage, E. & Naffrechoux, M. (1969). Influence of a consistent minority on the responses of a majority in a colour perception task. *Sociometry, 32,* 365-380.

Mugny, G. & Papastamou, S. (1980). When rigidity does not fail: Individualisation and psychologisation as resistances to the diffusion of minority innovations. *European Journal of Social Psychology, 10,* 43-62.

Nemeth, G.J. & Brilmayer, A.G. (1987). Negotiation versus influence. *European Journal of Social Psychology, 17,* 45-56.

Nicholson, M., Cole, S.G. & Rocklin, T. (1985). Conformity in the Asch situation: A comparison between contemporary British and US university students. *British Journal of Social Psychology, 24,* 59-63.

Paicheler, G. (1976). Norms and attitude change: 1. Polarisation and styles of behaviour. *European Journal of Social Psychology, 6,* 405-427.

Perez, J.A., Papastamou, S. & Mugny, G. (1995). 'Zeitgeist' and minority influence – where is the causality: A comment on Clark (1990). *European Journal of Social Psychology, 25,* 703-710.

Sampson, E.E. (1991). *Social worlds, personal lives: An introduction to social psychology.* New York: Harcourt Brace Jovanovich.

Sherif, M. (1935). A study of some social factors in perception. *Archives of Psychology, 27,* no. 187.

Sistrunk, F. & McDavid, J.W. (1971). Sex variable in conforming behaviour. *Journal of Personality and Social Psychology, 17,* 200-207.

Smith, P.B. & Bond, M.H. (1993). *Social psychology across cultures: Analysis and perspectives.* Hemel Hempstead: Harvester Wheatsheaf.

Turner, J.C. (1991). *Social influence.* Buckingham: Open University Press.

van Avermaet, E. (1996). Social influence in small groups. In M. Hewstone, W. Stroebe & G.M. Stephenson (Eds.), *Introduction to social psychology* (2nd ed.). Oxford: Blackwell.

Zimbardo, P.G. & Leippe, M. (1991). *The psychology of attitude change and social influence.* New York: McGraw-Hill.

Zimbardo, P.G., McDermott, M., Jansz, J. & Metaal, M. (1995). *Psychology: A European text.* London: Harper Collins.

▶ **Introduction**

It's your first day at university, you're excited, apprehensive and not sure what to do. You go to your first psychology lecture. The lecturer begins by telling you the rules. He assigns seats in the lecture theatre and you go where you're told. You must not talk in lectures, you require permission to leave early and you must bring your textbook to every lecture. So far, so good, apart from the weight of the textbook.

Then the lecturer's demands become less reasonable. 'You must use a pencil to take notes. Take your watch off. Keep both hands on the desktop at all times.' Finally, you are told, 'Stick two fingers up your nose and quack like a duck'.

This is a demonstration sometimes used by psychology lecturers in the USA (Halonen, 1986). Would you obey the lecturer and end up quacking with two fingers up your nose? You'd probably be surprised how many students do just that.

This is a rather silly example but it illustrates one of the main issues examined in this chapter. How far would people go if ordered to do something by those in authority? Would they obey orders which they thought immoral? For example, would they torture and kill defenceless men, women and children? Would they take their own lives if ordered to do so? Under certain circumstances people have done all these things.

This chapter looks at obedience, a major form of social influence.

Chapter summary

- Unit 1 considers the view that certain people are prone to obedience because of their personality type.
- Unit 2 outlines and assesses experimental studies of obedience.
- Unit 3 examines resistance to authority – why some people refuse to obey those who have the right to give orders.

Unit 1 Obeying others

KEY ISSUES

1 **What is obedience?**
2 **Can obedience be seen as a problem?**
3 **Is there an 'obedient personality'?**

Stanley Milgram, one of the leading researchers into the psychology of obedience, notes that conformity and obedience have an important factor in common. Both involve changes in a person's behaviour due to social pressure. Both are forms of social influence. However, they differ from one another in important ways.

- Obedience involves a direct requirement to change behaviour in response to authority whereas conformity is a change in behaviour in response to group norms.
- Obedience involves people of different social status – those in authority and those subject to authority. Conformity usually occurs in groups whose members have a similar social status, for example peer groups.
- Obedience results from the direct exercise of power – those in charge usually have the power to ensure that their directives are followed. Conformity occurs primarily from a desire for acceptance within the group.

Milgram illustrates the difference between obedience and conformity with the experience of a new recruit in the army. 'He scrupulously carries out the orders of his superiors. At the same time he adopts the habits, routines and language of his peers. The former represents obedience and the latter conformity.' Thus a person *obeys* when they 'comply with authority', they *conform* when they 'go along with their peers who have no special right to direct their behaviour' (Milgram, 1974).

1.1 Obedience – is it a problem?

People usually obey others for one of two main reasons. First, because they see the authority of others as right and lawful – as *legitimate authority*. In this case, they are likely to obey willingly. Second, they may obey others because they are forced to, or because they fear the consequences of not obeying. In this case, they are likely to see the authority of others as illegitimate, and attempts to enforce obedience as *coercion*.

The question of whether obedience can be a problem is to some extent a political one. Right-wing political philosophies see obedience as essential to the wellbeing of society. Conservatives often blame society's ills, such as crime and delinquency, on a decline of obedience resulting from a 'breakdown of authority'. Fascists prized obedience as a great virtue, admiring strong government and emphasising the importance of order in society. Hitler, in a speech in 1928, stated, 'We must teach the people to recognise authority and leadership', and in 1933 he exhorted his storm-troopers to 'submit to this overwhelming need to obey'. Fascist rulers were commonly referred to simply as 'the Leader': Mussolini was 'Il Duce', Hitler was the 'Führer' – both terms meant leader.

By contrast, more liberal political perspectives see obedience as potentially dangerous, especially when, in their view, obedience to so-called legitimate authority results in evil and inhumane actions. Liberals prefer to stress the importance of each person making their own individual decisions. They are more likely to question the requests and demands of authority figures.

Milgram accepts the necessity for some kind of legitimate authority. He points out that we happily and reasonably accept the authority of others in their specific domains. As he put it, 'We expose our throats to a man with a razor blade in the barber's shop, but would not do so in a shoe store' (Milgram, 1974). In all societies, from the smallest hunting and gathering bands to the largest nation states, there is some system of authority. It ranges from the authority of parents, teachers and employers, to the authority of the state represented in institutions such as parliament and the police. It is difficult to see how human society could operate without some degree of obedience to some system of authority.

While accepting this view, social psychologists recognise that obedience can lead to actions which they regard as unreasonable, morally wrong and even dangerous. American psychologists often refer to this type of obedience as 'destructive obedience'. Much of the early research was concerned with obedience to Nazi policies of genocide during the Second World War. It asked why people obeyed orders which violated the most basic moral codes of humane behaviour.

1.2 Personality or situation?

This section contrasts two views of obedience. The first states that some people are more prone than others to obey because of the nature of their personalities. The second states that those who obey do so because of the situation in which they find themselves.

The authoritarian personality

Theodore Adorno (1950) and his colleagues started their research shortly after World War II. They began by investigating anti-Semitism (prejudice against Jews) in order to understand the treatment of Jews in Nazi Germany. They claimed that people with a certain personality type – which they called the authoritarian personality – were more prone to obedience than others. On a personality questionnaire, people with this personality type emphatically agreed with statements such as 'Obedience and respect for authority are the most important virtues children should learn'. They were submissive to those in authority and inclined towards unquestioning obedience. They looked up to their 'superiors' and often treated those beneath them with contempt. They believed in a rigid social structure with everybody in their place, and tended to be prejudiced against minority groups.

Adorno claimed that people with authoritarian personalities

had childhoods which were dominated by a strict and punitive father who demanded absolute obedience. They developed a defence mechanism of *displacement*, targeting the anger they felt for their father at safer targets such as minority groups. They were conditioned to value strength and perceive the world to be full of people who need to be defeated, as they were defeated in childhood. They learned to fear and obey authority from an early age.

Evaluation Adorno used the idea of the authoritarian personality to explain obedience to authority in fascist societies. He argued that fascism encouraged the development of this type of personality. This led to hostility towards minority groups, particularly Jews, and to the obeying of orders to oppress and murder Jewish people.

Despite later research which supports the existence of authoritarian personalities, critics have argued that Adorno's theory is hardly sufficient to explain the slaughter of millions of Jews in Nazi Germany. First, fascism developed in Germany some ten years before the persecution of the Jews began. This is hardly enough time for German families to adopt the child-rearing practices needed to produce authoritarian personalities, or for their children to reach adulthood and obey the orders of the Nazi leadership. Second, Adorno's theories cannot explain why whole communities share the same prejudices and obey the same orders, or why attitudes and behaviour change rapidly over short periods of time (Zimbardo et al., 1995). Third, evidence suggests that Nazi officials were not so much authoritarian as merely bureaucratic. Hannah Arendt (1963) studied the trial of Adolf Eichmann who was judged to be responsible for the murder of millions of Jews in Nazi Germany. She found his obedience to authority differed little from that of officials in any bureaucratic organisation. He was simply a cog, albeit a major one, in a massive bureaucratic machine, obeying the orders of his superiors just like any good bureaucrat. He appeared ordinary, even dull and boring, fitting neatly into the stereotype of the bureaucrat. Arendt referred to his behaviour, and similar actions, as the 'banality of evil'. In this sense, evil can be seen as a commonplace response to the demands of authority. In Arendt's words, it is 'terrifyingly normal'.

In situations such as Hitler's Germany, the demand for obedience was overpowering. There was tremendous pressure for people to obey, whatever their personality type. Even without such pressure, there is evidence that obedience to authority is a normal part of social situations and has nothing necessarily to do with personality type.

Key terms

Obedience *Obeying the requests and demands of others.*

Legitimate authority *Authority which is considered right. It is often supported by the law.*

Coercion *Forced obedience. The authority of those who enforce coercion is considered illegitimate and wrong.*

Authoritarian personality *A personality type which results in people being more likely to respect authority figures and to obey them without question.*

Displacement *Directing the anger and frustration from the source which caused them on to another, usually less threatening, target such as minority groups.*

Summary

1 Obedience and conformity are both forms of social influence. However, whereas obedience results from pressure to comply with authority, conformity results from pressure to behave in terms of group norms.

2 According to Adorno, people with authoritarian personalities are more prone to obedience.

3 Situational explanations see obedience as a product of the situation rather than a reflection of personality.

Activity 1   Obeying orders

Item A   The final solution

In 1941, Rudolf Hoess was placed in charge of the extermination camp at Auschwitz. He received his orders from the head of the SS in Berlin who, in turn, received his orders directly from the Fuhrer, Adolf Hitler. Hoess was told:

'The Fuhrer has ordered the final solution of the Jewish question and we – the SS – have to carry out this order. It will be onerous and difficult and will require your full personal commitment without regard for any difficulties that may arise.'

Auschwitz, 1945

Hoess took his orders very seriously. He wrote, 'On receiving this grave order, I returned at once to Auschwitz'.

Five years later, Hoess made the following statement during his trial for war crimes in 1946.

'The final solution of the Jewish question meant the complete extermination of all Jews in Europe. I was ordered to establish extermination facilities at Auschwitz in June 1941.

I visited Treblinka to find out how they carried out their extermination. The camp commandant at Treblinka told me he had liquidated 80,000 in the course of half a year.

He used monoxide gas and I did not think his methods were very efficient. So when I set up the extermination building at Auschwitz, I used Zyklon B, which was crystallised prussic acid which we dropped into the death chamber from a small opening. It took from three to fifteen minutes to kill all the people in the death chamber, depending on climatic conditions. We knew when the people were dead because their screaming stopped. We usually waited about half an hour before we opened the doors and removed the bodies. After the bodies were removed our special commandos took off the rings and extracted the gold from the teeth of the corpses.

Another improvement we made over Treblinka was that we built our gas chambers to accommodate 2,000 people at one time, whereas at Treblinka their ten gas chambers only accommodated 200 people each.'

Quotations from Noakes & Pridham, 1988 and Brooman, 1985.

Item B   My Lai

The My Lai massacre took place on 16 March 1968 during the Vietnam War. Under the command of Lieutenant William Calley, US Army Charlie Company 'swept through' the small South Vietnamese village of My Lai. Calley ordered his men to shoot the villagers, whom he suspected of being enemy sympathisers. The official body count was 128 but unofficial estimates put the figure at 500. They were unarmed civilians and included women, children and old people.

One American soldier was asked to explain why he personally killed over 50 Vietnamese during the massacre. 'Why did I do it? Because I felt like I was ordered to do it, and it seemed like I was doing the right thing.'

Adapted from *The New York Times*, 25.11.1969

Item C   What would you have done?

Many Americans were outraged when Lieutenant William Calley was tried and convicted for his part in the killing of Vietnamese civilians at My Lai. These Americans believed he was simply carrying out the policy set forth by his superiors. In a national sample, 51% said that if they had been soldiers in Vietnam and were ordered to kill innocent civilians, they would have done so. Given their view that one must obey orders, these people saw the Army's legal case against Calley as a betrayal. But other people in the sample took a different view, holding that we must each accept ultimate responsibility for our own actions.

Lieutenant William Calley

Adapted from Rubin & McNeil, 1987

Questions

1 Read Item A. Hoess was concerned about 'efficiency' and 'improvement' in his 'extermination facility'. What does this suggest about the way he saw his work?

2 On the basis of Items A, B and C, which best explains the behaviour of those who murdered innocent civilians –

personality or situation?

3 People often say one thing and do another. Why is this important to bear in mind when interpreting the data from the national sample in Item C?

Unit 2 Experimental studies of obedience

KEY ISSUES

1 **What do experimental studies reveal about obedience?**

2 **What are the problems of studying obedience in laboratory situations?**

A number of experimental studies have investigated the degree to which obedience arises from the situation people find themselves in. It is easy to see how people are likely to obey commands they dislike or feel are morally wrong if the penalty for disobedience is imprisonment or death. But what if they are not forced? Will people still obey, even if obedience goes against their ethical values?

The answer appears to be yes. Contrary to popular belief, the high level of obedience Hitler's regime commanded in Germany and Austria (as well as in many occupied territories) was not in the main due to direct force. Evidence suggests that there was a mass willingness on behalf of tens of thousands of people to cooperate with the Nazi regime and obey Hitler's edicts, even to the extent of shopping neighbours to the Gestapo (the Nazi secret police) and helping to round up Jews to be sent to Auschwitz and other extermination camps (Goldhagen, 1996). This was commonly interpreted on the Allied side as being due to the German 'national character', which was depicted as authoritarian, militaristic and obedient. The American psychologist Stanley Milgram was sceptical of this idea, and thought it likely that obedience owed more to the situation than to culture or national character. He suspected that Americans, despite their perception of themselves as rugged individualists, would be just as likely to obey orders to harm others given the 'right' situation. It was this idea that Milgram set out to investigate in a series of experiments conducted in the early 1960s.

2.1 Stanley Milgram

The participants in Milgram's first experiment were forty men, aged between twenty and fifty, whose jobs ranged from unskilled labourers to school teachers and engineers (Milgram, 1963). They were recruited by a deceptive newspaper advertisement which asked for volunteers for a 'study of memory' rather than for the obedience experiment that Milgram conducted (see p 195). They were paid $4 plus travelling expenses for taking part in the experiment.

When the participants arrived they were told that the experiment was designed to investigate whether punishment improves learning. Each participant was told they would either play the role of 'teacher', or the role of 'learner'. The teacher would give the

learner tests and deliver an electric shock – the punishment – for each incorrect answer. Each participant was introduced to another person – a mild-mannered, middle-aged man they thought was a fellow participant but who was in fact a 'stooge', a confederate working with Milgram. Then the participants and the confederate drew lots for their roles as teacher and learner but the draw was rigged – the genuine participants were always allocated the role of teacher while the confederate always played the role of learner. Several versions of the experiment were used. The following describes the first experiment.

The participants watched as the confederate was strapped into a chair – 'to prevent excessive movement' – and attached to electrodes – to deliver the electric shock. In practice no shock was delivered. The confederate was asked whether he had any medical conditions and announced he had a heart ailment.

The participant was then led into another room and seated in front of a large generator. He was told that this generator could administer shocks to the confederate via the electrodes which had been attached to him. The confederate was out of sight in the next room but communication was made possible via an intercom. The participant was instructed to ask the confederate questions about word pairs. Each time the confederate made a mistake, the participant was told to administer an electric shock, increasing the voltage by 15 volts for each incorrect answer. The generator had a row of switches which indicated shocks from 15 volts up to 450 volts. The switches were labelled 'Slight Shock' to 'Danger – Severe Shock', with the final two switches being labelled XXX. The participant was given a sample electric shock of 45 volts to demonstrate that the generator was indeed capable of delivering a dose of electricity. This shock came from a hidden

The experimenter (right) and a participant (left) attach electrodes to the confederate's wrists.

battery – the generator was a mock-up and incapable of generating electricity.

During the experiment the confederate kept making mistakes. He protested about the shocks, crying out in pain and saying that his heart was bothering him. Many of the participants were visibly upset. Some were laughing nervously – an indication of emotional disturbance. Signs of tension included trembling, stuttering, biting lips and digging fingernails into palms of hands. Three participants had uncontrollable seizures, one of which was severe enough to halt the experiment. They frequently asked the experimenter whether they should continue to administer shocks, many pleading to be allowed to stop.

The experimenter remained calm and responded with a standardised set of verbal prods.

1   Please continue.
2   The experiment requires you to continue.
3   It is absolutely essential that you continue.
4   You have no other choice, you *must* go on.

Only if the participant refused to continue after the fourth and final prod was the experiment terminated.

The results of the experiment were as follows. All the participants gave shocks up to and including the level of 'Intense Shock' as labelled on the generator. 65% of the participants continued to the maximum of 450 volts – they obeyed the instructions to the letter.

Follow-up experiments

In a series of follow-up experiments, Milgram (1974) investigated factors which may vary the level of obedience. They included the following.

Proximity of the victim The presence of the confederate in another room resulted in a psychological as well as a physical distance between him and the participant. The common phrase is 'out of sight, out of mind'. Participants could not see the suffering of their victim. They were less willing to follow orders when they could see the confederate and least willing when they were required to force his hand onto the electrode – then obedience fell from 65% to 30%.

Milgram (1974) draws a comparison with a bomber pilot to illustrate the importance of proximity. The pilot 'can reasonably suppose that his weapons will inflict suffering and death, yet this knowledge is divested of affect (emotion) and does not arouse in him an emotional response to the suffering he causes'. Distance prevents him from seeing the death and destruction his bombs produce.

Proximity of experimenter When the experimenter was in the same room as the participant, 'breathing down his neck' as it were, the level of obedience was high. If the experimenter was in another room, giving instructions over the telephone, obedience fell to 20.5%. In this situation, participants often said they were administering shocks when in fact they weren't doing so.

Perceived authority Because the experiment was conducted at Yale, a prestigious Ivy League university, the participants perceived it as very important. Because of the status of the university, they were convinced of the integrity of the experimenter. These factors encouraged them to obey the experimenter and continue with the experiment. When the

experiment was conducted in a run-down office building and the experimenter did not wear a scientist's lab coat, obedience fell to 47.5%. Some of the participants questioned the legitimacy of the experimenter. This did not happen at Yale.

Whether or not people obey depends on how they perceive the person giving the orders. In one experiment, the experimenter and the confederate changed places. The experimenter told the participant to stop the shocks while the confederate told him to continue. In this situation all the participants refused to give further shocks. The demands of the experimenter – the authority figure – were clearly more influential.

Social support If a participant wanted to disobey the experimenter, he was more likely to do so if he was with other participants who supported his views. In one experiment Milgram introduced two confederates who refused to continue. The participants' obedience fell to 10%.

Individual differences Obedience depends in part on individual differences – differences in people's personalities, experiences, backgrounds and so on. Milgram found that participants who had gone on to higher education were less obedient, possibly because they had been taught to think for themselves and were more likely to be in occupations where they gave rather than received orders. He also found that participants with a military background tended to be more obedient, possibly because they had been trained to obey orders. Gender appeared to make no difference to levels of obedience. Milgram repeated his experiment using 40 female participants – 65% continued to the highest voltage level.

2.2 Methods

Milgram claimed that his experiments indicate that in the 'right' situation ordinary people will obey orders from those in authority, even if obedience goes against deeply held moral beliefs. A number of Milgram's critics reject this claim. They argue that his findings reflect flaws in the design of his experiment. They believe that the methods Milgram used in his research produced the behaviour he observed. In other words, the behaviour of his participants does not reflect how people would normally behave in response to orders from an authority figure.

Milgram's methodology has been criticised on two main grounds – *internal validity* and *external validity*.

Internal validity

An experiment has internal validity if it measures what it is intended to measure. Milgram's experiments were designed to measure obedience to authority. If they actually measured obedience, then they are internally valid. But did they measure what they were intended to measure?

Did Milgram's participants really believe that they were inflicting painful electric shocks on a middle-aged man with a heart condition? As with all laboratory experiments, participants may define the situation as 'artificial', 'unreal' and 'false'. As a result, they may see through Milgram's deception and realise they are not really inflicting painful shocks. They may 'play along' to please the experimenter and to earn their fees. They may pretend to show signs of distress – trembling, stuttering and groaning – in order to add realism to their performance (Orne &

Holland, 1968). If this is the case, then Milgram's experiments are not measuring obedience to authority – they are not internally valid.

Milgram rejects these criticisms claiming that, 'with few exceptions subjects (participants) were convinced of the reality of the experimental situation' (Milgram, 1963). A questionnaire given to participants a year after the experiment asked if they believed they were really inflicting painful shocks. 56.1% 'fully believed', 24% 'had some doubts' but on balance believed, 11.4% had doubts but thought probably not, 6.1% 'just weren't sure' and only 2.4% were 'certain' the shocks were not real.

Were the signs of distress shown by the participants genuine? The answer is probably yes judging from the observations of those who watched the experiments. This is how one observer described a participant.

'I observed a mature and initially poised businessman enter the laboratory smiling and confident. Within 20 minutes he was reduced to a twitching, stuttering wreck, who was rapidly approaching a point of nervous collapse' (Milgram, 1963).

Participants interviewed after the experiment gave every indication that their distress was real. During the experiment, several had expressed their tension in terms of nervous laughter. They were at pains to point out that this did *not* mean they enjoyed inflicting shocks.

Milgram claims that his experiments were internally valid. But, even if this claim is accepted, can his findings be applied beyond the four walls of the laboratory? In other words, can his findings be generalised?

External validity

External validity refers to the extent to which the findings of a research study can be generalised to other settings, other people and other times. Can Milgram's findings be generalised to other settings outside the laboratory and outside the USA? Can they be generalised to other people? For example, do the findings of Milgram's first experiment apply to people other than American males between the ages of 20 and 50? And, do the findings apply to other time periods apart from the 1960s when Milgram conducted his experiments?

The laboratory setting Both the setting and the relationships involved in experiments are very different from the world outside the laboratory. In particular, the experimenter/ participant relationship is distinct from all other relationships. Participants agree to do what the experimenter asks them within a limited time in a laboratory situation. They assume that the experimenter will not harm them and will take full responsibility for whatever happens in the experiment. Given this unique relationship and setting, it is not surprising that most of the participants in Milgram's experiments did what they were told and obeyed the experimenter. As a result, it is not possible to generalise from Milgram's findings since they simply reflect the experimenter/participant relationship (Orne & Holland, 1968).

Milgram (1992) makes the following response to this argument. He states that the relationship between experimenter and participant is little different from the relationship between any authority figure and those subject to their authority. Since the relationships are essentially the same, it is possible to generalise from the laboratory to the wider society. In view of this, Milgram

Key terms

Internal validity *The extent to which an experiment measures what it is intended to measure.*

External validity *The extent to which the findings of an experiment can be generalised; the extent to which they apply outside the laboratory.*

claims that his experiments have high external validity.

People, settings and times As noted earlier, Milgram repeated his first experiment with 40 female participants. Sixty-five per cent continued to the highest voltage level, the same percentage as his male participants. This suggests that in terms of gender his findings can be generalised. Do they apply to people in other societies with different cultures? This question is examined in detail in Section 2.6. Various versions of Milgram's experiments have been conducted in a number of countries. Complete obedience – continuing to the highest voltage level – ranges from 16% to 90%, compared to 65% for Milgram's studies of US males and females. These differences may reflect differences in the experimental design and procedures and/or differences in culture between the participants. In view of this, it is not possible to say with any degree of certainty whether Milgram's findings can be generalised to other societies.

Nor is it possible to say whether Milgram's findings can be generalised to other time periods. Milgram's experiments were conducted in the 1960s. In the USA, the last version of his experiments was published in 1976. Because of changing ethical standards, researchers are no longer able to conduct this type of research. (The ethical issues raised by Milgram's research are examined in the following chapter.)

No firm conclusions can be reached about the external validity of Milgram's experiments. However, a number of studies using different methods and approaches have provided some support for his findings. Two of these studies will now be examined.

2.3 Obedience in a job interview

There is a further question about the external validity of Milgram's research. The participants had been told they were taking part in a memory and learning experiment. Then, with no warning, they were sat down in front of a shock generator and told to give shocks to an apparently unwilling victim. They had very little time to think about the situation and to consider what they should do. If they had the time – as they probably would in everyday life – would they have behaved in the same way? A possible answer to this question is given by the second experiment described below.

Two Dutch psychologists, Meeus and Raaijmakers (1987), designed a series of experiments which help to answer these questions. The experiments were a variation on Milgram's research. However, rather than inflicting physical harm, the participants were required to inflict psychological harm. They were asked to interview applicants for a job. Unknown to the participants, the applicants were confederates of the experimenter. At the time, unemployment in Holland was high – failing the interview would be a serious blow to the applicants who were all presented to the participants as unemployed. At various points in the interview, participants were told to make 'stress remarks' to put the applicant under pressure, for example, 'If you continue like this you'll fail the test' and 'This job is too difficult for you. You are more suited to lower functions'. Participants were told the job required people who could handle stress, and that it was therefore necessary to put the applicants under stress to ensure they would be able to cope with the demands of the job.

There were 15 'stress remarks' which increased steadily in severity, just as the shock levels in Milgram's experiments. Participants were instructed to make *all* the remarks – they must continue no matter how much the applicant complained or appeared to suffer. They were prodded by the experimenter, as in the Milgram experiments, and told it was necessary to see how the applicant performed under stress.

At the start of the interview, applicants appeared confident, assured and at ease. As the interview developed they became increasingly distressed. They complained that the remarks were ruining their chances of getting a job they desperately needed. They pleaded with the interviewer to stop making abusive remarks, they became angry and refused to answer further questions and finally fell into a state of despair. As a result, they failed to get the job.

Despite finding the interview distasteful, unfair and humiliating for the applicant, 22 out of the 24 participants continued to the end. They obeyed the experimenter – the authority figure. In a control group without a prodding experimenter, *none* of the participants continued to the end.

As noted earlier, one of the criticisms of Milgram's experiments was that the participants had little opportunity to consider their actions. As such, the experiments lacked external validity – in real life people usually have time to think about what they should do. To counter this criticism, Meeus and Raaijmakers conducted a further experiment. They sent participants a letter detailing the interview procedure a week before the experiment. This gave them plenty of time outside the laboratory in their normal surroundings to decide whether they would go ahead and behave in this way. Despite this time to consider, the same proportion of participants continued to the end of the experiment as those in the 'no-warning' experiment. This suggests that, at least in this respect, the experiment was externally valid – in other words the findings could be generalised to situations outside the laboratory (Meeus & Raaijmakers, 1987).

2.4   Obedience in a hospital

So far, this unit has examined studies of obedience conducted in laboratories. Because laboratories are to some extent artificial and unreal settings, these studies are open to the criticism of lacking both internal and external validity. The following study of obedience is a field experiment – an experiment conducted in a normal, everyday social setting.

The experiment was conducted by Hofling and his colleagues (Hofling et al., 1966). The setting was a number of psychiatric hospitals in the USA. The participants were 22 staff nurses on night duty. An unknown 'doctor' (actually a confederate of Hofling) telephoned each staff nurse with instructions to give medication to a patient. The medication was a drug with a maximum daily dosage of 10mg. This was clearly stated on the label. The doctor asked the nurses to administer 20mg, twice the recommended maximum. The doctor said that he would sign the necessary authorisation papers when he arrived at the hospital in

about 10 minutes time.

Twenty-one out of the twenty-two nurses obeyed the telephoned instruction and prepared the medication before they were stopped and the situation explained to them. In doing so, they broke a number of important hospital rules. First, they accepted instructions over the telephone, something which is forbidden as they cannot be certain that the caller is a genuine doctor. Second, they accepted instructions from a doctor they had never heard of, which is forbidden for the same reason. Third, the medication was an unauthorised drug for the wards in question. Fourth, doubling the maximum dosage might seriously endanger the patients.

Why were the nurses prepared to obey the doctor? In their role as nurses, it is the norm to accept orders from the higher authority of a doctor. In addition, the doctor who telephoned promised to take responsibility by signing the authorisation papers. When questioned later, the nurses said that doctors often telephoned instructions and got very annoyed if nurses attempted to stick to hospital regulations.

Hofling interviewed 12 experienced nurses asking them what they would have done in this situation. Ten said they would refuse to follow the doctor's instructions. He also interviewed 21 student nurses, asking the same question. All of them stated that they would disobey the doctor. This is important as it suggests that what people say in an interview may be very different from what they do in everyday life.

Hofling's research is important because it studied obedience in a real-life setting. As such, it is more realistic than the relatively artificial context of the laboratory.

2.5   Explaining obedience

This section examines theories which have been put forward to explain obedience.

Seeing authority as legitimate

People tend to obey others if they recognise their authority as morally right and/or legally based. This response to legitimate authority is learned in a variety of situations, for example in the family, school and workplace. It is particularly obvious in organisations with a clearly marked hierarchy of authority such as the army and the civil service. Although the pressures to obey are not as severe as in totalitarian societies such as Nazi Germany, they are still powerful. Disobedience may result in a reprimand, demotion or loss of employment.

Obedience to legitimate authority can become 'second nature' – unthinking and taken for granted. It can also lead to the removal of individual responsibility – since people are only following orders they cannot be held personally responsible for the consequences. Their job is simply to translate the order into action as efficiently as possible. In this respect, obedience has nothing necessarily to do with personality. Instead, it is the result of a social situation – learning to obey and being subject to legitimate authority.

Milgram saw obedience as an essential part of all social life. In his words, 'Obedience is as basic an element in the structure of social life as one can point to. Some system of authority is a requirement of all communal living, and it is only the man living in isolation who is not forced to respond, through defiance or submission, to the commands of others' (Milgram, 1974).

Obedience to authority is learned from an early age, it is reinforced in schools and required in the workplace. Its importance can be seen clearly from both Milgram's and Hofling's experiments.

Milgram's experimenter was in charge, he was an authority figure who directed the participants. His integrity and status were indicated by the prestige of the institution – Yale University; by the significance of the experiment – an important scientific investigation; and by the uniform he wore – a lab coat. When these factors were removed and the experiment was conducted in a rundown office building, the participants who administered the maximum shock dropped from 65% to 47.5%.

The nurses in Hofling's experiment were used to the hierarchy of authority in the hospital. Under normal circumstances there was no question that doctors gave orders and nurses obeyed. Nor was there much question that doctors could bend the rules, judging from what the nurses said after the experiment.

The perception of authority as legitimate provides a major explanation for obedience.

Allocation of responsibility

During Milgram's experiments, a number of participants pestered the experimenter to take responsibility for the situation. They typically asked, 'Who is going to take the responsibility if anything happens to that gentleman?' They were determined to absolve themselves of any personal responsibility and to see themselves as simply carrying out orders from a higher authority. Milgram called this 'being another person's agent', a situation known as the *agentic state*. During the debrief one participant who had administered the maximum shock indicated that he wouldn't have been overconcerned if the victim died – he was just doing a job he was told to do.

In Hofling's hospital experiment, personal responsibility was partly removed from the nurses. The doctor promised to sign the authorisation papers when he arrived at the hospital ten minutes after his phone call.

There is considerable evidence both from experiments and real life that the removal of personal responsibility encourages obedience. Time and time again, in war crimes trials from World War II in the 1940s to the civil wars in the former Yugoslavia in the 1990s, those on trial stated they were simply following orders, doing their job, and therefore not personally responsible for their actions.

The just world hypothesis

If people are ordered to inflict harm on others, they may justify their actions with the *just world hypothesis*. Lerner (1980) argues that people have a need to believe that the world is fair and just, and that everybody gets what they deserve. Victims are often said to deserve their fate. For example, some people see AIDS as God's punishment of gays for their 'deviant' sexual behaviour. Nazi propaganda stated in no uncertain terms that the Jews deserved everything they got. They were portrayed as responsible for practically every ill of German society, from inflation, to unemployment, to crime, to disease. This is known as *victim derogation*.

Inflicting pain on others can result in *cognitive dissonance* – a clash between two contradictory attitudes held by the same person. Festinger (1957) suggested that if a person holds two conflicting views, or if their actions contradict their beliefs, then a state of tension results which must be reduced. People need consistency, they strive to match their attitudes and behaviour.

Many of Milgram's participants experienced cognitive dissonance. They saw themselves as kind and decent people, yet found themselves inflicting pain on another human being. This produced a contradiction between their self-perception and their behaviour. The resulting tension led to cognitive dissonance. Rather than changing their self-perception and seeing themselves as cruel and inhumane, they were more likely to derogate the victim and see his suffering as deserved.

The just world hypothesis can resolve the contradictions which produce cognitive dissonance. It can state that bad things happen to those who deserve them. In this respect, it can encourage following orders to inflict pain on others.

Dehumanisation

Dehumanisation means denying people their humanity. They may be seen as less than human, or as an impersonal object, or as something that doesn't really exist. Dehumanisation can encourage people to obey orders which involve harming others.

There are many techniques for dehumanising the victim. One of the simplest is to forget about them. For example, one of Milgram's participants stated, 'You really begin to forget that there's a guy out there, even though you can hear him … I just concentrated on pressing the switches and reading the words' (Milgram, 1974). Another method is to remove a person's individuality. Victims of torture sometimes have their heads covered with bags, so that the torturers cannot see their victims' faces and are not moved by their humanity. Defining people as less than human can provide justification for inhuman treatment. For example, slaves have often been seen as a lower form of human life.

Language is an important part of this process. Veterans of the Vietnam war speak of 'search and destroy' missions and 'sweeping through' enemy villages. Often this involved the murder of innocent civilians. When confronted with this reality, the veterans were uncomfortable and preferred their own sanitised terms. Similarly, the Nazis spoke of 'the final solution' which really meant the genocide of the Jewish people. In the

Key terms

Agentic state *Being another person's agent and, as a result, not being personally responsible for the consequences of following orders given by that person.*

Just world hypothesis *The idea that people need to believe that the world is just and fair and that everybody gets what they deserve.*

Victim derogation *Reducing the dignity and worth of a victim, so making them appear more deserving of their suffering.*

Cognitive dissonance *A clash between two conflicting beliefs held by a person, or a contradiction between their beliefs and behaviour. It results in a state of tension.*

Dehumanisation *Denying people their humanity – seeing them as less than human or as impersonal objects. It means that normal standards for treating human beings can be ignored.*

Foot-in-the-door effect *The first step in a commitment to a path of action.*

civil war in the former Yugoslavia, the slaughter of thousands of men, women and children was glossed with the phrase 'ethnic cleansing'. And Nato officials often referred to the deaths of civilians as a result of their air strikes in Serbia as 'collateral damage'. In Milgram's words, 'Euphemisms come to dominate language as a means of guarding the person against the full moral implications of his acts' (Milgram, 1974).

Dehumanisation means that normal standards for treating human beings can be ignored, morality can be suspended, and orders which result in harm to others can be accepted and carried out and justified.

Gradual commitment

Milgram's participants were encouraged to obey the experimenter by the gradual steps they were asked to take. They started with a practice session, then went on to the real thing, beginning with the 15 volt switch and gradually moving up the voltage scale. The initial act of obedience – administering 15 volts – was not too difficult. The increases were gradual – in 15 volt increments – each step only slightly worse than the one before. What difference would an extra 15 volts make? Not a lot. However, a jump from 15 to 450 volts is something else. It is unlikely that the participants would have taken this step.

The first step in this gradual commitment is known as the *foot-in-the-door effect* (Freedman & Fraser, 1966). Agreeing to a small, seemingly harmless effect can pave the way to obeying larger, more harmful orders.

Activity 2   Why obedience?

Item A   Learning to obey

Children are taught to obey from an early age. They are told what to wear, how to eat and drink, how to go to the toilet and so on. Lessons learned during childhood often last a lifetime. As the following quotation suggests, this may well be essential for the wellbeing of human society. 'Every day society is submitted to a terrible invasion: within it a multitude of small barbarians is born. They would quickly overthrow the whole social order and all the institutions of society if they were not well-disciplined and educated.'

R. Pinot quoted in Goodman, 1967

Item B   Mass suicide

In 1978, 913 members of an American religious cult, the People's Temple, were found dead, deep in the jungle in Guyana. They had moved there four years earlier from San Francisco and set up an agricultural commune called Jonestown. The cult leader, the Reverend Jim Jones, had ordered his followers to take their own lives as a sign of their religious dedication. They drank a mixture of Kool-Aid (a soft drink) and cyanide. According to the few survivors, most people took their lives willingly, with mothers giving the cyanide to their children, then drinking it themselves.

Adapted from *Chronicle of America*, 1989

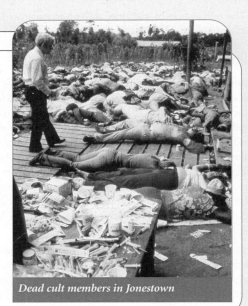
Dead cult members in Jonestown

Item C   Authority, obedience and blame

After Germany's defeat in 1945, 21 leading Nazis were put on trial for war crimes at Nuremberg. All pleaded their innocence, none accepted personal blame. When presented with incriminating evidence, most claimed they were simply following orders issued by a higher authority. Former Nazi SS officer Adolf Eichmann admitted at his trial in 1960 that he had played a part in 'liquidating' the Jews. In his defence he claimed he was simply doing his job, following orders, and was 'only a little sausage' in the Nazi war machine. The historian Klaus Fischer described him as a 'normal' human being 'who followed orders without question and served his employer loyally and efficiently'. Looking back on his time as Commandant of Auschwitz concentration camp, Rudolph Hoess wrote, 'Unknowingly, I was a cog in the chain of the great extermination machine of the Third Reich'. Apart from their 'work', most of these men appeared to live normal lives, with families and friends, and saw themselves as decent, law-abiding citizens.

Adapted from Lee 1989 and Fischer 1995

Item E   'Gooks'

Vietnamese prisoners led by US marines during the Vietnam war. The Americans referred to the Vietnamese as 'gooks'.

Item D   'My Struggle'

Mein Kampf ('My Struggle') was written by Adolf Hitler. Published in 1925, it became a bestseller in Germany. Hitler wrote: 'Was there any form of filth or crime without at least one Jew involved in it? If you cut such a sore, you find – like a maggot in a rotting body – a Jew. By defending myself against the Jew, I am fighting for the work of the Lord.'

This cartoon appeared in the German magazine Der Sturmer ('The Stormer') in 1934. It shows Jews draining the blood of innocent German children.

Questions

1   With reference to Item A, briefly discuss the view that,
    a) Obedience is learned from an early age.
    b) Obedience is necessary for human society.

2   Use the idea of legitimate authority to explain the mass suicide described in Item B.

3   Read Item C. Explain the relationship between responsibility, obedience and authority.

4   Read Item D. Use the ideas of the just world hypothesis and cognitive dissonance to explain obedience to orders to commit atrocities against Jewish people.

Item F   Gradual commitment

The 1967-1974 Greek military regime had great success in taking ordinary civilians and making them into official torturers. The military rulers selected stable, well-adjusted fishermen, farmers, carpenters, civil servants, shoemakers, cooks, lorry drivers, and small businessmen for 'special training.' During their training, the men were gradually introduced to brutality. They were often kept from eating, urinating, and defecating for days at a time. They were ordered to eat lighted cigarettes. They were 'forced to run while beaten until there were drops of sweat hanging from the ceiling' (Haritos-Fatouros, 1988).

At the end of the training, the apprentice torturers had to swear on their knees their undying allegiance and obedience to the military rulers. After enduring torture themselves, they first watched more experienced torturers and then gradually joined in unbelievably sadistic torture of citizens who were suspected of being disloyal to the military rulers. Through these carefully orchestrated indoctrination procedures, ordinary citizens were turned into obedient and efficient torturers.

Adapted from Lord, 1997

Indonesian secret police torturing an East Timorese man

5   Look at Item E.
    a) How might the term 'gook' help to dehumanise the Vietnamese?
    b) How might this make it easier for American soldiers to obey orders during the Vietnam war?

6   Explain the part played by gradual commitment in ensuring that the torturers in Item F obeyed orders.

2.6   Culture and obedience

Most of the studies of obedience have been conducted in the USA. Many have been conducted in laboratory settings where the participants have tended to be white American middle-class males. Can the results of these studies be generalised to other groups within the same society or to other societies? For example, can they be generalised to ethnic groups within the USA, such as African Americans and Hispanics, or to countries outside the USA, particularly non-Western societies?

This leads to the question of *culture*. Culture is the learned, shared behaviour of members of society and includes social norms, values and beliefs. Culture varies from society to society.

To some extent, each society has its own distinctive norms, values and beliefs which provide guidelines and directives for the behaviour of its members.

Within each society, particular groups have their own *subculture*. They share some of the norms and values of the wider society but also have their own norms and values. For example, many Hispanics in the USA speak Spanish and have distinctive tastes in food and music.

To what extent will cultures and subcultures affect behaviour in terms of obedience, and, in particular, laboratory experiments on obedience? The short answer is we don't really know. However, it is very unlikely they will have no effect.

Milgram's experiments have been conducted in a number of

countries. Complete obedience – where participants continued to the maximum shock level – ranged from over 90% in Spain, to over 80% in Italy, Germany and Austria, to 73% in Jordan, 50% in the UK, and 40% for Australian males and only 16% for Australian females. To some researchers, these results generally support Milgram's findings. They indicate that his findings are not limited to the USA, that they are not simply a product of American culture. Other researchers disagree. They see the findings from various countries as very different. Complete obedience ranges from 90% to 16% compared to 65% for Milgram's studies of US males and females.

Not all the experiments conducted outside the USA are exact replications of Milgram's research – the samples and the procedures are not exactly the same. For example, the Jordanian research, where complete obedience was 73%, was conducted by a female experimenter and the participants were children, aged 6 to 16 of both sexes (Shanab & Yahya, 1977). In the USA, Milgram found the same level of complete obedience for males and females – 65%. In Australia, the figure for male participants was 40%, for female participants, 16%. Part of this gender difference may be due to the fact that Australian women were asked to give shocks to a female 'victim', whereas the 'victims' for Australian men and Milgram's participants were male (Kilham & Mann, 1974).

It is not possible to say whether the variation in findings between countries is due to differences in experimental design or to differences in culture. The answer may well be both (Smith & Bond, 1993).

Levels of obedience in laboratory settings depend in part on the meanings given to laboratories, science and scientists. And these meanings might differ from culture to culture. In the West, science and scientists usually have high status. As a result, a scientist in a laboratory situation may well command a high level of obedience, as Milgram's experiments indicate. This may not apply to other societies. For example, after the 1979 revolution in Iran, universities were closed and scientists who were trained in the West were at best regarded with suspicion. Fathali Moghaddam, who was there at the time, writes, 'In this context, the scientist in the white lab coat would have made a pathetic authority figure, but the mullah (religious leader) would have made a very powerful one' (Moghaddam et al., 1993).

Moving outside the laboratory, there is plenty of evidence to

Summary

1. Milgram's experiments indicate that most people will obey authority figures when placed in the 'right' situation. Obedience in such situations is likely even if it results in harm to others.

2. Critics of Milgram argue that his experiments lacked both internal validity and external validity.

3. Support for Milgram's findings comes from experiments in Holland where participants had time to consider whether or not to obey orders and from a field experiment in American hospitals – a real life situation – where nurses obeyed orders with potentially harmful consequences.

4. Obedience is often a response to legitimate authority – authority regarded as morally right and/or legal.

5. People are more likely to obey if they can absolve themselves of responsibility for their actions.

6. Where obedience results in harm to others, people are more likely to obey if a) their actions can be justified by the just world hypothesis – the world is fair and people get what they deserve; b) their 'victims' can be dehumanised – deprived of their human characteristics; c) their commitment is gradual.

7. Studies of obedience have been largely based on American culture. Because of this, we cannot be sure whether or not the results can be applied to other cultures.

indicate that culture has an important influence on obedience. Studies of obedience training of children in different cultures shows considerable variation in the types and levels of obedience required (Berry et al., 1992). And as cultures change, so do expected levels of obedience. This can be seen by comparing family relationships in the West in the 19th century with those of today. The authoritarian Victorian husband and father is, for most women and children, a thing of the past.

The psychology of obedience has been largely based on studies conducted in American society by American social psychologists. A considerable amount of research is needed before we know whether or not these findings apply to different societies with different cultures.

Unit 3 Resistance to authority

KEY ISSUES

1 How important is the example and support of others for resisting authority?

2 Do individual differences play a part in resistance?

3 What part can conformity to group norms play in resistance?

Units 1 and 2 may have given the impression that resistance to authority is a rare occurrence. It isn't. For example, many individuals conscripted into the armed forces, such as conscientious objectors, refuse to join. During the Vietnam War, thousands of American 'draft dodgers' avoided conscription, either through opposition to the war or simply for self-preservation. During the Nazi regime, many German citizens sheltered Jews and helped to smuggle them out of the country. Millions of people have joined together to overthrow established authority as in the French revolution of 1789 and the Russian revolution of 1917. And it is important to remember that 35% of Milgram's participants refused to go further than the 'intense shock' level, despite being told they 'must go on'.

3.1 Social support

There is evidence to indicate that when a person is provided with social support and/or role models for resisting authority, they are more likely to disobey directives from above. In other words, if an individual joins with others to resist, or is presented with the example of others resisting, then disobedience is more likely. Often both kinds of social support – joining with others and the presence of role models for resistance – occur in the same social situation.

Milgram's experiments In one experiment, Milgram assigned two confederates to join the participants in the role of teacher. The first confederate refused to continue beyond the 150 volt shock, the second beyond the 210 volt shock. In this situation, only 10% of the participants obeyed the experimenter and continued to the highest voltage level. Those who refused to go further were supported by the role models provided by the confederates.

The MHRC experiment The importance of social support can be seen from an experiment designed to encourage resistance to authority (Gamson et al.,1982). Participants were contacted by a non-existent company, MHRC – Manufacturers' Human Relations Consultants – and asked to take part in discussions about how legal cases are affected by the views of the local community. They were placed in groups of nine and asked to discuss the following case. They gave MHRC permission to videotape their discussions.

Mr C was manager of a petrol station. The oil company which owned the station hired a private detective to investigate his lifestyle. Mr C was living with a woman but they were not married. The company cancelled his franchise on the station, claiming that his behaviour offended the moral standards of the local community and would result in loss of business. Mr C sued the oil company for breach of contract and invasion of privacy.

After a general discussion, the experimenter – who called himself the coordinator – asked three members of each group to argue that Mr C's domestic arrangements had caused them offence. A further three participants from each group were then asked to do the same. Finally, each group member was asked to speak individually. They were told to say that Mr C's behaviour was offensive, that he should lose his franchise and that they intended to boycott the service station. The coordinator then asked them to sign affidavits – written statements taken under oath – allowing MHRC to edit the videotapes as they saw fit and to use them as evidence in court.

Most of the participants objected strongly to this procedure. They realised that their 'evidence' was being distorted and insisted on an assurance that the court would be told that these weren't their real views. There were 33 groups in the experiment. In 16 groups, every member refused to sign the affidavit, in 9 a majority refused and in the remaining 8 a minority refused. Most participants therefore resisted authority.

Why did so many participants disobey the coordinator? First, the experiment was designed to encourage resistance. Mr C's treatment by MHRC was clearly unacceptable to most fair-minded people. Judging from the results of a questionnaire given before the discussions, most participants saw nothing wrong with his behaviour. In addition, asking the participants to argue against their own views then directing them to sign affidavits allowing MHRC to use their statements as evidence in court clearly violated normal standards of behaviour. Second, the participants had the example and support of other group members for resistance. During the discussions they were given breaks which provided ample opportunity to share their views

with others and question the morality of the coordinator's directives. During these breaks, the decision to disobey was formulated and often became a group norm.

Moving from small-scale experiments to the wider society, there is considerable evidence that resistance to authority is often a collective act involving role models for resistance and support from like-minded others. This can be seen in strikes, protests, demonstrations, riots and revolutions.

3.2 Attitudes and individual differences

As discussed earlier, Milgram found that individual differences – differences in attitudes, experiences and backgrounds – influenced whether or not people resisted authority. One of his participants, Gretchen Brandt, refused to go beyond the 210 volt level. She was raised in Nazi Germany and told the experimenter, 'Perhaps we have seen too much pain'. Another participant, who had lived in Holland during the Nazi occupation, also refused to continue to the maximum voltage. These participants had been sickened by the suffering they had seen during the Nazi regime and regarded the pain apparently inflicted in Milgram's experiments as morally unacceptable. Compared to the participants who obeyed, they were calm and self-assured – they were in no doubt that their refusal was right.

In the MHRC experiment, most of the groups who disobeyed contained members with previous experience of dissent – they had participated in strikes, protests and demonstrations against authority. They often provided role models for other group members.

Participants' attitudes towards authority were assessed by a questionnaire given at the start of the MHRC experiment. There was a close link between anti-authority attitudes and disobedience on the one hand, and pro-authority attitudes and obedience on the other. Thus members of groups with a high level of pro-authority attitudes were most likely to obey and sign the affidavit.

Attitudes on their own, however, do not provide a sufficient explanation for obedience and resistance. Almost all of Milgram's participants were disturbed about the pain they thought they had inflicted – after the experiment many expressed dismay about their behaviour. But the pressure of the situation led them to shelve their attitudes and beliefs and do as they were told. Situational forces and constraints often outweigh attitudes and beliefs.

3.3 The role of conformity in disobedience

The previous chapter indicated the power of the group to enforce conformity to group norms and group standards. How far was the disobedience of participants in the MHRC experiment due to conformity to group norms rather than resistance to authority? There is evidence which suggests that for some participants, their refusal to obey the coordinator was due mainly to social pressures to conform to group norms. When faced with the choice of obedience or conformity, many participants 'were uncertain at this point, waiting to see what others would do, delaying decision as long as possible. Ultimately, they were faced with an unavoidable choice – to sign or not to sign – and loyalty to the group became one major factor in their decision.' One participant stood up to the coordinator, making it clear where the strongest pressure lay. 'I didn't personally say anything

I didn't believe, but I'm not going to sign this either, if the rest of the group isn't signing' (Gamson et al., 1982).

Evaluation

Studies of resistance to authority indicate there are many factors involved. It is difficult to tease out these factors and weigh their influence. For example, just how important were social support, individual differences and conformity to the results of the MHRC experiment?

Much of the research on resistance to authority is based on laboratory experiments. To what extent can conclusions based on such artificial social situations be generalised to the real world? As the following activity indicates, this world is a lot messier than controlled experiments which have been set up to assess the importance of specific variables.

Key terms

Social support *Support provided by others for an individual.*

Individual differences *Differences in personality, attitudes, experiences and social factors (eg, gender, ethnicity, social class and culture) between people.*

Summary

1. It appears easier for groups rather than individuals to resist authority. This is probably due to the influence of social support.

2. Individual differences help to explain why some rather than others resist authority.

3. In a group context, conformity to group norms can increase resistance.

Activity 3   Resisting authority

Item A   Tiananmen Square

In April 1989, hundreds of thousands of students, supported by people from all walks of life, gathered in Tiananmen Square in Beijing. They were demanding democratic reforms and protesting against the autocratic leadership of the People's Republic of China. The demonstration developed into an occupation of the Square and the demonstrators ignored government orders to disperse and return to their homes.

On May 20th the government ordered the army to clear the Square. For nearly two weeks the troops, many of them young, inexperienced conscripts, could not – or chose not to – obey those orders. Late in the night of June 23rd, seasoned troops, backed by tanks and armoured cars were sent in. They fired indiscriminately, killing many hundreds, perhaps thousands.

Adapted from Spence & Chin, 1996

A student blocks the path of a column of tanks in Tiananmen Square

Item B   Conscientious objection

On August 18 1916, at an army barracks at Warley in Essex, 26-year-old Clifford Allen, a pacifist, was court-martialled for refusing to agree to any form of military or non-combatant service. He told the officers trying him, 'I believe in the inherent worth and sanctity of every human personality, irrespective of the nation to which a man belongs'.

Adapted from Gilbert, 1994

Item C   Resistance groups

Hans and Sophie were brother and sister. They were members of the White Rose, a resistance group which opposed Hitler's rule in Nazi Germany. They distributed leaflets which were highly critical of the Nazi regime. In 1943 they were arrested by the Gestapo, Hitler's secret police. Their sister Inge wrote the following account of Hans and Sophie's last days.

'Everyone who came into contact with Hans and Sophie – the other prisoners, the pastors at the prison, the guards, and even the Gestapo officers – were deeply moved by their courage and their noble bearing. Their calm and composure made for a strange contrast to the hectic tension of that place. Their activities worried party and government officials right up to the top levels.

Two days after their arrest, it became clear to them that they could expect the death sentence. There was only one thing to do: remain prudent and rational, involve as few people as possible, and embody, in all clarity, the freedom of the human spirit.

When the last morning came, Hans asked his cellmate to bid goodbye to our parents. Then he gave him his hand, kindly, almost ceremoniously, and said, 'We want to say goodbye while we're still alone'. With that, he turned around without a word and wrote something on the white prison wall. There was silence. He had barely put the pencil down when the guard came to handcuff him and lead him into court. The words on the wall were Goethe's words, words which his father had often murmured while pacing back and forth, the pathos of which had sometimes made Hans smile: *Allen Gewalten zum Trutz sich erhalten* (To stand defiant before overwhelming power).

When Sophie left her cell for the last time, a piece of paper remained behind – an indictment, in one word, Freedom.'

Adapted from Steinhoff, Pechel & Showalter, 1991.

References

Adorno, T.W., Frenkel-Brunswik, E., Levinson, D.J. & Stanford, R.M. (1950). *The authoritarian personality.* New York: Harper.

Arendt, H. (1963). *Eichmann in Jerusalem: A report on the banality of evil.* New York: Viking.

Berry, J.W., Poortinga, Y.H., Segall, M.H. & Dasen, P.R. (Eds.) (1992). *Cross-cultural psychology: Research and applications.* Cambridge: Cambridge University Press.

Brooman, J. (1985). *Hitler's Germany.* Harlow: Longman.

Chronicle of America. (1989). Farnborough: J L International Publishing.

Festinger, L. (1957). *A theory of cognitive dissonance.* Stanford, CA: Stanford Univerity Press.

Fischer, K.P. (1995). *Nazi Germany: A new history.* London: Constable.

Freedman, J.L. & Fraser, S.C. (1966). Compliance without pressure: The foot-in-the-door technique. *Journal of Personality and Social Psychology, 4,* 195-202.

Gamson, W.B., Fireman, B. & Rytina, S. (1982). *Encounters with unjust authority.* Homewood, ILL: Dorsey Press.

Gilbert, M. (1994). *First World War.* London: BCA.

Goldhagen, D.J. (1996). *Hitler's willing executioners: Ordinary Germans and the Holocaust.* Boston: Little Brown.

Goodman, M.E. (1967). *The individual and culture.* Homewood: Dorsey.

Halonen, J.S. (1986). *Teaching critical thinking in psychology.* Milwaukee, WI: Alverno Productions.

Haritos-Fatouros, M. (1988). The official torturer: A learning model for obedience to the authority of violence. *Journal of Applied Social Psychology, 18,* 1107-1120.

Hofling, K.C., Brotzman, E., Dalrymple, S., Graves, N. & Pierce, C.M. (1966). An experimental study in the nurse-physician relationship. *Journal of Nervous and Mental Disorders, 143,* 171-180.

Kilham, W. & Mann, L. (1974). Level of destructive obedience as a function of transmitter and executant roles in the Milgram obedience paradigm. *Journal of Personality and Social Psychology, 29,* 696-702.

Lee, S. (1989). *Nazi Germany.* Oxford: Heinemann.

Lerner, M.J. (1980). *The belief in a just world: A fundamental delusion.* New York: Plenum.

Lord, C.G. (1997). *Social psychology.* Fort Worth: Harcourt Brace.

Meeus, W.H.J. & Raaijmakers, Q.A.W. (1987). Administrative obedience as a social phenomenon. In W. Doise & S. Moscovici (Eds.), *Current issues in European social psychology* (Vol.2). Cambridge: Cambridge University Press.

Milgram, S. (1963). Behavioral study of obedience. *Journal of Abnormal and Social Psychology, 67,* 371-378.

Milgram, S. (1965). Some conditions of obedience and disobedience to authority. *Human Relations, 18,* 57-76.

Milgram, S. (1974). *Obedience to authority.* London: Tavistock.

Milgram, S. (1992). *The individual in a social world* (2nd ed.). New York: McGraw-Hill.

Moghaddam, F.M., Taylor, D.M. & Wright, S.C. (1993). *Social psychology in cross-cultural perspective.* New York: W. H. Freeman.

Noakes, J. & Pridham, G. (Eds.) (1988). *Nazism 1919-1945.* Exeter: University of Exeter Press.

Orne, M.T. & Holland, C.C. (1968). On the ecological validity of laboratory experiments. *International Journal of Psychology, 6,* 282-293.

Rubin, Z. & McNeil, E.B. (1987). *Psychology: Being human* (4th ed.). New York: Harper & Row.

Shanab, M.E. & Yahya, K.A. (1977). A behavioural study of obedience in children. *Journal of Personality and Social Psychology, 35,* 530-536.

Smith, P.B. & Bond, M.H. (1993). *Social psychology across cultures: Analysis and perspectives.* Hemel Hempstead: Harvester Wheatsheaf.

Spence, J. & Chin, A. (1996). *The Chinese century.* London: Harper Collins.

Steinhoff, J., Pechel, D. & Showalter, D. (1991). *Voices from the Third Reich: An oral history.* London: Grafton Books.

Zimbardo, P.G., McDermott, M., Jansz, J. & Metaal, N. (1995). *Psychology: A European text.* London: Harper Collins.

Introduction

Ethics are a set of moral principles, a set of beliefs about what is right and wrong. In terms of research, ethics are the moral principles which guide research. Psychological associations in many countries now have a set of ethical guidelines for conducting research. Psychology departments in universities usually have an ethics committee to ensure that research conducted by members of the department is in line with these guidelines.

There is a growing awareness that those who participate in research have rights and that researchers have responsibilities and obligations. For example, should participants be informed about the purpose of the research and what exactly their participation involves? Should researchers make every effort to ensure that participants come to no physical or psychological harm? Is it ever justifiable to deceive participants about the purpose of the research and the true nature of the tasks they may be asked to perform? These are some of the questions this chapter examines.

Chapter summary

- Unit 1 looks at the development of ethical guidelines for research. It outlines recent guidelines, focusing on those of the British Psychological Society.

- Unit 2 examines the ethics of Milgram's obedience research.
- Unit 3 considers the ethical issues raised by Zimbardo's prison simulation experiment.

Unit 1 Ethical guidelines for research

KEY ISSUES

1 How have ethical guidelines for research developed?
2 What are the main ethical issues in research with human participants?

1.1 The development of ethical guidelines

The Nuremberg Code

After World War II (1939-1945) Nazi doctors stood trial at Nuremberg for experiments they conducted on prisoners in German concentration camps. The world was horrified by the revelations of their 'research'. Jews, Gypsies, Poles and Russians were subjected to appalling treatment in the name of science. They were thrown into icy water to see how they would react to extreme cold. Every detail of their behaviour was clinically and carefully recorded – how they writhed in pain, foamed at the mouth and went into death rattles. Other experiments included infecting prisoners with malaria, typhoid and jaundice, dosing or injecting them with a variety of poisons, and placing them in decompression chambers which sometimes resulted in ruptured lungs and death (Fischer, 1995). On August 19th, 1947, seven of the Nazi doctors received death sentences and the remaining sixteen were imprisoned.

One positive outcome of these horrific experiments was the Nuremberg Code, a code of ethics which forms the basis for research in medicine and psychology and the social sciences in general. The Code outlined the responsibilities and obligations of researchers and the rights of participants. These include:

- Participation in research should be voluntary.
- Participants should be informed of any risks involved.
- They should be free to withdraw from an experiment at any point *and* made aware of this right from the start.
- Participants should be told about the purpose of the research and given details about their involvement.
- Researchers should make sure participants come to no physical or psychological harm.
- Experiments should be stopped immediately if such harm is occurring (Homan, 1991).

Human rights

The Nazis used Jews, Gypsies, Poles and Russians in their experiments because they regarded them as a lower form of humanity. They also used them because, in the words of one doctor, they were the cheapest experimental animals, cheaper even than rats (Fischer, 1995). Clearly, this is an extreme example of a disregard for human rights. A further positive outcome of the atrocities of the Second World War was the United Nations' Universal Declaration of Human Rights in 1948. Article 1 states that, 'All human beings are born free and equal in dignity and rights'. Article 5 states that, 'No one shall be subjected to torture or to cruel, inhuman or degrading treatment or punishment'.

The UN Declaration reflected an increasing concern with human rights which has continued to the present day. This concern is mirrored in the codes of ethics for medical and social science research, including psychology. For example, the British Psychological Society's code states that participants 'should be able to expect to be treated with the highest standards of consideration and respect' (BPS, 1998).

From 'subjects' to 'participants'

The growing concern with the dignity and rights of all human beings is reflected in the change from 'subjects' to 'participants'. Those who took part in research used to be known as 'subjects'; today they are increasingly referred to as 'participants'. 'Subjects' implies that people are subordinate to others, that they are under the control and authority of others. As the British Psychological Society (BPS) notes, the term 'subject' can seem impersonal, disrespectful and even derogatory (BPS, 1998).

The term 'subject' can also imply that people can be seen and treated as 'objects' in experimental research. This reflected psychology's concern with science and the scientific method. The natural sciences, such as physics and chemistry, study the behaviour of matter. Matter is manipulated in controlled experiments in order to discover the laws which underlie its behaviour. Psychology has often applied the same approach to human beings. In the past, though to a lesser extent today, 'subjects' were manipulated in experiments in order to discover the principles underlying human behaviour.

Psychologists are increasingly realising that people who participate in experiments are very different from the passive objects which are manipulated in natural science experiments. For example, interviews with people who have taken part in psychology experiments have shown that they often work out what is expected from them and do their best to give experimenters what they want (Silverman, 1977). Now the 'passive subject' of the psychology experiment is more likely to be seen as the 'active participant'.

This view places participants in a new light. Increasingly, they are seen not as objects to be manipulated but as people who are actively involved and cooperating with the experimenter. In the words of the British Psychological Society, 'Good psychological research is possible only if there is mutual respect and confidence between investigators and participants' (BPS, 1998). This focus on respect leads to an increasing concern with the rights of participants and the responsibilities of researchers.

Codes of conduct for research

During the 1960s and 1970s, there were growing demands for explicit and detailed ethical guidelines for psychological research. These demands were triggered by a number of controversial experiments, in particular, Milgram's (1963) obedience experiments (see pp 179-181) and Zimbardo's prison simulation study (Haney, Banks & Zimbardo, 1973; see pp 169-170). Participants in both studies experienced considerable stress. They were instructed to do things which, under normal circumstances, they would probably see as unacceptable. And, in the case of Milgram's research, participants were deceived about the purpose of the research and the nature of the tasks they were instructed to perform.

Ethical issues were now on the agenda. Milgram and Zimbardo were stongly criticised by some of their colleagues and strongly supported by others. Partly as a result of this debate, professional associations of psychologists in a number of countries produced codes of conduct for research with human participants. In 1978, the British Psychological Society published its *Ethical principles for research on human subjects*. This was revised in 1990, further amended in 1992, and republished in 1993 and 1998 with the title *Ethical principles for conducting research with human participants*. It is noticeable that 'on' has changed to 'with' and 'subjects' to 'participants'.

Ethical considerations are now a major concern in research. The BPS (1998) states that, 'In all circumstances, investigators must consider the ethical implications and psychological consequences for the participants in their research. The essential principle is that the investigation should be considered from the standpoint of all participants; foreseeable threats to their psychological wellbeing, health, values or dignity should be eliminated.'

Psychological associations such as the BPS now have committees which are responsible for ethical issues and for reviewing and updating codes of conduct. In addition, psychology departments in universities usually have ethics committees which examine research proposals to ensure they are in line with codes of conduct.

1.2   The BPS ethical principles

This section looks at codes of conduct for research, focusing on the British Psychological Society's *Ethical principles for conducting research with human participants* (1998).

Informed consent

Participants must give their consent to take part in research and this consent must be 'informed'. This means that information must be made available on which to base a decision to participate or not. According to the BPS, 'The investigator should inform the participants of all aspects of the research … that might reasonably be expected to influence willingness to participate' (BPS, 1998).

In practice, this means participants should be told:

- They are volunteers – they have a free choice whether or not to participate in the research and are free to withdraw whenever they wish, even if they have been paid to take part.
- The objectives of the research – in general terms, what the investigator is looking at.
- The experiences they will undergo during the actual research.
- The expectation that there is no risk – participation is not expected to lead to psychological or physical harm.

In a nutshell, participants should be told what they are letting themselves in for. Only then are they in a position to give informed consent.

Special safeguards are needed for certain participants. In the case of young people under 16, consent should also be obtained from their parents. In the case of people who have difficulties with communication and understanding, every attempt must be made to obtain 'real consent'. Where this is not possible, approval must be obtained from those 'well-placed to appreciate the participant's reaction, such as the person's family' and from an independent advisor (BPS, 1998). When people are detained in institutions such as prisons or psychiatric hospitals, care must be taken to ensure their consent is freely given. The same applies to participants over whom the researcher has authority and influence – his or her students, clients or employees. These relationships must not be used to place pressure on them to participate in the research.

Finally, if there is any possibility of 'harm, unusual discomfort, or other negative consequences' resulting from participation, the investigator must inform not only participants but also independent advisors. All must give their consent (BPS, 1998).

A major problem with informed consent is the possibility that the researcher will 'give the game away' – reveal what they expect to find. Participants may then act in terms of these expectations and so invalidate the experiment – they will not be responding to the factors which the experiment is designed to examine. As a result, a case can be made for withholding information. This case will be examined in the following section.

Deception

Deception means that information is withheld from participants, they are misled about the purpose of the study and the events that will take place during an experiment. According to the BPS, 'Intentional deception of the participants over the purpose and general nature of the investigation should be avoided whenever possible'. In particular, deception is unacceptable if it leads to 'discomfort, anger or objections from the participants' when the deception is revealed after the research has been completed (BPS, 1998).

However, both the BPS and the American Psychological Association agree that in certain cases deception is unavoidable. For example, the BPS states that, 'It may be impossible to study some psychological processes without withholding information about the true object of the study or deliberately misleading the participants' (BPS, 1998). In such cases the researcher must 1) make sure that alternative procedures which avoid deception are not available; 2) consult with colleagues about how participants might be affected by the deception; 3) reveal the deception to participants immediately after the research has been completed.

Opinion on the use of deception in research is divided. Some feel that it is wrong and, no matter how useful, should be avoided (Baumrind, 1979). However well-intentioned, deception involves lies and manipulation. Some researchers argue that it shows a disrespect for participants and views them as objects to be manipulated at will (Kelman, 1967). And informed consent is not possible if deception is involved – participants will have no idea what they are letting themselves in for.

Others argue that deception is often essential. Many experiments just would not work without it. For example, participants in Asch's experiments on conformity were told they were taking part in a study of perception – the way people judge line lengths – rather than study of social influence. They were led to believe that the other members of the experimental group were participants like themselves rather than confederates. It is difficult to see how this experiment could have been conducted successfully without deception (see pp 164-165). A similar case can be made for Sherif's use of deception in his autokinetic experiment. If the participants had been told that the light was actually stationary, the experiment would not have worked (see pp 163-164).

Those who support the use of deception do so on the assumption that it is harmless, trivial and short-lived. It is short-lived, as in most cases participants are told about the deception immediately after the experiment. It is trivial in the sense that most participants see it as unimportant. It is harmless as there is no evidence of any long-term harm to participants (Elms, 1982). In fact, the vast majority of participants enjoy taking part in experiments which involve deception and often express admiration for the researcher for staging a skilful deception (Christensen, 1988).

Protection from harm

The BPS ethical guidelines state that, 'Investigators have a primary responsibility to protect participants from physical and mental harm during the investigation' (BPS, 1998). However, no investigation is entirely free from risk. The guiding principle is that risk should be no greater than the risks participants are exposed to in their normal lifestyles.

Participants should be encouraged to contact the investigator after the research if they have any worries or concerns. As Latané and Darley (1970) note in Activity 1, Item C, participants 'experienced stress and conflict' during the seizure experiment. This stress and conflict may continue after the experiment along with self-doubt and low self-esteem for those participants who did not offer help to an apparently dying student. If the research results 'in undesirable consequences for participants, the investigator has the responsibility to detect and remove these consequences' (BPS, 1998). However, this is easier said than done, especially if participants are ashamed of their behaviour during an experiment and wish to conceal their shame.

As noted in the previous section, there is no evidence of any long-term harm to participants in psychological research (Elms, 1982). However, people's responses to questionnaires and comments in interviews about their experience of participating in research cannot be taken at face value. They may disguise their true feelings for a variety of reasons.

Confidentiality Protection from harm also involves confidentiality. Participants may be asked personal and private questions. They must be told that there is no compulsion to answer these questions, and, if they do answer, their replies will be treated in confidence. If the research is published, they should remain anonymous. If this cannot be guaranteed, they should be told in advance and have the right to withdraw.

During experiments, participants may behave in ways they don't wish to be made public. The same safeguards apply – there should be no way they can be identified. Without such safeguards, participants may experience worry and stress.

Research outside the laboratory where the investigator observes behaviour 'must respect the privacy and psychological wellbeing of the individuals studied'. Invasion of privacy can result in unease or distress. According to the BPS, unless people have given their consent, they should only be observed in situations where they would expect to be observed by strangers (BPS, 1998). This largely limits observational research to public places.

Withdrawal from investigations Participants should have the right to withdraw from an investigation at any time. This applies even if they have been paid to take part. They should be told this at the start of the investigation. No attempt should be made to encourage or persuade them to remain should they wish to withdraw. This is an important right since staying against their will may result in considerable stress.

Debriefing

Debriefing involves a full disclosure – telling it all – after the investigation is complete. Typically, researchers discuss the aims of the research with participants, making sure they understand how they have contributed to meeting those aims. Any deception is disclosed, explained and justified. Attempts are made to undo any negative effects of the research experience. For example, if participants experience guilt, anxiety or lowered self-esteem as a result of their behaviour during an experiment, they are given reassurance and support. Researchers attempt to remove any feelings of discomfort and distress and ask participants to get back in touch should such feelings continue.

Codes of conduct for research state that all participants have a right to a debriefing session after the investigation has been completed. But does debriefing work? A review of the research on debriefing indicates that if it is done with 'care, effort and vigilance', then it does work (Holmes, 1976). However, others are not so sure. Participants may be reluctant to express negative feelings during debriefing. They may feel embarrassed, they may not wish to upset the researcher, and as a result their negative feelings may continue (Fisher & Fyrberg, 1994).

Key terms

Informed consent *A voluntary decision to participate in research based on information about the aims of the research and the tasks the participants will be asked to perform.*

Deception *Purposely misleading participants about the aims of the research and/or the nature of the tasks they are asked to perform. This is done by withholding information and/or providing false information.*

Debriefing *The procedure at the end of the research which involves a full disclosure of the aims of the research and the reasons for the tasks which participants have performed. Any deception is explained and justified. Attempts are made to undo any negative effects of the research experience.*

Summary

1. In terms of research, ethics are the moral principles which guide research. They involve the rights of participants and the responsibilities of researchers.

2. Ethical guidelines for research in psychology were influenced by the concern for human rights following World War II. This concern was reflected in the Nuremburg Code and the Universal Declaration of Human Rights.

3. Increasingly, participants are seen not as objects to be manipulated but as people who cooperate with researchers. This is reflected in the change in terminology from 'subjects' to 'participants'. It indicates increased respect for those who take part in research.

4. Demands for ethical guidelines for psychological research were triggered by controversial experiments in the 1960s and 1970s, in particular Milgram's obedience experiments and Zimbardo's prison simulation study.

5. The main ethical principles for conducting research with human participants are:
   - Informed consent
   - Avoidance of deception if at all possible
   - Protection of participants from physical and psychological harm
   - Confidentiality and respect for privacy
   - The right to withdraw from investigations at any time
   - Debriefing.

Activity 1   Deception

Item A   Acceptable deception?

Item B   The bystander effect

Darley and Latané designed an experiment to investigate the 'bystander effect'. Their hypothesis was the greater the number of bystanders who witness an emergency, the less likely any one of them is to help. The participants were students. Each sat in a separate room discussing university life over an intercom with one or more students in other rooms. Then one of the participants appeared to have a seizure and cried out, 'I'm gonna die er er I'm gonna die, er help'. In fact, there was only one real participant, all the others were pre-recorded voices. When participants believed they were the only ones listening to the student having a seizure, 85% left the experimental room and offered help within a minute and 100% offered help within $2^{1}/2$ minutes. When participants believed there was another student listening, fewer offered help and took longer to do so. When participants believed there were four other students listening, even fewer offered help and took even longer – 31% helped in the first minute and after 6 minutes (when the experiment ended) only 62% had offered help.

Adapted from Darley & Latané, 1968

Item C   The debrief

After the experiment outlined in Item B, the participants were told about the deception and the purpose of the research. According to Latané and Darley, this is how they felt. 'Although the subjects (participants) experienced stress and conflict during the experiment, their general reactions to it were highly positive. On a questionnaire administered after the experimenter had discussed the nature and purpose of the experiment, every single subject found the experiment either "interesting" or "very interesting" and was willing to participate in similar experiments in the future. All subjects felt they understood what the experiment was about and indicated that they thought the deceptions were necessary and justified.'

From Latané & Darley, 1970

Questions

1   a) How would you feel if you were the participant in Item A?
    b) Assuming that the experiment was to investigate reactions to a big lottery win, do you feel the deception is justified?

2   With reference to Item C, provide brief arguments to a) support and b) reject the experimenters' claim that the deception in Item B was necessary and justified.

Activity 2   Ethics and research

Item A   Little Albert

Little Albert was a healthy, well-balanced baby. John Watson and Rosalie Rayner felt they would 'do him relatively little harm' by carrying out the following experiment in 1919 when Albert was 11 months old. They wanted to see if emotional responses could be learned, in particular, could fear be learned.

Albert was presented with a white rat – he showed no fear of the rat. Could he be conditioned to fear it? A four foot steel bar was suspended near Albert's head and struck with a hammer. On the third strike he 'broke into a sudden crying fit'. The rat was then presented to Albert and as he reached out to touch it, the bar was struck. This was done several times. Then the rat was presented to Albert without the bar being struck. The result was dramatic. 'The instant the rat was shown, the baby began to cry. Almost instantly he turned sharply to the left, fell over on left side, raised himself on all fours and began to crawl away so rapidly that he was caught with difficulty before reaching the edge of the table'. Watson and Rayner were extremely pleased with this result. In their words, 'This was as convincing a case of a completely conditioned fear response as could have been theoretically pictured'. However, no attempt was made to decondition Little Albert, ie to remove his fear of rats.

Adapted from Watson & Rayner, 1920

Item B   Invasion of privacy?

Evidence for a study of the relationship between stress and the invasion of 'personal space' was obtained by observation in a men's public toilet. The observer hid in a cubicle and used a periscope to watch the urinals. As expected, men took longer to urinate when a confederate occupied an adjoining urinal.

Adapted from Middlemist et al., 1976

Questions

1   Read Item A. What aspects of this experiment would be considered unethical in terms of today's standards?

2   Are the research methods in Item B justifiable? Give reasons for your answer.

Unit 2 The ethics of Milgram's obedience research

KEY ISSUES

1   **What ethical issues were raised by Milgram's experiments?**

2   **How did Milgram defend himself against his critics?**

This unit examines the ethical issues involved in Milgram's experiments designed to study obedience to authority. These experiments are outlined on pp 179-181. Some commentators have described them as amongst the most unethical in psychological research.

2.1   Deception

Milgram's experiments were masterpieces of deception. They were elaborate, stage-managed hoaxes. The props were excellent, the performances of the experimenter and the confederate were accomplished.

The deception began even before the participants were selected. Figure 1 is a copy of a newspaper advertisement placed by Milgram. It asked for 'men to help us complete a scientific study of memory and learning'. In fact, the research was a study of obedience.

The stage was set at the beginning of the experiment. The participants were falsely informed that:

'We want to find out just what effect different people have on each other as teachers and learners, and also what effect *punishment* will have on learning in this situation. Therefore, I'm going to ask one of you to be the teacher here tonight and the other one to be the learner' (Milgram, 1963).

Participants then drew slips of paper from a hat to see who would be a teacher and a learner. The draw was fixed so the participant was always a teacher and a confederate the learner.

The 'punishment' was a series of electric shocks of increasing severity given by the teacher (the participant) to the learner (the confederate). Unknown to the participant, the shocks were not real.

At the start of the experiment the confederate was strapped into an 'electric chair'. Electrodes were attached to his wrist and electrode paste applied to 'avoid blisters and burns'. The performance was convincing.

The apparatus used in Milgram's experiments was realistic. This is how Milgram (1963) described the 'shock generator'.

> 'The instrument panel consists of 30 lever switches set in a horizontal line. Each switch is clearly labelled with a voltage designation that ranges from 15 to 450 volts.
>
> Upon depressing a switch: a pilot light corresponding to each switch is illuminated in bright red; an electric buzzing is heard; an electric blue light, labelled "voltage energizer", flashes; the dial on the voltage meter swings to the right; various relay clicks are sounded.
>
> The upper left-hand corner of the generator is labelled Shock Generator, Type ZLB, Dyson Instrument Company, Waltham, Mass. Output 15 Volts – 450 Volts.
>
> Details of the instrument were carefully handled to insure an appearance of authenticity. The panel was engraved by precision industrial engravers, and all components were of high quality. No subject in the experiment suspected that the instrument was merely a simulated shock generator.'

Just to make sure the deception worked, participants were given a 'sample shock' from a battery wired into the 'generator'.

In one experiment, the participants heard what they assumed to be the learner's cries of protest and pain as the voltage level increased. Exclamations of 'Ugh!' were followed by shouted protests and later by agonised screams. This deception was accomplished by an audio-tape which had been carefully prepared before the experiment (see Table 1 for a transcript of this tape).

Milgram's experiments were based on deception from

Figure 1 Milgram's newspaper advertisement

Public Announcement

WE WILL PAY YOU $4.00 FOR ONE HOUR OF YOUR TIME

Persons Needed for a Study of Memory

* We will pay five hundred New Haven men to help us complete a scientific study of memory and learning. The study is being done at Yale University.

* Each person who participates will be paid $4.00 (plus 50c carfare) for approximately 1 hour's time. We need you for only one hour: there are no further obligations. You may choose the time you would like to come (evenings, weekdays, or weekends).

* No special training, education, or experience is needed. We want:

Factory workers	Businessmen	Construction workers
City employees	Clerks	Salespeople
Laborers	Professional people	White-collar workers
Barbers	Telephone workers	Others

All persons must be between the ages of 20 and 50. High school and college students cannot be used.

* If you meet these qualifications, fill out the coupon below and mail it now to Professor Stanley Milgram, Department of Psychology, Yale University, New Haven. You will be notified later of the specific time and place of study. We reserve the right to decline any application.

* You will be paid $4.00 (plus 50c carfare) as soon as you arrive at the laboratory.

— — — — — — — — — — — — — — — — — — — —

TO: PROF. STANLEY MILGRAM, DEPARTMENT OF PSYCHOLOGY, YALE UNIVERSITY, NEW HAVEN, CONN. I want to take part in this study of memory and learning. I am between the ages of 20 and 50. I will be paid $4.00 (plus 50c carfare) if I participate.

NAME (Please print)..

ADDRESS..

TELEPHONE NO .... Best time to call you ....

AGE .... OCCUPATION .... SEX ....

CAN YOU COME:

WEEKDAYS .... EVENINGS .... WEEKENDS ....

beginning to end. Everything was false – the initial advert, the briefing before the experiments began, the equipment and the behaviour of the confederate. And, according to Milgram (1963) 'with a few exceptions', the deception worked. Nearly all the participants 'were convinced of the reality of the experimental situation' and that 'they were administering shocks to another person'.

Criticism and defence Milgram has been criticised for

The 'shock generator'

Participant receives 'sample shock'

deceiving the participants in his experiments. He makes two main points in his defence. First, without deceptions – or 'technical illusions' as he prefers to call them – the experiments would not have worked. In Milgram's words, 'illusion is used when necessary in order to set the stage for the revelation of certain difficult-to-get-at truths'. Thus, for example, if participants were aware that the shocks weren't real and that the learner was really a confederate, then these 'truths' could not have been revealed.

Second, Milgram claimed that if participants later accept that deception has been necessary and worthwhile, then it is justified. In Milgram's words, 'The central moral justification for allowing a procedure of the sort used in my experiment is that it is judged acceptable by those who have taken part in it' (Milgram, 1974). Judging from the debriefing sessions which followed Milgram's experiments, most participants found the deception acceptable – 83.7% said they were 'glad to have been in the experiment', only 1.3% said they wished they had not been involved.

2.2   Informed consent

Deception means that informed consent is not possible. This is particularly so in Milgram's experiments where the deception was widespread and carefully planned. Informed consent needs information, not misinformation.

Milgram admits that his participants were 'misinformed', a term he prefers to 'deceived'. However, he argues that since misinformation is essential for experiments such as his, there are two ways of dealing with the problem of consent. First, *prior general consent,* that is obtaining the consent of participants to take part in an experiment and telling them that they may be misinformed about its purpose. Second, *presumptive consent* which means asking 'reasonable people', who are not taking part, whether the experiment is acceptable and how they think the participants would react. If they think everything is OK, then they have given presumptive consent.

2.3   Protection of participants

The ethical guidelines of the British Psychological Society state that, 'Investigators have a primary responsibility to protect participants from physical and mental harm during the investigation' (BPS, 1998). How do Milgam's experiments measure up to this?

Table 1 shows the learner's (confederate's) responses to various shock levels. Above 330 volts there was an ominous silence – the learner ceased to respond. This could suggest he had either passed out or was dead.

Many of the participants were visibly shaken by their experiences. This is how an observer, watching through one-way glass, describes one of them. 'I observed a mature and initially poised businessman enter the laboratory smiling and confident. Within 20 minutes he was reduced to a twitching, stuttering wreck, who was rapidly approaching a point of nervous collapse. He constantly pulled on his earlobe, and twisted his hands. At one point he pushed his fist into his forehead and muttered: "Oh God, let's stop it". And yet he continued to respond to every word of the experimenter, and obeyed to the end' (Milgram, 1963).

Milgram describes what he calls 'signs of extreme tension' in

Table 1	Learner's responses
75 volts	Ugh!
90 volts	Ugh!
105 volts	Ugh! *(louder)*
120 volts	Ugh! Hey this really hurts.
135 volts	Ugh!!
150 volts	Ugh!!! Experimenter! That's all. Get me out of here. My heart's bothering me. Let me out of here! You have no right to keep me here! Let me out! Let me out of here! Let me out! Let me out of here! My heart's bothering me. Let me out! Let me out!
210 volts	Ugh!! Experimenter! Get me out of here. I've had enough. I won't be in the experiment any more.
225 volts	Ugh!
240 volts	Ugh!
255 volts	Ugh! Get me out of here.
270 volts	*(Agonised scream)* Let me out of here. Let me out of here. Let me out of here. Let me out. Do you hear? Let me out of here.
285 volts	*(Agonised scream)*
300 volts	*(Agonised scream)* I absolutely refuse to answer any more. Get me out of here. You can't hold me here. Get me out. Get me out of here.
315 volts	*(Intensely agonised scream)* I told you I refuse to answer. I'm no longer part of this experiment.
330 volts	*(Intense and prolonged agonised scream)* Let me out of here. Let me out of here. My heart's bothering me. Let me out, I tell you. *(Hysterically)* Let me out of here. Let me out of here. You have no right to hold me here. Let me out! Let me out! Let me out of here! Let me out!

Adapted from Milgram, 1974

the participants. 'Many subjects (participants) showed signs of nervousness in the experimental situation, and especially upon administering the more powerful shocks. In a large number of cases the degree of tension reached extremes that are rarely seen in sociopsychological laboratory studies. Subjects were observed to sweat, tremble, stutter, bite their lips, groan, and dig their fingernails into their flesh. These were characteristic rather than exceptional responses to the experiment'.

'One sign of tension was the regular occurrence of nervous laughing fits. Fourteen of the 40 subjects showed definite signs of nervous laughter and smiling. The laughter seemed entirely out of place, even bizarre. Full-blown, uncontrollable seizures were observed for 3 subjects. On one occasion we observed a seizure so violently convulsive that it was necessary to call a halt to the experiment. The subject, a 46-year-old encyclopaedia salesman, was seriously embarrassed by his untoward and uncontrollable behaviour' (Milgram, 1963).

Short-term and long-term effects Clearly, in the short term, many participants were extremely distressed. But does this amount to 'psychological harm'? And what about the long term

– did participants experience any lasting harm?

Milgram has been severely criticised for putting participants through this experience (Baumrind, 1964). In his defence he says 1) he didn't expect it to happen and 2) there was no long-term harm.

Milgram had discussed his experiments at length with colleagues beforehand. None had expected the participants to reach the shock level where the learner protested and showed pain. The 'extreme tension' that resulted was neither anticipated nor intended.

While admitting the obvious short-term distress, Milgram argued there was no evidence of any long-term harm. He hired a psychiatrist to interview 40 participants one year after the experiments. There was no indication of any harmful effects – most felt their participation had been rewarding and informative. However, what people say in an interview does not always reveal their true feelings. What about the small minority who said they wished they had never taken part? And could all the participants live happily with the knowledge that they were capable of inflicting pain – in some cases extreme pain – on a fellow human being? These questions will be examined further in the section on debriefing.

2.4 The right to withdraw

The British Psychological Society states that at the start of an investigation, researchers 'should make plain to participants their right to withdraw from the research at any time', whether they are being paid for participating or not (BPS, 1998). What opportunities did Milgram's participants have to withdraw from his experiments?

First, Milgram refers to his participants as 'volunteers'. This is perhaps stretching the meaning of the word since they had little idea what they were 'volunteering' for. There was no informed consent on which to base a free choice.

Second, Milgram does admit that once participants have agreed to take part, there is an obligation not to withdraw. However, even though they accepted payment, the participants were told, 'Of course, as in all experiments, the money is yours simply for coming to the laboratory. From this point on, no matter what happens, the money is yours' (Milgram, 1963). However, they were not explicitly told they were free to withdraw at any time. In fact, the whole point of the research was to encourage them to stay until the end. This can clearly be seen by the following procedures.

The experimenter made it very difficult for the participants to withdraw. Participants who appeared unwilling to continue with the experiment were encouraged, cajoled or bullied (depending on your point of view) to carry on. Here's how Milgram (1963) described the procedures.

'At various points in the experiment the subject may turn to the experimenter for advice on whether he should continue to administer shocks. Or he may indicate that he does not wish to go on. It was important to standardise the experimenter's responses to these inquiries and reactions.'

'If the subject indicated his unwillingness to go on, the experimenter responded with a sequence of "prods", using as many as necessary to bring the subject into line.'

Prod 1: Please continue. Or Please go on.

Prod 2: The experiment requires that you continue.

Prod 3: It is absolutely essential that you continue.

Prod 4: You have no other choice, you *must* go on.

The prods were always made in sequence: Only if Prod 1 had been unsuccessful, could Prod 2 be used. If the subject refused to obey the experimenters after Prod 4, the experiment was terminated. The experimenter's tone of voice was at all times firm, but not impolite. The sequence was begun anew on each occasion that the subject balked or showed reluctance to follow orders.'

Given that the whole point of the experiments was to see how far participants would go in response to orders, there is justification for the prods. But, at the same time, the prods made it difficult for them to withdraw. Prod 4, in fact, forbids withdrawal – 'You have no other choice, you *must* go on'.

2.5 Debriefing

The British Psychological Society states that participants should be debriefed after an investigation. They should be given sufficient information to understand the purpose of the research. Any deception should be revealed. They should have the opportunity to discuss their experiences with the researcher in order to clear up any misunderstandings. This also allows the researcher to pick up on any 'negative effects' of the research experience and, hopefully, remove them (BPS, 1998).

In terms of this aspect of ethical conduct, Milgram comes out well. After each experiment, the participants were interviewed and given a battery of psychological tests to make sure they hadn't experienced any negative effects. The aim was to ensure that they left the laboratory 'in a state of wellbeing'. Participants were told that their behaviour during the experiment was perfectly normal and that they shouldn't feel ashamed or blame themselves. They were told the shocks were not real, and it was smiles all round as they met, shook hands with and chatted to their 'victim' (the confederate). Every effort was made 'to reduce any tension that arose as a result of the experiment' (Milgram, 1963). The debrief, or 'dehoax' as Milgram called it, was careful and thorough. As mentioned earlier, 40 participants were interviewed by a psychiatrist one year after the experiment. No long-lasting harmful effects were discovered.

At the debriefing, the experimenter explained the purpose of the research to the participants. He said their contribution provided important insights into the dangers of 'blind obedience'. Later the participants were sent a summary of the results and a questionnaire asking them what they felt about their participation. 83.7% said they were 'very glad' or 'glad' to have taken part and only 1.3% said they were 'sorry' or 'very sorry'. 74% indicated that they had learned something of real personal significance from their experience.

2.6 Conclusion

Milgram's research has been branded as unethical for what others see as deliberate deception, a lack of informed consent, a disregard of the right to withdraw, and a failure to protect participants from psychological harm. As the previous sections indicate, Milgram has defended himself on all these counts. His final defence rests on the importance of the research.

Milgram argues that the significance of his findings justifies the methods he used. He therefore suggests that, up to a point, the end justifies the means. In his words, 'If this experiment serves to jar people out of their complacency, it will have served its end' (Milgram, 1974). Milgram points to the wider significance of his findings. 'If an anonymous experimenter can successfully command adults to subdue a 50-year-old man and force on him painful electric shocks against his protests, one can only wonder what government, with its vastly greater authority and prestige, can command of its subjects' (Milgram, 1965).

Some researchers agree with Milgram. For example, Erikson (1968) believes that Milgram made 'a momentous and meaningful contribution to our knowledge of human behaviour'. However, the psychiatrist Bruno Bettelheim states, 'These experiments are so vile, the intention with which they were engaged in is so vile, that nothing these experiments show has any value' (quoted in Miller, 1986). Ironically, Bettelheim experienced the very thing that inspired Milgram's research – he had been interned in a German concentration camp.

Milgram's experiments led to a long and heated debate about ethical issues in research. Shortly after the publication of his first paper in 1963, he was suspended from the American Psychological Association. After an investigation, the Association decided his research was ethically acceptable. Throughout the 1960s and early 1970s there were many replications (repetitions) of Milgram's experiments. However, times were changing. The last replication in the USA was published in 1976. Given the present ethical guidelines, it is very unlikely that Milgram's experiments could be conducted today.

A final note Milgram was horrified by the slaughter of millions in the Nazi death camps during the 1930s and 1940s. He designed his experiments to investigate the extent to which ordinary people would obey orders to cause pain and suffering to others. He hoped that the findings of his research would show the world just how easily 'ordinary', 'decent' people can harm others. He believed that his experiments would make people think twice about obeying those in authority, especially if obedience meant harming others. In this respect, it is ironic that he should be condemned by some for causing his participants to suffer.

Summary

1   Milgram's experiments have been seen as unethical because:

- Participants were not in a position to give informed consent
- The experiments involved widespread deception
- Participants experienced psychological harm, at least in the short term
- They were discouraged from withdrawing, and in some cases ordered not to withdraw, from the experiments.

2   In his defence, Milgram argued that:

- Informed consent was not possible as participants had to be misled for the experiments to work
- Deception was essential in order to reveal 'difficult-to-get-at truths'
- There was no evidence that participants suffered any long-term harm
- Ordering participants not to withdraw was an essential part of the experiments – after all, the whole point of the research was to study obedience
- Most of the participants saw the experiments as worthwhile and were pleased to have taken part
- The importance of the findings justifies the methods used.

Unit 3 The ethics of Zimbardo's prison experiment

KEY ISSUES

1   **What ethical issues were raised by Zimbardo's prison simulation experiment?**

2   **What arguments did Zimbardo make in defence of his research procedures?**

Informed consent

Like Milgram, Zimbardo placed a newspaper advertisement asking for 'volunteers' to take part in an experiment (see pp 169-170 for an outline of Zimbardo's study). Participants were offered $15 a day and told the experiment was to last for two weeks. Unlike Milgram, Zimbardo openly stated the aim of his research – 'a psychological study of prison life' (Haney, Banks & Zimbardo, 1973).

The participants were told they would be randomly assigned to the roles of prisoner or guard. They signed a contract which stated that those playing the role of prisoner agreed to a suspension of their 'basic civil rights', except for the right to freedom from physical abuse. They were informed that they had no right to privacy and, as prisoners, they would be harassed.

No instructions were given about how to play the role of prisoner or what to expect during the experiment.

Those assigned to the role of guards were told they must 'maintain the reasonable degree of order within the prison necessary for effective functioning'. Apart from being told they must not use physical force, no details of how to play their role were given.

According to Zimbardo, the only breach of the principle of informed consent was the arrest of the prisoners in their homes at the start of the experiment. There were two reasons for this breach. First, the local police only gave their approval for the mock arrests a few minutes before the experiment took place. As a result, there was not time to inform the participants that they were going to be 'arrested' at home. Second, the researchers wanted the arrests to come as a surprise in order to add realism to the experiment.

Official approval Zimbardo made every effort to gain official approval for his research. Before the experiment was carried out, it was approved by the Psychology Department at Stanford University, by the University Committee of Human Experimentation and the Office of Naval Research which sponsored the research.

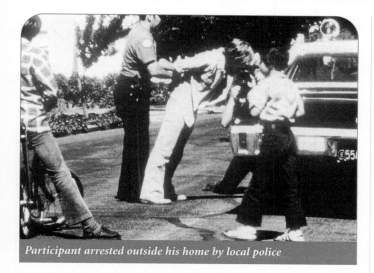

Participant arrested outside his home by local police

Deception

As noted above, the researchers failed to inform the prisoners about their arrest. As Zimbardo admitted, this can be seen as deception.

Zimbardo was just as interested in the behaviour of the guards as he was in the behaviour of the prisoners. However, the participants who played the role of guards believed he was primarily interested in the behaviour of the prisoners. Zimbardo made no attempt to correct this false impression.

Apart from the information in the contract, participants were given little or no indication of what to expect. In other words, they were kept in the dark. As it turned out, the researchers themselves failed to predict how the experiment would develop. However, it can be reasonably argued that telling the participants what to expect would lead to *expectancy bias*. Participants may behave in terms of the researchers' expectations which would lead to invalid results.

Protection from harm

Zimbardo made every effort to ensure the participants were psychologically and physically fit to take part in the experiment. Seventy-five people replied to his advertisement. Each person was interviewed and completed a lengthy questionnaire about their 'physical and mental history'. Twenty-one were selected to take part in the experiment. They were judged to be the 'most stable (physically and mentally)' and the 'most mature'.

The aim of the experiment was to create and maintain 'a psychological state of imprisonment'. For ethical reasons, many aspects of prison life which might harm the prisoners were forbidden – physical punishment, racism and rape. However, the experiment was designed to simulate the social relationships and psychology of prison life – power, control, oppression, humiliation and powerlessness. And this is how things got out of hand.

The guards behaviour became increasingly 'negative, hostile, insulting and dehumanising'. Five of the prisoners had to be 'released' because of 'extreme emotional depression, crying, rage and acute anxiety'. One of them developed a 'psychosomatic rash' which covered large parts of his body. The experiment was planned to last for two weeks. After six days the researchers decided to end it. In Zimbardo's words, 'we had to close down our mock prison because what we saw was

frightening'.

There is no doubt that the prisoners were suffering during the experiment. They were deteriorating rapidly, both psychologically and physically. In addition, the proceedings may have caused harm to the guards. Zimbardo recognised this. In his words, 'Volunteer prisoners suffered physical and psychological abuse hour after hour for days, while volunteer guards were exposed to the new self-knowledge that they enjoyed being powerful and had abused this power to make other human beings suffer' (Zimbardo, 1973).

It was the failure to protect the prisoners from harm which resulted in considerable criticism of the prison simulation experiment. Some critics argued that the researchers should have anticipated what happened and should not have conducted the research in the first place (Savin, 1973). Zimbardo argued that there was no way of predicting such extreme behaviour. In addition, the 'release' of five prisoners, then the abandonment of the experiment after six days, indicates that steps were taken to protect the participants from harm.

Debriefing

Thorough debriefing sessions were held with participants on a one-to-one basis and in groups. They completed questionnaires on their experience of the research, then further questionnaires after several weeks, several months and then every year. Zimbardo (1973) concluded, 'We are sufficiently convinced that the suffering we observed, and were responsible for … did not extend beyond the confines of that basement prison'. In other words, the participants did not experience any long-term harm – the debriefing revealed 'no lasting negative effects'. The participants were 'basically healthy and they readily bounced

Guards and prisoner

back from that highly charged situation' (Zimbardo et al., 1995).

Conclusion

Do the benefits of the prison simulation experiment outweigh the costs? Can the suffering of the prisoners be justified? Some critics answer these questions with a resounding no (Savin, 1973). However, the researchers disagree. None of the participants showed any ill-effects *after* the experiment. They were fully debriefed by professional counsellors who explained the aims of the experiment and what had been learned from it. And the participants appreciated what they had learned. In Zimbardo's words, 'The participants had all learned an important lesson: to never underestimate the power of socially negotiated situations and interpersonal influences to overwhelm

Key term

Expectancy bias *Invalid findings resulting from participants acting in terms of researchers' expectations of how they will behave.*

the personalities and intentions of even the brightest, most emotionally resilient and moral among us' (Zimbardo et al., 1995).

Summary

1. Zimbardo argued that he and his colleagues made every attempt to ensure that the prison simulation experiment was ethically sound.

- Informed consent was obtained
- Deception was minimised
- Every effort was made to protect the participants
- What happened could not be predicted
- There was no indication of lasting harm to the participants
- The findings were valuable and provided a lesson in what can happen in the wider society.

2. Critics argued that what happened during the experiment should have been anticipated and, however valuable the findings, the end does not justify the means.

References

Baumrind, D. (1964). Some thoughts on ethics of research: After reading Milgram's 'Behavioral Study of Obedience'. *American Psychologist, 19,* 421-423.

Baumrind, D. (1979). The costs of deception. *IRB: A Review of Human Subjects Research, 6,* 1-4.

BPS (British Psychological Society). (1998). *Code of conduct, ethical principles and guidelines.* Leicester: BPS.

Christensen, L. (1988). Deception in psychological research: When is its use justified? *Personality and Social Psychology Bulletin, 14,* 664-675.

Darley, J.M. & Latané, B. (1968). Bystander intervention in emergencies: Diffusion of responsibility. *Journal of Personality and Social Psychology, 8,* 377-383.

Elms, A.C. (1982). Keeping deception honest: justifying conditions for social scientific research strategies. In T.L. Beauchamp & R. Faden (Eds.), *Ethical issues in social science research.* Baltimore, MD: Johns Hopkins University Press.

Erikson, M. (1968). The inhumanity of ordinary people. *International Journal of Psychiatry, 6,* 278-9.

Fischer, K.P. (1995). *Nazi Germany: A new history.* London: Constable.

Fisher, C.B. & Fyrberg, D. (1994). Participant partners: College students weigh the costs and benefits of deceptive research. *American Psychologist, 49,* 417-427.

Gross, R.D. (1994). *Key studies in psychology* (2nd ed.). London: Hodder & Stoughton.

Haney, C., Banks, C. & Zimbardo, P. (1973). Interpersonal dynamics in a simulated prison. *International Journal of Criminology and Penology, 1,* 69-97.

Holmes, D.S. (1976a). Debriefing after psychological experiments 1. Effectiveness of postdeception dehoaxing. *American Psychologist, 31,* 858-867.

Holmes, D.S. (1976b). Debriefing after psychological experiments II. Effectiveness of postexperimental desensitising. *American Psychologist, 31,* 868-875.

Homan, R. (1991). *The ethics of social research.* Harlow: Longman.

Kelman, H.C. (1967). Human use of human subjects: The problem of deception in social psychological experiments. *Psychological Bulletin, 67,* 1-11.

Latané, B. & Darley, J.M. (1970). *The unresponsive bystander: Why doesn't he help?* Englewood Cliffs, NJ: Prentice Hall.

Middlemist, R.D., Knowles, E.S. & Matter, C.F. (1976). Personal space invasions in the lavatory: Suggestive evidence for arousal. *Journal of Personality and Social Psychology, 33,* 541-546.

Milgram, S. (1963). Behavioral study of obedience. *Journal of Abnormal and Social Psychology, 67,* 371-378.

Milgram, S. (1965). Some conditions of obedience and disobedience to authority. *Human Relations, 18,* 57-76.

Milgram, S. (1974). *Obedience to authority: An experimental view.* New York: Harper & Row.

Miller. A.G. (1986). *The obedience experiments: A case study of controversy in social science.* New York: Praeger.

Savin, H.B. (1973). Professors and psychological researchers: Conflicting values in conflicting roles. *Cognition, 2,* 147-149.

Silverman, I. (1977). *The human subject in the psychological laboratory.* New York: Pergamon.

Watson, J.B. & Rayner, R. (1920). Conditioned emotional reactions. *Journal of Experimental Psychology, 3,* 1-14.

Zimbardo, P.G. (1973). On the ethics of intervention in human psychological research: With special reference to the Stanford prison experiment. *Cognition, 2,* 243-256.

Zimbardo, P.G., McDermott, M., Jansz, J. & Metaal, M. (1995). *Psychology: A European text.* London: Harper Collins.

▶ Introduction

In their research, psychologists use a range of different methods which produce a variety of different types of data. This chapter looks at a number of these methods and assesses their advantages and disadvantages.

Chapter summary

- Unit 1 distinguishes between quantitative and qualitative data.
- Unit 2 looks at the three main types of experiments – laboratory, field and natural experiments.
- Unit 3 examines investigations using correlational analysis.
- Units 4, 5 and 6 look at non-experimental research methods – observation, questionnaire surveys and interviews.

Unit 1 Quantitative and qualitative data

KEY ISSUES

1. What is the difference between quantitative and qualitative research methods?
2. What kinds of data does each produce?

Psychologists use research methods to gather data. Data can be *quantitative* – in the form of numbers, or *qualitative* – in the form of a description.

Research methods such as laboratory experiments and questionnaire surveys are more likely to produce quantitative data. Methods such as unstructured, in-depth interviews and participant observation (where the researcher joins the group they are observing) are more likely to produce qualitative data – a detailed description of behaviour.

The distinction between quantitative and qualitative data is illustrated in Activity 1. To appreciate the difference, it is a good idea to read Items A and B now, then answer the questions when you have read this unit.

Some researchers argue that unless human behaviour is expressed in the form of numbers, it cannot be accurately measured. Without accurate measurement, conclusions will be based on impressions and will be little more than opinions. Accurate measurement is essential if cause and effect relationships are to be established. Some researchers argue that

the establishment of cause and effect relationships is the basis of science. They believe that for psychology to be a science, quantitative data is essential.

Other researchers tend to favour qualitative research methods. They argue that qualitative data has greater depth, it is more meaningful, it produces a richer and more detailed picture of behaviour. In particular, they believe it is more likely to give a picture of life from the point of view of the people they are studying. It is more likely to capture subtleties, nuances and shades of meaning than the numerical data provided by quantitative methods.

In practice, many researchers use both quantitative and qualitative methods. They recognise the strengths and weaknesses of each and see the different types of data as suitable for different purposes. For example, the findings produced by a participant observation study might form the basis for a laboratory experiment. And quantitative and qualitative data can be used together as 1) a means of checking the other and 2) building up a more complete picture of human behaviour.

Key terms

Quantitative data *Data in the form of numbers.*

Qualitative data *Descriptive data.*

Unit 2 Experiments

KEY ISSUES

1. What are the main types of experiment?
2. What are the advantages and disadvantages of each?

2.1 Laboratory experiments

The following experiment, which was briefly outlined in

Chapter 1 (see p 20), illustrates the main features of a laboratory experiment.

A researcher wishes to find out the effect of light on plant growth. In order to do this, it is necessary to identify and control all the variables or factors which affect plant growth. This is difficult to do outside a laboratory since variables such as temperature and humidity cannot be controlled. Within a laboratory, there is a greater chance of controlling such variables.

Activity 1   Quantitative and qualitative data

The following items are taken from *Violence against wives* (Dobash & Dobash, 1980). The study was based on in-depth interviews with 109 women who had experienced battering. During each interview a number of specific questions were asked which provided data which could be quantified.

Item A   Qualitative data

He punched me, he kicked me, he pulled me by the hair. My face hit a step. He had his bare feet, you know, with being in bed, and he just jumped up and he pulled on his trousers and he was kicking me. If he had his shoes oh, God knows what kind of face I would have had. As it was, I had a cracked cheek-bone, two teeth knocked out, cracked ribs, broken nose, two beautiful black eyes – it wasn't even a black eye, my whole cheek was just purple from one eye to the other. And he had got me by the neck and, you know, he was trying, in fact, practically succeeded in strangling me. I was choking, I was actually at the blacking-out stage. I was trying to pull his fingers away, with me trying to pull his fingers away, I scratched myself, you know, trying to get his fingers off. He hit me and I felt my head, you know, hitting the back of the lock of the door. I started to scream and I felt as if I'd been screaming for ages. When I came to, he was pulling me up the stairs by the hair, I mean, I think it was the pain of him pulling me up the stairs by the hair that brought me round again.

Item B   Quantitative data

Types of injuries resulting from the first, worst, and last violent episode*

| Injuries | Violent episode | | | | | |
| | First | | Worst | | Last | |
	Number	%	Number	%	Number	%
Bruises to face and/or body	101	74	182	64	148	70
Abrasions	0	0	2	1	3	1
Burns	0	0	4	1	5	3
Cuts	18	13	48	17	27	13
Hair torn out	5	3	13	5	10	5
Fractured bones or broken teeth	6	5	11	4	9	4
Internal injuries, miscarriages	4	3	8	3	2	1
Knocked unconscious	2	1	14	5	7	3
Total	136	100	282	100	211	100

* We recorded up to five *different* types of physical injuries in any single violent episode. These figures reflect only the *different* types of injuries, and not the number of times a particular type of injury was received.

Question

What are the advantages and disadvantages of the types of data in Items A and B?

The researcher conducts the following experiment. Every variable except light is held constant – kept the same. For example, plants of the same species and size are kept at the same temperature and humidity; they are grown in the same type of soil and given the same amount of water. Only the light is varied. For example, one group of plants is exposed to the same type and intensity of light for a longer period of time than another group. Since nothing else varies, any difference in growth between the two groups of plants is due to differences in the amount of light they receive.

From this simple example, some of the main features of a laboratory experiment can be identified.

- **Control** The researcher has a greater chance of controlling the variables. One variable is manipulated and changed (the duration of exposure to light), the other variables are held constant (the same temperature, humidity etc).
- **The independent variable** This is the variable that is manipulated by the researcher. In the above example, the independent variable is the duration of exposure to light.
- **The dependent variable** This is the variable that is measured by the researcher. In the above example, the dependent variable is growth. The purpose of the experiment is to see if the dependent variable is affected by the independent

variable. In psychology experiments, the dependent variable is usually the performance of the participants.

- **Cause and effect** In an experiment it is possible to establish a cause and effect relationship between the independent variable and the dependent variable. In terms of the above example, variations in exposure to light cause variations in growth.
- **Quantification** Experiments usually produce quantitative data – data in the form of numbers, for example, 4 hours and 30 minutes, 5 millimetres, and so on.
- **Objective measurement** Ideally, measurement in experiments should be objective. This means it is not affected by personal judgements. For instance, the duration of exposure to light can be measured quantitatively in hours, minutes and seconds, plant growth in millimetres, and so on. These quantitative measurements are unlikely to be affected by personal judgements.
- **Replication** This means repeating the experiment under exactly the same conditions by the same or other researchers. If the variables have been controlled and if the measurements are objective and the data quantified, then replication is possible. If the same results are then obtained, then there is a greater likelihood that the findings of the experiment are reliable.

The laboratory experiment in psychology

The laboratory experiment has dominated large areas of research in psychology. For instance, it has been particularly important in memory research, as the first three chapters indicate. The following example provides an illustration of a laboratory experiment in memory research.

A researcher wishes to investigate the effect of noise on memory. Noise is the independent variable which is manipulated. The dependent variable is the performance of participants on a memory test. One group of participants takes the test in a quiet room, another group in a room with loud music playing. There are two *conditions* – a quiet condition and a noisy condition. Quietness and noisiness are two values or levels of the independent variable.

Apart from the independent variable – level of noise – the researcher attempts to keep all other variables constant. For example, lighting, temperature and the size of rooms are the same. Participants are given the same instructions, the same test, and the same amount of time in which to do it.

The performance of the participants in the two conditions is measured. If participants in the quiet condition perform differently on the memory test that those in the noisy condition, then this suggests that noise affects memory.

It is important to ensure that the only difference between the two conditions is the difference in the value of the independent variable – in this case the level of the noise. If any other variables intrude – for example, if one room was hotter than the other, or if one group of participants had been partying all night and had hangovers – then the researcher would not know if the results were due to the independent variable or one of these other variables. As a result the experiment has been confounded or ruined. Uncontrolled variables which affect the results are known as *confounding variables*.

Summary The experiment is an investigation into the effect of an independent variable on a dependent variable. In its simplest form, there are two conditions, in which participants are presented with one value of the independent variable in one condition, and the other value of the independent variable in the other condition. The performance of the participants – the dependent variable – in condition 1 is measured and compared with the performance of the participants in condition 2. The only way to know whether the independent variable has had an effect on the dependent variable is by making sure that all variables which might confound the experiment have been controlled or eliminated.

Advantages of laboratory experiments

Control The laboratory experiment gives the researcher a greater opportunity to control variables than any other research method.

Cause and effect By controlling variables and reducing or even eliminating the effect of confounding variables, the researcher can be more confident about establishing cause and effect relationships between the independent variable and the dependent variable.

Replication Because laboratory experiments are conducted under controlled conditions, they are easier to replicate than studies conducted using other research methods.

Quantification It is easier to quantify the results of an

Key terms

Variables *Factors which affect behaviour. Variables can vary or change. For example, temperature can increase or decrease.*

Control of variables *The ability to control the value of variables. The researcher can keep them constant (the same) or change their value.*

Cause and effect relationship *When one variable is shown to cause a change in another variable.*

Independent variable *The variable that is manipulated by the researcher to see if it has an effect on the dependent variable.*

Dependent variable *The variable that is measured by the researcher – in psychology this is usually the performance of the participants.*

Replication *Repeating an experiment in exactly the same way to see if its results are reliable.*

Confounding variables *Uncontrolled variables which interfere with the experiment and affect the dependent variable.*

experiment in the controlled conditions of a laboratory. It is then possible to use statistical tests to indicate how likely it is that the results are due to the action of the independent variable.

Time and money Laboratory experiments are often less expensive and time-consuming than other research methods. This is particularly true for the study of events that rarely occur in everyday life such as an eyewitness observing a robbery. Showing participants a film of a robbery in the laboratory is far less expensive and time-consuming than waiting for a similar event to occur in real life.

Specialised equipment Laboratories provide the opportunity to use specialised equipment which may be unavailable or difficult to use in other research settings – for example, instruments for measuring brain activity.

Disadvantages of laboratory experiments

Psychology and science Laboratory experiments were developed by the natural sciences – physics, chemistry and biology. They enable the scientist to show that, under controlled conditions, matter always reacts in the same way to an external stimulus. For example, water always boils at the same temperature. Matter is compelled to react in this way because it has no consciousness. It has no awareness, meanings or motives which direct its behaviour.

Although most psychologists see psychology as a science, they differ over how far the methods of the natural sciences are appropriate for the study of human beings. Some are in favour of laboratory experiments. Others are less sure. They argue that there is a fundamental difference between the subject matter of psychology and the natural sciences. In particular, human beings have consciousness, matter does not. As a result, human beings can give different meanings to situations and act in terms of those meanings rather than simply reacting to the situation itself. Assume the loud music played in the memory experiment described earlier was classical music. Participants will give meaning to the music – some may like classical music, others may not; some may have particular associations with the music. As a result, they are not simply reacting to the noise level. And the meaning they give to the music may affect their performance on the memory test. Considerations such as these do not affect water boiling at a particular temperature.

Some psychologists argue that the laboratory experiment is not appropriate for the study of human beings. Since every aspect of the experiment will be given meanings by the participants, it is not possible to say with any certainty what is directing the participants' actions. This argument lies behind some of the following objections to the use of laboratory experiments in psychology.

Demand characteristics These are cues or clues in an experiment that convey the researcher's hypothesis to the participant. For example, participants try to make sense of experiments and give meaning to the tasks they perform. They may try to guess what the experiment is about and how the researcher expects them to behave. They may act in terms of these expectations and try to please the researcher (Orne, 1962). If they do this, they are responding to demand characteristics rather than to the independent variable.

The researcher/participant relationship In a laboratory experiment, the relationship between the researcher and the participant is distinct from all other relationships outside the laboratory. Participants assume that the researcher will take full responsibility for whatever happens in the experiment. As a result of this unique relationship, participants may behave in ways they would never dream of outside the laboratory (Orne & Holland, 1968). This is one of the criticisms of the Milgram obedience experiments (see pp 179-181). The willingness of some of the participants to deliver supposedly high-voltage shocks to an apparently helpless 'victim', may well reflect the researcher/participant relationship. This relationship may be unique to experimental situations.

Evaluation apprehension Some participants may experience *evaluation apprehension* – they may be worried about how they appear to the researcher and what the researcher might think about them. For example, they may try to look good and behave in ways which are socially acceptable. This is known as the *social desirability effect*.

Laboratory experiments are designed to measure response to independent variables. If participants are concerned about how they appear to the researcher, then this might affect their response to the independent variable.

Investigator or experimenter effects This refers to the ways in which researchers influence the behaviour of participants. For example, a smile, a frown, or a questioning look from the experimenter might encourage participants to behave in particular ways. The same applies to the characteristics of the experimenter – whether they are male or female, black or white, attractive or unattractive, cheerful or solemn, and so on. All these factors may affect the participants' behaviour.

Researchers sometimes expect and hope that experiments will produce certain results. These hopes and expectations may influence participants. For example, a smile when their behaviour matches the expected findings may encourage participants to continue to behave in that way (Rosenthal, 1966).

Artificiality Both the laboratory setting and the tasks participants are asked to perform can appear artificial and unrealistic.

In a laboratory experiment, participants are removed from their everyday settings. They are directed by an experimenter, often in the company of complete strangers. For many people, this is a brand new experience far removed from their everyday lives. It can appear artificial and 'unreal'.

Sometimes the tasks participants are asked to perform appear meaningless. For example, learning nonsense syllables in memory experiments may make little sense to participants. However, not all experimental tasks are as artificial as this. Some experiments attempt to simulate life outside the laboratory – for example, experiments on eyewitness testimony which show participants a film of an accident or a robbery. But even this is a long way from the real thing.

Ecological validity This refers to the extent to which the findings of an experiment can be generalised to settings outside the laboratory. Critics argue that participants are unlikely to behave normally and naturally in a laboratory because of the artificiality of the setting and the tasks. As a result, it is unlikely that their behaviour in the laboratory will reflect their behaviour in other settings. If this is the case, then laboratory experiments will tend to have low ecological validity – it is unlikely that their findings will apply to other settings.

Samples Who are the participants who take part in laboratory experiments? Particularly in the USA, they tend to be white, middle-class, male undergraduate students in their late teens and early twenties. Can the results of experiments based on this type of sample be generalised to other cultures, other places and other times? According to some researchers, the answer is no (Sears, 1986).

There is considerable evidence that a wide range of social factors such as gender, social class, ethnicity, age and culture affect the way people behave and see the world. It can be argued that unless these factors are represented in samples, then generalisations from laboratory experiments are unjustified.

Culture Human beings live in different societies with different cultures – different norms, values, beliefs and attitudes. As a result, they may respond to the same experiment in different ways. For example, a number of researchers have argued that the Strange Situation, a procedure developed in the USA, is not appropriate for classifying and measuring infant attachment across cultures (see pp 54-55). Similar criticisms can be made of many laboratory experiments which have been designed in Western societies. They may be inappropriate for use in other societies with different cultures.

Key terms

Demand characteristics *The cues in an experiment which convey the researcher's hypothesis to the participants.*

Evaluation apprehension *A concern by participants that they are being judged and evaluated by the researcher.*

Social desirability effect *The tendency for participants to behave in ways which are socially acceptable and desirable.*

Investigator or experimenter effects *Ways in which the expectations, behaviour, appearance and social characteristics of the researcher affect the behaviour of participants.*

Ecological validity *The extent to which the findings of an experiment can be generalised to settings outside the laboratory.*

Limitations There are many types of behaviour which are difficult, if not impossible to study in laboratory experiments. For example, complex social behaviours like falling in love; frightening or dangerous situations such as stalking or physical assault; and mental or cognitive events such as dreaming or imagining are difficult to reproduce in a laboratory setting. And in some cases, such as physical assault, it would be unethical to do so.

Ethical issues Laboratory experiments raise a number of ethical issues. As outlined in Chapter 15, the British Psychological Society states that researchers should obtain the informed consent of participants and, wherever possible, avoid deceiving them. This raises a problem. If participants are told everything about the experiment before taking part, this may invalidate the whole experiment. For example, if participants are aware of how they are expected to behave, they may well act accordingly. Some researchers argue that deception is sometimes necessary to avoid the effect of demand characteristics. Others reject this view, seeing deception as unethical.

Activity 2 Eyewitness testimony

Participants watched a film about a car accident. They described what happened, as if they were eyewitnesses giving evidence. They were divided into three groups and each group was asked a slightly different question. The questions and answers are shown below.

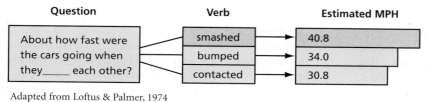

Question	Verb	Estimated MPH
About how fast were the cars going when they _____ each other?	smashed	40.8
	bumped	34.0
	contacted	30.8

Adapted from Loftus & Palmer, 1974

Questions

1 What is the independent variable in this experiment?

2 What is the dependent variable in this experiment?

3 What data is quantified?

4 How many conditions are there? What are they?

5 What cause and effect relationship is suggested by the results?

2.2 Field experiments

Field experiments are conducted outside the laboratory in normal social situations such as the classroom, the workplace, the hospital or the street. The researcher still manipulates the independent variable and measures the dependent variable. However, compared to the laboratory experiment, the researcher has far less control over variables which might affect the participants' behaviour. For example, if the field experiment was conducted on the street, the researcher cannot control the weather or the number of people present.

Hofling et al's (1966) study of obedience in the hospital outlined in Chapter 14 (p182) is an example of a field experiment. The participants were 22 staff nurses on night duty in psychiatric hospitals in the USA. They were telephoned by an unknown 'doctor' (a confederate of Hofling) and instructed to give medication to a patient. All but one of the nurses obeyed this instruction and prepared the medication before they were stopped and the situation explained to them. In doing so, they broke a number of hospital rules. For example, they were forbidden to accept instructions over the telephone and from an unknown doctor.

Field experiments may have certain advantages over other research methods such as interviews. After completing his experiment, Hofling interviewed 12 experienced nurses and asked them what they would have done in this situation. Ten said they would refuse to follow the doctor's instructions. Hofling also interviewed 21 student nurses. All of them said they would disobey the doctor. This suggests that what people say in an interview may be very different from what they do in everyday life.

Activity 3 indicates a further advantage of the field experiment. It suggests that the way people behave in their natural settings may be different from the way they perform in a laboratory experiment.

Advantages of field experiments

Realism Since they are conducted in normal social settings, field experiments are often more realistic and true to life than laboratory experiments. As a result, participants are more likely to behave normally and naturally. Because of this, some researchers believe that field experiments have higher ecological validity than laboratory experiments – that there is a greater likelihood of generalising their findings to other settings.

Other research methods Compared to other research methods, evidence suggests that the data from field experiments may have higher validity. As the hospital experiment indicates, interview data may not give a true picture of how people actually behave in real life. And, as the subway experiment suggests, the way people behave in the laboratory does not necessarily reflect their behaviour in more natural settings.

Demand characteristics Compared to laboratory experiments, it is less likely that demand characteristics will affect participants' behaviour. The participants don't know they are taking part in an experiment. As a result, they will not be aware of the purpose of the experiment. In addition, they will be unlikely to respond in terms of the researcher/participant relationship; they will be less likely to be influenced by investigator effects.

Disadvantages of field experiments

Control of variables Field experiments do not provide the control available in the laboratory. For example, in the subway experiment, the researchers had no control over the number or ethnicity of the commuters in the train compartment. As a result, there is a greater chance of uncontrolled variables affecting participants' behaviour.

Replication Because many variables cannot be controlled, it is difficult to replicate field experiments precisely. For example, it is not possible to exactly reproduce the 103 trials in the subway experiment.

Time and money Field experiments are often more time-consuming and expensive than laboratory experiments. However, compared to observational research (discussed in Unit 4), they usually cost less and take less time.

Sampling The researcher often has little control of the sample of participants who take part in a field experiment. For example, in the subway experiment, apart from selecting the route, the researcher had no control over who was present in the compartment.

Specialised equipment Often, it is not possible to use technical equipment in field experiments – for example equipment to measure physiological changes.

Ethical issues Participants in field experiments are unable to give informed consent – they don't even know they are taking part in an experiment. As a result, they are deceived. In many cases, participants in field experiments are not debriefed after the experiment. Sometimes, a debrief can do more harm than good.

Ethical guidelines for research in psychology state that participants should be protected from psychological harm. In the hospital experiment, the researchers later explained the situation to the nurses. However, the nurses still had to live with the realisation that they had been prepared to give their patients an overdose of a drug which might have caused serious injury.

2.3 Natural experiments

A natural experiment is the study of the effects of a naturally occurring event. It is not set up and controlled by the researcher. The difference in the situation before and after the event is taken to be the independent variable and its effect on behaviour, the dependent variable. The eruption of Mount St Helens in the USA in 1980 provides an example (see p99). Although there were warnings, the exact time of the eruption could not be predicted, nor was the scale and power of the blast anticipated. Sixty people were killed and the blast of hot gas, ash and rock destroyed an area of 150 square miles.

Psychologists studied the behaviour of people in the small agricultural town of Othello near the disaster area. After the eruption they found a 198% increase in stress-related illness, a 235% increase in the diagnosis of mental health problems and an 18.6% increase in the death rate. Crisis calls to the emergency services increased dramatically, as did appointments

Activity 3   Field experiments

Item A   Helping on the New York subway

The following field experiment was designed to examine 'helping behaviour'. It was conducted on subway trains in New York City during a 7$\frac{1}{2}$ minute journey between Harlem and the Bronx. Students played the role of 'victims' who were either drunk or ill, black or white. The students were male, between 26-35 years of age, three were white and one was black. In the drunk condition, the victim smelled of alcohol and carried a bottle in a brown paper bag. In the ill condition, the victim carried a black cane. In both conditions, the victims were dressed identically and collapsed – apparently drunk or ill – in a train compartment. There were between 40 and 45 passengers in the compartment and 8 or 9 close to the victim. Around 45% of the passengers were black, 55% white.

Adapted from Piliavin et al., 1969

Questions

1   Why is this a field study?

2   How is the independent variable manipulated in this study?

3   What variables cannot be controlled in this study?

4   Judging by Item B, why is it important to conduct field experiments as well as laboratory experiments?

Item B   The results

The New York subway

Help for the victim was provided by one or more passengers in 81 of the 103 trials. This is high compared with previous laboratory experiments which indicated a much lower rate of assistance. Evidence from laboratory experiments also suggested that as the number of bystanders increases, the likelihood that any individual would help decreases (Darley & Latané, 1968 – see p193). There was no evidence to support this from the subway experiment. If anything, the opposite occurred.

The 'ill' victim was more likely to be helped than the 'drunk' victim. In the ill condition, ethnicity appeared to make no difference to helping. In the drunk condition, the victim was more likely to be helped by a member of his own ethnic group.

Adapted from Piliavin et al., 1969

at the local mental health clinic (Adams & Adams, 1984).

Natural experiments usually look at behaviour before and after a naturally occurring event. In the case of the Mount St Helens experiment, researchers noted differences in behaviour before and after the eruption. They assumed that changes in behaviour resulted from the eruption.

The researcher has no control over the variables in a natural experiment. As a result, it is difficult to establish cause and effect relationships with any degree of certainty. This can be seen clearly from Activity 4 which looks at the possible effects of zero tolerance policing on crime rates.

Advantages of natural experiments

Realism Natural experiments are realistic – they are based on real-life events. They avoid the artificiality of laboratory experiments.

Demand characteristics and investigator effects Natural experiments minimise demand characteristics and investigator effects. In many cases, the researcher is not present when the event occurs. And, in many cases, participants have no idea their behaviour is being studied.

Research opportunities Often natural experiments give researchers the opportunity to study events that could not be simulated in a laboratory experiment or created in a field experiment. The Mount St Helens eruption is an obvious example.

Ethical issues It can be argued that natural experiments are ethically sound for the following reasons. The events on which they are based would happen anyway and researchers are unlikely to have much effect on the behaviour of those they are studying.

Disadvantages of natural experiments

Lack of control Researchers have no control over the variables in a natural experiment. They simply study what naturally happens.

Cause and effect Because of this lack of control, the researcher is unlikely to establish cause and effect relationships with any degree of certainty. As the example of zero tolerance policing indicates, there are many possible causes for the drop in the crime rate.

Replication and generalisation It is not possible to replicate natural experiments. The events on which they are based are one-off situations which will not occur again with exactly the same characteristics. As a result, it is difficult to make generalisations from natural experiments.

Ethical issues There may be ethical problems in certain situations. For example, people's experience of natural disasters can be traumatic. They don't want an intrusive researcher asking questions if they are still in shock after an earthquake; and after they have got over the initial shock, they might not want to be reminded of the situation as they attempt to rebuild their lives.

Activity 4   Zero tolerance policing

In 1994, William J Bratton was appointed police commissioner for New York City. He introduced the policy of zero tolerance policing. This meant that the police clamped down on all types of crime, however petty and insignificant. No longer did they turn a blind eye to people riding bikes on the sidewalk, urinating in public, petty drug dealers, graffiti, beggars and street prostitution. In Brattons' words, 'If you don't stop the small offenders, it emboldens the really bad guys. It creates an atmosphere of lawlessness.' Within two years of the

Stop-and-search in Harlem, New York City

introduction of zero tolerance, homicides in New York City were halved and robberies dropped by a third. Everybody was impressed, but was this due to zero tolerance policing?

The USA experienced a crime wave from 1990 to 1993. This coincided with an economic recession and high unemployment. Since then, 10.5 million new jobs have been created in the USA. In addition, there has been a decline in the crack-cocaine epidemic and longer prison sentences have kept many criminals locked up and off the streets for much longer periods.

Zero tolerance policing was later introduced in Washington DC. There was little change in the crime rate. In some American cities which did not introduce zero tolerance policing, the reduction in the crime rate was similar to that of New York City.

Adapted from Chaudhary & Walker, 1996

Questions

1 Some researchers assume that zero tolerance policing resulted in a reduction in the crime rate. What are the possible uncontrolled variables which suggest that this might not be the case?

2 Why is it difficult to establish cause and effect relationships from natural experiments?

2.4 Quasi-experiments

Natural experiments are an example of *quasi-experiments*. Quasi means almost. In a quasi-experiment, the researcher lacks the degree of control found in true experiments.

Quasi-experiments usually take place in natural settings outside the laboratory. In such settings, the researcher may be unable to control important variables. First, the researcher may be unable to control the independent variable. This can be seen clearly from natural experiments. In terms of the examples given in this section, the researcher is unable to control a natural disaster or a policy of zero tolerance policing. In a true experiment, the researcher would be able to systematically manipulate the independent variable and control a range of other variables which might affect the participants' behaviour. As the activity on zero tolerance policing shows, this is not possible in a natural experiment. A number of uncontrolled factors, other than zero tolerance policing, may have affected the reduction in the crime rate. Because of this, the researcher cannot be confident about establishing cause and effect relationships.

Second, in a natural setting, the researcher is often unable to select participants and assign them to one condition or another. For example, in the New York subway experiment, the researchers simply relied on participants who happened to be in the train compartment. In a true experiment, participants are randomly assigned to the different conditions. It is assumed that random assignment will cancel out differences between the participants. As a result, differences in their behaviour in the various conditions are seen to reflect different levels of the independent variable. In a quasi-experiment, differences in behaviour may be due to differences between the groups of participants. Again, this makes it difficult to establish cause and effect relationships.

In summary, quasi-experiments lack the controls of a true experiment – in particular, they lack control of the independent variable and/or participants are not randomly assigned to different conditions. Despite this, quasi-experiments can produce valuable data. Their findings can suggest cause and effect relationships. And these findings are often supported by evidence from other studies. In addition, because they often take place in natural settings, quasi-experiments avoid the criticism of artificiality and lack of realism which is sometimes levelled at laboratory experiments.

Summary

1. Supporters of laboratory experiments argue that their value lies in:

- Control of variables
- Establishing cause and effect relationships
- Objective measurement
- Ease of replication.

2. There are a number of possible disadvantages to laboratory experiments. They include:

- Demand characteristics
- Investigator effects
- Low ecological validity
- Inappropriateness for different cultures
- Limited to certain types of behaviour.

3. Compared to laboratory experiments, field experiments are likely to have the following advantages:

- Greater realism
- Less likely to be affected by demand characteristics and investigator effects

and the following disadvantages:

- Less control of variables
- More difficult to replicate
- More costly and time-consuming
- Less control of samples
- Often not possible to use technical equipment.

4. Natural experiments have the following advantages:

- Realism
- Minimal demand characteristics and investigator effects
- Unique research opportunities

and the following disadvantages:

- No control over variables
- Cannot establish cause and effect relationships
- Cannot be replicated
- Difficult to generalise.

5. Quasi-experiments lack the controls of true experiments. The researcher is sometimes unable to control the independent variable and may be unable to randomly assign participants to different conditions.

Unit 3 Investigations using correlational analysis

KEY ISSUES

1. What is correlational analysis?
2. What are its advantages and disadvantages?

Correlational analysis is a technique for analysing data rather than a research method as such. Thus, correlational analysis can be used for analysing data produced by different research methods – by laboratory and field experiments, questionnaire surveys, interviews and so on.

Correlational analysis is a statistical technique which measures the strength of relationships between two or more variables. As such, it requires quantitative data – data in the form of numbers. For example, correlational analysis can be used to measure the relationship between the amount of revision – measured in hours and minutes – and examination performance – measured in the number of marks.

It is possible to obtain a numerical measure of the strength of the relationship between variables. This measure is known as the correlational coefficient. Correlational coefficients vary between −1 (perfect negative correlation) to +1 (perfect positive correlation) with 0 showing no correlation at all between the variables.

A positive correlation refers to a relationship where an increase in one variable is accompanied by an increase in another variable. For example, an increase in revision is accompanied by an increase in examination marks. A negative correlation refers to a relationship in which an increase in one variable is accompanied by a decrease in another variable. For example, an increase in visits to the pub is accompanied by a decrease in examination marks. A correlation of zero indicates no relationship between the variables. For example, there may be a zero correlation between hair colour and examination marks. (Correlational analysis is examined in more detail in Chapter 18).

Correlation and causation If there is a high positive or negative correlation between two variables, this does not necessarily mean that one causes the other. For example, there is often a high positive correlation between the sales of cold drinks and the yellowness of grass, yet neither of these factors is causing the other. The explanation for this correlation lies with a 'hidden third factor', namely the temperature. On hot summer days the grass tends to turn to yellow and everyone wants cold drinks.

Correlational analysis in psychological research

Correlational analysis is widely used in psychology. The following example indicates some of the advantages and disadvantages of this technique.

Life events, stress and illness Life events are significant changes in a person's life which disrupt their normal routines. Examples include marriage, the death of a close relative and moving house. As outlined in Chapter 8 (pp 100-101), Holmes and Rahe (1967) argued that life events produce high levels of stress. They devised the Social Readjustment Rating Scale (SRRS) in which 43 life events were ranked in terms of the degree of 'social readjustment' they required. Each life event was assigned a number of 'life change units' from 100 (death of husband or wife) to 11 (minor violations of the law such as a speeding ticket). A person's 'stress score' is the sum of the life change units of events they have experienced during a period of 12 months.

Correlational analysis was then used to discover whether there was a relationship between stress scores and incidence of future illness. A survey of studies using the SRRS indicates a correlation coefficient of 0.3 (Sarafino, 1994). This suggests a relationship, but not a particularly strong one.

Does a high 'stress score' produce a greater chance of illness? Not necessarily. Some illnesses can develop

undetected over long periods of time. Some of the life events included in the SRRS may result from the early stages of an illness rather than causing that illness. Possible examples are changes in eating and sleeping habits, trouble with in-laws or the boss, and sex difficulties, all of which may be a response to a developing illness (Brown, 1986).

This example shows why correlational analysis cannot establish cause and effect relationships. It indicates three possibilities. First, high stress scores might lead to illness. Second, illness might lead to high stress scores. Third, both high stress scores and illness might result from some other unknown factor.

Advantages of correlational analysis

Strength of relationships Correlational analysis measures the strength of relationships between variables. It can be applied to numerical data produced by a range of research methods.

Further research Correlational analysis can identify relationships between variables. This may open up new lines of research. Further experimental research may indicate the probability of the relationship being causal or not.

Disadvantages of correlational analysis

Causation A high correlation between two variables cannot, on its own, show that one variable is causing the other. The correlation may be caused by a third factor. Even if a causal relationship exists, correlation does not show the direction of causation – for example A might cause B or B might cause A.

Summary

1   Correlational analysis provides a numerical measure of the strength of the relationship between variables. It is widely used in psychological research.

2   A high correlation between two variables does not necessarily indicate a cause and effect relationship.

Unit 4 Observational research

KEY ISSUES

1. **What are the main types of observational research?**
2. **What are their advantages and disadvantages?**

4.1 Naturalistic observation

Naturalistic observation refers to the observation of behaviour in its natural setting. The researcher makes no attempt to influence the behaviour of those being observed. In fact, researchers do their best not to intervene and manipulate variables. The aim is to observe naturally occurring behaviour.

Naturalistic observation is widely used in zoology and ethology where non-human animals are observed in their natural habitat. It is also used to study human behaviour.

Naturalistic observation may be *disclosed* – where the observer informs the people he or she is studying that they are being observed. Or, it may be *undisclosed* – where the observer remains hidden and/or attempts to disguise the real reason for their presence.

Naturalistic observation is sometimes defined as *non-participant observation*. This means that researchers do not participate in the behaviour they are observing and, most of the time, those they are observing are unaware of the researcher's presence. It is possible to observe human behaviour in this way – for example the researcher may find an inconspicuous place on a street, in a shopping centre or a museum from which to observe undetected. Alternatively, behaviour can be filmed using hidden video cameras.

Naturalistic observation tends to be limited to public places and specific aspects of behaviour. For example, it might be used to study behaviour at a pelican crossing. The researcher might note who waits for the 'green man' before crossing the road. At first sight, this seems a rather trivial study. However, if the findings showed that males and young people were more likely to cross on red than females and older people, this may indicate gender and age differences in risk taking. And if this finding was reflected in risk taking in a range of other situations, then it ceases to be trivial and may indicate general tendencies in human behaviour.

Systematic observation Naturalistic observations are often conducted systematically. The researcher may use a *behaviour schedule* – a checklist of precisely defined behaviours which are recorded as and when they occur. For example, a behaviour schedule for aggressive behaviours in a primary school playground included the following categories: bite, chase, hit, push-pull and wrestle (Strayer & Strayer, 1976). These behaviours were ticked off systematically as they occurred. This provides quantitative data which can be directly compared with the results of similar studies using the same behaviour schedule. However, there are a number of problems with this approach. First, only behaviours which fit the categories on the schedule are recorded. Second, the researcher has no information about the meaning of these behaviours to those concerned. For example, is a 'hit' in the playground study an aggressive or a playful act?

Advantages of naturalistic observation

Realism and natural behaviour The researcher is able to observe behaviour which occurs naturally in a real-life setting. No attempt is made to change that behaviour. As a result, it is likely that people will behave normally.

Low demand characteristics and investigator effects When people are unaware they are being observed, their behaviour will not be influenced by demand characteristics or investigator effects.

New ideas Naturalistic observation can provide new ideas for research which can be examined systematically in later studies.

Testing existing findings Naturalistic observation can be used to discover whether the findings of laboratory experiments are reflected in real-life situations.

Disadvantages of naturalistic observation

Lack of control The researcher has no control over the variables – for example, the number and social characteristics of the participants. As a result, cause and effect relationships cannot be established. Observations can describe behaviour but are unlikely to tell us why it took place.

Observer bias As Chapter 3 on eyewitness testimony has shown, observers interpret what they see, they are selective in what they notice, and they tend to see what they expect to see. Observer bias can be reduced by using a behaviour schedule. However, this places limits on the behaviour recorded and discourages observation of behaviour not listed on the schedule.

Meanings Naturalistic observation provides little information about the meanings which direct the behaviour of those observed. This raises problems for the analysis and interpretation of observational findings.

Limitations Naturalistic observation tends to be limited to public places and specific aspects of behaviour. It is unlikely to provide a picture of the way of life of a group of people.

Ethical issues In many cases, people have no idea they are being observed. As a result, they have no opportunity to give informed consent. According to the British Psychological Society's ethical guidelines for research, unless people give their consent, observational research is only acceptable in places where they would expect to be observed by strangers (BPS, 1998). However, a glance from a stranger is very different from the close scrutiny of naturalistic observation. People may well object to this scrutiny as an invasion of their privacy. They may also object to being filmed by hidden video cameras.

4.2 Controlled observation

Controlled observation takes place in a natural setting, but the researcher intervenes and manipulates certain aspects of the situation. An illustration of controlled observation is provided in Activity 5, which looks at the behaviour of macaque monkeys.

Certain features of their natural environment were changed in order to study the extent to which the monkeys could learn new behaviour patterns. It is important that the environment remains unaltered apart from the changes introduced by the researcher. This means that any changes in behaviour are probably due to the changes introduced by the observer. And, because they remain in their normal environment, the monkeys can respond to these changes as naturally as possible.

Advantages of controlled observation

Natural setting Controlled observation allows researchers to study behaviour in natural settings.

Focus Controlled observation enables researchers to focus on what they want to study. In the case of the macaques, intervention meant the researchers were able to observe the extent to which new behaviour patterns could be learned. Without intervention, they might observe the macaques for years without seeing any significant change in behaviour.

Disadvantages of controlled observation

Disturbing natural settings Intervention means that the natural setting has been disturbed – in this respect it is no longer natural. For example, the macaques were provided with a new supply of food. And, for the first time in their existence, they no longer had to forage for food.

4.3 Participant observation

How do we really know how people behave in their normal, everyday settings? One way is to join them – to participate in their daily activities and observe what they say and do. This research method is known as *participant observation*. It was used by Erving Goffman (1968) when he took on the role of a member of staff in order to study the experience of patients in a

Activity 5   Controlled observation

Japanese macaques washing potatoes

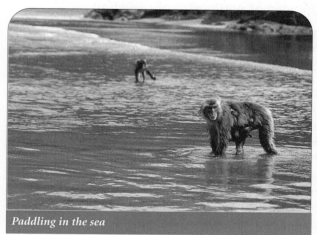

Paddling in the sea

For a number of years Japanese researchers have been studying the behaviour of macaque monkeys on islands in northern Japan. On one island, the macaques lived in the forest in the interior. The researchers tried to discover whether they could change the behaviour of the monkeys. They began by dumping potatoes in a clearing in the forest. The macaques picked them up, sniffed them inquisitively and tasted them. Gradually they changed their eating habits, and potatoes, a food previously unknown to them, became their main diet. The researchers then began moving the potatoes towards the shoreline, and the macaques followed. The potatoes were regularly dumped on the beach and the troupe took up residence there rather than in the forest. Then, without any encouragement from the researchers, a number of brand new behaviour patterns developed.

   Some of the macaques began washing potatoes in the sea before eating them, a practice which was soon adopted by the whole group. Some of the younger monkeys began paddling in the sea then took the plunge and learned how to swim. Their elders followed suit and swimming became normal behaviour for the whole troupe. Finally, some of the more adventurous youngsters began diving into the sea from rocks on the shoreline. Other members of the troupe imitated them but some of the older macaques decided that this time they would not follow the lead of the youngsters.

Adapted from Kawamura, 1963

Questions

1   Why is this a controlled observation?
2   Why is it important that it be conducted in the macaques' natural environment?

psychiatric hospital in Washington DC. It was also used by the white journalist John Howard Griffin (1960), who dyed his skin black in order to discover what it was like to live as an African American in the southern states of the USA.

   Supporters of participant observation see it as an important means of obtaining rich qualitative data. It provides an opportunity to observe people in their natural settings as opposed to the artificial surroundings of the laboratory. It enables researchers to see what people actually do, as opposed to what they say they do when interviewed. It provides an opportunity to capture the meanings which direct behaviour in everyday life.

Gaining entry Participant observation only works if the researcher can gain entry into the group and obtain some degree of acceptance and trust. Researchers sometimes inform those they are studying about their research. For example, William Whyte (1955), told the Italian-American gang he observed in Boston, Massachusetts, that he was studying the area – they assumed he was gathering material for a book. Sometimes researchers disguise their real purpose for joining the group. This is known as covert (hidden) research. For example, Festinger et al. (1956) found that the only way to observe a small religious sect was to pretend to be a 'true believer' and become a member of the group.

Conducting research As far as possible, researchers try not to influence the behaviour of those they observe. Most researchers simply watch and listen and attempt to blend into the background.

   Participant observation is often informal, unplanned and unstructured – it consists of 'hanging around'. In his study of pilfering from the docks in St Johns, Newfoundland, Mars (1982) wandered round the wharves and sheds chatting to the dockers, and hung round the bars with them in the evening.

   Recording data can be difficult. Researchers usually write up the day's findings each evening, when events are still fresh in their mind. However, this relies on the researcher's memory which is inevitably partial and selective.

   Participant observation can be a long and difficult process. Some researchers spend over a year 'in the field', often cut off from the normal social supports of family and friends.

Some of the advantages and disadvantages of participant observation can be seen from Activity 6.

Advantages of participant observation

Normal behaviour Since those observed are in their normal, everyday environment, they are likely to behave naturally. The presence of an observer may affect their behaviour. However, most participant observers believe that once they have gained acceptance and trust, people revert to their normal behaviour.

Insight and new directions Observation can provide fresh insights and new directions for research as the quote from Whyte (1955) indicates (see Activity 6, Item A).

Insider's view By watching and listening, the participant observer has the chance to discover how people see the world in which they live – their meanings, concerns and priorities.

Qualitative data Participant observation can provide a rich source of qualitative data – from detailed accounts of conversations in bars and on streetcorners to vivid descriptions of people's feelings as they experience the ups and downs of everyday life.

Practicality Sometimes the only way to study a group is to join it. The Italian-American gang studied by Whyte were suspicious of outsiders. Only when he gained their trust and acceptance did he obtain any worthwhile data.

Disadvantages of participant observation

Observer bias Researchers interpret the behaviour of those they observe. They watch and listen and try to make sense of the behaviour of others. To some extent, these observations will be affected by the researcher's own beliefs, values and sympathies.

Observer effects The presence of the researcher will, to some degree, affect the behaviour of those observed. As Hargreaves' (1967) study indicates, some teachers changed their behaviour in his presence (see Activity 6, Item B).

Sample size Sample sizes are small. The researcher can only be at one place at one time and can only obtain an in-depth picture of a small group of people.

Quantitative data The type of data obtained by participant observation does not lend itself to quantification. Descriptions of everyday life are difficult to translate into numbers.

Replication Because participant observation relies so heavily on the interpretive skills and personal qualities of the observer, it is

Activity 6   Participant observation

Item A   Cornerville

The following extract is taken from William Whyte's study of an Italian-American gang in Boston in an area he called 'Cornerville'.

'As I sat and listened, I learned the answers to questions that I would not even have had the sense to ask if I had been getting my information solely on an interviewing basis. When I had established my position on the street corner, the data simply came to me without very active efforts on my part.'

Adapted from Whyte, 1955

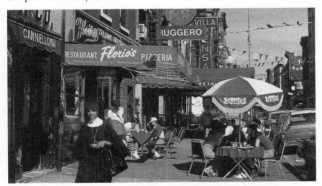

Whyte's research was carried out in the Italian-American community of South Boston. Many east coast American cities have large Italian communities. This picture shows 'Little Italy' in New York.

Question

What are the advantages and disadvantages of participant observation indicated by Items A, B and C?

Item B   In the classroom

The following extract is taken from David Hargreaves' study of an all-boys secondary school in England. He sat at the back of the classroom to observe lessons. Later, he talked to some of the boys about the behaviour of the teachers. This is what they said.

'When you're in he tries to act calmly as though he's a little angel and all that.'

'They put on a show for you. They put the good act on, smiles and all that, and when you've gone out …'

'Like if Mr O's getting mad 'cos someone's ripped a book or something, but if you're in he seems to drop it. If you weren't there, he'd get real mad.'

Adapted from Hargreaves, 1967

Item C   On the street

Elliot Liebow studied African-American 'streetcorner men' – unemployed men who hung round on street corners – in Washington DC. He chose participant observation because he wanted 'an inside view, a clear first-hand picture of the life of ordinary people, on their grounds and on their terms'. Liebow claims that, 'Taking this inside view makes it easier to avoid structuring the material in ways that might be alien to the material itself'.

Adapted from Liebow, 1967

difficult to replicate. Participant observation is often unsystematic – there are no fixed procedures. Again, this makes replication difficult, if not impossible.

Generalisation Small samples make if difficult to generalise. Also, because participant observation studies look at people at particular times and in particular settings, it is difficult to generalise to other times and settings.

Time, money and personal cost Participant observation is often costly and time-consuming. Researchers can spend over a year 'in the field'. There are also personal costs – time away from friends and family and sometimes high levels of stress and even danger. For example, Haralambos (1994) was threatened with guns on more than one occasion during his research on the south side of Chicago.

Ethical issues Covert (hidden) observation involves deception – people don't know they are being observed. Even when researchers reveal the reasons for their presence, they rarely tell the whole truth. Often those observed have insufficient information to give fully informed consent.

Key terms

Naturalistic observation *Observation of behaviour in its normal social setting. Usually, the researcher does not participate in this behaviour and those observed are unaware of the researcher's presence.*

Behaviour schedule *A checklist of precisely defined behaviours which are recorded as and when they occur.*

Controlled observation *The researcher controls one or more of the factors in a natural setting and observes the behaviour that results.*

Participant observation *Observation of behaviour in its normal social setting. The researcher participates in the activities of those observed.*

Summary

1 Naturalistic observation has the following advantages:

- Realism and natural behaviour
- Low demand characteristics and investigator effects
- It can generate new ideas
- It can be used to test existing findings

and the following disadvantages:

- Lack of control of variables
- Observer bias
- Little information about meanings
- Tends to be limited to public places and specific aspects of behaviour
- Ethical problems.

2 Controlled observation allows researchers to observe behaviour in natural settings and to focus on what they want to study. However, intervention by the researcher disturbs the setting.

3 Participant observation has the following advantages:

- Realism and natural behaviour
- Insight and new directions for research
- Provides a rich source of qualitative data
- Can be the only practical way of studying certain groups

and the following disadvantages:

- Observer bias
- Observer effects
- Small samples
- Lack of quantitative data
- Difficult to replicate
- Difficult to generalise from findings
- Often time-consuming, with high financial and personal costs
- Ethical problems.

Unit 5 Questionnaire surveys

KEY ISSUES

1. What are questionnaire surveys?
2. What are they used for?

5.1 Surveys

A *survey* is the systematic collection of the same type of data from a large number of people. This data is usually collected by means of a *questionnaire* – a printed list of questions. In most cases, everybody in the survey is asked the same questions. The type of data collected by surveys is illustrated by the following examples. Twenty-six per cent of all households in 1997 had a home computer. In 1997, *Sugar* was the most popular magazine for 11-14 year old girls – it was read by 47% of the age group. In 1998, 61% of households participated in the Saturday draw of the National Lottery. (All figures are for the UK and taken from *Social Trends*, 1999).

Nearly all surveys are based on a sample of the population to

be investigated – the Census is an exception, it requires information on all members of a society. 'Population' refers to everybody in the group to be studied. The population might be 16-19 year old students, manual workers, divorced men, single women and so on. A sample is a selection of part of the population. Samples are necessary because researchers rarely have the time and money to study everybody in the population.

Most researchers try to select a sample which is representative of the population. This means that the sample should have the same characteristics as the population as a whole. For example, if a sample of 16-19 year old students contained only females who were taking A level psychology, it would not be representative. With a representative sample, the researcher can be more confident of generalising from the survey findings, that is applying them to the population as a whole. (Sampling techniques are examined in the following chapter.)

Surveys are sometimes divided into two types – the *descriptive* and the *analytic survey* (Oppenheim, 1992).

Descriptive surveys, as their name suggests, simply describe aspects of the population under study. The information they provide is often based on the question 'How many?' For example, 'How many people attend church on Sundays?' or 'How many people intend to vote Liberal Democrat in the next general election?'

Analytic surveys are designed to discover relationships between variables – for example, the relationship between age, gender and church attendance. Correlational analysis is often used to calculate the strength of these relationships, but as noted earlier, this type of analysis cannot establish cause and effect relationships.

5.2 Questionnaires

The questionnaire is the main method of collecting data for surveys. It consists of a list of pre-set questions.

Types of questions There are two main types of questions used in questionnaires – *closed* and *open questions*. In closed questions, the various responses are fixed by the researcher. Respondents – those who answer the questions – are required to give 'yes' or 'no' answers or to choose between a fixed number of alternatives. The following example is taken from the annual British Social Attitudes Survey. It shows the percentage of respondents who selected each alternative.

How often do you …		
Make a special effort to sort glass or tins or plastic or newspapers and so on for recycling?		%
	Always	19
	Often	23
	Sometimes	30
	Never	21
	Not available where I live	6

From Jowell et al., 1994

Closed questions are easy to quantify and therefore appropriate for correlational analysis. However, they limit the respondent's choice and freedom of expression.

Open questions allow respondents to answer in their own words. They are particularly appropriate for finding out respondents' opinions and their views of their own behaviour. For example, the question 'Why did you vote Liberal Democrat?' allows respondents to give their own views in their own way.

Open questions are more difficult to quantify. Researchers have to *code* the answers – interpret and classify them – in order to state, for example, that 40% of respondents voted Liberal Democrat because of the party's policy on education. (The design of questionnaires and the analysis of questionnaire data is discussed in more detail in the following two chapters).

Administering questionnaires Questionnaires can be administered – given to respondents – in a number of ways. They can be sent through the post or printed in newspapers and magazines. They can be handed to the respondent and collected later. They can be read out and filled in by the researcher as the respondent answers verbally. In this case, they take the form of structured interviews. This involves the problem of interviewer effects which is discussed in the following unit.

Advantages of questionnaire surveys

Time and money Questionnaires are a fast, efficient and relatively inexpensive method of collecting data.

Large samples Because questionnaires are fast and cheap, questionnaire surveys can be based on far larger samples than are available to other research methods.

Quantitative data Particularly in the case of closed questions, questionnaire data is easy to quantify. As a result, it is suitable for statistical analysis.

Generalisation If the sample is representative, it is possible to generalise from the findings of a questionnaire survey.

Replication Since the questions are standardised and selection procedures for the sample are usually explicit, questionnaire surveys are easy to replicate.

Disadvantages of questionnaire surveys

Response rate The response rate – the percentage of people in the sample who actually complete the questionnaire – is sometimes low – often well below 50% for postal questionnaires and well below 5% for questionnaires in newspapers and magazines. This may destroy the representativeness of the sample. Those who do not complete the questionnaire may differ in important respects from those who do.

Limitations on response Questionnaires often place limits on what respondents wish to say, particularly in the case of closed questions.

Key terms

Questionnaire *A list of pre-set questions.*

Questionnaire survey *The collection of the same type of data from a large number of people by means of a questionnaire.*

Descriptive survey *The collection of data which can be used to describe a population.*

Analytic survey *A survey designed to discover relationships between variables.*

Closed questions *Questions where the various responses are fixed by the researcher.*

Open questions *Questions where the responses are not fixed – respondents can answer them in their own way.*

Coding questionnaires *Classifying answers into different types.*

Summary

Questionnaire surveys have the following advantages:

- Fast, efficient, relatively inexpensive
- Large samples
- Provide quantitative data
- Easy to replicate

and the following disadvantages:

- Sometimes low response rate
- Limited possible responses
- Demand characteristics
- Refusal to reveal sensitive information
- Possible ambiguity of questions.

Demand characteristics Respondents may give answers which they think the researcher expects or wants. There may also be social desirability effects – respondents may try to present themselves in the best possible light.

Sensitive areas Respondents may refuse to reveal information which they find embarrassing, eg sexual behaviour, or which may cause them problems if reported to the authorities, eg criminal behaviour.

Ambiguity of questions Questions may be open to different interpretations. If respondents interpret questions differently, then their answers are not directly comparable.

Unit 6 Interviews

KEY ISSUES

1. **What are the main types of interview?**
2. **What are their advantages and disadvantages?**

Interviews involve the researcher asking the respondent questions. However, some interviews are more like a discussion or a conversation than a question and answer session. Interviews fall between two extremes – *structured interviews* and *unstructured interviews*. In the middle are *semi-structured interviews* which are a mixture of the two types.

6.1 Structured interviews

A structured interview is simply a questionnaire which is read out to the respondent. The interviewer writes down the answers. All respondents are given the same questions in the same order. Structured interviews are sometimes known as *formal interviews* because there is little opportunity for informal conversation. They are also known as *directive interviews* because the interviewer directs the proceedings. Structured interviews have many of the same advantages and disadvantages as questionnaires.

Advantages of structured interviews

Focus They allow researchers to focus on exactly what they want to find out.

Time and money Most are relatively short and inexpensive.

Quantifiable data Much of the data is easily quantified.

Replication Since respondents are asked the same questions in the same order, they are easy to replicate.

Comparable data Assuming the questions mean the same thing to all respondents, the data can be directly compared since all respondents are answering the same questions.

Interviewer assistance The interviewer is on hand to clear up any ambiguity or misunderstanding with the questions.

Disadvantages of structured interviews

Lack of flexibility The questions are predetermined which leaves little room for respondents to develop their answers or move into areas which interest them. As a result, there is less chance of the richer qualitative data that unstructured interviews often produce.

Investigator or interviewer effects Because they are answered in the presence of an interviewer, there is a greater chance of investigator effects than in a questionnaire survey. For example, with certain questions respondents might give different answers to male and female interviewers. However, investigator effects are probably less likely than in unstructured interviews.

6.2 Unstructured interviews

Unstructured interviews are more like a conversation. They are sometimes called *informal interviews* because the atmosphere is relatively relaxed and friendly. They are sometimes known as *non-directive interviews* because the interviewer is usually less directive and, at times, the respondent decides which direction the interview will take. And, they are sometimes called *in-depth interviews* because they tend to 'dig more deeply' into the respondent's beliefs, attitudes and feelings.

As part of their training, interviewers are encouraged to develop *rapport* – a friendly and understanding relationship with the respondent. However, they must maintain a certain distance or the respondent may be unduly influenced if they become too friendly. When conducting an unstructured interview, interviewers are taught to be non-directive – they must avoid asking leading questions and allow respondents to express themselves in their own way. This does not mean they have a chat about something and nothing. Interviewers have certain topics they wish to cover and, at times, they must steer respondents towards these topics.

Advantages of unstructured interviews

Respondent's viewpoint Opportunities are provided for respondents to give their own point of view in their own way. They are able to talk about things which interest them, rather than simply responding to pre-set questions. This can produce new and important insights.

Qualitative data Unstructured interviews can produce rich and detailed qualitative data, especially when the respondent feels the interviewer is sympathetic and understanding.

Developing answers The interviewer has the opportunity to develop the respondent's answers by asking further questions. Interviewers can 'dig deeper'.

Sensitive areas Unstructured interviews are particularly suitable for covering sensitive areas because they provide an opportunity for trust to develop between interviewer and respondent. For example, postal questionnaire surveys were used in London to find out why people did not apply for welfare benefits to which they were entitled. The response rate was very low, partly due to fear and suspicion of authority. Research indicated that the best way to obtain answers was to use unstructured interviews, with skilled interviewers who could develop rapport (Fielding, 1993).

Disadvantages of unstructured interviews

Investigator or interviewer effects Unstructured interviews involve a face-to-face relationship between interviewer and respondent, and often the discussion of intimate personal details. Because of this they are 'wide open' to interviewer effects. For example, the interviewer's beliefs and values can affect the respondent's answers (see Item B, Activity 7). So can the personal qualities of the interviewer – for example, whether they have a sense of humour or a concern for others. And so can the social characteristics of the interviewer – their gender, ethnicity, age, social class and so on (see Item C, Activity 7). And, in a face-to-face situation, social desirability effects may also influence the respondent's answers.

Lack of comparable data Because of a lack of structure and the fact that interviews can take very different directions, it is difficult to directly compare the data from unstructured interviews.

Lack of quantitative data It is difficult to code and quantify much of the qualitative data produced by unstructured interviews.

Replication and generalisation Because each interview is different, and because each involves a unique social

relationship, it is not possible to exactly replicate an unstructured interview. And, for the same reasons, it is difficult to generalise from unstructured interviews.

Summary

1. Structured interviews have the following advantages:
   - Directly focused
   - Relatively short and inexpensive
   - Quantitative data
   - Comparable data
   - Easy to replicate
   - Interviewer assistance

   and the following disadvantages:
   - Lack of flexibility
   - Interviewer effects (though less than unstructured interviews).

2. Unstructured interviews have the following advantages:
   - Provide respondent's viewpoint
   - Rich, detailed qualitative data
   - Allow the interviewer to develop respondent's answers
   - Suitable for sensitive areas

   and the following disadvantages:
   - Interviewer effects and social desirability effects
   - Lack of quantitative data
   - Lack of comparable data
   - Difficult to replicate and generalise from.

Key terms

Structured interview *A pre-set list of questions which is read out to the respondent by the interviewer.*

Unstructured interview *Questions and discussion about particular topics. The questions are not pre-set, the direction of the interview is not pre-determined.*

Activity 7   Interviews

Item A   Three interviews

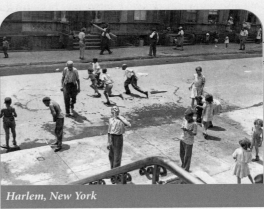
Harlem, New York

Interview 1 An eight-year-old black boy from Harlem in New York is interviewed by a 'friendly' white interviewer who presents him with a toy jet plane and asks him to describe it. The setting is formal. There are long silences followed by short two or three word answers, which hardly provide an adequate description of the plane.

Interview 2 Another black boy from Harlem is interviewed. Again the setting is formal but this time the interviewer is black and raised in Harlem. The boy responds in much the same way as the boy in the first interview.

Interview 3 The boy and the interviewer are the same as in the second interview. This time the interviewer sits on the floor, the boy is provided with a supply of crisps and his best friend is invited along. The change is dramatic. The boy is enthusiastic, talkative, and gives a detailed description of the toy plane.

Adapted from Labov, 1973

Item B   Interviewer effects (1)

In 1914, 2000 destitute men ('down-and-outs' with no means of support) were questioned by two interviewers in the USA. They were asked, among other things, to explain their situation. One of the interviewers was a strong supporter of prohibition – forbidding by law the manufacture and sale of alcoholic drinks. There was a strong tendency for the men he interviewed to blame their situation on alcohol. The second interviewer was a strong supporter of socialist political views. He believed that private industry should be brought into public ownership and that making a profit should take second place to the welfare of the workers. The men that he interviewed were much more likely to explain their misfortune in terms of the industrial situation.

Adapted from Deming, 1971

Item C   Interviewer effects (2)

Eight hundred and forty African Americans were interviewed in North Carolina during the 1960s. All the interviewers were female, 13 were African American, 9 were white. Important differences were revealed between the responses obtained by black and white interviewers. For example, a significantly higher proportion of those interviewed by blacks said they approved of civil rights demonstrations and school desegregation. In addition, more respondents refused to give answers to these questions when faced by a white interviewer.

Adapted from Williams, 1971

Questions

1   Suggest reasons for the similarities and differences between the three interviews in Item A.

2   a)   Explain the responses to the two interviewers in Item B.

   b)   What problem does this raise for researchers?

3   Suggest reasons for the different responses obtained by black and white interviewers in Item C.

6.3   Conclusion

Over a century ago, the German philosopher Wilhelm Dilthey distinguished between what he called 'scientific psychology' and 'humanistic psychology'. The prime objective of scientific psychology is to be scientific at all costs. It adopted the methods of the natural sciences – particularly the laboratory experiment – and applied them to human behaviour. The prime objective of humanistic psychology is to be as true as possible to the complexities and subtleties of human nature. And if this means losing the scientific status of psychology, then so be it.

Even today, we see 'scientifically-minded' psychologists preferring experimental methods, believing that only by controlling variables, objective measurement and replication can cause and effect relationships be established. On the other hand, 'humanistically-minded' psychologists tend to prefer non-experimental methods such as unstructured interviews and participant observation where the sheer richness and diversity of human experience can be explored. Each group remains highly critical of the other.

However, things are not locked into a stalemate. Many psychologists fall between these extremes. They recognise that no one method is entirely satisfactory – all have their strengths and weaknesses. Some argue that if a variety of methods are applied to the same question, and broadly similar results are obtained, then researchers can be more confident about their findings. This use of different methods is known as *triangulation*. It enables researchers to overcome the limitations imposed by any one method and can result in a deeper understanding of human behaviour.

References

Adams, P.R. & Adams, G.R. (1984). Mount Saint Helen's ashfall: Evidence for a disaster stress reaction. *American Psychologist, 39,* 252-260.

BPS (British Psychological Society). (1998). *Code of conduct, ethical principles and guidelines.* Leicester: BPS.

Brown, R. (1986). *Social psychology: The second edition.* New York: Free Press.

Chaundhary, V. & Walker, M. (1996). The petty crime war. *The Guardian,* 21.11.96.

Deming, W.E. (1971). On errors in surveys. In B.J. Franklin & H.W. Osborne (Eds.), *Research methods.* Belmont: Wadsworth.

Dobash, R.E. & Dobash, R. (1980). *Violence against wives.* Wells: Open Books.

Festinger, L., Riecken, H.W. & Schachter, S. (1956). *When prophecy fails.* Minneapolis: University of Minnesota Press.

Fielding, M. (1993). Qualitative interviewing. In N. Gilbert (Ed.), *Researching social life.* London: Sage.

Goffman, E. (1968). *Asylums.* Harmondsworth: Penguin.

Griffin, J.H. (1960). *Black like me.* New York: Signet.

Haralambos, M. (1994). *Right on: From blues to soul in black America.* Ormskirk: Causeway Press.

Hargreaves, D.H. *Social relations in a secondary school.* London: Routledge & Kegan Paul.

Hofling, K.C., Brotzman, E., Balrymple, S., Graves, N. & Pierce, C.M. (1966). An experimental study in the nurse-physician relationship. *Journal of Nervous and Mental Disorders, 143,* 171-180.

Holmes, T.H. & Rahe, R.H. (1967). The social readjustment rating scale. *Journal of Psychosomatic Research, 11,* 213-218.

Jowell, R., Curtice, J., Brook, L. & Ahrendt, D. (Eds.) (1994). *British social attitudes: The 11th report.* Aldershot: Dartmouth.

Kawamura, S. (1963). The process of sub-culture propagation among Japanese macaques. In C.H. Southwick (Ed.), *Primate social behaviour.* New York: Van Nostrand.

Labov, W. (1973). The logic of nonstandard English. In N. Keddie (Ed.), *Tinker, tailor … the myth of cultural deprivation.* Harmondsworth: Penguin.

Liebow, E. (1967). *Tally's corner.* Boston: Little Brown.

Loftus, E.F. & Palmer, J.C. (1974). Reconstruction of automobile destruction: An example of the interaction between language and memory. *Journal of Verbal Learning and Verbal Behavior, 13,* 585-589.

Mars, G. (1982). *Cheats at work: An anthropology of workplace crime.* London: Allen & Unwin.

Oppenheim, A.N. (1992). *Questionnaire design, interviewing and attitude measurement.* London: Pinter.

Orne, M.T. (1962). On the social psychology of the psychology experiment: With particular reference to demand characteristics and their implications. *American Psychologist, 17,* 776-783.

Orne, M.T. & Holland, C.C. (1968). On the ecological validity of laboratory deceptions. *International Journal of Psychiatry, 6,* 282-293.

Piliavin, I.M., Rodin, J. & Piliavin, J. (1969). Good Samaritanism: An underground phenomenon? *Journal of Personality and Social Psychology, 13,* 289-299.

Rosenthal, R. (1966). Covert communication in the psychological experiment. *Psychological Bulletin, 67,* 356-367.

Sarafino, E.P. (1994). *Health psychology: Biopsychological interactions* (2nd ed.). New York: John Wiley.

Sears, D.O. (1986). College sophomores in the laboratory: Influences of a narrow data base on psychology's view of human nature. *Journal of Personality and Social Psychology, 51,* 515-530.

Social Trends. (1999). London: the Stationery Office.

Strayer, F.F. & Strayer, J. (1976). An ethological analysis of social antagonism and dominance relations among preschool children. *Child Development, 47,* 980-989.

Whyte, W.F. (1955). *Street corner society* (2nd ed.). Chicago: University of Chicago Press.

Williams, J.A. Jr. (1971). Interviewer-respondent interaction. In B.J. Franklin, & H.W. Osborne (Eds.), *Research methods.* Belmont: Wadsworth.

Research studies require careful planning and organisation. The organisation of a study is called the research design. This chapter looks at research design and how studies may be carried out or implemented.

Chapter summary

- **Unit 1** looks at aims and hypotheses in research studies.
- **Unit 2** examines some of the main features of research design, focusing on experiments.
- **Unit 3** outlines the main sampling procedures used to select participants for research.

- **Unit 4** examines ways in which the relationship between researchers and participants can affect research.
- **Unit 5** looks at the design of naturalistic observations, questionnaire surveys and interviews.

Unit 1 Aims and hypotheses

KEY ISSUES

1. How can aims be formulated?
2. What are the different types of hypotheses and why are they used?

1.1 Formulation of aims

No research study takes place without an aim in mind. Where does the aim for a research project come from? Sometimes it reflects the researcher's personal interests, observations and concerns. For example, Stanley Milgram was horrified by the slaughter of the Holocaust. He wanted to know why apparently normal people followed orders which resulted in the deaths of millions of innocent people.

Often the aims of research derive from other researchers' theories and studies. For example, Bowlby's theory of maternal deprivation and Freud's idea of repressed memories have formed the basis for a large number of studies. Later research builds on the findings of earlier research and develops existing knowledge. For example, Milgram's obedience experiments have been repeated in various societies in order to see how culture affected their findings.

Sometimes research seeks to discover a solution to a practical problem. For example, the aim of some childcare studies is to improve day care facilities. And many studies of stress aim to provide methods for managing and reducing stress.

Once researchers have decided on an area to investigate, for example obedience or memory, they need to state the purpose of their research in a clear and precise way. For example, it is not sufficient to say, 'I'm going to study memory'. This is only a first step. In practice, most worthwhile studies have a much more specific aim, for example, 'This study aims to investigate the effects of noise on memory'.

It is important to ensure that the aim is realistic in terms of available resources, and that it is ethically acceptable. For

example, if research funds were low, a study of attachment behaviour in six different cultures would probably be unrealistic. And, in terms of today's ethical guidelines, a replication of Milgram's obedience experiments would be considered unacceptable.

1.2 Hypotheses

Many research studies focus the aim more narrowly by translating it into a hypothesis. This turns the aim into a testable statement. For example, Darley and Latané (1968) designed an experiment to test the hypothesis that the greater the number of bystanders who witness an emergency, the less likely any one of them is to help (see p193). The hypothesis is usually a prediction of what the researcher expects to happen. The research study is therefore a means of testing whether or not the hypothesis is supported by the findings.

Alternative and null hypotheses

In an experiment where the researcher is manipulating an independent variable (eg noise) and measuring a dependent variable (eg participants' performance on a memory test), it is customary to state two contradictory hypotheses – the *alternative hypothesis* and the *null hypothesis*. (In an experiment, the alternative hypothesis is also known as the *experimental hypothesis*.)

These two hypotheses cover the two possible outcomes of the experiment. Either the independent variable will have an effect on the dependent variable, or it will not. The alternative (or experimental) hypothesis states that it will. The null hypothesis states that it will not.

In terms of the effect of noise on memory experiment outlined in the previous chapter (see p203), the two hypotheses could be presented like this:

- The alternative hypothesis states that noise will have an effect on performance of the memory task.
- The null hypothesis states that noise will not have an effect

on performance of the memory task.

By stating both hypotheses, the researcher is spelling out the options. One of these options must be true. One of the hypotheses has to be correct.

Statistical tests are generally used to decide between the hypotheses. The researcher can reject the null hypothesis and accept the alternative hypothesis only if they can be more than 95% sure that the results are due to the action of the independent variable. If they are not this sure, they must reject the alternative hypothesis and accept the null hypothesis.

Most experiments have an alternative and null hypothesis. Correlational studies usually have both an alternative hypothesis and a null hypothesis (which predicts no correlation). Qualitative studies always have an aim but may not have an actual hypothesis.

Directional and non-directional hypotheses

In formulating the alternative hypothesis there is an additional decision that must be made – whether the hypothesis is directional or non-directional.

A *directional hypothesis* not only predicts that the independent variable will have an effect, it predicts what that effect will be. In the effect of noise on memory experiment, for example, a directional hypothesis will not just state that loud noise will have an effect on performance of the memory task, it

will predict that loud noise will have the effect of impairing performance on the task.

A *non-directional hypothesis* simply states that the independent variable will have an effect and does not predict the direction of the effect. In the above example, it simply says that noise will have an effect on performance of the memory task.

The researcher must decide which form of the alternative hypothesis to use in each particular experiment. They cannot cheat and use both! The directional form has the advantage of being more precise, but the researcher must give good reasons why a directional hypothesis is being used. By and large, researchers can only use a directional hypothesis if they are confident of the direction of the effect of the independent variable. If they are not confident, they *must* use a non-directional hypothesis.

Some researchers do not think psychologists can ever be sufficiently confident to use a directional hypothesis. This might be a bit extreme. In the effect of noise on memory experiment, a directional hypothesis may well be justified since it is reasonable to assume that if loud noise has any effect, it will act as a distraction. However, in a study into whether people do better in exams in the morning or the afternoon, a non-directional hypothesis would probably be more appropriate.

It is important to note that this choice of two forms of hypothesis only applies to the alternative hypothesis. The null hypothesis is always a straight statement that the independent variable will not have an effect (or, in the case of a correlational study, that there will be no relationship between the variables).

Key terms

Null hypothesis *A hypothesis which states that the independent variable will have no effect on the dependent variable.*

Alternative hypothesis *In an experiment, a hypothesis which states that the independent variable will have an effect on the dependent variable.*

Directional hypothesis *A form of alternative hypothesis which states the direction of the effect of the independent variable.*

Non-directional hypothesis *A form of alternative hypothesis which does not state the direction of the effect of the independent variable.*

Summary

1 Research studies begin with a general aim which is increasingly focused.

2 In many studies, the aim is translated into a hypothesis which turns the aim into a testable statement.

3 If the researcher is more than 95% sure that the independent variable has had an effect, the alternative hypothesis can be accepted. If not, the null hypothesis must be accepted.

Unit 2 Research design

KEY ISSUES

1. How are variables operationalised?
2. How might pilot studies improve research design?
3. What are the main features of experimental design?
4. How are reliability and validity assessed and improved?
5. How do ethical issues affect research design?

2.1 Operationalisation

In an experiment, the researcher manipulates the independent variable to discover its effect on the dependent variable. In order to do this, it is necessary to *operationalise* these variables. This

means defining the variables in such a way that they can be manipulated and precisely measured. For example, in the effect of noise on memory experiment, noise can be operationalised as so many decibels, and memory can be operationalised as performance on a memory test. Each operational definition provides quantitative data – numbers of decibels and scores on the memory test. Without operational definitions, it is not possible to measure the results of an experiment with any degree of precision. Nor is it possible to replicate the experiment since this requires the use of the same measuring instruments.

Sometimes it is more difficult to operationalise variables. Consider the following hypothesis: the more favouritism an adult shows to a child, the more the child will like the adult. Operationalising variables such as 'favouritism' and 'liking' requires considerable ingenuity. And when such variables are operationalised, are they actually measuring what they are intended to measure? For example, psychologists have operationalised aggression as delivering electric shocks, honking car horns, and pressing a button to make it difficult for others to complete a task. Are all these behaviours measuring the same thing? Despite these problems, it is often necessary to operationalise variables in order to do research.

2.2 Pilot studies

Pilot studies are sometimes carried out before the full-scale research project begins. They are a small-scale version of the real thing. Based on a small sample, they are usually quick, easy to conduct and inexpensive.

Pilot studies are used to make sure the research design works. For example, a questionnaire can be piloted with a small sample to make sure that the instructions are clear and that the questions make sense and mean the same thing to all the participants. Any errors in the design of the questionnaire can hopefully be corrected before the main research begins.

Pilot studies can also be helpful in operationalising variables. The previous chapter looked at a naturalistic observation of aggressive behaviour in a primary school playground (see p210). Aggressive behaviour was operationalised by using a behaviour schedule which included the following items: bit, chase, hit, push-pull and wrestle (Strayer & Strayer, 1976). Preliminary observation of children in the playground may result in a more comprehensive schedule – for example, the addition of further items such as pinching. It may also indicate the importance of verbal aggression and lead the researcher to add examples of this to the schedule. And, as a final check, the improved schedule can be piloted before the actual research begins.

Pilot studies can reveal demand characteristics and provide an opportunity for the researcher to reduce them. For example, participants may guess the hypothesis under investigation and behave accordingly. A debrief after the pilot study may reveal this and lead to design changes which reduce demand characteristics. If changes are made, then it is advisable to pilot the new design.

Finally, a pilot study may show that the research design is completely impractical and send the researcher back to the drawing board.

2.3 Participant design

One of the most important features of experimental design is the way participants are allocated to groups when they take part in an experiment. This is called the *participant design*. The main purpose of participant design is to ensure that individual differences between the participants do not confound the results of the experiment. Suppose that in the effect of noise on memory experiment, participants in the quiet condition have normal hearing, while those in the noisy condition have impaired hearing. Clearly, this difference in hearing ability will affect the results. It becomes a confounding variable. The researcher cannot be sure whether a difference in performance between the two groups is due to the independent variable (noise level), or to the difference in hearing ability, or to both.

Individuals differ in many ways – personality, intelligence,

physical skills, experience, sexual orientation, age, gender, social class, ethnicity, nationality and culture. Any, some, or all of these factors can affect their performance in an experiment. The researcher must find some way of eliminating, or at least minimising, the effects of individual differences in order to make sure that it is the effect of the independent variable that is being measured.

The three main types of participant design will now be examined.

Repeated measures design

The repeated measures design uses the same participants in each condition. For example, in the effect of noise on memory experiment, the *same* participants would be used in the quiet and noisy conditions. This eliminates the effect of individual differences since the same people are tested in each condition. As a result, a participant's performance in condition 1 can be directly compared with their performance in condition 2.

The repeated measures design has the added advantage of reducing the number of participants required. More participants would be needed if different participants were used in each of the two conditions. However, there are disadvantages to the repeated measures design.

There may be practical difficulties. For example, in the effect of noise on memory experiment, the researcher would need two memory tests of equivalent difficulty. And, if there was a period of time between the conditions, it is not always possible to get all the participants back!

Demand characteristics can be high as participants may realise what the experiment is about once they begin the second condition and see how it differs from the first. This is particularly true of experiments involving deception.

Similar problems arise if the experiment is studying the effectiveness of two training techniques – it is not easy for participants to unlearn what they have learned in the first condition. In these circumstances, two groups of participants are needed, one to do each condition.

Order effects This refers to the effects created by the order of the conditions. Because each participant does each condition, their performance in the second condition may be influenced by their performance in the first condition. They may learn a skill in the first condition which improves their performance in the second condition. This is called a *practice* or *transfer* effect. On the other hand, participants may get tired or bored by the time they do the second condition and this might impair their performance. Unless order effects are eliminated, they will become confounding variables.

Counterbalancing This technique aims to eliminate order effects. The order in which the participants do the conditions is counterbalanced. Some do condition 1 first, others start with condition 2. Counterbalancing only works if the effect of doing condition 1 then condition 2 is the same as doing them in the reverse order. It is difficult to be sure that this is the case.

Matched participants design

This participant design uses a different group of participants for each condition. Each participant in condition 1 is matched with a participant in condition 2 in terms of one or more variables.

For example, they may be matched in terms of intelligence. The two participants with the highest IQ are randomly assigned, one to condition 1, the other to condition 2. The same applies to the two participants with the next highest IQ, and so on. This ensures that the groups are directly comparable in terms of IQ.

Sometimes participants are matched in terms of their performance on the experimental task. For example, in the effect of noise on memory experiment, the researcher may decide to match the participants in terms of memory skills. They are given a preliminary memory test and then assigned to groups on the basis of their scores. This means that their scores in the actual experiment should reflect noise level rather than memory ability.

The matched participants design has several advantages. It eliminates order and practice effects, and ensures that participants do not become fatigued by doing both conditions. It also saves the researcher from finding two sets of different but equivalent materials. For example, if a matched participants design was used in the effect of noise on memory experiment, only one memory test, not two, would be needed.

The main disadvantage is knowing what to match the participants for. It is all very well matching them for memory ability in a memory experiment, but what if hearing sensitivity, age, gender, ethnicity, IQ and so on affect performance? It would be extremely difficult and time-consuming to find participants who could be matched on a range of individual differences. And, even if this were possible, the researcher cannot be sure they have been matched on the right things. In addition, if matching involved a test before the experiment, this can be a source of demand characteristics.

Independent groups design

In this participant design, there are different participants in each

Key terms

Repeated measures design *The same participants are used in all the conditions. Also known as related samples, related measures and within-group design.*

Matched participants design *Different participants are used in each condition but they are matched in terms of one or more variables, for example intelligence and memory ability. Also known as matched pairs and matched groups design.*

Independent groups design *Different participants are used in each condition. They are randomly allocated to the conditions. Also known as independent measures, independent participant and between-groups design.*

Order effects *The effect of the order of the conditions on the performance of the participants in the repeated measures design.*

Practice or transfer effect *An example of an order effect in which a skill learned in the first condition can affect performance in later conditions.*

Counterbalancing *A technique which aims to eliminate order effects.*

Random assignment *The random allocation of participants to each condition. Each participant has an equal chance of being assigned to each condition.*

condition but no attempt is made to match them. Instead, participants are randomly assigned to each condition, for example by tossing a coin or using a random number table. This means that each participant has an equal chance of being assigned to each of the conditions. The assumption is that reasonably comparable groups will emerge entirely by chance, provided the sample is fairly large. As a result, individual differences should cancel each other out and therefore have little effect on the results.

The independent groups design has a number of advantages. It avoids order effects. It is less costly and time-consuming than the matched participants design. However, control over individual differences is left to chance. This may have the desired effect of producing comparable groups of participants by cancelling out differences between them. But it may not. Using large samples and randomly allocating participants to conditions increases the likelihood of producing comparable groups, but it does not guarantee it.

2.4 Controlling variables

The previous section looked at three types of participant design which aim to control the effects of individual differences on the results of experiments. This section takes a wider view of the problem of controlling variables.

Extraneous variables

In an experiment an independent variable is manipulated to see if it has an effect on a dependent variable – the performance of the participants. However, there are many other variables which might have an effect on the dependent variable. These are known as *extraneous variables*. In order to measure the effect of the independent variable, it is essential that the extraneous variables are controlled. If this isn't done, then extraneous variables may spoil or confound the experiment. In other words, they may become *confounding variables*.

Systematic variation Some extraneous variables operate systematically, that is they vary from one condition to the next and so affect condition 1 differently from the way they affect condition 2. As a result, they may become confounding variables. For example, in the effect of noise on memory experiment, suppose participants in the noisy condition were in a hot room, while those in the quiet condition were in a cool room. Any difference in performance between the two sets of participants could be due to noise *or* temperature. Temperature may have become a confounding variable.

Similarly, suppose the participants in the noisy condition were 6th form students, and those in the quiet condition were pensioners. The researcher would not know whether the performance of the two groups was due to the action of the independent variable (noise level) or to their age. Age may have become a confounding variable.

Extraneous variables which operate systematically must be controlled in order to prevent the experiment from being spoiled or confounded. Ways of controlling extraneous variables are discussed on p222.

Random errors Other extraneous variables do not operate systematically – they do not affect all the participants in a particular condition. Some participants in condition 1 might be affected by them and some participants in condition 2. These unsystematic effects are sometimes known as *random errors*. For example, a participant in one condition may have stomach ache. The researcher may sneeze in front of another participant. A wasp may buzz round the head of a third participant. Random errors do not confound the experiment because they do not make condition 1 consistently different from condition 2. However, they may still have some effect.

The effect of random errors can be indicated by having a control condition in the experiment to which the independent variable is not applied. The performance of the participants in the control group can be regarded as due to random errors, and their performance can then be compared to that of the experimental group. Many experiments in psychology compare an experimental group with a control group in this way.

The purpose of statistical testing is to estimate how likely it is that random errors have affected the dependent variable. If the test indicates that their effect was small, ie there is less than a 5% chance that they caused the change in the dependent variable, then the researcher can conclude that the results were due to the action of the independent variable, and accept the experimental hypothesis. Although it is not possible to get rid of random errors, statistical testing is a way of dealing with them.

Types of extraneous variables

There are three main types of extraneous variables which can affect the results of an experiment. They are *participant variables*, *situational variables* and *investigator variables*.

Participant variables refer to differences between the participants which might affect their performance. They include individual differences such as personality, intelligence, age and a range of social characteristics such as ethnicity and social class. They also include factors such as how participants feel on the day of the experiment and how much attention they give to the tasks they are performing.

Situational variables refer to the setting and circumstances of the research which may affect the performance of the participants. They include things like heat, light, noise, time of day and size of room. They also include the instructions given to participants and the procedures they follow.

Investigator variables refer to the personal and social characteristics and the behaviour of the researcher which may affect the performance of the participants. For example, the personality and appearance of the researcher and their age, gender, ethnicity and social class.

Controlling participant variables

Section 2.3 looked at the control of participant variables. Participant variables are controlled by participant design. There are three main types of participant design used in experiments – repeated measures design, matched participants design and independent groups design. Each type of participant design attempts to ensure that there are no consistent differences between the participants in the various conditions. The idea is to minimise the effects of individual differences on the performance of the participants. However, as noted earlier, there are problems with all three types of experimental design.

Controlling situational variables

Situational variables can be controlled in three main ways:

standardisation, randomisation and counterbalancing.

Standardisation This refers to keeping variables constant, that is the same. For example, in a laboratory experiment, factors such as light, temperature and the time of day can be kept constant for all participants in all conditions. It is assumed that if everybody experiences constant situational variables, then these variables won't change their performance in the various conditions.

The procedures which participants follow and the tasks they perform must be the same in each condition. Participants must be given the same instructions and the same length of time to complete the tasks. Any variations in these factors can affect the performance of the participants and confound the experiment.

However, too much standardisation can be a problem. For example, if the researcher attempted to control every aspect of the environment, then the situation might become so artificial that there would be little chance of generalising the findings beyond the laboratory walls.

Randomisation Even in the highly controlled setting of a laboratory, it is not always possible to standardise situational variables. For example, it may not be possible to test all participants at the same time of day. In this case, randomisation offers an alternative to standardisation. Participants are randomly allocated to different times of the day. Here, the researcher assumes that random allocation will cancel out the effect of testing at different time periods.

Sometimes experiments are conducted outside the laboratory. For example, they may be conducted in participants' homes. This prevents standardisation of a number of situational variables, for example lighting and temperature. Rather than trying to control these variables, the researcher assumes that if participants in each condition experience a similar *range* of lighting and temperature, then these situational variables will cancel each other out. In order to be fairly sure that this happens, large samples are needed. This adds time and expense, but it can result in a more realistic experiment.

Counterbalancing can be used to deliberately cancel out situational variables. For example, if participants are being tested at different times of day, half the participants in condition

Key terms

Extraneous variables *Variables other than the independent variables which may affect the dependent variable.*

Confounding variables *Extraneous variables which affect the dependent variable in a systematic way and confound the experiment.*

Random errors *Extraneous variables which do not affect the dependent variable in a systematic way, but may still have some effect.*

Participant variables *Differences between participants which may affect their performance.*

Situational variables *The setting or circumstances of the research which may affect the performance of the participants.*

Investigator variables *The personal and social characteristics and the behaviour of the researcher which may affect the performance of the participants.*

1 perform the experiment in the morning and half in the afternoon. The same applies to the participants in condition 2. The assumption is that this will cancel out the effect of testing at different times of day.

All three techniques of controlling situational variables may be used in one experiment. Instructions and procedures are usually standardised. In a repeated measures design, order effects can be eliminated by counterbalancing. Other situational variables may be dealt with by a mixture of standardisation and randomising according to the circumstances and the researcher's judgement. Designing experiments is quite an art.

Controlling investigator variables

Counterbalancing can also be used to control investigator variables. For example, if there were two researchers, a cheerful young woman for condition 1 and a solemn older man for condition 2, then participants may respond differently to each. However, if half the participants in each condition were dealt with by each researcher, then this may cancel out any effects of the different researchers' characteristics.

Investigator variables and their control are examined in more detail in Unit 4.

2.5 Reliability and validity

Reliability

Researchers aim to produce results which are both reliable and valid. Results are reliable if they are consistent. For example, if researchers replicate an experiment, using the same methods of observation and measurement, and obtain the same results, then both the methods and the data they produce are seen as reliable. Reliability matters – researchers can only trust results if they are reliable. However, reliability does not mean that the results are accurate. Nor does it mean that the methods are measuring what they are intended to measure. Take the following example.

A milometer in a car produces consistent readings between two towns. Every time the journey is made, it measures the same distance – 25 miles. This measurement is reliable because it is consistent. However, it is not accurate – the actual distance is 30 miles. The milometer is faulty.

And, the milometer may not be measuring what it is intended to measure, ie distance. It may be measuring something completely different. For example, due to incorrect wiring, it might be measuring fuel consumption.

In terms of this example, the measuring instrument is reliable – it produces consistent measurements – but it is not valid. A valid measuring instrument produces accurate measurements and measures what it is supposed to measure.

Assessing reliability

There are various methods of checking reliability.

Replication This refers to repeating a research study under exactly the same conditions. For example, in a laboratory experiment, it means using the same procedures in the same setting. Participants are given the same instructions and required to perform the same tasks. The sample is the same – for example in both experiments participants are 18-20 year old, middle-class British females. If the same results are obtained, then those results are seen as reliable.

Exact replication is practically impossible. Participants will not be exactly the same as those in the first experiment. The same usually applies to the researcher and the setting. However, if a later experiment is basically similar to an earlier experiment and produces similar results, then many researchers accept the results as reliable (Shaughnessy & Zechmeister, 1997).

In practice, few researchers attempt exact replications, mainly because it does little to advance their careers. For example, psychology journals rarely publish replications. To make a name for themselves, researchers need to publish new and exciting research, rather than simply repeating what went before (Graziano & Raulin, 1997).

A number of techniques have been developed for assessing the reliability of particular research methods. Some of these will be examined in Unit 5.

Validity

The results of a research study may be reliable but this does not necessarily mean they are valid. Valid results are accurate. A valid measuring instrument produces accurate measurements of what it is intended to measure. Returning to the example of the use of a behaviour schedule for measuring aggression in a school playground (see p220), the schedule may produce results which are reliable but not valid. All the observers may obtain the same results – a reliable measure – but what they record as aggression may simply be non-aggressive play. If so, they are not measuring aggression. Their measurements are not valid because their measuring instrument – the behaviour schedule – is not measuring what it is designed to measure.

Research studies can be assessed in terms of *internal validity* and *external validity*.

Internal validity

Internal validity is the extent to which the findings of an experiment can be attributed to the effect of the independent variable. An experiment is internally valid when the findings have not been affected by confounding variables. In other words, the findings are due to the action of the independent variable. For example, in the effect of noise on memory experiment, if participants' performance on the memory test (the dependent variable) was due to variation in the noise level (the independent variable), then the experiment is internally valid. However, if their performance was affected by extraneous variables, such as differences in room temperature between the conditions, then the experiment does not have internal validity.

Establishing internal validity In order to establish internal validity, the researcher must control extraneous variables which might affect the dependent variable. In other words, the researcher must prevent extraneous variables from becoming confounding variables. Many of the techniques which aim to do this have already been examined. They include participant designs, such as the repeated measures design, which aim to prevent individual differences between participants from confounding the results. They include controlling situational variables and investigator variables. And they include attempts to reduce demand characteristics, investigator effects and social desirability effects (examined in Unit 4). The greater the control of extraneous variables, the more confident the researcher can be that the experiment is internally valid.

External validity

External validity refers to the extent to which research findings can be generalised. Simply because a research study has internal validity does not mean its results can be generalised. For example, an experiment may have internal validity but its findings may not apply to people beyond the laboratory walls.

A research study has high external validity if its findings can be generalised to other populations, other settings and other times.

Populations Can the findings be generalised to similar populations to those used in the research study? For example, if the study was based on a sample of female undergraduates, can the findings be applied to all female undergraduates? Can the findings be generalised further – for example, to male undergraduates, or more widely to people of different age, ethnic and social class groups? The term *population validity* refers to the extent to which findings can be generalised to other populations.

Settings Can the findings be generalised to other settings and situations? For example, can the findings of the New York subway experiment on helping behaviour be generalised to other settings such as the street, the school playground and the workplace? The term *ecological validity* refers to the extent to which findings can be generalised to other settings. (Ecological validity is sometimes used to mean external validity though, strictly speaking, it refers to settings.)

Times Can the findings be generalised to other times? For example, are the findings of studies conducted in the 1950s, such as Asch's conformity experiments in the USA, still valid today? As noted in Chapter 13, nonconformity was widely discouraged in 1950s' America (see p166). The term *temporal validity* may be used to refer to the extent to which findings can be generalised to other times.

The highest level of external validity is when findings can be generalised to all populations, all settings, and all times.

Establishing external validity

How can researchers increase the external validity of their studies? How do they know the extent of the external validity of their research?

Sampling In general, researchers assume that the more representative the sample, the more likely the results can be generalised to a wider population. For example, if the sample reflects the general population in terms of a range of factors such as age, gender, ethnicity and social class, then the results of the study are more likely to have high population validity – they are more likely to apply to the population as a whole. (Sampling methods are examined in Unit 3.)

Partial replication This refers to repeating a study with a change in one or more of the variables, for example a change in the sample, setting or time (Shaughnessy & Zechmeister, 1997). Milgram partially replicated his original obedience experiment using female rather than male participants. The results were similar, indicating that, in terms of gender, the experiment had high population validity. Partial replications of Milgram's experiment were conducted using samples from different countries. The results varied indicating that, in these cases, population validity was lower (see pp 185-186). Milgram also used a partial replication by changing the setting from a laboratory in Yale University to a rundown office building. Here

the results indicated fairly low ecological validity – obedience was much lower in the office building (see p183).

Realism Some researchers assume that the more realistic a research study, the higher its external validity. From this viewpoint, laboratory experiments are often seen as artificial and unrealistic. Because of this, it is unlikely that participants' behaviour in the laboratory will reflect their behaviour in the world outside. As a result, laboratory experiments are seen to have low external validity.

However, greater realism does not necessarily mean higher external validity. For example, field experiments are usually more realistic than laboratory experiments since they are conducted in 'natural' settings. But this does not automatically mean that their results have higher ecological validity. As noted earlier, the findings of the New York subway experiment may not generalise to other settings.

Triangulation This is a term used to compare the results of research studies using different investigators and different methods (O'Connell Davidson & Layder, 1994). Triangulation can be used to assess the external validity of research results. For example, if laboratory experiments, field experiments, observational research, questionnaire surveys and interviews on the same topic produce similar results, then the researcher can be more confident about generalising from those results. In other words, triangulation of methods which produce similar results may indicate high external validity.

2.6 Ethical issues

When designing their research, investigators must make sure it complies with ethical guidelines. Ethical issues in psychological research are discussed in detail in Chapter 15. This section

Key terms

Reliability *Measurements and findings are reliable if they are consistent.*

Replication *Repeating a research study under exactly the same conditions.*

Partial replication *Repeating a research study with a change in one or more of the variables, eg a different type of sample or setting.*

Validity *Measurements and findings are valid if they are accurate.*

Internal validity *The extent to which the findings of an experiment can be attributed to the effect of the independent variable.*

External validity *The extent to which research findings can be generalised to other populations, settings and times.*

Population validity *The extent to which research findings can be generalised to other populations.*

Ecological validity *The extent to which research findings can be generalised to other settings.*

Temporal validity *The extent to which research findings can be generalised to other times.*

Triangulation *Comparing the results of research studies which use different researchers and different methods.*

summarises and develops some of the points made earlier. It is based on the British Psychological Society's ethical guidelines for research with human participants (BPS, 1998).

Protection from harm Researchers must protect participants from physical and psychological harm. They must not offend participants' values or undermine their dignity. No risk, stress or harm greater than that normally encountered in everyday life should be permitted. If researchers are in any doubt about this, they must consult with independent judges, drawn from the same population as the participants, and ask them how they would feel about taking part in the study. This is especially important if the participants are of different age, gender, social class, ethnicity or culture to the researcher.

Informed consent Participants must be given sufficient information on which to base a decision whether or not to take part in the research. In particular, they must be informed about any aspects of the study which might influence their willingness to participate. In the case of young people under 16, researchers must obtain both their consent and that of their parents or guardians. In the case of adults with 'impairments in understanding or communication', the researcher should consult a member of the person's family, their doctor or obtain approval from independent advisors.

Care must be taken to make sure consent is freely given. This is particularly important when participants are in institutions such as prisons or psychiatric hospitals and in the case of students who are asked to participate in experiments as part of their course requirements. There is a danger of coercion when participants are not volunteers – they may be pressured to take part.

Deception Whenever possible, deception should be avoided. Some researchers insist that deception is never justified, as it demeans the participant and turns psychological research into a con trick (eg Baumrind, 1979; Korn, 1987). Others argue that deception is sometimes justified – without it certain experiments simply would not work. When deception is used, the researcher should check with independent judges, for example members of an ethics committee, to make sure it won't cause the participants distress.

Debriefing Participants must be fully debriefed after the research. Any deception must be revealed. Participants who have experienced guilt, anxiety or stress as a result of the research should be reassured and supported immediately after completion of the study. Immediate debriefing is especially important when deception has been used.

Withdrawal from investigation Participants have the right to withdraw from an investigation at any time, whether or not they have been paid to take part. They should be informed of this right at the start of the investigation. Participants also have the right to withdraw their results, even after the research has been completed.

Confidentiality Participants' identity must not be revealed. Often

research deals with personal and sensitive areas. Researchers must make it clear that participants cannot be identified when research results are published.

Privacy In studies based on observation, the researcher must respect the privacy of those observed. Unless they give their consent, observational research should be limited to settings where people normally expect to be observed by strangers.

Giving advice If researchers believe that participants have physical or psychological problems which might threaten their future wellbeing, they have a responsibility to inform them. However, researchers should not lay claim to competence they do not possess or pose as experts.

Psychological research and society What use should be made of psychological research? This is an ethical question which the British Psychological Society does not address in its ethical guidelines. For Hans Eysenck (1969) in his *Technology of consent*, psychology should make its expertise available to the powers that be to engineer a more ordered and obedient society. For George Miller, in his *Psychology as a means of promoting human welfare* (1969), psychology should never become a tool in the hands of the powerful. Instead, it should 'give itself away' to citizens for use in their own lives, and to defend themselves against attempts by government, business and advertisers to manipulate them. The ethics of 'What is psychology for?' and 'Who are psychologists working for?' are perhaps even more important than the ethics of research procedures.

Summary

1. Variables in a research study need to be operationalised in order to measure changes in the independent variable and the dependent variable.

2. Pilot studies can be used to improve research designs.

3. Wherever possible, researchers must control extraneous variables and prevent them from becoming confounding variables.

4. Participant design aims to control the effects of extraneous variables arising from differences between participants.

5. Replication can be used to assess the reliability of the findings of a research study.

6. The results of research may be reliable, but this does not necessarily mean they are valid.

7. Internal validity is threatened by extraneous variables.

8. External validity can be improved by effective sampling techniques and assessed by partial replication and triangulation.

9. Research design and implementation should comply with ethical guidelines for research.

Unit 3 Sampling procedures

KEY ISSUES

1. What are the main methods of sampling?

2. What are their advantages and disadvantages?

Sampling refers to the way participants are selected for research studies. Sampling is important if the researcher wishes to generalise the findings of a particular study to a larger population. In order to do this, the sample must be representative of the wider population.

The term population refers to the total number of people in the group to be studied. The population might be teenage boys, middle-class housewives, bus drivers, divorced men, African Caribbeans living in Britain, and so on. The term *target population* is used to refer to the population to be investigated.

Ideally, the researcher should study the entire target population. In practice, this is usually impracticable – it would cost too much and take too long. Researchers therefore select a sample from the target population. If they are going to generalise from their findings to the population as a whole, then the sample must represent that population. For example, if the study was based on teenage boys in Britain, the sample should be drawn from different social classes, different ethnic groups and different parts of the country. A sample of boys drawn solely from middle-class households would produce a biased sample – it would not represent the target population.

There are various ways of selecting samples. The main ways are outlined below.

Opportunity samples

Also known as convenience samples, *opportunity samples* are the most common sampling technique used in psychological research. Opportunity samples are made up of anyone who is available to take part in the research – anyone who is handy and convenient. Since most researchers are based in university psychology departments, opportunity samples are usually composed of undergraduate students, and, more often than not, students taking psychology courses. According to one estimate, around 75% of the participants in British and American studies are students (Valentine, 1992).

Students may be convenient but they are hardly representative of the population as a whole. They tend to be young, middle-class, male (though in recent years this is changing), white, and more intelligent and literate than the general population. And, because of the popularity of psychology in the USA, the students in research studies tend to be American. Studies using opportunity samples have been criticised for lacking external validity. Students are a narrow and distinctive band of the population as a whole. As a result, generalisations from studies based on opportunity samples of students must be treated with considerable caution.

The use of students in research also raises ethical issues. Students taking psychology courses are often asked to participate in research as part of the course requirements. They are usually offered alternatives, such as writing papers, but these are often hard work compared to taking part in research. As a result, there is pressure for students to participate. Some researchers regard this as unethical (Korn, 1988).

Random samples

A *random sample* gives every member of the target population an equal chance of being selected for the sample. Every name is given a number and a list of random numbers is then used to select the sample. Ideally, this will result in a representative sample, assuming the sample is large enough. However, this cannot be guaranteed. Because the sample is random, a disproportionate number of, for example, men or young people might be selected. If the target population is the general population, researchers often select a random sample from the electoral register. This automatically excludes those not old enough to vote. And certain groups, such as the poor, are under-represented on the electoral register because many have not registered to vote.

In many cases, it is difficult to obtain a list of members of the target population from which to select a random sample. For example, lists of people with criminal records or psychological disorders are not readily available.

In practice, researchers do not randomly sample entire target populations. If this were possible, they'd end up with people from all over the country which would make their research too costly and time-consuming. Instead, they often choose a particular place – a university, a town, or a district – and draw a random sample from the local telephone directory or electoral register. However, care is needed. For example, if the sample is intended to represent the population as a whole, then choosing a retirement resort like Bournemouth can result in an over-representation of wealthy, elderly and white people.

Despite all these difficulties, a random sample does avoid the possibility of researchers selecting a sample which supports their hypothesis. And random samples are more likely to represent the target population than the opportunity samples so often used in psychological research.

Stratified samples

A random sample does not necessarily produce a representative sample. A *stratified sample* offers a partial solution to this problem. It allows researchers to make sure that certain aspects of the target population which are relevant to their research are reflected in the sample. The population is divided into separate 'strata' in terms of one or more characteristics, for example age, gender, ethnicity and social class. A random sample which reflects the proportion of those characteristics in the target population is then drawn from the strata. For example, if the aim is to reflect gender divisions in the UK, then 51% of the sample will be randomly selected from the female stratum and 49% from the male stratum. In terms of gender, the sample will be representative of the population as a whole.

Quota samples

Quota samples are similar to stratified samples. They are often used by market researchers. For example, the researcher may require 20 women between the ages of 30 and 45 to fill her quota. If she was using a questionnaire in a town centre, she would probably select the first available people who met her requirements that passed by. This is the main difference between quota and stratified samples – in a quota sample, participants are not selected randomly.

Quota sampling has certain advantages. It is quicker, cheaper and easier than stratified sampling. However, it can lead to a more biased sample. For example, stopping people on the street during working hours would exclude many people in paid employment.

Snowball sampling

Sometimes researchers have great difficulty in obtaining a sample. First, lists of members of the target population may not be available. Second, members of the target population might not wish to be identified – for example, burglars, heroin users, prostitutes or members of a Masonic Lodge. One possibility is to use an existing network of members of the target population.

This is the basis of *snowball sampling*, so-called because it is like rolling a snowball.

Snowballing works like this. The researcher finds a member of the target population. They are asked to find another person who fits the sample, and so on until the sample is complete.

Snowballing has the obvious advantage of providing a sample where other methods might fail. However, it is unlikely to provide a representative sample since it relies on personal networks and personal recommendations.

Volunteer sampling

Snowballing is an example of *volunteer sampling* which involves people volunteering to participate in research. Researchers sometimes advertise for volunteers on university notice boards or in newspapers – see Milgram's advertisement on p195. Sometimes questionnaires are included in newspapers or magazines.

Volunteer sampling is a quick, cheap and easy way of obtaining participants but it is not without its problems. The participants are self-selected – they choose themselves – and, as a result, they may differ in important respects from those who did not volunteer. As a result, they may not be representative of the population being investigated. According to Rosenthal (1965), volunteers tend to be more intelligent, younger, less conventional, less authoritarian, more sociable, and more in need of social approval than the general population. Because of this, generalisations from volunteer samples should be treated with caution.

Cross-cultural samples

In recent years, psychologists have become increasingly aware of the dangers of generalising their findings across cultures. Findings from a study based on a sample of white, male, middle-class, American undergraduate students cannot be automatically generalised to other cultures whose members have different norms, values, attitudes and beliefs.

Samples based on members of different cultures show this clearly. They indicate the limits to the external validity of much of the research conducted in Western societies. This has been shown when Ainsworth's Strange Situation and Milgram's obedience experiments have been used in different societies (see pp 54-55; 185-186). Culture can make a significant difference to people's responses to laboratory and field experiments. Because of this, increasing numbers of psychologists are calling for *cross-cultural samples* – samples drawn from members of different cultures (Moghaddam et al., 1993; Smith & Bond, 1993).

Critics have made similar points about the under-representation of a range of social groups in samples. Such groups include women, the working class, ethnic minorities, the disabled and gays. As a result, psychologists have been accused of bias in selecting and generalising from their samples. Some researchers see the under-representation of women as an example of *androcentrism* (seeing the world through male eyes), and the under-representation of other cultures as an example of *ethnocentrism* (seeing the world through the eyes of your own culture).

Conclusion

Without a representative sample of the target population, researchers cannot generalise their findings with any degree of confidence. As a result, the external validity of their research is likely to be low.

Psychologists have tended to rely on opportunity samples of undergraduate students. This is a serious drawback. These samples may only represent the people who make them up – that is undergraduate students. This suggests that many of the findings about human behaviour which psychologists claim to have discovered may have limited application. Fortunately, psychologists are increasingly aware of this possibility as can be seen with the growing calls for more cross-cultural research.

Key terms

Sample *The selection of part of a larger population in order to indicate what the larger population is like.*

Target population *The population under investigation from which the sample is drawn.*

Representative sample *A sample that represents the larger population.*

Biased sample *A sample that does not represent the target population.*

Opportunity sample *A sample made up of anybody who is available.*

Random sample *A sample which is randomly selected from the target population.*

Stratified sample *A sample which reflects the proportion of certain characteristics in the target population. Members of the sample are randomly selected.*

Quota sample *Similar to a stratified sample except that participants are not randomly selected.*

Snowball sample *A sample drawn from introductions provided by members of the target population.*

Volunteer sample *A sample drawn from people who volunteer to take part in the research.*

Cross-cultural sample *A sample drawn from members of different cultures.*

Summary

1. Samples are necessary because researchers are rarely able to study the whole target population.

2. Researchers can only be confident in generalising from their findings if the sample is representative.

3. Most psychological research is based on opportunity samples which are unlikely to be representative of wider populations.

Activity 1   Problems with samples

Item A   A self-selected sample

Shere Hite's *The Hite report on the family* (1994), based on a questionnaire survey, presented some dramatic figures about the 'dark side' of family life. According to the survey, more than one in four women 'have no memory of affection by their father'. Four out of ten fathers frighten their sons with their violent tempers. 31% of girls and young women 'report sexual harassment or abuse by a male family member'. Hite distributed 100,000 questionnaires in magazines such as *Penthouse* in America, *Women against fundamentalism* in Britain and *Nouvelles questions feminists* in France. Her statistics come from the 3% who responded.

Adapted from Kellner, 1994

Will the readership of 'Penthouse' provide a representative sample?

Item B   A student sample

In a study of eyewitness testimony, Loftus and Burns (1982) showed participants two filmed versions of a crime. In one version, the robbers made a clean getaway without any violence. In the other version, a small boy was shot in the face as the robbers escaped. Loftus and Burns found that the inclusion of violence in the film impaired participants' memory for other details occurring up to two minutes before the shooting happened.

This experiment was conducted at the University of Washington. The sample consisted of 226 students who volunteered to take part in order to fulfil a course requirement.

Adapted from Loftus and Burns, 1982

Questions

1   Why should we question Hite's findings in Item A?

2   Critically assess the sample in Item B.

Unit 4   The relationship between researcher and participants

KEY ISSUES

1. **How might the relationship between researcher and participants affect the results of research?**
2. **What can be done to control this possibility?**

Most research studies involve a social relationship between researchers and participants. In any social relationship, those involved will influence each other's behaviour. Social relationships in a research study are unusual, particularly from the participants' viewpoint. Many have never been the focus of research. How will this affect their behaviour? This unit looks at how the relationship between researchers and participants might affect the findings of research studies.

A special relationship

According to Orne (1962), in a laboratory experiment, the relationship between the researcher and the participant is distinct from all other relationships outside the laboratory. Participants agree to do what the researcher asks them within a limited period of time in a strange place. Some might withdraw from the experiment, but most continue to the end. They assume that the researcher will not harm them and will take full responsibility for what happens during the experiment. In view of this special relationship and unusual setting, it is not

surprising that participants sometimes behave in ways that are very different from their behaviour outside the laboratory.

This raises serious questions about the internal validity of laboratory experiments. Are participants responding to the independent variable or to the special relationship with the researcher? In other words, is the experiment measuring what it is supposed to measure? For example, are Milgram's experiments measuring obedience or do their findings simply reflect the researcher/participant relationship? (Orne & Holland, 1968)

Consider the following experiments. In one experiment, participants picked up snakes which they had been told were poisonous. In another experiment, they picked coins out of an acid solution which they were told would burn their hands (Orne, 1969). They were willing to do this because they believed the researcher would protect them from harm – and they were right! These experiments contained cues which informed the participants that there was no real danger. And they behaved accordingly. These cues are known as *demand characteristics*.

Demand characteristics

Demand characteristics are the cues or clues in an investigation that convey the researcher's hypothesis to the participant (Orne, 1962). In doing so, they influence the participants' behaviour. When entering a laboratory, participants try to make sense of the situation. Often this involves asking themselves what the experiment is all about. In answering this question, they may well try to guess the researcher's hypothesis. (Sometimes the term demand characteristic is used more generally to refer to any aspect of the researcher's behaviour or the research design which indicates to participants how they are expected to behave.)

The following experiment conducted by Orne and Scheibe (1964) shows how demand characteristics can operate. Two groups of participants were asked to sit for four hours in a small but comfortable room. The first group were told they were taking part in a sensory deprivation experiment. They signed a form which released the researcher from any liability for what might happen. They were provided with a 'panic button' which they could press if the experience became too much for them. At the end of four hours, the participants reported finding the experiment extremely stressful. The second group were simply asked to sit in the room for four hours. They were told nothing about sensory deprivation, and given no panic button to press or release form to sign. Although a little bored, they experienced no stress.

The first group experienced stress simply because they expected to – there was nothing essentially stressful about sitting in a comfortable room for four hours. However, the way the experiment was set up gave participants clues about how they ought to feel. They believed they knew what the researcher's hypothesis was and behaved accordingly. This experiment shows how cues in the research setting can become demand characteristics.

This can have serious consequences for research. In an experiment, participants may be responding to demand characteristics rather than the independent variable. If so, demand characteristics become confounding variables and reduce the internal validity of the experiment.

Investigator effects

Researchers are human beings with their own hopes and expectations. In terms of their research, they hope and expect that the results will turn out as predicted and support their hypothesis. They are often emotionally involved in their work – they have put considerable time and energy into their research and their career may depend on the expected outcome. As a result, they might influence participants' behaviour to support their hypothesis. However, they usually have little or no awareness of doing this.

The various ways in which researchers influence the behaviour of participants are known as *investigator effects*. In the context of experiments, they are sometimes known as *experimenter effects*.

Consider the following experiment conducted by Rosenthal and Fode (1963a). Two groups of participants were given identical sets of photographs of people. They were asked to judge how successful the people were on a scale of -10 (total failure) to +10 (extremely successful). Researchers who conducted the experiment with the first group were told that the participants would rate the pictures positively. Researchers with the second group were told the participants would rate the pictures negatively. And this is exactly what happened! It appears that the researchers' expectations were communicated to the participants who then made judgements in line with these

expectations. This is known as the *expectancy effect*. It is an example of a *self-fulfilling prophecy* – an expectation that is conveyed to others who then act to make it come true.

Expectancy effects are another example of demand characteristics. They are particularly likely to occur in the enclosed setting of a laboratory where the researcher is in direct communication with participants. In this context, the researcher's manner and tone of voice, a nod, a smile, or a frown, can influence participants' behaviour. This type of influence can also operate in the face-to-face situation of an unstructured, in-depth interview.

Individual differences No two researchers are the same. They may differ in terms of personality, age, gender, ethnicity, social class, and so on. To some extent, their personal and social characteristics will have some effect on the behaviour of participants.

As the previous chapter indicated, African American respondents may give different answers to black and white interviewers (see Activity 7, Item C, p 217). Self-conscious researchers are often anxious, fidgety and less courteous. Female researchers tend to be more friendly to male participants. The same applies to male researchers with female participants – they are likely to use a different tone of voice and lean closer towards them (Rosenthal, 1967). All these differences between researchers can have some effect on the behaviour of participants.

Participant effects

Just as researchers can affect the outcome of a research study, so can participants.

Evaluation apprehension This refers to the concern felt by participants that they are being judged or evaluated by the researcher (Rosenberg, 1969). Many participants want to make a good impression and present themselves in the best possible light. As a result, they may hide certain aspects of their normal behaviour which they think might be interpreted in a negative way. This can have serious consequences for research. For example, respondents in an interview may give answers they think are socially desirable. This is known as the *social desirability effect*. It can be clearly seen from the following example.

Interviews were conducted in New York to investigate the relationship between psychological disorders and ethnicity. People were asked whether or not they had experienced a list of symptoms associated with psychological disorders. Compared with Jewish people, Irish Americans and African Americans, Puerto Ricans reported experiencing more of the symptoms and therefore appeared to have a higher rate of psychological disorders. However, it was then found that the symptoms were regarded as less undesirable by Puerto Ricans than by members of other ethnic groups. As a result, they were more likely to admit to them (Phillips, 1971).

The Hawthorne effect The following research was conducted at the Hawthorne plant of the Western Electricity Company in Cicero, Illinois (Roethlisberger & Dickson, 1939). Factors affecting the productivity of five female workers were investigated. Variables such as lighting and heating, the length of rest periods and the value of bonus payments were systematically manipulated. But, no matter what changes were made, productivity remained consistently high even when working conditions and bonus payments worsened.

One interpretation of these results is known as the *Hawthorne effect* (named after the plant). It states that participants' behaviour is affected by their awareness that others are interested in them. The workers knew they were taking part in an experiment, they were flattered by the interest shown in them and did their best to please the researchers. As a result, they were not responding to changes in the various independent variables – lighting, bonus payments and so on. Instead they were responding to the attention being paid to them.

Individual differences Like researchers, participants vary in terms of their personal and social characteristics. These factors can affect their behaviour in a research situation. For example, some participants are cooperative and do their best to help the researcher; others do just the opposite – the 'screw you effect' (Masling, 1966). Some might be suspicious or even fearful of the researcher. All these factors can affect participants' behaviour in the presence of a researcher.

Controlling demand characteristics, investigator and participant effects

Clearly researchers wish to reduce and ideally eliminate these effects. A number of techniques have been developed for this purpose. Some are examined below, others are outlined in the following unit which looks at the design of various research methods.

Blind procedures In some studies, participants know the general aim of the research. However, demand characteristics can be reduced by concealing from them which condition they are in. This is known as the *single-blind procedure*. However, it does not stop participants from guessing the condition and acting accordingly. It doesn't really matter whether their guess is right or wrong. It will still affect their behaviour.

With a *double-blind procedure* research assistants are used to direct the experiment. Neither they, nor the participants, know which condition the participants are in. This technique is often used in drug studies. Participants in the experimental group are given the drug, those in the control group are given a pill which looks identical but does not contain the drug. Neither the research assistant nor the participants know which pill is being taken.

Deception One of the most common techniques for reducing demand characteristics is to deceive participants. For example, Milgram deliberately misled his participants by telling them they were taking part in 'a study of memory and learning' when, in fact, they were taking part in an obedience experiment (see pp 194-195). Today, most researchers would regard such blatant deception as unethical. However, in some circumstances, researchers see it as acceptable to withhold the aim of the research from participants. Again, however, this does not prevent participants from guessing the aim and acting accordingly.

Automation One of the most effective ways of reducing investigator effects is to remove the researcher from the scene of the experiment. For example, instructions to participants can be tape recorded or presented on a computer screen. In this respect, the experiment is 'automated'.

Alternative research methods Many of the effects discussed in this unit apply particularly to laboratory studies. Here

participants are aware they are the focus of research and they usually communicate directly with the researcher. Field experiments and naturalistic observations often avoid these problems.

Conclusion

Despite various techniques to control demand characteristics, investigator effects and participant effects, it is generally agreed that they cannot be eliminated. They threaten both the internal and external validity of research studies. They threaten internal validity because participants may be responding to demand characteristics rather than the independent variable. As a result, the findings of the experiment cannot be generalised – they are limited to the experimental situation. Some researchers have even suggested that laboratory experiments should be removed from the repertoire of research methods in psychology. For example, Orne (1962) is sceptical about the possibility of laboratory experiments producing anything approaching real-life behaviour.

However, many researchers reject this view. While accepting that experiments have their problems, they still see them as an important research method. Experimental research has provided valuable insights which are often supported by triangulation – by the use of data produced by other research methods.

Key terms

Demand characteristics *The cues in a research study which convey the hypothesis to the participants.*

Investigator or experimenter effects *Ways in which researchers influence the behaviour of participants.*

Expectancy effects *The tendency for participants to behave in ways the researcher expects them to behave.*

Evaluation apprehension *A concern felt by participants that they are being judged by the researcher.*

Hawthorne effect *The effect on participants' behaviour of their awareness that others are interested in them.*

Single-blind procedure *Concealing from participants the condition they are in.*

Double-blind procedure *Concealing from both participants and research assistants which condition the participants are in.*

Summary

1. Social relationships between researchers and participants will affect the behaviour of participants in a research study.

2. This is particularly so in the enclosed situation of a laboratory experiment where researchers and participants communicate directly.

3. Various aspects of this communication can become confounding variables which threaten both the internal and external validity of research studies.

4. While it is possible to reduce demand characteristics and investigator and participant effects, there is general agreement that they cannot be eliminated.

Activity 2   Influencing responses

Item A   Clever Hans

Clever Hans was a performing horse who amazed his audiences in Berlin during the early years of the 20th century. Spectators would ask him to solve mathematical problems and he gave the answer by tapping his hoof. And, practically every time, he got the answer right. How did he do it? When asking a question, spectators would lean forward very slightly or move their eyes up and down without being aware of it. When Hans reached the correct answer by tapping his hoof, the spectator would straighten up or glance up. This signalled to Hans that it was time to stop.

Adapted from Goodwin, 1998

Clever Hans and his owner

Questions

1 What parallels can be drawn between Clever Hans's performance and investigator effects?

2 Use the idea of social desirability effects to explain the difference between the two sets of figures in Item B.

3 Use the idea of investigator effects to explain the behaviour of the two groups of rats in Item C.

Item B   Social desirability

Survey after survey has revealed a high level of church attendance in the USA, far higher than the UK. Yet figures produced by the churches in America sometimes tell a rather different story. For example, a survey conducted by Gallup indicates that 35% of Episcopalians in the USA had been to church in the last 7 days. Yet figures from the churches showed that only 16% actually did so.

Adapted from Bruce, 1995

Item C   Bright rats and dull rats

Members of two groups of students were each given five rats and asked to train them on a T-maze task. Students in the first condition were told that their rats were bred to be 'maze-bright'; those in the second condition were told that their rats were 'maze-dull'. In fact, the two groups of rats were randomly selected from the same stock – they only difference between them was in the minds of the students.

The 'maze-bright' rats made more correct responses, and they made them more quickly, than the 'maze-dull' rats. Results from a questionnaire after the experiment indicated that students with the 'maze-bright' rats rated their rats as cleaner, tamer, more pleasant and more intelligent than did students with 'maze-dull' rats. They also estimated that they handled their rats more gently and more often.

Adapted from Rosenthal & Fode, 1963 (b)

Unit 5 Designing naturalistic observations, questionnaire surveys and interviews

KEY ISSUES

1. **How might research studies using these methods be designed?**

2. **What problems are involved and how might they be overcome?**

5.1   Designing naturalistic observations

Naturalistic observation is the observation of behaviour in a natural setting, that is a setting in which the behaviour normally occurs. Examples include the street, the school playground, the workplace or a shopping centre. Events are allowed to occur naturally – they are not manipulated or controlled by the observer. The researcher tries to remain unobtrusive – usually those observed are not aware of the researcher. As a result, the researcher's presence does not affect the behaviour of those observed.

Aim and hypothesis

As with all research studies, the researcher begins with an aim – for example:

'The aim of the study is to observe gender differences in the behaviour of primary school children in the school playground.'

Sometimes this aim can be refined further and expressed as a hypothesis:

'It is predicted that girls will be more cooperative in their play, and boys more competitive.'

Because naturalistic observation does not involve the manipulation of variables or permit cause-and-effect relationships to be established, it is not usually necessary to state a null hypothesis.

Sampling procedures

Having decided on the aim of the study, the researcher must now select a sample of people to observe. The size of the sample will depend in part on the resources – time and money – available. Ideally the sample will be representative of the wider population. How typical of primary school children will a sample drawn from the school round the corner be? Probably not very typical – most primary schools are neighbourhood schools often drawing children from particular social class and ethnic groups. In order to reflect such social differences, the researcher might select samples from a number of schools in different areas.

Time sampling This refers to the intervals at which observations are made. For example, the researcher may decide to observe children in the playground for ten minutes during morning, lunchtime and afternoon breaks. Systematic time sampling allows the observations of different researchers to be directly compared and means the study can be replicated using the same procedures.

The importance of time sampling can be seen from the following example. A researcher wishes to observe the behaviour of people using a pelican crossing. It is important to observe behaviour at different times of the day and night. First, there are different volumes of traffic at different time periods. Second, there are different types of people using the crossing at different times. At mid-morning during a weekday, those observed will be unrepresentative since most employed people will be at work. Those in the street at midnight will be even more unrepresentative.

Event sampling Here the researcher decides which events or behaviours are going to be sampled. In any situation, a wide range of behaviours can occur. The researcher decides which of these are relevant to the study and records them on a checklist or behaviour schedule each time they occur.

Situation sampling This refers to sampling the behaviour to be observed in different circumstances and locations. As noted earlier, samples for an observation of primary school children's play might be drawn from different schools with children of different ethnic and social class backgrounds. In addition, children from this age group might be observed playing in different settings – in the street, the park or at home. Situation sampling can increase the external validity of a study. If the same behaviour is observed in different settings with children of different backgrounds, then the researcher can be more confident of generalising from the study's findings.

The behaviour schedule

The researcher needs to decide which behaviours are relevant to the study and how to identify and measure them. Returning to the study of children playing, the researcher will need to clearly identify which behaviours indicate cooperative play and which indicate competitive play. A pilot study – an initial observation of children playing – will be useful in this respect. The researcher may identify behaviours such as:

- Shares toy with another child

- Gives toy to another child
- Explains to another child how to use toy

as examples of *cooperative* play, and behaviours like:

- Refuses to share toy
- Takes toy from another child
- Warns another child not to touch.

as examples of *competitive* play.

Once these behaviours have been identified and precisely defined, they are entered on a behaviour schedule or checklist. The observer can then simply tick them off as and when they occur. Usually, researchers devise a behaviour schedule which suits their particular study. However, some 'off the shelf' schedules are available – for example the Bales' Interaction Process Analysis (Bales, 1950) for verbal behaviour in small group interactions.

Rather than simply measuring the frequency of behaviours, the researcher might also want to measure their intensity. For example, if aggressive behaviour is being observed, the researcher might want to measure the level of aggression. This may involve rating how loudly one person shouted at another or how hard they pushed them. This type of rating is open to the observer's interpretation. For example, one observer might think a shove is a normal part of everyday life and give it a rating of 3 out of 10. Another observer might interpret it as a sign of real aggression and give it a rating of 8 out of 10.

Reliability How reliable are the results of naturalistic observations? One way to answer this question is to use the same behaviour schedule with two or more observers and test for *inter-observer reliability*, ie the degree of consistency between the observers' results. As a general rule, if there is 85% or above agreement, then inter-observer reliability is seen as high (Shaughnessy & Zechmeister, 1997). However, this does not necessarily mean the results are valid. For example, two observers might make the same errors because behaviours have been inadequately defined on the schedule.

Some form of mechanical recording – video, audio or photographic – can serve as a means of checking the reliability of observations. However, recording behaviour without consent raises ethical issues.

Observing others

In naturalistic observations, the researcher usually tries to be unobtrusive, but this is not always easy. Ticking boxes on a behaviour schedule is fairly straightforward if the researcher sits in a café watching people using a pelican crossing. But how can the researcher remain inconspicuous observing children in a playground? The problem is magnified if the researcher wants to get close enough to hear what people are saying.

Key terms

Time sampling *Sampling behaviour at specific times and for specific lengths of time.*

Event sampling *Sampling specific behaviours from a range of behaviours.*

Situation sampling *Sampling the same behaviour in different situations and locations.*

Inter-observer reliability *The degree of consistency between the observations of different researchers.*

A possible solution is for the researcher to openly observe people. This is known as *disclosed observation* (as opposed to *undisclosed observation*). However, disclosed observation may influence people's behaviour. They may become self-conscious. This may result in demand characteristics if they ask questions such as, 'What am I supposed to be doing?' and 'How am I expected to behave?' This may result in unnatural behaviour – quite different from the kind of behaviour naturalistic observations are designed to record. However, many researchers believe that people revert to their normal behaviour once they get used to the presence of an observer.

Ethical issues Observing people without their consent can be seen as an invasion of privacy. The British Psychological Society's ethical guidelines state that naturalistic observation without consent is only acceptable in public places where people expect to be seen by strangers (BPS, 1998). The street is an obvious public place, but what about a pub or a club? The definition of a public place is not clear-cut.

5.2 Designing questionnaire surveys

A questionnaire is a list of questions. A questionnaire survey involves collecting information from a sample of people by means of a questionnaire. Those who answer the questionnaire are known as respondents.

Aim and hypothesis

As with all research studies, the researcher begins with an aim. The choice of aim will affect the design of the questionnaire – in particular the choice of questions. Oppenheim (1992) identifies two main types of survey in terms of the data they produce. Descriptive surveys record attitudes and behaviours and simply collect information on 'how many' – for example 40% of respondents prefer westerns to thrillers. Analytic surveys are designed to test hypotheses. For example, the hypothesis might state that film preference is related to social characteristics. In this case, respondents might be asked a series of questions which identify their social class, ethnicity, gender, age group, sexual orientation, religion and so on. This will allow the researcher to discover possible relationships between social factors and film preferences.

Sampling procedures

Having decided on the aim of the survey, the researcher must now decide on who will take part and how to select them. Ideally, the sample should be representative of the target population in order to generalise from the findings of the survey. If the aim of the study is a descriptive survey of the adult population, then a random sample drawn from the electoral register will probably be adequate. However, if the study is an analytic survey designed to test a hypothesis, then a stratified sample may well be more appropriate. For example, if the researcher is examining the relationship between film preference, gender and age, then a stratified sample, which includes gender and age groups in proportion to their numbers in the general population, will probably be selected.

Opportunity samples – samples drawn from whoever is convenient – are unlikely to be representative. However, they may be useful as a basis for a pilot study. For example, an opportunity sample may indicate a strong relationship between social class and film preference. This may lead the researcher to

use a stratified sample in which one of the strata is social class. (Sampling procedures are examined in more detail in Unit 3.)

Administering the survey

Concerns about sampling may influence how the questionnaire is administered. Postal questionnaires have a low response rate. As a result, they are unlikely to provide a representative sample. The same applies to questionnaires reproduced in newspapers and magazines. First, the readership is unlikely to be representative. Second, those who answer the questionnaire are unlikely to be representative of the readership – they are likely to differ in important respects from those who do not respond.

Questionnaires administered by an interviewer – structured interviews – have a much higher response rate. However, they are more expensive and more likely to produce investigator effects (see Unit 4). But, they have the advantage of allowing the interviewer to correct any misunderstandings respondents might have with the questions.

Designing questions

Designing questions is quite an art. In general, they should be clear, simple and mean the same thing to all respondents. And, obviously, they should provide the information which the researcher requires. Here are some things to avoid.

- **Leading questions** These questions encourage respondents to give particular answers. For example, 'Any sensible person would want to ban fox hunting. Do you agree?' Some respondents might agree simply to appear sensible.
- **Ambiguity** Questions which can be interpreted in various ways should be avoided. For example, 'Do you drink coffee often?' can mean different things to different respondents. How often is often? Questions should be clear and precise. For example, 'How many cups of coffee do you drink a day?'
- **Loaded questions** These are questions which contain emotive language. For example, 'Do you think right-wing extremists should be allowed to stand for Parliament?' Emotive language can encourage respondents to give particular answers.
- **Jargon** Technical jargon should be avoided, simply because most respondents will not know what it means. For example, phrases like 'role conflict' and 'role ambiguity' are likely to confuse many people.
- **Double-barrelled questions** These contain two options within a single question. For example, 'Do you think crime is due to bad housing and poor education?' A respondent who blames bad housing but not poor education would have difficulty answering this question. It should be rewritten as two separate questions.
- **Negatives** The use of negatives can often confuse respondents. For example, 'Would you not trust a secondhand car salesman?'
- **Complex questions** Respondents can get lost with long, complex questions. For example, 'While equal opportunity legislation may reduce discrimination against minority groups, it may have the reverse effect by antagonising those who are responsible for discrimination, so reinforcing the very behaviour it was designed to eradicate. Do you agree?'
- **Impossible questions** Some questions are just impossible to answer accurately. For example, 'How many Mars bars have you eaten in the last five years?' Probably, the only

respondents who are able to provide an accurate answer are those who can't stand Mars bars – and never eat them!

Even apparently straightforward questions may be misunderstood. A man who had an extremely busy sex life answered 'no' to the question 'Are you sexually active?' In his words, 'I just lie there' (Zimbardo et al., 1995). There is always a danger of misunderstanding, but care in framing questions can reduce this.

It is always advisable to pilot a questionnaire, using people drawn from the same target population as the respondents. This can highlight any problems with the questions – whether they can be answered, whether they will be answered (some respondents may refuse to answer sensitive questions) and whether they will mean the same thing to all respondents. In addition, the pilot study may indicate whether respondents will answer truthfully. If this leads to a revision of the questionnaire, it is advisable to pilot the new version.

The format of questions

Questions can be *closed* or *open*.

Closed questions Closed or fixed-response questions provide the respondent with a set of possible responses which are fixed by the researcher. For example, the respondent may be asked to select from the following alternatives.

☐ Married
☐ Cohabiting
☐ Single
☐ Separated
☐ Divorced
☐ Widowed

Respondents may be asked to give their opinion by selecting an answer from alternatives provided. For example, 'What do you think of the service provided by state-run hospitals?'

☐ Very good
☐ Fairly good
☐ Neither good nor bad
☐ Not very good
☐ Not good at all

Another variation is to ask respondents to rank the alternatives provided. An example of this type of question is given below.

Which do you feel are the most important factors in choosing a university? Please rank the following in order of importance to you. Number them from 1= most important, to 7= least important.

Closeness to a town or city.
Good academic reputation.
Good chance of getting a job after graduation.
Attractive campus.
Good social facilities.
Good accommodation.
Availability of real ale.

From Newell, 1993

This type of question limits the respondent's range of choice. One way round this is to add a further alternative: 'Other factors, please specify'.

Closed questions have a number of advantages. The responses are easily quantified – put into a numerical form. For example, 55% of respondents chose their university because it had a good academic reputation. Closed questions are easy to code – to classify the answers into particular types. In fact, they are pre-coded – the categories are pre-set and the respondent simply has to choose one or rank some. Ease of quantification and coding means that a questionnaire consisting of closed questions is relatively quick and easy to process and analyse. However, closed questions can limit respondents' choices. Although the researcher can add, 'Other factors, please specify', the respondent does not have the freedom to express their answers in their own way.

Open questions This freedom is provided by open or free-response questions. Here the researcher simply asks a question, for example, 'What are your views on abortion?' and leaves space on the questionnaire for respondents to write in their answer. Often people do not have a clear-cut view. For example, they might favour abortion in cases of rape and where the child might be born with severe disabilities, but they may reject abortion as an option for all parents. Open questions allow respondents to qualify their answers, to give shades of opinion, and to express themselves in their own way. However, open questions are often difficult to code. The kind of answers they produce do not fit easily into a particular category.

Reliability and validity

Reliability Reliability of coding can be assessed by giving two or more researchers the same questions to code. If there is a high level of agreement, then the coding is seen as reliable.

Validity Is the data obtained from questionnaire surveys valid? In other words, are respondents giving accurate answers, are they telling the truth? To what degree does social desirability affect their responses? Are their answers influenced by how they think they ought to behave and what they think they ought to believe? Where evidence from other sources about respondents' behaviour is available, it is possible to check on the validity of their answers. One study found that 40% of respondents gave inaccurate answers about their contributions to a charity, 25% provided inaccurate information about whether they had registered to vote and had voted in a recent election, and 17% lied about their age (Parry & Crossley, 1950).

Respondents may be unwilling to give honest answers about sensitive issues, as indicated by the 17% who lied about their age in the above example. Respondents often shy away from answering questions about sexual behaviour. Guaranteeing anonymity may help the sensitive to overcome their inhibitions, but may not prevent the boastful from bragging about their supposed 'exploits'.

Respondents are sometimes influenced by social desirability – their answers may reflect how they think they ought to behave rather than how they actually behave. In the above example, those who gave inaccurate answers about their contributions to charity may have deviated from the truth and given a socially desirable answer in order to 'look good'.

When respondents are asked what they would do in particular situations, do their answers reflect what they'd actually do? In Milgram's first obedience experiment, 65% of men aged 20-50 applied shocks to the highest level. Before conducting the experiment, Milgram asked a similar group of men what they would do. Most said they would not continue to the highest level (Milgram, 1974).

The evidence presented in this section raises serious questions about the validity of questionnaire data.

Ethical issues

Confidentiality should be guaranteed and this should be made clear to all respondents. When the results are coded and published, there should be no way of identifying the respondents. Both the aims of the research and the uses to which the data will be put should be made clear. Questionnaire surveys are often used by big businesses to promote their products. For example, a Burger King survey indicated that 75% of respondents preferred their Whoppers to Big Macs. However, a McDonald's survey reported that 85% of respondents preferred Big Macs (see Activity 3, Item B). Clever phrasing of the questions by both companies produced the desired results (Goodwin, 1998).

5.3 Designing interviews

Interviews range from structured interviews, which consist of a questionnaire read out by an interviewer, to unstructured interviews which are more like a conversation. The semi-structured interview is mid-way between these two extremes.

Structured interviews

The design of structured interviews is similar to the design of questionnaires. The various do's and don'ts of question design apply to both. The key difference is the presence of an interviewer.

As with questionnaires, each respondent in a structured interview is presented with the same questions in the same order. Ideally, each respondent should experience an identical interview. In this way, they are responding to the actual questions rather than differences between the questions, their order, and the interviewer.

Interviews are face-to-face encounters. Different interviewers may produce different responses from respondents. In order to minimise investigator effects, the following approach is often recommended. Interviewers should be pleasant, friendly and businesslike. They should not become emotionally involved. Questions should be phrased in a neutral way. Interviewers should not communicate their feelings about respondents' answers – for example, they should not express approval or disapproval. The interviewer should always be in control. For example, if the respondent is allowed to direct the interview, then the result will be different interviews for each respondent. As a result, the data will not be directly comparable. In the words of one researcher, 'losing control of the interview is almost always a methodological disaster' (Hessler, 1992). The goal of a standardised interview for each respondent is lost.

The above outline of how to conduct an interview is found in many 'traditional', 'orthodox' textbooks on research methods. Although it applies particularly to structured interviews, some of its guidelines are also recommended for unstructured interviews. However, not all researchers agree with the use of this approach for unstructured interviews.

Unstructured interviews

Unstructured interviews are not standardised. The interviewer has a number of topics to cover, but the questions are usually not pre-set. Unstructured interviews are less formal, more open-ended, flexible and free-flowing than structured interviews. They are sometimes called in-depth interviews because the aim is to 'dig deeper', to find out exactly what the respondent means, and to give respondents the opportunity to develop their answers and to express themselves freely. Some researchers argue that this means that an unstructured interview must be conducted very differently from a structured interview.

Conducting unstructured interviews One of the keys to a successful unstructured interview is the relationship between interviewer and respondent. According to many researchers, trust is essential for honest, sincere answers, especially on sensitive topics. The respondent needs to feel that the interviewer is sympathetic and understanding and is interested in what they have to say (Glesne & Peshkin, 1992).

This approach is not always possible. Diane Scully's *Understanding sexual violence* (1990) was based on interviews with convicted rapists. She found some of the men 'personally repulsive' and some of the stories they told 'horrible'. Unable to take a warm and caring approach, she adopted a neutral, non-judgemental position. In her words, 'no one tells his or her secrets to a visibly hostile and disapproving person'. To some extent, she gained the trust of the respondents by hiding her true feelings. Some might see this as unethical, but without it there was little chance of obtaining valid data.

Unstructured interviews are often spontaneous and unpredictable. Although the interviewer guides them to some extent – for example covering topics relevant to the research – the type of control used in structured interviews is absent. Respondents must be allowed to express their answers in their own way. However, interviewers are allowed to probe – to ask respondents to clarify, qualify and develop their answers.

Unstructured interviews are largely non-directive. This means that the interviewer is not constantly directing the course of the interview. At times, as in a normal conversation, respondents must be allowed to direct the interview into areas which interest them.

Investigator effects

As noted in the previous chapter, the personal and social characteristics of the interviewer can affect the respondent's answers (see pp 215-217). For example, middle-aged female interviewers may obtain far more information from retired women than young male interviewers. In fact, the young man may not even get past the door (van Kammen & Stouthamer-Loeber, 1998). Some researchers have suggested matching interviewers and respondents in terms of age, gender, ethnicity and social class on the assumption that respondents are more likely to 'open up' to people like themselves.

Unstructured interviews are wide open to demand characteristics, investigator effects and social desirability effects. They are face-to-face relationships in which respondents are often asked to divulge very personal information. In this kind of relationship, demand characteristics can flourish – some respondents can be easily led into saying what the researcher wants to hear (see Activity 3, Item C). And, faced with an interviewer, social desirability effects are likely. However, these effects may well be reduced if the interviewer appears sympathetic, understanding and non-judgemental – respondents may feel more able to admit their faults and weaknesses and the less desirable aspects of their behaviour.

Validity and reliability

Because of the free-ranging, conversational and unpredictable nature of unstructured interviews, their reliability is low. Two different interviewers may well obtain very different data from the same respondent. By comparison, structured interviews are generally seen as having greater reliability.

However, some researchers argue that what unstructured interviews lose in reliability, they gain in validity. Compared to structured interviews, they are more likely to produce richer data, to capture shades of opinion and reveal the meanings which direct behaviour. In these respects, unstructured interviews are more likely to produce valid data.

Summary

1. Naturalistic observation is the observation of behaviour in its natural setting. Usually, those observed are unaware of the observer's presence.

2. Various sampling procedures can be used – time sampling, event sampling and situation sampling.

3. A behaviour schedule is often used to record behaviours.

4. Questionnaire surveys are designed to survey relatively large numbers of people. Representative samples are normally used in order to generalise the findings to the target population.

5. Questions in the survey require careful construction.

6. There are doubts about the validity of some questionnaire data.

7. Interviews are particularly susceptible to demand characteristics, investigator effects and social desirability effects.

8. Although the reliability of unstructured interviews is low, some researchers see their potential for producing valid data as high.

Activity 3   Conducting research

Item A   Naturalistic observation

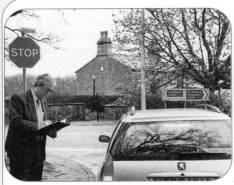

A researcher observed the behaviour of car drivers at a stop sign. He stood at the intersection next to the stop sign, holding a clipboard. He soon noticed that all the cars came to a complete halt. He then concealed himself and found that although many of the drivers slowed down, they went across the intersection without stopping.

Adapted from Underwood & Shaughnessy, 1975

Item B   Whopper or Big Mac?

Burger King conducted a questionnaire survey comparing their Whoppers to McDonald's Big Macs. The key question asked, 'Do you prefer your hamburgers flame-broiled or fried?' Seventy-five per cent of the respondents said they preferred flame-broiled – the process used for Whoppers. On the basis of this response, Burger King claimed that most people preferred Whoppers to Big Macs.

Another survey asked, 'Do you prefer a hamburger that is grilled on a hot, stainless-steel grill or by passing the raw meat through an open gas flame'. Over half the respondents selected the first option – the McDonald's method. When the question contained the information that flame-broiled burgers – the Whoppers – were reheated in a microwave oven before being served, 85% said they preferred Big Macs.

Adapted from Goodwin, 1998

Item C   Demand characteristics

During the late 1960s many African Americans rejected the idea that 'white is right' and stopped trying to copy white Americans. Being black became something to be proud of rather than ashamed. The researcher believed that this outlook was reflected in African-American 'soul' music. The following extract quotes a small part of an interview with Jay Butler, a black disc jockey from Detroit.

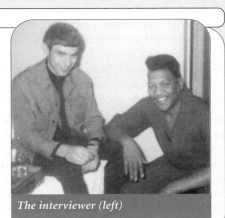

The interviewer (left)

Interviewer   The song *Take me as I am* by Solomon Burke. What's it about?

Jay Butler   It's just about a guy and his woman and he's telling her not to try and change him, to take him as he is.

Interviewer   But don't you think it could have a deeper meaning, that it's saying accept me as a black man, not as a poor substitute for a white man?

Jay Butler Yeah. You got a point there. The black community wants to be accepted as black American. I don't wanna be a white American, I wanna be a black American. It's like the Detroit Emeralds' song *I'm an ordinary man, take me the way I am.* There's a two-fold meaning in all these soul songs. Take Solomon Burke's *Take me as I am.* This song might be about a guy and his girl, but it means more at this period of time. Back in the 1950s we were trying to be accepted by white Americans on their terms. Now accept me as I am, accept my nappy (tightly curled) hair, accept me period.

Adapted from Haralambos, 1994

Questions

1 What does Item A indicate about investigator effects?

2 a) Briefly explain why different results were obtained by the two surveys in Item B.

   b) What lessons does this contain for constructing questions?

3 How might demand characteristics have influenced the respondent's answers in Item C?

References

Bales, R.F. (1950). *Interaction process analysis: A method for the study of small groups.* Reading, Mass: Addison-Wesley.

Baumrind, D. (1979). The costs of deception. *IRB: A Review of Human Subjects Research, 6,* 1-4.

BPS (British Psychological Society). (1998). *Code of conduct, ethical principles and guidelines.* Leicester: BPS.

Bruce, S. (1995). Religion and the Sociology of Religion in M. Haralambos (Ed.). *Developments in Sociology, Vol 11.* Ormskirk: Causeway.

Darley, J.M. & Latané, B. (1968). Bystander intervention in emergencies: Diffusion of responsibility. *Journal of Personality and Social Psychology, 8,* 377-383.

Eysenck, H. (1969). The technology of consent. *New Scientist, 42,* 688-690.

Glesne, C. & Peshkin, A. (1992). *Becoming qualitative researchers: An introduction.* New York: Longman.

Goodwin, C.J. (1998). *Research in psychology: Methods and design* (2nd ed.). New York: John Wiley & Sons.

Graziano, A.M. & Raulin, M.L. (1997). *Research methods: A process of inquiry* (3rd ed.). New York: Longman.

Haralambos, M. (1994). *Right on: From blues to soul in black America.* Ormskirk: Causeway.

Hessler, R. (1992). *Social research methods.* St. Paul: West Publishing.

Kellner, P. (1994). The figures are Shere nonsense. *Sunday Times,* 27.2.94.

Korn, J.H. (1987). Judgements of acceptability of deception in psychological research. *Journal of General Psychology, 14,* 205-216.

Korn, J.H. (1988). Students' roles, rights, and responsibilities as research participants. *Teaching of Psychology, 15,* 74-78.

Loftus, E.F. & Burns, T.E. (1982). Mental shock can produce retrograde amnesia. *Memory and Cognition, 10,* 318-323.

Masling, J. (1966). Role-related behaviour of the subject and psychologist and its effect upon psychological data. In D. Levine (Ed.), *Nebraska Symposium on Motivation.* Lincoln: University of Nebraska Press.

Milgram, S. (1974). *Obedience to authority: An experimental view.* New York: Harper & Row.

Miller, G. (1969). Psychology as a means of promoting human welfare. *American Psychologist, 24,* 1063-1075.

Moghaddam, F.M., Taylor, D.M. & Wright, S.C. (1993). *Social psychology in cross-cultural perspective.* New York: W.H. Freeman.

Newell, R. (1993). Questionnaires. In N. Gilbert (Ed.), *Researching social life.* London: Sage.

O'Connell Davidson, J. & Layder, D. (1994). *Methods, sex and madness.* London: Routledge.

Oppenheim, A.N. (1992). *Questionnaire design, interviewing and attitude measurement.* London: Pinter.

Orne, M.T. (1962). On the social psychology of the psychology experiment: With particular reference to demand characteristics and their implications. *American Psychologist, 17,* 776-783.

Orne, M.T. (1969). Demand characteristics and the concept of quasi-controls. In R. Rosenthal & R.L. Rosnow (Eds.), *Artifact in behavioral research.* New York: Academic Press.

Orne, M.T. & Holland, C.C. (1968). On the ecological validity of laboratory deceptions. *International Journal of Psychiatry, 6,* 282-293.

Orne, M.T. & Scheibe, K.E. (1964). The contribution of nondeprivation factors in the production of sensory deprivation effects. *Journal of Abnormal and Social Psychology, 68,* 3-12.

Parry, H.J. & Crossley, H.M. (1950). Validity of responses to survey questions. *Public Opinion Quarterly, 14,* 61-80.

Phillips, D.L. (1971). *Knowledge from what?* Chicago: Rand McNally.

Roethlisberger, F.J. & Dickson, W.J. (1939). *Management and the worker.* Cambridge, Mass: Harvard University Press.

Rosenberg, M.J. (1969). The conditions and consequences of evaluation apprehension. In R. Rosenthal & R.L. Rosnow (Eds.), *Artifact in behavioral research.* New York: Academic Press.

Rosenthal, R. (1965). The volunteer subject. *Human Relations, 18,* 389-406.

Rosenthal, R. (1967). Covert communication in the psychological experiment. *Psychological Bulletin, 67,* 356-367.

Rosenthal, R. & Fode, K.L. (1963a). Three experiments in experimenter bias. *Psychological Reports, 12,* 491-511.

Rosenthal, R. & Fode, K.L. (1963b). The effect of experimenter bias on the performance of the albino rat. *Behavioral Science, 8,* 183-189.

Scully, D. (1990). *Understanding sexual violence.* London: Harper Collins.

Shaughnessy, J.J. & Zechmeister, E.B. (1997). *Research methods in psychology* (4th ed.). New York: McGraw-Hill.

Smith, P.B. & Bond, M.H. (1993). *Social psychology across cultures: Analysis and perspectives.* Hemel Hempstead: Harvester Wheatsheaf.

Strayer, F.F. & Strayer, J. (1976). An ethological analysis of social antagonism and dominance relations among preschool children. *Child Development, 47,* 980-989.

Underwood, B.J. & Shaughnessy, J.J. (1975). *Experimentation in psychology.* New York: Wiley.

Valentine, E.R. (1992). *Conceptual issues in psychology* (2nd ed.). London: Routledge.

van Kammen, W.B. & Stouthamer-Loeber, M. (1998). Practice aspects of interview data collection and data management. In L. Bickman & D.J. Rog (Eds.). *Handbook of applied social research methods.* Thousand Oaks, CA: Sage.

Zimbardo, P., McDermott, M., Jansz, J. & Metall, N. (1995). *Psychology: A European text.* London: Harper Collins.

18 Data analysis

▶ **Introduction**

The previous two chapters looked at methods of data collection. This chapter looks at ways of analysing data once it has been collected. Analysis involves categorising and classifying the data, looking for relationships or links between the data, identifying themes running through the data, and discovering meanings underlying the data. In general, analysis involves making sense of data.

This chapter looks at ways of analysing qualitative and quantitative data.

Chapter summary

- Unit 1 examines various methods of analysing qualitative data.

- Units 2, 3 and 4 outline statistical methods of analysing quantitative data.

Unit 1 The analysis of qualitative data

KEY ISSUES

1. **What is qualitative data?**
2. **What are the main methods of analysing qualitative data?**

Qualitative data refers to information collected by researchers which is not in the form of numbers. It includes information from interviews, questionnaires and observational research which has not been collected in, or translated into, a numerical form. Examples of qualitative data include a passage from an interview in which a respondent describes their work experience, a written answer to a questionnaire in which a respondent outlines their views on child rearing practices, and data from participant observation of students in a classroom.

Content analysis

Content analysis has been widely used in media research. It has been used for analysing the content of television and radio programmes, books, newspapers, magazines and comics, and popular songs and nursery rhymes. Many of the techniques used in content analysis have been applied to the analysis of qualitative data from interviews, questionnaires and observations.

The following example illustrates typical features of content analysis. It is based on an analysis of gender roles in six reading schemes, including the *Janet and John* and *Ladybird* series, which were widely used in primary schools during the 1960s (Lobban, 1974).

First, a sample of the materials to be analysed is examined. In terms of the above example, three books from each of the series might be selected.

Second, categories are created in terms of which the data can be classified and organised. The categories reflect the purpose of the research – in this case an analysis of gender roles. Categories developed from the reading schemes included

objects, activities and roles that are linked to girls, those that are linked to boys, and those that are linked to both.

Third, a larger sample is selected and the researcher classifies data from the books in terms of the various categories. Table 1 presents the results of this analysis for the six reading schemes.

Themes The classification of data into categories is usually only a first step. Once this has been done, further analysis can take place. For example, the researcher might look for themes which are common to many of the categories in Table 1. The following themes might be identified from the way boys and girls are presented in the reading schemes.

- Boys are presented as more adventurous than girls
- As physically stronger
- As having more choices
- Girls are presented as more caring than boys
- As more interested in domestic matters
- As followers rather than leaders.

The researcher may then widen the focus and, for example, relate these themes to adult roles such as the mother-housewife role and gender divisions in the labour market. For instance, women are concentrated in the caring professions – nursing, social work and primary school teaching. Men outnumber women in leadership roles such as managers. The researcher may then ask how the themes identified in the reading schemes form a part of gender socialisation – the way boys learn to be men and girls learn to be women. For example, how do these themes steer men and women into 'men's jobs' and 'women's jobs'?

Observational research

In many ways the analysis of data from naturalistic observation uses the same methods as content analysis. The example of observation of aggression in the school playground was outlined earlier – see p210. Based on preliminary observations, a behaviour schedule was drawn up with categories such as 'pushing' and 'hitting', and these behaviours were recorded as and when they occurred. This is a fairly straightforward procedure that usually produces quantitative

Table 1	Gender roles that occurred in three or more of the six schemes				
Gender for which role was allocated	Toys and Pets	Activities	Taking the lead in activities that both boys and girls take part in	Learning a new skill	Adult roles presented
Girls only	1 Doll 2 Skipping rope 3 Doll's pram	1 Preparing the tea 2 Playing with dolls 3 Taking care of younger siblings	1 Hopping 2 Shopping with parents 3 Skipping	1 Taking care of younger siblings	1 Mother 2 Aunt 3 Grandmother
Boys only	1 Car 2 Train 3 Aeroplane 4 Boat 5 Football	1 Playing with cars 2 Playing with trains 3 Playing football 4 Lifting or pulling heavy objects 5 Playing cricket 6 Watching adult males in occupational roles 7 Heavy gardening	1 Going exploring alone 2 Climbing trees 3 Building things 4 Taking care of pets 5 Sailing boats 6 Flying kites 7 Washing and polishing Dad's car	1 Taking care of pets 2 Making/building 3 Saving/rescuing people or pets 4 Playing sports	1 Father 2 Uncle 3 Grandfather 4 Postman 5 Farmer 6 Fisherman 7 Business owner 8 Policeman 9 Builder 10 Bus driver 11 Bus conductor 12 Train driver 13 Railway porter
Girls and boys	1 Book 2 Ball 3 Paints 4 Bucket and spade 5 Dog 6 Cat 7 Shop	1 Playing with pets 2 Writing 3 Reading 4 Going to the seaside 5 Going on a family outing			1 Teacher 2 Shop assistant

Adapted from Lobban, 1974

data. However, it is fairly limited in scope. It is suitable for the behaviour of pedestrians at pelican crossings and drivers at traffic lights which can be readily observed, classified and counted. But it is not particularly suitable for more complex behaviour patterns. It can be argued that behaviour schedules fail to capture the richness of life as it is lived, that they are unable to discover the meanings which direct behaviour. How is it possible to analyse more complex behaviour patterns observed in natural contexts?

Behaviour in a mental hospital Erving Goffman's classic study, *Asylums* (1968), is an investigation of the behaviour of inmates in a mental hospital in Washington DC. Goffman spent a year in the hospital in the role of a member of staff. As a participant observer, he watched and listened, and amassed a vast quantity of data. How could he make sense of it all?

Goffman did not decide in advance what was relevant. He did not start with pre-set categories in which to classify the data. Instead, he simply watched and listened. Categories, themes and patterns gradually emerged from his observations. Here is an example of how he organised and made sense of his data.

Goffman identified a pattern of behaviour which he called the *mortification process*. He recognised this process time and time again during his stay at the mental hospital. It consisted of 'a series of abasements, degradations, humiliations, and profanities of self' in terms of which inmates were stripped of their former identities and treated as 'mental cases' who had little social significance and 'were hardly capable of acting like a fully-fledged person at all'. The idea of a mortification process

connected a range of apparently unconnected behaviours, it identified a common theme underlying those behaviours, and made sense of them.

On entry to mental hospitals, inmates are often stripped of various supports which help them to maintain their former self-concepts. Their clothes, an important symbol of identity, are sometimes removed. Their possessions, a further symbol of identity, may be taken away and stored for the duration of their stay. They may be washed, disinfected and have their hair cut. They may be issued with a new 'identity kit' such as regulation clothes and toilet articles. Such standardised articles tend to remove individuality.

Once the entry phase is over, the inmate settles down to a range of 'mortifying experiences'. Each day is strictly timetabled into a set of compulsory activities controlled by the staff. Inmates are allowed little freedom of movement, few opportunities for self-expression, and little chance to show initiative or take decisions. Their actions are scrutinised and assessed by the staff in terms of the rules and regulations of the institution. A demeaning system of rewards and privileges is administered to encourage obedience and 'appropriate behaviour'. Watching TV, an extra cup of coffee or a cigarette are awarded for 'good behaviour', or withheld from those who don't 'toe the line'. Many of the behaviours demanded from inmates are degrading – for example, in some mental hospitals, a spoon is the only utensil provided for them to eat with.

Goffman found that his idea of a mortification process identified a theme running through a large number of apparently differing behaviours. It connected those behaviours and made sense of them. Time and time again the mortification process told inmates they were less than human.

Goffman's study is generally regarded as a classic. However, it relies heavily on his interpretation of the behaviour he observed. Did he get it right? Here are Goffman's thoughts about this question.

'I want to warn that my view is probably too much that of a middle-class male; perhaps I suffered vicariously about conditions that lower-class patients handled with little pain. Also, unlike some patients, I came to the hospital with no great respect for the discipline of psychiatry' (Goffman, 1968).

Discovering meanings

The analysis of qualitative data often aims to discover the meanings which underlie what people say and do. There is no simple recipe for doing this. It relies heavily on the interpretive skills of the researcher, and is best illustrated by example.

Look at the newspaper headlines in Figure 1. They refer to men and women infected with AIDS through blood transfusions and mother to child transmission of AIDS in the womb.

What meanings lie behind these headlines? One interpretation runs as follows. The word 'innocent' crops up again and again. This suggests that the people concerned do not deserve to be infected – it is not their fault. As one headline states, they come from 'ordinary families', and this kind of thing does not, and should not, happen to 'ordinary people'. This implies that unlike 'ordinary people', 'typical' AIDS victims are not so 'innocent' – in some way they deserve their fate, in some way they are guilty for what happens to them.

Here is another example of interpreting meanings, from the Glasgow University Media Group's (1976) analysis of the reporting of industrial disputes on television news. Trade unionists were typically asked, 'What are you doing to end the strike?' whereas the typical question put to managers was, 'How much production or exports have you lost?' The assumption appears to be that unions cause strikes. Shop stewards were often accused by TV interviewers of 'acting irresponsibly', 'destroying the company' and 'cutting their own throats'. The implication is that the blame for strikes lies with workers and trade unions. Other factors which may have caused the strike, such as bad management, low wages despite high profits, or high inflation, were largely ignored. This type of analysis looks

Figure 1 Newspaper headlines

We must help the innocent AIDS victims

EXPRESS GOES INTO ACTION TO PROTECT THE INNOCENT

Now innocents demand millions

Agony of innocent mum

CURSE HITS ORDINARY FAMILIES

FURY OF THE INNOCENTS

The AIDS innocents
Trauma of youngsters facing prejudice in the playground

Innocent AIDS victim leaves legacy of hope

Innocent victims face cash blow
An innocent victim tells of his agony

Adapted from Kitzinger, 1993

closely at the words and phrases people use and the assumptions that lie behind them. In this case, the researchers concluded that the view that unions cause industrial problems underpinned television news coverage.

The interpretation of meanings is a long way from the 'hard' empirical data and number crunching of many laboratory experiments. Researchers may provide evidence to support the meanings they claim to have discovered. But, in many cases, they are a long way from demonstrating that their interpretations are correct. Despite this, the search for meanings is important. Meanings guide and direct human behaviour. And the analysis of meanings that underlie qualitative data is often convincing, plausible and insightful.

Summary

1 The analysis of qualitative data often starts with categorising and classifying the data.

2 The researcher may then look for themes and patterns which run through and link the data.

3 There is no simple way of discovering and interpreting the meanings which underlie behaviour. This type of analysis relies on the interpretive skills of the researcher.

Unit 2 Quantitative data

KEY ISSUES

1. What is quantitative data?
2. How can quantitative data be presented?

Many research methods, particularly experiments and questionnaires, are designed to provide *quantitative data*. Quantitative data takes the form of measurements or scores in the form of numbers. There are four main types or *levels* of measurement.

2.1 Levels of measurement

Nominal level of measurement This is the simplest *level of*

measurement. The data it provides is known as nominal data. The researcher identifies categories of objects or behaviours, and simply counts how many instances there are in each category.

For example, an investigation of a fruit bowl reveals 6 apples, 3 oranges, 15 grapes and 2 bananas. The types of fruit are the categories, and the researcher counts how many there are of each type of fruit.

People's behaviour can be recorded as nominal data. In the observation of children's aggressive behaviour in the playground (see p210), a behaviour schedule was drawn up and a tally made of how many times each type of behaviour occurred – see Table 2. Collecting nominal data simply involves counting the number of instances in each category.

Activity 1 — Analysing qualitative data

Item A — Gender roles in reading schemes

Questions

1 What do the pictures in Item A suggest about gender roles?

2 What attitudes and strategies for living may lie behind the lyrics in Item B?

Item B — African-American blues songs

I've been down so long

I've been down so long,
That down don't bother me,
I'm gonna take all of my troubles,
And toss them in the deep blue sea.

Born under a bad sign

Born under a bad sign,
Been down since I began to crawl,
If it wasn't for bad luck,
You know I wouldn't have no luck at all.

Blues singer Albert King who recorded these songs.

Table 2 — Behaviour schedule for 10 minute observation of children at play

Behaviour	Number of occurrences
Bit	1
Chased	3
Hit	2
Pushed/pulled	5
Wrestled	2

Ordinal level of measurement Ordinal data is ordered or ranked according to its position on a scale.

Positions in a race provide an example of ordinal scale measures. The runners are ordered in terms of their finishing positions – 1st, 2nd, 3rd, and so on.

Ordinal data is also provided by attitude scales, where a respondent rates items, for example types of soft drink, in order of preference.

Ordinal scales simply provide a rank order. They do not measure how far apart the items on the scale are. For example, they do not state the time between the runners or how much more a respondent liked drink A compared with drink B.

Interval level of measurement Interval measurements go one step further than ordinal scales. They place items on a scale with fixed intervals, for example temperature in degrees Celsius. It is now possible not only to rank items but also to show how far apart they are.

Temperature provides a good example. If town A has a temperature of 40°C, town B has a temperature of 30°C, and town C of 20°C, this tells us not only the order of the three towns in terms of temperature, but also the difference in temperature between them.

However, it is not possible to say that town A is twice as hot as town C. This is because the zero point on the Celsius scale is not a true or absolute zero. In other words, a temperature of 0°C does not mean no temperature at all since lower temperatures, eg minus 5°C, are possible.

Ratio level of measurement A ratio scale is simply an interval scale with a true or absolute zero point below which no values can occur. This provides a baseline for comparing scores. Time is a good example of this. Suppose participant A takes 25 seconds to complete a task, participant B takes 50 seconds, and participant C takes 75 seconds. It is possible to say that B took twice as long as A to complete the task, and C took three times as long as A. This is possible because the scale starts at zero seconds.

In psychological research, ratio scales are simply regarded as a form of interval scale.

Key terms

Quantitative data *Measurements or scores in the form of numbers.*

Nominal level of measurement *A count of the number of instances in each category.*

Ordinal level of measurement *Placing data into a rank order.*

Interval level of measurement *Placing data on a scale with fixed intervals.*

Ratio level of measurement *Placing data on an interval scale with an absolute zero point.*

Activity 2   Levels of measurement

Item A   Girl bands

Female and male teenagers were asked whether or not they liked girl bands.

	Likes girl bands	Dislikes girl bands
Female	42	12
Male	37	18

(Taken from a student research project.)

The Corrs

Item B   Soaps

A respondent is asked to rank a list of 5 television soaps in order of preference (the favourite earning a score of 5, the least favourite a score of 1). The following result was obtained.

Emmerdale	5
Coronation Street	4
Brookside	3
Neighbours	2
EastEnders	1

(Taken from a student research project.)

Questions

1   Why is the data in Item A a nominal level of measurement?

2   Why is the data in Item B an ordinal level of measurement?

3   What kind of data is shown in Item C?

Item C   War of the ghosts

A replication of the *War of the ghosts* experiment (see p35) produced the following results. Condition 1 shows the number of correctly recorded details from the story recalled by each participant immediately after hearing the story. Condition 2 shows the number of correctly recorded details a week later.

Participant Number	Condition 1 (immediate recall)	Condition 2 (recall 1 week later)
1	33	25
2	18	4
3	27	15
4	11	14
5	19	8
6	22	15
7	7	3
8	31	22
9	22	12
10	9	8
11	26	18
12	15	6

2.2   Frequency distributions

Measurements of participants' behaviour obtained directly from a research study are called *raw scores*. They have not yet been organised or processed. Raw nominal scores are often quite easy to interpret. Look at Item A in Activity 2. It is quite clear from this data that girl groups are popular with both teenage boys and teenage girls, and are especially popular with girls. Raw ordinal scores are often fairly straightforward too. It is fairly clear what the scores in Item B show.

Raw interval and ratio scores are often less clear. Look at the data in Activity 2 Item C. It is not very easy to see any pattern in these raw scores, or to get much impression of what effect (if any) time has on recall of details from the *War of the ghosts* story.

In order to get a clearer picture of raw results, they can be rearranged into a *frequency distribution*. The total number of times each score occurs is called its *frequency*. A frequency distribution is a table showing the frequencies of all the scores.

Suppose a study was conducted into the number of hours a sample of 10 male and 10 female psychology students spent revising the day before an AS level exam – see Table 3. For convenience, all figures are rounded up or down to the nearest hour.

A frequency distribution of this data would look like this:

Table 4 shows that two males did approximately 1 hours revision; one male and one female did approximately 2 hours, and so on. The frequency distribution provides a clearer picture of the layout of the scores. It shows that male students varied more widely in their revision times than female students.

Table 3   Revision time (in hours)

Males	Females
5	4
4	5
3	3
6	4
1	2
2	3
3	4
5	3
8	4
1	5

Table 4	Frequency distribution of revision time	
Revision time (hours)	Males	Females
1	2	0
2	1	1
3	2	3
4	1	4
5	2	2
6	1	0
7	0	0
8	1	0

Grouped frequency distributions

A frequency distribution does not have to show each individual score. If, for example, there are over 100 scores, the table would be too large and confusing. A clearer picture is produced by grouping scores into *class intervals* – in Table 5 the class intervals used are 1-2, 3-4, and so on.

Grouped frequency distribution of the data in Table 3 would look like this:

Table 5	Grouped frequency distribution of revision time	
Revision time (hours)	Males	Females
1-2	3	1
3-4	3	7
5-6	3	2
7-8	1	0

Grouped frequency distributions often provide a simpler and clearer picture. For example, the data from the *War of the ghosts* experiment in Activity 2, Item C would be a lot clearer presented in the form of a grouped frequency distribution table.

2.3   Pictorial presentation of frequency distributions

Many people find numerical data easier to understand if it is presented in a pictorial form. This section looks at ways of presenting frequency distributions in the form of charts, graphs and diagrams.

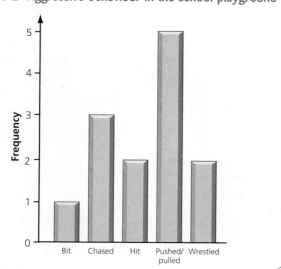

Figure 2   Aggressive behaviour in the school playground

Bar charts

Bar charts provide a simple and effective way of presenting and comparing data, particularly nominal data. The bar chart in Figure 2 illustrates data from the behaviour schedule shown in Table 2 on p241. The height of each bar gives the frequency of each type of behaviour.

The bar chart in Figure 2 illustrates, at a glance, the frequency distribution of the five types of aggressive behaviour. Because each bar represents a different category of data, the bars are presented separately with spaces between them. Different categories of data are known as *discrete data*. The bars can be drawn in any order.

Histograms

Histograms are mainly used to present frequency distributions of interval and ratio data. They can also be used for grouped frequency distributions. The horizontal axis is a *continuous* scale, for example of time as shown in Figure 3. On a histogram there are no spaces between the bars. A histogram showing the frequencies of revision times for female students, taken from Table 4, would look like this:

Figure 3   Frequencies of revision times for females

Frequency polygons

Frequency polygons are an alternative way of presenting the same information shown on a histogram. They are often used to

Figure 4   Frequencies of revision times for males and females compare two or more sets of data. A frequency polygon is drawn by plotting the frequencies of each score, then joining the successive points with straight lines. Figure 4 shows the frequency polygons for the revision times of male and female students, taken from Table 4.

It allows a direct comparison of the frequency distributions of male and female revision times to be made.

Stem and leaf diagrams

A *stem and leaf diagram* is a quick and efficient way of displaying *actual* data in the form of a frequency distribution. Table 6 shows the raw scores from condition 1 of the replication of the *War of ghosts* experiment (see Activity 2, Item C, p242).

Table 6	Raw scores

33
18
27
11
19
22
7
31
22
9
26
15

> To create a stem and leaf diagram, all the scores between 0 and 9 are laid out in a horizontal line from the smallest to the largest. Scores from 10 to 19 are placed on a second line; those from 20 to 29 on a third line, and so on. This is shown below.

7	9		
11	15	18	19
22	22	26	27
31	33		

To convert Table 6 into a stem and leaf diagram, the scores 7 and 9 must be thought of as 07 and 09. For each line of the diagram, the stem is the first digit of the score and the numbers on the leaves are the second digits of each score. The frequency of scores for each line can be noted, as shown in Table 7.

Table 7	Stem and leaf diagram

Stem	Leaves				Frequency
0	7	9			2
1	1	5	8	9	4
2	2	2	6	7	4
3	1	3			2

The stem and leaf diagram groups scores together as in a grouped frequency distribution, while retaining information on individual scores. When laid on its side, a stem and leaf diagram looks like a histogram for a grouped frequency distribution.

Key terms

Raw scores *Unprocessed scores taken directly from a study.*

Frequency *The total number of times a score occurs.*

Frequency distribution *The distribution of the frequencies of all scores.*

Grouped frequency distribution *A frequency distribution in which scores are grouped into class intervals.*

Bar chart *A chart in which the height of each bar shows the frequency of each score.*

Histogram *A type of bar chart showing a grouped frequency distribution or continuous data.*

Frequency polygon *A graph which shows a frequency distribution as frequencies joined by straight lines.*

Stem and leaf diagram *A diagram which shows grouped frequency distribution. It also shows individual scores.*

Activity 3 Eyewitness testimony

The following experiment was designed to investigate eyewitness testimony.

Two groups of nine participants were asked to watch a video of an event staged in a bank. The first group saw a man paying in money to a bank clerk. The second group saw a man with a gun threatening a customer. Both events lasted exactly 8 seconds. The participants' estimates (in seconds) of the length of these events is shown below.

Condition 1 (man paying in money)	Condition 2 (man with gun)
10	20
12	24
11	23
10	22
11	20
11	23
12	25
13	19
9	23

1 a) Draw up a frequency distribution (see Table 4) of the data in conditions 1 and 2.

   b) Draw up a grouped frequency distribution (see Table 5) of the data in conditions 1 and 2, using suitable class intervals.

   c) What does each frequency distribution tell you?

2 a) Draw a histogram for each condition (see Figure 3).

   b) Draw frequency polygons of the two frequency distributions (see Figure 4).

   c) What does each graph tell you about the results obtained in the experiment?

3 a) Draw up a stem and leaf diagram of the data in the two conditions, noting the frequency (see Table 7).

   b) Describe the advantages of a stem and leaf diagram.

Summary

1 Quantitative data takes the form of scores or measurements.

2 There are four main levels of measurement – nominal, ordinal, interval and ratio.

3 Raw interval and ratio scores are easier to interpret when arranged into a frequency distribution.

4 There are various ways of presenting frequency distributions. They can be presented as individual scores or grouped scores, and in tables or in graphical form.

Unit 3 Analysing quantitative data

KEY ISSUES

1. What is central tendency? What are the advantages and disadvantages of each measure of central tendency?

2. How is the spread (dispersion) of scores measured? What are the advantages and disadvantages of each measure?

In an experiment, an independent variable is manipulated to see if it has an effect on the performance of the participants – the dependent variable. Two sets of scores are obtained – one from each condition. These two sets of scores need to be compared to see if there is any noticeable difference between them. In order to compare two sets of scores, it is necessary to summarise them. A set of scores can be summarised by:

1) a measure of *central tendency*, that is, a single score that represents the whole set;

2) a measure of the *spread* or *dispersion* of the scores.

   With this information it is possible to compare two or more sets of scores.

3.1 Measures of central tendency

There are three measures of central tendency – the *mode*, the *median* and the *mean*.

- The mode is the most common score.
- The median is found by arranging the scores from lowest to highest, and taking the middle score. If there is an even number of scores, the median is given by the average of the two middle scores.
- The mean is found by adding up the total of all the scores and dividing by the number of scores.

The following formula is used to work out the mean.

$$\text{Mean} \; = \; \frac{\text{total of all scores}}{\text{number of scores}}$$

This formula can be written using the following symbols.

$$\bar{x} \; = \; \frac{\sum x}{n}$$

where $\bar{x}$ (pronounced 'x bar') is the mean,

   $\sum$ (the Greek letter sigma) stands for 'the sum of',

   x represents each score,

   n is the number of scores.

   Data from Table 8 can be used to show how the mode, median and mean are worked out. The table shows the number of minutes taken to solve a puzzle by participants working in normal and very hot temperatures.

Table 8	Time taken to solve a puzzle		
Participant number	**Condition 1 normal (minutes)**	**Participant number**	**Condition 2 hot (minutes)**
P1	7	P6	11
P2	5	P7	7
P3	4	P8	8
P4	5	P9	12
P5	2	P10	9

   Table 9 shows the mode, median and mean for the data in conditions 1 and 2.

Mode, median and mean – advantages and disadvantages

Mode The mode is the most frequently occurring score or item

Table 9 Mode, median and mean

Condition 1

Mode
Scores: 7, 5, 4, 5, 2
The mode is the most common score.
Mode = 5 minutes

Median
Arrange the scores in order:
2, 4, 5, 5, 7
The median is the middle score.
Median = 5 minutes

Mean

$$\bar{x} = \frac{\sum x}{n}$$

$$= \frac{7+5+4+5+2}{5}$$

$$= \frac{23}{5}$$

$$= 4.6 \text{ minutes}$$

Condition 2

Mode
scores: 11, 7, 8, 12, 9
There is no mode.

Median
Scores in order:
7, 8, 9, 11, 12

Median = 9 minutes

Mean

$$\bar{x} = \frac{\sum x}{n}$$

$$= \frac{11+7+8+12+9}{5}$$

$$= \frac{47}{5}$$

$$= 9.4 \text{ minutes}$$

Both the mean and the median show that participants in the hot condition take roughly twice as long to solve the puzzles.

of data. It is the only measure that can be used for nominal data. For example, the mode for the types of behaviour shown in Table 2 is 'pushed/pulled' which occurs 5 times. (The mean cannot be used for nominal data – it would make no sense to average the behaviours in Table 2 because they are different kinds of behaviour. Nor could the median be used because there is no order to the data.)

Sometimes, the mode does not provide an overall summary of a set of scores. For example, the most frequently occurring score may be the highest or the lowest score, and is located away from the centre of the distribution.

Median The median is the middle score or measurement. It can be used for ordinal, interval and ratio data. It is more likely to provide a measure of central tendency than the mode. However, it can give a misleading impression when scores are clustered in low and high groups. For example, the median for the following scores is six.

1   2   3   6   27   48   63

Key terms

Mode *The most common score.*

Median *The middle score when the scores are arranged from lowest to highest.*

Mean *The total of all scores divided by the number of scores.*

Central tendency *A typical or representative score which tends to be found near the centre of the distribution of scores.*

Rogue score *An extreme score which can result in the mean giving a misleading impression. Also called an outlier.*

Mean The mean provides a typical score for interval and ratio data. However, a single extreme score – known as a *rogue score* or *outlier* – results in the mean giving a misleading impression of central tendency. Suppose that in the example in Table 8, participant 1 took 67 minutes to complete the puzzle. The mean for condition 1 now shoots up to 16.6. This gives the impression that people solve puzzles faster in a hot room, when in fact most do not. When rogue scores affect the mean, the median can often give a better measure of central tendency.

3.2 Dispersion

In order to summarise a set of scores, a measure of central tendency is important, but on its own it is not enough. Consider the following sets of scores.

Table 10 Sets of scores

Set A	35	48	49	50	50	54	57
Set B	2	25	47	50	50	79	90

The mean of each set it 49, the mode 50, and the median 50, yet these are clearly very different sets of data. The main difference between them is the spread of the scores. Set A spreads from 35 to 57, while set B has a much larger spread from 2 to 90.

The spread of scores is also known as *dispersion* or *variability*. In order to clearly summarise a set of scores, it is as important to measure spread or dispersion as it is to measure central tendency.

This can be done a number of ways.

The range

This is the simplest and most obvious way to measure the dispersion of a set of scores. It is obtained by subtracting the lowest score from the highest. The range of a Set A is 57–35=22. The range of Set B is 90-2=88. This shows how much greater the spread of scores in Set B is. There are problems with the range, however.

First, although with a small range we can see that the scores are tightly clustered, with a large range, we do not know how the scores are dispersed. Set B, for example, has one very low score, three near the mean, and two high scores. The range gives us no information about this.

Second, the range is vulnerable to rogue scores or outliers. Suppose the last score in Set A was not 57 but 136, this would bump up the range of Set A to 101, giving a misleading impression of the real dispersion of scores in Set A.

Interquartile range

The *interquartile range* avoids the problem of rogue scores by ignoring the highest 25% and the lowest 25% of the scores. It is a measure of the range of the middle 50% of the scores. This is shown in Figure 5 using scores from Set A.

The interquartile range is the difference between the upper and lower quartiles. To find the lower quartile, use the formula $\frac{1}{4}(n+1)$ where n = the number of scores. For the scores in Set A, this is $\frac{1}{4}(7+1) = 2$. The lower quartile is the second score which is 48. To find the upper quartile, use the formula $\frac{3}{4}$

Figure 5 The interquartile range

| 35 | 48 | 49 | 50 | 50 | 54 | 57 |

Median

Lower quartile

Upper quartile

The interquartile range = upper quartile minus lower quartile.

(n+1). For the scores in Set A, this is $^3/_4$ (7+1) = 6. The upper quartile is the sixth score which is 54.

The interquartile range for the scores is Set A is 54−48 = 6.

The interquartile range is especially valuable with ordinal data, and has the advantage of not being distorted by rogue scores. However, it does lose a lot of information, since 50% of the scores are discarded.

Box plots

Box plots are used to show the range and interquartile range of a set of scores. Box plots are also known as *box and whisker plots*. Figure 6 shows a box plot for the scores in Set A and Set B.

Figure 6 Box plots for Set A and Set B

The 'boxes' show the interquartile range of the scores. The 'whiskers' show the range of the data from the lowest score on the left to the highest score on the right. The vertical line in the boxes shows the median.

Box plots provide a clear image of the dispersion of different sets of scores, enabling direct comparisons to be made. They lose less information than the interquartile range, since highest and lowest scores are indicated by the whiskers.

Key terms

Range *A measure of spread or dispersion of scores given by taking the lowest score from the highest.*

Interquartile range *The range of the middle 50% of the scores.*

Box plot *A way of showing both the range and the interquartile range on the same diagram. Also known as a box and whisker plot.*

Standard deviation

We have already looked at two measures of spread – the range and the interquartile range. The range measures the spread of all scores. It can be affected by rogue scores, or outliers, and can be misleading. The interquartile range only

measures the spread of the middle 50% of the scores.

A third measure, called *standard deviation*, is more precise. It gets round the problems of range and interquartile range. Standard deviation measures the average deviation (difference) of each score or item of data from the mean. Every score is involved in the calculation. Standard deviation involves the mean of a set of scores. Because of this, it can only be used with interval and ratio data. Nominal and ordinal data do not have means.

Standard deviation (sd) is given by the formulae:

$$sd = \sqrt{\frac{\sum(x-\bar{x})^2}{n}} \quad \text{or} \quad sd = \sqrt{\frac{\sum x^2}{n} - \bar{x}^2}$$

where n is the number of items of data and

$(x - \bar{x})$ is the difference between each score or item of data and the mean.

Look at the sets of scores in Table 11. They show the number of seconds taken by participants to complete a task without alcohol (condition 1) and with alcohol (condition 2).

Standard deviation can be calculated using the formulae shown above, or by using a statistical calculator. Tables 13 and 14 (see p248) show two methods for calculating standard deviation using the scores from Table 11.

Use whichever method you find easiest to perform calculations.

Table 11 Times (in seconds) to complete a task

Condition 1 (without alcohol)	Condition 2 (with alcohol)
3	3
4	6
4	6
5	9
5	9
5	9
6	11
6	13
7	15

The results of the numerical analysis from Tables 13 and 14 can be summarised as:

Table 12 Summary

	Mean	Standard deviation
Condition 1	5 seconds	1.15 seconds
Condition 2	9 seconds	3.50 seconds

Table 14 provides the following information. The means tell us that the participants in condition 2 (with alcohol) took nearly twice as long to complete the task as the participants in condition 1 (without alcohol).

The standard deviations tell us that the spread of scores in condition 2 was much greater than the spread in condition 1. Scores in condition 1 are clustered around the mean; those in condition 2 are more widely spread out.

These findings indicate that alcohol has two effects.

- First, it increases the average time taken to perform a task.
- Second, it exaggerates differences in task performance – slowing some people down a lot, and others hardly at all.

Standard deviation is the most commonly used measure of dispersion for interval and ratio data. It gives an indication of how far the average participant deviates from the mean. As Table 12 indicates, it provides a precise and useful summary of the spread of data.

The normal distribution

Look at Figure 7 which shows the distributions of marks obtained by the same group of students in three different psychology exams. The distributions are shown as *frequency curves*. Frequency curves are often used instead of frequency polygons in order to represent a large number of scores.

The first diagram shows a *positive skew*. This is caused by many students getting low scores – the exam may have been too hard.

The third diagram shows a *negative skew*. This is caused by many students getting high scores – the exam may have been too easy.

The second diagram shows a *normal distribution* of marks. The exam is well matched to the ability of the students.

The mode is always at the highest point in the curve. The median always divides the area into two equal parts. If the data in a distribution is skewed, it is better to use the median as a measure of central tendency, and the interquartile range as a measure of spread (dispersion). The reasons for this can be seen by looking at the skewed distribution diagrams in Figure 7.

For the normal distribution the mode = median = mean.

When interval or ratio scores are clustered symmetrically around the mean, a special frequency distribution is produced. This is called the *normal distribution*. The normal distribution is important in nature. Many naturally occurring phenomena are normally distributed – for example, the heights of women in the UK, the number of branches on yew trees, and so on. Some would say that psychological features like IQ are normally distributed too (see p121).

An interesting feature of a set of data that is normally distributed is the relationship between the area below the curve (which represents the number of scores or items of data), the mean, and the standard deviation.

This relationship is shown in Figure 8.

Since the data is symmetrically distributed about the mean, 50% of the area lies on either side of the mean.

Roughly 68% of the area, 34% being either side of the mean, lies within a standard deviation of the mean, that is from $\bar{x} - sd$ to $\bar{x} + sd$.

Roughly 95% of the area, 47.5% being either side of the mean, lies within 2 standard deviations of the mean, that is from $\bar{x} - 2sd$ to $\bar{x} + 2sd$.

Roughly 99.8% of the area, 49.9% being either side of the mean, lies within 3 standard deviations of the mean, that is from $\bar{x} - 3sd$ to $\bar{x} + 3sd$.

Table 13   Standard deviation – method 1

Using $sd = \sqrt{\dfrac{\sum(x-\bar{x})^2}{n}}$

Condition 1
First calculate the mean.

$$\bar{x} = \frac{\sum x}{n} = \frac{45}{9} = 5$$

The mean is 5 seconds.

x	$x - \bar{x}$	$(x-\bar{x})^2$
3	-2	4
4	-1	1
4	-1	1
5	0	0
5	0	0
5	0	0
6	1	1
6	1	1
7	2	4
$\sum x = 45$		$\sum(x-\bar{x})^2 = 12$

$$sd = \sqrt{\frac{\sum(x-\bar{x})^2}{n}}$$

$$= \sqrt{\frac{12}{9}}$$

=1.15 seconds, to 2 decimal places

Condition 1 has a mean of 5 seconds and a standard deviation of 1.15 seconds.

Condition 2
First calculate the mean.

$$\bar{x} = \frac{\sum x}{n} = \frac{81}{9} = 9$$

The mean is 9 seconds.

x	$x - \bar{x}$	$(x-\bar{x})^2$
3	-6	36
6	-3	9
6	-3	9
9	0	0
9	0	0
9	0	0
11	2	4
13	4	16
15	6	36
$\sum x = 81$		$\sum(x-\bar{x})^2 = 110$

$$sd = \sqrt{\frac{\sum(x-\bar{x})^2}{n}}$$

$$= \sqrt{\frac{110}{9}}$$

=3.50 seconds, to 2 decimal places

Condition 2 has a mean of 9 seconds and a standard deviation of 3.50 seconds

Table 14   Standard deviation – method 2

Using $sd = \sqrt{\dfrac{\sum x^2}{n} - \bar{x}^2}$

Condition 1
First calculate the mean.

$$\bar{x} = \frac{\sum x}{n} = \frac{45}{9} = 5$$

The mean is 5 seconds.

x	x^2
3	9
4	16
4	16
5	25
5	25
5	25
6	36
6	36
7	49
$\sum x = 45$	$\sum x^2 = 237$

$$sd = \sqrt{\frac{\sum x^2}{n} - \bar{x}^2}$$

$$= \sqrt{\frac{237}{9} - 5^2}$$

$$= \sqrt{1.33...}$$

= 1.15 seconds, to 2 decimal places

Condition 1 has a mean of 5 seconds and a standard deviation of 1.15 seconds.

Condition 2
First calculate the mean.

$$\bar{x} = \frac{\sum x}{n} = \frac{81}{9} = 9$$

The mean is 9 seconds.

x	x^2
3	9
6	36
6	36
9	81
9	81
9	81
11	121
13	169
15	225
$\sum x = 81$	$\sum x^2 = 839$

$$sd = \sqrt{\frac{\sum x^2}{n} - \bar{x}^2}$$

$$= \sqrt{\frac{839}{9} - 9^2}$$

$$= \sqrt{12.22...}$$

=3.50 seconds, to 2 decimal places

Condition 2 has a mean of 9 seconds and a standard deviation of 3.50 seconds

Activity 4   Caffeine and concentration

The data below is taken from an investigation into the effect of caffeine on concentration.

The participants in condition 1 were given no caffeine. Those in condition 2 drank five cups of strong coffee. The scores show the number of maths problems each participant solved correctly in 10 minutes.

Participant number	Condition 1 (no coffee)	Condition 2 (coffee)
1	5	9
2	4	3
3	3	1
4	2	1
5	7	7
6	3	5
7	4	1
8	5	9
9	4	2
10	6	7

(Taken from a student research project.)

Questions

1 a) Calculate the mean and median for both conditions.
   b) How reliable is the mean as a measure of central tendency in each case?

2 Calculate the range and standard deviation of the scores for each condition.

3 Use the means and standard deviations to analyse the effect of caffeine on concentration.

The above information can be used for analysing any normal distribution. For example, suppose the heights of men in Manchester are normally distributed, about a mean height of 70 inches, with a standard deviation of 2 inches. This information allows us to build up an accurate picture of the heights of men in Manchester. For example, Figure 8 shows that:

68% of men are between 68 and 72 inches tall.

$50 - 47.5 = 2.5\%$ of men are shorter than 66 inches.

0.1%, 1 in 1000, are taller than 76 inches.

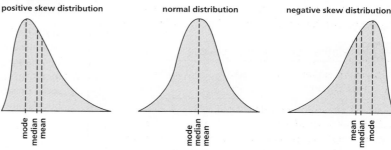

Figure 7 Frequency curves

positive skew distribution   normal distribution   negative skew distribution

mode median mean   mode median mean   mean median mode

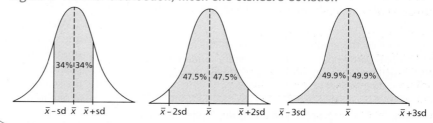

Figure 8 Normal distribution, mean and standard deviation

34% 34%   47.5% 47.5%   49.9% 49.9%

$\bar{x} - sd$ $\bar{x}$ $\bar{x} + sd$ $\bar{x} - 2sd$ $\bar{x}$ $\bar{x} + 2sd$ $\bar{x} - 3sd$ $\bar{x}$ $\bar{x} + 3sd$

Key terms

Standard deviation *A measure of the average deviation of each score from the mean.*

Normal distribution *A frequency distribution in which the scores are symmetrically arranged around the mean.*

Skewed distribution *A frequency distribution in which the scores are asymmetrical (not symmetrically arranged around the mean).*

Summary

1 There are two main measures for summarising quantitative data.
   • A measure of central tendency – a single score that represents the whole set of scores.
   • A measure of the spread or dispersion of the scores.

2 The range provides a simple measure of dispersion. It is the difference between the lowest and highest scores. However, when the range is used, rogue scores can give a misleading impression of the overall spread of the data.

3 The interquartile range overcomes this problem by measuring the range of the middle 50% of a set of scores. However, in doing so, it loses 50% of the scores.

4 Standard deviation is a more precise measure of dispersion. Every score is involved in the calculation.

Unit 4 Correlation

KEY ISSUES

1. What is correlation?
2. What is a scattergraph?
3. How may a correlation coefficient be calculated?

The idea of correlation was introduced in Chapter 16 – see pp 208-209. Correlation is the relationship between two sets of data. A correlation exists when two different measures vary together. For example, there is a correlation between intelligence, measured by scores on an IQ test, and examination results, measured by GCSE grades, if the two measures vary together.

Investigations into the relationship between the crime rate and the unemployment rate, between smoking and the incidence of cancer, and between age and income, may all reveal correlations.

4.1 The scattergraph

A study is conducted into students' performance in a maths test (maximum score 10) and their performance in a physics exam (maximum score 100%). The results are shown in Table 15.

Table 15 Maths and physics scores

Participant	Maths score	Physics score
1	10	77
2	8	63
3	9	68
4	2	37
5	9	42
6	7	56

These results can be drawn on a *scattergraph*, as shown in Figure 9.

Each cross on the graph represents the maths *and* physics scores of one participant. It is not necessary to identify the participants by numbering the crosses. It is the overall *trend*

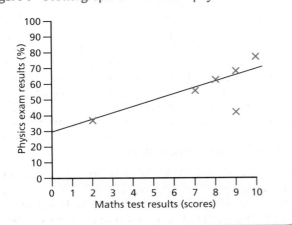

Figure 9 Scattergraph of maths and physics scores

which matters. A *line of best fit* can be drawn, by eye, to show the trend. It does not have to go through the origin of the graph, ie the zero. The line of best fit shows the relationship between the two sets of data. It can be seen immediately that students who did well on the maths test tended to do well on the physics exam.

This suggests that the maths test is a good predictor of performance in physics, and could be used by the school or college to estimate how well applicants for the physics course are likely to get on.

The scattergraph in Figure 9 shows a *positive correlation*. As scores on one variable (the maths test) increase, so do scores on the other variable (the physics exam).

A *negative correlation* exists when the scores on one variable increase and the scores on the other variable decrease. For example, the more pints students drink the night before the physics exam, the lower their marks.

A *zero correlation* exists when there is no relationship between the variables. For example, there is a zero correlation between marks in the physics exam and the heights of students.

4.2 Correlation coefficients

The strengths of the relationship between two sets of data can be measured with a *correlation coefficient*. A *perfect positive correlation* has a coefficient of +1. As the scores on one variable increase, so do the scores on the other variable, in exactly the same proportion – for example, the number of litres of petrol bought and the price paid.

A *perfect negative correlation* has a coefficient of –1, for example the amount of money spent on petrol and the amount of money left in your pocket. When there is no correlation, the coefficient is 0.

Correlation coefficients are illustrated in Figure 10.

With a strong correlation, it is possible to use the scores on one variable to predict the scores on the other variable. The stronger the correlation, the more reliable the prediction. In Figure 9, the scattergraph suggests that the relationship between the scores on the maths test and the physics exam is sufficiently strong to use the maths test to predict performance in physics.

Calculating a correlation coefficient

Spearman's coefficient of rank correlation is a useful way of quantifying the strength of the correlation between variables.

Spearman's coefficient of rank correlation, r_s, is calculated using the following formula

$$r_s = 1 - \frac{6 \sum d^2}{n(n^2 - 1)}$$

where d is the difference in the rank of the score in each set of data (that is, d = rank in set 1 – rank in set 2) and n is the number of items of data. Table 16 shows the rank orders for the maths and physics scores.

To rank the scores, the lowest score is given the rank of 1 (eg the score of 2 in maths), the next lowest is given the rank of 2

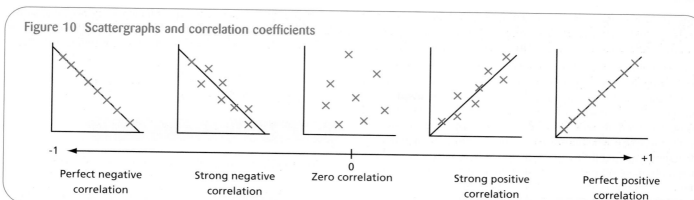

Figure 10 Scattergraphs and correlation coefficients

-1 ← ——————————— 0 ——————————— → +1

Perfect negative correlation   Strong negative correlation   Zero correlation   Strong positive correlation   Perfect positive correlation

Table 16 Rank order of scores

Participant	Maths score	Physics score	Rank order (maths)	Rank order (physics)	d	d²
1	10	77	6	6	0	0
2	8	63	3	4	-1	1
3	9	68	4.5	5	-0.5	0.25
4	2	37	1	1	0	0
5	9	42	4.5	2	2.5	6.25
6	7	56	2	3	-1	1

$$\sum d^2 = 8.5$$

(eg the score of 7 in maths), and so on. When there are equal scores (eg two scores of 9 in maths) the scores are given the next two available ranks (in this example, ranks 4 and 5). The ranks are then divided between the equal scores – in this example both scores are given the rank of 4.5. Since ranks 4 and 5 have now been occupied, the next score gets the rank of 6.

As Table 16 shows, the difference (d) between each pair of ranks is calculated. Each value of d is then squared (d^2). This makes all the values positive.

Using this example, Spearman's coefficient of correlation (r_s) is calculated as follows.

$$r_s = 1 - \frac{6 \sum d^2}{n(n^2-1)}$$

$$= 1 - \left(\frac{6 \times 8.5}{6(6^2-1)} \right)$$

$$= 1 - \left(\frac{6 \times 8.5}{6(36-1)} \right)$$

$$= 1 - \left(\frac{6 \times 8.5}{6 \times 35} \right)$$

$$= 1 - \frac{51}{210}$$

$$= 1 - 0.242...$$

$$= 0.76 \text{ to 2 decimal places}$$

Spearman's coefficient of rank correlation for the relationship between maths and physics scores is 0.76. This is a strong positive correlation.

Correlation coefficients of:

  0.5 to 1 for positive correlation and

  – 0.5 to –1 for negative correlation

are considered to provide reliable predicted values. They indicate reasonably strong correlations. The closer the values of r_s to 1 and –1 respectively, the stronger the correlations, and the higher the reliability of prediction.

One weakness of Spearman's coefficient of rank correlation is that it only indicates linear correlation – that is, relationships which go in one direction only. Some correlations are non-linear – they may begin as positive and then become negative (or vice versa). This is illustrated in Figure 11 which shows the relationship between how enjoyable people found a party and the number of guests present.

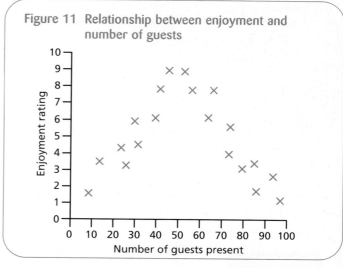

Figure 11 Relationship between enjoyment and number of guests

As more people arrive, the party becomes more lively and enjoyable. However, the party then becomes increasingly crowded and less and less enjoyable. The Spearman coefficient of rank correlation gives a zero correlation for these two sets of data. This gives the mistaken impression that there is no correlation when, in fact, there is quite a striking one – it is just that it is non-linear. It is important to draw a scattergraph in order to see what the correlation coefficient is telling us.

Correlation and causation

Correlations, no matter how strong, do not necessarily indicate cause and effect relationships (see p209). For example, people's enjoyment of the party may have nothing to do with the number of guests, despite the correlation shown in Figure 11. The enjoyment rating might have declined because of the host's choice of music. She might have replaced dance music with her favourite Cliff Richard CDs after half the guests had arrived.

Even if there is a cause and effect relationship, correlation does not indicate the direction of causation – it does not show what causes what. For example, there may be a correlation between schizophrenia and imbalances of dopamine. However, this does not tell us whether the dopamine imbalance causes schizophrenia, or whether schizophrenia causes the dopamine imbalance. And, returning to the point made in the previous paragraph, there may be an unknown third factor which causes both.

Even a very strong correlation coefficient does not necessarily show any real relationship between the variables. Snedecor (1946) provides a delightful example of a near perfect negative correlation of –0.98 between the birth rate in the UK and the production of pig iron in the USA between 1875 and 1920. Despite this impressive correlation coefficient, it is highly unlikely that these factors are related.

Key terms

Correlation *The relationship between two or more variables or sets of data.*

Positive correlation *As scores on one variable increase, so do scores on the other variable.*

Negative correlation *As scores on one variable increase, scores on the other variable decrease.*

Correlation coefficient *A measure of the strength of the correlation.*

Scattergraph *A graph which illustrates the relationship between two or more variables. Also known as scattergram and scatter plot.*

Summary

1. Correlations can be illustrated on a scattergraph and measured using a correlation coefficient.

2. Spearman's coefficient of rank correlation is a simple and useful method of producing correlation coefficients. However, it cannot measure non-linear correlations.

3. Correlations do not necessarily indicate cause and effect relationships.

Activity 5   Oasis and Blur

Item A   Student ratings

Students were asked to rate two bands on a scale of 1 to 10, with ten being the highest rating. The results are shown below.

Ratings for two bands

Participant	Oasis rating	Blur rating
1	4	9
2	5	7
3	10	2
4	8	3
5	9	5
6	1	9
7	5	5
8	3	6
9	8	2
10	7	7

(Taken from a student research project.)

Oasis

Blur

Questions

1 a) Draw a scattergraph of the data.
   b) What does the graph show?
2 a) Calculate Spearman's coefficient of rank correlation for the data.
   b) What does the correlation show?

References

Glasgow University Media Group (1980). *Bad news.* London: Routledge.

Goffman, E. (1968). *Asylums.* Harmondsworth: Penguin.

Kitzinger, J. (1993). Understanding AIDS. In J. Eldridge (Ed.), *Getting the message: News, truth and power.* London: Routledge.

Lobban, G. (1974). Data report on British reading schemes. *Times Educational Supplement*, 1.3.1974.

Snedecor, G.W. (1946). *Statistical methods* (4th ed.). Ames: Iowa State College Press.

(19) Social cognition

▶ ## Introduction

Every day of our lives we are involved in 'people watching'. We look at other people's appearances, we listen to what they say, and we observe their behaviour. On the basis of this, we make all sorts of judgements about them. We form impressions about other people's personality or character. We decide where someone seems to fit in society. We judge how they behave and compare it to what we would have done in a similar situation.

Social cognition is the name given to this process of perceiving and evaluating our social world. It refers to the way we categorise, organise, interpret and make sense of incoming social information. In particular, it refers to the way we deal with information about ourselves, our social relationships, and the behaviour of others.

Social cognition is not an objective process. It is often biased and subject to errors. Sometimes our views of others are based on prejudice. Sometimes we just get things wrong. Despite these problems, social cognition is vital for social life. This chapter looks at the positive and negative sides of social cognition.

Chapter summary

- Unit 1 explores the attribution of causality and describes errors and biases in the attribution process.
- Unit 2 defines the concepts of schema, stereotyping and social representations and

outlines social and cultural influences on social perception.
- Unit 3 looks at theories of the origins, maintenance and reduction of prejudice and discrimination.

Unit 1 Attribution of causality

KEY ISSUES

1 Why do we try to attribute causality to people's behaviour?

2 How are attributions of causality made?

3 What errors commonly occur in the attribution process?

1.1 The attribution process

As social beings, we appear to have a need to find meaning in our immediate environment. Bartlett (1932) described how people exert 'effort after meaning' as they explore and reflect upon their social world. One of the major things that individuals reflect upon is what causes other people to act as they do. We want to know this so we can judge how best to respond to them. The process of working out what causes social behaviour is known as the *attribution of causality*.

According to Fritz Heider (1958), the founder of attribution theory, there are two major kinds of attribution that observers make when they decide on the causes of other people's behaviour (known as 'actors' in attribution theory). The first is called a *person* or *dispositional* or *internal* attribution. This is made when the observer decides that something within the actor – like their personality – caused them behave as they did. The other kind is called a *situation* or *environmental* or *external* attribution. This is made when the observer concludes that

something outside the actor is the cause of their behaviour. These outside factors might be things like an order given to the actor by an authority figure or a set of customs and rules that they feel impelled to follow.

Heider believed that people have a tendency to make person rather than situation attributions. In other words, they are more likely to look for the causes of behaviour within the person rather than the external environment.

Some attribution theorists (eg Heider, 1958; Kelley, 1967) claim that when an individual makes an attribution for social behaviour they act in a similar way to a scientist investigating the natural world. Scientists search for causes through a process of careful observation, using rules and methods to test theories about causality. In everyday life, we also seem to use rules to make attributions about the causes of other people's behaviour. These rules are based upon a mixture of observation and our previous experience.

But this image of people as 'lay scientists' has been criticised. Ordinary people in social situations attribute causes almost automatically and sometimes in ways that are inaccurate and biased. This happens because the process of making attributions occurs as we interact with other people and is affected by all sorts of factors, such as our mood, the kind of relationship we have with the people around us, the activity we are currently engaged in, and so on. We typically act more like a politician than a scientist – we are more concerned with how far our explanations of other people's behaviour fit with our own interests and plans than we are with their accuracy and objectivity.

Key terms

Person or **dispositional** or **internal attribution** *A judgement that something within the person, like personality or mood, caused their behaviour.*

Situation or **environmental** or **external attribution** *A judgement that something outside the person, like an order or situational constraint, caused their behaviour.*

All of the major theories of causal attribution try to explain the rules observers use when they make attributions. This unit outlines and assesses the following theories: Jones and Davis' *correspondent inference theory*, Kelley's *covariation* and *schema models* and Weiner's *achievement attribution model*.

1.2   Theories of causal attribution

Jones and Davis' correspondent inference theory

Jones and Davis' (1965) theory develops Heider's idea that observers have a general tendency to make person or dispositional attributions (ie where the cause of behaviour is attributed to something 'within' the actor). Heider claimed that we tend to make dispositional attributions because they make the world seem to be a stable and predictable place. For example, if we tend to attribute the causes of someone's behaviour to something within them, like their personality, we feel we can also predict how that person will behave over a range of situations, how they are likely to behave in the future, and so on. But if we tend to attribute causes to something 'outside' the person, such as the situation, we will make separate attributions for the behaviour that occurs in each and every situation we observe. The world will then appear to be a much less stable and predictable place!

Jones and Davis set out to look at the grounds we use to make dispositional attributions. There are some forms of behaviour that we expect from people simply because of the job they do or their social role (eg we expect parents to be 'grown up', teachers to be 'responsible', doctors to be 'caring'). When people act in ways that fit with our expectations we tend to make situation attributions, because we assume that they are simply behaving 'as they should' and not perhaps as they would really like to do. However, when someone does something that is uncommon or unexpected (eg a parent acts 'like a child') we are more likely to conclude that they are acting *intentionally* and not because of the constraints of their social role. When this occurs, we make a special kind of person attribution called a *correspondent inference*. This is an inference that the actor's behaviour corresponds to their underlying character. Jones and Davis' theory then states that there are a number of principles which observers draw upon to arrive at correspondent inferences.

Non-common effects One of the main ways observers make attributions is by examining situations in which actors have a choice between two or more courses of action. Consider the following. Sarah has a choice between two jobs (see Figure 1). The first job is in advertising. It offers high pay and good promotion prospects, it will enable her to use her artistic talents and will involve living in Edinburgh. The second job is in nursery education. It is based in Manchester and offers her the

opportunity to work with and care for children. The pay is average and there are few promotion prospects. The only thing the two jobs have in common is a good pension scheme. It would be difficult to say why Sarah chose one job rather than the other because the jobs have so little in common. Her choice would produce many non-common effects. In other words, most of the effects produced by one course of action would not be produced by the other course of action. As a result, it would be difficult to attribute a cause to her choice.

Jane also has a choice between two jobs (see Figure 1). Both jobs are in advertising and based in London, both offer good pay and promotion prospects and will enable her to develop her artistic talents. The main difference is that one company is a charity for the homeless, the other produces garden furniture. In this case, the only non-common effect is raising money for the homeless or selling garden furniture. It appears that Jane's choice of job is based on a choice between these two alternatives.

Jones and Davis argue that when there are a large number of non-common effects, it is difficult to make an attribution about people's choice of action (as in Sarah's case). However, when the number of non-common effects is small, (as in Jane's case), then the choice made is more likely to tell us something about the person. For example, if Jane chose to work for the charity, she may well be seen as a caring person and this would account for her choice. When there are few non-common effects, there is a greater likelihood of making a person or a dispositional attribution.

Figure 1   Non-common effects

Sarah

Advertising
High pay
Good promotion prospects
Use of artistic talents
Based in Edinburgh

Good pension scheme

Nursery Education
Average pay
Few promotion prospects
Work with and care for children
Based in Manchester

Many non-common effects

■ Common effects   ■ Non-common effects

Jane

Charity for homeless

Advertising
Good pay and promotion prospects
Use of artistic talents
Based in London

Selling garden furniture

Few non-common effects

Freely-chosen behaviour When an actor appears to have chosen to behave in a particular way of their own free will, observers will tend to see the actor's behaviour as indicative of the kind of person they are.

Social desirability In general, actions that are socially undesirable, such as rudeness or aggression, tend to 'stand out' more than *socially desirable* actions, which we usually expect and take for granted from others. The queue jumper stands out, whereas those who stand patiently in line often remain unnoticed – their behaviour conforms with our expectations. Socially undesirable actions provide us with more information on which to base a correspondent inference. This means that observers are more likely to attribute undesirable actions to the person.

Social role Actions that form part of someone's *social role* tend not to stand out. They are just 'part of the job'. Action out of role, however, can be a great deal more informative. Jones, Davis and Gergen (1961), found that bogus interviewees who acted inappropriately in a tape-recorded 'job interview' attracted more correspondent inferences from listeners than those who behaved appropriately. Listeners concluded that anyone who was prepared to act unusually in a formal situation must be a fairly unusual person. As a result, they tended to make a person attribution for their behaviour.

Evaluation

Advantages Jones and Davis' theory of correspondent inferences is based on a great deal of experimental work. They offer hard evidence for their claims that observers draw upon a number of principles (freely chosen behaviour, non-common effects, social desirability, social role) to check observed behaviour against inferences of the actor's underlying character.

Disadvantages Do people really make correspondent inferences by rigidly applying a limited set of principles in this way? They may well do some of the time, but observers often jump to conclusions about the causes of other people's behaviour without doing any of the analysis suggested by Jones and Davis. For example, when someone behaves in a way that is clumsy, we often attribute this clumsiness to them as a person (ie a person attribution), even though we are well aware that they acted unintentionally (Eiser, 1986). On these sorts of occasions, there are other factors informing an observer's attributions. These include the prior experiences and beliefs of the observer, including the kinds of stereotypes they hold, as well as their

Key terms

Correspondent inference *An attribution that someone's behaviour corresponds to and is therefore caused by their underlying character.*

Non-common effects *The effects produced by one course of action that would not be produced by an alternative course of action.*

Social desirability *Actions which we take for granted or expect from others and thus do not tend to 'stand out'. Actions which are accepted and seen as desirable.*

Social role *Actions which form part of someone's role. These too tend not to 'stand out'.*

membership of different social groups (Hogg & Vaughan, 1995). For example, an observer might make an attribution of a woman's, a gay person's or an American's behaviour on the basis of stereotypes in terms of which they see each group. The next unit outlines how these kind of factors strongly influence the way observers perceive others.

Kelley's covariation model

Kelley's (1967) model of attribution attempts to describe how observers infer the causes of an actor's behaviour by drawing on three types of information:

Consensus The degree to which other actors would respond in a similar way to the same stimulus.

Consistency How stable the behaviour appears to be – the degree to which the actor has responded in the same way to the same stimulus on other occasions.

Distinctiveness The degree to which the person has behaved in the same way to other similar stimuli.

Observers then make their attribution by combining information about consensus, consistency and distinctiveness. For example, Emily has just started a new job that involves regular contact with a particular manager. Emily feels that the manager is treating her in an unhelpful and discourteous way. She wonders what might be causing this behaviour. Emily then notices that other managers in the company do not behave in this way (consensus information), that this particular manager is consistently unhelpful and discourteous to her, whatever the situation (consistency information), and behaves in the same way towards other people (distinctiveness information). Given this information, Emily is likely to make a person attribution – this manager is simply a rude and boorish individual and these characteristics account for his behaviour.

Like Heider, Kelley believed that when ordinary people make attributions in this way they act rather like scientists. Kelley took this belief to its extreme, claiming that the attribution process operated rather like a statistical test. He thought that observers sift through social information looking for similarities and repeated patterns in behaviour ('covariation') from which causal inferences could be made.

Experimental evidence The best known application of Kelley's model is an experiment by McArthur (1972). McArthur gave participants descriptions of different actions and then asked them to state the causes of the action. For a statement such as 'John laughed at the comedian', three kinds of attribution are possible. A *person attribution* would conclude that John laughs because he is a jovial kind of person. A *stimulus attribution* would conclude that there is something funny about this particular comedian which makes John laugh. Finally, a *circumstance attribution* would conclude that there is something special about the current circumstances which makes John laugh.

By manipulating the kinds of additional information available to participants about John and the comedian, McArthur showed how observers draw upon Kelley's dimensions to ask three sorts of questions:

- Do other people laugh at the comedian? (consensus information)
- Has John laughed at the same comedian on other occasions and under different circumstances, eg on stage as well as on

television? (consistency information)
- Does John laugh at other comedians? (distinctiveness information)

If observers were made aware than it is only John who laughs at the comedian (low consensus) and he has done so on previous occasions (high consistency), but he also tends to laugh at most other comedians (low distinctiveness), they usually made a *person attribution*, reasoning that it was something about John himself that resulted in his laughter.

If, however, observers were told that many other people laughed along with John (high consensus), whilst John himself has laughed at this comedian in the past (high consistency), and that he is rarely quite so tickled by other comedians (high distinctiveness), they were likely to make a *stimulus attribution* and conclude that it was the comic genius of this particular comedian which caused John's hysterics.

Finally, when observers were told that only John laughed at the comedian (low consensus), that he has not done so on previous occasions (low consistency) and that in general John does not tend to laugh at comedians (high distinctiveness), they tended to make a *circumstance attribution*, having concluded that there must be something special about the current circumstance which caused John's laughter (perhaps John was watching the comic with a new girlfriend and anxious to make a good impression).

Table 1 summarises Kelley's covariation model.

| Table 1 | Kelley's covariation model of attributions |

	Person attribution	Stimulus attribution	Circumstance attribution
Consensus	Low	High	Low
Consistency	High	High	Low
Distinctiveness	Low	High	High

Based on Kelley, 1967

Evaluation

Advantages Kelley's model is different from Jones and Davis' work in that it explores three different possible attributions – person, stimulus and circumstance – rather than the usual person vs situation attributions. It is also designed to account for situations where multiple sets of information gathered over time are drawn upon by observers.

Disadvantages The process that Kelley describes involves a great deal of mental effort or 'cognitive expensiveness' on the part of the observer. On many occasions observers may simply arrive at their conclusions without bothering to make all the mental calculations that Kelley describes. For example, we expect certain kinds of behaviour, like being successful, to result from internal factors, such as ability or perseverance. Because we expect this, in these cases we tend to make person attributions. Our expectations and beliefs allow us to make a 'shortcut' in the attribution process (Lupfer, Clark & Hutcherson, 1990). In fact on many occasions we simply don't bother to look at all the available information, we just concentrate on the bits that seem most important or relevant to us at the time (Nisbett & Ross, 1980).

But some situations do take us by surprise. When this happens our expectations are thrown up in the air, and it is likely that we will need to do the analysis that Kelley outlines in order to infer causes. Equally, if particularly unpleasant outcomes are involved, then we will probably put the effort in to do some serious analysis. So in both of these cases, Kelley's model may be a good description of what observers do.

Finally, much of the experimental work which has developed Kelley's model (eg McArthur's studies) lacks ecological validity. Just because people can apply Kelley's principles to 'prepackaged' material in experimental situations – such as John and the comedian – does not mean they actually do use these principles in their everyday lives.

Key terms

Stimulus attribution *An attribution that other people have caused the behaviour in question.*

Circumstance attribution *An attribution that there is something special about the current circumstances which has caused the behaviour in question.*

Kelley's causal schemas

In response to criticisms of the covariation model, Kelley (1972) developed a separate theory to explain what happens when observers lack information about consensus, consistency and distinctiveness. Under these circumstances observers draw upon 'ready-made' explanations. These are cognitively stored in the form of *causal schemas* (see Unit 2). A causal schema is a set of beliefs or ideas about the likely causes of certain kinds of behaviour. Observers develop schemas through experience and then draw upon them as required. Kelley described two kinds of causal schema, along with two principles which can be applied to each schema.

A *multiple sufficient causes schema* applies to situations where a number of causes could all plausibly have led to the same behaviour. It emphasises that one cause will do just as well as any other to explain the situation. For example, the contestants on the television programme Big Brother may have taken part for any number of reasons, such as wanting to be on TV, a desire to discover something about themselves, or just plain exhibitionism. A second schema, the *multiple necessary causes schema,* also deals with situations where there are a number of causes, but emphasises that two or more of them are necessary to produce the behaviour in question. For example, a wannabe pop star may have talent, but we are likely to conclude that they will also need a good manager and massive financial backing to succeed.

The *discounting principle* is usually applied to the multiple sufficient causes schema, but can also be applied to the multiple necessary causes schema. It is applied when we suspect that one of the possible causes far outweighs the others in importance. We might reason that wanting the £70,000 pound prize was likely to be the most important cause for Big Brother contestants, and discount the other causes.

The *augmentation principle* applies when other possible causes appear to work against a particular outcome. For example, if the wannabe pop star succeeds despite having a poor manager and little financial backing, then there is a greater likelihood that talent accounts for their success. The possibility that talent is the cause is augmented or increased.

Big Brother contestants – although they may have many reasons for wanting to take part, we might discount these and suspect that the £70,000 prize was the most important.

Evaluation

Advantages The causal schema model offers a reasonable explanation of how observers make attributions without having to expend the considerable cognitive effort suggested by the covariation model. It also explains what may happen when information about consensus, consistency and distinctiveness is incomplete.

Disadvantages The causal schema model has not proved as popular as the covariation model and remains little tested. It may also not apply well cross-culturally. Some African cultures, for example, make a distinction between proximal and distal causes (Moghaddam et al., 1993). A house may collapse because of any number of proximal reasons (poor foundations, a storm). But these causes are understood to be brought about by an ultimate or distal cause, such the actions of a supernatural power. Kelley's schema model explains very little about such causal reasoning in which an ultimate, often supernatural, cause produces a number of other, lower level causes.

Key term

Causal schema *A set of beliefs or ideas about the likely causes of certain kinds of behaviour.*

Weiner's achievement attribution theory

Weiner's work (1979; 1986) has explored the kinds of attributions observers make to explain the causes of success or failure. The theory states that following perceived success or failure at some task, such as an examination or sports match, individuals experience either a positive or a negative emotional reaction. This reaction leads them to search for the causes of the performance by sorting through whatever social information is available. They then make an attribution based around one of four factors – ability, effort, task difficulty and luck. Any one of these attributions can either reinforce or alter the individual's

expectations about how they may perform in the future. Low expectations generally diminish motivation, whilst high expectations result in increased motivation.

Weiner's argument is illustrated by the following example. Examination failure might involve an initial judgement of performance ('I've blown it') followed by emotional arousal ('This is a real disaster') prompting an attributional search. This may result in the student attributing their failure to poor preparation ('I didn't revise properly'). An attribution like this may make the student resolve to revise properly in the future, and increase their motivation to succeed ('I'm going to try harder next time'). However, a different kind of attribution – such as 'I'm not very bright' – may have other effects. It may reduce the student's expectations about their likely future examination performance ('I don't expect to do well'), which will in turn affect their motivation ('There's no point trying').

Attributions about a person's success or failure can be made by themselves and by others. For example, both a student and their teacher may make attributions for the student's examination performance. And, if the teacher's attribution is communicated to the student, then this may affect the student's motivation to succeed in future examinations. Weiner suggests that there are three related dimensions that are used to make attributions for achievement.

Internal/external refers to the degree to which a cause is 'internal' (person) or 'external' (situation/environmental) to the actor concerned. A student may believe that they have failed an exam because of their abilities (internal cause) or because they were distracted by a noise in the examination room (external cause).

Stability/instability refers to the degree to which the cause is seen as a something which is likely to remain a cause of similar events in the future. If a student believes they have failed an exam because they have little academic ability, this will be seen as a fairly stable cause which is likely to result in future exam failures. But failure caused by a noise in the examination room would be a temporary, or unstable, cause, and therefore unlikely to affect future examination performance.

Controllable/uncontrollable refers to whether or not the cause is seen as being under control of the person involved. If a student attributes examination failure to lack of revision, then this is controllable – the student can revise thoroughly next time. However, if failure is attributed to lack of ability, then this is largely uncontrollable – the student cannot readily increase their intelligence.

Weiner's attributions for achievement can be combined in various ways. They offer eight different explanations for performance (see Table 2). For example, a student may attribute their examination success to internal, controllable and stable factors, such as the effort they put into revision. It is internal because the effort comes from the student, it is controllable because the student can plan and direct their revision, it is stable because it is typical of the effort usually put into revision. This kind of attribution is highly motivating because it suggests to the student that there is no barrier to a repeat performance in the future. However, if the student concluded that their success was based on external, uncontrollable and unstable factors – it was due to luck – then this kind of attribution is not particularly motivating since they cannot do anything about it. In this way, the attribution selected can have an important effect on future motivation and performance.

When people try to explain their own success or failure, they tend to choose attributions which place them in the best possible light. For example, they prefer to make internal rather than external attributions for academic success. This may be because it is far more motivating to believe that they are responsible for their success and are not purely at the mercy of circumstances. Conversely, when it comes to explaining failure, it is more reassuring to believe that external factors somehow undermined their own ability to succeed. (Augoustinos & Walker, 1995).

Evaluation

Methodology The achievement attribution model is well supported by evidence from empirical studies. However, most of this evidence comes from laboratory experiments where both the settings and the tasks can appear artificial and contrived. For example, participants are sometimes presented with stories and asked to attribute causes to the actions of those involved. Will participants use the same procedures for making attributions in everyday life? In other words, can the findings of experiments be generalised beyond the laboratory walls? Despite these doubts about ecological validity, there is a large body of evidence to support the achievement attribution model (Hewstone & Fincham, 1996).

Attribution and motivation A major strength of Weiner's model is that it makes a connection between the attribution process and motivation. Weiner shows that the kinds of attributions people make on a routine, daily basis may have long-term effects on their future behaviour. The link to motivation also shows that emotions are involved in the attribution process. Making attributions is not just about the kinds of cool mental calculations suggested by Jones and Davis or Kelley.

Applications Weiner's model has some interesting and useful applications. For example, studies have shown that happily married couples tend to see positive behaviours in their partners as internal, stable and controllable. Negative behaviours are explained away as external, unstable and uncontrollable, so removing blame from their partners. Unhappy couples tend to do just the opposite, thereby blaming their partners for the unhappy marriage (Fincham & O'Leary, 1983). This suggests that unhappy marriages can be improved by changes in attribution, a finding that can be usefully applied by marriage guidance counsellors.

Culture Cross-cultural studies have supported the applicability of Weiner's model across cultures (Schuster et al., 1989). However, it was found that Indian participants made more external, unstable and uncontrollable attributions than participants from other cultures. Moghaddam (1998) notes that this may be due to a sense of 'fatalism' prevalent in Indian culture (ie, a sense that the individual's power to control events is limited). Cultural differences certainly exist in how personal control is viewed. Western societies tend to see personal control over events as something each individual should strive to achieve (Crawford, 1984).

Table 2   Possible causes of achievement

| | Internal | | External | |
	Stable	Unstable	Stable	Unstable
Controllable	Typical effort exerted	Unusual effort exerted	Consistent help or hindrance from others	Unusual help or hindrance from others
Uncontrollable	Ability	Mood	Task difficulty	Luck

Adapted from Weiner, 1979

Krantz and Rude (1984) report that whilst individuals from different cultures use the same three dimensions to infer causes, the way they are used may differ. For example, Westerners tend to use internal or person attributions to explain success, whilst the opposite may be true for Japanese, who are more likely to explain success in terms of external or situational factors (Shikanai, 1984).

Key terms

Stability *The degree to which a cause of success or failure is seen to endure over time.*

Controllability *The degree to which a cause of success or failure is seen to be under the control of the individual.*

Overall evaluation of attribution theories

The major contributions to the study of attribution (Jones and Davis, Kelley, Weiner) all follow Heider in making a basic distinction between person and situation attributions. But there are important differences between their approaches.

Jones and Davis look in detail at how observers make person attributions, and the grounds they use to do this (eg non-common effects, social role). Jones and Davis emphasise that uncommon behaviour is more likely to result in a person attribution than behaviour that we would usually expect from an actor given their social role.

Kelley's covariation model concentrates on the decision-making process involved in making attributions and looks at the use of particular types of information (ie, consensus, distinctiveness, consistency) to arrive at person, stimulus or circumstance attributions. Kelley's causal schema model suggests how these kinds of decisions are made when full information is not available.

Weiner's achievement attribution theory shows how we interpret our own and other people's successes and failures. Weiner links the attribution process to emotion and motivation. This recognises that attribution is not just about mental calculation – it can also be a highly emotional experience.

But all these theories suffer from a common weakness. They are all based around the idea of the 'naive scientist' who applies a limited number of principles to explain the causes of behaviour. Now, the question is whether people actually make attributions in this way in their everyday lives. Sure, they might do so in an experiment, that is, they might go along with the way the experiment is set up and behave in the way the theories suggest. But these experiments often lack ecological validity –

they don't look or feel much like real life. For example, the information about John and the comedian has little significance to participants, it is irrelevant to their ordinary concerns, and the whole laboratory situation is artificial compared to their everyday lives (Edwards & Potter, 1992).

What is also missing from these attribution theories is any description of the observer and the actor (Moghaddam, 1998). In real life, things like someone's gender, age, ethnic or class background, ability or disability can matter a great deal to us. These characteristics of an actor can affect how we explain their behaviour. For example, Deaux and Emswiller (1974) found that when judging the performance of actors on a task, observers tend to make person attributions, such as skill, for 'majority group' actors (eg males, whites) and situation attributions, such as luck, for 'minority group' actors (eg females, blacks).

What this shows is that observers often make attributions based upon stereotypes – stereotypes of men and women, ethnic groups, age groups and so on. For example, 'She did that because she's a woman' is an attribution which draws on the supposed characteristics of women contained in a gender stereotype. Attributions based on stereotypes offer a picture of an unthinking, blinkered, unconsidered response rather than the analytical response of 'man the scientist' described by most attribution theorists. To understand such attributions, we need to turn to schema theory, which is considered in Unit 2.

Activity 1   The Cantona kick

On Saturday 26 January 1995, Manchester United were playing Crystal Palace. Eric Cantona of United was having an unhappy afternoon. From the outset he complained about the tackling he received. In the 48th minute his notoriously short fuse was ignited. Shaw of Crystal Palace fouled him and seconds later Cantona kicked Shaw as the pair went for a high clearance. Out came the red card and off went Cantona for the fifth time in 16 months.

As he walked along the touchline to the dressing room, a 20-year-old Palace fan raced to the front of the stand hurling abuse at the Frenchman. According to another Palace fan he made obscene gestures, shouted 'You fucking French git', and a string of other insults. Cantona immediately leapt at his abuser with a two-footed flying kick. He then threw several punches before police, stewards, team officials and other players pulled the pair apart.

Gifted footballer though he is, Cantona again demonstrated the fatal flaw in his temperament which eventually saw him quit league football in France after a series of run-ins with the authorities. In last season's European Cup he was shown the red card at the end of a game in Istanbul for calling the referee a cheat, having already punched the Turkish team's reserve goalkeeper as he sat on the bench.

Cantona was charged with common assault for his attack on the Crystal Palace fan. He was given 120 hours community service. Referring to the fan's behaviour, the judge stated, 'Such conduct would provoke the most stoic, and we believe Mr Cantona reacted in a way that was out of character'.

Adapted from the *Guardian*, 16.1.1995; 27.1.1995; 1.4.1995

Questions

1 Provide a person or dispositional attribution for Cantona's assault.

2 Provide a situation or environmental attribution for Cantona's assault.

3 Using Jones and Davis' theory, explain why Cantona's kick aimed at the fan is more informative to us than his kick aimed at the Palace player.

4 Describe the questions that we would need to ask about this situation in order to do a Kelley-style covariation analysis of Cantona's kick.

1.3 Errors and biases in attribution

So far we have looked at various theories which claim to explain how the attribution process works. In this section we ask, How good are attributions?. Do they provide accurate accounts of the causes of actions and events? Or are they sometimes, or even often, just plain wrong? Social psychologists refer to attributions which appear to get it wrong as *errors*.

Alternatively, if attributions aren't precisely 'wrong', they may be *biased*. Biased attributions tend to emphasise certain explanations rather than others. Attributions may also be *self-serving*, placing the person making the attribution in a good light and protecting them from blame. Some social psychologists prefer the term bias to error. Stating something is an error implies the psychologist knows the truth. However, it is possible to identify bias without saying an attribution is incorrect.

The fundamental attribution error

The basis of *fundamental attribution error* lies in a tendency – originally noted by Heider – for observers to make person or dispositional attributions for actors' behaviour rather than situation attributions (Ross, 1977). That is, they overestimate the importance of information about the person and underestimate the importance of information about the situation.

This tendency remains even when observers have been informed about possible situational or environmental causes, such as being told that the actor was simply following the instructions given to them by an experimenter (Jones & Harris, 1967). Observers tend, for example, to attribute the causes of road accidents far more to drivers than to general driving conditions or to vehicle fault, even though they may be well aware of the importance of these situational factors (Barjonet, 1980).

A number of explanations have been suggested for the fundamental attribution error.

Focus of attention People tend to focus on the person rather than the situation. This is partly because they are often unaware of situational or background information. Experimental evidence indicates that the less people know about situational factors, the more likely they are to make person attributions (Gilbert & Malone, 1995).

Linguistic factors It has been suggested that the structure of the English language encourages person rather than situation attributions. It is fairly easy to describe a person and their actions in the same terms, for example as kind, friendly, mean or dishonest, but applying the same terms to a situation is inappropriate. For example, it is easy to describe a person and their actions as dishonest, but a dishonest situation makes little sense. As a result, the rules of English may encourage person rather than situation attributions (Nisbett & Ross, 1980).

Cultural factors In recent years, a growing number of researchers have argued that the fundamental attribution error is a reflection of the culture people belong to. In other words, it is not universal, it is only found in particular cultures.

There is evidence that the fundamental attribution error is largely absent in North American children, yet becomes progressively more apparent with age (White, 1988). Why might older North Americans make more person attributions? One explanation is that the fundamental attribution error is the result of being socialised into a particular culture. Like many Western societies, there is considerable emphasis on the individual rather than the group or collective in North America. This is known as *individualism*. The individual is seen as autonomous, as not dependent on others, and as the centre of all action and responsibility (Sampson, 1993). A person who is brought up with these culturally accepted ways of thinking and behaving will be more likely to make person attributions.

The fundamental attribution error may then be better understood as a cultural rather than a cognitive bias. In other words, it is due to culture rather than errors in thinking. Cross-cultural evidence supports this. Miller (1984) found that adult Indian Hindus tend to make far less person attributions than adult North Americans. Their culture places far more emphasis on the group, on collective rather than individual responsibility.

The following study provides further support for a cultural explanation of the fundamental attribution error. The researchers studied reports of two mass murders in the *New York Times* (an English language newspaper), and the *World Journal* (a Chinese language newspaper), both published in the USA. One of the mass murders was committed by a Chinese university student, the other by a white postal worker. Journalists writing in English made far more person attributions than those writing in Chinese. For example, they described the Chinese murderer as a 'darkly disturbed man' with a 'sinister edge', seeing these personal

characteristics as explaining his actions. In contrast, the Chinese reporters focused on situation attributions describing the murderer as 'not getting along with his advisor' at university and being 'isolated from the Chinese community'. The researchers argue that these differences in attribution are due to differences in culture (Morris & Peng, 1994).

Key terms

Fundamental attribution error *The tendency to make person attributions rather than situation attributions when explaining behaviour.*

Individualism *A cultural belief that the individual is an autonomous agent, not dependent on others, who directly controls and is responsible for their own actions.*

Actor-observer effect

The fundamental attribution error does not apply to the same extent to people's attributions of their own behaviour. Whilst observers tend to attribute person or dispositional causes for the behaviour of others, when it comes to accounting for their own behaviour they are far more likely to attribute situation causes (Jones & Nisbett, 1972). This is known as the *actor-observer effect*.

In the classic demonstration of the effect, Nisbett et al. (1973) asked observers to predict the future behaviour of actors who had been asked to volunteer to help at a charity function. In order to do this, observers tended to speculate about the kind of person each actor was. In other words, they used person attributions as the basis for their predictions. Yet when the actors were asked about how they themselves would behave in the future (ie, would they be likely to volunteer for charity work?), they tended to think about what they might do in each particular situation being described. Actors, then, used situation attributions as the basis for predicting their own behaviour.

Various explanations have been suggested for the actor-observer effect.

Different perspectives When we are explaining our own behaviour we literally see ourselves differently than observers do. When we look at the actions of others, we focus on the actor; when we are acting, we focus on the situation. Experiments in which participants are given the opportunity to view a video recording of themselves in conversation, shot from the perspective of the other speaker, show that this tends to reduce the actor-observer effect (Storms, 1973). In this situation, actors are more likely to attribute person causes to their own behaviour. Formerly they were seeing the situation, now they are actually seeing themselves.

Different information The actor-observer effect may arise because actors have more information about themselves than observers do. Actors have background information about the situation, their relationship with those involved, the role they are playing, their duties and responsibilities, the demands on their time, and so on. As a result, they tend to make situation attributions to account for their own behaviour. Those observing the actor are unlikely to have this background information. As a result, they are more likely to make a person attribution (Greenwald & Banaji, 1989).

Cultural factors As with the fundamental attribution error, there is evidence that the actor-observer effect is not present in all cultures (Fletcher & Ward, 1988). For example, the individualism of North American culture promotes a view of people as autonomous – as free agents. As a result, they see their behaviour as based on choice, as flexible and unpredictable. They see themselves adapting to different situations and therefore tend to make situation attributions for their own behaviour (Baxter & Goldberg, 1988). This suggests that the actor-observer effect reflects culturally accepted ways of making causal attributions rather than some form of cognitive bias that is present in all human beings.

Self-serving biases

Some kinds of biased attributions appear to have positive benefits for the observer. They seem to make the observer feel better about themself. These kinds of biases are known as *self-serving biases*. They include the following.

False consensus effect This is based on the view that most people are like us, that our behaviour is typical. People tend to overestimate the degree to which others share their attitudes and opinions. They assume that in a given situation others are likely to behave in the same way as themselves and for the same reasons. This can create errors in attribution because it assumes a high consensus that might not exist.

As a practical display of the false consensus effect, Ross et al. (1977) asked university students to parade around campus wearing a sandwich-board bearing the letters **REPENT**. Exactly 50% of the students agreed to take part in the experiment, and 50% refused. However, both groups estimated that the majority of students would make the same decision as themselves – an estimate based on false consensus. Members of each group gave a situation attribution to account for their own decisions. They saw their action as a normal and reasonable response to the situation. However, they gave a person attribution to explain the behaviour of the 'minority' they believed would make the opposite decision to themselves. These people were seen as 'oddballs', a characteristic which explained their 'unreasonable' behaviour (Ross et al., 1977).

This experiment indicates how the false consensus effect can be self-serving. We assume that the majority will behave like us. We see our behaviour as reasonable. We assume that only a minority of 'oddballs' will behave differently. This puts us in a positive light.

False consensus may be caused by the tendency to seek out 'like minds' – people who think and behave like us – as friends and colleagues. This may then generate a false sense of consensus with 'most people'. The assumption is that if our friends are like us, most people are like us. False consensus may also serve to justify opinions and behaviour – if others are like us, then our opinions and behaviour must be right. In this respect, false consensus can be seen as a self-serving bias.

False uniqueness effect This is the tendency to overrate our own abilities in comparison to those of others (Marks, 1984). It is often expressed by car drivers, who believe themselves to be more skilled and safer than their fellow motorists (Svenson, 1981). Ross and Sicoly (1979) found that individuals working within groups tend to overestimate their own contribution to the group's performance when compared with that attributed to them by fellow workers. The false uniqueness effect may arise because information about our own abilities is more easily accessible than information about the abilities of others. Alternatively, it may simply enhance our self-esteem to believe that we are somewhat superior to the crowd.

Whereas the false consensus effect assumes high consensus – most people are like us – the false uniqueness effect assumes low consensus – we are unique. Both can, in particular circumstances, lead us to attributions which protect and/or enhance our sense of self, our self-esteem. People may, therefore, switch from one to the other, given the situation. If, for example, they are heavy drinkers, they may assume that this behaviour is widespread (high consensus) and therefore normal and not a problem. If they are involved in a motoring accident, they may then assume that their driving ability is superior (low consensus) and blame the accident on other drivers.

Self-enhancement and self-protection biases These biases have the effect of improving or maintaining the self-esteem of the individual (Miller & Ross, 1975). The *self-enhancement bias* is a tendency to take credit for success by attributing an internal cause – a person attribution – whereas the *self-protection bias* is a tendency to deny all responsibility for failure by attributing external causes – a situation attribution. For example, self-enhancement bias can be seen in attributions of exam success – I deserved it, I worked hard. Self-protection bias can be seen in attributions of exam failure – it was a terrible paper, the teacher didn't prepare us properly, I felt ill.

Explanations There are a number of explanations for self-serving biases.

- First, people have a need for high self-esteem – to feel good about themselves. Self-serving biases lead to self-enhancement which, in turn, produces a 'feel-good' effect.
- Second, people wish to present themselves to others in the best possible light. Self-serving biases award personal credit for success and remove personal blame from failure. They can be seen as a strategy for the successful presentation of self to others.
- Third, most people expect to succeed. In addition, they tend to exaggerate the amount of effort they themselves have put into a successful outcome. These factors encourage them to take personal credit for success.
- Fourth, self-serving biases may be more common in Western societies. In Western culture, success and failure tend to be credited or blamed on the self. This reflects the emphasis on individualism – the independent self, the unique individual, who is responsible for their own actions, for their own successes and failures. As a result, self-serving biases are particularly important – they enhance and protect the self.

In many non-Western cultures there is greater emphasis on the group, on collective rather than individual responsibility. In such cultures, the self is more interdependent – fitting in with and belonging to the group. As a result, there is a greater emphasis on modesty, self-effacement and humility (Moghaddam, 1998). This is particularly apparent in attributions of success and failure. In the West, success is usually explained in terms of individual ability and effort – a self-serving person attribution. By comparison, in Japan, people tend to attribute success to the ease of the task – a situation attribution – and failure to a lack of effort – a person attribution (Shikanai, 1984).

In one respect, Japanese attributions can be seen as self-serving – for example, modesty brings a positive evaluation of self. And, people in all societies appear to need a positive sense of self (Moghaddam, 1998). However, these attributions are very different from the self-serving biases common in the West. Western self-serving biases, many of which have been identified by North American psychologists, may be largely due to and limited to Western culture.

Key terms

Actor-observer effect *A tendency to attribute situation causes for one's own behaviour, and person causes for other people's behaviour.*

Self-serving bias *Biased attributions which have a positive benefit for the observer – they make the observer feel better about themself.*

False consensus effect *An overestimation of the degree to which others share our opinions and attitudes and would behave like us in the same situation.*

False uniqueness effect *An overestimation of our own abilities in comparison to others.*

Self-enhancement bias *A tendency to take the credit for success by attributing it to an internal or person cause.*

Self-protection bias *A tendency to deny all responsibility for failure by attributing it to an external or situation cause.*

Summary

1   Causal attributions are explanations that people give for their own behaviour and the behaviour of others.

2   Heider distinguished between person and situation attributions. He claimed that there is a general tendency to make person attributions.

3   Jones and Davis' correspondent inference theory states that when making a person attribution, observers infer that the actor's behaviour corresponds with their underlying character or personality.

4   Kelley's covariation model states that observers infer the causes of an actor's behaviour by combining a range of information from different sources. In particular, they look for repeated patterns of behaviour on which to base attributions.

5   Kelley's causal schema model states that observers have a set of ready-made explanations which they use to make attributions when they have insufficient information.

6   Weiner's achievement attribution theory seeks to explain the reasoning behind attributions which explain success and failure. It suggests that such attributions can affect people's motivation to achieve.

7   Many of the theories of attribution see people as naive scientists collecting and analysing information in order to make attributions. This may reflect their behaviour in experiments. However, in everyday life attributions may be largely unthinking and unconsidered – for example, they may be based on taken-for-granted stereotypes.

8   A number of errors and biases have been identified in the attribution process. They include the fundamental attribution error, the actor-observer effect, and a number of self-serving biases.

9   These errors and biases have often been identified and confirmed from experiments using Western participants. They may not apply to other cultures – they may not be universal.

Activity 2   Errors and biases

Item A   The fundamental attribution error

Joan Miller (1984) presented participants in Chicago, USA and Mysore, India with descriptions of behaviour and asked them to give reasons for the behaviour. She found that Americans were more likely to give person attributions, while Indians were more likely to give situation attributions. Here is an example.

The behaviour A lawyer was on his way to court. He was riding a motorcycle with a passenger. The rear tyre burst and the passenger fell off and struck his head on the pavement. The lawyer took the injured man to the local hospital and then went to court to attend to his duties. He left the passenger without consulting a doctor about the seriousness of his injuries or finding out whether the hospital had the expertise to deal with the injuries. The passenger eventually died.

The attributions The participants were asked to explain the lawyer's behaviour.

American attributions

1   He was obviously irresponsible.
2   He must be in a state of shock.
3   He was aggressive in pursuing his career success.

Indian attributions

1   It was his duty to be in court for the client he was representing.
2   He might have become nervous or confused.
3   The injured man might not have looked as seriously injured as he was.

Adapted from Miller, 1984

Item B	The actor-observer effect

A study by Schoeneman and Rubanowitz (1985) looked at letters in the advice columns in newspapers and magazines and the replies from the 'agony aunts'. The study found strong evidence of the actor-observer effect.

Item C	Self-serving biases

A study examined the attributions students made about their examination performance. Before each exam they were asked what grade they expected. After each exam they were asked to give reasons for their performance. Students who attained or surpassed their expected grade explained their success in terms of ability and hard work. Those who fell below their expected grade blamed luck or the difficulty of the examination.

Adapted from Bernstein, Stephan & Davis, 1979

Dear Ann Landers:
I'm writing you in desperation, hoping you can help me with a problem I'm having with my mother.

A little over a year ago, I moved in with my boyfriend despite my mother's protests. She has never liked Kevin. I'll admit he's far from perfect and we've had our problems. He's an alcoholic, has a bad temper, is mentally abusive, is a compulsive liar and cannot hold a job. I am in debt over my head because of him but my biggest problem is that my mother is obsessed with my situation. I understand her concern, but I can take only so much ...

OVER-MOTHERED
IN MICHIGAN

Dear Over-Mothered:
Your mother didn't write to me. You did. So you're the one who is going to get the advice. Get into counselling at once and find out why you insist on hanging on to an alcoholic, abusive, unemployed liar ...

Questions

1 The fundamental attribution error is a reflection of culture rather than a universal way of thinking. Discuss with reference to Item A.

2 What evidence of the actor-observer effect is provided by Item B?

3 How can the explanations of exam performance in Item C be seen as 'self-serving'?

Unit 2 Social perception

KEY ISSUES

1 **What are schemas?**

2 **How does social and cultural stereotyping operate?**

3 **What are social representations?**

The attribution theories outlined in Unit 1 suggest that people observe and explain the social world in a rational and logical way. Evidence is assessed and analysed and conclusions drawn to explain the behaviour of self and others. Research into social perception provides a number of alternative views of the way people interpret and explain the social world. This unit examines some of these views.

2.1 Schema theory

Definition

A *social schema* is a mental file or pigeonhole which stores knowledge about a concept (eg, 'romantic love' or 'authority') or about a particular stimulus (eg, different types of people or different kinds of commonly occurring situations). This knowledge describes the different elements that are typically involved with the concept or stimulus. It might tell us, for example, that being romantic involves constantly thinking about a loved one, being attentive to their every need, feeling unbelievably happy, and so on. Schemas also provide us with expectations. When we fall in love, we expect to feel wonderful and fulfilled. These expectations in turn lead us to selectively attend to those features of the world that fit with our existing schema. When in love, we may concentrate on our own feelings and pay little attention to the other more mundane features of life.

Because schemas contain both knowledge and expectations, they can be used to provide ready-made explanations for behaviour. One of the applications of schema theory to the study of attributions is Kelley's causal schema model (see Unit 1). The schema approach to attributions suggests that observers routinely draw upon the knowledge stored in schemas to understand and explain social behaviour. This is thought to involve far less mental time and effort than the extensive cognitive processes suggested by many attribution theorists. In fact schema theorists, such as Taylor (1981), propose that people act like 'cognitive misers'. That is, in our everyday lives we expend as little effort as possible on cognitive acts like attribution. We prefer to take 'shortcuts'. One useful shortcut is through categorisation.

Categorisation

Categorisation is the act of classifying a person or situation into a given category on the basis of relevant social information. For example, a person can be classified according to their gender, age, ethnicity, social status, and so on. Categories are built around a *prototype* (Fiske &Taylor, 1991). Prototypes are perceptions of the 'average figure' which best represents a particular category, for example the typical school headteacher or the typical truck driver. When we categorise, we use social schemas to compare the person to a set of likely prototypes or exemplars. If the person sufficiently resembles a given prototype, we will categorise them accordingly.

Categorising people according to social schemas means that observers have a tendency towards stereotyping because they are using an often sketchy idea of what a 'typical' member of any social category is like. And since schemas influence the way we actually perceive others, observers are likely to home in on and emphasise any similarities a person has to a particular prototype and ignore other potentially relevant features. Thus a British observer of a French person might assume that because they are drinking wine they also 'typically' enjoy rich cuisine, are highly cultured and so on, irrespective of whether this particular individual shows any signs of such tastes or attributes. This tendency to selectively attend to those features of a person that confirm our existing stereotypes is known as the *confirmatory bias*.

Key terms

Prototype *An image of the typical person or thing that best represents a particular category.*

Confirmatory bias *A tendency to only attend to those features of people which fit existing stereotypes, thereby confirming those stereotypes.*

Types of schemas

Schema theorists have identified several different kinds of social schemas.

Person schemas contain a prototype of a particular kind of person. This prototype will usually consist of a personality trait (eg, neurotic, anxious, extrovert) and some general information about likely characteristics. For example, a person schema of a 'shy' person will describe someone who is 'anxious' along with information such as 'not usually very talkative', 'tends to avoid social situations' etc.

Self schemas are descriptions of ourselves. We possess a number of self-schemas, each of which describes a different aspect of our identity – for example 'me as a family member', 'me as a professional individual', 'me as a British person'. We use these self schemas constantly to decide how we should behave, what we think about a given issue, and so on.

Role schemas contain prototypes about particular roles in society (eg, parent, child, doctor, patient). They include the kinds of behaviour expected from someone who adopts a particular role.

Event or script schemas contain a 'cognitive script' which describes a sequence of events found in a common social activity. For example, a cognitive script describing a meal in a restaurant will outline a sequence of events beginning with waiting to be seated and progressing through ordering, eating the meal, paying the bill and ending with leaving (having remembered to leave a tip). Schank and Abelson (1977) argue that much of our knowledge of how to behave in social settings is contained in this script-like or episodic way.

Can schemas be changed?

Social schemas – particularly role schemas – seem to be quite resistant to change. If observers are confronted with people who appear to contradict a given schema, instead of questioning their own beliefs, the observers tend to make sense of this contradictory information by accommodating it *within* the schema. Hewstone et al. (1992) found that secondary school pupils had strong negative stereotypes of the police – a prejudiced social schema. They then assessed the impact of regular visits to the schools by police liaison officers, who were generally well regarded by the pupils. The pupils, however, dealt with this apparent contradiction by categorising the liaison officers as 'non-typical members' of their existing police schema rather than altering their beliefs about the police as a whole. That is, they saw them as exceptions. This suggests that schemas are strongly resistant to contradictory evidence.

Evaluation

Advantages Schema theory sheds important light on how social perception is influenced by prior beliefs. It provides detail about the cognitive mechanisms which lead us to selectively attend to those aspects of the world which fit with our existing categories, scripts and stereotypes. The model of the person as a 'cognitive miser' helps explain how we manage to deal efficiently with a considerable mass of social information at any one time. But the model also implies that much of the time we are lazy and biased when it comes to understanding the world around us.

Schema theory makes an important contribution to understanding the attribution process. It suggests that wherever we can, we make 'shortcuts' in our attributions. We do this by drawing upon already existing descriptions of people and their likely behaviour. This means that under normal circumstances we are unlikely to make any of the complex attributional assessments suggested by Jones and Davis or Kelley.

Disadvantages However schema theory has its own problems. It does not explain how schemas are initially formed or how we come to acquire them (Augostinous & Walker, 1995). It also does not offer much of an explanation as to how we choose between potentially relevant schemas when we are categorising ourselves and other people (Spears et al., 1999). For example, you might categorise someone you have just met according to their age, their gender, or their ethnicity, or by how friendly they appear, or the way they dress. Schema theory suggests that you choose whichever category makes the job easiest (ie, whichever schema reduces the mental work the most).

The very idea of a schema itself may be problematic. To cover all the possible situations or people we might encounter in our lives, we would need to have thousands, if not hundreds of thousands of different schemas. Imagine how much cognitive effort would be needed if we had to find the right 'mental pigeon hole' each time we categorise somebody or something!

Some social psychologists have therefore suggested that schema theory is simply studying the wrong thing. There is one place where all of the categories that we will ever need already exist, 'ready made' for us. That place is in the language we use to communicate with one another (Billig, 1996). An important recent approach called *discursive psychology* studies how people use language to make attributions and categorisations (Edwards & Potter, 1992; Potter, 1997). The basis of this approach is that language is central to all forms of social interaction. When we make an attribution or categorise someone, we draw upon language to do so. For example, if I hear someone being described as 'friendly', this suggests a number of other words typically used and associated with 'friendly' – for example, 'easy-going', 'cheerful' and 'pleasant'. Together, these words provide a picture of a type of person. I do not need a cognitive schema to tell me this, just a knowledge of what sorts of things are typically associated in everyday conversation with being friendly.

For schema theory thinking is a private activity, whereas for discursive psychology thinking is a very public part of how we interact with one another through common language. Discursive psychology is a genuinely social approach to studying social perception, whilst schema theory is a firmly cognitive approach.

Key term

Discursive psychology *An approach which studies how people use language to make attributions and categorisations as part of everyday social interaction.*

2.2   Social and cultural stereotyping

Definition

The term stereotype was introduced by the journalist Walter Lippman in his book *Public Opinion*, published in 1922. He described stereotypes as 'the little pictures we carry around within our heads'. Social psychologists define stereotypes as widely held beliefs about the characteristics of members of social groups. Simply because they belong to a particular group, people are seen to have certain attitudes and behaviours. They are pictured as certain types of people.

Stereotypes are generalisations – they tend to be applied to all members of a group. For example, all Germans may be seen as efficient, all black people as good athletes, and all students as layabouts. Stereotypes can be positive or negative, they can offer a favourable or unfavourable image of a group. For example, nurses are usually pictured as kind, caring and self-sacrificing, whereas traders dealing in stocks and shares are often portrayed as money-grabbing and selfish.

Functions of stereotypes

Individual functions Stereotypes serve the individual function of saving mental energy. They are a way in which individuals as 'cognitive misers' cut down on the cognitive effort involved in social perception (Fiske & Taylor, 1991).

Stereotypes categorise groups of people. They identify certain characteristics and apply them to all members of the group. They ignore variety within the group, providing shorthand and simple descriptions of the group as a whole. Allport (1958) described stereotyping as 'the law of least effort'. Often stereotypes spring to mind immediately – they are 'activated' as soon as we encounter members of a particular social group. The stereotype then provides a ready-made description of members of that social group. As such, stereotypes can direct our attention. Once a stereotype is activated, it identifies which stimuli out of a mass of possible stimuli we pay attention to. In this way, stereotypes save mental energy.

In addition to saving on cognitive effort, stereotypes have an important role in the way individuals interpret social information. For example, Duncan (1976) showed white participants a video of two actors arguing, culminating in one actor shoving another. When the actor who did the shoving was black, the behaviour was categorised as a violent act. When the actor responsible for the shove was white, the behaviour was categorised as playfulness. This is because the stereotype defines blacks as prone to violence.

Social functions The social functions of stereotypes refer to the part they play in the wider society. Stereotypes present a description and an evaluation of members of social groups. *Social identity theory* (see Unit 3) states that when people identify with a social group, they make a sharp distinction between that group – the *in-group* – and other groups – the *out-groups* (Tajfel & Turner, 1979). People's sense of identity derives in part from their group membership – for example, from their class, ethnic, gender and religious groups. Since people strive for a positive identity, they will tend to see their in-groups in a positive light and to judge them as superior to out-groups. As a result, they are likely to develop positive stereotypes of in-groups and negative stereotypes of out-groups.

In terms of social identity theory, the major social function of stereotypes is to provide group members with a positive social identity. This function is served by upgrading in-group members by means of positive stereotypes and downgrading out-group members by means of negative stereotypes. In addition, by defining all in-group members as similar, stereotypes function to maintain in-group cohesiveness and solidarity.

Stereotypes have been seen as a means by which powerful groups reinforce social divisions which are beneficial to them (Spears et al., 1997). In terms of this argument, stereotypes function to maintain the position of the powerful and to keep the less powerful in their place. For example, if stereotypes of ethnic minorities define them as inferior, then this can explain and justify their disadvantaged position in society and so help to maintain the power of the majority. Similarly, stereotypes of women have often been used to keep them in their place. For example, the traditional stereotype of women as mothers and housewives preoccupied with 'feminine concerns' and domestic matters has been used to argue against allowing them to vote and to block their access to higher education and high status occupations. In this way stereotypes can serve to maintain male power.

Stereotypes have been used to justify and legitimate actions which might otherwise appear cruel and inhumane. During the era of slavery in the USA, stereotypes of African Americans as 'lazy', 'simply-minded' and 'less than human' served to justify the harsh treatment of black slaves.

Stereotypes often form part of a wider *ideology*. An ideology is a set of beliefs and claims about how the world is and how it ought to be. Some sociologists argue that ideologies direct the way people think about themselves and the society they live in. In societies where there are significant inequalities between class, gender and ethnic groups and marked differences in wealth, power and status, the ruling groups attempt to impose their ideology on others. If successful, this reinforces their position by making it appear normal, legitimate, and even inevitable. Others in society will tend to see themselves in terms of the stereotypes contained in the ruling ideology. For example, feminists argue that in male-dominated societies, women tend to see themselves as passive and dependent, in line with male stereotypes of femininity. This distorted view of the nature of women is an example of *false consciousness* – a false view of reality.

In terms of this argument, one of the functions of stereotypes is the contribution they make to ruling ideology and the promotion of false consciousness. Augoustinos (1999) argues that research into stereotyping should pay more attention to the broader social, cultural and ideological influences in society which produce false consciousness.

Key terms

Social identity *The aspects of a person's self-image that come from the groups they belong to and identify with.*

In-group *A group to which a person belongs and identifies with.*

Out-group *A group to which a person does not belong and does not identify with.*

Ideology *A systematic set of beliefs and claims about how the world is and how it ought to be which is shared by a particular group or by society as a whole.*

False consciousness *A false or distorted view of reality.*

Origins of stereotypes

This section looks at the origins of stereotypes – how they arise, where they come from.

'Grain of truth' hypothesis Allport (1958) suggested that stereotypes may originate from a 'grain of truth'. However, he argued that once a stereotype is established, that 'grain of truth' is blown out of all proportion. Campbell (1967) developed this idea. He proposed that stereotypes originate either from our own experience or through communicating with other people. For example, if I have a stereotype of German people as humourless and efficient, either I must have met a German person in the past who had these characteristics, or I must have talked to someone who had actually done so. Now this is not to say that all Germans are humourless and efficient, only that such a person has existed. However, because people are able to draw upon a real example of someone who fits the stereotype, they convince themselves that there must be a 'grain of truth' to it.

Evaluation For many social psychologists, the 'grain of truth' hypothesis has little to support it.

- First, it fails to explain how a 'grain of truth' becomes a full-blown stereotype. How and why does a stereotype become so prominent and so widely shared? To some extent the idea of illusory correlation, examined in the following section, answers this question.
- Second, it fails to explain why particular items out of a wide range of behaviour have been selected to form a stereotype. Again, the idea of illusory correlation helps to explain this.

- Third, there might be no 'grain of truth' in the first place. The way people perceive a trait or characteristic in others may reflect their culture – their shared values, attitudes and perceptions – rather than any objective, 'real' truth. For example, a common Western stereotype of Japanese people portrays them as subservient – bowing and scraping to authority. This perception may simply reflect Western culture and may be a misunderstanding of Japanese manners (Oakes, Haslam & Turner, 1994).

Illusory correlation The term *illusory correlation* refers to either a perceived relationship between two things that does not exist, or a relationship that is overestimated. Illusory correlations are most likely to occur when the things being correlated – people, behaviour, events – stand out, when they appear conspicuous and distinctive. One of the ways things appear distinctive is when they are infrequent. People can appear distinctive when they are in a minority. Behaviour is conspicuous when it is unusual. Events stand out when they are infrequent.

Consider the following experiment conducted by Hamilton and Gifford (1976). Participants were given statements which they were told described the behaviour of members of two groups, groups A and B. Group A – the majority group – had more members than group B – the minority group. Two-thirds of the statements for each group described desirable behaviour (eg, helping an elderly neighbour) and one-third of the statements for each group described undesirable behaviour (eg, being late for work). In other words, the proportion of desirable and undesirable behaviour was the same for each group. Given this, participants should *not* form a more favourable impression of one group. But they did.

After they had read all the statements, the participants were asked to recall how many times members of each group behaved in desirable and undesirable ways. The results are shown in Figure 2. The participants overestimated the number of times members of group B and undesirable behaviours were paired. Members of group B and undesirable behaviours were less frequent than members of group A and desirable behaviours. As a result, they appeared distinctive, they stood out. Because of this, the participants tended to associate group B with bad behaviour. In fact, the proportion of bad behaviour was the same for both groups. The participants had therefore produced an illusory correlation.

Illusory correlations can then become the source of stereotypes in the following way. Members of a minority group, compared to the general population, are fewer in number. Violent behaviour, because it is not a part of most people's everyday experience, is infrequent. Both therefore stand out. As a result, violent behaviour by members of a minority group seems to stand out more than violence committed by members of the majority. This can be seen in countries such as Britain and America, where violent crime is often associated with black people. Evidence from the USA indicates that many white

Key terms

'Grain of truth' hypothesis *The idea that stereotypes must be based on a real example of someone who fits the description of the stereotype in question.*

Illusory correlation *A perceived relationship between two things that does not exist, or is overestimated.*

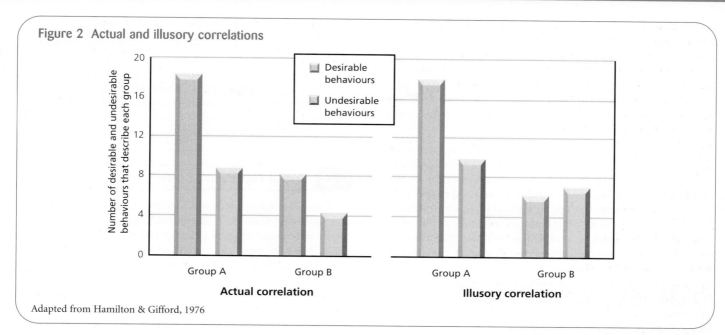

Figure 2 Actual and illusory correlations

Legend:
- Desirable behaviours
- Undesirable behaviours

Y-axis: Number of desirable and undesirable behaviours that describe each group

Actual correlation: Group A, Group B
Illusory correlation: Group A, Group B

Adapted from Hamilton & Gifford, 1976

people overestimate the amount of violent crime committed by African Americans (Hamilton & Sherman, 1989). This illusory correlation reinforces stereotypes of black people. In doing so it makes those stereotypes resistant to change. At the same time, illusory correlations may actually distract people from the real sources of much violent crime (for example, widespread unemployment and drug addiction).

Group membership and stereotypes Social identity theory starts from the idea that stereotypes result, in part, from the human ability to categorise. Stereotypes are categories of groups of people. However, as outlined earlier, social identity theory sees group membership as the main reason why stereotypes arise. A person's self-image derives in part from the groups to which they belong and identify with. Since people prefer a positive self-image, they will tend to see their in-groups in a positive light and to downgrade out-groups by comparison. The result is positive in-group stereotypes and negative out-group stereotypes. (See Unit 3 for a more detailed outline of social identity theory.)

Social and cultural change Why do particular stereotypes arise? One answer to this question is that their origin lies in the wider society and culture – new stereotypes arise in response to social and cultural change (Brown, 1995).

One of the earliest studies of stereotypes was conducted by Katz and Braly in America in 1932. They asked 100 white students at Princeton University to select 5 out of a list of 84 attributes that they felt were most characteristic of Germans, English, Jews, African Americans, Turks, Japanese, Italians, Chinese Americans and Irish. Eighteen years later, in 1950, G.M.Gilbert repeated the experiment in the same university (Gilbert, 1951). Table 3 shows the images of Italians from the two studies.

Commenting on this table, Gilbert wrote, 'The artistic and hot-tempered Italian, representing a cross between the temperamental maestro and the cheerful organ grinder, is still with us; but he is only a faded image of his former self' (quoted in Allport, 1958). The study was repeated in 1967, again using Princeton students, by Karlins et al. A number of interesting points emerged from the three studies. First, stereotypes change. For example, in 1951 Japanese were seen as sly, extremely nationalistic and treacherous; in 1967 they were pictured as industrious, ambitious and efficient. Second, stereotypes can be shaped by events. The negative stereotypes of Japanese in 1951 reflected their role in World War II, and in particular their bombing of the American Pacific fleet at Pearl Harbour in 1941 (see Activity 3). Third, people may be less willing to stereotype than before. A number of students in the 1950 and 1967 studies objected to taking part. They saw it as unreasonable to characterise ethnic and national groups with whom they had little or no contact.

These studies suggest that the content of particular stereotypes reflects the wider society and culture. Social and cultural change results in changes to existing stereotypes and the emergence of new stereotypes. And, in some cases, the content of stereotypes can be pinpointed to an actual event, as the Japanese bombing of Pearl Harbour indicates.

Evaluation

Much of the work on stereotypes, particularly the early research, was conducted in the USA. It was strongly influenced by the values of the researchers. They assumed that stereotypes were 'bad'. Stereotypes were seen as 'inaccurate', 'unjustified' and 'irrational'. They should be condemned and eliminated since they harmed relationships between groups (Smith & Bond, 1993).

| Table 3 | Traits attributed to Italians |

| | (percentages of students) | | |
	1932	1950	Difference
Artistic	53	28	-25
Impulsive	44	19	-25
Passionate	37	25	-12
Quick-tempered	35	15	-20
Musical	32	22	-10
Imaginative	30	20	-10
Very religious	21	33	+12

From Allport, 1958

Stereotypes were seen as a problem because of the policy of cultural integration – the 'melting pot' ideology – which existed in the US at that time. 'The idea is that newcomers to America should divest themselves of their heritage cultures, become stirred into the melting pot and surface as quickly as possible as "Americans"' (Moghaddam et al., 1993). Stereotypes were seen as unfortunate biases that could prevent people from becoming assimilated into North American culture.

While accepting that under certain circumstances stereotypes could be harmful, European researchers took a rather different view. First, they were more likely to see stereotyping as a normal cognitive process rather than a flawed and destructive way of thinking. Stereotypes picture social groups as different and distinctive. In this respect, they can reflect the reality of multi-cultural societies. Second, European researchers were more ready to see positive aspects of stereotyping. In particular, stereotypes can picture groups in a favourable light. As such they can provide a positive identity for group members. As Taylor and Lalonde (1987) argue, 'stereotypes can be an important mechanism for recognising and expressing pride in ethnic distinctiveness'. And stereotypes can encourage

'outsiders' to view other groups in a positive light.

Stereotyping is no longer seen as necessarily and uniformly 'wicked' and 'evil'. This opens the door to looking at stereotyping as a normal process of thinking and at stereotypes as a normal part of culture (Moghaddam et al., 1993). Social representations theory, examined in the following section, attempts to do just this. It looks at stereotypes as part of the wider social and cultural influences on social perception.

2.3   Social representations

Social representations theory is a major alternative to schema and attribution theories. It attempts to provide a more social theory of how we interpret and understand our social world. Social representations are shared views or explanations of the world. The study of social representations was initiated by Serge Moscovici (1976; 1981). In contrast to those approaches to social cognition which draw heavily upon cognitive psychology (eg, schema theory), social representation theory has its roots in sociology. One of the founding fathers of sociology, Emile

---

Activity 3   Stereotyping

Item A   Racial stereotypes

After being shown this picture, one participant described it to a second participant, who then described it to a third, and so on. After six descriptions, over half the final participants reported that the black person, not the white person was holding the razor. Some even had the black person waving the razor in a threatening manner.

Adapted from Allport & Postman, 1947

Questions

1   Explain the results of the experiment in Item A, using the idea of stereotypes.

2   Look at Item B.

a) Describe the changes in American stereotypes of Japanese.

b) Suggest reasons for these changes.

Item B   American stereotypes of Japanese

1932	1950	1967
intelligent	treacherous	industrious
industrious	sly	ambitious
progressive	extremely nationalistic	efficient

Adapted from Katz & Braly, 1933; Gilbert, 1951; Karlins, Coffman & Walters, 1969

The cover of an American magazine published five days after the Japanese bombed the American fleet at Pearl Harbour in 1941.

A response by an American cartoonist to the torture and execution of American airmen who had bailed out from damaged planes during a bombing raid over Japan. (Tojo was the Japanese Prime Minister during World War II.)

Durkheim, advocated the study of knowledge shared by different segments of society. He called this shared knowledge *collective representations*.

Collective or *social representations* can range from the knowledge held by members of a political party about the state of the nation to the everyday know-how held by workers about their job. It can also include religious beliefs and cultural myths (for example, 'urban myths' such as alligators living in New York sewers and 'conspiracy theories' such as the United Nations being the 'real' world government – a popular belief amongst some right-wing US groups). Moscovici argued that these representations had never been properly studied and consequently that we have little idea of how they are generated and how people come to share them collectively.

Moscovici (1981) defined a social representation as:

'a set of concepts, statements and explanations originating in daily life in the course of inter-individual communications. They are the equivalent, in our society, of the myths and belief systems in traditional societies; they might even be said to be the contemporary version of common sense.'

By this he meant that social representations originate in everyday interaction. They are stories, ideas and explanations that are passed around between people as they talk and gossip to one another in the course of daily life. Once enough people share a given social representation it passes for common sense. Moscovici (1976) studied how ideas about psychoanalysis became popular in France. He noted that people took it as a matter of course that individuals might suffer from 'complexes' or be 'neurotic', whereas a few years before such ideas were entirely unheard of. People had come to share a body of knowledge – a social representation – in terms of which it was entirely reasonable and sensible to explain the behaviour of individuals in psychoanalytic terms. This suggests that social representations are dynamic, they are constantly changing.

What makes the social representations approach different to other theories of social cognition is that it takes a genuinely social view of how people develop knowledge. Moscovici proposes that social representations are held collectively by a group. These groups can include anything from a local darts team to a whole society. Social representations appear 'real' to all group members who share them – that is, a believable and accurate description of the world. For example, a popular social representation amongst some groups is that aliens are conducting experiments on abducted humans. People who share this social representation will tend to regard reports of alien abduction as a 'real', possibly even routine, aspect of everyday life. People who do not share this social representation may find such reports outlandish and simply unbelievable.

Moscovici argued that social representations determine how we see the world and explain otherwise inexplicable events. They do this by locating an unfamiliar object, person or event within a existing familiar context. This process is known as *conventionalisation*.

Not all knowledge, however, comes in the form of social representations. Moscovici (1984) believed that scientific knowledge is based on facts and hard evidence. But many of us are not able to draw upon first-hand knowledge of science. What we actually tend to use are social representations based on popular ideas about science. Moscovici and Hewstone (1983) use the example of scientific research into hemispheric lateralisation of brain functioning (the splitting of functions between the left and right side of the brain). Scientists see some evidence for lateralisation of function. But social representations based around this idea, made popular in magazine articles and television programmes, hold that there is major distinction between the two halves of the brain. One side of the brain is 'emotional', the other is 'rational'. The idea of lateralisation was blown out of all proportion in the public mind.

Key terms

Social representations *The shared knowledge held by particular groups within society or by society as a whole.*

Conventionalisation *A process of making unfamiliar objects, persons or events appear conventional by considering them in a familiar context.*

Anchoring and objectification

Social representations are shared collectively by members of a group. Before this can happen, a representation must first be formed. Moscovici describes two major mechanisms through which social representations are formed and transformed: *anchoring* and *objectification*.

Anchoring occurs when an unfamiliar object, person or event confronts us. We immediately compare the object to our existing sets of social representations for describing the world (Moscovici, 1984). Like social schemas, social representations are organised around prototypes – typical examples of a given category. By comparing the new object with an existing prototype we can make educated guesses as to some of the new object's likely characteristics. This enables us to classify the object by 'anchoring' it alongside our existing knowledge. For example, people who start to use electronic mail (email) often write very formal messages. This is because they have anchored this unfamiliar practice alongside their social representation of letter writing and formal communication. Once the object is anchored, it comes to take on some of the characteristics of the surrounding social representations.

Wagner et al. (1995) studied social representations of human conception. They found that a great many people anchor 'sperm' and 'ova' amongst their social representations of gender. This results in the association of male characteristics (eg, aggressive, strong) with 'sperm', whilst 'ovum' become associated with female characteristics (eg, passive, weak). There is of course no good scientific reason for doing this. What happens is that people use their pre-existing ideas of the differences between women and men to understand the differences between sperm and ova and their behaviour during conception.

Objectification occurs when a newly anchored object, person or event is transformed into a common sense, objective reality. When we have anchored the notion of sperm and ovum alongside our social representations of gender, we begin to think of these ideas as objectively representing the real process of conception. We think of core images such as fast, aggressive sperm 'chasing' after weak, passive ova in a desperate race to be first to 'penetrate' the cell wall of an ovum. Note that this way of understanding conception is not necessarily technically correct – it is an explanation based on our pre-existing ideas about gender which has become real for us, or *objectified*. Because it seems to us self-evident that conception involves complementary differences between men and women, it comes to appear equally commonsensical to believe that sperm and ova really do behave in 'male' and 'female' ways.

Moscovici and Hewstone (1983) describe three ways in which objectified social representations may be built up. *Personification* is when a social representation becomes associated with a figurehead or 'great person'. Many people associate ideas about psychoanalysis with Freud, which makes these ideas appear more coherent and recognisable. *Figuration* is the association of an abstract idea with a key metaphor. During the 1970s, popular representations of the European Economic Community's agricultural policy used metaphors such as milk and wine 'lakes' and sugar and butter 'mountains' to make the policies appear wasteful and excessive. *Ontologisation* is where an abstract idea is seen as having a material existence. Throughout history, for example, people have tended to see madness not as a vague concept defining odd behaviour, but as having a literal physical existence, from excited movements of 'animal spirits' within the bodies of mad people to the current preoccupation with finding a gene for schizophrenia.

Key terms

Anchoring *The association of an unfamiliar person, object or event with existing social representations.*

Objectification *The transformation of an anchored person, object or event into a common sense, objective reality.*

Studies of social representations

Research into social representations has used a variety of methods, ranging from interviews to questionnaire surveys and experiments. Two of the best known studies of social representations are by Herzlich (1973) and Jodelet (1991).

Claudine Herzlich's (1973) study of health and illness amongst Parisians used extended interviews to explore how participants explained health and illness. She found that they tended to think about health in a number of different ways. Some considered health as being simply the absence of illness. Others thought of their own health as an 'asset' or 'reserve' that might sometimes be built up or sometimes squandered. Still others described health as a matter of 'equilibrium', a fundamental balance and harmony between all aspects of life.

Herzlich identified three distinct metaphors used by her participants when talking about health. She argued that each metaphor was the basis for a distinct social representation. 'Illness as destroyer' described illness as something that could interfere with or ruin one's life. This representation tended to be used by people who stressed their social and professional responsibilities. 'Illness as liberator' described illness as something that removed the pressure of life from the ill person, freeing them temporarily from their responsibilities. 'Illness as

occupation' described illness as a challenge, something the ill person had to devote all their time and energy fighting. This research shows that different groups may share different social representations of the same thing, in this case 'health'.

Denise Jodelet's (1991) work on social representations of mental illness was based on observation and interviews in a small French rural community. A form of 'care in the community' programme had been running in the village for many years. Patients who were attending a nearby care institution actually lived in the village. Jodelet found that the villagers had initially tried to understand the mentally-ill residents by anchoring them alongside their existing social representation of *bredin* ('rogues'). This social representation usually described tramps, 'idiots' and people with mild disabilities. But the villagers disagreed amongst themselves about the degree to which each individual patient should be regarded as one of the *bredin*. Part of the problem was that the villagers often disagreed on what a proper *bredin* should be like in the first place. The message of Jodelet's work is that although social representations are shared, there can be considerable variation in what each person actually makes of the social representation.

Evaluation

Advantages Social representations theory is probably the most sophisticated approach to social cognition. Like schema theory, it emphasises how pre-existing information influences an individual's perception of the world. It also stresses the importance of categorisation in the form of anchoring. However, it goes beyond this to argue that explanations and descriptions of the world are shared collectively by groups who experience them as 'real'. Group members experience social representations not as theoretical explanations, but as real things that have a concrete existence.

The social representations approach uses a range of methods, including both qualitative and quantitative techniques. Herzlich's (1973) study of social representations of health and illness was based on extended, in-depth interviews. Jodelet's (1991) research on mental illness used interviews and observation. Some researchers argue that qualitative techniques are more likely to capture participants' view of the world than quantitative methods.

Augoustinos and Walker (1995) suggest that many aspects of social cognition, such as attributional biases and stereotyping, can be better understood by taking into account the kinds of social representations a person holds. For example, cultural differences in the fundamental attribution error (see Unit 1) can be understood as rooted in different forms of collectively held social representations about the individual. In Jodelet's work the villagers stereotyped the mentally ill by drawing on a pre-existing social representation that existed in their own local culture.

Disadvantages The social representations approach has been criticised for its vagueness (Farr, 1987; Jahoda, 1988). Moscovici's writing is often difficult to follow, and does not outline social representations theory in a clear way. For example, the concepts of anchoring and objectification look very similar. It is difficult to think how they could be studied separately, since the process of anchoring always seems to involve some objectification and vice versa.

Social representations theory fails to provide adequate answers to a number of important questions.

- First, why does one individual sometimes have different social representations about the same thing? For example, McKinlay and Potter (1987) argue that individuals can usually offer several different explanations for the same event. This does not imply, however, that they believe all of them. In a study of racism in New Zealand, Wetherell and Potter (1992) found that, during interviews, white New Zealanders tended to offer explanations of cultural differences which presented them as liberal, well-meaning individuals. But at other times, when not being interviewed by social psychologists, the same individuals would give other explanations of cultural differences which were more racist in tone. This suggests that people are aware of different representations and the representation that they present depends on the social circumstances, eg, who they're talking to.
- Second, why do people in the same society or the same group within society have different social representations?

For example, why did Herzlich's participants have different social representations of health? How do these different representations come about? Stainton Rogers (1991) suggests that we need to relate social representations of health to wider cultural and historical shifts in how people understand their own health.

- Third, how do social representations become shared? Billig (1991) claims that although the social representations approach is more 'social' than most research in social cognition, it still treats thinking as though it were a private act that occurs in isolation. It is more appropriate, he suggests, to treat thinking as a public act which occurs as people argue and discuss ideas with each other. In this way people become aware of other points of view and sometimes modify their own position through interaction with others. Discursive psychology has attempted to study social representations through analysing how people argue and debate ideas with one another in everyday conversation. For example, Billig (1992) looked at how families discuss and argue about the royal family and its relevance to modern Britain.

Activity 4 — Social representations of the body's immune system

Item A — Representations of the body

Popular books on health used to describe illness using illustrations like the above. They emphasised that the body could be overwhelmed or 'invaded' by germs.

Item B — Popular scientific social representations

Immunology is the study of the immune system, a part of the body which protects organisms from infection by harmful microbes and parasites. In humans, the immune system is made up by a huge number of immune cells and molecules (mostly white blood cells) which respond to infections.

Immunologists have a distinctive way of describing these cells and what they do. One type of white blood cell, a T-lymphocyte, is given the technical scientific name of 'killer cell'. It is the 'immune system's special combat unit in the war against cancer'. Killer cells 'strike', 'attack' and 'assault': 'The killer cells are relentless. Docking with infected cells, they shoot lethal proteins at the cell membrane. Holes form where the protein molecules hit, and the cell, dying, leaks out its insides.'

At other times, a slightly different language is used. Every cell in the human body requires 'proof of identity'. These constitute 'the cell's identity papers, protecting it against the body's own police force, the immune system'. This police force is 'programmed to distinguish between bona fide residents and illegal aliens – an ability fundamental to the body's powers of self-defence.' Immune system cells store 'vast criminal records' of bacterial cells.

Adapted from Martin, 1990; 1992

Item C — Anchoring and objectification of the immune system

Here is how some ordinary people try to explain what is going on in their own immune system:

- 'Antibodies protect your body from anything that's going to do you harm, you know, that's going to make you sick. Like an army I guess, that keeps some sort of balance in your body, and keeps and controls things that enter your body that shouldn't be there.'

- 'It's funny, when you think of the inside of your body, I think about outer space. It's like the only things that looks like this, you know, they're that far away from you. It's weird because outer space is like way out there, and your body is just right here, but it's about the same, it's the same thing.'

- 'So AIDS would seem to just render you helpless to things that, in the past you had, like maybe, if you think of a big medieval city that all of a sudden doesn't have any walls or any moat, anything can come along and just knock you out.'

Adapted from Martin, 1994

Questions

1   How is illness depicted in the social representation of the body in Item A?

2   Describe the two social representations the scientists in Item B seem to hold about how the immune system works.

3   How has the immune system become objectified for each of the three people in Item C?

Summary

1   Schemas are like mental files which store information. They provide 'ready-made' categories, understandings and explanations. They also contain expectations. Schemas directly influence social perception.

2   Schemas reduce cognitive effort by providing mental 'short-cuts' and 'ready-made' answers.

3   Stereotypes are often seen as distorted mental pictures which are applied to members of a group. More recently, they have been seen as a type of social schema.

4   Stereotypes have both individual and social functions. On the individual level they serve to reduce cognitive effort. On the social level they can serve to justify and maintain the position of the powerful.

5   Explanations for the origin of stereotypes include the 'grain of truth' hypothesis, the idea of illusory correlation, and social identity theory.

6   Social representations are collectively held beliefs and explanations.

7   Unfamiliar objects, persons or events are anchored to existing social representations, where they are then objectified into new social representations.

8   Social representations theory emphasises how pre-existing information influences social perception. It argues that social representations are experienced as 'real'.

9   Most theories of social perception overestimate the cognitive dimension and seriously underestimate the social dimension – they focus on individual thinking rather than the social production of knowledge.

Unit 3 Prejudice and discrimination

KEY ISSUES

1   **What are prejudice and discrimination?**

2   **What explanations have social psychologists offered for prejudice and discrimination?**

3.1 Definitions

Prejudice

As used by social psychologists, a *prejudice* is an attitude towards a group. Prejudice literally means prejudgement. In this sense, members of a group are prejudged – a judgement is made before others have even met them. That judgement can be positive or negative. In practice, psychologists have tended to focus on negative prejudices. For example, Baron and Byrne (1997) define prejudice as 'a negative attitude towards the members of specific social groups, based solely on their membership in these groups'.

Attitudes involve emotions. If a person is prejudiced towards a particular group, they may dislike, despise or even hate members of that group. It is this emotional or affective component which is the key characteristic of prejudice. Prejudice can also involve a predisposition or tendency to act in certain ways. For example, if people have negative feelings towards certain groups, they may well be predisposed to avoid contact with members of those groups.

Prejudice is usually seen as having two main components:

1 **The cognitive component** – an image or perception of a group, in other words a stereotype. (Cognitive refers to perceptions, ideas and beliefs as distinct from emotions.)

2 **The affective component** – strong feelings (usually negative) towards the group. (The word affect refers to the emotions.)

Discrimination

Social psychologists use the term *discrimination* to refer to particular treatment of people simply because they are seen to belong to certain groups. Discrimination can be positive or negative – treating people favourably or unfavourably on the basis of group membership. For example, giving a person a job because their skin is white is an example of positive discrimination; refusing them a job because their skin is black is an example of negative discrimination. In practice, social psychologists usually define discrimination as negative behaviour. For example, Baron and Byrne (1997) define discrimination as 'negative behaviours directed towards people who are the object of prejudice'.

What is the connection between prejudice and discrimination? Prejudice is an attitude which may or may not be expressed in behaviour. Whether or not it is translated into discrimination depends on a number of factors. One of the most obvious is the law. For example, in the UK the Race Relations Act and the Sex Discrimination Act make discrimination on the basis of race and gender illegal. Other factors include fear of retaliation from those who are discriminated against, social pressure from those who object to discrimination and a feeling that discrimination is wrong even though prejudices are held. Factors such as these may prevent prejudice from being expressed in the form of discrimination.

Turning the argument around, discrimination is not necessarily an expression of prejudice. People who discriminate against members of particular groups may not be prejudiced against them. They may, for example, discriminate simply because the law requires them to do so, as in Apartheid South Africa and Nazi Germany. The Nuremberg Laws passed in Nazi Germany in 1935 stated that Jews were no longer German citizens, and as a result could not vote or hold public office (Lancaster & Lancaster, 1995). As a result, all German citizens, whatever their feelings about Jews, were required by law to discriminate against them.

As noted above, prejudices are not always expressed in behaviour, they do not automatically lead to discrimination. The following study indicates some of the difficulties in pinpointing the relationship between prejudice and discrimination.

In the early 1930s, Richard LaPiere, a social psychologist at Stanford University, travelled 10,000 miles across the USA with a young Chinese-American couple (LaPiere, 1934). At the time there was widespread prejudice against Asians and there were no laws preventing racial discrimination in public accommodation. They visited 250 hotels, restaurants and campsites and only once were they refused service. After the trip, LaPiere sent a letter to all the places they had visited asking, 'Will you accept members of the Chinese race as guests in your establishment?' 92% said 'no', 7% said 'uncertain, depends on the circumstances' and only 1% said 'yes'. It appears that prejudice was widespread, but rarely expressed as discrimination.

There are, however, a number of problems with this study, some of which LaPiere recognised. They include:

1 The person who answered the letter – usually the owner or the manager – may not have been the same person who served the guests.

2 It may have been the presence of a white American academic that resulted in the service.

3 Those who replied to the letter may not have been prejudiced. Their response may have reflected a belief that most of their guests were prejudiced and would therefore object to the presence of Chinese Americans.

4 The Chinese-American couple spoke excellent English and, in LaPiere's words, were 'skilful smilers'. They were a polite, well-dressed and attractive couple. This may well have played a part in their acceptance as guests.

Since LaPiere's study, there has been a large amount of research into the relationship between attitudes (such as prejudice) and behaviour (such as discrimination). This research indicates that attitudes only predict behaviour under specific conditions. For example, if LaPiere had asked a much more specific question in his letter such as, 'Would you accept a well-educated, well-dressed, polite Chinese-American couple accompanied by a white American university lecturer as guests?' then the answers he received may well have been very different – and more in line with the behaviour he encountered.

Racism Most social psychological studies of prejudice have been concerned with *racism*. Racism is a general term used to cover prejudice and discrimination against groups seen as racially different. Traditionally, racist beliefs have assumed that there is a biological basis for so-called 'racial differences'. For example, such beliefs assumed that some 'races' were more intelligent than others, and that this difference was genetically based.

In recent years, researchers have noted the appearance of *new racism*. Rather than seeing differences between so-called racial groups as genetically based, new racism sees these differences as based on culture. In terms of new racism, prejudice and discrimination against Blacks and Asians in Britain are justified because they have alien cultures which threaten the 'British way of life' (Taylor et al., 1995).

Racism can exist in various forms. On the individual level, it can take the form of an individual's prejudiced beliefs and discriminatory actions. On the cultural level, it can take the form of shared beliefs, for example negative stereotypes of so-called racial groups. On the societal level, it can take the form of *institutional racism* where racism is built into the policies and practices of society's institutions.

Institutional racism is most obvious in societies such as Nazi Germany and Apartheid South Africa where racism was 'institutionalised' in the legal, political, educational and economic systems. However, a number of researchers argue that institutional racism is present in modern Western societies. For example, the police force in the United Kingdom has been described as institutionally racist. This does not mean that every police officer is racist. It means that racism forms a part of the policies and practices of the police force, that racism is an in-built, taken-for-granted feature of the police force as an institution.

Key terms

Prejudice *An attitude held towards members of a specific social group.*

Discrimination *Particular actions directed towards members of a specific social group. These actions may or may not be based on prejudice.*

Racism *Negative prejudice and discrimination directed towards members of a so-called 'racial group.*

Institutional racism *A form of racism in which the policies and practices of society's institutions are racist.*

3.2   Theories of the origins and maintenance of prejudice and discrimination

Psychologists have developed a range of theories to explain the origin and maintenance of prejudice and discrimination. This section focuses on three: the *authoritarian personality*, *realistic conflict theory* and *social identity theory*.

Personality and prejudice

Some people appear to be more prejudiced than others. Could this result from their personalities? Taking the argument one step further, can the origin of prejudice be located in certain types of personality? This was the argument put forward by Theodor Adorno and his colleagues (1950) who claimed to have discovered the existence of an *authoritarian personality*. This personality type was said to predispose people to prejudice and discrimination.

According to Adorno et al. (1950), people's social attitudes are 'an expression of deep-lying trends in personality'. Taking a psychoanalytic view, Adorno suggested that an individual's personality is heavily influenced by the way they were raised by their parents. Most people develop 'normally' because their parents balance discipline and freedom. However, when discipline is harsh and compliance to social norms rigorously enforced, this balance is upset. In such families, the father is usually the disciplinarian, with the mother playing a submissive role. The children grow up to hate and fear their fathers. But, such feelings are unacceptable to them and would be severely punished if the children expressed them. They are therefore *repressed*. They are then redirected and projected on to groups who are seen as weaker and inferior and who deviate from accepted norms of behaviour. The result is the authoritarian personality which is predisposed to prejudice and discrimination.

To identify the authoritarian personality Adorno et al. devised a measure of authoritarian tendencies. Participants had to state their level of agreement with a number of statements. These statements included:

1   Obedience and respect for authority are the most important virtues that children should learn.

2   A person who has bad manners, habits and breeding can hardly expect to get along with decent people.

3   Most of our social problems would be solved if we could somehow get rid of the immoral, crooked and feeble-

minded people.

4   People can be divided into two distinct classes: the weak and the strong.

5   Human nature being what it is, there will always be war and conflict.

Participants were also questioned about their upbringing. According to Adorno et al., there was a link between authoritarianism and having received a harsh, strict upbringing. As a result of childhood experiences, authoritarian personalities see the world in terms of us and them, good and bad, superior and inferior, with a clearly demarcated system of social inequality with everybody in their place. They are deferential and look up to those they see as above them and look down on and treat with contempt those they see as below them. They displace their hatred on to those who are weaker than themselves, particularly minority groups such as Jews, blacks and gays who, in their eyes, have broken social norms. The authoritarian personality is predisposed to prejudice and discrimination.

Evaluation

Adorno et al's claim that there is a link between authoritarianism and prejudice has been supported by a number of studies – for example, prejudice against the mentally ill and people with AIDS (Brown, 1986). However, both the methodology and the conclusions of Adorno et al's research have been questioned.

Methodology First, the methodology has been criticised. The statements on the questionnaire were written in such a way that agreement always indicated authoritarianism. There were no statements provided where agreement indicated a lack of authoritarianism. Therefore, we cannot be sure whether those who agreed with most of the statements were actually more authoritarian or simply more inclined to agree with what was put before them (Brown, 1965). In other words, were they merely 'yes-people'?

In addition, the original sample, from which the questionnaire was developed, has been criticised. It consisted of over 2000, largely middle-class, non-Jewish, white Americans from California. As such, the sample was biased – it was not representative of the population as a whole (Brown, 1995).

Social norms Second, even if the authoritarian personality exists, the theory leaves a lot to be explained. Individual personality types cannot explain how whole societies, such as Nazi Germany in the 1930s and 40s, can become prejudiced (Billig, 1976). If prejudice is a personality characteristic, then some people would be much more prejudiced than others. But many groups appear to be remarkably uniform in their prejudices. This suggests, as Pettigrew (1959) argues, that conformity to group norms rather than personality type is responsible for prejudice. Pettigrew compared four towns in the northern states of America with four towns in the southern states. Available evidence indicated that white southerners were more prejudiced against African Americans than white northerners. Was this due to a higher incidence of authoritarian personalities in the south or was it the result of different cultural norms? Using the questionnaire developed by Adorno et al., Pettigrew found that southerners were no more authoritarian than northerners – though he did find that authoritarian individuals in *both* regions were more prejudiced. Pettigrew argued that differences between north and south were due to differences in norms – prejudice was more acceptable and accepted in the south. He also found that the most conformist southerners (according to a personality questionnaire) were the most prejudiced, while the most conformist northerners were the least prejudiced.

Social change Third, history shows that prejudices appear and disappear, often with remarkable rapidity. This would be difficult to explain if prejudice was a part of personality. The anti-Japanese attitudes in the United States during World War II led to the internment of thousands of Japanese-Americans. This is far more likely to be due to the change in international relations that followed the Japanese bombing of the American fleet in Pearl Harbour than to the personalities of individual Americans (Vivian & Brown, 1995). However, in defence of the personality theorists, it could be argued that those with authoritarian personalities simply select a new target – they redirect their prejudice towards other groups.

Key terms

Authoritarian personality *A personality type which predisposes the individual towards prejudice and discrimination.*

Repression *A mental process by which experiences, memories and impulses which might produce anxiety or guilt are directed into the unconscious.*

Projection *The redirection of repressed feelings and emotions onto others.*

Realistic conflict theory and prejudice

This theory states that there are real conflicts of interest between social groups. Prejudice and discrimination either arise or are increased by competition for scarce resources. Resources are scarce when there aren't enough of them to go around. Scarce resources include jobs, houses, income, status, land, political power and educational opportunities. John Dollard's (1938) study of a small American industrial town was one of the first to show the relationship between economic competition and prejudice. At first there was no prejudice against recently arrived German immigrants. However, when jobs grew scarce, prejudice against the immigrants developed.

In a situation of realistic conflict, competing groups often develop negative stereotypes of one another. These stereotypes are used to justify discrimination against particular groups. For example, the position of women has long been justified and explained by a series of stereotypes. These stereotypes come to the fore when women compete with men for scarce resources such as political power, income and jobs. In the UK, women were barred from voting until 1918. Writing in *The Girl's Own Paper* in 1896, Frederick Ryland makes it clear why they were unfit to vote. 'The truth is that the intelligence of women is not political. The factory-girl class will be the most important class of women voters. Political power in many large cities would be in the hands of young, ill-educated, giddy girls.' Similar stereotypes have been used to explain why women were 'unsuitable' for higher education and professional and managerial positions, but highly 'suitable' for domestic labour and a range of low skill, low status occupations. Men gain by

keeping women down. Negative stereotypes of women maintain male power by justifying the traditional lowly position of women and the discrimination they suffer at the hands of men.

The Robber's Cave experiment In a classic study, Muzafer Sherif et al. (1961) designed an experiment to investigate the relationships between competition and prejudice and discrimination. The participants were twenty-two white, middle-class, well-adjusted eleven and twelve-year-old boys at a summer camp at Robber's Cave State Park in Oklahoma. They were randomly assigned to two groups. The groups were kept apart for most of the first week, each living in their own cabin. The researchers designed activities to increase group cohesiveness and identity. Treasure hunts, building projects and preparing group meals involved teamwork and developed a sense of group-belonging. Typical group-defining behaviour emerged such as adopting group names – the Rattlers and the Eagles – and making group flags.

At the end of the first week the boys had developed a group coherence and a group identity. The two groups were then introduced to one another. They immediately showed signs of territoriality, for example one group refused to share a swimming hole they had found. Each group rapidly developed a sense of an in-group and out-group and talked in terms of 'us and them'. The camp counsellors – the researchers – organised a tournament between the two groups. It consisted of ten team games including tug-of-war, baseball and football. There were prizes for each member of the winning group – four-bladed knives and medals. Even before the tournament began competition developed into conflict. The Eagles burned the Rattlers' flag and the counsellors had to break up a fight between the two groups. The Eagles won the tournament and the scarce resources – the prizes. Not to be outdone, the Rattlers stole the prizes from their rivals.

During the final week of the experiment solidarity had steadily increased within each group. Boys rated their own in-group members as far better than the other group. And boys who had previously held low-ranking positions found themselves highly valued by other members of their group. Stereotypes rapidly developed. In-group members were seen as 'tough', 'brave' and 'friendly', out-group members were denounced as 'bums', 'cheats' and 'cowards'. This experiment shows how competition for scarce resources can generate stereotypes, prejudice and discrimination. It also shows how competition can degenerate into hostility and open conflict. And this all happened in a couple of weeks!

Evaluation

Advantages Realistic conflict theory offers a social view of prejudice. It links the emergence of prejudice to shifts in the economic and political relationships between groups. This makes the theory far more sensitive to historical changes and the broader social context than personality based theories. However, there is evidence that competition between groups does not always result in prejudice and discrimination.

Disadvantages Tyerman and Spencer (1983) studied English boy scouts at their annual camp. They were divided into four groups and competed against each other in a series of games, not unlike the boys in Sherif et al's study. The main difference was that the English boys all knew each other before they went to camp and those friendships were maintained throughout their stay. As a result, competition was friendly, in-groups and out-groups were absent, competition did not become conflict and prejudice and discrimination did not develop. It appears that competition for scarce resources only results in prejudice and discrimination under particular conditions. Competing groups must develop, along with separate group identities. If there are overarching alliances and identifications between the groups, then prejudice and discrimination will probably not develop.

A more serious problem is that in many cases it is difficult to judge whether a conflict of interest between groups is real or imagined (Brown, 1986). Clearly it has to be perceived as real by group members for prejudice and discrimination to develop. But consider the following case. One of the main reasons for high levels of unemployment in former East Germany is the uncompetitiveness of their industry due to overstaffing and outdated machinery. It is this, rather than the presence of foreign workers, which has put many East Germans out of work. As such, there is little *real* conflict of interest between the two groups. Despite this, many Germans see themselves in competition with foreign workers and this perception has led to prejudice and discrimination.

Finally, as Tajfel et al. (1971) found in a series of experiments, it is not even necessary for competition to exist between groups for prejudice to emerge. They found that merely being categorised as a member of the same group led to a tendency for people to favour their fellow group members (the in-group) over people categorised as belonging to another group (the out-group). This finding became the basis for social identity theory, examined in the following section.

Activity 5   Realistic conflict

Item A   Changing prejudices

Chinese labourers working on the Central Pacific Railroad

During the 19th century in the USA, prejudice and discrimination against Chinese immigrants fluctuated considerably. When they joined the gold rush in California in 1848, they were described by the white miners as 'depraved, vicious, bloodthirsty and inhuman'. A few years later, 12,000 Chinese coolies were shipped over to work on the Central Pacific Railroad. They accepted the long hours and the dangerous and backbreaking work which few whites were prepared to do. One of the directors of the railroad, Charles Crocker, wrote, 'They are equal to the best white men. They are very trusty, very intelligent and they live up to their contracts'. After the Civil War ended in 1865, thousands of ex-soldiers poured into an already crowded job market. This was followed by a wave of prejudice against the Chinese. They were now 'criminal, conniving, crafty, and stupid'.

Adapted from Jacobs & Landau, 1971

Item B   Reporting the Gulf War

The Gulf War (1990-91) was fought between Iraq, led by Saddam Hussein, and the Allies (USA, Britain and a number of other countries) led by the American president George Bush. The following table shows some of the words and phrases used by the British media to describe each side.

Mad dogs and Englishmen

We have	They have
Army, Navy and Air Force	A war machine
Reporting guidelines	Censorship
Press briefings	Propaganda
We	**They**
Take out	Destroy
Suppress	Destroy
Eliminate	Kill
Neutralise	Kill
Dig in	Cower in their foxholes
We Launch	**They Launch**
First strikes	Sneak missile attacks
Pre-emptively	Without provocation
Our boys are ...	**Theirs are ...**
Professional	Brainwashed
Lion-hearts	Paper tigers
Cautious	Cowardly
Confident	Desperate
Heroes	Cornered
Dare-devils	Cannon fodder
Young knights of the skies	Bastards of Baghdad
Loyal	Blindly obedient
Desert rats	Mad dogs
Resolute	Ruthless
Brave	Fanatical
Our planes ...	**Their planes ...**
Suffer a high rate of attrition	Are shot out of the sky
Fail to return from missions	Are zapped
Our missiles cause ...	**Their missiles cause ...**
Collateral damage	Civilian casualties
George Bush is ...	**Saddam Hussein is ...**
At peace with himself	Demented
Resolute	Defiant
Statesmanlike	An evil tyrant
Assured	A crackpot monster

Adapted from *The Guardian*, 23.1.1991

Social identity theory and prejudice

During the 1950s, the dominant approach in psychology was that prejudice was caused by an abnormal, authoritarian personality. In 1969, Henri Tajfel wrote a classic article called *Cognitive aspects of prejudice* which argued fiercely against this view. Tajfel was a Jewish émigré who had narrowly survived the Holocaust which had claimed the lives of most of his relatives. He subsequently became a social psychologist and his entire career was driven by the question of how prejudice, like that displayed by the Nazis against Jews, was possible.

Tajfel's starting point was that human beings are motivated to make sense of their social world. In order to do this, they engage in the processes of *categorisation, assimilation*, and the *search for coherence*.

Categorisation This is a process of classifying people, objects and events into different categories. Categorisation is seen as a basic and essential aspect of human thinking. On the basis of evidence from experimental work, Tajfel (1969) noted that people tend to *overestimate* the differences between things placed in *different* categories, and to *underestimate* the differences between things placed in the *same* category. As a result, they are likely to see people in groups other than their own as very different from themselves. At the same time, they are likely to see people in another group as very similar to each other. In a nutshell, 'they're not like us' and 'they're all the same'. This view of others provides the basis for stereotypes.

Assimilation This refers to learning the norms, values, attitudes and beliefs of society or particular groups within society. People tend to learn from those around them, from the groups to which they belong such as their ethnic group, social class group and so on. As a result, they are likely to assimilate the outlook of their particular group and see the world 'through the eyes' of the group.

Search for coherence People search for coherence – an understanding of the world that makes sense, that seems reasonable, that fits together. According to Tajfel (1969), people are continuously adjusting to new situations and this can threaten coherence. In order to make sense of these situations, they tend to draw on the values, attitudes and outlooks of their own groups.

The above processes help to explain how people's outlook is shaped by their membership of social groups, but they do not, on their own, provide an explanation of prejudice.

Social identity theory In order to explain the origin of prejudice, Tajfel (1981) proposed *social identity theory*. His earlier work on categorisation, assimilation and the search for coherence suggested that group identity and stereotyping arise naturally from the way people seek to make sense of their social world. In social identity theory, Tajfel went further and put forward two additional points. First, that membership of social groups provides people with much of their *personal identity*. Second, that people strive for *self-esteem*.

According to social identity theory, prejudice and discrimination are only possible if people are categorised into groups. This leads them to identify with certain groups and from this they develop a sense of in-groups and out-groups.

Group identification provides people with their social identity. Tajfel and Turner (1979) define social identity as 'those aspects of an individual's self-image that derive from the social categories to which he [sic] perceives himself belonging'. These social categories are groups based on class, ethnicity, nationality, occupation, gender, sexual orientation, religion, region, and so on. Part of an individual's self-image or personal identity therefore comes from their social identity.

Social identity theory assumes that people prefer to see themselves in a positive light. They will therefore strive for a positive self-image. Since part of their self-image comes from their social identity, they will tend to see the groups they belong to in a positive light. They compare their own group to those of others. As a result, they will favour their in-group – *in-group favouritism* – and develop negative views of out-groups – *negative out-group bias*. Prejudice and discrimination therefore result from group identification and the need for a positive self-image.

Minimal groups Support for this view came from a series of experiments conducted by Tajfel and his colleagues. The participants were complete strangers. Throughout the experiments they had no contact with each other – the tasks they were given were performed alone. They were randomly divided into two groups. The basis for this division was meaningless – there was nothing to distinguish one group from the other except for the labels attached to the groups. For example, in one experiment participants were allocated to groups by the toss of a coin. Tajfel called these groups *minimal groups* since the things which held them together were minimal. Would such minimal groups result in the formation of in-groups and out-groups and in-group favouritism and negative out-group bias?

In one experiment the participants were asked to allocate money to members of both groups. They favoured their own group even if this cost them money. For example, if they had a choice of giving *either* £2 to their group and £1 to the other group *or* £3 to their group and £4 to the other group, they would choose the first option. This meant they would lose £1 but get more than the other group. Even in the case of minimal groups, in-groups and out-groups were formed and in-group favouritism and negative out-group bias developed. Participants identified with 'their group', showed a clear preference for it, and discriminated against the other group. As a result, their self-esteem was boosted and this contributed to a positive self-image. This happened over a short period of time in minimal groups. Given this, it is much more likely to occur in the outside world where groups have much more in common, where they share norms, values, aims and aspirations, and are linked by gender, ethnicity, nationality and so on.

Social identity theory arrives at the very gloomy conclusion that prejudice is inevitable. The very fact of being part of a group, however minimal, leads a person to develop prejudice and act in a discriminatory way.

Social change Social identity theory also contains a theory of social change. A conflict can occur between a person's social identity and their need to preserve self-esteem. For example, a powerful group can impose a negative social identity on others (see Activity 6, Item B). This may motivate members of the less powerful group to take one or more of the following forms of action (Tajfel, 1981).

Individual mobility This involves 'exiting' the current group and attempting to join another, higher status group. An individual who strives to advance their career and mix in the 'right social circles' may achieve such mobility.

Social creativity This involves an attempt to change the current status of the group by either finding a more favourable basis of comparison with out-groups (for example, by changing a negative group image into a positive image), or finding a new out-group altogether to compare itself to. Examples of social creativity include the idea of 'gay pride' and the black civil rights movement in the USA in the 1960s who adopted the slogan 'black is beautiful'.

Social competition This is the most 'direct' way of changing categories, through political activism, revolution or terrorism. Social competition is an attempt to overturn the existing status quo through direct intergroup conflict. Examples of social competition include conflict between Catholics and Protestants in Northern Ireland, Palestinians and Israelis in the Middle East and ethnic riots in Britain and the USA.

Evaluation

Advantages Social identity theory neatly combines explanations for stereotypes, prejudice and discrimination. All three are seen to result from a need for a positive identity. Preference for the in-group leads to the creation of positive in-group stereotypes and to prejudice and discrimination in favour of in-group members. And it leads to the reverse for out-groups – negative stereotypes and negative prejudice and discrimination against out-group members.

Disadvantages However, there is a lot that social identity theory does not explain. Relationships between groups are not simply based on a need for people to see their own group in a positive light. They are also, for example, based on a struggle for scarce resources such as money, material goods and power. And this struggle can generate prejudice and discrimination, as realistic conflict theory indicates. Although social identity theory does consider such wider social issues, they are not central to the theory.

Social identity theory focuses on individuals as members of social groups. In doing so, it tends to downplay the importance of relationships between groups in the wider social and historical context (Billig, 1991; Wetherell & Potter, 1992). For example, an explanation of prejudice and discrimination against African Americans requires, among other things, a historical perspective from slavery to the present day, and an analysis of the distribution of power in society.

Social identity theory finds it difficult to explain extreme forms of prejudice (Brown & Lunt, 2002). For example, how can a theory based on attitudes, such as in-group favouritism, explain the systematic slaughter of millions in Nazi death camps? Tajfel

(1981) originally made a distinction between 'prejudice', which he saw as following from categorisation, and 'bigotry', which was prejudice taken to extreme forms. He claimed that social identity theory could explain prejudice, but bigotry was too complex a phenomenon to be explained by any single theory. However, this distinction has been forgotten in later work (Billig, 2001).

Experimental research has tended to focus on two groups – an in-group and an out-group. In this situation, it is fairly easy to create group polarisation and an 'us and them' situation. When a third group is introduced, there is less bias against out-groups and therefore less out-group prejudice (Augoustinos & Walker, 1995). Social identity theory needs developing in order to explain situations involving three or more groups.

Finally, much of the research on social identity theory has been based on experiments.   Relatively little research has been conducted in actual social settings. The 'real world' is more complex and 'messy' than the laboratory and often involves situations where more than two groups are present. For example, the conflicts in the former Yugoslavia involved a number of different groups – Serbs, Croats, Bosnian Muslims and Western peacekeepers. And, relationships between these groups changed. Social identity theory, as it stands, would have difficulty explaining this kind of multi-group conflict.

Key terms

Categorisation *The process of classifying people, objects and events into different categories.*

Assimilation *Learning the norms, values, attitudes and beliefs of society or particular groups within society.*

Coherence *An understanding of the world that makes sense, that fits together.*

In-group favouritism *Favouritism shown by a person towards members of the group to which they themselves belong.*

Negative out-group bias *A bias shown by a person against members of groups to which they do not belong.*

Minimal groups *Experimental groups formed at random. The things which hold such groups together are 'minimal'.*

Summary

1. Prejudice is an attitude towards a group. It can be positive or negative.

2. There are two main components of prejudice – the cognitive and the affective.

3. Adorno et al's theory of the authoritarian personality emphasises the role of childhood upbringing in producing a prejudiced personality.

4. Realistic conflict theory states that prejudice emerges from real conflicts of interest between groups over scarce resources.

5. Social identity theory states that prejudice develops from group membership. People strive for a positive identity. As a result, they will tend to favour their in-group and view out-groups in a negative light.

6. No one theory is likely to explain all the aspects of prejudice and discrimination.

Item A   Creating prejudice

Jane Elliott, a school teacher in an all-white farming community in Iowa, wanted to show her primary school children what prejudice and discrimination felt like. One day she told the class that blue-eyed children were 'better' and more intelligent than brown-eyed children. Elliott treated the blue-eyed children more favourably and gave them extra privileges. She seated them at the front of the class and gave them five more minutes at break. She responded positively to the answers from blue-eyed children and took every opportunity to criticise the brown-eyed children.

Two distinct groups of children were created. Relationships between the groups rapidly deteriorated – fights broke out between children who were formerly friends. Within a day the 'inferior' group actually saw itself as inferior – these children described themselves as 'stupid', 'bad' and 'mean'. The 'superior' group discriminated against their former friends, refusing to play with them. Referring to the 'superior' group, Elliott stated, 'What had been marvellously cooperative, thoughtful children became nasty, vicious, discriminating little third-graders'.

Adapted from Elliott, 1977

Item B   'The white man's burden'

The following extract is taken from the autobiography of Miriam Makeba, a black South African singer who grew up under the Apartheid regime.

The whites have to justify the rape of our land, and so they claim that we are inferior. We are not worthy of God's gifts. It says so in the Bible. They lay claim to our land and our lives and then, to add insult to injury, they patronise us. They say we are ignorant children. Our salvation and welfare are – alas! – 'the white man's burden'.

And, after a while a terrible thing happens. For many of my people, the message begins to sink in. Day after day we are treated like dirt and told we are inferior. It is drummed into our heads. Your self-respect disappears. You begin to hate everything that is black.

No dogs, cycles or natives!

Adapted from Makeba & Hall, 1988

Item C   They all look the same

The BBC television football commentator John Motson yesterday sparked off a race row after suggesting during a radio interview that it was difficult to tell black players apart.

Talking on Radio 5's *Sportsweek* programme, Mr Motson, who has covered league and international games for more than 20 years, stated 'There are teams where you have got players who, from a distance, look almost identical. And, of course, with more black players coming in to the game, they would not mind me saying that that can be very confusing.'

His remarks drew criticism from politicians. Richard Allan, Liberal Democrat community affairs spokesman, said such attitudes were wrong and outdated. 'It is unfortunate that with so many of our top sports personalities coming from the ethnic communities and doing so well flying the flag for Britain we still suffer from these racial stereotypes.'

In response, John Motson stated, 'Some of the black players would appreciate that it can be more difficult when a lot of black players are on the pitch. I am not a racist. It was not meant that way at all. I am just saying if there are five or six black players in the team and several of them are going for the ball it can be difficult. The comments were perfectly innocent.'

Adapted from *The Guardian*, 5.1.1998

Leicester City players celebrate a goal.

Questions

1   Use social identity theory to explain the children's behaviour in Item A.

2   When an in-group is considerably more powerful than an out-group, it can, at least in part, shape the identity of out-group members. Discuss this view with reference to Item B.

3   a)   Use the idea of out-group categorisation to explain John Motson's 'problems' in Item C.

    b)   Is it fair to describe him as 'racist'?

Unit 4 Reducing prejudice and discrimination

KEY ISSUES

1 Can prejudice and discrimination be reduced?
2 What are the main strategies for their reduction?

4.1 Introduction

This unit examines possibilities for reducing prejudice and discrimination. Judging from the theories outlined in the previous unit, the prospects for this are not good, though there are some glimmers of hope. A brief review of these theories shows why.

Personality theories Adorno et al. (1950) claim that the authoritarian personality predisposes people to prejudice and discrimination. It results from a childhood characterised by harsh discipline and strict compliance with social norms. Typically, the father is the disciplinarian and the dominant figure in the family. However, more recent evidence indicates that family life is becoming increasingly democratic and the 'Victorian father' has largely disappeared (Haralambos & Holborn, 2000). If this is the case, we can expect a reduction in authoritarian personalities and with it, a reduction in prejudice and discrimination.

Realistic conflict theory states that prejudice and discrimination result from real conflicts of interest between social groups. Today's society gives little or no indication of any reduction in competition for scarce resources. Individuals compete for educational qualifications, occupational groups compete for income, companies compete for market share. And, in an increasingly global economy, economic competition is played out on a worldwide stage. Given this, realistic conflict theory appears to offer little hope for a reduction in prejudice and discrimination.

On the other hand, there is a possibility that an increasingly global society may generate common goals – for example, seeking solutions to worldwide problems such as pollution. This may lead to global cooperation and a reduction in conflicts of interest. And this, in turn, may lead to a reduction in prejudice and discrimination.

Social identity theory states that part of our personal identity comes from our group membership. Because of our need for self-esteem we favour our own groups at the expense of others. The result is in-group favouritism and negative out-group bias. Since this applies even to minimal groups, social identity theory appears to hold out little hope for an end to prejudice and discrimination.

On the other hand, there is a possibility that in an increasingly global society, people's social identity may become more and more global. They may see themselves as part of humanity, an all-inclusive in-group. And this may lead to a reduction in prejudice and discrimination.

The following sections examine the possibilities for reducing, or even eliminating, prejudice and discrimination.

4.2 The contact hypothesis

The *contact hypothesis* states that positive contact between members of different groups will reduce prejudice and discrimination. Perceptions of out-group homogeneity ('they're all the same') will tend to disappear as people realise that out-group members are as diverse as people in their own groups. Hostility will tend to disappear as friendly relationships are established between members of different groups. However, research has indicated that contact can only reduce prejudice and discrimination under certain conditions. Often contact can have just the opposite effect – it can increase prejudice and discrimination. This can be seen from the following examples.

In 1954, the US Supreme Court ordered an end to segregated schools. No longer could schools be designated 'black' schools and 'white' schools. It was hoped that this would reduce inter-racial prejudice. More often than not the opposite happened. A survey of research on school integration showed that 53% of studies found that prejudice increased and 34% found no change (Stephan, 1978).

Sherif et al's (1961) study of the boys at summer camp produced similar results. The second phase of the experiment attempted to reduce hostility between the two groups by bringing them together in non-competitive situations. For example, they were sat next to each other at movies and meals. If anything, hostility between the groups increased.

Research indicates that contact must be coupled with other factors in order to reduce prejudice and discrimination. These factors will now be examined.

Superordinate goals Realistic conflict theory states that prejudice and discrimination result from a real conflict of interest between groups. It follows that if this conflict of interest can be superseded by common goals which serve the interests of both groups, then prejudice and discrimination should be reduced. This is the idea of *superordinate goals* – goals which are shared by both groups, which require the cooperation of both groups for their attainment, and which benefit all. This is illustrated by Sherif et al's (1961) summer camp experiment.

In the final phase of Sherif's et al's experiment, the researchers attempted to create superordinate goals. For example, they arranged for the camp truck to break down. The only way to get it back to camp was for both groups to pull it by a rope attached to the front bumper. The researchers sabotaged the camp water supply and the only way to restore it was for both groups to cooperate. As a result of these and similar tasks, there was a marked reduction in hostility between the two groups and a development of friendships across group boundaries. Superordinate goals made the boys realise that they were all in the same boat and had better pull together for the benefit of all.

There are many 'real-world' examples of the effect of common goals. In 1993, a huge earthquake in central India killed an estimated 30,000 people. In the face of this shared disaster, the religious and social divisions between Hindus and Muslims largely disappeared. As one rescuer said, 'It doesn't matter to me whether this house belongs to a Hindu or a Muslim. Whoever it is, they need our help' (Brown, 1995).

Equal status Consider the following situation. Before the abolition of Apartheid in South Africa, contact between blacks and whites was usually based on unequal relationships. Blacks were cooks, cleaners, maids and gardeners, often serving whites. Contact in this situation is unlikely to reduce prejudice since one group has low status and subservient roles which tend to reinforce prejudicial attitudes.

Contact will be more likely to reduce prejudice and discrimination if group members share the same status. For example, the boys in Sherif's experiment were roughly equal in terms of status and power. They were similar in age, they were all white and all middle class. If, for example, there were wide class differences between the two groups, then the hostility between them would have been more difficult to reduce. Equal status contact prevents other social differences from dividing the groups.

The significance of equal status contact can be seen from the following experiment. Researchers set up a summer camp in which all the responsibilities, duties and roles were shared equally by blacks and whites (Clore, 1976). There were four camp directors – a white male, a white female, a black male and a black female. There were three black and three white youngsters, plus one black and one white counsellor, on each campsite. Power and status were equally divided between blacks and whites. By the end of the summer there was a marked decrease in prejudice among the young people attending the camp.

Generalisation Consider the following. Two groups are prejudiced towards each other. Individual members of these two groups meet and get on extremely well. They see each other as people like themselves and their prejudices disappear. Yet they remain prejudiced against the groups to which the other belongs. Why? The answer is they see each other as individuals rather than as representatives of groups. And they can retain their prejudices against the group by seeing the individuals they meet as the exception rather than the rule – these individuals are different from the rest. If group prejudice and discrimination are to be reduced, individuals in positive contact situations must be seen as typical of their group. In other words, a *generalisation* of positive attitudes must be made from specific group members to the group as a whole.

The above points are illustrated by a study of male police officers with female work partners in Washington DC. The men were quite satisfied with their female partners yet maintained their prejudice against women police officers, believing that no more should be employed. In this respect they were no different than their male colleagues with male partners. Their positive experience of a female partner was not generalised to female police officers as a whole. They regarded their partner as an exception (Milton, 1972).

In terms of the contact hypothesis, contact between individuals only serves to reduce prejudice in the wider society when positive attitudes can be generalised from individuals to the groups to which they belong.

Acquaintance potential In order to reduce prejudice and discrimination, contact should have *acquaintance potential* – it should provide the opportunity for people to get fully acquainted. Ideally, contact should be informal, friendly and on a one-to-one basis, so that people can get to know each other as individuals, rather than remaining segregated in their own groups. This encourages a generalisation of positive attitudes from the contact situation to the out-group as a whole (Cook, 1962).

Normative support There is a greater chance of reducing prejudice in a setting where the norms encourage group equality. For example, if those in power, such as employers, establish norms which favour tolerance and understanding, their employees will tend to modify their behaviour accordingly (Aronson et al., 1999). Similarly, if laws are passed which ban discrimination on the grounds of race or gender, this provides a legal framework which is conducive to reducing prejudice.

This section has shown that contact can lead to a reduction in prejudice and discrimination – but only if the conditions are appropriate. These conditions can be contrived in field experiments, such as the summer camp experiments, and in the artificial context of the laboratory. However, such combinations of appropriate conditions rarely occur in the wider society. But occasionally they do, as the following section shows.

Key terms

Superordinate goals *Common goals which serve the interests of two or more social groups.*

Equal status contact *Contact between individuals who share the same status or prestige.*

Generalisation of attitudes *Generalising attitudes about particular individuals to the groups to which they belong.*

Acquaintance potential *The opportunity for people to get well acquainted and develop meaningful relationships.*

Normative support *Support for behaviour provided by social norms.*

4.3 The jigsaw classroom

This section looks at a specific example of a situation in which superordinate goals produced cooperation rather than competition between social groups. This reduced conflicts of interest and, as realistic conflict theory predicts, it also reduced prejudice and discrimination.

Think of a typical classroom situation. The students are competing with each other and their status is unequal – some are ranked at the top of the class, others at the bottom. This situation is hardly designed to reduce prejudice and discrimination. In fact, it has the potential to increase both. This is what happened in 1971 when the school system in Austin, Texas, was desegregated. There was open conflict between the various ethnic groups as whites, African Americans and Mexican Americans were brought together in the same schools.

The situation was made worse by the fact that the previous schooling of many ethnic minority students had not equipped them to compete on equal terms with white students. Research indicated a general decrease in self-esteem amongst minority group students after school desegregation. Many lagged behind their white counterparts and appeared less intelligent and less motivated. This only served to confirm the prejudices of the white students.

Things got so bad that Elliot Aronson, a social psychologist from the University of Texas, was invited to Austin and given a free hand to solve the problem. His solution was the *jigsaw classroom*.

The jigsaw classroom was designed to reduce prejudice and raise self-esteem. Students were placed in groups of six, with the membership of the groups reflecting the ethnic composition of the school. For example, if the school was one third white, one third African American and one third Mexican American, then there would be two students from each ethnic group in the classroom groups.

Each student in the six-person groups was given part of the information needed to complete a project or prepare for a test. For example, if they were studying George Washington, the first American President, each would be given part of his biography. Students were to learn their part of the information and teach it to the other five members of their group. All six parts were essential to complete a project or for examination success. Hence the term jigsaw classroom – there were six pieces in the jigsaw which must be put together.

Rather than competing, students were now cooperating. They depended on each other and shared a common goal. Students now had equal status – each member of the group was responsible for a vital piece of the information needed by all. Because of this, each group member was seen as important, was listened to and given respect. The result was a significant decrease in prejudice and discrimination and, particularly for minority group students, an increase in self-esteem and an improvement in examination performance.

Jigsaw classrooms spread rapidly across the USA and beyond. By the mid-1980s, over 25,000 teachers in the USA were using jigsaw classrooms or a similar form of cooperative learning (Aronson et al., 1999).

Is there a generalisation of non-prejudiced attitudes from the classroom to the wider society? This is a difficult question to answer. The following rather pessimistic response comes from Martin, a white pupil in a North American school where blacks and whites had been successfully integrated.

Interviewer: Has being in a school like Wexler changed white kids' *ideas* about what blacks are like?

Martin: It's still the same stereotype. Parents tell you what to believe, and then you probably believe it. (Schofield, 1982)

4.4　Categorisation

According to social identity theory, categorising people into groups produces in-groups and out-groups and results in in-group favouritism. This, in turn, can lead to prejudice and discrimination against out-groups. This suggests two obvious solutions for the elimination of prejudice and discrimination. Both involve a radical recategorisation of people. The first is the creation of an all inclusive in-group composed of the entire human race. The second is the abolition of all groups and with it the removal of all group identities. Every human being will now be seen as an individual.

Recategorisation This refers to changing the category within which people are grouped together. Laboratory experiments indicate that if members of two groups come to see each other as part of a single group, then they will see each other in a more favourable light. This was also shown in a study of American high schools with a multi-ethnic student population, eg students from African-American, Hispanic, Chinese, Vietnamese, Mexican-American and Caucasian (white) backgrounds. The more the students saw themselves as a single student body, the more positive were their feelings towards the various ethnic groups that made up the school population (Gaertner et al., 1989, 1993).

This is known as the *common in-group identity model*, in which a number of different groups form a larger, more inclusive in-group. However, it is important to note that this process does not remove in-groups, it simply enlarges them. But, if it serves to reduce some forms of prejudice, as the study of American high schools indicates, then it can be seen as a positive process.

History has provided many examples of common in-group identity as former out-groups come to see themselves as part of a larger social entity. This often happens in times of war when a nation unites in the face of a common foe. Groups often come together when they see their interests as shared. This happened in the 1980s, when Jesse Jackson formed the Rainbow Coalition to represent ethnic minorities in the USA. It can be seen on an international scale with the formation and expansion of the European Union. Whether it will ever happen on a global scale, only time will tell. The United Nations is hardly a major factor in people's social identity. However, there is a growing awareness of global problems, such as global warming, which may provide superordinate goals for the human race. And this may encourage people to see *humanity* as an increasingly important part of their social identity.

Decategorisation This refers to the removal of all categories. Group identities disappear and people see themselves and each other as individuals. What effect might this have on prejudice and discrimination?

Gaertner et al. (1989, 1993) designed an experiment to answer this question. They began with two groups of three students. They then encouraged the students to recategorise themselves as six unique individuals. The result was a considerable reduction of former in-group bias. However, the students now thought less highly of former in-group members. When the two groups were combined to form a single group, they then thought *more* highly of former out-group members.

These results can be explained in terms of social identity theory. When the individual was part of the combined group, they identified with the group. Since part of their personal identity came from group membership, they were encouraged to view other group members in a positive light in order to raise their own self-esteem. However, when they saw themselves as individuals, this association of others with the self was lost. A person's self-concept was less dependent on group membership, therefore there was less reason to view others in a positive light. And there was less reason to view former out-group members in a negative light.

This experiment suggests that, on balance, it may be preferable for people to see themselves as individuals rather than members of groups. Most social scientists see individualism as an ongoing trend in modern society. If they are right, then this may lead to a reduction in prejudice and discrimination.

Key terms

Recategorisation *Changing the category within which people are grouped. Usually refers to the creation of a larger, more inclusive group.*

Decategorisation *The removal of all categories. As a result, people see themselves and others as individuals rather than group members.*

4.5 Fighting back

Prejudice and discrimination are about power. Some have the power to translate their prejudices into action and discriminate against others. In order to reduce prejudice and discrimination, one strategy is to fight power with power.

Social identity theory is one of the few theories which takes account of this strategy. It states that social competition – political activism, revolution or even terrorism – is likely to occur when a group feels that it cannot gain a positive social identity by any other means. But social competition remains the least researched aspect of the theory (Reicher, 1996).

So far this unit has focused on laboratory experiments and small-scale social settings such as classrooms. This section takes a brief look at the ways of reducing prejudice and discrimination which cannot be reproduced in the laboratory – various forms of direct action including demonstrations, political protest, civil disobedience, boycotts, strikes, riots and armed rebellion.

Civil rights protest In December 1955 in Montgomery, Alabama, Mrs Rosa Parks, an African-American woman, refused to give up her seat on a bus to a white man. Blacks were allocated seats at the rear of buses and expected to give them to whites if the white section was full. Mrs Parks' act of defiance was the beginning of direct action against segregation and discrimination. It resulted in the Montgomery bus boycott, organised by Dr Martin Luther King, in which thousands of African Americans walked to work for over six months. The case was taken to court and segregation on Montgomery buses was declared illegal.

1960 saw the beginning of 'sit-ins'. Four African-American students in Greensboro, North Carolina, sat down at the all-white lunch counter in Woolworth's and asked politely to be served. They were refused, but continued to 'sit-in'. This prompted direct action on a massive scale against segregation in public places. In 1963, there were over 2,000 demonstrations in the southern states with hundreds of thousands participating.

African-American protest was dramatised in 1963 by the march on Washington of nearly a quarter of a million people, culminating in Dr King's 'I have a dream' speech. Responding to the steady build-up of pressure, the Federal Government passed the Civil Rights Act in 1964 which declared racial segregation and discrimination illegal in employment, education, voting and justice (Haralambos, 1994).

The Suffragette movement In the United Kingdom, women did not have the right to vote until 1918. They had to fight for it. The Suffragettes, a woman's organisation with their motto, 'Deeds not words', took direct action in their campaign for political equality with men. Many were arrested and those who went on hunger strike in prison were brutally force-fed. In 1912, the Suffragettes organised mass window smashing in London and then moved on to more violent tactics such as bombing and arson. They set fire to buildings, bombed post boxes and slashed valuable paintings in art galleries. Their actions led to violent clashes with the police.

In 1918 women over 30 were given the vote. In 1928 the Equal Franchise Act reduced the voting age for women to 21. Although there were many factors involved in ending political discrimination against women, most historians agree that direct action by the Suffragettes played an important part. (Lancaster & Lancaster, 1995).

Apartheid When the interests of the powerful are threatened, they often make concessions. If the threat is sufficiently powerful, as in South Africa, they can even relinquish their power. Faced with the threat of civil war, the dominant white minority in South Africa finally gave non-whites the right to vote in 1992. This brought an end to Apartheid, one of the most brutal, systematic and rigid forms of racial segregation and discrimination ever invented.

Conclusion Fighting back is probably the most effective way of ending discrimination. It often leads to changes in the law which make discrimination illegal. If laws are enforced, this leads to changes in behaviour which can result in changes in attitudes, in particular the reduction or even elimination of prejudice. It has often been argued that it is impossible to legislate against prejudice. But, as Gordon Allport (1958) states, 'Legislation aims not at controlling prejudice, but only its expression. But when expression changes, thoughts too, in the long run, are likely to fall into line.'

Summary

1. Each of the main theories suggests different ways to reduce prejudice and discrimination.

2. Contact between groups can increase prejudice and discrimination. Only under specific conditions can it lead to a reduction.

3. These conditions include superordinate goals and equal status contact.

4. Recategorising and decategorising social groups can lead to a reduction in prejudice and discrimination.

5. Minority groups can successfully oppose prejudice and discrimination. This can lead to laws which ban discrimination. This, in turn, can lead to changes in social norms and a reduction of prejudice.

Activity 7   Reducing prejudice and discrimination

Item A   Contact

"I WISH WE COULD HAVE MET
UNDER DIFFERENT CIRCUMSTANCES . . ."

Item B   One race

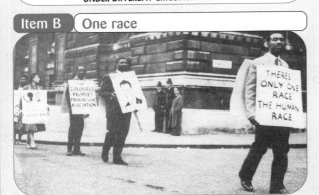

Item C   One individual

The American golfer Tiger Woods describes himself as a Cablinasian. His father is half African-American, a quarter Native-American and a quarter Caucasian (white). His mother is half Thai and half Chinese. According to Woods, 'I'm just who I am – whoever you see in front of you. Growing up, I came up with this name – I'm a Cablinasian.'

Adapted from *The Guardian*, 24.4.1997

Item D   Global problems

At Kyoto in Japan, 160 governments agreed to cut global gas emissions by an average of 5.2% within 15 years.

Adapted from *The Guardian*, 12.12.1997

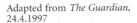

Item E   Asteroid threatens Earth

In March 1998 the International Astronomical Union warned that there was a small chance that an asteroid might hit the Earth in 2028, killing millions of people. If it hit a deep ocean, coastal regions would be devastated by a tidal wave hundreds of feet high. If it hit land, the explosion would destroy everything within thousands of square miles and – more seriously – throw enough dust into the atmosphere to blot out the sun and trigger a cosmic winter worldwide. Unofficial estimates put the odds of a collision at about one in a thousand.

Adapted from *The Financial Times*, 13.3.1998

Item F   Gay power

In New York 30 years ago, it was illegal even to serve drinks to gays. Then, on 28 July 1969, a bottle was thrown at police by a gay woman in a Greenwich Village bar and the Gay Rights Movement began. The incident was followed by three days of rioting. Today, the New York Police Department employs a growing number of openly gay men and women. They are in charge of protecting gay bars, not raiding them as they had in the past.

In 1994, hundreds of thousands of gay people paraded in London to celebrate 25 years of Gay Pride. One man recalled the first parade. 'We were jeered and spat at and you just knew the police wanted to have a go.' Now the marchers were cheered and clapped. As buses passed, they waved and whistled and the passengers responded in kind.

Adapted from *The Guardian* 4.3.1996, 5.3.1996, 15.7.1997.

Questions

1 The contact in Item A may result in reducing prejudice. Why?

2 How might the categories shown in Items B and C reduce prejudice and discrimination?

3 Look at Items D and E. How might they lead to a reduction in prejudice and discrimination?

4 The best strategy for reducing prejudice and discrimination is for those who experience them to fight back. Briefly discuss with reference to Item F.

References

Adorno, T.W., Frenkel-Brunswik, E., Levinson, D.J. & Sanford, R.M. (1950). *The authoritarian personality*. New York: Harper.

Allport, G.W. (1958). *The nature of prejudice*, New York: Doubleday Anchor.

Allport, G.W. & Postman, L. (1947). *The psychology of rumor*. New York: H. Holt & Company.

Aronson, E., Wilson, T.D. & Akert, R.M. (1999). *Social psychology* (3rd ed.). New York: Addison Wesley Longman.

Augoustinos, M. & Walker, I. (1995). *Social cognition: An integrated introduction*. London: Sage.

Augoustinos, M. (1999). Ideology, false consciousness and psychology. *Theory & Psychology, 9*, 295-312.

Barjonet, P.E. (1980). L'influence sociale et des representations des causes de l'accident de la route. *Travail Humain, 43*, 243-253.

Baron, R.A. & Byrne, D. (1997). *Social psychology* (8th ed.). Boston: Allyn and Bacon.

Bartlett, F. (1932). *Remembering: A study in experimental and social psychology*. Cambridge: Cambridge University Press.

Baxter, T.L. & Goldberg, L.R. (1988) Perceived behavioral consistency underlying trait attributions to oneself and another: An extension of the actor-observer effect. *Personality and Social Psychology Bulletin, 13*, 437-447.

Bernstein, W.M., Stephan, W.G., & Davis, M.H. (1979). Explaining attributions for achievement: A path analytic approach. *Journal of Personality and Social Psychology, 37*, 1810-1821.

Billig, M. (1976). *Social psychology and intergroups relations*. London: Academic Press.

Billig, M. (1991). *Ideology, rhetoric and opinions*. London: Sage.

Billig, M. (1992). *Talking about the royal family*. London: Sage.

Billig, M. (1996). *Arguing and thinking: A rhetorical approach to social psychology* (2nd ed.). Cambridge: Cambridge University Press.

Billig, M. (2001). Cognitive aspects of prejudice and the psychology of bigotry. *British Journal of Social Psychology*, forthcoming.

Brown, R. (1965). *Social psychology* (1st ed.). New York: Macmillan.

Brown, R. (1986) *Social psychology* (2nd ed.). New York: Free Press.

Brown, R. (1995). *Prejudice: Its social psychology*. Oxford: Blackwell.

Brown, S.D. & Lunt, P. (2002). A genealogy of the social identity tradition. *British Journal of Social Psychology*, forthcoming.

Campbell, D.T. (1967). Stereotypes and the perception of group differences. *American Psychologist, 22*, 817-829.

Clore, G.L. (1976). Interpersonal attraction: An overview. In J.W. Thilbaut, J.T. Spence & R.C. Carson (Eds.), *Contemporary topics in social psychology*. Morristown, NJ: General Learning Press.

Cook, S.W. (1962). The systematic analysis of socially significant events. *Journal of Social Issues, 18*, 66-84.

Crawford. R. (1984). A cultural account of 'health': Control, release, and the social body. In J.B. McKinlay (Ed.), *Issues in the political economy of health care*. New York: Tavistock.

Deaux, K. & Emswiller, T. (1974). Explanations of successful performance on sex-linked tasks: What is skill for the male is luck for the female. *Journal of Personality and Social Psychology, 29*, 80-85.

Dollard, J. (1938) Hostility and fear in social life. *Social Forces, 17*, 15-26.

Duncan, B.L. (1976). Differential social perception and attribution of intergroup violence: Testing the lower limits of stereotyping of blacks. *Journal of Personality and Social Psychology, 34*, 590-598.

Edwards, D. & Potter, J. (1992). *Discursive psychology*. London: Sage.

Eiser, J.R. (1986). *Social psychology: Attitudes, cognition and social behaviour. Cambridge*: Cambridge University Press.

Elliott, J. (1977). The power and pathology of prejudice. In P.G. Zimbardo & F.L. Ruch (Eds.), *Psychology and life*. New York: Scott Foreman.

Farr, R. (1987). Social representations: A French tradition of research. *Journal for the Theory of Social Behaviour, 17*, 343-369.

Fincham, F.D. & O'Leary, K.D. (1983). Causal inferences for spouse behaviour in maritally distressed and nondistressed couples. *Journal of Social and Clinical Psychology, 1*, 42-57.

Fiske, S.T. & Taylor, S.E. (1991). *Social cognition* (2nd ed.). New York: McGraw-Hill.

Fletcher, G.F.O. & Ward, C. (1988). Attribution theory and processes: A cross-cultural perspective. In M.H. Bond (Ed.), *The cross-cultural challenge to social psychology*. Newbury Park, CA: Sage.

Gaertner, S.L., Mann, J., Murrell, A. and Dovidio, J.F. (1989) Reducing intergroup bias: the benefits of recategorisation. *Journal of Personality and Social Psychology, 57*, 239-249.

Gaertner, S.L., Rust, M.C., Dovidio, J.F., Bachman, B.A. and Anastasio, P.A. (1993) The contact hypothesis: the role of a common ingroup identity on reducing intergroup bias. *Small Groups Research, 25*(2), 224-249.

Gilbert, G.M. (1951). Stereotype persistence and change among college students. *Journal of Abnormal and Social Psychology, 46*, 245-254.

Gilbert, D.T. & Malone, P.S. (1995). The correspondence bias. *Psychological Bulletin, 117*, 21-38.

Greenwald, A.G. & Banaji, M.R. (1989). The self as a memory system: Powerful, but ordinary. *Journal of Personality and Social Psychology, 57*, 41-54.

Hamilton, D.L. & Gifford, R.K. (1976). Illusory correlation in interpersonal perception: a cognitive basis of stereotypic judgements. *Journal of Experimental Social Psychology, 12*, 392-407.

Hamilton, D.L. & Sherman, S.J. (1989). Illusory correlations: Implications for stereotype theory and research. In D. Bar-Tal, C.F. Graumann, A.W. Kruglanski, & W. Stroebe (Eds.), *Stereotypes and prejudice: Changing conceptions*. New York: Springer-Verlag.

Haralambos, M. (1994). *Right on: From blues to soul in Black America*. Ormskirk: Causeway Press.

Haralambos, M. & Holborn, M. (2000) *Sociology: Themes and perspectives* (5th ed.). London: Collins Educational.

Heider, F. (1958). *The psychology of interpersonal relations*. New York: John Wiley.

Herzlich, C. (1973). *Health and illness*. London: Academic Press.

Hewstone, M. & Fincham, F. (1996). Attribution theory and research: Basic issues and applications. In M. Hewstone, W. Stroebe & G.M. Stephenson (Eds.), *Introduction to social psychology* (2nd ed.). Oxford: Blackwell.

Hewstone, M., Hopkins, N. & Routh, D.A. (1992). Cognitive models of stereotype change: Generalisation and subtyping in young people's views of the police. *European Journal of Social Psychology, 22,* 219-234.

Hogg, M.A. & Vaughan, G.M. (1995). *Social psychology: An introduction.* London: Prentice Hall/Harvester Wheatsheaf.

Jacobs, P. & Landau, S. (1971). *To serve the devil.* New York: Vintage Books.

Jacoby, R. & Glauberman, N. (Eds.) (1995). *The bell curve debate.* New York: Times Books.

Jahoda, G. (1988). Critical notes and reflections on 'social representations'. *European Journal of Social Psychology, 18,* 195-209.

Jodelet, D. (1991). *Madness and social representations.* Hemel Hempstead: Harvester Wheatsheaf.

Jones, E.E. & Davis, K.E. (1965). From acts to dispositions: The attribution process in social perception. In L. Berkowitz (Ed.), *Advances in experimental social psychology* (Vol. 2). New York: Academic Press.

Jones, E.E., Davis, K.E., & Gergen, K.J. (1961). Role playing variations and their informational value for person perception. *Journal of Abnormal and Social Psychology, 63,* 302-10.

Jones, E.E. & Harris, V.A. (1967). The attribution of attitudes. *Journal of Experimental Social Psychology, 3,* 1-24.

Jones, E.E. & Nisbett, R.E. (1972). The actor and the observer: Divergent perceptions of the causes of behaviour. In E.E. Jones, D.E. Kanouse, H.H. Kelley, R.E. Nisbett, S. Valins, & B. Weiner (Eds.), Attribution: *Perceiving the causes of behaviour.* Morristown, NJ: General Learning Press.

Karlins, M., Coffman, T.L. & Walters, G. (1969). On the fading of social stereotypes: Studies in three generations of college students. *Journal of Personality and Social Psychology, 13,* 1-16.

Katz, D. & Braly, K.W. (1933). Racial stereotypes of 100 college students. *Journal of Abnormal and Social Psychology, 28,* 280-290.

Kelley, H.H. (1967). Attribution theory in social psychology. In D. Levine (Ed.), *Nebraska symposium on motivation* (Vol. 15). Lincoln, Nebraska: University Of Nebraska Press.

Kelley, H.H. (1972). Causal schemata and the attribution process. In E.E. Jones, D.E. Karouse, H.H. Kelley, R.E. Nisbett, S. Valins & B. Weiner (Eds.), *Attribution: Perceiving the causes of behaviour.* Morriston, NJ: General Learning Press.

Krantz, S.E. & Rude, S. (1984). Depressive attributions: Selection of different causes or assignment of dimensional meanings. *Journal of Personality and Social Psychology, 47,* 193-203.

Lancaster, T. & Lancaster, S. (1995). *Britain and the world: The 20th century.* Ormskirk: Causeway Press.

LaPiere, R.T. (1934) Attitudes vs. actions. *Social Forces, 13,* 230-237.

Lupfer, M.B., Clark, L.F. & Hutcherson, H.W. (1990). Impact of context on spontaneous trait and situational attributions. *Journal of Personality and Social Psychology, 58,* 239-249.

Makeba, M. & Hall, J. (1988). *My story.* Bloomsbury: London.

Marks, G. (1984). Thinking one's abilities are unique and one's opinions are common. *Personality and Social Psychology Bulletin, 10,* 203-208.

Martin, E. (1990). Towards an anthropology of immunology: The body as nation state. *Medical Anthropology Quarterly, 4,* 410-23

Martin, E. (1992). The end of the body? *American Ethnologist, 19,* 121-40.

Martin, E. (1994). *Flexible bodies: Tracking immunity in American culture from the days of polio to the age of AIDS.* Boston: Beacon.

McArthur, L.A. (1972). The how and what of why: Some determinants and consequences of causal attribution. *Journal of Personality and Social Psychology, 2,* 171-93.

McKinlay, A. & Potter, J. (1987). Social representations: A conceptual critique. *Journal for the Theory of Social Behaviour, 17,* 471-478.

Miller, D.T. & Ross, M. (1975). Self-servicing biases in the attribution of causality: Fact or fiction? *Psychological Bulletin, 82,* 213-25.

Miller, J.G. (1984). Culture and the development of everyday social explanation. *Journal of Personality and Social Psychology, 46,* 961-978.

Moghaddam, F.M., Taylore, D.M., & Wright, S.C. (1993). *Social psychology in cross-cultural perspective.* New York: Freeman.

Moghaddam, F.M. (1998). *Social psychology: Exploring universals in social behaviour.* New York: Freeman.

Morris, M.W. & Peng, K. (1994). Culture and cause: American and Chinese attributions for social and physical events. *Journal of Personality and Social Psychology, 67,* 395-415.

Moscovici, S. (1976). La psychanalyse: *Son image et son public.* (2nd ed.). Paris: Presses Universitaires de France.

Moscovici, S. (1981). On social representation. In J. Forgas (Ed.), *Social cognition: Perspectives on everyday understanding.* London: Academic Press.

Moscovici, S. (1984). The phenomenon of social representations. In R.M. Farr & S. Moscovici (Eds.), *Social representations.* Cambridge: Cambridge University Press.

Moscovici, S. & Hewstone, M. (1983). Social representations and social explanations: From the 'naïve' to the 'amateur' scientist. In M. Hewstone (Ed.), *Attribution theory: Social and functional extensions.* Oxford: Blackwell.

Nisbett, R.E., Caputo, C., Legant, P., & Maracek, J. (1973). Behavior as seen by the actor and as seen by the observer. *Journal of Personality and Social Psychology, 27,* 154-64.

Nisbett, R.E. & Ross, L. (1980). *Human inference: Strategies and shortcomings of human judgement.* Englewood Cliffs, NJ: Prentice Hall.

Oakes, P.J., Haslam, S.A. & Turner, J.C. (1994). *Stereotyping and social reality.* Oxford: Blackwell.

Pettigrew, T.F. (1959) Regional difference in anti-negro prejudice. *Journal of Abnormal and Social Psychology, 59,* 28-56.

Potter, J. (1998). Discursive social psychology: *From attitudes to evaluations, European Review of Social Psychology, 9,* 233-266.

Reicher, S.D. (1996). 'The battle of Westminster': Developing the social identity model of crowd behaviour in order to explain the initiation and development of collective conflict. *European Journal of Social Psychology, 26,* 115-134.

Ross, L. (1977). The intuitive psychologist and his shortcomings: Distortions in the attribution process. In L. Berkowitz (Ed.), *Advances in experimental social psychology* (Vol.10). New York: Academic Press.

Ross, L., Greene, D., & House, P. (1977). The false consensus phenomenon: An attributional bias in self-perception and social perception processes. *Journal of Experimental Social Psychology, 13,* 279-301.

Ross, M. & Sicoly, F. (1979). Egocentric biases in availability and attribution. *Journal of Personality and Social Psychology, 37,* 322-37.

Sampson, E.E. (1993). *Celebrating the other: A dialogic account of human nature.* Hemel Hempstead: Harvester Wheatsheaf.

Schank, R. & Abelson, R.P. (1977). *Scripts, plans, goals and understanding.* Hillsdale, NJ: Lawrence Erlbaum.

Schoeneman, T.J. & Rubanowitz, D.E. (1985). Attributions in the advice columns: Actors and observers, causes and reasons. *Personality and Social Psychology Bulletin, 11,* 315-325.

Schofield, J.W. (1982). *Black and white in school: Trust, tension, or tolerance.* New York: Praeger.

Schuster, B., Forsterlung F., & Weiner, B. (1989). Perceiving the causes of success and failure: A cross-cultural examination of attributional concepts. *Journal of Cross-Cultural Psychology, 20,* 191-213.

Sherif, M., Harvey, O.J., Hood, W. & Sherif, C. (1961). *Intergroup conflict and cooperation: The Robber's Cave experiment.* Norman: University of Oklahoma, Institute of Intergroup Relations.

Shikanai, K. (1984). Effects of self-esteem and one's own performance on attribution of others' success and failure. *Japanese Journal of Experimental Social Psychology, 24,* 37-46.

Smith, P.B. & Bond, M.H. (1993). *Social psychology across cultures: Analysis and perspectives.* London: Harvester Wheatsheaf.

Spears, R., Haslam, S.A. & Jansen, R. (1999). The effect of cognitive load on social categorization in the category confusion paradigm. *European Journal of Social Psychology, 29,* 621-639.

Spears, R., Oakes, P.J., Ellemers, N., & Haslam, S.A. (Eds.) (1997). *The social psychology of stereotyping and group life.* Oxford: Blackwell.

Stainton Rogers, W. (1991). *Explaining health and illness: An exploration of diversity.* Hemel Hempstead: Harvester Wheatsheaf.

Stephan, W.G. (1978). School desegregation: An evaluation of predictions made in Brown vs. Board of Education. *Psychological Bulletin, 85,* 217-238.

Storms, M.D. (1973). Videotape and the attribution process. *Journal of Personality and Social Psychology, 27,* 165-175.

Svenson, O. (1981). Are we all less risky and more skilful than our fellow drivers? *Acta Psychologica, 47,* 143-148.

Tajfel, H. (1969). Cognitive aspects of prejudice. *Journal of Social Issues, 25,* 79-97.

Tajfel, H. (1981). *Human groups and social categories: Studies in social psychology.* Cambridge: Cambridge University Press.

Tajfel, H. & Turner, J.C. (1979). An integrative theory of intergroup conflict. In W.G. Austin & S. Worchel (Eds.), *The social psychology of intergroup relations.* Monterey, CA: Brooks/Cole.

Tajfel, H., Billig, M., Bundy, R.P., & Flament, C. (1971). Social categorization and intergroup behaviour. *European Journal of Social Psychology, 1,* 149-178.

Taylor, D.M., & Lalonde, R.N. (1987). Ethnic stereotypes: A psychological analysis. In L. Diedger (ed.), *Ethnic Canada: Identities and inequalities.* Toronto: Copp, Clark, Pitman.

Taylor, P., Richardson, J., Yeo, A., Marsh, I., Trobe, K. & Pilkington, A. (1995). *Sociology in focus.* Ormskirk: Causeway.

Taylor, S.E. (1981). The interface of cognitive and social psychology. In J. Harvey (Ed.), *Cognition, social behaviour and the environment.* Hillsdale, NJ: Erlbaum.

Tyerman, A. & Spencer, C. (1983). A critical test of Sherif's Robbers Cave experiments: Intergroup competition and cooperation between groups of well-acquainted individuals. *Small Group Behaviour, 14,* 515-531.

Vivian, J. & Brown, R. (1995). Prejudice and intergroup conflict. In M. Argyle & A.M. Colman (Eds.), *Social Psychology.* London: Longman.

Wagner, W., Elejabarrieta, F., & Lahnsteiner, I. (1995). How the sperm dominates the ovum: Objectification by metaphor in the social representation of conception. *European Journal of Social Psychology, 25,* 671-688.

Weiner, B. (1979). A theory of motivation for some classroom experiences. *Journal of Educational Psychology, 71,* 3-25.

Weiner, B. (1986). *An attributional theory of motivation and emotion.* New York: Springer-Verlag.

Wetherell, M. & Potter, J. (1992). *Mapping the language of racism: Discourse and the legitimation of exploitation.* Hemel Hempstead: Harvester Wheatsheaf.

White, P.A. (1988). *Causal processing: Origins and development. Psychological Bulletin, 104,* 36-52.

20 Relationships

▶ **Introduction**

'Any ongoing association between two or more individuals is considered a relationship.'
(Reis, 1996)

Humans are a social species. This means that relationships play a decisive role in our lives. Many of our most profound emotions – both good and bad – are experienced in the context of relationships. Myers (1992) claims that the evidence for a link between positive close relationships and happiness is so strong that it can be considered a 'deep truth'. Without relationships – with friends, family, colleagues and partners – many of us would feel that life has no meaning. Indeed, on this depressing note, there is convincing evidence that people who lack satisfying relationships risk poor mental and physical health (Lynch, 1977; Martin, 1998). Large-scale longitudinal studies, in which thousands of people are studied for a number of years, have found that people who are comparatively isolated from meaningful relationships are twice as likely to die during the course of the study than those with strong relationships (Berkman & Breslow, 1983; Berkman & Syme, 1979).

This chapter looks at how relationships are formed, maintained and dissolved, and how they are influenced by culture.

Chapter summary

- **Unit 1 outlines and assesses theories which seek to explain the formation of relationships.**
- **Unit 2 looks at theories and findings relating to the maintenance of relationships, and to their dissolution or breakdown, and summarises**

- social psychological work on love.
- **Unit 3 examines the question of the role of culture in shaping relationships, and discusses two forms of understudied relationship: 'electronic' relationships, and gay and lesbian relationships.**

Unit 1 The formation of relationships

KEY ISSUES

1 **What are the main theories of relationship formation?**
2 **What are their strengths and weaknesses?**

1.1 Thinking about relationship formation

Given the many people that we could potentially get to know, how come we only actually form relationships with a very small percentage of these? What is it, in other words, that leads us to form relationships? Is there some force, like gravity or magnetism, which causes some people to like one another, and not others?

Imagine a random cluster of people who are 'thrown' together. They have nothing in common except that they are all not involved in relationships. From this imagined 'new beginning' we can examine the relationships that do develop, and see if there are any *patterns*. To give a silly example, do tall people mix with tall people according to the 'birds of a feather flock together' hypothesis, or do tall mix with short according to the 'opposites attract' hypothesis? We would then want to work out what causes these patterns.

Notice that this way of thinking assumes that the formation of relationships is driven by causes which ordinary people are not necessarily aware of, but that can be discovered by

psychologists. Psychologists, in other words, do not typically accept 'common sense' explanations such as 'I became friends with Julie because I like her'. They might try to look instead for what causes this 'liking' of Julie. We now turn to some of these proposed causes, starting with the controversial role of physical attractiveness.

1.2 Physical attractiveness and the matching hypothesis

Often the first thing we notice about people is their physical attractiveness. This is an area that has preoccupied many social psychologists, and is often presented as a key factor in relationship formation, particularly in the formation of romantic or sexual relationships ('mate selection'). Although it is common sense that physical attractiveness has an impact on relationship formation, common sense also tells us that factors like character or personality play a key role. Indeed, folk wisdom tells us not to judge a book by its cover, implying that physical attractiveness is a comparatively superficial and deceptive thing. But could this be an example of common sense missing the true causes? Elliot Aronson suggested this when he said of early social psychologists that they were reluctant to study physical attraction since they were afraid of what they might find. So what did they find?

Testing the matching hypothesis

Walster et al. (1966) randomly paired over 700 first year

Minnesota students into 'blind-date' couples for a university dance (in fact, the pairing was not quite random, since in each case it was ensured that the man in the paired couple was taller than the woman). They were interested in testing a theory first suggested by Erving Goffman called the *matching hypothesis*. This theory predicts:

1 that people aspire to be in a romantic relationship with a partner who has a high level of *social desirability*. Somebody is 'socially desirable' if they have generally wished-for qualities such as a nice personality, wealth, status, intelligence, social skills, good looks, and so on.

2 this aspiration is tempered by the *perceived probability of attaining it*. In other words, we can't all expect to get the most desirable individual as our partner, and so we settle for someone who is roughly as socially desirable as we are.

If such considerations do indeed shape our desires, then it is likely that couples that do form will be roughly *matched* in terms of their social desirability.

Each of the 752 students in Walster et al's study had previously completed questionnaires measuring qualities such as personality, intelligence, attitudes and social skills. Their physical attractiveness was quickly and roughly assessed on entry to the dance. In line with the matching hypothesis, the prediction made was that participants would like their randomly allocated dancing partners more if they were well matched as a couple in terms of social desirability. During an intermission in the dance, participants were given a questionnaire asking how much they liked their partner, and whether they would like to see them again. To the surprise of the researchers, the predicted hypothesis was not supported. In fact, the only important factor in determining how much a partner was liked was their physical attractiveness. Regardless of social skills, intelligence or personality, it seems the better looking the dancing partner, the more he or she was liked (the effect occurred for both males and females).

As discussed in a review by Berscheid and Hatfield (1974), this finding of the inordinate importance of physical attractiveness in determining overall attractiveness has been backed up by several other studies (eg, Tesser & Brodie, 1971).

Evaluation of Walster et al's test of the matching hypothesis

The Walster et al. (1966) study is a classic in social psychology. Instead of taking place in the artificial environment of a laboratory, Walster et al. turned a 'real-life' event into a controlled study. However, we must be careful not to *overgeneralise* the importance of attraction on the basis of studies like these.

First, they concern only the very first stage of potential relationships. In later stages other factors are important.

Second, whilst we can almost instantly assess how physically attractive somebody is, other 'information' about them – such as their character or their intelligence – may take longer to reveal itself. 'Blind-date' studies set up a situation – a relatively noisy dance – which enhances the importance of physical attractiveness at the expense of other qualities. You are not likely to detect your dancing partner's subtle interpretation of great Russian literature whilst strutting your stuff on the dancefloor!

In short, in the absence of any other information about someone, it is unsurprising that people base their judgements on what they do have available.

Third, such studies by no means refute the matching hypothesis. Recall that this hypothesis holds that people will aspire to something as a result of its desirability combined with their perceived probability of attaining it. We might recognise that Brad Pitt is desirable, but we also recognise that we stand no chance of having him to ourselves – and so content ourselves with Paddy Brit from down the road. Hence a true test of the matching hypothesis must distinguish between *idealistic* choices ('in your dreams!') and realistic choices, since the process of matching will probably only occur in realistic choices. In reality, most of us realise that we would get rejected by the Brad Pitts of this world. The Walster et al. study, however, cuts out the possibility of being rejected by the desirable other since each person is magically allocated a partner, rather than having to go through the potentially embarrassing process of asking for a dance.

Fourth, other studies that do allow for rejection have provided support for the matching hypothesis. Huston (1973) asked male participants to choose a date from a selection of women judged of high, medium and low physical attractiveness. Generally, men preferred to date a highly physically attractive woman, but this was especially so when they were guaranteed acceptance from them. As we would expect from the matching hypothesis, men who were not guaranteed acceptance tended to believe that the better looking women would be more likely to reject them.

Key terms

Matching hypothesis *States that people aspire to be in a relationship with a partner who is socially desirable, but that this aspiration is balanced against the perceived probability of attaining it.*

Social desirability *A person is socially desirable if they have generally wished-for qualities such as a nice personality, wealth, status, intelligence, social skills and good looks.*

1.3 Evolutionary explanations

In asking *why* physical attractiveness seems to be so important in the formation of relationships, evolutionary psychologists draw upon a mass of biological knowledge, accumulated since Darwin's theory of evolution, which shows that natural selection operates to produce behaviour that will *maximise the reproductive success* of the organism (see pp 600-603 and 779-780). Like all species, humans are thought to work with an inherited, genetically organised repertoire of tactics and strategies that help to ensure survival and reproduction. If a man is 'turned on' by a healthy, young and attractive woman, the story goes, this will serve to enhance his chances of producing successful offspring, since youth and good looks are good signs of healthy reproductive potential. Singh (1993), for example, argues that men find a specific 'waist to hip ratio' attractive in women, where the waist is thinner than the hips: a ratio that bodes well for child-birth. From this perspective, the connection between good looks and attraction does not need to be learned, for it has been genetically *fixed* so that the attraction response occurs automatically.

Note that this example deals with what *males* find attractive. An important claim of evolutionary psychologists is that because men and women bring very different physiological mechanisms to the business of reproduction, so they have evolved separate strategies and tactics for maximising their reproductive success. Two such differences are:

- Males produce millions of sperm, whilst females produce comparatively few eggs.
- Males, in principle, need contribute very little in order to reproduce (only one of many sperm needs to fertilise a receptive egg), whereas females must go through a difficult and lengthy period of pregnancy, childbirth and lactation (producing milk and suckling the young).

These differences mean that any given female can have, in principle, far fewer children than any given male, and must 'invest' more biological energy into the children she has. It thus makes sense for females and males to operate with different strategies. Not only this, it is possible that the strategies of males and females may be at crossed purposes. Berkow (1989), for example, presents the argument that human females have evolved the strategy of aiming to pair sexually with carefully chosen, reliable males with good resources (since the number of children she can have is limited, and much of her time and energy will be spent in giving birth to, and rearing them). Males, by contrast, are genetically inclined to pair frequently with as many different females as possible. Both are seen as following the common evolutionary principle of maximising reproductive success, but given the different biological 'starting points', different paths are taken to the same end. The outcome of this is thought to be that males show a preference for young and attractive partners, whilst females desire partners who can provide material wealth and support, and are preoccupied with long-term relationships (Buss, 1988).

A major questionnaire study by Buss et al. (1990) involving over 10,000 participants from 37 different cultures found strong evidence that indeed females do rank things like 'good financial prospects', 'ambition' and 'industriousness' higher as attractive qualities in a mate than do males, whilst males rate 'physical attractiveness' as more important than do females. Also, males were generally found to prefer younger females, and females older men. Another study involving over 10,000 participants from the United States in a National Survey of Families and Households (Sprecher et al., 1994) backed up this finding that youth and physical attractiveness are ranked as more important by males than females, whilst earning potential matters more to females than males.

Evaluation of the evolutionary approach

The advantage of this approach is that it is firmly grounded in respectable biological science. But five related criticisms are typically raised.

Determinism If our relationship to rivals or mates is fixed in our biology, this means that we have little or no *choice* about the way we respond to these others: our emotional responses of pleasure or pain are more or less automatic. But for many people the choice of a partner or a friend involves a good deal of deliberation and weighing up of pros and cons.

Reductionism Such evolutionary arguments always involve the same simplifying moves. First complex social behaviour is reduced to sexual behaviour. Then sexual behaviour is reduced to a reproductive strategy. The meaning of life is simplified down to the spreading of genes. In the process simplifying generalisations are made about what males and females desire, and those desires are themselves then reduced to a single, monotonous motive: maximising reproductive success. In fact life, for most people, is more complicated and more richly diverse. But this diversity is typically avoided in evolutionary accounts. Gay men, for example, have been found (by Sergios and Cody, 1985, using Walster et al's 1966 'blind date' technique) to be just as interested in the good-looks of strangers as are heterosexual men and women, presumably without the interest in reproduction!

Speculation Although the arguments sound convincing and very scientific, in fact the genetic bases have not (yet?) been identified. It is important to remember that we are dealing with theoretical speculation and not fact.

Underplaying culture, history and socialisation Much to do with human relationships is learned and socially constructed, rather than fixed (see Unit 3). It is notable, for instance, that the findings of Buss et al. (1990) and Sprecher et al. (1994) that women typically desire earning potential whilst men desire youth and beauty would be predicted from both an evolutionary and a socialisation perspective. In other words, if, because of the way a society is arranged, women are economically dependent upon men, then it would go 'against the grain' if a woman did not desire to secure a man who could support her. We might predict from a socialisation perspective, however, that as societies become more 'gender equal', so desires will become more similar. The evolutionary perspective would predict no such change.

Essentialism and sexism Evolutionary theories are often accused of sexism, since they treat what many would consider typical selfish male sexual behaviour as if it was natural and normal. This reinforces Western patriarchal stereotypes by treating them as *essential* (natural and unchangeable) rather than simply as one (sexist) way of organising relationships. For example, from a feminist perspective, the type of gender-divided society described above (where men are 'bread-winners' and women 'trophies', 'home-makers' and 'baby-producers') is a sexist society that should be changed. In implying that such gender division is the natural and inevitable result of 'hard-wired' desires, evolutionists are seen as dressing up their sexism and political conservatism in scientific clothing.

Key term

Reproductive success *An organism that is able to reproduce itself efficiently helps to maintain the population of the species. Any feature of the organism that evolves to increase the chances of reproduction in a competitive environment increases reproductive success.*

1.4   The reinforcement/affect explanation

The *reinforcement/affect theory* (Byrne, 1971) is based on *conditioning* (see pp 610-616 and 792-794). Relationship formation is explained by the simple principle that we are attracted by what we like and repulsed by what we dislike.

'Affect' (emotion or feeling ranging from pleasure to pain) is the 'motor' of relationship formation since we 'like' things that generate positive affect, and 'dislike' negative affect. If true, relationships should always follow the path of maximum pleasure and minimum pain: 'It is simple but true, that we tend to like others when our emotions are positive and to dislike them when we are experiencing negative feelings, no matter what caused the emotions' (Baron & Byrne, 1997).

Hence familiarity, whether we know it or not, and all else being equal, generates positive affect. Unless something else causes negative affect, this will cause us to like those we see frequently, even though *they* were not strictly the cause of the positive affect. For example, Lott (1974) found that people who just happen to be present when we are rewarded are subsequently liked. The positive affect acted as a *reinforcer* – hence reinforcement/affect theory. Griffit and Guay (1969) found that participants who are told after a test that they are very creative expressed more liking both for the experimenter and for a bystander. Baron and Byrne (1997) present a lot of evidence which shows that we are attracted to those who are associated with positive things like our favourite music, happy films, and good news on the radio. Rozin, Millman and Nemeroff (1986) even found that a laundered shirt thought to have been worn by a disliked person was considered less desirable than the same shirt thought to have been worn by a liked person!

Evaluation of reinforcement/affect theory

Reinforcement/affect theory is concerned with socialisation and learning rather than with evolution. Like the evolutionary approach it is impressively scientific, giving clear definitions of terms, and laying out clear predictions, and it is supported by much evidence. Whereas evolutionary psychologists tend to argue that what we find pleasurable (a sexy mate) and painful (a threatening rival) has *already been fixed* through evolution, the reinforcement/affect model argues that we like things and people that have been *associated with* previous pleasures and dislike things and people *associated with* pain and distress. It hence covers much ground ignored by the evolutionary approach. However, there are a number of problems with reinforcement/affect theory. They include:

Reductionism and determinism For reinforcement/affect theorists, relationships are ultimately *reduced* down to the motor of the repetition of pleasurable behaviour and the avoidance of painful behaviour. This has the advantage of simplicity, but the disadvantage of over-simplification. It downplays the role of *thought* or cognition (as opposed to affect) in the formation of relationships. And it implies that we have no genuine *choice* – in other words it suggests that behaviour is *determined* by forces outside our control.

Limited application Reinforcement/affect theory seems to apply only to those relationships that we *choose* (ie, to voluntary as opposed to involuntary relationships). It is weak when it comes to family relationships, which we typically don't choose, and work relationships. Relationships with our mothers and fathers – or with our bosses for that matter – are not usually formed simply because they are associated with positive emotions. Generally, the theory underestimates the role that *culture* plays in shaping our relationships into pre-given patterns (see Unit 3).

Assumption of selfishness or 'hedonism' The reinforcement/affect approach presents a very self-centred picture of human beings. We like people for the pleasures we can get out of them and the pains they can help us to avoid. But do we really go through life like monstrous little hedonists aiming only for selfish pleasure and to further our own interests? If these were the only forces in play we would surely live in a pretty chaotic and disorderly world. Most of us recognise, for instance, that there must be 'give and take' in a relationship, as discussed in Unit 2.

Key term

Reinforcement/affect theory *A theory based on conditioning which holds that we are attracted to things and people that generate or are associated with positive affect (emotion), and repulsed by things and people that generate or are associated with negative affect.*

Activity 1   Relationship formation in theory

Item A   An evolutionary perspective

'Men seek to propagate widely, whereas women seek to propagate wisely.'
Robert Hinde

'She's beautiful and therefore to be woo'd.'
William Shakespeare

Item B   The reinforcement/affect model

In a study by Griffit and Veitch (1971), statements by strangers were presented to participants who were in either physically uncomfortable conditions (hot and crowded), or physically comfortable conditions. Results indicated that in the more uncomfortable conditions, the strangers were liked less.

Adapted from Hogg & Vaughan, 1995

May and Hamilton (1980) aroused affect with background music that had been rated by undergraduates as pleasant or unpleasant. Other participants – female undergraduates – were asked to make judgements about male strangers based on their photos. Each participant was shown the same photos. While they were making these judgements the researchers played either no music, pleasant music (rock), or unpleasant music (avant-garde classical) in the background. The women were asked to indicate how much they liked each man on the basis of his photograph. Compared to the no-music condition, students listening to the pleasant rock music liked the strangers better and even thought they were more physically attractive. The most negative evaluations of the strangers were made by participants listening to the unpleasant music.

Adapted from Baron & Byrne, 1997

Item C   Oscillating Wildley between both perspectives

'Beauty is a form of Genius – is, higher, indeed, than Genius, as it needs no explanation. It cannot be questioned. It has its divine right of sovereignty. It makes princes of those that have it… People say sometimes that Beauty is only superficial. That may be so. But at least it is not so superficial as Thought is… It is only shallow people who do not judge by appearances.'

From Oscar Wilde

Questions

1   Explain Item A from an evolutionary perspective.

2   Explain Item B from a reinforcement/affect perspective.

3   Explain Item C from both perspectives.

1.5   Other factors relevant to relationship formation

Proximity

Do people marry the boy or girl next door? There is evidence that *proximity*, or being physically near to people, is an important factor in the development of relationships.

Festinger, Schachter and Back (1950) took advantage of a situation where married college students in the United States were randomly allocated apartments in 17 University buildings. They asked each student to name their three closest friends, and found that 65% of friends lived in the same building and that 41% of next door neighbours were friends (compared to only 10% who lived on opposite sides of a hall). Those who had apartments at the foot of stairways or close to a mailbox had the most friends of all, since, the proximity argument goes, they physically came into contact with more people. Byrne and Buehler (1955) similarly found that students are more likely to become friends with those who sit next to them in class. Hence a key factor in relationship formation, so simple it is often overlooked, is proximity or physical 'nearness' .

Familiarity

Many studies have found that repeated exposure to things – faces, words, or whatever – leads these to be rated more positively (Moreland & Zajonc, 1982). This, of course, is a trick regularly used by advertisers, whose main mission is often simply to expose their product or brand name to an audience as often as possible. In a simple test of this 'mere exposure effect',

Mita et al. (1977) showed their participants two photographs of themselves: one a mirror image of the other. Most preferred the mirror image, whilst their close friends preferred the original photo. This fits the prediction that we are attracted to familiar things, since we, unlike our friends, are typically most familiar with the image of ourselves we see in the mirror. Interestingly, Bornstein and D'Agostino (1992) found that the mere exposure effect worked best when the viewer was presented stimuli at a speed too fast for conscious awareness (ie *subliminally*).

Similarity

Many studies have found that we are far more likely to form relationships with people who are similar to ourselves. Friends, for example, are likely to be of the same age, personality, race, marital status and sex (Hays, 1988). In a classic study, Newcomb (1956) gave out a battery of attitude questionnaires to 34 male college students from the USA. They were provided with free university accommodation in exchange for taking part in the study. Their attitudes to issues like religion, race relations and sexuality were collected before they met one another. After 15 weeks of living in the same housing block, Newcomb found that students expressed more liking for colleagues who shared their attitudes.

Newcomb enquired into who liked who in the group on a weekly basis. At first proximity seemed to matter most (people expressed liking for those who lived closest to them). But, by the end of the study, *similarity* had become the decisive factor. This study was particularly powerful since it followed an earlier one (Newcomb & Svehla, 1937) which had found a high degree of similarity of attitudes amongst a sample of married couples. This first study, however, was unable to tell us whether couples' attitudes became more similar as a *result* of marriage, or whether shared attitudes were a *cause* of the liking that led to marriage. The second study suggests the latter explanation.

The attraction paradigm Byrne (1971) refined the relationship between similarity and attraction using his *attraction paradigm*. Participants were presented with completed attitude questionnaires and asked whether they would like or dislike the stranger who completed them. In fact, the questionnaires had been completed by the experimenters, who varied the degree to which the fake stranger agreed or disagreed with the views of the participant (who had filled in their own questionnaire earlier!). The results of this experiment indicated that we like people in proportion to the amount of attitudes we share in common. For example, more liking is expressed for people who share three quarters of our attitudes than for those who share only half.

Byrne (1971) explains this similarity pattern using his reinforcement/affect theory. He argues that similarity increases attraction because it leads to positive affect by bolstering our view of things. Being agreed with, in other words, is a positively reinforcing experience, and having this positive affect leads us to like the person who agreed with us by holding similar views. Similarity may also be attractive since it can: a) reduce anxiety (Schachter, 1959), b) validate our beliefs (Rubin, 1973), c) provide the common ground necessary both for communication and for d), joint action (Rusbult & van Lange, 1996).

Self-disclosure and reciprocity

Self-disclosure (disclosing intimate information) has been shown to influence attraction in three ways (Collins & Miller, 1994):

- Effect 1 – Those who engage in 'intimate disclosures' (like explaining how you feel) are generally liked more than those who don't (or do so less).
- Effect 2 – People disclose more to those they like in the first place.
- Effect 3 – The act of self-disclosure makes us like the person we are speaking to.

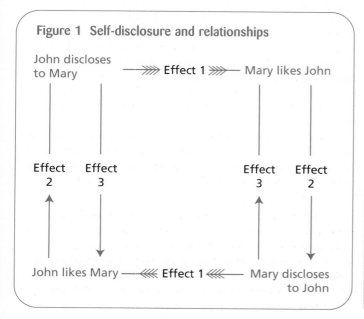

Figure 1 Self-disclosure and relationships

John discloses to Mary ⟫⟫ Effect 1 ⟫⟫ Mary likes John

Effect 2   Effect 3   Effect 3   Effect 2

John likes Mary ⟪⟪ Effect 1 ⟪⟪ Mary discloses to John

Figure 1 indicates that self-disclosure works best when it is *reciprocal* (as when John tells Mary about his work anxieties and Mary reciprocates by disclosing how sad she is about her father's illness). Curtis and Miller (1986) conducted a study to test more generally the 'reciprocity principle' – that we like people better if we think they like us. They observed strangers interacting together. Some of the participants had been told that the person they were talking to liked them (condition A). Others were told the stranger had evaluated them negatively (condition B). Although in fact no such evaluations had been made, participants in condition A made more eye contact, spoke more warmly and positively, and were generally more friendly in their interactions. However, it seems we especially like those who are critical of us at first, but then come to like us (Aronson & Linder, 1965).

Key terms

Proximity *Sometimes called 'propinquity', proximity means simply 'nearness in space'. It can be an important influence on who forms relationships with whom.*

Familiarity *There is evidence that we like those with whom we are familiar. If no other forces are in play, familiarity may be an important factor in relationship formation.*

Similarity *There is convincing evidence suggesting that people who are similar to one another are more likely to be attracted and form relationships.*

Self-disclosure *Telling other people intimate or personal information about ourselves.*

Reciprocity *Something is 'reciprocated' if it is returned in kind. A smile is reciprocated with a smile, a gift with a gift, an insult with an insult, or a self-disclosure with a self-disclosure. People tend to like reciprocation in relationships.*

1.6 Evaluation and conclusion

For critically-minded people, the above list of how relationships are formed may appear somewhat partial and even a bit trivial. This is paradoxically because social psychologists have concentrated on trying to discover general laws and principles that apply to everybody. This has confined them to experimental studies that are good at simplifying and clarifying the causal connections between narrowly defined variables, but poor at grasping the richness and complexity involved in relationships. The situation is summed up by the Sufi proverb about the man who looks for his lost key only in the small pool of light shed by a street lamp, and not in the dark bushes where it is likely to be found. To be fair, many interesting things have been found, but what is lacking is an agreed overall picture.

Byrne's attraction paradigm, for example, is very artificial. It strips away the context within which we usually meet people, and the subtle reciprocal process we usually go through in finding out one another's viewpoints. Is it so surprising that people base their judgements of liking on attitude similarity when they are given no other information with which to form a judgement? Byrne's findings on similarity, although robust, by no means exclude the other possibility, favoured by Winch (1958), that we are also attracted to people with qualities which are complementary to our own.

There has also been a focus on a very limited variety of relationships. The studies tend to focus on relationships between young friends – the type of relationship that can be entered into and exited from *voluntarily* without much fuss. Most relationships are not like this. Family relationships, for example, are largely *involuntary* – most of us are stuck with them – and the various theories of relationship formation do not apply very well to these. Nor do they apply very well to the formation of most *work relationships*, which are often hierarchical and involve clear relations of power (such as teacher/student, employer/employee, manager/worker).

Finally, most of the classic research discussed in Unit 1 was conducted in North America using US students as participants. There is a danger in generalising from such a limited population. The way US students think about attraction or similarity may not be the way other people do.

Summary

1 Various factors are involved in the formation of relationships, including physical attraction, proximity, familiarity, similarity, self-disclosure and reciprocity.

2 The importance of physical attractiveness was established by the Walster et al. (1966) study, although this cannot be taken as having disproved the 'matching hypothesis'.

3 The two dominant theories in the field are the reinforcement/affect theory (which holds that the above factors cause the formation of relationships because they generate positive affect) and the evolutionary approach (which explains social relationships in terms of reproductive strategies which have evolved to enhance the organism's chances of successfully mating, conceiving and passing on genes).

4 Both the evolutionary, and the reinforcement/affect perspective tend towards determinism and reductionism.

5 Research on relationships has been criticised for sacrificing the complexity of what goes on in actual social interactions for the simplicity of controllable experimental conditions.

Unit 2 Maintenance and dissolution of relationships

KEY ISSUES

1 **What are the main theories explaining the maintenance of relationships?**

2 **What is love, and how do we know?**

3 **What makes relationships break up?**

2.1 The maintenance of relationships

This section deals with theories and findings about what makes for stable relationships. The two main forms of explanation discussed in Unit 1 – evolutionary theory and reinforcement/affect theory – both hold that people are motivated to form relationships out of self-interest. But for a relationship to last, according to this selfish logic, both parties need to 'get something' from the 'deal'. A relationship must involve give and take. Talk of 'give and take' is talk of *exchange*, and *exchange theories*, of various kinds, have been central to the social psychology of relationship maintenance.

Exchange theory

Social exchange theory (Homans, 1961) is the most basic version of exchange theory. All human relationships are seen as business transactions wherein the 'merchants' – motivated by self-interest – strive to get the best possible deal (the best 'outcome'). The best outcome is to make a 'profit' (ie an outcome wherein rewards are higher than costs). The so-called *minimax strategy* thus states that we aim for the outcome of minimum costs and maximum rewards in our dealings with others. Homans was well aware that his theory is not the way most of us would *like* to think of ourselves. He liked to think of his theory as brutally honest and provocative.

Anything that is valued can be exchanged. For example, if an ugly rich man values beauty in a woman and a beautiful poor woman values money in a man, then we can see a relationship between the two as an exchange. Homans was a behaviourist and so, as in the reinforcement/affect theory, the bottom line is that we repeat that which rewards us, and avoid that which punishes us with 'costs'. This means, importantly, that what counts as a reward or a cost cannot be defined in advance: if you find it unpleasant, it is a cost, if pleasant, a reward. There is no reason to assume that everyone will find the same *value* in the same things. Indeed the same person may value the same thing differently at different times (food is valued more when hungry, for example). 'Cost' for Homans is in fact a little more complicated, since it also includes what he calls 'value foregone'. For example, spending your time with X means that you are foregoing spending that time with Y and Z, and this hidden cost needs to be taken into account when making your 'outcome' calculation.

Social exchange theory enables us to predict that, all else being equal, an individual will stay in a relationship only as long as it generates sufficiently positive outcomes. However, as value is 'subjective', we cannot know in advance what will count as a *sufficiently positive outcome*, and each individual judges this on the basis of their experience. This is a problem for testing the theory, since it makes it difficult to objectively measure 'value'.

Equity theory

Equity theory (Messick & Cook, 1983, Walster, Walster & Berscheid, 1978) states that people are unhappy in a relationship that they perceive as being unfair. The theory holds that an exchange is judged as fair if the ratio of perceived inputs (costs) to rewards is the same for both. So if Nick is seen to put a lot in and get a lot out of his relationship with Simon, and Simon is seen to put little in but get little out, then this is still 'fair' because the ratio of inputs to outcomes (costs to rewards) is the same. A 'fair' relationship is a stable relationship because it is balanced. Of course, if Nick is seen to put a lot in and get only a little out, and Simon is seen to put a little in and get a lot out, then this would not be fair (Nick would be *underbenefited* and Simon *overbenefited*). In these examples I say 'is seen' because it is the subjectively perceived inputs and outcomes that matter, since there is no objective measure of what is a cost or a reward in a relationship.

Equity theory differs from exchange theory in holding that people strive for fairness in relationships, and not just personal gain. It predicts not only that those who get a bad deal from 'one-sided' relationships will be unhappy (the underbenefited), but also the overbenefited who get an unfair good deal will be unhappy (since the theory holds that we aim for fairness). Such a relationship would be out of balance and hence potentially unstable. The overbenefited should feel uncomfortable and guilty, and the underbenefited should feel hurt and hard-done-by (Sprecher, 1986). There are two ways to restore equilibrium to an unstable (unfair) relationship. Either:

1   The inputs and outcomes must be changed (Nick could put less in or Simon could put more in), or

2   The participants must change their perception of the situation (Simon might convince Nick that actually Simon does put a lot into the relationship).

Buunk and van Yperen (1991) have indeed found that married people who perceive their relationships as equitable were most content with them and those who felt underbenefited were least satisfied (those who felt overbenefited fell in the middle). They also found evidence that women in their sample tended to restore equity (when underbenefited) by having affairs. In an earlier large-scale study (736 participants), van Yperen and Buunk (1990) found the same predicted relationship between satisfaction and equity, but found that being overbenefited led to dissatisfaction only for women. They also found that twice as many women as men felt underbenefited, and more men than women felt overbenefited. Taken together, these findings suggest that women may be more concerned with equity in relationships than men.

Exchange vs communal relationships Clark and Mills (1993) argue, however, that close relationships like marriages and intimate friendships are not governed by rules of equity. They argue for a difference between:

Exchange relationships – where things are exchanged in a 'business like' way according to equity rules, ie a benefit for a benefit, and

Communal relationships – where people care about the happiness and needs of the other and are less concerned about equity.

Clark and her colleagues ran experiments where participants met an attractive stranger and were told either that this stranger is new to the area and looking for friends, or that they are married and briefly visiting the area. Participants in the second group tended to treat the stranger according to equity concerns whilst those in the first group interacted in a more communal way (extending kindness with no expectation of repayment).

Close relationships Aron et al. (1991) claim that equity becomes less of a concern the closer a relationship gets. In exchange relationships, what is at issue are the goods being exchanged (we are typically less interested in the shopkeeper than in the product we buy from them), and fairness is required. In communal relationships, such equity concerns may even *interfere* with what is at issue – namely the relationship itself. Hence we may signal our intimacy by displaying that we are *not* concerned with our 'costs' and 'benefits' (eg, we take the price-tag off gifts between friends). In fact, we often like to display that we are less interested in the *product* our lover gives us as a present, than in the fact that they gave us a *gift*. It is the 'thought' that counts, we say, and that thought is about the relationship. Indeed, in a close *relationship*, returning a favour or reciprocating a gift too quickly can be seen as a sign of ingratitude (Bourdieu, 1991). But this does not necessarily mean that equity is no longer a useful concept. It could be that being more relaxed about the *speed* of reciprocity is a sign that the relationship has moved to another, more committed, level (Batson, 1993).

Interdependence theory

Once a relationship is formed, people who were at one time independent of one another become increasingly *interdependent* on one another. What one feels, says or does may depend on what the other feels, says or does. It is often the case that this intertwining of lives leads to the blurring of boundaries between self and partner, so that a new 'joint' identity emerges (Aron et al. 1991). Interdependence theory (eg Thibaut & Kelley, 1959, Rusbult & van Lange, 1996) studies the *forms* that interdependence takes. The basic form of interdependence is the exchange relationship described above, where individuals are motivated by self-interest and interact to maximise their own outcomes (MaxOwn). Thibaut and Kelley (1959) called this the *given matrix*. But other forms of interdependence also occur which need not be driven by immediate self-interest, such as:

- Cooperation – a motivation to maximise *both* people's outcomes (MaxJoint)
- Altruism – a motivation to selflessly provide for the other (MaxOther)
- Nihilism – a motivation to minimise outcomes for both (MinJoint).

As these depart from the 'given matrix', Thibaut and Kelley (1959) refer to them as 'effective matrices'. Which 'effective matrix' is adopted (and there are many more than the three above) depends on the situation. Interpersonal situations are seen to vary in respect to four properties:

1   **Degree of dependence** To what extent are a person's positive

and negative outcomes dependent on their partner's actions? For instance, to rely upon the actions of a partner to satisfy important needs is to be dependent. There is evidence that those who are dependent are less likely to end their relationship, more likely to be jealous, and more likely to express commitment (Rusbult & van Lange, 1996). This is hence an important factor in relationship stability.

2   **Mutuality of dependence** Are both partners equally dependent on one another (mutual dependence), or does one need the relationship more than the other to achieve their outcomes (unilateral dependence)? Mutually dependent relationships tend to be more stable (Rusbult & van Lange, 1996). There is also evidence for a 'principle of least interest', where the partner who is less interested in the relationship continuing is more likely to dictate the terms of the relationship (Huston et al., 1986).

3   **Correspondence of outcomes** To what extent do both partners value the same outcomes? Do their wishes and preferences correspond or conflict? Where they conflict, relationships are more likely to be stormy, competitive and hostile (Rusbult & van Lange, 1996).

4   **Basis for dependence** Do both partners feel that they jointly control their outcomes ('it's up to us'), or do they feel that their fate depends on the whim of the other? The latter is more likely to lead to an interdependence situation governed by principles of exchange as opposed to cooperation.

In asking 'what makes for a stable relationship?' interdependence theory distinguishes between *satisfaction level* and *level of dependence*. One person may be perfectly satisfied with a relationship, but still leave it for a better alternative ('satisfied but not dependent'), whilst another may be unsatisfied yet their relationship remains stable since they depend on it and have no alternatives. This 'dependent but not satisfied' pattern is often tragically the case with wives who remain with abusive husbands (Rusbult & van Lange, 1996). The following two concepts from Thibaut and Kelley (1959) are central to interdependence theory:

- Satisfaction and Comparison Level: When judging how *satisfying* and attractive a relationship is, people are thought to *compare* their relationship against their expectations and past experiences. This is called their *comparison level* (CL).
- Dependence and Comparison Level for Alternatives: When deciding whether to *remain* in a relationship they take *dependency* into account by drawing upon their *comparison level for alternatives* (CL-alt), defined by Thibaut and Kelley (1959) as 'the lowest level of outcomes a member will accept in the light of available alternative opportunities'.

Rusbult (1983) adds a third factor, *investment,* to her 'investment model' of what leads to commitment in relationships. Hence commitment depends upon:

1   The degree to which the relationship is *satisfying* (determined by the CL)

2   The degree of *dependence* on the relationship (determined by the CL-alt)

3   The *investment size* ('how much time, effort and resources have I put in to this relationship?')

Rusbult's version of interdependence theory therefore suggests that the more someone has put into a relationship, the more committed that person will feel. 'Investments' include things like time, energy, personal information as well as material things like

shared possessions and children. Once invested, such things cannot be easily 'taken out', and so are mostly lost if a relationship ends. Hence Rusbult claims that the greater our investment, the greater our commitment to the relationship in order to protect that investment. As you might expect, concern with better alternatives becomes less important as more investments are made in an existing relationship. This makes sense of why people involved in romantic relationships tend to find other potential partners less attractive (Simpson, Gangstad & Lerma, 1990).

2.2 Evaluation of exchange, equity and interdependence theory

- Social exchange theory is positive because it provokes us into seeing the extent to which economic concepts such as exchange, cost, profit and investment have a deep influence on our relationships. It shares with reinforcement/affect theory, and with evolutionary theory, the notion that we are motivated by self-interest. It differs in that it holds that we rationally *calculate* the most rewarding course of action (as opposed to being 'driven' by learned or innate affect). It paints a cynical picture of people as parasites, rationally calculating ways to take as much as they can from others, whilst giving nothing back, unless it benefits them to do so.

- Interdependence theory and equity theory view relationships as potentially *symbiotic* (mutually benefiting) rather than simply *parasitical*. Equity theory holds that people are motivated to make things *fair,* and interdependence theory gives detailed attention to the ways in which people in relationships become dependent upon one another to satisfy their needs. Both view relationships over a longer time-scale. In the long-term, it is more rational (and more in our self-interest) to be symbiotic than parasitical, since ultimately the parasite *depends upon* its host.

- A key problem with exchange and equity theory is that each overgeneralises – they tend to see behaviour as universal and general rather than particular and specific. We do indeed engage in self-centred *exchanges*, but not in *all* spheres of our lives. Likewise we do indeed worry about *fairness*, but not in *all* spheres of our lives. A master, for example, may take everything from a slave (even his life), and give almost nothing in return. And yet the relationship between two masters may be based on strict rules of equity. Although interdependence theory points in more fruitful directions, social psychologists have generally been less successful at the more difficult task of showing how these different specific ways of acting are linked together.

- The problem with Rusbult's investment model is that, in practice, it reduces the unpredictable complexity of ordinary life down to a handful of simplified variables like 'satisfaction', 'commitment' and 'investment'. In fact, each of these is a highly complex concept and, despite the cleverest experimental design, they are not independent of one another (finding another person attractive may itself decrease perceived investment size in a marriage). Rather than being causal factors which 'underlie' relationships, things like commitment and satisfaction can be seen as part of the stories people tell themselves, and one another, about what they are doing, where they are going, and why (Curt, 1994).

- All three theories are ultimately based upon the idea that we rationally calculate courses of action that maximise our self-interest. Self-interest is hence at the heart of these approaches, yet it is difficult to *define* self-interest in advance, since, as we have seen, it is a *subjective* and flexible concept.

- A final problem is that these theories give insufficient

attention to the role of culture in influencing perceptions of 'fairness' and 'self-interest' in different relationships, and of what counts as 'valuable' inputs and outcomes. The influence of culture on relationships is examined in Unit 3.

Activity 2 Giving and taking

Pippa sat gazing out of the kitchen window thinking about her marriage to Ernie. When they'd married ten years ago she'd felt so proud of him. What a relief it had been to make the difficult decision of choosing Ernie over Gavin. She remembered her surprise when Ernie had proposed to her one rainy afternoon in Stratford. She'd been seeing Gavin for over a year and had no idea of Ernie's feelings. Although he was sweet, Gavin didn't seem to be going anywhere, and had a lot of problems with his self-esteem. 'What are you doing with me?', he'd ask her, 'you're beautiful, sexy, rich and well educated, and me... I'm none of those things.' At first she had told him not to be so silly, but after a while she began to believe that he was right. Gavin used to do everything for her. He'd pick her up at work everyday, cook her meals and attend to her every whim. Whilst in the beginning she'd found this flattering and endearing, she came to resent it as time went on. Also Melanie, Pippa's best friend, couldn't stand Gavin, and somehow this influenced Pippa's feelings. Melanie would complain about Pippa's 'low standards' and say that this was because she had been treated badly by lovers in the past. So she accepted tall, dark and handsome Ernie, and all was fine in their little flat for the first year or so. But, she sighed to herself, 'happy ever after' it was not. Here she is with two screaming kids, a pile of washing up, a week's worth of laundry, and unlike Gavin, Ernie never seems to lift a finger to help. When he's not out looking for work, he's down the pub, in front of the telly, or out watching Arsenal. What little money they have, she earns by waiting at table in a greasy-spoon cafe. 'It's just not fair', she moans.

Questions

Using the key concepts from the theories, explain the above story from the perspective of:

1   exchange theory

2   equity theory

3   interdependence theory.

2.3 Love

The concept of love is at the core of many major religions, including Christianity. This is a fact that John Lennon was enthusiastically aware of when he and the other Beatles offered up the anthem *All you need is love*. For many, including several psychologists, love represents an almost miraculous reversal of the usual, monotonous story of self-interest. Hence Lewis (1960) drew a distinction between 'love' based on need and self-interest ('deficit love') and genuine love which is given freely ('gift love'). Maslow (1962) made a similar distinction between D-love (a basically selfish love based upon a psychological deficiency) and B-love (a 'true' love given freely by a 'self-actualised' person). The same message of true love as selfless giving is implied in Sperling's (1985) distinction between 'desperate love' and 'mature love'.

Actual empirical studies into the nature of love have revealed a more complicated picture. The early work of Zick Rubin

(1970) distinguished 'liking' from 'loving', the latter containing three components: *attachment* (involving passion and possessiveness), *caring* (involving concern for the other) and *intimacy* (involving the reciprocal exchange of personal information, feelings and actions). Berscheid and Walster (1974) developed this into a distinction between:

- *Passionate love*: which involves strong, consuming arousal, and is typical of the initial stages of a love relationship.

- *Companionate love*: which is an extension of 'liking', but with more interdependency.

Lee's (1973) work on 'love styles' complicated matters by identifying three distinct *ways of loving*, each of which can combine with the others to generate a rich menu of 'love styles'.

Eros – love is based on an image of an ideal lover. It starts with strong, immediate attraction and involves intense and satisfying lovemaking.

Ludus – love is a kind of game where partners are often 'played off' one another. An element of uncertainty is often introduced to 'spice up' the game.

Storge – love develops slowly but deeply and is very 'companionate'.

Mania – a combination of *eros* and *ludus* yields an obsessional and jealous love which is passionate and consuming.

Agape – a combination of *eros* and *storge* yields a deeply devoted and selfless love that always places the needs of the loved one before those of the lover.

Pragma – a combination of *ludus* and *storge* yields a practical and strategic love that calculates its self-interest carefully before choosing a lover.

This typology, as measured by Hendrick and Hendrick's (1992) *love attitudes* scale, has given rise to some interesting findings, such as that men are typically more *erotic* and *ludic*, and women more *storgic*, *pragmatic* and *manic*. Religious

people tend to endorse storge, pragma and agape and reject ludus and mania, and those with high self-esteem are more likely to endorse eros and reject mania (Hendrick & Hendrick, 1992).

Currently the most popular theory is that of Sternberg (1986), who proposed a triangular model with *intimacy* at one vertex of the triangle, *commitment* at a second, and *passion* at the third (these are similar to Rubin's components of intimacy, caring and attachment, described above). A balanced combination of all three yields the ideal love that Sternberg calls *consummate love*. If *passion* is missing the outcome is *companionate love* (intimacy + commitment), whereas if *only* passion is present *infatuation* is the result. If only commitment is missing, the outcome is *romantic love* (intimacy + passion), which is roughly equivalent to Berscheid and Walster's (1974) 'passionate love'. If only intimacy is present, we have something approximating Rubin's (1970) 'liking'. The various other combinations are shown in the diagram in Activity 3.

Activity 3   Love triangles and love styles

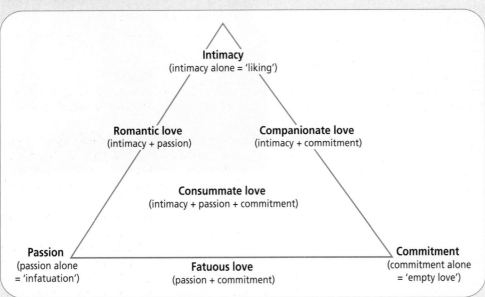

Questions

1   Study Sternberg's 'love triangle'. Which, if any, of Sternberg's love types correspond to Lee's 'love styles'? How are they similar and different?

2   How might the same person experience different types of love at different times?

3   How might two people in the same relationship each experience different types of love?

4   Suggest advantages and disadvantages of Sternberg's and Lee's theories.

2.4   Evaluation of love research

These various theories of love are thought provoking, and some useful typologies have been proposed, each of which has been supported with empirical data. However:

- The theories remain largely descriptive (they do not explain love).
- There is no agreed way of deciding which offers the best description.
- None of these theories adequately addresses the possibility of cultural and historical variation in the experience of love. This is a problem since the meaning and personal significance of 'love' can be radically different in different times and places. For the ancient Greeks one of the highest forms of love was that between a boy and an older man (and

this was often sexual – Vernant, 1996); within Hindu India there is a strong tradition of arranged marriage wherein it is not unusual to marry somebody you have never met; and for Shiite Muslim men it is not unusual to have four wives and a large string of 'temporary wives' (Moghaddam, 1998). In twelfth century France, ladies and viscountesses gathered in court society to reach judgements about questions of love – the Countess of Champagne and others, for example, decided in such a court that true love between married couples cannot exist! (Stendhal, 1980). Ugandans, Senegalese and USA engineering students tend to think of love as a calming force to be thought about carefully whilst South Africans (black and white) are more likely to think of it as a powerful passionate force (Smith & Bond, 1993). The statement 'lovers should freely confess everything of personal significance to each other' was agreed with by 75%

of Germans, 53% of North Americans, and only 25% of Japanese (Simmons et al., 1986, 1989). LeVine et al. (1995) found that when asked the question: 'If a man (woman) had all the other qualities you desired, would you marry this person even if you were not in love with him (her)' around 50% of young people in India and Pakistan replied 'yes' compared with only 3.5% in the USA and 7.3% in the UK.

2.5 Relationship dissolution

Between a half and a third of all marriages in Western societies end in divorce (Holmes, 2000). Given the investments and commitments put into such relationships, it is no surprise that their dissolution is often experienced as highly traumatic by all concerned, children included. So why so much breakup? Huston and Vangelisti (1991) found that married couples report a steep drop in satisfaction shortly after marriage. Worse, this decline in satisfaction appears to continue for at least 10 years, and often longer (Glen & Weaver, 1988).

But as interdependence theory suggests, satisfaction is not the only factor. Holmes (2000) draws upon data to suggest that the rise in divorce rate followed the weakening of external barriers to dissolution: divorce in the Western world is now easier and more socially acceptable, and hence makes less of a 'statement'. People, especially financially independent and well-educated women, are now less likely to stay in an unhappy marriage. Also, Holmes (2000) reports that having 'good alternatives' to a marriage is a better predictor of dissolution than is dissatisfaction. It seems that the key player in determining a breakup is the one who is dissatisfied and has 'other options'.

Spirals of escalating negativity

Holmes (2000) discusses evidence that suggests that dissatisfied couples are more likely to engage in 'negative reciprocity' or 'tit for tat' behaviour. This can make a bad situation worse and escalate a conflict, speeding a relationship to dissolution. An example is the *transgression-complaint-defence set*, where one person does something 'wrong' (eg, forgets to make the bed or some other *transgression*), the other complains ('that's typical lazy behaviour!') leading the other to defend ('you're always nagging me!'). This constructs an unhappy situation where partners treat each other as opponents 'cross-complaining' to one another, and refusing to 'hear' the other's version. Another pattern which forecasts a decline in satisfaction is the *demand/withdraw set*, where one partner (usually the male) responds to a demand by withdrawing and avoiding the situation. This may have the short-term advantage of avoiding an escalation of negativity, but it has the long-term disadvantage of reducing communication.

An important aspect of situations of spiralling conflict are the *construals* made by the participants, who come to *view* each other more as enemies in conflict than cooperating friends. Gottman (1979) coined the phrase *negative mindreading* to convey the way in which unhappy partners read negative motives into their partner's actions. He also found such couples engage in 'character assassination', where the negative actions of their partner are interpreted as 'just the kind of thing such a nasty person does'.

Research on construals or 'social cognition' has been developed within an attribution theory framework (Bradbury &

Fincham, 1990). Compared to satisfied partners, unsatisfied couples make *distress maintaining attributions*. That is, when something negative happens (Melinda forgets to make the bed, for instance), *satisfied* couples tend to minimise this by attributing it to 'specific', 'unstable' and 'situational' causes ('she was in a rush to get to the interview'), whereas *unsatisfied* couples tend to maximise it by making 'global', 'stable' and 'internal' attributions ('that's typical of lazy good-for-nothings like Melinda'). On the other hand, when something positive happens (Mark buys Melinda flowers), *satisfied* couples tend to maximise this with 'global', 'stable' and 'internal' attributions ('that's typical of the kind of thoughtful, loving man Mark is') whereas *unsatisfied* couples tend to minimise it with 'specific', 'unstable' and 'situational' causes ('he's feeling guilty for being so insensitive last night, and is trying to get into my good books'). Such findings are relevant to both the maintenance and the dissolution of relationships, since such patterns of attribution predict future satisfaction (Bradbury & Fincham 1990).

Key term

Escalating negativity *Negative feelings and actions of one partner in a relationship have a tendency to be reciprocated with negative feelings and actions of the other. This can lead to an escalation or rapid increase in negativity.*

Phases of dissolution

Although each breakup is unique, there appear to be some general patterns. Duck (1986) has proposed five phases of dissolution.

1 In the *breakdown phase* at least one of the partners gets unhappy about the relationship. This must reach a point where they tell themselves, 'I can't stand this anymore'. Once this 'threshold' is reached they move to the second *intrapsychic phase*.

2 'Intrapsychic' means 'in the head'. At this stage the unhappy partner broods over the relationship, rehearsing dissatisfactions 'in their head', but keeping it to themselves. This phase ends when they start to complain openly, not to their partner, but to other people. They cross a second threshold when, having thought about it themselves, and having got some support from friends, they can tell themselves 'I'd be justified in leaving...'.

3 The *dyadic phase* involves the difficult task of confronting the partner with these dissatisfactions, and raising the question of the future of 'the relationship' (eg, trying to negotiate the grounds for a new shared story: 'I care for you, but I really don't think this is going anywhere'). If 'repairs' are not made – if a new 'success story' is not agreed upon – then the threshold between this phase and the next is represented by a statement such as 'I'm serious about splitting up'.

4 This ushers in the *social phase* where family and friends are told about the breakup and the social network changes accordingly (some friends supporting one partner's story, some the other, some both).

5 Finally, there is the *grave-dressing phase* where the now dead relationship is 'buried', and given a place in the continuing story of each ex's personal history.

How the part is played – active and passive, breaker and breakee

Duck's phases represent the typical 'plot' of a breakup story, but by no means apply to everyone (the stories would be different in different cultures, and for different relationships). Many people simply leave a relationship and say very little (Lee, 1984), and many relationships split in a cloud of rage and passion because of infidelity and jealousy.

As Rusbult and Zembrodt (1983) make clear, not everyone responds in the same way to the crisis of dissolution. Some, wishing to be the author of their own story, take an *active* role in steering things (either to salvage the relationship or to speed up its end), and some take a *passive* role (either waiting loyally for things to improve, or simply neglecting things so that the relationship declines without them needing to do anything explicit). The tendency to behave passively is perhaps a way of avoiding being judged badly for actively spoiling things.

The person who is left when a romantic relationship breaks up (the 'breakee') may also play a very different role to the person who leaves (the 'breaker'). Akert (1992), found that breakees tend to be considerably more upset about the ending of a relationship than breakers. In a study of 344 USA college students, Akert found that breakees suffer from more physical symptoms like upset stomachs, disrupted sleeping and eating, and stress, and also more depression and anger.

Some relationships are ended by both parties, and Akert found that those who mutually agreed to split tended to be more upset than breakers, but less than breakees. Also, in general, men were found to make more complete (or drastic) breaks than women – who tended to want to keep some contact with their ex-partners. Kiecolt-Glaser (1987, 1988) also found that divorce or separation weakens the body's immune system and that, for both men and women, this situation is worse for the breakee than the breaker.

Rules

Argyle and Henderson (1985) argued that relationships are held together in part by the following of informal rules. In a study of broken friendships they found that the breaking of 'third party rules' was considered an important cause for the end of friendship. Examples of such rules include being jealous of a friend's other relationships and breaking a confidence. The rules tend to 'show up' only when broken – for example not offering help in a time of need, or criticising in public.

Evaluation of relationship dissolution work

Social psychological work on the breaking up of relationships has developed fairly recently, particularly in the United States. What is positive about this work is that it shows an awareness of the *complexity* involved in breakups (meaning that many factors are involved, and that each case involves a unique combination of factors). *Interdependence theory* is particularly good at dealing with such complexity, since it recognises the extent to which the identities and actions of people in relationships become intertwined and difficult to separate.

Some of the key concepts are well designed to deal with this complexity. For example, the *transgression-complaint-defence set* and the *demand/withdraw set* encourage us to view the interactions of two people as tightly interdependent, as in a dance like a waltz or tango. Much psychology, by contrast, deals merely with the thoughts, feelings and behaviours of *individual* people, missing completely the dynamic of the 'dance' itself.

A problem with this research is that it deals primarily with married couples from the United States. This is largely because of a social pressure (backed up with funding) to deal with the perceived 'problem' of marital breakups. Being *problem driven* in this way, the research runs the risk of *marginalising* every other kind of relationship.

The same pros and cons apply to the work on phases of dissolution. Duck's (1986) phases are merely a *typical* pattern, and exceptions are frequently encountered. Argyle and Henderson's (1985) research on relationship *rules* could be very usefully applied to discovering whether rules apply not just to the maintenance of relationships, but also to their breakup. If

Summary

1. Social exchange theory argues that people use the minimax strategy of minimum costs, maximum rewards.

2. Equity theory holds that people become unhappy in a relationship which they perceive as being unfair. Clark and Mills distinguish *exchange relationships* (governed by equity rules) from *communal relationships* (concerned with care and need more than with equity).

3. Interdependence theory studies the forms that interdependence takes and identifies the *degree*, *mutuality* and *basis of dependence*, and *correspondence of outcomes*, as ways in which interdependence situations can vary. Rusbult's *investment model* holds that commitment to a relationship is influenced by three factors: *satisfaction* (determined by 'comparison level'), *dependence* (determined by 'comparison level for alternatives'), and *investment size*.

4. Love has been distinguished from liking; divided into 'passionate' and 'companionate' varieties; arranged into 'styles' of loving; and presented as a triangle of *intimacy*, *commitment* and *passion*.

5. Relationships take a turn for the worse when couples generate 'spirals of escalating negativity' by engaging in 'negative reciprocity' and making 'distress maintaining attributions'.

6. Duck's model of phases of *dissolution* proposes that romantic relationships breakup through five stages: the *breakdown phase*, the *intrapsychic phase*, the *dyadic phase*, the *social phase* and the *grave-dressing phase*.

7. Rusbult and Zembrodt distinguish between those who take an *active* role, and those who are *passive* in the breakup of a relationship.

8. 'Breakees' seem to have a harder time, both physically and mentally, than 'breakers' when the relationship breaks down.

so, it may be that different 'breakup rules' apply in different kinds of relationship.

Finally, there is currently a lot of excitement about work such as that by Kiecolt-Glaser et al. (1987, 1988) which studies the impact of divorce or separation on the immune systems of those involved. There is clear evidence that our immune systems are far more sensitive to social psychological factors than had previously been thought. This adds the exciting possibility of connecting biological, psychological and social factors together in what is called a bio-psycho-social alliance. This will make the study of relationships fundamental to many other fields of research, especially those dealing with health issues.

Unit 3 Cultural and subcultural differences in relationships

KEY ISSUES

1 **What influence does culture have on relationships?**

2 **How has politics entered into science in the study of gay and lesbian relationships?**

3 **Will the internet change our ways of relating?**

3.1 Culture and relationships

'One of the strongest field recollections of this writer was his meeting, among the Bororo of central Brazil, of a man of about thirty years old: unclean, ill-fed, sad and lonesome. When asked if the man was seriously ill the natives' answer came as a shock: What was wrong with him? – nothing at all, he was just a bachelor, and true enough, in a society where labour is systematically shared between man and woman and where only the married status permits the man to benefit from the fruits of woman's work, including delousing, body painting, and hair-plucking as well as vegetable food and cooked food (since the Bororo woman tills the soil and makes pots), a bachelor is really only half a human being.' (Lévi-Strauss, 1956).

The above quotation shows how even experienced anthropologists like Lévi-Strauss can be shocked by the extent of cultural variation in relationships. There is a tendency to 'take-for-granted' one's own local cultural norms and values and to assume that they are somehow 'natural' and global – hence the 'culture shock' that can come from an encounter with different ways of living and thinking about relationships.

Unfortunately, as we have seen, much psychological work is based on relationships between young, white, North American, heterosexual, college students. The assumption made is that if we can discover consistent patterns in the way students relate together, then we can find out something *universal* about relationships – something applicable to *everyone*. The dream is to 'strip away' the veils of culture, so that we can see the laws that govern the 'natural' person's relationships.

But are these students really 'free' of culture? Clearly not. Students, and also the psychologists who study them, are socialised within a given culture and within a society with its own issues and priorities, and its own taken-for-granted 'reality'. Research on marital satisfaction, for instance, is powerfully shaped by the perceived 'crisis' in Western marriages, and boosted by funding aimed to solve this 'social problem'. Such research routinely assumes a heterosexual and monogamous 'normality' which, arguably, only appears 'natural' because it is taken-for-granted. Moghaddam et al. (1993), for instance, state that the concentration amongst social psychologists on romantic couples and first time acquaintances is the result of a 'Western cultural perspective'. For most cultures, kinship relationships would be the most important kind of relationships to study. Kinship relationships tend to be relatively permanent rather than impermanent (ie, we are born into our relationship with our relatives, and continue these all our lives) and hence it makes little sense to divide them into phases like 'attraction/formation', 'maintenance' and 'dissolution'.

Ethnocentrism This raises the danger that one particular (local) form of relationship common to one particular cultural or subcultural group might wrongly become the (global) standard against which the relationships of all other people are judged. An *ethnocentric* starting point is very likely to result in an *ethnocentric* conclusion ('ethnocentrism', according to the classic definition of Sumner, is 'the view of things in which one's own group is the centre of everything, and all others are

A nuclear family

An extended family

scaled and rated with reference to it', Sumner, 1940). In this way, politics enters into science, since ethnocentric findings are not objective, and can serve to alienate and even oppress those others who are made to appear 'unnatural' or 'abnormal'. It is thus scientifically and ethically important to develop a sensitivity to cultural differences, including subcultures within one's own culture (the UK is host to a variety of different ethnic, religious, economic and political groups with more or less distinct subcultures) and the practices of geographically separate cultures.

The emic and the etic – or the particular and the universal

The issue of *cultural diversity* raises the problem that relationships may not be natural objects that obey the kind of physical laws discovered by scientists. Much of the research in the previous two units implies that relationships go through phases of formation, maintenance and dissolution much as a caterpillar will become a pupa and then a butterfly (Berry, 1989, named such general universals *etics*). This could be a misleading comparison, since our relationships may be more like songs or buildings – ie, *humanly made* – than natural objects. They are in part specific *cultural* products (Berry called these non-universal particulars *emics*).

This raises the second issue of *diversity* in relationships. Like our buildings and our songs, our relationships were different in the historical past, are different in other societies and cultures, and will be different in the future. Amidst all this difference there may well be some underlying similarity, but this should be *discovered* and not *assumed*.

The following comment about relationships comes from a young Asian woman attending a Further Education College in East London:

'Everyone sees it as alright for white and black [girls] to talk with as many boys as they like and muck about with as many boys as they like and wear whatever kind of clothes they like and it's no problem. But if an Asian does it she's a slut or a slag straight away and I think that's so sad' (from Marshall & Stenner, 1997).

To make sense of this young woman's experience of relationships it is necessary to consider various emic factors such as:

1   The multi-ethnic context within which she lives, and the history of how this came about.

2   The influence of cultural tradition on how relationships should be organised (she is from a background where arranged marriages are the norm, and where parents and brothers keep a careful watch over what friendships – particularly with young men – are being formed).

Key terms

Ethnocentrism *Thinking of one's own social group or culture as the centre of everything, and judging all others from this point of view.*

Emic *Something that is specific to a particular culture.*

Etic *Something that is universal, that is found in all cultures.*

3   The historical fact that this young woman, having been born in London, has a very different set of experiences than her parents, who were born in Bangladesh.

4   The different meaning attached to being a young woman compared to a young man, and how this question of 'gender' is also influenced by 'ethnicity' (think of the usage of terms like 'slag' and 'slut' – which serve to regulate the 'proper' behaviour of young women).

3.2   Dimensions of cultural difference

As a way of simplifying cultural diversity, several researchers have attempted to identify dimensions along which relationships may vary between cultures. Hofstede (1983) identified four such dimensions:

1   **Individualism-collectivism** In *individualist* cultures (like USA and Great Britain, according to Hofstede's findings), each person is expected to be relatively autonomous, to make their own decisions and to fend for themselves (and their immediate family). The 'I' comes before the 'we'. In *collectivist* cultures (like Guatemala and Panama), people are tightly integrated into a cohesive social network, and this 'we' comes before any particular 'I'. It is in individualist cultures that 'love' tends to be seen as a matter of personal choice and desire. In collectivist cultures, marriage first of all joins *families* not individuals, with the bride often having a clear 'price'. This relates to the useful dimension for thinking about types of relationship briefly mentioned in Unit 1: *voluntary/involuntary*. Much of the material discussed in Units 1 and 2 is ethnocentric to the extent that it applies only to relationships that are entered into *voluntarily*. Yet, for instance, the most common method of 'mate selection' in the world is the *arranged marriage*, where often the will and desire of the couple is not of primary importance. *Voluntary* relationships tend to be more common in *individualist* cultures.

2   **Masculinity/femininity** 'Masculine' cultures (like Japan and Venezuela) promote assertiveness, achievement and heroism and accentuate the difference between men and women, whilst 'feminine' cultures (like Holland and Sweden) value warm and harmonious personal relationships and quality of life and put less emphasis on differentiating between genders.

3   **Power distance** Cultures high in power distance (Malaysia and Guatemala) accept that power in society is unequally distributed and is backed up by force. They show deference and respect to those with more power. Low power distance cultures are more egalitarian and less accepting of conspicuous power inequalities.

4   **Uncertainty avoidance** Cultures high in uncertainty avoidance (like Greece and Portugal) treat what is different as dangerous, whilst low uncertainty avoidance cultures (like Denmark and Jamaica) treat what is different as interesting.

Trompenaars (1993) also identified an *individualism-collectivism* dimension, but added several others, such as *universalism-particularism* and *neutral versus emotional relationship orientations*. He was interested in work relationships and found that cultures that value *universalism* (such as Germany) believe that rules are rules, and should apply to everyone, irrespective of who they are in particular.

Particularist cultures (such as Japan) are happy to bend rules for particular individuals, such as family members. Regarding the second dimension, Italy is an example of a culture where emotions are readily expressed in most interactions, whereas in Great Britain, relationship orientations are typically more *neutral* (except when drunk!).

Taking some of these dimensions we might predict that the principle of equity (see Unit 2) is more important in individualist cultures which are universalist (and, perhaps, low in power distance). There is some evidence to support this. Berman et al. (1985) compared how Indian and American students preferred to allocate resources in pretend work situations. They found that most American students preferred to allocate extra pay to the best workers (which fits equity theory), whereas students from India gave the extra pay to the most needy worker. The Americans, in other words, were more *universalist* (each should be rewarded on the basis of their contribution, not on the basis of *particulars* like how 'needy' this particular person is). This also suggests that equity theory applies more to individualist cultures (like the USA – where if an individual contributes, then that individual should gain) than to collectivist cultures (like India – where a needy one is still part of the collective and should be provided for, as in *communal* relationships discussed in Unit 2).

Argyle et al. (1986) studied the *rules* of relationships in different cultures and found that the 'do not criticise friends in public' rule is more important in Japan and Hong Kong than in Italy or Great Britain. As Goodwin (1999) suggests, this is likely to be due to the collectivism of Japan and Hong Kong, where there is strong pressure 'to avoid loss of face and to maintain group harmony'.

Evaluation of work on cultural dimensions

The various attempts to discover underlying 'dimensions' on which cultures vary represent a practical way of dealing with the otherwise bewildering mass of information on 'cultural differences'. However, there are problems with classifying cultures in terms of dimensions, and then using these classifications to explain relationships.

- First, identifying dimensions such as *individualism-collectivism* inevitably leads to simplification. To label an entire culture as 'individualistic' is a crude and sweeping generalisation which covers up the richness and variety that characterises all cultures.
- Second, such dimensions *appear* to provide an explanation when really what we have is a partial description that is too often used as an 'explain all'.
- Third, members of any culture can have their *moments* of both collectivism or individualism – their behaviour does not fall neatly into a single category.
- Fourth, when a culture is found to be, say, 'masculine', this does not mean that each individual in that culture is masculine. It means that *on average* the 'culture' comes out with a masculine score when completed questionnaires from many individuals from that culture are analysed. We risk then 'generalising' on the basis of this average score.
- Fifth, many of the dimensions are not independent of one another, but seem to reflect an underlying *modernisation*. For instance, wealthy post-industrial countries tend, as a rule, to be more individualist, universalist, feminine and egalitarian.

Activity 4 — Cultural differences and ethnocentrism

Item A — Brothers and sisters

Cheyenne women and children.

The brother-sister relationship amongst the Cheyenne is one of formal respect and restraint. Although they may play together as small children, after puberty they must shed all expressions of familiarity. There can be no physical contacts or joking between them. Indeed they may not even speak to each other. There is an indirect way around this tabu, however. A man who goes to his brother-in-law's tipi to borrow something, for instance, may find that the brother-in-law is not at home. He does not tell his sister what he wants, but he can tell her little baby of his request. After a while his sister, having overheard his wish, puts the article in a place where it can be seen. He picks it up and departs. He has obtained what he wants without violating the rules of right conduct.

Adapted from E.A. Hoebel, 1960

Item B — Tongan families

In Tonga, the individual is surrounded and supported by relatives from birth to old age. Theirs is a kinship system with strong rights and obligations that apply even to distant relatives. For example, no Tongan can refuse to give a meal – or a home – to needy relatives, no matter how far removed. If a kinsman asks for a mat, for money, or even for a 'loan' of the family's sewing machine, he cannot be refused. When a Tongan child is orphaned, a relative immediately adopts him – regardless of any inconvenience or expense.

Adapted from M. Douglas, 1964

After getting to this point in the chapter, you should be in a pretty good position to make a favourable impression the next time you meet someone. Suppose you want Claudia to like you. You should hang around her so that you become familiar, act in ways that are rewarding to her, and emphasise your similarity to her. You should let her know you like her, but if you want to be especially clever, you should at first be a little critical, and then compliment her profusely. We make no guarantee that you and Claudia will become best friends, but all else being equal, these techniques work fairly well.

Adapted from E. Aronson, et al., 1997

Questions

1 Make a guess at classifying Items A, B and C (providing reasons for your decisions) in terms of:

   a) Individualism-collectivism
   b) Voluntary-involuntary

2 Item C is taken from a North American textbook and the 'advice' offered is very much directed at USA college students. Do you think the advice offered is *generalisable* to all people? Give reasons for your answer.

3.3 **Understudied relationships**

Gay and lesbian relationships

The study of 'sexual orientation' is one area where politics and science mix uncomfortably. In the late 19th century, 'sexologists' – scientists of sexuality – effectively created the concept of the 'homosexual' as a label for a kind of disease. To sexually desire people of the same sex as oneself came to be thought of as a 'condition' that can be 'cured' and whose causes can be potentially tracked down. Homosexuality featured in the DSM (the classification manual of the American Psychiatric Association) as a sexual deviation until as recently as 1973. In this way, sexologists and psychiatrists were reflecting the values and prejudices of their culture: values which took it for granted that 'homosexuality' was 'queer', 'dangerous' and 'dirty'. Until the 1960s, homosexuality was illegal in the UK, and people were forced to act secretly and to 'pass' as heterosexual, or else to face public condemnation and shame. What 'science' added to this 'hot' prejudice was the impression of 'cold', objective neutrality. The prejudice and undisguised hatred came to appear as reasonable and based on fact. Desire for the same sex became, in a word, *pathologised* – made into a disease.

As the twentieth century Western World became increasingly liberal in its surface attitudes, so homosexuality came to be viewed less as a disease and more as a lifestyle choice. It was largely decriminalised (although the age of sexual consent, set at 18 since 1995, is still higher than for heterosexuals in the UK) and depathologised (removed from the DSM), although negative attitudes and hostility are still common. Kitzinger (1987) points out that from the 1960s onwards a new category of people became the targets of pathologisation: *homophobes* (those who have the 'psychological problem' of hating homosexuals). All of this goes to show how what passes as 'knowledge' has a tendency to shift with cultural values.

But this 'shift' was not painless. As with any political movement against oppression, it involved struggle and sacrifice. Part of that struggle was a redefinition of terms: the use of the words 'gay' and 'lesbian' instead of 'homosexual', for example, is for many gay people a means of resisting a pathological label. Many have gone further and describe themselves as 'queer', thereby celebrating what was once seen as negative by proudly rejecting what is seen as the boring, uniform and unadventurous strictures of 'straight' culture. In the 1980s, gay pop stars like Boy George, Marilyn and Holly Johnson of Frankie goes to Hollywood became cultural icons for a youth culture amongst whom the word 'straight' was a form of insult. Intolerance, violence and hatred is still rife in many sectors of society, of course, but today gay people have become a vibrant cultural and political force, gathering in large numbers in cosmopolitan urban centers such as London, San Francisco and Sydney.

In a report based on the *National Survey of Sexual Attitudes and Lifestyles*, Wellings et al. (1994) state that 6.1% of the men, and 3.4% of the women in their UK sample had engaged in 'same sex' activity. However these figures were almost double for Londoners, indicating migration of gays and lesbians to the capital (the figures are also higher for those who went to boarding school). Such figures as these (see also Table 1 for more detail) should always be taken with caution, since people do not always respond truthfully to questionnaires, and sometimes there is no simple truth, since one's sexual preferences can change. Interestingly, Wellings et al. (1994) found that the probability of women making a 'homosexual debut' (having a first lesbian experience) is constant up to the fifth decade, whilst once men have reached thirty, they are thereafter unlikely to have a first gay experience. Lesbian women also reported fewer sexual partners than gay men.

Table 1   **Percentages of men and women reporting different kinds of sexual attraction and sexual experience**

	Sexual attraction		Sexual experience	
	Men	Women	Men	Women
Only heterosexual	93.3	93.6	92.3	95.1
Mostly heterosexual	4.0	3.8	3.9	2.2
Both hetero and homosexual	0.5	0.2	0.3	0.1
Mostly homosexual	0.5	0.2	0.6	0.2
Only homosexual	0.5	0.3	0.4	0.1
None	0.8	1.2	2.0	1.6
Refused to answer	0.5	0.7	0.6	0.7

Data from Wellings et al., 1994

Whilst much research over the past 30 years has stressed the basic similarity of gay and straight relationships, Kitzinger and Coyle (1995) argue that homosexual relationships are in several ways distinct, and that some should be positively viewed as a challenge to heterosexual lifestyles. Gay people, they claim, are less likely to live together than heterosexuals, are less likely to be 'sexually exclusive' and are more likely to be creative in their sex-roles, distancing themselves from traditional 'husband-wife' arrangements.

This is backed up by work by Hickson (1990) with gay men in the UK, amongst whom 'it remains common for men to combine regular relationships with other regular liasons or with casual encounters.... it is clear from this empirical work that sexual exclusivity is neither a reality, nor an ideal, for most coupled gay men'. This work involved interviewing 387 gay men about the rules they use in managing their 'extra-relational' affairs. An interesting finding was that what seemed to matter was not so much the *content* of the rule, but simply *that there was a rule*. Consider, to end this section, the following pairs of rules:

a 'My partner can bonk women but not men.'
b 'Generally, not to have sex with women as it's found more threatening.'

a 'If we pick someone up it must always be in our flat and never theirs.'
b 'Never at home.'

a 'We should tell each other.'
b 'Not to talk about it.'

'Electronic' relationships

Human beings are tool-using creatures, but sometimes it seems that our technologies influence us as much as we use them. Technologies mediate our relationships to each other and to the world, transforming our powers of action, our ways of being, and our ways of thinking. It is hence crucial for social psychologists to think about mediation. Mediation means coming between one thing and another. For example, television comes between the audience and what is happening in the studio. In doing so, the medium of television creates a new form of communication and transmits a new type of message. Language itself is an ancient form of technology that 'mediates' between people. This text that you are reading is a form of media just as much as newer forms of technology such as the internet. New technologies are at first strange, but we quickly take them for granted such that we barely notice their presence. But once established, a new mediating technology typically takes over and transforms large parts of our daily lives (not without our help, of course). Think for a while of life before TV, radio and recorded music. How much have these things changed how we live? There is no doubt that our technologies participate in changing who and what we are by shaping and changing how we do things, and sometimes even what we do.

Activity 5   Forms of mediation

Item A   Speaking face to face

Item B   Speaking on the telephone

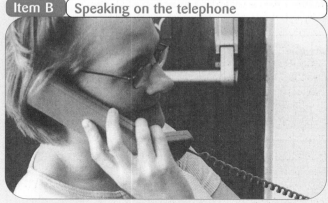

Item C   Sending a letter

Item D   Sending an email

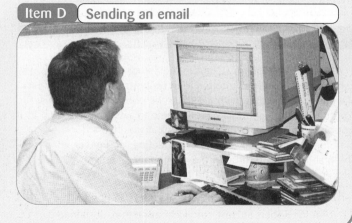

Question

Look at the above forms of communication which mediate the relationship between yourself and a friend. Briefly suggest how each type of technology affects your communication.

The internet is in the process of becoming a dominant technology of mediation. Things that used to happen elsewhere are increasingly happening on the internet as well, and sometimes instead. Many of us now shop, teach, learn, have fun, make friends, protest and even have sex on the internet. Again, at first this seems strange to us, and it is no surprise to hear people doubting the genuineness of such experiences and criticising the 'handful of computer nerds' that they imagine partaking. It is also no surprise to hear the repeated refrain that such technologies 'don't change basic human nature'. But as happened for many people with writing and TV, it may be that there will come a point when we imagine that something has not truly happened *unless* it takes place on the internet! History tells us that it is unwise to underestimate.

There are various forms of *computer mediated communication* (CMC), which can broadly be divided into the asynchronous (such as email, newsgroups and discussion forums which do not take place in 'real time') and the synchronous (such as Internet Relay Chat where users who are simultaneously logged on can have a 'real time' turn-by-turn exchange). Currently popular are forums that allow participants to communicate in a 3-d virtual world-space (such as a virtual conference room or virtual bar). Each participant can be 'represented' in this space by an 'avatar' that can move around, encounter other avatars, and express basic feelings.

Examples of avatars

Allbright and Conran (1996) in their study of electronic romantic relationships quote a man (Robert) describing his first 'face to face' meeting with a woman he considered to be his 'on-line' romantic partner: 'Well, I hate to say it, but as soon as I got off the plane and got my first look it was like a door slamming shut. I'll never forget that feeling, and never got over the first impression through the relationship. She was a lot bigger than what I thought she had led me to believe.'

This quotation, taken at face value, illustrates four things:

1   That for Robert at least, 'physical attraction' remained a vitally important factor in choosing a partner, despite the fact

that he 'hates to say it'.

2   That in the absence of direct information about his partner's attractiveness, he had built up an attractive 'mental picture' of her, hence his disappointment with the 'reality'.

3   That, according to Robert, his partner had collaborated with him in building this false picture (she 'led him to believe'), indicating that she too was aware of the importance of physical attraction.

4   That this new information permanently modified his view of the relationship (he 'never got over it').

Key terms

Mediation *Coming between one thing and another.*

Computer mediated communication (CMC) *Communication which is mediated through computer technology.*

'Cues filtered out' models

The 'problems' illustrated by Robert's story were caused in part by the fact that this couple changed the medium of their relationship from CMC to 'face to face'. A variety of what Culnan and Markus (1987) call *cues filtered out* models have been proposed to explain such differences between media. Imagine a mediating technology as a filter or sieve. Of all the possible types of information available to us about someone (what they look like, sound like, walk like, smell like, what their surroundings are like, their family background, their plans, their non-verbal signals, etc) only a limited few are selected, and the rest are 'filtered out'. The telephone filters out everything but the voice. But each person's voice is still characteristic of them, and can convey information about mood, social class etc, as well as whatever is said. CMC, in most cases (although this is changing fast), filters out everything but the written word.

Reduced social cues The *reduced social cues* model (Sproull & Kiesler, 1986), for instance, concentrates on information about a communication provided by the social context. Such cues may be either static (a big desk and large office signify power and prestige, for instance) or *dynamic* (a frown or a smile provide ongoing cues about what a person feels). In email communication, they argue, dynamic cues are filtered out (since there is a time gap between sending and receiving) and static cues are greatly reduced. This constitutes an unusual communication situation (with very few social cues), and Sproull and Kiesler argue that it sometimes leads people to lose some of their inhibitions and engage in *flaming* (swearing and abusing people, expressing negative emotions by WRITING IN CAPITALS AND EXCLAIMING A LOT!!!!!). However, people have come up with clever ways of re-introducing some of these lost cues. For example many people use a **CHARACTERISTIC FONT** to personalise their CMC; use 'emoticon' signs (like ☹ and ☺) and abbreviations (like 'lol' for 'loads of laughs') to inform of mood; send electronic pictures to supply visual information;

or select an avatar (an image) to represent them on-screen.

The hyperpersonal model (Walther, 1996) gives another slant to Robert's story. Instead of *depersonalising* relationships, the lack of cues in CMC can sometimes lead to *hyperpersonal* interactions. In a sense, the gaps that are left by the filtered out cues can be 'filled in' by our imagination, leading to elaborate fantasies which can be treated as real by the participants. In this case, CMC involves:

- an idealised perception of others,
- an idealised and optimised presentation of self, and
- an intensification loop.

Hence Robert fantasised an ideal picture of his partner, who in turn generated an ideal picture of herself, designed to fit and fuel his fantasy, which in turn intensifies, through a feedback loop, the plausibility of these fantastic pictures (and no doubt Robert presented himself in ideal form to fit the fantasies of his partner).

The fact that CMC can both depersonalise and hyperpersonalise alerts us to the fact that such technologies do not generate their effects alone, but require our participation. The same technology can function very differently depending on who uses it, how, and why. In sum, it seems that relationships of one kind or another are more fundamental than meets the eye. Technologies mediate our relationships to each other and to things, shaping and patterning them in subtle but important ways. But this shaping and patterning ultimately depends on the relationship we people adopt to our technologies.

Key terms

Depersonalisation *In everyday face-to-face personal interactions there are many cues that subtly help to coordinate our interactions, such as tone of voice, facial expression and the sheer physical presence of the other. These help to make the interaction a personal interaction. With much computer mediated interaction these cues are not present. According to some, this can lead to depersonalisation. We 'forget' that we are dealing with another human being with a face and a voice and feelings.*

Hyperpersonalisation *The opposite of depersonalisation. One effect of engaging in relatively cue-less computer mediated interaction is that we can 'fill in the gaps' with our own imagination, leading to fantasies of intimacy and closeness that lead to very personal interactions.*

Summary

1 It is very important to consider the full diversity of relationships, as much social psychology to date has limited itself to a narrow range of relationships. A cross-cultural perspective is valuable here.

2 Ethnocentrism is taking one's own group's view of things to be the centre of everything, and ranking others from that perspective. It is ethnocentric, for example, to imagine that a Western conception of love is normal and natural, and any other conception is abnormal and unnatural.

3 Etics are behaviours that are found universally. Emics are behaviours that are found in one or a few societies. Psychologists have traditionally studied etics, but much that is of importance in human relationships is emic.

4 Various dimensions of cultural difference have been identified, including individualism-collectivism, masculinity-femininity, power distance, uncertainty avoidance, universalism-particularism and neutral-emotional. Such dimensions are useful, but we should be wary of generalising on the basis of them.

5 The scientific study of homosexual relationships has been a hot political issue, since early science served to pathologise gay people.

6 Relationships conducted via the internet are understudied. There are good reasons to think that mediating technologies have a profound shaping influence on how we relate.

References

Akert, R.M. (1992). Terminating romantic relationships: The role of personal responsibility and gender. Unpublished Manuscript. Wellsley College.

Allbright, J. M. & Conran, T. (1996). On-line love: Sex, gender and relationships in cyberspace. Unpublished manuscript.

Argyle, M. & Henderson, M. (1985). *The anatomy of relationships*. Harmondsworth: Penguin.

Argyle, M., Henderson, M., Iizuka, Y. & Contarello, A. (1986). Cross-cultural variations in relationship rules. *International Journal of Psychology, 21*, 287-315.

Argyle, M., Henderson, M., Bond, M., Iizuka, Y. & Contarello, A. (1986). Cross-cultural variations in relationship rules. *International Journal of Psychology, 21*, 287-315.

Aron, A., Aron, E. N., Tudor, M. & Nelson, G. (1991). Close relationships as including other in the self. *Journal of Personality and Social Psychology, 60*, 241-253.

Aronson, E. & Linder, D. (1965). Gain and loss of esteem as determinants of interpersonal attractiveness. *Journal of Experimental Social Psychology, 1*, 156-171.

Aronson, E., Wilson, T. D. & Akert, R. M. (1997). *Social psychology*. New York: Longman.

Baron, R. A. & Byrne, D. (1997). *Social psychology*. Boston, MA: Allyn and Bacon.

Batson, C.D. (1993). Communal and exchange relationships: What is the difference? *Personality and Social Psychology Bulletin, 19*, 677-683.

Berscheid, E. & Hatfield, E. (1974). Physical attractiveness. In L. Berkowitz (Ed.), *Advances in experimental social psychology*. New York: Academic Press.

Berscheid, E. & Walster, E. (1974). A little bit about love. In R. L. Huston (Ed.), *Foundations of interpersonal attraction*. New York: Academic Press.

Berkman, L. & Breslow, L. (1983). *Health and ways of living: Findings from the Alameda County study*. Oxford: Oxford University Press.

Berkman, L. F. & Syme, S. L. (1979). Social networks, host resistance and mortality: A nine year follow-up of the Alameda County residents. *American Journal of Epidemiology, 109*, 186-204.

Berkow, J. H. (1989). *Darwin, sex and status: Biological approaches to mind and culture.* Toronto: University of Toronto Press.

Berman, J., Murphy-Berman, V. & Singh, P. (1985). Cross cultural similarities and differences in perceptions of fairness. *Journal of Cross-Cultural Psychology, 16,* 55-67.

Berry, J. (1989). Imposed etics derived emics: The operationalisation of a compelling idea. *International Journal of Psychology, 24,* 721-35.

Bornstein, R.F. & D'Agostino, P.R. (1992). Stimulus recognition and the mere exposure effect. *Journal of Personality and Social Psychology, 63,* 545-552.

Bourdieu, P. (1991). *Outline for a theory of practice.* Cambridge: Cambridge University Press.

Bradbury, T. N. & Fincham, F. D. (1990). Attributions in marriage: Review and critique. *Psychological Bulletin, 107,* 3-33.

Buss, D. M. (1988). Love acts: The evolutionary biology of love. In R. J. Sternberg & M. L. Barnes (Eds.), *The psychology of love.* New Haven: Yale University Press.

Buss, D.M., Abbott, M., Angleitner., et al (1990). International preferences in selecting mates. *Journal of Cross-Cultural Psychology, 21:* 5-47.

Buunk, B. P. & van Yperen, N. W. (1991). Referential comparisons, relational comparisons and exchange orientation: Their relation to marital satisfaction. *Personality and Social Psychology Bulletin, 17,* 710-718.

Byrne, D. & Buehler, J. A. (1955). A note on the influence of propinquity upon acquaintanceships. *Journal of Abnormal and Social Psychology, 51,* 147-148.

Byrne, D. (1971). *The attraction paradigm.* New York: Academic Press.

Clark, M. S. & Mills, J. (1993). The difference between communal and exchange relationships: What it is and is not. *Personality and Social Psychology Bulletin, 19,* 684-691.

Collins, N.L. & Miller, L.C. (1994). Self-disclosure and liking: A meta-analytic review. *Psychological Bulletin, 116,* 457-475.

Culnan, M. J. & Markus, M. L. (1987). Information technologies. In F. M. Jablin., L. L. Putnam., K. H. Roberts & L. W. Porter (Eds.), *Handbook of organizational communication: An interdisciplinary perspective.* London: Sage.

Curt, B. C. (1994). *Textuality and tectonics: Troubling social and psychological science.* Buckingham: Open University Press.

Curtis, R. C. & Miller, K. (1986). Believing another likes or dislikes you: Behaviours making the beliefs come true. *Journal of Personality and Social Psychology, 51,* 284-290.

Duck, S. (1986). *Human relationships: An introduction to social psychology.* London: Sage.

Festinger, L., Schachter, S. & Back, K. (1950). *Social pressures in informal groups: A study of a housing community.* New York: Harper.

Glenn, N.D. & Weaver, C.M. (1988). The changing relationship of marital status to reported happiness. *Journal of Marriage and the Family, 50,* 317-324.

Goodwin, R. (1999). *Personal relationships across cultures.* London: Routledge.

Gotman, J. M. (1979). *Marital interaction: Experimental investigations.* New York: Academic Press.

Griffit, W. B. & Guay, P. (1969). Object evaluation and conditioned affect. *Journal of Experimental Research in Psychology, 4,* 1-8.

Hays, R. B. (1988). Friendship. In S. Duck (Ed.), *Handbook of personal relationships.* Chichester: Wiley.

Hendrick, S. S. & Hendrick, C. (1992). *Romantic love.* London: Sage.

Hickson, F. (1990). Sexual exclusivity, non-exclusivity and HIV, *Project Sigma Working Paper Number 31.*

Hofstede, G. (1983). Dimensions of national cultures in fifty cultures and three regions. In J.B. Deregowski, S. Dziurawiec & R.C. Annis (Eds.). *Explorations in cross-cultural psychology.* Lisse: Swets and Zweitlinger.

Hogg, M. A. & Vaughan, G. M. (1995). *Social psychology: An introduction.* Hemel Hempstead: Prentice Hall/Harvester Wheatsheaf.

Holmes, J. G. (2000). Social relationships: The nature and function of relational schemas.*The European Journal of Social Psychology, 30,* 447-485.

Homans, G. C. (1961). *Social behaviour: Its elementary forms.* New York: Harcourt, Brace and World.

Huston, T.L. (1973) Ambiguity of acceptance, social desirability and dating choice. *Journal of Experimental Social Psychology, 9,* 32-42.

Huston, T. L., McHale, S. & Crouter, A. (1986). When the honeymoon's over: Changes in the marriage relationship over the first year. In R. Gilmour & S. Duck (Eds.), *The emerging field of interpersonal relationships.* Hillsdale, NJ: Erlbaum.

Huston, T. L. & Vangelisti, A. L. (1991). Socioemotional behaviour and satisfaction in marital relationships: A longitudinal study. *Journal of Personality and Social Psychology, 61,* 721-733.

Kiecolt-Glaser, J. K. (1987). Marital quality, marital disruption, and immune function. *Journal of Psychosomatic Medicine, 49,* 13.

Kiecolt-Glaser, J. K. (1988). Marital discord and immunity in males. *Journal of Psychosomatic Medicine, 50,* 213.

Kitzinger, C. (1987). *The social construction of lesbianism.* London: Sage.

Kitzinger, C. & Coyle, A. (1995). Lesbian and gay couples: Speaking of difference. *Psychologist, 8,* 64-69.

Lee, J. A. (1973). *The colours of love: An exploration of the ways of loving.* Ontario: New Press.

Lee, J. A. (1984). Sequences in separation: A framework for investigating endings of the personal (romantic) relationship. *Journal of Social and Personal Relationships, 1,* 49-74.

LeVine, R., Sato, S., Hashimoto, T. & Varma, J. (1995). Love and marriage in eleven cultures. *Journal of Cross-Cultural Psychology, 26,* 554-571.

Lévi-Strauss, C. (1956). The Family. In H.L. Shapiro (Ed.), *Man, culture and society.* London: Oxford University Press.

Lewis, C.S. (1960). *The four loves.* New York: Harcourt, Brace and World.

Lott, A. J. & Lott, B. E. (1974). The role of reward in the formation of positive interpersonal attitudes. In T. L. Huston (Ed.), *Foundations of interpersonal attraction.* New York: Academic Press.

Lynch, J. J. (1977). *The Broken heart: Medical consequences of loneliness.* New York: Basic Books.

Marshall, H. & Stenner, P. (1997). Friends and lovers. In J.Roche & S. Tucker (Eds.), *Youth in society.* London: Sage.

Martin, P. (1998). *The sickening mind: Brain, behaviour, immunity and disease.* London: Harper Collins.

Maslow, A.H. (1962). *Toward a psychology of being.* Princeton, NJ: Van Norstrand.

May, J.L. & Hamilton, P.A. (1980). Effects of musically evoked affect on women's interpersonal attraction and perceptual judgements of physical attractiveness of men. *Motivation and Emotion, 4,* 217-228.

Messick, D. M. & Cook, K. S. (Eds.) (1983). *Equity theory: Psychological and sociological perspectives.* New York: Praeger.

Mita, T.H., Dermer, M. & Knight, J. (1977). Reversed facial images and the mere-exposure hypothesis. *Journal of Personality and Social Psychology, 35,* 597-601.

Moghaddam, F. M., Taylor, D. M. & Wright, S. C. (1993). *Social psychology in cross-cultural perspective.* New York: Freeman and Co.

Moghaddam, F. M. (1998). *Social psychology: Exploring universals across cultures.* New York: Freeman and Co.

Moreland, R. L. & Zajonc, R. B. (1982). Exposure effects in person perception: Familiarity, similarity, and attraction. *Journal of Experimental Social Psychology, 18,* 395-415.

Myers, D.G. (1992). *The pursuit of happiness: Who is happy and why?* New York: Morrow.

Newcomb, T. M. (1956). *The prediction of interpersonal attraction. Psychological Review, 60,* 393-404.

Newcombe, T.M. & Svehla, G. (1937). Intra-family relationships in attitudes. *Sociometry, 1,* 180-205.

Reis, H. T. (1996). Relationships. In A. S. R. Manstead & M. Hewstone et al. (Eds.), *The Blackwell encyclopedia of social psychology*. Oxford: Blackwell.

Rozin, P. Millman, M. & Nemeroff, C. (1986). Operation of the laws of sympathetic magic in disgust and other domains. *Journal of Personality and Social Psychology, 50*, 703-712.

Rubin, R.G. (1973). How strong is the feminine drive to high position? *American Psychologist, 28*, 621-623.

Rubin, Z. (1970). Measurement of romantic love. *Journal of Personality and Social Psychology, 16*, 265-273.

Rusbult, C. E. (1983). A longitudinal test of the investment model: The development (and deterioration) of satisfaction and commitment in heterosexual involvements. *Journal of Personality and Social Psychology, 45*, 101-117.

Rusbult, C. E. & Zembrodt, I. M. (1983). Responses to dissatisfaction in romantic involvements: A multidimensional scaling analysis. *Journal of Experimental Social Psychology, 43*, 1230-1242.

Rusbult, C. E. & van Lange, P. A. M. (1996). Interdependence processes. In E. T. Higgins & A. Kruglanski (Eds.), *Social psychology: Handbook of basic principles*. New York: Guilford.

Schachter, S. (1959). *The psychology of affiliation*. Stanford CA: Stanford University Press.

Sergios, P. A. & Cody, J. (1985). Physical attractiveness and social assertiveness skills in male homosexual dating behavior and partner selection. *Journal of Social Psychology, 125*, 505-514.

Simmons, C. H., von Kolke, A. & Shimuzu, H. (1986). Attitudes toward romantic love among American, German and Japanese students. *Journal of Social Psychology, 126*, 327-36.

Simmons, C. H., Wehner, E. A. & Kay, K. A. (1989). Differences in attitude toward romantic love of French and American college students. *Journal of Social Psychology, 129*, 793-9.

Simpson, J.A., Gangstad, S.W. & Lerma, M. (1990). Perception of physical attractiveness: Mechanisms involved in the maintenance of romantic relationships. *Journal of Personality and Social Psychology, 59*, 1192-1201.

Singh, D. (1993). Adaptive significance of female physical attractiveness: Role of waist-to-hip ratio. *Journal of Personality and Social Psychology, 65*, 293-307.

Smith, P. B. & Bond, M. H. (1993). *Social psychology across cultures: Analysis and perspectives*. Hemel Hempstead: Harvester Wheatsheaf.

Sperling, M.B. (1985). Fusional love relations: The developmental origins of love. *Journal of Personality Assessment, 49*, 324-328.

Sprecher, S. (1986). The relation between inequity and emotion in close relationships. *Social Psychology Quarterly, 49*, 309-321.

Sprecher, S., Sullivan, Q. & Hatfield, E. (1994) Mate selection preferences: Gender differences examined in a national sample. *Journal of Personality and Social Psychology, 66*, 1074-1080.

Sproull, L. & Kiesler, S. (1986). Reducing social context cues: Electronic mail in organizational communication. *Management Science, 32*, 1492-1512.

Stendhal, M. H. (1980). *Love*. Harmondsworth: Penguin Books.

Sternberg, R. J. (1986). A triangular theory of love. *Psychological Review, 93*, 199-135.

Sumner, W.G. (1940). *Folkways*. Boston, MA: Ginn.

Tesser, A. & Brodie, M. (1971). A note on the evaluation of a "computer date". *Psychonomic Science, 23*, 300.

Thibaut, J. T. & Kelley, H. H. (1959). *The social psychology of groups*. New York: Wiley.

Trompenaars, F. (1993). *Riding the waves of culture: Understanding cultural diversity in business*. London: Nicholas Brealey.

Vernant, J. P. (1996). *Myth and society in ancient Greece*. New York: Zone Books.

Walster, E., Walster, G. W. & Berscheid, E. (1978). *Equity theory and research*. Boston, MA: Allyn and Bacon.

Walster, E., Aronson, V., Abrahams, D. & Rottman, L. (1966). Importance of physical attraction in dating behaviour. *Journal of Personality and Social Psychology, 5*, 508-516.

Walther, J. B. (1996). Computer mediated communication: Impersonal, interpersonal and hyperpersonal interaction. *Communication Research, 23*, 3-43.

Wellings, K., Field, J., Johnson, A.M. & Wadsworth, J. (1994). *Sexual behaviour in England*. Harmondsworth: Penguin.

Winch, R.F. (1958). *Mate selection: A study in complementary needs*. New York: Harper Row.

21 Prosocial and antisocial behaviour

■ Introduction

In *Imagine*, John Lennon asks us to imagine a world where there is 'nothing to kill or die for', with 'all the people living life in peace'. The world is a long way from this dream – there are wars between nations and within nations, and violence on the street and in the home. This chapter begins by looking at the nature and causes of aggression – why do people behave in an aggressive and sometimes violent manner?

Aggression is often seen as antisocial behaviour. The other side of the coin is prosocial behaviour – helping others being an obvious example. Why do we help others – out of the goodness of our heart or for our own selfish reasons? This question is examined in the second part of the chapter.

Finally, what effects, if any, do the mass media have on prosocial and antisocial behaviour? For example, does violence on the television screen lead to violence off the screen? The third part of this chapter shows that things are a lot more complex than this apparently simple question suggests.

Chapter summary

- Unit 1 looks at the nature and causes of aggression.
- Unit 2 explores prosocial behaviour and bystander behaviour.
- Unit 3 discusses media effects on prosocial and antisocial behaviour.

Unit 1 Nature and causes of aggression

KEY ISSUES

1 How is aggression defined and measured?
2 What are the main social psychological theories of aggression?
3 What are the effects of environmental stressors on aggression?

1.1 What is aggression?

Aggression is not easy to define. Many psychologists define aggression as behaviour that is *intended* to harm others. The emphasis here is on intention. In other words, the aggressor must mean to harm somebody. This harm can be physical – intending to cause bodily harm – or psychological – intending to cause psychological pain. In this way Aronson et al. (1997) state that 'aggressive action is behaviour aimed at causing either physical or psychological pain'.

When aggression is defined like this, the following actions can be seen as aggressive behaviour. Biting, scratching, hitting, attacking others with a weapon such as a knife or gun, in fact any form of physical violence where the intention is to harm another. Also included are actions which do not involve physical violence but are intended to cause pain. These include verbal behaviour, such as threats, insults and sarcasm, and facial expressions and postures which are intended to communicate aggression.

So far, so good, but defining aggression is not as simple as the definition in the first paragraph suggests. Some psychologists have made a distinction between *hostile* or *antisocial aggression*, where the primary aim is to hurt others, and *instrumental aggression*, where the primary aim is not to hurt others but to attain some other goal. Examples of instrumental aggression include a parent smacking a child with the aim of improving his or her behaviour, or a rugby player who injures an opponent through a rough tackle. In these cases, aggression is a means to an end. The primary intention is not to harm others.

There are two further kinds of aggressive behaviour identified by psychologists. *Prosocial aggression* is aggressive behaviour which is performed to prevent or offset greater harm. For example, a bystander who intervenes forcefully to break up a fight may use moderate aggression to prevent more substantial harm occurring. *Sanctioned aggression* is aggressive behaviour that is usually permitted or excused. This is because the outcome of the behaviour is seen as outweighing or justifying the aggression. That is, the end justifies the means – for example, a wife who murders her husband claiming self-defence after years of physical abuse. Most societies normally grant certain groups like the police or the military the right to engage in sanctioned aggression, so long as it is seen to be committed in the course of legitimate duties.

Measuring aggression

When measuring anything, it is essential to know exactly what is being measured. Given the various types of aggression identified above, it is important to know which type is being measured in order to evaluate and compare different studies. For example, if one researcher based their measurements on hostile aggression and another on instrumental aggression, are they measuring the same thing?

In an attempt to get around this problem, most social psychological studies have focused exclusively on physical acts of aggression which involve causing pain to others. They have tried to produce aggressive behaviour in the laboratory. Experiments have been devised in which the behaviour to be measured is an analogue or substitute for 'real life' aggression.

The most common analogue has been the use of buttons or knobs which actually, or supposedly (as far as the participants were concerned) delivered an electric shock to another person. Lubek (1979) estimated that around 65% of all social psychological studies of aggression used this analogue.

There are a number of problems with such experiments. The first involves ethical issues. Many would see it as unacceptable to put pressure on participants to inflict pain on others. Where the shocks are not real, yet the participants believe they are, then it is unacceptable to mislead – or lie – to the participants. Second, there is evidence that some participants do not believe that they are really inflicting pain. If that is the case, this may have an effect on the way the participant behaves. They may behave more aggressively than they would in 'real life' because they know that they are in no danger of causing any actual harm. Third, the experimental situation is artificial, even bizarre. In everyday life, who in their right mind would sit in front of a 'shock box' and deliver electric shocks to a fellow human being? In view of this, to what extent can we generalise from the laboratory to the world outside?

Table 1 shows some of the ways that social psychologists have attempted to measure aggression. The table raises two main problems. First, are they all measuring the same thing, ie the same type of aggression? Second, even if they are, will different methods of measurement produce different results?

Table 1   Measurements of aggression

- Punching an inflatable plastic doll (Bandura et al., 1961)
- Pushing a button which delivers an electric shock to someone else (Berkowitz & LePage, 1967)
- Pencil-and-paper ratings by teachers and classmates of a child's level of aggressiveness (Eron, 1982)
- Written self-report by institutionalised teenage boys about their prior aggressive behaviour (Leyens et al., 1975)
- A verbal expression of willingness to use violence in an experimental laboratory setting (Geen, 1978)

Adapted from Hogg & Vaughn, 1995

Key terms

Hostile or antisocial aggression *Behaviour in which the primary aim is to inflict harm on others.*

Instrumental aggression *Behaviour which involves harm to others but only as a means to some other end or goal.*

Prosocial aggression *Aggressive behaviour which aims to prevent the occurrence of some greater harm.*

Sanctioned aggression *Aggressive behaviour which is either legal or permitted because the ultimate outcome is seen as desirable or justifiable.*

Activity 1   Defining aggression

Item A   Psychological definitions

- Aggression is any series of actions whose goal is to injure another organism (Selg, 1973).
- Aggression is an act whose direct purpose is to cause damage or injury, although this may be incidental to the aggressor's overall purpose (Schott, 1975).
- Aggression is injurious and destructive behaviour that is socially defined as aggressive on the basis of a variety of factors (Bandura, 1973).
- Aggression is a name for all kinds of different actions which tend to vary historically and across culture (Stainton Rogers et al., 1995).

Questions

1   State the benefits and drawbacks of each of the psychological definitions of aggression in Item A.

2   What problems did you find in devising your own definition of aggression?

Item B   Personal definition

Try to devise your own definition of aggression. Your definition should be one sentence long. It should be able to cover all the kinds of behaviour and circumstances that you would normally think of as 'aggressive'. Once you have devised a definition see if it can be used to cover the following situations:

- A schoolboy who bullies other children in the playground to extort their dinner money
- A mother who slaps her child after he has just run out into the road
- An exchange of abuse between two drivers following an overtaking incident
- A drunken brawl between rival groups of young men at a night club
- A wife who murders her husband after enduring years of physical and emotional abuse
- A politician who authorises military action against another country.

1.2 Social psychological explanations of aggression

Social psychological theories of aggression suggest that aggressive behaviour arises through an interaction of the individual with a particular kind of situation that in some way 'triggers' or generates aggression.

Frustration-aggression hypothesis

This hypothesis dominated aggression research for several decades. Dollard et al. (1939) suggested that aggression is a specific response that individuals make to *frustration*. They described frustration as an unpleasant state which an individual experiences when their attempts to attain some goal are blocked (see Figure 1). The theory claims that frustration always leads to aggression and that every aggressive act is the result of some form of frustration.

For example, if Susan's attempts to study for an examination are thwarted by her noisy neighbours, she will express this frustration with some form of aggression, such as hammering violently on the wall or going next door to confront her neighbours. The theory also states that aggression can sometimes be displaced – turned towards somebody or something that is not necessarily the cause of the initial frustration. For example, Susan might displace her aggression by shouting at her brother, or by kicking the furniture.

Evaluation The frustration-aggression hypothesis has been widely criticised. It has been pointed out that frustration does not always result in aggression. The frustrated individual may well burst into tears, become depressed, or simply withdraw from the situation. This is not surprising given that there are constraints on aggressive behaviour in all human societies. There are also innumerable examples of aggression which does not arise from frustration, for example, 'cold-blooded' acts of premeditated murder committed by a paid killer.

In response to these criticisms, Miller et al. (1941) revised the hypothesis slightly, stating that frustration leads to a range of responses, with aggression being the most common but not the only possible response. However, this revised hypothesis still fails to answer why there should be such a wide variation amongst individuals in response to frustration. To answer this, we need to know why one person becomes aggressive when frustrated, but another simply shrugs their shoulders and remains calm.

Even though the frustration-aggression hypothesis has overstated the link between frustration and aggression, many researchers still see it as the most important idea in social-psychological research on aggression (Moghaddam, 1998).

Relative deprivation theory

One of the problems with the frustration-aggression hypothesis is identifying the causes of frustration. Common sense suggests that people at the bottom of the social system will experience most hardship, and this will lead to high levels of frustration and aggression. Put simply, deprivation leads to frustration which leads to aggression.

This argument ignores the fact that people define and assess deprivation from their own viewpoints. Thus one person's poverty is another person's reasonable standard of living. This idea forms the basis of *relative deprivation theory*. Relative deprivation is a perception held by an individual or a group that they have less than they deserve, or less than they have been led to expect. For example, relative deprivation exists when people see a gap between their present standard of living and the standard of living they feel they *should* be enjoying. It is the relative part of relative deprivation that is seen to lead to frustration, aggression and social unrest (Brown, 1995).

Consider the following example. In 1967 and 1968, inner-city black ghettoes across the USA exploded in a series of riots. The phrase, 'a revolution in rising expectations' was a widely used shorthand explanation for these events. In Jesse Jackson's words, the riots occurred 'in the middle of rising expectations and the increased, though inadequate, social spending'. People's expectations for improvement had risen, these expectations had not been met, the result was relative deprivation which led to widespread rioting. The most serious rioting did not occur in the poorest areas but in Watts in Los Angeles and in Detroit, areas of considerable poverty but not as bad as many other inner-city areas. According to the official report on the riots, the 'typical rioter' was better educated than his non-rioting counterpart and 'he feels strongly that he *deserves* a better job' (National Advisory Commission on Civil Disorders, 1968).

Relative deprivation often occurs when things are improving. For example, the revolutions in Eastern Europe occurred when the grip of the Soviet Union was loosening. Similarly, the breakup of the former Yugoslavia occurred when its citizens began to hope for and expect something better (Aronson et al., 1997).

Evaluation Relative deprivation theory makes the distinction

Key term

Relative deprivation *A perception held by an individual or a group that they have less than they deserve, or less than they expect. In this sense deprivation is relative – it is in the eye of the beholder.*

Figure 1 Frustration-aggression hypothesis

Individual attempts to attain goal → Goal blocked → Frustration → Aggression

between actual deprivation and relative deprivation. This distinction is important. Evidence suggests that it is relative deprivation that leads to frustration. However, when it comes to explaining aggression, relative deprivation theory has the same problems as the frustration-aggression hypothesis – in particular, frustration does not necessarily lead to aggression.

Cue-arousal theory

Cue-arousal theory builds on the frustration-aggression hypothesis (Berkowitz, 1964, 1974). It adds the idea that frustration first leads to anger (see Figure 3). Being angry makes the individual more likely to act aggressively, but does not automatically lead to aggression. What makes the difference is whether or not there is a stimulus present in the situation which acts as a *cue* to aggressive behaviour. To act as a cue, the stimulus must be associated with aggression by the angry person.

Say that Carl is struggling to carry a tray full of drinks in a crowded bar when his arm is violently jogged, spilling several of the drinks. Carl would experience some frustration leading to immediate anger – his goal of successfully buying a round of drinks has been interrupted when nearly attained. If the person who jogged him then turns round and apologies in a tone that Carl takes to be sarcastic, this will act as a cue to turn Carl's anger into outright aggression. The important point here is that there are many things in the situation which could act as a cue (perhaps loud music or being in a crowded space), but only those which Carl has learnt in the past to associate with aggression (in this case, speaking sarcastically) will actually cue Carl to express his anger as aggressive behaviour.

The weapons effect The problem of identifying exactly which stimuli can act as cues for aggression was explored by Berkowitz and LePage (1967). They set out to test the idea that certain objects, such as knives or guns, act as clear cues to aggression for most people. They called this the *weapons effect*. Berkowitz and LePage studied the effect by asking participants to carry out a task. They were evaluated on the task by being given a number of electric shocks ranging from 1 (very satisfactory) to 7 (very poor). The purpose of the evaluation, however, was simply to produce different levels of anger in the participants – the number of shocks had actually nothing to do with their performance. Some participants ('angered' group) were given more shocks than others ('non-angered' group).

In the second part of the experiment the roles were reversed, with participants evaluating the performance of other people on the task, using the same shock procedure. During this second part, a shotgun and a revolver were left on a table near to the person carrying out the task. Participants were told that they belonged to the person they were evaluating but that they

should ignore the weapons. The idea was that the weapons would cue aggressive behaviour from participants. This would then be measured by counting the number of shocks they gave as evaluation. The 'angered' group gave an average number of 6 shocks, whilst the 'non-angered' group gave on average only 2 shocks, despite the performance they were evaluating being the same in each case (see Figure 2). The researchers also used a control group in which 'angered' and 'non-angered' participants performed evaluations *without* weapons being present. The 'angered' group gave more shocks than the 'non-angered' group but less than the 'angered' participants gave when weapons were present. Berkowitz and LePage claimed that this showed that weapons could act as cues for aggression for individuals in an angry state.

Evaluation The weapons effect is the clearest demonstration of cue-arousal theory. However, many researchers have failed to find evidence for this effect in their own experiments (Page & Scheidt, 1971; Turner & Simons, 1974). This may be because the presence of a weapon might make participants think twice about acting aggressively for fear of being harmed themselves. There are also likely to be important cultural differences. In the USA – where the original research was conducted – guns are carried more frequently than in many other parts of the world. Reactions of individuals to the sight of guns are likely to vary from society to society. This makes Berkowitz's results and the theory itself difficult to generalise.

Finally, there are a number of problems with the experiment itself. First, it has low ecological validity – the setting (the laboratory) and the task (delivering electric shocks) are a long way from everyday life. And, unlike most real-life situations, the 'victim' has no opportunity to retaliate. Second, there is

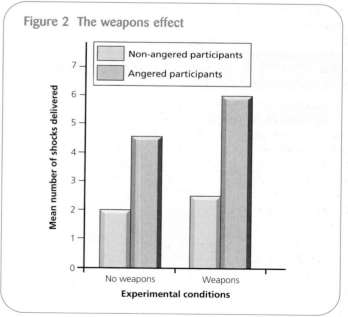

Figure 2 The weapons effect

Figure 3 Cue-arousal theory

Individual attempts to attain goal → Goal Blocked → Frustration → Anger → Cue (eg. weapons effect) → Aggression evidence from electric shock experiments that some participants believe they are not really hurting the 'victim'. Results from these participants are not directly comparable to the results from those who believe they are inflicting pain (Baron & Byrne, 1997).

Key term

The weapons effect *The cueing of aggression by the presence of a weapon.*

Excitation-transfer effect

Imagine that it's mid-morning. You have just downed a fourth cup of strong coffee. You start to feel a little edgy and irritable. You snap at people without much provocation. The reason for this is that your body is flooded with caffeine, causing your heart to beat a little faster and giving the sensation of general arousal. The idea that arousal caused by one source can be unwittingly transferred to a new situation has been offered as an explanation for aggressive behaviour by Zillmann's (1979) *excitation-transfer model.*

Arousal can be generated in a variety of ways – by drugs such as caffeine, by exercise, by driving in rush hour traffic, and so on. According to the excitation transfer model, arousal takes time to die down. It may continue when a person moves on to a new situation. As a result, the aroused person is more likely to respond to provocation with aggressive behaviour.

Zillmann et al. (1972) conducted a series of experiments in which participants were first provoked by verbal abuse and later offered the opportunity to give electric shocks to the person who

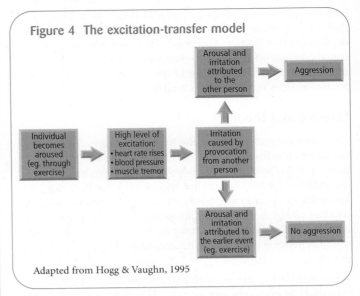

Figure 4   The excitation-transfer model

Adapted from Hogg & Vaughn, 1995

provoked them. In between, participants either exercised vigorously on a cycling machine or sat quietly watching slides. Participants who had exercised tended to give far more shocks than did those who watched slides. The 'exercise' group had apparently transferred their physical arousal from one situation to another.

Evaluation The excitation-transfer model appears to provide a reasonable explanation for what happens when people who are already 'hyped-up' in some way go on to engage in aggressive behaviour. It does not, however, explain situations where people knowingly set out to commit aggressive acts which they have planned in a cold and calculating manner. The model has been criticised for suggesting that aggression is produced in an unthinking, automatic way. It is as though we get carried along

Activity 2   Frustration and aggression

Item A   Lynchings and the price of cotton

Adapted from Hovland & Sears, 1940

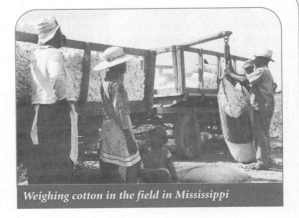

Weighing cotton in the field in Mississippi

This graph shows a) the price of cotton in the southern states of the USA between 1882 and 1930 and b) the number of African Americans lynched in those states. During this period, the economy of the South was largely based on cotton. The graph showing the price of cotton shows the highest price at the top of the graph. The graph showing lynching shows the highest number of lynchings at the bottom of the graph.

Item B — Rebellion at Auschwitz

Auschwitz was one of the death camps set up by the Nazis. In 1944, 12,000 people at this camp were killed in the gas chambers every day. Primo Levi, who survived Auschwitz, states that the few cases of rebellion did not involve the masses who suffered most, but 'prisoners who were privileged in some way'.

Adapted from Levi, 1986

Auschwitz, January 1945

Item D — The aggression machine

The aggression machine was invented by the American psychologist Arnold Buss. Participants were told they could deliver shocks of varying intensities to another person by pushing buttons on the machine. In fact no shocks were delivered. Before its invention, studies of aggression were based on asking participants how they would respond to imaginary situations, or their *verbal* reactions to frustrating experiences set up by the experimenter. Now the aggression machine provided a harmless way of studying physical aggression. Researchers argued that as far as the participants were concerned, they were actually causing pain to others. And they could select the level of pain. Here, at last, was a safe way of measuring physical aggression under controlled laboratory conditions. This was the promise of the aggression machine.

Adapted from Baron & Byrne, 1977

Item C — Road rage in Reading

Police say road rage is increasing on the streets of Reading after the latest incident in which a shotgun was pointed at a woman motorist. A bare-chested man pointed the gun out of the window of the car he was in after it pulled level with the woman who had stopped to let a fire engine pass. The woman estimated the gun was pointed at her for about five seconds before the white Rover sped off. This latest road rage incident came just as police released details of an earlier attack, which they described as 'one of the worst cases in Reading'. It involved the driver of a Range Rover who chased an Escort containing a family. The Range Rover hit the Escort several times before the driver got out and attacked the driver of the Escort and then punched in a side window of the car. A police spokeswoman is stunned by both attacks. She said, 'It appears road rage is getting worse in general across the country. I don't think it is just a case of it being reported more. It is just part of the general deterioration of people's behaviour. And I don't believe that hot weather is a good excuse, either.'

Adapted from the *Reading Evening Post*, 28.6.1996

Road rage

Questions

1   a) Briefly summarise the graphs in Item A.

    b) Use the frustration-aggression hypothesis to explain the correlation between the price of cotton and the number of lynchings.

2   Read Item B. Use relative deprivation theory to explain why privileged prisoners were more likely to rebel.

3   Read Item C. Briefly explain 'road rage' in terms of the following theories: frustration-aggression, cue-arousal and excitation-transfer.

4   Read Item D. What are the advantages and disadvantages of using the aggression machine to study aggression?

by our aroused state, and without thinking, lash out at other people.

In response to this criticism, Zillmann (1988, 1994) reformulated the model in the following way. Yes, we can be carried along by our aroused state – strong emotions can make us less rational and less self-conscious in our actions. But, cognition – thoughts – may also affect emotion. Sometimes we can *reappraise* or reassess the situation we are in. For example, we may suddenly realise that we are feeling irritable because of the coffee and not because of the way people around us are behaving. So provocation may not automatically result in an aroused person behaving aggressively if they can reappraise the way they are feeling (see Figure 4).

Social learning theory

Social learning theory developed from behaviourism. According to the behaviourists, behaviour that is reinforced – rewarded – is likely to be repeated and learned. Behaviour is positively reinforced if it brings about the desired outcome. Behaviour is negatively reinforced if it prevents undesirable outcomes. For example, aggression is positively reinforced when a child obtains a toy by hitting another child. Aggression is negatively reinforced when a child prevents other children from taking his or her toys by threatening to hit them. In both cases, aggressive behaviour is rewarded and likely to be learned.

Social learning theory emphasises that learning occurs in a social context. As well as learning behaviour *directly*, by being personally rewarded, people also learn behaviour *indirectly* by observing what happens to other people. Albert Bandura (1977) calls this *learning by vicarious experience* or *observational learning*. An infant, for example, may observe an older sister getting what she wants by throwing a temper tantrum. The younger child may then imitate this behaviour in similar situations. In doing so, they are *modelling* their own behaviour on that of their sister.

Modelling behaviour There are three main stages to the modelling of any form of behaviour: *acquisition, instigation* and *regulation*. Say that Paul watches his older brother stealing car radios. He will rapidly learn through observation the best way to break into a car, disconnect the radio and flee the scene. The behaviour is now acquired. Paul may then progress to actually taking part in the thefts, perhaps initially serving as look-out and then going on to break into cars on his own. This is the instigation phase. But simply having taken part in the thefts does not mean that Paul will necessarily continue with the behaviour. This will depend on whether his behaviour is reinforced either directly (eg, being able to sell the car radios; not getting caught) or indirectly (eg, pressure to carry on from brother and friends). Reinforcement determines the maintenance or regulation of behaviour.

The 'Bobo doll' studies To study the process of modelling aggressive behaviour, Bandura and colleagues performed a number of studies involving children observing an adult behaving aggressively towards an inflatable toy. These studies are now part of the folklore of psychology and are often misinterpreted, so it is worth spelling out exactly what Bandura did and what the results actually were.

Experiment 1 (Bandura et al., 1961). In this experiment, nursery school children were asked by an experimenter to play by themselves in a playroom containing a range of toys, including a 'Bobo doll' – a five foot high, inflatable plastic doll which bounces back upright when hit. An adult, who the children had not met, then entered the room and was invited by the experimenter to play with the toys. The experimenter then left the room. At first, the adult played quietly, but then attacked the Bobo doll. They punched the doll, threw it to the ground and sat on it whilst saying phrases such as 'sock him in the nose', 'hit him down', 'kick him' and 'pow'. At this point, the experimenter returned and, in the most bizarre part of the experiment, deliberately frustrated the child by taking them to another room and showing them a 'varied array of attractive toys'. Once the child showed interest in playing with the toys, they were told that these were reserved for other, better children. The child was then taken to a further room which contained both aggressive toys (eg, dart guns, tether balls), nonaggressive toys (eg, crayons, dolls) and the Bobo doll.

Bandura found that children who had seen the Bobo doll being mistreated earlier reproduced this behaviour. They hit the doll, sat on it, threw it around, just like the adult they had observed earlier. And they repeated the phrases used by the adult. By contrast, a control group who had not been exposed to the aggressive behaviour tended not to act in these ways. They did however play with the aggressive toys, and some behaved aggressively, but not in the same way as the children in the experimental condition. The overall finding of this experiment is that children can learn and then perform unusually aggressive behaviour through direct observation of an adult model.

Experiment 2 (Bandura et al., 1963a). This experiment used much the same procedure as experiment 1, but with an important difference. Six groups of nursery children took part. Groups one and two watched either a male or a female adult behaving aggressively, as before. Groups three and four saw a film of the same male or female adults behaving in exactly the same way. Group five watched a cartoon of 'Herman the Cat' behaving aggressively towards the Bobo doll. Group six, the control group, saw no aggression at all in the first part of the experiment.

The groups of children who had seen the real-life or the filmed aggression exhibited nearly twice as many instances of aggression in the second part of the experiment as the control group. There was no significant difference between the amount of aggression shown by the groups who saw either of the films and the groups who saw the real-life aggression. So it did not matter whether the filmed aggression had been 'realistic' or cartoon-like. It was also found that boys tended to behave more aggressively than girls. Overall, the findings of this experiment suggest that filmed aggression is just as powerful an influence on young children as real-life aggression.

Experiment 3 (Bandura et al., 1963b). This experiment used a similar procedure. Four groups of nursery children took part. Three groups watched a film showing two adult models – Rocky and Johnny – playing together. Group one saw Rocky behaving aggressively towards Johnny. At the end Rocky appears victorious, and leaves with all the toys. Group two saw a slightly different film where Rocky is punished for his aggression. He is spanked and 'thoroughly thrashed' by Johnny, who leaves with the toys. Group three saw Rocky and Johnny playing nonagressively, and group four watched no film at all. Each group was then taken to play in a room containing the same toys that were present in the film.

The findings of this experiment are not clear-cut. The group of children who saw Rocky being rewarded tended to imitate his behaviour more than the children who saw him being punished. However, there was no difference in the amount of imitation between the children who had seen Rocky punished and the groups who had either seen the nonaggressive film or no film at all. This suggests that seeing Rocky punished did not deter children from imitating his behaviour. More importantly, the total levels of aggression across all groups were roughly similar. Overall, the findings of this experiment suggest that seeing aggressive behaviour being rewarded does not unduly influence aggression in children.

Evaluation Social learning theory offers a powerful framework for understanding how aggressive behaviour is acquired, instigated and regulated. It offers a theoretical basis for understanding how children, in particular, may vicariously learn aggressive behaviour from a range of possible models – for example, actors on television, peers, adult role models.

Social learning theory has been successfully applied to offending behaviour. Feldman (1994) used Bandura's ideas to discuss how offenders acquire aggressive or criminal behaviour from immediate peers. He emphasised that offending behaviour needs to be understood in terms of the social context in which it is acquired and regulated (eg, family, local community) rather than solely in terms of personal disposition.

However, the Bobo doll studies on which Bandura's theory is based have been criticised on numerous grounds.

- Because the experiments do not involve harm to another human being – merely an inflatable doll – they do not provide a good example of aggression (Joseph et al., 1977).
- The Bobo doll 'invited' aggression. Sometimes known as a 'punching doll', it was designed to be hit, it was 'made for punching'. Can this type of 'playful' aggression be compared to 'real' aggression?
- Aggression is often described as antinormative or antisocial behaviour. It is possible that observing an adult mistreating the doll suggests to the children that, in this particular case, such behaviour is acceptable and normative. Remember that in experiment 1 the adult model's behaviour is not challenged or even acknowledged by the experimenter!
- In a similar study, the children who behaved most aggressively tended to be those who were rated as generally more aggressive by both their peers and their teachers (Johnston et al., 1977). This suggests that many experimental procedures may simply 'trigger' pre-existing aggressive tendencies.
- Finally, it is worth noting that all the children who took part in experiments 1 to 3 were from the Stanford University nursery. They were the children of Bandura's own colleagues and students – not the most representative of samples!

The above criticisms suggest that the ecological validity of Bandura's experiments is low. Critics have argued that 'aggression' against a Bobo doll in a laboratory setting is very different from aggression in the 'real' world. As a result, there are problems generalising Bandura's findings to the wider society.

Bandura has also been criticised for suggesting that children passively absorb the events they see around them, including those on television (Baron & Richardson, 1994). But Bandura (1973) does make an important distinction between *learning* aggression and actually *performing* in an aggressive way.

Children may learn all sorts of things from the media, but this does not necessarily mean that they will act them out. When interviewing the children in experiment 3, Bandura found they knew perfectly well that Rocky's behaviour was wrong. He was described by the children as 'wicked', 'mean', and 'rough and bossy'. What the children were attracted to was his success at getting all the toys rather than his rough treatment of Johnny. This suggests it was the results or goals of the aggression rather than the aggression itself which really influenced the children.

Social learning theory and culture

Culture is the learned, shared behaviour of members of a particular society. *Socialisation* is the process by which people learn the culture of their society. They are socialised by their parents, relatives, neighbours, peers, teachers, and by the mass media.

Culture includes norms, values, attitudes and beliefs. Culture therefore includes norms, values, attitudes and beliefs about aggression. People learn about aggression as part of their socialisation. What they learn will, to some extent, guide and direct their behaviour. Since cultures vary from society to society, so will definitions of aggression, attitudes towards aggression, norms governing aggression and the value attached to aggressive behaviour.

These points seem fairly obvious, but until recently they have been largely ignored by psychologists studying aggression. But, as Activity 3 indicates, they are important points. They show how aggression can be learned in a social context. They show how aggression can vary from society to society. They show how aggression can be shaped by culture.

Activity 3 shows clearly that some cultures encourage the expression of aggression, others do not. The Yanomamo and the !Kung represent opposite ends of the spectrum.

What counts as an aggressive act also varies from culture to culture. As noted in Activity 3, the Yanomamo see crop failure or illness as acts of aggression by their enemies. In Western society, such events are unlikely to be seen in this light.

The way aggression is expressed is influenced by culture. In some societies, aggression can take the form of sorcery – for example, in Haiti, believers in Voodoo sometimes cast spells to harm others.

The above examples indicate the importance of taking culture into account when explaining human aggression (Moghaddam et al., 1993).

Evaluation The idea of culture adds a new dimension to the study of aggression. It indicates that when, where, how and why aggression is expressed is influenced by culture and varies from culture to culture. It shows how aspects of aggression are learned in social contexts – as part of the socialisation process.

However, social learning theory fails to explain the origins of aggressive behaviour. Why are the Yanomamo so aggressive? To say they have learned to be aggressive because they have been socialised into a culture that values aggression is only part of the answer. Why does Yanomamo culture value aggression? An answer to this question requires an historical view of the circumstances that led to the development of this value. An example of this approach is given in Activity 4.

Activity 3   Culture and aggression

Item A   The Yanomamo

Yanomamo in a ritual display of strength to guests arriving for a feast

The Yanomamo live in the tropical rainforests of the Upper Amazon on the borders of Venezuela and Brazil. Numbering around 20,000, they are a fierce and violent people. Elders teach the children to admire and live up to these qualities.

There is almost constant warfare between villages, and fighting within villages is frequent. Men proudly display their battle scars and a man's love for his wife is measured by the harshness of the beatings she receives. Bravery is idealised, disputes are settled by violent confrontation, and a man's status is largely determined by his aggression. If a person falls sick or crops fail, members of an enemy village are usually blamed. War often results – revenge is necessary to maintain honour and respect.

Almost half the men over 25 have killed at least one person – around one third of the male population die violent deaths.

Adapted from Chagnon, 1988

Item B   The !Kung

!Kung family

The !Kung of the Kalahari Desert in southern Africa have been described as 'the harmless people'. Controversy is avoided, physical violence is rare, conflicts are resolved through negotiation or withdrawal. They respond to threats from neighbouring communities by retreating deeper into the desert rather than fighting back. Bravery or aggressiveness are not valued, they are not idealised as a sign of masculinity.

Adapted from Moghaddam et al., 1993

Questions

1   Read Items A and B. With reference to aggression, briefly outline the differences between the Yanomamo and the !Kung.

2   How does social learning theory and the idea of culture help to explain these differences?

Deindividuation

Social psychology has a longstanding interest in crowds and aggression. In a classic early work, Gustav Le Bon (1895) wrote at length about the 'mob violence' during the French Revolution in the late eighteenth century. Le Bon noted that individuals are capable of extraordinary acts of aggression and violence when part of a crowd. These same individuals would be very unlikely to behave in this way under different circumstances.

Le Bon believed the explanation for this difference was to do with the unique properties of crowds. Individuals become less identifiable when they are part of a crowd. No one person stands out. This makes people feel anonymous and hence less accountable for their own actions.

Le Bon claimed that crowds generate a kind of primitive or uncivilised state. Individuals lose their self-control – they are at the mercy of uncontrollable impulses and whims. As a result, crowds tend to be highly impulsive and suggestible. They tend to look towards a leader – such as Napoleon – to give them direction.

These ideas were taken up by Festinger et al. (1952), who coined the phrase *deindividuation*. This refers to situations where individuals experience themselves as an anonymous 'part

of the crowd'. They feel merged with one another and consequently less aware of themselves as an individual. This may result in a loss of personal responsibility and fear of public disapproval. As a result, the normal constraints on behaviour are reduced. In particular, people may lose the inhibitions which prevent them from acting aggressively.

Experimental evidence A number of experiments have supported the view that deindividuation can lead to aggression. In one experiment, female participants were asked to deliver shocks to a woman as part of a 'learning experiment'. One group of participants wore bulky clothing and hoods which covered their faces, they were never called by name, and they were placed in a dimly lit room. A second group wore their regular clothes plus large name tags, they were frequently called by name, and they were placed in a brightly lit room. The shocks delivered by the hooded group were twice as severe as those given by the other group (Zimbardo, 1970).

In an experiment conducted in Germany, children were divided randomly into five-a-side teams to play handball. In each case, one team played in their normal clothes, the other team played in orange shirts. Those who wore orange shirts played significantly more aggressively than those who wore their everyday clothes (Rehm et al., 1987).

Activity 4   Aggression, social change and culture

Item A   The Iroquois

The Iroquois lived in northwestern USA. For hundreds of years they were at peace with their neighbours – they were regarded as a peaceful, non-aggressive people. By the 17th century the 'fur trade' was in full swing. Tribes in the area had become dependent on metal goods, guns and cloth traded by the French in return for furs. Their territories were trapped and hunted to exhaustion and tribes fought each other to acquire new land.

Within a fairly short time, the Iroquois changed from a peaceful to a warlike people. Their warriors became renowned for their ferocity and aggression. A man's status increasingly depended on his prowess in war. And their neighbours, the Huron, were now their rivals and their enemies as they competed for land and furs.

Adapted from Hunt, 1940

An Iroquois warrior drawn in the 18th century

Questions

1   Briefly explain why the Iroquois changed from a peaceful to a warlike people.

2   Why is it important to look at social change when explaining the influence of culture on aggression?

Real-world evidence There are plenty of real-world examples of the relationship between deindividuation and aggression. Mullen (1986) analysed newspaper reports of lynching and mob violence in the USA between 1899 and 1946. He found that the more people in the mob, the greater their savagery and viciousness and the more prolonged it tended to be. Mann (1981) analysed 21 reports of suicide in American newspapers from the 1960s and 70s. In ten cases, he identified a 'baiting crowd' – a crowd which baits the individual threatening suicide with shouts of 'jump' and the like. Baiting was more likely to occur at night, when the crowd was large (over 300 people), and when there was some distance between the crowd and the person threatening suicide – for example, a crowd at ground level and the individual on the top of a tall building.

Deindividuation and self-awareness The above evidence appears to provide support for the view that people are less conscious of their identity and less self-aware when they are part of a group or a crowd. As a result, they lose their usual inhibitions and this can make them more aggressive. However, there is evidence that in certain situations, aggressive behaviour does not result from a reduction in self-awareness. This apparently conflicting evidence makes sense in terms of Prentice-Dunn and Rogers' (1983) distinction between *public* and *private self-awareness*.

Public self-awareness This is the individual's sense of being visible to other people. As part of a crowd, in a dimly-lit room, or wearing a hood or a mask, people are less visible and less likely to be identified. They feel anonymous and this reduces their public self-awareness. As a result, they feel there is a greater chance of 'getting away' with behaviour that might otherwise be punished – for example, people who took advantage of the civil emergency during the Los Angeles earthquake in 1994 to loot goods from damaged shops.

The anonymity that results from a lowering of public awareness reduces the power of social norms – people sometimes do things they would normally feel too embarrassed or too afraid of doing. Some researchers see this as disinhibition – a lowering of inhibition – rather than deindividuation. For example, Diener (1980) argues that deindividuation only occurs when private self-awareness is reduced – when individuals 'lose' themselves in the group.

Private self-awareness This is the individual's own sense of self-awareness – their awareness of their own actions, inner thoughts and feelings. Immersed in a crowd, sharing a collective experience, swept up in the emotions of the group, people tend to focus on what is going on around them rather than themselves. There is a loss of personal identity – people 'forget themselves'. When this happens they tend to become more impulsive and less rational. They go along with what other people are doing because, to some extent, they are unable to think for themselves. For some researchers, this is real deindividuation – it is a loss of private self-awareness.

A decrease in either public self-awareness or private self-awareness may result in aggressive behaviour. But the important point is this. When public self-awareness is reduced, people are still capable of making rational choices. They are less likely to do this when private self-awareness is reduced.

Evaluation of deindividuation theory

The evidence There are plenty of examples of a link between deindividuation and aggression from both the psychological laboratory and the real world. But there are also plenty of examples of deindividuation either reducing, or having no effect on, aggression (Mummendey, 1996). Responses to disasters such as floods and earthquakes show that large groups of people can act in a selfless and altruistic way when caring for survivors. Religious festivals often involve large crowds expressing goodwill to each other and to humankind in general.

Deindividuation doesn't necessarily lead to aggression. Under certain circumstances, it can increase the possibility of aggression, it can make its expression more likely.

Emergent norm theory Deindividuation theory suggests that people in crowd situations lose their inhibitions and are no longer guided by social norms. Some researchers believe that new norms emerge in crowd situations (Turner, 1974). This idea is known as *emergent norm theory*. If people become aggressive, it is because they are being directed by norms which apply to crowd behaviour in specific situations – for example, stone throwing in demonstrations against authority. Members of a crowd reinforce each other's behaviour, seeing themselves behaving appropriately in that situation. Emergent norm theory provides an alternative explanation for aggressive behaviour in crowds.

Social identity theory There is a big difference between a crowd gathered to watch a person threatening suicide and a crowd gathered for a demonstration. The first crowd is made up of individuals with little in common – apart from the fact that they happened to be at a certain place at a certain time. The second crowd has a common cause and a common enemy – for example, anti-capitalist demonstrators vs the state; the Anti-Nazi League vs the National Front. To some degree, these crowds have a shared social identity.

Rather than losing their identity, people sometimes come together *because* of their shared social identity (Tajfel & Turner,

1979). They have a common purpose and their behaviour is directed by group norms. When a common enemy is identified, violence may result. However, this violence is not unrestrained and undirected – it is not simply a normless release of frustration and aggression. This can be seen from Reicher's analysis of a riot which occurred in the African Caribbean area of St Pauls in Bristol in 1980. The rioters were selective – they chose their targets. They directed their aggression at symbols of the state – the police and banks. They looted and burned shops and businesses owned by people from outside St Pauls. They felt a strong sense of social identity (Reicher, 1984).

Activity 5 — Deindividuation and aggression

Item A — Warpaint

Watchful Fox, a warrior of the Native American Sauk and Fox tribe

A study of 24 cultures indicated that warriors who went into battle with their faces painted were more likely to kill or torture captured enemies.

Adapted from Watson, 1973

Item B — Ku Klux Klan

The Ku Klux Klan – a racist organisation in the USA whose members have mutilated and murdered African Americans.

Item C — Crowds

Pop festival

Members of the Anti-Nazi League protesting against a National Front march

Item D Political violence

Palestinians throwing stones at a Jewish settlement in the Gaza Strip

Questions

1 Explain the findings outlined in Item A.

2 How might the uniform of the Ku Klux Klan encourage aggression?

3 Deindividuation might occur in both the situations pictured in Item C.

 a) Why might it occur?

 b) Which situation is more likely to lead to aggression? Why?

4 Briefly explain the behaviour pictured in Item D in terms of a) emergent norm theory and b) social identity theory.

Item E Football violence

Euro 2000. English soccer fans throw chairs at German fans in Charleroi.

Research indicates that football violence is not simply the 'mindless aggression' portrayed by the media. Violence is usually organised well before a match starts. The aggression is 'ritualised', it follows rules which are often designed to prevent physical harm. For example, when home fans 'see off' opposing fans after the match, the norm is to hurl insults but avoid catching them. Football violence is usually a well-staged performance.

Adapted from Marsh et al., 1978

5 Use Item E to criticise the view that aggression results from a failure to follow norms due to a loss of identity and self-awareness.

The social construction of aggression

Social constructionism is a recent approach to studying social behaviour. The basis of this approach is neatly summed up by one of the major contributors, Rom Harré:

'There has been a tendency among both philosophers and psychologists to abstract an entity – call it 'anger', 'love', 'grief', or 'anxiety' – and to try to study it. But what there is are angry people, upsetting scenes, sentimental episodes, grieving families and funerals, anxious parents pacing at midnight, and so on. There is a concrete world of contexts and activities. We reify and abstract from that concreteness at our peril.'(Harré, 1986)

According to Harré, psychologists have tended to examine topics like aggression in a very peculiar way. They have defined it in abstract terms and studied it in the laboratory just like natural scientists study a mineral or a newly discovered plant. Of course aggression is nothing like that! It is something people define, something they express in particular ways, in particular situations, in the company of particular people. It cannot be wrenched out of context and recreated in the laboratory for observation and measurement. Harré argues that psychologists should be studying real-world instances of aggression – 'the concrete world of contexts and activities', the actual occasions on which people become aggressive, the sorts of things they do and their reasons for doing them. This is because aggression, like all behaviours, is socially constructed – it is constructed by

particular people in particular social contexts.

When actual occasions are studied it becomes apparent that aggression is a complex social phenomenon. Different social groups have very different ideas about what counts as 'aggression'. For example, Marsh, Rosser and Harré (1978) studied football hooliganism. They found that the aggression is highly structured or 'ritualised' amongst gangs of football hooligans. For instance, aggression after a match tends to follow a common pattern of verbal insults between rival groups, followed by threatening but generally non-violent chases and confrontations. Marsh et al. pointed out that the hooligans were drawing on informal sets of rules about how to act aggressively. These informal rules were shared by the group, and developed over time. But members of the group did not passively follow them – they used them as guidelines to give meaning to their own behaviour and to interpret other people's behaviour. From a social constructionist view, only by observing behaviour in its social context is it possible to understand football violence.

Cross-cultural studies of aggression support the social constructionist view. As the section on culture indicated, definitions of aggression, expressions of aggression, norms governing aggression and the value attached to aggressive behaviour vary from culture to culture. This suggests that aggression is socially constructed and can only be fully understood from its cultural context.

1.3   The effects of environmental stressors on aggressive behaviour

The physical environment can have significant effects on human behaviour. The amount of light, the time of day or the weather can all affect our physiological state, our mood, and the way we think. This section examines three environmental stressors – heat, noise and crowding. They may result in heightened physiological and psychological arousal. This can lead to aggressive behaviour.

Temperature

Think of the 'hot' words and phrases used to describe people and behaviour – 'fiery tempered', 'hot-blooded', 'hot under the collar', 'tempers flare', 'steamed up', 'hot and bothered'. These phrases suggest a relationship between heat and aggression. A large number of studies have investigated the possibility of a connection between temperature and aggressive behaviour.

The long hot summer thesis During the late 1960s and early 1970s, a series of riots and civil unrest occurred in the USA during the summer months. The phrase 'long hot summer' was on everybody's lips as they made a connection between social unrest and hot weather. Carlsmith and Anderson (1979) looked at disturbances in 79 US cities between 1967 and 1971. They found a straightforward relationship: the hotter the weather, the greater the likelihood of a riot. The critical temperature seems to be between 27-32 degrees Centigrade (80-90 degrees Fahrenheit).

There appears to be a similar relationship between temperature and violent crime (though not nonviolent crime). In cities across the USA the hotter it is, the higher the level of violent crime – see Figure 5. Studies from other parts of the world have produced similar results (Anderson, 1989).

Field experiments support the idea of a relationship between temperature and aggression. In one experiment, conducted in Phoenix, Arizona, a confederate pretended to stall her car when the traffic lights turned green, so blocking the motorists behind. The hotter the temperature, the more likely the blocked motorists were to honk their horns aggressively. However, this only applied to drivers with their windows down – presumably because they did not have air conditioning (Kenrick & MacFarlane, 1986).

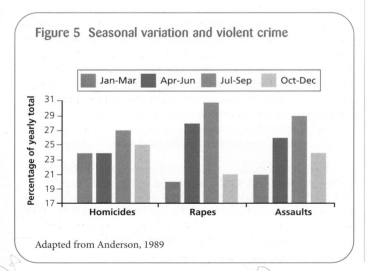

Figure 5   Seasonal variation and violent crime

Adapted from Anderson, 1989

'Too hot to handle' Laboratory studies have questioned the apparently straightforward relationship of more heat, more aggression. In one experiment, participants were placed in comfortable, hot, or very hot rooms. Those in the hot room showed more aggression to a confederate than those in the other two rooms. It appears that under extreme conditions, all people want to do is escape from the situation. When discomfort is sufficiently high, aggression appears to decline as people become preoccupied with escape (Baron & Bell, 1976).

Baron and Bell provide the following explanation. As the temperature rises, people experience *negative affect* – they feel bad. This predisposes them to aggressive behaviour, which can be triggered by a frustrating experience – for example, being stuck at a green light in Phoenix, Arizona. A rise in temperature to extreme levels leads to a further rise in negative affect, but to a decline in aggression. At this point people are too uncomfortable or exhausted to react aggressively when frustrated – they just want 'out', hence the term *negative affect escape model*. There appears to be a 'bell-shaped' or curvilinear relationship between mood and temperature – see Figure 6. So although there may be a straightforward or linear relationship between temperature and negative affect, there is a 'peak temperature' for aggression.

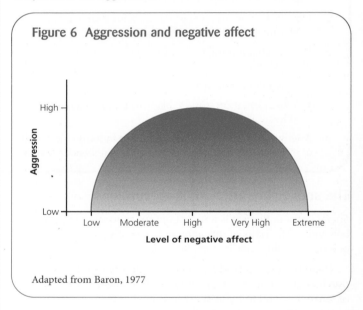

Figure 6   Aggression and negative affect

Adapted from Baron, 1977

Evaluation The negative affect escape model may work in the laboratory but it is not clear how well it works in the outside world. Participants can 'escape' from the laboratory. Escape may not be that easy in real-life situations. This may explain examples of extreme heat contributing to aggression in the real world (Geen, 1990).

The relationship between temperature and aggression is not as clear-cut as either the linear model (more heat, more aggression) or the curvilinear model (Figure 5) suggest. Other variables may affect the relationship as the following examples indicate.

- The apparent rise in violent crime during summer months may be due to factors other than temperature. People are out on the streets more in summer – there is greater social contact hence more opportunity for assault, rape and homicide. Homicide peaks in the hottest days of summer, and during the Christmas holidays – some of the coldest days of the year. A social contact explanation fits – people see more of each other over Christmas, particularly friends and relatives. Victims of homicide are usually known to the killer (Moghaddam, 1998).

- Regional differences in crime rates appear to support the view that there is a relationship between violent crime and temperature. For example, in the USA the homicide rate is higher in the hotter southern states than in the cooler northern states. However, there are many differences, apart from temperature, between these regions which may account for this. For example, Nisbett (1993) argues there is a 'culture of honour' in the south which states that any threat to a person's property or reputation must be dealt with by violence.

Noise

Noise has been defined as 'an unwanted sound, one that brings about a negative response' (Baron & Byrne, 1997). In other words, it's a sound we don't want and don't like. Sounds which are experienced as too loud and as unpredictable usually produce a negative response. Predictable sounds, such as the ticking of a clock, tend not to (Bell et al., 1990).

Noise typically produces stress. In a classic early study, Cohen et al. (1980) studied the stress levels of children living under the flight path of Los Angeles airport. In comparison with a matched sample of children living in quieter environments, the children near the airport showed more signs of chronic, long-term stress.

Laboratory studies also reveal the negative effects of noise. Glass and Singer (1972) asked participants to work on arithmetic sums whilst being exposed to very loud random bursts of noise. Rather surprisingly, the participants were able to complete the tasks, but when asked to then do a proof-reading task in a quiet environment, they performed particularly badly. The likely explanation is that whilst exposed to noise, they tried to overcome the problem and carry on with what they were doing. But the noise had an effect – they became more aroused and frustrated. This showed up when they no longer had to concentrate to shut out the noise. Another interesting finding from the study is that when participants were told they could turn off the noise by pressing a button, they made far less mistakes on the second task. It seems that having control over noise reduced their level of arousal.

Is there a relationship between noise and aggression? The following experiment, using a Buss 'aggression machine' (see p68), was designed to answer this question (Donnerstein & Wilson, 1976). In the first part, half the participants were angered by having an essay they had written harshly criticised by a confederate. The other participants had their essays praised. All participants were then given the opportunity to give the confederate electric shocks when she made mistakes on a learning task. During this part of the experiment, the participants wore headphones which transmitted low-intensity (slightly unpleasant) or high-intensity (very unpleasant) noise. Participants who had been angered gave significantly more and longer shocks if they heard high intensity noise. Those who had received praise were not affected by the intensity of the noise. This experiment suggests that noise must be combined with a further negative stimulus before it produces aggression. In another experiment, participants were told they could shut off the noise whenever they wished. In this situation, the intensity

of the noise had no affect on aggression. It appears that a belief that noise can be controlled reduces the arousal and frustration it might otherwise produce (Donnerstein & Wilson, 1976).

Crowding

Crowding is the unpleasant sensation that too many people are sharing the same space. Crowding is a subjective state. It depends upon how comfortable we feel in the close presence of others.

Density is an objective measure of the number of people who occupy a given space. An underground train with seventy passengers in the same carriage is more densely occupied than one with seventeen passengers.

The most common finding in studies of density and aggressive behaviour is that people's reaction to the same level of density depends upon their personal perceptions of crowding (Stokols, 1972). What is unbearably crowded for one person may be only moderately disagreeable for another.

There is some evidence that aggression results from the arousal and frustration caused by crowding. As with temperature, there may be a curvilinear relationship between crowding and aggressive behaviour (Matthews et al., 1979). When the crowd starts to swell, people become uncomfortable and irritated, and disposed to aggression. But once a certain level of density is reached, they become too uncomfortable to react aggressively. However, evidence of a link between aggression and density is inconclusive. Some studies indicate higher density leads to aggression, while some studies have found no link at all (Mummendey, 1996). One laboratory study found that increased density for males led to increased feelings of aggression, but just the opposite occurred for females (Stokols et al., 1973).

As noted earlier, perception of crowding varies from one person to another. There are a number of reasons for this.

Intensification Increases in density of people may intensify someone's usual reaction to the situation (Freedman, 1975). For example, if I dislike commuting by train, then an increase in the number of passengers may lead me to feel crowded and quite likely aroused and frustrated. But if I enjoy a night out dancing, then a packed dance floor at a club may actually increase my enjoyment.

Stimulus overload Situations where we have to deal with a large number of people at once are stressful because there are a lot of stimuli to manage (Cohen, 1978). A parent accompanying a group of young children on a school trip is likely to find the experience highly stressful because they have to constantly attend to what a number of children are doing. A family trip to the same destination may be much less stressful because of the decreased stimulus demands.

Perceived control When we believe that we have the ability to leave a crowded situation, this has an effect on our perception of crowding. Sherrod (1974) performed an experiment similar to Glass and Singer (1972), where level of crowd density rather than noise was used as an environmental stressor during a problem-solving task. As with the noise study, when participants were told they could control the interference (by leaving the room), the effects of the stressor were minimised.

Culture and gender There is some evidence of cultural variation in the amount of space which people feel they need around them before becoming uncomfortable. South Americans, for example, supposedly require less distance between people during polite social interaction than North Americans (Hall, 1959). There are also marked gender differences. Men become aggressive far more readily than women in response to the same crowd density (Freedman et al., 1972).

Evaluation and conclusion

The findings of research into the relationship between crowding and aggression are inconclusive. There are two main reasons for this. They apply to the findings of all research on the relationship between environmental stressors and aggression.

- First, what matters is how a person perceives the potential stressor, rather than the actual nature of the stressor itself. One person may perceive a certain density as crowding – an unpleasant sensation – while another might experience it as exciting, cosy and so on.
- Second, there are all sorts of other variables which affect the relationship between environmental stressors and aggression. For example, negative affect rather than arousal seems to be the important link between temperature and aggression. High population densities in inner city areas have been

linked to high rates of violent crime. But this ignores the many variables often found in inner city areas which may well influence the crime rate. These include poverty, substandard housing, high levels of unemployment, low educational attainment and low paid, low status, low skill occupations. When these factors are taken into account the link between high density and crime disappears (Winsborough, 1965) and the link between temperature and crime appears slight (Baron & Richardson, 1994).

Key terms

Environmental stressors *Aspects of the physical environment which can produce stress.*

Negative affect *A negative emotion which is experienced as unpleasant.*

Crowding *An unpleasant sensation that too many people are sharing the same space.*

Density *A measure of the number of people occupying a given space.*

Summary

1. Aggression can be defined in various ways. Research in psychology is usually based on the following definition – 'aggressive action is behaviour aimed at causing either physical or psychological pain' (Aronson et al., 1997).

2. Most laboratory research has been based on experiments which have used analogues for aggression, such as electric shocks. These experiments lack ecological validity.

3. The frustration-aggression hypothesis states that frustration leads to aggression. This aggression is sometimes displaced – directed towards somebody or something which did not cause the initial frustration.

4. Relative deprivation is a perception held by an individual or group that they have less than they deserve, or less than they have been led to expect. Relative deprivation may lead to frustration and aggression.

5. Cue arousal theory suggests that aggression is more likely if there is a stimulus present – for example, a gun – which acts as a cue for aggressive behaviour. The weapons effect is an example of cue arousal.

6. The excitation-transfer model states that physical and psychological arousal makes a person more likely to respond to provocation with aggressive behaviour.

7. Social learning theory sees aggression as learned by observational learning and reinforcement.

8. A cultural approach states that when, where, how and why aggression is expressed is influenced by culture and varies from culture to culture.

9. Deindividuation theory states that when people become less aware of themselves as individuals, they tend to become impulsive and less rational, and therefore more prone to aggressive behaviour.

10. The social constructionist approach states that aggression is socially constructed and can only be understood within its social context.

11. Environmental stressors like temperature, noise and crowding can increase arousal. This may or may not lead to aggressive behaviour, depending on the nature of the situation and how the individual perceives it.

Activity 6   Environmental stressors and aggression

Item A   Temperature

An analysis of data from 826 major league baseball games in the USA showed that as the temperature increased, so did the likelihood of the pitcher hitting the batter with the ball. It appeared that balls were often aimed at the batter's head. They travelled at up to 90 miles per hour. The results of this study are shown in the bar chart.

Adapted from Reifman et al., 1991

The St. Louis Cardinals vs the Montreal Expos

Item B   Noise

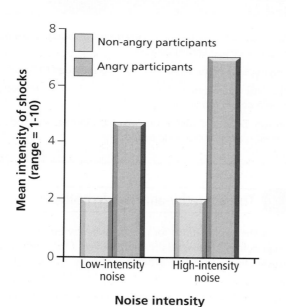

The bar chart shows the effects of noise and anger on the intensity of electric shocks given to a confederate in an experiment.

Adapted from Donnerstein & Wilson, 1976

Item C   Density

Dancing to the Ministry of Sound

A crowded commuter train

Questions

1   Provide an explanation of the findings in Item A.

2   What does Item B suggest about the relationship between noise and aggression?

3   High density is not necessarily experienced as crowding. Explain with some reference to Item C.

Unit 2 Altruism and bystander behaviour

KEY ISSUES

1 **What are prosocial behaviour, helping behaviour and altruistic behaviour?**

2 **What are the main theories of helping behaviour?**

3 **What are the main explanations of bystander behaviour?**

Consider the following.

- Between 1939 and 1945, at great personal danger, Oskar Schindler saved 4000 Jewish men, women and children from Hitler's death camps.
- Six customers in a supermarket in Fredericksburg, Virginia, watched while a 17-year-old youth viciously beat a female clerk. No one called the police or tried to help her (Aronson et al., 1997).
- A man was robbed, beaten, stripped and left for dead on the road from Jerusalem to Jericho. A priest saw him and passed by on the other side of the road. A Levite did the same. A Samaritan saw the man, stopped, bandaged his wounds, took him to a nearby inn and cared for him.

These are fairly dramatic examples of helping and not helping. Everyday instances are usually much less dramatic.

This unit looks at why people decide to help or not to help others. Why do they sometimes stand by and do nothing? Why do they sometimes risk their own life to help another person?

2.1 Definitions

Prosocial behaviour This is a general term for a variety of behaviour which is seen as beneficial to other people. It includes acts as varied as helping, rescuing, protecting, sharing, cooperating, and befriending.

What counts as prosocial behaviour depends on the values of the particular society being considered. In countries with the death penalty, prison staff involved in executions may be seen to be acting in a prosocial way – their action may be viewed as protecting and therefore benefiting society as a whole.

Helping behaviour This refers to behaviour which is intended to help another person – for example, a motorist who stops to assist another motorist whose car has broken down. The main point here is that the person who helps does so intentionally. Unintentional help does not fit the definition. For instance, if a passenger on a crowded bus vacates their seat to get off and it is immediately taken by an elderly person, their action incidentally benefits someone else. This is not an example of helping behaviour.

The motivation behind helping behaviour may be selfish or unselfish. For example, a man may give up his seat on the bus to an elderly person out of the kindness of his heart or to impress his girlfriend. Whatever the reason, the act is still helping behaviour.

Altruism or altruistic behaviour is a form of helping behaviour which is motivated by a desire to benefit another person rather than oneself. It is unselfish behaviour concerned with the welfare and wellbeing of others. Mother Theresa is sometimes seen as a personification of altruism – she dedicated her life to the poor and downtrodden in India.

Egoism or egoistic behaviour is helping behaviour which is motivated by a desire to benefit oneself rather than others. It is selfish behaviour concerned with the wellbeing of self. For example, a male nurse who regularly helps his female colleagues with heavy lifting may be motivated by the regular boosts to his ego and masculine identity that this provides. Helping may simply be a means to this end.

In practice, it is difficult to distinguish between altruistic and egoistic helping. First, it involves discovering the motives which direct behaviour – even a trained observer cannot be sure. Second, the many possible benefits to the helper make it difficult to identify 'pure' acts of altruism. Mother Theresa presumably gained considerable satisfaction from her good deeds. The cynical amongst us could easily interpret her behaviour as egoistic.

Key terms

Prosocial behaviour *A general term for a variety of behaviour which is seen to benefit others.*

Helping behaviour *Behaviour which is intended to help others.*

Altruistic behaviour *Helping behaviour which is intended to benefit others rather than oneself.*

Egoistic behaviour *Behaviour which is motivated by a desire to benefit oneself rather than others.*

2.2 The empathy-altruism hypothesis

Most of the explanations for prosocial behaviour argue that human beings are essentially selfish. Even if they appear to be altruistic, they are in fact acting egoistically – their motive for helping is to benefit self rather than to benefit others.

Daniel Batson (1991) argues that under certain circumstances, people's motives for helping others are altruistic. They help because their concern is mainly for the other person. They act primarily out of a desire to minimise the other's distress.

According to Batson, altruism is made possible by *empathy* – the ability to experience the emotions of another person by imagining ourselves in their situation. As a result, we experience their distress – their discomfort, sadness, or pain – and are more likely to help them from a genuine spirit of altruism. The *empathy-altruism hypothesis* states that the higher the level of empathy, the more likely altruistic behaviour is to occur.

Experimental evidence

Batson and his colleagues conducted a series of experiments in which participants were given the opportunity to act either altruistically or egoistically. In one experiment, participants could either help someone in trouble or escape from the situation (Batson et al., 1981). They observed a fellow participant – in fact, a confederate – being wired up to receive supposedly mild electric shocks as part of a 'learning experiment'. The female participants watched 'Elaine', the male participants watched 'Charlie'. During the experiment, Elaine (or Charlie) indicates considerable distress and tells of a childhood trauma involving electric shocks. The experimenter then asked the participant whether they would be prepared to help Elaine by changing places with her.

Batson and his colleagues systematically varied aspects of the experiment. In the 'easy escape condition', participants were told they could leave after watching only part of the experiment, and so escape from the distressing situation. In the 'difficult escape condition', they were told to stay until the experiment finished. The researchers assumed that if altruism existed, then some of the participants would help regardless of whether it was easy or difficult to escape.

In a second variation, participants were told about Elaine's attitudes. In one condition, they were told that her attitudes were similar to their own – the 'high attitude similarity condition'. The researchers assumed that this would increase empathy, and therefore altruism, because participants would see Elaine as similar to themselves. In the other condition, participants were told that Elaine's attitudes were different from their own – the 'low attitude similarity condition'. It was assumed that this would reduce empathy and therefore encourage an egoistic motivation.

The results of these experiments generally supported the empathy-altruism hypothesis. First, they suggest that altruism exists. Even in the easy escape/dissimilar attitudes condition, the least likely situation for altruism, 18% of the participants stayed and helped Elaine. In all the other conditions, as Figure 7 shows, the helping rate was much higher. Significantly, in the easy escape/similar attitudes condition, 90% of the participants helped Elaine. This supports Batson's argument that similar attitudes encourage empathy, and empathy is a key factor in motivating altruism.

Evaluation

Batson and his colleagues have made a strong case for the existence of altruism. This case is backed by a large body of experimental evidence. However, it is possible to see altruism as selfish egoistic behaviour. This view is taken by the *negative-state relief model* (Cialdini et al., 1987).

Briefly, this model states that helping is motivated by the relief of negative feelings. Empathy means sharing the distress and discomfort of the other person. This leads to negative feelings – the potential helper feels upset. Helping the other person can bring relief from these negative feelings. Put simply, people help others in order to make themselves feel better. This is egoistic rather than altruistic behaviour. As the next section indicates, there is experimental evidence to support this view. The empathy-altruism and negative-state relief models are illustrated in Figure 8.

Helping others involves time and effort. There is evidence that people assess these costs when deciding whether or not to help others. They may have altruistic motives, but their behaviour may be egoistic because of the costs involved. In one

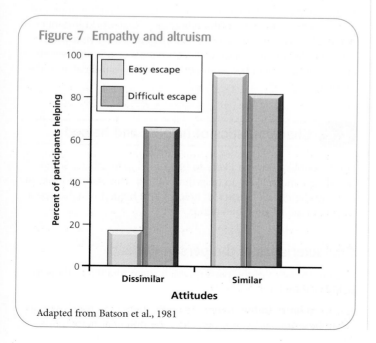

Figure 7 Empathy and altruism

Adapted from Batson et al., 1981

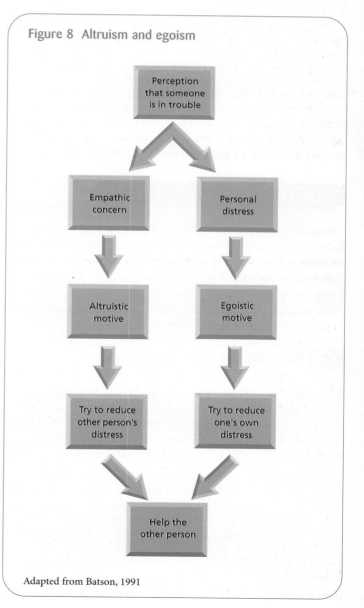

Figure 8 Altruism and egoism

Adapted from Batson, 1991

experiment, participants were asked to help with a project for the homeless (Shaw et al., 1994). Some were told this would involve a relatively large commitment (three meetings with a homeless person), others that the commitment would be small (an hour writing letters for contributions). The participants were then asked to select one of two messages about the project – either an emotional, empathy-inducing message about the hardship and pain of homelessness, or an impersonal 'just the facts' message. Those who thought the commitment would be small opted to see the emotional message, whilst those who thought the commitment would be large opted for the factual message. It appears that those who believed that helping would involve a large commitment were trying to *avoid* empathy. They know they will feel more disposed to help once they have seen the emotional message. Since they wish to avoid the high costs of helping, they choose the 'facts only' message. This is less likely to arouse empathy, and so less likely to result in helping.

Batson accepts this point – people may reject the option of helping other if they judge the costs as too high. He also accepts that helping behaviour is often directed by egoistic motives. However, he maintains that altruism is the basis of some helping behaviour (Batson, 1991).

Much of the evidence in this debate is drawn from laboratory experiments. Things get a lot more complicated in real-world situations where considerations of family, friends, money, jobs – to name but a few – affect people's behaviour. In this context, the power of social norms is greater than in the relative anonymity of the laboratory. In the outside world, social norms indicate who, when and where to help; they indicate what is expected and what is acceptable. From this point of view, helping behaviour is directed by social norms rather than motivated by altruism or the relief of negative states.

Key terms

Empathy *The ability to experience the emotions of another person. Often the term is used to imply sympathy for the other person.*

Negative state relief *Relieving negative feelings – for example, reducing or removing a feeling of distress.*

2.3   The negative state relief model

This model, introduced earlier, was developed by Robert Cialdini and his colleagues (Cialdini, et al., 1987). It states that the primary motive for helping others is to help ourselves. When people are in negative mood states, they can improve their mood by helping others. Take the following example.

Jackie and James have been shopping for clothes. Jackie is in a good mood because she's found just what she wants, James is in a bad mood because he hasn't. They pass a man slumped in a doorway with a handwritten sign asking for loose change. Jackie's good mood disappears, as she feels sad at the sight of this poor person. She gives him 50p and immediately feels better. James's bad mood stays with him as he approaches the man in the doorway. He also donates 50p and begins to feel more cheerful.

According to the negative state relief model, it doesn't matter whether the negative feelings preceded the sight of the person who was helped (as in James's case), or was actually caused by the sight of the person who was helped (as in Jackie's case). What matters, is that helping provides negative state relief – it makes the helper feel better.

However, experimental evidence suggests that helping isn't the only way to relieve negative feelings. Cialdini devised an interesting variation on Batson's 'Elaine' and 'Charlie' experiment. Participants were offered an unexpected financial reward during the experiment. This apparently reduced the tendency of members of the high empathy group to help Elaine (or Charlie). Cialdini argues that this finding supports the negative state relief model. The negative mood produced by Elaine's plight was replaced by pleasure from the financial reward. As a result, there was no need for many participants to relieve their negative feelings by helping Elaine (Cialdini et al., 1987).

Evaluation

Like the empathy-altruism hypothesis, Cialdini's negative state relief model is supported by a large body of experimental evidence. However, a number of laboratory studies do not support the model. The following study by Batson et al. (1989) provides an example.

The first part of the experiment showed Elaine and Charlie in the situation described earlier. Participants were then shown a film. Half were told the film wouldn't change their present mood, the other half were told the film would significantly improve their mood. According to the negative-state relief model, the helping behaviour of this last group should decrease. Their mood has been elevated by the film, so why help Elaine and Charlie to relieve their negative state? In fact, those who expected their mood to improve did not decrease their helping behaviour. A similar number of participants from each of the groups volunteered to help Elaine and Charlie.

Since there is evidence to support both the empathy-altruism hypothesis and the negative state relief model, each may explain some, but not all, helping behaviour. As noted earlier, much of this evidence comes from the laboratory. Real-world instances of helping behaviour are far more complex and involve a wide variety of factors which may affect whether or not one person chooses to help another. Some of this variety is indicated in the following section.

2.4   Characteristics of helpers and helped

Some people are more likely to be helped than others. Some people are more likely to help than others. This section looks at some of the characteristics of helpers and helped which appear to encourage helping behaviour.

Characteristics of the person in need

Characteristics of the person which seem to attract others to help them include:

- **A similarity to the helper** When the person in need appears to be a similar type of person to the potential helper, this tends to arouse feelings of empathy in the helper, leading them to offer help (Krebs, 1975). For example, there is evidence that people are more likely to help members of their own ethnic group and those with the same sexual orientation as themselves (Shaw et al., 1994).

- **A physically attractive appearance** People seen as physically attractive tend to be helped more (Benson et al., 1976).
- **An appearance of needing help** People who seem to have an obvious need for help, particularly those seen as less able than the helper, are more likely to receive an offer of assistance (Piliavin et al., 1981). Examples include a child in distress and an elderly person unable to carry their shopping.
- **An appearance of deserving help** The 'just world' hypothesis suggests that we all have a need to believe that people get what they deserve. If a person is seen to have brought about their own misfortune – for example, injured themselves whilst drunk, or become destitute as a result of gambling – they are less likely to be helped. It's their fault – they don't deserve help. However, if their injury results from a mugging, or their destitution from redundancy, they are more likely to be helped. They don't deserve their misfortune – they deserve to be helped.

- **An appearance that help will be effective** If help promises to be effective, then it is more likely to be offered (Miller, 1977). For example, charitable donations for refugees were more likely if the donation was a) restricted to a particular family and b) the family's need was short term. This gave the impression that help would be effective (Warren & Walker, 1991).

Characteristics of a 'helpful' person

Characteristics which appear to encourage people to act as helpers include:

- **A sense of competence** If a person feels competent to deal with an emergency, they are more likely to help. This is particularly so if they have a skill that will help the person in need – for example, first-aid training, being a good swimmer (Korte, 1971).
- **A relationship to the person in need** A prior relationship, if only of a few minutes standing, makes a person more likely to help (Moriarty, 1975).
- **A sense of social responsibility** People with a strong sense of social responsibility see it as their duty to help others (Bierhoff et al., 1991).

Activity 7 — Why help others?

Item A — Altruism and self-interest

One day, while travelling in a coach, Abraham Lincoln and a companion were questioning the existence of altruism. Lincoln maintained that self-interest was the basis of helping. They were interrupted by a shrieking whine from a sow who was trying to save her piglets from drowning in a creek. Lincoln went to her assistance and lifted the piglets to the safety of the bank.

'Now, Abe, where does selfishness come in on this little episode?' 'Why, bless your soul, Ed,' Lincoln replied. 'That was the very essence of selfishness. I should have had no peace of mind all day had I gone on and left that suffering old sow worrying over those pigs. I did it to get peace of mind, don't you see?'

Adapted from Aronson et al., 1997

Item B — Homeless

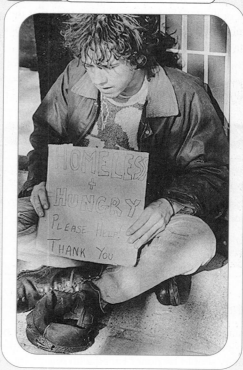

Questions

1. A major problem with researching helping behaviour is the discovery of motives. Briefly discuss with reference to Item A.

2. Explain Lincoln's behaviour in Item A in terms of:

   a) The empathy-altruism hypothesis

   b) The negative-state relief model.

3. Suggest reasons why some people may help the person in Item B while others may not.

2.5   Bystander behaviour

What makes a person help someone who is obviously in distress. Picture the following situations:

* A child falls off her bike and hurts her knee.
* A man collapses on the pavement holding his chest.
* A woman is robbed by two attackers.

These are emergency situations. You are a bystander. Would you help?

This section looks at *bystander behaviour* – the behaviour of people standing or passing by when an emergency occurs. This may result in *bystander intervention*, a form of prosocial behaviour where the bystander intervenes to help the person in distress. Or it may result in *bystander apathy* where the observer chooses not to intervene and ignores the person in distress.

The study of bystander behaviour began in earnest with the murder of a women, Catherine (Kitty) Genovese, in New York in 1964. She was stabbed repeatedly by an attacker over a period of half an hour whilst returning home from work. Around 38 of her neighbours heard her screams and cries for help, but none went to investigate, or called the police until it was too late. The incident was widely reported with newspapers making much of the 'apathy' and 'indifference' of the neighbours.

These reports led two social psychologists – Bibb Latané and John Darley – to investigate bystander behaviour. They were impressed by the fact that 'not just one or two, but 38 people had watched and done nothing' (Latané, 1987). This led to the idea of the *bystander effect* which states that the greater the number of bystanders who witness an emergency, the less likely any one of them is to help.

This section examines the two main models of bystander intervention – Latané and Darley's *cognitive model* and Piliavin et al's *bystander-calculus model*.

Key terms

Bystander intervention *A form of prosocial behaviour where a bystander intervenes to help a person in distress.*

Bystander apathy *The bystander decides not to intervene and does nothing to help the person in distress.*

Bystander effect *The greater the number of bystanders who witness an emergency, the less likely any one of them is to help.*

Latané and Darley's cognitive model

Bystanders often experience uncertainty in emergency situations. The situations are unusual, they often involve danger. What exactly should be done? Faced with uncertainty, people tend to look to others for advice and guidance. According to Latané and Darley (1970), the greater the number of bystanders present, the less likely any one of them is to help the person in distress. This makes sense of the behaviour of the 38 bystanders in the Kitty Genovese murder.

Latané and Darley conducted a number of experiments to test their views. They include the following.

The epileptic fit Participants sat in separate booths discussing aspects of university life over an intercom. In fact, there was only one participant, all the others were prerecorded voices. One of the 'participants' said he suffered from epilepsy and was later heard apparently having a fit. He made choking sounds, cried out that he was going to die, then fell silent. Would the real participants help?

When they believed they were the only ones listening, 85% helped within one minute. When they believed there was another participant listening, only 62% helped within one minute. And when they believed there were four others listening, only 31% helped within one minute. This provided experimental support for the idea of the bystander effect (Darley & Latané, 1968).

The smoke-filled room Participants have agreed to take part in a study on the problems of urban life. They are placed in a room and asked to fill out a questionnaire. White smoke starts pouring out from a vent in the wall. Would the participants define this as an emergency? Would they do anything about it? When left on their own 75% of the participants reported the smoke. When they were with one other person, only 38% took action. And when they were with two confederates who completely ignored the smoke, only 10% reported the situation. Judging from the behaviour of the confederates, there was nothing to worry about – there was no emergency (Latané & Darley, 1970).

The filing cabinet accident As in the above experiment, participants were asked to fill out a questionnaire. They heard a loud crash from the next room and a cry of pain, followed by moaning. It appeared that a woman had been injured while struggling to open a filing cabinet. When on there own, 70% of participants went to investigate. This dropped to 40% when they were with one other participant, and to only 7% when they were with a confederate who assured them that there was no cause for concern (Latané & Rodin, 1969).

On the basis of these and other experiments, Latané and Darley developed their cognitive model of bystander intervention. This model states that a person must go through five stages in order to intervene.

1   **Noticing the event** Clearly a bystander won't intervene if they haven't even noticed an event. Failure to notice can be due to a variety of factors. In one experiment, people who were in a hurry often walked by without noticing a man who was clearly in distress, slumped in a shop doorway coughing and groaning (Darley & Batson, 1973).

2   **Interpreting the event as an emergency** Before offering help, a bystander needs to interpret the event as an emergency. In this situation, they often look to others for guidance and follow their lead. If all the bystanders do this, it can appear as if there's nothing wrong because nobody appears concerned. As a result, there is no point in intervening and offering help. This is known as *pluralistic ignorance* – bystanders mislead each other by their apparently unconcerned response.

3   **Assuming responsibility** Once a bystander has established that an emergency exists, will they take on the responsibility for helping? As noted earlier, the bystander effect states that the greater the number of bystanders, the less likely they are to assume this responsibility.

4   **Knowing how to help** Does the bystander know how to help – for example, can they provide medical help, comfort, or

call on somebody who can help?

5   **Intervening and helping** If the answer is 'Yes, I know how to help', then they are in a position to decide whether or not to actually intervene and help.

Latané and Darley identify a number of processes that can affect various parts of this decision-making chain and lead to bystander apathy. They include:

- **Diffusion of responsibility** If there are other bystanders present, then the individual feels that the burden of responsibility for 'doing something' does not fall entirely on them. Instead, it is seen as diffused or spread amongst all the bystanders. For example, in the epileptic fit experiment, each participant may have assumed that somebody else had intervened. Similarly, the 38 witnesses to Kitty Genovese's murder probably assumed that someone else would intervene – either by helping directly or by phoning the police. Each bystander's sense of responsibility appears to decrease in line with the increase in the number of bystanders.

- **Audience inhibition** A bystander on their own is not inhibited by the presence of others. However, further bystanders provide an audience which can inhibit intervention by any one individual. Faced with others, people are afraid of making a blunder, of overreacting, of taking inappropriate action. They fear embarrassment, public ridicule, looking foolish. This helps to explain why the lone bystander is more likely to intervene.

- **Social influence** Audience inhibition is an example of social influence. The influence of others can have a powerful effect on an individual's behaviour. As noted earlier, people often look to others for guidance in an unusual situation. In the smoke-filled room experiment, 90% of participants followed the lead of the two confederates who carried on as normal. The presence of bystanders can lead to pluralistic ignorance, as each misleads others by their apparent lack of concern.

Evaluation

Latané and Darley's cognitive model is supported by a wide range of experimental evidence and real-world data. Situations which don't fit with their findings do not necessarily contradict the model. For example, bystanders do not appear to be inhibited by others if they have special expertise to offer, eg if they are medically trained, or if they know the other bystanders (Latané & Rodin, 1969). These findings refine rather than contradict the model. For example, they indicate circumstances in which diffusion of responsibility and audience inhibition do not operate.

However, the cognitive model, like all models, simplifies complex situations. In the real world, a multitude of factors influence bystander behaviour. Some of these are listed on pp 328-329. The cognitive model does not account for many of these factors. An appreciation of the complexity of real world situations can be gained from the following reconsideration of the Kitty Genovese murder.

Latané and Darley's research was a response to the murder of Kitty Genovese. But their experiments ignored important aspects of this crime. First, the attack was not simply an 'emergency situation' – it was a specific example of male violence against women. Genovese was stabbed repeatedly

and raped. Second, violence against women in 1964 was seen somewhat differently than it is today – 'wife battering' was not documented, wives could not legally claim to have been raped by husbands. This may have made bystanders less sensitive to what was happening. In fact one witness stated that his reason for not intervening was that he thought it was simply a 'lover's quarrel'. Latané and Darley's experiments ignored gender relations. They investigated bystander apathy as a general phenomenon. A more insightful approach might have been to investigate violence against women and the effects *this* has on observers.

Key terms

Diffusion of responsibility *The spreading out of responsibility. In terms of bystander behaviour, each bystander's sense of responsibility for the victim is reduced in proportion to the increase in the number of bystanders.*

Audience inhibition *The inhibition of an individual's behaviour produced by an audience. In terms of bystander behaviour, an audience of other bystanders may prevent the individual from intervening.*

Pluralistic ignorance *A situation where a number of people do not know what is happening. In terms of bystander behaviour, bystanders mislead each other about the situation because of their apparent lack of concern.*

The bystander-calculus model

Piliavin et al. (1981) devised the *bystander-calculus model* in an attempt to explain some of the physiological and cognitive factors which are involved in bystander behaviour. The model proposes that when a bystander observes an emergency situation, they pass through three distinct stages before deciding whether or not to intervene. At stage 3, they calculate the costs and benefits of intervention, hence the term bystander-calculus model. This model is also known as the *arousal: cost-reward model*.

Stage 1 Arousal The first response to an emergency is physiological. The bystander's heart rate often drops rapidly. This reaction – called an *orienting reaction* – sends an immediate warning signal to the bystander, leading them to pause to consider what is going on. Almost immediately, a second physiological reaction leading to increased arousal takes place. This is a *defensive reaction* which prepares the body to take action. Piliavin et al. found that the higher the arousal level, the more likely the bystander was to intervene.

Stage 2 Labelling People interpret their aroused state in a range of different ways, for example as anger, anxiety or intense joy. The interpretation they choose – that is, the label they choose for the sensations they feel in their body – depends to a large extent on the situation. Piliavin et al. suggest that in an emergency situation the most common way that bystanders label their arousal is as *personal distress* – 'this upsets me'. Piliavin et al. then claim that this makes a bystander more likely to intervene in an attempt to try to reduce their own distress. This claim is very similar to the negative-stage relief model discussed on p81.

Stage 3 Evaluation Having labelled their arousal as distress, the bystander then calculates the costs and benefits of helping. Costs include time and effort (the greater they are, the less likely bystanders are to intervene), the possibility of physical danger (as in the Kitty Genovese murder) and psychological distress (such as aversion to the sight of blood).

There are two further sets of costs that the bystander takes into account – *empathy costs* and *personal costs*. Empathy costs are related to the feelings of distress which the bystander feels when they witness the plight of another. Not intervening means that the bystander is unable to reduce their empathy and the distress it causes. Similarity between victim and bystander increases empathy and therefore the level of distress. Personal costs are feelings of self-blame or loss of respect from others which can result from a failure to help. The possibility of personal costs increases with the severity of the situation.

In summary, the bystander-calculus model states that whether or not a bystander will actually help depends upon:

- Their level of arousal
- The way that arousal is labelled
- A calculation of the costs and benefits of intervening.

Evaluation

There are a number of advantages to the bystander calculus model. First, it introduces a physiological dimension – arousal. Second, it brings in the idea of a cost-benefit analysis. In this respect, it spells out the final stage of decision-making more clearly than Latané and Darley's cognitive model.

However, the model does appear a bit too mechanical. The bystander is pictured as systematically calculating the costs and benefits of intervention. This is in sharp contrast to the reports of many bystanders who intervene – 'I just did it without thinking'.

The bystander calculus model presents the bystander as directed by egoistic motives, as concerned above all else with self-interest. This leaves no room for the possibility of altruism. In later writings, Piliavin admitted that more recent research indicated that 'true altruism – acting with the goal of benefiting another – does exist and is part of human nature' (Piliavin & Charng, 1990).

Activity 8   Bystander behaviour

Item A   The bystander effect

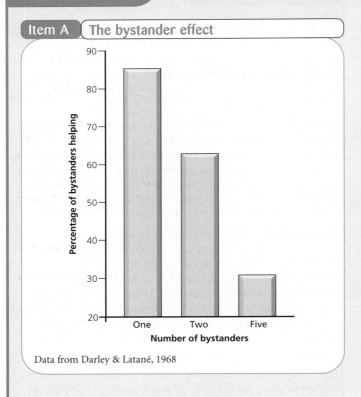

Data from Darley & Latané, 1968

Item B   Five steps to helping

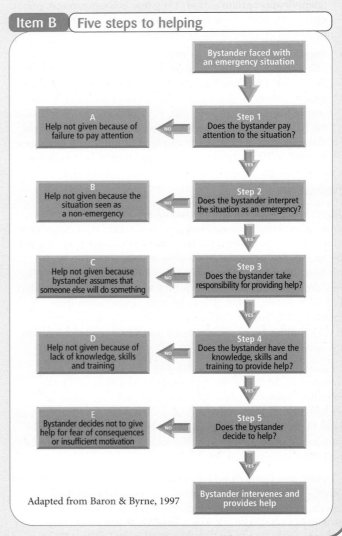

Adapted from Baron & Byrne, 1997

Item C The costs of helping

Jane Piliavin and her colleagues conducted a number of field experiments on bystander behaviour using New York subway trains. In one study, confederates, in various conditions – black, white, ill or drunk – collapsed in a carriage. Bystanders were more likely to help the 'ill' victim than the drunk 'victim'. In the ill condition, ethnicity made no difference to helping. In the drunk condition, the victim was more likely to be helped by a member of their own ethnic group.

In a further study, the victim either collapsed and bled from the mouth, or collapsed with no bleeding. Bystanders were more likely to help when no blood appeared.

Adapted from Piliavin et al., 1969 and Piliavin & Piliavin, 1972

Questions

1. a) Briefly summarise the results of the experiment shown in Item A.

   b) Explain the results using the following ideas:

   i) diffusion of responsibility

   ii) audience inhibition

   iii) pluralistic ignorance.

2. Below are a number of reasons why bystanders might fail to intervene in an emergency situation. Match each reason with one of the 5 boxes labelled A to E in Item B.

   i) I'll look like a fool.

   ii) It's only a family quarrel.

   iii) I was late for an appointment and didn't even notice.

   iv) I've got no medical training.

   v) Someone else will call an ambulance.

   vi) Nothing wrong with him – he's just drunk.

   vii) There's blood everywhere – I might catch AIDS.

3. Explain the results outlined in Item C using the bystander-calculus model.

2.6 Social learning theory and culture

Theories of helping behaviour and bystander intervention have tended to focus on the act of helping. This is a fairly narrow focus. It largely ignores the wider society. It leaves out the whole question of culture. This section begins with a social learning theory explanation of helping behaviour. It then widens the focus to include the relationship between culture and helping behaviour.

In terms of social learning theory, helping behaviour is learned as part of the socialisation process – the process by which people learn the culture of their society. Behaviour which is defined as appropriate and acceptable by cultural values is positively reinforced. Such behaviour provides a template for modelling – a way of learning by observing and imitating the behaviour of others.

Culture includes *values* – beliefs about what is worthwhile and worth striving for – and *norms* – standards of acceptable and appropriate behaviour. Helping behaviour reflects values and is directed by norms. Since culture varies from society to society, so, to some extent, will helping behaviour.

All cultures contain norms and beliefs about helping others. Margaret Mead's (1942) study of New Guinea tribes provides an illustration. She describes the Arapesh as caring, considerate and responsive to the needs of others. By comparison, the Mundugumor are selfish, aggressive and unresponsive to the needs of others. Mead attributes the differences in behaviour to the cultures of the two societies.

Individualistic vs collectivistic societies

Researchers sometimes make a distinction between individualistic and collectivistic societies. In individualistic societies, the focus is on the individual – on individual achievement and individual responsibility. People tend to be self-contained and self-centred. By comparison, in collectivistic societies there is more emphasis on the group, on a person's social or group identity rather than their personal identity. The focus is on cooperation rather than competition.

These differences will affect helping behaviour. There is more emphasis on mutual support in collectivistic societies. A higher value tends to be placed on helping others. Social norms stress the importance of duty to others rather than the rights of the individual. Because people have a strong social identity – as members of a village, clan, extended family, or neighbourhood – helping others is, to some extent, helping themselves, as everybody shares a social identity.

By comparison, the emphasis in individualistic societies is on self-help. The focus on individual achievement and independence means that individuals are largely responsible for their own care and wellbeing. The focus on self can be seen clearly in capitalist market economies, in particular the USA. There decisions about whether or not to help others are often based on self-interest – what's in it for me? (Lord, 1997).

The above generalisations are rather broad but there is evidence to support them. Studies of small-scale collectivistic societies such as Native Americans and Australian Aborigines indicate that helping behaviour is more widespread than in the West. The same applies to Israeli kibbutzim. Compared to children raised in cities in the West, children from the kibbutzim cooperate more on tasks and continue to help each other even when individual achievement is rewarded (Mann, 1980).

A study of children aged 3-11 in six countries showed significant differences in helping behaviour (Whiting & Whiting, 1975; Whiting & Edwards, 1988). Children from Kenya, Mexico and the Philippines received the highest scores on a scale of helping behaviour. Children from the USA, generally regarded as the most individualistic society in the world, received the lowest scores. The researchers argue that helping behaviour is learned during childhood. They found that children with high scores came from societies where they were involved with the responsibilities of family life – looking after young children, doing household chores or working on the family farm. These were duties which did not receive material or financial rewards. By comparison, the emphasis for children in the USA is on individual achievement – for example, doing well at school. When they do help their parents – washing the car, babysitting – they are often paid for doing so. Children in the West have relatively few helping duties. As a result, there is less emphasis on helping behaviour during their socialisation.

Altruistic vs egoistic helping

According to some researchers, altruism is more widespread in collectivistic societies (Moghaddam, 1998). The Moose (pronounced moh-say) provide evidence for this claim. They are a village people from West Africa living in an area with little water or farming land. Although one of the poorest people in the world, they are extremely generous. They give land which is not in use to anyone who asks, even a stranger. They share water with anyone who needs it, even though it does not rain for six

months of the year. When someone needs help, they freely provide their labour without keeping records of how much work was completed by each person. Sometimes they travel to the cities to sell their labour. However, when they return to their village, they often share most of their earnings (Fiske, 1990).

According to Fathali Moghaddam, 'Humankind in fact shows a great variety of prosocial behaviours, from absolute egoism to true altruism. The major source of such variations is culture' (Moghaddam, 1998).

Evaluation

Social learning theory and the idea of culture make two simple points which have been largely ignored by theories of helping behaviour. First, helping behaviour is learned. Second, helping behaviour varies from culture to culture. As Fiske (1991) states, 'If we want to know how and when people will be altruistic or otherwise prosocial, we have to understand the culture of the people in question'. However, this does not tell us why helping behaviour varies from culture to culture. Why, for example, is helping behaviour amongst the Moose so different from helping behaviour in the USA? To answer this question, we need to look at the history of the two societies in order to discover how their norms of helping behaviour developed.

Summary

1. There are various types of prosocial behaviour. They include helping behaviour which can be divided into altruistic and egoistic helping.

2. The empathy-altruism hypothesis states that the higher the level of empathy, the more likely altruistic behaviour is to occur. This hypothesis claims that genuine altruism exists.

3. The negative state relief model states that the primary motive for helping others is to relieve negative feelings. It sees helping behaviour as based on egoistic motives.

4. People are more likely to be helped if they appear to have certain characteristics, eg similarity to the helpers. Conversely, helpers tend to have certain characteristics, eg a sense of social responsibility.

5. Latané and Darley conducted a number of experiments which indicated the existence of a bystander effect. Their cognitive model identifies five stages a bystander must go through in order to intervene.

6. Bystander apathy may result from diffusion of responsibility, audience inhibition and/or pluralistic ignorance.

7. The bystander-calculus model states that bystanders must go through three stages in order to intervene – 1) arousal 2) labelling (interpreting their arousal as distress) 3) evaluation – calculating the costs and benefits of helping.

8. Social learning theory states that helping behaviour is learned as part of the socialisation process.

9. Helping behaviour reflects cultural values and is directed by cultural norms. Since culture varies from society to society, so will helping behaviour.

Unit 3 Media influences on prosocial and antisocial behaviour

KEY ISSUES

1 **Does the media influence behaviour?**

2 **What effects, if any, does television have on antisocial and prosocial behaviour?**

The first part of this unit examines some of the research on the relationship between the media and antisocial behaviour. It focuses on the portrayal of violence on television and the effect this may have on the audience. The unit begins with a word of warning – research into the relationship between the media and behaviour is full of pitfalls. The methodological problems are immense and the results are inconclusive.

3.1 A word of warning

The mass media includes all forms of communication to a mass audience – for example, television, cinema, radio, newspapers and magazines. Debates about the power of the media to influence its audience have been around for a long time. More recently, these debates have tended to focus on the portrayal of acts of violence on television. Their primary concern is the effects of television violence, particularly on the more 'vulnerable' and 'impressionable' members of society such as children. Surprisingly, given the amount of research which has been done, there is still no clear understanding of how the media influences individuals. The debate becomes a hot political topic at regular intervals, usually following the publication of a new study or the reporting of a 'copycat' crime which appears to mirror a media portrayal of violence.

Defining violence Why has so little progress been made in understanding the effects of media violence? One of the main problems is defining and measuring violence. First, the term 'violence' can cover a vast range of very different acts. For example, in one study on television violence, violent acts included using physical force against oneself or others, threatening to hurt or kill others, and accidents and natural disasters involving injury or death (Gerbner & Gross, 1976). These are very different actions and events which involve a range of very different meanings, intentions and motives. This can be seen from the following examples: a 'cold-blooded' murder, a fatal skiing accident, bombing an enemy position, killing somebody in self-defence. Many studies simply count the number of violent actions that appear on television over a given time period and lump them together in a grand total. This ignores the many different forms that 'violence' can take.

Context and meaning Second, the context in which so-called violent acts are portrayed can be very different and affect the meaning given to such acts. For example, physical violence is portrayed in cartoons such as *Tom and Jerry*, in soaps such as *Coronation Street*, in series such as *The Bill*, in films such as *The Matrix* and *Scary Movie* and in news and documentary programmes. Clearly the context will affect the meaning and therefore the effect. 'Real' violence on the news can hardly be compared to the 'fun' – and for many funny – violence in *Scary*

Movie. Again, simply adding up the acts of violence ignores the variety of meanings that may be given to apparently similar acts in different contexts.

Audience response Studies based on counting produce data that, on the face of it, are alarming. For example, British viewers watch an average of 1.68 acts of violence on TV every hour (Cumberbatch, 1987). American children see 8,000 murders and more than 100,000 other acts of violence on TV by the time they finish elementary school (DeAngelis, 1993). Such studies tend to picture viewers as sponges, passively soaking up what they see. They suggest that this vast output of 'violence' must have an effect on the viewer. Often, however, little attempt is made to say *how* that effect actually occurs – ie the psychological processes involved – and how it might be translated into behaviour. Sometimes conclusions can be extremely simplistic – a diet of TV violence will increase aggressive and violent behaviour. However, research has indicated that things are not nearly so simple. Viewers are not merely a mass of identical and passive sponges. Their response to the media is influenced by a range of factors including their personal experiences, age, gender, sexual orientation, ethnicity, social class and culture. They actively and creatively engage with and think about the programmes they watch. Different viewers tend to interpret the same programmes in very different ways (Livingstone, 1997).

3.2 Studies of television violence

Whilst research has been carried out to investigate the influence of a variety of media on audiences, most studies have concentrated on television and have been concerned with the portrayal of violence. These studies have used a variety of methods including laboratory, field, and natural experiments.

Laboratory experiments

Laboratory experiments into television violence usually take two groups of participants and expose the experimental group to violent programmes, whilst showing the control group neutral, non-violent programmes. Aggressive behaviour is then measured in both experimental and control group members at a later point. This method is broadly based on Bandura et al's (1963a) 'Bobo doll' studies, which showed that children exposed to video footage of adults behaving aggressively will themselves display aggression. Laboratory studies have generally shown that exposure to violent programmes does result in increased aggressive behaviour.

For example, Liebert and Baron (1972) showed one group of children an episode of a TV police drama featuring high levels of violence. They also showed a control group of children an equally exciting TV sporting event, which did not feature violence. After the viewing session, the children were allowed to play with a further group of children, who had seen neither programme. Children who had seen the violent programme tended to behave more aggressively than those who watched the non-violent programme.

Care should be taken when interpreting these findings. They are based on the average length of time the children behaved aggressively. Some children in the experimental group in such studies may not behave aggressively.

Josephson (1987) found that watching violent programmes tended to have most impact on children who are already prone to violence (based on reports by teachers). The violent film may simply have triggered their aggressive tendencies. In a similar experiment, children watched a violent film, whilst a control group watched a film about a bicycle race. Both sets of children then took part in a game of indoor hockey. Those who had been rated as aggressive and who had watched the violent film behaved most aggressively. In this case, the film may have sent an implicit message to the children who tend to behave aggressively that it was OK on this occasion to behave in a violent way.

Evaluation

Laboratory studies of television violence have the same problems as other kinds of psychological experiments.

- They tend to be unrealistic and artificial. Often the programmes are specially made and quite unlike typical television programmes which depict violence – for example, there is often no plot, no character development, no moral theme. This makes it difficult to generalise the experimental results.

- Freedman (1984) suggests that because the experimenter does not often comment on the programmes, there is a possibility that participants will interpret this as implicit approval of the violent images. This may lead to experimenter effects, where the participant's responses are influenced by their perception of what the experimenter wants to see and hear.

- Laboratory studies are limited to studying short-term effects. They are unable to assess the effects of long-term exposure to media violence.

- Sample sizes are often small. This makes generalisation difficult.

- Often the experimental and control groups have not been properly matched – for example, in terms of social class. As a result, it is not clear whether differences in behaviour between the two groups reflect this or their different experiences in the laboratory.

Field experiments

Field experiments are conducted in real-world settings such as the workplace, home, or school. They can avoid some of the artificiality of the laboratory. In a famous experiment, Feshbach and Singer (1971) studied 652 boys, aged 8-18, living in residential institutions – three private schools and two boys' homes. The boys were randomly divided into two groups. The first group watched only violent programmes for 6 weeks, the second group only non-violent programmes. Surprisingly, the boys who watched non-violent programmes showed more aggression towards others than those who watched violent programmes. This result was interpreted as evidence for a *catharsis* view of aggression – those who watched violent programmes could 'let off steam' safely by empathising with the violence. Those who watched non-violent programmes did not

have this opportunity, leading them to express their feelings in actual physical aggression.

Other field experiments have produced different findings. For example, American and British teenage delinquents in residential institutions were shown violent and non-violent films. Those who watched the non-violent films appeared to behave less aggressively. The violent films appeared to increase aggression, but *only* in boys who had a record of violent behaviour (Parke et al., 1977).

The findings of field experiments are inconclusive. Sometimes the control group reveals more aggression, sometimes there appears to be no effect on either group. In general, field experiments indicate that exposure to violent films appears to produce an increase in aggressive behaviour, at least in the short term. However, the effect is usually weaker in the more natural surroundings of the field experiment than in the laboratory (Wood et al., 1991).

Evaluation Field experiments have the advantage of providing a natural setting. On balance, this should allow participants to behave in a more normal way than in the laboratory.

However, field experiments are less easy to control. All sorts of uncontrolled variables can affect the findings – for example, the weather, the time of day. As a result, the findings of field experiments can be difficult to interpret. For example, the boys who watched the non-violent programmes in the Feshbach and Singer study may have acted more aggressively because they were banned from watching their favourite programmes – which involved violence.

Field experiments on the effects of media violence are often criticised for their methodological failings. For example, the researchers who observed and recorded the boys' behaviour over the 6 week period in Feshbach and Singer's study, knew which programmes each boy had watched. This may well have biased their observations. And male teenagers in custodial institutions in the Parke et al. study are hardly representative of the adolescent population.

Natural experiments

Natural experiments study the effects of a naturally occurring event – for example, the introduction of television. The researcher looks at behaviour before and after the event and assumes that any change in this behaviour may be due to the event.

A natural experiment on the effects of television was conducted during the 1980s in three small communities in Canada (Williams, 1986). The first community had no television, the second had a single channel, and the third had several channels. After television was introduced into the first community, the behaviour of elementary-school children became more aggressive – judging from observations of their behaviour in the playground over a two-year period. But, there was no change in the behaviour of similar children in the other two communities. This indicates that the introduction of television *may* have led to an increase in aggressive behaviour.

An interesting natural experiment was conducted in the 1990s on the introduction of television to the remote island of St Helena in the South Atlantic (Charlton, 2000). Children's behaviour in classrooms and playgrounds was observed for two years before television arrived and for five years afterwards. The researchers found no increase in antisocial behaviour after the introduction of television. In fact, the evidence suggested that, if anything, there was a slight increase in prosocial behaviour.

An historical study examined the introduction of television to a number of towns in the USA in the 1950s (Hennigan et al., 1982). The researchers compared the levels of crime before and after the introduction of television. Levels of violent crime remained largely unchanged. However, there did appear to be a small increase in non-violent theft. The researchers suggested that this may be due to a sense of relative deprivation felt by viewers who saw programmes which depicted wealthy characters leading glamorous lifestyles. A comparison with similar sized communities which already had television revealed very similar crime rates. It appears from this research that television has little, if any, effect on crime.

Evaluation Natural experiments, as their name indicates, allow researchers to study behaviour as it occurs naturally. The situation is not set up by the researcher, as in a field experiment. However, this means the researcher has no control over the variables involved. As a result, cause and effect relationships are difficult to establish. For example, the increase in aggressive behaviour of the children in the Canadian study may have been due to a variety of factors – the introduction of television may have been completely coincidental.

Natural experiments often involve one-off situations which are not typical and therefore difficult to generalise from. For example, the St Helena study involves an isolated, close-knit community. As older students there pointed out to the researchers, antisocial behaviour is difficult 'because everyone knows you and watches you'. In a different situation, the introduction of television may have had a different effect.

Correlation studies

Correlation studies collect information on viewing patterns and measures of aggression from large samples of participants. They then compare the two sets of information to assess whether there is any correlation, that is a significant statistical relationship between the two. For example, Belson (1978) organised interviews with over 1,500 boys aged 12-17 in London to assess their television viewing habits and to measure their aggressiveness. It was found that those who tended to watch more violent programmes also committed more violent acts. This may mean that television violence encourages violent behaviour. Or it may simply mean that violent people prefer to watch violent programmes.

Similarly, a survey of 624 13-16 year-olds found a correlation between frequency of watching violent television programmes and aggressive attitudes and behaviour (McLeod et al., 1972). Again, this may simply mean that violent people like violent TV.

Evaluation Correlational studies simply show a statistical relationship. They do not necessarily indicate a cause and effect relationship. In other words, just because two variables correlate does not mean that one causes the other.

Many correlational studies of the possible effects of TV violence are very simplistic. Often, they fail to consider a range of variables such as age, gender, class and ethnicity. When these variables are taken into account, they usually have a stronger relationship to aggressive behaviour than viewing habits (Newburn & Hagell, 1995).

Longitudinal studies

Correlational studies which use longitudinal data have a better chance of identifying cause and effect relationships. Longitudinal studies examine the same participants over time. They provide an opportunity to examine possible long-term effects of television viewing.

Milavasky et al. (1982) surveyed around 2,400 school children aged 7-12 and 12-16. They gathered information on viewing habits and on aggressive behaviour, using questionnaires and interviews. The research was conducted in six waves, producing longitudinal data over a four year period. There were some low correlations between TV violence and aggressive behaviour at certain periods, but overall the relationship was insignificant. It appeared that watching violence on TV had little or no effect on behaviour. The researchers found that factors such as low socio-economic status and high levels of family and school violence rather than viewing habits seemed to be related to high levels of aggression.

A rather different picture emerges from Leonard Eron's longitudinal study of aggressiveness from aged 8 to aged 30 (Eron, 1987). He claims that the best predictor of a young man's aggressiveness at 19 is the amount of television violence he watched at aged 8. Similarly, the more TV he watched at 8, the more likely he was to have a serious criminal record at 30. The same pattern applies to women though the levels of aggressiveness and criminal behaviour are lower.

This does not, of course, show that TV violence leads to violent behaviour. It may be that violent children prefer violent programmes. Eron found evidence that 8-year-old boys who watched large amounts of TV violence were more aggressive than their peers, and that they preferred such programmes and selected them. However, Eron argues that 1) they were more open to influence from TV violence and 2) as a result of watching large amounts over the years, they were more likely to engage in antisocial behaviour in later life.

Evaluation The findings of longitudinal studies are still correlational and still inconclusive. However, they do offer the opportunity of looking at the long-term influence of TV violence. And they do provide a means of weighing the effect of a range of variables on aggressive behaviour.

3.3 Effects of television on antisocial behaviour

A number of different psychological mechanisms have been suggested which may mediate the effects of viewing television programmes with a violent content. These mechanisms are believed to process the imagery viewed on screen and, as a result, to influence behaviour.

Arousal

Psychological arousal can result from viewing violent imagery. According to the excitation-transfer model (see p 314), this arousal may be carried over into a new situation where it can dispose the aroused individual to react aggressively if they are provoked. Zillmann and Bryant (1984) found that individuals who viewed high levels of violent pornography tended to react with aggression when they were then subjected to a frustrating experience. However, the link between television violence and emotional arousal does not appear to be particularly strong (Bryant & Zillmann, 1994).

Desensitisation

Many studies of television violence claim that watching violent programmes may *desensitise* viewers to actual violence. Individuals desensitised to violence will not find aggressive acts particularly disturbing or unusual. They are therefore less likely to be restrained by social norms against aggression. Although this claim is often made in the popular reporting of research, there is little hard evidence to support it. Belson (1978) found that teenage boys who had been exposed to violent programmes were not desensitised in their reactions to either directly experienced violence or news reports of violent events.

The 'zombie' effect

Another effect often claimed is that widespread exposure to television can make viewers – particularly children – into 'mindless', uncritical individuals who are unable to distinguish fantasy from reality. Gauntlett (1995) calls this the 'zombie' effect. As with desensitisation, there is little evidence to support the claim. Neumann (1991) presented evidence that television neither reduces children's attention spans nor blurs their ability to think clearly. Buckingham (1996) found that children could make clear and confident distinctions between what happens on television and what happens in the real world.

Cultivation

Cultivation refers to the process by which the mass media, particularly television, construct a false or distorted version of social reality (Gerbner et al., 1986). This may change viewers' perception of the world, particularly if their exposure to television is high. For example, the rates of violence portrayed on TV are far greater than those in the wider society. This portrayal may result in exaggerated fears of violent crime and a picture of the world as a threatening and dangerous place. As a result, people might be more likely to behave aggressively and even arm themselves in situations they see as threatening. The problem with this argument is what comes first. Does television violence actually create a distorted picture of social reality, or does it merely reinforce the attitudes that already exist?

Imitation

Social learning theory states that children will often imitate the actions of adult models. Bandura's classic Bobo doll experiments showed that, under certain circumstances, children who see an adult hit the doll with a mallet will imitate this behaviour (see pages 69-70).

It is imitating a particular form of media violence that is most often reported. For example, when John Hinckley shot US President Reagan, he appeared to imitate a scene from the film *Taxi Driver*. Some press reports claimed that the two children who murdered the toddler James Bulger imitated certain aspects of the violence in the horror film *Child's Play 3* (see Activity 9).

However, it cannot be proved that viewing a portrayal of a violent act on television directly causes a re-enactment of that act in real life. Even when a violent act closely mirrors a media depiction, this may have little significance. For example, three gunmen behaving like characters in the movie *Scream* held up two restaurants in Omaha, Nebraska. They may well have robbed the restaurants without seeing the film – behaving like characters in *Scream* may simply have added spice to their venture.

Catharsis

Catharsis refers to the release of tension and anxiety resulting in a calming effect. The idea of catharsis was used by Feshbach and Singer (1971) to explain their finding that the boys who watched violent films behaved less aggressively than those who watched non-violent films. In terms of catharsis theory, images of violence can serve as a release for pent-up aggression and therefore have a positive effect on behaviour.

Conclusion

The results of research on the effects of television violence are inconclusive. In a sentence – nobody knows how TV violence affects viewers. But this does not mean that years of research have been a waste of time. Knowing we don't know is important. It can question the views of those who pronounce and pontificate about the dangers of TV violence and demand its removal from our screens. It can counter simplistic arguments which state little more than TV violence must cause real violence. Often such arguments are based on prejudice and blind faith. Conversely, it can counter the claim that TV violence has no effect at all. Again, there is no conclusive evidence to show this. As the first section in this unit implied, the findings of research into media effects should be stamped with a word of 'warning'.

Key terms

Arousal *A heightened state of mental and physical alertness.*

Desensitisation *A decrease in sensitivity. In the context of the media, a failure to be disturbed by violent behaviour. Desensitisation is seen to result from high levels of exposure to images of violence.*

The 'zombie' effect *The claim that widespread exposure to television can make viewers, particularly children, into 'mindless', uncritical individuals who have difficulty distinguishing fantasy from reality.*

Cultivation *The process by which the media, particularly television, create a false or distorted view of social reality.*

Catharsis *The release of tension and anxiety resulting in a calming effect.*

Activity 9   Child's Play

Item A   The judge's view

In November 1993, two 11-year-old boys from Merseyside were found guilty of murdering a two-year-old. The 'horror' video *Child's Play 3* had been rented by the father of one of the boys shortly before the murder. There were certain similarities between the scenes in the video and the killing of the child. But there was no evidence that either boy had seen the video. Despite this, the judge at the trial stated, 'I suspect that exposure to violent video films may in part be an explanation'.

Adapted from the *Guardian*, 26.11.1993

Item B   The police view

Merseyside detectives who had interviewed the boys for several weeks before the trial rejected any suggestions that the 'horror' videos had influenced the boys' behaviour. One detective said, 'I don't know where the judge got that idea from. I couldn't believe it when I heard him. We went through something like 200 titles rented by the family. There were some you or I wouldn't want to see, but nothing – no scene, plot or dialogue – where you could put your finger on the freeze button and say that influenced a boy to go out and commit murder.'

Quoted in the *Independent*, 26.11.1993

Item C   Reaction in Parliament

In the Commons, the Conservative MP Sir Ivan Lawrence QC called for action to curb 'the constant diet of violence and depravity' fed to youngsters through television, videos and computer pornography. Sir Ivan, chairman of the Home Affairs Select Committee, said it was becoming 'daily more obvious' that this was a major reason for the rise in juvenile crime.

Quoted in the *Independent*, 26.11.1993

Item D   Press editorial

More and more children are growing up in a moral vacuum, which for so many is being filled with fetid junk from the lower depths of popular culture – video nasties, crude comics and violent television.

The *Daily Express*, 26.11.1993

Item F   Moral panics

At the turn of the century, there was great concern about violent images in Penny Dreadful comics. In the 1950s, panic that horror comics would lead to children copying the things they saw, led to the Children and Young Persons (Harmful Publications) Act 1956. Ten years ago, there was a huge panic about films such as *Drillerkiller*, which also led to a new law. There's been a recurrent moral panic about violent images which looks to a mythical golden age of tranquil behaviour.

T. Newburn, Policy Studies Institute, quoted in the *Guardian*, 16.11.1993

Item E   The *Sun's* reaction

The *Sun*, 26.11.1993

Questions

1   Read Items A to E.

   a) Judging from the evidence, is there any justification for the reaction of the judge, the MP and the *Sun*?

   b) Why do you think they reacted this way?

   c) From what you have read in this unit about the effects of TV violence, what advice would you give the judge and the MP?

2   Read Item F. What does it suggest about the concern over TV violence?

Activity 10 Violence and video games

Item A | Is there a link?

The Columbine High School shootings in Colorado in 1999 drew widespread attention to graphic violence in video games. Teenagers Dylan Klebold and Eric Harris shot dead 12 classmates and a teacher before killing themselves. A recording they left behind describes how the slaughter would be just like their favourite video game, *Doom*. This is an extremely violent game used in the training of US marines.

A study led by Dr Craig Anderson looked at the effect of violent video games on people already prone to aggression. He states that, 'Our study reveals that young men who are habitually aggressive may be especially vulnerable to the aggression-enhancing effects of repeated exposure to violent games'.

Violent video games are sometimes seen as more harmful than television violence because they are interactive, they are realistic, they are particularly engrossing and they often require the player to identify with the aggressor.

Adapted from McVeigh, 2001

Playing 'Mortal Combat'

Item B | We can't be sure

Psychologist Mark Griffiths summarises research into the effects of violent video games on behaviour. These are his main points.

Laboratory studies For ethical reasons, laboratory experiments can only study aggression in fantasy and role play. The results fit the catharsis hypothesis rather than confirming the view that violent games cause aggressive behaviour.

Observational studies A number of studies have examined children's behaviour before and after playing a violent video game. These studies suggest that in the short term, such games tend to increase children's aggressive behaviour. However, this says nothing about possible long-term effects.

Other studies These studies have used a mixture of self-reports, experiments and observation. Many support the catharsis hypothesis – that violent video games release aggressive impulses in socially acceptable ways. The children are 'letting off steam', 'getting it off their chest'. Again, this research says little or nothing about possible long-term effects.

Adapted from Griffiths, 1997

Questions

1 Suggest why there is so much concern about violent video games.

2 Why do we know so little about the effects of violent video games?

3.4 | Effects of television on prosocial behaviour

Introduction

Prosocial behaviour refers to behaviour which is valued by society or has positive consequences for other people – for example, helping, rescuing, sharing, befriending. Studies of social learning have shown that prosocial behaviour can be learned by imitating a model in much the same way that antisocial behaviour is learned. Midlarsky et al. (1973) showed that if children watch a model perform an act of helping, and also see the model rewarded for their behaviour, they are likely to imitate that behaviour. Findings like this have led researchers to explore how far television can positively influence its audience. Although viewers are exposed to a great deal of violence and aggression, they are also exposed to a considerable amount of prosocial behaviour. An analysis of US television found that 97% of 'prime time' entertainment

programmes during a four week period contain at least one prosocial act (Lee, 1988).

Research findings

Research on the effects of prosocial programmes has focused on children. Coates et al. (1976) studied nursery school children who watched TV programmes containing prosocial themes for 15 minutes each day over a four day period. As a result, some of the children were more likely to encourage others who they saw acting prosocially. This effect was, however, limited to those children who did not usually act in this way. Friedrich and Stein (1973) also showed nursery school children prosocial programmes over the course of a week. They found that children learned from the programmes in as much as they could describe a range of prosocial behaviours and give instances of their use. There was no evidence, though, that the programmes had any effect on the actual behaviour of the children.

A great deal of research has been conducted to evaluate the

impact of children's programmes which are deliberately designed to promote prosocial behaviour, such as *Sesame Street*. Children who view *Sesame Street* on a regular basis (either at home or in school) show increased abilities to learn from the exercises contained on the programme (eg, counting, letter recognition), as well as being better prepared for school life and better able to maintain peer relationships (Lesser, 1974). A study by Johnston and Ettema (1986) looked at the effects of *Freestyle*, a television drama series aimed at 9-12 year olds which contained anti-sexist themes. The researchers found that girls were affected more by the programme than boys (eg, they expressed changes in attitudes and beliefs) and that supplementing the programme with classroom discussions typically doubled its impact on all pupils. It was also found that the prosocial themes were more effective when they were placed in the context of dramatic action. This would suggest that programmes that 'preach' a message of prosocial behaviour to their audience are less effective than those which embed it within long running plots and established characters, for example, *EastEnders, Coronation Street, Star Trek: The Next Generation.*

Conclusion

From an analysis of 190 studies of the effects of television on prosocial behaviour, Susan Hearold (1986) suggests the following.

- Most studies show that prosocial behaviour is encouraged by the use of positive role models and prosocial messages and themes.
- Judging from the findings of laboratory and field experiments, the effects of prosocial programmes on children's behaviour are significantly greater than the effects of antisocial programmes.
- Producers of children's television programmes should focus on 'accentuating the positive', with more shows emphasising prosocial themes and presenting positive role models.

Many have welcomed these points. However, research evidence is primarily limited to short-term effects. Experiments typically show children prosocial programmes and look at their behaviour shortly afterwards. There is little evidence of any long-term effects.

Television viewers – including children – are increasingly sophisticated in how they watch television and the programmes they select (Livingstone, 1997). Children are very good at spotting when they are being 'lectured to'. Programmes which are too obvious in their attempts to encourage prosocial behaviour may not have their intended effect.

Summary

1. The findings of studies on the effects of television violence are inconclusive and sometimes contradictory.

2. This is partly due to the problems of defining and measuring violence both on and off the screen.

3. The main methods used to study the effects of television violence are laboratory, field and natural experiments, correlation studies and longitudinal studies. Each has its drawbacks.

4. Television violence may result in one or more of the following processes.

   - Arousal
   - Cultivation
   - Desensitisation
   - Imitation
   - The 'zombie' effect
   - Catharsis

5. Research has indicated that television programmes with prosocial themes and positive role models are likely to encourage prosocial behaviour in children.

6. However, the evidence is primarily limited to short-term effects.

References

Anderson, C.A. (1989). Temperature and aggression: The ubiquitous effects of heat on the occurrence of human violence. *Psychological Bulletin, 106,* 74-96.

Aronson, E., Wilson, T.D. & Akert, R.M. (1997). *Social psychology* (3rd ed.). New York: Longman.

Bandura, A. (1973). *Aggression: A social learning analysis.* Englewood Cliffs, NJ: Prentice Hall.

Bandura, A. (1977). *Social learning theory.* Englewood Cliffs, NJ: Prentice Hall.

Bandura, A., Ross, D. & Ross, S.A. (1961). Transmission of aggression through imitation of aggressive models. *Journal of Abnormal and Social Psychology, 63,* 575-582.

Bandura, A., Ross, D. & Ross, S.A. (1963a). Imitation of film-mediated aggressive models. *Journal of Abnormal and Social Psychology, 66,* 3-11.

Bandura, A., Ross, D. & Ross, S.A. (1963b). Vicarious reinforcement and imitative learning. *Journal of Abnormal and Social Psychology, 66,* 601-607.

Baron, R.A. (1977). *Human aggression.* New York: Plenum.

Baron, R.A. & Bell, P.A. (1976). Aggression and heat: The influence of ambient temperature, negative affect, and a cooling drink on physical aggression. *Journal of Personality and Social Psychology, 33,* 245-255.

Baron, R.A. & Byrne, D. (1997). *Social psychology* (8th ed.). Boston: Allyn & Bacon.

Baron, R.A. & Richardson, D.R. (1994). *Human aggression* (2nd ed.). New York: Plenum.

Batson, C.D. (1991). *The altruism question: Towards a social psychological answer.* Hillsdale, NJ: Erlbaum.

Batson, C.D., Batson, J.G., Griffit, C.A., Barrientos, S., Brandt, J.R., Sprengelmeyer, P. & Bayly, M.J. (1989). Negative-state relief and the empathy-altruism hypothesis. *Journal of Personality and Social Psychology, 56*, 922-933.

Batson, C.D., Duncan, B.D., Ackerman, P., Buckley, T. & Biech, K. (1981). Is empathic emotion a source of altruistic motivation? *Journal of Personality and Social Psychology, 40*, 290-302.

Bell, P.A., Fisher, J.D., Baum, A. & Green, T.E. (1990). *Environmental psychology* (3rd ed.). New York: Holt, Rinehart and Winston.

Belson, W.A. (1978). *Television violence and the adolescent boy.* Westmead: Saxon.

Benson, P.K., Karabenic, S.A. & Lerner, R.M. (1976). Pretty pleases: The effects of physical attractiveness on race, sex and receiving help. *Journal of Experimental Social Psychology, 12*, 409-415.

Berkowitz, L. (1964). Aggressive cues in aggressive behaviour and hostility catharsis. *Psychological Review, 71*, 104-122.

Berkowitz, L. (1974). Some determinants of impulsive aggression: The role of mediated associations with reinforcements of aggression. *Psychological Review, 81*, 165-176.

Berkowitz, L. & LePage, A. (1967). Weapons as aggressive-eliciting stimuli. *Journal of Personality and Social Psychology, 7*, 202-207.

Bierhoff, H.W., Klein, R. & Kramp, P. (1991). Evidence for the altruistic personality from data on accident research. *Journal of Personality, 59*, 263-280.

Brown, R. (1995). *Prejudice: Its social psychology.* Oxford: Blackwell.

Bryant, J. & Zillman; D. (Eds.) (1994). *Media effects: Advances in theory and research.* Hove: Erlbaum.

Buckingham, D. (1996). *Moving images: Understanding children's emotional responses to television.* Manchester: Manchester University Press.

Carlsmith. J. & Anderson, C. (1979). Ambient temperature and the occurrence of collective violence: A new analysis. *Journal of Personality and Social Psychology, 37*, 337-344.

Chagnon, N. (1988). Life histories, blood revenge, and warfare in a tribal population. *Science, 266*, 225-253.

Charlton, T. (2000). TV is not bad for children – official. *Observer,* 29.10.2000.

Cialdini, R.B., Schaller, M., Houlihan, D., Arps, K., Fultz, J., & Beaman, A.L. (1987). Empathy-based helping: Is it selflessly or selfishly motivated? *Journal of Personality and Social Psychology, 52*, 749-758.

Coates, B., Pusser, H., Ellison, S. & Goodman, I. (1976). The influence of 'Sesame Street' and 'Mister Rogers' Neighborhood on children's social behavior in the preschool. *Child Development, 47* 138-144.

Cohen, S. (1978). Environmental load and the allocation of attention. In A. Baum, J.S. Singer & S. Valins (Eds.), *Advances in environmental psychology* (vol 1). Hillsdale, NJ: Erlbaum.

Cohen, S., Evans, G.W., Krantz, D.S., & Stokols, D. (1980). Physiological, motivational, and cognitive effects of aircraft noise on children. *American Psychologist, 35*, 231-243.

Cumberbatch, G. (1987). *The portrayal of violence on British television: A content analysis.* London: BBC Publications.

Darley, J.M. & Batson, C.D. (1973). From Jerusalem to Jericho: A study of situational and dispositional variables in helping behaviour. *Journal of Personality and Social Psychology, 27*, 100-108.

Darley, J.M. & Latané, B. (1968). Bystander intervention in emergencies: Diffusion of responsibility. *Journal of Personality and Social Psychology, 8*, 377-383.

DeAngelis, T. (1993). *APA Monitor,* August.

Diener, E. (1980). Deindividuation: The absence of self-awareness and self-regulation in group members. In P. Paulas (Ed.), *The psychology of group influence.* Hillsdale, NJ: Erlbaum.

Dollard, J., Doob, L.W., Miller, N.E., Mowrer, O.H. & Sears, R.T. (1939). *Frustration and aggression.* New Haven: Yale University Press.

Donnerstein, E. & Wilson, D.W. (1976). The effects of noise and perceived control upon ongoing and subsequent aggressive behaviour. *Journal of Personality and Social Psychology, 34*, 774-781.

Eron, L.D. (1982). Parent-child interaction, television violence, and aggression in children. *American Psychologist, 37*, 197-211.

Eron, L.D. (1987). The development of aggressive behavior from the perspective of a developing behaviorism. *American Psychologist, 42*, 435-442.

Feldman, P. (1994). *The psychology of crime.* Cambridge: Cambridge University Press.

Feshbach, S. & Singer, R.D. (1971). *Television and aggression: An experimental field study.* San Francisco, CA: Jossey-Bass.

Festinger, L., Pepitone, A. & Newcomb, T. (1952). Some consequences of deindividuation in a group. *Journal of Abnormal and Social Psychology, 47*, 382-389.

Fiske, A.P. (1990). Relativity within Moose ('Mossi') culture: Four incommensurable models for social relationships. *Ethos, 18*, 180-204.

Fiske, A.P. (1991). The cultural relativity of selfish individualism. In M.C. Clark (Ed.), *Prosocial behavior.* Newbury Park, CA: Sage.

Freedman, J.L. (1984). Effects of television violence on aggressiveness. *Psychological Bulletin, 92*, 227-246.

Freedman, J.L. (1975). *Crowding and behavior.* San Francisco, CA: Freeman.

Freedman, J.L., Levy, A.S., Buchanan, R.W. & Price, J. (1972). Crowding and human aggressiveness. *Journal of Experimental Social Psychology, 8*, 528-548.

Friedrich, L.K. & Stein, A.H. (1973). Aggressive and prosocial television programs and the natural behaviour of preschool children. *Monographs of the Society for Research in Child Development, 38, Serial No. 151.*

Gauntlett, D. (1995). *Moving experiences: Understanding television's influences and effects.* London: John Libbey.

Geen, R.G. (1978). Some effects of observing violence on the behaviour of the observer. In B.A. Maher (Ed.), *Process in experimental personality research* (vol. 8). New York: Academic Press.

Geen, R.G. (1990). *Human aggression.* Milton Keynes: Open University Press.

Gerbner, G. & Gross, L. (1976). Living with television: The violence profile. *Journal of Communication, 26*, 173-199.

Gerbner, G., Gross, L., Morgan, M. & Signorielli, N. (1986). Living with television: The dynamics of the cultivation process. In J. Bryant & D. Zillmann (Eds.), *Perspectives on media effects.* Hillsdale, NJ: Erlbaum.

Glass, D.C. & Singer, J.E. (1972). Urban stress: *Experiments on noise and social stressors.* New York: Academic Press.

Griffiths, M. (1997). Video games and aggression. *The Psychologist,* September.

Hall, E.T. (1959). *The silent language.* Garden City: Doubleday.

Harré, R. (1986). An outline of the social constructionist viewpoint. In R. Harré (Ed.), *The social construction of emotions.* Oxford: Blackwell.

Hearold, S. (1986). A synthesis of 1043 effects of television on social behavior. In G. Comstock (Ed.), *Public communication and behavior.* Orlando, FL: Academic Press.

Hennigan, K.M., Heath, L., Wharton, J.D., Del Rosario, M.L., Cook, T.D. & Calder, B.J. (1982). Impact of the introduction of television on crime in the United States. Empirical findings and theoretical implications. *Journal of Personality and Social Psychology, 42*, 461-477.

Hogg, M.A. & Vaughn, G.M. (1995). *Social psychology: An introduction.* London: Prentice Hall/Harvester Wheatsheaf.

Hovland, C.I. & Sears, R.R. (1940). Minor studies in aggression: 6. Correlation of lynchings with economic indices. *Journal of Psychology, 9*, 301-310.

Hunt, G.T. (1940). *The wars of the Iroquois.* Madison: University of Wisconsin Press.

Johnston, A., DeLuca, D., Murtaugh, K., & Diener, E. (1977). Validation of a laboratory play measure of child aggression. *Child Development, 48*, 324-327.

Johnston, J. & Ettema, J.S. (1986). Using television to best advantage: Research for pro-social television. In J. Bryant & D. Zillman (Eds.), *Perspectives on media effects.* Hillsdale, NJ: Lawrence Erlbaum.

Joseph, J.M., Kane, T.R., Nacci, P.L. & Tedeschi, J.T. (1977). Perceived aggression: A re-evaluation of the Bandura modelling paradigm. *Journal of Social Psychology, 103*, 277-289.

Josephson, W.D. (1987). Television violence and children's aggression: Testing the priming, social script and disinhibition prediction. *Journal of Personality and Social Psychology, 53*, 882-890.

Kenrick, D.T. & MacFarlane, S.W. (1986). Ambient temperature and horn honking: A field study of the heat/aggression relationship. *Environment and Behavior, 18*, 179-191.

Korte, C. (1971). Effects of individual responsibility and group communication on help-giving in an emergency. *Human Relations, 24*, 149-159.

Krebs, D. (1975). Empathy and altruism. Journal of Personality and *Social Psychology, 32*, 1134-1146.

Latané, B. (1987). From student to colleague: Retracing a decade. In N.E. Grunberg, R.E. Nisbett, J. Rodin & J.E. Singer (Eds.), *A distinctive approach to psychological research: The influence of Stanley Schachter.* Hillsdale, NJ: Erlbaum.

Latané, B. & Darley, J.M. (1970). *The unresponsive bystander: Why doesn't he help?* Englewood Cliffs, NJ: Prestice Hall.

Latané, B. & Rodin, J. (1969). A lady in distress: Inhibiting effects of friends and strangers on bystander intervention. *Journal of Experimental Social Psychology, 37*, 822-832.

Le Bon, G. (1895). *The crowd.* New York: Viking Press.

Lee, B. (1988). Pro-social content on prime-time television. In S. Oskamp (Ed.), *Television as a social issue.* Newbury Park, CA: Sage.

Lesser, G. (1974). *Children and television: Lessons from Sesame Street.* New York: Random House.

Levi, P. (1986). *"Survival in Auschwitz";* and *"The Reawakening: Two memoirs."* New York: Summit Books.

Leyens, J.P., Camino, L., Parke, R.D., & Berkowitz, L. (1975). Effects of movie violence on aggression in a field setting and as a function of group dominance and cohesion. *Journal of Personality and Social Psychology, 32*, 346-360.

Liebert, R.M. & Baron, R.A. (1972). Some immediate effects of televised violence on children's behavior. *Developmental Psychology, 6*, 469-475.

Livingstone, S. (1997). *Making sense of television: The psychology of audience interpretation.* London: Routledge.

Lord, C.G. (1997). *Social psychology.* Fort Worth, TX: Harcourt Brace.

Lubek, I. (1979). A brief social psychological analysis of research on aggression in social psychology. In A. Buss (Ed.), *Psychology in social context.* New York: Irvington.

Mann, L. (1980). Cross-cultural studies of small groups. In H.C. Triandis & R.W. Brislin (Eds.), *Handbook of cross-cultural psychology.* Boston: Allyn & Bacon.

Mann, L. (1981). The baiting crowd in episodes of threatened suicide.

Journal of Personality and Social Psychology, 41, 703-709.

Marsh, P., Rosser, E. & Harré, R. (1978). *The rules of disorder.* London: Routledge & Kegan Paul.

Matthews, P., Paulus, P. & Baron, R.A. (1979). Physical aggression after being crowded. *Journal of Nonverbal Behavior, 4*, 5-17.

McLeod, J., Atkin, C. & Chaffee, S. (1972). Adolescents, parents and television use: Adolescent self-report measures from Maryland and Wisconsin samples. In G.A. Comstock and E.A. Rubenstein (Eds.), *Television and social behavior.* Washington DC: US Government Printing Office.

McVeigh, T. (2001). Games stunt teen brains. *Observer,* 19.8.2001.

Mead, M. (1942). *Growing up in New Guinea.* Harmondsworth: Penguin.

Midlarsky, E., Bryan, J.H. & Brickam, P. (1973). Aversive approval: Interactive effects of modelling and reinforcement on altruistic behaviour. *Child Development, 44*, 321-328.

Milavasky, R.J., Kessler, R.C., Stipp, H.H. & Rubens, W.S. (1982). *Television and aggression: A panel study.* New York: Academic Press.

Miller, D.T. (1977). Altruism and threat to a belief in a just world. *Journal of Experimental Social Psychology, 13*, 113-124.

Miller, N.E., Sears, R.T., Mowrer, O.H., Doob, L.W. & Dolard, J. (1941). The frustration-aggression hypothesis. *Psychological Review, 48*, 337-342.

Moghaddam, F.M. (1998). *Social psychology: Exploring universals across cultures.* New York: W.H. Freeman.

Moghaddam, F.M., Taylor, D.M. & Wright, S.C. (1993). *Social psychology in cross-cultural perspective.* New York: Freeman.

Moriarty, T. (1975). Crime, commitment and the responsive bystander: Two field experiments. *Journal of Personality and Social Psychology, 31*, 370-376.

Mullen, B. (1986). Atrocity as a function of lynch mob composition: A self-attention perspective. *Journal of Personality and Social Psychology, 12*, 197.

Mummendey, A. (1996). Aggressive behaviour. In M. Hewstone, W. Stroebe & G.M. Stephenson (Eds.), *Introduction to social psychology* (2nd ed.). Oxford: Blackwell.

National Advisory Commission on Civil Disorders (1968). *Report of the National Advisory Commission on Civil Disorders.* New York: Bantam Books.

Neuman, S.B. (1991). *Literacy in the television age.* Norwood, NJ: Ablex.

Newburn, T. & Hagell, A. (1995). Violence on the screen. *Sociology Review,* February.

Nisbett, R.E. (1993). Violence and U.S. regional culture. *American Psychologist, 48*, 441-449.

Page, M.M. & Scheidt, R. (1971). The elusive weapons effect: Demand awareness, evaluation and slightly sophisticated subjects. *Journal of Personality and Social Psychology, 20*, 304-318.

Parke, R.D., Berkowitz, L., Leyens, J.P., West, S. & Sebastian, R.J. (1977). Some effects of violent and nonviolent movies on the behaviour of juvenile delinquents. In I. Berkowitz (Ed.), *Advances in experimental psychology, 10*, New York: Academic Press.

Piliavin, I.M., Dovidio, J.F., Gaertner, S. & Clark, R.D. (1981). *Emergency intervention.* New York: Academic Press.

Piliavin, I.M., Rodin, J. & Piliavin, J. (1969). Good Samaritanism: An underground phenomenon? *Journal of Personality and Social Psychology, 13*, 289-299.

Piliavin, J.A. & Charng, H. (1990). Altruism: A review of recent theory and research. *Annual Review of Sociology, 16*, 27-65.

Piliavin, J.A. & Piliavin, I.M. (1972). Effect of blood on reactions to a victim. *Journal of Personality and Social Psychology, 23*, 353-361.

Prentice-Dunn, S. & Rogers, R.W. (1983). Deindividuation in aggression. In R.G. Green & E.I. Donnerstein (Eds.), *Aggression, theoretical and empirical reviews* (vol 2). New York: Academic Press.

Rehm, J., Steinleitner, M. & Lilli, W. (1987). Wearing uniforms and aggression: A field experiment. *European Journal of Social Psychology, 17,* 357-360.

Reicher, S.D. (1984). Social influence in the crowd: Attitudinal and behavioural effects of deindividuation in conditions of high and low group salience. *British Journal of Social Psychology, 23,* 341-350.

Reifman, A.S., Larrick, R.P. & Fein, S. (1991). Temper and temperature on the diamond: The heat-aggression relationship in major league baseball. *Personality and Social Psychology Bulletin, 17,* 580-585.

Schott, F. (1975). What is aggression? In H. Selg (Ed.), The making of human aggression: A psychological approach. London: Quartet.

Selg, H. (1973). The frustration-aggression hypothesis. In H. Selg (Ed.), *The making of human aggression: A psychological approach.* London: Quartet.

Shaw, L.L., Batson, C.D. & Todd, R.M. (1994). Empathy avoidance: Forestalling feeling for another in order to escape the motivational consequences. *Journal of Personality and Social Psychology, 67,* 879-887.

Sherrod, D.R. (1974). Crowding, perceived control and behavioral aftereffects. *Journal of Applied Social Psychology, 4,* 171-186.

Stainton Rogers, R., Stenner, P., Stainton Rogers, W. & Gleeson, K. (1995). *Social psychology: A critical agenda.* Oxford: Polity.

Stokols, D. (1972). On the distinction between density and crowding: Some implications for future research. *Psychological Review, 79,* 275-278.

Stokols, D., Rall, M., Pinner, B. & Schopler, J. (1973). Physical, social and personal determinants of the perception of crowding. *Environmental and Behaviour, 5,* 87-115.

Tajfel, H. & Turner, J.C. (1979). An intergrative theory of intergroup conflict. In W.G. Austin & S, Worchel (Eds.), *The social psychology of intergroup relations.* Monterey, CA: Brooks/Cole.

Turner, C.W. & Simons, L.S. (1974). Effects of subject sophistication and apprehensive evaluation on aggressive responses to weapons. *Journal of Personality and Social Psychology, 30,* 341-348.

Turner, R.H. (1974). Collective behavior. In R.E.L. Faris (Ed.), *Handbook of modern sociology.* Chicago, IL: Rand-McNally.

Warren, P.E. & Walker, I. (1991). Empathy, effectiveness and donations to charity: Social psychology's contribution. *British Journal of Social Psychology, 30,* 325-337.

Watson, R.I. (1973). Investigation into deindividuation using a cross-cultural survey technique. *Journal of Personality and Social Psychology, 25,* 342-345.

Williams, T.M. (1986). *The impact of television: A natural experiment in three communities.* Orlando, FL: Academic Press.

Whiting, B.B. & Edwards, C.P. (1988). *Children of different worlds: The foundations of social behavior.* Cambridge, MA: Harvard University Press.

Whiting, B.B. & Whiting, J.W. (1975). *Children of six countries: A psychological analysis.* Cambridge, MA: Harvard University Press.

Winsborough, H. (1965). The social consequences of high population density. *Law and Contemporary Problems, 30,* 120-126.

Wood, W., Wong, F.Y. & Chachere, J.G. (1991). Effects of media violence on viewers' aggression in unconstrained social interaction. *Psychological Bulletin, 109,* 371-383.

Zillmann, D. (1979). *Hostility and aggression.* Hillsdale, NJ: Erlbaum.

Zillmann, D. (1988). Cognition-excitation interdependence in aggressive behaviour. *Aggressive Behavior, 14,* 51-64.

Zillmann, D. (1994). Cognition-excitation interdependencies in the escalation of anger and angry aggression. In M. Potegal & J.F. Knutson (Eds.), *Dynamics of aggression: Biological and social processes in dyads and groups.* Hillsdale, NJ: Erlbaum.

Zillmann, D. & Bryant, J. (1984). Effects of massive exposure to pornography. In M.N. Malamuth & E. Donnerstein (Eds.), *Pornography and sexual aggression.* New York: Academic Press.

Zillmann, D., Katcher, A.H. & Milavsky, B. (1972). Excitation transfer from physical exercise to subsequent aggressive behaviour. *Journal of Experimental Social Psychology, 8,* 247-259.

Zimbardo, P.G. (1970). The human choice: Individuation, reason, and order versus deindividuation, impulse and chaos. In W.J. Arnold & D. Levine (Eds.), *Nebraska Symposium on Motivation,* vol XVII. Lincoln: University of Nebraska Press.

22 Brain and behaviour

Introduction

The human brain is a vastly complicated network of cells. It processes information by relaying electrical messages from one cell to another. In this way, it receives information, processes and stores information, and selects and executes responses. A product of all this processing is what we recognise as behaviour. Complex human behaviours are possible only because we possess a large brain, much of which is concerned with higher functions such as thinking, consciousness and language. These brain functions are mainly studied in humans, but others such as memory and sensory perception can also be studied in animals. This chapter illustrates some techniques for investigating the workings of the brain, what can happen when the brain is damaged, and the extent to which functions are located in particular brain areas.

Chapter summary

- **Unit 1 introduces some techniques used to investigate brain function.**
- **Unit 2 looks at the organisation of the brain, especially areas of the cortex with particular functional responsibilities.**

- **Unit 3 looks at differences between the two brain hemispheres and the extent to which functions such as language are located in one hemisphere or the other.**

Unit 1 Methods of investigating the brain

K KEY ISSUES

1 What are the main methods of investigating the brain?

2 What can these methods tell us about the structure, organisation and function of the brain?

3 What are the advantages and disadvantages of each technique?

A variety of techniques have been developed to investigate the brain. The purpose of these techniques is to discover how the brain works, what the different parts of the brain do (their *functions*), and how these parts are connected together. This unit outlines techniques used to examine the appearance and the internal structure of the brain, then looks at techniques used to investigate its functions.

1.1 Anatomical methods

Cell appearance and function

The detailed structure of the brain can be examined by shaving off very fine slices or sections, and studying each region in turn, using a microscope. The brain is not a porridge of identical cells – different regions of the brain contain cells of different shapes, sizes and characteristics. The anatomist Brodmann in 1909 produced a detailed map of the surface of the human brain purely on the basis of the appearances of cells in different zones, to which he gave numbers (Figure 1). With minor modifications his classification is still used today.

Figure 1 A brain atlas

A map of the human brain surface based on cell classification

Modern techniques use stains which are applied to sections of brain tissue, allowing different components to be highlighted when viewed under a microscope. One stain may just colour cell bodies (the information processing units), while another may just stain cell axons (which transmit information from one cell to another). From stained sections nuclei can be identified – a nucleus is a small group of similar cells, packed together and forming a functional unit, that is, a unit with a particular function or job. For example, nuclei in the hypothalamus – a small structure at the base of the brain – can be identified from their different cells types. They each have a different role – for example, they may be involved in the control of eating, drinking, temperature regulation, or aggression. Therefore, a group of cells which look alike often act together to perform a particular function.

The brain atlas How can each brain structure be located within the complex depths of the brain? This is possible using a *brain atlas*, which contains pictures of successive slices of brain, from top to bottom (in the *horizontal* plane), from the side to the midline (the *sagittal* plane) or from front to back (the *coronal* plane) as shown in Figure 2. Every structure within the brain can therefore be located precisely in 3-dimensional coordinates called *stereotaxic coordinates*. These are used extensively in techniques that investigate function (described in later sections) in which it is crucial to be able to pinpoint the locations of particular brain structures.

Figure 2 Stereotaxic coordinates

Terminology for describing locations in the brain including the 3 stereotaxic planes

Evaluation of anatomical methods

Advantages The anatomical approach is valuable because groups of cells which look similar are often functionally related. This allows us to define the boundaries of particular functional zones. Atlases are very precise – they pinpoint the locations of brain structures and have supported the development of other techniques for investigating brain function.

Disadvantages It is not possible to say, purely by looking at brain tissue, what it does. Some cells are similar in size and appearance but may do quite different things.

Investigating brain function

Techniques can be divided into *invasive* and *non-invasive procedures*. Invasive procedures require some intervention within the living brain – for example, an electrode in the form of a thin wire can be inserted into the brain to record the electrical activity of neurons. Non-invasive procedures do not require entry into the brain – for example, scanning enables activity within the brain to be viewed without direct intervention. In many cases, a technique can be applied in either way – for example, the brain can be electrically stimulated via an inserted electrode (invasively) or via the application of a strong magnetic field to the outside of the head (non-invasively).

Key terms

Key terms

Nucleus *A small collection of similar cells working together to form a functional unit.*

Stereotaxic *The 3-dimensional coordinate system used to pinpoint any location within the brain.*

Invasive technique *A technique that involves some manipulation inside the brain itself.*

Non-invasive technique *A technique involving manipulations from outside the head.*

1.2 Electrical stimulation of the brain

Neurons communicate by sending volleys of electrical signals called action potentials, from one neuron to another. All information in the brain is electrical in nature, just as electrical signals form the information that passes from one part of a computer to another. Direct electrical stimulation can be applied to the brain, having either of two effects: stimulation can mimic natural electrical activity, or it can interrupt it. We will see examples of both.

Local stimulation It is possible to fix a tiny electrode permanently in the brain of an animal while it is freely moving about. The placement, at a precise stereotaxic location, is made while the animal is asleep under deep anaesthesia. Low voltage electrical stimulation can then be delivered to the brain when the animal is behaving, similar to the activity that naturally occurs in that structure associated with a particular behaviour. Stimulation in the brain stem may cause a sleeping cat to wake, for example. In various nuclei in the hypothalamus, electrical stimulation can produce biting attacks, feeding, drinking or escape behaviours. In one particular region, the lateral hypothalamus, stimulation is a very effective reward – a rat will work to exhaustion pressing a lever to receive bursts of stimulation. Humans given the same stimulation report feelings of ecstatic pleasure. This effect might also be related to the 'rush' of excitement that is experienced after taking a drug such as crack cocaine. Studies of reward networks enable research to be carried out on drugs which are commonly abused, and to develop drugs to treat depression, a mood change which may be related to dysfunction in reward systems.

Stimulation and memory The neurosurgeon Penfield (Penfield & Rasmussen, 1950) used an electric probe to stimulate the brains of patients undergoing neurosurgery. In this case, the local low-level stimulation appeared to trigger memory retrieval; that is, the artificial electrical stimulus reproduced the natural brain activity that would normally occur when the patient remembered an event. He found that when particular places on the brain surface were stimulated (especially in the temporal lobe), patients would report hearing songs or remembering personal events that had taken place many years previously. However, re-stimulating the same spot could produce different reports, raising doubts about how well memories are individually localised.

Disruptive brain stimulation Brain electrical stimulation can have a wide range of effects, and may sometimes intercept natural activity, jamming up a neural system. Stimulation techniques have been used to deliberately interrupt the activity of a brain structure in an attempt to clarify its function. In other words, a behaviour that would usually be emitted as a result of normal activity in that structure might be cancelled or delayed via the application of a burst of stimulation.

Hebb (1949), investigating short-term memory, argued that loops of cells circulating messages to one another worked *together* to register and maintain memory over short periods of time – so-called short-term memory. STM is the kind of memory that we use to remember a telephone number for just long enough to dial it. Hebb found that when patients underwent therapy for depression involving the application of a strong electric shock to the head (ECT – electroconvulsive therapy), they would forget all that happened just prior to the shock. However, more established longer-term memories were not destroyed by the shock, suggesting that they are held in a different, more permanent store. This may explain a phenomenon seen in epilepsy. A *grand mal* epileptic fit is the result of a massive electrical discharge from many brain cells, all firing simultaneously. People usually forget what happened just before the fit – for example, they may not remember where they are. But again, longer-term memories are less affected. The epileptic discharge seems to interrupt the neural circuits that are actively processing new memories when the fit occurs.

Magnetic stimulation of the brain The brain can also be stimulated non-invasively via a powerful magnetic coil which circles the head. The stimulus accurately targets a particular brain area. Unlike an epileptic discharge, which produces massive stimulation all over the brain, the effect is to create a brief temporary disruption in one small area alone. This method is known as Transcranial Magnetic Stimulation (TMS). It can be used to study the way that motor responses begin. As a participant is just about to make a movement, electrical stimulation targeted at the motor cortex can interrupt it, enabling experimenters to study the sequence of activity in the brain that occurs in structures involved in the initiation of motor movement. TMS can also be used to interrupt a range of perceptual, cognitive and motor processes in the brain (Rushworth & Walsh, 1999).

Evaluation of brain stimulation techniques

Advantages Brain stimulation is a powerful tool with which to investigate motivational systems and reward. In some structures, stimulation acts as a powerful reward and can have clear and predictable effects in changing behaviour, indicating localisation of brain functions associated with reward and pleasure. Interruptive stimulation via magnetic induction can be focused very precisely from outside the brain and could be extremely useful in future, avoiding the need for surgical procedures in animals, and allowing detailed study of human brain systems.

Disadvantages Electrodes implanted in the brain cannot remain for long periods of time in humans or animals. Electrical stimulation is always artificial and can never precisely mimic normal physiological activity. Where behaviour is disrupted by stimulation, this could be the result of alteration to any one of several functional brain systems.

1.3 | Recording electrical activity in the brain

Another way of examining what particular parts of the brain are doing is to record the electrical activity taking place in a particular region of the brain – in a large cluster of neurons or in single neurons.

Recording from blocks of neurons It is sometimes possible to get an overall measure of activity by recording from many neurons (perhaps many millions of neurons) simultaneously, a procedure known as *multi-unit recording*. (The word *unit* is often used to mean 'neuron'.) The most common example in humans is the measurement of the EEG (electroencephalogram).

Activity 1 | Electrical stimulation

A bullfight

In 1975, the Spanish physiologist Delgado played the part of matador in a Spanish Plaza del Toros – bullfighting arena – armed only with an electrical transmitter. The bull that he was 'fighting' had an electrode implanted in the brain prior to the bullfight. Each time the bull charged towards him, Delgado pressed a button that caused a burst of electrical stimulation in a part of the bull's brain. The stimulation stopped the bull in its tracks.

Questions

1 Why do you think the stimulation stopped the bull?

2 Delgado claimed to be delivering a disrupting stimulus that blocked an 'aggression centre' in the brain. Can we be sure?

3 How might the stimulation have affected (a) aggression, (b) motor control, (c) attention or (d) pleasure? How could a change in any one of these functions have been brought about by the stimulation and therefore influenced the behaviour of the bull?

Electro refers to the fact that electrical voltage is being measured, *encephalo* means the recordings are from the brain, and *gram* means that the results are printed as a record. Electrodes are attached to the outside of the head. Each picks up the tiny voltage changes occurring within the brain beneath it, and the voltage from the electrodes is printed out as continuous wavering lines on a machine called a *polygraph* (poly = many, and graph = to draw). To an experienced observer, the wave patterns in these lines indicate a great deal about changing activity in the brain, although the EEG is a blunt instrument insofar as each electrode picks up from a wide area and it is hard to relate waveforms to activity in particular brain areas.

The EEG can be used to examine changes in normal brain activity during sleeping and waking (see Chapter 6). It can also diagnose pathological changes that are caused by illness, such as the presence of an epileptic focus – a hot spot of over-activity which can trigger an epileptic fit.

In animals, implanted electrodes, located permanently in the brain, can be used to record from whole blocks of tissue. Unlike human EEG studies, the source of a waveform is known, and changes in waveform can be linked to changes in behaviours. For example, a distinctive waveform called *theta rhythm* occurs in the hippocampus (in the temporal lobe) when the animal engages in exploratory behaviour, suggesting a role for hippocampus in information gathering (see Chapter 24).

Sometimes it is possible to record activity in the brain which is produced or 'evoked' by a particular stimulus such as a simple bright light flash, a flash of a pattern, or a sound (Figure 3). These voltage changes are known as *evoked potentials* or *event-related potentials (ERPs)*. Here the recording of brain activity is not continuous. Each stimulus presentation is recorded as a separate event, and a brief recording of brain activity is triggered at the moment each stimulus is presented. So, if the stimulus is a light flash, the brain's electrical response is recorded for 1-2 seconds after the flash occurs. Responses are usually averaged across many presentations, giving the type of uniform waveform shown in Figure 4. Waveforms are described in terms of whether they include positive voltages (P waves shown as downward pen deflections) and negative voltage

waves (N waves, upward deflections). Particular waveforms appear when the participant is engaged in certain behaviours. For example, when they must pay careful attention to the stimulus, a large positive wave often appears in the frontal lobe. The functioning of specific sensory pathways can be examined using this technique.

Magnetoencephalography (MEG) Electrical activity within the brain causes small magnetic fields (dipoles) to be created around it. These are very weak but using MEG recording, a recently-developed technique, they can be amplified and recorded, giving results similar to the EEG. Activity can be traced from one area to others as waves of activity sweep across the brain. While a participant is engaged in an activity, such as naming a picture, a MEG recording will show the whole sequence of events – from the areas of the brain that first become active, to those becoming active later, eventually reaching the motor systems that generate response outputs. Salmelin et al. (1994) used this technique to trace activity taking place when a participant names a picture. This technique therefore allows patterns of brain activity to be monitored across time, and across the whole brain. It is limited insofar as not all brain activity creates recordable magnetic dipoles.

Recording from single neurons Unlike multi-unit recordings, which tell us about activity in large blocks of neurons, *single-unit recording* tells us what a particular neuron is doing. Neurons produce bursts of electrical signals when they become active in transmitting information, and these can be recorded using a fine wire microelectrode. Figure 4 shows recordings made from single neurons in the primary visual cortex of cats, by the Nobel Prize winners David Hubel and Torston Wiesel, while the animals saw carefully controlled visual stimuli such as dots or lines. A burst of activity occurred in response to a particular stimulus, for example a line at a particular angle. The neurons are said to be 'tuned' to particular features. In Figure 4 the neuron's tuning (a preference for vertical lines) is represented by the coloured bar. When a stimulus (white bar) is presented horizontally the neuron shows no burst of activity (top panel). When the stimulus gets closer to its tuning preference (middle panel) some activity is recorded. Only when the stimulus line coincides exactly with the tuning preference (lower panel) is a rapid burst of activity seen. Hubel and Wiesel believed that this type of *feature detection* forms the basis of object identification in the brain. High level neurons would take these simple lines and edges and piece them together to represent more complex features and whole objects. The model predicts that at the very highest level of perception, specialised cells must 'recognise' particular complex stimuli – for example, a 'grandmother' cell would become active whenever grandma's face appears. It is likely that the processing of some stimuli occurs in this way, since cells have been found in the temporal lobes that respond to complex objects and faces (Desimone, 1991). However, it would be impossible for individual cells to act as detectors for recognising all stimuli (bucket cell, table cell, bicycle cell, and so on) – we recognise many more objects than we have cells in the brain, let alone in the visual cortex!

Single units can be recorded while an animal is free to move about. Some units in the temporal lobe hippocampus fire selectively when an animal is in a particular place in a familiar environment, suggesting a role for such 'place cells' in spatial navigation (see Chapter 24).

Single unit recordings are generally used in studies of non-

Figure 3   A visual evoked potential (VEP)

1.5 seconds

Voltage change in the visual cortex when a visual stimulus is presented

Figure 4   Tuning of a visual neuron

Recording from a single visual neuron by Hubel and Wiesel. In the left panels, the white line is the stimulus presented to the eye, and the vertical line shows the preferred stimulus orientation of the neuron being recorded from in the brain. Right panels show the activity of the neuron when the stimulus is presented.

human animals, although they can be made in human patients whose brains are exposed for surgery (Kropotov & Ponomarev, 1991).

Evaluation of recording techniques

Advantages Recording techniques have provided a large volume of valuable data, indicating the way that information is processed by individual neurons. For example, before Hubel and Wiesel, no models existed as to how edges and lines are processed within the visual system.

Disadvantages It is difficult to identify the reason why a neuron becomes active when a particular stimulus is presented. For example, a neuron responding to a figure of a cat may be a sensory unit (responding to 'cat' features), a memory unit (relating the input to a stored image), or a response unit (relating to the intention to stroke or escape from the cat). Models based purely on physiological recordings sometimes encounter problems – Hubel and Wiesel's model of vision relies on there being a neuron in the brain corresponding to every complex stimulus which we recognise, but this is clearly impossible – we recognise many more objects than we have neurons in the brain. Some techniques are limited – the MEG technique is only useful for activity which generates recordable magnetic fields.

1.4   Chemical manipulation

Since brain activity involves chemical changes in neurons, brain functions can be influenced and investigated using drugs which increase or decrease chemical activity in particular neuronal pathways. Because there is very precise chemical coding in neurotransmitter systems, it is possible to use a drug to enhance or block a particular pathway. The effect on behaviour gives clues as to the functional role of that pathway. Drugs enhancing activity in a neuronal pathway are called *agonists*, those reducing activity are *antagonists*.

Drugs taken by mouth or injection enter the blood stream and travel to the brain. In animals, they can be injected directly into the brain through a small cannula (a fine metal tube) that is surgically implanted using stereotaxic coordinates with its tip in the target structure, ensuring that the drug is delivered only to that particular structure. Studies in humans and animals have identified several important brain systems. The anti-anxiety drug diazepam is effective when injected directly into the amygdala, indicating that this is an important brain site where it exerts its action. Similarly injecting the anti-schizophrenic drug, Haloperidol, into a nucleus deep in the frontal lobe, the *nucleus accumbens*, reduces experimentally-induced schizophrenic-like symptoms in rats. Haloperidol is an antagonist for the neurotransmitter dopamine (DA) which is prevalent in the nucleus accumbens, which is probably a major site where the drug acts in humans to suppress schizophrenic symptoms. Alzheimer's disease, or *Senile Dementia of the Alzheimer-Type* (SDAT), commonly occurs with increasing age and involves a complete breakdown of cognitive functions including memory loss. This may be the result of losing neurons in another forebrain nucleus, the nucleus basalis, which uses the neurotransmitter acetyl choline (ACh). Certainly, ACh antagonists, such as scopolamine, can produce memory losses, while ACh stimulants and choline-rich diets can sometimes improve memory functions in some Alzheimer's patients.

It is often not possible to study neurotransmitter activity directly in humans, and extrapolation from animal studies can be difficult. At post-mortem, the brains of schizophrenic or Alzheimer's disease patients can be studied to assess the numbers of specific receptor types in the brain in order to test hypotheses developed in animals, though most patients will have been on medication for many years making data hard to interpret. The use of scanning techniques (see Unit 2) may in future help to identify early changes in the chemistry of the brain associated with these diseases before symptoms develop.

Evaluation of chemical manipulation

Advantages Centrally injected drugs can identify very specifically the neural structures or pathways involved in behaviours, including pathological behaviours like those seen in schizophrenic or Alzheimer's patients. This information can contribute to the development of better drug treatments.

Disadvantages Many behaviours are probably not precisely chemically coded in the brain, and many involve multiple brain systems. A drug may affect several systems at once. Animal studies are sometimes difficult to extrapolate to human disease processes – animals and humans differ in the way their behavioural repertoires change in response to chemical changes in the brain.

Key terms

Neurotransmitters *Chemicals used by neurons for communication (eg dopamine, acetyl choline).*

Agonist *A drug which enhances activity in a chemical pathway in the brain.*

Antagonist *A drug which reduces activity within a chemical pathway in the brain.*

1.5 Evidence from damaged brains

The *lesion technique* involves the analysis of the consequences of brain damage. In animal studies, researchers can produce carefully localised damage to particular brain structures by (a) removing (ablating) tissue, (b) damaging (lesioning) tissue via the brief application of heat, electrical current, or a laser beam, (c) by cutting the connections between structures or (d) injecting a neurotoxin, a targeted chemical which attacks only those cells using a particular neurotransmitter. Such procedures are only carried out under deep anaesthesia.

One of the first to use the lesion technique experimentally, in the 1920s, was Karl Lashley, an American psychologist, who began to search for the places in the brain where he supposed memories must be stored. He hypothesised that if an animal had learned a particular route through a maze, and the route is 'stored' in one cortical area, removal of that one small area should destroy the memory for the route – the animal would simply forget the route, but nothing else. Removal of any other area would have no effect on the route memory. Lashley made lesions in the brains of maze-trained rats, ranging from large lesions in some animals to small lesions in others, in many different cortical areas. The animals were retrained in the maze until they relearned the task. Lashley found that the number of training trials needed to relearn was *not* related to the lesion site – that is, the particular area of the cortex lesioned – but rather to the amount of cortex removed. The bigger the lesion, *wherever* in the cortex it was placed, the bigger the deficit, and the more relearning required. After many years of experimenting, he concluded that no one 'memory area' could be found. In summary, Lashley concluded that there is no memory trace, or engram, in one particular area, but that all of the cortex acts together (his *Law of Mass Action*), and all areas are equally involved in any complex behaviour (his *Law of Equipotentiality*).

Probably Lashley was partly right, though his laws are no longer accepted. Most behaviours are complex and require the integrated action of many brain areas, to a lesser or greater degree. Probably the tasks that Lashley used needed involvement of many brain areas – running a maze requires the use of visual cues, motor responses, spatial memory, motivation to succeed and so on. Had Lashley used simpler discrimination tasks he would have found greater localisation. In other words, simpler tasks are more likely to be dealt with in particular 'local' areas of the brain which specialise in certain functions. For example, in a choice task in which an animal must run toward a circle stimulus but not to a triangle, performance would be greatly disrupted by small lesions which just removed the primary visual cortex. In recent decades, work using smaller lesions has revealed quite a high degree of functional localisation within the brain.

The logic of the lesion technique The lesion technique assumes that any skill that the participant can perform before the damage, but which they cannot perform afterwards, is the function of the area damaged.

This may not always be true – removing a component from a computer might stop it working but will not necessarily tell us what that component was doing in the working computer. Take the following example. Assume that a brain lesion in rats causes them to become hyperactive (running about frantically). Is the function of the damaged area to 'inhibit activity', so that activity

is 'released' from inhibition when the structure is removed? Removing any one of several components in a computer will produce a snowy screen, but it would be wrong to conclude that all of those components function to 'inhibit screen snow'! Furthermore, damage to any one of several structures in the rat's brain might produce similar effects. Using the computer analogy again, removing either the power supply, or some wires, the transformer, or the on-off switch will all have the same effect though they do quite different jobs.

On the other hand, we should not be too pessimistic. In many complex systems, removal of a component can be informative – in a cassette recorder, removal of one ear piece from headphones will result in the loss of sound to one ear, while the removal of a 'record' button will leave all play functions intact, but prevent the making of new recordings. In terms of brain function, the lesion approach has produced some interesting findings, both in animals where brain damage can be made fairly precisely, but also in humans despite the fact that damage caused by injuries and illnesses in humans is often haphazard and not neatly localised in particular brain areas.

Behavioural testing of brain damage in animals Testing before and after lesion damage can be used to highlight the resulting deficits – the poor performance that results from the brain tissue loss. How is it possible to do this in animals, for example to test their memory or attention before and after the injury?

An animal's spatial memory can be tested using a radial arm maze (Figure 5), in which the animal has to forage among the arms of the maze for a food reward without making revisit errors. Animals will do this with little training.

Figure 5 The radial arm maze

food

food

food

On the radial arm maze, an animal has to run down each arm once in order to take a food reward (hidden in a shallow well). Repeat arm visits are errors. Animals learn very rapidly to make error-less choices to all maze arms, as though foraging for food in their natural environment. Animals with damage to the hippocampus make many error re-visits.

Human brain damage

Accidents, illnesses and injuries are important sources of data for neuropsychologists. Sadly, wars have provided many human participants for experimental analysis. The effects of injuries to the brain have provided valuable information on the likely functions of brain regions, particularly since the development of tests that tell us precisely which functions have been lost (see also Chapter 23).

Figure 6 The Poppelreuter Overlapping Figures Test

Patients with visual and language difficulties have problems separating the four figures, and naming them.

Humans sustain brain injuries in many ways, usually through blows to the head in traffic accidents, tumour growth in the brain, a stroke due to a blocked blood vessel in the brain, oxygen deprivation (for example through inhaling smoke or carbon monoxide), and long-term alcohol abuse (Joseph & Heckers, 1997).

Humans who sustain brain injuries will often have widespread damage throughout the brain, rather than localised damage within one area. For example, stroke patients suffer brain damage both as a result of blood starvation in the areas supplied by the blocked blood vessel, and locally around the burst if bleeding occurs. Patients with closed-head injuries may have no outward signs of damage, but may have widespread lesions due to the twisting and jarring of the brain during their accident.

Testing human patients after brain damage When testing humans, opportunities exist which are not available with animals. Human testing is conducted either with a test battery – a collection of different tests – or a specific test that is aimed at identifying the function that is suspected to be deficient. Examples of general tests of intelligence, memory and comprehension are the WAIS (Wisconsin Adult Intelligence Scale), and Benton and Wechsler scales. These have sub-scales, separately measuring verbal and non-verbal skills, and showing specifically the areas in which the patient is deficient, such as memory, attention, reasoning, and so on. Specific tests for damage to particular brain regions are sorting and reasoning tasks (frontal lobes), Rey figure and sequential memory tasks (temporal), constructional and spatial tasks (parietal) and colour naming (occipital). Visual object extraction can be tested using the Poppelreuter test shown in Figure 6.

Evaluation of the lesion approach

Advantages The lesion approach shows relationships between brain damage and the effects that it produces. Careful testing can reveal deficits in humans and animals that can be localised to particular neural structures. This can provide the basis for other types of study.

Disadvantages In many cases, human brain damage is widespread, affecting many structures. It cannot always be assumed that a behaviour that appears 'missing' after brain damage is purely the functional responsibility of the area(s) damaged – effects may be due to effects on distant structures, for example where damage to one area prevents the undamaged functions of another area from being expressed. Also, we generally test abilities after brain damage but not before. Therefore, it is often uncertain whether stubbornness, forgetfulness or low IQ in a brain-damaged patient result from their brain lesion, or whether they were as poor before they sustained the injury.

Activity 2 The parts and the whole

Imagine that aliens are seeing a motor car for the first time. They are fascinated by the way in which humans transport themselves in metal boxes which move. They are interested to know how these moving boxes work. They decide to undertake a study which consists of removing one bit at a time, to see what effect this has on the function of the car.

Questions

1   What could the aliens learn about the 'functions' of different parts of the car by removing each of them (eg steering wheel, wheels, engine, brakes, lights)?

2   What might they report back
(a) correctly or
(b) incorrectly to their planet after using the 'lesion' technique?

3   What does this example suggest about the uses and limitations of the lesion technique for examining the functions of the brain?

1.6 Human brain scanning and imaging

One way of examining brain function and detecting brain abnormalities is to watch the brain in action. In recent years, technology has progressed rapidly so that activities deep in the brain can be imaged in detail, sometimes as they actually take place. There are various kinds of brain scanning and imaging. In some cases, the brain is 'photographed' but in depth – the inner structures of the brain can be visualised. In others, physiological functions can be monitored. In very fast scanners, with good computer software, the brain can be imaged in real time as things are actually happening.

Scanning-imaging techniques

CAT scans *Computerised Axial Tomography (CT or CAT)* This was the first of the new technologies, appearing in the 1970s. (*Tomography* comes from the Greek word tomos meaning a slice). The participant lays on a surface which can be slid into a circular scanner, which surrounds their head. They are painlessly bombarded with X-rays, from a variety of different angles. Different amounts of X-radiation pass through the brain, depending on the type of tissue that the rays encounter. Some types of brain tissue are denser than others, and the denser the tissue, the fewer X-rays pass through. From the pattern of radiation that passes through different regions, a picture can be built up using computer imaging. Dense bone tissue appears white, blood as dark grey, and brain tissue light grey. The fluid filled cavities within the brain are the least dense, and appear black. This technique is similar to that used in hospital X-ray units to obtain X-rays of the chest and lungs. Several CT slices can be taken at different levels through the brain, and these can be 'stacked' using computer graphics to create a 3-D image. CT scans have diagnosed serious abnormalities in the brains of many professional boxers.

MRI scans *Magnetic Resonance Imaging (MRI)* The participant is surrounded by very powerful magnets, creating a strong electric field (50,000 times the earth's magnetic field strength), and radio waves are then passed through the head. Radio waves cause molecules in the brain to vibrate and emit their own waves, which are recorded by sensors. The radio waves can be adjusted to show up a particular kind of brain tissue, such as soft tissue The image can best be seen when 'enhanced' with colour to show the softer tissues in lighter colours, and three dimensional views of the brain can be built up using computer imaging.

Evaluation of scanning-imaging techniques

Advantages These are non-invasive techniques, ie they do not involve physical entry into the brain. They can provide images that can be used to identify damaged regions of brain, for experimental investigations. Areas of old brain damage can be distinguished from new brain damage.

Disadvantages CT scans require the use of X-rays, which can be harmful. MRI requires the patient to spend a long time in a noisy environment as magnets rotate about them. Patients with metal in the body, such as heart pacemakers, cannot be tested using MRI because of the strong magnetic fields involved. The resolution on CT scans is poor – this technique cannot discriminate two objects that are separated by less than about 5mm, and some small lesions go undetected by CT. MRI produces clearer images and a greater resolution (about 0.1 mm).

Physiological functional imaging

This refers to the continuous recording of the activity of the brain while the participant is engaged in an activity. It monitors a physiological change, such as the rate at which a brain nutrient (a chemical, or blood gas such as oxygen) is being used by active brain areas.

PET scans *Positron Emission Tomography (PET)* The participant is injected with a substance such as glucose, which circulates throughout the body including the brain. So that the glucose can be detected, it is first 'labelled' with a radioactive chemical (ie each molecule of glucose has a radioactive marker attached to it). In the brain, active cells take up the labelled glucose (since glucose is used by cells for energy), and the PET scan 'maps' the areas of the brain where the radioactivity is most concentrated. This is done via sensitive detectors which record particles, called positrons, emitted by the radioactive markers. The results are displayed as an image like a photograph (Figure 7).

Maguire et al. (1997) investigated spatial skills in taxi drivers. Taxi drivers in London describe their intricate knowledge of complex routes through London as 'the knowledge'. Maguire et al. found that when imagining particular routes, their PET scans showed that a particular brain structure – the hippocampus of the right hemisphere – became especially active. This is important, because the hippocampus has previously been shown in animals to be involved in spatial encoding of the environment and route-finding. Similarly, if a participant imagines a colour, activity will be seen in the corresponding part of the brain (Visual area 4 in the temporal lobe) where colour information is processed. The same applies to motor

Figure 7 A PET scan

HEARING   SEEING

SPEAKING   THINKING

PET scans during different tasks

activity. For example, moving a finger will be 'reflected' in the images of the motor parts of the cortex which become active at the moment that the movement is made.

Single positron emission computerised tomography (SPECT) is a new form of PET scanning that uses a slower-decaying radioactive isotope, allowing a longer period for the collection of data.

PET scanning can also be used to identify the locations of particular neurotransmitter receptors in the brain via the use of radioactive ligands. Ligands are chemicals which attach to receptors. The scan enables assessment of the density of receptors and can indicate too few or too many receptors in illnesses such as schizophrenia and depression.

fMRI *Functional MRI (fMRI)* This, like PET scanning, also takes advantage of the fact that local blood flow through a region of brain increases when that brain area becomes active. It uses a variant on the standard MRI technique described above, but instead of just revealing brain structure, this technique also highlights the regions of the brain that are especially active by superimposing a functional layer of imaging on the structural scan of the brain. The scanner monitors activity by detecting the ratio of oxygenated to deoxygenated haemoglobin in the blood. Haemoglobin in blood picks up oxygen from the lungs and transports it about the body, including the brain. When blood passes through an active area of brain, a strange thing happens: the blood flow increases due to the cell activity, but the brain tissue cannot soak up all the extra oxygen that is supplied. This means that blood leaving an active area actually contains a larger proportion of oxygenated haemoglobin than deoxygenated. So fMRI shows areas having *greater* than normal levels of oxygenated haemoglobin, which are the *most* active regions. The participant is recorded in an experimental condition and in a control condition. For example, if the experiment is concerned with regions of the brain most involved in music perception, the experimental condition will involve being scanned while listening to music, while in the control condition they may listen to a voice or some random noise.

Evaluation of functional imaging

Advantages For the first time it is possible to have accurate images of the brain in action. The involvement of specific areas in behaviours can be identified with great accuracy. fMRI involves no injection of radioactive chemical. It can be used to investigate a wide range of sensory experiences, and methods have been found to enable participants to interact with a variety of displays, such as computer generated scenes, while being scanned. fMRI is a cheaper procedure than PET. Repeated recordings can be made from a single individual using fMRI.

Disadvantages For PET scans, a radioactive chemical has to be injected and the recording has to be completed within the short period in which the radioactivity decays. Data from several participants must be added together to give a reliable image, and adjustments must be made for different head sizes when combining participants' data. PET scan images do not reveal fine detail. The cooperation of the participant is necessary, and young or hyperactive children may be unable to lie still in an MRI or PET scanner.

Care is needed in interpreting results. The fact that a brain region 'lights up' in a scan image does not necessarily mean that it is the only region that plays a critical role in the performance of the task. The use of impressive technologies does not remove the need for careful analyses of behaviour and behaviour-brain relationships (Gabrieli, 1998).

Piecing the picture together

No one technique or approach tells us everything about the function of a brain structure. Only by placing together information from a wide variety of approaches can we identify the nature of the information processing that takes place there. It is rather like piecing together the pieces of a jigsaw puzzle. Each piece alone means little, but when many pieces are placed together, a picture begins to appear. From the various examples above, the role of the temporal lobe hippocampus in spatial behaviour is indicated by deficits in radial maze performance after hippocampal lesions in rats, single unit recordings that

Summary

1. No one technique provides a complete description of the functions of particular brain structures.

2. Anatomical methods produce a detailed map of the brain based on the appearance of cells in different areas. Brain atlases precisely identify the location of brain structures. However, they are not able to identify the functions of brain structures.

3. Areas of the brain can be stimulated electrically to mimic their normal functions. This gives an indication of the functions of different brain areas. However, electrical stimulation is artificial and cannot precisely mimic normal brain activity.

4. Recording electrical activity in the brain can also indicate the functions of particular brain structures. Single-unit recordings reveal the activity of a single neuron. However, it is difficult to identify the exact function of a neuron – it may become active for a variety of reasons.

5. The use of drugs has helped to identify several important brain systems. However, a drug may affect several systems at once.

6. The lesion technique assumes that any behaviour lost as a result of brain damage provides an indication of the function of the damaged area. This may be the case. However, damage in one area may affect other, undamaged, areas. As a result, it is not possible to say with certainty that damage in a particular area indicates the functions of that area.

7. Brain scanning and imaging provide 'pictures' of brain structures and activity. Functional imaging is particularly valuable since it provides accurate images of the brain in action. As a result, it can link specific brain areas to particular behaviours. However, caution is needed in interpreting results. Just because one area is particularly active does not exclude the possibility that other areas are involved.

reveal 'place cells' in the structure, and characteristic rhythms recorded in the structure when the animal is exploring its environment. These data are further complemented by human PET scanning that shows the hippocampus becomes especially active when someone is performing a spatial memory task. Each technique tells us more about the type of information being handled and how it is used. New imaging techniques have great potential, and may enable us to relate structure and function more precisely than ever before.

Key terms

Brain imaging *Building up a picture or model of the brain from X-ray like scanning.*

Functional imaging *Using images from brain scans and physiological measures to identify the regions of the brain currently active.*

Unit 2 Localisation of function in the cerebral cortex

KEY ISSUES

1   **What are the main functions of the frontal, occipital, temporal and parietal lobes of the brain?**

2   **To what extent are these functions localised within specific brain areas?**

3   **To what extent are they distributed across and between brain areas?**

2.1   The brain as a controller of behaviour

The evolution of human society, technology and communication has only been possible because humans possess such a large brain. It allows us to plan ahead and solve complex problems. Crucial to this development is the enlargement of the cerebral cortex – the surface of the brain – where many complex computations take place.

Often the brain is spoken about as though it is merely a powerful computer. But is this an appropriate way to view the brain? Computers can appear to be intelligent – they certainly perform calculations very quickly. But even the most powerful computers fall far short of the complexity and power of the human brain. A computer has recently been programmed to play chess so well that it beats chess masters. But the way it does so is quite different from human chess playing – the computer rapidly calculates all of the possible permutations of moves that could be made, and charts a route through the billions of possibilities in order to maximise the likelihood of success. Humans use insightful behaviours that the machine does not possess. Remember too that such a computer only plays chess – it cannot shop, write letters, hold conversations, discuss morality, play soccer, think, read, plan, express love or anger, or do the many other things that are controlled by our one brain.

It is probably an impossible task to understand exactly how a brain functions – we would need computers more complex than the brain itself to be able to account for all the electrical activity taking place in it. However, just as we don't need to be computer scientists to understand how a computer works in terms of inputs (keyboard, joystick, mouse), outputs (monitor screen, sounds, printing) and memory (diskettes, CD, ROM and RAM microchips), it may be possible to understand the brain in terms of systems or modules that are linked together, each having a responsibility for particular jobs or functions. This is the concept of *localisation of function* – the idea that specific functions have particular locations in the brain, that they are 'localised' in certain areas.

2.2   Functions: information processing in brain systems

What does 'function' mean when we apply the word to the brain? Put simply, it means the job each part of the brain does. It is fairly easy to identify the function of some organs of the body. For example, the heart 'pumps' blood. This analogy between the heart and a mechanical pump gives us a quick but accurate description of a complex process. It is more difficult to label brain structures as having psychological functions.

The term *brain function* implies that we can identify and label the particular role that each brain region plays in organising behaviour. We can think of the brain as an *input-processing-output* device which receives inputs, organises them and stores information in memory, and programs output responses by sending command signals to muscles and body organs. In other words, function refers to the kind of information processing that takes place within a brain structure. The whole brain acts in concert to organise behaviour, but we can identify the special responsibilities of different regions of the brain. Some systems and structures in the brain are more involved than others in organising particular kinds of behaviour – seeing, hearing, remembering, paying attention, directing motor responses – because psychological functions are to some extent 'localised' in specialised brain regions. But be careful: don't expect to find one single 'box' in the brain that we can label 'memory', for example. Memory is composed of several processes, and various parts of the brain are involved in remembering. The same applies to all other complex behaviours. We will consider language in this context in Unit 3.

Double-dissociation of function How can we decide whether brain structures form parts of the same or different processing systems? If damage to one structure, let's call it A, causes memory loss but has no effect on seeing, but damage to another structure, B, causes visual problems but no memory loss, we can assume that they form parts of rather separate brain systems. This is known as *double-dissociation of function* – meaning that each part is dissociated (separated) from the other. But can we separate vision and memory completely? No. We recognise an object (vision) because we have seen it before (memory), and therefore we should not be surprised to find another structure, let's say C, which is involved in BOTH vision and memory.

Take the following example. A patient with damage in their cerebral cortex is shown a picture of a cow and asked to identify it. They can see all the features of the cow separately (head, hoof, tail and so on) but they do not recognise the whole object as a cow. What kind of problem do they have? A visual problem, a memory problem, or both? This condition is known as *associative agnosia*. The patient does have some idea of the shape and category of an object – they might misidentify a cow as a pig, but not a boat, for example. Their basic perceptual abilities are intact because they can see the parts of the cow perfectly well. Their memory works, because they can say what a cow is 'a farmyard animal'. But they seem unable to link incoming visual information to stored meanings in memory. Often the damage that causes associative agnosia is *bilateral* (in both the left and right cortex), around the border between the occipital and temporal lobes. Examples such as this show how separate functions – in this case, memory and vision – must be linked together.

Key terms

Brain lobe *A label given to each of four major regions of brain cortex (occipital, parietal, temporal and frontal).*

Bilateral *On both sides of the brain.*

Unilateral *On one side of the brain.*

Agnosia *The inability to recognise objects.*

Double-dissociation of function *Contrasting the behavioural effects of pairs of brain structures in order to clarify their individual functions.*

2.3 The functions of the four main brain lobes in humans

This section draws largely on what is known about brain function from studies of patients with brain damage. It considers the main functional responsibilities of the four main cortical lobes of the human brain.

The *cortex* is where much higher processing takes place in humans. Although it began to develop in fairly primitive animals such as reptiles, it has grown to relatively vast proportions in mammals, especially in primates and most of all in humans

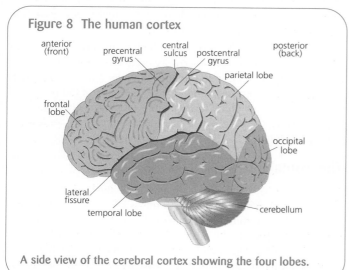

Figure 8   The human cortex

anterior (front) · precentral gyrus · central sulcus · postcentral gyrus · posterior (back) · parietal lobe · frontal lobe · occipital lobe · lateral fissure · temporal lobe · cerebellum

A side view of the cerebral cortex showing the four lobes.

where it forms a large proportion of the adult brain. If stretched flat, your cortex would cover an area of about 2400 cm². The surface is actually folded up giving a walnut-like appearance. The hills and valleys are known as *convolutions*. A hill is a *gyrus* (plural, gyri) and a valley a *sulcus* (plural, sulci), very deep sulci being called *fissures*. Humans' wide range of complex behaviours requires a large cortical volume, but there are limits. During recent evolution the human brain could not expand indefinitely like an inflating balloon because, at birth, the head has to pass through a narrow birth canal. The convoluted brain surface overcomes this problem because it allows a large cortical area to be folded up into a small volume.

Unlike structures deep in the brain, where damage can often be fatal, superficial damage to the cortex, such as occurs after a blow to the head or penetrating injury, can often leave the victim functioning normally, except for a particular functional loss – a particular skill or ability is missing. The study of such losses is fascinating and can often tell us a great deal about how the brain is organised.

The occipital lobe

The *occipital lobe* is situated at the back of the brain and is especially concerned with vision. Information travels in the optic nerve from the eye to the *primary visual cortex* or *Area 17*. Primary implies that it is linked to a particular function – in this case, vision. It is the first cortical area to receive input from the eye via the optic nerve, and it is the region where the process of pattern perception begins. Single neurons in the primary visual cortex are sensitive to lines and edges (see Unit 1). In humans, the primary visual cortex is about the size of a credit card. If someone has been unlucky enough to suffer a gunshot wound, stroke, or other brain damage that destroys all of the primary visual cortex on both sides of the brain, they will be 'blind' in the sense that they will not perceive objects. They may perceive light-dark differences and movement by using other brain pathways, but they will lose all pattern perception.

In front of the primary visual cortex is *secondary visual cortex*, an area in which further processing takes place, refining and making more sense of visual information from the eye. Information is then sent to higher cortical areas with more and more sophisticated functions, so that higher order information (such as colour and movement) can be extracted, and visual information linked and integrated with other senses. Two pathways in particular arise in the primary visual cortex and project forward – a northern pathway, travelling to the parietal area, and a southern pathway travelling to the temporal lobe (see Figure 9). In the temporal lobe, visual form processing takes place, among other things. The parietal route is often thought to allow spatial encoding, although some believe that its major role is coordinating visual information with complex hand movements required to grasp objects (Milner & Goodale, 1996).

The parietal lobe

The *parietal lobe* is *association cortex*. This means that its activity is not related narrowly to one particular sense – it has a more general and higher level involvement in behaviour. It is more difficult to characterise than primary visual cortex, but it is probably concerned with higher perception (of the geometry of complex objects), spatial behaviours and the control of skilled action sequences such as grasping objects. This lobe is sent

Figure 9 Pathways from the occipital lobe

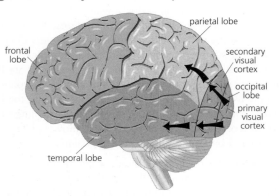

Two major pathways project forward from the primary visual cortex

Figure 10 Spatial disorientation after head injury

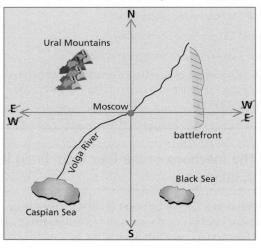

information via neural pathways from many other brain areas. A clinical condition known as *acalculia* – the inability to do mathematical calculations – is associated with parietal damage. Interestingly, post-mortem analysis of the brain of the famous scientist Albert Einstein revealed that he possessed a surprisingly large parietal area.

Damage to the posterior (or back) part of the parietal lobe results in difficulties with spatial localisation, knowing where objects are positioned in relation to one-another, and apraxias which involve poor control of skilled motor actions. Damage to the right parietal lobe often causes a complete lack of awareness of objects in the left half of the visual field (see Figure 11) and of the left side of the body, a phenomenon known as *contralateral* or *contra-lesional neglect*. Damage to the left parietal area rarely produces such a strong effect, suggesting that left and right parietal areas function differently.

Parietal damage therefore gives rise to a constellation of different effects, but the following examples illustrate the types of deficit – loss of functions – most commonly observed.

The electrician An electrician who regularly wired up houses suddenly suffered a stroke. He had been used to deciding where to route electric wires and organise circuits from one room to another. After the stroke, he was unable to imagine the 3-D structure of a house and completely unable to work out a wiring circuit. The stroke was in the right parietal lobe. (Source: Dr Allan Dodds).

The soldier The Russian neuropsychologist, Alexander Luria, found numerous examples of patients with injuries to the parietal cortex who made interesting spatial errors. Figure 10 shows the results of Luria's testing of a man with a gunshot wound to the right hemisphere, mainly in the parietal cortex. The patient had been a soldier during World War II in the former Soviet Union. He was asked to draw a map of the region in which he had been fighting. Before his injury, he had an excellent knowledge of the region. The parietal cortex damage affected his ability to remember spatial relationships. The true map of the area is shown at the top in Figure 10. The patient's drawing below is completely disorganised. As well as reversing most of the locations, he was unable to distinguish east from west.

The neglect patient A patient with a wound in the right parietal lobe was reported to neglect the left hand side of his body, dressing only the right side and shaving only the right side of his face. He could detect a nurse approaching from the right hand side of his hospital bed, but not from the left. He neglected the left side of a picture and left food uneaten on the left side of his plate. When putting on trousers, he appeared to lose the left trouser leg completely, and endeavoured to place both legs into the right one (McFie & Zangwill, 1960).

At the front edge of the parietal cortex is the postcentral gyrus (see Figure 8). This is somatosensory cortex, meaning that it receives sensory input from the body surface. The whole body is represented, but disproportionately so that parts of the body such as the fingers which have greatest touch sensitivity have large areas devoted to them, while the back and legs are less well represented.

The frontal lobe

The *frontal lobe* is sometimes thought to be the seat of reasoning and intelligence, though this is controversial. Higher functions such as thinking and creativity involve many brain regions, but certainly the prefrontal part of the frontal lobe seems especially important for complex behaviours such as anticipating the future, planning ahead, and problem solving. Often these are referred to as *executive functions*, because they

Figure 11 Drawing by a patient with right parietal damage (left visual field neglect)

Actual drawing   **Patient's copy**

Figure 12 The frontal lobe

dorsolateral prefrontal cortex

premotor cortex

primary motor cortex

orbital frontal cortex (part hidden)

are similar to the functions of a business executive – predicting, planning, changing direction, and making inferences. These abilities are slow to develop in humans – infants and young children will often behave as if unaware that 'If I do X, then Y will follow...' (Parents often act as 'frontal lobes' for children!)

The anterior (or forward) part of the frontal lobe, the prefrontal area, is subdivided into different regions (Figure 12) having their own localised functions. The *dorsolateral area* is involved in a range of cognitive processes including temporal processing (remembering across time intervals), and an area around the orbit of the eye, the *orbital frontal cortex*, is concerned with motor programming, particularly with carrying out sequences of actions and inhibiting (withholding) unwanted motor responses. A region found only in the left frontal lobe – Broca's area – is responsible for language production. Patients with damage in this area suffer *production aphasia*, producing speech which is slow and telegraphic ('I... go... walk', for example). Language functions are discussed in more detail in Unit 3.

Key terms

Primary cortex *Cortex dedicated to one particular sense or to motor output.*

Association cortex *Cortex which is not specific, in which the senses merge and can be integrated.*

Neglect *A clinical condition in which some information is not attended to.*

Contralateral or contralesional neglect *Failure to pay attention to stimuli on the opposite side of sensory space to the side of the brain lesion.*

The prefrontal cortex is therefore important for several related behaviours, so that frontal damage can have dramatic behavioural effects.

Prefrontal cortex is important for 'executive' functions. This area is much larger in humans compared with lower species, reflecting the complexity of human life and the decision and thinking processes that humans must use to survive.

The following are examples of the effects of damage to the frontal lobe:

Perseveration A man with damage in the orbital frontal cortex was cutting a hedge with clippers. He came to a region of hedge where a telegraph wire ran down through the leaves. He cut through the wire with the clippers. Asked afterwards why he did this, he said that he had realised that he should cut the hedge not the wire but '... I could not help it; once I had begun clipping, I just couldn't stop'. Damage to the orbital frontal cortex had removed the ability to interrupt an ongoing plan or sequence, and withheld the motor response. This type of behaviour is sometimes referred to as *perseveration*.

Impulsiveness Phineus Gage was employed by a railway company in the mid-1850s. His job was blasting rock to make way for railway tracks. On one occasion, he was busy pouring explosive into a hole in a rock and thumping it in with a tamping rod, a metal rod weighing several kilograms. Unfortunately for him, but fortunately for brain sciences, the explosive suddenly ignited. The explosion blasted the tamping rod up through his left cheek, and out through the top of his skull, damaging most of the frontal lobes of the brain (see Figure 13). He survived the injury and, apart from being paralysed on one side of his face, he was able to function normally. However, after the accident, he was a changed personality '... not Phineus Gage any longer', as one person commented. He was suddenly rude, impulsive, over-sexual and irresponsible. This type of behaviour is sometimes said to result from *disinhibition* – the removal of inhibitions. Frontal patients often show shallow emotions, even showing little response to pain; their facial expressions are blank and head and eye movements are few. They are unself-critical and show little concern for the past or future.

The motor strip

Also located in the frontal lobe, behind the prefrontal cortex, is a strip of motor cortex (the precentral gyrus) known as *primary*

Figure 13 The skull of Phineus Gage

This reconstruction shows the tamping iron which penetrated Gage's skull and caused massive damage to his frontal lobes.

Figure 14 The primary motor cortex

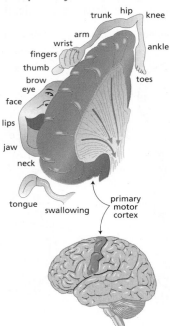

The drawings of areas of the body indicate the amount of motor cortex directing movement in those areas.

motor cortex (see Figure 12). 'Primary' means that this region is the main motor area (devoted to motor control). The motor strip is laid out in an organised fashion, representing the entire body (see Figure 14). Electrical stimulation of this cortex with a fine electrical probe produces motor movements, showing that pathways originating in the motor strip project down to the spinal cord and then to the muscles. Notice in Figure 14 that areas of the body are disproportionately represented. This is how you look to your motor cortex! The body parts best represented include the hand and face, for which the most precise control is required – the face has 40 separate muscles which enable us to produce a wide range of facial expressions using subtle combinations of movements. The motor cortex acts in concert with several cortical and subcortical structures, plus the cerebellum which also influences movements (see Figure 8).

The temporal lobe

The temporal lobe has both primary and association functions. One region of this lobe is concerned with hearing, the *primary auditory area*, on the upper ridge of the temporal cortex. Other areas are concerned with 'higher' auditory and visual processing, with language comprehension and with memory. Tucked inside the inner wall of the temporal lobe is the *hippocampus*, which has important roles in spatial processing and memory (see Unit 1 and Chapter 24).

The following example of the effects of damage to the temporal lobe gives an indication of one of its functions.

HM – these are his initials, by which he is known to neuropsychologists – was born in the USA in 1926. On his 16th birthday, he began to have serious epileptic fits. His epilepsy

Key terms

Perseveration *The inability to cease doing something or change behaviour.*

Disinhibition *The impulsive tendency to initiate new behaviours, even when these are unacceptable or embarrassing.*

Anterior *toward the front.*

Posterior *toward the back.*

showed no sign of improvement so when he was 27, radical surgery was carried out. His operation, performed by Dr William Scoville, removed the inner surfaces of both right and left temporal lobes. His epileptic attacks reduced in frequency afterwards, but he suffered serious memory impairments. Although he could remember details of houses that he had lived in many years previously, he thought he still lived there. He suffered severe *anterograde amnesia* (amnesia = memory loss, and antero = forward or future): that is, he had memory loss for new information, for events happening after his surgery. He did not know who cared for him, or what he had eaten for his previous meal. At various times he estimated his age to be 10 to 26 years less than it was (Corkin, 1984).

2.4 Primary and association cortex

We have seen that there are two main types of cortex. First, there are primary cortices such as the primary visual area and the primary auditory area. These are sometimes referred to as *projection* cortices because they are the first regions of cortex to which sensory information is projected from the eye and ear. The primary motor cortex is also primary, because it is concerned only with motor control. All these areas are narrowly devoted to a particular function. Areas or cortex surrounding primary cortex are known as secondary cortex – they are also quite narrowly focused and extend the functions of primary cortex. However, a different type of cortex, including the parietal cortex, prefrontal cortex and the lower part of the temporal cortex, is known as *association cortex*. These areas receive information passed on from primary and secondary cortex, for processing at a more sophisticated level. The term association cortex was originally used because it was assumed that the senses, for example seeing and hearing, were brought together – *associated* – in these areas, though this is a rather simplistic idea. Certainly association areas deal with high level processing such as perceptual categorisation.

Association cortex forms about 80% of the human cortex. We have much more association cortex than other primates such as monkeys or chimpanzees. But it is difficult to compare species by measuring their brain sizes or volumes. Elephants have bigger brains than rats, not necessarily because they are more intelligent but just because they are bigger animals – more brain is required for more body. It is possible to overcome this problem by calculating an *encephalisation quotient* (EQ). This indicates the amount of brain that an animal possesses over and above that which is expected based on their body size. Table 1 shows that humans have an especially high EQ, three times that of a chimpanzee, for example.

Table 1	Encephalisation quotients
Human	7.44
Dolphin	5.31
Chimpanzee	2.49
Elephant	1.87
Dog	1.17
Cat	1.00
Rabbit	0.40

From Macphail, 1982

Humans' excess brain volume is largely a result of extra association cortex, such as frontal and parietal cortex (Rilling & Insell, 1999). However, size is not everything. It is the way that the human brain is organised which gives us our human features. In a microcephalic individual the brain fails to develop properly, sometimes resulting in a brain smaller than that of a chimpanzee, yet they can still have abilities, such as the ability to use language, which chimpanzees do not possess. The development of so much association cortex in the human brain has an evolutionary advantage – processing capacity is greatly increased, allowing the development of sophisticated behaviours related to thinking and social behaviour.

Figure 15 Association cortex in the human brain

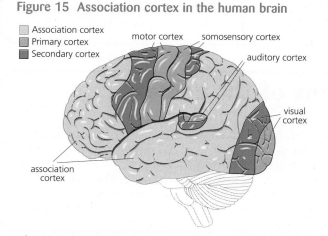

- Association cortex
- Primary cortex
- Secondary cortex

motor cortex   somosensory cortex

auditory cortex

visual cortex

association cortex

Only 20% of the human brain is dedicated to purely sensory or purely motor functions. 80% is association cortex where information is subjected to higher processing and interpretation.

2.5 Distributed processing

As a result of research in recent decades, the concept of strict localisation of function has often been questioned. We have seen that in some regions of the brain particular functions predominate – major memory impairments occur after temporal lobe lesions but not after occipital lesions, whereas total loss of visual pattern perception occurs after occipital but not temporal lesions. Nevertheless, in most behaviours, especially complex behaviours, many brain areas need to interact with one another. Almost any function within the brain is bound to call up information from a wide area. Unit 3 shows how language processing involves interactions among several centres in the left

Figure 16 Networks of neurons

A parallel-distributed neural network. It shows connections between neurons which form words and associations between words. The strength of the connections increases with rehearsal and use.

hemisphere – visual processing of written words, auditory processing of spoken words, processing of meaning in Wernicke's area and the programming of speech outputs via Broca's area and the motor cortex. We saw how Lashley was unable to localise memory in one 'engram', and that multiple systems are needed to process the information used to solve maze problems. And we saw how the processing of visual stimuli requires a synthesis of the component parts (for example, of a drawing of an animal) and a linkage with an object vocabulary in memory for correct recognition to occur.

A single brain area cannot be expected to 'hold' all of the information that it needs to perform its functions. Another interesting example is the hippocampus, discussed above in relation to spatial encoding and memory – knowing where you are and how you got there. The hippocampus cannot do this in isolation. Since spatial memory involves the use of visual, auditory and motor information (and more) the hippocampus must rely on information coming from many areas of the brain. Indeed, its pivotal position in spatial functions may stem from its

marshalling information for storage in, and later retrieval from, other brain areas.

Developments in computer programming have led to an alternative theoretical approach to the distribution of information within networks of neurons, which might apply to any or all of the networks described previously. Such models, termed *parallel-distributed processing*, view the brain as a vast net of neurons all of which can potentially communicate with all others. Connections between neurons become stronger the more their connections are activated. After many inputs – for example sensory experiences, and learning about the consequences of behaviour – a pattern develops in which some neuronal paths become strongly connected, while those used less often weaken. Such a network can be programmed by computer and shown to be capable of learning. An example of such a neural net is shown in Figure 16. Although some nets have been shown to learn (and make mistakes!) in a way that is also characteristic of real human or animal learning, it remains to be seen whether real brains develop their interconnections in this way.

Summary

1. The human brain can be thought of in terms of computer terminology, though its complexity and versatility far outweigh that of the most complex computer.

2. Areas of the cortex can be seen as performing functions, insofar as particular areas make different contributions to the processing of information. This is known as localisation of function.

3. These areas are extensively connected, but separate subsystems can be identified.

4. Occipital cortex is the primary area for processing visual information – its destruction leads to a total inability to perceive and identify objects using vision.

5. Parietal cortex is involved in spatial perception, also in reaching for and grasping objects – damage can lead to sensory neglect and deficits (losses) in motor coordination.

6. Frontal cortex is involved in executive decision-making, for example planning and problem solving. Damage results in impulsiveness and the inappropriate repetition of behaviours.

7. The primary motor cortex is the main motor area. It is concerned with movement and controls the muscles.

8. Temporal cortex contains the primary auditory processing area, high level visual processing and some memory functions – damage can lead to visual, memory and language disorders.

9. Primary cortex specialises in particular functions – for example, the primary visual area and the primary auditory area. Secondary cortex extends the functions of primary cortex.

10. Association cortex deals with higher-level processing.

11. Recent research has questioned the idea of strict localisation of function. The concept of parallel-distributed functioning sees the brain as a vast set of neurons whose interconnections can be strengthened with use. Such a neural network has been simulated and shown to be capable of complex learning.

Activity 3   Using the functions of the cortex

Different types of occupation demand the use and development of particular skills. From what you know of the functions of the main four brain lobes, assess how each contributes to the skills required by the following jobs. Decide which regions of the brain are likely to be most engaged in each type of work.

1 actor	4 taxi driver
2 gymnast	5 detective
3 fashion designer	6 scientist/mathematician

Activity 4 Lateralisation of function

Many people find that when they are doing one 'left-hemisphere' task such as speaking it is more difficult to do other left-hemisphere tasks simultaneously, such as balancing on the right leg. Try the following experiment. Tap with your left hand for one minute as fast as you can, and then for one minute with the right. Get someone to count the number of taps per minute. Now do the same but while you are reading from a book. In most cases, tapping speed with the right hand will be reduced while reading, because the right hand is controlled by the left hemisphere where, for most people, the language centres are also located. However, left-hand tapping should remain unaffected, because left-handed tapping is being controlled by the right hemisphere. Now try this with some left-handed participants. What would you expect? Try the same in right handers, but using an interfering right-hemisphere task – for example a spatial task such as reading a map. Provide an explanation for the results.

Local versus global processing

Studies in split-brain patients have suggested that local information (fine detail) is best processed by the left hemisphere, while the global features of an object – the overall figure, or *Gestalt* – are best processed in the right hemisphere. In one study, a patient with a left-hemisphere lesion reproduced the global elements of a figure, while ignoring the detail, but a patient with a right-hemisphere lesion did the reverse (Figure 22).

Other abilities which seem to be at least partially lateralised in the left hemisphere include the perception of time, fine movement control, and analytical/sequential analysis, whereas the right hemisphere seems specialised for music perception, and the recognition of unfamiliar faces.

Characterisation of the two brain hemispheres

Table 2 lists some of the distinctions that have been made between the brain hemispheres. The right hemisphere is portrayed as an artistic, free-thinking, emotional hemisphere which processes whole figures in a global fashion, whereas the left hemisphere is calculating, rational, scientific and processes fine detail one bit at a time. It is easy to get carried away with this apparently strong distinction. Some theorists have attempted to classify people as right- or left-hemisphere responders. This is amusing but oversimplified. In those individuals – most of us – whose brains are not split, there is constant interplay between the hemispheres, and all behaviours inevitably call on functions in both hemispheres of the brain.

Table 2 Hemispheric differences

Studies have suggested the following division of lateralised functions.

Right hemisphere	Left hemisphere
Spatial	Non-spatial
Nonlinguistic	Linguistic
Artistic	Scientific
Emotional	Rational
Whole figure perception	Detail and component perception
Creative	Deductive
Music	Words

Adapted from Ornstein, 1986

Figure 22 Local and global processing

Target stimulus	Right-hemisphere patients	Left-hemisphere patients

3.5 How might asymmetries be explained?

Why did cerebral asymmetries arise in the first place? Cerebral asymmetries have presumably developed in response to selective pressures: those individuals having the most efficient brains would have been more likely to survive than those with inefficient brains. What benefits might result from having a function located in a particular region of brain, say in one cerebral hemisphere, rather than divided across two?

In evolutionary terms, it might be surprising if the two cerebral hemispheres did exactly the same thing since this would involve unnecessary duplication. If an area in one hemisphere develops a particular specialisation (such as face processing) it would be unnecessary to use up brain tissue in duplicating that area on the opposite side of the brain. However, it seems that for most functions, such duplication has occurred, since the two sides of the brain are far more similar than they are different.

In some cases, there may be an advantage to having a single system carrying out a single function. For example, one of the functions most obviously lateralised is speech. Speech involves rapid communication that might have suffered if speech areas in the two hemispheres had to send messages across the corpus callosum to one another. It has been suggested that stuttering occurs in people who have language areas in each hemisphere, and that these systems compete to produce output. MRI scanning has shown that the planum temporale, usually larger in the left hemisphere, is roughly symmetrical in children who suffer from dyslexia, suggesting that their language problems might arise from a lack of specialisation between the hemispheres (Gazzaniga et al., 1998).

Alternatively, it may be that duplicating functions in the brain is an advantage – if brain injury occurs, it is possible to make use of a back-up system. Probably there is considerable redundancy within the brain, which makes recovery of function possible, even in individuals with quite extensive brain damage. In non-brain damaged individuals, the hemispheres may be complementary insofar as it seems to be an advantage to use both sides of the brain rather than placing too much reliance on one. Like two people having a discussion, it might be useful to have the two hemispheres contributing to thinking, but from a slightly different angle. Having structures in the two hemispheres which carry out similar, but slightly different functions, may provide 'added value', enabling the development of abilities that combine slightly different modes of processing. What is clear is that in most practical tasks both hemispheres are involved, acting in concert, taking the major or minor role depending on changing requirements from one moment to the next.

Annett's right-shift theory One influential theory, put forward by Annett (1985), might explain the relationship between left and right handedness, speech lateralisation and the lateralisation of cognitive functions. Annett noticed that primates such as gorillas and monkeys just as often show left-hand preference as right, but only in humans is the distribution of hand preference shifted toward the right. Therefore, humans might inherit a gene (called the rs+ gene) which acts to encourage the development of language in the left hemisphere, and this in turn may encourage right-hand preferences, perhaps because the left hand becomes slightly weakened. The right shift gene has not been found, but there is evidence for the idea. Because we all inherit pairs of chromosomes (one from each parent) we could receive none, one of two of these rs+ genes. In theory, individuals who have just one copy of the gene are mildly right-handed (though they can still use their left hand quite well, for writing their name, for example) whereas many of those who have two copies of the gene (rs++) are 'too' right-handed – they pack too much into a dominant left hemisphere, which means that they do not use both hemispheres effectively and simultaneously. Extreme right-handers score slightly lower on standard intelligence tests than ambidextrals – people who can use both hands accurately despite having a right bias. So, it may be best to get just one copy of the rs+ gene.

3.6 Callosal agenesis

What happens if the corpus callosum fails to develop? In some individuals with *callosal agenesis*, this is what happens (genesis = creation, so agenesis = not created). You might expect that they would show all the effects of hemispheric disconnection – 'divided consciousness' and so on – because the two halves of the brain are functionally separated. In fact, they show very few of these effects. It takes a little longer for visual information to travel between the two halves of the brain and motor responses might be slightly slower, but generally, they are unaffected. Why? There are many situations – after injury, or after poor development – when the brain finds alternative ways of performing functions. There are pathways other than the callosum between the hemispheres. Pathways connecting the hemispheres are called *commisures* (com = together, mis = put). The anterior commisure (toward the front of the brain) and the posterior commisures may overdevelop to compensate for the absence of the corpus callosum. A great deal of compensation can occur in the brains of agenesis patients (Fischer et al., 1992). These other commisures are especially

well developed in animals which have a very small or absent corpus callosum, such as the kangaroo and other Australian marsupials.

3.7 Split brain and split mind?

Speculation about the consequences of splitting the human brain is not new. One of the earliest experimental psychologists, Gustav Fechner, pondered this issue in 1860, and concluded that probably the two cerebral hemispheres were capable of separate conscious experience – that a separate mind exists within each. While the split-brain patients might at first seem a perfect test for this hypothesis, we should remember that sectioning the corpus callosum does not entirely separate the hemispheres. But the vast amount of work on split-brain patients indicates that in some respects, Fechner was right. Split-brain patients will sometimes experience conflict, when one hand does one thing and the other intervenes to prevent it – if the left hand chooses one dress and the right hand another, it implies that the two hemispheres experience different moods and preferences. Nevertheless, this kind of competition occurs without splitting the brain. Despite the fact that our two hemispheres normally operate together, rapidly swapping and sharing information, we have the option of behaving in alternative ways, perhaps dictated by whichever hemisphere seems to dominate our behaviour at the time. The splitting of the brain may simply accentuate a division that is already present in all of us.

3.8 Language: linking areas of association cortex

Language is unique to humans. Chimpanzees are capable of associating written words with the objects they represent, and some experimenters have suggested that a rudimentary grammar is possible – some well-trained chimps can piece together primitive short sentences. However, no animal has the remarkable language abilities of humans. Humans possess unique skills that enable the rapid acquisition of language in the early years of life. Having language goes hand in hand with a high degree of brain specialisation – lateral asymmetry in the two cerebral hemispheres, and strong hand preferences. As we shall see, these are not tied tightly together, since hand preference does not always predict the side of the brain on which language functions will be located, but nevertheless the emergence of these human features are likely to be related.

Language, in most people, is represented in the left brain hemisphere. A great deal is known about the contributions of different cortical areas to language – both to language comprehension and speech production. Why is language located in one hemisphere? First, language is a behaviour requiring rapid sequences of behaviour, and having language structures in both hemispheres would introduce delays as information passed between hemispheres. Second, the left hemisphere is specialised for sequential analysis, which may be especially useful for language processing since, unlike vision, language involves the sequential analysis of inputs and the production of words. Third, the output function of language – the production of words – may be best coming from one single source, in case the hemispheres compete for what to say. Perhaps this is why, unlike limb movements which are controlled by the motor cortex on the contralateral side of the brain, it is the left motor cortex which controls the movements of the mouth and tongue used in producing speech.

Language and speech functions are located in specific centres in the frontal and temporal lobes. In about 97% of the population, particularly in right-handed people, they are located in the left hemisphere. However, the association between handedness and language location is not strong. In left handers (7% of the population), 50% of them also have left-hemisphere language and just a few right handers have right hemisphere language. A test known as the Wada test can identify which side has the language centres. In this test, an awake participant has an anaesthetic drug (sodium amytal) injected into the carotid artery, on either the right or the left side of the brain. The carotids are the main blood vessels which supply the cerebral hemispheres. The participant is asked to speak (count, for example) while the anaesthetic is injected. If the language centres are on the left, injection into the left carotid will stop the flow of speech, and vice-versa.

Brain damage and human language function

In 1865, the French neurologist Paul Broca treated a patient with very limited language. The patient was called 'Tan' because this was one of the few words he could pronounce. (The brain of Tan was recently rediscovered among the preserved specimens in bottles in the hospital in which Broca worked). The brain had a particular area of damage – an area in the left hemisphere, close to the motor strip. Subsequent work has confirmed how important this area (now known as Broca's area) is for speech production.

A second major cortical area in the left hemisphere, known as Wernicke's area, is associated with language comprehension. It is in the planum temporale which is the area known to be larger in the left hemisphere than the right. Broca's and Wernicke's areas are connected by fibres in a pathway called the *arcuate fasciculus* (Figure 23).

Disrupting language

Electrical stimulation of language areas (Figure 24) provides further evidence for brain localisation of language and complements other techniques such as the study of language function after brain damage.

Figure 23 Language areas

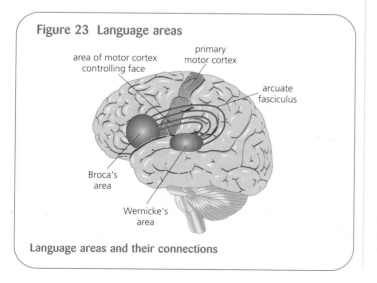

area of motor cortex controlling face

primary motor cortex

arcuate fasciculus

Broca's area

Wernicke's area

Language areas and their connections

Figure 24 Points where stimulation disrupts language

Stimulation in the left hemisphere at points shown by the triangles disrupts speech. These points cluster in the same two major areas in which damage produces aphasias (language loss).

Language deficits (losses) are known as *aphasias* (meaning no language) though many people prefer the term *dysphasia*, meaning language dysfunction, since most aphasic patients do have some language. However, the type of language dysfunction seen after injury to Broca's and Wernicke's area is very different. Damage to Broca's area produces slow speech, lacking prepositions and 'joining words' such as 'to', 'with' and 'then', so a patient may say 'go... train... station'. This deficit is known as Broca's or production aphasia. In contrast, damage to Wernicke's area produces fast and fluent speech, but speech which is disorganised and incomprehensible – a 'salad' of fluent words which have no structure or content and make little sense. The individual with this type of aphasia is unable to comprehend speech, neither their own nor others'. This type of aphasia is known as *receptive aphasia*. A third kind, *conduction aphasia*, which occurs rarely, involves the patient being able to understand speech and produce speech, but they cannot repeat the words they hear.

3.9 Disconnection syndromes

How might conduction aphasia be explained? Conduction aphasia is an example of a *disconnection syndrome*. In this case, it appears that both of the major language centres are undamaged, so both function normally. However, there is a lack of communication between them. If damage interrupts the connections between Broca's and Wernicke's areas, the patient can still understand speech (Wernicke's area is intact) and produce speech (Broca's area is intact) but the words they hear cannot be forwarded to Broca's area to be repeated.

Another syndrome concerns the function of the *angular gyrus*, which connects the visual cortex to structures such as Wernicke's area that interpret the visual input. Without this connection, a syndrome results called *alexia without agraphia* or *pure word blindness*. The patient can write words but they cannot read the words that they themselves have written. Words can be written because the output stream (for example, Broca's area and the motor cortex) is intact, but the input stream (visual cortex to Wernicke's area) has been cut.

In summary, language functions need (a) auditory and visual

input (to hear and read words), (b) motor movements of the eyes when scanning written text, (c) memory with which to compare incoming information, and (d) motor outputs to the mouth to produce speech. So although we can say that an area such as Broca's is a 'language area', because it does have special responsibility for a particular aspect of language, its function depends upon inputs and outputs via connections with many other language and 'non-language' brain structures.

Key terms

Aphasia *Language loss, but usually partial.*

Dysphasia *Disturbance of language function.*

Conduction aphasia *Inability to repeat words heard.*

Disconnection syndrome *A deficit arising not from damage to functional areas but to the severing of neuronal pathways through which they communicate.*

Summary

1 The brain's hemispheres are more similar than they are different. Information arriving in one is rapidly transferred to the other via the corpus callosum.

2 Some brain functions are lateralised – they are located, or more strongly represented, in one hemisphere rather than the other.

3 Most available information about lateralisation of function has come from studies of a small number of split-brain patients whose hemispheres have been split by a total section of the corpus callosum. Conclusions drawn from such a small sample must be regarded with caution.

4 The left hemisphere is specialised for language and the right for emotion and spatial perception. However, both hemispheres are probably involved in most behaviours.

5 There are several structures in the left hemisphere involved in language processing. They operate as a network. Broca's area in the frontal lobe is crucial for speech production. Wernicke's area in the temporo-parietal area is crucial for speech perception.

6 Disconnection between language areas can leave each intact while preventing communication between them. This leads to disconnection syndromes.

References

Ali, N. & Camino, C. R. (1997). Hemispheric lateralization of perception and memory for emotional verbal stimuli in normal individuals. *Neuropsychology, 11*, 114-119.

Annett, M. (1985). *Left, right, hand and brain: The right-shift theory.* Hillsdale, NJ: Erlbaum.

Corkin, S. (1984). Lasting consequences of bilateral medial temporal lobectomy: Clinical course and experimental findings in HM. *Seminars in Neurology, 4*, 249-259.

Davidson, R., Fedio, P., Smith, B., Aureille, E. & Martin, I. (1992). Lateralised mediation of arousal and habituation: Differential bilateral electrodermal activity in unilateral temporal lobectomy patients. *Neuropsychologia, 30*, 1053-1063.

Desimone, R. (1991). Face-selective cells in the temporal cortex of monkeys. *Journal of Cognitive Neuroscience, 3*, 1-8.

Efron, R. (1990). *The decline and fall of hemispheric specialization.* Hillsdale, NJ: Lawrence Erlbaum Associates.

Fischer, M., Ryan, S., & Dobyns, W. (1992). Mechanisms of interhemispheric transfer and patterns of cognitive function in acallosal patients of normal intelligence. *Archives of Neurology, 49*, 271-277.

Gabrieli, J. D. E. (1998). Cognitive neuroscience of human memory. *Annual Review of Psychology, 49*, 87-115.

Gazzaniga, M. S. (1970). *The bisected brain.* New York: Appleton-Century-Crofts.

Gazzaniga, M. S., Ivry, R. B. & Mangun, G. R. (1998). *Cognitive neuroscience: The biology of the mind.* New York: Norton.

Hebb, D. O. (1949). *The organization of behavior: A neuropsychological theory.* New York: Wiley.

Joseph, R. & Heckers, S. (1997). Neuropsychiatry, neuropsychology, and clinical neuroscience: Emotion, evolution, cognition, language, memory, brain damage and abnormal behavior. *Psychosomatics, 38*, 81-89.

Kropotov, J. & Ponomarev, V. A. (1991). Subcortical neuronal correlates of component P300 in man. *Electroencephalography and Clinical Neurophysiology, 78*, 40-49.

Lashley, K. S. (1950) In search of the engram. *Symposia of the Society for Experimental Biology, 4*, 454-482.

Luria, A. R. (1973). *The working brain.* London: Penguin.

Macphail, E. M. (1982). *Brain and intelligence in vertebrates.* Oxford: Clarendon Press.

Maguire, E. A., Frackowiak, R. S. J. & Frith, C. D. (1997). Recalling routes around London: Activation of the right hippocampus in taxi drivers. *Journal of Neuroscience, 17*, 7013-7110.

McFie, J. & Zangwill, O. L. (1960). Visual-constructive disabilities associated with lesions of the left cerebral hemisphere. *Brain, 83*, 243-260.

Milner, A. D. & Goodale, M. A. (1996). *The visual brain in action.* Oxford Psychology Series, No. 27. Oxford: Oxford University Press.

Ornstein, R. E. (1986). *The psychology of consciousness.* (revised edition). New York: Viking Penguin.

Penfield, W. & Rasmussen, T. (1950). *The cerebral cortex of man.* New York: Macmillan.

Rilling, J. K. & Insell, T. R. (1999). The primate neocortex in comparative perspective using magnetic resonance imaging. *Journal of Human Evolution, 37*, 191-223.

Rushworth, M. F. S. & Walsh, V. (1999). TMS in Neuropsychology. *Neuropsychologia (Special Issue), 37*, 125-251.

Salmelin, R., Hari, R., Lounasmaa, O. V. & Sams, M. (1994). Dynamics of brain activation during picture naming. *Nature, 368*, 463-465.

Sperry, R. (1964). The great cerebral commissure. *Scientific American, 210*, 42-52.

23 Biological rhythms, sleep and dreaming

▶ **Introduction**

This chapter concerns cyclic behaviours, those occurring at regular intervals. The daily cycle of sleeping and waking is the most familiar cycle that we experience, but it is only one of the 'rhythms of life'. There are many other ways in which we experience cyclic variations in behaviour. Often we are not aware of cycles, for example fluctuating body temperature. Some cycles are short, such as eating-fasting or the sleep-wake cycle, while others are longer – the monthly menstrual cycle in females for example. Some individuals' behaviour appears to undergo variations with the seasons of the year – depressive illness is more common in winter. Cycle-related illnesses might be avoided or treated if we knew more about biological rhythms.

The daily cycle of conscious waking and unconscious sleeping is intriguing because it is not clear why we sleep at all. Why spend one third of our lives in a non-conscious state? During sleep, we cycle in and out of dream sleep. But what is dreaming, and does it have a purpose? The nature and control of sleeping and dreaming are also considered in this chapter.

Chapter summary

- Unit 1 looks at the variety of bodily rhythms that occur over different time spans, and the effects of disturbing these rhythms via travel or 24 hour working.
- Unit 2 considers sleeping: what is sleep and

what purpose does it serve?
- Unit 3 examines the special sleep state of dreaming: what are dreams, is there a purpose to dreaming, and what explanations have psychologists given for dream experiences?

Unit 1 Bodily rhythms

KEY ISSUES

1 What is a biological rhythm and what behaviours change under the influence of such rhythms?

2 How do endogenous (internal) clocks and environmental (external) factors interact to control cycles?

3 What consequences can arise from disturbances to daily rhythms, such as night shift working?

1.1 What is a biological rhythm or cycle?

Much behaviour is cyclic. In other words it occurs regularly – in cycles with regular intervals between each cycle. For most people, around 16 waking hours of the day alternate with around 8 sleeping hours. During the sleeping hours we cycle in and out of dream sleep every 90 minutes – a cycle within a cycle. The waking day has cycles of eating, meals occurring at roughly 4-hourly intervals. The female menstrual cycle is monthly.

Often it is hard to say why a cycle occurs over a particular interval. Why do we eat 3 times in the waking day, and is this necessary or desirable? Sometimes cycles are linked to regular changes in the physical environment – for example the day-night activity coincides with a single rotation of the earth, and seasonal changes with the earth's orbiting around the sun. The

year is divided into seasons that produce systematic changes in weather and temperature – days gradually lengthen between December and June and then shorten again, systematically varying temperature and our exposure to sunlight. Are these changes in the environment responsible for our cyclic behavioural changes? Or do we have some kind of internal biological 'clock' which directs our cycles of behaviour?

After observing the daily activity patterns of rats, Richter (1922) was one of the first to put forward the revolutionary suggestion that cycles or rhythms could be *endogenous* (meaning that they are generated internally). Before Richter, psychologists had assumed that behaviour only changed in direct response to environmental stimuli – that cycles or rhythms are *exogenous* or externally generated.

Different types of rhythms or cycles

Table 1   Types of rhythm

Ultradian rhythm	A rhythm occurring more than once within a day.
Circadian rhythm	A rhythm tuned roughly to the 24 hour clock.
Infradian rhythm	A rhythm occurring across many days.
Circannual rhythm	A rhythm occurring approximately yearly.

Ultradian rhythms

Ultradian rhythms occur more than once in a 24 hour period. They do not necessarily occur right across the 24 hour day – most occur during either the waking or the sleeping phase of the activity cycle. An example of an ultradian rhythm is the 90-minute cycle between REM (dreaming) sleep and slow wave sleep that occurs during the night (described in detail in Units 2 and 3). During the waking day, eating occurs over roughly 4-hour intervals, and recreational drug-taking, cigarette smoking and coffee drinking are cyclic due to the need to sustain the stimulant effects that progressively wear off after each 'shot'. Other ultradian rhythms include urination at intervals, and invisible cycles such as the release of hormones from the liver. Animals which engage in 'patrolling' systematically explore their home territory several times in a day or night, and animals fed at particular times of the day reliably increase their activity levels just prior to feeding times. Sometimes it is hard to know whether fluctuations are really cycles – in humans, the ability to pay careful attention to a task varies from highs in mid-morning and mid-afternoon, with a distinct post-lunch dip in the early afternoon, and early morning and late evening dips in concentration level. Brain systems have been identified which regulate ultradian rhythms – nuclei in the hypothalamus seem to have an important role since lesions there can disrupt or abolish ultradian rhythms.

Circadian rhythms

Circadian rhythms occur on an approximately 24 hour cycle. The term circa means approximately – as we shall see, endogenous rhythms (internal clocks) are not tied precisely to the 24 hour clock. The most obvious circadian rhythm is the sleep-wake cycle (see Units 2 and 3). An animal maintained in an artificial environment, with constant temperature and illumination, typically maintains its usual day-night activity cycle, but this often runs fast or slow, in the absence of the usual cues (lightness-darkness, or temperature) that normally tie the daily rhythm to the 24 hour clock (Figure 1).

In humans, temperature drops during the evening, falling to as low as 36.7° during the night (hence the shivers after all-night parties!). It rises in the morning prior to waking, reaching 37.1°

in mid-afternoon (Figure 2). This temperature peak is accompanied by peaks in other physiological functions such as heart rate, blood pressure, and breathing rate. This may often be the most active part of the day. However, the same peaks occur when the daily activity cycle is reversed, indicating that they are regulated by an internal 'clock' (sometimes called an *oscillator*). Sometimes, a change in one cycle is accompanied by changes in others, suggesting that they are regulated by the same underlying oscillator. Sensitivity to drugs, release of hormones, and pain sensitivity all vary systematically across the day, though these are hidden rhythms – we are not aware of them. We may be aware of their consequences – for example, clotting factors in the blood peak in the early morning, which is when heart attacks are most common, while the onset of birth labour is common at night, when the female hormone prolactin reaches its peak.

Figure 2   Temperature variation across the day

Mean rectal temperature of nine adults (Morris et al., 1990)

There are large individual differences in circadian rhythms. Some of these follow a common pattern – for example, our internal clocks slow as we get older. But within a cross-section of people, rhythms are expressed differently – there are 'larks' who can work effectively in the early morning and 'owls' who function best in the late evening and at night (Kerkhof, 1985).

Infradian rhythms

These cycle over a period greater than 24 hours. Examples are the menstrual cycle which is variable between individual women, but is lunar (approximately following the 28 day moon cycle). A feature of the menstrual cycle for up to 40% of women is the phenomenon known as *premenstrual syndrome* (PMS), involving stress and irritability, poor concentration, loss of appetite and headaches for a few days before the onset of menstrual bleeding.

Since many infradian rhythms are seasonally based, approximately following the calendar year, they are referred to as *circannual* (approximately annual) rhythms.

Circannual rhythms

There are many circannual rhythms that we can observe, particularly in animals. The hibernation cycle in animals such as squirrels and hedgehogs, and the migration cycle of some species of birds are examples. We know that migratory behaviours in birds are endogenous because even when they are kept in a constant environment with no clues to the season,

Figure 1   Activity cycle in a constant environment

Activity record of a flying squirrel kept in constant darkness. The coloured lines indicate periods of activity as measured by a running wheel (De Coursey, 1960).

they become restless at migratory times of the year. And when released, they make flying movements in the correct migratory compass direction, south in winter and north in summer (Gwinner, 1986).

What determines the length of rhythms?

A variety of factors affect the length of cycles. For ultradian cycles one factor is an animal's body size since in smaller animals, which have a faster metabolic rate, these cycles repeat more rapidly. When animals' circadian rhythms are examined in a constant environment, for some species the natural rhythm comes out slightly shorter than 24 hours, sometimes longer. This depends on whether the environment is constantly dark or constantly light, and whether that species is naturally active in darkness (such as the rat) or in the light (as many bird species). Even when all these factors are taken into account, there are individual differences that are hard to explain, although it is rare to find day-to-day variation within one individual – each animal's daily cycle period is fixed, probably due to its being inherited genetically. Similarly among humans, for many of the cycles discussed here, there is considerable individual variation in cycle length determined by age, preferences, lifestyle and other individual differences that are not well understood.

Relationships between rhythms

Long-term and short-term rhythms seem to be relatively independent of one another. Clearly, it would be possible for a circannual rhythm to be 'built up' from shorter cycles, but this is not usually the case. For example in animals, damage to the hypothalamus that disrupts circadian rhythms generally leaves many shorter ultradian and longer circannual rhythms unaffected. We should not assume that there is only one circadian clock. In one study, hypothalamic damage which disrupted the sleep-wake cycle in squirrel monkeys did not affect their daily rhythm in temperature, so a second clock must have remained intact (Fuller et al., 1981).

Key terms

Endogenous *Occurring within the body (endo=inside).*

Exogenous *Occurring outside the body, in the environment (exo = outside).*

1.2 Endogenous clocks and environmental factors

What sensory cues are used to train or time biological rhythms? Where control is exerted from within by endogenous processes, these are referred to as *pacemakers*, just as an electric heart pacemaker ensures that the heartbeat is triggered at regular intervals. Where control is exerted from outside by exogenous environmental stimuli, these are known as *Zeitgebers* (in German, Zeit = time, and geben = to give). As we have seen, the existence of biological pacemakers and their powerful influence makes it likely that the basic rhythms of daily activity are largely fixed and inherited. The circadian clock is extremely robust – it runs to time even when challenged with periods of unconsciousness induced by anaesthesia, with food or water deprivation, alcohol, tranquillisers, brain damage or with long periods of forced activity.

Key terms

Pacemaker *An internal (endogenous) process that controls a biological rhythm.*

Zeitgeber *An external (exogenous) event which sets or modifies an internal biological clock.*

The physiology of the circadian rhythm

There is no doubt that our daily behavioural routines are closely linked to the day-night cycle. But are they tied to the light-dark cycle, or do humans also have an internally running biological clock? In order to investigate this, it is necessary to place humans in the situation described above for animals, in which the environment remains constant, devoid of cues that signal time of day. Imagine spending several weeks underground. Would you stick to a 24 hour routine? Well probably you would, almost. Humans do have an internal clock, but one that runs more slowly than the 24 hour clock. Over time, a subterranean person will shift their cycle by about 1 hour per day, so that after 2 weeks, they will be awake at (what on the surface is) night and sleeping during the (surface) daytime. This tells us that our underlying circadian rhythm, our biological clock, is normally reset or *entrained* to synchronise with the external environment by sensory factors – in this case, the daily cycle of light and darkness. This is why we use the term 'circadian rhythm', meaning *approximately* 24 hours.

Designing isolation studies for humans is not easy. Not everyone wants to spend months in constant environmental conditions, particularly in constant illumination. In fact, the period of the human circadian oscillator seems to vary according to whether lights are left on or off for fixed periods of time, or whether the participant is left to control their own light hours. The true length of the human circadian rhythm, independent of the lighting factor, can be determined by placing participants on a 28 hour light-dark cycle. Such a long cycle is so far from the usual 24 hours that it is impossible to adjust to it, leaving the endogenous rhythm to run free. When this is done, the human clock is found to be longer than 24 hours, but there is disagreement over by how much. Estimates vary from 12 minutes to one hour.

External and internal influences come into conflict when we change our routine, for example staying up all night at a party. We are not slaves either to the external environment, or to our internal clocks. We can override the tendency to fall asleep. However, this does not mean that we have delayed the cycle – after an all-night party, you will find yourself beginning to feel slightly more awake in the light of morning. The sleep-wake rhythm has been overridden but not stopped, and the light stimulus in the morning still keeps the rhythm in train. People living in polar regions, where they experience periods of the year with continuous light, or continuous darkness, appear to regulate their daily cycles via social activities and do not rely on light at all.

In babies, rhythmic cycles of activity occur before birth. Can we assume from this that the baby has its own rhythmic cycle? On one hand, the baby's cycle may have been entrained during months of exposure to its mother's activity-sleep cycles. But in fact, the baby's cycles of activity are quite different from the mother's – small babies spend much of their time drifting in and out of sleep – so that mother and baby are not 'synchronised'.

Babies have their own cycles, though these may be modified by those of their mothers.

1.3 The pineal gland, SCN, and melatonin

What external factors influence the daily cycle? As noted above, one of the most important, at least in terrestrial animals, is light.

In lower animals such as birds and reptiles, a brain structure that plays an important role is the *pineal gland* (or pineal body). This gland sits just behind the thalamus on the top of the brain stem astride the midline, and secretes the hormone melatonin (see Figure 3). In lower species the pineal is relatively exposed on the upper surface of the brain, receiving diffuse direct light stimulation, because a small amount of light passes through the thin layer of overlying cranial bone. Pineal light receptors are similar to the photoreceptors in the eye. The pineal has its own pacemaker activity, but the light receptors influence its secretions of melatonin (which it manufactures from the neurotransmitter, serotonin). Melatonin circulates in the blood. The distribution of melatonin-sensitive receptors in the bodies of lower animals is not known, but this hormone is known to have a synchronising effect in sleep, regulating systems in the brain stem in some birds.

No such pineal light receptors exist in mammals. The main clock in humans appears to be located in the suprachiasmic nuclei (SCN) of the hypothalamus, located just above the optic chiasm (see Figure 3).

Figure 3   The SCN and pineal gland

SCN

hypothalamus

pineal gland

The SCN consists of a pair of nuclei, which by brain nuclei standards are small, containing only 10,000 neurons each. It receives a small off-shoot projection of optic nerve fibres from the primary optic tract. This tract provides the equivalent of pineal light stimulation – if the pathway connecting the retina and SCN is cut, light no longer regulates circadian rhythms, and no longer influences melatonin secretion. This is not a result of blindness, because if retinal fibres are cut after the SCN, the animal cannot see, but the circadian rhythms still continue. In rats, mild electrical stimulation of the SCN has the effect of shifting the phase of circadian rhythms (advancing or retarding the clock, depending on the time of day), and SCN lesions abolish the day-night activity cycle.

A rather strange study, carried out in 1998 by Campbell and

Murphy, involved giving participants 3 hours of bright light directed at the skin behind their knee. The light was carefully shielded so that the participants could not see it. This was apparently sufficient to reset the participants' circadian rhythm, indicating that chemical changes in the blood can influence the SCN in addition to neuronal pathways from the retina.

The SCN may also have an indirect role in the control of longer-term rhythms since SCN lesions in male hamsters also disrupt their circannual breeding cycle. Usually, male hamsters secrete the male sex hormone, testosterone, in the summer mating season when days are light and long. But without the SCN to detect day length, lesioned hamsters secrete testosterone continuously (Rusak & Morin, 1976).

The role of melatonin in mammals is easily demonstrated – daily injections given at a regular fixed time to rats kept in constant dim light will maintain their 24 hour circadian rhythm. Melatonin release occurs naturally mainly at night, so the effect of light is to inhibit melatonin release.

Although melatonin has been found to influence the reproductive cycle of hamsters, whether it has such effects in humans is debatable. However, a number of studies have shown that light exposure affects human reproduction. The onset of menstruation (the first menstrual period, or *menarche*) is more likely to occur in winter than in summer, and occurs earlier in blind than sighted girls. The conception rate in Finland increases during the very long days of summer, and sexual maturity occurs particularly early in the tropics where there is relatively more sunlight.

Key terms

Pineal gland   *Controls daily rhythms in birds and reptiles.*

Melatonin *Hormone released by the pineal gland during the night.*

Suprachiasmatic nucleus (SCN)   *A brain nucleus which enables light to influence the human daily rhythm.*

1.4 Disrupted cycles

Rapid adjustment to our circadian rhythm is required when we travel across world time zones, for example flying to the east or west. Daily cycles need to become entrained to a new time zone, as the new cycle of light-darkness and the new cycle of sleep-activity gradually pull the internal clock into line. Adjustments of 1-2 hours either way are not especially traumatic. It takes approximately one day to adjust for every one-hour time zone traversed (Moline et al., 1992) so it is not too hard to adapt to a one hour shift in cycle, as occurs when we put clocks forward one hour in spring and back in autumn. However, when people fly long distances and undergo severe shifts, such as a complete 12 hour reversal, they typically feel badly disoriented, fatigued, have difficulty concentrating, and fall asleep at unexpected times. This is known as *jet lag*.

Jet lag

Imagine that you leave London at 12.00 midday and arrive in San Francisco 12 hours later, midnight UK time. Because San Francisco is 8 hours behind UK time, you will have gained 8 hours. You will arrive there at 4.00 pm local time, but with your internal clock geared up to start sleeping – your body temperature will be dropping, your general level of arousal will be declining, and your digestion will have slowed. Yet your friends in San Francisco will have a full evening ahead, with visits and a meal planned! In fact, travelling westward is generally easier than travelling eastward, presumably because the 25 hour human clock can more easily adjust to 'gaining' hours (extending the natural day: called *phase delay*) than 'losing' them (called *phase advance*). (See Activity 1.)

Shift work

People whose jobs involve shift work have similar difficulties of adjustment to those of international travellers. However, they face a different problem – for them, Zeitgebers, such as the onset of dawn and night time, remain the same. As a result, they are forced to adjust their natural sleep-wake patterns to the demands of shift work, in spite of the cues and triggers of Zeitgebers which suggest the opposite – for example, when they are required to work at night.

Adjustments in sleep-wake patterns are made more difficult because night-shift workers usually sleep less during the day than they would at night. Things are made worse if they revert to their usual daily activity cycle at weekends – they are socialising with friends when their body tells them they 'should be sleeping'.

Studies have shown that shift-work can result in:
* Sleep disturbances
* Fatigue
* Digestive problems
* Lack of concentration.

In the workplace, this can lead to a reduction in productivity and job satisfaction, and a higher accident rate (Pinel, 1997).

Shift work can be organised in various ways. A standard arrangement is three eight-hour shifts. In this way, production can be maintained for 24 hours a day. Workers can either remain on the same shift, for example they stay on the 'night shift' (10 p.m. to 6.0 a.m.), or they rotate through the three shifts. They can change shifts over different periods – for example, every week, every three weeks, and so on. Shifts can be rotated clockwise, for example moving forwards from the 'night shift' to the 'early shift', or anticlockwise, for example moving backwards from the 'early shift' to the 'night shift'.

Research indicates that the following shift patterns are most beneficial to both workers and employers.

* Rotation rather than remaining on the same shift.
* Changing shifts every three weeks or so rather than every week.
* Changing in a clockwise rather than anticlockwise direction.

Monk and Folkard (1985) examined different patterns of shift work and found that changing shifts was more beneficial than remaining on one shift for a long period of time. Workers who rotated shifts felt better and made fewer mistakes, and the accident rate was lower. This is surprising since we might expect that it would be better to get used to a particular shift and stick to it. Monk and Folkard argued that shift rotation prevents an accumulation of sleep deprivation.

A study of a chemical plant in Utah in the USA indicated that workers took about 16 days to adjust to a change in shifts (Czeisler et al., 1982). The researchers recommended a change from the existing 7 day shift rotation to a 21 day rotation. They also suggested that workers move forward in time rather than backwards when changing shifts. In other words, shift rotation should be clockwise rather than anticlockwise, resulting in phase delay rather than phase advance. As indicated with jet lag, the 25 hour human clock appears to adjust more easily to phase delay rather than phase advance.

As a result of these two changes both workers and the company benefited. Job satisfaction increased, productivity rose, the accident rate declined, and workers reported improvements in their health and more enjoyment during their leisure time.

1.5 Seasonal affective disorder (SAD)

You probably think that you feel happier in the summer than in the winter. Most people do. Low levels of natural sunlight in winter might be a factor in inducing a particular kind of depression – so-called *seasonal affective disorder* or SAD. This disorder appears to be particularly common in the polar regions which are in almost total darkness during winter months, although this has not been confirmed in all studies. Exposure to at least one hour of bright artificial sunlight in their homes during winter can often relieve depression in SAD patients, perhaps because the light stimulates the SCN thereby inhibiting melatonin release. Reducing the amount of circulating melatonin seems to relieve depression, either because melatonin itself can cause depression directly, or perhaps indirectly via its effect on another neurotransmitter. One possibility is serotonin, which is a member of the same family of neurotransmitters as melatonin. Serotonin is known to play a role in depression – antidepressant drugs such as Prozac relieve depression by increasing the level of serotonin activity in the brain. Light stimulation may produce a similar effect.

Most melatonin is released during the night, so that a night-time dose of illumination – which interrupts the melatonin flow – has been suggested as being more effective in relieving SAD than a day-time dose, despite the fact that the individual must be woken up at 2.00 am for the treatment. Recent research, however, has suggested that intense light doses at any time of day can be helpful, and since early morning doses are particularly effective the intense light may have a Zeitgeber effect, causing the circadian rhythm to be better regulated (Eastman et al., 1998).

Melatonin therapy

People with tumours in the pineal gland often have great difficulty falling asleep and staying asleep. Melatonin therapy can be used to train biological rhythms in such cases, and to artificially restore a disrupted rhythm. Adapting to a new time zone takes time, and experiments have shown that feelings of sleepiness around the 'old' bed time only abate when the melatonin cycle has adapted (Dijk & Cajochen, 1997). Melatonin capsules, which produce sleepiness 2-3 hours later, are sometimes used by people who have to adjust to falling asleep at an unusual time of day, when in a new international time zone or adapting to a new work schedule. However, a note of caution – short-term use of melatonin is probably harmless, but the effects of long-term use have not been fully investigated. Melatonin can affect a number of body processes, including reproductive cycles, and it should be used with care.

Summary

1 Ultradian, circadian, and infradian/circannual rhythms influence many biological systems and behavioural cycles.

2 Rhythms are largely controlled by endogenous biological clocks. The circadian clock runs roughly to the 24 hour clock, and circannual clocks in migratory or hibernating animals, to a 12-monthly cycle. Circadian clocks are kept in synchrony with environmental changes via external triggers known as Zeitgebers.

3 Light influences daily rhythms in lower animals by stimulating the pineal gland.

4 Human cycles are influenced by signals from the eye to the suprachiasmic nucleus (SCN). Stimulation by light inhibits melatonin release.

5 Cycles are seriously disrupted by shift work and jet lag.

6 Moving east-west is easier to cope with than west-east travel, perhaps because the internal human clock cycles every 25 hours, making it easier to accommodate to a lengthening day than a shortening day.

7 Depression in some people may relate to excessive melatonin release in winter. Some may benefit from light supplementation.

Activity 1   Cycles

Item A   A biological clock

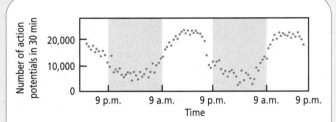

This chart shows the activity of single cells (neurons) in the suprachiasmatic nucleus (SCN) of a rat's hypothalamus. It illustrates the regular changes from day to night in the firing rate of these neurons.

Item B   Jet lag – westbound

This chart shows how many days it took a sample of 14 individuals to adjust to jet lag on a westbound flight.

Item C   Jet lag – eastbound

This chart shows how many days it took a sample of 14 individuals to adjust to jet lag on a eastbound flight.

Questions

1 Look at Item A. What evidence does it contain which indicates the existence of an internal biological clock?

2 Describe and explain what the chart in Item B shows.

3 a) Compare Items B and C.
   b) Give a reason for the differences between them.

Activity 2 The 24 hour society

A 24 hour supermarket in Rio de Janeiro

Compared with 100 years ago, humans sleep about 1.5 hours less. The invention of the electric light has meant that people can extend the hours of lightness. Recently, this trend has become more extreme as our society adopts 24 hour working. Electronic communication means that the world is accessible 24 hours per day; supermarkets and garages advertise that they open 24 hours. Of course no-one works 24 hours, but shift-working is necessary for 24 hour working. Some have suggested ways of adapting people to irregular hours by (a) taking melatonin tablets, (b) selective exposure to light, and (c) selecting people according to the suitability of their own personal daily rhythms.

Questions

1   How might adaptation to the 24 hour clock vary from one individual to another?

2   How might
    a) taking melatonin tablets and
    b) selective exposure to light, help people adapt to irregular hours?

Unit 2 Sleep

KEY ISSUES

1 **What is sleep?**

2 **How has sleep been investigated biologically?**

3 **What theories attempt to explain the functions of sleep?**

2.1 What are we doing when we sleep?

At first glance, sleep might seem like doing nothing – a time when behaviour is suspended. However, studies have shown that sleep is a very active time for the brain. We spend about one third of our lives sleeping, suggesting that sleep is probably important and has some purpose or function.

Sleep research is one branch of a wider research area concerned with the nature of consciousness. At the simplest level, we can think of sleep as non-consciousness, insofar as we are not awake or responsible for our actions. However, this does *not* mean that there are two states: one of being unconscious and asleep (when the brain shuts down), and another of being conscious and awake (when the brain is active). Research has shown that there are many levels of consciousness during both waking and sleeping. Sleep is not a single state or level – in one night we pass through several cycles of sleep states or *stages*.

Sleep is always under active control by the brain and is certainly not a matter of 'doing nothing'.

In Unit 1, we saw how brain mechanisms exert control over the diurnal sleeping-waking cycle. This internal clock urges sleep but it competes with brain arousal generated by sensory inputs. Sometimes at an all-night party, we may stay awake during usual sleeping time, stimulated by noise and bright lights, while other times, the clock will win, and we nod off despite the noise and lights.

Experience during sleep is difficult to study directly because we cannot verify the accuracy of people's subjective reports. Sleep research took a great step forward in the 1950s when William Dement first measured the electrical activity taking place in the sleeping brain, by recording the electroencephalogram (EEG) (see Dement, 1990). The recordings made since then, in sleep laboratories throughout the world, have greatly enhanced our understanding of the variety of sleep stages, including the stage when most dreaming occurs. Of course, the EEG cannot tell us what someone is experiencing while sleeping and dreaming.

The EEG and sleep stages

The EEG is recorded using a machine called a polygraph. Small electrodes glued to the scalp pick up the changes in electrical activity in the brain beneath them. The electrodes are connected to the polygraph, which amplifies the signals and prints them out, so that the activity within the brain can be recorded as continuous ink traces on a moving paper printout (see Figures 4 and 5). In a sleep laboratory, other measurements are taken, such as muscular tension and heart rate. A participant taking part in a sleep study goes to bed wired up with electrodes glued to the head and face, but somehow they usually manage to sleep. While they sleep, a video camera and the polygraph record their night's activity and brain electrical changes. Depending on the aims of the study, some intervention may be necessary, such as playing them tape recordings as stimuli or perhaps waking them up at intervals to ask for reports on the content of their dreams.

Figure 4   Recording the EEG

A sleeping participant with electrodes attached to record brain activity. The output from each electrode is displayed as a wavy line on the polygraph.

A typical night's sleep

An uninterrupted night's sleep tends to follow a similar pattern. From falling asleep at night to waking in the morning may feel like one continuous state – sleep. But in fact, throughout the night, an individual passes through a series of sleep stages, classified according to the kinds of waveform seen in the polygraph EEG record. Most researchers identify five stages of sleep: slow-wave sleep stages 1-4 and a separate stage called REM.

The waking EEG of an alert individual is shown at the top of Figure 5, and consists of waves that are small, irregular and frequent. This waveform is known as the *beta* wave. Note the way in which waveforms on the polygraph are described. The up-down deflection of the pen is known as the *amplitude* of the wave – this represents the size of voltage changes. The beta wave is of *low amplitude* – the height of the waves is low. The *frequency* of a waveform is the rate at which the pen moves up and down – swings per second. The beta wave is therefore of *high frequency*, because successive wave peaks occur close together in time, 13-30 times per second (ie, 13-30 Hz where Hz stands for 'Hertz', or 'cycles per second'). It is also said to be

Figure 5   A typical night's sleep

This figure shows the stages passed through in a typical night's sleep. The EEG recordings on the left show electrical changes in the brain during different sleep stages.

desynchronised, since there is no obvious regularity to the wave pattern.

Prior to falling asleep, an individual feels pleasantly drowsy and relaxed. In this stage the waveform changes to the alpha pattern. Alpha is high amplitude with a low frequency of 8-12 Hz – the alpha wave peaks about 8-12 times per second. This is a *synchronised* waveform, having regular peaks – pulses of activity produced by many neurons firing simultaneously. Some dream-like, 'unreal' experiences can begin to occur when alpha appears though this is not yet true sleep. Sleeping proper then begins.

Stage 1 This involves an even slower waveform, known as *theta* (5-7 Hz). It is relatively easy to wake someone at this stage, and often they will claim not to have been asleep.

Stage 2 This stage is the first point at which the person is truly sound asleep and the body relaxed. Electrical activity consists of larger and slower waves, interrupted sometimes by large spiky waves, known as *K-complexes,* which seem to occur in the sleeper's brain in response to unexpected stimulation such as a sudden noise. In stage 2, the slow waveform is occasionally interrupted for short intervals of 0.5-2 seconds by bursts of higher frequency activity (12-14 Hz). These high frequency bursts are often spindle shaped, so they are referred to as *sleep spindles.*

Stage 3 In stage 3, *delta* waves occur. These are large slow waves, about 0.5-2 Hz, wandering waves of low amplitude. The individual is now in a deep sleep with heart rate, respiration and metabolic rate all very slow.

Stage 4 This is the deepest stage of slow wave sleep. Delta waves occur at high amplitudes, and muscles are totally relaxed. Metabolism is extremely slow and the sleeper's arousal threshold is at its highest – it is very difficult to wake them. Interestingly, this is the stage in which such things as night wetting and soiling occur, also night terrors (severe nightmares often having a suffocating or crushing quality), and somnambulism or sleep-walking. Stages 3 and 4 tend to occur in the early part of the night (see Figure 5).

Rapid eye movement (REM) sleep

Every 90 minutes or so, a strange phenomenon occurs. If you were an assistant working in a sleep laboratory, you would occasionally notice that the sleeping participant's EEG would speed up – as though they had woken up. However, they are certainly not awake – they are deeply asleep, very difficult to wake, and immobile. This is *REM sleep* – called 'rapid eye movement' sleep because rapid movements of the eyes can be seen beneath the closed eyelids. It is also called *paradoxical sleep*, since it 'paradoxically' produces what looks like a waking EEG at a time when the individual is soundly asleep. REM sleep accounts for about 20% of total sleeping time. In one study, people woken in this stage reported dreaming on 74% of occasions (Aserinsky & Kleitman, 1953).

During a night's sleep, it is usual to pass through 4-6 sleep cycles, the deepest levels of slow wave sleep occurring in the early part of the night with longer REM periods later (see Figure 5). REM periods last for 20-40 minutes.

Cognitive activity in sleep

The brain is extremely active during sleep – examples are the sleeper alternating between REM and non-REM stages at regular intervals, and dream-related activity in the brain during REM periods. But what kinds of cognitive processing – thinking and planning – take place? There are many examples, some of which may appear surprising.

Key terms

Electroencephalogram *The recording of changes in brain activity using a polygraph.*

Amplitude *The size (height) of a waveform.*

Frequency *The number of wave peaks per second.*

Slow wave or non-REM sleep *Sleep in stages 1-4, with slow regular waves in the EEG.*

REM sleep or paradoxical sleep *A sleep stage in which the eyes move rapidly, and high frequency waves occur in the EEG.*

First, some individuals can wake at a pre-set time in the morning, as though setting an internal alarm clock. This is known as *intentional waking*, and suggests that the brain is actively monitoring time while the individual is sleeping. Second, a sleeper can show signs of arousal when listening to the sound of their own name. If a tape recording of names is played to them, a K-complex wave and a small electrodermal reaction occurs when their own name is played, but not when non-significant names are played. (The electrodermal response is a change in the electrical conductance of the skin – a measure of mild emotional arousal, also called the galvanic skin response or GSR). This effect shows that during sleep, the brain is able to detect stimuli of special importance. Such selective attention applies to other significant sounds – often parents will wake to the sound of their own baby's cry but not that of someone else's baby.

2.2 Theories of sleep

The sheer universality of sleep in all birds and mammals suggests that it is important. Humans spend a third of their lives asleep, and so we might reasonably assume that sleep is essential. However, some people appear to need very little sleep. Meddis (1979) reported a retired nurse who was busy and cheerful despite sleeping for just one hour each night. This person cannot be described as sleep-deprived – she simply had a low sleep requirement.

However, for an average sleeper, several days of poor sleeping or total sleep deprivation will cause them to feel irritable and unwell. Experimental sleep deprivation studies typically find that after 2-3 nights' sleep loss, an individual performs poorly on tasks requiring sustained attention, and after 4-6 nights, they begin to suffer confusion and delusions that verge on a psychological disorder. But these psychological changes quickly disappear when the participant is allowed to sleep. When

Activity 3 The Bowery-El phonomenon

A station on the Bowery Elevated Railroad

The Bowery-El phenomenon is named after a railway – the Bowery Elevated Railroad. This railway rattled past Third Avenue, New York at night on a noisy elevated track, at particular scheduled times. It did this for many years and residents living nearby were used to it. When the track was pulled down and the train no longer ran, people awakened at the time it would normally have passed. Some phoned the police in alarm. They said, 'Something odd is happening – we are hearing strange noises'.

Adapted from Pribram, 1971

Questions

1 Is it accurate to describe sleep as 'a period of doing nothing'? Give reasons for your answer.

2 What does the Bowery-El example tell us about selective attention during sleep?

experimenters have investigated physiological changes following sleep loss, it has proved surprisingly difficult to identify any particular deficit – sleep deprivation appears to have no lasting ill effects.

Why, then, did sleep evolve in the first place? Why did sleeping-waking patterns develop, why do they vary among species, and why have humans adopted a diurnal sleeping-waking pattern? There are four main types of theory explaining why sleep is necessary.

- First, sleep *protects* against injury and predation during the dangerous hours of darkness.
- Second, sleep *conserves* energy at times when it is difficult to move about and eat.

These are both ecological theories, emphasising evolution and adaptation to the environment.

- Third, *restoration theory*, which states that sleep is necessary to restore biological functions (like recharging run-down batteries).
- Fourth, sleep is required because it promotes learning by affecting memory selection and storage.

There is evidence for and against all of these explanations.

Protection

According to this form of *evolutionary* or *ecological theory*, humans have inherited night-time sleeping from earlier generations because it has adaptive benefits. This is a *circadian theory* in the sense that it is based on the daily sleeping-waking cycle. The theory states that sleeping during darkness promoted survival by reducing several sources of risk. Since humans have poor night vision, nocturnal activity would have carried dangers such as attack from predatory animals, and injury due to collisions with obstacles. By sleeping, such dangers would be avoided. Sleepers would therefore have survival advantages over non-sleepers. As a result, sleeping at night is a behaviour that would have been passed on from one generation to the next.

Animals that sleep for long hours each day, such as cats (lions, tigers) and bats, are generally those which throughout their evolution have faced little threat while sleeping, being well protected or secreted in caves or burrows. Animals such as sheep and horses are particularly vulnerable – they cannot hide themselves very easily and are more likely to fall prey to predators while asleep. As a result, such animals sleep for only short periods. For example, horses sleep for about 3 hours a day, whereas African lions often sleep for 2 or 3 days after they have gorged themselves on a kill.

Evaluation If sleep occurs purely for protection, it is not clear why some species bother to sleep at all. Sleep is not without its hazards – a sleeping animal is always more vulnerable than one that is awake. Rather than risking naps, some animals might derive more benefit from remaining permanently alert to predators and in a ready state for escape.

The universality of sleeping suggests a need to sleep irrespective of such factors as vulnerability to predation. Further evidence for this comes from the dolphin, an aquatic animal which needs to surface for air periodically. It would drown if it slept for long periods under water. In one species, the bottle-nosed dolphin, the brain hemispheres take it in turn to sleep – this animal is really 'half asleep'! In another species, the Indus dolphin, the problem is solved by taking many short naps,

spread across the day. The need for sleep seems irresistible – it is not just a matter of keeping out of trouble.

Conservation

Conservation theory proposes that sleep conserves energy at times of the day when an animal does not need to engage in activities necessary for survival. Nocturnal animals (nocturnal = active during darkness) sleep during daylight, being adapted to hunting and feeding at night. In humans, the reverse is true – remaining inactive at night time conserved energy at a time of the day when it was difficult for our ancestors to work, look for mates, or forage for food. According to this theory, just as hibernating animals' heart rate, breathing rate, brain activity and heat generation are reduced to a minimum during the unproductive winter months, sleep in humans also represents a form of hibernation that enables energy to be conserved during the unproductive hours of darkness. This is a second form of evolutionary or ecological theory because it emphasises adaptation to the demands of the environment.

Body temperature falls during sleep, which is bound to conserve energy. For animals such as mammals (including humans) which maintain a constant body temperature, a large proportion of the energy intake each day is used up just keeping the body warm. When food is in short supply, animals conserve energy by increasing their sleep time or decreasing their body temperature as conservation theory would predict (Berger & Phillips, 1995).

Evaluation Clearly, sleeping does promote energy conservation. But is this the main function of sleep? As Meddis (1979) points out, the amount of time spent asleep in a particular species reflects not one factor, but a trade-off between various factors. These include the amount of time that the animal must devote to searching for food plus the dangers associated with sleeping.

Animals which eat highly nutritious meals quickly sleep for long periods – meat-eating cats such as lions and tigers sleep for 14-16 hours each day. Animals which graze for food sleep very little – horses sleep for only 3 hours per day. In addition to its vulnerability, the horse's feeding needs are such that it cannot afford to take long periods of sleep. Compared with small burrowing animals, the horse requires more food which takes longer to obtain – grass is not very nutritious and large quantities must be eaten to supply the necessary nutrition. Therefore, for the horse, energy conservation does not appear to be the main priority. Small animals may sleep for longer because they have high metabolic rates – for them, long periods without activity would be especially beneficial in conserving energy. All of this evidence suggests that while sleep conserves energy, this factor competes with others so that time spent sleeping is tailored to the needs and life styles of individual species.

Restoration

Restoration, repair or *recuperation theories* propose that sleep is necessary to reverse the wear and tear occurring during waking life. These theories assume that waking life disrupts the body's homeostasis or balance, and that sleep in some way restores it. For example, waste chemical build-up in the muscles during the day may disperse overnight, restoring optimal levels. A particular sleep stage may enable the replenishment of neurotransmitter chemicals that are depleted or used up during waking – rather like recharging a battery. The *sensitivity* of some receptors to their neurotransmitter chemicals is thought to build up during the day and fall during the night. Cells might be repaired, or energy levels replenished. Restoration theories either emphasise a need for restoration following *psychological/brain activity* (the need for sleep may be greater at times of stress or mental activity) or after *physical/muscular activity* (the need for sleep may be greater after strenuous physical exercise or illness).

Psychological restoration Subjectively we feel refreshed after a good night's sleep especially if we have been busy or anxious, implying that sleep has a role in psychological restoration. Shakespeare wrote that sleep 'knits up the ravel'd sleeve of care'. If sleep does promote psychological restoration, people ought to sleep more when experiencing stress, for example, and there is evidence that mild stress causes people to sleep longer (Hicks & Garcia, 1987). However, severe stress is associated with insomnia (inability to sleep) – in part perhaps because sleep loss itself causes stress, setting up a vicious cycle (Rosch, 1996). It is not clear, therefore, whether sleep promotes psychological restoration.

Physical restoration The fact that sleep often increases during illness suggests a role in physical recuperation and cell repair. Newborn babies spend about 50% of their time in REM sleep, and for premature infants, born weeks before their due date, the figure is 80%. Since early infancy is a period of rapid growth and construction, REM sleep may be associated with growth and development of the nervous system. In old age, there is a diminished need for growth, which is perhaps why REM sleep diminishes. Brain neurotransmitter levels might be restored during REM (Stern & Morgane, 1974). However, stages other than REM might be involved. Oswald's (1980) restoration theory argued that repair and recovery of the brain occurs during REM, while during non-REM or *orthodox sleep*, hormonal activities are restorative for the rest of the body. He pointed out that stages 3 and 4 of non-REM sleep tend to occur at the start of the night when we are most tired, and they tend to occur in large amounts for a few nights after strenuous exercise such as running a marathon. Consistent with this theory is that growth hormone is released into the blood during non-REM sleep. This hormone has a role in the synthesis of proteins, an important process in the restoration of body tissue.

Horne (1988) distinguished 'core' sleep (stage 4 non-REM and REM sleep) from 'optional' sleep (other slow wave sleep stages). Because it is necessary for brain restoration, core sleep is prioritised in the early part of the night. And it occurs across animal species, unlike the amount of optional sleep which varies according to species-specific factors such as safety while sleeping, and the degree to which sleep conserves energy.

Inconsistent with restoration theories is the fact that a lack of exercise, such as in immobilised patients, does not reduce sleeping time or the proportion of time spend in REM or non-REM stage 4 sleep.

Restoration theories emphasising physical exertion imply that very active species of animal would sleep for longer than inactive ones, because the active species have more energy expenditure to recover. But the evidence for this is not clear-cut. For example, the giant sloth, one of the most sluggish animals, sleeps for 20 hours per day. Conversely, as we saw above, some humans lead an active life despite having only 1-2 hours of sleep per night. Strenuous exercise in humans, according to the restoration model, would increase the amount of restoration needed, and therefore increase sleeping time. However, the effect is at best small (Horne & Minard, 1985). As you have probably experienced, falling asleep is easier when you are physically exhausted, but you do not actually sleep for longer.

Sleep deprivation studies have been used to evaluate restoration theories.

Sleep deprivation studies – animals

A technique used until recently to selectively deprive animals of REM sleep was the 'flower pot technique'. An animal such as a rat was placed on an upturned flower pot in a pool of water. Each time the animal entered REM sleep, the muscles relaxed and the neck drooped, bringing the snout into contact with the surrounding water and waking the animal up. Animals became generally sleep-deprived, but REM sleep especially was prevented. Studies using this technique showed that sleep deprivation has severe effects. After a few days, body temperature and metabolic rate increased. Over longer periods of time, more serious problems occurred – the animals became less disease resistant, brain activity was reduced, and in extreme cases the animal died (Everson, 1995). These effects may be caused by a lack of physical restoration – the body has been denied the opportunity to restore its processes. On the other hand, they may result from the stress involved in the deprivation procedure used in the experiment.

Sleep deprivation studies – humans

It ought to be easy to shed light on the functions of sleep states in humans by depriving them of sleep and studying the consequences. In 1965, a 17-year-old American, Randy Gardner, established a world record by staying awake continuously for 11 days. Extensive testing during this time revealed only small difficulties with blurred vision, garbled speech, some perceptual confusions and a slight paranoia about the experimenters. Afterwards, he slept for 14 hours and suffered no lasting ill effects.

Gardner is not unusual. Most studies involving physiological measurements (reflexes, blood pressure, respiration, heart rate, EEG) and cognitive tests (thinking, abstract reasoning and comprehension) have concluded that sleep deprivation, even exceeding 200 hours, produces few marked effects. The main effect appears to be a decrease in performance on tasks requiring vigilance – such as a radar operator's task, watching a screen for several hours to detect occasional signals. Tired radar operators in war time would miss approaching aircraft, due to minor lapses of attention, known as *microsleeps*. Eyelids droop and the eyes de-focus for 2-3 seconds. Sleep-deprived car drivers experience a similar effect, particularly when driving on boring motorways. This might support restoration theory, if the cause of these effects could be shown to be poor recovery by the brain. On the other hand, such problems may simply arise from a strong tendency to sleep, not a lack of restoration as such. However, recent research by Dement and Vaughan (2000) suggests that most of us do not sleep enough. As a result, we build up a 'sleep debt' and this leads to general fatigue, low motivation and other harmful effects.

During the first nights after the wake-athon, Randy Gardner showed a phenomenon often seen in sleep deprived participants – a 'rebound' effect. This is a temporary large increase in stage 4 non-REM and REM sleep when participants deprived of sleep are finally allowed a period of uninterrupted sleep. It is as though, for these stages, the brain needs to catch up on lost time. In terms of overall sleep time, catch-up is minimal – after only one day, Gardner returned to his usual 8 hours sleep per night. But stage 4 non-REM and REM sleep seem to be more 'necessary' than other stages and need to be restored (Horne, 1988).

Selective deprivation of REM sleep produces a similar effect. This is achieved by waking participants each time their sleeping EEG records shows signs of fast activity. REM sleep deprivation causes participants to become irritable, aggressive, and unable to concentrate when given boring tasks. These effects are not seen in a control group, woken in stages 3 or 4 (May & Kline, 1987). Participants deprived of REM sleep show a strong rebound tendency – after several nights they immediately drop into REM on falling asleep, and become increasingly difficult to rouse (Webb & Craddick, 1993). This suggests that REM is an important stage which the brain actively attempts to restore.

On the other hand, there is evidence that people seem to manage without REM sleep. Several classes of drug prescribed for depression and anxiety, such as the tricyclic antidepressants, suppress REM. People taking these drugs for many months have very little REM sleep, yet they appear to show no ill effects as a result.

Evaluation Sleep deprivation studies using animals appear to provide support for restoration theory. However, it is not clear whether the ill effects are due to sleep deprivation or to the stress resulting from the methods used to prevent sleep.

In humans, restorative functions (eg, adjustment of neurotransmitter levels) could occur during periods of inactivity and relaxation in the waking day, so it is unclear why such processes need to occur during sleep. Psychological disturbances are apparent after relatively short periods of sleep deprivation. Catch-up of REM and stage 4 non-REM sleep (the rebound effect) suggests that these are more important than other stages, and that they require restoration. However, not all participants show the rebound effect. Recovery of overall sleep time is minimal after long periods of deprivation, and recovery from psychological ill-effects occurs quickly. Although restoration theory does have some support, it remains unclear exactly what the restorative processes are. And it also remains unclear why some individuals appear to function well with a very low (1-2 hour) sleep requirement.

Memory consolidation and learning

This theory assumes that information is not fully processed during the waking day. The waking brain is distracted, too busy dealing with incoming and outgoing messages to select important information for storage in longer-term permanent memory stores. This may be better done during sleep. Studies have shown that more information is retained if participants sleep between learning and recall, than if they remain awake.

Rats spend longer in REM sleep on nights after being trained in a maze, and longest when learning is progressing most quickly. This suggests that REM sleep is needed to consolidate the new memories. Deprivation of REM sleep interferes with performance on a task that was learned the previous day. Smith and Rose (1997) found that rats trained to swim to a platform hidden beneath the surface of a pool of milky water forgot the location of the platform if they were deprived of REM sleep. The activation of spatial memory in animals during REM sleep is suggested by the appearance of theta rhythm (7.7 Hz) in the

hippocampus, a rhythm that occurs in waking life when acquiring new information. In REM sleep, this may represent the calling up of newly acquired information from the hippocampus so that it can be 'filed away' appropriately in longer-term stores in the cortex. This may need to be done during sleep when there are fewer processing demands on the brain.

Most studies of humans indicate that REM sleep deprivation has little effect on learning. However, Karni et al. (1994) found that while participants were being trained to make accurate judgements about the angle of lines briefly flashed in the periphery of the visual field, the usual day-to-day improvement in performance failed to occur in those deprived of REM sleep. Participants deprived of stage 3 and 4 non-REM sleep showed the usual improvement. This suggests that perceptual learning can be stored and/or organised during REM sleep.

Winston (1997) has suggested that in humans, memory consolidation may involve memories of complex behaviours specific to (and adaptive for) the human species. Such behaviours include interpersonal relationships and problem solving, enabling the development of strategies to cope with future challenges. Interview studies have shown that dreams tend to feature recent events – patients interviewed in hospital tend to incorporate doctors and hospitals, as though the day's activities are being recalled or reviewed in some way. The large proportion of sleeping time spent in REM in small babies may reflect the fact that so much of their experience is new and unexpected, and therefore in need of a great deal of filing and organisation in the absence of much previous experience.

Evaluation It is not clear why memory consolidation should occur during sleep any more than in quiet periods during waking life. While there is evidence for consolidation theory, many studies involving human learning and REM sleep deprivation have been inconclusive. REM may assist in the process of consolidation, particularly of complex skills, but it is probably not essential.

It would be wrong to think that there is a single explanation for sleeping. Competing theories are not necessarily incompatible. Sleep may have evolved for a variety of reasons, and may perform a variety of functions both in humans and across species.

Key terms

Protection theory *An ecological theory stating that night sleeping in humans evolved to protect against the dangers of darkness.*

Conservation theory *An ecological theory proposing that sleep conserves energy during the unproductive hours of darkness.*

Restoration theory *States that sleep enables the restoration of bodily states (eg, muscle chemicals, brain neurotransmitter levels) or psychological functions that are reduced or disturbed during wakefulness.*

Rebound effect *A temporary increase in the amount of REM and stage 4 sleep following sleep deprivation.*

Memory consolidation *The laying down of recent memories in longer-term memory stores.*

Summary

1 Sleep is a behaviour. It is actively controlled by the brain which continues to monitor events in the external world during sleeping.

2 Sleep may have evolved as a protection against predation during the dangerous hours of darkness. However, this is unlikely to be its major or only function.

3 Sleep may have evolved because it allowed energy to be conserved for use in the most productive hours of the day.

4 Sleep may have a function in restoring the body – reversing muscular changes, or restoring brain neurotransmitter levels. However, there is little evidence of lasting physiological or psychological changes after a long period of sleep deprivation.

5 REM sleep may have a role in enhancing learning by allowing memory consolidation.

6 It is unlikely that sleep evolved for a single purpose – it may have different functions and benefits.

Activity 4 Sleeping patterns

19.9 hrs Bat☐

14.5 hrs Cat☐

8.0 hrs Human

3.8 hrs Sheep

Question

Suggest reasons for the different sleeping times of the above animals.

Unit 3 Dreaming

KEY ISSUES

1 **What are dreams?**

2 **Does dreaming have a purpose?**

3 **What neurobiological and psychological explanations have been given for dreaming?**

3.1 Dreams and dreaming

In *Hamlet*, William Shakespeare's words 'to sleep, perchance to dream' imply that dreaming is sporadic – that although we may dream when sleeping, we do not always do so. Some mornings – maybe often – you will wake thinking that you had no dreams that night. Other times, you will wake to a vivid, emotional dream that leaves you frightened or exhausted.

As outlined in Unit 2, a sleep cycle on any night consists of a regular pattern of slow wave non-REM sleep, alternating every 90 minutes with periods of REM. People woken during REM periods report dreaming on nearly 80% of occasions. It is therefore reasonable to think that, whether we remember it or not, we have four or five separate bursts of dreaming each night.

Perspectives on dreams

Most of the time we pay little attention to dreams – they are occasionally interesting and memorable, but more often rather haphazard, vague, random phenomena which seem to have little meaning. Dreams have been variously regarded as:

- Narratives that are symbolic but which can give revealing insights into our unconscious – guides to inner emotions, a window on an inner world, and a reflection of deep-seated worries and forbidden desires.
- Having a significant impact on life events (Shakespeare's plays and the Bible are full of examples of premonitions and revelations being made known to dreamers).
- Performing biological functions, perhaps reorganising brain activity and assisting waking thinking processes. In some way, this can only occur when the rest of the brain is inactive, rather as a library might close while the catalogue is up-dated.

- Simply an emptying out of the brain's dustbin – just an unconnected and disorganised sequence of unrelated junk which can be brought forward into semi-awareness before being discarded.
- The brain just 'free running' with a succession of random fragmentary thoughts and images.

Of course, dreams could have more than one purpose. If we accept that some dreams provide meaningful insights into our inner thoughts and worries, others may only reflect random brain activity.

Studying dreams

Only half of the population remembers their dreams regularly. However, most people like to talk about their dreams and read significance into them. It is not surprising that many people throughout history have attempted to explain or interpret dream contents.

For psychologists, the study of dreams is difficult because they are subjective – they cannot be directly observed, recorded or measured. Because of this, they cannot be verified as an accurate record of what took place at the time. Dreaming is known to occur mainly, though not exclusively, during REM episodes, so it is possible to gain some insight into dream content by waking up sleeping participants when REM appears, in order to quiz them immediately about their dreams. Other studies have used the diary method, in which careful records are made of remembered dream content over several weeks. People often remember more dreams than usual if they use this method.

Studies have shown that most people dream about familiar places, objects and people. Content is often related to personal anxieties – athletes will dream about winning and losing competitions, and hungry people dream about food. Most of the emotional content is negative – pain, anger and anxiety are reported in over 60% of dream records, but positive emotions in less than 20%. Compared with women, men tend to report many more dreams involving sex and aggression. Dreams are largely audio-visual (in colour, or black and white) though people who are completely blind have rich, vivid auditory dreams. Tastes and smells are not reported.

Because dream reports are subjective, we cannot be sure that they represent a true *memory* of dream events. A reported dream sequence – the plot – could be mainly the product of our imagination. In waking life, the brain is constantly having to make sense of incoming information, often partial information. Applied to dreams, this might explain why they are reported as adventures – on waking, we may link together some random fragments of night-time imagery to form a coherent story. When people are asked to make up dreams, they can do so very convincingly (Cavallero et al., 1992). The brain is capable of great creativity! You may have woken after dreaming about a ringing telephone, only to find that your telephone is actually ringing. In this case, the real event was cleverly inserted into the script of the dream, and initially misinterpreted as a dream event. When sleep researchers sprayed cold water on sleeping participants' faces, they typically awoke claiming to have dreamed about water-related events such as walking through rain (Dement & Wolpert, 1958). Dream reports vary widely in terms of vividness, emotional content, and organisation.

Time perception seems to be preserved during dreams. People woken after variable lengths of REM and asked 'How long have you been dreaming?' usually give an accurate answer, at least up to about 15 minutes, after which they lost track of time. Dream events therefore occur in near real time.

Lucid dreaming

Sometimes a dreamer feels as though they are awake during a dream – as though they are able to influence the content of a dream and alter its course. The lucid dreamer may have difficulty deciding whether they are awake or asleep. They may need to test themselves, for example by performing impossible imaginary actions (such as flying) in order to *confirm* that they are actually dreaming. Compared to non-lucid dreams, lucid dreams are more like waking experience, containing less imagery and disguise. The dreamer feels as though they are in active control – they can still use their imagination and are not simply attending to the dream situation. Lucid dreams are more easily recalled, in greater detail, than non-lucid dreams. Sleep researchers can ask lucid dreamers to use a particular pattern of eye movements to indicate the point at which a lucid dream begins, suggesting that the lucid dreamer is in quite close contact with the waking world.

Key terms

Subjective experiences *Experiences reportable by and available only to the person concerned.*

Objective phenomena *Phenomena that can be observed, recorded and measured by an observer.*

Lucid dreams *Dreams having a real quality, in which the dreamer feels in control of the situation.*

Chuang Tzu and the butterfly

The strange division between dreams and waking experience has intrigued many cultures. The subjective nature of dreaming, and the contradictions, confusion and uncertainty surrounding the idea of consciousness, are well illustrated by the following poem by Chuang Tzu.

> Once upon a time, I, Chuang Tzu, dreamt I was a butterfly
> Fluttering hither and thither, to all intents and purposes a butterfly.
> … Suddenly I awoke, and there I lay, myself again.
> Now I do not know whether I was then a man dreaming I was a butterfly,
> Or whether I am now a butterfly dreaming I am a man.
> (Chuang Tzu, 1935)

REM sleep and dreaming

Despite the fact that REM is often termed *dream sleep*, not all dreaming occurs during REM periods, and not all REM periods involve dreaming. In one experiment, participants in a sleep laboratory who were woken during REM periods reported vivid dreams on 74% of occasions, but when woken in non-REM periods, dreaming was also reported on 7% of occasions (Aserinsky & Kleitman, 1953). Some put this last figure as high as 15%. Selective deprivation of REM sleep does not therefore result in complete dream deprivation. However, REM deprivation probably eliminates particular types of dream – those dependent on vivid visual imagery, which are most often reported when people are woken from REM sleep. Non-REM dreams are apparently of the 'thinking-about-problems' type.

Rapid eye movements Whether the rapid eye movements that occur in REM sleep are related to dream content is unclear. Some researchers claim that eye movements represent the scanning of visual events as though the dreamer is watching their own dream (Imeri et al., 1994). In one instance, a participant in a sleep laboratory was seen to make alternating eye movements, to left and right. On being woken they reported dreaming of watching a tennis match. In another instance, a dreamer made a series of eye movements in a triangular pattern, and on waking reported drawing a triangle. However, eye movements are not usually sufficiently systematic or regular to be related to a particular dream report, and since we do not know exactly what dream imagery consists of, it is difficult to know what pattern of eye movements to look for! Many studies have concluded that rapid eye movements are unrelated to dream imagery, since the movements occur in short bursts, and have an apparently random pattern with parameters (speed and frequency) that are quite unlike the more organised targeted eye movements used for visual exploration when awake.

3.2 Brain mechanisms involved in dreaming

Several brain neurotransmitters are involved in the regulation of sleep, but acetyl choline (used by structures in the pons, and at the base of the forebrain) appears to be involved in the form of brain 'arousal' that is associated with REM sleep. A nucleus in the pons called *nucleus pontis gigantocellularis* consists of very large neurons which use acetyl choline as their transmitter. They become particularly active during REM sleep. These neurons seem to be the origin of large bursts of electrical activity called *PGO waves* (ponto-geniculo-occipital waves) that sweep forward from the pons to the thalamus and then to visual cortex during REM sleep (see Figure 6). These waves are thought to be related to the visual imagery component of dreams. Alternatively, they may perhaps provoke the bursts of eye movements that characterise REM.

The onset of REM is accompanied by other physiological changes – heart rate and breathing become faster and more irregular, and sexual arousal occurs, indicated by penile erection in males and increased vaginal blood flow in females. However, in other respects, dreaming is psychological activity that occurs in the *absence* of bodily activity – people do not move about while dreaming. Neurons located in the brain-stem exert a strong inhibitory influence on the motor system during REM, blocking activity in the spinal motor neurons that normally activate muscles, so preventing dreams from being acted out. Sometimes in humans, damage to the pons produces *REM behaviour disorder*, in which the individual thrashes about during REM periods. A similar abnormality occurs in cats with small lesions in the pons. Instead of becoming paralysed during paradoxical sleep, they can be seen 'batting' at imaginary objects, as though playing with an imaginary mouse. Yet they are still asleep in the sense of being unresponsive to lights and sounds. They appear to be acting on their dream imagery, as though motor inhibition has been removed. This is perhaps the strongest evidence we have that animals, like humans, dream about events.

Many people make the mistake of thinking that sleep-walking and sleep-talking are dream phenomena. In fact, since the skeletal muscles are paralysed during REM, sleep-walking and sleep-talking are not possible during REM and only occur in slow wave sleep stages (non-REM stages 3 and 4).

Figure 6 PGO waves

2 seconds

PGO waves originate in the pons and travel to the lateral geniculate nucleus, then to the occipital cortex.

Hemispheric differences in dreaming

Dreaming is often illogical and schematic, which suggests that it might depend more upon activity in the right-brain hemisphere (generally associated with non-logical processes) than the left-brain hemisphere. Penfield and Jasper (1954), stimulating the brains of awake patients undergoing surgery for epilepsy, found that stimulating the temporal lobe could produce dream-like experiences, particularly in the right hemisphere. One patient reported that 'it was a woman calling something but I cannot make out the name … someone was speaking to another and he mentioned a name, but I could not understand it … it was just like a dream'. In lucid dreams, which are more logical and rational than non-lucid dreams, the left brain hemisphere may be activated, at least in the period just before waking (Walsh & Vaughan, 1992).

3.3 Theories of dreaming

As outlined in Unit 2, participants selectively deprived of REM sleep show a variety of adverse effects – typically they become irritable and anxious, agitated, and show poorer concentration. Whether this is related to reduced dreaming time is unknown. A certain amount of REM sleep is apparently 'needed'. When allowed to resume non-interrupted sleep, most sleep-deprived participants will, for two days or so, drop into REM more quickly and remain in REM for longer than usual periods. If dreaming were to have beneficial psychological effects, this might explain why the loss of REM sleep needs to be compensated.

Dreaming as a by-product of REM

A number of theories assume that dreaming is a by-product or side-effect of REM sleep. In other words, the main purpose of REM sleep is something other than dreaming.

Functional explanations include the suggestion that the increased metabolism occurring in the brain during REM – particularly in humans, who as a species have large brains – may be necessary to maintain brain temperature. During REM sleep, the body cools in relation to the external temperature – probably why we sleep under duvets! While this may not be dangerous for the body, the brain could become dangerously cold without the increased metabolism associated with REM arousal.

Other explanations suggest that a purpose of REM activity is to prepare the brain for waking, or for sudden activation in the case of being woken in dangerous circumstances. A short period of waking often occurs in animals shortly after a REM period, perhaps enabling them to check the safety of their nest site. A further explanation states that REM provides exercise for the extraocular muscles – those which move the eye ball in the orbit. Maurice (1998) suggested rapid movements of the eyes in REM sleep ensure a circulation of fresh fluid around the surface of the eye, maintaining a good supply of oxygen.

Evaluation there is little or no direct empirical evidence for these theories. However, they serve to remind us that dreaming may not be the primary function of REM. These theories assume that dreams are just accidental by-products of REM sleep.

Neurobiological theories of dreaming

Reverse learning

Interview studies have shown that dreams tend to feature recent events – patients interviewed in hospital tend to incorporate doctors and hospitals, as though the day's activities are being recalled or reviewed in some way. As outlined in Unit 2, REM activity may reflect the 'off-line' sorting out of new information for placement in long-term memory stores.

Crick and Mitchison (1983) argue that unwanted information can build up in memory systems, as a result of experience, and cause information overload. Consequently, unwanted connections need to be flushed out. They argue that this occurs during REM, when information can be sifted and selectively eliminated by the weakening of unwanted connections between neurons. This is sometimes referred to as *reverse learning*.

The purpose of dreaming is therefore to aid forgetting. Without this nightly clear-out, daytime thinking would be disrupted by obsessional thoughts and bizarre associations. Interestingly, as noted in Unit 2, such thoughts are known to occur following prolonged REM deprivation when participants can show bizarre behaviours. For such memory theories of REM, the actual content of the dream is irrelevant – dreaming experience is merely a by-product of a biological process. Dreams are seen as 'aimless meanderings' which do not warrant interpretation. This contrasts sharply with Freud's assumption (see below) that dreams reflect unconscious life dilemmas and wish-fulfilment. Indeed, Crick and Mitchison would argue that analysing dream content is counterproductive because it involves reinstating information that the dream was intended to eliminate.

Evaluation Reverse learning theory helps to explain the bizarre imagery and thoughts that occur following periods of sleep deprivation. However, if memory elimination is the primary function of REM sleep, it is unclear why babies prior to birth spend 50-80% of their sleeping time in REM, given that they have a minimal requirement for reverse learning. However, the theory does not rule out the involvement of REM and dreaming in other processes.

Activation-synthesis

Hobson and McCarley's (1977) *activation-synthesis hypothesis* suggests that an underlying biological clock *activates* neural systems randomly during sleep, like an off-line computer. The activation is similar to brain activation in the waking state, stimulating activity in wide regions of the visual, auditory and motor cortex. However, during dreams, the triggered experience is random. Fragments of experience are generated which are not coherent or related. During sleep, as in waking life, centres in the brain such as the association areas of the cortex do their best to *synthesise* this information – assembling and making sense of these fragments, based on the individual's past experience. But, since the original signals are randomly generated, it is impossible for the brain's higher centres to make logical sense of them. The result of this failure is dreams.

Evaluation Neurons have been detected in the cat brain which fire randomly during REM sleep. However, the concept of synthesis relies on the researcher's interpretation of the coherence or otherwise of dream fragments that are reported by participants. We cannot be sure whether the self-reports are accurate or if the researcher's interpretations are correct, particularly given the often bizarre sequences that people experience in dreams. This model contrasts with Freud's insofar as activation-synthesis assumes that the basis of dreaming is random brain activity, and unrelated to unconscious wishes and anxieties.

Psychological theories of dreaming

Problem solving

Cartwright (1993) adopts a cognitive approach, arguing that dealing with problems in the bizarre context of dreams might assist people to find creative solutions to difficulties in waking life, because the dream is less constrained by logic than waking thought processes. Therefore, dreams serve as problem-solving exercises and represent an extension of waking thought processes, helping us to deal with challenges associated with work and personal relationships.

The theory assumes that dream content reflects the actual meaning of the dream – it is not hidden beneath obscure symbolism, although a dream may contain metaphorical references. For example, 'car-racing' may represent competition with work colleagues, but the car is not a sexual symbol, as Freud might have supposed.

Cartwright examined the dreams of women undergoing divorce. She found that women who dreamed about divorce coped better with their situation than those who did not. Studies have shown that participants deprived of REM sleep are less able to develop constructive solutions to problems. In addition, there is evidence that when crises occur that require problem solving, people drop into REM sleep more quickly and remain in REM for longer.

Evaluation Evidence from REM studies is consistent with the theory, but it does not prove the theory. Evidence from the dreams of people in crises suggests that a possible function of dreaming is to contribute to the identification of real life problems and their solutions.

Psychoanalysis and dreams

The most famous theory of dreams is based on Freud's theory of psychoanalysis. Freud saw dreams arising from the unconscious part of the mind. In *Interpretation of dreams* (1900), he wrote that dreams provide the 'royal road to a knowledge of the unconscious activities of the mind'.

According to Freud, human beings are motivated by two main drives which are rooted in the unconscious. The life drive is expressed in desires for sexual and sensual pleasure. The aggressive drive gives rise to feelings of aggression towards others and towards the self. Only if these drives are kept in check and expressed in acceptable ways can society exist in a peaceful and ordered form.

The most important mechanism for keeping drives in check is *repression*. It contains sexual and aggressive impulses within the subconscious and prevents them from entering the conscious mind. In this way, sexual and aggressive thoughts and behaviour which are forbidden by society are prevented from finding expression. Repression also protects individuals by preventing unacceptable impulses and desires from reaching conscious awareness and producing anxiety and guilt.

However, repression cannot completely remove the motivation to satisfy forbidden desires. It keeps them out of conscious awareness but it doesn't make them go away. Repressed desires that have no means of expression can be psychologically harmful – according to Freud they cause neuroses (anxiety disorders). One way in which they can find expression and gratification is in the form of dreams.

At a simple level, dreams are attempts at *wish fulfilment*. In a proverb quoted by Freud, 'Pigs dream of acorns, and geese dream of maize'. By gobbling up their favourite food in dreams, pigs and geese fulfil their wishes. But few dreams are simple, straightforward examples of wish fulfilment. According to Freud, most deal with the fulfilment of forbidden and unacceptable wishes – the gratification of desires and impulses that have been repressed to the unconscious and hidden from the individual. For example, a dream may fulfil the desire of a boy to possess his mother both as a comforter and as a sexual partner.

Because wish fulfilment often involves forbidden and unacceptable thoughts and behaviour, it is expressed in a disguised form in dreams. Expressed openly and directly, it would threaten the individual and continually wake them up in horror. For example, an individual with sexual anxieties may dream of climbing stairs or being chased by snakes rather than dreaming of actual sexual encounters. Climbing stairs represents sexual intercourse and a snake represents a penis. Freud referred to this imagery or symbolism as the *manifest content* of dreams. This is the way the dream is experienced and recounted. However, this is a censored version of the 'real' dream. The actual content of the dream, its real meaning, is known as the *latent content*. Censorship protects the sleeper. It allows repressed desires and impulses to be expressed symbolically so avoiding the guilt or anxiety that would result if they were expressed openly.

Dreams can therefore be seen as psychological safety valves. They release the tension which results from repressing forbidden desires and unacceptable impulses. And they release it in a harmless and non-threatening way. Dreams are veiled in symbolism and cloaked in imagery – their true meaning is disguised. As a result, they can act as a safety valve without threat to the individual.

Evaluation Freud's theory of dreams has been widely criticised.

- His view that the dream represents wish fulfilment has been questioned. Many dreams do not appear to be either disguised or open wish fulfilment. In one study, participants were made extremely thirsty before they went to sleep. None reported dreams about drinking – there was no indication of wish fulfilment to relieve their thirst (Dement & Wolpert, 1958).

- Freud's view that the content of dreams is heavily censored and disguised has been criticised. Disturbing events and experiences, such as witnessing a serious injury, often recur

Key terms

Reverse learning *Removing information from memory during dreaming to prevent information overload.*

Activation-synthesis *The random activation of neural systems during dreaming and the synthesis of the information that results from this activation.*

Wish fulfilment *As used by Freud, the satisfaction of a wish on a symbolic or fantasy level.*

Repression *The containment of unacceptable and forbidden impulses and desires in the unconscious, so preventing them from reaching conscious awareness.*

Manifest content *The content of dreams as they are experienced and recounted by the dreamer.*

Latent content *The actual content of dreams which underlies the symbolism and imagery. The true meaning of the dream.*

in the same form in dreams without any disguise or masking. Many dreams are not cloaked in imagery to protect the dreamer. However, Freud accepted this. His theory stated that only repressed material is heavily disguised.

- Another common criticism of Freud is that the content of dreams mirrors events during a person's waking hours rather than a disguised expression of unacceptable desires (Foulkes, 1971). Again, Freud accepted that dreams often incorporate events of the previous day.

- Freud's theory is based upon the interpretation of dreams. It is not possible to verify interpretations. For example, is

Summary

1	Dreaming occurs mainly during periods of rapid eye movement (REM) sleep. This occurs at 90 minute intervals through the night.
2	Mechanisms in the pons (brain stem) produce PGO waves during REM sleep which may generate dream imagery.
3	The motor system is inhibited during REM sleep, perhaps to prevent the acting-out of dreams.
4	The neurotransmitter acetyl choline may be involved in the formation of imagery during REM periods.
5	A number of theories assume that dreaming is a by-product of REM sleep.
6	Reverse learning theory states that dreaming eliminates information from memory in order to prevent information overload.
7	The activation-synthesis hypothesis states that neural systems are activated randomly during sleep. The information generated by this process is synthesised. This synthesis produces dreams.
8	Cartwright's problem-solving theory states that dreams may serve as problem-solving exercises to find creative solutions to everyday problems.
9	Freud's theory sees the main function of dreams as the fulfilment of unacceptable desires and impulses. Dreams provide symbolic wish fulfilment.

climbing stairs a metaphor for sexual intercourse or is it simply climbing stairs? As Freud himself once remarked, 'sometimes a cigar is only a cigar'.

On a positive note, Freud's theory of dreams has proved one of the most exciting and creative theories in psychology. It has generated an enormous amount of research, speculation and controversy. But, there is no way that Freud's theory can be proved or disproved. Many psychologists now see his ideas as little more than an interesting aspect of the history of psychology. However, some recent biological evidence is consistent with some of Freud's ideas. A study of patients suffering from strokes reveals that they lose their capacity to dream if there is damage to areas of the higher forebrain governing desires (Solms, 1999). This suggests that Freud's claim that there is a link between dreaming and desire might have some truth in it after all.

References

Aserinsky, E. & Kleitman, N. (1953). Regularly occurring periods of eye mobility and concomitant phenomena during sleep. *Science, 118*, 273-274.

Berger, R.J. & Phillips, N.H. (1995). Energy conservation and sleep. *Behavioural Brain Research, 69*, 65-73.

Campbell, S.S. & Murphy, P.J. (1998). Extraocular circadian phototransduction in humans, *Science, 279*, 396-399.

Cartwright, R.D. (1993).Who needs their dreams? The usefulness of dreams in psychotherapy. *Journal of the American Academy of Psychoanalysis, 21*, 539-547.

Cavellero, C., Cicogna, P., Natale, V. & Occhionero, M. (1992). Slow wave sleep dreaming. *Sleep, 15*, 562-566.

Crick, F. & Mitchison, G. (1983). The function of dream sleep. *Nature, 304*, 111-114.

Czeisler, C.A., Moore-Ede, M.C. & Coleman,R.M. (1982). Rotating shift work schedules that disrupt sleep are improved by applying circadian principles. *Science, 217*, 461-463.

De Coursey, P. (1960). Phase control of activity in a rodent. *Cold Spring Harbor Symposia on Quantitative Biology, 25*, 49-55.

Dement, W.C. (1990). A personal history of sleep disorders medicine. *Journal of Clinical Neurophysiology, 7*, 17-47.

Dement, W.C. & Vaughan, C. (2000). *The promise of sleep*. London: Macmillan.

Dement, W.C. & Wolpert, E.A. (1958). The relationship of eye-movements, body motility, and external stimuli to dream content. *Journal of Experimental Psychology, 55*, 543-553.

Dijk, D.J. & Cajochen, C. (1997). Melatonin and the circadian regulation of sleep initiation, consolidation, structure, and the sleep EEG. *Journal of Biological Rhythms, 12*, 627-635.

Eastman, C.I., Young, M.A., Fogg, L.F., Liu, L. & Measden, P.M. (1998). Bright light treatment of winter depression. *Archives of General Psychiatry, 55*, 883-889.

Everson, C.A. (1995). Functional consequences of sustained sleep deprivation in the rat. *Behavioural Brain Research, 69*, 43-54.

Foulkes, D. (1971). Longitudinal studies of dreams in children. In J. Masserman (Ed.), *Science and psychoanalysis*. New York: Grune & Stratton.

Freud, S. (1900). *The interpretation of dreams*. London: Hogarth Press.

Fuller, C.A., Lydic, R., Sulzman, F.M., Albers, H.E., Tepper, B. & Moore-Ede, M.C. (1981). Circadian rhythm of body temperature persists after suprachiasmatic lesions in the squirrel monkey. *American Journal of Physiology, 241*, R385-R391.

Gwinner, E. (1986). Circannual rhythms in the control of avian rhythms. *Advances in the Study of Behavior, 16*, 191-228.

Hicks, R.A. & Garcia, E.R. (1987). Level of stress and sleep duration. *Perceptual and Motor Skills, 64*, 44-46.

Hobson, J.A., & McCarley, R.W. (1977). The brain as a dream state generator. An activation-synthesis hypothesis of the dream process. *American Journal of Psychiatry, 134*, 1335-1348.

Horne, J.A. (1988). *Why we sleep: The functions of sleep in humans and other mammals*. Oxford: Oxford University Press.

Horne, J.A., & Minard, A. (1985). Sleep and sleepiness following a behaviourally 'active' day. *Ergonomics, 28*, 567-575.

Imeri, L., De Simoni, M., Giglio, R., Clavenna, A. & Marcia, M. (1994). Changes in the serotonergic system during the sleep-wake cycle. *Neuroscience, 58*, 353-359.

Karni, A., Tanne, D., Rubenstein, B.S., Askenasy, J.J., & Sagi, D. (1994). Dependence on REM sleep of overnight improvement of a perceptual skill. *Science, 265*, 679-682.

Kerkhof, F.A. (1985). Inter-individual differences in the human circadian system: A review. *Biological Psychology, 20*, 83-112.

Maurice, D.M.(1998). The Von Sallman lecture of 1996: An ophthalmological explanation of REM sleep. *Experimental Eye Research, 66*, 139-145.

May, J. & Kline, P. (1987). Measuring the effects upon cognitive abilities of sleep loss during continuous operations. *British Journal of Psychology, 78*, 443-455.

Meddis, R. (1979). The evolution and function of sleep. In D.A. Oakley & H.C. Plotkin (Eds.), *Brain, behaviour and evolution*. London: Methuen.

Moline, M., Pollak, K., Monk, T., Lester, T. & Wagner, D. (1992). Age-related differences in recovery from simulated jet lag. *Sleep, 15*, 28-40.

Monk, T.H. & Folkard, S. (1985). Shiftwork and performance. In S. Folkard and T.H. Monk (Eds.), *Hours of work*. Wiley: Chichester.

Morris, M., Lack, L. & Dawson, D. (1990). Sleep-onset insomniacs have delayed temperature rhythms. *Sleep, 13*, 1-14.

Oswald, I. (1980). *Sleep* (4th ed.). Harmondsworth: Penguin Books.

Penfield, W. & Jasper, H. (1954). *Epilepsy and the functional anatomy of the human brain*. Boston: Little, Brown.

Pinel, J.P.J. (1997). *Biopsychology* (3rd ed.). Boston: Allyn and Bacon.

Pribram, K.H. (1971). *Languages of the brain: Experimental para-doxes and principles in neuropsychology*. Englewood Cliffs, NJ: Prentice-Hall.

Richter, C.P. (1922). A behavioristic study of the activity of the rat. *Comparative Psychology Monographs, 1*, 1-55.

Rosch, P.J. (1996). Stress and sleep: Some startling and sobering statistics. *Stress-medicine, 12*, 207-210.

Rusak, B. & Morin, L.P. (1976). Testicular responses to photoperiod are blocked by lesions of the suprachiasmatic nuclei in golden hamsters. *Biology of Reproduction, 15*, 366-374.

Smith, C. & Rose, G.M. (1997). Post-training paradoxical sleep in rats is increased after spatial learning in the Morris water maze. *Behavioral Neuroscience, 111*, 1197-1204.

Solms, M. (1999, 29 Jan.). Wishes, perchance to dream. *Times Higher Educational Supplement*.

Stern, W.C. & Morgane, P.J. (1974). Theoretical view of REM sleep: Maintenance of catecholamine systems in the central nervous system. *Behavioral Biology, 11*, 1-32.

Walsh, R.N. & Vaughan, F. (1992). Lucid dreaming: Some trans-personal implications. *Journal of Transpersonal Psychology, 24*, 193-200.

Webb, D.E. & Craddick, R.A. (1993). Unconscious cathexis of dream symbols as measured by the Kahn Test of Symbol Arrangement. *Perceptual and Motor Skills, 77*, 547-554.

Winson, J. (1997). The meaning of dreams. *Scientific American, 7*, 58-67.

▶ Introduction

What motivates behaviour? In other words, what causes people to behave the way they do? To take an apparently simple question: What motivates people to eat and drink? The answers to this question are far from simple. This chapter examines various theories which claim to explain eating and drinking behaviour, and motivated behaviour in general. The focus is the biopsychology of motivation – the role of biological systems in motivating behaviour.

What is emotion and how are emotions such as happiness and anger generated? Again the answers are far from simple. This chapter examines various theories of emotion. It focuses on the role of the nervous system in initiating, regulating and controlling emotional states.

Chapter summary

- Unit 1 looks at mechanisms in the brain which regulate the motivational states of hunger and thirst.
- Unit 2 reviews the theories put forward to account for motivation and how motivation arises.
- Unit 3 considers emotion, and the role of brain structures and environmental factors in generating emotional states.

Unit 1 Brain mechanisms controlling hunger and thirst

KEY ISSUES

1 Why is it important to maintain physiological equilibrium in the body?
2 What are the main theories explaining the regulation of eating and drinking?

1.1 Why be motivated?

All animals have to cope with the fact that their external environment is constantly changing. They have to adapt to change from moment to moment so that the internal environment of the body is maintained in a fairly constant state. Sometimes this can be achieved via *adaptive behaviours* – lighting a fire to keep warm in cold weather and shedding clothes when it's hot. The body is equipped with motivational systems that automatically regulate internal processes, such as maintaining levels of nutrients – either by making internal physiological adjustments or by changing behaviours. If the level of a nutrient deviates significantly, upward or downward from its optimum (ideal) level, the level is adjusted back toward optimum via physiological feedback, and via learned behavioural responses. Walter Cannon, in the 1920s, gave this state of balance, which the body tries to sustain, the name *homeostasis* (homos means 'the same').

Balance has to be maintained actively within the body, as in other controlled systems. For example, think about how a central heating system works. A central boiler heats water which is piped around the house into radiators which warm the air. Air temperature is monitored by a thermostat – a thermometer which sends signals to control the boiler, switching it on when the temperature falls below a lower fixed point and off again when the temperature rises above an upper fixed point. There are good reasons for keeping a house within a comfortable temperature range, since very low temperatures might cause water pipes to burst and high temperatures might kill all the plants in the house. In just the same way, the body's physiological systems are regulated to operate most efficiently and avoid damage.

This unit looks at two *motivational states* – hunger and thirst. It asks what motivates animals and humans to start and stop eating and drinking.

One way of achieving homeostasis or balance is to provide essential nutrients in the correct proportions. This is one of the main factors that keeps the body in optimal condition. Compared to other animals, humans eat a far wider range of foods. Our meals consist of fats, carbohydrates, proteins, vitamins, minerals, and water, all of which are subject to control. But control is made difficult by the fact that these occur together in the same foods, in various mixtures and proportions. We should therefore expect motivational systems which control the intake of food to be complex.

Maintenance of homeostatic balances requires a constant interplay between the peripheral nervous system and the endocrine system on the one hand, and the central nervous system (control centres in the brain) on the other. The role of these systems in the regulation of eating and drinking is examined in the following two sections.

Key terms

Adaptive behaviours *Behaviours which promote survival.*

Motivation *Activation of behaviour, particularly behaviours directed toward achieving goals and adapting to change.*

Optimum *An ideal level at which processes operate most efficiently.*

Homeostasis *A state of balance or equilibrium which the body strives to maintain.*

Regulation of food intake

Regulation and control of food intake is affected by various factors. These include energy storage and energy output, and also *metabolism* – the speed at which the body's chemical processes which result in energy production take place. Understanding heat regulation in the example of a central heating system is simple, because just one signal – temperature – is needed to control the system. Eating is more complex because we need to know which nutrient levels are monitored, where the monitoring devices are located and how they work, and how nutrient levels in the body signal adjustments in eating. In short, to explain how eating behaviour is motivated, we need to know 1) what factors cause us to start eating and 2) what factors cause us to stop eating.

1.2   Central theories of eating control

Central theories assume that mechanisms in the brain monitor nutrient levels, and start and stop eating.

Hypothalamic nuclei

As noted in previous chapters, the *hypothalamus* acts as a regulatory centre for many behaviours (see Figure 1). Each of its nuclei appears to be involved in a separate aspect of regulation – of aggression, diurnal rhythms, temperature control, food and water intake, sexual behaviour, salt balance, and so on. Two particular nuclei have been traditionally linked to eating behaviour – the *lateral hypothalamus* (LH), which was said to act as a *hunger centre*, 'switching on' eating, and the *ventromedial hypothalamus* (VMH), a *satiety centre*, which has been said to 'switch off' eating (satiety means feeling full up). These two centres were thought to inhibit one another – when one was active, the other was suppressed. This model caused great excitement in the 1950s because it offered the prospect of simple cures for eating disorders such as anorexia and obesity – it was just a matter of finding out how to turn these centres on or off.

The model is sometimes known as the *dual-centre hypothesis* because it identifies two eating control centres – a hunger centre (the LH) and a satiety centre (the VMH).

Evidence for this dual-centre model came from studies in which rats with implanted stimulating electrodes in the LH began feeding when electrical stimulation was applied, while stimulation of the VMH stopped feeding in a hungry animal. Conversely, animals with lesions in the LH starved because they failed to initiate eating when food was available (a condition called *aphagia*), while those with lesions in the VMH went on eating insatiably (*hyperphagia*) until they became extremely obese. Tumours in these areas in people often produce similar effects. Tumours destroying the LH lead to anorexia, while those in the VMH cause weight gain at a rate of 10 kg per month. Further evidence for VMH as a satiety centre came from studies of blood glucose. Some cells within the VMH are sensitive to the levels of sugar circulating in the blood and so high sugar levels could trigger the VMH to 'turn off' feeding. Selective destruction of the VMH cells which are sensitive to glucose gives rise to massive weight gain. (We will return to this model later in the discussion of glucostatic theory).

Key terms

Hypothalamus *A collection of small nuclei at the base of the forebrain, often involved in detecting change and sending out regulatory signals.*

Hunger centre *A brain nucleus or structure which detects hunger signals and promotes eating.*

Satiety centre *A brain nucleus or structure which detects satiety signals and suppresses eating.*

Anorexia *An eating disorder where body weight is very low.*

Obesity *An eating disorder where body weight is too high.*

Aphagia *Eating too little or not at all.*

Hyperphagia *Overeating.*

Figure 1   The hypothalamus

lateral hypothalamus (LH)

ventromedial hypothalamus (VMH)

The hypothalamus is situated at the base of the forebrain. It consists of a cluster of nuclei, each linked to a different regulatory process.

Criticisms of the dual-centre hypothesis

Research has since shown that the situation is more complicated than the dual-centre model suggests. The LH and VMH are no longer regarded simply as switches which turn eating motivation on or off. The following evidence indicated that the hypothalamus does not act alone in regulating eating behaviour. It suggests that the motivation to eat is a complex process controlled by various structures in the brain, and other organs such as the liver, all of which are connected and interrelated.

The LH hunger centre model An animal with a lesioned (cut or damaged) LH seems to pay no attention to food-related stimuli such as the sight or smell of food. However, if food is placed in its mouth, it will eat. This does not mean that the LH has no role in controlling eating. But it indicates that the LH does not work alone. The lack of attention to food-related stimuli after LH lesions suggests that the LH may influence cells in the forebrain, making them more sensitive to the taste, smell and sight of food (Critchley & Rolls, 1996). In addition, when LH-lesioned animals are carefully handled and tube-fed, they eventually recover eating control, but they adjust to a lower 'set point' and maintain a low body weight. Again this suggests that the LH does not act alone in motivating eating behaviour. Experimental evidence shows that stimulation of various other sites in the brain – for example, the frontal cortex, amygdala and thalamus – can also initiate eating. In conclusion, the LH does appear to have a role in stimulating eating, but it is not a unique hunger centre – it is probably regulated from elsewhere, and influences eating via other brain structures.

The VMH satiety model Evidence suggests similar conclusions about the VMH. Its role in reducing or ending the motivation to eat appears to be shared by other brain structures. True, animals overeat when the VMH is lesioned, but only if food is palatable. Given bitter or untasty food, they eat less – in other words, the lesion makes them more finicky rather than more hungry. They are also less prepared to work for food (for example by pressing a bar to obtain food pellets) than control animals. (A similar effect is seen in obese humans.) They seem to eat more meals rather than larger meals. Furthermore, VMH-lesioned animals fed on palatable food such as laboratory pellets, after a *dynamic phase* of massive weight gain in which they might triple or quadruple their weight, reach a *static phase* in which food intake and weight stabilise. At some point, therefore, they do 'stop' overfeeding, despite the absence of the VMH. This does not mean that the VMH has no role in terminating eating in normal conditions, only that other mechanisms are also involved. It might be that at a particular weight, the sheer discomfort of a large body mass has a negative feedback effect, and eating stops.

Animals with VMH lesions may put on weight for reasons other than excessive eating. Studies have shown that they have high levels of the hormone insulin circulating in the blood. One effect of insulin is to increase fat storage. The VMH-lesioned animal therefore stores a high percentage of each meal as body fat. In fact, even when their food intake is restricted, they continue to gain weight. This is further evidence that the VMH is not just related to *eating* as such. We can conclude that the VMH is not a simple eating-off switch, but influences many regulatory systems.

Other feeding-related brain centres

The paraventricular nucleus (PVN) receives many inputs (involving several neurotransmitters) and appears to influence fat, protein and carbohydrate consumption, specific food selection, and in particular meal size – PVN-lesioned animals seem insensitive to the feedback signals at the end of a meal that say 'that's enough' (Leibowitz et al., 1981). The amygdala, which is a small nucleus in the temporal lobe, may have a role in labelling particular foods as rewarding (Fukuda & Ono, 1993). This effect might be reinforced via the chemical neurotransmitter dopamine, which is released in the lateral hypothalamus when something particularly tasty is eaten.

In conclusion, a simple dual-centre control system consisting of 'eating-start' and 'eating-stop' switches is too simplistic. On the other hand, both the LH and VMH seem to have important roles in regulating hunger and eating behaviours. Motivation to eat (and then later, to stop) depends upon a variety of factors, including hormone levels and the levels of sugar, fats and nutrients in the blood. Feedback to the brain might be channelled to the LH and VMH, which may integrate signals from several sources, promoting or restraining eating behaviour.

1.3 Peripheral feedback theories of eating control

Peripheral theories argue that the trigger signals to start and stop eating are independent of the brain, and rely on mechanisms in the organs of the body such as the liver and stomach.

Stomach feedback

Some of the earliest models of hunger assumed that feedback from the stomach plays a major role in eating control. No doubt you have experienced the sound and feel of a growling, hungry stomach around lunch time. The physiologist Cannon had his cooperative research assistant, Washburn, swallow a balloon that could be inflated or deflated, thus expanding or contracting the stomach. Washburn reported feeling hungry when the balloon was deflated and the stomach became smaller (Cannon & Washburn, 1912). Cannon concluded that stomach distension or shrinking is a major source of feedback for all aspects of feeding – when a meal is eaten, the swelling of the stomach creates feelings of satiety, but when food progressively empties from the stomach, the contracted stomach sends messages to the brain indicating a need to eat.

> Figure 2
>
>
>
> The rat on the left has a VMH lesion. The rat on the right is normal.

We now know that this explanation is simplistic. There are other ways of providing feedback signals for hunger and satiety. Cannon himself said that he was referring to hunger as hunger 'pangs' and not the more general wish to eat. In fact, Cannon was not entirely wrong – feedback from receptors in the gut and stomach does contribute to feelings of hunger (Davidson, 1993) and there is no doubt that feedback from a grossly bloated stomach stops eating. Dieters are encouraged to fill up on stomach-distending fibrous but non-fattening foods such as vegetables to reduce the craving to eat. Certainly, signals from the stomach to the LH might encourage eating, and signals to the VMH might discourage eating. There is evidence for this idea. When food is artificially introduced into the gut via a tube, activity in LH neurons decreases while VMH activity increases – a naturally full stomach would presumably do the same thing.

However, signals arising from the stomach have a minor influence on the regulation of eating, since hunger feelings are reported by people whose stomachs have been completely removed. Experience tells you that distension of the stomach does not necessarily end hunger feelings. Although your stomach may feel 'full up' after a main course of meat and potatoes, there is often a strong urge to begin eating again when the lemon meringue pie appears! We will look at other stomach factors in a later section.

Figure 3 Cannon and Washburn's experiment

to clock

balloon/stomach contractions

time

hunger pangs

air pressure recorder

balloon

response key

Whenever Washburn felt a hunger pang he pressed the response key. His hunger pangs coincided with stomach contractions.

1.4 Glucostatic theory

Sugar (blood glucose) is an essential fuel that enables cells to function. Meyer (1953) proposed that a falling level of blood sugar is the crucial signal indicating that food is required, triggering food seeking and eating behaviours. Certainly people report feeling hungry when their blood sugar level drops. And injecting a small amount of glucose directly into the blood stream in rats delays the point at which they next start eating. According to this view, when food is eaten and blood sugar levels rise, a terminator signal to the VMH stops feeding. The signal could come from the liver, which detects sugar levels and may communicate this information to the hypothalamus. A theory that assumes blood sugar (glucose) levels to be the main controller of food intake is called a *glucostatic theory* (static = to maintain constant). Cells that are specialised for monitoring glucose levels, in the liver, LH, or VMH, are called *glucostats*.

The glucostatic model is often referred to as a peripheral model as opposed to a central model, since the signals probably originate in the liver, not in the brain – peripheral means on the fringe, not central. But brain mechanisms need peripheral inputs to fully monitor the state of nutrients in the body. Therefore a strong distinction between peripheral and central models is not appropriate – detection of sugar levels can occur as blood passes through the brain within nuclei such as the LH and VMH, but there are such fast connections between the gut, the liver and the hypothalamus that in practice all of these act together.

A problem with the simple glucostatic model is that blood glucose levels do not vary much. When levels fall, the liver compensates by releasing glycogen (stored sugar) which is converted back to glucose, keeping the level fairly stable. How then does hunger ever occur? More important seems to be the body's *usage* of sugar. Glucostats seem especially sensitive to the difference between blood glucose concentrations in the arteries (the blood vessels which take blood to the tissues) and the veins (which take blood back to the heart). This difference is known as the artero-venous (A-V) difference. It is greatest when glucose is being used up by the body – when it is being drawn out of the circulating blood into the tissues, especially the muscles. This large A-V difference only occurs in the phase when food is being absorbed into the blood – known as the *absorption* phase, when we feel satiety. So, a big A-V difference means that we feel full. Some time after a meal, when the supply of glucose from food to the blood has dried up – in the *fasting* phase – the A-V difference is small because little glucose is being transported from the blood into the muscles. This is when the individual begins to feel hungry again. The A-V difference at any one moment reflects not only food eaten but energy expended across the day.

Usually we eat at similar 'meal times' each day. This tells us that stopping and starting eating is not purely controlled by physiological signals. However, the typical interval between meals (for most people, 3-5 hours across the waking day) allows time for an absorption and a fasting phase, and thus for hunger to build up when a meal is due. Sustained activity on a particular day – such as playing sport for an afternoon – uses energy, depletes the supply of glucose, and increases feelings of hunger. This is why people will often want a high-sugar snack of fruit or biscuits after playing sport, as a fill-in before the next meal time comes around.

The A-V version of the glucostatic theory is probably the most successful in accounting for the regulation of food intake, particularly feelings of hunger as meal times approach. But it only accounts for short-term effects. Other longer-term factors also influence food intake and energy balance. Eating just a little more, or a little less, each day over many weeks has long term consequences. Energy from food that is surplus to requirements is stored up for the future, accumulating in the body in the form of fat. Balancing intake against output in the longer term therefore requires a different, more gradual mechanism, related to body weight. Meyer (1953) proposed that the feedback signals which are used to adjust food intake over the long-term are provided by the levels of fat in the body.

Key terms

Feedback *A signal from the body (for example, indicating sugar level) is sent to a regulator that restores the system to balance when the signal is too high or too low.*

Glucostatic theory *States that eating is mainly regulated according to blood glucose level.*

Glucostats *Cells specialised to monitor glucose levels.*

Artero-venous (A-V) difference *The difference in sugar concentration in the arteries (blood vessels taking blood to the muscles and tissues) and veins (returning blood from the muscles and tissues).*

Absorption phase *The phase of the digestion cycle when the stomach is full of food and glucose is being absorbed into the blood.*

Fasting phase *The phase of digestion when the stomach is empty; fatty acids provide a temporary energy source instead of glucose.*

1.5 Lipostatic 'set point' theory

The levels of fat in the body and circulating in the blood seem to be important factors in determining the long-term regulation of body weight. This type of theory is a *lipostatic theory* (lipids = fats). Cells called *adipocytes* form the *adipose tissues* or fatty tissues of the body. Particular cells, some of which are found in the hypothalamus, act as a sort of comparator – they compare the circulating concentration of fat in the blood with their own stored fat level.

Fat levels in the blood could be one of the many influences on short-term eating behaviour. Fats (fatty acids) are released into the blood as an energy source during the fasting phase of digestion, long after a meal when the gut is empty and the glucose supply has dried up. The level of fats falls again when eating occurs. Therefore, a low blood fat level could act as a satiety signal to the brain. However, most researchers think that the effect of fat signals on stopping and starting eating is small. Glucose-related signals are seen as more important.

Signals arising from fat levels are likely to be most relevant to the longer-term control of body weight, via adjustments made not in the brain but in the liver. The liver contains cells that monitor blood fat levels, so it can decide either to (a) burn up fats and use them for energy purposes, or (b) store fats in the body. The latter is an excellent way of storing energy for long-term use since fats can later be broken down to form sugars and used as energy if food supplies become scarce. In an environment in which food supply is unpredictable, this has survival value.

However, accumulated body fat is not always broken down. Some individuals lay down excessive amounts, maintaining a high body weight even when exercising regularly to burn off energy. This is because body weight is to some degree genetically inherited – one study in Denmark found that the body weights of 540 adopted children showed a higher correlation with those of their biological family than those of their adopted family (Stunkard et al., 1986). This experimental design eliminates the simple explanation that parents' and children's weights correlate simply because they share the same diets. An internal *set point* seems to be an important genetic determinant of food intake and weight control in the long-term. A particular set weight is *defended*, meaning that below this weight food intake is increased, while above it intake decreases. The system is rather finely balanced. Eating just one extra portion of butter or margarine per day has the effect of adding over 2 kg to body weight per year. This indicates that gradual changes in the short-term control of eating behaviour can have cumulative effects, altering long-term control and energy balance.

Leptin

Where genetic differences have been investigated between animals, naturally obese mice have been found to possess a particular *obesity gene*. The normal version of the gene produces a particular protein, known as *leptin*, which circulates in the blood and seems to signal the current state of fat supplies to the rest of the body (including the brain). Leptin level increases as the amount of fat stored in the body increases. When the level of leptin in the blood is high, hunger decreases, activity levels increase and metabolism speeds up so that more fat is burned off as energy. Animals with the abnormal obesity gene fail to produce leptin, so the body behaves as though it has no fat. On the face of it, injections of leptin might be seen as an instant cure for obesity in humans, but unfortunately obesity in humans is rarely if at all caused by an obesity gene that reduces leptin levels. In fact, leptin levels are too high in obese humans – it is not that they lack leptin but perhaps that, for some other genetic reason, the brain cells which should respond to leptin are insensitive to it (Clement et al., 1998).

Key terms

Lipostatic theory *States that eating behaviour is regulated according to levels of fat in the body.*

Adipose tissue *Fatty tissue composed of cells called adipocytes.*

Set point *A body weight that is determined biologically and which the body actively tries to maintain.*

Leptin *A protein that circulates in the blood and may signal fat storage levels to the rest of the body.*

1.6 Incentive value theory

Incentive value refers to the characteristics of foods, such as taste, appearance and variety, that alter their attractiveness. When a range of foods is offered, both rats and people eat more calories than when just one or two types of food are available. Probably a liking for variety has a biological advantage of varying our diet. Humans and other animals will eat purely for taste – eating sweet foods even when fully satiated on less exciting foods such as vegetables, fish and meat. Non-human animals rarely encounter natural sources of concentrated sugar. However humans, by eating a small amount of sweet food such as chocolates or cream cakes, can ingest many times the amount of sugar that other animals would obtain from their diets of leaves, roots or meat.

In fact, all human sugar intake via sweet foods is superfluous –

we obtain all the glucose we need from a balanced diet, without added sugars. Our liking for sweet foods and the availability of sugar in concentrated forms probably makes humans particularly vulnerable to obesity. Some 25% of the population of the USA are obese – more than 30% above the recommended weight for their body height, thus carrying an abnormally high proportion of body fat. Unfortunately, instead of producing a negative feedback homeostatic effect, eating some foods has a feed-forward incentive effect, increasing their desirability. For most of us, eating just a few salted peanuts or potato crisps tends to make us want more. And these foods are seriously fattening.

1.7 The role of learning and feedback

Learning Learning is involved in food intake regulation. People tend to adjust their intake of various foods in order to maintain a relatively constant calorie supply. In other words, we learn to associate foods with the amount of energy which they supply. Given the delay between food ingestion and the appearance of nutrients in the blood, it is probably necessary for the brain to do some makeshift calculations about likely nutritional intake from such factors as smell, taste, texture and bulk, learned from past experience.

Feedback The presence of food in the mouth is important in several respects. Firstly, the enjoyment of eating is removed when food is pumped directly into the stomach. However, in studies in which participants have regulated the delivery of food via a tube to their own stomachs, they do this in such a way as to maintain body weight. This shows that tasting, chewing and swallowing are not essential to food regulation. Normally, we probably do monitor the food taken in by the size of a mouthful and the number of mouthfuls taken in a meal, using both as a rough guide as to bulk. Oral factors are therefore one source of possible feedback that can terminate eating. However, we can't be sure. In animal studies, it is possible to arrange for so-called *sham feeding*, in which the oesophagus (which normally carries food from the mouth to the stomach) is re-routed outside the body, so the swallowed food passes out of the body, not reaching the stomach. In these circumstances, animals eat much more than normal. Clearly, oral feedback alone does not inhibit feeding.

We saw earlier that stomach distension was not a major

source of feedback that stops eating. But perhaps the presence of nutrients in the gut produces chemical feedback? When food passes out of the stomach into the duodenum, a hormone, CCK-8 (cholecystokinin) is released which inhibits further stomach emptying. Its presence in the blood stream might be one of those many signals to the VMH to decrease eating. Certainly, injections of CCK suppress eating, though it is not clear whether this effect is simply due to the unpleasant nauseous effects of CCK. If this hormone is injected into rats while they taste a novel flavour, the rats will avoid that flavour in future, indicating that CCK is aversive – they have learned to associate the flavour with an unpleasant feeling (Chen et al., 1993).

In short, we have seen how many factors can influence eating behaviour: some (like the A-V glucose difference) are most important in relation to the experience of hunger and satiety across a day, while others such as fat level may make longer-term adjustments to food intake, and energy usage and storage. Simple feedback from the mouth and stomach may enable the brain to calculate roughly, on the basis of learning from past experience, when enough food has been eaten during a meal to meet the body's likely energy requirements. Such influences may be exerted via signals that arrive at the LH and VMH in the hypothalamus. Table 1 shows some of the major factors that could 'signal' hunger and satiety, and thereby control eating.

Table 1 Factors influencing eating

Encourage eating	Discourage
High activity in LH	High activity in VMH
Low levels of arterial blood glucose (small A-V difference)	High level of arterial blood (large A-V difference)
High levels of fatty acids in blood	Low levels of fatty acids in blood
Low set point reached for stored fats	High set point reached for stored fats
Empty stomach	Distended stomach
Low leptin level	High leptin level
High palatability of food	Low palatability of food

Activity 1   Why, when and what do we eat?

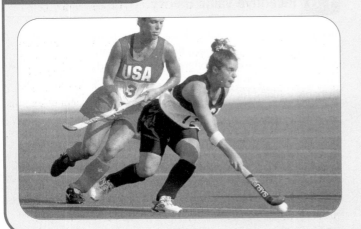

You have just come home after playing hockey all afternoon (4.30 pm). You say you are 'starving' and eat an apple. You eat at your usual meal time (6.00 pm): today you choose fish, chips and peas followed by two helpings of ice cream. You say that you are 'full up' (6.30 pm).

Questions

1 Why was the apple at 4.30 pm a satisfying 'filler'?

2 What physiological 'signals' might have given rise to feelings of hunger at 4.30 pm and satiety at 6.30 pm?

3 Despite feeling 'full' after your main meal, why couldn't you resist the ice cream?

1.8 Regulation of body fluids

Water is an extremely important body constituent. Two thirds of all the water in the body is contained in cells. The rest is in blood, the cerebrospinal fluid which bathes the brain and spinal cord, and in interstitial fluid – the fluid between cells. Loss of fluid from the body can be life-threatening. It is possible to live for 2-3 months without food, but only a few days without water. When cells of the body lose water, they become incapable of performing many of their functions. Too much water, and the cell walls may expand and rupture, giving rise to a life-threatening situation. Changes in fluid balance can occur for a variety of reasons – for example, as a result of fluid loss after bleeding, sweating, vomiting or diarrhoea, and as a result of evaporation from the skin.

This section looks how the body's fluids are regulated and how drinking is motivated.

Deprivation-induced drinking

Common-sense suggests that the motivation to drink is due to a reduction of the body's fluids. In other words, when the level of body fluids is low, the result is thirst which motivates drinking. This restores the body's fluids to their optimum (ideal) level. Much of the research on drinking is based on this idea which is known as *deprivation-induced drinking*. Drinking is therefore seen to be induced or motivated by a deprivation or lack of bodily fluids.

There are two main systems regulating deprivation-induced drinking. One responds to a reduction of fluids inside the cells – *intracellular fluid*. This reduction is called *cellular dehydration*. The second system responds to a reduction of fluids outside the cells – *extracellular fluid* – in particular, to a reduction in blood volume. This reduction is called *hypovolemia*.

Cellular dehydration

How does cellular dehydration occur? In other words, how is the level of fluid in the cells reduced? The simple answer is that water is drawn out of the cells into the other bodily fluids – that is, intracellular fluids pass through the cells into extracellular fluids.

Bodily fluids are composed of *solutes* – substances dissolved in liquids. Normally, the proportion of solutes in intracellular and extracellular fluids is the same. However, if the proportion of solutes in the fluid outside the cells is higher than the proportion inside the cells, then water will be drawn from the cells into the extracellular fluid. This process is illustrated in Figure 4. The dots indicate the proportion of solutes inside and outside the cell. The arrow shows water being drawn out of the cell. The pressure that draws water through the cell membrane is known as *osmotic pressure*. The motivation to drink as a result of this is known as *osmotic thirst*. Drinking serves to re-establish the balance between the fluids inside and outside the cells. When in balance, both fluids have the same concentration of solutes and, as a result, there is no osmotic pressure.

The main solute in body fluids is sodium (sodium is a constituent of salt – sodium chloride). After a salty meal of fish and chips, or a snack of salted nuts, people feel thirsty. Salt does not pass easily into the cells and as a result, there is a concentration of sodium solutes in the extracellular fluids, the fluids outside the cells. This draws water out of the cells,

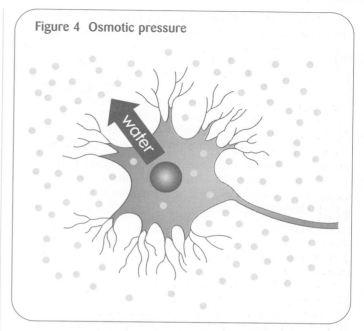

Figure 4 Osmotic pressure

resulting in cellular dehydration.

Detecting cellular dehydration How is cellular dehydration monitored? Much of the research has focused on locating the cells which detect cellular dehydration. These cells are called *osmoreceptors*.

Research indicates that osmoreceptors in the lateral preoptic area of hypothalamus play a part in drinking. For example, the injection of minute quantities of a saline (salt) solution into this area caused drinking in rats (Andrews et al., 1992).

Inducing thirst How do the osmoreceptors actually produce a feeling of thirst and so motivate drinking? First, they send signals which activate neurons in the brain which create the experience of thirst. Second, they increase the release of a hormone *antidiuretic hormone* (ADH). This hormone increases thirst and conserves water in the body by preventing the kidneys from releasing it by decreasing their production of urine.

Hypovolemia

The above section examined deprivation-induced drinking as a response to cellular dehydration – a reduction in cellular fluids. This section looks at deprivation-induced drinking as a response to hypovolemia – a reduction in blood volume. This type of thirst is known as *volumetric thirst*. The term volumetric refers to the need to measure the body's blood volume in order to regulate drinking.

Detectors that monitor blood volume are located in the heart, where they measure blood pressure, and in the kidneys where they measure blood flow. Volumetric thirst can be triggered by either set of detectors. In both case, a message is sent in the brain by the release of the hormone *angiotensin*. This activates an area in the hypothalamus (the median preoptic nucleus) which motivates drinking. Very small quantities of angiotensin injected into this area in rats result in drinking (Epstein et al., 1970).

Spontaneous drinking

Animals and humans drink far more than they need. Most drinking occurs without water deficits (lack of water) in the body. Drinking which is above and beyond the requirement to restore the fluid balance in the body is called *spontaneous drinking*. Various reasons have been suggested for this.

Pleasure Drinking is usually a pleasurable experience. People enjoy tasty drinks – colas, fruit juices, sodas, milk. They also enjoy drinks containing drugs which produce pleasurable effects – alcoholic beverages and drinks containing caffeine such as coffee and tea. Experiments with rats show that the amount of water they consume grows rapidly with the addition of a small quantity of the sweetener saccharin (Rolls et al., 1978).

Social effects People drink more in company. Socialising is a strong stimulus to drinking – many more pints of beer are consumed on Saturday nights than are needed to restore the body's fluid balance.

Food intake Water is needed to digest food and transform it into energy. For example, rats drink about 70% of their water intake during meals. They drink very little when they are deprived of food.

Learning Drinking often involves anticipation of future needs. Animals learn to drink to prevent future water deficits. In much the same way, joggers learn that drinking before running, especially on a hot day, can prevent water deficits on route.

Stopping drinking

What motivates animals and humans to stop drinking? Set-point theories suggest that once bodily fluids are restored to their optimum level (the set point), then drinking will stop. However, there are a number of problems with this view.

- First, it cannot account for spontaneous drinking, ie drinking which is not required to make up water deficits.
- Second, when deprivation-induced drinking to restore fluid deficits occurs, it usually stops before the fluid has been absorbed into the body from the digestive system. As with eating, receptors in the mouth or digestive tract may be

capable of relating the amount of water taken in to bodily needs, and terminating drinking at the appropriate point. This is supported by evidence that direct injection of water into the stomach, bypassing the mouth, results in over-drinking. The stomach also appears to play a role. This has been demonstrated by arranging for the water which an animal drinks to bypass the stomach by using a tube which redirects all water outside the body. In this case, the animal will go on drinking continuously. Therefore, as with eating, stomach distension (swelling) may call a halt when an uncomfortably large volume has been taken in.

Key terms

Deprivation-induced drinking *Drinking that is motivated or induced by a deprivation or lack of bodily fluids.*

Intracellular fluids *Fluids inside the cells.*

Extracellular fluids *Bodily fluids outside the cells.*

Cellular dehydration *A reduction of intracellular fluids.*

Hypovolemia *A reduction of extracellular fluids, particularly of blood volume.*

Solutes *Substances dissolved in liquids.*

Osmotic pressure *Pressure that draws fluid through the cell membrane.*

Osmotic thirst *The motivation to drink as a result of osmotic pressure.*

Osmoreceptors *Cells which detect cellular dehydration.*

Volumetric thirst *The motivation to drink as a result of hypovolemia.*

Spontaneous drinking *Drinking beyond the level needed to restore the body's fluid balance.*

Summary

1. Homeostasis refers to the tendency for physiological processes to maintain balance or equilibrium.

2. The motivation of physiological states such as hunger and thirst is a complex process. These states are not regulated by a simple 'on/off' mechanism.

3. The lateral hypothalamus (LH) plays a role in promoting feeding, the ventromedial hypothalamus (VMH) in ceasing feeding, but several other brain centres are also involved.

4. The initiation and cessation of food seeking and eating are probably triggered by glucose (sugar) levels in the blood – in particular the artero-venous difference in glucose content.

5. Cessation of eating probably depends upon a range of other factors, including peripheral feedback from the mouth and stomach.

6. Long-term control of food intake involves many systems, stored fat levels being particularly important.

7. Feedback from the mouth and stomach on the bulk of food eaten is likely to provide a rough estimate of nutritional intake.

8. Most theories assume that the motivation to drink is based on the need to restore the body's fluid levels.

9. Such theories fail to explain spontaneous drinking.

Activity 2   Spontaneous drinking

Item A   Anticipatory drinking

Drinking is greater with a high-protein diet. Proteins draw large amounts of water out of the body into the digestive system. The drinking behaviour of rats placed on a high-protein diet was observed. At first, drinking increased some time after each meal. Later, they drank considerable amounts of water during, rather than after, the meal. It appeared that the rats anticipated their fluid requirements and learned to drink more during the meal in order to prevent future water deficits.

Adapted from Fitzsimons & LeMagnen, 1969

The bar chart shows the results of an experiment using three groups of rats. Each group was given fluid to drink for one hour. Those in the first group were given water, those in the second group were given flavoured water, and those in the third group were given a different flavour of water every 15 minutes for one hour.

Item B   Fluid consumption

Adapted from Rolls et al., 1980

Question

There is more to drinking than restoring bodily fluid deficits. Discuss with reference to Items A and B.

Unit 2 Theories of motivation

KEY ISSUES

1 **What are the main theories of motivation?**
2 **What are their strengths and weaknesses?**

If we ask, 'what motivates behaviour?' we are asking a big question: 'why do we behave at all?' Motivation is concerned with all the processes that trigger behaviours, and that direct and sustain them. The motivation to be successful in business is rather different from the motivation to eat, or to avoid pain, but these have some features in common – they all involve directed behaviours aimed at particular goals or targets; they are behaviours which are often pursued with great energy, vigour, determination and persistence; they can be seen to have survival benefits and to meet personal needs. Motivation theory seeks to explain how and why human and non-human animals are motivated to behave in particular ways.

2.1   Instinct theories

Prior to the 19th century, it had been assumed that non-human animal behaviour consisted of actions based on *instinct*, while human behaviour was directed by reason and free will. Charles Darwin's theory of evolution overturned this idea, since it argued there were basic similarities underlying the behaviour of all species. As a result, human behaviour was seen to be guided and directed by instinct.

Instincts are inborn, genetically determined programmes that are expressed in the same way in all members of a species, and which have survival value. The migratory habits of birds which take them many thousands of miles, using a variety of guidance systems, cannot be explained by simple learning. Over many generations, this complex sequence of behaviour presumably became innate because the migrating bird had an advantage over the non-migrator. It moved to a warm climate as opposed to remaining in the same place with the risk of dying from cold and lack of food.

Migrating birds

William James (1890) proposed a wide range of human instincts, some shared with lower animals such as the need to eat, drink and reproduce, some exclusively human such as assertiveness, curiosity, jealousy, love, and sociability. Excited psychologists 'discovered' more and more instinctive human behaviours – thousands of them – until the whole exercise became ridiculous.

Evaluation There are a number of problems with instinct theory. They include the following.

- First, in its earlier versions, it largely ignored the role of learning. However, later theorists accepted that instincts could be modified by learning.
- Second, the argument is circular. Consider the logic of the following. People often express jealousy in their behaviour. Why? Because they have an instinct for jealousy. How do we know? Because they often express jealousy in their behaviour. And so the argument goes round in circles, explaining nothing.
- Third, the vast number of instincts 'discovered' – at one point, around 15,000 human instincts had been identified (Tolman, 1932). However, there was no direct, independent evidence for their existence.

Key term

Instinct *An inborn, genetically determined pattern of behaviour which motivates and directs members of a species to behave in a particular way.*

2.2 Drive theories

Unhappy with the poor explanatory power of the concept of instinct, psychologists in the 1920s developed the concept of *drive*. Drive refers to an internal state of the organism which promotes and energises particular classes of behaviour, for example, hunger, thirst, sex, and curiosity. Some theorists contrast *primary drives*, relating to primary biological functions such as hunger, thirst, sleep, pain avoidance and the maintenance of temperature, with *secondary drives* said to be acquired via learning, such as the need for social contact and exploration. Others contrast *homeostatic* or *regulatory drives*, which restore energy or fluid deficits (hunger, thirst), with *non-regulatory drives* which are not necessary for homeostatic balance (sex, curiosity).

Homeostatic drive theory

The idea of homeostasis was introduced by Walter B. Cannon in the 1920s. It assumes that the body's internal environment must be kept constant in order to ensure physical wellbeing and survival. Systems have developed to regulate the body's internal processes in order to maintain homeostasis – ie, a state of balance or equilibrium. These systems monitor and maintain fluid, energy and temperature levels. For example, if fluid levels are above or below the optimum (ideal) level, they are returned to the optimum level and homeostasis is restored.

Homeostatic drive theory states that physiological imbalances activate internal or homeostatic drives. For example, there are internal drives for food (hunger) and for water (thirst). These drives continue to operate until homeostasis is restored. For example, the drive for water motivates drinking behaviour until the body's fluid has returned to the optimum level.

Homeostatic drive theory is a physiological theory. It assumes that physiological systems such as the central nervous system – in particular the brain – and the endocrine system, via various hormones, monitor and regulate the body's internal processes and maintain homeostasis.

But how does the concept of drive translate into behaviour? How does it relate to learning and changes in behaviour? How can it account for motivations which are not directly concerned with the body's internal processes? Answers to these questions require a theory of motivation which combines both physiological and psychological approaches. One attempt to do this is *drive reduction theory*.

Hull's drive reduction theory

The American behaviourist Clark Hull (1943) argued that the basis of all motivation and learning is *drive reduction*. According to Hull, a drive is an internal state of bodily arousal and tension. Drive states are unpleasant – they produce negative feelings. Many behaviours are motivated to reduce the arousal and negative feelings produced by drive states. For example, eating and drinking reduce the hunger drive and the thirst drive. Once *drive* reduction has been achieved, arousal is reduced and the behaviour stops.

How does the idea of drive reduction explain learning? Behaviours which reduce drive states are rewarding – they reduce unpleasant feelings. In other words, these behaviours are positively reinforced because they lead to drive reduction. They are therefore likely to be learned and repeated. For example, one way to encourage a rat to learn the correct route through a maze is to deprive it of food, and place food at the end point of the maze. Obtaining food reduces the hunger drive, decreases unpleasant feelings of tension and arousal and provides positive reinforcement. As a result, the animal will be motivated to learn the route through the maze.

All motivated behaviours are seen to stem from a few basic homeostatic or *primary drives*. This view is illustrated by the following example from attachment theory. Hunger is a primary drive. When a baby is hungry it enters a drive state and is motivated to find some way to reduce the discomfort that hunger brings. At this stage, the baby can do little more than howl but that is often sufficient to encourage an adult – usually the mother – to feed it. This results in drive reduction and the child soon learns that food is a reward or positive reinforcer. Food is a *primary reinforcer* because it is reinforcing in itself. The person who supplies the food is associated with the food and becomes a *secondary reinforcer*. After a while, the mere presence of the mother is a source of comfort and security to the child, and as a result, the child develops an attachment to her. Attachment is a *secondary drive* that the child learns because the mother is so strongly associated with food (Dollard & Miller, 1950). In this way, motivated behaviours which do not directly satisfy bodily needs, are learned.

Evaluation

Today, drive reduction theory is generally regarded as a brave, but largely unsuccessful, attempt to explain motivation. The following points outline the main criticisms of the theory.

- First, are all motivated behaviours developed from primary drives which meet basic bodily needs? It is difficult to see how behaviours like watching a movie, participating in a sporting event, reading a book or playing the guitar are derived from primary drives such as hunger and thirst.

- Second, is drive reduction the main motivation for behaviour? Drive reduction theory assumes that all animals, including human beings, are motivated to reduce tension and arousal. This suggests that peace and quiet are preferable to states of tension and arousal. However, evidence suggests that people often actively seek activities which raise their levels of tension and arousal – for example, watching and participating in sporting events; the thrills and excitement of the fairground such as roller-coaster riding; watching thrillers and horror movies. Drive reduction theory is unable to explain the attraction of these behaviours (Gleitman et al., 1999).

- Third, can drive reduction theory satisfactorily explain the motivation for eating and drinking? At first sight, drive reduction theory offers a reasonable explanation – hunger and thirst are unpleasant drives so food and drink provide positive rewards by reducing these drives. However, in both animals and humans, there is more to eating and drinking than satisfying hunger and thirst. For example, rats will drink saccharin-sweetened water well beyond that point needed to restore their fluid levels (Sheffield & Roby, 1950). And people will eat tasty puddings despite the fact that their hunger drive has been reduced. In such cases, those involved continue to consume simply because they like the food and drink on offer. Incentive theory (see below) provides an explanation for such behaviours, drive reduction theory does not.

- Fourth, can motivated behaviour occur without drive reduction and positive reinforcement? For example, can rats learn a maze without food rewards which reduce their hunger drive? Experiments have shown that rats can learn a maze without external rewards such as food. It appears that spatial learning in animals does not depend on drive reduction and reinforcement (Tolman, 1948).

- Fifth, the argument used in drive reduction theory is circular. It assumes that there are a number of drives ranging from sex and curiosity drives to hunger and thirst drives. But how do we know these drives exist? The argument runs as follows: an animal eats in order to reduce its hunger drive. We know a hunger drive exists because the animal eats.

  In order to break the circularity, we need to look for evidence of internal drive states that can be measured, for example a group of neurons which become active when an animal is deprived of something (eg, water) and which decrease their activity when the appropriate reinforcer is presented (ie, when the animal drinks). As outlined in the previous unit, such centres exist in the hypothalamus, promoting drinking and eating, so there is some physiological support for the drive-reduction model. However, this only applies to primary, homeostatic drives such as hunger and thirst. And, as noted earlier, there is a further problem – animals sometimes continue to eat and drink beyond the point needed to restore their energy and fluid levels.

- Sixth, there is evidence that behaviour can be motivated by directly stimulating areas in the brain. This increases rather than decreases drive and arousal. This evidence is examined in the following section.

Key terms

Drive *An internal state which motivates particular types of behaviour.*

Homeostatic drive/regulatory drive *A drive which regulates the body's internal processes in order to maintain homeostasis – a state of balance or equilibrium. Examples include hunger and thirst drives.*

Non-regulatory drive *A drive which is not directed to the restoration of equilibrium.*

Drive reduction *The reduction of a drive state, for example reducing hunger.*

Primary drive *An innate drive arising from a biological need such as hunger or thirst.*

Secondary drive *An acquired or learned drive which is not directly related to a biological need.*

Positive reinforcer *A reward. Rewarding behaviour leads to that behaviour being learned and repeated.*

Primary reinforcer *A positive reinforcer that is rewarding in itself, for example, food.*

Secondary reinforcer *Something that is associated with a primary reinforcer often enough that it becomes a reward itself.*

2.3 Physiological approaches

Electrical self-stimulation of the brain (ESB)

Is there a physiological basis for motivation? There is evidence that when particular areas of the brain are activated, they can motivate certain behaviours. These areas are sometimes known as *pleasure centres* or *reward pathways* because they provide pleasure or rewards.

Quite by accident, Olds and Milner (1954) discovered that small groups of neurons in the brain act as centres for reinforcement. When an electrode is placed in these centres, an animal will work continuously to obtain *electrical self-stimulation of the brain* (ESB). Olds and Milner placed rats in a

Figure 5 ESB

lever

electrical stimulator

A rat is trained to press a lever for a reward. In this case, the reward is a brief burst of electrical stimulation delivered to a brain centre via a fine wire electrode.

Skinner box so they could press a bar to obtain stimulation (see Figure 5). They found that bar-pressing for ESB is frantic – sometimes hundreds of times per minute. Animals will press to exhaustion and hungry animals will press for ESB in preference to eating.

ESB apparently mimics the activity that normally occurs in these areas when normal rewards are experienced (food, drink, sex and drug effects), although there is a difference – no drive-reduction effects are observed with ESB. There are no constraints or 'brakes' on ESB (such as the gut distension or rising glucose levels that limit eating) so that ESB does not extinguish – the behaviour it motivates does not end, except with exhaustion. In fact, far from reducing drive, ESB increases it.

ESB centres are distributed in wide areas of the forebrain, but they overlap considerably with those involved in eating and drinking. One such reward pathway is the *medial forebrain bundle* (MFB) – see Figure 6 – which passes close to the lateral hypothalamus, an area involved in the initiation of feeding (see Unit 1).

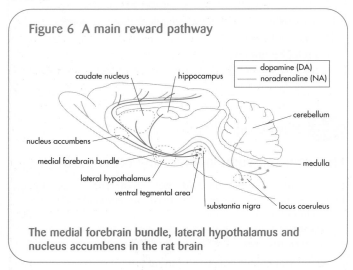

Figure 6   A main reward pathway

The medial forebrain bundle, lateral hypothalamus and nucleus accumbens in the rat brain

The existence of reward pathways explains why stimuli used as rewards do not need to reduce homeostatic drives. In experiments rats learn to perform tasks when rewarded with saccharin pellets. But these are not nutritious – they do not reduce the hunger drive. In order to motivate eating, it is only necessary that the pellets create activity in reward pathways. Drugs, such as crack cocaine, which create pleasurable highs probably have the same, but more dramatic, effects.

Incentive or expectancy theory

An incentive is something that encourages behaviour. It is based on the expectation of a desirable outcome. For example, if the smell or appearance of food is pleasant, then this can be an incentive to eat because of the expectation of a pleasant taste. Incentive or expectancy theory emphasises external factors that provide motivation – such factors *pull* people in particular directions. By comparison drive theory emphasises internal factors which *push* people in particular directions.

Expectation is important. To be presented with food that cannot be reached and eaten is, for a hungry individual, a frustrating and negative event. If food is presented and we know for certain that it is available to eat, then that expectancy can become highly reinforcing. In the words of A.A. Milne's honey-

loving bear, Winnie the Pooh, eating honey is not the best thing in the world; the best moment of all is 'just before you start eating the honey'.

Incentives are stimuli that produce motivated behaviour that is not directed by an internal need or drive. Drive reduction theory cannot explain incentives. For example, it cannot explain why non-nutritious foods such as saccharin are rewarding. Reward pathways can be excited by any pleasurable event or its expectation, such as eating pleasant-tasting food or the anticipation of doing so.

Optimal arousal theory

Drive reduction theory states that the main motivation for behaviour is to reduce the tension and arousal produced by drives. As noted earlier, one of the main criticisms of drive reduction theory is that many behaviours appear to be motivated by a desire to increase rather than reduce arousal. Optimal arousal theory deals with this criticism. It assumes that each individual has their own optimal level of arousal, which they strive to maintain. When arousal is too high they become anxious and seek to avoid stimulation but if the level is too low they become bored and seek out stimulation to increase it (Fowler, 1965).

Arousal is the general level of activity or activation of the brain and nervous system. For example, high levels of arousal produce alertness accompanied by increased heart rate, blood pressure, muscle tension and respiration.

There is evidence which suggests that low levels of arousal lead to a craving for stimulation. Consider the following sensory deprivation experiment. Participants were placed in a floatation chamber, floating on water, supported by air cuffs, with ears blocked and eyes masked so they could receive no external stimulation. In such situations, people develop hallucinations as the brain generates stimulation and arousal. Students who were paid well for remaining in an isolation chamber were able to stand it for 2-3 days only.

Studies of monkeys indicate that they sometimes attempt to generate arousal rather than reduce it. In other words, they seek out stimulation rather than try to avoid it. Research by Harlow (1950) shows that rhesus monkeys will spend considerable time working out how to open latches attached to a board. They received no external reward (such as food) for opening the latches. Apparently, they learned to open them 'just for the fun of it'. One interpretation of this behaviour is that the monkeys were bored and they looked for stimulation in order to restore their arousal to the optimal level.

Optimal arousal theory has difficulty explaining why some people seek out arousing experiences while others tend to avoid them. Individuals who seek out exciting activities are known as *sensation-seekers*. In terms of optimal arousal theory, their usual level of arousal should be low. Some support for this view is provided by studies of children in classrooms who draw attention to themselves by clowning around and misbehaving. There is evidence that the arousal levels of these children are normally low (Nelson, 1992).

Differences in personality may be related to differences in people's optimal level of arousal. One way of distinguishing personality types is to place them on a dimension ranging from introversion to extraversion (Eysenck, 1970). This dimension has been measured with a personality questionnaire. The introvert has a very reactive nervous system, and is quickly and highly aroused by relatively ordinary, everyday events. The extreme extravert is someone with an initially low level of arousal, who craves a lot of company, changes cars, houses and partners relatively often and is attracted to dangerous sports such as skydiving. Illegal drug use, high coffee intake and cigarette smoking are more common in extraverts, presumably because these have arousing stimulant effects. In summary, the extreme extravert is a sensation-seeker. Personality may provide part of the explanation for differences in people's optimal levels of arousal.

Evaluation

Optimal arousal theory has a number of advantages.

- First, it provides an explanation for increasing as well as decreasing arousal.
- Second, it accepts that a variety of behaviours can increase or decrease arousal. For example, boredom can be overcome in many different ways. Note the contrast with drive reduction theory which tends to see particular behaviours directed towards the reduction of particular drives – for example, the hunger drive promotes behaviours specifically directed towards obtaining food.

However, optimal arousal theory has a number of disadvantages.

- A variety of indicators have been developed for measuring arousal. They include heart rate, blood pressure, degree of sweating, and respiration level. However, it has proved difficult to develop measures of arousal which can be applied to everyone. For example, some people may sweat heavily and have high blood pressure and these may have

Key terms

Pleasure centres/reward pathways *Areas of the brain which produce pleasure when stimulated.*

Electrical self-stimulation of the brain (ESB) *Self-stimulation of pleasure centres produced by a brief burst of electricity.*

Medial forebrain bundle *A collection of neurons whose axons pass through the hypothalamus where electrical self-stimulation is especially rewarding.*

Arousal *The general level of activity or activation of the brain and nervous system.*

Incentive *Stimuli that produce motivated behaviour which is not directed by an internal need or drive.*

Sensation-seekers *Individuals who seek out exciting activities which raise their level of arousal.*

Introvert *A person with a highly reactive nervous system who is quickly aroused by relatively ordinary, everyday events.*

Extravert *A person who craves excitement in order to raise their arousal level.*

Activity 3   Pleasure-seeking

Item A   Sky-diving

Item B   Curiosity

Young rhesus monkeys attempting to open a latch 'just for the fun of it'.

Item C   Sweet taste

A rat pressing a lever for saccharin pellets

Questions

1 How might drive reduction theory have problems explaining Items A, B and C?

2 How might optimal arousal theory explain Items A and B?

3 How might incentive or expectancy theory explain Item C?

little to do with their arousal level. As a result, it has proved difficult to assess optimal arousal levels.

- Researchers have tended to measure optimal arousal level in terms of behaviour. Thus if people can be classified in terms of their behaviour as sensation-seekers, then they are seen to have high optimal levels of arousal. However, this results in a circular argument. If they like fast cars and dangerous sports they have high optimal arousal levels. How do we know this? Because they like fast cars and dangerous sports. To break out of this circular argument, we need an independent measure of arousal.

2.4 Psychological theories

Psychological theories of motivation, as their name suggests, emphasise psychological rather than biological factors. They tend to focus on motivated behaviours which are not directed towards the satisfaction of biological needs or the reduction of biological drives. In addition, they focus on human motivation rather than attempting to explain motivation in both human and non-human animals.

Maslow's hierarchy of needs

In the 1950s, Abraham Maslow (1908-1970) developed one of the most famous psychological theories of human motivation. He believed that human beings are motivated to satisfy a series of needs. These needs are hierarchical in the sense that lower-level needs must at least be partly satisfied before the needs above them can motivate behaviour (see Figure 7). For example, if physiological needs, such as the need for food and water, are not met, then there is little chance of satisfying higher-level needs. For instance, in time of famine, people will be preoccupied with finding food and have little time or energy to direct to other needs.

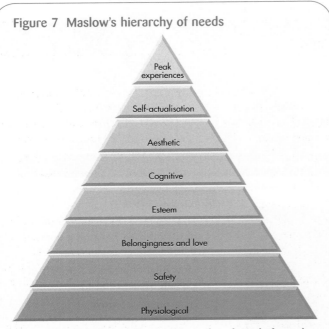

Figure 7   Maslow's hierarchy of needs

Peak experiences
Self-actualisation
Aesthetic
Cognitive
Esteem
Belongingness and love
Safety
Physiological

Maslow identified the following hierarchy of needs from the most basic – physiological needs – through to the highest level – peak experiences.

Physiological These include the need for food, water, oxygen, sleep and sexual expression.

Safety The need for protection, security, comfort and freedom from fear.

Belongingness and love The need for acceptance from others, a sense of belonging to a group, and the need to give and receive love.

Esteem The need for a sense of self-worth, and for respect, approval and recognition from others. The need to feel competent and capable.

Cognitive The need for knowledge and understanding in order to find meaning in life and to grow intellectually. The need for novelty and to satisfy curiosity.

Aesthetic The need to find beauty, order and symmetry in life and in the world.

Self-actualisation The need to realise one's potential, to achieve fulfilment and fully develop all the positive aspects of oneself. At this level, the individual is spontaneous, open, and independent of environmental pressures. Maslow believed that only 1% of the population achieve this ultimate level of personal growth.

Peak experiences The self-actualised person is more likely to have peak experiences – profound and significant moments in life resulting in 'a feeling of great ecstasy and awe' (Maslow, 1970). Peak experiences may come from watching a sunset, looking at a great work of art, or listening to a symphony.

Maslow distinguished between *deficiency needs* and *growth needs*. Deficiency needs are those in the lower part of the hierarchy. They motivate people when there is a deficiency or lack of something – for example, a lack of food or a lack of security. Growth needs are found in the higher levels of the hierarchy. Their satisfaction contributes to personal growth and fulfilment, in other words, to self-actualisation. Growth needs make people human, their satisfaction creates truly human beings.

Evaluation

In its favour, Maslow's theory does attempt to account for the more complex human motivations, some of which are largely ignored by the theories presented earlier in the unit. Despite this, his theory has been widely criticised.

- First, the ranking of needs in the hierarchy has been criticised. When people are asked to list their own needs in order of importance, the order rarely matches Maslow's hierarchy (Mills, 1985).
- Second, Maslow's claim that lower-level needs must be largely satisfied before higher-level needs can motivate behaviour has been criticised. Maslow admitted that there are exceptions – for example, 'starving artists' who tend to ignore physiological needs in order to pursue their art. But, there are plenty of other examples which question Maslow's claim. For example, parents who give food to their children in time of famine are meeting higher-level needs (love) at the expense of lower-level needs (food).
- Third, Maslow sees self-actualisation as a positive achievement – the height of truly human self-expression. His list of self-actualisers includes Albert Einstein, Martin Luther King, Abraham Lincoln and Ludwig van Beethoven, people

who have fulfilled their potential, and who personify a range of admirable characteristics. But what about the likes of Adolf Hitler and Saddam Hussein – self-made men who rose to great heights and may well have realised their potential for evil? Shouldn't they be seen as self-actualised? (Gleitman et al., 1999).

- Fourth, Maslow's hierarchy may be limited to the USA or at best to Western society. In other words, it may be culture-bound. American culture emphasises the individual – individual achievement, individual responsibility, self-fulfilment, self-sufficiency, self-determination. Self-actualisation fits neatly into this focus. By comparison, non-Western, collectivist cultures place more emphasis on the group rather than the individual, on collective rather than individual achievement and responsibility. Maslow's hierarchy of needs may be inappropriate for non-Western cultures (Moghaddam, 1998).

- Fifth, a major problem with research into motivation is the identification of motives. This is particularly so for higher level needs. How do we *know* whether people's behaviour is motivated by self-actualisation needs, aesthetic needs, belongingness needs and so on? The answer is, we can't be sure. Nor can we be sure that people can accurately report their own needs hierarchy. Research data on motives is at best inconclusive, at worst little more than guesswork.

In addition, several motivations can be attributed to a single behaviour. Is somebody cooking a tasty meal for their partner because they are hungry, seeking approval, fearing their partner's rejection, because they want to enjoy an aesthetic experience, or to achieve personal fulfilment – or all of these things simultaneously?

As a result of these problems, there is little direct evidence to either support or reject Maslow's theory.

Summary

1. Instinct theories see motivated behaviours resulting from genetically-based directives. However, there is no independent evidence for instincts in humans.

2. Drive theories see inborn and learned drives as the basis for motivated behaviours.

3. Drive reduction theory argues that many behaviours are motivated to reduce the arousal and negative feelings produced by drive states. However, the theory fails to explain many aspects of motivation – for example, it cannot explain the motivation for activities that raise arousal.

4. Behaviour can be motivated by the activation of pleasure centres or reward pathways in the brain.

5. Incentive or expectancy theory states that behaviour is motivated by the expectation of a rewarding outcome.

6. Optimal arousal theory assumes that each individual has their own optimal level of arousal which they are motivated to maintain.

7. Maslow's hierarchy of needs theory states that lower-level needs must be largely satisfied before higher-level needs can motivate behaviour. It is extremely difficult to identify the motives which direct behaviour. As a result, there is little concrete evidence either to support or reject Maslow's theory.

Unit 3 Emotion

KEY ISSUES

1. **What are the main physiological theories of emotion?**
2. **What part do brain structures play in emotion?**
3. **What role does facial expression play in emotion?**

3.1 How do we recognise emotion?

We all know when we feel emotional – fearful, angry, sad, excited. The emotion is usually pretty obvious in these extreme states, often accompanied by grimacing, scowling, crying or laughing. But emotion does not only refer to extreme states – mild emotional states are also important, such as relief and apprehension. Emotions are often related to expectations and uncertainty about rewards and punishments. Charles Dickens'

Mr Micawber, who constantly teeters on the brink of financial disaster, says that 'happiness' is when income exceeds expenditure, but when expenditure exceeds income, the result is 'misery'. Emotional feelings are internal, but they are usually influenced by external environmental events.

Even psychologists researching emotion cannot define it precisely. A comprehensive definition was attempted by Kleinginna and Kleinginna (1981). They define emotion in a general way, as a complex set of interactions among objective and subjective factors – objective events in the world, and our subjective feelings about them which are mediated by the nervous system and hormonal changes. Emotions (a) give rise to affective experiences, such as feelings of arousal, pleasure and displeasure; (b) generate cognitive processes such as the labelling of an experience as happy, or sad, and (c) cause physiological adjustments throughout the body such as speeding or slowing the heart rate. Factors (a) (b) and (c) combine to cause (d) behaviour that is usually expressive, goal-directed and adaptive. For example, running away from a predator is expressive of fear, it is directed toward a goal (to escape danger) and it is adaptive (it can prevent injury or death).

This definition is similar to that of motivation. As we saw in the last unit, emotion is hard to separate from motivation since motivated behaviours are invariably accompanied by emotion – escaping from a threat involves fear, winning a race is accompanied by elation. Some have argued that emotional feelings tend to occur during an event, or after it, as the behaviour finishes (after escaping, after winning), whereas motivation causes the behaviour in the first place.

How many emotions are there?

Most theorists believe that there are between 6 and 10 basic *primary* emotions. Complex emotions such as guilt and contempt may result from combinations of two or more primary emotions. The primary emotions are assumed to have evolved over many generations because they have proved adaptive and promoted survival. Plutchik (1984) has proposed that humans have an innate set of 8 primary emotions (see Figure 8). These consist of 4 pairs of opposite emotions (shown inside the 'emotion wheel'), adjacent emotions combining to form secondary emotions (outside the wheel), while more complex emotions result from more remote combinations.

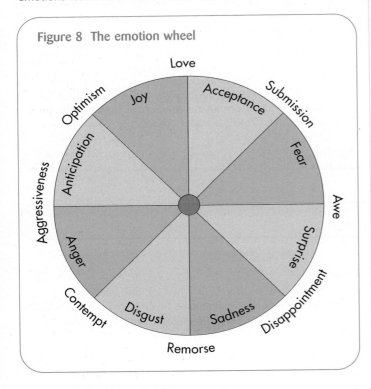

Figure 8 The emotion wheel

What is emotional behaviour?

Emotional behaviours include running away from a danger, banging a fist in temper when frustrated, or crying when sad. But in humans especially, emotional behaviours are often not so obvious and demonstrative. Silence can be highly emotionally charged, and involve high arousal. Human emotional behaviours often involve facial expressions, which communicate our feelings to others. As we shall see later, these might also be used as feedback cues to label our emotions. Since we possess some 40 facial muscles, a variety of expressions can be formed which can express a wide range of subtle emotional states.

However it is important to note that facial expressions can be misleading – expressions are used as social communications, and may not truly reflect underlying feelings.

Arousal and emotion

Emotion involves feelings, or *affect*, for example of happiness or anger. These involve physiological changes including physiological arousal. Arousal is associated with a high level of activity in the Ascending Reticular Activating System (ARAS, the reticular formation in the brainstem) and in the sympathetic branch of the autonomic nervous system (ANS). Activity in the sympathetic ANS affects many physiological processes: heart rate (the pulse starts racing, perhaps with heart palpitations, in panic and fear situations), palmar sweating (the hands especially become sticky with sweat), nervous perspiration, changes in blood flow to the gut and stomach leading to changes in digestion (experienced as 'butterflies in the stomach') and a dry mouth, due to the inhibition of the parasympathetic branch of the nervous system which causes salivation. We associate these bodily states with emotion.

Key terms

Affect *Positive or negative feelings.*

ARAS *Ascending reticular activation system, in the core of the brain stem, which causes general arousal when activated.*

Measurement of emotion

Self-report questionnaires Emotional states can be measured using questionnaires, for example the Mood Adjective Check List in which individuals rate themselves on measures such as angry, energetic, elated, or suspicious. The State-Trait Anxiety Inventory (Spielberger et al., 1970) provides measures of both the current state of anxiety and longer-term proneness to anxiety. These are self-report questionnaires, scores from which enable individuals to be rated by comparison with the general population. But questionnaire measures suffer from the drawback that there is no way of assessing whether participants' self-reports are accurate.

Physiological measures Often used in studies of emotion, these include a range of indicators that reflect the level of activity within the autonomic nervous system, central nervous system and skeletal muscles, and general level of arousal. Measures include heart rate, blood pressure, muscular tension, respiration depth and rate, brain activity, and skin conductance (galvanic skin response). (Electrical conductance across the skin increases when an individual becomes anxious, because of the release of electrolytes in perspiration, so conductance is measured as the GSR or galvanic skin response). Sometimes several measures can be recorded simultaneously using a polygraph recorder – this is commonly used in lie detection, on the assumption that lying will be accompanied by emotional physiological reactions. However, measures of emotion are fraught with difficulties. In particular, individuals differ enormously in the type and magnitude of physiological change which they show when they change emotional state.

3.2 Peripheral theories of emotion

Peripheral theories see the peripheral nervous system (PNS) as the source of emotions. The PNS consists of two divisions: 1) the autonomic nervous system which controls basic bodily functions such as the heart rate, breathing, and activity in the stomach and intestines and 2) the somatic nervous system which connects the central nervous system (the brain and the spinal cord) with the organs and with the muscles of the body.

According to peripheral theories, feedback to the brain from the body's organs and muscles generates emotions. In particular, arousal in the PNS feeds back to the brain where it is experienced as emotion.

The James-Lange theory

William James in the USA in 1884, and a Danish psychologist, Carl Lange in 1885, came up with this theory almost simultaneously, and so it carries both their names. James summarised the theory as follows: 'We feel sorry because we cry, angry because we strike, afraid because we tremble'. Imagine that you are running from a hungry bear. Are you running because you know the bear is dangerous, or do you feel fearful because you are running? According to the James-Lange model, what we normally speak of as emotion is sensing our body's reactions to stimuli that elicit activity in the peripheral nervous system. In the case of the bear, our brain registers the behaviours (running away and pounding heart) and interprets this as fear. To put it simply, we are fearful *because* we are running.

Most people would expect the opposite, but there is some sense to this suggestion. After all a dog will run from a frightening stimulus, just as a human does, but it cannot use a verbal label such as 'fear' as its reason for running. In humans, certain types of stimulus may direct sequences of behaviour and autonomic responses, which we can only categorise and label as they occur, or after they have occurred. Behaving quickly and thinking later would have obvious survival value – during evolution, animals that waited for cognitive appraisal of a threat before running may well have become a predator's lunch. Certainly, humans can infer emotion from bodily changes with statements like, 'I feel anxious, but I don't know why'. In one study, in which autonomic arousal was produced using the drug adrenaline, some participants did report feeling 'as if fearful or angry'. The theory depends upon our being able to identify the feeling of emotion which we experience on the basis of feedback from the body – in particular feedback from the viscera (internal organs such as the heart, liver, stomach, spleen, and intestines).

Evaluation of the James-Lange Theory

Points against The physiologist Walter Cannon (1927) led the criticism of this theory, putting forward five main points.

- First, the same visceral changes occur in many different emotional states, and also in states that we would not label as emotional. For example, both sexual attraction and fear involve speeding of the heart rate and deepening respiration. In addition, the visceral organs of the body, such as stomach, spleen and liver, are rather insensitive structures producing general physiological responses that lack the subtlety needed to discriminate and label emotions.
- Second, the physiological effects that occur, particularly in 'emergency' states which threaten danger, do so relatively slowly whereas the perception of threat is immediate. Should you narrowly miss having an accident, it is only after the event that the heart begins to race and your limbs feel jelly-like.
- Third, the James-Lange theory would predict that simple direct manipulation of the viscera, or simple exercise would produce emotional states. According to the theory, a cross-country run should produce emotional states, since it increases heart rate, but there is no evidence for exercise alone causing emotions similar to fear or elation. Strenuous regular exercise has been said to improve depression. The autonomic arousal caused by exercise can have some influence on mood, although this effect could equally be due to the release of opiate-like chemicals (endorphins) in the brain during exercise.
- Fourth, Cannon cited an experiment by Marañon (1924) in which participants were injected with the drug adrenaline (which causes arousal in the ANS). They reported the physiological effects of arousal (heart racing and so on) but, in many cases, no emotional changes.
- Fifth, the James-Lange theory would predict that people with damage to the spinal cord that cuts off stimulation travelling from the viscera to the brain would no longer feel emotional. But there are reports that they do. In one notable case, a participant with a lesion high up the spinal cord, which severed almost all the cord and cut off almost all autonomic feedback, reported being so angry with one of his tutors that he wanted to 'run over him a few times' with his wheelchair!

Points in favour Not all researchers agree with these criticisms. Regarding the first criticism, some have argued that different emotions can show subtly different patterns of autonomic arousal. For example, while both fear and happiness produce speeding of the heart, fear provokes a much faster acceleration. This makes sense because of the responses required in each case – fear provokes a flight or escape response, for which a rapid speeding of the heart and increased circulation of blood to muscles is beneficial, but this is not the case for happiness. Many people show heart rate acceleration when angry or fearful, but deceleration when showing disgust (Levenson, 1992). The fifth criticism is also open to dispute – the data from such studies are not conclusive, since spinal lesions never eliminate body sensation completely. Even a lesion at the neck leaves some sensory (cranial nerve) inputs to the brain intact, so some feedback is still present. Consistent with James-Lange, some studies have suggested that high lesions lead to a reduction in emotion (Lowe & Carroll, 1985). We will see later that facial feedback studies also offer some support for the theory.

Summary On balance the evidence is against the James-Lange theory as an explanation of the *causes* of emotion. However,

Key terms

Peripheral theories *Theories which argue that arousal within the peripheral nervous system is the source of emotions.*

Viscera *Internal organs such as the heart, liver, stomach, spleen and intestines.*

this does not mean that feedback from the body does not affect emotions. Running from danger may not cause fear, but it may well heighten the experience of fear. Much research has focused on emotions such as anger, fear and elation, which are often accompanied by physiological and behavioural changes. These changes, if not causing emotion, probably enhance or heighten existing emotions. However, this argument may not apply to less 'extreme' and less 'active' emotional states such as envy or shame.

3.3   Central theories of emotion

The James-Lange theory sees the peripheral nervous system as the main source of emotional behaviours and feelings. Central theories see the brain as the source of emotions. They identify specific brain centres which are seen to generate and direct emotional states and behaviours.

The Cannon-Bard theory

In 1927, Walter Cannon put forward a theory that was developed by Bard in 1934. They argued that the cerebral cortex normally exerts an inhibitory or restraining effect downward on subcortical emotion centres in the brain, particularly the thalamus. When emotionally significant stimuli reach the cortex – for example, fear resulting from the threat of injury – this inhibition is removed. The thalamus sends signals to the rest of the body – skeletal muscles, and the autonomic nervous system – that initiate appropriate emotional behaviours such as fight or escape, plus physiological changes such as increased heart rate, that enable the individual to deal with threatening situations.

In contrast to James-Lange where emotions *followed* actions, the Cannon-Bard theory states that emotional feelings and the initiation of appropriate responses occur simultaneously. According to Cannon-Bard, there is no direct causal relationship between the experience of emotion and the responses produced by the peripheral nervous system. James-Lange states that the perception of a threat produces physiological reactions which generate feelings of fear. Cannon-Bard states that the perception of a threat produces feelings of fear and physiological reactions at the same time, and that the two responses occur independently of each another.

Evaluation of Cannon-Bard

- As noted earlier, it is unlikely that feelings of emotion and physiological changes are independent. There is evidence that activity in the peripheral nervous system in response to emotional stimuli can affect emotional experience (Pinel, 1997).
- Is the thalamus central to emotion? Certainly tumours that damage the thalamus have been reported to produce serious emotional disturbances, although this can also be said of many other brain structures. In fact, structures such as the hypothalamus and others in the limbic system (see below) are more clearly related to specific emotions than the thalamus. In summary, Cannon and Bard were right to point to centres in the brain, including the cortex, as having important initiating or coordinating roles in the feeling and

the expression of emotion, but the assumption that the thalamus plays the central coordinating role was wrong.

3.4   Cognitive theories of emotion

The Schachter-Singer labelling theory

Consider the following. A person's heart is pounding. Are they experiencing fear, excitement, anger or elation? The particular emotion they feel will depend on their *cognitive appraisal* or interpretation of the situation. If the situation is interpreted as dangerous, then the person will experience fear; if the situation is seen as competitive, as in a world championship snooker game, then the person will feel excitement. The bodily reaction – in this case the pounding heart – creates a general feeling of emotionality which is then labelled and experienced as a particular emotion. This argument forms the basis of the Schachter-Singer *cognitive labelling theory*.

Schachter and Singer (1962) argued that:

- Autonomic responses – responses of the autonomic nervous system such as increasing heart rate – are important aspects of emotion.
- The responses precede and accompany the emotion, but they do not define or identify it.
- The emotional state is labelled – for example, as happiness or anger – via cognitive appraisal.

How does this work in practice? If a person is being insulted, they feel emotion. This emotionality is due to a racing heart, sweating, and deep breathing that result from autonomic activation. Cognitive appraisal labels the emotion as anger. This appraisal is based on an interpretation of the insults and on knowledge and memories about the situation and those involved.

Experimental evidence To investigate their theory, Schachter and Singer designed an experiment in which participants experienced a state of arousal produced by an injection of adrenaline. They then attempted to vary the participants' cognitive appraisal of the situation so that some would label their arousal state as happiness and others would label it as anger. If the experiment produced these results, then this would provide evidence to support cognitive labelling theory.

The participants were divided into four groups. They were told they were to be given an injection of a vitamin supplement, 'suproxin', and that the experiment was designed to study the effects of the vitamin on vision.

Group 1 (the 'informed group') were warned about possible side-effects – to expect their hands to start shaking, their heart to pound, that their face may get warm and flushed and their mouth dry. These are the expected effects of adrenaline. This group had a ready-made explanation for their arousal – they knew what they would feel and why.

Group 2 (the 'ignorant group') were told that the injection would have no side-effects. They were given no explanation for the physiological effects they would shortly experience.

Group 3 (the 'misinformed group') were given an incorrect description of the effects of adrenaline. They were told that their feet would feel numb, that they would experience an itching sensation and a slight headache.

Group 4 (the control group) were given an injection of a saline solution which has no physiological effects. Like Group 2, they were told to expect no side-effects.

Schachter and Singer then attempted to generate cognitive labels in terms of which participants would define and experience their emotions. After receiving their injections, participants from each group were placed in one of two situations. The first situation was designed to produce 'euphoria' – a feeling of well-being, of happiness. Participants entered a room individually where they were joined by a man they thought was a fellow participant. In fact he was a confederate – a skilled actor who was working with the experimenters. He laughed and joked, made paper aeroplanes and flew them, scrumpled paper into balls and used them to play a game of basketball, and generally clowned around.

The second situation was designed to produce anger. The actor began by complaining about the injections, saying that they were unfair. Participants were given questionnaires and required to answer personal and sometimes embarrassing questions about themselves and their families. The actor became increasingly angry about this 'invasion of privacy' and finally stormed out of the room, apparently in a rage. (Participants from Group 3 – the 'misinformed group' did not take part in the anger situation because it was originally seen as a control condition.)

Participants' emotions were identified and measured by their behaviour – observed from behind a one-way mirror – and self-reports obtained by questionnaires. In the euphoria situation, the self-report scores of the 'ignorant group' and the 'misinformed group' indicated twice as much happiness as the 'informed group'. The behavioural observations indicated a similar pattern, though not to the same extent. In the anger situation, the experimenters had to rely on behavioural measures since the participants – who were students – were afraid of expressing anger to the experimenters for fear of losing the marks they'd been offered for taking part in the experiment. On the basis of their behaviour, participants in the 'ignorant group' expressed considerably more anger than those in the 'informed group'.

Schachter and Singer claimed that the results of this experiment are generally as their theory would predict. Participants in groups 1, 2, and 3 had received the same injection. The majority experienced similar levels of arousal. Despite this, those in the euphoria situation labelled their arousal as happiness, those in the anger situation as anger, and each group behaved accordingly. The same physiological effects were labelled *differently* and, as a result, the participants experienced different emotions.

In addition, those in the 'ignorant' and 'misinformed' groups experienced a higher level of happiness or, in the case of the 'ignorant group' anger, then those in the 'informed group'. Unlike members of the informed group who had been provided with an explanation for their arousal state (the side-effects of their injection), those in the other two groups had no such ready-made explanation. As a result, they were more likely to be influenced by the actions of the actor and to label their emotions in terms of his behaviour.

Evaluation of cognitive labelling theory

A number of criticisms have been made both of the original experiment and of the theory itself. The criticisms of the experiment will now be examined, followed by an evaluation of the theory.

- First, adrenaline does not affect everybody in the same way. Five of the participants said they experienced no physiological effects and were eliminated from the study. This raises doubts about the findings and questions whether they can be generalised.
- Second, participants under the influence of adrenaline might simply have been more prone to *imitate* the actor's behaviour in the 'happy' and 'angry' rooms. In other words, the participants were acting out emotions rather than feeling them.
- Third, the study assumed that the labelling of emotions is based solely on external events – in this case, the actor's behaviour. But in real life, labelling involves memory, past experience and prior emotional state. The study did not take such factors into account.
- Fourth, the experiment has low ecological validity. The experimental setting, the injection, and the actor's behaviour are contrived, and far removed from the experience of emotions in everyday life.
- Fifth, replications have largely failed to confirm the results of the experiment. However, complete replications are rare, partly because the original experiment involved deception of the participants which is now regarded as unethical.

Similar experiments indicated that participants found the experience of adrenaline unpleasant. This tended to produce negative emotions even in 'happy' situations (Maslach, 1979; Marshall & Zimbardo, 1979). However there is some experimental evidence which may support Schachter and Singer's findings. For example, Sinclair et al. (1994) found that emotions experienced by participants after bursts of exercise could be influenced by cognitions manipulated by the experimenters.

Apart from criticisms of their method, Schachter and Singer's theory has also been questioned. The theory states that there is general, non-specific arousal which becomes labelled as a particular emotion, for example, as joy, anger, or sadness.

- First, as noted earlier, there is some evidence that different emotions are linked to particular physiological changes rather than to 'general' arousal.
- Second, the theory suggests that the higher the level of arousal, the more intense the emotion. But studies have shown that reducing arousal – for example, by using beta blocker drugs to reduce heart rate – does not appear to reduce emotional feelings.
- Third, the theory assumes that arousal precedes cognitive appraisal. The opposite – that cognitive appraisal comes first – may be the case, at least in certain circumstances.

In their favour, however, Schachter and Singer brought cognitive appraisal to the forefront of research on emotion.

Key terms

Cognitive theories *Theories which see cognition – thought, interpretation and assessment – as central to the experience of emotion.*

Cognitive appraisal *Assessing and evaluating the situation.*

Lazarus' cognitive appraisal theory

In contrast to the theories outlined so far, Richard Lazarus (1982) argued that cognitive appraisal always precedes emotion. That is, the expressed emotion follows only after a person has assessed the situation. Assessment of the situation is made according to its implications for the person's own well-being – how it might affect them personally. This is called *primary appraisal*. It determines the type and intensity of the emotion that will be felt. Sadness, for example, arises from the loss of something or somebody that the individual regards as especially meaningful to them, and which they cannot regain or retrieve. *Secondary appraisal* then determines the response. This is the way that emotion is expressed in behaviour. For example, feeling anger toward a parent might be expressed quite differently from anger towards a police officer. The anger may be the same but the response is different.

Lazarus based his theory on a number of experiments. In one experiment, participants were shown films of events designed to stimulate emotions, for example a safety film showing accidents in the workplace. The films were accompanied by various soundtracks, each designed to produce a different appraisal of the events. In the safety at work film, one of the soundtracks indicated that those involved were actors, leading the participants to assume that the accidents were not real. This

appraisal is an example of what Lazarus called *denial* – an appraisal which states 'it wasn't true, it wasn't really happening'. As a result, the anxiety of the participants who appraised the film in this way was substantially less than those who saw the accidents it portrayed as real.

Lazarus (1982) concluded that, 'Cognitive appraisal (of meaning and significance) underlies and is an integrated feature of all emotional states'. Critics of this view argue that although cognition and emotion often work together, emotions can be generated without cognitive appraisal, without being preceded by a cognitive process.

Emotion without cognition?

Just as emotion in animals occurs without cognitive labelling, humans too have been regarded by some theorists as possessing emotional states that are entirely independent of appraisal and cognition.

Zajonc (1980) examined studies in which stimuli such as pictures or music were presented to participants for very short time periods or while they were engaged in other tasks. When participants were later asked to select those they preferred from a wider range of stimuli, they tended to choose those already presented to them rather than additional new items. Apparently, the participants had no memory of the items previously presented to them. Zajonc argues that this indicates that emotions can occur without cognitive appraisal.

Lazarus (1982) admits that people are sometimes unaware of cognitive appraisal – it may occur on an unconscious level. But he insists that it still occurs and still precedes the expression of emotion. The problem is that he has no direct evidence for this claim.

Panksepp (1982) believes that emotional states are in-wired,

Activity 4   Theories of emotion

Question

Each of the diagrams presents a simplified version of one of the four theories outlined in this section – James-Lange, Cannon-Bard, Schachter-Singer, Lazarus. Match each diagram with a theory and briefly explain your choices.

genetically-based action patterns that can be activated in the absence of cognition. According to this theory, there are four basic emotions – fear, rage, panic and expectancy – each having its own in-wired circuitry, its own chemical coding via specific neurotransmitters, and its own coordinated command system within the brain. Certainly rage behaviour can be elicited in cats via direct electrical stimulation near the hypothalamus in the absence of any other stimulus and therefore independent of any cognitive processing. LeDoux (1996) has also argued for the independence of emotion and cognition (see Section 3.5).

In summary, most researchers now believe that emotional experience is usually preceded by cognitive processing, particularly in the case of strong emotional responses to meaningful stimuli. But they admit this is not inevitable and in some circumstances it is *possible* for emotion to occur before any cognitive evaluation has taken place. This may apply to some emotions such as anger, but is unlikely to apply to more subtle emotions such as pride, envy or disappointment.

3.5 Brain mechanisms of emotion

Studies of brain mechanisms in emotion have tended to focus on aggression, probably because aggression involves behavioural responses in animals that are clear and measurable. Animals' aggressive repertoire – snarling and fighting – has obvious parallels with the expression of aggression in humans. As a result, some researchers argue that animal data can often be applied to humans.

Changes in emotionality – particularly increased aggression – are common after severe damage to the brain in humans. In some cases, the aggression may be secondary to the brain injury. For example, an individual who has had a motorbike accident and damaged a large region of the brain and who is unable to communicate and make accurate movements may become extremely frustrated. Aggressive outbursts may reflect that frustration, and not damage to a brain aggression centre as such. On the other hand, damage to localised regions of the brain can cause extreme aggression, while electrical stimulation or lesions of particular brain areas in animals can either induce rage or tranquillity.

All branches of the nervous system and the endocrine system contribute to emotion, but here we are mainly concerned with systems within the brain. Some brain systems are non-specific, relating to general arousal (such as the ARAS), while other centres are associated with particular emotional behaviours such as aggression.

Brain centres controlling emotion

There are several connected structures in the brain that are associated with the control of emotional behaviours, in particular the structures which form the Papez loop (Figure 9). These include the amygdala, hypothalamus, cingulate gyrus, septum and hippocampus. The Papez loop (pronounced 'payps') is named after a famous anatomist, James Papez, who first suggested that this group of structures form an integrated loop concerned with emotion.

The model was later elaborated by MacLean (1949). MacLean viewed the brain as having three main levels: the hindbrain

(controlling basic physiological functions), the limbic system (controlling emotion) and the forebrain (higher cognitive functions). The limbic system includes the structures in the Papez loop. This emotion model is sometimes referred to as the Papez-MacLean model. It is generally accepted that the limbic system is responsible for integrating aspects of emotional behaviour. The Papez loop consists of several structures in which damage or electrical stimulation can give rise to emotional changes, particularly in aggression. Also, the Papez structures are well connected within the brain, with both cortical and subcortical structures. They receive inputs from the relevant sensory pathways. As a result, the Papez loop is well placed to play a central role in the regulation and control of emotional states (LeDoux, 1993).

Figure 9 The Papez loop

cingulate gyrus

fornix

septum

hypothalamus

amygdala

hippocampus

Among the structures forming the Papez loop, the amygdala has been seen as particularly prominent in recent years. In a highly aggressive species such as the lynx, removal of the amygdala can render the animal docile. LeDoux (1996) in his book *The emotional brain*, points to a number of studies of amygdala lesions and stimulation in monkeys and the effects of human amygdala damage which highlight its role, particularly in the control of aggression. He argues that emotional responses can be elicited independently of the cortex – in other words, without conscious thought. LeDoux sees these pre-cognitive emotional responses as adaptive in situations where cognitive appraisal would introduce a dangerous delay in responding to threat.

In primates, damage to parts of the amygdala (and to the closely associated structure, the septum) can have dramatic effects on social relations, including a 'taming' effect – monkeys given such lesions become less fearful and more interactive with humans. However, because they typically misinterpret aggressive and social signals from other monkeys, they can be over-aggressive to members of their own species, and they rarely survive. In laboratory studies of a monkey troupe, an amygdala lesion in the most dominant and aggressive monkey resulted in its dropping down the social hierarchy (Pribram, 1962). Amygdala removal has been carried out on troublesome domestic pets, but damage to regions of the limbic system or frontal lobes can have unpredictable effects. In some it leads to quietening and in others to heightened aggression. This is important because it indicates that there are opposing centres in the brain, some eliciting aggression, others suppressing it. Rabies is a disease which leads to violent fury, as a result of damage caused by the disease to parts of the temporal lobe including the hippocampus and amygdala.

Kluver and Bucy (1939) found that lesions of the front pole of the temporal lobe in monkeys (also damaging the amygdala) could produce significant changes in emotion – the animals showed a variety of symptoms including increased sexuality, and absence of fear. They would try to pick up a lighted match, and show no response to a stimulus such as a snake which provokes terror in normal monkeys. They became placid, tame and apparently lost the ability to display rage.

In humans, temporal lobe epilepsy (*overactivity* in the temporal lobe) can provoke heightened emotional reactions, including extreme aggression in about 10% of patients. Theories that assume extreme violence in humans to be due to abnormalities in these control systems are known as *loss-of-control* theories. The implication is that control could be restored by lesioning or stimulating an appropriate part of the brain. Aggressive behaviour in epileptic patients may be controllable via removal of the amygdala (Groves & Schlesinger, 1979). Some have advocated the use of frontal or temporal lobe surgery for violent offenders, though *psychosurgery* in the service of behavioural control remains a highly controversial ethical issue.

Of course, it is not always possible to extrapolate from animal studies of a limited number of emotions (fear, aggression, rage) to humans, who have such a wide range of subtle emotions and feelings which cannot be investigated by observing animals' emotional behaviours. Nevertheless, animal-human comparisons can be made in relation to such emotional disorders as explosive aggression.

Rage due to septum or amygdala damage in animals and humans

Animals After septal lesions, animals will viciously bite a pencil touched against their skin while a normal animal may jump, or move away, showing only mild interest. The septal lesion appears to remove an inhibition – the animal is prone to sudden outbursts with only the slightest provocation.

Humans A man suffering from extreme aggression was seen by a psychologist. He would often fly into a rage at breakfast, pick up his plate and hurl it at his wife. He might justify this by complaining that an egg was cold or the bacon too hot. Anything that was said to him he would interpret as hostile. He was suffering from damage to the amygdala. There are several examples of septal or amygdala damage being found at post-mortem examinations in the brain of men who have suddenly gone out on shooting sprees, murdering passers-by for no apparent reason. In a celebrated case in America, Charles Whitman who killed 15 people, including himself, from a tower in the University of Texas, was found to be suffering from a tumour near the amygdala (Carlson, 1986). Brain damage is not always found in such people, but damage in limbic structures such as the septum, amygdala and hypothalamus is not uncommon.

Electrical stimulation of the hypothalamus

As we saw in Chapter 4, Delgado found that electrical stimulation of the brain could apparently inhibit aggression in a

charging bull. In another experiment, Delgado (1981) also showed that stimulation in the anterior and medial hypothalamus, part of the Papez loop, could provoke all the outward expressions of aggressive behaviour in cats – raising the hair, arching the back, snarling, baring the teeth and hissing. However, the cats did not attack or attempt to bite or scratch their handlers, nor would they bite a nearby rat (Figure 10). This behaviour is termed *sham rage*.

Predatory aggression (involved in hunting) is probably quite different from the aggression which occurs between members of the same species, over mates and territory. In cats, stimulation of some lateral regions of the hypothalamus could provoke actual attacks on other cats, while stimulation in parts of the medial forebrain (near or in hypothalamic centres that are involved in feeding) could provoke predatory aggression on mice. The centres in the brain that initiate these behaviours are, of course, dependent upon sensory inputs from other systems. Experimental stimulation via an electrode only mimics the activity that would normally occur in that brain region when natural aggression occurs. The fact that brain stimulation will not elicit attack responses in a blindfolded animal shows that what appear to be 'aggression centres' are not independent centres – they rely on sensory inputs.

Figure 10 Sham rage

The cat makes an undirected attack expression when the hypothalamus is stimulated.

In summary, aggressive behaviour in human beings and animals can be caused by specific damage to the brain. This damage could (a) directly stimulate the release of unprovoked aggressive outbursts, (b) heighten response to provocation, or (c) remove inhibition from aggressive responding, thereby exaggerating aggressive responses.

The cortex and emotion

Cognitive theorists such as Lazarus (1982) argue that emotional feelings derive primarily from cognitive appraisal – from the interpretation of events and other stimuli. This involves high level information processing throughout the brain, particularly within the cortex.

Prefrontal cortex damage in humans frequently leads to emotional changes. Some patients are disinhibited – they lose their inhibitions. They threaten and pick fights on the slightest provocation. Damasio (1994) has reported patients with frontal damage who show an apparent absence of emotionality. However, such effects may depend on the side of the brain on which the injury occurs. As outlined in Chapter 22, there is evidence that the two brain hemispheres differ, the right hemisphere being particularly associated with initiating emotion, since right hemisphere damage is more likely than left damage to cause a neutral, emotionless state. Some believe that all emotional processing takes place in the right hemisphere (Silberman & Weingartner, 1986), while others believe that the right is especially involved in sadness and other negative mood states.

In a study by Ley and Bryden (1982), participants were briefly shown sketches of faces that depicted different emotional expressions such as happiness, or sadness, or milder emotional expressions. These stimuli were displayed either to the right visual field (left hemisphere) or left visual field (right hemisphere), followed by a probe stimulus which was presented in the centre of the visual field (going to both hemispheres). Participants were asked to judge whether the emotion shown in the central picture was the same or different from the emotion displayed earlier to the left or right visual field. Judgements were found to be easier when the first stimulus was presented in the left visual field (travelling to the right hemisphere). No differences were seen when the faces portrayed mild emotional states. It would seem that the right hemisphere recognises only strong or distinctive facial expressions.

Conclusion

Findings from research investigating the role of brain structures in emotion can be used to support various theories of emotion. There is evidence that some brain centres operate individually and directly cause a particular emotion. There is also evidence that regions in the cortex first evaluate the situation (cognitive appraisal) and then provoke emotional responses via their inputs to the structures of the Papez loop.

This section has focused on the brain. Clearly, brain outputs have effects on the peripheral nervous system, producing hormonal release and other physiological changes. But, the brain cannot be seen as independent in the control of emotion. The current view is that cognitive appraisal (in the cortex and related structures) influences centres in the brain which control the expression of emotional states (that is, the subcortex and Papez loop) and that these emotional states can be heightened by physiological responses directed by the autonomic nervous system.

Key terms

Papez loop *An interconnected series of brain structures, including the amygdala, hypothalamus and septum, which regulate and control emotions.*

Cortex *The surface area of the brain involved in cognition and higher-level processing.*

Sham rage *Exaggerated aggressive responses in animals which do not lead to attack.*

3.6 Expressing and recognising emotions

Facial expression is one of the main ways in which emotions are expressed, communicated and recognised. In the 19th century, Charles Darwin claimed that people all over the world used similar facial expressions to portray similar emotions. Later researchers argued that facial expressions were learned and varied from culture to culture. For example, the facial expression of happiness was assumed to vary from one culture to the next.

Paul Ekman and his colleagues have spent many years studying facial expressions. His research has shown that across the world, people adopt very similar facial expressions to express similar emotions – confirming Darwin's observation made many years earlier (Ekman, 1993). This suggests that humans inherit, rather than learn, an in-built vocabulary of facial expressions for emotions. Ekman showed pictures of white Westerners expressing seven emotions to participants in the USA, Brazil, Chile, Argentina and Japan. He found that in all these cultures, there was a high level of agreement about which emotion was conveyed by each facial expression. Although the

Figure 11 Universal facial expressions

Anger

Sadness

Happiness

Fear

Disgust

Surprise

Contempt

experiences that give rise to emotions vary among cultures, Ekman's research suggests that the ways in which emotions are expressed facially and perceived are common to all.

But have these cultures learned to recognise white Western facial expressions as a result of exposure to Western films and pictures? Ekman conducted a study in which white facial expressions were shown to members of an isolated, preliterate culture in New Guinea – the Fore culture. Although totally unfamiliar with Western facial expressions, they successfully identified expressions of the main emotions and did so with reference to the situations in which they themselves would experience the emotion. For example, the fearful expression was described as 'when being chased by a wild boar' (Ekman & Friesen, 1971).

Evaluation Ekman's research can be criticised on the grounds that it used still photographs of posed expressions. When someone is asked to 'pose' an emotional expression – 'look as though you are sad' for example – they may exaggerate, or produce a stereotyped expression that might be different from the expression that they would make spontaneously when actually feeling that emotion. Human expressions are dynamic – they involve many facial movements which cannot be seen in a static picture. In addition, Ekman always provided his participants with a list of emotions (surprise, happiness, fear and so on), which they were asked to match to the appropriate picture. This limits their choice. Studies in which participants made their assessments by writing a description resulted in much more disagreement about the emotion each expression represented.

Facial feedback theory

Ekman found that when people are asked to form different facial expressions, each expression produces a different pattern of arousal within the nervous system. This suggests that facial expressions can influence emotional experience. This view forms the basis of *facial feedback theory* (Tomkins, 1995).

Facial feedback theory assumes that facial expressions can heighten or enhance existing emotions – a person smiles because they are happy and the fact that they are smiling makes them feel even happier. A more extreme version of the theory states that facial expressions can actually create emotions. Like the James-Lange theory of emotion, it states that rather than smiling because they are happy, people are happy because they are smiling.

There is evidence to support both versions of the facial feedback theory. For example, Strack et al. (1988) asked participants to rate funny cartoons while holding a pencil in their teeth (forcing a smiling expression) or between their lips (which prevents smiling). Those who were forced to smile rated the cartoons as funnier. We do appear to listen to our bodies to some extent when labelling emotional states.

Summary

1. Emotion has various dimensions – cognitive, affective and physiological. As a result, it is difficult to define and measure.

2. The James-Lange theory states that arousal within the peripheral nervous system feeds back to the brain where it is experienced as emotion. Specific types of arousal produce specific emotions.

3. According to the Cannon-Bard theory, the brain is the source of emotions. In response to a stimulus, the brain generates emotions and physiological reactions at one and the same time.

4. The Schachter-Singer cognitive labelling theory states that emotions start from general, non-specific arousal within the autonomic nervous system. This emotional state is then labelled and experienced as a specific emotion via a process of cognitive appraisal.

5. Richard Lazarus argued that cognitive appraisal always precedes emotion. The way a situation is assessed and interpreted determines the type and intensity of the emotion.

6. All branches of the nervous system and the endocrine system are involved in emotion.

7. Various brain centres have been associated with emotion. In particular, the Papez loop, which includes the amygdala and hypothalamus, plays a central role in the regulation and control of emotional states.

8. The current view is that cognitive appraisal in the cortex influences brain centres – such as the Papez loop – which control the expression of emotional states.

9. There is some evidence, based on facial expressions, that the expression and recognition of emotions are to some extent inborn.

10. Facial feedback theory states that facial expressions of emotion can heighten the experience of existing emotions, or actually generate emotions.

References

Andrews, K.M., McGowan, J.K., Gallitano, A. & Grossman, S.P. (1992). Water intake during chronic preoptic infusions of osmotically active or inert solutions. *Physiology and Behaviour*, 52, 241-245.

Cannon, W.B. (1927). The James-Lange theory of emotion: A critical examination and an alternative theory. *American Journal of Psychology*, 39, 106-124.

Cannon, W.B. & Washburn, A.L. (1912). *An explanation of hunger.* Cambridge, MA: The University Press.

Carlson, N.R. (1986). *Physiology of behaviour* (3rd ed.). Boston: Allyn & Bacon.

Chen, D.Y., Deutsch, J.A., Gonzales, M.F. & Gu, Y. (1993). The induction and suppression of c-fos expression in the rat brain by cholecystokinin and its antagonist L364, 718. *Neuroscience Letters*, 149, 91-94.

Clement, K., Vaisse, C., Lahlou, N., Cabrol, S., Pelloux, V., Cassuto, D., Gourmelen, M., Dina, C., Chambaz, J., Lacorte, J.-M., Basdevant,A., Bougneres, P., Labouc, Y., Froguel, P. & Guy-Brand, B. (1998). A mutation in the human leptin receptor gene causes obesity and pituitary dysfunction. *Nature, 392*, 398-401.

Critchley, H.D. & Rolls, E.T. (1996). Hunger and satiety modify the responses of olfactory and visual neurons in the primate orbitofrontal cortex. *Journal of Neurophysiology, 75*, 1673-1686.

Damasio, A.R. (1994). *Descartes' error: Emotion, reason, and the human brain.* New York: G.P. Putnam.

Davidson, T.L. (1993). The nature and function of interoceptive signals to feed: Toward integration of physiological and learning perspectives. *Psychological Review, 100*, 640-665

Delgado, J.M.R. (1981). Neuronal constellations in aggressive behaviour. In L.Valzelli and L. Morgese (Eds.), *Aggression and violence: A psycho/biological and clinical approach.* Milan: Edizioni Saint Vincent.

Dollard, J. & Miller, N.E. (1950). *Personality and psychotherapy.* New York: McGraw-Hill.

Ekman, P. (1993). Facial expression and emotion. *American Psychologist, 48*, 384-392.

Ekman, P. & Friesen, W.V. (1971). Constants across cultures in the face and emotion. *Journal of Personality and Social Psychology, 17*, 124-129.

Epstein, A.N., Fitzsimons, J.T. & Rolls, B.J. (1970). Drinking induced by injection of angiotensin into the brain of the rat. *Journal of Physiology, 210*, 457-474.

Eysenck, H.J. (1970). *The structure of human personality* (3rd ed.). London: Methuen.

Fitzsimons, J.T. & LeMagnen, J. (1969). Eating as a regulatory control of drinking in the rat. *Journal of Comparative and Physiological Psychology, 67*, 273-283.

Fowler, H. (1965). *Curiosity and exploratory behaviour.* New York: Macmillan.

Fukuda, T. & Ono, T. (1993). Amygdala-hypothalamic control of feeding behaviour in monkeys: Single cell responses before and after reversible blockade of temporal cortex or amygdala projections. *Behavioural Brain Research, 55*, 288-341.

Gleitman, H., Fridlund, A.J. & Reisberg, D. (1999). *Psychology* (5th ed.). New York: W.W. Norton.

Groves, P. & Schlesinger, K. (1979). *Introduction to biological psychology.* Dubuque, Iowa: W.C. Brown.

Harlow, H.E. (1950). Learning and satiation of response in intrinsically motivated complex puzzle performance in monkeys. *Journal of Comparative and Physiological Psychology, 43*, 289-294.

Hull, C.L. (1943). *Principles of behaviour.* New York: Appleton-Century-Crofts.

James, W. (1890). *Principles of psychology.* New York: Henry Holt.

Kleinginna, P.R. & Kleinginna, A.M. (1981). A categorised list of motivational definitions with a suggestion for a consensual definition. *Motivation and Emotions, 5*, 263-291.

Kluver, H. & Bucy, P.C. (1939). Preliminary analysis of functions of the temporal lobes in monkeys. *Archives of Neurology and Psychiatry, 42*, 979-1000.

Lazarus, R.S. (1982). Thoughts on the relations between emotion and cognition. *American Psychologist, 37*, 1019-1024.

LeDoux, J.E. (1993). Emotional memory systems in the brain. *Behavioural Brain Research, 58*, 69-79.

LeDoux, J.E. (1996). *The emotional brain.* New York: Simon and Schuster.

Leibowitz, S.F., Hammer, N.J. & Chang, K. (1981). Hypothalamic paraventricular nucleus lesions produced overeating and obesity in the rat. *Physiology and Behaviour, 27*, 1031-1040.

Levenson, R. (1992). Autonomic nervous system differences among emotions. *Psychological Science, 3*, 23-27.

Ley, R.G. & Bryden, M.P. (1982). A dissociation of right and left hemispheric effects for recognising emotional tone and verbal content. *Brain and Cognition, 1*, 3-9.

Lowe, J. & Carroll, D. (1985). The effects of spinal injury on the intensity of emotional experience. *British Journal of Clinical Psychology, 24*, 135-136.

MacLean, P.D. (1949). Psychosomatic disease and the 'visceral brain': Recent developments bearing on the Papez theory of emotion. *Psychosomatic Medicine, 11*, 338-353.

Marañon, G. (1924). Contribution a l'etude de l'action emotive de l'adrenaline. *Revue Francaise d'Endocrinologie, 2*, 301-325.

Marshall, G.D. & Zimbardo, P.G. (1979). Affective consequences of inadequately explained physiological arousal. *Journal of Personality and Social Psychology, 37*, 970-988.

Maslach, C. (1979). Negative emotional biasing of unexplained physiological arousal. *Journal of Personality and Social Psychology, 37*, 953-969.

Maslow, A.H. (1970). *Motivation and personality*, 2nd Edition. New York: Harper and Row.

Meyer, J.D. (1953). Glucostatic mechanism of regulation of food intake. *New England Journal of Medicine, 249*, 13-16.

Mills, A.S. (1985). Participation motivations for outdoor recreation: A test of Maslow's theory. *Journal of Leisure Research, 17*, 184-199.

Moghaddam, F.M. (1998). *Social psychology: Exploring universals across cultures.* New York: W.H. Freeman.

Nelson, J.G. (1992). Class clowns as a function of the type T psychobiological personality. *Personality and Individual Differences, 13*, 1247-1248.

Olds, J. & Milner, P. (1954). Positive reinforcement produced by electrical stimulation of septal areas and other regions of rat brains. *Journal of Comparative and Physiological Psychology, 47*, 419-427.

Panksepp, J. (1982). Toward a general psychobiological theory of emotions. *Behavioural and Brain Sciences, 5*, 407-467.

Pinel, J.P.J. (1997). *Biopsychology* (3rd ed.). Boston: Allyn and Bacon.

Plutchik, R. (1984). Emotions: A general psychoevolutionary theory. In K.Schemer & P. Ekman (Eds.), *Approaches to emotion.* Hillsdale, NJ: Erlbaum.

Pribram, K.H. (1962). Interrelations of psychology and the neurological disciplines. In S. Koch (Ed.), *Psychology: A study of a science.* Volume 4. New York: McGraw-Hill.

Rolls, B.J., Wood, R.J. & Stevens, R.M. (1978). Effects of palatability on body fluid homeostasis. *Physiology and Behaviour, 20*, 15-19.

Rolls, B.J., Wood, R., Rolls, E.T., Lind, H., Ling, R. & Ledingham, J.G. (1980). Thirst following water deprivation in humans. *American Journal of Physiology, 239*, 476-482.

Schachter, S. & Singer, J. (1962). Cognitive, social and physiological determinants of emotional state. *Psychological Review, 69*, 379-399.

Sheffield, F.D. & Roby, T.B. (1950). Reward value of a non-nutritive sweet taste. *Journal of Comparative and Physiological Psychology, 43*, 471-481.

Silberman, E.K. & Weingartner, H. (1986). Hemispheric lateralisation of functions related to emotion. *Brain and Cognition, 5*, 322-353.

Sinclair, R.C. Hoffman, C., Mark, M.M. Martin, L.L. et al., (1994). Construct accessibility and the misattribution of arousal: Schachter and Singer revisited. *Psychological Science, 5*, 15-19.

Spielberger, C.D., Gorsuch, R.L. & Lushene, R.E. (1970). *The State-Trait Anxiety Inventory (STAI)* Form X. Palo Alto, CA: Consulting Psychologists Press.

Strack, F., Martin, L.L. & Stepper, S. (1988). Inhibiting and facilitating conditions of the human smile: A nonobtrusive test of the facial feedback hypothesis. *Journal of Personality and Social Psychology, 54,* 768-777.

Stunkard, A.J., Sorensen, T.I.A., Hanis, C., Teasdale, T.W., Chakraborty, R., Schull, W.J. & Schulsinger, F. (1986). An adoption study of human obesity. *New England Journal of Medicine, 314,* 193-198.

Tolman, E.C. (1932). *Purposive behaviour in animals and men.* New York: Appleton-Century-Crofts.

Tolman, E.C. (1948). Cognitive maps in rats and men. *Psychological Review, 55,* 189-208.

Tomkins, S.S. (1995). *Exploring affect: The selected writings of Sylvan S. Tomkins.* New York: Cambridge University Press.

Zajonc, R.B. (1980). Feeling and thinking: Preferences need no inferences. *American Psychologist, 35,* 151-175.

25 Attention and pattern recognition

Introduction

We are constantly bombarded with a huge amount of information through our senses. We cannot process all of this information, so we need to select what we are going to attend to. This process of selective attention can be seen from the following examples.

While you are reading this, there is probably some noise going on nearby. If you are concentrating on reading, you will be able to 'block out' the noise, as long as it does not become too loud and intrusive. At other times, you might want to divide your attention between two tasks. For example, you might want to read a book and listen to music at the same time. How well can you do this?

Sometimes, people are not aware that they are focusing attention on one or more tasks. In other words, they are processing information automatically. What are the advantages and disadvantages of automatic processing?

In general, people recognise patterns – words, objects and faces – quickly and efficiently. How are they able to do this?

This chapter looks at the answers psychologists have given to the above questions.

Chapter summary

- **Unit 1 examines theories of focused attention.**
- **Unit 2 looks at theories of divided attention.**
- **Unit 3 examines theories of automatic processing.**

- **Unit 4 discusses theories of action slips.**
- **Unit 5 looks at explanations of pattern recognition, including face recognition.**

Unit 1 Focused attention

KEY ISSUES

1 What is focused or selective attention?
2 What are the main theories of focused auditory attention?

1.1 Defining and researching attention

Attention is the system with which we select and process a limited amount of information from the enormous amount available to us through our senses, our memories and other cognitive processes. Since our information processing systems have a limited capacity, one of the main purposes of an attention system is to prevent our processing systems from becoming overloaded. Selection is vital for this. Without it, we would be unable to focus, for example, on a particular sight or sound.

Focused attention This refers to directing attention on to one thing. The efficiency with which people are able to concentrate on one thing and not be distracted by something else is measured using a *focused attention task*. This involves presenting two different stimuli at the same time. Participants are instructed to attend to one of the stimuli while ignoring the other. For example, a common method for investigating auditory

attention is for participants to wear stereo headphones with a different 'message' played to each ear. They are instructed to attend to one of the messages while ignoring the other. Experiments using this type of procedure can tell us how effectively people are able to direct their attention and select particular stimuli. They also indicate the extent to which unattended stimuli are processed.

Divided attention refers to the capacity to perform two tasks at the same time. It is studied by presenting participants with two tasks simultaneously and asking them to attend to both. For example, they may be asked to attend to two different messages played through headphones, so *dividing* their attention between the two. These tests tell us about processing limitations. For example, it is easier to attend to two stimuli if participants use different processes than if they use the same process. For instance, it is easier to read and listen to music than to listen to two pieces of music at the same time because reading and listening involve two different processes, while listening is a single process.

Whenever a task involves presenting different auditory information either as a focused or divided attention task, this is called a *dichotic listening* task.

Much of the research on attention has concentrated on *auditory* attention, using audio-tape technology developed in the 1950s. This unit looks at focused auditory attention. The following unit looks at divided auditory attention.

Key terms

Focused attention task *A task that measures the degree to which attention can be focused on one stimulus.*

Divided attention task *A task that requires participants to attend to two stimuli simultaneously.*

Dichotic listening task *A task that presents two sets of auditory information simultaneously – one set to each ear. This can be either a focused or divided attention task.*

1.2 The 'cocktail party effect'

Colin Cherry (1953) observed what he called the 'cocktail party phenomenon'. He noticed that at a crowded party, he was able to listen to one person speaking to him even though several people were speaking at the same time in other parts of the room. This observation led Cherry to conduct a series of experiments to investigate the 'cocktail party effect' – how are we able to focus on one conversation when there are other conversations going on around us?

Cherry conducted a number of experiments using the *shadowing technique*. Shadowing involves listening to, and repeating, an auditory message as it is heard. In one experiment, Cherry played participants a different message to each ear. They were instructed to shadow one of the messages. Cherry found that this led to very little information being extracted from the unattended message – the message played to the other ear. In this type of study, participants can typically process the unattended message sufficiently to report whether the voice was male or female, but cannot identify what was said or even the language spoken.

In this type of focused attention task, participants are able to detect certain physical characteristics of the unattended message. They perform a very basic *sensory analysis* of the sound – an analysis using the senses, in this case the sense of hearing. For example, if a pure tone is inserted into the unattended message, it is nearly always detected. However, non-physical characteristics of the unattended message, in particular its meaning, are not recalled.

This suggests that unattended auditory information receives virtually no processing. It raises one of the important questions concerning attention – what happens to the information that is not attended to? Is it processed or is it filtered out before it is processed? These alternatives are reflected in *early selection* and *late selection* theories of attention. Early selection theories suggest that unattended information is filtered out at an early stage, and so it receives little or no processing. Late selection theories suggest that all stimuli receive some processing, and the decision about what information to attend to is made after that processing has been completed.

Some theories suggest that information passes through an *attentional bottleneck*, which somehow filters and sorts out what we do and do not pay attention to. Different *bottleneck theories* present very different views about when the filtering occurs and what happens to the unattended stimuli.

Activity 1   Focused attention

Headphone A   **Headphone B**

Attended message - male voice
I walked down the lane past the duck pond. It was snowing.

Unattended message - female voice
I opened the gate. Path the down walked I. Het regende hard.

(Het regende hard is Dutch for It is raining hard.)

In the above dichotic listening task, different information is transmitted simultaneously to each ear. Participants were asked to shadow – attend to – the message transmitted by headphone A.

Questions

1   Judging from Cherry's experiments, what would the participant recall from the attended message?

2   a) What would the participant recall from the unattended message?
    b) Why would they not recall anything else from the unattended message?

Key terms

Shadowing *Repeating a message out loud as you hear it.*

Sensory analysis *An analysis using the senses which detects certain physical characteristics of the stimuli.*

Early selection model *A model of attention that suggests that unattended stimuli receive no processing other than basic sensory analysis.*

Late selection model *A model of attention that suggests that the decision about what to attend to is made after all stimuli have been processed beyond the basic sensory level.*

Attentional bottleneck *A limited capacity processor that can only deal with a small amount of information at a time.*

1.3 Broadbent's theory of attention

Donald Broadbent (1954) presented one of the first early selection theories. It was based in part on his own research. In one experiment, the participants heard three pairs of digits *dichotically*. This means that three digits were presented in the participants' left ear at the same time as a different three digits were presented in the right ear (see Figure 1). The digits were presented once. Participants were then asked to recall them in any order. Broadbent found that participants tended to recall digits from one ear and then the other. On average, they recalled 65% of the digits. When participants were asked to recall the digits in the order that they had been presented, that is pair-by-pair rather than ear-by-ear, the accuracy of recall dropped to 15%. This means that, on average, participants were able to recall just one of the six digits.

Figure 1 Recalling digits

Channel 1 **251** → ← **748** Channel 2

Ear-by-ear recall 251 748. One channel change.

Pair-by-pair recall 27 54 18. Five channel changes.

Broadbent (1958) accounted for these findings, and for Cherry's shadowing experiments, by producing a model of attention. According to Broadbent, each ear is like a separate channel and only one channel can be attended to at once. Information is registered at the sensory level, but can only be processed and given meaning after it has passed through a filter. The pair-by-pair method of recalling the digits in the above experiment is more difficult than the ear-by-ear method because it involves changing from one channel to the other channel several times. Recalling the three digits from one ear and then three from the other ear requires changing channel only once. Broadbent suggested that changing channels takes time, so information might be missed while the channel is being changed. It's like

hopping between two channels on TV – while you're changing channel, you miss some of the information. Because of this, the attentional system prefers to deal with one channel and then the other. When forced to operate in a different way, as in Broadbent's second condition, the attentional system becomes much less efficient at dealing with the incoming stimuli.

This model is often referred to as *Broadbent's filter theory*. Its main features are:

1 Stimuli enter a sensory 'buffer', where they are held for a short time. If not attended to and processed, information fades away very quickly.
2 One channel of information at a time is allowed through an attentional filter to be processed. The decision about which channel to allow through the filter is based on sensory information (eg, whether it is a person's voice or another sound, whether it is loud or quiet, whether it is heard in one ear or the other).
3 Other channels of information are filtered out at the sensory level. They may never be processed because they may fade away while another channel is being dealt with.

Broadbent's filter theory is an example of an *early selection* model. The information to be attended to is selected or filtered at an early stage. Only after this initial selection does 'deeper' processing take place – for example, processing in terms of meaning.

Broadbent's filter theory is also an example of a *limited capacity* model. It suggests that the amount of information that can be dealt with by the auditory system is limited. Because of this, early selection is essential to prevent the system from becoming overloaded. Without the filter, there would be times when the system would be overwhelmed with the mass and variety of sounds from the outside world.

Evaluation

Broadbent's filter model can account for the findings of his own experiments and those of Cherry. It was not long, however, before his model was challenged. Although the paired-digit experiment supports Broadbent's theory, a slight alteration to the stimuli completely changes the result. Gray and Wedderburn (1960) used the same technique as Broadbent, but instead of presenting pairs of digits, participants heard combinations of digits and words. For example, 'it 9 raining' might be presented to one ear, at the same time as '4 is 2' is presented to the other ear. In this task, participants were instructed to report all the items that had been presented. Broadbent's model predicts that participants would report the message from one ear followed by the other ear. Gray and Wedderburn, however, found that participants would typically recall 'it is raining 4 9 2'. This means that they are alternating between the channels. Broadbent's theory states that this is very difficult and that the attentional system deals with one channel at a time. Gray and Wedderburn showed that the attentional system can successfully alternate between channels and can select channels based on the *meaning* of the information. Broadbent argued that the selection of information preceded processing in terms of meaning, but Gray and Wedderburn showed that this was not always the case.

Anne Treisman (1960) used a similar procedure. However, unlike Gray and Wedderburn, she instructed participants to shadow a specified ear and ignore the message in the other ear.

Like Gray and Wedderburn, Treisman found that participants followed the meaningful message from one ear to the other, contrary to instructions. This is very important. Again it suggests that the selection of information to be attended to can be based on meaning. This would not be possible unless *all* the information has been processed to some extent.

Treisman's findings indicate that the unattended message is processed more thoroughly than Broadbent's model suggests. Her findings also indicate that it is possible to successfully alternate between attentional channels, that is from one ear to the other. Broadbent's model does not allow for this.

Using her findings, and the findings of Gray and Wedderburn, Treisman proposed her own theory of attention.

Activity 2   Words and numbers

The 2 runs →

← 4 dog 7

Questions

1   According to Gray and Wedderburn, in what way would participants recall what they heard in this dichotic listening task?

2   What criticisms of Broadbent's model does this suggest?

1.4   Treisman's attenuator theory

Anne Treisman (1960) presented an alternative version of the early selection model. Like Broadbent, she argued that the auditory system has a limited capacity. As a result, auditory information requires selection at an early stage so that the system is not overloaded. However, selection does not mean that unattended information is entirely blocked out, as Broadbent's filter theory suggests. Instead, selection *attenuates* the information – weakens it in some way.

Like Broadbent, Treisman suggests that there is a selective filter. However, compared to Broadbent's filter, her filter is 'leaky' – unattended information leaks or permeates through in a weakened form.

There is plenty of evidence which appears to support the idea of a 'leaky' filter which attenuates information. Cherry (1953) noted that if people are involved in conversation at one side of a crowded room, they may well detect a mention of their name in a conversation at the other side of the room. Similarly, in a focused attention experiment in which each participant's name was mentioned in the unattended message, 35% recalled hearing their name (Moray, 1959). Treisman herself conducted a number of experiments which appear to support her attenuator theory. For example, participants in a focused attention task, who were fluent in both English and French, were asked to shadow a message in English in one ear, while ignoring a message in French in the other ear. Around half realised that the two messages said exactly the same thing (Treisman, 1964).

How does the selection process operate in Treisman's model? Why is some attentuated or 'weakened' information given further processing while other information is ignored? Treisman suggests a number of possibilities. If the attentuated information is particularly relevant to the person concerned, for example their name, then it is more likely to receive further processing. When an attenuated message signals danger, it is more likely to be picked up. A mother engaged in conversation will often stop short when she hears her young child shout 'mum' in a frightened voice.

Attenuated information can come to the fore when people expect to hear it. For example, if a sentence begins with the words, 'She sang a…', the listener expects to hear the word 'song'.

Evaluation

Treisman's model has a number of advantages compared to Broadbent's filter model.

- First, it provides an explanation for findings which cannot be accounted for by Broadbent's model – for example, people hearing their own name in an unattended message.
- Second, it indicates the importance of meaning in the selection of information to be attended to.
- Third, it suggests how unattended information can break through and become the focus of attention.

Despite these advantages, there are problems with Treisman's model. In particular, it is not clear how attenuation works. Does attenuation reduce the amount of information available for further processing? Or, does it somehow weaken the information by 'turning down its volume', so making it more difficult to attend to and less likely to receive further processing? There are no clearcut answers to these questions.

This lack of clarity and precision is a weakness of Treisman's model.

1.5   Early selection models – a critique

Broadbent and Treisman's theories present early selection models of auditory attention. Each model sees a filter making decisions about what to attend to at a very early stage. This is an extremely complex task. It is also a vital task – our survival depends on the filter making appropriate decisions.

But how is effective decision-making possible when processing capacity is so limited and so little is known about the incoming information? Decisions in Broadbent's model are made largely on the physical characteristics – the actual sounds – of the information. Decisions in Treisman's model are made partly on the basis of the meaning of attenuated information. How can effective decisions be made from such limited and low grade information?

It is far from clear how an early selection filter can make such complex decisions and, apparently, make the right decisions most of the time. The filter, as pictured in early selection models, is given an impossible task (Zimbardo et al., 1995).

One solution to this problem is the late selection model. In this model, the decision about what information to select and attend to is made at a much later stage. Two late selection models will now be examined.

1.6 Deutsch and Deutsch's response selection theory

Antony and Diana Deutsch (1963) present a late selection model of auditory attention. They argue that effective selection is only possible after incoming information has been given meaning. All incoming information is processed to some extent – it is categorised and recognised, and its importance is assessed. This occurs without conscious awareness – we don't know we're doing it. We become aware of information if it is judged to be sufficiently important. This is the stage where the filter appears and selection occurs. The decision about what to attend to is therefore moved to a later stage after incoming information has been given meaning and significance. As a result, this model is known as a *late selection* model.

Deutsch and Deutsch's theory appears to give a picture of an *unlimited capacity* system – *all* incoming information is processed for meaning. Why then have a filter selecting at a late stage? The idea of a filter in the previous models was to prevent overloading in a limited capacity system. The filter in Deutsch and Deutsch's model serves a different purpose. There is no limit to the amount of information that can be processed and in this sense the system cannot be overloaded. However, a filter for selection is necessary because human beings are limited in the number of *responses* they can make at any one time. We cannot respond to all the incoming information. Selection for response is therefore essential. Our survival can depend on making the right response and making it quickly. Hence Deutsch and Deutsch's model has been called *response selection theory*.

Evaluation

Points in favour Response selection theory has the advantage of providing an explanation for how complex and important selection decisions are possible. All incoming auditory information is processed for meaning. This provides a basis for effective decision-making. But, how do we know that incoming information is processed for meaning before selection occurs? The theory states that pre-selection processing is unconscious – we are not aware it is taking place. There is, however, some evidence to support unconscious processing.

Von Wright et al. (1975) asked English-speaking participants to listen to long lists of words. Whenever the Finnish word for 'suitable' was presented, the participants received an electric shock. They were then asked to shadow a message in one ear while a second, unshadowed message was presented to the other ear. When the Finnish word for 'suitable', or any word that sounded like it, was presented in the unshadowed message,

participants sometimes showed a change in galvanic skin response – a sign of stress. This suggests that some participants had unconsciously processed the unshadowed message.

In another experiment, participants were asked to shadow sentences in one ear and ignore what was presented simultaneously to the other ear. Some of the sentences contained an ambiguous word. For example, the word 'bank' in 'The man walked by the bank' could mean the NatWest on the high street or a river bank. At the same time, a word related to the ambiguous word – for example, money or river – was presented to the unattended ear. When asked to recall the ambiguous sentences, participants were influenced by the unattended message. For example, if the word river was presented, they were likely to interpret 'bank' as a river bank. This suggested that the unattended message was unconsciously processed for meaning (Lackner & Garrett, 1972).

Points against Although there is evidence for *some* unconscious processing, this does not mean that *all* incoming information is processed for meaning before selection takes place. According to researchers such as Treisman, this would overload the attentional system. Treisman supports her view with the following experiment.

Participants were asked to shadow one message while a second message was presented to the other ear. Whenever they heard a particular word – the ' target word' – in the shadowed message, they were asked to say it out loud and tap the table. Whenever they heard the target word in the unshadowed message, they were asked just to tap the table. Eighty-seven per cent of the target words were detected in the attended (shadowed) message and only eight per cent in the unattended (unshadowed) message (Treisman & Geffen, 1967). Deutsch and Deutsch's model would predict that the detection of target words would be similar for both messages. Treisman's model would predict that the unattended message would be attenuated and therefore fewer target words would be detected.

Deutsch and Deutsch (1967) interpreted these findings differently. Their model states that information only reaches conscious awareness when it is judged to be important. Since participants were told to shadow only one message, that message was judged to be important. Deutsch and Deutsch argued that targets were being *perceived* in both messages, but the attentional system was choosing to *respond* to the targets in the shadowed message because that message was judged to be more important. They pointed out that participants were asked to make two responses to the target word in the shadowed message (say it out loud and tap) and only one (tap) for the unshadowed message. This makes the shadowed message appear more important and results in more target words being responded to.

In response to this criticism, Treisman and Riley (1969) conducted a further experiment. They asked participants to briefly stop shadowing and simply tap whenever the target word was detected in *either* message. In other words, they were asked to make the *same* response to both messages. This time 76% of target words were detected in the shadowed message and 33% in the unshadowed message. Treisman and Riley argue that this finding supports the attenuator model. Fewer words are detected in the unshadowed message because this message is attenuated due to the limited capacity of the auditory perceptual system.

1.7 Johnston and Heinz's theory

Johnston and Heinz (1978) present a more flexible theory of selective attention. Rather than coming down on the side of early or late selection, they combine the two models. Thus selection can be early or late depending on the circumstances. Johnston and Heinz assume that:

- The more stages of processing that occur before selection takes place, the greater the demands on processing capacity.
- Selection is made as early as possible in order to minimise the demands on processing capacity.
- Analysis of the physical characteristics of incoming auditory information is made continuously. However, analysis in terms of meaning only occurs when sufficient processing capacity is available.
- The amount of processing needed depends on the requirements of the task. In other words, selection can be made at various stages of processing – early or late – depending on the amount of processing needed.

Support for Johnston and Heinz's theory is provided by the following experiment (Johnston & Heinz, 1978). Participants were presented with pairs of words simultaneously – one word in each ear. They were asked to repeat particular target words. In condition 1, the target words were spoken in a male voice, the non-target words in a female voice. In terms of physical characteristics, there was a clear distinction between the two types of words. Target words were easy to detect in condition 1 – participants simply had to listen for the male voice.

In condition 2, all the words were spoken by the same male voice. In physical terms, there was little to distinguish between target and non-target words. The words in condition 2 required greater processing – more attention had to be given to the meaning of *all* the words. Fewer target words were detected in condition 2.

Then the participants were given a surprise recall test. They were asked to recall the non-target words. They had *not* been told to attend to these words. This time, more non-target words were identified in condition 2. This suggests that greater processing had occurred in condition 2. Because non-target words had received more processing, they were more readily recalled.

The results of this experiment suggest that the amount of processing depends on the type of task. In condition 1, selection occurred at an early stage. In condition 2, further stages of processes were required, so selection occurred at a later stage. This experiment supports Johnston and Heinz's claim that selection can be early or late depending on the nature of the task.

Evaluation Johnston and Heinz's theory is supported by evidence from their own experimental research. It also appears to explain much of the data from experiments on focused attention conducted by other researchers. However, as the next section indicates, these experiments might be seriously flawed.

1.8 Methodological issues

Many of the experiments on focused attention treat each ear as a separate channel. For example, shadowing experiments send different messages to each ear. When researchers interpret the findings of these experiments, they assume that each ear operates as a separate channel. But, people do not use their ears like this in everyday life. As a result, many of the experiments on auditory attention are artificial, they do not reflect the way focused attention operates in the 'real' world. As such, they lack ecological validity. This means that the findings from experimental research cannot be generalised to situations outside the laboratory.

There are further problems with experiments using the shadowing technique. Participants are not usually asked about the non-shadowed message until the end of the experiment. This might mean that they did process information from the unattended message, but just forgot it by the time they were asked. In support of this view, Norman (1969) found that participants were able to report the last few words of the unshadowed message when they were unexpectedly stopped during the shadowing task.

Summary

1. Most theories of focused or selective auditory attention assume that the attentional system has limited processing capacity. As a result, selection is essential to prevent the system from becoming overloaded.

2. Broadbent's theory is an early selection model. It states that auditory information is selected or filtered at an early stage on the basis of its sensory characteristics – the physical characteristics of the sound. Only after selection does processing in terms of meaning occur.

3. Treisman's attenuator theory presents an alternative early selection model. Rather than information being filtered out, it is attenuated or weakened at an early stage. Attenuated information may then be ignored or given further processing.

4. Deutsch and Deutsch's response selection theory is a late selection model. It states that all incoming information is processed to some extent in terms of meaning. Only then – at a fairly late stage – can the importance of information be assessed. Information is selected for further processing on the basis of its importance.

5. Johnston and Heinz's theory states that selection can be early or late depending on the amount of processing required by each particular task.

6. Experiments on focused attention have been criticised for lacking ecological validity. If this is so, their findings cannot be generalised to situations outside the laboratory.

Unit 2 Divided attention

KEY ISSUES

1 How can we do two things at once?
2 What are the main theories of divided attention?
3 Are the theories supported by research evidence?

2.1 Dividing attention

Divided attention refers to dividing attention between two or more tasks. Sometimes, people find it easy to divide their attention and successfully perform more than one task at the same time. For example, an experienced driver can drive a car and hold a conversation at the same time. An accomplished musician can play a piano and sing. A footballer can control the ball at his feet while running and also look to see where team-mates are. Most people seem able to read a book and listen to music at the same time. Other tasks, however, are much more difficult to perform simultaneously. It is difficult, for example, to listen to the news on the radio while reading a book without there being severe disruption of performance of one of these two tasks.

Why are some tasks more difficult to perform together than others? How do we manage to divide our attention between tasks? The following sections describe the main theories of divided attention.

2.2 Theories of divided attention

Welford's bottleneck theory

Welford (1952) suggested that the attentional system contains a bottleneck that makes it difficult to make simultaneous decisions about two tasks. This idea is very similar to Broadbent's bottleneck theory of focused attention. The evidence for this idea came from studies of the *psychological refractory period*. If you are asked to respond to two stimuli in very quick succession, the response time to the second stimulus will be slowed slightly. According to Welford, this is because the second stimulus occurs while the system is still dealing with the first one. When the second stimulus appears, the system is not ready for it. The response to the second stimulus is slowed by the bottleneck. This delay is known as the psychological refractory period. The attentional system cannot deal immediately with two things if they are presented very close together in time.

A typical task used to investigate the psychological refractory period involves two stimuli – eg, two lights – and two responses – eg, two buttons. Whenever a light comes on, the participant has to press the corresponding button as quickly as possible. If the two lights come on within a very short time, the response time to the second light is longer. The psychological refractory period can be explained by the bottleneck in the system described by Welford, but it could also be explained in much simpler terms. The effects might be due to the unfamiliarity of the task. People do not often have to monitor lights and press

two buttons in quick succession, so their ability to divide attention between two tasks might be affected by this. However, Pashler (1990) found that the psychological refractory period effect is still found even after extensive practice on the task, so it is not a task unfamiliarity effect. Even when participants have pressed the buttons thousands of times, the psychological refractory period is still evident.

Pashler's experiments showed that the psychological refractory period is important, and that the bottleneck in the attentional system does affect the ability to attend to two things at the same time. There are, however, other factors that influence the ability to divide attention between two tasks. These additional factors are described in other theories of divided attention.

Key term

Psychological refractory period *When two responses have to be made in rapid succession, the second one is slower.*

Central capacity theories

Central capacity theories of divided attention start from the idea that there is a fixed or finite amount of attentional capacity. Resources from this fixed capacity are allocated to the two tasks. If the tasks require more than the available attentional resources, then the performance of one or both tasks will be disrupted.

Kahneman's central allocation theory

Kahneman (1973) began with the idea that there is a *central processor* that allocates attentional resources to tasks. These resources are finite – there is a limited amount available. However, they can be allocated flexibly. The *allocation policy*, that is the way that the system decides to allocate attention to different tasks, is dependent upon a number of factors. Walking along a quiet street, for instance, places a small demand upon the attentional resource. Another task can easily be performed at the same time, for example, looking in shop windows, tossing and catching a ball, or even reading a newspaper. If, however, the quiet street is located in a neighbourhood where people let their dogs roam free, there might be randomly placed hazards on the footpath. As the location of these hazards is not predictable, a greater attentional resource would be needed to successfully negotiate the street without stepping in anything nasty. As the attentional demands of the walking task increase, there are fewer resources left over to allow other tasks, such as newspaper reading. So, part of the allocation policy depends upon the tasks themselves and what they involve.

According to Kahneman, all tasks require a certain level of attention – they all draw on the central capacity. The level of attention allocated to a task depends upon the task itself, and the level of experience and familiarity with that task. Well-practised skills require less attention to be allocated to them. A child learning to walk allocates a very high level of attention to walking. For an adult, walking requires very little attention.

Kahneman's theory is able to explain the results observed in the listening tasks presented earlier in the chapter. Shadowing a message requires a great deal of attentional capacity, so there might not be enough left to allow a second message to be monitored in anything but a very superficial way.

Kahneman's model predicts that skills can be practised and developed so that they demand less attentional capacity. When this happens, skills can become automatic. Theories of automatic processing are outlined in Unit 3.

Key terms

Central processor *A system that allocates attentional resources to tasks.*

Allocation policy *The factors influencing how the central processor allocates resources.*

Norman and Bobrow's theory

Norman and Bobrow (1975) extended Kahneman's theory to include the distinction between *resource-limited* and *data-limited* processes. Resource-limited processes are affected by the amount of processing capacity available. As mentioned earlier, shadowing a message in one ear may greatly reduce the resources left to process a message in the other ear. Data-limited processes are affected by the information being presented. If, for instance, the message does not have very good sound quality, then having extra processing capacity will not help. The only thing that would improve processing of this message would be to improve its sound quality.

The detection of a simple tone, like a single musical note or a beep, requires fewer processing resources than the identification of a word. The identification of a word is resource-limited, but it may also be data-limited if the word is not recorded clearly. The detection of a tone, on the other hand, is purely data-limited – the tone may not be sounded clearly enough to be heard. It is not resource-limited, as few resources are needed to detect the tone.

This simple distinction has been criticised because there are no independent measures of whether a process is data-limited or resource-limited. It is assumed that resource-limited processes are affected by the reduction in processing capacity. When a process is affected by the reduction in processing capacity, it is then labelled as a resource-limited process. Because of this circularity, the Norman and Bobrow extension to Kahneman's theory has not been widely accepted.

Evaluation of central capacity theories

Kahneman's theory predicts that task difficulty is the important factor in determining divided-attention task performance. Difficulty in this sense refers to the load placed on the attentional capacity. The more that tasks demand from the attentional resource, the more difficult it will be to perform those tasks together. However, it appears that difficulty effects are often overwhelmed by similarity effects. Tasks might not be very demanding of capacity, but if two tasks are similar, then it might be very difficult to divide attention between those tasks.

For example, Segal and Fusella (1970) investigated the ability to detect visual or auditory stimuli while forming visual or auditory images. Participants were asked to imagine a picture of something, or to imagine a particular sound. While they had this visual or auditory image in their heads, they were asked to perform a task involving visual stimuli, or a task involving auditory stimuli. Segal and Fusella found that visual imagery reduced the detection of visual stimuli, but not auditory stimuli. And auditory imagery impaired detection of auditory stimuli but not visual stimuli.

To give a real life example, it is much easier to listen to music and to what someone is saying to you than it is to listen to two people talking to you at the same time. Why should particular tasks interfere with some tasks more than others? This cannot be explained in terms of the required attentional capacity.

A further problem with central capacity theory is the measurement of attentional capacity. No effective measure is available. There is a tendency to assume that if performance on divided attention tasks is impaired, then this indicates that attentional capacity has reached its limit. However, there are other reasons, such as task similarity, which can account for this.

Modular or multichannel theories

Allport (1989) rejects the view of a single, general-purpose, central capacity processor. Instead, he proposes a modular or multichannel system in which there are various modules or channels dealing with particular skills. For example, there might be a visual attentional module, an auditory attentional module, and so on, with each module having its own separate capacity.

This view of the attentional system provides an explanation for similarity effects. For example, a divided attention task that involves two visual activities may overload the visual attentional module. However, two tasks of a similar difficulty, one visual and the other auditory, may be well performed because they draw attention from different modules.

Evaluation Modular theories have the advantage of providing an explanation for similarity effects. Evidence from brain imaging provides some support for modular theories since it indicates that different attentional processes (visual, auditory, etc) take place in different parts of the brain.

However, modular theories have been criticised because it is not clear how many modules there are. Is there one module for each sensory system or are there several? For example, the auditory system could have a subsystem for attending to speech and a different subsystem for music. If there are a large number of subsystems, then the attentional system could run into problems coordinating the outputs of all the subsystems.

As with central capacity theories, modular theories have the problem of measuring capacity. The capacity of the various modules is not clear.

Conclusion

The factors influencing divided attention are fairly clear – psychological refractory period, task difficulty, task similarity – but there is no one theory that fully explains how these factors interact with each other to make it easier or more difficult to divide attention between tasks.

Summary

1 The attentional system cannot deal immediately with two stimuli in rapid succession. There is a delay – the psychological refractory period – in dealing with the second stimulus.

2 Central capacity theories state that there is a fixed or finite amount of attentional capacity that can be allocated to tasks.

3 It is not clear how the central capacity can be measured.

4 Central capacity theories are unable to explain similarity effects.

5 Modular theories state that the attentional system contains various modules specialising in particular skills.

6 Modular theories provide an explanation for similarity effects. However, it is not clear how many modules there are, what their capacity is, or how they are coordinated.

Unit 3 Automatic processing

KEY ISSUES

1 How does automatic processing help divided attention?

2 What is the difference between automatic and controlled processes?

3 What are the main theories of how processes become automatic?

3.1 Automatic processes

It becomes easier to divide attention between two tasks and to do two things at once if one of the tasks becomes automatic. *Automatic processes* involve no conscious control. They are fast and place very little demand on the attentional system. As a result, they do not reduce the capacity for performing other tasks at the same time. Processes that are not automatic are called *controlled processes*. These demand conscious control, and so there is a limit to how many of these processes can be performed simultaneously. This also means that they will be slower than automatic processing.

The distinction between controlled and automatic processes is easily demonstrated with a description of the *Stroop effect*. Stroop (1935) asked participants to name the colour of ink in which a series of words was printed. In one condition, the words were themselves colour words printed in an incompatible colour of ink (eg, the word 'red' printed in blue ink). Stroop found that when the words were the names of colours, it took participants longer to name the colour of the ink in which the words were printed. This is because, for adults, reading is an automatic process, but naming colours is a controlled process. The interference between the word and the colour of the ink occurs because the faster automatic process (reading the word) is completed before the slower, controlled process (naming the ink colour). As a result, the automatic process of identifying the word 'red' interferes with the controlled process of identifying the colour 'blue'. The Stroop effect is the classic example of the distinction between automatic and controlled processes and of an automatic process interfering with a controlled process.

Activity 3 A version of the Stroop effect

Item A

←RIGHT	↑LEFT	→DOWN	↓UP
↑LEFT	←DOWN	↓RIGHT	→UP
↓UP	→LEFT	←DOWN	↑RIGHT
←UP	↓RIGHT	↑LEFT	→DOWN

Item B

↑BLUE	→YELLOW	←GREEN	↓RED
←YELLOW	↓BLUE	↑RED	→GREEN
→RED	←BLUE	↓YELLOW	↑BLUE
↓GREEN	↑GREEN	←RED	→BLUE

Questions

1 In Item A, work along each row saying aloud which direction each arrow points in (up, down, left, or right).

2 Now do the same in Item B.

3 a) Which task did you find more difficult – Item A or Item B?

   b) How can this be explained in terms of automatic and controlled processing?

Very few processes satisfy all of the criteria for being automatic. Some automatic processes are not available to consciousness, eg, recognising speech, whilst others have become automatic, but could be consciously controlled, eg, tying your shoelaces.

Processes do not start off as automatic processes. They begin as controlled processes and then become automatic. One example of this has already been mentioned – reading. For adults, reading is an automatic process, and this produces the Stroop effect. For children who have not learned to read, or for whom reading involves a step-by-step sounding out of words, the Stroop effect does not operate. Reading becomes automatic as we become better at it.

3.2 Theories of automatic processing

How do processes become automatic? One view is that the steps involved in a process become combined into bigger steps, which are, in turn, integrated into even bigger steps. Eventually, entire processes become single procedures rather than a long series of smaller steps.

Bryan and Harter (1899) found that telegraph operators began by learning how to transmit single letters. Once the single letters had been learned and automatised, the transmission of words became automatic, followed by the automatisation of entire phrases. In this way, smaller steps were combined into larger steps. Similarly, touch-typists become skilled at pressing the correct keys in the correct order, so the processes involved in typing words become automatic. For example, a touch typist does not think about the locations of the letters 't', 'h' and 'e'. Typing the word 'the' becomes automatic through extensive practice.

Logan's instance theory

Logan (1988) proposed what he called *instance theory*. He suggested that we learn to associate particular responses with particular events, or instances. For example, a child learning to do sums applies a counting procedure to deal with pairs of numbers. If a child is asked for the first time what the sum 5 + 4 equals, they will usually begin with five, and count upwards four numbers until the right answer is reached. With repeated practice, the child will store in memory the fact that 5 + 4 = 9, and the counting procedure will no longer be needed for this sum. In other words, adding 4 to 5 has become automatic. As more instances are encountered and learned, the need for conscious counting procedures is largely removed. Most adults can instantly answer the question 'what is 8 x 2?' without laboriously adding together eight twos. This is because, Logan argues, the instance has been encoded in memory – the process has become automatic. Logan's theory is fairly useful for explaining certain specific responses to stimuli.

Shiffrin and Schneider's theory

Shiffrin and Schneider (1977) suggest that controlled processes require attention and so are limited in how much information can be processed at once. Controlled processes are flexible and can be changed to meet changing circumstances. Automatic processes, on the other hand, use very little attention and so can process lots more information at once. However, they are very difficult to change once they have been learned.

Shiffrin and Schneider (1977) conducted a series of experiments to investigate automatic processing. They used a visual search method in which participants were asked to search for letters amongst other letters. In their initial task, participants were shown sets of letters. They were asked to spot, as quickly as possible, any letter from the part of the alphabet between B and L. Participants had to search for these target letters in amongst letters from the part of the alphabet between Q and Z. The participants' speed of search increased during 2100 trials, suggesting that with practice the task made less use of controlled processing and more use of automatic processing – participants were able to spot the target letters more easily without having to think about the alphabet every time.

In the second part of the experiment, the letter sets were swapped over. Now, the letters between Q and Z were targets and the letters from B to L distractors. In the first part of the experiment, participants had spent 2100 trials searching for letters B to L, and this had become largely automatic. Now, they were being asked to look for letters Q to Z. As mentioned earlier, Shiffrin and Schneider had suggested that automatic processes were inflexible and very difficult to alter once they had been learned. When the letter sets were swapped over, participants took almost 1000 trials before attaining the speed they had reached at the very beginning of the first task. The automatic processing that had been learned when searching for letters B to L made it extremely difficult to stop searching for those letters and search for different ones. Automatic processing is rigid and inflexible – it is difficult to modify or change.

Evaluation Shiffrin and Schneider have been criticised for not explaining how processes become automatic. Their finding that practice can lead to automatic processing does not explain whether the same processes are being performed more efficiently or whether new, faster processes are being used in their place (Cheng, 1985).

Shiffrin and Schneider have also been criticised for suggesting that processing is *either* automatic *or* controlled. Other researchers argue that processing can be a mixture of both these extremes – partly automatic and partly controlled.

Norman and Shallice's theory

Norman and Shallice (1986) point out that most of our routine behaviour is organised into *schemas* – mental representations of familiar actions. Whenever we need to perform a familiar action, the appropriate schema will be activated to guide us through the process, step-by-step. There is a separate schema for each well-learned type of action, for example, making a pot of tea, brushing your teeth, and so on. Once a schema starts to operate, it will automatically continue to its conclusion. This is the automatic part of processing.

Norman and Shallice suggest that automatic processes would frequently disrupt behaviour if they were left unchecked. For example, if there are two very similar schemas, there must be a way of making sure that the correct one is used. According to Norman and Shallice, a system called *contention scheduling* is used. This routine system makes sure that the appropriate schema is used, by switching off all similar schemas. For example, if you go into the kitchen to make a pot of tea, you need the 'tea-making' schema to start up. Other similar schemas such as 'toast-making' which are similar to the 'tea-making' schema need to be prevented from being triggered by the situation – the act of going into the kitchen. Contention scheduling is a semi-automatic system that does this.

Sometimes, we need to change our habits or most frequent behaviours. For instance, if we usually walk in one direction when we leave our front door in the morning, the schema will automatically start up every morning, triggered by the situation. If, one morning, we needed to go in a different direction to keep an appointment, we need to use a third system – the *supervisory attentional system* – to consciously control our behaviour and to respond flexibly.

So, Norman and Shallice suggest three different systems for controlling actions:

- Automatic schemas that store information about well-learned familiar routines.
- Contention scheduling: A partially automatic system that chooses between competing schemas.
- Supervisory attentional system: A consciously controlled system that overrides contention scheduling to allow us to behave in ways different from our normal routines and habits.

One of the aims of Norman and Shallice's model is to explain how automatic processes are kept under control. Why is this necessary? As mentioned above, automatic processes can cause inappropriate behaviour. To prevent this, we need to be able to override automatic processes and consciously control our actions.

Evaluation Norman and Shallice's ideas about the interaction between automatic schemas and consciously controlled behaviour are important. They suggested that people sometimes make mistakes because an inappropriate schema has become activated, or because the supervisory attentional system has failed to override the automatic schemas at a crucial moment. These ideas led to the development of theories of action slips, discussed in the next unit.

Key terms

Schemas *Mental representations of familiar and well-learned routines that operate automatically.*

Contention scheduling *A partially automatic system for choosing the correct schema from a number of similar schemas.*

Supervisory attentional system *A consciously controlled system for overriding automatic processing and allowing flexible responses.*

Summary

1 Instance theory states that processes become automatic when particular responses are associated with particular events or instances. These responses are stored in memory and retrieved when the appropriate event occurs.

2 According to Shiffrin and Schneider automatic processing requires no attention. It is fast and can process large quantities of information. However, it is rigid and inflexible and, therefore, difficult to modify or change. Controlled processes require attention, they are flexible, but can only process limited amounts of information at any one time.

3 It is not clear whether automatic processes merely perform existing processes more quickly and efficiently or whether they replace existing processes with new, faster and more efficient processes.

4 Norman and Shallice suggest that well-learned, habitual behaviour is controlled by schemas that operate automatically in response to the situation. A contention scheduling system selects which schema is to operate at any one time. A supervisory attentional system consciously controls behaviour by overriding contention scheduling when we need to change our behaviours from our normal routines and habits.

Unit 4 Action slips

KEY ISSUES

1 **What is an action slip?**

2 **What are the main explanations of action slips?**

3 **How might over-reliance on automatic processing be dangerous?**

4.1 Action slips

An *action slip* occurs when an action is performed that was not intended. Examples include forgetting that there is already sugar in your tea and adding another spoonful; leaving the house and heading for college when you should be going in the opposite direction towards the dentist's surgery.

Types of action slips

Reason (1979) asked 35 participants to keep diaries of their action slips over a two-week period. Of the 433 slips recorded, Reason categorised 94% into the following five types.

Storage failure (40%) Intentions or actions are forgotten or only partially recalled. For example, one participant said that they had started to pour a second kettle of boiling water into a teapot of freshly made tea. They had no recollection of having just made it.

Test failure (20%) When an action involves a series of stages, failure to monitor what is going to happen when one stage finishes and the next one begins. For example, one participant said: 'I meant to get my car out, but as I passed through the back porch on my way to the garage I stopped to put on my wellington boots and gardening jacket as if to work in the garden'. The action of going to the garage reached a crucial stage – passing through the back porch – and because this stage in the process was not monitored effectively, going to the garden took over from the intended action of going to the garage.

Subroutine failure (18%) This involves either omitting or mis-ordering the stages in a sequence of actions. Reason gives the following example of an omission 'I picked up my coat to go out when the phone rang. I answered it and then went out of the front door without my coat', and of mis-ordering: 'While running water into a bucket from the kitchen tap, I put the lid back on the bucket before turning off the tap'.

Discrimination failure (11%) This involves failing to distinguish between similar objects, for example, mistaking shaving cream for toothpaste.

Programme assembly failure (5%) This involves combining actions inappropriately. For example, 'I unwrapped a sweet, put the paper in my mouth and threw the sweet into the waste bucket'.

This type of diary study relies entirely on self-report. As Reason was studying action slips, it would not be too surprising if some of the participants performed an additional action slip – failing to write down the details of an action slip that had occurred. In addition, there may have been other slips that the participants did not notice.

4.2   Theories of action slips

Reason's theory of action slips

Reason (1979) identified two forms of processing. First, there is an automatic mode that controls performance according to pre-arranged sequences of instructions. This type of processing is fast, but inflexible and difficult to change (as shown by Shiffrin and Schneider, see p177). Second, there is a conscious control mode based on a central processor or attentional system. This is slow, but is sometimes needed to override the automatic mode. The conscious control mode is very flexible.

In everyday life, automatic processes control most of our

behaviour, and usually these processes are sufficient for us to get by. However, Reason says that there are *critical decision points*. These are points at which the conscious control mode must be used to choose between two similar and competing responses. For instance, in the example given earlier, the man who started to put on his gardening clothes when he intended to take his car out of the garage had reached a critical decision point – the kitchen porch gave access to both garden and garage – and he had failed to use conscious control to select the appropriate response.

Reason points out that when action slips occur they tend to take the form of well-practised behavioural sequences. The intention of going to the garage is replaced by the well-practised action of getting ready to do some gardening. Habit plays an important part. When conscious control is not used at a critical decision point to select the correct motor program, the motor program that takes over instead will tend to be one that is frequently used.

Reason argues that the different types of action slip reported in his diary study can be explained in terms of critical decision points being missed, and a 'strong' motor program taking over from the one that was intended to be used.

In a laboratory study, Reason demonstrated the role of habit strength in producing action slips. This is illustrated by the experiment outlined in Activity 4.

Key term

Critical decision point   *The point in a sequence of actions at which a decision must be made about how to appropriately continue that sequence.*

Activity 4   Action slips in action

1   Read these questions out loud, as quickly as possible, and answer each one quickly:
What do we call the tree that grows from acorns?
What do we call a funny story?
What sound does a frog make?
What is *Pepsi*'s major competitor?
What is another word for cape?
What do you call the white of an egg?

2   What did you answer to the last question? Did you answer 'yolk'? The correct answers to these questions are 'oak', 'joke', 'croak', 'Coke', 'cloak' and 'albumen'. The yolk is the yellow part of an egg!

3   Try asking the same questions to a few people. Note down how many answered 'yolk' to the question 'What do you call the white of an egg?' Ask some other people only the last question, and see how many of them answer 'yolk'.

4   When Reason (1992) conducted this experiment, he found that 85% of participants incorrectly answered 'yolk' to the question 'what do you call the white of an egg?' When people were asked that question on its own, only 5% answered 'yolk'. How can these results be explained in terms of automatic and controlled processing?

Reason (1992) explained the results of the experiment described in Activity 4 as follows. The fact that the answers to the other questions all rhyme with 'oak' sets up a 'mini habit' in participants to say words that rhyme. As the questions are asked, the automatic mode takes over and starts to quickly produce answers that rhyme with 'oak'. When the last question is asked, the automatic mode finds an answer that rhymes with 'oak' and

has something to do with eggs: 'yolk'. Reason called this the *oak-yolk effect*. In order to stop this from happening, the conscious control mode needs to step in and stop the automatic mode. However, the automatic mode is faster, so the conscious control mode does not get there quickly enough to prevent the incorrect answer. Most people, if they experience this effect, say 'yolk' and then instantly realise that they have got it wrong. This is because the conscious control mode has tried to interfere, but has got there too late.

Evaluation The interaction between automatic and controlled processes helps to explain the types of everyday action slips reported by the participants in Reason's diary study. The need for conscious control to override automatic processing at critical decision points explains why action slips are often made when we are preoccupied and not concentrating.

The laboratory study reported by Reason (1992) has been criticised for lacking ecological validity. If this is the case, then the findings of laboratory experiments cannot be generalised to other settings and situations. Critics argue that the types of action slips induced in the laboratory are often very different from the slips that people make in everyday life. Sellen and Norman (1992) claim that action slips usually occur when people are preoccupied and not concentrating on what they are doing. Laboratory studies like Reason's typically encourage people to focus on the task in hand, rather than recreating or simulating the situations in which action slips occur in everyday life. However, Reason's (1992) laboratory study was intended to demonstrate the role of habit in action slips. Reason agrees that everyday action slips tend to occur when people are distracted so that conscious control fails to take over at crucial moments.

Sellen and Norman's schema theory

According to Sellen and Norman (1992) behaviours are determined by schemas or plans that are organised in a hierarchy. At the top of the hierarchy there is a schema that represents the overall goal of an action – eg, the goal is to make a cup of tea. Below that, there are lower level schemas for the actions involved in reaching that goal – eg, going into the kitchen, filling the kettle with water, getting milk from the fridge. Schemas for the separate actions often have to be activated in the correct order.

A schema dictates what action will be performed next when it is activated. The activation of a schema is brought about by the appropriate *triggering conditions* being present – eg, pouring the water into the teapot when the kettle boils. According to this theory, action slips occur because the wrong schema might receive activation at the start – eg, the 'making a cup of tea' schema might not be fully activated, and the action of going into the kitchen results in the activation of other kitchen-related schemas. For example, a weakly activated 'tea' schema might suddenly be overruled by a 'getting something to eat' schema. This problem will be especially apparent when two or more schemas share similar stages – eg, going to the fridge may be a stage in both tea-making and yoghurt-eating schemas.

Sellen and Norman's theory can be used to explain the different types of action slip described by Reason (1979). For example, a test failure can occur when an inappropriate schema suddenly takes over from the correct one because they share stages. In Reason's example, the person intending to go into the garage but who puts on wellington boots instead has done this because of the faulty activation of the 'garage' schema and the inappropriate activation of the 'garden' schema. At points such as this, where actions have elements in common, attentional control is needed to make sure that the switch from one schema to another is made smoothly and correctly. If attentional control is not applied at the right time, then the wrong schema could be activated and an action slip performed. A failure to apply

attentional control at the right moment can be caused by the person being distracted or preoccupied. If the conscious control system is thinking about something else, then it won't be able to step in at the right moment and select the correct schema to activate.

This suggests that behaviour is at its most efficient when there is an interaction between controlled and automatic processes and when controlled processes are concentrated on the task in hand. Automatic processes are efficient because they are tried and tested, they require minimal thought and usually get the job done. However, they have their limitations, they can lead to errors. As a result, they must be subject to some supervision from controlled processes for error-free efficient behaviour.

Evaluation Sellen and Norman's theory of action slips provides an explanation of how action slips arise from the interaction between conscious and automatic control. The idea that behaviour is consciously controlled or automatic is simplistic. It is improbable that there is a single attentional system – rather there may be several different systems that control different aspects of behaviour. This point was made by Norman and Shallice (1986) when they distinguished between automatic, partially automatic and consciously controlled systems (see pp 422-423).

Key term

Triggering conditions *The conditions that must be present to trigger a schema into action.*

4.3 Behavioural efficiency

As automatic processes can produce action slips, maybe people would make fewer action slips if automatic processing were used less. Remember, however, that automatic processing allows us to use processing capacity to attend to other things. And it is much faster than controlled processing. Also, automatic activities can suffer if they are attended to and consciously controlled. For example, if you try to consciously control the way that you walk, you find yourself walking very strangely. Sports people, such as golfers, know that once a process has become automatic, it is often best to leave it that way. If a golfer begins to consciously control the way that they swing a golf club, their game might suffer.

As there are advantages and disadvantages to using automatic and controlled processing it appears that the best strategy for everyday use is for controlled and automatic processing to interact. A reliance on automatic processing, unsupervised by controlled processing, may have serious consequences. It may result in a phenomenon known as *mindlessness*.

Mindlessness

Langer (1989) uses the term *mindlessness* to refer to action slips that are the result of actions becoming routine and automatic. In an experimental example of this, Barshi and Healy (1993) showed that checklists, like those used by pilots before take-off, can be very dangerous if they become too routine and automatic. They asked participants to check through pages of simple sums, in which the same 10 sums were repeated again and again. Within the pages there were five mistakes (eg, 6 × 4 = 20). Participants were asked to spot the mistakes. For half of the participants, the same 10 sums were repeated several times in the same order. For the other half, the 10 sums were in a different order in each repetition. The participants in the fixed order condition missed 23% of the mistakes, compared with just 9% in the other condition.

For the participants in the fixed order condition, the checking task had become routine and automatic, so they failed to spot almost a quarter of the errors. Barshi and Healy suggested that the use of the same checklist, in the same order, again and again could have catastrophic results for airline pilots.

Langer (1989) reported the real-life effects of this. In 1982 an airline pilot and co-pilot went through a routine checklist before take-off. They had done this hundreds of times before. They routinely noted that the de-icer was switched to 'off', as it should have been under normal circumstances, but not under the icy conditions of that day. The plane crashed, killing 74 passengers. In 1983, an airliner landed without its landing gear down because the standard checklist had been used and the co-pilot had mindlessly verified that the landing gear had been lowered. He was responding in an automatic way without really noticing what the instrument panel was saying.

These two examples clearly illustrate the dangers of automatic processing. They indicate the importance of combining controlled and automatic processing.

Theories of action slips – evaluation

The factors that determine whether automatic or controlled processing will be used have not been fully explained. Theorists have correctly suggested that action slips tend to occur most frequently on well-practised actions, because these are the

activities that are most likely to become automatic. However, action slips are more likely to occur with actions that are of minor importance than those that are seen to be very important. For example, a well-rehearsed juggler could use the automatic mode to juggle razor-sharp knives, but the possible consequences of an action slip ensure that the juggler does not rely on automatic processing. The theories of action slips outlined in this unit do not explain why more important activities are less likely to be automatic and, therefore, less likely to be prone to action slips. Of course, the juggler's attentional system is affected by the motivation not to lose any fingers. Theories of action slips and more general theories of attention neglect the role of motivation in everyday attention.

Summary

1   Automatic processing is fast and efficient. It conserves processing resources. However, it is more likely than controlled processing to lead to action slips.

2   Normal routines are largely directed by automatic processes. Action slips often occur when there is a critical decision point and controlled processing fails to override automatic processes. When this happens, behaviour continues according to habit.

3   Sellen and Norman explain action slips in terms of schemas. For example, if a schema is not fully activated, an action slip may result.

4   Mindlessness occurs when actions become too routine and automatic. This can lead to action slips.

5   Theories of action slips tend to ignore motivation.

Unit 5 Pattern recognition

KEY ISSUES

1   **Why is pattern recognition important?**

2   **What are the main theories of pattern recognition?**

3   **How are people's faces recognised?**

5.1   Pattern recognition

The importance of pattern recognition

The ability to recognise patterns in the world around us is very important. Patterns don't just mean abstract designs – they refer to any consistent visual shape that has meaning. Each letter printed on this page is a pattern. Every person's face is a pattern. Clearly, the recognition of these patterns is a vital skill. Without it, we could not read, and we could not recognise anyone's face.

Three main types of theory have been proposed to explain pattern recognition. They are *template matching*, *prototypes*, and *feature theories*. This section will examine these theories.

Template matching

Template matching is a very simple theory. It states that we

compare the pattern that we are looking at to a set of templates stored in memory. When we find the template that matches the perceived pattern, the pattern is recognised. This theory does not work for a number of reasons.

In order for a pattern to be recognised, it has to match its template exactly. There is no room for variation in a pattern. For example, we are able to recognise all of the following patterns:

A a A a A a

Although these patterns are different, they are easily recognised as forms of the letter 'a'. In order for template matching to work, we would need to have a different template stored in memory for each of these forms, as well as for the many other forms in which the letter 'a' can be represented. There would need to be an infinite number of templates to allow us to recognise all possible variations in letters. Similarly, for each person's face, we would need a different template to allow us to recognise them from different angles, when they were wearing a hat or sunglasses, and so on. This would present the brain with enormous storage problems. There simply wouldn't be space to store all these templates.

Even if there were room for all these templates to be stored, it would take a long time to search through them all in order to identify a pattern. Since we are able to identify patterns very quickly, this again suggests that pattern recognition is not based on template matching.

Prototype theories

Template matching theory argues that an exact match is necessary for pattern recognition. *Prototype theory* states that patterns are recognised by comparing them to prototypes stored in memory. For example, there is a prototype of the letter 'a' that provides a representation of all the variations of a written or printed 'a'. Prototypes are not as precise and specific as templates – they are not an exact match. Instead, they provide a general representation in terms of which similar patterns can be recognised.

Research indicates that patterns are recognised even when people have never seen a pattern that exactly matches the prototype. For example, Reed (1972) showed participants series of faces, some of which are shown in Figure 2. The faces differed on four dimensions: eye separation, height of mouth, height of forehead and nose length. Participants were asked to divide the faces into two categories, using their own criteria.

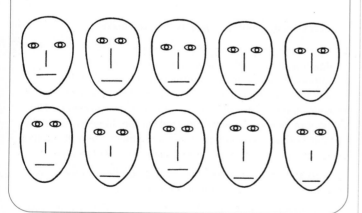

Figure 2 Examples of Reed's faces

When they were later shown faces that had an average value for each of the four dimensions, participants found it very easy to categorise them, even though they did not have a combination of features that they had seen before. Reed investigated how participants had categorised the faces, and concluded that no details of individual faces were held in memory. It appeared that each new face was compared to an average of the dimensions of the previous sets of faces shown. In other words, the participants created prototypes of faces and compared each new face to the prototype in order to categorise it. When the average face was presented, it matched the participant's idea of the prototype so closely that it was very easily categorised.

Evaluation Far fewer prototypes than templates would be

required for pattern recognition. This overcomes the storage problems that would occur if vast numbers of templates were needed. Prototype theories provide a general explanation of how variations of the same pattern are recognised. However, they do not explain how patterns are compared to prototypes, or how closely a pattern has to resemble a prototype in order to be recognised.

Feature detection theories

Feature detection theories start with the idea that patterns have distinctive features (Selfridge, 1959). Recognising a pattern begins with the identification of its features or parts. For example, the key features of a face are eyes, nose, mouth, and so on.

Feature detection theories see pattern recognition as a step-by-step process. First, the features of a pattern are extracted. For example, a capital 'H' consists of two straight vertical lines and one straight horizontal line. These features are recognised by comparison with similar features held in memory. For example, the straight, vertical and horizontal lines that make up the letter 'H' are identified on the basis of information about lines held in memory. Further information in memory is then used to combine the key features which are recognised as making up the letter 'H'.

Evaluation – supporting evidence The following evidence provides support for feature detection theories.

- Research indicates that people take longer to identify a pattern when it shares features with other patterns around it. For example, Neisser (1964) found that participants detected the letter 'Z' more quickly when it was surrounded with letters made up of curved lines (eg, O, Q, U) than when it was amongst letters made up of straight lines (eg, T, L, W). It appears that the more similar the features, the more difficult it is to identify the pattern. This suggests that the identification of features plays a part in pattern recognition.
- There is also biological support for feature detection theories. Hubel and Wiesel (1962, 1965, 1979) used single-cell recording techniques with animals – typically monkeys or cats. They carefully measured the responses of individual brain cells (neurons) in the visual cortex – the part of the brain responsible for dealing with visual stimuli. They showed that individual neurons respond best to particular types of lines. For example, one neuron might respond strongly when a vertical line is presented, but will not respond at all to a horizontal line. Other investigations found neurons that respond to corners and angles of different orientations. In some areas of the visual cortex, certain neurons respond particularly strongly to specific shapes such as a hand or a face.

The neurons described in the above paragraph are sometimes called *feature detectors*. They appear to specialise in the detection of particular features. This provides support for feature detection theories of pattern recognition. (For a more detailed description of biological theories of feature detection, see pp 348-349.)

Evaluation – criticisms Although there is some evidence that feature detection plays a part in pattern recognition, it is clear that other factors are also important.

- Identifying a list of features is not sufficient to recognise a pattern. Identification requires the relationship between features to be specified. For example, the features of the letter 'T' are one vertical and one horizontal line. These features can be presented as 'L', which is clearly not recognisable as a letter 'T'. Feature detection theories tend to focus on the features of a pattern rather than the relationship between the features (Eysenck & Keane, 2000).
- Experimental evidence does not always support the finding that letters with similar features tend to be confused. In one experiment, participants were shown individual letters in rapid succession and asked to name them. Letters with similar features such as 'N' and 'Z' were *not* confused. Feature detection theory predicts that they would be confused (Harvey, Roberts & Gervais, 1983).
- People recognise three-dimensional objects even though many of their features are hidden from view. For example, they recognise a cup when they cannot see the handle; they recognise a car when only the rear end is visible. Because objects are three-dimensional, parts are always hidden from view. With its emphasis on feature detection, feature detection theory has difficulty explaining why three-dimensional objects are easily recognised.
- Feature detection theory implies that the more features there are in a pattern, and the more complex those features, the longer it would take to recognise the pattern. There is no evidence for this.
- Feature detection theories, along with template matching and prototype theories, tend to ignore the importance of context in pattern recognition. Consider the following phrase with a missing letter. 'A b_ttle of beer'. The context, in this case the letters surrounding the missing letter and the link with beer, provide clues for the completion of the word. Context is important for pattern recognition but is largely ignored by the theories in this section. It is examined in Section 5.2.

Key terms

Feature detection theories *Theories of pattern recognition in which features of objects are examined then compared to features stored in memory. An object is recognised when sufficient features are matched.*

Feature detectors *Neurons in the visual cortex that specialise in detecting particular features.*

Biederman's recognition-by-components theory

Biederman (1987, 1990) says that objects can be regarded as consisting of different-shaped three-dimensional building blocks arranged in different ways. He called the blocks *geons* (short for geometric icons). Examples of geons are blocks, cylinders, spheres, arcs and wedges. Biederman says that there are about 36 different geons, and that these are combined in various ways to make up objects. For example, a cup is made up of an arc connected to the side of a cylinder, a suitcase is a rectangular block with an arc attached to one side of it, and so on (see

Figure 3). Recognition of objects involves the extraction of the component geons. These are then matched with stored representations to see which one best fits the geon-based information from the visual object. *Recognition-by-components theory* is a type of three-dimensional feature theory.

Figure 3   Geons

Geons

Objects

Examples of geons and objects they can make

Evaluation At first sight, Biederman's recognition-by-components theory provides a reasonable and plausible explanation of object recognition. A small number of geons provides the basis for recognising a vast array of objects. The amount of storage capacity required for the 36 geons is small. Yet this compact geon kit provides a flexible system of building blocks which can be applied to a wide variety of objects.

Despite its attractiveness, there are a number of problems with recognition-by-components theory.

- The theory fails to take account of the importance of colour and texture in object recognition. For example, colour is important for identifying fruits and vegetables. And people find it more difficult to recognise an object if it appears in an unusual colour – for instance, a green postbox.
- The theory does not explain how we can recognise objects that are the same shape but which have different colours. How, for example, are we able to tell the difference between a carrot and a parsnip? Biederman's theory concentrates on shape, and says nothing about colour.
- We often process the overall shape of an object before we analyse any of its parts. We can sometimes identify an object from its overall shape rather than by analysing its constituent geons (Kimchi, 1992).
- Some objects (eg, clouds) do not contain any geons, yet we can easily recognise them.

- The role of prior knowledge and experience is ignored. For example, Biederman explains how we can recognise cups, but how do we recognise which is *our* cup?
- There is no evidence that there are 36 geons (Eysenck & Keane, 2000).
- Cave and Kosslyn (1993) showed that pictures of objects were just as easy to recognise when broken down into 'unnatural'

parts as when the picture was broken down into geons. Recognition by components theory would predict that objects should be easier to recognise when the individual geons are intact, as in the left-hand picture in Figure 4, than when the geons are split into parts, as in the right-hand picture.

Key terms

Recognition-by-components theory *Biederman's theory that objects are recognised by extracting individual component parts.*

Geons (geometric icons) *According to Biederman, the basic building-block shapes from which all objects are comprised.*

Figure 4   An example of Cave and Kosslyn's stimuli

Activity 5   Incomplete patterns

Item A   Partly hidden

[Image of a partly hidden truck]

Item B   Missing letters

How much information do we need to recognise written words? F-r -x-mpl-, th-s s-nt-nc- h-s n- v-w-ls, b-t y-- c-n st-ll r--d -t.

Questions

1 The truck in Item A is easily recognisable. How can this be used to argue against (a) template theories, (b) prototype theories and, (c) feature theories?

2   Read the sentence in Item B.
   a) Assuming that you can read it, how does this cast doubt on template and feature theories of pattern recognition?
   b) How might an awareness of context help to 'fill in' the blanks?

5.2   The importance of context

Bottom-up processing Feature detection theories and recognition-by-components theory assume that pattern recognition begins with an analysis of the component parts of an object – that is the parts which make up an object. For example, feature detection theories state that the key features of a pattern are first extracted and then combined. The pattern is then recognised. This is known as *bottom-up processing* or *data-driven processing*.

Theories which emphasise bottom-up processing pay little attention to the context in which a pattern occurs. Context can be very important for pattern recognition. Consider the following objects – cake fork, cheese knife, olive stoner, garlic crusher, pastry cutter, pastry brush, zester, juicer. They may well be recognised more easily if they were seen in context – in the cutlery drawer or in the kitchen cupboard, or actually in use in the kitchen.

Top-down processing Also known as *concept-driven processing*, this involves the use of context for pattern recognition. When recognising objects, people draw on their knowledge and expectations of the context. In the above example, they draw on

their knowledge and expectations of kitchens in order to recognise the various kitchen implements. That is, they start from the top (the context) and zero in on the particular pattern (the object).

The importance of top-down processing to pattern recognition can be seen from the missing-letter sentence in Activity 5. The sentence can be read because we have knowledge and expectations about what the missing letters are likely to be and what word is likely to follow on from other words. Although the features of the missing letters are not there to be analysed, context can be used to work out what the letters should be and to 'fill-in' the blank spaces.

A large amount of the evidence concerning the role of context in pattern recognition comes from research into reading processes. The evidence suggests that there is much more to reading processes than the bottom-up analysis of letters and words. If we were to read entirely by extracting features of letters, we would need to detect about 5,000 features per minute. This would require an enormous amount of processing resources, and could not account for the speed with which most adults read (Matlin, 1998).

Support for the use of top-down processing is provided by the *word superiority effect*. This is the fact that a single letter that is part of a word can be recognised much more easily than the same letter presented as part of a non-word. For example, the letter *r* in *work* can be recognised much more quickly than the *r* in *korw* (Reicher, 1969). This suggests that prior knowledge that the word 'work' contains an *r* allows faster identification of the letter than would be expected through bottom-up feature analysis.

Sometimes, the same set of features can be interpreted in different ways depending on the context in which it is presented. For example, read the following sentence.

THE MAN RAN.

The second letter of the first word is recognised as 'H'. The second letter of the second word is recognised as 'A'. In terms of features, though, these two letters are identical. Why are they recognised as different letters? Feature theories do not explain this. Theories based on top-down processing do.

Other patterns can also be recognised more quickly if presented in context. Palmer (1975) asked participants to identify pictures of objects that were shown very briefly. Some participants were initially shown a picture showing a familiar scene, such as a kitchen. Following this, they were very briefly shown a picture of an object that was either associated with the kitchen, such as a loaf of bread, or would not normally be expected to be found in the kitchen, such as a drum. Palmer found that participants were much better at identifying the object when it was something that

was associated with the kitchen.

In another condition, Palmer asked participants to identify the objects without first having been shown the picture of the kitchen scene. Participants found it much more difficult to identify the loaf of bread when recognition of it was not primed by the presentation of the associated scene. Both groups of participants had seen the same picture of a loaf of bread for the same duration. If pattern recognition is a bottom-up process, both groups should have been equally likely to recognise the loaf of bread. However, where context allowed top-down processing to be used, participants were more likely to identify the loaf.

So far, this unit has focused on theories of two-dimensional pattern recognition, using letters and pictures as examples. How do people process and recognise more complex patterns? Specifically, how do they recognise people's faces?

Key terms

Top-down processing *Cognitive processing that first takes account of context, knowledge and expectation.*

Bottom-up processing *Cognitive processing that deals first with the characteristics or component parts of a stimulus.*

Word-superiority effect *The finding that an individual letter can be more easily recognised if it is part of a word rather than part of a non-word.*

Activity 6   Context effects in word recognition

Item A   An experiment on word recognition

Rueckl and Oden (1986) found that context is important in word recognition. They presented participants with a word that contained either a clearly identifiable letter (*r* or *n*) or a symbol part way between the two letters (see the stimuli along the bottom of the graph in Item B). In each case, the stimulus letter pattern was embedded in the word 'bea-s', so that there were five stimuli ranging between 'n' and 'r'.

Altering the sentence in which the word was contained changed the context in which the stimuli were presented. There were four different versions of the sentence (the dash could be replaced by any of the five letter patterns):

The lion tamer raised bea-s to supplement his income.
The zookeeper raised bea-s to supplement his income.
The botanist raised bea-s to supplement his income.
The dairy farmer raised bea-s to supplement his income.

The idea is that a lion tamer or a zookeeper will be more likely to raise bears and botanists and dairy farmers would be more likely to raise beans. On each trial, the participant saw one sentence for one second. Then the two test words ('beans' and 'bears') were shown, and participants were asked which one they had seen.

Item B   Rueckl and Oden's results

The graph give the percentage of participants who said they saw the word *bears*. It shows that participants were more likely to see bears when the subject of the sentence was lion tamer or zookeeper, rather than botanist or dairy farmer.

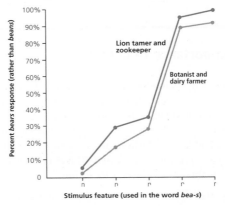

Adapted from Rueckl & Oden, 1986

Questions

1   Summarise the results shown on the graph in Item B.

2   Briefly explain the results.

3   How can the results be used to support the idea that top-down processes are important in pattern recognition?

5.3   Face recognition

Face recognition is the most common method of recognising and identifying familiar people. There has been a lot of research into the processes involved in recognising faces, and more is known about these processes than about recognition of other patterns or objects.

Template matching

Some theorists of face recognition have considered template theories, but, as outlined earlier, such explanations have severe shortcomings. In particular, a separate template would be needed for each possible view of a person's face.

Feature theories

Feature theories state that the description of a person's face is stored as a list of features with which the seen face is compared. Such a list might include hair colour, hair style, shape of face, shape of nose, shape of lips, colour of eyes, skin tone, whether the person wears glasses or has a moustache, and so on.

When a face is seen, the features can be matched against stored lists. If the seen features match the features on a stored list, then the face will be recognised as familiar. This type of feature-based model is flexible, in that it allows the face to be recognised from different angles, unlike a template model.

Features do seem to play a role in face recognition. Police forces often make use of Identikit methods in which witnesses are asked to build up a picture of a suspect's face on a feature-by-feature basis.

Configuration

There are, however, some problems with a simple feature-based model. First, people find it difficult to recognise inverted faces, despite the fact they contain the same features as a non-inverted face (Valentine, 1988). Second, a 'scrambled' face like the one shown in Figure 5 is harder to recognise than a normal face. The scrambled face of the singer Robbie Williams has all the same features as his normal face, but they are arranged differently – they have a different *configuration*.

Also, as Figure 6 shows, varying the configuration of a fixed set of features can radically alter the overall appearance of a face. In Figure 6, each pair of faces (1 and 2; 3 and 4; 5 and 6; 7 and 8) differs only in the configuration of their internal

Figure 5   A scrambled face

Figure 6   The importance of configuration

features. This suggests that a simple list of features is not specific enough to account for face recognition (Sergent, 1984).

Rhodes, Brennan and Carey (1987) demonstrated the importance of the configuration of features. They found that caricatures of faces were more recognisable than accurate line drawings of the same face. This, they suggested, is because caricatures emphasise the features and the configurations of features that make the face different from the 'average' face. Emphasising these differences in a caricature makes the face easier to recognise.

Activity 7   Recognising caricatures

Famous people

Questions

1   Look at the caricatures. Assuming that you can recognise Tony Blair, Sir Elton John and Courteney Cox Arquette, why are they so easily recognisable?

2   Why does our ability to recognise caricatures cast doubt on template theories of face recognition?

Bruce and Young's model of face recognition

Research findings indicate that a number of important factors need to be incorporated into any model of face recognition. These findings are summarised below.

- There is evidence that facial expression is processed separately from the face. There are patients with neurological damage who can identify facial expressions (happiness, sadness, anger, etc) but who cannot identify faces. There are other patients who show the reverse pattern (Bruce & Young, 1986).
- The ability to lip-read has been shown to be independent of face recognition. Some individuals who have suffered brain damage can recognise faces but not lip-read, while others cannot lip-read but can recognise faces.
- People make certain kinds of error in recognising faces. For example, they sometimes find the face familiar but are unable to retrieve any further information about the person from memory. Sometimes, people are able to retrieve information about the person (eg, that the face is that of an actor), but are unable to retrieve the name. When people are able to correctly name a face they are always able to retrieve information about the person. For example, you would never see the face of Liam Gallagher of the band *Oasis* and say 'That's Liam Gallagher, but I have no idea who Liam Gallagher is'. Young, Hay and Ellis (1985) found

that of over 1000 errors in face recognition there were 190 occasions on which a participant could remember information about a person, but could not think of their name. There were no occasions on which a participant could name a face while knowing nothing about the person.

Bruce and Young (1986) incorporated these findings into a model of face recognition. Their model is illustrated in Figure 7. Each box represents either a separate processing stage or a memory store. The arrows indicate the transmission of information between these stages and stores.

The model begins with the visual processing of the face, or *structural encoding*. This produces various representations of the face, first as it is seen from the viewer's perspective, and then as a representation independent of the facial expression. As mentioned earlier, facial expression is processed separately, so there is a separate *expression analysis* box.

Facial speech analysis is the part of the system that deals with lip-reading. Visual information from lip movements helps us to make sense of what people are saying to us. It is easier to understand speech when we can see the speaker's lips. This is why it's sometimes more difficult to understand what someone says on the telephone. It is also the reason why radio broadcasters need to speak very clearly.

Directed visual processing is included because we can direct attention to particular facial features. For example, if we know that the friend we are meeting at the busy railway station has long blonde hair, we might look specifically for that feature, ignoring faces that do not have it.

The structural encoding unit passes information on to the *face recognition units*. Each unit contains stored information about the face of a familiar person. The more a seen face resembles a face stored in a face recognition unit, the greater the stimulation of that unit. Face recognition units are linked to both the *cognitive system* and the *person identity nodes*.

The cognitive system is a store of information about people, and is part of *semantic memory* in which knowledge about the world is stored. The cognitive system might, for example, help us to decide that a person is old, because we know that old people tend to have wrinkled faces.

The person identity nodes are responsible for recognising the person. The face recognition units allow us to judge that a face is familiar and the person identity nodes use information from the cognitive system to recognise the person. The person identity nodes provide information about the person, such as their occupation, interests, friends, and so on.

When a person identity node has been activated, *name generation* allows us to retrieve the person's name and thus put a name to the face.

The structure of this model captures the kinds of errors that people make, and those that they never make. For example, it is clear from this model that the name cannot be generated without semantic information about the person first being accessed. The name 'Liam Gallagher' cannot be retrieved from the *name generation* system without the face first being recognised, and the appropriate *person identity* node being activated. In short, this model doesn't allow Liam Gallagher's face to be named without knowing who Liam Gallagher *is*.

Figure 7 Bruce and Young's model of face recognition

Adapted from Eysenck & Keane (2000)

Evaluation

Advantages There are a number of advantages to the Bruce and Young model.

- There is evidence from neuropsychological patients that supports the Bruce and Young model. The model predicts that a face cannot be named without some other information about the person also being available. Patients with brain damage show this pattern. There are also patients in whom the opposite pattern is evident – they can remember who people *are* and produce accurate information about them, but simply cannot recall their name. Flude, Ellis and Kay (1989) report that a patient was able to correctly retrieve people's occupations 85% of the time when shown their faces, but could only retrieve their name 15% of the time. This provides support for the idea that people's names are stored separately from other information about the person.

- The model also predicts that decisions about whether a face is familiar should be faster than decisions about whether, for instance, the person is an actor. This is because a feeling of familiarity is generated when the face recognition unit is activated, whereas information about the person is accessed from the person identity node, which cannot be activated until *after* the face recognition unit has been activated. Young et al. (1986) found that participants could, indeed, make faster decisions about familiarity than about other types of information about the person. This supports the model.

  Young, Hay and Ellis (1985) found that participants often reported a feeling of familiarity, combined with an inability to recall any other information about the person. This is due to the face recognition unit being activated, but the information not being passed on to the appropriate person identity node. In other words, the model can explain why we sometimes find someone's face familiar, but can't 'place them'.

- There is evidence from neuropsychological patients to support the idea that the ability to analyse facial expression is independent of the ability to recognise faces, as the model predicts (Young et al. 1993).

Disadvantages There are a number of findings which the Bruce and Young model fails to explain.

- Experiments have shown that a person's face is more easily recognised if it is seen immediately after the face of a second person with whom it is associated (Bruce & Valentine, 1986). For example, the face of Stan Laurel will be recognised more quickly if the face of Oliver Hardy is shown before it. The Bruce and Young model cannot explain this.

- Second, the Bruce and Young model assumes that names are stored separately from other information about the person. Whilst, in all normal cases, a name cannot be retrieved without information being known about the person, there are rare patients with neurological damage who are able to match faces to names of famous people while being unable to retrieve any autobiographical information about the person. This inability to retrieve autobiographical information suggests that the person identity nodes are damaged. This should prevent information about the name from being retrieved, and so the patient should not be able to match faces to names in this way (de Haan, Young & Newcombe, 1991).

Burton, Bruce and Johnston (1990) and later Burton and Bruce (1992) developed the Bruce and Young model to account for these findings. This revised model is outlined in the following section.

The interactive activation model of face recognition

This model is shown in Figure 8. It assumes that there are three sources of information:

- *Face recognition units*: These are activated by the presentation of any familiar face.
- *Person identity nodes*: These are connected to the semantic system.
- *Semantic information units*: Information about the person, including their name.

Figure 8   Interactive activation model of face recognition

Adapted from Burton et al., 1990

Each unit is linked to other units that it is associated with (eg, each face recognition unit is linked directly to the appropriate person identity node). Person identity nodes are linked to semantic information. For example, in Figure 8, the person identity node for Leonardo Di Caprio is linked to the semantic information that he is a film star. In the full model, the person identity node for Leonardo Di Caprio is linked to all semantic information about him – he is an actor, American, the star of *The Beach*, *Romeo and Juliet*, *Titanic*, and so on.

In the interactive activation model, face recognition occurs if the excitation in the person identity node reaches a certain threshold level. A unit that is excited will transmit excitation to all of the units that it is linked to. There are also inhibitory links, so that, for example, when one person identity node becomes more excited, all of the other person identity nodes will become less excited.

This model has been successful in explaining aspects of face recognition which the earlier Bruce and Young model failed to explain. For example, when the face of Prince Charles is seen, it will excite the person identity node for Prince Charles. This will pass excitation to the appropriate semantic information node (in Figure 8, 'royalty'). This, in turn, passes excitation *back* to the Prince Charles person identity node, but also passes excitation to the person identity node for Prince William (since he is also a 'royal'). The passing back and forth of information in this way continues until the system 'levels out' at a certain level of activation. When the system levels out, the result will be that the Prince Charles person identity node is activated the most, but the

Prince William person identity node will have some activation, although not enough to reach the threshold. If the face of Prince William is then shown, it will then be recognised more quickly because the person identity node still has some activation left over from when Prince Charles's face was shown. In this way, faces are recognised more quickly when an associated face has preceded them. This finding could not be explained by the Bruce and Young model.

The interactive activation model also explains why names are harder to access than other information even though they are stored in the same system, rather than a different system as suggested by Bruce and Young. Burton and Bruce (1992) pointed out that a person's name is connected with only one person identity node, while other types of semantic information (eg, actor) will be linked to many person identity nodes. Because of this, names receive less excitation, while more general concepts like actor will receive excitation from lots of person identity nodes. It is not necessary to assume that names are stored separately and treated differently from other types of information in order to explain why names are more difficult to access. The fact that a name is a usually a unique identifier for a person explains why other semantic information is accessed before the name.

The interactive activation model provides a more complete explanation of the research findings into face recognition than the Bruce and Young model.

Summary

1. Attempts to explain the processes involved in pattern recognition have included template theories, prototype theories, feature theories, and recognition by components theory.

2. Template theories argue that stimuli are matched against patterns stored in memory. This would require an almost infinite number of templates for pattern recognition to be successful.

3. Prototype theories suggest that stimuli are compared to a prototype stored in memory. These theories do not explain how the comparison is made, or how similar to the prototype the stimulus has to be.

4. Feature theories state that patterns are made up of features that can be individually identified and compared to lists of features stored in memory. Feature theories fail to explain how relationships between features are recognised.

5. Biederman's recognition-by-components model suggests that three-dimensional objects are recognised by extracting the geons (shapes) that comprise them. This model does not explain how objects with similar shapes are differentiated.

6. Theories of pattern recognition tend to overlook the importance of context. Patterns, including objects, can be recognised more quickly when they are presented in context.

7. Approaches to face recognition have included template theories and feature theories. Template theories are too inflexible, but there is evidence that features play a role in face recognition.

8. A list of features is not specific enough – the configuration of features is also important for face recognition.

9. Bruce and Young's model of face recognition incorporated a number of processing stages. This model explained some findings, but was unable to explain others, such as the fact that a face will be recognised more quickly if it has been preceded by another face that is associated with it.

10. The interactive activation model of face recognition improved upon the Bruce and Young model by explaining more of the research findings.

References

Allport, D.A. (1989). Visual attention. In M.I. Posner (Ed.), *Foundations of cognitive science*. Cambridge, MA: MIT Press.

Barshi, I. & Healy, A. F. (1993). Checklist procedures and the cost of automaticity. *Memory and Cognition, 21*, 496-505.

Biederman, I. (1987). Recognition-by-components: A theory of human image understanding. *Psychological Review, 94*, 115-147.

Biederman, I. (1990). Higher-level vision. In D.N. Osherson, S. Kosslyn & J. Hollerbach (Eds.), *An invitation to cognitive science: Visual cognition and action*. Cambridge, MA: MIT Press.

Broadbent, D. E. (1954). The role of auditory localization in attention and memory span. *Journal of Experimental Psychology, 47*, 191-196.

Broadbent, D. E. (1958). *Perception and communication*. Oxford: Pergamon.

Bruce, V. & Valentine, T. (1986). When a nod's as good as a wink: The role of dynamic information in face recognition. In M. Gruneberg, P. Morris & R. Sykes (Eds.), *Practical aspects of memory: Current research and issues (Vol. 1)*. Chichester, UK: John Wiley.

Bruce, V. & Young, A. W. (1986). Understanding face recognition. *British Journal of Psychology, 77*, 305-327.

Bryan, W. L. & Harter, N. (1899). Studies on the telegraphic language. *Psychological Review, 4*, 27-53.

Burton, A. M. & Bruce, V. (1992). I recognize your face but I can't remember your name: A simple explanation? *British Journal of Psychology, 83*, 45-60.

Burton, A. M., Bruce, V. & Johnston, R. A. (1990). Understanding face recognition with an interactive activation model. *British Journal of Psychology, 81*, 361-380.

Cave, C. B. & Kosslyn, S. M. (1993). The role of parts and spatial relations in object identification. *Perception, 22*, 229-248.

Cheng, P. W. (1985). Restructuring versus automaticity: Alternative accounts of skill acquisition. *Psychological Review, 92*, 414-423.

Cherry, E. C. (1953). Some experiments on the recognition of speech with one and two ears. *Journal of the Acoustical Society of America, 25*, 975-979.

De Haan, E. H. F., Young, A. W. & Newcombe, F. (1991). A dissociation between the sense of familiarity and access to semantic information concerning familiar people. *European Journal of Cognitive Psychology, 3*, 51-67.

Deutsch, J. A. & Deutsch, D. (1963). Attention: some theoretical considerations. *Psychological Review, 70*, 80-90.

Deutsch, J.A. & Deutsch, D. (1967). Comments on "Selective attention: Perception or response?" *Quarterly Journal of Experimental Psychology, 19*, 362-363.

Eysenck, M. W. & Keane, M. T. (2000). *Cognitive psychology: A student's handbook*. Hove: LEA.

Flude, B. M., Ellis, A. W. & Kay, J. (1989). Face processing and name retrieval in an anomic aphasia: Names are stored separately from semantic information about people. *Brain and Cognition, 11*, 60-72.

Gray, J. A. & Wedderburn, A. A. (1960). Grouping strategies with simultaneous stimuli. *Quarterly Journal of Experimental Psychology, 12*, 180-184.

Harvey, L. O., Roberts, J. O. & Gervais, M. J. (1983). The spatial frequency basis of internal representations. In H.-G. Geissler, H. F. J. M. Buffart, E. L. J. Leeuwenberg & V. Sarris (Eds.), *Modern issues in perception*. Rotterdam: North-Holland.

Hubel, D. H. & Wiesel, T. N. (1962). Receptive fields, binocular interaction and functional architecture in the cat's visual cortex. *Journal of Physiology, 160*, 106-154.

Hubel, D. H. & Wiesel, T. N. (1965). Receptive fields of single neurons in two non-striate visual areas, 18 and 19 of the cat. *Journal of Neurophysiology, 28*, 229-289.

Hubel, D. H. & Wiesel, T. N. (1979). Brain mechanisms of vision. *Scientific American, 241*, 130-144.

Johnston, W. A. & Heinz, S. P. (1978). Flexibility and capacity demands of attention. *Journal of Experimental Psychology: General, 107*, 420-435.

Kahneman, D. (1973). *Attention and effort*. Englewood Cliffs, NJ: Prentice Hall.

Kimchi, R. (1992). Primacy of wholistic processing and global/local paradigm: A critical review. Psychological Bulletin, 112, 24-38.

Lackner, J.R. & Garrett, M.F. (1972). Resolving ambiguity: Effects of biasing context in the unattended ear. *Cognition, 1*, 359-372.

Langer, E. J. (1989). *Mindfulness*. New York: Addison-Wesley.

Logan, G. D. (1988). Toward an instance theory of automatisation. *Psychological Review, 95*, 492-527.

Matlin, M. W. (1998). *Cognition*, (4th ed.). Fort Worth: Harcourt Brace.

Moray, N. (1959). Attention in dichotic listening: Affective cues and the influence of instructions. *Quarterly Journal of Experimental Psychology, 11*, 56-60.

Neisser, U. (1964). Visual search. *Scientific American, 210*, 94-101.

Norman, D.A. (1969). Memory while shadowing. *Quarterly Journal of Experimental Psychology, 21*, 85-93.

Norman, D. A. & Bobrow, D. T. (1975). On data-limited and resource-limited processes. *Cognitive Psychology, 7*, 44-64.

Norman, D. A. & Shallice, T. (1986). Attention to action: Willed and automatic control of behavior. In R. J. Davidson, D. E. Schwartz & D. Shapiro (Eds.), *Consciousness and self-regulation: Advances in research and theory, vol. 4*. New York: Plenum Press.

Palmer, S.E. (1975). The effects of contextual scenes on the identification of objects. *Memory & Cognition, 3*, 519-526.

Pashler, H. (1990). Do response modality effects support multiprocessor models of divided attention? *Journal of Experimental Psychology: Human Perception and Performance, 16*, 826-842.

Reason, J. T. (1979). Actions not as planned: The price of automatisation. In G. Underwood & R. Stevens (Eds.), *Aspects of consciousness: Vol. 1. Psychological issues*. London: Academic Press.

Reason, J. T. (1992). Cognitive underspecification: Its variety and consequences. In B. J. Baars (Ed.), *Experimental slips and human error: Exploring the architecture of volition*. New York: Plenum Press.

Reed, S. K. (1972). Pattern recognition and categorization. *Cognitive Psychology, 3*, 382-407.

Reicher, G. M. (1969). Perceptual recognition as a function of meaningfulness of stimuli material. *Journal of Experimental Psychology, 81*, 275-280.

Rhodes, G., Brennan, S. & Carey, S. (1987). Identification and ratings of caricatures: Implications for mental representations of faces. *Cognitive Psychology, 19*, 473-497.

Rueckl, J. G. & Oden, G. C. (1986). The integration of contextual and featural information during word identification. *Journal of Memory and Language, 25*, 445-460.

Schneider, W. & Shiffrin, R. M. (1977). Controlled and automatic human information processing: I. Detection, search, and attention. *Psychological Review, 84*, 1-66.

Segal, S.J. & Fusella, V. (1970). Influence of imaged pictures and sounds on detection of visual and auditory signals. *Journal of Experimental Psychology, 83*, 458-464.

Selfridge, O. G. (1959). Pandemonium: A paradigm for learning. In *Symposium on the mechanisation of thought processes*. London: HMSO.

Sellen, A. J. & Norman, D. A. (1992). The psychology of slips. In B. J. Baars (Ed.), *Experimental slips and human error: Exploring the architecture of volition*. New York: Plenum Press.

Sergent, J. (1984). An investigation into component and configurational processes underlying face perception. *British Journal of Psychology, 75*, 221-242.

Shiffrin, R.M. & Schneider, W. (1977). Controlled and automatic human information processing: II. Perceptual learning, automatic attending, and a general theory. *Psychological Review, 84*, 127-190.

Stroop, J.R. (1935). Studies of interference in serial verbal reactions. *Journal of Experimental Psychology, 18*, 643-662.

Treisman, A.M. (1964). Verbal cues, language, and meaning in selective attention. *American Journal of Psychology, 77*, 206-219.

Treisman, A.M. (1988). Features and objects: The fourteenth Bartlett memorial lecture. *Quarterly Journal of Experimental Psychology, 40A*, 201-237.

Treisman, A.M. & Geffen, G. (1967). Selective attention: Perception or response? *Quarterly Journal of Experimental Psychology, 19*, 1-18.

Treisman, A.M. & Riley, J.G.A. (1969). Is selective attention selective perception or selective response: A further test. *Journal of Experimental Psychology, 79*, 27-34.

Valentine, T. (1988). Upside-down faces: A review of the effects of inversion upon face recognition. *British Journal of Psychology, 79*, 471-491.

Von Wright, J. M., Anderson, K. & Stenman, U. (1975). Generalisation of conditioned G.S.R.s in dichotic listening. In P. M. A. Rabbitt & S. Dornic (Eds.), *Attention and Performance V*. London: Academic Press.

Welford, A. T. (1952). The psychological refractory period and the timing of high-speed performance. *British Journal of Psychology, 43*, 2-19.

Young, A. W., Hay, D. C. & Ellis, A. W. (1985). The faces that launched a thousand slips: Everyday difficulties and errors in recognising people. *British Journal of Psychology, 76*, 495-523.

Young, A. W., McWeeny, K. H., Hay, D. C. & Ellis, A. W. (1986b). Matching familiar and unfamiliar faces on identity and expression. *Psychological Research, 48*, 63-68.

Young, A. W., Newcombe, F., de Haan, E. H. F., Small, M. & Hay, D. C.

(1993). Face perception after brain injury: Selective impairments affecting identity and expression. *Brain, 116*, 941-959.

Zimbardo, P.G., McDermott, M., Junsz, J. & Metaal, N. (1995). *Psychology: A European text*. London: Harper Collins.

Introduction

The ability to make sense of the world around us is very important. We use our senses to take in information from the world, but this isn't enough. We need to be able to organise and interpret the information. It is this organisation and interpretation that is referred to as perception. Psychologists have studied the processes involved in visual perception more than any other sensory system. This chapter focuses on visual perception.

What is the structure of the visual system? How does it work? How do we process colour and visual features? How do we make sense of the information that comes in through our eyes? How much does perception depend on our prior experiences and knowledge? How do children develop visual perception? Is the ability to organise and interpret the visual world something that we are born with, or is it learned through experience? These questions are examined in this chapter.

Chapter summary

- Unit 1 examines the structure and function of the visual system.
- Unit 2 looks at different theories of perceptual organisation.
- Unit 3 reviews explanations of perceptual development, including the nature-nurture debate.

Unit 1 Structure and function of the visual system

KEY ISSUES

1 What is the difference between sensation and perception?
2 What is the structure of the visual system?
3 How do we perceive contrast, colour and features?

1.1 Sensation and perception

The distinction between *sensation* and *perception* is an important one in psychology. *Sensation* refers to the collection of information from the environment through the senses. In the case of vision, sensation involves light rays entering the eye and stimulating cells at the back of the eye. *Perception* is the process by which the brain makes sense of the sensory information entering through the eye. Gregory (1966) suggests that 'perception is not simply determined by stimulus patterns; rather it is a dynamic searching for the best interpretation of the available data'. Sensation is the collection of data from the environment and perception is the interpretation of the data.

Key terms

Sensation *The collection of data from the environment through the sense organs.*

Perception *The organisation and interpretation of the information collected by the sense organs.*

1.2 The visual system

The eye is the sense organ that collects visual information from the environment. It is estimated that at least 80% of sensory input arrives through the eye, so for those people who possess all of their sensory abilities, the eye is a very important organ. The structure of the eye is shown in Figure 1.

Figure 1 Diagram of the eye

eye muscle
vitreous humour
ligament
iris
pupil
fovea
aqueous humour
blind spot
lens
cornea
ciliary muscle
optic nerve
sclera (the white of the eye)
retina

Visual sensation begins with light rays entering the eye through the *cornea*, which is the tough transparent membrane on the front of the eye. If you look at someone's eye from the side, you'll be able to see the cornea bulging out. Behind the cornea is the *aqueous humour* – a watery fluid that provides nutrients to the cornea. The cornea needs to be supplied in this way because it cannot be served by blood vessels, as it has to remain totally transparent. Light then passes through the *pupil* – an opening controlled by muscles called the *iris* – and through the *lens*, which changes shape to focus the light rays through the *vitreous humour* – the transparent jelly filling the interior of the eye – on to the *retina* at the back of the eye. The retina is the part of the eye containing the cells that are sensitive to light. The lens thickens to focus on close objects and becomes thinner to focus on objects that are further away. The muscles that change the shape of the lens are called *ciliary muscles*.

When the image from the object being looked at passes through the lens, it is turned upside down (see Figure 2). We do not, however, perceive the world as being upside down because the brain transforms the inverted sensation into a right-way-up perception.

Figure 2   Inversion of the visual stimulus

Key terms

Cornea *Tough transparent membrane in the front of the eye.*

Aqueous humour *Watery fluid behind the cornea.*

Pupil *The circular opening in the front of the eye.*

Iris *The muscles that control the pupil.*

Lens *This focuses light onto the retina by changing shape.*

Vitreous humour *Transparent jelly filling the interior of the eye.*

Retina *The part of the back of the eye sensitive to light.*

Ciliary muscles *Muscles used to change the shape of the lens.*

The pupil

The pupils of the eyes control the amount of light that enters the eye. In bright light, the muscles of the iris cause the pupil to contract to as little as 2 mm in diameter to reduce the amount of light entering. In dim light the iris causes the pupil to dilate – or open – to as much as 8mm in diameter to allow as much light as possible to enter. When you leave a dark room and walk out into bright sunlight, you will be dazzled for a few seconds. This happens because your pupils need to contract to adapt to the change in conditions. The dazzling effect disappears once the pupils have contracted enough to suit the bright sunlight.

Pupils also dilate when we are interested in something, when we see someone who we find attractive, when we are afraid or disturbed, or when we are under the influence of certain drugs.

The retina

The retina is at the back of the eye. A diagram of the retina is shown in Figure 3. It is partly made up of a layer of light-sensitive cells called *photoreceptors*. These are the cells that are stimulated by the light that passes into the eye. There are two types of photoreceptors – *rods* and *cones*.

Figure 3   A section through the retina

Cones are, as the name suggests, cone-shaped. They are sensitive to colour, and function best in bright light. They make up the *photopic system*. Cones are located mainly in the centre of the retina, with fewer towards the periphery. There are about 6 million cones in the retina.

There are about 120 million rods in the retina. Rods are long, thin cells that work best in dim light. They make up the *scotopic system*. They are able to detect movement, but cannot detect colour. At night, we mainly rely on rods for our vision, which is why our night vision is not very good at distinguishing colours. Try looking at the colours of cars that pass you in the street at night and you'll see why witnesses to night-time hit-and-run accidents are often only able to say that the car was 'dark' or 'light-coloured'.

Because rods are concentrated towards the edges on the retina, they are good at picking up movement in the periphery of vision. When you see something move 'out of the corner of your eye' it is because rods have detected it.

When we move from a brightly lit place into a dark one, the rods need to take over from the cones. This can take a little while, which is partly why it takes time to adapt to dark conditions. This adjustment of the eye to deal with dark conditions is called *dark adaptation*.

The retina contains the *fovea* (see Figure 1). This is the part of the retina that has the highest *visual acuity* – the sharpest focus.

The fovea deals with the part of the visual world that we are looking directly at and focusing on. The fovea is made up almost entirely of cones. They are packed very closely together to give a sharp, detailed image. There are about 50,000 cones in the fovea, packed into about 1 square millimetre of space.

The area of the retina outside the fovea is made up of cones and rods, with fewer cones located towards the periphery.

The rods and cones pass information to the *bipolar cells*, which in turn pass information onto the *ganglion cells* that form the *optic nerve*, the nerve that carries the information from the eye to the brain (see Figure 3). In order for the light to reach the rods and cones, it has to pass through layers of other cells and through the blood vessels that serve the retina. If you stare at a clear blue sky, or a similar visual field, you will be able to see the blood moving through the blood vessels that lie in front of the rods and cones.

There is a point in the retina that contains no photoreceptors – ie, no rods or cones. This is the point at which the optic nerve leaves the eye. It is called the *blindspot*. We do not usually notice the area of blindness in our visual field for two reasons. First, the brain compensates for this gap in the retina by 'filling in' the information. Second, because we usually look through two eyes, the blindspots in both eyes do not correspond to the same point in the visual world. In other words, what one eye does not see, the other usually does. You can investigate the existence of your own blindspots by working through Activity 1.

Key terms

Photoreceptors *Light-sensitive cells in the retina that are stimulated by the light that passes into the eye.*

Rods *Long, thin cells that work best in dim light. They are able to detect movement, but cannot detect colour.*

Scotopic system *The visual system for seeing in dim light*

Cones *Cone-shaped cells that are sensitive to colour and function best in bright light.*

Photopic system *The cone-based system of seeing in brightly lit conditions.*

Fovea *The part of the retina that deals with the part of the visual world that we are looking directly at and focusing on. The fovea provides the sharpest focus.*

Visual acuity *The ability to see the details of a stimulus.*

Bipolar cells *Cells located in the retina that pass information from the rods and cones to the ganglion cells.*

Ganglion cells *Cells that form the optic nerve which carries information to the brain.*

Optic nerve *The nerve that carries the information from the eye to the brain.*

Blindspot *The point in the retina at which the optic nerve joins the eye.*

Activity 1   Find your blindspot

Questions

1   Close your left eye and stare directly at the square. Move the page slowly towards or away from you, always focusing on the square. Suddenly, the circle will ' disappear'.

2   Why does this happen?

3   Why doesn't this work if you keep both eyes open?

The visual pathways

From the retina, the visual information is coded as electrical activity, and is passed along the optic nerve into the brain. The visual system is not like a camera – there are no pictures in the brain, only patterns of electrochemical activity. The visual pathways in the brain are shown in Figure 4.

The optic nerves from the two eyes cross over at a point in the brain called the *optic chiasm*. At this point, information from the eyes crosses over. Information from the left visual field travels to the right-hand side of the brain and vice versa (see Figure 4). Information is then passed into the *lateral geniculate body* – the part of the brain where impulses from the optic nerves are relayed to the *visual cortex*. The visual cortex is located at the back of the brain.

When information reaches the visual cortex, the visual pathway is divided into two streams that appear to serve different functions.

•   The *parietal pathway* ends at the *parietal lobe*, located just

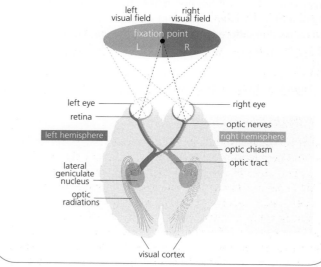

Figure 4   Visual pathways in the brain

left visual field   right visual field
fixation point
L   R
left eye   right eye
retina   optic nerves
left hemisphere   right hemisphere
optic chiasm
optic tract
lateral geniculate nucleus
optic radiations
visual cortex

above the ears. This system seems to make use of visual information to guide our movements, such as reaching and grabbing.

- The *temporal pathway* terminates at the *temporal lobe*, just beneath the temples. This uses visual information to identify what it is we're looking at.

The presence of these two pathways indicates that visual perception is used for two distinct purposes: to identify objects, and to interact with the environment.

Processing of contrast

Objects are mainly defined by their edges and borders. These are indicated by changes in brightness from one surface to another. In order to perceive the objects in the world around us, we need to be able to detect these differences in brightness from one surface to another. The change in brightness from one surface to another is called *contrast*. Rather than just detecting brightness levels, the visual system is set up to exaggerate the contrast, so making it easier to detect objects.

For example, if you look at a television screen when the television is switched off, it will appear to be a mid-grey colour. When the television is switched on, some of the objects on the screen appear black. However, the screen cannot actually be darker when it is switched on – it cannot emit *less* light than when it was off! The perception of black is caused by contrast between the grey screen and the areas of brightness surrounding it. This is an example of the way in which the visual system exaggerates contrast to aid perception.

Another example is shown in Figure 5, below. Each of the solid grey bands appears to be brighter near its border with the darker band to its left, and darker near its boundary with the lighter band to its right.

How does the visual system do this? Photoreceptors have lateral (sideways) connections to other, nearby photoreceptors. When two nearby photoreceptors receive different amounts of light, the photoreceptor that receives more light inhibits (suppresses) the signal sent to the brain by the other photoreceptor. This makes it seem as though there is less light reaching that photoreceptor than there really is. As a result, the contrast between the outputs from the two cells is exaggerated. This process is known as *lateral inhibition*. If we see the brighter edge of an object against a darker background, lateral inhibition makes the contrast between the object and the background seem greater than it really is, enhancing the difference and making the edge of the object more noticeable.

Figure 5   Exaggeration of contrast

Colour vision

Cones are thought to be responsible for colour vision. A number of different theories have attempted to explain how this works.

Trichromatic theory Helmholtz (1885) suggested that there are three different types of cone, each sensitive to a different wavelength of light – that is, to different colours. *Trichromatic* means 'three colours'. The three colours that Helmholtz suggested are red, blue, and green. Because other colours (eg, yellow) are made up of different combinations of red, blue and green light, we are able to perceive different colours because different combinations of cones will become stimulated. For example, yellow contains a mixture of red and green wavelengths. These stimulate red and green cones allowing us to perceive yellow.

This idea is supported by evidence from different types of colour blindness. For example, someone who lacks 'red' cones in their retina will be unable to see red. It isn't clear, however, why someone who is unable to see the colour red is able to perceive yellow.

Some colours that we can perceive are not just combinations of red, blue and green light. For instance, we are able to see silver. It is likely that we do this by combining our natural colour recognition processes with the learned concept of things being 'metallic'.

Opponent process theory Hering (1878) noticed that although we sometimes see colours that are 'bluish-red' or 'yellowish-green', we never see 'yellowish-blue' or 'reddish-green'. Hering also noted that afterimages often appear. If you stare at a small red circle for a minute or so, and then quickly look at a plain white surface, you will see a green circle appear in front of your eyes. Hering suggested that the perceptions of red and green are separate and opposing processes, as are the perceptions of yellow and blue. This idea was supported by Svaetichin (1956) who identified cells in the retina that worked on this colour-opponent basis. For each colour pair, red-green or blue-yellow, one colour of the pair is produced when the receptor is building up activity, and the other colour is produced when the receptor is reducing activity. The two phases cannot occur at the same time. That is why we never see a reddish-green.

A more recent version of *opponent process theory* assumes that the opponent process takes place not in the receptors themselves, but in coding mechanisms closer to the brain.

The two theories – trichromatic theory and opponent process theory – are not necessarily mutually exclusive – each might explain a different process involved in colour vision. Evidence which supports trichromatic theory suggests that there are three types of cones, responsive to different wavelengths of light. Evidence which supports opponent process theory suggests that the ganglion cells operate some kind of 'on-off' process. Some cells respond with a burst of activity when stimulated with one wavelength of light, but are switched 'off' with a different wavelength. This suggests that there is an opponent process taking place, not in the cones, but in the ganglion cells.

Hurvich (1981) argues that there is a two-stage process of colour vision. Each theory explains one stage of this process. The three types of colour receptor respond to different colours of light, and these responses are encoded into opponent signals further along the visual system. The output from the ganglion cells determines what colour is perceived.

Key terms

Trichromatic theory *The theory that colour vision is made up of combinations of activity from three different types of cone, each responsive to different colours of light: red, green, and blue.*

Opponent process theory *The theory that ganglion cells are activated by one wavelength of light and are inhibited by its opposing wavelength.*

Processing of features

In order to identify objects, we need to be able to identify not just areas of contrast, but the orientation of contrasting areas. The angles of lines and edges of objects are important in helping us to perceive the world accurately.

Hubel and Wiesel (1962) conducted Nobel Prize-winning research that showed how the visual system detects the orientation of features. They recorded the electrical activity of individual neurons in the visual cortex of cats and monkeys. They found that different neurons responded best to regions of dark and light presented at different orientations. For example, one neuron might respond most to a vertical line, but not respond at all to the presentation of a horizontal line. Other neurons responded most to a dark bar against a light background, while others responded maximally to a light bar against a dark background (see Figure 4, p349).

With detailed investigation, Hubel and Wiesel found that whole columns of neurons in the visual cortex were responsive to the same orientations. For example, in one column all the neurons would respond best to a vertical bar. In the next column, the neurons would show the greatest response to a bar rotated 5 degrees from the vertical, and so on. Because these neurons seem to be set up to respond to specific features, Hubel and Wiesel called them *feature detectors*. They divided these cells into three types:

- *Simple cells* respond to a line or a straight edge of a particular orientation.
- *Complex cells* also respond a line or straight edge of a particular orientation, but will continue to respond if the line moves, as long as it remains in the same orientation.
- *Hypercomplex cells* respond to lines of a particular orientation and length.

Feature detectors have the capacity to keep track of the relative orientations of areas of light and dark across the whole visual scene. They provide essential information for recognising and identifying objects.

Summary

1 Visual perception is the process of the brain organising and interpreting the information collected by the eyes.

2 Visual perception begins with light entering the eye and striking the retina. Photoreceptors (rods and cones) convert the light into electrochemical activity that the brain can process.

3 The neural pathways in the brain that process the information include the parietal pathway that processes visual information for movement, and the temporal pathway that deals with visual information to recognise objects that are being looked at.

4 Lateral inhibition helps us to perceive contrast between areas of differing brightness.

5 There are cones in the retina that respond best to red, green, or blue light. There are also ganglion cells that are responsive to particular colours of light. These two processes combine to produce colour vision.

6 There are special feature detectors in the visual cortex that respond best to specific orientations of lines and edges. These may provide the first step in recognising objects.

Activity 2   Contrast detection

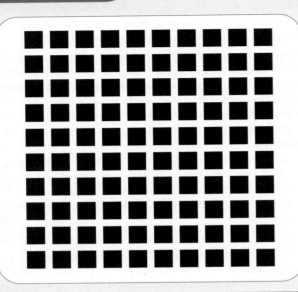

Questions

1   Look at the drawing. Do you see grey areas appearing at the intersection of the white lines?

2   What happens when you try to look directly at one of these grey areas?

3   Use the idea of lateral inhibition to explain why these effects occur.

Unit 2 Perceptual organisation

KEY ISSUES

1   **What is meant by 'top-down' and 'bottom-up' processing?**

2   **How is sensation converted into perception?**

3   **How do theories of visual perception explain perceptual organisation?**

2.1 'Top-down' and 'bottom-up' processing

Perception is the process of making sense of the sensations created by light entering the eye and striking the retina. In making sense of these sensations, there are two extreme possibilities:

1   The sensory information is enough to allow us to perceive the world. There is very little need for processing of the raw light information. In other words, 'sensation' and 'perception' are virtually the same thing. Perception is 'data-driven' – the incoming stimuli determine what we perceive. This is referred to as *bottom-up processing* because it emphasises the importance of the incoming stimuli over any higher cognitive processes. What we see is mainly due to what's actually there.

2   The idea of *top-down processing* starts from the opposite extreme. It states that in order to convert sensation into perception we need to apply our existing knowledge and experience of the world. Sensory information is not enough to allow us to perceive the world. We don't just passively register sensation like a camera – what we see depends largely on what we expect to see. Perception is 'conceptually-driven' – the conversion of sensation into perception is determined by factors such as context, expectation and knowledge. This view is known as 'top-down' processing because it emphasises the importance of higher cognitive processes to perception.

The idea of top-down and bottom-up processing was summed up by William James in 1890 when he wrote: 'Whilst part of what we perceive comes through our senses from the object before us, another part (and it may be the larger part) always comes out of our own mind'.

Theories of visual perception tend to emphasise the importance of either top-down or bottom-up processing. Some of these theories will now be examined.

Key terms

Top-down processing *Cognitive processing that takes account, first, of context, knowledge and expectation.*

Bottom-up processing *Cognitive processing that deals first with the characteristics of a stimulus.*

2.2 'Top-down' theories of visual perception

Constructivist theory

Constructivist theory is a top-down theory. It is called constructivist theory because it states that perception is *constructed*. This means it is built up from information derived from the senses – sensations – plus existing knowledge and expectations drawn from past experience.

According to constructivist theory, how do we see what we see? Picture the following objects – a ball-point pen, a cigarette lighter, an electric kettle, a telephone and a credit card. These are common, everyday objects, instantly recognised and identified. But how might they appear to people who have never seen them before – to people living in England during the Middle Ages or Native Americans in the Amazon rain forest who have had no previous contact with Western society? Their perception of the objects listed above would probably be very different from that seen through the eyes of people in the West today.

In terms of constructivist theory, recognising and identifying an object is based in part on knowledge and past experience. Drawing on information contained in long-term memory, objects like a ball-point pen are perceived as such because we have seen them before, used them before, and have past knowledge of them. Our view of them is not simply based on the physical properties of the objects – their shape, texture, colour, and so on. In other words, the information we receive from our senses, for example the visual information received from looking at a ball-point pen, is not sufficient to make sense of the object. Meaning is given to the object, and this meaning is drawn from memory. In this way sensation – information which comes directly from the senses – becomes perception.

Perceptual set theory

A *perceptual set* is a readiness or predisposition to perceive a stimulus in a particular way (Allport, 1955). Perceptual set theory is a top-down theory because it states that perception is constructed from knowledge and expectations drawn from past experience.

The following experiment (Palmer, 1975) provides support for perceptual set theory. Participants were presented with a picture of a kitchen then very briefly shown three pictures – a loaf, a mailbox and a drum (see Figure 6). The experiment was conducted in the USA hence the picture (B) of an American-style mail box. Participants were more likely to identify the loaf of bread because it was more appropriate to the context – the picture of the kitchen – which they had previously been shown. They made a 'best guess' based on visual information and their knowledge and expectations of articles that were likely to be found in kitchens. This suggests that perception is constructed both from visual information and a perceptual set – a readiness, based on past experience, to perceive a stimulus in a particular way.

Figure 6 Perception and context

Adapted from Palmer, 1975

Hypothesis theory

Richard Gregory (1970, 1980) argues that perception involves a process of forming and testing hypotheses. Sensation on its own isn't enough because it is always ambiguous. Perception is therefore a problem-solving activity – an *intelligent* activity.

Gregory's theory is known as the *hypothesis theory* of perception. When we see something, we make an 'educated guess' based on available data – information drawn from the senses and information from memory. This 'best guess' or 'best interpretation' forms our perception of an object, and of everything else that we see. Hypothesis theory is an example of a top-down theory.

The main points of Gregory's hypothesis theory are as follows.

- Perception is an active and constructive process, not just a passive acceptance of sensations.
- Signals received from photoreceptors are interpreted in terms of knowledge and expectations derived from past experience.
- From this information, hypotheses – informed guesses or inferences – are made and tested. In this way sensations are translated, transformed and constructed into perceptions. Meaning is *given* to visual sensations.
- Hypotheses are 'best guesses' based on available information. Because of this they will sometimes be incorrect. As a result, perceptions are prone to errors and we are sometimes misled by what we *think* we see.

Further evidence in favour of and against constructivist theory is examined in later sections.

2.3 Bottom-up theories

Gibson's theory of direct perception

Between 1950 and 1979, J.J. Gibson developed a theory of perception called *direct perception*. He rejected the idea that prior knowledge and experience is needed to make sense of the visual information entering the eye. Gibson said that, far from being inadequate, the light that enters the eye is extremely rich in information, and perception involves picking up the information contained in the light. A light source will emit several million rays of light, which are reflected from objects into our eyes. Rays are reflected by walls and the floor, and by the surface that the object is standing on. This visual information is received *directly* and requires little or none of the processing suggested by Gregory's top-down processing theory.

Gibson's theory can be summarised as follows:

- The visual world is made up of surfaces under illumination. These surfaces reflect millions of light rays into the eyes.
- Because light travels in straight lines, it carries information about the environment that it has passed through, and about any surface that it has been reflected from.
- The light is structured by the surfaces that it has been reflected from, and forms an *optic array*.
- Perception involves picking up this rich, unambiguous information with little or no top-down processing.
- Gibson referred to his theory as an *ecological approach* to perception. He emphasised that visual perception isn't just for looking at objects and being a passive receiver of information. Its main purpose is to allow animals, including people, to interact with their environment. Whenever people move, the optic array changes and it is these changes that help them to directly perceive the relationships between objects in the visual world.
- Gibson's focus was the patterns of light reaching the eye and the potential information about the environment contained in those patterns.

Key terms

Direct perception *Gibson's view that perception does not involve any existing knowledge. All of the information needed to convert sensation into perception is contained in the light entering the eye.*

Optic array *Light that has been structured by being reflected from surfaces.*

Ecological approach *The idea that the role of perception is to allow an animal to interact with its environment.*

The role of invariants in perception

One of the most important parts of Gibson's theory is called an *invariant*. Many aspects of the visual world are invariant – they do not change, they remain the same. However, because we are constantly moving, the patterns of light entering the eye are constantly changing. How can we perceive the world as it is when visual information is constantly changing? We are able to do this because the patterns of light do not change in a random way. As a result, much of the visual information we receive is invariant information – it is regular and unchanging. This allows us to correctly perceive the shape of objects, the size of objects and their distance from us. Gibson argued that invariant information is very important because it allows us to perceive the world as it is. Examples of invariant information will now be examined.

Texture gradients Gibson emphasised that the world is made up of surfaces under illumination. Surfaces have different textures, and these textures can help us to perceive depth and distance. Imagine that you are standing on a gravel path that stretches off into the distance. The path has a specific texture – if you look down at your feet, you will be able to see each individual piece of gravel. If you look off into the distance, the texture will no longer be seen – the path will look a uniform shade of grey. The same effect occurs with any textured object. The further away the surface being looked at, the less distinct its texture will be.

These *texture gradients* also provide information about the shapes of objects. For example, Figure 7 shows how the shape

of an object can be detected from a change in its texture gradient on different parts of its surface.

Figure 7 Texture gradient and surface shape

Texture gradient is an example of an invariant because information from texture gradients always follows the same rule – the greater the distance, the less distinct the texture. Because this information is invariant, it acts as a powerful cue to the spatial layout of objects and their distance from us.

The horizon ratio relation If two objects that have the same physical size are positioned at different distances from an observer, how is the observer able to perceive that they are the same size?

If objects are located outdoors, in a natural environment, there will usually be a visible horizon. Sedgwick (1973) pointed out that if two objects are the same size, but are different distances from the observer, the proportion of the objects that is above the horizon will always be the same. If, however, the objects are different sizes, then the proportion of each object that is above the horizon will be different. This invariant information may help us to perceive the relative sizes of objects and their relative distance from us.

Optic flow Because observers move around their environment, the optic array is constantly changing. Gibson argued that changes in the optic array provide powerful information about the observer's position relative to other objects and about the observer's movements.

As we move around, there is always *optic flow* in the visual array. The importance of optic flow is illustrated by the following example. During the Second World War, Gibson was involved in finding ways to train pilots quickly and of identifying people who had the potential to be successful pilots. Flying planes involves judgements about distance and depth, particularly when landing. Gibson realised that the visual information available to pilots when coming in to land is provided in the form of optic flow patterns. Figure 8 shows the optic flow patterns available to a pilot approaching a runway. Visual information appears to flow from a fixed point in the distance which the plane is heading towards. This is known as the *pole* of the optic flow field. As the plane approaches the pole, texture information emerges from that point and expands outwards, flowing towards, past, under and over the plane. As objects emerge from the pole of the optic flow field, they appear to be moving relatively slowly towards the plane. As they come nearer, they seem to speed up until they 'flash past' as they pass by the plane. Gibson claimed that optic flow patterns provide invariant information which allow pilots to judge their direction, speed and altitude.

Figure 8 Pilot's optic flow patterns

Gibson (1979) said that the relationship between optic flow and movement was:

- Optic flow indicates movement. Absence of optic flow means that the observer and everything else is stationary.
- Information flowing from the pole towards the observer indicates that the observer is approaching the pole, or some object is approaching the observer. Optic flow towards the pole indicates that the observer is moving away from the pole, or that some object is moving away from the observer into the distance.
- If the pole changes, then there must have been a change in direction.

Gibson's ideas about texture gradients and optic flow patterns provide an explanation of how we perceive depth and distance and how we are able to perceive the ways in which objects are positioned in the world, relative to each other, and to ourselves.

Affordances

Gibson's main emphasis was on the role of movement in perception and on the role of perception in allowing the observer to interact with the environment. However, a complete theory of visual perception needs to explain how we are able to recognise what we are looking at. While optic flow patterns might tell us we are approaching an object, and how far away it is, they don't tell us *what* that object is.

Gibson claimed that all of the information to allow us to recognise and identify objects and their uses is available in the environment. He said that objects and surfaces contain information about their potential uses, and this information is directly perceivable – we don't need to use stored knowledge to know that we can sit on a chair, we can perceive this use directly. Gibson called this information *affordances*. Affordances are the meanings that the environment has for the perceiver and

what the environment has to offer. They guide behaviour and tell the perceiver what is or is not possible.

In Gibson's terminology, the meaning of an object is what it 'affords'. For example, a chair affords sitting. This is its potential use or affordance. In this sense:

- A flat, substantial surface affords 'walking on'.
- A flat surface at knee level affords 'sitting'.
- A door-handle affords 'pulling'.
- A doorbell affords 'pressing'.
- Water affords 'drinking'.

A single object can give rise to more than one affordance. For instance, an orange affords 'eating' if hungry, but it also affords 'grasping and throwing' if feeling playful or angry. An apple tree may afford food, or afford shelter in a rainstorm.

Gibson's central point is that all of these affordances can be perceived in an entirely bottom-up way. There is no need for knowledge about objects and their uses – no need for top-down processing. The uses of objects are directly perceived because all of the information needed to make sense of the visual environment is present in the visual input.

Key terms

Invariants *Aspects of the visual world which do not change. The systematic relationships between features of the visual world.*

Texture gradient *The changing patterns of surfaces in the visual world. Texture gradients can tell us about distance, and help us to perceive the shapes of objects.*

Horizon ratio *If two objects are the same size, but are different distances from the observer, the proportion of the objects that is above the horizon will always be the same. This invariant ratio provides a cue to distance.*

Optic flow *The changing patterns of the optic array as we move around the environment.*

Pole *The point from which the optic flow appears to arise.*

Affordances *The features of surfaces and objects that allow their uses to be directly perceived.*

2.4 Top-down and bottom-up explanations of perceptual organisation

Before evaluating constructivist theory and Gibson's direct perception theory, it is important to consider the range of perceptual abilities that we have, and see how well the competing theories explain them.

Depth perception

Although the retina is two-dimensional, we are able to convert this into a three-dimensional image in order to perceive depth and distance. How do we do this?

There are several different types of cue available to help us to perceive depth. Some have already been described – texture gradients and optic flow. Other cues are available. While

Gibson's direct theory of perception states that all of the cues can be directly perceived, the constructivists disagree. They argue that the ability to perceive depth is learned through experience.

Depth cues Cues to depth can be divided into two types. *Binocular cues* require the use of two eyes – they are no longer available when we close one eye. *Monocular cues* require the use of only one eye.

Binocular depth cues

Convergence When you focus on an object, your eyes turn inwards towards your nose. The closer the object to your face, the more your eyes need to turn inwards. The muscles that move the eyes send signals to the brain. These signals provide information about the extent of *convergence* of the eyes. This, in turn, provides an indication of depth.

Stereopsis Each eye has a slightly different viewpoint, simply because they are located in different positions. If you look at an object and close each eye alternately, you will see that the image seems to 'jump' from one place to another. The closer the object is to your eyes, the greater the difference, or disparity between what your two eyes see. If you look at a distant object, the disparity between the two images will be extremely small. So *stereopsis* only works as a useful cue to depth over short distances.

Monocular depth cues

Linear perspective Lines that are parallel will appear to converge – come closer together – as they recede into the distance. If you look along a straight road, it will appear that the sides of the road converge. This works over short distances too. If you sit at one end of a rectangular table, the sides of the table will appear to converge.

Interposition If one object blocks our view of part of another object, we perceive the partially obscured object as being further away.

Height in the visual field Objects that are on the ground and are higher up in the visual field will appear to be further away than objects lower down in the visual field.

Familiar size With familiar objects, we have an idea about how big they usually are. We can use the size of the image formed on the retina to make a judgement about how far away the object is.

Texture gradient Surfaces are textured and this can help us to judge depth and distance. For example, the further away the surface is, the less distinct its texture will appear.

Aerial perspective Because dust particles in the air diffuse the light travelling towards us, distant objects will appear to be a bit fuzzy and less distinct than objects that are nearer.

Shadow Because light travels in straight lines, and we assume that light comes from above, we can use the pattern of light and shade to make judgements about depth. In Figure 9, which half of the avocado contains the stone, and which half contains the hole left by the stone? When you've decided, turn the page upside down. You'll see that the depth perception is based on the assumption that light comes from above.

Figure 9 Shadow as a cue to depth perception

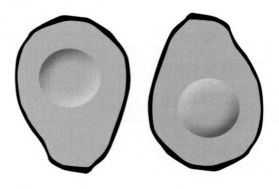

Motion parallax This cue depends on movement. If you move your head from side to side, the objects closer to you will appear to move more than objects that are further away. If you're travelling by car, and you look out of the side window, objects next to the road will flash past. Objects that are in the distance will appear to move more slowly. This is *motion parallax*. By judging the movements of objects relative to us, we can judge how far away they are.

Key terms

Binocular cues *Cues to depth that require the use of both eyes.*

Monocular cues *Cues to depth that require the use of only one eye.*

Convergence *A binocular depth cue that makes use of the extent to which our eyes turn inwards to focus on an object.*

Stereopsis *A binocular depth cue that uses the fact that our eyes see slightly different images.*

Linear perspective *A monocular depth cue that parallel lines will appear to converge as they recede into the distance.*

Interposition *A monocular depth cue that nearer objects will obscure parts of more distant objects.*

Height in the visual field *A monocular depth cue. More distant objects appear closer to the horizon than closer objects.*

Familiar size *Because we know the size of familiar objects, we can judge their distance from us from their apparent size. This is a monocular depth cue.*

Aerial perspective *A monocular depth cue that more distant objects will appear to be slightly fuzzy.*

Motion parallax *The movement of an object's image over the retina.*

Perception of movement

The ability to perceive movement depends on the visual system being able to detect systematic changes in the visual stimulus. When we look at a moving object we don't perceive it as a series of jerky images, we perceive smooth, continuous movement.

There is evidence that movement of an object can be used to tell us about the object's shape. Johansson (1975) dressed actors in black and attached small lights to their shoulders, knees, elbows, wrists, ankles and hips. Participants were then asked to observe these patterns of lights in a dark room. When the actors stood still, participants perceived the pattern of lights as a random, two-dimensional image. They couldn't make any sense of it. When the actors started to move around, the participants were immediately able to perceive a human figure. The participants were able to accurately describe the posture of the actors, and say what they were doing. Cutting and Kozlowski (1977) found that 65% of the time, participants were able to correctly guess the sex of the actors from the way they walked.

This ability to detect and respond to movement and use it to make judgements about object shape is an important perceptual skill. In fact, the visual system sometimes detects movement when there is no movement there.

Apparent motion

The phi phenomenon The illusion of movement can be created by displaying a series of still images. This is exactly what happens when we watch a movie at the cinema. The movie reel is made up a series of still photographs that are projected at 24 frames a second. When the presentation is this rapid, we don't perceive the individual pictures, we perceive motion. The same principle is, of course, used in animation. Cartoons and stop-motion animations like *Wallace and Gromit* use this principle.

Wertheimer (1912) investigated apparent motion in the laboratory. He presented two vertical lines, one beside the other. Presentation of the lines was alternated, so as one line appeared, the other disappeared. Wertheimer found that when the delay between the disappearance of one line and the appearance of the other was reduced to one-twentieth of a second, observers reported that they had perceived one vertical line that moved from one position to the other.

This perception of apparent movement is known as the *phi phenomenon*. As well as providing the basis for movies and animation, the apparent motion produced by alternately displaying two stimuli is used in neon signs to create the impression of movement.

The autokinetic effect This is the perception of movement when there is not only no movement, but there is no changing stimulus to create the impression of movement. If a single, stationary light is viewed in a dark room, the light will appear to move.

Key terms

Phi phenomenon *The perception of apparent movement created by a rapid succession of stimuli.*

Autokinetic effect *The perception that a light in a darkened room will appear to move.*

Explanations of movement perception

Top-down explanations Bruce and Green (1985) suggest that the impression of apparent movement and the perception of real movement are very similar, psychologically. This, they argue, means that the perception of movement can be explained in terms of the brain integrating the rapid succession of separate images that the world generates. In other words, there might be a sense in which the brain takes a series of 'snapshots' of the world and compares each one to the previous one in order to detect movement. This is a top-down explanation because it relies heavily on the processing of information and the application of existing knowledge about shapes of objects and what an apparent change in shape might signify in terms of movement of the object.

Bottom-up explanations We have already discussed Gibson's views about optic flow and the close link between movement and perception. Clocksin (1980) suggests that motion can be perceived directly and can help us to perceive the shapes of objects. This, again, emphasises the role of movement in perception. As an object moves, it will temporarily obscure other objects in the visual world. As a simple example, imagine a small remote-controlled car driving along a black-and-white tiled floor. As the car moves, its front edge will cover up some of the squares and its rear edge will uncover other squares. This change in the background texture that is obscured by a moving object provides a *local movement signal* and tells us that something is moving. The pattern of covering and obscuring of background texture can also tell us about the shape of the moving object.

This type of explanation does not, however, explain the phi phenomenon or the autokinetic effect – it does not explain the perception of movement when no movement occurs.

Key term

Local movement signal *A changing in background resulting from a moving object.*

Visual constancies

As we move our eyes around the visual field, it is remarkable that the world appears as a stable, unchanging place. With every small movement of our eyes, the pattern of activation produced in the retina changes and shifts. Despite this, we seem able to make sense of the world – it doesn't all seem to move around every time we move our eyes. So, although the retinal image changes, our perception remains the same – it stays constant. There are different types of *visual constancies*. Each of them refers to a different way in which our perceptions remain stable although the retinal image changes.

Shape constancy When we look at the same object from different angles, the image that it forms on our retinas changes. For example, when you hold a book vertically at arms' length in front of your face, the rectangular book will form a rectangular retinal image, as in the left-hand picture in Figure 10. If, however, you hold the same book at arm's length, but lie it flat, the retinal image is no longer rectangular. It becomes a trapezoidal shape, as in the right-hand picture in Figure 10. Despite the fact that the shape of the retinal image has changed, we still perceive the book as being rectangular. This is *shape constancy*. Although the retinal image changes shape, the shape that we perceive remains constant.

Figure 10 Changing retinal images

Size constancy Size constancy refers to the fact that our perception of an object remains the same even though the size of the retinal image changes. For example, when we watch someone walking off into the distance, the image on the retina shrinks. We don't draw the conclusion that the person must be shrinking. Rather, we perceive the person as remaining the same size, but getting further away from us.

Lightness constancy This is the perception of an object as being evenly illuminated, even though different amounts of light might be reflected into our eyes from different parts of its surface. For example, in Figure 11 the tiled area is perceived as being made up of light squares and dark squares. All the light squares appear to be the same shade of grey, and all the dark squares appear to be the same shade. The pattern is perceived as being a regular pattern of alternating light and dark squares, like a chess board. However, the level of light reaching our eye from the 'light' square in the centre of the shadow is actually *identical* to the 'dark' squares outside the shadow. The 'light' square in the centre of the shadow is exactly the same shade of grey as the 'dark' squares outside the shadow area.

Colour constancy If you look at a banana on a sunny day, it will look yellow. If you take it into a room lit by electric light, it will still look yellow, despite the fact that the wavelength of light being reflected from it is now very different. This is *colour constancy*. Objects do not appear to change colour, even though the light being reflected from the object will be very different under different conditions.

Figure 11 Lightness constancy

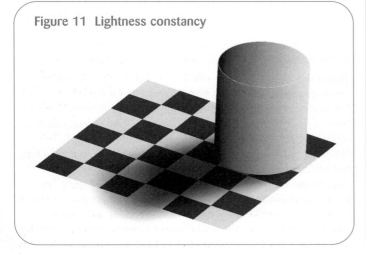

Explanations of visual constancies

Top-down explanations The constructivists argue that all of the visual constancies are due to the application of stored knowledge. We have stored knowledge about objects, so when we see a book, we are able to infer that it is rectangular. We also have stored knowledge that tells us that objects usually do not change shape or size as they move. A change in the size or shape of the retinal image means that we are looking at the same object from a different angle, or that the object is now a different distance from us.

We also have vast experience about light and the way that shadows are cast, so we have stored knowledge that tells us that the levels of light reaching our eyes might mislead us. We know that the same object will reflect different wavelengths of light under different conditions, so we make adjustments to allow us to perceive light and colour consistently.

Bottom-up explanations Gibson argues that the information contained in the optic array is sufficient for us to determine that we are looking at an object from a particular angle. We'll be able to determine that we are looking at a rectangular object lying flat because the pattern of light will be different from when we look at the same object straight on. Information from texture gradients will help us to make this judgement.

We can judge how far away an object is by making use of texture gradients, optic flow, and the horizon ratio, described earlier. In other words, visual constancies are due to our ability to directly perceive all of the visual characteristics of the world by picking up on the rich, elaborate information contained in the optic array.

Visual illusions

Sometimes, there is a mismatch between our perception and what it is that we're looking at. Perception is most likely to be error-prone when the viewing conditions are less than ideal, due to poor lighting, unusual angle of viewing, and so on.

It is difficult to investigate errors in perception by using real-life stimuli, as it is hard to precisely control the viewing conditions. Instead, research has mainly concentrated on artificially constructed figures that can be presented to people in a laboratory setting. The Ames distorted room is one of the most famous illusions based on the failure of size constancy.

The Ames distorted room This is a room that is carefully constructed to provide misleading cues about depth. Figure 12 is a photograph of two people standing in such a room. This isn't a trick photograph – if you were standing in the position of the camera and peering into the Ames room with one eye, this is precisely what you would see.

The person on the left of the picture appears to be much smaller than the person on the right. This is because the two people appear to be the same distance away and the retinal image of the person on the left is smaller. If any two objects are the same distance from us, and one projects a smaller retinal image, then that object will be perceived as smaller.

Figure 12 The Ames distorted room

Although the room appears to be square, it isn't. Depth cues have been manipulated to make the room appear to be normal when it is actually shaped as shown in Figure 13.

The illusion is so powerful that if the two people swapped places, they would appear to grow or shrink as they crossed the room! The false depth cues prevent size constancy from operating. So a change in the size of the retinal image is perceived as meaning that the person has changed size, rather than moved further away or come closer.

Figure 13 True shape of the Ames room

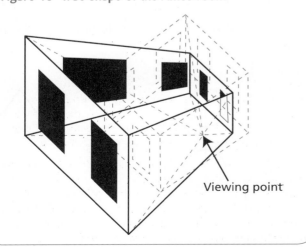

Viewing point

Two-dimensional illusions

These can be categorised into four main types:

Ambiguous figures These are figures that can be perceived in two different ways. Each perception provides a plausible interpretation, so the brain tends to switch back and forth between them. An example of this is the Necker cube shown in Figure 14. Look at the cube. You should find that it seems to change its orientation as you look at it. At one moment, the shaded surface of the cube will seem to be the front of the cube, in the next moment it will appear to be the back of the cube.

Figure 14 The Necker cube

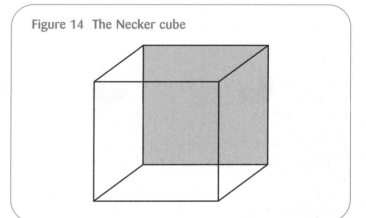

Paradoxical figures If you look closely at the paradoxical figure shown in Figure 15, you will see that it would be impossible to construct the three-dimensional object that it seems to be at first glance.

Figure 15 A paradoxical figure

Fictitious figures These are illusory figures that we perceive, even though they don't actually exist. Figure 16 illustrates the Kanisza Square. We perceive a white square that appears to be partially obscuring the black circles at its corners. It is such a powerful illusion that if you look at a point half way along the 'edge' of the square, you will perceive a difference in brightness between the 'inside' and the 'outside' of the square. There is, of course, no square there at all.

Distortions Some of the classic visual illusions are distortion illusions. These are designed to produce a misperception of the stimulus so that things appear not as they truly are. In the Müller-Lyer illusion shown in Figure 17, the vertical line on the left appears to be longer than the vertical line on the right. They are, in fact, exactly the same length. In the Ponzo Illusion, the horizontal line at the top appears to be longer than the horizontal line at the bottom, even though they are, again, the same length.

Figure 16 Kanisza square

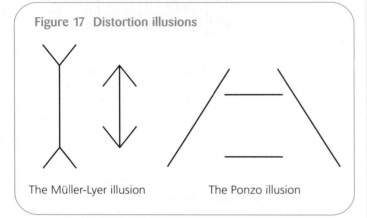

Figure 17 Distortion illusions

The Müller-Lyer illusion   The Ponzo illusion

Explanations of visual illusions

Top-down explanations Gregory (1970, 1980) argues that illusions like the Müller-Lyer illusion and the Ponzo illusion occur because people try to apply their knowledge of the three-dimensional world to two-dimensional line drawings. As a result, we see what we expect to see. In particular, we try to make use of visual constancies. If a drawing can be interpreted as representing distance, then we try to apply size constancy to make judgements about the relative sizes of parts of the drawing. For example, the Ponzo illusion can be interpreted as representing a road or a railway line going off into the distance (see Figure 17). If the two converging lines were the rails of a railway line, and the horizontal lines were objects lying across the track, then size constancy would be applied as follows:

* The two horizontal lines form the same size retinal images.
* The upper horizontal line appears to be further away along the railway line.
* If two objects produce the same size retinal image, if one appears to be further away, then it must be bigger.
* Therefore, the upper horizontal line is perceived as being longer.

This is a fairly straightforward explanation. The same type of explanation applied to the Müller-Lyer illusion is a little more complicated. Gregory argues that the Müller-Lyer illusion can be

seen as simple perspective drawings. The outward fins on the left-hand line can be perceived as representing an internal corner of a room, and the inward fins as the exterior corner of a building, as in Figure 18.

Because the walls of the room come towards us from the vertical line, while the outside walls of the building go away from us from the vertical line, it appears as though the interior corner of the room is further away from us than the outside corner of the building. Because the two vertical lines form the same size retinal image, the one that seems to be further away is perceived as being longer. Gregory argues that the cues we use to judge depth are applied automatically, even though we are aware that the drawing is two-dimensional. Gregory's explanation of the illusion is supported by the fact that the Müller-Lyer lines take on a three-dimensional appearance when presented by cutting slits out of a piece of card and illuminating it from behind in a darkened room.

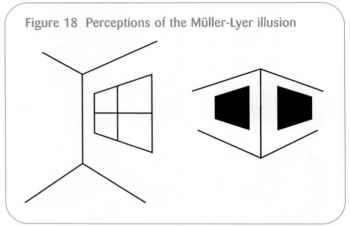

Figure 18 Perceptions of the Müller-Lyer illusion

However, there are criticisms of Gregory's explanation of the Müller-Lyer illusion.

* In Figure 18, the corner of the building actually looks as though it's further away than the internal corner of the room.
* The illusion still works if the fins that provide the three-dimensional cues are replaced by circles so that the figure cannot be interpreted as representing a three-dimensional object. It could just be that the left-hand line is seen as being longer or shorter because it is part of a larger or a smaller object. Figure 19 illustrates this point.

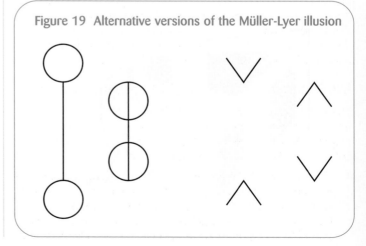

Figure 19 Alternative versions of the Müller-Lyer illusion

Activity 3   Visual illusion

Item A   Arrangement of CD cases

Item B   Ambiguous image

Questions

1 a) Take three CD cases, and position them as shown in Item A. Make sure that the distance from the hinge of the left-hand case to that of the middle case is the same as the distance from the hinge of the middle case to the one on the right.

  b) View the arrangement from the angle shown in Item A. What do you observe? Explain why this is a version of the Müller-Lyer illusion.

  c) Why does this cast doubt on Gibson's argument that visual illusions have no relevance to real-world perception?

2 a) Look at the picture in Item B. This is an ambiguous figure – it can be viewed as either a young woman or an old woman.

  b) Once you are able to 'see' the two interpretations, can you see them both at the same time, or can you only see one at a time by switching between them?

  c) Explain this in terms of Gregory's view that perception involves testing hypotheses.

• Coren and Girgus (1972) found that the illusion was less effective when the fins were a different colour from the vertical lines. Matlin and Foley (1997) suggest that this leads us to judge the lines more carefully as they are separate from the fins. As a result, we are less likely to judge the lines' lengths in relation to the overall size of the figure. This supports the view that the illusion is due to a judgement of the overall size of the figure rather than misapplied size constancy.

Bottom-up explanations Gibson argues that illusions like the Müller-Lyer illusion are artificially constructed to fool people, and that the study of illusions like these has no bearing on an explanation of visual perception in the real world. There is, however, evidence that some visual illusions do have effect in real-life situations outside the laboratory – see Activity 3 for a demonstration. Gibson's theory of direct perception fails to explain why visual illusions operate in the real world.

Evaluation of top-down and bottom-up theories

The constructivist approach There is clear evidence that perception involves an element of top-down processing, particularly when identifying objects. There are, however, criticisms of the constructivist approach.

• Gregory argued that perception involves testing hypotheses – it is based on 'educated guesses' about what we are looking at. If this is so, then why is our processing of visual information nearly always correct? Guesswork suggests we should be wrong more often than we are, that identification

of objects should be more unreliable than it is.

• If perception is based on hypotheses, why do illusions like the Müller-Lyer illusion still work even though we know what the true state of affairs is? Even when we *know* that the lines are the same length, why do they still *look* different?

• Much of the evidence supporting constructivist theory has come from laboratory experiments. These experiments have been criticised as artificial. In many cases, the stimuli and tasks used in the laboratory fail to reflect everyday experience. Visual illusions which present ambiguous, paradoxical, fictitious and distorted figures are rarely mirrored in everyday life. Studies such as Palmer's pictures of kitchens and extremely brief presentations of objects are not often duplicated in everyday tasks. And actors in a darkened room with lights attached to their clothing are not an everyday sight.

• Experiments such as these appear to be designed to support top-down processing. The stimuli require considerable interpretation to make sense of them, so supporting the idea that perception is constructed. Often the stimuli are deliberately designed to be ambiguous and to confuse, so supporting the constructivist view that perception is a 'best guess' and, as such, can mislead and produce errors. Sometimes the stimuli are presented very briefly which encourages interpretation and inferences, that is the formation of hypotheses. A brief glimpse reduces the effect of bottom-up processing. If the object is no longer visible, there is no opportunity to collect further information from the environment.

- The above criticisms do not mean that constructivist theory should be dismissed. As outlined earlier, there is evidence to support it. However, the criticisms suggest that constructivist theory has exaggerated the importance of top-down processing.

Gibson's theory of direct perception

Gibson's theory has been valuable in a number of ways.

- It emphasises the relationship between the perceiver and their environment. In doing so, Gibson was able to focus attention on the role of movement in perception. We do not live in a world of single, separate stimuli that we look at one-at-a-time for a brief duration.
- The concepts of optic flow and texture gradients provide a consistent explanation of the perception of movement and the interaction between an animal and its environment.
- Gibson was right that the visual world provides much more information than was previously thought to be available. The experimental work conducted by the constructivists tended to use briefly presented visual displays, while the observer remained still. We do not stand stock still when looking at things. The Ames room only works because the observer has to look through a little hole. It removes the role of the observer's movement in perception that Gibson saw as very important.
- Direct perception only works in the real world. Gibson believed that pictures were perceived indirectly, because pictures are two-dimensional and do not provide the same richness of light information. This, he argues, explains why the constructivists' experiments using pictures of objects produce evidence for the involvement of top-down processing.
- Norman (1988) points out the idea of affordances can be used by designers to make things easier to use. This supports the idea of direct perception. According to Norman, 'affordances provide strong clues to the operation of things. Plates [on doors] are for pushing. Knobs are for turning. Slots are for inserting things into....When affordances are taken advantage of, the user knows what to do just by looking: no picture, label, or instruction is required. Complex things may require explanation, but simple things should not.'

There are also a number of criticisms of Gibson's theory.

- Marr (1982) says that the detection of edges and surfaces requires a great deal of information processing. So, far from being able to remove the role of information processing from perception, Marr argues that the very things that Gibson is talking about involve complex information processing.
- Gibson does not explain why visual perception is sometimes inaccurate. Presumably, this would involve the optic array being misleading in some way. Gibson does not explain why or how this might occur.
- Gibson does not explain how we identify specific instances of objects. What is it that tells me that the cup on the table is *my* cup? How do I know which is *my* coat, *my* car?
- Gibson assumes that there is no need for stored knowledge, but this does not seem very plausible. As Bruce et al. (1996) say, 'We find it unconvincing to explain a person returning after 10 years to their grandparents' home and seeing that a tree has been cut down as having detected directly an event specified by a transformation in the optic array'.
- Direct perception fails to explain visual illusions. These

occur in real life – they are not just concocted in experiments conducted by constructivists.

Integration of top-down and bottom-up approaches

The relative importance of top-down and bottom-up processes varies in different situations. When viewing conditions worsen, there may be more need to form hypotheses about what's being looked at. In making these guesses, the importance of existing knowledge will come to the fore. Gibson tended to emphasise optimal viewing conditions, while the constructivists sometimes used poor viewing conditions, for example, by showing stimuli for brief periods of time.

Top-down processes are more important when the stimuli are ambiguous, when they are not clear-cut. This is illustrated in an extreme form by visual illusions. When stimuli are ambiguous, they require more interpretation, more use of knowledge from memory, more top-down processing. If you hadn't been to the USA, or seen American mail boxes in movies, would you recognise the mail box illustrated in Figure 6?

Why the differences between constructivist and direct perception theorists? Why not combine the two theories and conclude that both top-down and bottom-up processes are important? A possible reason is that the researchers have been investigating different things (Milner & Goodale, 1998).

In Unit 1, we discussed the existence of two different visual pathways in the brain, which seem to use visual information for different purposes. The distinction was made between two different aspects of perception.

- **Perception for recognition** This is what the constructivists concentrate on. They were mainly concerned with the way in which we identify objects.
- **Perception for action** Gibson emphasises the importance of the relationship between movement and perception. His theory describes how we use visual information to allow us to move around and interact with the environment.

In other words, the constructivists and Gibson seem to have been looking at different aspects of perception, dealt with to some extent by different systems.

A number of researchers have attempted to integrate constructivist and direct perception theories, arguing that perception involves both top-down and bottom-up processes. The relative importance of each process will depend on the nature of the stimulus, for example whether it is clear-cut or ambiguous.

Neisser's (1976) theory states that perception involves a combination of bottom-up and top-down processes. It outlines a four stage process for perceiving an object.

- First, a general, global glance. This is a bottom-up process providing visual information.
- Second, generating a hypothesis based on knowledge and expectations. This is a top-down process.
- Third, testing this hypothesis. This may require additional visual information which involves looking for further details. This stage combines top-down and bottom-up processes.
- Fourth, obtaining a match between the hypothesis and the visual information. The object has now been identified.

Although Neisser's theory is rather sketchy, it may well be 'on the right lines' (Eysenck & Keane, 1995).

Summary

1 Constructivist theories of perception emphasise top-down processing. They state that visual perception is based on visual information plus knowledge and expectations drawn from long-term memory.

2 Theories of direct perception are bottom-up theories. They state that sensory information is sufficient to perceive the world.

3 Gregory's hypothesis theory states that perception involves forming hypotheses based on prior knowledge and experience.

4 Gibson's theory of direct perception states that all the information needed for perception is directly perceived in the patterns of light entering the eye.

5 Cues to depth perception include binocular cues, requiring the use of both eyes, and monocular cues, needing just one eye.

6 Visual constancies are perceptions of objects that remain stable even though the retinal image of the object changes when the viewpoint changes.

7 Constructivists explain depth perception and visual constancies as the application of knowledge and experiences about the nature of objects.

8 Gibson argues that depth perception and visual constancies are due to the rich information contained in the patterns of light entering the eye.

9 Constructivists argue that two-dimensional illusions are due to the misapplication of visual constancies.

10 Gibson argues that two-dimensional illusions are tricks created to fool people and do not help us to understand real-world perception.

11 The relative importance of top-down and bottom-up processing might change with viewing conditions, for example, bottom-up processing is more important when viewing conditions are good.

12 The constructivist view has been criticised for suggesting that perception should be more error-prone than it actually is. Experiments which have provided evidence to support constructivist theory have been criticised as artificial, as having little relevance to everyday life.

13 Gibson's theory of direct perception has been criticised for not explaining how perception might sometimes be inaccurate, and how we are able to recognise specific instances of objects, such as our own cup.

14 Despite these criticisms, there is evidence to support both theories. Many researchers now argue that perception involves both top-down and bottom-up processes.

Unit 3 Perceptual development

KEY ISSUES

1 **How does visual perception develop in young babies?**

2 **What are the main theories explaining this development?**

3 **To what extent does culture affect visual perception?**

3.1 The nature-nurture debate

Visual perception involves an amazing set of abilities. We are able to convert the sensation of light falling on the retina of the eye into a rich, three-dimensional, full-colour view of the world. Our perception of the world remains stable, even though the pattern of sensation is always changing and shifting.

Are we born with these perceptual skills, or do they have to be learned through experience? There are two extreme views on this issue.

- **Empiricism** This view states that perceptual abilities are acquired through experience and interaction with the environment. They are learned rather than inborn.

- **Nativism** This view states that perceptual skills are inborn. They are biologically programmed to develop in a certain way. Learning and experience are of minor importance.

These positions reflect the two extremes of the *nature-nurture debate*. The nature or nativist side of this debate states that abilities are largely innate, that they are genetically programmed to develop in a certain way. The nurture or empiricist side states that abilities are largely learned as part of our upbringing, as a result of interaction with the social and physical environment.

Key terms

Empiricism *The view that perceptual skills are developed through learning and experience of the environment.*

Nativism *The view that perceptual skills are innate and programmed to develop in a certain way.*

3.2 Neonate studies

A *neonate* is a newborn baby. Studying the perceptual abilities of infants can tell us a great deal about visual perception in the early stages of life, and the ways in which different types of perceptual ability develop. During the first few months of life, there are rapid and marked changes in perceptual skills.

It is, however, difficult to study perception in newborn infants for a number of reasons.

- First, babies are unable to understand verbal instructions, and cannot answer questions. A baby cannot say what it is perceiving or which type of stimulus it finds the most pleasant to look at.
- Second, there is very little that newborn babies can do. They don't have good control over motor movements, and certainly can't point to objects to indicate a preference.
- Third, very young babies' lives consist of a cycle of eating, sleeping and crying. It is difficult to find a time in between when the baby is awake, alert and willing to be tested.

Assuming that the neonate is cooperating, there are various ways of drawing inferences about what kind of stimuli babies can distinguish and which they prefer. A number of techniques have been developed.

- **The preference technique** This was developed by Fantz (1956). The idea is that if a baby is shown two stimuli, and it spends more time looking at one, then this might mean that the baby can tell the difference between the two stimuli and that it prefers one to the other.
- **Habituation** In this method, a specific stimulus is shown to the baby. If the same stimulus is shown for a long time, or is shown repeatedly, the baby will become used to it and stop paying attention and looking at it. This is known as *habituation*. If a different stimulus is then presented and the infant shows interest and starts looking at it, this might mean that the infant has detected that there has been a change in the visual stimulus. This renewed interest following habituation is called *dishabituation*.
- **Sucking rate** The rate and intensity with which a baby sucks a dummy gives an indication of its level of interest in the stimulus presented to it. Infants tend to suck a dummy faster if they are stimulated and interested in something. This can be used as a measure of habituation. If the sucking rate declines as the infant becomes habituated to one stimulus, but speeds up when a new stimulus is presented, this suggests that the infant has detected a change in the stimulus and is showing renewed interest.
- **Conditioned head rotation** If a pleasant reward is provided every time a baby turns its head towards a particular stimulus, and if the baby continues to do this when the stimulus is presented from a different angle, then this suggests that the baby can still distinguish the stimulus.
- **Physiological changes** Heart rate and breathing rate can be taken as measures of interest. Decreases in heart rate or breathing rate might indicate habituation to a stimulus, while increases might indicate that the baby is able to detect that the stimulus has changed and is expressing renewed interest.
- **Brain activity** If different parts of the brain become activated in response to different stimuli, it might mean that the baby can distinguish between them.

It is important to note that these methods are based on a number of assumptions. It has to be assumed, for instance, that the time spent looking at a stimulus gives an indication of preference. And, it has to be assumed that physiological changes, such as changes in heart and breathing rates, and behavioural changes, such as the rate and intensity of sucking, indicate different levels of interest. Because of all these assumptions, caution is needed when drawing conclusions from research into neonate perception.

Key terms

Neonate *A newborn baby.*

Habituation *The process of becoming bored with a stimulus and ceasing to look at it.*

Dishabituation *Following habituation, dishabituation is the renewed interest shown when a new stimulus is presented.*

Habituation technique *The method of using habituation and dishabituation to show that an infant is able to detect the difference between two stimuli.*

Research into neonate perception

Colour vision The receptors in the retina of the eye that provide colour vision are called cones. Bornstein et al. (1992) found that the cones required for perceiving red and green are clearly present in the retinas of one-month-old babies, and may have been present from birth.

Adams (1989) claims that four-day-old infants are able to distinguish red from green and that babies as young as three days prefer coloured stimuli to black-and-white stimuli. Infants as young as four months appear to show the same colour preferences as adults, as they prefer to look at blue and red rather than yellow (Banks & Salapatek, 1983).

Visual acuity Until about 40 years ago, medical textbooks stated that the perceptual abilities of newborn infants were very poorly developed. It is now clear that this simply isn't true. *Visual acuity* is the ability to see the details of stimuli in sharp focus. In adults, the usual standard for measuring visual acuity is '20/20 vision'. A person with 20/20 vision can identify an object 20 feet away that the average person can also identify at 20 feet. A person with 20/100 vision would need to be within 20 feet of an object that the average person would be able to identify at 100 feet. At birth, an infant's visual acuity is somewhere between 20/200 and 20/800. In other words, the visual world is not very clear to the neonate. Visual acuity does improve quite quickly, and by the age of one year, most infants' visual acuity is 20/20 (Haith, 1990).

Bee (2000) suggests that the poor visual acuity of newborns is not necessarily a negative thing. In the early part of life, the infant only needs to be able to see close-up objects like breasts, bottles, cot toys, and parents' faces.

Tracking movement *Tracking* is the ability to follow a moving object by moving the eyes. This is a very important skill to develop. In order for the neonate to learn about objects and learn to recognise them, it is important to keep them in view. If the object moves, the eyes need to move to keep the object in view. This is, of course, especially important if the viewer is unable to move around because they haven't yet developed the appropriate motor skills.

Aslin (1987) showed that tracking improves very quickly from inefficient beginnings. Before the age of about 6 weeks, infants are able to track objects briefly if the object is moving slowly. After about 6-10 weeks, the baby is able to track objects much more efficiently. Figure 20 shows the tracking skills of infants at six weeks and at 10 weeks. The thick grey line shows the path of a moving line. The thinner green line represents one infant's eye movements at 6 weeks, and again at 10 weeks. As you can see, at 6 weeks, the baby was able to track the line with a series of jerky eye movements. At 10 weeks, the movements had become much smoother and the tracking much more accurate.

Figure 20 Eye movements in tracking

6-Week-Old

10-Week-Old

——— stimulus
——— tracking movement

It is quite apparent that basic visual skills are present from very early in life. Acuity improves rapidly during the first few months, as does tracking ability. Colour vision is also operating from very early in life. One thing is certain – the newborn infant is not blind.

Key terms

Visual acuity *A measure of the level of detail that can be perceived in a stimulus from a certain distance. Acuity of 20/20 indicates the ability to see a stimulus from 20 feet that the average person would also see from 20 feet.*

Tracking *The ability to follow a moving object with the eyes.*

Complex perceptual skills

Beyond the basic skills of being able to focus and move the eyes to track objects, research has been conducted into infants' abilities to discriminate patterns, including faces, and to perceive objects and depth.

Pattern and face perception

Fantz (1961) showed patterns to infants and measured how long they spent looking at each type of pattern. The patterns included a face, a piece of printed text, a bullseye shape and plain and striped squares (see Figure 21).

Figure 21 Example images used in Fantz's experiments

Fantz's findings were as follows:

- Babies as young as two days old spent longer looking at patterned surfaces than plain ones. Striped, bullseye, or checked patterns were preferred to plain squares, triangles, or discs.
- They preferred symmetrical patterns to asymmetrical ones.
- From about four days to six months old, babies preferred patterns that resembled faces, even faces with the features arranged in a scrambled order. For example, in Figure 22, babies spent longer looking at Face A than Face B, and Face B was looked at for longer than Face C.

Figure 22 Face-like patterns

A   B   C

Fantz argued that infants seem to have a natural preference for faces. Some studies have confirmed that infants spend longer looking at faces than other types of pattern (Dannemiller & Stephens, 1988), but others have not (Cohen et al., 1979). It is possible that infants simply prefer to look at more complex stimuli, and this is why Fantz found they spent longer looking at the 'face patterns'. Maybe because faces are a common type of complex stimulus in the infant's environment, they like to look at them. Small (1990) claims that, if a baby has no experience of faces, then they do not show a preference for looking at faces.

There is evidence that infants are able to recognise particular faces at very early ages. Walton et al. (1992) videotaped the faces of mothers of newborn babies and matched them with the faces of other women who had the same eye colour, hair colour, complexion and hair style. Each baby was shown one face at a time. The face was shown as long as the baby continued to suck a dummy. The idea was that if the baby liked the face, it would show a sucking response. Once the baby stopped sucking, it was assumed that the baby had lost interest in the face. Judging from the sucking response, babies as young as one or two days showed a clear preference for their mother's face over the face of another woman who looked very similar.

There is evidence that some facial features are more important than others to the neonate's face recognition. Pascalis et al. (1995) showed that newborn babies could not discriminate the mother's face from that of an unfamiliar woman if the hairline was obscured by a headscarf or a hat. This suggests that, before the age of about 2 months, babies tend to concentrate their face perception efforts on the edges of the face rather than features like the eyes, nose, or mouth. From about 2-3 months of age, the infant starts to concentrate more on the central features, especially the eyes. After about 4 months, covering the hairline no longer prevents the infant from discriminating the mother's face from other faces.

Depth perception

A classic study of the ability of infants to perceive depth was conducted by Gibson and Walk (1960). They used a *visual cliff*, as shown in Figure 23. The apparatus consists of a special table. One half of the table's surface is made up of black-and-white tiles. The other half is clear glass with the black-and-white tile pattern several feet below the glass. There is no danger to the baby.

Figure 23 Gibson and Walk's 'visual cliff'

Gibson and Walk found that babies who were six months old were very reluctant to crawl over the 'cliff', even when encouraged to do so by their mothers. This indicated that six-month-old babies were able to perceive depth. They could see that the 'cliff' had depth and that there was a drop from the edge of the cliff down to the black-and-white pattern below.

Younger children who were unable to crawl showed a different response. Campos et al. (1970) placed infants of 2, 3 and 5 months of age directly onto the glass over the deep side of the 'cliff'. Their heart rates slowed down, indicating that they were interested in what was going on rather than frightened. This study indicated that infants younger than six months of age haven't yet learned to fear and avoid the cliff, suggesting that the avoidance behaviour displayed by the six-month-old infants was learned as they learned to crawl.

Although two-month old babies do not display avoidance behaviour on a visual cliff because they cannot crawl, they do show avoidance of other stimuli requiring the ability to perceive depth. Bower et al. (1970) found that babies as young as 6 days

showed avoidance behaviour of a cube or ball that loomed towards their face. When the cube came close, they threw up their arms, moved their head back, or opened their eyes very wide. All of these are defensive behaviours, showing that the babies were able to perceive that the distance between the cube and their face had suddenly reduced. Similarly, Yonas and Owsley (1987) found that three-month-old infants flinched when shown a film of an object apparently heading directly towards them. There must be some ability to perceive depth for this to occur. The presence of depth perception in very young infants might lend support to the nativist view – that depth perception is innate.

Visual constancies

As discussed in Unit 2, visual constancies are important in allowing us to maintain a stable perception of the world in the face of changing visual images. In order to perceive the world reliably, we need to apply these constancies. Are they learned, or are we born with the ability to do this?

Shape constancy This is the ability to recognise that the shape of an object remains the same even though it is viewed from different angles. Bower (1966) conducted a classic study on shape constancy. He trained two-month-old babies to turn their heads when they saw a particular rectangle. He then showed them slightly different views of the same rectangle, either tilted or turned slightly, and tested whether the infants would respond to these images in the same way. Even though the shape of the retinal image had changed, two-month-old babies continued to turn their heads towards the rectangle when it was presented at different angles. They did seem to show shape constancy.

Size constancy This is the ability to recognise that an object has not changed in size because the retinal image changes in size. When we see a person walking off into the distance, we do not perceive them as having shrunk.

Bower (1965) used an ingenious technique to investigate whether babies would show size constancy. Babies between 40 and 60 days old were conditioned to make a head-turning response when a 30cm cube – a cube with sides 30 cm long – was presented to them at a distance of 1 metre. If the babies turned their head when this cube was present, an adult popped up in front of them and played 'peek-a-boo'.

Bower then presented four different stimuli in various orders.

1 The original 30cm cube, presented 1 metre away from the baby.

2 The same 30cm cube, presented at a distance of 3 metres.

3 A 90cm cube presented 1 metre away.

4 A 90cm cube presented 3 metres away.

These stimuli were carefully selected to make sure that the size of the retinal image produced by the 30cm cube presented 1 metre away would be exactly the same size as that produced by the 90 cm cube at 3 metres' distance.

Bower noted how many head-turning responses were made to each of the four stimuli:

- 98 responses were made to the original stimulus.
- 58 responses were made to the original cube presented at a longer distance (producing a smaller retinal image than the original stimulus).

- 54 responses were made to the 90cm cube presented 1 metre away (producing a larger retinal image then the original cube.
- 22 responses were made to the 90cm cube presented 3 metres away (producing the same size retinal image as the original cube).

It is clear that the babies in Bower's study were not just responding to the size of the retinal image. If they were, they would have responded equally to stimulus 1 and stimulus 4. They do seem to show some, limited, size constancy ability, and were apparently able to detect the same 30 cm cube when it was displayed further away from them.

In a later study, Yonas et al. (1982) tested the ability of five and seven-month-old infants to apply size constancy to faces. To eliminate binocular depth cues, each infant had a patch placed over one eye. They were then shown photographs of large and small faces. If similar stimuli were shown to adults, they would realise that only the large face might be close enough to touch. Size constancy would be applied, and the small faces would be perceived as being further away. The five-month-old infants were as likely to reach out for the small faces as the large ones, but the seven-month-old infants reached more often for the large faces, indicating that they were using size constancy to judge that the small faces were further away.

Explanations of perceptual development

The research described in this unit has provided a range of evidence about the remarkable perceptual skills that neonates possess. Their ability to recognise patterns, to respond to specific faces, to perceive depth and show shape and size constancy from a very early age is impressive. But what does this tell us about whether perceptual skills are innate or learned? To what extent does the evidence support nativist or empiricist views?

Evidence in favour of nativism

A range of evidence supports the idea that perceptual abilities are innate.

- Neonates as young as two or three days show preferences for looking at patterned objects and for looking at faces. These preferences do not appear to be learned.
- Depth perception abilities are evident from an early age, including avoidance behaviour of approaching objects. However, avoidance behaviour of 'cliffs' seems to develop to coincide with the development of crawling.
- Babies who are born late show more consistent reactions to the 'looming objects' than babies who are born on time or prematurely, even when they have all had the same number of weeks of experience since birth. This indicates that maturational age, not experience and learning, is the important factor in displaying avoidance behaviour of objects that appear to be approaching quickly. This suggests that avoidance behaviour is biologically programmed to appear at a certain time (Yonas, 1981).
- The findings on size and shape constancy suggest that these abilities may have a genetic basis since they appear at an early age.

Evidence in favour of empiricism

There is evidence that at least some minimal level of experience is necessary for the perceptual system to develop and function fully.

- Animals deprived of light show deterioration of the entire visual system, and decreased perceptual abilities (Hubel & Wiesel, 1963). Riesen (1965) found that chimpanzees who were kept in the dark from birth experienced damage to the cells in the retina and visual cortex. Chimpanzees who were made to wear translucent goggles, which allowed some light stimulation to reach their eyes, showed an ability to distinguish changes in brightness, but were unable to track a moving object with their eyes when the goggles were removed. This suggests that interaction with the environment is important for the visual system to develop fully.
- Even if perceptual abilities have a genetic basis, infants have to learn how to use those abilities. For example, they learn to recognise their mother's face.

Nativism or empiricism?

It is clear that visual perception develops as a result of both innate abilities and learning. Research showing that neonates are able to make discriminations between patterns strongly suggests that there may be some innate predisposition for this ability. However, the infant will learn to use this ability to make discriminations between *specific* patterns, faces and objects – and these will be the ones that are important in the child's environment. In other words, if innate abilities are shaped by the environment, both nativist and empiricist approaches are needed to understand the development of visual perception.

As a result of this, the focus of research in perceptual development has shifted away from trying to decide whether perceptual development is the result of *either* innate factors *or* environmental learning. Instead, more emphasis has been placed on questions like these.

- What are the patterns of change in perception as the child grows older?
- How does the child's environment influence these changes?
- How are basic sensory skills combined to allow perception to take place?

One of the important researchers in this area is Eleanor Gibson (1969). She makes use of some of the concepts developed with her husband, J.J. Gibson, whose ideas were described in Unit 2. Her approach focuses on the ways in which perception changes and develops, and seeks to provide a fuller explanation of the types of skills needed as perception develops. For example, she argues that the awareness of the meaning of perceptual information develops as the child learns to pay attention to all of the affordances of objects – to all their potential uses.

This approach captures the richness and variation of perceptual development, rather than trying to decide whether perceptual development is explained by empiricism or nativism.

3.3   Cross-cultural studies of visual perception

Cross-cultural studies can provide insight into the ways in which different environments influence the development of visual perception.

Studies using visual illusions

Empiricism If visual perception is influenced by learning, then

Activity 4   Environmental effects in perceptual development

Item A   A world of stripes

Blakemore and Cooper (1970) raised kittens in complete darkness for the first five months of their lives, except for five hours each day when the kitten was placed inside a cylinder painted with vertical stripes. The kitten could see only the stripes because it was wearing a collar that prevented it from seeing its own body.

After five months, kittens raised in this way were unable to perceive horizontal lines, and lacked feature detectors in the cortex that responded to horizontal lines. The opposite was found with kittens raised in a cylinder painted with horizontal stripes.

Questions

1 What do these findings suggest about the role of the environment in perception?

2 Do they support a nativist or empiricist view of perception, or a combination of the two views?

---

people from different cultures, living in different social and physical environments should, to some extent, perceive things differently. They should, for example, be more susceptible or less susceptible to (likely to be fooled by) visual illusions.

Early studies by Rivers (1901, 1905) supported this view. He found that non-Western peoples (from Papua New Guinea and Southern India) were less susceptible to the Müller-Lyer illusion than Western people (English adults and children).

Segall et al. (1966) re-examined Rivers' findings using adults and children from 14 'non-European' samples, mostly from Africa, and three 'European' samples, two from the USA, and one from South Africa of people of European descent living in Johannesburg. In all, 1,878 people were surveyed. As with the Rivers study, the results showed that members of the 'non-European' sample were less susceptible to the Müller-Lyer illusion than the 'European' sample.

To explain their findings, Segall et al. developed the *carpentered-world hypothesis*. This hypothesis states that Western people live in a world of carpentered structures – a world of buildings made up of straight lines, right angles and rectangles. This encourages people to interpret obtuse and acute angles as deriving from right-angled rectangular objects. This tendency is learned from their built environment and it becomes automatic fairly early in life. As a result, they are more susceptible to the Müller-Lyer illusion which they tend to interpret in the form of buildings (see p205 for a fuller explanation of this tendency).

This conclusion supports the empiricist view – that to a large extent visual perception is learned, that different learning experiences in different cultures and environments will produce different visual perceptions.

Nativism This interpretation of Segall's et al's findings has been challenged from a nativist view which argues that differences in perception result from differences in biology rather than culture

and environment.

Pollack and Silvar (1967) found a correlation between the ability to detect contours (outlines of shapes) and susceptibility to the Müller-Lyer illusion. The less able participants were to detect contours, the less susceptible they were to the illusion. The same researchers also showed that people with denser retinal pigmentation, found particularly in darker-skinned people, have greater difficulty in detecting contours (Silvar & Pollack, 1967). Pollack and Silvar therefore argued that biological differences might account for what Segall et al. had explained in terms of cultural differences.

Some support for this view was provided by a study which presented the Müller-Lyer illusion to samples drawn from Australian aborigines, Inuit (Eskimos), and people from Scotland, Sierra Leone and New Guinea (Berry, 1971). Again, it appeared that people with denser retinal pigmentation and a darker skin were less susceptible to the illusion, and that the explanation lay in biology rather than culture.

Back to empiricism A number of studies have challenged this explanation, and returned to the view that differences in susceptibility to illusions are due to culture. The most impressive piece of research was conducted in the USA and Zambia by Stewart (1973). She used the Müller-Lyer and Sander illusions (see Figure 24).

This illusion gives the impression that the two diagonal lines that cross the parallelograms are of different lengths – in fact, they are the same length.

She presented these illusions to 60 African Americans and 60 White Americans from aged 6 to 17, selected randomly from three schools in Evanston, Illinois. Boys and girls were equally represented. They shared the same carpentered environment. Only the race of the children varied. In Zambia the sample was drawn from all-black children. This time the environment varied from unschooled children living in an uncarpentered rural area

Figure 24 The Sander illusion

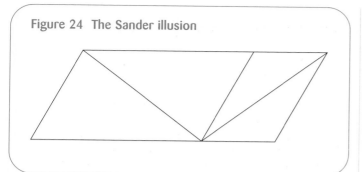

in the Zambezi Valley, to middle-class children living in Lusaka, the capital of Zambia, a carpentered area. This time, race was held constant and the extent of carpenteredness was varied. Stewart's main finding was that susceptibility to illusions rose as the degree of carpenteredness rose. Her findings are summarised in Table 1.

Table 1 Susceptibility to illusions

	Zambezi Valley uncarpentered	Lusaka carpentered	Evanston black	Evanston white
Müller-Lyer	4.63	5.81	6.10	6.10
Sander	4.24	5.33	5.59	5.40

Average number of responses showing susceptibility to illusions

Conclusion The weight of evidence supports the empiricist view that, at least in terms of susceptibility to illusions, culture and the environment influence visual perception. Segall et al. (1990) draw the following conclusion – 'After a quarter century of cross-cultural research on visual perception, it may be stated with confidence that people perceive in ways that are shaped by the inferences they have learned to make in order to function most effectively in the particular ecological settings in which they live. Thus, environment and culture shape our perceptual habits.'

Culture and size constancy

Size constancy refers to the fact that perception of an object remains the same even though the size of the retinal image changes. For example, when a person walks into the distance, the image on the retina shrinks but the person is not perceived as physically shrinking. Is size constancy influenced by culture and the environment?

Colin Turnbull (1961) studied the BaMbuti people who live in the dense Ituri Forest in the Democratic Republic of the Congo (formerly Zaire). At the end of his study, Turnbull took one of the BaMbuti, Kenge, out of the forest. Kenge had lived all his life in a forested environment. They drove to the top of a hill and looked down on the rolling grasslands below. Several miles away, a herd of buffalo were grazing. 'What insects are those?' asked Kenge. Turnbull was puzzled. 'At first I hardly understood, then I realised that in the forest vision is so limited that there is no great need to make an automatic allowance for distance when judging size. Kenge was looking for the first time over apparently unending miles of unfamiliar grasslands, with not a tree worth the name to give him any basis for comparison.'

When Turnbull told Kenge the 'insects' were buffalo, Kenge

roared with laughter and told him not to tell lies. As they drove closer, Kenge kept his face glued to the window. As they passed the buffalo, his only comment was they were not real buffalo, and he was not going to get out of the car. Turnbull was unable to discover what Kenge thought was happening.

Evaluation This story is often quoted in psychology textbooks as an example of how culture and environment affect perception. It is claimed that because Kenge had spent his whole life in a dense jungle with no opportunity to see for any great distance, he was unable to use size constancy. This is one possible explanation.

However, there are other explanations.

- First, Kenge may have been unable to use size constancy in this situation because there was 'not a tree worth the name' to provide a guide for judging size and distance. This is not the same as saying that Kenge was unable to use size constancy. He may have been unable to use it in this situation because there was nothing in the environment on which he could base a judgement. In this case the problem may be a lack of *familiar size*. With familiar objects we know how big they are and can use the size of the image formed in the retina to make a judgement of how far away they are. Since familiar size is influenced by objects in the environment, this explanation still supports the view that culture shapes perception.

- Second, as Vernon (1970) points out, size constancy doesn't work as well over long distances. If you look from the top of a tall building, the cars on the road below do look like toy cars. Size constancy doesn't seem to be as effective when there is a large distance between the viewer and the object.

Key term

Carpentered environment *A man-made environment containing many straight lines and right-angles.*

Culture and perception of pictures

Does culture affect the way people perceive pictures? Will people from different cultures perceive pictures differently? If the interpretation of pictures differs from culture to culture, then this suggests that, to some extent, visual perception is learned.

William Hudson (1960) began systematic research into these questions. He developed a pictorial perception test consisting of a series of pictures which contained a number of depth cues. These cues included:

- **Familiar size** The larger of two known objects is drawn considerably smaller to indicate it is further away – for example, the elephant and the antelope in Figure 25.
- **Overlap** Parts of nearer objects overlap and obscure parts of objects that are further away. For example, the man and the antelope obscuring part of the hills in Figure 25.
- **Perspective** For example, the convergence of lines which are known to be parallel in order to indicate distance.

Hudson's pictures have been shown across Africa to many peoples with different cultures and languages. Participants were asked to name the objects in the pictures, to describe what the people were doing, and the relations between the objects, for example which objects are closest to the man in Figure 25.

Figure 25 Example of Hudson's drawings

Figure 26 Two squares

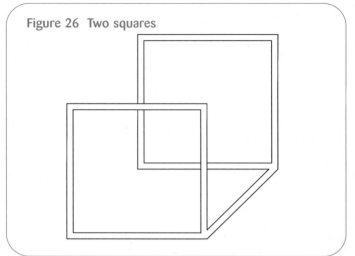

Participants who used depth clues and made 'correct' interpretations (eg the antelope was closest to the man) were said to have three-dimensional perception; those who did not and gave 'incorrect' interpretations (eg the elephant was closest to the man) were said to have two-dimensional vision. Many African participants, particularly those who had not been exposed to Western culture, were classified as having two-dimensional vision. They found it difficult to perceive depth in the pictures.

Support for Hudson's findings was provided by Deregowski (1972). Primary school boys and unskilled workers in Zambia were given Hudson's picture test and classified as having either two-dimensional or three-dimensional perception. They were then shown the drawing in Figure 26 which most Westerners see as three-dimensional. The Zambian participants were asked to look at the drawing and construct a model to represent it from sticks and clay. Almost all the participants who had been classified as three-dimensional perceivers made a three-dimensional model. Those classified as two-dimensional perceivers – ie they did not perceive depth in pictures – tended to build flat models.

Evaluation

The picture tests described in this section appear to support the empiricist view – that perception is learned and varies from culture to culture. Had the various African participants grown up in Western society, they would have interpreted the pictures in the same way as Western participants. Perceiving pictures as three-dimensional is therefore learned. But before reaching this conclusion, a number of points must be considered.

* Hudson's pictures omitted texture gradient – an important depth clue. When texture gradient was added to the pictures, African participants were more likely to perceive the pictures as three-dimensional (Berry et al., 1992). In addition, when the pictures were in colour, non-Western participants were more likely to recognise objects (Hagen & Jones, 1978).
* The pictures used in cross-cultural studies are drawn by Western artists. Researchers have tended to assume that Western art presents an accurate, realistic and correct view of the world. Participants who do not perceive these pictures

Summary

1. The nature-nurture debate centres on whether perceptual skills are innate – the nativist view – or whether they are learned through experience – the empiricist view.

2. Neonate studies have investigated the perceptual skills of newborn babies, using a range of research techiques including sucking responses and time spent looking at an object.

3. Studies of neonates show that they possess some remarkable perceptual skills, and that these develop very quickly in the early part of life.

4. Neonates seem to possess colour vision, and while their visual acuity is initially very poor, it quickly improves.

5. Neonates show early preference for looking at certain types of pattern – patterns that resemble faces seem to attract most interest.

6. Studies show that perception develops at an early age, but avoidance of 'visual cliffs' does not develop until the infant starts to crawl.

7. The focus has shifted from trying to find out whether the nativist or empiricist approach is correct towards investigating the relative importance of each to perceptual development.

8. Cross-cultural studies have been conducted to investigate the degree to which perception is influenced by culture and environment.

9. Cross-cultural research using illusions suggests that visual perception is largely shaped by culture and the environment.

10. Evidence from the perception of pictures in different cultures leads to a similar conclusion. However, picture perception tests must be treated with caution, particularly when Western-style art is used as a basis for judging the perceptual skills of non-Western peoples.

as three-dimensional are said to perceive them 'incorrectly'. However, the same accusation may be levelled at Westerners who 'misinterpret' non-Western art (see Activity 5, Item A).

- Art from different cultures uses different stylistic conventions. For example, linear perspective has been widely used in Western art for only a few hundred years. Unfamiliarity with artistic conventions may tell us more about stylistic preference than perception (Serpell, 1976). In other words, researchers may have mistakenly seen a preference for a particular style as indicating a difference in perception.

Activity 5   Art and culture

Item A   Tsimshian art

This highly stylised picture of a bear was drawn by a Tsimshian, a Native American people from the Pacific coast of British Columbia, Canada. It is an example of a 'split drawing', a style found in many non-Western cultures.

Item B   Elephants

Hudson (1960) showed this picture to African children and adults. All but one preferred the picture on the left – the 'split drawing'. The person who did not prefer this drawing thought the elephant was jumping about in a dangerous manner.

Item C   A fishing boat?

A BaMbuti hunter in the Ituri forest

For the first time in his life Kenge, a BaMbuti man, had left the dense tropical forest in Central Africa. Colin Turnbull, the researcher who accompanied Kenge, writes: 'I pointed out a boat in the middle of the lake. It was a large fishing boat with a number of people in it. Kenge at first refused to believe it. He thought it was a floating piece of wood.'

Adapted from Turnbull, 1961

Questions

1   What can Items A and B tell us about cultural differences in perception?

2   Suggest reasons for Kenge's behaviour in Item C.

References

Adams, R.J. (1989). Obstetrical medication and the human newborn: The influence of alphaprodine hydrochloride on visual behavior. *Developmental Medicine and Child Neurology*, 31, 650-656.

Allport, F.H. (1955). *Theories of perception and the concept of structure*. New York: Wiley.

Aslin, R.N. (1987). Motor aspects of visual development in infancy. In P. Salapatek and L. Cohen (Eds.), *Handbook of infant perception,*

Vol 1: From sensation to perception. Orlando: Academic Press.

Banks, M.S. & Salapatek, P. (1983). Infant visual perception. In P.H. Mussen (Ed.), *Handbook of child development*, (4th ed.). New York: Wiley.

Bee, H. (2000). *The developing child* (9th ed.). Boston: Allyn & Bacon.

Berry, J.W. (1971). Müller-Lyer susceptibility: Culture, ecology, or race? *International Journal of Psychology*, 6, 193-197.

Berry, J.W., Poortinga, Y.H., Segall, M.H. & Dasen, P.R. (1992). *Cross-cultural psychology: Research and applications*. New York: Cambridge University Press.

Blakemore, C. & Cooper, C.R. (1970). The development of the brain depends on the visual environment. *Nature*, 228, 477-8.

Bornstein, M.H., Tamis-LeMonda, C.S., Tal, J., Ludermann, P., Toda, S., Rahn, C. W., Pecheux, M., Azuma, H. & Vardi, D. (1992). Maternal responsiveness to infants in three societies: The United States, France and Japan. *Child Development*, 63, 808-21.

Bower, T.G.R. (1965). Stimulus variables determining space perception in infants. *Science*, 149, 88-9.

Bower, T.G.R. (1966). The visual world of infants. *Scientific American*, 215, 80-92.

Bower, T.G.R., Broughton, J.M. & Moore, M.K. (1970). Infant response to approaching objects: An indication of response to distal variation. *Perception and Psychophysics*, 9, 193-196.

Bruce, V., & Green, P. (1985). *Visual perception: Physiology, psychology and ecology*. Hove: Psychology Press.

Bruce, V., Green, P.R. & Georgeson, M.A. (1996). *Visual perception: Physiology, psychology and ecology* (3rd ed.). Hove: Psychology Press.

Campos, J.J., Langer, A. & Krowitz, A. (1970). Cardiac response on the cliff in pre-locomotor human infants. *Science*, 170, 196-7.

Clocksin, W.F. (1980). Perception of surface slant and edge labels from optical flow: A computational approach. *Perception*, 9, 253-271.

Cohen, L.B., DeLoache, J.S. & Strauss, M.S. (1979). Infant visual perception. In J. Osofsky (Ed.), *Handbook of infant development*. New York: Wiley.

Coren, S. & Girgus, J.S. (1972). Visual spatial illusions: Many explanations. Science, 179, 503-504.

Cutting, J.E. & Kozlowski, L.T. (1977). Recognising friends by their walk: Gait perception without familiarity cues. *Bulletin of the Psychonomic Society*, 9, 353-356.

Dannemiller, J.L. & Stephens, B.R. (1988). A critical test of infant pattern preference models. *Child Development*, 59, 210-216.

Deregowski, J. (1972). Pictorial perception and culture. *Scientific American*, 227, 82-8.

Eysenck, M.W. & Keane, M.T. (1995). *Cognitive psychology: A student's handbook*. Hove: LEA.

Fantz, R.L. (1956). A method for studying early visual development. *Perceptual and Motor Skills*, 6, 13-15.

Fantz, R.L. (1961). The origin of form perception. *Scientific American*, 204(5), 66-72.

Gibson, E. (1969). *Principles of perceptual learning and development*. New York: Prentice-Hall

Gibson, E.J. & Walk, P.D. (1960). The visual cliff. *Scientific American*, 202, 64-71.

Gibson, J.J. (1979). *The perception of the visual world*. Boston: Houghton-Mifflin.

Gregory, R.L. (1966). *Eye and brain*. New York: McGraw Hill.

Gregory, R.L. (1970). *The intelligent eye*. London: Weidenfeld & Nicolson.

Gregory, R.L. (1980). Perceptions as hypotheses. *Philosophical Transactions of the Royal Society of London*, Series B, 290, 181-187.

Hagen, M. & Jones, R. (1978). Cultural effect on pictorial perception: How many words is one picture really worth?. In R. Walk and H. Pick (Eds.), *Perception and experience*. New York: Plenum Press.

Haith, M.M. (1990). *Rules that babies look by*. Hillsdale, NJ: Erlbaum.

Helmholtz, H.L.F. von (1885). *Sensations of tone*. London: Longman.

Hering, E. (1878). *Outlines of a theory of the light sense* (translation). Cambridge, MA: Harvard University Press.

Hubel, D.H. & Wiesel, T.N. (1962). Receptive fields, binocular interaction and functional architecture in the cat's visual cortex. *Journal of Physiology*, 195, 215-243.

Hubel, D.H. & Wiesel, T.N. (1963). Receptive fields of cells in striate cortex of very young, visually inexperienced kittens. *Journal of Neurophysiology*, 26, 994-1002.

Hudson, W. (1960). Pictorial depth perception in sub-cultural groups in Africa. *Journal of Social Psychology*, 52, 183-208.

Hurvich, L.M. (1981). *Colour vision*. Sunderland, MA: Sinauer Associates.

James, W. (1890). *Principles of psychology*. New York: Holt.

Johansson, G. (1975). Visual motion perception. *Scientific American*, 232, 76-89.

Marr, D. (1982). *Vision: A computational investigation into the human representation and processing of visual information*. San Francisco: W.H. Freeman.

Matlin, M.W. & Foley, H.J. (1997). *Sensation and perception* (4th ed.). Boston: Allyn & Bacon.

Milner, A.D. & Goodale, M.A. (1998). The visual brain in action. *Psyche*, 4, 1-14.

Neisser, U. (1976). *Cognition and reality*. San Francisco: W.H. Freeman.

Norman, D.A. (1988). *The psychology of everyday things*. New York: Basic Books.

Palmer, S.E. (1975). The effects of contextual scenes on the identification of objects. *Memory and Cognition*, 3. 519-526.

Pascalis, O., deSchonen, S., Morton, J., Deruelle, C. & Fabre-Grenet, M. (1995). Mother's face recognition by neonates: A replication and an extension. *Infant Behaviour and Development*, 18, 79-85.

Pollack, R.H. & Silvar, S.D. (1967). Magnitude of the Müller-Lyer illusion in children as a function of pigmentation of the Fundus oculi. *Psychonomic Science*, 8, 83-84.

Rivers, W.H.R. (1901). Visual spatial perception. In A. C. Haddom (Ed.), *Reports of the Cambridge anthropological expedition to the Torres Straits, 2(1)*. Cambridge: Cambridge University Press.

Rivers, W.H.R. (1905). Observations on the senses of the Todas. *British Journal of Psychology*, 1, 321-396.

Sedgwick, H.A. (1973). *The visible horizon*. Ph.D. thesis, Cornell University.

Segall, M.H., Campbell, D.T. & Herskovits, M.J. (1966). *The influence of culture on visual perception*. Indianapolis: Bobbs-Merrill.

Segall, M.H., Dasen, P.R., Berry, J.W. & Poortinga, Y.H. (1990). Human behaviour in global perspective: *An introduction to cross-cultural psychology*. Boston: Allyn and Bacon.

Serpell, R.S. (1976). *Culture's influence on behaviour*. London: Methuen.

Silvar, S.D. & Pollack, R.H. (1967). Racial differences in pigmentation of the Fundus oculi. *Psychonomic Science*, 7, 159-160.

Small, M.Y. (1990). *Cognitive development*. San Diego: Harcourt Brace, Jovanovich.

Stewart, V.M. (1973). Tests of the 'carpentered world' hypothesis by race and environment in America and Zambia. *International Journal of Psychology*, 8, 83-94.

Svaetichin, G. (1956). Spectral response curves from single cones. *Acta Physiologica Scandinavica, 39*, (suppl. 134), 17-46.

Turnbull, C. (1961). *The forest people: A study of Pygmies of the Congo*. New York: Simon & Schuster.

Vernon, M.D. (1970). *Perception through experience*. London: Methuen.

Walton, G.E., Bower N.J.A. & Bower, T.G.R (1992). Recognition of familiar faces by newborns. *Infant Behaviour and Development, 15*, 265-9.

Wertheimer, M. (1912). Experimentelle studien über das sehen von bewegung. *Zeitschrift für Psychologie*, 61, 161-265.

Yonas, A. & Owsley, C. (1987). Development of visual space perception. In P. Salapatek and L. Cohen (Eds.), *Handbook of infant perception, Volume 2: From perception to cognition*. Orlando: Academic Press.

Yonas, A. (1981). Infants' responses to optical information for collision. In R.N. Aslin, J.R. Alberts and M.R. Peterson (Eds.), *Development of perception: Psychobiological perspectives, Volume 2, the visual system*. New York: Academic Press.

Yonas, A., Pettersen, L. & Granrud, C.E. (1982). Infants' sensitivity to familiar size as information for distance. *Child Development, 53*, 1285-1290.

27 Language, thought and problem-solving

▶ **Introduction**

What makes us human? Answers to this question often include the ability to use language and the ability to think. Our use of language enables us to communicate an infinitely diverse set of ideas, thoughts, feelings and emotions to other people.

As language is so complex, it is clear that if we could not think, we would not be able to use language. Perhaps the opposite is true. Perhaps if we did not possess language skills, then we would not be able to think and solve problems as we do. How are language and thought related? Does language influence thought or thought influence language? Do they influence each other or are they largely unaffected by each other?

How do we acquire language as children? Are we biologically 'wired' for language acquisition, or is language-learning merely a process of imitation, with infants learning from their elders?

What kinds of thought processes are used to solve puzzles and make decisions? Are people good at judging the probabilities of events occurring, or are they prone to making mistakes?

These are the main issues discussed in this chapter.

Chapter summary

- Unit 1 discusses the relationship between language and thought.
- Unit 2 looks at social and cultural aspects of language.
- Unit 3 examines theories of the acquisition of language.

- Unit 4 looks at theoretical accounts of problem-solving.
- Unit 5 considers some of the factors influencing decision-making and risk-taking.

Unit 1 Language and culture

KEY ISSUES

1 What is the relationship between and language thought ?

2 What evidence is there that language influences thought?

3 What is the evidence that thought influences language?

1.1 Language and culture

Culture is the learned, shared behaviour of members of society. It includes social norms, values and beliefs that direct the behaviours of members of society and influence the way they think about the world around them. To some degree, people from different cultures will understand the world in different ways.

Language is an important part of culture. It is learned and shared by members of society and often varies from culture to culture. Do different languages affect the way people think

about and interpret the world? For example, do English-speakers and French-speakers think differently because of the words they use and the structure of their language? Does the same apply to people who speak different versions of the same language, for example different dialects of English?

There are five possible relationships between language and thought:

- First, thought and language are one and the same.
- Second, language and thought are completely separate processes that never affect each other.
- Third, language shapes the way we think. The words and phrases we use and the rules that structure language influence the way we think.
- Fourth, language is a reflection of thought. It is a device that translates thoughts into sounds – speech – in order to communicate these thoughts.
- Fifth, language and thought influence each other.

The first two possibilities will now be briefly dealt with. The remaining three possibilities are discussed in detail in this unit.

First, language and thought are one and the same. This idea was proposed by the behaviourist John Watson (1913). He believed that thinking involves speaking silently to oneself. This is accompanied by movements of the larynx – an organ in the throat that holds the vocal cords. This idea has been refuted by researchers paralysing their larynx and finding that they could still think (Smith et al., 1947). In addition, research has shown that deaf mutes who have not learned sign language think in much the same way as people who can hear and speak (Furth, 1966). The available evidence indicates that language and thought are *not* one and the same.

Second, language and thought are independent processes. A number of psychologists believe that the central nervous system is modular. It consists of modules – systems of neurons – each of which functions independently, but is linked to and coordinated with other modules (Fodor, 1983). From this point of view language and thought can be seen as independent but coordinated modules.

No researcher argues that language and thought are completely separate. However, there is evidence that to some extent they operate independently. For example, Pinker (1994) points out that we have all had the experience of speaking or writing a sentence and feeling that it wasn't quite what we meant to say. In other words, language and thought are not one and the same because sometimes language fails to adequately reflect our thoughts. This does not, mean, however, that language and thought are completely separate, that they never influence each other.

1.2 The linguistic relativity hypothesis

The *linguistic relativity hypothesis* states that the form of our language influences or determines the structure of our thought processes. It affects the way we perceive the world, it shapes our world view.

The linguistic relativity hypothesis developed out of the ideas of Edward Sapir – an American linguist who specialised in studying Native American languages – and Benjamin Lee Whorf – an amateur linguist and Sapir's student in the late 1920s. As a result, the linguistic relativity hypothesis is often known as the Sapir-Whorf linguistic relativity hypothesis.

Sapir (1929) suggested that the structure of the language that we speak influences how we perceive the world – our world view. This idea was developed by Whorf (1940), who said that:

> 'We dissect nature along lines laid down by our native languages. The categories and types that we isolate from the world of phenomena we do not find there because they stare every observer in the face; on the contrary, the world is presented in a kaleidoscopic flux of impressions which has to be organised by our minds – and this means largely by the linguistic systems in our minds. We cut nature up, organise it into concepts, and ascribe significances as we do, largely because we are parties to an agreement to organise it in this way – an agreement that holds throughout our speech community and is codified in the patterns of our language.'

Whorf is suggesting that the language we use is directly responsible for shaping our thoughts about the world. Sapir was more cautious. He saw language influencing rather then determining thought.

These two versions of the linguistic relativity hypothesis became known as the 'strong' and 'weak' versions, to which Miller and McNeill (1969) add a third 'weakest' version that suggests that language differences affect processing on certain tasks where linguistic encoding is important, for example on memory tasks.

Whorf (1956) carried out an extensive analysis of Native American languages, from which he drew his conclusions. Some of his evidence will now be examined.

Vocabulary of languages Compared to English-speakers, the Hopi of the southwestern USA have a different way of classifying objects and events. In English, chair, dog, flame and lightning are all treated as nouns. The Hopi classify events by their duration, so that brief events – like lightning, puff of smoke and flame – are treated as verbs, and more long-lasting events and objects – such as dogs and chairs – are treated as nouns. According to Whorf, this is 'strange to our modes of thought'. He is suggesting that Hopi speakers think about the world differently because their language classifies the world differently.

Hopi performing a raindance

Apart from birds, the Hopi have only one word ('masa'ytaka') for everything that flies, for example, aeroplanes, kites, insects, and pilots. This might seem clumsy and confusing since it apparently fails to discriminate between very different flying objects. In a famous example, Whorf argues that our use of the word 'snow' would seem equally indiscriminate to the Inuit (Eskimos) who use different words for different types of snow, such as falling snow, snow on the ground, slushy snow, snow that is safe to stand on, and so on.

Are the Hopi's perceptions of flying objects different from those of English-speakers? Are Inuits' perceptions of snow different from English-speakers? The linguistic relativity hypothesis suggests that they are.

Grammar of language A language's grammar may also affect the way its speakers think. While the English language makes a clear distinction between past, present and future tenses, Whorf reports that Hopi has no words that directly relate to time. As a result, he argues the Hopi have a very different sense of time from English-speakers. Whorf states that Hopi-speakers do not think of time as passing by in fixed intervals such as minutes and hours. Rather, they seem to judge 'how long ago' something happened by the number of events that occurred between then and the present.

Whorf argues that if Hopi language does not refer to 'time' as we view it, then Hopi-speakers must think about the world very differently from English-speakers.

Structure of sentences Sentence structure within a language may also affect the speaker's world view. Two frequently used examples from Whorf's work illustrate this possibility.

- The Nootka of Vancouver Island express the statement 'the boat is grounded on the beach' as 'tlih-is-ma' which translates directly as 'it is on the beach pointwise as an event of canoe motion'.
- In Apache, the phrase 'it is a dripping spring' is expressed as 'to no-ga', which translates directly 'as water, or springs, whiteness moves downward'.

As Whorf puts it: 'How unlike our way of thinking!' In other words, speakers of different languages do not just construct sentences differently, they *think* differently, too.

Evaluation of Whorf

- Whorf's work has been very influential. The evidence he produces in support of the linguistic relativity hypothesis is fascinating and seductive. For many, he makes a compelling case for the view that language shapes thought. However, there are problems with his analysis.
- Some critics argue that Whorf does no more than indicate the possibility that language determines thought. He does not show that speakers of Hopi, Apache, Nootka, or any other language think differently just because they express ideas in different ways. As Pinker (1994) points out, Whorf's

conclusions are based on a circular argument – Hopi speak differently, so they must think differently. How do we know they think differently? Because they speak differently!

- Whorf's translations are questionable. Alternative translations sometimes suggest that the structure of Native American languages is much closer to English than Whorf claims. For example, 'as water, or springs, whiteness moves downward' could be equally well translated as 'clear stuff – water – is falling'. This is more similar to the structure of English than Whorf's translation from the Apache (Pinker, 1994).
- Whorf's knowledge of Native American languages is incomplete. For example, Malotki (1983) reports that Hopi does have words corresponding to time and can describe time elaborately. However, despite criticising Whorf's ignorance of Hopi, Malotki admits that he did not study the same Hopi dialect that Whorf did.
- The following section on testing the linguistic relativity hypothesis provides further evaluation of Whorf.

Key term

Linguistic relativity hypothesis *There are three versions of the linguistic relativity hypothesis. The strong version states that language determines thought. The weak version says that language influences thought. The weakest version claims that language influences certain thought processes in which language plays an important part, for example memory.*

Activity 1   The Great Eskimo Vocabulary Hoax

Item A   The environment

Question

The so-called Great Eskimo Vocabulary Hoax illustrates some of the problems with the evidence and reasoning Whorf used to support the linguistic relativity hypothesis. Discuss.

Item B   The Hoax

The American anthropologist Franz Boas (1911) reported that the Inuit (Eskimo) have four words for snow. Whorf stated they have 'several'. Slowly but surely, the number grew, reaching a peak of around 200 in the 1980s. Pullum (1989) described this meteoric rise as The Great Eskimo Vocabulary Hoax. The number 'magically' multiplied as the story was repeated. Why?

First, this vast array of snow words makes sense in terms of Inuit culture and lifestyle. For most of the year the landscape is snowbound and precise distinctions between different types of snow are vital for the Inuit way of life.

Second, it makes sense in terms of the linguistic relativity hypothesis. A large number of words for snow influences Inuit perceptions of snow. It means that the Inuit could make finer distinctions between types of snow compared to English-speakers. Again, this is vital for their way of life.

But do the Inuit have a variety of words for types of snow? According to Harley (1995), they only have two words – 'qanik' for snow in the air and 'aput' for snow on the ground. And, according to Pinker (1994), English may have even more words than Inuit, for example sleet, slush and blizzard.

There are further complications. First, there are various groups of Inuit, each with their own dialect. Second, there is the problem of translation from Inuit to English. And third, types of snow can be distinguished by phrases – for example, light powdery snow – rather than single words.

1.3 Testing the linguistic relativity hypothesis

According to the linguistic relativity hypothesis, differences between languages will affect how speakers think about, perceive, and remember the world. This hypothesis is very difficult to test experimentally, although attempts have been made. Some of this research will now be examined.

Colour words and discrimination

Researchers have investigated the ways in which different languages code and name the colours of the spectrum. The linguistic relativity hypothesis predicts that in languages that do not have a name for a particular colour, speakers of that language will be less likely to discriminate that colour from others.

Brown and Lenneberg (1954) found some support for the linguistic relativity hypothesis. They found that Zuni speakers in New Mexico made more mistakes in recognising yellows and oranges than English speakers. This could be explained by the fact that Zuni has a single word to describe yellows and oranges.

Other evidence, however, does not support the linguistic relativity hypothesis. Rosch (1974) studied speakers of Dani, a New Guinea Highland language that has only two terms for colours: dark and light. The speakers were, however, able to recognise a range of colours. This means, for example, that they could recognise a shade of red they had been shown earlier even though their language contains no word for 'red'. As the Dani performed this task very similarly to American participants, it suggests that the perception and memory of colour are not determined by language.

More recent evidence supports a weak version of the linguistic relativity hypothesis. Davies and Corbett (1997) and Davies (1998) found that Setswana-speakers (in Botswana), who have a single word ('botala') for blue and green were more likely to group blue and green colour chips together than English speakers. This suggests that language influences perceptions of colour. However, Russian speakers have different words for light blue ('goluboj') and dark blue ('sinij'), but are no more likely to group dark blue and light blue separately than English speakers. Davies and Corbett (1997) conclude that there are strong universal influences on colour perception, but these universal influences can be moderated by cultural influences such as language. This suggests support for a weak version of the linguistic relativity hypothesis.

There is also evidence that basic, or 'focal', colours can be learned before the verbal labels are learned. Bornstein (1976) found that four-month-old children were able to detect small changes in the wavelength of light – so they can perceive different colours of light. This suggests that infants who have not yet learned to speak are still able to categorise visible light into blues, yellows, greens and reds. These categories are very similar to the ones used by adults when they give names to colours. This is important because it suggests that thought about colour precedes language. If this is the case, then language cannot determine thought in the way suggested by the strong linguistic relativity hypothesis.

Grammatical differences between languages

In the Navaho language, there are verbs that refer to handling objects (eg, to carry). The form of the verb is altered depending on the type of object being handled. If a Navaho-speaker asked you to hand them an object, the form of the verb would depend on the shape and form of the object. If the object were long and flexible, like a piece of string, the Navaho-speaker would say 'sanleh'. If it were a long rigid object, like a stick, they would say 'santiih'. If the object were flat and flexible, like a piece of paper or cloth, the request would be 'sanilcoos'. English does not make these types of distinction.

Carroll and Casagrande (1958) compared the development of shape recognition in Navaho Indian children who spoke mainly Navaho, Navaho children who spoke mainly English, and American children who spoke only English. They suggested that if language influenced the cognitive development of these groups of children, then the predominantly Navaho speakers should have better-developed shape recognition than both the predominantly English-speaking Navaho children, and the English-speaking American children.

Each child was shown a pair of objects that differed in size, shape and colour (eg, a yellow stick and a piece of blue rope). The child was then shown another object (eg, a yellow rope) and asked to say which of the other two objects it would be best matched with. In this example, the yellow rope could be matched on the basis of colour with the yellow stick, or on the basis of shape with the blue rope.

The children who spoke mainly Navaho were more likely to match the objects on the basis of shape than the Navaho children who spoke mainly English. Surprisingly, the children who spoke only English also showed a tendency to group the objects by shape. Carroll and Casagrande examined their results carefully and suggested that the American children had a very different cultural background from Navaho children, and were given toys from an early age that emphasise the importance of shape relative to colour. Because of this, they conclude that the tendency of a child to match objects on the basis of shape or material rather than colour increases with age and may be enhanced by either of two kinds of experiences:

- Because of the role of shape and material in Navaho grammar, it is vital for the speaker to quickly develop the ability to discriminate between the shape and material of objects in order to be understood.
- Practice with toys and other objects involving fitting different shapes together encourages children to focus on shape rather than colour.

Carroll and Casagrande suggest that Navaho provides support for the linguistic relativity hypothesis, but there are other factors (eg, childhood experiences) that also influence the way that shapes are thought about. This is further support for a weak version of the linguistic relativity hypothesis.

Counterfactual thinking

Bloom (1981) argued that English speakers are able to reason counterfactually because the English language allows them to do so. For example, we can reason that 'If I had gone to the library I would have met Mike'. Chinese does not allow this type of grammatical structure, so Chinese-speakers should be unable to reason counterfactually.

Bloom wrote some stories that contained this type of counterfactual reasoning. For example: 'Bier could not read Chinese, but if he had been able to do so, he would have discovered A. What would most have influenced him would have been B'. He gave this type of story to American and Chinese students, in their own languages. They were asked to read the stories and say whether A, B, and so on, had actually occurred. American students gave the correct answer 98% of the time, but Chinese-speakers were correct only 7% of the time. Bloom argued that Chinese-speakers have difficulty reasoning counterfactually because of the language that they speak.

However, Au (1984) and Liu (1985) point out that the Chinese versions of the stories were written in a very stilted, unfamiliar Chinese – they were bad translations from English. Also, some of the stories were ambiguous, and it appeared that the Chinese students were *better* at detecting the ambiguities than the American students were. When these problems were resolved, the Chinese students were able to reason counterfactually, although counterfactual statements in Chinese are more complex and take longer to construct.

The Bloom study cannot be used to support the strong version of the linguistic relativity hypothesis, but it suggests that the way in which a language expresses concepts influences the thought processes involved. The more simply an idea can be expressed in language, the easier it will be to think about that idea. This is the weakest version of the linguistic relativity hypothesis.

Evaluation of the evidence

Experimental research suggests the following. There is no clear evidence to support the strong version of the linguistic relativity hypothesis – that language determines thought. There is some evidence to support the weak version – that language influences thought. And there is some evidence to support the weakest version that language influences processing on tasks that are heavily dependent on language.

However, there is a problem with looking at the relationship between language and thought in isolation from culture and the environment. Consider the following possibility. Assume that the Inuit have a variety of words for snow. Their adaptation to a largely snowbound environment requires them to discriminate between different types of snow. Their culture prioritises this requirement. It states that snow is important and types of snow require differentiating for different tasks, for example building an igloo. As a result, words for different types of snow develop. From this point of view, language does not shape thought and perception. Instead language and thought are both shaped by culture and the environment. To some extent, language may feed back on thought and, in this respect, influences thought. But, it can be argued that both language and thought stem from the wider cultural and environmental framework (Westen, 1996).

1.4 Thought influencing language

Part of the evidence used to support the linguistic relativity hypothesis – that language influences thought – can also be used to support the opposite view – that thought influences language. Why, for example, do the Hanuxoo of the Phillipines have 92 names for different types of rice, and why are there so

many words related to camels in Arabic? It can be argued that these words have developed because the things they refer to are so important to these people in their adaptation to the environment. The Hanuxoo depend on rice for their survival – it is their basic foodstuff. For the traditional way of life of Arabs in North Africa and the Middle East, the camel is central. It can be argued that people think a lot about things that are important to them and develop words to communicate these thoughts. For example, the Hanuxoo think about different types of rice and translate these thoughts into words. In this respect, thought influences language rather than language influencing thought.

Even if this view is accepted, it is still possible that language influences thought, although this influence is secondary. Once created by thought, language may feed back on thought and make it easier to think in certain ways. Thus, Hunt and Agnoli (1991) state 'Different languages lend themselves to the transmission of different types of messages'. It is, therefore, easier to think in certain ways about certain things – for example, rice and camels – in some languages than in others. However, following the argument of this section, thought comes first, it is primary, and language is secondary.

Piaget's views on thought and language

The views of the Swiss psychologist Jean Piaget (1926) are in many ways the opposite of the linguistic relativity hypothesis. Piaget believed that knowledge was the precursor to language. He thought that language develops to allow the child to express the conceptual knowledge that has been acquired. The view that knowledge precedes language led to the idea that a child's language use will reflect their cognitive development. As children mature, their thought processes become more sophisticated and subtle – and their language becomes more sophisticated and subtle to reflect this. According to Piaget, the fact that children learn the word 'bigger' after they have learned the word 'big' indicates that they have a tendency to think in absolute terms at first, and later develop the ability to think about things comparatively.

Piaget suggests that children cannot really understand the expression of a concept in language unless they have first developed and understood the underlying mental concept. For example, a child does not really know what the word 'bigger' means unless they have an internal representation of the concept of relative size. One implication of Piaget's view is that teaching language skills to children will not help them unless their cognitive development has already reached the appropriate stage.

Support for Piaget's view Sinclair de Zwart (1967) investigated whether training children to use descriptive language would help them to perform Piagetian conservation tasks. *Conservation* refers to the understanding that objects remain the same in relation to some fundamental characteristic such as mass, number or volume, even following changes in shape or arrangement. For example, Piaget observed that up until about seven years of age, children usually think that a tall thin glass contains more water than a short wide glass, even though they contain the same amount of water (see p496). Sinclair de Zwart found that training children to use more descriptive language does not alter their cognition – they can use the appropriate language, but still don't conserve. For example, they don't realise that different shaped glasses contain the same amounts of water even though they have been taught the words to express this. Unless their cognitive development has reached the appropriate stage, language cannot help them to conserve. In this sense, thought precedes language. (See pp 491-501 for an outline of Piaget's theory.)

Evaluation of Piaget's view Although findings like those of Sinclair de Zwart support Piaget's view, there are some major criticisms of his ideas.

- There is no clear evidence that the underlying concepts in thought have to be formed before language can develop. Around the age of 16-18 months, children's vocabulary expands rapidly. This seems to have little relationship to conceptual development.

- Bellugi et al., (1991) found that individuals affected by a rare genetic condition called Williams syndrome had very low IQs but completely normal language. Yamada (1990) reports an individual with severe cognitive impairment and restricted short-term memory who was able to construct complex sentences and perform a variety of linguistic tasks. If language cannot develop until the underlying thought processes have been acquired, how can these individuals develop normal language with impaired cognitive processes?

Key term

Conservation *The understanding that objects that are different shapes or have different arrangements can have the same mass, number or volume.*

1.5 Language and thought shape each other

Vygotsky's theory

The Russian psychologist Lev Vygotsky (1934) provided a very different view of the relationship between language and thought. He argues that language and thought develop independently but become interwoven in the course of the child's development. Speech develops from babbling and has a social purpose – to communicate with other people. As children develop, they are encouraged by their parents to use words and to construct verbal messages. However, early speech is not linked to thought.

Pre-linguistic thinking is used by the child to store, organise and restructure its experiences of the world. Vygotsky argues that these early thought processes do not make use of language.

Vygotsky differs from Piaget in his ideas about what happens later in the development of thought and language. According to Vygotsky, at about the age of 2 years pre-linguistic thought and pre-intellectual language become joined. In his words, 'thought becomes verbal and speech rational'. From this point, language serves two distinct purposes:

- To monitor and direct some internal thought processes in the form of 'inner speech'.
- To interact and communicate with other people using 'external speech'.

So, internal 'speech' is used to aid thought, and external speech is used to communicate. Between the ages of about two and seven years, children find it difficult to separate these two functions of language. Because of this, 'inner speech' becomes externalised in the form of *egocentric speech*.

Egocentric speech In egocentric speech, the child talks about what is on their mind, regardless of whether anyone is listening or understanding. The interpretation of egocentric speech was a major difference between Piaget and Vygotsky.

- Piaget thought that egocentric speech, which he called 'verbal incontinence', reflected the child's inability to restrain speech and was nothing more than a sort of running commentary on the child's own activities. As such, egocentric speech was not very important.

- Vygotsky believed that egocentric speech was the child 'thinking aloud' – a view which small children will themselves confirm. He reports how egocentric speech may alter the course of an activity. A five-and-a-half year-old child was drawing a tram when the point of his pencil broke. The child muttered to himself 'it's broken', put the pencil aside, picked up some paints and began painting a *broken* tram, continuing to talk to himself from time to time. This shows how egocentric speech can actually affect thought and behaviour. It suggests that egocentric speech is more important than Piaget originally thought.

By about seven years of age, egocentric speech disappears. At first, Piaget and Vygotsky disagreed about what happens to it.

- Piaget originally thought that the child's running commentary was replaced by communicative speech as the child learned to restrain its own egocentric speech and communicate directly with others.

- Vygotsky argued that egocentric speech became internalised, so rather than children thinking aloud, they started to think 'inside their own head'. Egocentric speech becomes 'inner speech' – the 'inner voice' which adults 'hear' in their head.

According to Vygotsky, inner speech provides a link between thought and the use of language. For instance, when trying to solve difficult problems both adults and children tend to think aloud. This is a return to the child's use of speech as a tool for thinking. Also, people who have little contact with others, for example those who live alone, often find themselves talking to themselves and thinking aloud. This is the same as the young child's use of egocentric speech.

The social use of language becomes clearer to the child as word meanings are learned and the ability to group experiences into categories improves. The increased ability to label experiences helps this external use of language to become more sophisticated. Vygotsky argues that much straightforward everyday thinking has no direct connection with language. And language can occur without thought – for instance, when we learn something 'off by heart', we can repeat it without thinking about the meaning of the words.

Vygotsky's main point is that thought and language exist independently but interact with each other in both inner and social speech. Rather than vanishing, egocentric speech became internalised as an 'inner voice' to aid thinking and problem-solving. Vygotsky's arguments concerning the role of egocentric speech eventually won over Piaget, who admitted that he had been wrong about this aspect of child development.

According to Vygotsky, language, in the form of 'inner speech', is used as a tool to facilitate thought. In particular, it provides an aid to problem-solving. Vygotsky's theory is similar to the weakest version of the linguistic relativity hypothesis. Both argue that language plays an active role in thinking. (See pp 501-503 for an outline of Vygotsky's theory.)

Summary

1. The linguistic relativity hypothesis states that thought is shaped to some degree by language. The strong version suggests that language determines thought, the weak version that language influences thought, and the weakest version that language influences processing of some tasks that make use of language.

2. There is no direct evidence to support the strong version. There is some experimental evidence to support the weak and weakest versions.

3. Piaget argues that language is a reflection of thought and that language development must be preceded by cognitive development. There is limited evidence to support this view.

4. Vygotsky states that language and thought develop independently and then become interwoven. Language, in the form of 'inner speech', is used to facilitate thought.

Unit 2 Social and cultural aspects of language

KEY ISSUES

1. **How do social and cultural factors affect language use?**

2. **Do speakers of different English dialects think differently?**

2.1 Language, class and ethnicity

In Unit 1, the linguistic relativity debate was examined by comparing speakers of different languages from different cultures. This unit examines varieties of the same language used by different groups within the same society.

Will different dialects of the same language affect the way speakers of each dialect think? Will membership of different social groups affect language use and the way people think? These questions will now be examined in terms of social class, ethnic group, and gender differences in the use of the English language.

Social class and language use

The British sociologist Basil Bernstein (1961) suggested that there are significant differences in the speech patterns of the working and middle classes. This may have important effects on the development of children's thinking and their educational progress. Bernstein claimed that different social class backgrounds produce different speech patterns. The following provides an example of these differences. A young child is playing noisily with pots and pans when the telephone rings. A working-class mother tells the child to 'be quiet'; a middle-class mother says 'I'd rather you made less noise for a minute, I want to talk on the telephone'. The first message is simple, requiring

little thought. The second message is more complex. The child is given the reason for the request, asked to consider the wishes of another person and asked to behave according to a time dimension – 'a minute'. Such speech patterns may provide greater mental stimulation for the middle-class child, possibly resulting in more complex thought processes.

Bernstein called the two speech patterns, the *restricted* code and the *elaborated code*. The restricted code is a kind of shorthand speech and has the following characteristics:

1. It is grammatically simple, with short, often unfinished sentences.

2. Simple and repetitive use of conjunctions (so, then, and, because).

3. Limited use of adjectives and adverbs.

4. Frequent use of pronouns (he, she, it) in place of nouns, with statements like 'She gave me it' rather than 'Alison gave me the toy'. The listener is expected to know what 'she' and 'it' refer to.

5. Basic, uninformative phrases such as 'you see', 'you know', 'isn't it' are frequent.

6. The emphasis is on describing the present rather than the past or future.

The elaborated code is grammatically more complex, and contains longer sentences. Meaning is much more explicit, with details and explanations provided rather than taken for granted. The elaborated code allows greater expression of thoughts and ideas, and places more emphasis on the past and the future. According to Bernstein, many members of the working class are limited to the restricted code whereas middle-class speakers can use both codes.

Why is this distinction between the restricted and elaborated codes important, and what does it have to do with the relationship between language and thought? Bernstein argued that differences in speech code can affect the educational attainment of children. First, working-class children are placed at a disadvantage in school because education tends to be conducted in an elaborated code. Second, speech patterns can affect a child's ability to reason, analyse and think logically. As a result, the restricted code may reduce the chances for working-class children to acquire some of the cognitive skills necessary to succeed in the educational system. In this respect, language may influence thought.

Bernstein does not suggest that there is anything wrong with the restricted code itself, just that its exclusive use might affect a child's educational progress. Other researchers take a different view. For example, the American psychologist Carl Bereiter et al. (1966) argue that the speech patterns of low-income groups in the USA are inferior in practically every respect to those of members of higher-income groups. He states that the speech of many low-income children 'is not merely an under-developed version of Standard English, but is a basically non-logical mode of expressive behaviour' (quoted in Labov, 1970). He concludes that the speech patterns of the lower class retard intellectual development, impede progress in school and directly contribute to educational failure.

Evaluation Bernstein's views provide a possible explanation for the relatively low attainment of working-class pupils. But is their educational progress limited by language? Many other explanations for low attainment have been suggested – for example, low expectations of working-class pupils' potential, and the consequences of low income – for example, poor housing, inadequate diet, frequent illness – on educational performance (Haralambos & Holborn, 2000).

The existence of a restricted code has been questioned. For example, Rosen (1972) argues that Bernstein provides few examples of working-class speech patterns. He states that, 'for all Bernstein's work, we know little about working-class language'.

Even if there are distinctive working-class speech patterns, do they limit cognitive development and impede educational progress? As Bernstein notes, education is conducted in terms of middle-class speech patterns. This in itself places working-class pupils at a disadvantage. Teachers may see these children's speech patterns as incorrect and inferior. This may result in lowering working-class pupils' self-esteem and in conflict between pupils and teachers. It may be this, rather than language itself, that limits educational progress.

Much of Bernstein's data came from interviews conducted by middle-class interviewers. Faced with a middle-class researcher, working-class children might feel inhibited, anxious and even hostile. Their responses may reflect this rather than any limitations in their speech patterns.

Key terms

Restricted code *A grammatically simple form of English, lacking in clear expression of ideas.*

Elaborated code *Grammatically more complex form of English, containing longer sentences and more explicit information.*

2.2 Ethnicity

Bernstein argued that social-class differences in speech patterns affect cognitive development. Similar points have been made about the speech patterns of certain ethnic groups. For example, the American psychologists Bereiter and Engelman (1966) claim that the dialect spoken by many African Americans from low-income backgrounds is an illogical, ungrammatical and substandard version of English. They point to the use of 'badly connected words or phrases' like 'They mine' or 'Me got juice'; to the use of double negatives in statements like 'I don't know nothing'; and the omission of the verb 'to be' in sentences like 'He a fool' instead of 'He is a fool'.

Bereiter and Engelman claim that African-American dialect restricts cognitive development and impedes rational thought. The American linguist William Labov (1970) rejects this view as being 'utter nonsense'. He makes the following points.

- First, Black English Vernacular (BEV), to use Labov's term, is not better or worse than Standard English, it is simply different. It has its own grammatical rules that make perfect sense to the speaker.

- Second, a number of languages use many of the same rules as BEV. For example, Russian and Arabic also omit the present tense of the verb 'to be'. These languages are never described as illogical or substandard. Labov argues that the use of this description for BEV is a reflection of prejudice rather than the quality of the dialect.

- Third, the claim that BEV limits rational thought is not supported by the evidence. Labov examines a statement from an African-American boy called Larry, explaining why nobody can go to heaven.

'You know, like some people say if you're good an' shit, your spirit goin' t'heaven … 'n if you bad, your spirit goin' to hell. Well, bullshit! Your spirit goin' to hell anyway, good or bad. …'Cause, you see, doesn' nobody really know that it's a God, y'know, 'cause I mean I have seen black gods, pink gods, white gods, all colour gods, and don't nobody know it's really a God. An' when they be sayin' if you good, you goin' t'heaven, tha's bullshit, 'cause you ain't goin' to no heaven, 'cause it ain't no heaven for you to go to.'

Labov translates this statement into Standard English as follows:

1 Everyone has a different idea of what God is like.

2 Therefore nobody really knows that God exists.

3 If there is a heaven, it was made by God.

4 If God doesn't exist he couldn't have made heaven.

5 Therefore heaven does not exist.

6 You can't go to somewhere that does not exist.

Labov sees this as clear evidence of logical thought and the ability to deal with high-level abstract concepts. Labov argues that those who condemn BEV as substandard simply don't understand it. He claims that low-income black children 'receive a great deal of verbal stimulation, hear more well-formed sentences than middle-class white children, and participate fully in a highly verbal culture; they have the same basic vocabulary, possess the same capacity for conceptual learning, and use the same logic as anyone else who learns to speak and understand English'.

- Fourth, Labov argues that the use of language is largely dependent on the social situation. He compares three interviews. In the first, an African-American boy is shown a toy jet plane by a 'friendly' white interviewer and asked to describe it. There are long silences followed by two or three-word answers. In the second interview, another African-American boy (named Leon) is asked similar questions by a black interviewer who speaks BEV. Leon's response is similar to that of the first boy. In the third interview, the same interviewer sits on the floor, Leon is joined by his best friend, Gregory, and they are provided with a large supply of crisps, making the interview into more of a party. In Labov's words, Leon changes from a 'monosyllabic, inept, ignorant, bumbling child' with 'nothing to say about anything' to an articulate, well-spoken young man who has so much to say that he keeps interrupting his friend.

  Labov argues that rather than language influencing thought, it is the social situation that influences language. In his first interview, Leon defined the situation as threatening – he is interviewed by an adult in a formal situation. As a result, his responses are minimal so as little as possible can be held against him. Labov claims that in a school situation, 'It should be immediately apparent that none of the standard tests will come anywhere near measuring Leon's verbal ability'.

- Fifth, it is not the so-called inadequacies of BEV that account for the low attainment levels of African-American pupils from low-income backgrounds. Instead, it is the fact that the education system is conducted in terms of Standard English, which places African-American children at a disadvantage. For example, Williams (1972) found that black children perform well on tests written in BEV, while white children do badly on such tests.

- Sixth, Labov's research provides no support for the linguistic relativity hypothesis. There is no evidence that BEV and Standard English provide different views of the world or shape thought processes differently.

2.3 Language and gender

So far this section has focused on dialects – different *versions* of the same language. This section looks at different *uses* of the same language. Deborah Tannen (1990, 1994) argues that there are important gender differences in the use of language. She claims that males and females share a common language but use that language differently.

According to Tannen, males typically use language as a means for communicating information, especially their own opinions. For females, language is the glue that holds relationships together. It is used to consult, to find out what other people think, to express interest in and care for others.

These differences start in childhood, and develop out of social interactions. Tannen (1990) says that

> 'The centre of a little girl's social life is her best friend. Girls' friendships are made and maintained by telling secrets. For grown women, too, the essence of friendship is talk, telling each other what they're thinking and feeling, and what happened that day….When asked who their best friends are, most women name other women they talk to regularly. When asked the same question, most men will say it's their wives. After that, many men name other men with whom they do things such as play tennis or baseball (but never just sit and talk) or a chum from high school whom they haven't spoken to in a year.'

Tannen sees gender difference in language use as a reflection of the way males and females see social relationships. Each tends to have a different view of 'how we should be a good person'. Each identifies with their own gender group. As a result, they *choose* to use language differently. They are quite capable of changing their use of language, but they simply don't want to.

Tannen claims that gender differences in language use are important. They can lead to misunderstandings between males and females, to problems in relationships and to conflict in the workplace.

Summary

1. Bernstein argues that the restricted code can limit children's ability to analyse and reason. As a result, it can limit their educational attainment. Bereiter and Engelman claimed that some dialects of English are inferior to Standard English and result in illogical thought.

2. Labov's account of Black English Vernacular indicates that it is not inferior but simply different from Standard English. He argues that any measurement of linguistic ability must take the social situation into account.

3. Research has shown that males and females use language differently. Males use language to inform, females to consult. For females, the social aspects of language are more important. These differences can lead to conflicts in relationships and in the workplace.

Activity 2 | Language, class and gender

Item A | Elaborated and restricted codes

Two five-year-olds, one from a working-class background, the other from a middle-class background, are given four pictures on which to base a story. In the first picture several boys are playing football. In the second, one of the boys kicks the ball and it breaks a window in a nearby house. The third picture shows a man and a woman looking out of the window. The final picture shows the boys running away in the opposite direction. The middle-class child clearly and accurately describes and analyses these events. The listener has no need to see the pictures in order to fully understand what they show. However, in order to make sense of the story told by the working-class child, the listener would need to see the pictures. The child fails to spell out the details of the story and fails to fully explain the relationship between the boys and the people in the house. Without the pictures his story is unclear and incomplete.

Bernstein uses this example to illustrate some of the differences he believes exist between working and middle-class speech patterns.

Adapted from Bernstein, 1970

Item B | Gender differences in communication

Deborah Tannen (1992) reports the following conversations that she had over dinner:

'To my right was a woman. As the dinner began, we introduced ourselves. After we told each other what departments we were in and what subjects we taught, she asked what my research was about. We talked about my research for a little while. Then I asked her about her research and she told me about it. Finally, we discussed the ways that our research overlapped. Later, as tends to happen at dinners, we branched out to others at the table. I asked a man across the table from me what department he was in and what he did. During the next half hour, I learned a lot about his job, his research, and his background. Shortly before the dinner ended, there was a lull, and he asked me what I did. When I said I was a linguist, he became excited and told me about a research project he had conducted that was related to neurolinguistics. He was still telling me about his research when we all got up to leave the table.'

Adapted from Tannen, 1990

Questions

1   a) What evidence does Item A provide for the existence of an elaborated and restricted code?

b) Why might the evidence in Item A say little or nothing about the children's linguistic skills?

2   What does Item B suggest about the differences between the ways that men and women use language?

Unit 3 Language acquisition

KEY ISSUES

1   **What is language?**

2   **What has research told us about children's language acquisition?**

3   **How do children learn their native language?**

3.1 | What is language?

Various researchers have attempted to list the features that characterise and define human language (eg, Hockett, 1960). In summary, the main features are: language is socially acquired, semantic (meaningful), syntactic (having rules about word order) and symbolic.

- The social acquisition of language means that language is acquired in social settings and that it is used for social purposes – to communicate with others.
- Semantic means that language is meaningful – individual words and groups of words convey meaning.

- Syntax refers to the fact that language has rules about the order of words. 'Raining is outside it' is syntactically incorrect – it breaks the rules of word order.
- Symbolic means that language stands for something. For example, the word 'book' stands for something with pages that people read. Unlike a picture which resembles something, language is arbitrary – the reason that the word 'book' stands for something is simply because people agree that it does.

3.2 | Research into children's language acquisition

Early perception of speech sounds

The language abilities of very young children are quite remarkable. For example, babies as young as three days old show a preference for human speech over other kinds of sounds (Butterfield & Siperstein, 1974).

Young infants are also able to distinguish between subtly different speech sounds that adult speakers of their language cannot detect. For instance, babies under the age of six months from all cultures are able to tell the difference between the different types of *t* sound that occur in Hindi (Werker & Tees, 1992), and Japanese babies are able to tell the difference between *l* and *r* sounds – something that adult Japanese speakers cannot do (Eimas, 1975).

Why do infants start off with the ability to hear all kinds of speech sounds, and then lose the ability to distinguish between some of them? Bates et al., (1992) suggest that, at around the age of 10-12 months, infants 'tune in' to the language sounds that they hear around them. By 9 months of age, babies used to hearing English prefer to listen to words that have the typical English pattern of stressing the first syllable (eg, 'alter', 'comet', or 'gentle') rather than words that have stress on the second syllable (eg, 'negate', 'comply', or 'sustain') (Jusczyk, Cutler & Redanz, 1993).

The different speech sounds that are used in the child's native language are 'picked up' and the subtle differences that aren't needed in that language are lost.

Early production of speech sounds

At around the age of two months, infants start to 'coo' – to produce vowel sounds (eg, 'aaaaa', 'ooooo'). At six or seven months, *babbling* develops, when consonant sounds are added to the vowel sounds to produce sounds like 'dadadada' and 'mumumumum'. This repetition of sounds is known as *echolalia*.

Infants the world over seem to babble in the same way – it doesn't seem to matter what language their parents speak. Infants' babbles are as likely to contain foreign-language sounds as sounds from their native language. Deaf infants also coo and babble in the same way as hearing infants (Lenneberg, 1967).

By around 9-10 months, babbling starts to become restricted to the sounds that infants hear in the language used around them, perhaps as they imitate the sounds they hear (Masataka, 1992).

Comprehension and production

At all stages of language development, children understand far more than they can produce. Even before children utter their first word, they are able to comprehend a great deal. Fenson et al. (1994) estimate that 10-month-old children are able to understand about 30 words, including words like 'mummy', 'daddy', 'no', 'bye' and 'bath'. By about the age of 13 months, it is estimated that children understand about 100 words, although they can only speak a few words.

First spoken words

At 12 months of age, the average child has a vocabulary of about 12 words. Words are acquired very slowly at first – it is quite common for a child to take six months to acquire a vocabulary of 30 words (Bee, 2000). Many of the child's early words tend to be names of people and objects encountered on a daily basis. About 50% of the words are for objects, including food, body parts, clothing, vehicles, toys, animals, people, and so on. Only about 13% of the words are for actions, including 'bye-bye', 'up', 'peepo', and so on (Nelson, 1973).

At around 16-24 months, the process speeds up dramatically.

During this *vocabulary explosion*, the child becomes more able to make a good guess about a word's meaning after one or two exposures to the word – a process called *fast mapping* (de Villiers & de Villiers, 1992). Having got the idea that things have names, the child is able to pick up those names more quickly, and has a vocabulary of 40-50 words at 16 months, 180 words at 20 months and 380 words at 28 months (Fenson et al., 1994).

Children continue to add words to their vocabulary at the incredible rate of about one new word every two hours (Pinker, 1994). Between 2½ and 5-6 years, vocabulary grows on average from 600 words to 15,000 words (Aitchison, 1998).

There is, of course, more to language than the acquisition of single words. Those words have to be used to convey meaningful messages.

Key terms

Babbling *The production of consonant and vowel sounds by infants.*

Echolalia *The repetitive sounds produced in babbling (eg, mummummum)*

Vocabulary explosion *The rapid acquisition of new words at around 16-24 months.*

Fast mapping *An increase in the speed of acquiring new words – usually after one or two exposures.*

Conveying meaning

Children between 12-18 months quickly develop the ability to express themselves by using *holophrases* – single words accompanied by gestures and intonation. For example, 'ball' accompanied by outstretched arms might mean 'give me the ball'. Following this period, the first two or three-word phrases appear.

At first, children tend to use mainly nouns and verbs to convey simple messages. Brown (1973) found that children arrange the words in the appropriate order to express an idea. For example, the child will say 'Kick Billy' to mean that someone is kicking Billy, and 'Billy kick' to mean that Billy is kicking something. Brown calls this type of speech *telegraphic speech* because it omits all but the crucial words. This type of speech does not make use of inflections like the plural '-s', or the verb endings '-ing' and '-ed'. The use of *inflections* in English speakers develops by about 3 years of age (Marcus et al., 1992).

When children learn how to use inflections, they tend to over-generalise them. For instance, when a child learns to say 'kicked', 'played' and 'laughed', they will also probably say 'goed', 'hitted' and 'thinked'. Similarly, when a child learns to add an '-s' to the end of words to make plurals, there is a tendency to generalise the rule to all words, including, for example, 'sheeps', 'mouses' and 'mans'.

These types of error make it very clear that the child is learning and applying rules, and not just imitating adults' speech – children do not copy the word 'sheeps' from anywhere, they seem to have created it for themselves by following the rule for making plural words.

Increasing complexity in speech

Between the ages of about 27 months and 36 months, vocabulary expands and the child produces more complex sentences. Very quickly, children start to use past tenses, plurals and auxiliary verbs (eg, 'is', 'does'). Negative statements are now used, and questions asked.

The *mean length of utterance (MLU)* is a measure of the average number of meaningful units in a child's spoken sentences. Each word is a unit, as is each inflection, so when a child says 'Doggy eating', this has a length of 3 units (Doggy, eat, -ing). As speech becomes less telegraphic, the MLU increases. Instead of saying 'Mummy there', the child will say 'Mummy is there' and later 'Mummy is there and I am here'. By the age of 24 months, children will be using sentences of about 4-5 units, and by the age of 30 months, sentences might contain as many as 8-10 units.

By about the age of 4 or 5, most children have acquired the basic rules that their language uses. This sets the child on their way to learn more and more about language. The English-speaking child, for example, has to learn about exceptions to the rules (eg, that the plural of 'mouse' is 'mice'), so there is still a long way to go.

Pragmatics: using language in context

So far, we have examined the development of vocabulary and the basic set of syntactic rules that underpin children's language development. The ultimate goal of language is to communicate and interact with other people. How do children learn to use appropriate phrases at appropriate times? How does telegraphic speech develop into the more easily comprehensible conversation of adults? How do children learn the rules of conversation?

Pragmatics refers to the rules specifying how language is to be used in different social contexts and situations. Before a child learns to speak, it is able to communicate through crying, smiling, or eye contact. Snow (1977) points out that these *proto-conversations* are largely one-sided. The infant tries to communicate, but success depends on an adult giving meaning to the infant's behaviour.

Although the child's utterances are not 'real' language, adults often treat them as such and answer the child as though they are conversing – in a sense, they are. This helps the child to learn that conversing involves taking turns, and to learn that they, themselves, can initiate and pursue communication with others.

If a child's parents can understand its non-verbal proto-communication, why does the child need to learn to speak? The child has to learn to communicate with people who have not spent time with them and so do not understand their proto-communication. Also, the child will want to express increasingly complex ideas, and to join in adult conversations. In order to interact successfully, all speakers of a language must share knowledge of syntactic, semantic and pragmatic rules.

The child uncovers pragmatic rules by interacting with others. Through simplifying language, and emphasising the relationship between words and objects, and the importance of taking turns, adults aid the child's development of conversational rules.

One important part of turn-taking in conversation is being able to anticipate when the other person is going to finish speaking. McTear (1985) found that this skill develops with experience. Two-year-old children take, on average, 1.5 seconds to respond to a conversational partner, while an adult takes just 0.8 seconds. The two-year-old is less able to anticipate when it is their turn to speak, so it takes a little longer. Language is, after all, about communication, and children learn the importance of this through interaction with parents and other adults in the early years of life.

Research has provided a lot of information about the way in which language develops in young children. This does not, however, explain *how* children are able to acquire the skills needed to build sentences or to converse. Some of the theories that have attempted to explain language acquisition are described in the next section.

3.3 Environmental theories of language acquisition

Environmental theories state that children acquire language from their environment – in particular, from their parents and others in their immediate surroundings. The emphasis is on learning rather than any inborn capacity for acquiring language. In other words, language acquisition is based on nurture rather than nature, it is a process of socialisation rather than the unfolding of a genetically-based capacity.

Imitation

Many people believe that children learn language by imitating their parents. This is only partly correct. Imitation must play some part in language acquisition because children learn the same language that their parents speak. However, children don't acquire language by merely imitating what they hear. If they did, they wouldn't be able to generate novel utterances – phrases or sentences they have never heard before. Also, children don't simply imitate the grammar used by adults. If they did, they would not make so many basic grammatical mistakes.

To underline the point, Fraser et al., (1963) showed that 2- and 3-year-old children were poor at imitating simple sentences. They usually omitted something (eg, 'I can see a cow' would be imitated as 'See cow' or 'Cow' and 'I am very tall' as 'I very tall').

The way in which children learn about the irregular parts of language also suggests that imitation is not a major driving force in language acquisition. For example, a child who once correctly said 'mice' might later say 'mouses'. Adults never say 'mouses' so the child is not imitating anyone. This suggests that the child is applying general rules rather than learning by imitation. 'Mouses' follows the general rule for plurals; 'mice' does not. Children frequently produce words that they are unlikely to have heard anyone say. An American 4-year-old described the television version of the Gulf War as 'If the watcher plane sees a bad guy, it radio-shacks to the bomber plane, and the bomber plane blewns it up' (Baron, 1992). Examples such as this suggest that imitation does not provide an adequate explanation for the ways in which children learn about and produce language.

Skinner's learning theory

The American psychologist B.F. Skinner applied his theory of *operant conditioning* to language acquisition. He believed that all behaviour is learned by reinforcement. *Positive reinforcement* encourages behaviours by means of rewards, for example, parents praising a child for correct language use. Behaviours that lead to desirable outcomes, such as praise, are likely to be repeated. *Negative reinforcement* encourages behaviours by removing unpleasant events when those behaviours occur. For example, when a child ceases to mispronounce a word, parents stop telling them off. The removal of parental displeasure encourages the child to pronounce the word correctly.

Skinner (1957) identifies two ways in which children produce sounds that are reinforced by their parents and others around them.

- Children make *echoic responses* – they imitate the sounds made by others around them.
- Children accidentally produce sounds that resemble words – for example, most babies accidentally produce the sound 'dad'.

Skinner divides the verbal responses into two categories, and explains how reinforcement helps the child to acquire language.

- *Tacts* are verbal labels for objects. These might initially be echoic responses or accidentally produced sounds that resemble the right word. The reinforcement for this behaviour is parental attention and pleasure. Parents may repeat the sound several times, which encourages the infant to do the same. Eventually, the child learns, for example, that the sound 'dad' produces positive reinforcement, and, later, that this word is a label for one parent. This reinforcement increases the likelihood that the sound will be repeated in the future in the presence of the same object or person.
- *Mands* are requests or demands. A child might say 'drink' when they want a drink. In addition to parental pleasure and repetition of the sound, a mand is reinforced by the delivery of the required object.

Reinforcement begins in this way to encourage the child to repeat single words. Later on, the same procedure continues to encourage two-word utterances, and then the construction of sentences.

Evaluation Skinner's theory sees imitation and reinforcement as the driving forces behind language acquisition. However, evidence suggests that neither of these processes is a major factor. As the previous section indicated, imitation does not appear central to language acquisition.

- If Skinner is correct, reinforcement should lead to constant improvement in language skills. For instance, if children imitate the word 'mice', this will result in positive reinforcement and repetition. Children usually begin by imitating 'mice', but then start saying 'mouses'. Later on, they revert to 'mice'. Skinner's learning theory cannot explain this pattern of language acquisition (Chomsky, 1957).
- The significance of negative reinforcement has also been questioned. Marcus (1993) argues that negative reinforcement has little effect on language acquisition. Generally, adults only correct children's utterances when they cannot be understood. When the meaning is clear, negative reinforcement is not often provided to correct syntax or grammar. When adults do correct a child's use of language, it usually makes little difference. In the following example, the adult tries to correct a child's use of the word 'holded'.

Child: My teacher holded the rabbits and we patted them.

Adult: Did you say teacher held the baby rabbits?

Child: Yes.

Adult: What did you say she did?

Child: She holded the baby rabbits and we patted them.

Adult: Did you say she held them tightly?

Child: No, she holded them loosely.

(From Bellugi, 1970)

- Skinner's theory fails to account for universal stages of language development. Children in every society appear to go through these stages. In terms of Skinner's theory, this would require universal patterns of reinforcement. It is highly unlikely that children around the world would receive the same degree of reinforcement throughout the stages of language development.
- Skinner's theory suggests that every sentence has to be learned before it can be said. This would require an unbelievable amount of learning. In addition, there is plenty of evidence that children can make novel, spontaneous and creative utterances – they can create sentences that they have never heard before.
- In short, Skinner's attempts to explain language acquisition by operant conditioning were largely unsuccessful. Language acquisition and use cannot be reduced to imitation and reinforcement. There are more productive theories than this.

Key terms

Operant conditioning *A form of learning based on the use of reinforcement.*

Positive reinforcement *The encouragement of behaviours by means of rewards.*

Negative reinforcement *The encouragement of behaviours by removing unpleasant events when those behaviours occur.*

Echoic response *A sound made by imitating others.*

Tact *A verbal label for an object or person.*

Mand *A verbal request or demand for something.*

3.4 Nativist theories of language acquisition

Compared to environmental theories, *nativist theories* emphasise inborn capacities for language acquisition. They accept that learning is an important factor but argue that children are born with a genetically-based mechanism which is essential for language acquisition and development. The most famous nativist theory was developed by the American linguist Noam Chomsky.

Chomsky's theory

Chomsky (1957) argues that Skinner's theory cannot explain the speed at which children learn language, nor the level of sophistication that they reach within a relatively short time period.

* First, children don't hear enough examples of language to reach this level.
* Second, they don't receive enough feedback to help them acquire language so quickly.

Chomsky says that there is more to learning language than imitation and reinforcement of adult speech. He makes the point that most verbal utterances are made up on the spot, and some may never have been spoken, or even heard, before. Such utterances cannot be simply imitations of adult speech.

According to Chomsky, children are not born as 'blank slates' requiring everything to be learned. Chomsky takes a *nativist* standpoint – he suggests that children are born with the capacity for language – they are biologically prepared to acquire language. All humans have basically the same brains and, in particular, language centres in the brain that equip them to grasp the essentials of language. In Chomsky's terminology, humans are born with a *language acquisition device* (LAD). The LAD is a set of biologically-based mental structures that allows humans to uncover the principles underlying *all* languages.

Universal grammar According to Chomsky (1980), all languages are based on a common set of rules which he calls *universal grammar*. The language acquisition device (LAD) provides children with an innate knowledge of the universal grammar. This gives them a basis for learning any language.

Chomsky distinguishes between *principles* and *parameters*. Principles are those features that all languages share, ie the universal grammar. Parameters are the relatively superficial differences between languages. With exposure to an actual language, the child learns the parameters – the particular rules (and exceptions to those rules) found in that language. The parameters become set, just as though a set of switches have been turned on. In this way, the child's inborn language blueprint becomes tailor-made and specialised to the language that the child is exposed to.

According to Chomsky, language development follows a biologically determined schedule and is, therefore, linked to biological growth. There are certain 'sensitive periods' that are important for language development. If the child is not exposed to language during these periods, language development might be impaired.

Chomsky's central point is that foundations of language are innate, and that each child has a basic language blueprint that comes into operation when the child is ready. The LAD allows children to grasp the underlying principles of language. Once they have learned these, they are well on the way to teaching themselves language and generating speech on the basis of the rules they have uncovered.

Transformational grammar According to Chomsky, language use requires the ability to transform meaning into words and words into meaning. He called the rules used for these processes *transformational grammar*.

Chomsky made a distinction between *deep structure* and *surface structure*. The surface structure of a sentence refers to its syntax – the actual words and phrases used and the order in which they occur. The deep structure corresponds to the underlying meaning of the sentence.

In English, two sentences can have the same deep structure, but different surface structures:

The boy kicked the ball.

The ball was kicked by the boy.

These two sentences have the same deep structure – they mean the same thing – but the surface structures – the actual words used – are different.

Sentences can also have similar surface structures, but very different deep structures:

He is easy to please.

He is eager to please.

Finally, the same surface structures can be transformed into different deep structures and so can have more than one meaning:

They are cooking apples.

Teachers should stop drinking in classrooms.

Chomsky argues that the transformational grammar is used to transform surface structure into deep structure and vice versa.

He claims that the ability to transform is built into the language acquisition device. Transformational grammar allows words to be translated into meaning and meaning to be translated into words. This enables people to produce and understand an infinite number of meaningful sentences, many of which they have never heard before.

Grammatical errors Chomsky's emphasis on the importance of rules provides an explanation for common errors that children make with irregular plural words. Although a child has the innate ability to uncover the rules, success depends on exposure to language. The child is equipped to learn, for instance, the rule for making words into plurals (add an -s). But, before the child uncovers the rule, they might hear the word 'mice' being used, and use it themselves. Once the rule has been learned the child might incorrectly pluralise 'mouse' as 'mouses'. Later, when the exceptions to the rule have been learned, the child's plural of 'mouse' will revert to the correct 'mice'. Again, it is unlikely that a child will have heard the word 'mouses', so Skinner's explanation of language learning in terms of imitation does not work.

So, while Skinner suggests that an infant's language skills are the reinforced imitation of adult models, Chomsky argues that the infant is born with a great deal of linguistic knowledge. This knowledge is used at the appropriate stages of physical and mental development to allow the child's language skills to 'grow' as they uncover the rules of language.

Evaluation of Chomsky

Advantages

- Lenneberg (1967) supports Chomsky's idea that language acquisition has a biological basis, and suggests that the brain is not fully specialised for a particular language until it is fully mature, at puberty. This, he argues, explains why children find it easy to learn their native tongue, and also why they find it easier than adults to learn a second language. According to Lenneberg, all normal children follow roughly the same stages of linguistic development, an idea known as the *critical period hypothesis*. Evidence suggests that this is so. As discussed in Section 3.2, children do not begin to babble for several months, do not produce

Activity 3 Language acquisition

Item A — One wug and two_____?

This is a wug.

Now there is another one. There are two of them. There are two _____

With this test, Berko (1958) found that children who had just begun to use the rule of forming plurals by adding an '-s' use the rule correctly for words they had never heard before. They said 'There are two wugs'.

Adapted from Berko, 1958

Item B — Correcting children

Child: Nobody don't like me.
Mother: No, say 'nobody likes me'.
Child: Nobody don't like me.
[eight repetitions of this exchange]
Mother: No, now listen carefully; say 'nobody likes me'.
Child: Oh! Nobody don't likes me.

Adapted from McNeill, 1970

Item C — Sign language

Before 1980, deaf Nicaraguans had little opportunity to meet other deaf people. There was no deaf community or common sign language, and the deaf were typically treated as though they were retarded. In 1980, a new government created schools for the deaf – for the first time, deaf people came into extended contact with one another. The schools aimed to teach them to speak Spanish, the official language of the country. Despite this policy, students started to communicate with one another using hand signs.

At first their signing system was unstructured and made up of the various signs and gestures that individuals had been using at home. Over the course of a few years, the signs became consistent, and a system of grammar emerged. All of this occurred with no formal teaching – simply through the students' desire to communicate.

The new grammar was created by the youngest members of the community. Most people who were over 10 years old when the grammar was created failed to contribute to its development and learned very little.

The sign language invented by the deaf children has since become the official sign language in Nicaragua. It is a true language, with units of meaning and rules about how those units can be combined.

Adapted from Senghas, 1994.

Questions

1. Why do Items A and B cast doubt on Skinner's explanation of language acquisition?

2. How well does the evidence in Item C support the ideas of (a) Skinner and (b) Chomsky?

meaningful words for the first year or so, and children in all cultures (and speaking all languages) show similar patterns of language development. The critical period hypothesis also implies that if language is not acquired during the critical period, it will be very difficult to learn it later on.

- Chomsky's theory explains aspects of language acquisition which other theories fail to explain. For example, it explains how children develop language and learn the rules of grammar with little correction by adults. And it explains why children say things that they have never heard before. Only by discovering the underlying rules of language could children develop these skills.

- As described in Section 3.2, very young infants are able to distinguish subtle differences in speech sounds that occur in all languages. This ability disappears very quickly. This suggests that there is an innate ability to detect different speech sounds, which disappears as the parameters of the child's native language become set.

Disadvantages

- Children might be born with an ability to acquire language, but they will only do so if exposed to language. Although Chomsky (1980) recognised this, critics argue that he underestimated the importance of exposure to language.

- Chomsky's suggestion that children learn language without being taught can only be taken so far. Bard and Sachs (1977) showed that children do not learn language by simply being exposed to it – they don't just teach themselves. They reported the case of a child born to deaf parents. The parents communicated with each other using sign language, but they wanted their child to grow up to use normal speech. Although the child was exposed to spoken language on radio and television, he did not learn to speak until the age of four. Then a speech therapist was employed and he learned language very quickly. This suggests that the child had reached a critical period for language acquisition, as Lenneberg argued. But it also suggests that social interaction with other speakers is necessary for learning to take place. Language encounters must be interactive if the innate 'readiness' to learn is to be converted into language development.

- If learning a language involves 'setting switches' to specific positions, then how can bilingual children have learned the

Key terms

Nativism *The view that certain skills are inborn and are not learned.*

Universal grammar *Chomsky's idea that all languages share a common set of rules.*

Language acquisition device (LAD) *An innate biological system that allows children to grasp the underlying principles of language.*

Transformational grammar *The rules for converting between deep and surface structure.*

Critical period hypothesis *Lenneberg's idea that all normal children should follow roughly the same stages of linguistic development and that language will be more difficult to learn once the critical period has ended.*

rules for two different languages? It seems unlikely that the parameters can be set to two different positions at once (Messer, 1999).

3.5 Social interaction and language acquisition

Social interactionists see meaningful social interaction rather than inborn capacities as central to the process of language acquisition. Bruner (1983) argued that Chomsky's biologically-based LAD and the idea of a universal grammar were not sufficient to explain language acquisition. He suggested instead that there was a *language acquisition socialisation system* (LASS).

According to Bruner, mother-child interactions are very important in helping the child work out the meaning of speech. Children do not acquire language by just *listening* to adults. They participate. They are not simply listening and learning syntax and grammar – they are communicating feelings, needs, intentions, requests and demands. Language acquisition builds on pre-linguistic communication, particularly between mother and child. This pre-linguistic communication is based on eye contact, facial expressions, smiles, giggles, grunts and various other 'noises'.

Adults interact with and support children with pre-linguistic communications. They do the same with linguistic communication. For example, adults look towards objects that words refer to and encourage the child to do the same. The child also learns about taking turns – which is crucial to conversation – through speech and games based on turn-taking.

Snow (1972) found that adults adapt their speech when speaking to very young children. They use short sentences with simple word orders. Utterances to young children contain simple concrete nouns and emphasise the present rather than the past or future. Interestingly, four-year-olds also use simpler language when they talk to two-year-olds than when they talk to adults (Tomasello & Mannle, 1985).

This simplification of adult speech when speaking to children has been called *motherese, parentese* or *baby talk register*. Motherese is part of the social interaction between parent and child and supports the child's understanding of language. According to social interactionists, language acquisition depends on a meaningful and supportive social context.

Evaluation The main problem with the social interactionist view is that social interactions are not independent of cognitive processes or biological development. Bruner's idea is important. There is evidence that language acquisition depends, at least in part, upon social interaction. But there is also evidence that social interaction can only lead to language acquisition if the child has the appropriate cognitive resources and has reached a certain level of biological development. In view of this, the social side of language acquisition cannot be considered separately from cognitive and biological development.

Do adults actually *teach* children to develop their language skills by the use of motherese in the context of meaningful interaction? Motherese is found in most, but not all, cultures. Exceptions include the Kaluli who treat young children as 'having no understanding'. They rarely talk to infants. Young children are often directed within one-line instructions which do not require or invite a response. However, despite the absence of motherese and the kind of infant/adult interaction found in most societies, Kaluli children acquire language at the same speed and level of sophistication as children in any other culture (Schieffelin & Ochs, 1983). This questions the central importance of social interaction to language acquisition.

Key terms

Language acquisition socialisation system (LASS) *Bruner's idea that children learn language through social interaction with adults.*

Motherese/parentese *The simplified form of speech used by adults to talk to young children.*

3.6 Cognitive development and language acquisition

Language acquisition might grow out of cognitive development rather than an innate ability to detect grammatical rules. Clark (1973a) argued that most of a child's early word meanings were related to previously acquired conceptual knowledge. Clark (1973b) showed that children were able to respond to instructions to put an object *in* a container at an earlier age than instructions to put an object *on* a container. According to Clark, this reflects the tendency of pre-linguistic children to put things in other things. From this viewpoint, children's language acquisition depends on their non-linguistic cognitive development. The development of concepts such as *in* precedes and influences linguistic development.

This view led to linguistic development being considered in terms of cognitive developmental theories, such as that of Piaget (see pp 467–468). The idea is that the driving force behind language acquisition is the development of intelligent thought. According to Piaget, cognitive development precedes language development, and, basically, children learn the language that they need to express their thoughts. Children therefore progress linguistically when their cognitive structures enable them to.

Evaluation It is not clear that particular aspects of cognitive development invariably precede linguistic development. Yarrow et al. (1975) report a weak relationship between measures of cognitive development and early language development. They note that some children with more advanced cognitive development have less advanced language skills. Gopnik (1984) argued that children used the word 'gone' to help them to develop the concept of objects. Piagetian theory states that the object concept *precedes* the use of the word 'gone', as objects can only be said to have 'gone' after the concept of objects has been established.

A second problem is that some children develop good syntactic skills but have a very poor vocabulary, and vice versa. The cognitive developmental view cannot explain why some language skills are acquired better than others. If cognitive development is the precursor to language, this should apply to all aspects of language. This problem is seen by some psychologists as a major stumbling block for the cognitive development view of language acquisition (Cromer, 1991).

Third, the cognitive development approach neglects the social factors influencing language acquisition. Dore (1985) comments that studying an individual's cognitive development is not a good basis for explaining something as social as linguistic development.

Conclusion

Theories that claim to explain language acquisition fall into two main groups.

- Nativist theories see an innate, biologically-based capacity as the driving force.
- Environmental theories see factors such as reinforcement and social interaction as primary.

Many researchers take a position between these extremes, arguing that language acquisition depends on both biological and environmental factors. For example, they suggest that a child has some kind of innate acquisition system that is activated through social interaction. This interpersonal interaction triggers human linguistic abilities and allows them to develop, albeit driven by an innate predisposition to learn.

Summary

1. Language acquisition follows similar patterns of development in different children, learning different languages, in different cultures.

2. Research evidence indicates that imitation alone cannot account for language acquisition.

3. Skinner claimed that language is acquired through a process of imitation and reinforcement. Evidence suggests that neither of these processes is central to language acquisition.

4. Chomsky argued that human infants have an inborn mechanism – the language acquisition device – which allows them to uncover the principles underlying all languages.

5. Chomsky has been criticised for underestimating the importance of social interaction and cognitive development to language acquisition.

6. Social interactionists see meaningful social interaction rather than inborn predispositions as central to language acquisition.

7. Some researchers see cognitive development as the driving force behind language acquisition.

8. Many researchers take the middle ground, arguing that some kind of innate acquisition system is activated through social interaction.

Activity 4 | Deprived of language

Genie was born and raised in Los Angeles. Throughout her childhood she was kept in a cupboard with hardly any contact with human beings apart from her father and brother who threw food in to her from time to time. She was forbidden to make any sounds at all and even managed to cry silently. When she was 13½, her mother escaped from the family prison, taking Genie with her. Genie could neither produce nor understand language. She was taught to speak and a team of psychologists studied her language development. Here is an example of her speech at age 18 after nearly five years of language tuition.

Genie :	Marsha give me square.
Researcher :	When?
Genie :	In the class. Marsha give me in the class. Marsha in the class.
Researcher :	Which class?
Genie :	One class, two class, three class.
Researcher :	What does Marsha do in class?
Genie :	Draw.
Researcher :	What does Marsha draw?
Genie :	Sun.

Genie's language development never reached the level of normal speakers and only people who knew her could understand much of what she was trying to say. According to Curtiss et al. (1975), Genie's inability to speak properly was due to the language centre in her brain failing to develop because of the lack of language stimulation in her early childhood.

Adapted from Curtiss et al., 1975

Questions

How well does Genie's experience support:

1 Chomsky's views on the acquisition of language?

2 The view that social interaction is essential for language acquisition?

3 Those who argue that language acquisition has both biological and social foundations?

4 The critical period hypothesis?

Unit 4 Problem-solving

KEY ISSUES

1 **What is problem-solving and why is it important?**

2 **What are the main explanations of problem-solving?**

4.1 | What is problem-solving?

Why do we need an ability to solve problems and to reason? In everyday life, we are usually able to function according to established routines and habits. However, unexpected problems sometimes occur and we need to adapt our behaviour to overcome them – this is what problem-solving really is. Because it can be difficult to observe people's problem-solving processes in their everyday lives, researchers have conducted laboratory studies to investigate the ways people tackle unfamiliar problems. Such studies have helped researchers develop theories of problem-solving.

4.2 | Theoretical accounts of problem-solving

The Gestaltist approach

The Gestaltists, a small group of German psychologists in the early years of the 20th century, conducted some of the earliest investigations into problem-solving. They challenged the behaviourist view that problem-solving was a matter of trial and error. *Gestalt* is a German word meaning 'whole', but this translation does not really encapsulate the meaning of the term, which is why the term gestalt is used instead of any English translation. The basic principles of the Gestaltist approach are 1) that humans perceive wholes or patterns rather than parts and 2) that the whole is greater than the sum of its individual parts. The Gestaltists therefore took a *holistic* view of thinking and problem-solving.

The Gestaltists believed that problem-solving behaviour can be *reproductive* or *productive*. This means that problem-solving does not just involve reproducing past behaviours – this sometimes hinders problem-solving in ways to be discussed later. It is also necessary to work out how to tackle an unfamiliar problem and to produce new behaviours to solve that problem. Productive problem-solving is characterised by *insight* and by *restructuring*, which are two of the Gestaltists' main ideas.

Key terms

Gestaltist approach *The idea that people view things as a whole rather than as a combination of parts.*

Reproductive problem-solving *The re-use of past behaviours to solve problems.*

Productive problem-solving *The generation of a new solution to a problem.*

Insight

Insight is a sudden realisation of the solution to a problem – a 'flash of inspiration'. Because this occurs suddenly, it is sometimes called the *Gestalt switch* and is said to be accompanied by an 'aha!' experience (you shout 'aha!' when you suddenly realise the solution).

This idea was first suggested by Köhler (1927). In one study, a chimpanzee used a long pole to reach through the bars of its cage and get a bunch of bananas. In a second study, the chimpanzee was given a short pole that was not long enough to reach the bananas. A second, longer pole was placed outside the cage, out of arm's reach, but within reach of the short pole. After unsuccessfully trying to reach the bananas with the short pole, the chimpanzee gazed about him, and then *suddenly* picked up the short pole again, and used it to pull the longer pole into the cage. It then used the longer pole to retrieve the bananas.

These findings suggest that problem-solving is based upon perception of a 'whole'. When confronted with these problems, the chimpanzees usually pause frequently to scrutinise the entire area and everything in it before suddenly, in one action, solving the problem. If the chimpanzees could speak, they would probably have said 'aha!' at the moment of insight.

There is more recent evidence that the solutions to problems do sometimes seem to occur suddenly. Before reading on, work through Activity 5.

Activity 5   Metcalfe's insight problems

Item A   Changing triangles

Move three of the circles to make the triangle point to the top of the page.

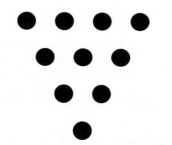

Item B   Anagrams

Solve these anagrams:

oosia	phmny
auevl	pmuoi
ttnua	rdcei
oapnr	tlcee
reckl	elcsa

Item C   Metcalfe's 'warmth ratings'

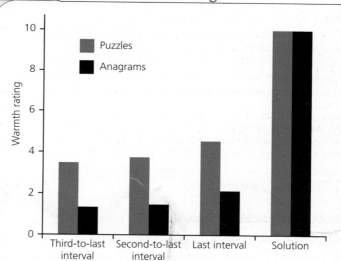

Metcalfe (1986) presented participants with problems similar to those in Items A and B. She asked them every 10 seconds to rate how close they felt themselves to be to the solution on a scale of 1-10. Metcalfe called these 'warmth ratings'. Item C is a graph of some of Metcalfe's results. It shows 'warmth ratings' for the last three intervals (30 seconds, 20 seconds and 10 seconds) before the correct solution.

Questions

1 a) Briefly describe the results in Item C.

   b) What support do they provide for the idea of 'insight'?

2 Solve the problems in Items A and B (the solutions are on p483). Assess your 'warmth rating' for each problem. Did you experience 'insight'?

As shown in Activity 5, Metcalfe (1986) found that participants showed little or no increase in 'warmth' until moments before solving the problem. In other, *routine problems* (eg, solving algebraic equations) which could be worked through step-by-step, participants' warmth ratings increased step-by-step. There was no evidence of a sudden insight or an 'aha!' experience with routine problems (Metcalfe & Weibe, 1987).

Metcalfe's studies indicate that certain types of problem are solved suddenly – there seems to be a sudden flash of inspiration. This supports the Gestaltist idea of insight. However, other types of problem are solved gradually in a step-by-step fashion.

Key term

Insight *The sudden realisation of the solution to a problem, often accompanied by an 'aha!' experience.*

Restructuring

According to the Gestaltists, insight requires changing, or *restructuring*, the way in which a problem is perceived or thought about. Maier (1931) produced the well-known 'two-string' or 'pendulum' problem. In this, two strings are suspended from the ceiling, and the goal is to tie them together. The strings are too far apart for a person to hold one and reach the other. In the room there are various objects including a chair, some paper and a pair of pliers. The solution involves using one of these objects in a novel way: tie the pliers to one string, swing it like a pendulum, and catch it on its backswing while holding the other string. Maier found that only 39% of participants solved this problem within a ten-minute limit.

Maier demonstrated restructuring by brushing against one string to start it swinging. Soon afterwards, most participants produced the pendulum solution, though few reported noticing the experimenter's actions. Maier claimed that this subtle hint aided restructuring of the problem.

Functional fixedness and einstellung

Functional fixedness is a tendency to only use objects and concepts in their usual ways. An inability to think about an object in a different way can lead to difficulties in problem-solving if the solution requires a novel use for the object. Maier's two-string problem illustrates this. Many participants had a fixed idea about the use of pliers. As a result, they were unable to see them as a weight on the end of a pendulum.

Difficulties resulting from functional fixedness are shown in the following experiment. Duncker (1945) gave participants a candle, a box of nails and several other objects, and asked them to attach the candle to the wall above a table, so that the wax did not drip onto the table when the candle was lit. Participants tried to nail the candle directly to the wall. Few thought of emptying the nails out of the box and using the box as a candle holder. Duncker suggested that participants were fixated on the box's function as a nail holder and could not re-conceptualise it as a candle holder. When he gave participants an empty box and the nails were loose on the table, they were much better at solving the problem. Thinking about the box as a 'box of nails' rather than as a 'box that has some nails in it' is an example of functional fixedness hindering problem-solving. This shows how the inappropriate use of past knowledge makes it difficult to solve a problem.

A related idea is that of *einstellung* or *negative set*. The idea of einstellung is that experience of certain types of problem can encourage people to use particular strategies. However, strategies that have been successful in the past may hinder the solution of similar problems in the future. Before reading further, complete Activity 6, which illustrates the idea of einstellung.

Luchins (1942) used the type of task in Activity 6 to demonstrate einstellung. As you worked through the activity, you probably realised that all of the problems could be solved using the same simple strategy (ie, fill up Jug A, use it to fill up Jug B, and then fill up Jug C twice). In all cases, this would produce the required amount of water. If you realised this, you probably applied it successfully to all the problems. However, the last four problems could be solved much more simply. In problems 7, 8, 9 and 10, Jug A was not needed at all. These problems can be solved by filling up Jug B and then pouring out the amount to fill Jug C.

Luchins found that 83% of participants who solved the first few problems continued to use the same strategy to solve the remaining problems, even though there was a much simpler solution. When participants had not encountered the first six problems, over 95% of participants used the simple solution to the later problems. The successful use of a strategy to solve a series of problems can result in that same strategy being used to solve similar problems, even when that is not the best strategy to use. This is what the Gestaltists meant by einstellung.

Evaluation The Gestaltists were the first to suggest that problem-solving entailed more than the reproduction of learned responses. They emphasised the creative aspects of problem-solving, with ideas such as insight. Using the ideas of functional fixedness and einstellung they showed that a reliance on past experience often hindered the problem-solving process.

The Gestaltists have been criticised for describing rather than explaining the processes involved in problem-solving. For example, they did not explain *how* insight occurs, or, indeed, how people actually solve problems. Newell and Simon (1972) developed a model that aimed to explain the actual cognitive processes involved in problem-solving.

Key terms

Functional fixedness *Knowledge of an object's normal use can prevent it from being used in a new way.*

Einstellung (or negative set) *People can become biased towards repeating previously successful strategies, even though those strategies are not the best ones to use.*

4.3   Newell and Simon's problem-space theory

Before reading on, complete Activity 7.

Activity 6 | Water jug problems

You are given three jugs of different capacities. Your task in each case is to measure out the precise amount of water given in the right-hand column. For example, this is how to do the first one. You need to measure out 100 pints of water and have three jugs of capacity 127 pints, 21 pints and 3 pints (some of these jugs are quite big!). Fill up the 127-pint jug, and then empty water from it into the 21-pint jug, leaving 106 pints in Jug A. Pour water from Jug A into Jug C, leaving 103 pints in Jug A. Empty Jug C, then refill it from Jug A. This leaves 100 pints in Jug A. Now you solve the rest of the problems.

Problem	Jug A	Jug B	Jug C	Required amount
1	127	21	3	100
2	163	14	25	99
3	126	12	5	104
4	68	14	11	32
5	145	31	9	96
6	82	17	14	37
7	51	24	3	21
8	98	46	6	40
9	118	56	6	50
10	91	42	9	31

Activity 7 | The Tower of Hanoi

Item A | The initial state

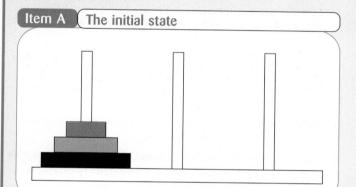

Item B | The goal state

Move the three disks from the left-hand peg (as in Item A) to the right-hand peg (as in Item B). You may only move one disk at a time by moving it to another peg. You may never place a larger disk on top of a smaller one.

Questions

1   How long did it take to solve the problem?

2   How many moves did it take?

3   What types of strategy did you use?

Solutions to the problems in Activity 5

1

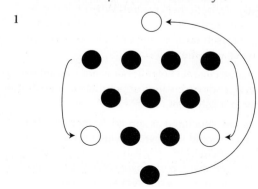

2

oasis	nymph
value	opium
taunt	cider
apron	elect
clerk	scale

The Tower of Hanoi problem is a good example to illustrate Newell and Simon's *problem-space theory*. According to Newell and Simon, problems can be solved through the exploration of different paths to a solution. This is literally true when finding your way through a maze – some paths lead towards the goal, others lead into dead-ends. Similarly, in the Tower of Hanoi problem, some moves advance you towards the goal, and others might lead you further away from the goal. In a maze, you can end up walking round in circles, in the Tower of Hanoi, you can end up repeating a short sequence of moves that keeps on returning you to the same position.

Newell and Simon suggested that a problem could be characterised as a set of states, from an initial state, through intermediate states to the goal state. One state can be transformed into the next by the performance of actions. In any given state there may be several options as to where to proceed next. When one option is chosen, it opens up new possibilities for the next action. In this way, progress is made through the puzzle toward its solution. For example, in the Tower of Hanoi, you can move a disk from one peg to another. This transforms the current state of the problem into a different state. From this state, another disk can be moved to produce another different state. The aim is to make moves and pass through various states of the problem until the goal state is reached.

In Newell and Simon's terminology, the *problem-space* consists of possible states and paths, only some of which lead to the goal state. Each problem has its own problem-space in which all of its permutations and possible routes to the solution are represented. For the Tower of Hanoi, the problem-space represents all of the possible states, and, which other states can be reached from them by moving one disk onto a different peg.

Newell and Simon's important point is that when people solve problems they build up the problem-space inside their heads, so they learn about the different states of the problem and how they can be reached. When someone tries to solve a problem like the Tower of Hanoi, they can imagine the next move and work out in their head whether it will lead towards the solution. As more moves are made, the problem-space becomes more complete and the path to the goal state becomes clearer.

When faced with a problem like the Tower of Hanoi, people have to work out the best way to tackle it. How do people choose which move to make next? With complex problems that have lots of different possible states, people use strategies to explore the problem-space and learn how to solve the problem.

- **Random trial-and-error** The simplest technique is to explore the problem randomly until the goal state is arrived at. This is very wasteful and inefficient. People might begin with this approach when faced with an unfamiliar problem, or if under stress, but it is not a good strategy for solving complex problems.
- **Hill climbing** This is another simple strategy in which possible moves are evaluated, then one chosen that appears to move closest to the goal state. The problem with this strategy is that only 'local highs' are often reached. These are positions from which progress cannot be made without first moving *away* from the goal state.
- **Means-ends analysis** Newell and Simon suggested that problems can be solved by breaking them down into smaller sections, or *sub-goals* and then working out how to solve the

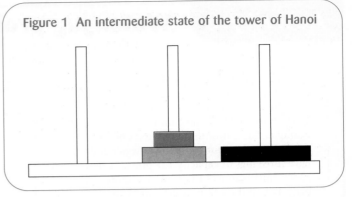

Figure 1   An intermediate state of the tower of Hanoi

sub-goal. For instance, in the Tower of Hanoi, you may reach the following state:

From this position, the goal state cannot be reached in one move. Means-ends analysis can be applied like this:

1   How does the current state differ from the goal state? The middle and smallest disks are on the wrong peg.

2   As the goal state cannot be achieved immediately, is there a sub-goal that will reduce the difference between the current state and the goal state? Yes, if the middle-sized disk can be moved onto the right-hand peg, this will produce a state closer to the goal state.

3   Can this sub-goal be achieved immediately? No, because the smallest disk is on top of the middle disk, preventing it from being moved.

4   The sub-goal of moving the middle disk onto the right-hand peg will have to wait. We need a different sub-goal. We need to move the smallest disk out of the way so that the middle disk can be moved.

5   We can achieve this sub-goal immediately by moving the smallest disk onto the left-hand peg.

6   Having moved the smallest disk out of the way, we can now achieve the previous sub-goal of moving the middle disk onto the right-hand peg. This moves us towards the goal state.

7   We are now left with the smallest disk on the left-hand peg. In order to reduce the difference between the current state and the goal state, we can create the sub-goal of moving the smallest disk onto the right-hand peg. There are no obstacles preventing this, so this sub-goal can be solved immediately. This also produces the goal state, so the problem is solved.

This example of means-ends analysis shows how this simple, well-organised strategy can help to solve problems. We can break problems down into sub-goals. Some sub-goals can be achieved immediately, but others cannot. When this happens, we create a new sub-goal that will allow us to return to and achieve our previous sub-goal. Eventually, all sub-goals are achieved, leaving us with the goal state.

Means-ends analysis can be helpful, but is not guaranteed to be successful. It depends on creating appropriate sub-goals and working out how to reach them.

If a problem can be structured as sub-goals, then problem-solving performance should improve. Having prior experience on similar tasks may help to identify sub-goals. Anzai and Simon (1979) observed that a participant solving a five disk Tower of Hanoi problem used a different strategy on each of four attempts. To begin with, the participant used random trial-

and-error to 'see what would happen' when different moves were made. The participant used general problem-solving strategies that could be applied to many different types of problem (eg, a loop-avoidance strategy to avoid 'going round in circles'). While using these general strategies to explore the problem-space, the participant was able to learn better sequences of moves that could be used in later attempts to solve the problem. In other words, by trying out general strategies, the participant could learn the particular characteristics of the Tower of Hanoi, including appropriate sub-goals and the ways to achieve them.

Problem-solving is a learning process. When trying to solve a new problem, we learn the 'tricks' to use on that particular problem – what works and what does not. General strategies help us to move towards the solution while we learn the strategies peculiar to that problem.

Key terms

Problem-space theory *Problems can be characterised as sets of states, from the initial state to the goal state. The problem-solver builds up the problem-space in their head as they explore the problem.*

Means-ends analysis *A strategy for progressing through the problem-space by identifying and solving sub-goals on the way to the goal state.*

Evaluation of the problem-space approach – advantages

- Problem-space accounts show that people have general strategies that can be applied to unfamiliar problems. They are not recollecting solutions to problems, they are actively constructing solutions. So, problem-solving appears to be productive, as the Gestaltists suggested.

- Problem-space theory represents a major contribution to understanding problem-solving. Its main theoretical contribution is that, unlike Gestalt psychology, it shows us how people examine the structure of problems and work out the best solution.

- Although puzzle problems may not resemble everyday

problems, problem-space theory gave researchers a solid foundation from which to work. Many of Newell and Simon's ideas about problem-solving are still widely used by researchers.

Limitations of problem-space research

- The puzzle problems used in research are often unfamiliar, whereas problem-solving in everyday life typically involves familiar problems and the use of a great deal of existing knowledge. For example, the problem, 'How can I get a good grade in my psychology exam?' can be tackled by using existing experience of exams, knowledge about how to revise, and so on. Everyday problems are more open-ended and social than puzzle problems.

- Puzzle problems contain all of the information required to solve them. They are self-contained, complete, and have unambiguous requirements. In the Tower of Hanoi, for example, the goal is to move the disks on to the right-hand peg, following the rules of the puzzle. In real life, the nature of the goal state might not be specified – this represents part of the problem. For example, you are having difficulties with your flat-mate. There are arguments over household chores, TV programmes, the volume of the CD player and, on top of all this, your personalities clash. You feel a need to do something about the situation. However, the goal state is not clear. Attempting to solve the problem might make it worse. There is no clear solution in sight. Should you try and find a new flat-mate, discuss the situation quietly and rationally with your existing flat-mate, write down some formal rules, or have a big bust-up? In puzzle problems the goal is stated and the rules are specified. Everyday problems are less clearly defined and more open.

- Problem-space theory provides a reasonable explanation of solving well-defined puzzles. It is less likely to explain the ill-defined problem situations that typically occur in everyday life. It needs to take account of the problem-solving skills used in the 'real world'. In particular, it needs to discover how people make decisions and judgements. This is considered in the next unit.

Summary

1. The Gestaltists suggested that problem-solving is reproductive and productive and involves restructuring and insight. Functional fixedness and einstellung have been shown to hinder problem-solving.

2. The Gestaltists were criticised for not explaining problem-solving processes.

3. Newell and Simon's problem-space theory looks at the cognitive processes underlying problem-solving and indicates how problems are solved by using various strategies.

4. General problem-solving strategies are used to uncover the problem-specific strategies.

5. Everyday problems are less well defined than puzzle problems.

Unit 5 Decision-making

KEY ISSUES

1 How do people make decisions?

2 What are heuristics, and how important are they?

5.1   Making decisions

Life involves making decisions all the time. We decide what to watch on television, whether to invite a friend for a meal, whether to travel by land, air or sea, whether to spend money or to save it, whether to buy one car or another. The list is endless. Our decisions are influenced by our estimations of the chances of success and, just as importantly, our estimations of any negative consequences. Decision-making is all about estimating the size of risks. It involves assessing alternatives and choosing between them.

We are often confronted with incomplete information on which to base a judgement. Consider buying a used car. Even with a test drive and a service record, there's still a lot we don't know about the car. People's decisions are often influenced by their expectations and beliefs. For example, they expect a used car to be reliable if they buy it from a reputable dealer.

Most of the time our decision-making processes serve us well. We are able to make sound decisions and reasonably accurate judgements, even when faced with incomplete information. Researchers are interested in finding out how we apply 'rules of thumb' to assess risks and estimate costs and benefits. They are also interested in why we sometimes make unsound decisions and inaccurate judgements.

5.2   Making judgements of probability

Decisions are often based on judgements of probability – for example, the probability of passing an exam, of receiving a pay rise, of it raining at the weekend, of the train being on time. Investigations of how good people are at estimating probabilities have revealed a number of flaws in the way probability-based decisions are made. Amos Tversky and Daniel Kahneman (1971, 1973, 1974) have proposed a number of *heuristics* or rules-of-thumb that people use to make judgements of probability. These allow us to make 'short-cuts' in our thinking. The main heuristics that have been identified are called the *representativeness heuristic*, the *availability heuristic*, and the *anchoring and adjustment heuristic*. The use of these heuristics often leads to errors of judgement. There are several flaws in the way people estimate probabilities, and applying different kinds of heuristics produces these errors.

Before reading further, work through Activity 8 and make a note of your answers. The answers are discussed in the following text.

Key term

Heuristics *Rules of thumb that people use to make judgements of probability.*

The representativeness heuristic

The *representativeness* or *similarity heuristic* is a method of judging how representative something is. Usually, this method is a helpful 'rule of thumb'. People often assume that various objects and events are typical or representative. For example, if they order bacon and eggs in a café, they assume that they will be similar to or representative of bacon and eggs they have eaten in the past. And they will probably be correct.

However, this method of making judgements can lead to errors. For example, it is now generally accepted that cigarette

Activity 8   Making judgements of probability

1   Birth orders

All the families with 6 children in a particular city were surveyed. In 72 of the families, the exact order of births of boys and girls was GBGBBG (G = girl, B = boy). What is your estimate of the number of families surveyed in which the exact order of births was BGBBBB?

2   Birthdays

There are 40 people in a room. How likely do you think it is that two people in the group will share the same birthday (same day and month, not necessarily the same year)?

3   Birth and sex

In a large hospital 30 babies are born every day; in a small hospital 10 babies are born every day. Overall, 50% of all babies born are boys. Over one year, each hospital records the days when more than 60% of the babies born are boys. Which hospital records more such days?

4   Engineers and lawyers

Imagine a group of 100 people consisting of 30 engineers and 70 lawyers.

One individual has been randomly selected from the group of 100 people:

Jack is a 45 year-old man. He is married and has four children. He is generally conservative, careful and ambitious. He shows no interest in political and social issues and spends most of his free time on his many hobbies, which include home carpentry, sailing and mathematical puzzles.

What is the probability that Jack is an engineer?

5   The letter *r*

Which are more common in English: words beginning with *r* or words with *r* as the third letter?

smoking can cause cancer. However, a person may know a heavy smoker who lived to be a hundred years old without any ill-effects. Based on this single case, which they assume to be representative, they reject the link between smoking and cancer.

Question 1 in Activity 8 illustrates how the representative heuristic can lead to an error in judgement. Most people estimate that the number of families with the birth order BGBBBB is less than 72. The best estimate of this sequence of births is 72, exactly the same as for GBGBBG. In fact, for any sequence of births, (even BBBBBB or GGGGGG), the probability is the same. The gender of each baby in the sequence is independent of the gender of the previous baby. The gender of one baby cannot (at least theoretically) affect the gender of the next baby to be born.

Kahneman and Tversky (1974) suggest that people judge the probability of an uncertain event occurring according to:

- The degree to which it appears similar to or representative of the population from which it is drawn. People believe that the birth-order GBGBBG is more similar to or representative of the numbers of males and females in the population.

- The degree to which it reflects the process by which it was produced (eg random generation). Whether a boy or a girl is born is a random event. The sequence GBGBBG looks more 'random' than the sequence BGBBBB, so people incorrectly believe that this sequence is more likely to occur by chance.

People tend to reason in this way, by thinking about whether something resembles a sequence of random events, rather than considering the true probability of the event occurring. When the National Lottery draw produces a sequence of numbers like 1, 2, 3, 4, 5, 6 many people think this is particularly unusual. When sequences like 2, 14, 23, 27, 39, 43 occur, people wrongly think this is more 'random' and so more likely to occur.

This tendency is seized upon by magicians and other party entertainers when they make correct predictions that seemingly unlikely events will occur. For example, the odds are 9-1 that 2 persons in a group of 40 will share the same birthday, and in a group of 14 people, there is more than 50% chance that two people will have a birthday within one day of each other (Krantz, 1992).

The small sample fallacy Tversky and Kahneman (1971) coined the term 'the law of small numbers'. This means that the characteristics of small samples are very unlikely to represent the characteristics of the wider population. They state that people frequently use the representativeness heuristic because they think that small samples will resemble the whole population from which that sample is drawn.

Tversky and Kahneman (1971) demonstrated this failure to take sample size into account by using the 'birth and sex' example in Activity 8, question 3. The correct answer to this problem is that the small hospital records more days on which 60% or more of the births are boys. For the small hospital, 60% or more is not particularly extreme, as an increase from 5 to 6 boys will increase the proportion from 50% to 60%. In the large hospital, an increase from 15 to 18 boys would be needed – an increase of three extra boys born. The smaller sample is less representative of the population than the large hospital, and so is more likely to deviate from the 'random' expectation. Large samples are more likely to resemble the population than small samples.

People also tend to use the representativeness heuristic when they know of anecdotal evidence based on a very small sample,

usually one person. When people are faced with statistical evidence, they sometimes use a 'man-who' argument (Nisbett & Ross, 1980). For example, when presented with statistics indicating that smoking causes cancer and shortens life expectancy, someone might refute the evidence by saying 'Well, I know a man who smoked 40 cigarettes a day and he lived to be 100'. This is an example of using a sample of one person as though they are representative of the whole population.

The assumption that a small sample will be representative of the population is known as the *small sample fallacy* (Poulton, 1994).

Base rates When people make judgements of how likely an event is to occur, they often ignore how often the item occurs in the population – the *base rate*. For example, Tversky and Kahneman (1973) found that when people were asked a question like Question 4 in Activity 8, they tended to judge the probability of the selected person being an engineer by comparing the person's characteristics to their view of a 'typical' engineer. In other words, they judged how representative the description was of an engineer. They ignored the base rate – the numbers of engineers and lawyers in the population. People tend to think that Jack is highly representative of engineers, and so is likely to be one. They ignore the base-rate information that engineers are relatively rare in the population, and so someone chosen at random will be more likely to be a lawyer (in Activity 4, in a population of 100, there were 30 engineers and 70 lawyers). When the proportions of engineers and lawyers in the question are changed, it makes no difference – people still ignore the base rate information and make a judgement on the basis of representativeness.

The tendency to ignore base rates has some real-world applications. For example, more two-storey hotels burn down than ten-storey hotels. Does this mean that you're safer if you stay in a ten-storey hotel? Not necessarily. More two-storey hotels burn down because there are more two-storey hotels to start with! Similarly, more first-born children go on to take A levels than second-born children. Does this mean that first-born children are more intelligent? Again, not necessarily. More first-born children take A levels because there are more first-born children in the population – many families only have one child.

The availability heuristic

Tversky and Kahneman (1973) suggested that people often make probability judgements according to the availability of similar occurrences in memory. A good example of this *availability heuristic* in action is the question 'Which is more common, words beginning with the letter *r* or words having the letter *r* as the third letter?' There are, in fact, many more words in English with *r* as the third letter, but it is easier to think of words beginning with *r*, so it seems as though there must be more of them. In experiments, over two-thirds of participants gave the incorrect answer. Examples of words beginning with *r* are more *available*.

Key terms

Representativeness heuristic *A method of making judgements based on the degree to which a particular instance or case is seen to be representative of a group of cases.*

Small sample fallacy *The assumption that small samples closely resemble the population from which they are drawn.*

Experiments such as this can be criticised as artificial and unrealistic. Few, if any, people would perform such tasks in everyday life. However, there are many examples of the availability heuristic operating in everyday situations. Married couples were interviewed individually and asked to assess their contribution to 20 tasks – for example, shopping for food, making breakfast, and cleaning (Ross & Sicoly, 1979). On 16 of the tasks, each said that they contributed more than their partner. In fact, on some tasks, each said that they contributed 80%. Clearly, in such cases, one partner's judgement is incorrect. This occurred because each individual's contribution was more available in their memory than their partner's.

Errors in judgement as a result of the availability hypothesis can have serious consequences. In the above example, it may lead to friction between partners as each claims to be making a greater contribution than the other. A study of doctors indicated that they were more likely to make a particular diagnosis if they had recently made a similar diagnosis (Weber et al., 1993). Again, the consequences of the availability heuristic could be serious.

Anchoring and adjustment

Tversky and Kahneman (1973) suggest that when people make a judgement they start by making a first guess. They then use this initial *anchor point* and *adjust* it on the basis of additional information. The *anchoring and adjustment heuristic* is related to the availability heuristic because information that is readily available is most likely to be used as the anchor. For example, if one person is asked whether the population of Leeds, West Yorkshire, is more than 100,000 and another person is asked whether the population of Leeds is less than 1,000,000, they will both probably say 'yes'. If we then ask them to estimate the population of Leeds, the person who 'starts' from 100,000 might guess 450,000, while the person who 'starts' from 1,000,000 might guess 800,000. They both rely too much on the anchor point, and although they adjust from it, they don't adjust enough (the population of Leeds is about 680,000).

The anchoring and adjustment heuristic often produces a reasonable answer, just like the representativeness and availability heuristics do, but it can also produce errors.

Studies have shown that people tend to adjust from an anchor point even when that anchor point is a random number. For instance, Tversky and Kahneman (1974) asked people to estimate the answers to a series of questions (eg, What percentage of United Nations delegates are from African countries?). As each question was asked, a roulette wheel was spun, generating a number between 1 and 100. Participants were asked whether the answer to the question was more or less than the number spun by the roulette wheel. They tended to use the roulette wheel's result as an anchor point and then adjust their answer from it. When the wheel produced a 10, participants would say that the proportion was higher than that, and might estimate the answer to be 25%. When the wheel produced a 65, participants would say that the answer was lower than that, and might estimate 45%. People adjusted their answer from the anchor point produced by the roulette wheel, but not by very much.

Real-life examples The anchoring and adjustment heuristic can be seen in a number of real-world settings. For example, if we go to a restaurant that has been recommended by a friend and we have a terrible time – the waiter is rude, the food badly cooked – this will anchor our judgement of that restaurant. If we

are told that our experience was very untypical, and we reluctantly return to that restaurant, our judgement will still be heavily based around that initial anchor point.

The same process can affect our judgements of people. If we read a newspaper article about a family with nine children living on social security and taking regular holidays abroad, this can anchor our judgements of people on benefit, even if we know that the family in the article are not typical. People anchor their judgements and generalise to other members of a category, even if they are fully aware that the example they have been given is not typical (Hamill et al., 1980).

The anchoring and adjustment hypothesis may lead to serious errors. For example, people who seek counselling about the likelihood of their children inheriting a genetic disorder start with their own estimate of the risk. They adjust this estimate on the basis of information provided by an expert counsellor, but their final estimate owes more to their original estimate. In other words, it is largely based on their initial anchor point (Shiloh, 1994).

Key terms

Availability heuristic *A method of making judgements based on the availability of information in memory.*

Anchoring and adjustment heuristic *Basing judgements on an initial estimate which is then adjusted up or down on the basis of additional information.*

Framing and risk

Other factors affecting decision-making are *framing* and *risk*. Framing refers to the way in which information is presented. Risk refers to the amount of risk seen to be involved in choosing one option rather than another. The way information is framed can affect the degree of risk people are prepared to take. It might lead to *risk aversion*, a desire to avoid risks, which will result in a low-risk decision. Framed in another way, the same information might lead to *risk-seeking*, resulting in a high-risk decision. This is shown in the following experiments by Tversky and Kahneman (1981).

Participants were given the following options.

Imagine that the United States is preparing for the outbreak of an unusual disease, which is expected to kill 600 people. Two alternative programs to combat the disease have been proposed. Assume that the exact scientific estimates of the consequences of the programmes are as follows:

- If Programme A is adopted, 200 people will be saved.
- If Programme B is adopted, there is a one-third probability that all 600 people will be saved and a two-thirds probability that no people will be saved.

Which of the two programmes would you choose?

Seventy-two per cent of the participants chose Programme A. They seemed to prefer the certain gain of saving 200 people to the uncertain gain of saving all 600 people. This suggests they experienced risk-aversion and, as a result, chose the low-risk option.

Exactly the same options were then presented in a second experiment using different participants, but this time the information was framed differently. Suppose that two further treatment programmes have been developed to combat the disease.

- If Programme A is adopted, 400 people will die.
- If Programme B is adopted, there is a one-third probability that nobody will die and a two-thirds probability that 600 people will die.

This time, 78% of the participants chose Programme B compared to only 28% in the first experiment. Yet Programme B in both experiments was the same – only the framing differed.

When the alternatives emphasise potential losses, most participants opted for risk taking. Research evidence indicates that people tend to choose options offering a large but uncertain loss rather than a smaller but certain loss.

Evaluation

Heuristics provide useful mental short-cuts for making judgements and decisions. Most of the time they work – if you go out of your house and see black clouds in the sky, you can use the representativeness heuristic to judge that it might well rain. The availability heuristic also works most of the time, because the examples that spring to mind are usually the most common ones which are tried and tested.

However, research suggests that people are not very efficient when it comes to making decisions based upon probabilities. This research is largely based on laboratory experiments. Gigerenzer (1993, 1996) argues that these experiments are artificial and unrealistic, and that people's everyday decision making is not as error-prone as the results suggest. He claims that laboratory studies of heuristics are artificially created to try and catch people out. Important information like base rates is often not sufficiently emphasised in the questions, so it's hardly surprising that people overlook it. People try to apply their knowledge about the real world rather then rely upon the statistical information provided in experiments. This often produces an incorrect decision in the laboratory. However, the use of everyday knowledge and experience when solving problems and making decisions in the real world is often reasonable and effective.

It is clear that the heuristics described by Tversky and Kahneman are useful in everyday decision-making. It is important to remember, however, that a 'rule of thumb' is nothing more than that, and that decision-making can be more effective if we realise that heuristics have limitations.

Key term

Framing *The way in which information is presented. This can affect people's risk-aversion or risk-seeking behaviour.*

Summary

1. Heuristics are 'rules of thumb' that help to make decisions. Errors in decision-making sometimes occur when people apply heuristics inappropriately.

2. Decisions based on the representativeness heuristic involve a judgement of the representativeness of a particular case or instance. Errors occur when sample size and base rates are ignored.

3. The availability heuristic is a method for judging probability based on the availability of information in memory. Errors can occur when the necessary information does not easily spring to mind.

4. The anchoring and adjustment heuristic involves establishing an anchor and then adjusting from it on the basis of additional information. The anchor often overrides the extent of the adjustments suggested by the additional information.

5. The extent to which people avoid or seek risk depends in part on the framing of the information.

6. A realisation that heuristics have limitations is necessary for effective decision-making.

References

Aitchison, J. (1998). *The articulate mammal*, (4th ed.). London: Routledge.

Anzai, Y. & Simon, H.A. (1979). The theory of learning by doing. *Psychological Review*, 86, 124-180.

Au, T. K. (1984). Counterfactuals: In reply to Alfred Bloom. *Cognition*, 17, 155-187.

Bard, B. & Sachs, J. (1977). Language acquisition patterns in two normal children of deaf parents. *Paper presented at the 2nd Annual Boston University Conference on Language Acquisition, October*.

Baron, N. S. (1992). *Growing up with language: How children learn to talk*. Reading, MA: Addison-Wesley.

Bates, E., O'Connell, B. & Janowsky, J. S. (1992). Language and communication in infancy. In J.D. Osofsky (Ed.), *Handbook of infant development*, (2nd ed.). New York: Wiley.

Bee, H. (2000). *The developing child*, (9th ed.). London: Allyn & Bacon.

Bellugi, U. (1970). Learning the language. *Psychology Today*, 4, 32-35.

Bellugi, U., Bihrle, A., Jernigan, T., Trauner, D. & Docherty, S. (1991). Neuropsychological, neurological and neuroanatomical profile of Williams syndrome. *American Journal of Medical Genetics Supplement*, 6, 115-25.

Bereiter, C. & Engelman, S. (1966). *Teaching disadvantaged children in pre-school*. Englewood Cliffs, NJ: Prentice Hall.

Bereiter, C., Engelman, S., Osborn, J. & Reidford, P.A. (1966). An academically oriented preschool for culturally deprived children. In F. Hechinger (Ed.), *Pre-school education today*. New York: Doubleday.

Berko, J. (1958). The child's learning of English morphology. *Word*, 14, 150-177.

Bernstein, B. (1961). Social class and linguistic development. In A.H.

Halsey, J. Floud & C.A. Anderson (Eds.), *Education, economy and society*. London: Collier-Macmillan.

Bernstein, B. (1970). A sociolinguistic approach to socialisation: With some reference to educability. In F. Williams (Ed.), *Language and poverty: Perspectives on a theme*. Chicago: Markham Publishing.

Bloom, A. H. (1981). *The linguistic shaping of thought: A study in the impact of language on thinking in China and the West*. Hillsdale, NJ: Erlbaum.

Boas, F. (1911). Introduction to the handbook of North American Indians (Vol. 1). *Bureau of American Ethnology Bulletin*, 40(1).

Bornstein, M.H. (1976). Infants are trichromats. *Journal of Experimental Child Psychology*, 19, 401-419.

Brown, R. & Lenneberg, E.H. (1954). A study in language and cognition. *Journal of Abnormal and Social Psychology*, 49, 454-462.

Brown, R. (1973). *A first language: The early stages*. Cambridge, MA: Harvard University Press.

Bruner, J. S. (1983). *Child's talk: Learning to use language*. New York: Norton.

Butterfield, E. C. & Siperstein, G. N. (1974). Influence of contingent auditory stimulation upon non-nutritional suckle. *Proceedings of the third symposium on oral sensation and perception: The mouth of the infant*. Springfield, IL: Charles C. Thomas.

Carroll, J. B. & Casagrande, J. B. (1958). The function of language classifications in behaviour. In E. E. Maccoby, T.M. Newcombe & E.L. Hartley (Eds.), *Readings in social psychology* (3rd ed.). New York: Holt, Rinehart and Winston.

Chomsky, N. (1957). *Syntactic structures*. The Hague: Mouton.

Chomsky, N. (1980). *Rules and representations*. Oxford : Blackwell.

Clark, E. V. (1973a). What's in a word? On the child's acquisition of semantics in his first language. In T. E. Moore (Ed.), *Cognitive development and the acquisition of language*. New York: Academic Press.

Clark, E. V. (1973b). Non-linguistic strategies and the acquisition of word meaning. *Cognition, 2*, 161-182.

Cromer, R. F. (1991). *Language and thought in normal and handicapped children*. Oxford: Blackwell.

Curtiss, S., Fromkin, V., Rigler, D., Rigler, M. & Krashen, S. (1975). An update on the linguistic development of Genie. In D.P. Dato (Ed.), *Developmental psycholinguistics: Theory and applications*. Washington, DC: US Department of Health and Human Services.

Davies, I. R. L. (1998). A study of colour grouping in three languages: A test of the linguistic relativity hypothesis. *British Journal of Psychology, 89*, 433-452.

Davies, I. R. L. & Corbett, G. G. (1997). A cross-cultural study of colour grouping: Evidence for weak linguistic relativity. *British Journal of Psychology, 88*, 493-517.

de Villiers, P. A. & de Villiers, J. G. (1992). Language development. In M.H. Bornstein & M.E. Lamb (Eds.), *Developmental psychology: An advanced textbook*, (3rd ed.). Hillsdale, NJ: Erlbaum.

Dore, J. (1985). Holophrases revisited: Their 'logical' development from dialogue. In M. D. Barrett (Ed.), *Children's language*, Vol. 1. New York: Gardner.

Duncker, K. (1945). On problem-solving. *Psychological Monographs, 58*, (Whole No. 270).

Eimas, P. D. (1975). Speech perception in early infancy. In L. B. Cohen and P. Salapatek (Eds.), *Infant perception: From sensation to cognition*, Vol. 2. New York: Academic Press.

Fenson, L., Dale, P. S., Reznick, J. S., Bates, E., Thal, D. J. & Pethick, S. J. (1994). Variability in early communicative development. *Monographs of the Society for Research in Child Development, 59*, (5, Serial No. 242).

Fodor, J. (1983). *The modularity of mind*. Cambridge, MA: MIT.

Fraser, C., Bellugi, U. & Brown, R. (1963). Control of grammar in imitation, comprehension, and production. *Journal of Verbal Learning and Verbal Behavior, 2*, 121-135.

Furth, H.G. (1966). *Thinking without language*. New York: Free Press.

Gigerenzer, G. (1993). The bounded rationality of probabilistic mental models. In K.I. Manktelow & D.E. Over (Eds.), *Rationality: Psychological and philosophical perspectives*. London: Routledge.

Gigerenzer, G. (1996). On narrow norms and vague heuristics: A reply to Kahneman and Tversky (1996). *Psychological Review, 103(3)*, 592, 596.

Gopnik, A. (1984). The acquisition of 'gone' and the development of the object concept. *Journal of Child Language, 11*, 273-292.

Hamill, R., Wilson, T.D. & Nisbett, R.E. (1980). Insensitivity to sample bias: Generalizing from atypical cases. *Journal of Personality & Social Psychology, 39*, 578-589.

Haralambos, M. & Holborn, M. (2000). *Sociology: Themes and perspectives* (5th ed.). London: Collins.

Harley, T. A. (1995). *The psychology of language: From data to theory*. Hove: Erlbaum.

Hockett, C. F. (1960). The origin of speech. *Scientific American, 203*, 89-96.

Hunt, E. & Agnoli, F. (1991). The Whorfian hypothesis: A cognitive psychological perspective. *Psychological Review, 98*, 377-389.

Jusczyk, P. W., Cutler, A. & Redanz, N.J. (1993). Infants' preference for predominant stress patterns of English words. *Child Development, 64*, 675-687.

Kahneman, D. & Tversky, A. (1974). Subjective probability: a judgement of representativeness. In C-A. S. Stael Von Holstein (Ed.), *The concept of probability in psychological experiments*. New York: Academic Press.

Köhler, W. (1927). *The mentality of apes* (2nd ed.). New York: Harcourt Brace.

Krantz, L. (1992). *What the odds are: A-to-Z odds on everything you hoped or feared could happen*. New York: Harper Perennial.

Labov, W. (1970). The logic of non-standard English. In F. Williams (Ed.). *Language and poverty*. Chicago: Markham.

Lenneberg, E. H. (1967). *The biological foundations of language*. New York: Wiley.

Liu, L. G. (1985). Reasoning counterfactually in Chinese: Are there any obstacles? *Cognition, 21*, 239-270.

Luchins, A. S. (1942). Mechanisation in problem-solving. The effect of Einstellung. *Psychological Monographs, 54*, (Whole No. 248).

Maier, N. R. F. (1931). Reasoning in humans II: The solution of a problem and its appearance in consciousness. *Journal of Comparative Psychology, 12*, 181-194.

Malotki, E. (1983). *Hopi time: A linguistic analysis of temporal concepts in the Hopi language*. Berlin: Mouton.

Marcus, G. F. (1993). Negative evidence in language acquisition. *Cognition, 46*, 53-85.

Marcus, G. F., Ullman, M., Pinker, S., Hollander, M., Rosen, T. J. & Xu, F. (1992). Overregularization in language acquisition. *Monographs of the Society for Research in Child Development, 57*, (Serial No. 228).

Masataka, N. (1992). Early ontogeny of vocal behaviour of Japanese infants in response to maternal speech. *Child Development, 63*, 1177-1185.

McNeill, D. (1970). *The acquisition of language: The study of developmental psycholinguistics*. New York: Harper and Row.

McTear, M. F. (1985). *Children's conversations*. Oxford: Ellis Horwood.

Messer, D. (1999). The development of communication and language. In D. Messer & S. Millar (Eds.). *Exploring developmental psychology*. London: Arnold.

Metcalfe, J. & Weibe, D. (1987). Intuition in insight and non-insight problem-solving. *Memory and Cognition*, 15, 238-246.

Metcalfe, J. (1986). Premonitions of insight predict impending error. *Journal of Experimental Psychology, Learning, Memory and Cognition, 12(4)*, 623-634.

Miller, G.A. & McNeill, D. (1969). Psycholinguistics. In G. Lindzey & E.Aronson (Eds.), *The handbook of social psychology*, Vol. 3. Reading MA: Addison-Wesley.

Nelson, K. (1973). Structure and strategy in learning to talk. *Monographs of the Society for Research in Child Development, 38*, 149.

Newell, A. & Simon, H. A. (1972). *Human problem-solving*. Englewood Cliffs, NJ: Prentice-Hall.

Nisbett, R. E. & Ross, L. (1980). *Human inference strategies and shortcomings of social judgement*. Englewood Cliffs, NJ: Prentice Hall.

Piaget, J. (1926). *The language and thought of the child*. New York: Basic Books.

Pinker, S. (1994). *The language instinct*. Harmondsworth: Allen Lane.

Poulton, E. C. (1994). *Behavioural decision theory: A new approach*. Cambridge: Cambridge University Press.

Pullum, G.K. (1989). The great Eskimo vocabulary hoax. *Natural Language and Linguistic Theory, 7*, 275-281.

Rosch, E. (1974). Linguistic relativity. In E. Silverstein (Ed.), *Human communication: Theoretical perspectives*. Hillsdale, NJ: Erlbaum.

Rosen, H. (1972). *Language and class: A critical look at the theories of Basil Bernstein*. Bristol: Falling Wall Press.

Ross, M. & Sicoly, F. (1979). Egocentric biases in availability and attribution. *Journal of Personality and Social Psychology, 37*, 322-336.

Sapir, E. (1929). The status of linguistics as a science. *Language, 5*, 207-214.

Schieffelin, B. & Ochs, E. (1983). A cultural perspective on the transition from prelinguistic to linguistic communication. In R. Golinkoff (Ed.), *The transition from prelinguistic to linguistic communication*. Hillsdale, NJ: Erlbaum.

Senghas, A. (1994). The development of Nicaraguan Sign Language via the language acquisition process. *Proceedings for the Boston University Conference on Language Development, 1994*.

Shiloh, S. (1994). Heuristics and biases in health decision making: Their expression in genetic counselling. In L. Heath, R.S. Tindale, J. Edwards, E.J. Posavac, F.B. Bryant,. E. Henderson-King, Y. Suarez-Balcazar & J. Myers (Eds.), *Applications of heuristics and biases to social issues*. New York: Plenum Press.

Sinclair de Zwart, H. (1967). *Acquisition du langage et dévelopement de la pensée*. Paris: Dunod.

Skinner, B. F. (1957). *Verbal behavior*. New York: Appleton-Century-Crofts.

Smith, S.M, Brown, H.O., Thomas, J.E.P & Goodman, L.S. (1947). The lack of cerebral effects of d-tubocurarine. *Anesthesiology, 8*, 1-14.

Snow, C. E. (1972). Mothers' speech to children learning language. *Child Development, 43*, 549-65.

Snow, C. E. (1977). The development of conversation between mothers and children. *Journal of Child Language, 4*, 1-22.

Tannen, D. (1990). *You just don't understand: Women and men in conversation*. London: Virago Press.

Tannen, D. (1994). *Talking from 9 to 5: Women and men at work: Language, sex and power*. London: Virago Press.

Tomasello, M. & Mannle, S. (1985). Pragmatics of sibling speech to one year-olds. *Child Development, 56*, 911-17.

Tversky, A. & Kahneman, D. (1971). Belief in the law of small numbers. *Psychological Bulletin, 76*, 31-48.

Tversky, A. & Kahneman, D. (1973). Availability: A heuristic for judging frequency and probability. *Cognitive Psychology, 5*, 207-232.

Tversky, A. & Kahneman, D. (1974). Judgment under uncertainty: Heuristics and biases. *Science, 185*, 1124-1131.

Tversky, A. & Kahneman, D. (1981). The framing of decisions and the psychology of choice. *Science, 211*, 453-458.

Vygotsky, L. S. (1934). *Thought and language*, edited and translated by E. Hanfmann & G. Vakar (1962). Cambridge, MA: MIT Press.

Watson, J.B. (1913). Psychology as the behaviourist views it. *Psychological Review, 20*, 158-177.

Weber, E. U., Bockenholt, U., Hilton, D. J. & Wallace, B. (1993). Determinants of diagnostic hypothesis generation: Effects of information, base rates and experience. *Journal of Experimental Psychology: Learning, Memory and Cognition, 19*, 1131-1164.

Werker, J. F. & Tees, R. C. (1992). The organization and reorganization of human speech perception. *Annual Review of Neuroscience, 15*, 377-402.

Westen, D. (1996). *Psychology: Mind, brain and culture*. Chichester: Wiley.

Whorf, B. L. (1940). Science and linguistics. *Technology Review, 42(6)*, 229-231, 247-248.

Whorf, B.L. (1956). *Language, thought and reality*. Cambridge MA: MIT Press.

Williams, R. L. (1972). *The BITCH test (Black Intelligence Test of Cultural Homgeneity)*. St. Louis: Washington University.

Yamada, J. E. (1990). *Laura: A case for the modularity of language*. Cambridge, MA: MIT Press.

Yarrow, L. J., Rubenstein, J. L. & Pedersen, F. A. (1975). *Infant and environment: Early cognitive and motivational development*. New York: Wiley.

28 Cognitive development

Cognitive abilities are the mental capacities people use to understand and make sense of the world around them. Cognitive development refers to the way these abilities take shape during childhood.

This chapter looks at three main aspects of children's cognitive development. Firstly, the development of their ability to solve problems or 'think'. Secondly, the development of their measured intelligence. Finally, the development of their ability to understand moral issues and to make moral judgements.

Chapter summary

- **Unit 1 looks at the development of children's thinking and understanding.**
- **Unit 2 looks at factors affecting children's performance on intelligence tests.**
- **Unit 3 looks at the development of moral understanding in children.**

Unit 1 Development of thinking

KEY ISSUES

1 **What are the main theories explaining how children's thinking and understanding develops?**

2 **What are the practical applications of these theories to education?**

This unit considers three main theories of the development of thinking and understanding in children. Firstly, that of Jean Piaget; secondly, that of Lev Vygotsky; thirdly, that of information processing theory.

1.1 Jean Piaget

The Swiss biologist and psychologist Jean Piaget (1896-1980) provided a highly influential theory of cognitive development. Working on intelligence testing in Paris in the 1920s, Piaget was struck by the fact that younger children gave different answers than older children, not because they were less intelligent, but because they were interpreting the questions differently.

Piaget realised that children's ability to think and understand matures through a series of stages. He called his new study of the stages of children's cognitive development *genetic epistemology* – genetic meaning origins and development, and epistemology meaning knowledge and understanding.

Piaget's theory is *interactionist*, stressing that the child is a dynamic organism, growing and developing psychologically through interaction with the environment. He believed that children are innately motivated by two processes – *organisation* of their thoughts, and *adaptation* to the environment.

Organisation In Piaget's view, the child's knowledge of the world is organised into *schemas*, structured patterns of knowledge and action. From birth the child has *action schemas*, enabling the child to know the world through acting upon it, recognising objects as 'suckable things', 'throwable things' and so on. During the second year, the child begins to think about actions, and *mental schemas* develop too. At all times, the child is motivated to keep their schemas organised, to incorporate new experiences into existing schemas, and to develop new schemas.

Mental schemas become more complex and integrated with one another throughout life. Adult schemas can include an in-depth knowledge of Shakespeare's sonnets or a mastery of rocket science. Schemas are never merely passive repositories of knowledge – they are always geared for action, guiding us to do things with our knowledge.

From the age of around 7 years, the child develops logical mental processes to organise and use the knowledge in their schemas. These logical mental processes are called *operations*.

Adaptation Piaget used the term adaptation to refer to the way the child learns as a result of their encounters and interactions with their environment.

Adaptation takes two possible forms. *Assimilation* is when the child learns something that readily slots into their existing schemas. *Accommodation* is when the child has to change their existing schemas in order to take in a new experience. Whether an experience is assimilated or accommodated depends on the level of development of the schemas, and whether they can handle the new information. It is through continual assimilation and accommodation of experience that knowledge and understanding of the world continues to develop.

Piaget called these innate motivations of adaptation and organisation *functional invariants* – functional because they serve a purpose, invariant because they are always present and active. In Piaget's view, adaptation and organisation require each other: it is through the action of these two functional invariants that the child is motivated to develop and learn.

Figure 1 Piaget's general theory

Equilibration Piaget proposed the existence of a third functional invariant called *equilibration* to keep the whole system in balance. Any change in any part of the system causes imbalance or disequilibrium. When that happens, equilibration re-establishes balance and harmony.

For example, new experiences that cannot be assimilated into existing schemas create disequilibrium. Equilibration causes the schemas to accommodate the new experience and restore equilibrium. Too much assimilation would be boring, and too much accommodation confusing. Equilibration keeps assimilation and accommodation in balance.

Key terms

Genetic epistemology *The study of the origins and development of thinking and knowledge in children.*

Interactionist *A term used to describe Piaget's theory because of the way it stresses the interaction between the individual and their environment.*

Functional invariants *Innate, universal and purposeful processes which keep us in productive interaction with our environments.*

Organisation *The functional invariant which motivates us to keep our schemas and operations ordered.*

Schemas *Organised patterns of action or knowledge.*

Operations *Mental processes emerging from around 7 years enabling the child to think logically.*

Adaptation *The functional invariant which motivates us to learn from our environment and change our schemas.*

Assimilation *A form of adaptation where new information is taken into existing schemas.*

Accommodation *A form of adaptation where schemas are modified or changed to take in new information.*

Equilibration *A third functional invariant which keeps the cognitive system in balance.*

Activity 1   Assimilation and accommodation

Item A   A bird schema

Joey

Charlotte is 4 years old. She has a bird schema which is based on pictures she has seen in books and on Joey, the budgerigar, a family pet.

Playing in the garden, she has no problem fitting a range of birds from sparrows to starlings into her bird schema. And, on visits to the zoo, she readily slots an array of exotic birds into her existing bird schema.

Item B   An aeroplane schema

One morning, when looking out of her bedroom window, Charlotte sees her first aeroplane. It appears to have wings and seems to be flying. However, it doesn't really fit her bird schema. She's fascinated but confused about this new thing. After talking to her parents, she develops a new schema. Now, these things in the sky, which aren't birds, fit readily into her aeroplane schema.

Questions

1   Which item is an example of a) assimilation and
    b) accommodation? Explain why.

2   How do the following ideas help to explain how Charlotte learns?

    a) adaptation   b) equilibration.

1.2 Stages of cognitive development

The child's cognitive development is not a smooth path of continuous progress, accumulating knowledge and experience. Cognitive development happens in stages, and at each stage the child reorganises the way they think.

Piaget identified four stages of cognitive development.

Stage 1 **The sensorimotor stage** (from birth to around 2 years): the child knows the world initially through sensation and action. Later, actions are internalised mentally as thoughts.

Stage 2 **The pre-operational stage** (from around 2-7 years): the child understands the world through visual appearances and non-logical assumptions.

Stage 3 **The concrete operational stage** (from around 7-11 years): the child develops a degree of logic and reason, but is limited to practical problems and specific examples.

Stage 4 **The formal operational stage** (from about 11 years): the child achieves mature thinking and is capable of abstract theorising and scientific reasoning.

This is not a rigid timetable. Individual children develop at different rates, due to their rate of physical development, and physical and social experience. Also there is overlap between the stages, which Piaget called *décalage* (French for 'time lag'), so that 7 year olds, for example, are likely to show a mixture of pre-operational and concrete operational abilities.

However, the sequence of stages is *invariant*, so all children go through them in the same order. Progress through the stages is motivated by equilibration. When the child has experiences they cannot explain in terms of the stage they are in, disequilibrium results. The child then acts to reorganise their internal schemas and operations to regain a new equilibrium by moving on to the next stage. The whole process of growing up can be seen as the child working through a series of disequilibria in pursuit of the ultimate equilibrium of adult understanding (Miller, 1983).

Piaget believed these stages are universal – they apply to all children in all societies and in all times. The possible exception was the formal operational stage, which Piaget (1972) suggested may be more common in Western scientific cultures.

The sensorimotor stage (birth to 2 years)

Piaget studied the sensorimotor phase by observing his own children in the 1930s. There are two principal features of this phase. First, children develop *object permanence*, the realisation that objects exist permanently even when the child cannot see them. Second, *action schemas*, by which the child knows the world through sensation and action, are supplemented and superseded by *mental representations*. This enables the child to think about actions and objects, plan what they are going to do, and predict what effect their actions will have.

Piaget (1936) divided the sensorimotor phase into six substages.

1 **Reflexes** (birth to 1 month): innate reflexes like sucking and grasping adapt through practice to become more flexible, enabling babies to suck and grasp objects of different size and shape. Babies recognise objects as suckable or graspable things, and begin to distinguish their own bodies from other objects.

2 **Primary circular reactions** (1-4 months): infants develop an interest in action for its own sake, repeating actions because it is satisfying to do so.

3 **Secondary circular reactions** (4-8 months): infants start to notice the effect their actions have on the world around them, and repeat actions out of interest to see what happens.

4 **Coordination of secondary schemas** (8-12 months): infants begin to combine actions into more complex action schemas, enabling them to deal with simple problems like removing a barrier to reach a desired toy. Crawling greatly assists in the exploration of the world (Bremner, 1998).

5 **Tertiary circular reactions** (12-18 months): children use trial and error to solve more complex problems and to develop new action schemas.

6 **Mental representation** (18-24 months): actions start being internalised or mentally represented as thoughts or mental schemas. These are more powerful and versatile than action schemas. Children can plan ahead without relying on trial and error. They are not restricted to immediate interaction with the world. They can learn something one day and not use their learning until another day. They can begin to use language.

Object permanence One key feature of the sensorimotor stage is the development of *object permanence* – the growing awareness that objects have a permanent existence even when out of sight (Piaget, 1937). In substage 1, babies see objects as part of their action schemas, and forget about them as soon as they move out of the visual field – literally a matter of 'out of sight, out of mind'. In substage 2, they will look where an object was last seen, but make no effort to search. In substage 3 they can retrieve a partially hidden object, and make some effort to look for an object if it is taken away. However, there is no real search stratagem and often infants ritually repeat an action to see if the object reappears. In substage 4 infants engage in active search for a hidden object, but only in the place where they saw the object hidden. Should the object be hidden again in a different place (*successive displacements*), they will still search in the first hiding place. In substage 5 they can search in new places but only if they saw the object put there. They can cope with successive displacements, but not with *invisible displacements* (not seeing the object being hidden). Only in substage 6 with the advent of mental representation is full object permanence attained, and children can work out where an object is even if they did not actually see it hidden there.

The sensorimotor stage – evaluation

Later research indicates that mental representations and object permanence develop earlier than Piaget suggested.

Object permanence According to Piaget, very young children should have no awareness of an object when it was out of sight. The following experiment questions this. Children as young as 20 days were shown an object. A screen was slowly moved in front of the object until it disappeared from view. In the first condition, the screen was removed and the object was still in place. In the second condition, the screen was removed and the object was gone (see Figure 2). The children's heart rate was higher in the second condition. This may indicate surprise. If so, it suggests that the children retained a mental representation of the object and therefore some awareness of object permanence. And this occurred at an earlier age than Piaget suggested (Bower, 1982).

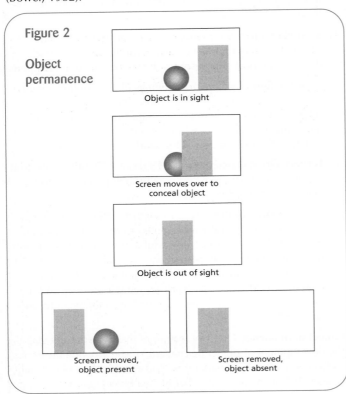

Figure 2

Object permanence

Object is in sight

Screen moves over to conceal object

Object is out of sight

Screen removed, object present

Screen removed, object absent

The following experiment again indicates that an understanding of object permanence develops at an early age. It is based on an 'impossible event', as shown in Figure 3. Carrots pass behind a screen from left to right. They are out of sight while they are behind the screen. This makes sense for the small carrot which is below the level of the window. But it doesn't make sense for the tall carrot which should be visible as it passes by the window. Researchers showed this procedure to 3-month-old children. They looked longer at the 'impossible event', which indicates that they found it more interesting than the 'possible event'. The researchers argue that this is because the children expected the tall carrot to appear in the window. This expectation can only be based on an understanding of object permanence – the tall carrot had disappeared, but they knew it was still there. The children apparently had a mental representation of the object – it was out of sight but *not* out of mind (Baillargeon & DeVos, 1991). Again, it appears that children develop an understanding of object permanence earlier than Piaget suggested.

Mental representations Piaget claimed that mental representations developed towards the end of the sensorimotor stage – between 18 and 24 months. However, there is evidence that mental representations develop at a much earlier age. The following experiment indicates that 6-week-old children can imitate behaviour they had seen the previous day. One group of children watched an adult make a facial gesture, for example stick out her tongue. A second group saw the same adult with a neutral expression. Next day, all the children saw the same adult with a neutral expression. Those who had seen her stick out her tongue were more likely to stick out their tongue. The

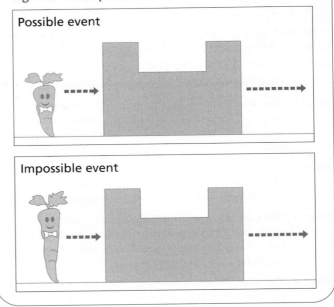

Figure 3   An impossible event

Possible event

Impossible event

researchers argue that this shows that the children must have a mental representation of facial gestures stored in memory (Meltzoff & Moore, 1994). If this is correct, then mental representations, albeit at a simple level, develop at an earlier age than Piaget claimed.

Conclusion In general, research has supported Piaget's view of the cognitive abilities that develop during the sensorimotor stage. However, more recent research indicates that many of these abilities develop at an earlier age than Piaget suggested (Smith et al., 1998).

Key terms

Décalage *Inconsistencies in children's cognitive abilities due to time lag between stages.*

Action schemas *Schemas based around sensation and action.*

Mental representations *Internalising and symbolising actions as thoughts, enabling the development of mental schemas.*

Object permanence *The development of the child's awareness that objects continue to exist even when out of sight.*

Successive displacements *Hiding an object in different places at different times.*

Invisible displacements *Hiding an object without the child actually seeing where it is hidden.*

The pre-operational stage (2 to 7 years)

From the age of about 2 years, children have mental schemas and can symbolise objects and actions in the mind as representational thought. Thought can be expressed through fantasy, play, drawing and language (Piaget & Inhelder, 1966). Language is important in enabling the child to talk about the world and communicate with others. However, children can only express what they can already think, and even then often only with difficulty (Piaget, 1923). (See pp 467-468 for Piaget's view of the relationship between language and thought.)

Activity 2   Object permanence

Item A   Jacqueline at 10 months

Piaget took Jacqueline's toy parrot and hid it under the mattress to her left side. Jacqueline found it easily. Piaget repeated the exercise, again Jacqueline found it. Then, in full view of the child, Piaget hid the parrot under the mattress to her right. Jacqueline looked under the mattress to her left.

Item B   Jacqueline at 19 months

With Jacqueline watching, Piaget placed a coin in his hand, put his hand under the blanket, and drew it out closed. Jacqueline opened his hand, and, not finding the coin, looked under the blanket to find it. Piaget repeated the exercise with the same result. Next, he put the coin in his hand, placed his hand under the cushion, and then under the coverlet, before withdrawing it, still closed. Jacqueline pushed his hand aside to look under the cushion. The coin was not there. Jacqueline immediately looked under the coverlet to find it.

Adapted from Piaget, 1937

Item C   Losing interest

The infant loses interest in the toy when it is hidden from view. An older infant would search for the toy or push the screen aside to reach it.

Item D   A jack-in-the-box

Questions

1   Using Piaget's substages, describe the development of Jacqueline's sense of object permanence between the ages of 10 months and 19 months.

2   At which substage would the infant actively search for the hidden toy in Item C?

3   Design an experiment using a jack-in-the-box (Item D) to discover when an understanding of object permanence develops. Explain the reasoning behind your experiment.

Piaget divided the pre-operational stage into two substages – the *pre-conceptual phase* (around 2 to 4 years), and the *intuitive phase* (around 4 to 7 years).

In the pre-conceptual phase, children's grasp of concepts is vague. They may, for example, think that if a dog is small enough it becomes a cat, or think all older girls are their sister Emily.

They are also prone to *animism*, where they attribute nature with human intentions, desires and feelings – for example, believing the sun exists to give us light, and that it goes down in the evening to let us sleep (Piaget, 1926).

In addition, pre-conceptual children do not grasp principles of organisation and classification (Piaget, 1959). They have difficulties with *seriation* – putting things into a sequential order. For example, they cannot arrange a series of sticks of different lengths in order from the shortest to the longest. They are also unable to categorise or classify objects, tending instead to put the blue ball and the yellow ball together because they are both balls, then add the yellow triangle because it's the same colour

as the second ball, and so on.

Egocentrism One of the most striking features of the pre-conceptual phase is that children can only see the world from their own point of view and cannot understand that things look different from other viewpoints. For example, Anna knows she has a sister, Katie, but may not grasp that Katie has a sister too (ie, Anna). This inability to grasp other viewpoints is called *egocentrism*.

Piaget's classic demonstration of egocentrism was the three mountains experiment (Piaget & Inhelder, 1956). Here, a child is seated one side of a model of mountain scenery, with a doll seated along a different side (see Figure 4). The child is shown a series of pictures of the mountain scene and asked to select the one which corresponds most closely to doll's view. They tend to choose the picture which corresponds to their own view. Piaget concluded that the child did not understand that the doll was at a different vantage point and would therefore 'see' a different view. The child was displaying egocentrism.

During the intuitive phase (4-7 years), animism and

Figure 4 The three mountains experiment

egocentrism decline, and children are able to organise and classify more consistently, but they are still not thinking logically, and cannot clearly explain their own thought processes. They show little sense of probability (Piaget & Inhelder, 1951). For example, they are unaware that if there are 10 blue marbles and 3 red marbles in a bag, it is more likely that a marble drawn out at random will be blue.

They are also hazy on tasks of *transitivity* or *transitive inference*. For example, if they know that stick A is longer than stick B, and are then shown that stick B is longer than stick C, they are unsure whether or not A is longer than C.

Centration Most characteristic of the intuitive phase, however, is *centration*. This refers to the child's inability to focus on more than one aspect or feature of a problem at any one time. One example of this is the child's confusion faced with *class inclusion* or *part-whole tasks* (Piaget, 1952). Given 10 white beads and 2 black ones, then asked if there are more white beads or beads, the child will tend to say there are more white ones. The child cannot maintain a simultaneous awareness of the whole (12 beads) and the parts (10 white and 2 black ones). They will tend to assume they were being asked if there were more white beads than black ones (Gardner, 1976).

Conservation The most famous example of centration is the child's failure to show *conservation*. This refers to the ability to understand that no matter how much things are rearranged, volume, quantity and number remain the same provided nothing has been added or taken away. To investigate pre-operational children's ability to conserve volume, Piaget and Inhelder (1941) presented them with three beakers, 2 short ones (A and B), and a tall thin one (C). Equal amounts of water were poured into A and B, and the child asked if there was the same amount in each. Typically the child would say 'yes'. Then the water in B was poured into beaker C, and the child was asked if there was the same amount in A and C. Typically, the child would say there was more in C, because the water level was higher (see Figure 5).

Piaget suggested that at this stage the child has no understanding of *reversibility, compensation,* or *identity*. In this experiment, reversibility is the realisation that the water could be poured back from C into B to arrive back at the starting point, so proving that the volume of water had not changed.

Figure 5 A conservation experiment

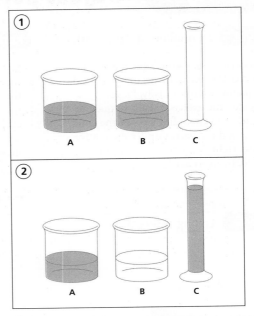

A and B have equal amouts of water. The contents of B is then poured into C.

Compensation is the ability to understand that although the water level is higher in C, the beaker is narrower, so the volume of water remains the same. Identity is the realisation that if nothing was added and nothing taken away, then the volume cannot have changed.

Piaget (1952) designed further experiments to investigate conservation of number and quantity. In one experiment, two rows of five buttons are laid out on a table. The rows are the same length. The child is asked if there is the same number of buttons in each row, and usually answers correctly. One row is then lengthened by increasing the spaces between the buttons. The question is repeated and the child typically answers that there are more buttons in the lengthened row (see Figure 6).

In another experiment, the child is shown two identical balls of plasticine. They are asked if there is the same amount of plasticine in each ball. They usually answer correctly. One ball is then flattened into a pancake. The question is repeated and the child typically answers that there is more plasticine in the pancake (see Figure 7).

Figure 6 Conservation of number

Figure 7 Conservation of quantity

The pre-operational stage – evaluation

Piaget claims that during the pre-conceptual phase (2-4 years), the child fails to grasp the principles of organisation and classification, and is unable to see the world from the viewpoint of others. During the intuitive phase (4-7 years), the child has difficulty with certain reasoning tasks, such as transitive inference and class inclusion tasks. Although the pre-operational child understands that objects have a permanent existence, they have yet to develop the ability to conserve. They fail to realise that if nothing is added or taken away, then the properties of objects, such as volume and number, are permanent too. Pre-operational thinking is dominated by appearances. The basic rule is: 'If it looks more, it is more'.

Piaget's work has led to an enormous amount of research on the so-called pre-operational child. This research has suggested that:

- Piaget underestimated children's abilities. For example, there is evidence that young children's ability to conserve is greater than Piaget assumed.

- Variations in experimental design can produce very different results. For example, one experiment may indicate that pre-operational children are egocentric, another experiment may indicate that they are not.

- The results of the same experiment can be interpreted in a number of ways. Because of this, any conclusions based on experimental findings must be treated with caution.

- Piaget's experiments were often badly designed. The tasks were sometimes inappropriate for children of the age group, the instructions unclear, the questions confusing and ambiguous, and the tasks themselves boring and irrelevant. When these problems were rectified in later experiments, children's performance improved and they appeared more able than Piaget's evidence indicated.

Egocentrism The results of experiments depend in part on the way participants interpret what they are asked to do. For example, they are more likely to succeed in a task if they see it as interesting and relevant rather than boring and irrelevant. They tend to do better if the task is within their experience and they can therefore relate to it.

Compare the following task with Piaget's three mountains task. Three-year-old children were asked to hide a baby boy doll from two toy police officers. They succeeded in hiding the doll so that neither of the police officers could see him. This requires an understanding of what the officers could see. In other words, the children took the viewpoint of the officers. This challenges Piaget's claim that children of this age are egocentric, that they are unable to take the viewpoint of others (Hughes cited in Donaldson, 1978).

Why did this study produce different results from the three mountains experiment? According to the researcher, the task 'made sense' to the children. As a result, they could relate to it. There are reasons for hiding from police officers, even for three-year-olds. What's the point of working out someone else's view of a group of mountains – there's no obvious reason for doing so. In addition, the task holds little interest for a child. When a task is meaningful, as in Item A in Activity 3, children are more likely to view a scene from another's standpoint (Donaldson, 1978).

Class inclusion tasks Piaget's experiments indicated that pre-operational children had difficulty with class-inclusion tasks – they were unable to understand part-whole relations. As noted earlier, when presented with 10 white beads and 2 black ones, and asked, 'Are there more white beads than beads?', the child is likely to say there are more white beads. But this answer may say more about the way the question is phrased than the child's cognitive ability (Smith et al., 1998). This type of question rarely occurs in everyday conversation. It sounds peculiar to an adult, never mind a child. And, as Item B in Activity 3 shows, a change in the wording of a class inclusion question may have a significant effect on the answer.

Conservation Participants in experiments try to make sense of the situation. And this effects their responses to tasks. In Piaget's conservation experiments, children were asked the same question twice – for example, 'Are there the same number of buttons in each row?' Rose and Blank (1974) found that his confused children. Repeating the question may have suggested that a) they had given the wrong answer at first, *or* b) a different answer was expected when the question was asked again. As a result, children may have given the answer they thought was expected, even if they believed it was wrong (see Item C, Activity 3).

When only *one* question was asked at the end of the experiment – for example after the row of buttons had been lengthened – this produced more correct answers. Experiments using this approach indicate that children are able to conserve at an earlier age than Piaget stated (Samuel & Bryant, 1984).

Interpreting the results of an experiment requires an understanding of the participants' viewpoint. Small children often use the word 'more' to mean any kind of increase (Gelman, 1978). So, when they say the plasticine ball is 'more' when it has been flattened into a pancake, this does not necessarily mean they cannot conserve quantity. They may simply be saying that the pancake occupies more space. In this sense, it is 'more'.

Conclusion The following quotation summarises present-day views of the pre-operational child. 'Piaget was right to point out difficulties that pre-operational children have with conservation and other reason tasks. But researchers since Piaget have found that, given appropriate wording and context, young children seem capable of demonstrating at least some of the abilities which Piaget thought only developed later. In the right social context, the child emerges as a more competent being than Piaget's work would suggest' (Smith et al., 1998).

Activity 3 looks at some important studies questioning Piaget's claims about the cognitive skills of pre-operational children.

The concrete operational stage (7 to 11 years)

In this stage children develop *mental operations*. That is, they begin to reason logically, and overcome the limitations of the pre-operational stage (Piaget, 1958, 1959). Egocentrism is left behind, children overcome centration and become *decentred*, they master principles of classification, seriation and class inclusion and, eventually, full conservation of volume, number and quantity.

Nevertheless, there are certain limitations to concrete operational thinking. The main one is children's inability to think abstractly and their dependence on concrete examples. For instance, they have difficulty with questions requiring transitive inference – for example, 'Joe is taller than Sam, John is taller than Joe, who is the tallest boy?'. Concrete operational

Activity 3 — Research into pre-operational abilities

Item A — Egocentrism

The following experiment on egocentrism was based on a sample of eight 3-year-olds and fourteen 4-year-olds. The children were shown three models. The first was a simple scene of a lake with a boat in it, a horse and a cow, and a house. The second was a version of Piaget's three mountains – another simple scene. The third was a complex scene with a variety of toy animals and people in various settings – for example, cowboys and Indians in a wood, and a woman feeding chickens.

Grover, a well-known puppet from *Sesame Street*, drove round each scene in his car. From time to time he stopped to look at the view. The children were given identical models of each scene on a turntable. They were told, 'When Grover stops to look out of his car, I want you to turn the scene that moves so you are looking at it in the same way Grover is'. The researcher then parked Grover at each of the three sides which presented a view different from the child's view. The percentage of correct responses were as follows:

	Scene 1	Scene 2	Scene 3
3-year-olds	80%	42%	79%
4-year-olds	80%	67%	93%

Adapted from Borke, 1975

Item B — Class inclusion

A sample of 6-year-old children were shown 4 toy cows. Three of the cows were black, one was white, all of them were lying on their sides, asleep. When asked the standard Piagetian question, 'Are there more black cows or more cows?', only 25% of the children answered correctly. However, when asked 'Are there more black cows or more sleeping cows?', 48% gave the correct answer.

Adapted from McGarrigle, cited in Donaldson, 1978

Item C — Conservation experiments

Three- and four-year-old children took part in a conservation experiment which involved asking the same question twice. They then observed another child taking part in the same experiment. The researcher asked, 'Why do you think the child answered in this way? Did she say that because that is what she really believed, or did she say it to please the adult?' When children gave an incorrect answer to the second question, many of the observers said they did so to please the adult. When they gave the correct answer, the observers often said they did so because they believed it. And many of the observers who said this had themselves given an incorrect answer to the second question.

Adapted from Siegal, 1991

Questions

1 a) Read Item A. Why were there more correct answers for Scenes 1 and 3?

   b) What does this suggest about the findings of Piaget's egocentrism experiments?

2 Judging from Item B, why should Piaget's conclusions drawn from class inclusion experiments be questioned?

3 Experiments don't always measure what they are intended to measure. Comment on this statement with reference to Item C.

Key terms

Animism *The belief that inanimate objects have human feelings and intentions.*

Seriation *The ability to organise objects into some kind of order, for example, order of size.*

Egocentrism *Seeing the world solely from your own viewpoint.*

Transitivity/transitive inference *Making logical deductions, for example, if A is cheaper than B, and B is cheaper than C, then A must be cheaper than C.*

Centration *The inability to focus on more than one feature or aspect of a problem at any one time.*

Class inclusion tasks *Part-whole tasks, which require the solver to think about the properties of the whole and of its parts simultaneously.*

Conservation *The ability to recognise that reorganising the appearance of materials and objects does not alter properties like volume, quantity and number. Conservation is possible when the child masters reversibility, compensation and identity.*

Reversibility *Understanding that procedures can be reversed to arrive back at the starting point, proving that nothing has really changed.*

Compensation *Understanding that different apparent changes can cancel each other out, proving that nothing has really changed.*

Identity *Understanding that if nothing was added or subtracted, then nothing has really changed.*

---

children may need dolls or pictures representing the three boys to help them solve the problem.

Concrete operational children deal with what is rather than what could be. They are likely to be intolerant of 'what if?' questions, for example, 'What if we could eat grass, what would the world be like?', dismissing such questions as irrelevant and not worth considering.

Their understanding of the world is piecemeal, fact-based and practical rather than theoretical (Gardner, 1976). They are not skilled at games like 'Twenty questions', tending to guess 'Is it a bird?' rather then logically working through 'Is it alive? Does it fly? Is it a bird?' (Bruner, 1966).

Evaluation In general, Piaget's views of the concrete operational stage have been supported by later research (Smith et al., 1998). However, as with earlier stages, Piaget tended to ignore the social and cultural context in which cognitive development takes place. Research indicates that this can have an important effect on cognitive skills. For example, Jahoda (1983) found that Zimbabwean 9-year-olds who helped in their parents' businesses had a sophisticated grasp of abstract principles of economics, while Price-Williams et al., (1969) found that Mexican children raised in pottery-making families could conserve quantity as early as 6 years old.

The formal operational stage (from 11 years)

The final stage, *formal operations*, begins around 11 years, and is fully developed by about 15 (Piaget, 1958). Formal operational adolescents are scientific in their thinking, use abstract logical reasoning and theorising, make hypotheses and test them systematically, and deduce conclusions from premises.

They use stratagems in 'Twenty questions', they can deal with proportions (eg, 12 is to 4 as 9 is to ...?), work out logical syllogisms (eg, 'All men are mortal; Socrates was a man, therefore ...?), and readily work out the answer to the 'Who is the tallest boy?' question in their heads.

At this stage, language plays an important role in thinking, and this means that instruction can play a more direct role than in earlier stages. Adolescents start to think about thought itself, and develop a taste for abstract intellectual games, including nonsense games and 'what if?' questions.

An experiment by Piaget and Inhelder (1956) illustrates the

difference between formal operations and earlier stages. The participant is given a sample of a liquid *g*, and 4 flasks containing colourless liquids (labelled 1-4). The task is to find which combination(s) of colourless liquids added to *g* produces a yellow colour. In fact, *g* is potassium iodide, which turns yellow when oxygenated water (in flask 3) and acid (in flask 1) are added. Flask 2 contains plain water which has no effect either way. Flask 4 contains alkaline that neutralises the acid in flask 1 (see Figure 8).

The correct combinations then are:

$g + 1 + 3$ = yellow; and $g + 1 + 3 + 2$ = yellow

All other combinations yield colourless solutions.

Figure 8

$g + 1 + 3$ = **yellow**

$g + 1 + 3 + 2$ = **yellow**

Typically, pre-operational children mix the liquids at random, without any kind of strategy, and hope for the best. Concrete operational children proceed by trial and error, and if they find one combination that works, they feel they have solved the problem and stop. Formal operational adolescents work out all the possible combinations and apply them systematically until they find all the answers. For them, the desire to understand the underlying principles of the task is as important as 'getting the right answer'.

Evaluation For once, subsequent research suggests that Piaget was over-estimating the abilities of young people at this age. Shayer et al., (1976) found that only 30% of British 16-year-olds had reached 'early formal operations'. In the USA, 18-year-old women were given formal operational tasks. Their success varied from 15% to 95% depending on the task (Martorano, 1977, cited in Smith et al., 1998). Research indicates that most adolescents and adults in Western societies only use formal operational thinking for certain tasks and in certain areas of their lives – for example, in their jobs (Segall et al., 1990). And in small-scale, non-literate societies, formal operational thinking is either limited to particular tasks, or, according to some researchers, completely absent (Smith et al., 1998).

In view of this, it is not clear whether formal operational thinking can be seen as a universal developmental stage. Young people in Western secondary schools are trained in this type of thinking. The tasks used by researchers reflect physics, chemistry and mathematics as they are taught in schools. The importance of training can be seen from Figure 9. The researchers coached students aged 10, 13 and 17 years, in three formal operational tasks. Coaching made a difference in all years, but particularly at 17.

Figure 9   Coaching and formal thought

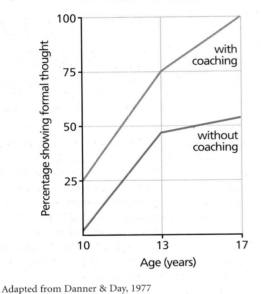

Adapted from Danner & Day, 1977

Piaget (1972) admits that formal operational thinking depends on experience and training. He revised his earlier figure (11-15 years) but still expected most young people to attain this stage between 15 and 20 years. Modern researchers tend to be more cautious. According to Smith et al. (1998), 'It seems that the period from 11-15 years signals the start of the possibility of formal operational thought, rather than its achievement'.

Key term

Decentred *When the child has overcome centration and can focus on several aspects of a situation at once.*

Piaget's theory – general evaluation

Methodology Piaget's methodology has been criticised for the following reasons. He rarely provides quantitative data. His samples are often very small – for example, his three children. He avoids standardised procedures and assessments – for example, structured interviews – in favour of flexible interviewing techniques which are difficult to replicate and

open to interviewer bias (Brainerd, 1978).

In Piaget's defence, flexible, unstructured interviews allow the interviewer to probe for further information and respond to a variety of answers. They are usually more informal and relaxed than structured interviews. As such, they may be more appropriate for finding out what children think. In addition, Piaget and his colleague, Bärbel Inhelder, pioneered experimental procedures like the three mountains and conservation experiments which later researchers could use to provide quantitative data from larger and more representative samples.

However, many of these experiments have been criticised for failing to produce valid data. According to some critics, the tasks were often boring, irrelevant and inappropriate for children, and the questions they were given were sometimes confusing and ambiguous. When these problems were rectified in later experiments, children often appeared more able and advanced than Piaget's evidence suggested (Smith et al., 1998).

Many of Piaget's concepts are difficult if not impossible to operationalise – to put into a form that can be measured. Critics see his theory as overloaded with hypothetical, metaphysical (non-observable) concepts that are difficult to understand, often vague, and even fictitious (Miller, 1983). For example, what exactly is equilibration, and what evidence is there that it actually exists?

Assessing ability Piaget has been criticised for failing to provide accurate assessments of children's ability. Judging from later research, he consistently underestimates the cognitive abilities of children in Stages 1 and 2. This research suggests that many of these abilities develop earlier than Piaget claims. These differences may be due to experimental design, as noted earlier. Given the right context and the right wording, children appear more competent than Piaget suggests (Smith et al., 1998). However, when it comes to Stage 4, Piaget has been criticised for overestimating the capabilities of adolescents.

Piaget's apparent underestimation of children's abilities may simply reflect the fact that he was interested in when children's cognitive skills were fully formed, whereas later researchers were more interested in when these skills first appear. The findings of both Piaget and later researchers may be right – one identifying when skills are fully developed, the others when they begin to emerge (Miller, 1983). However, this fails to explain why Piaget appears to have incorrectly estimated both the age of onset and the proportion of people attaining formal operational thought.

Universal stages Piaget argued that all children in all societies went through the same stages of cognitive development. The only possible exception was Stage 4. There are two main criticisms of this view. First, do these stages really exist? Second, if they do, can they be applied universally, ie to children in all societies?

First, later research has 'stretched' Piaget's stages. For example, children perform concrete operational tasks earlier than Piaget suggested, and most adolescents appear to develop formal operational thinking later than he suggested. Even so, a modified version of his stages might still be appropriate. But do the various aspects of each stage remain linked – do they occur together? For example, do the various aspects of concrete operational thought, such as conservation, classification, seriation and decline of egocentrism, stay linked together? The evidence indicates they do not, which suggests that a clearly identifiable stage does not exist. This linkage is only apparent for Stage 1, the sensorimotor stage (Smith et al., 1998).

Despite these criticisms, a number of researchers have accepted the broad outlines of Piaget's stages. Piaget based his stages on data from Western societies. Can they be applied cross-culturally? In other words, are they applicable to children in all societies? Most researchers agree that there are probably 'basic developmental processes' that occur in all societies (Segall et al., 1990). However, it is unlikely that these processes fit into neat and tidy universal stages. The way they are expressed depends on culture – on beliefs, values, experience and training. In terms of this argument, all adolescents, for example, develop the basic *competence* for formal operational thought. However, they will only learn to express it if their culture defines it as important and provides opportunities to develop it (Keats, 1985).

Social and emotional factors Piaget presented the child as an *individual* thinking organism, interacting with their environment and learning from their own experience. For Piaget, the child is a scientist, forming concepts and solving problems, assimilating and accommodating in an unemotional and calculating manner. This view of the child is reflected in many of the experiments designed to measure cognitive development. They take place in the cold and clinical surroundings of the laboratory. The child is given problems to solve as an individual. Piaget has been criticised for underestimating 1) the role of emotion as a motivating force in cognitive development (Cowan, 1978) and 2) the role of social factors in facilitating learning (Segall et al., 1990).

Conclusion Overall, Piaget stands as one of the great pioneers, providing 20th century psychology with its principal framework for understanding the cognitive development of the child. He had links with the psychoanalytic movement, and many of his ideas echo those of Freud.

- Both provide a dynamic theory of the child's progression through a series of stages, emphasising the role of the child as an active player in their own psychological development.

- Both reject the biological determinist 'child as genetically programmed' view held by nativists, and the environmental determinist 'child as empty vessel' view held by the behaviourists.

- Both Piaget and Freud see maturation as an interaction between growth and experience.

- Both have been criticised for being too theoretical and for failing to produce hard empirical data to substantiate their claims. In reply it can be argued that the job of a pioneer is not to produce a bullet-proof system, but to produce a fertile and fruitful theory, provide new ideas and frameworks of understanding, open doors and stimulate research. As a pioneer, Piaget, like Freud, scores highly.

1.3   L.S. Vygotsky

A radical alternative to Piaget's view of cognitive development was provided by the Russian literary critic and psychologist Lev Semenovich Vygotsky (1896-1934).

Unlike Piaget, Vygotsky (1934) insisted that the psychology of the individual can only be properly understood in a social, cultural and historical context. In his view, the child is born into a culture in which everything already has significance and meaning, so cognitive development involves understanding these significances and meanings. This understanding is achieved through social interaction with others, and most of this is achieved through language.

Vygotsky was a Marxist. Like Karl Marx (1818-1883), he believed that human beings are first and foremost social beings, born into a social context. Our individual psychology, our consciousness and even our sense of personal identity arise within this social context. Ironically, the Soviet Russian government in the 1930s, although supposedly 'Marxist', favoured a more behaviourist psychology, and was not at all happy with Vygotsky's ideas. When he died of tuberculosis at 38, his work was 'shelved', and only resurfaced in the Soviet Union in the 1950s, to be translated and exported abroad from the 1960s. Consequently, although Vygotsky knew of Piaget's work in the 1930s, Piaget only read Vygotsky in the 1960s.

Cognitive development is social

Vygotsky distinguished between lower functions of human psychology like recognition and sensation, and higher functions like thinking and understanding. He accepted that lower functions develop more or less individually through interaction with the environment, as Piaget had suggested, but insisted that higher functions can only develop through interaction with other people. This interaction is conducted largely through language.

Through linguistic interaction, the child 'plugs into' the wider culture and comes to understand the frameworks of symbols and meanings of the culture. In the same way, the child also acquires the tools of thinking. Through linguistic interaction, the child learns various cognitive skills – for example, how to organise and classify objects in a logical manner. This means that the child's individual understanding and skills are internalised from social communication with others. In Vygotsky's (1966) words, 'Any function of the child's cultural development appears on the stage twice, on two planes, first on the social plane and then on the psychological.'

Spontaneous and deliberate action From the moment of birth, infants find themselves engaged in social interactions, and their actions, initially mere reflexes, are given meaning by others. The baby smiles (probably due to wind!) and parents treat it as an intentional act of communication and respond by smiling back. The baby is raised in a framework of communication and meaning, where their own actions are given meaning by others.

As the child develops, so an awareness of the meaning of their own actions starts to become apparent to them. At this point, the child can begin to exercise *deliberate control* over actions that were originally *spontaneous reflexes* that just 'happened' (Shotter, 1976; Newson, 1979). The whole of childhood and adolescence can be seen as progress towards greater and greater control and social awareness of one's own actions, until the adult is regarded as a fully competent member of society.

Instruction Unlike Piaget, who saw cognitive development as a largely individual matter, where the child moves on to the next stage when their cognitive apparatus is 'ready', Vygotsky saw an important role for *instruction* by others in the child's cognitive development. Instructors may be parents or teachers, or more knowledgeable children of the same age or older. The point is that for Vygotsky, children learn largely by being taught by somebody else.

Scaffolding Vygotsky did not provide a theory of how instruction actually works. Since the 1970s, the American psychologist Jerome Bruner and his colleagues have explained instruction in terms of *scaffolding* (Wood et al., 1976). Scaffolding describes the way instructors structure the child's learning into parts and provide a framework to help organise the child's skills and understanding. Once the child shows mastery of the task in hand, the scaffolding is no longer needed.

Scaffolding involves engaging the child's interest, simplifying tasks, maintaining motivation, highlighting important features to focus the child's attention, and demonstrating or explaining the solution to the child.

Research suggest that the most effective instructors use a variety of stratagems to help the child master the problem, from general verbal encouragement to direct demonstration of 'how to do it' (Wood et al., 1978). Effective instructors also tend to stay one step ahead of the child, encourage the strengthening of new skills, and discourage relapses into immature behaviours (Moss, 1992). The following example illustrates scaffolded learning.

Greenfield and Lave (1982) found that Zinacanteco Mexican women introduce new girls to weaving in a series of stages. First, the girls spent much time simply watching; then they worked cooperatively with their instructor before being allowed to work alone. The instructors graded the tasks they set the girls so as not to overload them, yet, interestingly, they minimised their own role as instructors and claimed the girls largely taught themselves.

The zone of proximal development

According to Vygotsky (1934), 'What a child can do in cooperation today, he can do alone tomorrow'. This idea formed the basis for a key concept in Vygotsky's theory – the *zone of proximal development* (ZPD).

The ZPD is the gap between what a child can do alone – their level of *actual development* – and what they can do with the help of an instructor – their level of *potential development*. A child's actual development is measured by tasks they can do unaided – without help or assistance. This is how a child's ability is usually tested – by psychologists in experiments and by teachers in examinations. A child's potential development is measured by how well they perform with the assistance of those who are more knowledgeable and/or able than themselves – parents, teachers, or members of their peer group.

Figure 10 The zone of proximal development

level of potential development

zone of proximal development

level of actual development

Through instruction, the child can progress beyond the level of actual development, through the ZPD, and attain the level of potential development. This now becomes their new level of actual development, and a new ZPD opens out before them.

The ZPD is an indicator of the 'teachability' of the child. Vygotsky suggested it gave a better measure of a child's capacity than any test of current ability, such as an intelligence test.

Phases in cognitive development

Vygotsky (1934) reported the following study on the development of concepts in children. Children of different ages were presented with a number of wooden blocks of different sizes, shapes and colours. No two blocks were the same. The blocks had been categorised into four groups, and each group assigned a nonsense label. For example, tall, large blocks, irrespective of shape or colour, were labelled 'lag'. Each block was labelled on the bottom, and the blocks were mixed up. The child was shown the label on the bottom of one block and asked to pick out the other blocks in the same category. When they had made their first attempt, the experimenter showed the child which ones had different labels to the first block, and let the child have another go, and so on. Vygotsky called this the method of double stimulation, as the children had to categorise the blocks and work out what concept – eg size, shape or colour – the label stood for.

Vygotsky identified three main phases in the concept formation of children.

1 Syncretic phase Very young children showed *syncretic grouping*, basically gathering blocks at random into a disorganised heap. These children had no real sense of what a category was, nor did they seem to think that the label had any specific meaning.

2 Complex phase Pre-school and primary school age children thought in *complexes*, that is, they showed awareness of similarities and differences in the blocks, but they tended to group the blocks by association or chains. They knew the label referred to some feature of the blocks, but the meaning did not seem to be very stable in their minds. This can be seen from the following example of thinking in complexes. A child using the work 'quah' for a duck on a pond, then proceeded to use 'quah' for other types of liquid (milk, bath water, etc), and also for other types of bird, calling a coin with an eagle on it 'quah', and then using 'quah' for other round objects (Vygotsky, 1934).

3 Conceptual phase Finally, in adolescence, abstract concepts are mastered, and the child has no difficulty in solving the blocks puzzle and working out what the nonsense labels must mean.

Evaluation of Vygotsky

Vygotsky presented a strongly reasoned alternative to Piaget's theory of cognitive development. His views have been influential not only within psychology, but also in education – see Section 1.5.

Vygotsky saw cognitive development as a social process. It is not just helped or facilitated by social interaction, it is actually created and constituted by it. It involves learning the collective skills and knowledge – the shared culture – of members of society. And learning takes place in the context of social interaction – in collaboration with others. The child is pictured as an apprentice learning from those with more experience and greater knowledge (Rogoff, 1990). This contrasts with Piaget's view of the child exploring the world as an individual, striving to understand how things work like a little scientist.

Many psychologists believe that Piaget underestimated the importance of social interaction in cognitive development (Shotter, 1976; Bruner, 1990). Conversely, others argue that Vygotsky may have underestimated the role of maturation in cognitive development – young children may not be 'ready' to learn certain things, no matter how good the instruction.

However, things are not so one-sided as this. In some respects, Piaget and Vygotsky are not that far apart. Both see the child as active in their own development. Piaget accepted that social interaction had a role in cognitive development, and Vygotsky's phases of concept development are not that dissimilar to Piaget's stages. Some psychologists are hopeful that a synthesis of Piaget's maturational theory and Vygotsky's social theory will be possible (Slavin, 1987; Doise & Mugny, 1984).

Key terms

Scaffolding *A method of instruction which involves organising the child's learning into parts, and providing a framework for the development of skills.*

Zone of proximal development (ZPD) *The gap between what the child can do on their own, and what they can achieve with guidance.*

1.4 The information processing approach

As its name suggests, the *information processing approach* to cognitive development focuses on the way children process information. Cognitive development is seen as a growth in processing capabilities – for example, an increase in processing capacity and speed. This approach developed from the 1970s, partly as a reaction to Piaget and Vygotsky.

The information processing (IP) approach draws on research from cognitive psychology, particularly research into memory and problem-solving. For example, research shows that older children perform better on memory tests than younger children – they remember more items from lists of numbers, letters or words (Dempster, 1981). In terms of cognitive development, this suggests an increase in processing capacity as children grow older. Similarly, older children can complete a range of tasks more quickly than younger children (Kail, 1991). This suggests that processing speed increases with age.

From this perspective, cognitive development can be seen as an increase in the efficiency of the information processing system. A number of explanations have been suggested for this increase in efficiency. They include the following.

- The brain itself as a biological organ develops. Physiological changes in the brain account for improvements in information processing and an increase in processing capacity.

- Experience also accounts for this improvement. For example, younger children have less experience of numbers, letters and words. As a result, their performance on memory tests using these items will be poorer than that of older children.

- Children learn new and more effective problem-solving strategies as they grow older. For example, the capacity of working memory can be increased by 'chunking' – grouping items into larger units or chunks.

The computer analogy

Many researchers who take an IP approach see the human mind as similar, in many ways, to a computer. The brain itself is the 'hardware', and thinking processes are the 'software'. An understanding of cognitive development requires an analysis and explanation of changes in both hardware and software. Does the hardware change – for example, are there physical changes in the brain? Does the software change – for example, are there changes in thinking strategies?

Some researchers actually use computers in an attempt to simulate human information processing. They try to program computers to solve a problem or complete a task in the same way a human does. If the computer can do this, and can even predict the human response to a new task, errors and all, then the program may provide a model of how the human mind processes information or 'thinks'.

The development of memory

Research into the development of memory provides an example of the IP approach to cognitive development. Children's memory improves as they grow older. Three factors seem particularly important – 1) the development and use of memory strategies, 2) a growing awareness of cognitive abilities, 3) greater knowledge and experience.

Memory strategies There is evidence that the development and use of memory strategies increases with age.

- **Rehearsal** Repeating information to yourself, in order to remember it, is used more frequently as children grow older (Keeny et al., 1967).

- **Chunking** The same applies to 'chunking' – grouping information into meaningful chunks in order to aid recall. It is used more frequently as children grow older (Kail, 1990).

- **Elaboration** This refers to increasing the complexity of processing – for example, processing words in terms of distinctive images. For instance, remembering the words broomstick, moon and woman by putting them into a sentence such as: The woman flew over the moon on her broomstick. Research indicates that elaboration increases with frequency and effectiveness with age. Older children are more likely to use this strategy and more likely to produce memorable images (Buckhalt et al., 1976).

Metacognition This refers to an awareness of cognitive abilities. In terms of memory, it refers to an awareness of capacity and of strategies for encoding and retrieving information. As children grow older, they become increasingly aware of the availability of memory strategies, their usefulness and which are most effective for particular tasks (Kreutzer et al., 1975). The development of metacognition allows children to organise their thoughts and plan their activities.

Knowledge and experience With age, children learn more and experience more. New information can be linked with existing information which makes it easier to learn and retrieve. This is illustrated by the following experiment. Seven to nine-year-olds were divided into two groups, those who knew a lot about soccer and those who knew little. They were asked to learn two sets of drawings – one of items related to soccer, the other of unrelated items. Recall for both groups was the same for unrelated items, but the group interested in soccer recalled more of the soccer-related items (Scheider & Bjorklund, 1992). This indicates that existing knowledge can be an aid to learning and retrieving new knowledge.

Alternative answers

Part of the significance of the information processing approach can be seen from a comparison with Piaget. Piaget's stages represent qualitatively different ways of thinking – they are quantum leaps in cognitive development. Why can't young children perform certain tasks such as seriation tasks and transitive inference tasks? According to Piaget, because they haven't reached that stage of cognitive development – they have yet to make the quantum leap. Experimental evidence appears to support this view. It suggests that the ability to successfully complete many tasks is related to particular stages.

However, information processing theory provides an alternative explanation for such findings. In a typical transitive inference task children are shown two sticks – stick A and stick B. A is longer than B. These sticks are removed. They are then shown stick B (again) and stick C. B is longer than C. They are then asked which is longest, stick A or stick C? In terms of Piaget's view, a failure to give the correct answer reflects the fact that a child is unable to make the appropriate inferences. And this inability is due to the fact that the child has yet to reach Stage 3 – the concrete operational stage.

However, from an information processing perspective, the child may be quite capable of making inferences but may simply have *forgotten* the information needed to do so. In terms of the above example, the child may have forgotten that stick A is longer than stick B. As a result, it is not possible to say whether A is longer than C.

Some researchers have changed the procedure of cognitive inference experiments. They gave children the opportunity to learn the information needed to make inferences. For example, in one experiment, 7-year-olds were trained in memory skills. This improved their performance in transitive reasoning (Bryant & Trabasso, 1971). This suggests that memory is as important, if not more important, than reasoning skills. Similarly, children may be unable to solve seriation problems because their working memory can't hold the necessary information long enough to answer the question. Unwary psychologists then wrongly conclude the child does not understand seriation (Case, 1985).

Piaget argued that there are fundamental differences between the way children in different age groups think. The IP approach questions this view. Age differences in performance on a range of tasks may be due to differences in information processing. And this may be due to differences in knowledge and experience, particularly knowledge of thinking strategies, and an awareness of when to use them. Younger children can be trained to use strategies to improve memory. The difference is that older children know when to use them. And they use them spontaneously, whereas younger children do not.

Case's theory of mental space

Some theorists see the IP approach as essentially different from Piaget (eg, Best, 1993). Others see the approaches as complementary – they can be usefully combined. For example, Robbie Case (1985) has developed a neo-Piagetian approach which combines aspects of information processing theory and Piaget.

According to Case, cognitive development can be seen as the growth in the capacity and efficiency of the information processing system. The reasons for this include:

- Physical changes in the brain which increase the speed of neural transmission. This allows information to be processed more quickly and efficiently.
- An increase in *mental space*. This is the space available for processing information. As the brain develops, the capacity of working memory increases, which allows more data to be processed.
- With practice, problem-solving strategies become increasingly automatic. For example, various memory strategies become 'second nature'. This releases mental space or cognitive capacity for other tasks.
- In particular, it frees space for metacognition. Children become increasingly aware of their cognitive abilities. They consciously organise their thoughts, plan, and select strategies for particular tasks.

Like Piaget, Case sees children's cognitive development moving through stages. Each stage represents a significant advance in information processing which has been made possible by the availability of mental space. Case identifies four stages which are broadly similar to those of Piaget.

- Sensorimotor stage
- Representational stage
- Logical stage
- Formal operational stage

Evaluation

Many developmental psychologists were exasperated with what they saw as the vague and fuzzy concepts used by Piaget and Vygotsky to explain how children think. As Klahr (1982) put it: 'For 40 years now we have had assimilation and accommodation, the mysterious and shadowy forces of equilibration, the "Batman and Robin" of the developmental processes … Why is it that after all this time, we know no more about them than when they first sprang upon the scene?'

Supporters of the information processing approach were unhappy with explaining cognitive development in terms of the presence or absence of some cognitive principle like conservation or egocentrism. Instead, they hoped that the IP approach would reveal exactly what is going on in children's minds when they are tackling problems.

Ironically, one of the pioneers of the IP approach was Piaget himself. In the 1960s, he tried to construct detailed mathematical models of children's logical processing when they were solving problems. Piaget also suggested that children's ability to solve problems depended as much on their general level of cognitive development – especially their memory capacity – as on the presence of specific cognitive principles like seriation or conservation (Piaget & Inhelder, 1968).

The IP approach presents a challenge to Piagetian theory. It offers little support for cognitive principles like assimilation, accommodation, equilibration, conservation and so on. Instead, it looks at the effect of general cognitive capacity (eg, working memory) on the one hand, and the development of specific problem-solving strategies on the other. Some researchers (eg, Case, 1985) see the IP approach as consistent with Piaget's stages; others (eg, Best, 1993) do not.

The IP approach relies heavily on tightly controlled laboratory experiments and computer simulation. As such, it is more concerned with fact gathering than with generating theory. This is both a strength and a weakness. On the one hand, it is rigorously scientific in its methods and produces hard quantitative data. On the other hand, its ecological validity is suspect. Can the results of laboratory experiments be generalised to everyday situations? Do the findings of artificial tasks, such as learning and recalling word lists, reflect children's thinking in everyday life?

The IP approach may pay too little attention to the major qualitative changes in children's thinking that interested Piaget. It does deal with broad issues such as the development of metacognition and increasingly sophisticated cognitive strategies. However, it tends to describe and measure these processes rather than explain them.

The IP approach takes the study of cognitive development in the opposite direction to Vygotsky. Social and cultural factors play little part. There is the danger that it sees the child as 'a cold, calculating chunk of hardware' (Dodge, 1991). It omits emotion, social relationships and all the other things that make a child human rather than a machine. Attempts have been made to bridge the gap between Vygotsky and the IP approach, with,

for example, the idea of 'socio-computationalism' (Frawley, 1998). But these attempts tend to reduce social influence to another kind of 'information'.

Information processing research has been criticised for reducing human cognition to computer models. Critics see this as a sterile approach since it leaves out so much that is human (Shaw & Bransford, 1977). Moreover, computer simulations do not guarantee that human thinking and computer information processing really are that similar. There is a danger that simulations may be telling us more about computers than children's minds.

Despite these criticisms, information processing is clearly an important part of cognition. The IP approach adds to our understanding of children's cognitive development, it questions some of the assumptions made by other approaches, and provides answers to some of the questions they raise (Bee, 2000).

Key terms

Simulation *An attempt to reproduce something in another form. In this case, a computer program which seeks to model human information processing.*

Metacognition *An awareness of cognitive abilities. Knowledge about thinking and problem-solving strategies.*

Mental space *Cognitive capacity.*

Activity 4   Problem-solving strategies

Item A   The orange juice problem

In this experiment, children were shown two sets of glasses. In each set, at least one glass contained water and one contained orange juice. The children were shown two empty jugs. They were told Set A would be poured into one

Set A

Set B

■ Orange Juice
□ Water

jug and Set B into the other jug. They were then asked which jug would taste more strongly of orange – 'more orangey'. The responses from four age groups are summarised in Item B, along with an analysis of their thinking strategies.

Item B   Experimental results

3 to 4-year-olds As long as there was at least one glass of orange in each set, this age group said both jugs tasted 'more orangey'. This strategy required very little information to be held in working memory – just the colour of the glasses in each set.

5 to 6-year-olds This group said the set with more glasses of orange would taste more orangey. This strategy requires more processing capacity as the children have to count the glasses of orange in each set. They then have to retain these numbers in working memory in order to compare them.

7 to 8-year-olds This group compared the number of glasses of water and orange in each set. If one set contained more

glasses of orange than glasses of water, then it was seen as more orangey. However, if both or neither sets had more glasses of orange, the children just guessed. Compared to the previous group, this strategy required more information to be held in working memory.

9 to 10-year-olds This group used a strategy which always provided the correct answer. They subtracted the number of glasses with water from the number of glasses with orange and chose the set with the largest remainder. This was the most complex strategy and required more processing capacity then the strategies adopted by the younger age groups.

Adapted from Noelting, 1980 and Case, 1985

1.5 Educational applications

This section looks at the application of theories of cognitive development to education. Although not designed for this purpose, each of the three theories outlined in previous sections has been developed as an approach to education.

Although they differ in important ways, they have certain things in common. They all reject the view that the child is a passive recipient of learning and that the purpose of education is to fill empty heads with appropriate knowledge. They all stress that the child is an active participant in their own education.

Piaget's approach

In Piaget's view, conceptual understanding has to be achieved by the child. It cannot be explicitly taught. Education should therefore be *child centred* – it should foster the child's mental development, not simply impose 'knowledge'.

Piaget (1933) considered child-centred education to be good for the child, and also good for society. During the 1930s, fascist and communist regimes in Europe were indoctrinating their school children, along with the rest of their populations, and telling them what to think. Piaget wanted children to learn how to think for themselves. As such, Piaget's view of education can be seen as liberal and individualist.

Piaget thought there were limits to teaching. Education should be geared to the child's stage of cognitive development – the natural rate of maturation should be respected and not artificially speeded up (Gardner, 1976). Because he left no direct 'theory of instruction' (Ginsberg, 1981), Piaget has been open to misinterpretation. For example, it is widely believed that Piaget thought children simply mature in their own time, and grow and learn at their own pace, with next to no instruction from teachers. Consistent with this view, Leach (1977), told teachers: 'The child is a scientist and an inventor: your job is merely to provide the laboratories, the facilities and a research assistant – you – when she needs one'.

In fact Piaget saw a much more active role for the teacher as a facilitator of learning. Brainerd (1983) identifies three main implications of Piaget's theory for education. First, the idea of *readiness*. Because cognitive development happens in a series of stages, it follows that the child will be ready to learn different things at different times. There is no point trying to teach children formal operational skills at the pre-operational stage. The teacher should therefore identify what stage of development the child has reached, then provide challenges and problems appropriate to that stage.

Second, teaching methods should encourage children to think, not just absorb knowledge. The teacher should create an appropriate environment for the child to learn in, and set tasks that create disequilibrium and cognitive conflict. This encourages the child to develop new schemas and operations as they struggle to solve problems (Inhelder et al., 1974). However, this does not mean that the child is simply left to get on with it – the teacher has an important role in guiding, advising and answering questions as the child works through the set tasks (McNally, 1974).

Third, the curriculum should be designed to encourage the development of the child's reasoning abilities. Pre-operational children need materials and opportunities to explore spatial properties, conservation, sorting, and so on. Concrete operational children need maths and science practical work, leading on to more theoretical science to foster conceptual thinking and lead them into formal operations.

Piaget (1932) also saw an important role for interaction with peers – children of the same age – to help overcome egocentrism through cooperative problem-solving, and to create cognitive conflict through discussion and argument. Later Piagetians put even more emphasis on this (Doise & Mugny, 1984).

Child-centred education In the 1960s, the Plowden Committee was set up to look at ways of improving primary education. The Plowden Report, published in 1967, incorporated a number of Piaget's ideas in its recommendations. It encouraged child-centred education, recognised that children developed at different rates, and argued that each child required individual attention. Where possible, children should discover knowledge for themselves. Teachers should provide opportunities for *discovery learning* which should be appropriate for each stage of development. The Plowden Report strongly influenced teacher training and classroom practice, particularly in primary schools.

Interest in Piaget's work helped foster moves towards 'progressive education' in the 1960s, with its enthusiasm for 'discovery learning'. Unfortunately, in some cases, discovery learning meant leaving the children to their own devices, with the result that precious little learning or discovering took place. The child-centred dream began to turn sour in 1976 when the 'progressive' William Tyndale primary school was exposed as more of a bedlam than a school.

There were other problems emerging. Some of these were practical, for example, how to be child-centred with a class of 30 children, and how to match child-centred education to the demands of national assessments and exams.

Other problems were ethical and even political. For example, did child-centred education favour middle-class children, who may be 'ready' earlier and hence get more attention? Did it draw attention away from the role of the school in children's education (Rutter et al., 1979), and 'blame' the child or their home background for any lack of progress? Did the Piagetian approach foster individualism and competitiveness in children, thus smuggling capitalist values into education?

Was there something dishonest about an approach to education that claimed the child was 'self-teaching' and autonomous, yet retained the subtle power to decide if they were developing 'properly' or not? Did the Piagetian approach impose a rigid set of expectations about what constituted proper cognitive development, thus denying any value in cultural or subcultural diversity? The list goes on. See Burman (1994) for further discussion. By the 1980s, child-centred education was coming under pressure from a Conservative government that wanted a return to more traditional teacher-led and teacher-centred forms of education.

Vygotsky's approach

Many educationalists looked for a middle way between child-centred education and the traditional teacher-led approach. They found Vygotsky's approach promising. The Vygotskyite approach retains the focus on the child's developing mind, but also sees an important role for instruction by adults or more knowledgeable peers.

Scaffolding The instructor 'scaffolds' the child's thinking within the zone of proximal development, using various strategies. These range from general encouragement to specific instruction and demonstration depending on how difficult the task is and how well the child is coping (Wood et al., 1978). According to Wertsch et al. (1980), scaffolding is something adults spontaneously do when communicating with children. They guide the child to look at important features of the task and work with them until they are ready to do it alone.

In a classroom setting, Hedegaard (1996) claimed that a teacher can provide scaffolding for the thinking of a whole class by guiding them through a series of activities – from initial exploration, observation and researching into a new topic, through symbolisation of their findings as charts, drawings or models, to final formulation of principles and concepts arising from their study.

Group work The Vygotskyite approach also sees a central role for cooperative group work with other children (Cowie et al., 1994). Evidence from various studies suggests that:

- Children's thinking and language skills are enhanced by small-group work (Bennett & Dunne, 1992).
- Children develop skills working in pairs that they continue to use when working alone (Blaye et al., 1991).
- Tutoring of a younger child by an older child benefits both children (Barron & Foot, 1991).

If Piaget's approach was liberal and individualistic, Vygotsky's approach can be seen as more socialist, as children work together for a common good (Sutherland, 1992).

Evaluation However, Vygotsky's approach has its problems too. Scaffolding can lead to the instructor being too directive, resulting in loss of motivation in the child (Deci et al., 1993). The child may exploit the situation with 'strategic incompetence' until the instructor completes the task for them (Goodnow, 1990). Group work with other children can present opportunities to mess about (Foot & Barron, 1990), and enables some children to freeload while others gain status and prestige from dominating proceedings (Salomon & Globerson, 1989).

The information processing approach

In recent years the IP approach has been gaining influence. Like the Piagetians, the IP approach sees the child as an individual problem solver, but, like the Vygotskyites, the IP approach acknowledges an important role for instruction.

Key objectives of the IP approach to education include the following.

- First, to help children develop strategies for using limited-capacity memory most effectively – for example, rehearsal, chunking and elaboration. Evidence suggests that children can develop these strategies faster through being taught.
- Second, to help children build up a knowledge base as an aid to processing new information. Research indicates that the linking of new information with existing information makes it easier to learn and recall.
- Third, to help children develop metacognition, that is, an understanding of how their minds work to process information. This helps them to develop problem-solving strategies and to select appropriate strategies for particular tasks.

Teachers need to analyse the tasks they set and foster the development of relevant strategies to enable the children to deal with those tasks. They must avoid overloading the children's cognitive capacities. They must be able to analyse the mistakes children make in order to identify inappropriate rules of thinking in order to correct them.

The IP approach ties in neatly with prevailing attitudes to education in Britain and the USA, where the computer – an electronic information processor – plays an increasingly central role as a teaching aid. IP is as individualistic as the Piagetian approach, and pays little attention to cultural or subcultural diversity. Unlike Piaget, however, it focuses on information and performance skills rather than conceptual understandings.

Some supporters of the IP approach are committed to accelerating the child's cognitive development, an idea which has caught on in a big way in recent years. To this end, children are increasingly assessed and examined. In the UK, children's progress is monitored by SATs tests from the age of 7, while in some American schools 'recess' (playtime) has been abolished as a waste of valuable study time. For some, the drive to accelerate cognitive development places too much pressure on children. This may be reflected in the increasing number being diagnosed with attention-deficit/hyperactivity disorder and treated with drugs like Ritalin – an estimated 2 million children in the USA (Leutwyler, 1996).

Key terms

Child-centred *An educational approach focusing on developing the child's cognitive skills through discovery learning rather than instruction.*

Discovery learning *A process by which children learn by discovering for themselves.*

Readiness *The idea that children are 'ready' to learn certain skills at particular stages of cognitive development.*

Summary

1 Piaget sees the child as an active participant in their cognitive development. The child is motivated by functional invariants – organisation, adaptation and equilibration.

2 The child's knowledge of the world is organised into schemas. Adaptation takes two forms – assimilation and accommodation. These are the processes by which a child learns. The whole system is kept in balance by equilibration.

3 In Piaget's theory, the child matures through four stages of cognitive development.

- In the sensorimotor stage (0-2 years), the child knows the world through action and sensation.

- In the pre-operational stage (2-7 years), the child knows the world through perception and visual appearance.

- In the concrete operational stage (7-11 years), the child understands the world through practical reasoning.

- In the formal operational stage (11 and over), the child understands the world through abstract reasoning and scientific logic.

4 Later research suggests that Piaget underestimated the abilities of children in the first three stages, but overestimated the abilities of adolescents in the formal operational stage.

5 Critics claim that Piaget's experiments were often badly designed. For example, instructions were sometimes unclear and questions confusing.

6 A major criticism of Piaget is that he tends to see the child as an isolated problem solver and does not pay enough attention to the role of social interaction.

7 Vygotsky's theory takes a more social approach. It states that social interaction and instruction play a crucial role in cognitive development. Instruction takes the form of scaffolding and works best within the child's zone of proximal development.

8 The information processing approach sees cognitive development as a growth in processing capabilities – for example, an increase in processing capacity and speed.

9 Processing efficiency increases with physiological changes in the brain, a growth in knowledge and experience, the development of new and more effective problem-solving strategies, and an increasing awareness of cognitive abilities (metacognition).

10 Each theory of cognitive development has implications for education.

- Piaget's work has provided the basis for child-centred education and discovery learning.

- Vygotsky's approach supports a more active role for 1) instruction through scaffolding, and 2) cooperative peer group work.

- The information processing approach aims to develop strategies for increasing processing capacity, speed and efficiency, with the aim of improving learning and problem-solving.

Activity 5   Education and cognitive development

Item A   Approaches to learning

'Each time one prematurely teaches a child something he could have discovered himself, that child is kept from inventing it and consequently from understanding it completely.' (Piaget, 1983)

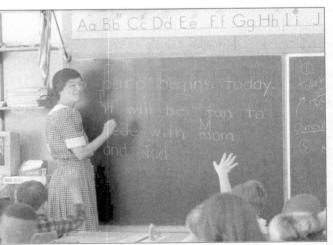

Item B — Teaching primary maths

There is a general pattern of development in the growth of children's thinking. These stages are well-marked but the ages differ among children. An awareness of this growth is important to teachers of mathematics. Teachers must be able to recognise at any time the kind of thinking that a child's work reveals. Our knowledge of the stages through which children's thinking passes should convince us of the necessity of allowing them ample opportunities for experimenting and constructing with a wide range of objects and materials, for making their own judgements, for expressing their findings in their own ways, and for thinking through for themselves the way to new discoveries and the solution to problems.

Adapted from Williams & Shuard, 1970

Questions

1   Judging from the pictures in Item A, which type of classroom would Piaget prefer? Give reasons for your answer.

2   Identify the influence of Piaget in Item B.

3   Identify the influence of Vygotsky in Item C.

Item C — Tutoring in problem solving

The problem was to build a pyramid with 6 levels out of 21 wooden blocks. Each level consisted of 4 interlocking blocks, with a solid block at the top. The tutor, an expert in this task, worked with 3, 4 and 5-year-old children. She directed the children when they needed help. There were three kinds of direction.

1   **Direct intervention** Showing the children how to do something, for example, actually joining two blocks.
2   **Verbal corrections** Telling the children when they did something wrong.
3   **Verbal directions** Reminding the child of the task requirements. For example, 'Can you make more blocks like this one?'

The table shows the results of this study. It indicates that the need for scaffolding reduces as the child grows older.

Type of intervention	Age 3	Age 4	Age 5
Direct intervention	12.0	6.0	3.0
Verbal corrections	3.0	5.0	4.5
Verbal directions	5.0	8.0	3.0
Total help received	20.0	19.0	10.5

Adapted from Wood et al., 1976

Unit 2   Development of measured intelligence

KEY ISSUES

1   **What are the main factors affecting performance on intelligence tests?**

2   **What are the main explanations for differences in IQ scores between so-called 'racial' groups?**

This unit looks at the development of measured intelligence. Measured intelligence refers to people's performance on intelligence tests. Intelligence tests are designed to discriminate between people, so that different people achieve different scores. In many Western societies, an individual's intelligence score is seen as highly significant – it may, for example, affect their educational and employment opportunities.

This unit looks at factors that may influence performance on intelligence tests. There are three main possible factors.

- First, genetic or inherited capacities or abilities.
- Second, environmental experience, such as education or diet.
- Third, there may be features of the tests themselves that produce certain results – they may be biased against certain groups of people.

Many psychologists believe that all three factors have some effect.

A particularly controversial aspect of intelligence testing is the claim that some *groups* of people are 'more intelligent' than others. This claim is based on differences in the average IQ scores of different class, ethnic and gender groups. This unit examines the evidence for so-called 'racial' differences in intelligence.

2.1   The background to intelligence testing

Intelligence testing was always an area of dispute and controversy. Right from the start it was a political issue. The founder of intelligence testing, Sir Francis Galton (1822-1911), was quite open that in measuring intelligence he wanted to confirm a number of his own beliefs.

- First, to show that intelligence was innate, and inherited through the male line.
- Second, to show that high intelligence guaranteed success in life. Galton fully expected to find that white British upper-class men were the most intelligent people in the world!
- Third, to confirm his political conviction that selective breeding of the human species was desirable.

Selective breeding would ensure that 'superior' intelligent stock was not contaminated by interbreeding with less intelligent groups. It would also restrict the reproduction of 'inferior' groups, such as the lower classes, non-whites, criminals, the mentally and physically unhealthy, and so on. Galton launched a political movement to promote selective breeding and sterilisation. He called this movement *eugenics*.

Galton's attempts in the 1880s to measure intelligence – by testing perception and reaction times – were unsuccessful. Although he never found the evidence to support his beliefs, Galton had a huge effect. To this day many people see intelligence as the most important measure of an individual, and as the key to success in life. The idea that it is innate remains widespread.

The eugenics movement flourished in northern Europe and the USA. Thousands were sterilised as 'unfit' right up until the 1930s and 40s. The Nazis took eugenics to its extreme and gassed mental patients, gays, Jews, Gypsies and others they considered 'undesirable'. Since then, eugenics has been markedly less popular, but still has some supporters.

The first successful intelligence test was designed by the French psychologist Alfred Binet (1857-1911). He believed that intelligence can only be measured by setting questions based on reasoning. Binet's first intelligence test (co-designed by Theodore Simon) was published in 1905.

Binet completely rejected the idea that intelligence is innate. He believed that intelligence is the result of learning and experience. To Binet, it was obvious that a child's intelligence increases over time – the same child is clearly more intelligent at 10 than they were at 3. His purpose in measuring intelligence was to identify school children who were lagging behind and needed extra help to catch up. Binet had no time for the idea that there were racial, class or gender differences in intelligence. He bitterly opposed eugenics.

The argument over how far intelligence is innate or due to environmental factors continues to this day.

2.2 Defining and measuring intelligence

Defining intelligence Binet (1905) defined intelligence as the ability 'to judge well, to comprehend well, to reason well'. Most psychologists would more or less agree. While such general definitions are widely acceptable, they are also rather vague. This creates difficulties when psychologists are trying to measure intelligence.

The measurement of intelligence

Binet's approach to measuring intelligence was to ask questions that required judgement, comprehension and reasoning to answer them. Most subsequent intelligence tests have taken the same approach. One of the most widely used tests in the 20th century – the Stanford-Binet test – was devised by Lewis Terman in 1916 and revised several times since. The Stanford-Binet test looks at four areas of intelligence – verbal reasoning, abstract and visual reasoning, quantitative (arithmetical) reasoning and short-term memory. Weschler's Adult Intelligence Scale (WAIS), first published in 1939, and Weschler's Intelligence Scale for Children (WISC) have also been widely used. For infants, the Bayley Scales of Infant Development, first published in 1969, tests sensory and motor skills.

A different approach to testing is to use neurological measures like brain activity and speed of performance. This has its supporters (eg, Jensen, 1998), but others are unconvinced by the reliability of these measures (Mackintosh, 2000).

Reliability and validity Reliability (consistency) appears to be good with most intelligence tests. Your score on a test this year is likely to be close to the score you'd get on a similar test next year. However, there are examples of people boosting their scores substantially through practice. Validity – whether the test is measuring what it sets out to measure – is more of a problem. Some argue that intelligence tests are mostly tests of short-term memory (Baddeley, 1976), others that intelligence tests merely measure your level of education.

IQ The most popular measure of intelligence is *intelligence quotient* or IQ. This was devised by the German psychologist Wilhelm Stern in 1911, and developed by the American psychologist Lewis Terman in 1916. To obtain a measure of IQ, the child's actual or chronological age (CA) is noted, and their mental age (MA) is measured. Mental age is given by comparing the child's performance on an intelligence test to the average performance of children of different ages. The child's mental age is then divided by their chronological age, and the result multiplied by 100.

$$IQ = \frac{MA}{CA} \times 100$$

So, if Anne is 5 years old (CA = 5), and her test performance is that of an average 5-year-old (MA = 5), then dividing MA by CA and multiplying by 100 gives her IQ:

$$\frac{5}{5} \times 100 = 100$$

Anne's IQ is exactly average for her age.

However, if Jane performs like an average 6-year-old when she is 5, then her CA = 5 and her MA = 6. This gives:

$$\frac{6}{5} \times 100 = 120$$

Jane's IQ is well above average.

For adults, IQ is not worked out in terms of mental ages, but by comparison with the distribution of intelligence scores among the adult population. Studies based on large and varied samples indicate that intelligence is normally distributed across the adult population. This is illustrated in Figure 11. The mean score is set at 100. An individual's IQ is where they fall on the normal distribution curve. An IQ of 90 to 110 is judged to be normal.

Figure 11 The distribution of IQ

0	100	200

Types of intelligence Psychologists have been divided over whether a person's abilities are underpinned by a level of general intelligence (g), or whether different skills draw on different specific intelligences (s). The idea of g suggests that some people are just more intelligent than others. The idea of s suggests that we all have our aptitudes and weaknesses.

An influential theory developed by Howard Gardner (1993) suggests seven types of intelligence: linguistic, logical-mathematical, spatial (including artistic and finding your way around), musical, body-kinaesthetic (including grace, sport and dexterity), inter-personal (social awareness) and intra-personal (understanding of yourself). Gardner has broadened the definition of intelligence to include more 'real-life' competences, not just the ability to do pen-and-paper tests. He found, for example, that people may do badly on tests of arithmetical ability, yet successfully complete complex calculations at the race track or in the supermarket. In Gardner's view, traditional IQ tests are very limited and tell us little about a person's mental capabilities.

Key term

Eugenics A political movement dedicated to 'improving' the human species by selective breeding, sterilisation of the 'unfit', and, as applied by the Nazis, by extermination.

2.3 The influence of genes

Most psychologists take the view that both genes and environment play some role in the development of measured intelligence. Biological inheritance provides the genotype, the individual genetic blueprint. But the way the individual actually turns out, the phenotype, is the product of interactions between genes and the environment.

Psychologists have attempted to discover how much of our intelligence is due to genetic inheritance. The main research method is the kinship study, which looks at similarities in intelligence between genetically related individuals. There are three types of kinship study – family studies, twin studies and adoption studies.

Family studies The very first kinship study was a family study conducted by Galton in 1869. Entitled *Hereditary genius*, it claimed to show that distinguished or eminent men are likely to be the sons of eminent fathers. This he explained as the result of inheritance of superior intelligence. It did not seem to cross Galton's mind that eminent Victorian gentlemen purchased exclusive educations for their sons – private school and Oxbridge, with all the associated contacts and opportunities – and that this might had something to do with their success.

This example illustrates the problem with family studies in general. Family members tend to share home environments as well as genes, so that family similarities in anything – intelligence, mental health, Catholicism, or support for Arsenal – are likely to owe more to the family environment than to genetic inheritance.

Twin studies A more sophisticated type of kinship study is the twin study. Identical (*monozygotic* or *MZ*) twins who share almost 100% of their genetic material are compared to fraternal (*dizygotic* or *DZ*) twins who share around 50% of their genetic material. If genetics played an important role in intelligence, we would expect the similarity (or *concordance*) within pairs of MZ twins to be higher than the concordance within pairs of DZ twins. If the concordance within pairs of twins remained high even if they were raised apart and did not share an environment, then this could be taken as strong evidence that intelligence was largely inherited.

Concordance is measured correlationally. Correlation coefficients for concordance vary from 0 (no correlation) to 1 (perfect correlation).

In the 1950s and 60s, the British psychologist Cyril Burt published a series of studies in which he calculated the concordance for MZ twins raised together to be 0.944, and for MZ twins raised apart to be 0.771. His findings were supported by a study by Shields (1962) showing the concordance for MZ twins raised apart to be 0.77. These consistently high correlations provided powerful evidence that intelligence was largely inherited. Burt estimated the 'heritability' of intelligence to be 80%, a figure adopted by Arthur Jensen (1969) and Hans Eysenck (1973).

However, there were problems with these studies. Evidence came to light that Burt had fixed his data to produce the high correlation he wanted (Kamin, 1974; Hearnshaw, 1979). Leon Kamin (1974) found that Shields omitted certain twin pairs from the study if their IQs were not similar. In addition, many of Shields's MZ twins were not really raised apart – they were raised in different branches of the same family, they maintained close contact with each other, and even went to school together. For the ten pairs of MZ twins in Shields' study who really were raised apart, the concordance was 0.47, a much lower figure.

In 1981, Thomas Bouchard and Matthew McGue published a review of 111 studies from around the world (excluding Burt's studies, but including Shields'). Some of the average concordances in their review were as follows:

MZ twins raised together	0.86
MZ twins raised apart	0.72
DZ twins raised together	0.60
Siblings raised together	0.47
Parent/child living together	0.42
Foster parent/child	0.31
Siblings raised apart	0.24
Parent/child separated	0.22
Cousins	0.15

Bouchard and McGue emphasise that these are average correlations, and that results from different studies sometimes vary quite widely. In part, this could be due to different researchers using different methods and different tests of intelligence. As a result, these figures should be treated cautiously. Nevertheless, Bouchard and McGue conclude that their review suggests that a significant proportion of intelligence is genetically inherited.

This conclusion is open to question. Concordance studies are based on certain assumptions which may not be valid. They assume, for example, that twins raised in the same environment have the same experiences. Hence if MZ twins raised together have a concordance of 0.86, while DZ twins raised together have a concordance of 0.60, the difference between the concordances must be due to genetic rather than environmental factors. In fact, this may not be so. Kamin (1981) suspects that pairs of MZ twins do have very similar environmental experiences, often being dressed alike and treated alike. But this is not true for pairs of DZ twins who often differ in appearance, personality and interests, and have different relationships with other family members. Sharing an environment does not mean having the same environmental experiences (Dunn & Plomin, 1990).

Studies of MZ twins raised apart appear to avoid this problem. Since they experience different environments, similarities between them are probably due to genetic factors. However, there are very few such studies. Bouchard and McGue's review covered only 65 pairs of MZ twins raised apart, from a mere three studies. This raises problems. For a start, it is dangerous to generalise from such a small sample. In addition, the studies themselves are open to question. One was the Shields (1962) study already referred to and another was Juel-Nielson (1965) which suffered similar defects. The third, Newman et al. (1937), had no means of genetic testing and could not be sure that the sample really were MZ twins. Moreover, MZ twins, even if raised apart, have already shared the important prenatal environment of the mother's womb, and similarities may owe as much to that as to shared genes (Howe, 1997).

Bouchard continues his work with the Minnesota Twin Study (1995). He has found remarkable similarities in MZ twins raised apart, including marrying people of the same name and supporting the same sports team. However, his sample consists of volunteers, many of whom have been reunited before the study, and who may have volunteered because they were intrigued by their similarities and liked publicity (Horgan, 1993). They may not be typical of separated MZ twins.

Leaving aside the many methodological problems, twin studies indicate that a significant proportion of intelligence is genetically inherited. However, in view of these problems, the evidence is suggestive rather than conclusive.

Adoption studies The third type of kinship study looks at the relationship between an adopted child's IQ and their biological parents on the one hand, and their adoptive parents on the other. Similarity of IQ with biological parents suggests a genetic influence, similarity with adoptive parents suggests an environmental influence.

The evidence is not clearcut. For example, the Texas Adoption Project found a correlation of 0.28 between the IQs of 469 adopted children and their biological mothers, and of 0.15 with their adoptive mothers (Horn, 1983). Although this suggests a genetic influence, it also suggests that this influence is fairly small. The results leave most of the children's IQ scores unexplained.

A longitudinal study of 245 children adopted before the age of one found a correlation between the child and both sets of parents – biological and adoptive. Common sense suggests that as the child grew older, they would become more like their adoptive parents. In terms of IQ, the opposite happened – by adolescence, there was no correlation with the adoptive parent. However, the correlation with the biological parent remained. In fact, there was no difference between the adopted children and a control group who remained with their biological parents. By adolescence, both groups had the same IQ correlation with their biological parents (Plomin et al., 1997). This study suggests that

genes have a strong influence on IQ.

However, other studies suggest a strong environmental influence. This is particularly apparent when there is a wide social class difference between the biological and adoptive parents. For example, Scarr and Kidd (1983) found that poor children adopted into middle-class homes showed IQ scores 10 to 15 points above those of their biological mothers. Some studies report as much as 20 points difference between adopted children and their biological parents (Howe, 1998).

Adoption studies are not easy to interpret. First, neither adoptive families nor adopted children are typical – they are not representative of the general population. Second, *selective placement* often takes place – children are adopted into families similar to their biological family in terms of social class, ethnicity, and so on. Because of this it is difficult to untangle the influence of biology and environment. For example, if children have similar IQs to their biological parents, is this due to similar genes or a similar environment in their adoptive family? Despite these problems, the available evidence suggests that the IQs of adopted children are more like those of their biological parents then their adoptive parents (Bee, 2000).

Molecular genetics

A new and different approach to investigating genetic effects on intelligence is through molecular genetics – research into genes themselves. One study analysed DNA samples from two groups – 'superbright' students (average IQ 136) and 'ordinary' students (average IQ 103). Thirty-three per cent of the 'superbright' group had a particular variant of the gene IGF2R on chromosome 6, compared to only 17% of the 'ordinary' group. The researchers suggested that the presence of this gene accounts for around 2% of the variation in IQ (Chorney et al., 1998).

Molecular genetics is still in its infancy. It is possible that the above study has identified a gene for intelligence. However, the correlation is not strong. Only 33% of the superbrights had the special variant – what about the other 67%? Where did their high IQ come from?

There are probably many genes influencing intelligence. In addition, these genes may only have their effect in particular

Key terms

Genotype *The genetic makeup of an individual.*

Phenotype *The characteristics of an individual which result from the interaction between their genotype and their environment.*

Monozygotic (MZ) twins *Twins who develop from one fertilised egg (zygote) and share nearly 100% of their genetic material. Often called 'identical' twins, although they do not always look similar.*

Dizygotic (DZ) twins *Twins who develop from two eggs fertilised simultaneously in the mother's womb. Sometimes called fraternal twins.*

Concordance *The degree of similarity between the members of a pair of twins.*

Selective placement *The placing of children into adoptive families that resemble their biological families.*

combinations. It may take a long time to sort out all the possible permutations.

2.4 Environmental influences on IQ

The previous section focused on genetic influences on measured intelligence. In doing so, it also provided examples of environmental influence. For example, some adoption studies indicate a strong environmental influence – especially where there are wide social class differences between the biological and adoptive parents.

Environmental influences refer to anything other than genes which affect a person's IQ. They may include a child's experience in the womb, their diet, their relationships with parents and siblings, the social class and ethnicity of their parents, the area in which they live, and a variety of other factors.

Social class

The class system is the major form of social inequality in Western industrial societies. There are various measures of social class, the most common being occupational status and income. Study after study has shown that, in general, the higher the parents' class position, the higher the IQ of their children. In fact, the best predictors of a child's IQ at age 4 are the family's class position and the level of the mother's education (Broman et al., 1975).

This can be seen from Figure 12 which shows the results for 11,800 white American children tested at aged 4. Both class position of the family and the level of education of the mother appear to make a significant difference to the child's IQ. Figure 12 shows that social class makes a difference to the child's IQ whatever the length of the mother's education. It also shows that the mother's education makes a difference whatever the social class. For example, in the lowest social class, the mean IQ for children whose mothers had 0-8 years of education was under 95, for those whose mothers had 12 years of education, their mean IQ was 100.

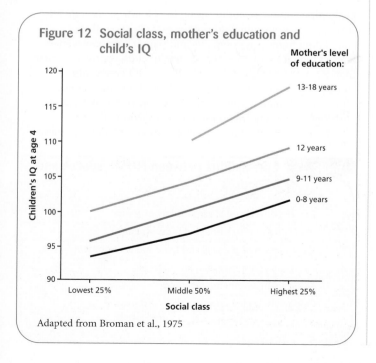

Figure 12 Social class, mother's education and child's IQ

Mother's level of education:

13-18 years
12 years
9-11 years
0-8 years

Children's IQ at age 4

Lowest 25%   Middle 50%   Highest 25%

Social class

Adapted from Broman et al., 1975

Social class differences are not found on infant IQ tests. They appear around 2 to 3 years of age and then steadily widen. This suggests that the advantages of being born at the top of the class system and the disadvantages of being born at the bottom are cumulative (Duncan, 1993).

Many of the factors specifically linked to IQ level are also linked to social class. For example, poor health during pregnancy, low birth weight, frequent childhood illness, poor nutrition and substandard housing are linked to low IQ and low social class position. The same applies to the 'risk factors' identified by the following study – they are more likely to be found in the lower levels of the class system.

Risk factors

The Rochester Longitudinal Study examined 152 children and their social environments. Conducted in New York City, the sample included families from all social classes and a number of ethnic groups. The researchers attempted to identify a number of *risk factors* which would result in low IQs. They tried to separate (isolate) these risk factors from other social factors such as class and ethnicity and genetic influences. The researchers claimed that the study showed that risk factors lowered IQs in *all* social classes and ethnic groups. And they also lowered IQs no matter what the genetic influences on the child's IQ (Sameroff et al., 1993).

The following risk factors were identified.

- **Minority group status** Child belongs to an ethnic minority group (African American or Puerto Rican).
- **Occupation** Head of household has low occupational status – eg, unemployed or low-skill job.
- **Maternal education** Mother did not complete high school.
- **Family size** Families with four or more children living at home.
- **Absence of father** Father not living in the family home.
- **Stressful life events** Family has 20 or more stressful life events before the child is 4 – eg, loss of job, serious physical illness, death in family.
- **Parents' views on child development** Parents have rigid attitudes about child's development.
- **Maternal anxiety** Mother suffers from a high level of anxiety.
- **Maternal mental health** Mother has a history of mental disorder.
- **Interaction** Mother has little positive interaction with child.

The children's IQ was measured at 4 years and 13 years of age. At 4 years of age, all 10 risk factors were significantly related to low IQs. At 13 years of age, 7 risk factors were related to low IQs – stressful life events, maternal anxiety and family interaction no longer appeared to affect IQ. At age 13, the average IQ of children with no risk factors was 115. The average IQ for children with 7 to 9 risk factors was 85 (see Figure 13).

The previous section showed that IQ is related to class position – in general, the lower the class position of the parents, the lower the child's IQ. Risk factors are also related to social class – the lower the parents' social class, the more risk factors are present. Does this mean that it is social class rather than risk factors that affects IQ? The researchers examined this question and found that risk factors lowered IQ independently of social class. Even in higher social classes, the more risk factors present, the more IQ was lowered.

An earlier section looked at the influence of genes on IQ.

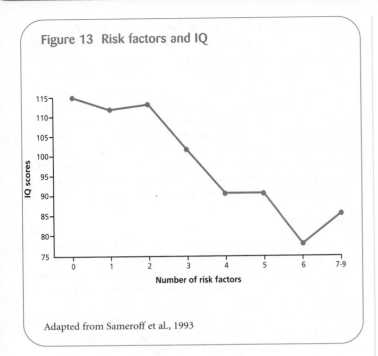

Figure 13 Risk factors and IQ

Adapted from Sameroff et al., 1993

Could it be genes rather than risk factors that lead to low IQ scores? In other words, could mothers with genes for low IQs pass these genes on to their children and *also produce* risk-filled environments? If so, could it be the genes rather than the environment which lead to low IQs? The researchers examined this question. They found that risk factors lowered IQ independently of the mother's IQ. In other words, risk factors had a major effect regardless of the mother's IQ.

The researchers conclude that risk factors explain 'one-third to one-half of IQ variance at 4 and 13 years' (Sameroff et al., 1993). If they are correct, this indicates that environmental factors have a powerful infuence on IQ.

Evaluation This is an important study. The sample size of 152 is relatively large. The sample is also varied, for example it includes members of all social classes. However, the sample is not representative. Around half the families included mothers with emotional problems. In addition, the risk factors are over-represented compared with the general population. Despite this, the researchers have identified a number of risk factors which correlate with low IQ. They have managed to isolate and measure the effects of certain risk factors. In particular, they have indicated that risk factors have a major effect whatever the IQ of the mother and the social class of the parents.

The link between risk factors and IQ is correlational. This means that risk factors do not necessarily cause low IQ. However, by isolating factors such as social class and mother's IQ, the researchers have strengthened the relationship between risk factors and IQ. This indicates a greater likelihood of risk factors affecting IQ.

Home environment and IQ

The previous study examined environmental factors which depress IQ. A number of studies have examined factors which appear to raise IQ. Several have used the Home Observation for Measurement of the Environment – the HOME scale. This scale attempts to measure the quality of stimulation in infants' home background and relate it to their IQ scores. Researchers visit the

family home, interview the mother and observe her interaction with the child.

The items on the HOME scale are as follows.

1 **Emotional and verbal responsivity of mother** For example, mother caresses or kisses child at least once during visit.

2 **Avoidance of restriction and punishment** For example, mother does not interfere with child's actions or restrict child's movements more than three times during visit.

3 **Organisation of physical and temporal environment** For example, child's play environment appears safe and free of hazards.

4 **Provision of appropriate play materials** For example, mother provides toys or interesting activities for child during interview.

5 **Maternal involvement with child** For example, mother tends to keep child within visual range and to look at the child often.

6 **Opportunities for variety in daily stimulation** For example, child eats at least one meal per day with mother and father (Elardo & Bradley, 1981).

In 1970, an 11 year longitudinal study using the HOME scale was begun in Little Rock, Arkansas. HOME scores were taken for 77 children during their first two years and related to their IQ at the age of 3. In general, the higher the HOME score, the higher the child's IQ. In particular, there was a strong correlation between items 1, 4, and 5 on the scale and IQ. Thus, the more responsive the mother, the greater her involvement with the child, and the better the provision of play materials, the higher the child's IQ score (Elardo et al., 1975).

Similar results were obtained from a follow-up study of 49 of the original sample at age 4. Table 1 shows the correlations between HOME scores obtained at 2 years and IQ scores obtained at 4 years. The researchers conclude that the home environment, and particularly the relationship between mother and child, have a significant effect on the child's IQ (Bradley & Caldwell, 1976).

Evaluation Although studies using the HOME scale indicate strong correlations, they do not necessarily show that stimulating home environments and parental responsiveness lead to high IQ scores. A genetic explanation is possible. First, high IQ parents might provide *both* high IQ genes *and* a stimulating home environment for their children. Second, children with high IQ genes may develop verbal skills at an early age, they may spend more time exploring their environment and they may 'demand' more attention. In these

Table 1	Correlations between HOME scores and IQ scores	
1	Emotional and verbal responsivity of mother	.50
2	Avoidance of restriction and punishment	.28
3	Organisation of physical and temporal environment	.33
4	Provision of appropriate play materials	.56
5	Maternal involvement with child	.55
6	Opportunities for variety in daily stimulation	.39

Adapted from Bradley & Caldwell, 1976

ways, they may encourage greater parental responsiveness and involvement (Bukatko & Daehler, 2001).

There is, however, evidence from adoption studies which supports the environmental argument. Children adopted by parents who are responsive and provide stimulating home environments tend to have a higher IQ than adopted children without these advantages (Plomin et al., 1985).

Changing IQs

If the environment influences IQ, then it should be possible to improve IQ scores by changing the environment. This is the thinking behind *enrichment programmes* which aim to enrich children's experience in order to boost their IQ.

Expectation and motivation A famous study conducted in a primary school in California suggests that teachers' expectations of children's ability can affect their IQ scores. The researchers Rosenthal and Jacobson (1968) selected a random sample of 20% of the student population and told the teachers that these children were 'bloomers' – that they were expected to show rapid intellectual growth. After one year, the group labelled as 'bloomers' showed significantly greater IQ gains than the student population as a whole. According to the researchers, teachers expected more from the 'bloomers' and communicated their expectations to these students, who responded by improving their performance.

This study suggests that an environmental change – teachers' expectations – can significantly improve children's IQs. However, attempts to replicate this study have produced varied results. Some studies show no expectancy effects, some show expectancy effects only with younger children, some only with older children. However, on balance, the evidence suggests that under certain circumstances, the expectancy effect does operate (Rogers, 1982).

Compensatory education What effect can education have on IQ? Can special educational programmes boost the IQ scores of those at the bottom of the class system? This is one of the aims of *compensatory education*. Operation Head Start was launched in the USA during the 1960s. It was a massive programme of preschool education involving half a million children from low-income families. These children were failing in droves in the school system. Their failure was seen to result from a lack of stimulation and 'richness' in their family life. Compensatory education is designed to make up or compensate for this supposed deficiency in their home background. It aims to *enrich* the children by providing the stimulation that was seen to be lacking in their family environment.

Children usually entered the Head Start programme at the age of 3 or 4. After a year, they had typically gained ten IQ points. However, this gain usually disappeared within a few years of starting elementary (primary) school. It appears that unless preschool programmes are followed on by further special programmes throughout the child's educational career, then the gains provided by Head Start will be lost (Zigler & Styfco, 1993). However, there is some evidence which may contradict this gloomy conclusion. One study found that some of the early IQ gains partly reappear in adolescence (Seitz, 1990).

It is difficult to assess the effects of Operation Head Start. It was a massive, sprawling operation and its programmes varied from one inner-city area to the next. Focusing on smaller scale

projects may provide a clearer picture of the relationship between IQ and compensatory education.

The Milwaukee Project A project in Milwaukee provided day care and compensatory education for infants from 3 months until entry to primary school. The children were selected from low-income, socially disadvantaged areas, and from mothers with low IQs (below 75). Their mothers were given training in parenting and home management skills. By the age of 4 the children's IQ averaged 112, compared with a control group averaging 85. At age 14, the experimental group averaged 100, the control group 90 (Garber, 1988). Although the gap had significantly narrowed, it does appear that at least part of the early gains in IQ had been maintained.

Social change Judging by the results of IQ tests, each generation appears to be more intelligent than the previous one. For example, in France there was an average gain of 21 IQ points between 1949 and 1974 (Flynn, 1987). As a result, IQ tests are regularly revised and 'restandardised' in order to reset the average IQ score to 100.

IQ scores have risen steadily over the past 50-60 years. This effect is known as the 'Flynn effect' after James Flynn who has been investigating the worldwide rise in IQ. His research indicates that IQ scores have risen by around 15 points every 30 years in 20 industrialised countries in North America, Europe and Asia (Flynn, 1999).

This has been seen as powerful evidence of the effect of environmental factors on IQ. There is no way that changes over such short periods of time can be due to changes in genes. The causes must be entirely environmental (Howe, 1997).

A whole range of environmental factors have been suggested to account for the Flynn effect. They include improvements in schooling, more time spent in education, changes in learning styles – less emphasis on rote-learning and more on problem solving – and changes in a range of other environmental factors such as smaller families, better diets, access to more information, improvements in communication, more complex toys, and increased urbanisation (Williams, 1998).

Key terms

Risk factors *Environmental factors which correlate with low IQ. They are seen to depress IQ.*

Enrichment programmes *Programmes which aim to enrich children's experience.*

Compensatory education *Educational programmes, usually for preschool children, which aim to compensate for supposed deficiencies in home background in order to give the children a head start in the school system.*

Flynn effect *A term used to describe the steady rise in IQ scores in modern industrial societies.*

2.5 IQ tests and IQ scores

So far, this unit has examined two factors which affect IQ scores – genes and the environment. There is ample evidence to indicate that both play a significant role. The third factor that accounts for variation in IQ scores is the tests themselves. Are IQ tests valid – in other words do they measure what they set out to measure? Do they provide an accurate measure of IQ? Or are they biased in favour of some and against others? The issues raised by these questions stand out most clearly when the relationship between IQ tests and culture is examined.

Culture, IQ and IQ tests

Look at the cartoon in Figure 14. Is this a fair test for the puzzled looking Westerner? Clearly the answer is 'no'.

Figure 14 Culture and IQ

'You can't build a hut, you don't know how to find edible roots and you know nothing about predicting the weather. In other words, you do *terribly* on our IQ test.'

In this case, the reason is fairly obvious – the Westerner is from a different culture and lacks the knowledge to complete the test. The test is not *culture-free* and as a result it is not *culture-fair*. Many psychologists believe that it is impossible to produce culture-fair tests, in other words tests which provide members of all cultures with an equal chance (Segall et al., 1990).

To some degree, the same applies to subcultural groups within society – for instance, ethnic groups and class groups. If, for example, IQ tests have been developed by, and standardised on, white middle-class people, then they may be biased against other groups in society.

Class subcultures and IQ

Consider the following classic study of canal-boat people who scraped a meagre living in the 1920s on the canals of England (Gordon, 1923). The children made occasional appearances in school and looked down on the mainstream way of life. They were generally regarded as lazy and stupid. And their average IQ score of 60 apparently reflected this view. But did the tests come anywhere near to measuring the children's intellectual ability? Or, were they simply measuring the children's patience and willingness to answer questions they considered irrelevant? Or, were the tests measuring their familiarity with mainstream culture which was different from their own? Or, more particularly, were they simply measuring the skills taught in schools? Many psychologists would argue that the tests came nowhere near to measuring the canal-boat children's intellectual ability (Segall et al., 1990).

A similar argument has been made about the use of IQ tests

with other groups in Western societies. The question of the relationship between IQ scores and so-called racial groups will be examined in a later section. This section will look at IQ and social class. Most research shows a strong positive correlation between class and IQ – in general, the higher a persons' class position, the higher their IQ. The previous section explained this in terms of the inequalities of class. For example, the risk factors which depress IQ are concentrated at the bottom of the class system and reflect basic inequalities in income, wealth, health and housing. In terms of the argument outlined in this section, class differences in IQ reflect IQ tests which are biased against those in the lower levels of the class system. In particular, they are testing skills which are less valued, less developed and less practised at lower levels. Similarly, the tests are based on knowledge which is less available at the lower levels of the class system.

According to Sternberg (1985), IQ tests measure *analytical intelligence* (reasoning skills). They largely fail to measure what he calls *creative intelligence* (new ideas, new ways of doing things) and *practical intelligence* (applying information to the real world, finding solutions to real-world problems).

According to Helen Bee (2000), both IQ tests and schools are 'designed by the majority culture to promote a particular form of intellectual activity – Sternberg's analytical intelligence'. And this kind of intellectual activity is more readily found in the middle classes. As a result, IQ tests are biased against the working class. From this point of view, social class differences in IQ scores are due to the way IQ tests are constructed.

Culture and IQ

Culture is the learned, shared behaviour of members of society. It consists of norms, values, beliefs, attitudes, priorities, perceptions and ways of seeing the world. Cultures vary from society to society.

IQ tests were invented in Western industrial societies. They were standardised on Western populations. To some degree they reflect Western culture. Is it possible to produce a *culture-free* IQ test – a test which is free from culture and is therefore applicable to members of every culture? Most psychologists would say 'no'. Is it possible to have a *culture-fair* test – an IQ test that may contain elements of culture but is not biased in favour of or against particular cultures? Again, most psychologists would say 'no'.

Western tests and non-Western people Consider the following examples of the use of Western IQ tests in non-Western cultures.

The Canadian psychologist Otto Klineberg (1971) gave an IQ test to Yakima Native American children living in Washington State, USA. The test consisted of placing different shaped wooden blocks into the appropriate holes in a wooden frame 'as quickly as possible'. The children had no problem with the test but produced low scores because they failed to finish within the required time. Klineberg argues that this test is not valid for the Yakima. It is a *culture-bound* test because it reflects Western priorities on speed which the Yakima do not share.

S.D. Porteus (1937) gave IQ tests to Australian Aborigines living in their own communities with little contact with mainstream society. They were reluctant to take the tests because they found it difficult to understand Porteus's request that they take them as individuals. Traditional Aboriginal culture states that problems should be solved by the group rather than by individuals. Important problems are discussed by the elders until a unanimous decision is reached. Again, the Western IQ test is culture-bound – it is based on Western values of individual achievement. As such, it is not a valid test for cultures which emphasise collective decision-making.

In the 1930s, IQ tests were given to Russian peasants who had had no schooling. One question contained four pictures – a saw, an axe, a shovel and a log. They were asked to pick out the three pictures that belonged together. The 'correct' answer was the saw, axe and shovel – they were all tools and therefore belonged to the same category. The peasants chose the axe, saw and log on the basis of which objects would be used together (Luria, 1971). Similarly, unschooled Kpelle farmers in Liberia in West Africa grouped objects by use rather than category – for example, a knife with an orange and a hoe with a potato. In their view, 'That is the way a wise man would do it'. When asked, 'How would a fool do it?' they grouped the objects into categories – tools such as knife and hoe; foods such as orange and potato. The Kpelle were quite capable of grouping objects into categories – a procedure required in many IQ questions. However, they didn't find it useful and saw it as a foolish procedure (Glick, 1975). IQ tests which require this procedure are culture-bound.

The cultural meaning of intelligence Intelligence means different things in different cultures. In the West, high intelligence involves being 'quick, analytic and abstract'. These skills are taught in schools and are highly valued in Western society. They form the basis of Western IQ tests. Other cultures have very different views of intelligence. In these cultures, children are taught and encouraged to develop different versions of 'intelligence'.

Among the Djerma-Sonhai who live in Niger in West Africa, intelligence refers to understanding, know-how and conformity to social norms. An intelligent child has a good memory, is obedient, understands many things, and does what is expected of them (Bisilliat et al., 1967). Among traditional Baganda villagers in Uganda in East Africa, an intelligent person is cautious, careful, stable and friendly (Wober, 1974). Many Native American cultures see intelligent thinking as slow, reflective and qualified. An intelligent person does not give a definite answer unless they are absolutely sure they are correct (Gleitman et al., 1999).

Western intelligence tests fail to measure many aspects of the types of intelligence outlined above. Having been brought up to develop the skills defined as intelligent in their own culture, members of non-Western societies are unlikely to obtain high scores on Western IQ tests. The failure to appreciate the significance of culture has led to what John Berry et al. (1992) describe as 'the long sad history of measuring the "intelligence" of peoples of various cultures'.

According to Robert LeVine (1970), 'Standard intelligence tests measure the current capacity of individuals to participate effectively in Western schools'. And this is just what they were originally designed to do. There have been attempts to produce culture-fair tests – tests which measure the same abilities in all cultures and result in the same distribution of IQ scores in all societies. So-called culture-fair tests have been unsuccessful. Often they produce larger cultural differences than standard tests. One supposedly culture-fair test, Raven's Progressive Matrices, is illustrated in Figure 15. Participants are asked to select the segment that correctly fits the larger pattern. However,

Figure 15 Raven's Progressive Matrices

Adapted from Raven (1962)

this requires a familiarity with two-dimensional representation of figures which does not exist in some cultures (Cole & Cole, 2001).

Most psychologists now believe that 'intelligence' or 'cognitive competence' can only be measured by tests which are appropriate to particular cultures. This is based on the view that it is impossible to create a culture-fair test. Tests should therefore be 'specially constructed and standardised for every distinct cultural group' (Biesheuvel, 1974).

Key terms

Culture-free tests *Tests which are free from culture.*

Culture-fair tests *Tests which provide members of all cultures with an equal chance.*

Culture-bound tests *Tests which are biased against members of one or more culture.*

2.6 'Race' and IQ

The idea that so-called 'racial groups' vary in terms of intelligence has a long history. For example, in the 19th century it was widely believed that the dominance of European colonial powers over their non-white subjects was due to the superior intelligence of the white race.

Some psychologists claim there is scientific backing for the view that 'racial groups' differ in intelligence. Most of the evidence used to support this claim comes from the USA. It provides the focus for this section.

The genetic argument

African-American children in the USA score, on average, 15 points lower than white (Caucasian) children on a range of IQ tests. A small number of researchers argue that this difference is largely due to heredity. In other words, differences in IQ test performance are due to genetic differences between these so-called 'racial' groups.

Activity 6   The !Kung

The !Kung live in the Kalahari Desert in Southern Africa. The following is a description of their traditional way of life. The !Kung live in small family bands rarely numbering more than 20 people. They are hunters and gatherers – the men hunt and the women gather edible roots and berries. The men are skilled hunters, recognising animals from their prints and tracking them from clues such as crushed grass and bent twigs. The women have a remarkable knowledge of what roots and berries are edible, where and when to find them, and how to prepare them.

The !Kung are nomadic – they roam from place to place in search of food and water. Their survival depends on remembering the location of water holes. They carry round maps of the territory in their heads. They have no tradition of writing or drawing and no familiarity with two-dimensional pictures. The closest they come to Western 'art' are decorative scars on women's foreheads and thighs. The cuts are made when they are young with a knife or an axe blade, then charcoal is rubbed in.

Adapted from Thomas, 1969 and Blurton-Jones & Konner, 1976

!Kung hunter

Questions

1   How might the !Kung define an intelligent person?

2   Why would Western IQ tests be unlikely to measure the 'intelligence' or cognitive abilities of the !Kung?

Arthur Jensen (1969; 1980) claims that 80% of the variation in IQ scores in a population is genetically based. Therefore, 80% of the difference between black and white IQ scores is due to genetic factors. The remaining 20% is seen to result from environmental factors. A similar view is put forward by Richard Herrnstein and Charles Murray in their controversial book *The bell curve* (1994). They are more cautious than Jensen, admitting that the evidence does not provide a precise figure for the contribution of genes and the environment. Despite this, they believe a significant part of black/white differences in IQ is due to genetic factors. There is evidence that the 15 point gap is narrowing, evidence which Herrnstein and Murray accept. However, they argue that black/white differences in genetically-based IQ remain, and will always remain.

Those who support the environmental view argue that African Americans are more likely than whites to live in poverty, to be unemployed, to have low-status, low-skill, low-income jobs and to experience a range of disadvantages as a result. Differences in IQ are due to these factors rather than heredity. Those who support the genetic view argue that when blacks and whites are matched in terms of occupational status, income, family size and a range of other factors, the IQ gap, though reduced, still remains. And the remaining gap must be due to genes rather than environment. This debate will be further examined shortly.

The idea of 'race'

Today, most researchers reject the idea of race in the biological sense. In other words, there is no basis for distinguishing between groups of people in terms of genetic differences. In fact, there is far more genetic diversity *within* so-called races than *between* them. Race is therefore a *social definition*. People construct so-called races and assume there are significant genetic differences between them. Few researchers accept this 'common-sense' view of 'race' (Taylor et al., 1995).

If race is a social definition, then it makes no sense to explain 'racial' differences in IQ in genetic terms.

Even if the possibility of genetically distinct races is accepted, then there are problems applying it to African Americans and White Americans. Biologically, they are not distinct populations. According to one estimate, 70% of African Americans have some white ancestry (Reed, 1969). Again, this makes the genetic argument for black/white differences in IQ scores difficult to sustain.

The environmental argument

From this point of view black/white differences in IQ are due to environmental factors. The following evidence supports this argument.

There are indications that the 15 point gap between blacks and whites declined during the 1970s and 80s to around 12 points, and by the 1990s, to less than 10 points (Williams & Ceci, 1997). This decline can only be due to environmental factors – genetic change cannot occur in such a short space of time.

A study looked at the IQ scores of several hundred children born to German women and American servicemen after the Second World War. They found no difference between the scores of children fathered by African Americans and whites – both groups averaged 97 (Eyferth et al., 1960).

Adoption studies in which black children are adopted by whites provide further evidence for the environmental view. One study looked at 101 African-American children from low-income homes adopted by middle-class white families. The average IQ of black children from a similar background was 85-90. Those adopted after they were one year old had IQs of 97-106, those adopted before the age of one averaged 110 (Scarr & Weinberg, 1976). Clearly, the family environment made a big difference to their IQ scores.

African-American children are more likely than white children to experience a range of environmental factors which are linked to low IQ. These include low class position of the family, poor health of the mother during pregnancy, low birth weight, frequent childhood illness, poor nutrition and substandard housing. The risk factors which depress IQ identified by the Rochester Longitudinal Study are more likely to be found in the lower levels of the class system (see pp 513-514). For many researchers most if not all of the IQ difference between blacks and whites are accounted for by these factors.

As noted earlier, when blacks and whites are matched in terms of environmental factors such as income and occupational status, the IQ gap is reduced but not eliminated. Supporters of the genetic view see the remaining gap as evidence of genetic differences between the two groups. However, it can be explained in environmental terms – in particular as a result of racism.

Racism For many generations, African Americans have suffered the intolerance and abuse of racism. Because of the colour of their skin, they have been defined as inferior, relegated to segregated substandard schools, barred from higher status occupations, and beaten, mutilated and even murdered for 'stepping out of line'. In view of this, it is not possible to directly compare 'matched' samples of blacks and whites. They may have similar incomes and occupations but only one group has a history of slavery, discrimination and oppression (Howe, 1997). In the words of one report, 'It would be rash indeed to assume that those experiences, and that historical legacy, have no impact on intellectual development' (Neisser et al., 1996).

Test bias The possibility that IQ tests are biased against African Americans may explain part of the difference in black and white scores. First, blacks are more likely than whites to be working class. As noted earlier, IQ tests may be biased against the working class – see p516.

Second, the tests may be culturally biased against African Americans. Some linguists argue that African Americans speak a different dialect from standard English (Labov, 1973; see pp 470-471). This may place them at a disadvantage on written tests. However, translating tests into black dialect appears to make little or no difference to their IQ scores (Quay, 1971). IQ tests tend to reward analytical intelligence. According to Sternberg, African American subculture emphasises practical intelligence – applying information to the real world and finding solutions to real-world problems (Sternberg & Suben, 1986). If this is correct, then standard IQ tests will place African Americans at a disadvantage. Finally, the very fact of taking an IQ test may place blacks at a further disadvantage. Because of the traditional stereotype of blacks as intellectually inferior, they may be placed under greater strain when taking an intelligence test (Steele, 1997). Evidence supporting this possibility is presented in Activity 7.

Comparing groups

This section has compared two groups – African Americans and White Americans. There is evidence that IQ differences between *individuals* can be partly accounted for by genetic factors. Is it reasonable to argue that IQ differences between *groups* can be explained in the same way? Many researchers would say 'no'. They argue that *within-group differences* are completely independent of *between-group differences* – one does not lead to the other.

Richard Lewontin (1976) illustrates this argument in terms of plant genetics – see Figure 16. Imagine two adjacent fields, one with fertile soil, the other with poor soil. They are both planted with corn and apart from the soil quality, the plants share the same environment. In each field, some of the plants will be taller than others. This can be explained by genetic factors because the environment is shared. However, the plants in the field with fertile soil will, on average, be taller than those in the field with poor soil. The explanation for this difference is environmental – the quality of the soil.

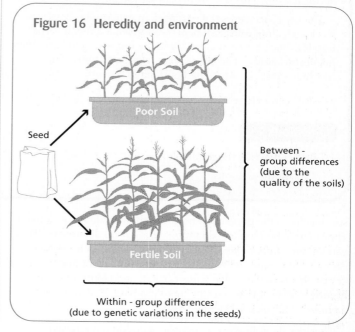

Figure 16 Heredity and environment

Seed

Poor Soil

Fertile Soil

Between - group differences (due to the quality of the soils)

Within - group differences (due to genetic variations in the seeds)

In terms of this argument, differences between individual plants in one group cannot explain differences between one group and the other. And the same applies to human beings. According to Lewontin (1976), it is incorrect to attribute differences in IQ between social groups to differences between individuals in one group. Logically, differences between social groups are due to environmental differences.

2.7 Heredity and environment

The evidence presented in this unit suggests that both genes and the environment contribute to IQ. Some psychologists have tried to find out how much each contributes.

Heritability When Arthur Jensen (1969) claimed that 80% of the variation in IQ scores between African Americans and White Americans was due to genetic differences, he was using the idea of *heritability*.

What exactly does heritability mean? It is *not* the proportion of intelligence that is inherited. It does not mean that inheritance contributes 80% of intelligence, and the environment contributes 20%. In genetics, heritability is a measure of the proportion of the variability of a trait in a given population that can be attributed to genetic differences. If Jensen's figures are correct, this means that 80% of the *variability* of IQ *within* the African-American population is due to genetic factors. And it means that 80% of the *variability* of IQ *within* the white population is due to genetic factors.

Estimates of heritability are *within-group* estimates – they refer

Activity 7   Stereotypes and test performance

African Americans have traditionally been viewed by mainstream society in terms of negative stereotypes. For example, they have been seen as intellectually inferior. This stereotype may reduce their performance on IQ tests. When taking a test, people experience greater pressure and anxiety when labelled with a stereotype which suggests they will perform badly. This is known as *stereotype threat*.

The bar chart shows the results of an experiment in which black and white college students were given a difficult verbal test. Half the participants were told the test would indicate their intellectual ability. The others were told the test was simply a laboratory exercise which had nothing to do with ability.

Adapted from Steele, 1997

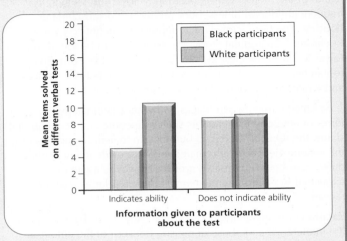

Questions

1   Briefly describe the results shown in the bar chart.

2   Explain these results.

3   Using the information in this activity, suggest why it is not possible to obtain matched groups of blacks and whites.

---

specifically to the population from which the estimate is derived. They cannot be used to explain *between-group* differences. They cannot, therefore, be used to explain differences in IQ between African Americans and white Americans. But, according to their critics, this is exactly what Jensen (1969) and Herrnstein and Murray (1994) did. As a result, there is a basic flaw in their argument (Bukatko & Daehler, 2001).

Consider the following. A sample of children are raised individually in barrels. The environment for each child is exactly the same. For this population, the heritability of IQ is 100%. Since their environments are identical, any variation in IQ must be due to genetic factors. Thus if the children's IQ varied between 70 and 130, then the entire *difference* of 60 points is due to genetic factors. If another sample of children were raised in widely differing environments, then the heritability of their intelligence would be much lower. Part of the variation in their IQ scores would be due to environmental differences.

Plomin (1990) suggests the heritability of IQ is around 30% for children and over 50% for adults. This is because there is more variation in the environments of children than there is in the environments of adults.

Based on evidence from around the world, most researchers today estimate that about half the variation in IQ within the population is due to heredity (Neisser et al., 1996). The environment and interactions between heredity and environment account for the remaining half.

Reaction range A useful way of thinking about the interaction of heredity and environment is the concept of *reaction range*. The idea is that genes fix upper and lower limits. Where a child's IQ falls within this range is determined by the environment. Thus a child with a very 'rich' environment – parents who are responsive and provide a stimulating environment – will be likely to have an IQ at the top of their reaction range.

According to Weinberg (1989), the reaction range for IQ scores is around 20 to 25 points. Thus the same child's IQ can

vary up to 25 points depending on whether they were raised in a very 'rich' or severely 'deprived' environment. The child's reaction range is due to their genes. Their IQ score *within* the reaction range is determined by their environment.

Genes shape environments Some researchers, for example, Sandra Scarr (1992), believe that genes are primarily responsible both for IQ scores and types of environment. For example, people with genes for a high IQ use their intelligence to create a high quality environment for themselves and their children. In this way, high IQ parents may provide high IQ genes *and* a stimulating home environment for their children.

Similarly, children with high IQ genes may receive more attention from adults. They may develop verbal skills at an earlier age and spend more time exploring their environment. This may encourage greater parental responsiveness and involvement. To some extent, therefore, children create their own environment. And, to some extent, this environment will reflect their IQ.

The politics of IQ Debates about the contribution of genes and environment to IQ are not just academic – they are also political. In *The Bell Curve: Intelligence and Class Structure in American Society*, Herrnstein and Murray (1994), argue that intelligence is becoming the key determinant of class position in the USA. They claim that 'success and failure in the American economy, and all that goes with it, are increasingly a matter of the genes that people inherit'. Those at the top tend to be the most intelligent, those at the bottom the least intelligent. Since this variation in IQ is largely based on genes, spending money on enrichment programmes and compensatory education will do little or nothing to change the situation. There is evidence that this kind of thinking has influenced government policy, particularly in the USA.

Most psychologists would reject this view, arguing that class, ethnic and so-called 'racial' differences in IQ are due to environmental factors. For example, they would argue that a 15 point difference in IQ between African American and White American children is quite easily explained by environmental factors. This view suggests a very different political agenda –

removing the environmental barriers that disadvantage certain groups in society.

Others see IQ in a very different light. For Heather (1976) and Gould (1981), IQ is, and always has been, a political tool to maintain class and ethnic inequalities in society, and justify the privileges of the white middle classes. In their view, nothing has changed since Galton's day.

Key terms

Heritability *A measure of the proportion of the variation of a trait (eg IQ) in a population that is due to genetic difference.*

Reaction range *The idea that genes fix upper and lower limits of an individual's IQ range. Where an individual's IQ falls within their reaction range is determined by the environment.*

Summary

1. There are three main factors affecting measured intelligence – genetic inheritance, environment and the way IQ tests are constructed.

2. Evidence for genetic influence comes mainly from kinship studies – family studies, twin studies and adoption studies. This evidence is suggestive rather than conclusive since it is difficult to separate genetic and environmental influences.

3. A range of environmental factors have been linked to IQ. They include social class, risk factors and home environment. However, the links are correlational which means that these factors do not necessarily influence IQ.

4. Changes in IQ scores over short time periods indicate environmental influence. There is evidence of this from some enrichment programmes and from the Flynn effect – IQ scores have risen steadily over the past 50-60 years in 20 modern industrial societies.

5. There is evidence that IQ tests may be biased against lower class and ethnic minority groups and non-Western cultures.

6. Many psychologists believe that it is impossible to construct a culture-fair test. IQ tests should be specially constructed and standardised for each culture.

7. A small number of researchers believe that the variation in IQ scores between so-called 'racial' groups is due in large part to genetic variation.

8. Most researchers argue that this difference is due to environmental factors. These factors include class differences, racism and test bias.

9. Today, most researchers estimate that about half the variation in IQ within the population is due to heredity.

Unit 3 Development of moral understanding

KEY ISSUES

1. **What are the main theories of moral understanding and prosocial reasoning?**

2. **How might gender and culture influence moral understanding?**

This unit looks at the development of *moral understanding* – the development of children's understanding of right and wrong. It focuses on cognitive theories of moral development – the way children think and reason about moral issues. It also examines the development of *prosocial reasoning* – the way children develop a concern for the wellbeing of others and a sense of duty and responsibility for others.

Four main theories are examined – those of Jean Piaget and Lawrence Kohlberg on moral development, Nancy Eisenberg on prosocial reasoning and Carol Gilligan on gender differences in moral development.

3.1 Jean Piaget

Piaget (1932) began with the idea that 'all morality consists in a system of rules'. An explanation of the development of moral understanding therefore requires an explanation of children's thinking about rules.

Piaget used two main methods for examining the development of moral understanding. First, he looked at children's games and how understandings of the rules changed as the children grew older. Second, he presented children with stories highlighting moral issues and noted how their moral judgements developed with age.

Rules of the game Piaget watched children aged between 3 and 12 playing marbles, and asked them to explain the rules to him. He found that children under the age of 5 were not playing according to any rules, nor did they really know what rules were.

Between the ages of 5 and 10, the children were playing by rules, but what was most striking was their attitude to those rules. They considered the rules to be absolutely fixed and unchangeable, being handed down from parents, time immemorial, or God. They believed that breaking the rules not only deserved punishment, but would inevitably be punished – although this did not stop the children from quite happily cheating if they got the chance!

From the age of about 10, children talked about the rules as existing by agreement in order to make the game possible, and acknowledged they could be changed by agreement too.

Moral stories Piaget presented children with pairs of short fictional stories containing moral dilemmas. Typically, the stories would tell of a child who creates some damage (often fairly mild) through being naughty, compared with another child who, although trying to be good, inadvertently creates mayhem. For example, one little boy tries to help his father by refilling his inkpot, but accidentally makes a big blot on the tablecloth, while another boy messes about with his father's inkpot and makes a small blot. The children were then asked which of the children in the stories was most naughty and most deserved to be punished.

Piaget found that children under the age of 10 usually responded more to the consequences of actions than the intentions of those involved. They were aware of the motivations of the children in the stories, of whether they were being intentionally good or bad. But, they still said the child who had done most damage deserved the severest punishment. From the age of around 10, children tended to judge the children in the stories on the basis of their intentions, not the consequences of their actions. They concluded that the child who caused damage with the best possible intentions was blameless.

On the basis of his findings, Piaget suggested a stage theory of moral development.

Stages of moral development

Stage 1 Premorality (from birth to around 5 years). Children have no discernible sense of morality or understanding of rules. Their play is not governed by rules – for example, they may pile up marbles, hide them, or throw them randomly, simply for the pleasure these activities bring. Since there are no rules, this type of play does not involve morality. Without rules, there can be no right or wrong. For example, there can be no cheating which can only occur when there are rules to break.

Stage 2 Heteronomy or moral realism (from around 5-10 years). Rules are fixed and non-negotiable. This is known as the *heteronomous stage* which means governed by others. Rules are seen to be handed down from above by authority figures such as parents or supernatural powers. This stage is also called the stage of *moral realism*, where children are unable to understand abstractions, and regard rules as objects that exist as surely as chairs and tables exist. Actions are evaluated on the basis of their consequences. Punishment is seen as deserved and inevitable if rules are broken (although, due to egocentrism, children do not always realise this should apply to them too).

Stage 3 Autonomy or moral relativism (around age 10 and over). At this stage, the child is increasingly autonomous – in control. Rules are less likely to be seen as handed down by authority figures. They are more likely to be seen as negotiated and based on agreement. As a result, they can be changed by consent. For example, the rules of marbles can be changed – what was once cheating can become fair play if everybody agrees. At this stage, actions are evaluated by intention rather than outcome. As noted earlier, the morality of spilling the ink is now judged by the intentions of the two boys rather than the amount spilled.

Explaining the development of moral understanding

So far, this section has presented a description rather than an explanation of the development of moral understanding. Why do children go through these stages? According to Piaget, there are two main reasons – first, general changes in cognitive development, second, increasing contact with peers.

Cognitive development Each stage in moral understanding corresponds to changes in cognitive development.

- Stage 1 coincides with the sensorimotor and pre-conceptual pre-operational stages of cognitive development. At this

stage, children have only a vague grasp of concepts and of principles of organisation. As a result, they are unlikely to appreciate rules and the morality that lies behind them.

- Stage 2 coincides with the intuitive pre-operational and the concrete operational stages of cognitive development. During these stages, children begin to reason logically but they mainly depend on concrete examples and have difficulty thinking abstractly. Reflecting these stages of cognitive development, rules are rules, they have a 'concrete' reality, they are fixed and unchangeable, they are 'set in concrete'.

- Stage 3 coincides with the formal operational stage. By now, egocentrism – seeing the world solely from one's own point of view – has largely disappeared. As a result, the child is able to appreciate the intentions and motives of others, and judge them accordingly. This ability is essential if actions are to be evaluated by intention.

Interaction with peers The move from moral realism to moral relativity is also explained by increasing interaction with peers – children of a similar age and situation. This encourages the child to consider the thoughts and feelings of others which can lead to an understanding of their intentions and motives. Piaget saw peer contact as crucial in overcoming egocentrism and helping the child move on to the autonomous stage of moral understanding. Negotiation with peers of equal status helps the child to understand that rules are negotiable rather than fixed and unchanging.

Evaluating Piaget's theory

There is considerable evidence to support Piaget's view that children's reasoning about moral issues becomes more complex and elaborate as they grow older. There is also evidence that more general cognitive development is related to changes in moral understanding. For example, the decline of egocentrism is related to the ability to appreciate the intentions of others. However, there are a number of criticisms of Piaget's views.

- First, he appears to have underestimated young children's ability to reason about moral issues.

- Second, the methods he used to obtain evidence of moral understanding are open to criticism.

- Third, he tended to see social rules and moral rules as one and the same. There are good reasons for seeing them as different.

Underestimating ability Costanzo et al., (1973) presented pre-school children with stories in which well-intentioned and ill-intentioned acts could lead to either positive or negative outcomes. They found that the children responded in quite a subtle way. They took intention into account if the outcome was positive, but not if the outcome was negative. Children did not think that a naughty child who inadvertently did some good deserved a reward, but felt that a well-intentioned child who created a mess deserved to be punished. This suggests that young children's understanding of moral issues is influenced by the likely reaction of their parents. They know from their own experience that they will probably be told off if they have naughty intent regardless of outcome, and also if they cause damage accidentally. This suggests that young children are quite sophisticated social thinkers in their moral reasoning.

Cameron et al., (1999) presented Canadian and Chinese children aged 7, 9 and 11 with one story in which someone tells a lie in order to offend someone, and another story where a lie is told to avoid giving offence. All the children found the first lie much worse than the second, again indicating that young children have a quite sophisticated grasp of moral issues.

The evidence provided by these studies suggests that Piaget underestimated children's ability to reason about moral issues.

Methodology The methods used in psychological experiments affect the evidence they produce. Kail (1990) pointed out that Piaget's moral dilemma stories may have been too taxing on young children's memories, and this may have affected their responses (although Piaget did ensure the children could remember the stories before he questioned them). For example, in Activity 8 a 'good' boy accidentally breaks 15 cups, whereas a 'naughty' boy accidentally breaks 1 cup in the process of wrongdoing. Most 5-year-olds believe that the 'good' boy deserves greater punishment. This may be because they have forgotten part of the story. When researchers make sure they are aware of all the details, many more 5-year-olds take intention into account when making moral judgements.

Karniol (1978) pointed out that in Piaget's stories, the accident often has a worse outcome than the intentionally naughty deed. This may distract children from attending to the intentions of the children in the stories, and prompt them to respond to the outcomes. When the outcomes are made the same – that is, equal damage – then children as young as 5 are more likely to make judgements based on intent.

The evidence provided by these studies suggests that Piaget's methods sometimes produced invalid data. In the examples given above, they produced data which led Piaget to underestimate young children's ability to reason about moral issues.

Social and moral rules According to Piaget, 'all morality consists in a system of rules'. Turiel (1983) was not convinced that children's understanding of the rules of games tells us much about their moral reasoning. Social rules (including the rules of games) are different from moral rules and children are aware of this. Moral rules are about right and wrong – for example, it is wrong to hit someone. Social rules do not necessarily involve morality and are often situational – it is alright to shout in the playground but not in the classroom. Turiel found that children clearly distinguished moral from social rules.

Despite these criticisms, Piaget provided the first systematic cognitive theory of the development of moral understanding. This formed the basis for Kohlberg's important and influential theory which will now be examined.

Key terms

Heteronomy *A stage of moral development in which the child sees rules as imposed by others.*

Moral realism *An alternative name for the heteronomous stage referring to the tendency to see rules as fixed and unchangeable objects.*

Autonomy *A stage of moral development in which the child is more self-governing and realises that they can negotiate with others about rules.*

Moral relativism *An alternative name for the autonomous stage referring to the tendency to see rules as negotiable and changeable, and to base judgements on a person's intentions.*

Activity 8 Developing morality

Item A — Two moral stories

Story 1 A little boy who is called John is in his room. He is called to dinner. He goes into the dining room. But behind the door there was a chair, and on the chair there was a tray with fifteen cups on it. John couldn't have known that there was all this behind the door. He goes in, the door knocks against the tray, bang go the fifteen cups and they all get broken!

Story 2 Once there was a little boy whose name was Henry. One day when his mother was out he tried to get some jam out of the cupboard. He climbed up on the chair and stretched out his arm. But the jam was too high up and he couldn't reach it and have any. But while he was trying to get it, he knocked over a cup. The cup fell down and broke.

Questions

1. At which stages of moral development are S and C?
2. Explain why you placed them at these stages.
3. What are the problems of using the moral dilemma story method for assessing children's moral understanding?

Item B — The responses of two children

Piaget:	Are those children both naughty, or is one not so naughty as the other?
S (aged 6):	Both just as naughty.
Piaget:	Would you punish them the same?
S:	No. The one who broke fifteen cups.
Piaget:	And would you punish the other one more, or less?
S:	The first broke lots of things, the other one fewer.
Piaget:	How would you punish them?
S:	The one who broke the fifteen cups: two slaps. The other one: one slap.
C (aged 9):	Well, the one who broke them as he was coming isn't naughty, 'cos he didn't know there was any cups. The other one wanted to take the jam and caught his arm on a cup.
Piaget:	Which one is the naughtiest?
C:	The one who wanted to take the jam.
Piaget:	How many cups did he break?
C:	One.
Piaget:	And the other boy?
C:	Fifteen.
Piaget:	Which one would you punish most?
C:	The boy who wanted to take the jam. He knew, he did it on purpose.

From Piaget, 1932

3.2   Lawrence Kohlberg

Lawrence Kohlberg (1927-1987) followed on from Piaget to produce the most influential theory of moral development to date. Like Piaget, Kohlberg suggested that moral understanding develops in a series of stages, that these stages are in a fixed sequence, that they are universal, and that moral understanding guides moral action. Again, like Piaget, Kohlberg was interested in the reasoning process that lies behind the moral decisions individuals make.

Unlike Piaget, however, Kohlberg used a much more standardised procedure of presenting children with moral dilemmas. This was followed by a battery of questions, enabling a complex scoring of the children's responses. Kohlberg was also interested in changes in moral understanding during adolescence and adulthood.

In his principal study, Kohlberg presented a series of nine moral dilemmas, each followed by twenty or so questions. The moral dilemmas included issues like whether a doctor should help a patient to die if the patient is terminally ill, in great pain, and wishes to die. The best known dilemma is the 'Heinz dilemma'. It is presented in Activity 9. I suggest you look at this activity now.

Activity 9   The Heinz dilemma

In Europe, a woman was near death from a special kind of cancer. There was one drug that the doctors thought might save her. It was a form of radium that a druggist in the same town had recently discovered. The drug was expensive to make, but the druggist was charging ten times what the drug cost him to make. He paid $200 for the radium and charged $2000 for a small dose of the drug. The sick woman's husband, Heinz, went to everyone he knew to borrow the money, but he could only get together about $1000 which is half what it cost. He told the druggist that his wife was dying, and asked him to sell it cheaper or let him pay later. But the druggist said, 'No, I discovered the drug and I'm going to make money from it'. So Heinz got desperate and broke into the man's store to steal the drug for his wife.

From Kohlberg & Elfenbein, 1975

Questions

1   These are the types of questions given to participants. Answer each question and give a reason for your answer.

Should Heinz steal the drug?

Why or why not?

Does he have a duty or obligation to steal it?

Should he steal the drug if he does not love his wife?

Should he steal it for a stranger?

It is illegal, is it also morally wrong?

2   Where do your responses fit in Kohlberg's stages of moral development shown in Table 2?

The participants in Kohlberg's study were 72 Chicago boys aged 10, 13, and 16. The study began in 1955. Six follow-up studies were carried out on the participants over the next 26 years, the final results being published by Colby et al., in 1983.

From the participants' responses, Kohlberg drew up a table of stages of moral development. He identified three levels of moral understanding, each divided into two stages, giving six stages in total. This is shown in Table 2.

At Level 1, the child bases judgements about right and wrong on sources of authority such as parents and teachers. These sources are external to the child – they issue rewards and punishments. Behaviour that is rewarded by others is judged to be right and behaviour punished by others is judged to be wrong.

At Level 2, the child internalises and conforms to the norms of the majority. Judgements about right and wrong are now based on the norms of the group to which the individual belongs – family, peer group and society as a whole. As a general rule, the individual does not analyse or question these norms.

At Level 3, a new kind of personal authority develops. Judgements about right and wrong are largely based on the individual's chosen morality. Their own ethical principles provide the guidelines for *individual* judgements and choices.

The results of Kohlberg's Chicago study are shown in Figure 17.

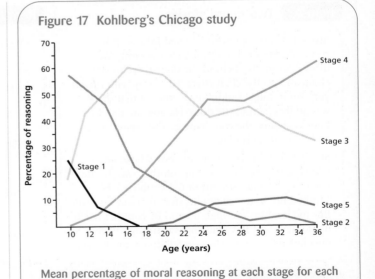

Figure 17   Kohlberg's Chicago study

Mean percentage of moral reasoning at each stage for each age group (adapted from Colby et al., 1983)

Figure 17 shows the extent to which participants' responses reflected the various levels, from age 10 to age 36. Moral reasoning at Stages 1 and 2 (the preconventional level), declined steadily with age. By age 18, most participants had reached Stage 3, by age 36, most were at Stage 4. The first evidence of

Table 2	Kohlberg's stages of moral development

LEVEL 1 PRECONVENTIONAL

Stage 1 Punishment and obedience orientation

The child's main reason for obeying rules is to avoid punishment from those in authority – usually parents and teachers.

Stage 2 Instrumental relativist orientation

The child is mainly motivated by a desire for rewards. Some concern is shown for others but the motive is primarily to benefit the child – 'I'll scratch your back if you scratch mine'.

LEVEL 2 CONVENTIONAL

Stage 3 Interpersonal concordance orientation

At this stage, the child sees 'good behaviour' as behaviour that pleases other people. The child conforms to gain the approval and avoid the disapproval of others. This is sometimes known as the 'good boy, nice girl' stage. 'Being good' means having good intentions and showing concern for others.

Stage 4 Law and order orientation

Here the emphasis is not so much on gaining approval and pleasing other people – as in Stage 3 – but more on acting out of a sense of duty and contributing to the group and to society as a whole. The individual believes that rules keep the social system going and must be obeyed for their own sake. An act is wrong if it breaks rules or does harm to others.

LEVEL 3 POSTCONVENTIONAL

Stage 5 Social contract orientation

Rules and regulations are still seen as important – in most cases they should be upheld in ensure fairness and impartiality. However, when rules conflict with deeply held moral principles, there is some justification for ignoring or trying to change them.

Stage 6 Universal ethical principles

At this stage, individuals are primarily concerned with living in accordance with deeply held moral principles – for example, universal principles of justice and human rights. These ethical principles override laws – the individual acts in terms of the principle rather than the law.

Stage 5 occurs around age 17 and rises slowly. However, relatively few participants reach Stage 5 and there is no evidence of Stage 6 responses. Colby and Kohlberg conclude that no more than 15% of people ever reach Stage 5, and that Stage 6 may be an ideal rather than a reality – except for such people as Jesus, Gandhi, Martin Luther King and maybe Kohlberg himself!

Why do people move from one level to another level of moral development? According to Kohlberg, the main reason is their increasing ability to take the perspective of others – to see the world through the eyes of others. At Level 1, children focus on personal needs – they are self-centred. As they grow older, they are exposed to others' points of view – in particular, the higher levels of reasoning of adults. This increases their ability to take the perspective of others – a necessary step if they are to recognise, appreciate and internalise the norms of family, peer groups and society as a whole.

Evaluating Kohlberg's theory

Supporting evidence There is evidence to support Kohlberg's theory as the following studies indicate.

- Kohlberg (1969) researched moral development in a number of countries including Britain, Mexico, Taiwan, Turkey and the USA. He found much the same pattern, though development appeared a little slower in non-industrial communities.

- A review of 44 studies conducted in 26 countries found that Stages 1 through to 4 appeared at more or less the same ages, in the same sequence, in almost all the studies. There was very little regression (going back) from higher stages to lower stages (Snarey, 1985).

Methodology Kohlberg's methodology has been widely criticised. The coding and classification of participants' responses to moral dilemmas involves considerable interpretation by the researcher. The resulting moral judgement scores have therefore been seen as unreliable. Kohlberg and his colleagues responded to this criticism by developing a new scoring system with explicit instructions on coding responses. This has resulted in high reliability – different researchers using the new system to code the same data produced similar results (Smith et al., 1998).

But are these results valid – do they provide an accurate measure of moral development? Some researchers have their doubts. They argue that the moral dilemmas presented to children are unrealistic – they do not reflect the child's experience. For example, the Heinz dilemma is far removed from the everyday life of a child. As a result, such dilemmas are unlikely to provide a valid measure of children's moral development. Some researchers have tried to get round this problem by presenting moral dilemmas set in situations with which children are familiar, for example, in the classroom (Damon, 1977).

Cultural differences It appears from the above evidence the Kohlberg's stages of moral development are universal – they apply to all cultures. However, Stage 5 seems to be limited to urban industrial societies. It has not been found in small-scale rural communities such as Alaskan Inuit, and rural areas of Guatemala, Kenya, New Guinea and Turkey. A number of researchers argue that Stage 5 is culturally biased. Stage 5 emphasises individual morality and responsibility – if social norms and laws conflict with personal morality then there is justification for ignoring or changing them. Some researchers claim that this reflects the focus on individualism and personal freedom and responsibility found in Western culture. Non-Western cultures place more emphasis on the social group – on collective responsibility (Snarey, 1985).

Rather than suggesting that people in non-Western cultures are inferior in terms of moral reasoning, many researchers argue they are simply different. If this is the case, then Kohlberg's Stage 5 cannot be applied universally. An alternative Stage 5 is needed to measure moral development in collectivist cultures. The following example from the Heinz dilemma illustrates this point. It comes from an interview with a man living in an Israeli kibbutz – a collective. The emphasis on collective responsibility comes through clearly.

'Should Moshe (Heinz) steal the drug? Why or why not?'

'Yes … I think that the community should be responsible for controlling this kind of situation. The medicine should be made available to all in need: the druggist should not have the right to decide on his own … the whole community or society should have the control of the drug.' (Snarey, 1985)

Many Asian cultures also emphasise the importance of collective good and social harmony. Ideally, disputes should be resolved by negotiation and reconciliation involving the community rather than by individuals fighting it out in law courts (Bukatko & Daehler, 2001).

Kohlberg's system, particularly at Stage 5, fails to take account of non-Western forms of moral reasoning. As a result, it is unlikely to provide valid measurements of moral development in non-Western cultures, at least beyond Stage 4. The relationship between culture and moral reasoning is discussed further in Section 3.5.

Gender bias Kohlberg's original sample from which he developed his scale of moral development consisted of 72 boys between the ages of 10 to 16. Does the fact it was an all-male sample matter? According to some researchers, it does. For example, Carol Gilligan (1982) argues that females tend to be more concerned with caregiving, relationships, and people's feelings than males. Kohlberg's scheme therefore reflects male morality and as a result is gender-biased. Gilligan accuses Kohlberg of assuming that male morality is the norm and of undervaluing a quite distinctive female reading of morality. Gilligan's views are examined in a later section. (For further criticism of gender bias see pp 728-729.)

Emotion Kohlberg's theory is about moral reasoning, it has little to say about emotion. It is about how people think rather than how they feel. A number of researchers have criticised this separation of emotion and reason. For example, Kagan (1984) found that very young children expressed shame and guilt for breaking rules, long before they are supposed to 'understand' morality.

The scope of moral reasoning Kohlberg has been criticised for taking a narrow view of moral reasoning. As he admits in his later writings, he has focused on moral reasoning about *justice* and *fairness* (Kohlberg et al., 1983). Other aspects of moral reasoning will shortly be examined – first, prosocial reasoning, then the claim that females develop a morality based on *care* and *responsibility*.

Conclusion Despite all the criticisms, Kohlberg's theory remains very influential. This is how Helen Bee (2000) evaluates his contribution. 'Over 1000 studies have explored or tested aspects of the theory, and several competing theories have been proposed. The remarkable thing is how well Kohlberg's ideas have stood up to this barrage of research and commentary. There does appear to be a clear set of stages in the development of moral reasoning, and these stages seem to be universal.'

3.3 Nancy Eisenberg and prosocial reasoning

Since the late 1970s, Nancy Eisenberg has explored a different way of looking at moral development. While Piaget and Kohlberg focused on the development of moral understanding of rules in a context of authority, wrongdoing and punishment, Eisenberg was more interested in how children develop a helping attitude to others.

Key terms

Moral reasoning *The assumptions, reasoning and analysis that lie behind the moral decisions individuals make.*

Moral dilemmas *A difficult choice between two or more courses of action which is made on the basis of the individual's morality.*

Preconventional level *Kohlberg's first level of moral reasoning. Morality is directed by the avoidance of punishments and the desire for rewards.*

Conventional level *Kohlberg's second level of moral reasoning. Morality is directed by the norms of the social group to which the individual belongs.*

Postconventional level *Kohlberg's third level of moral reasoning. Morality is increasingly directed by the individual's chosen morality.*

This section examines Eisenberg's views on *prosocial reasoning* – the thinking and reasoning that is involved in making decisions about whether to help, take care of, or share with other people, when this may prove costly to oneself (Eisenberg & Fabes, 1998).

Feeling plays an important role in Eisenberg's approach. In her view, prosocial reasoning arises from the development of compassion and empathy – awareness of others' feelings to the point of being able to share them. She suggests this arises from experience of *role play* and the development of *role-taking* skills (Eisenberg, 1987). As children grow older, they play an increasing number of roles – for example, daughter, friend, student, team member. They also become increasingly skilled at taking the role of others – being aware of the role others are playing by putting themselves in their place. This helps to develop empathy which involves appreciating the feelings of others.

In her research, Eisenberg et al. (1983) set children dilemmas where one child's need is in conflict with another's. An example concerns a child called Mary or Eric – Eisenberg changed the gender to match the participant in order to encourage identification with the main character. Mary is on her way to a birthday party, and meets a child injured in a fall. The dilemma is whether Mary goes on to the party or stays to help the injured child and thus misses the jellies, cakes and party games. The dilemmas are designed to find out if the participant, through identifying with the main character in the story, was willing to act selfishly (putting their own interests first and not wanting to miss the party), or altruistically (putting the interests of the injured child first and being prepared to miss the party).

Although no child was ever totally consistent in their responses to the dilemmas, Eisenberg et al. were able to identify five stages of prosocial reasoning from their findings.

Stage 1 Hedonistic orientation Children's prime concern is for themselves. What appears to be prosocial behaviour is motivated to increase their own gain in the long run – I'd help because she'd help me next time'.

Stage 2 Needs orientation The child is beginning to recognise the needs of others and will help a hurt child, but they are responding to the demands of the situation, rather than to any real sense of empathy. Typical reasons for helping are, 'She needs help', 'She's hurt'.

Stage 3 Stereotyped approval-focused orientation The child acts to gain approval by doing what they think is expected from them. For example, 'Mary should help because the other girl would like Mary'.

Stage 4 Empathic orientation The young person shows empathy and concern for others. 'I'm trying to put myself in her shoes.'

Stage 5 Internalised orientation The individual has a clear and articulate sense of duties and responsibilities. They maintain their self respect by living up to the values of care and responsibility for others which they have internalised.

Stages 1 and 2 are common in early childhood (up to the age of 7 or so); Stage 3 can begin before 7 and last until adolescence; Stage 4 and, more rarely, Stage 5 emerge at adolescence.

Eisenberg's research indicates that prosocial reasoning moves through a series of stages as children grow older. It begins with a self-centred, personal gain. It moves on to a growing awareness of prosocial norms and values, and increasing empathy for others.

However, Eisenberg (1983) found that empathy is not consistent. Children operate league tables of who they are most likely to help – preferring to help family, friends, people they know and people of similar ethnic or religious groups.

Evaluating Eisenberg's theory

Widening the focus Eisenberg has widened the idea of morality to include prosocial reasoning. Kohlberg's view of moral reasoning was based on ethics of justice and fairness. This view was criticised as narrow.

Kohlberg was also criticised for ignoring the role of emotion in moral reasoning. Eisenberg makes good this omission by showing how emotion is involved in explanations and justifications of prosocial behaviour.

Cultural differences Evidence from Western industrialised societies indicates that children go through the same stages of prosocial reasoning at around the same age. For example, children from the USA, Germany, Poland and Italy follow similar patterns of development (Boehnke et al., 1989).

However, there are important cultural differences in prosocial reasoning, a point Eisenberg herself recognised. For example, primary school children raised in an Israeli kibbutz showed aspects of Stage 5 – internalised orientation. In the story about Mary, many of them reasoned that, 'She has a duty to help others'. Israeli kibbutzim are collectives which emphasise cooperation, sharing and responsibility for others. It appears that the values of the kibbutz have a significant influence on prosocial reasoning (Eisenberg et al., 1990).

The importance of culture can be seen from a comparison with the Maisin people who live in coastal regions of Papua New Guinea. Maisin children are taught to be concerned about the needs of particular individuals rather than the group as a whole. They maintain a Stage 2 need orientation into adolescence and even into adulthood (Tietjen, 1986). Clearly prosocial reasoning is strongly influenced by culture.

3.4   Gender differences in moral development

Are there gender differences in moral development? And, if so, what do these differences mean?

A study by Kohlberg and Kramer (1969) indicated that women were more likely to be at Stage 3, whereas men were more likely to be at Stage 4. Similar gender patterns have been found in some, but by no means all, studies. Does this mean that men are more mature and sophisticated in terms of their moral understanding? Are they morally 'superior'? Kohlberg did not even suggest this. However, a number of researchers have attacked both his approach and the implications that can be drawn from his findings.

What accounts for gender differences in moral understanding? According to Carol Gilligan (1982), Kohlberg's theory is *androcentric* – biased in favour of males. She argues that there are distinctive male and female views of morality. She accuses Kohlberg as accepting male morality as a standard. By doing this, he obscures, undervalues and downgrades female morality. Gilligan claims that in moral reasoning experiments, females are asked to respond to moral dilemmas which are scored in terms of male morality. As a result, females are likely to obtain lower moral judgement scores and be placed in lower stages.

Gender differences

According to Gilligan, males tend to have a *justice orientation* and females a *care orientation*. Males are socialised to be independent and to achieve. As a result, they are concerned with justice – a fair return for individual effort and achievement, and equality of opportunity so they have a fair and equal chance to achieve. Conflicts of interest should be settled fairly in terms of legal principles on which the justice system is based.

By comparison, females are socialised to be caring, to be concerned about their duties and responsibilities for others. As a result of this, women are often placed at Stage 3 in Kohlberg's scheme which emphasises concern for the welfare of others, trying to please others, and living up to what others expect of you. With their emphasis on justice, men are more likely to be placed at Stage 4 – law and order orientation. In Gilligan's view, this means that 'the very traits that have traditionally defined the "goodness" of women are those that mark them deficient in moral development'.

According to Gilligan, Kohlberg's system values detachment in moral judgement. The postconventional level, the highest level of moral reasoning, is partly defined in terms of detachment – standing back from the situation in order to assess it in terms of general moral principles. Women, with their care orientation, tend to emphasise attachment – direct concern for particular people and how to help them. For example, women may respond to the Heinz dilemma by considering the effects it may have on the wife if Heinz goes to jail, and who will look after her if she has a relapse (Gilligan, 1982). In Kohlberg's system, this is Stage 3 reasoning. Gilligan, however, sees it as evidence of a different kind of moral reasoning which Kohlberg did not recognise or value.

Moral reasoning – a female view

Gilligan (1982) conducted informal interviews with 29 American women, aged between 15 and 33, all of whom were considering whether to abort an unwanted pregnancy. She found all of the women saw themselves as involved in relationships, rather than as isolated autonomous agents. In Gilligan's view, the women's reasoning was directed by a care orientation rather than the more masculine justice orientation.

From her findings, Gilligan suggested three stages in the development of the care orientation.

Stage 1 Survival and self-interest Here care was directed towards the self. Women at this stage thought mostly about their own needs, for example, what they had to do in order to be loved. Some considered having the baby in order to be loved by it. Others saw having the baby as a restriction on their freedom.

Stage 2 Responsibility and self-sacrifice Here care was directed towards others. Women were willing to put others' interests – the baby's, or their partner's – before their own. They considered giving birth out of duty to the baby, or aborting out of duty to a partner who was unwilling to be a father.

Stage 3 Care and relationships Here the woman was concerned to balance everyone's interests and arrive at a solution that was best for all. Care was directed to everyone concerned, including herself.

Gilligan (1982) defined the care orientation as 'a responsibility to discern and alleviate the real and recognisable trouble of this world'. She identified four main features of the care orientation.

- First, it stresses relationships rather than rights.
- Second, it stresses the consequences of moral actions, not rigid moral principles.
- Third, it is more willing to accept excuses for bad actions, rather than automatically damning them as inexcusable.
- Fourth, it puts moral dilemmas and problems into contexts, rather than treating them like logical or legal puzzles to be solved.

Gilligan accepted that the care orientation was not exclusive to women, but claimed that empirical evidence shows it as more characteristic of women's moral understanding. She accepted that Kohlberg gave a perfectly good account of the justice orientation, and claimed that her work provided the corresponding three levels for the care orientation. Gilligan did not claim that the care orientation was better or wiser, but insisted that it was wrong for it to be overlooked or devalued.

Evaluating Gilligan's theory

Women and Kohlberg's system The evidence for Gilligan's claim that women are likely to come out at a lower stage on Kohlberg's system is inconclusive. Some studies found they do (eg, Holstein, 1976), other studies found little difference between the sexes (eg, Walker, 1984). A review of 80 studies using Kohlberg's system found no significant differences when men and women were matched in terms of variables such as occupational status and educational attainment (Walker, 1995).

Gender and moral orientation Does the care orientation largely direct female moral reasoning, and the justice orientation direct male moral reasoning? Again, the evidence is not clear-cut. Gilligan's own research suggests that the care orientation provides the main focus for women's moral reasoning. But her sample was very small (29 women), it was unrepresentative, and the situation was unusual – all the women were considering an abortion. However, other studies do provide support for her claim. For example, Eisenberg (1987) found that 10 to 12-year-old girls gave more caring and empathetic responses than boys. Caring responses may, however, be due to demand characteristics – participants may respond in this way because they think that's what the researcher expects or wants (Eisenberg & Lennon, 1983).

A number of studies have found no significant gender differences in the use of care or justice orientations. A study of 80 Canadian children found that most used both orientations and that gender differences were very slight (Walker et al., 1987). A further study, based on a large sample of males and females, age 5-63 found the only evidence of gender differences was for adults on real-life, as opposed to fictional, dilemmas (Walker, 1989).

Class and ethnicity Gilligan has been criticised for ignoring class and ethnicity in her research (Tong, 1992). If gender makes a difference to moral reasoning, then why not class and ethnicity? Stack (1986) suggests that all oppressed groups generate an orientation of care. If this is so, it is not specifically a gender issue.

Feminism Some feminists have accused Gilligan of undermining the women's movement by confirming sexual stereotypes – women as caring, nurturant and emotional, with little interest in justice or abstract thought (Sayers, 1986).

Much Anglo-American feminism in the 1960s and 70s took a sociological view that men and women are the products of social conditioning and that masculinity and femininity are social constructs. Any inequalities or even differences between

---

Activity 10 Gender differences in moral reasoning

Carol Gilligan interviewed 80 participants, aged 14-77, in the USA. Of these, 46 were female, 34 were male. Gilligan asked them about moral dilemmas they had faced in their own lives, and did a content analysis of their accounts.

Some participants explained and justified their actions using only one orientation ('care only' or 'justice only'), some used both orientations but favoured one ('care focused' or 'justice focused'), while some made equal use of both orientations ('care and justice balanced'). The findings are shown in the chart.

Adapted from Gilligan & Attanucci, 1988

	Care only or care focused	Care and justice balanced	Justice only or justice focused
female	12	12	10
male	1	15	30

Question

What evidence do these findings provide for gender differences in moral understanding?

the sexes were socially and politically imposed and therefore could be challenged and changed. An alternative perspective, emerging from France, took the view that the sexes were equal but different, and that the liberation of women must include a recognition and celebration of their difference, not a dismissal of all women's qualities as being merely the product of socialisation. As a 'difference' feminist, Gilligan has come under attack from the more mainstream feminist tradition in the English-speaking world.

Conclusion Despite all the criticism, Gilligan has broadened the scope of research into moral reasoning. Many researchers now regard schemes based solely on a justice orientation as too narrow. (For further evaluation of Gilligan's theory see pp 482-483.)

Key terms

Androcentrism *A male view of the world which results in bias in favour of males.*

Justice orientation *A view of morality which focuses on justice and fairness.*

Care orientation *A view of morality which focuses on care and responsibility for others.*

3.5 Culture and moral understanding

The relationship between culture and moral understanding has been discussed on a number of occasions in this unit. Culture is the learned, shared behaviour of members of society. It includes norms, values, attitudes and beliefs, all of which have a moral dimension. And it includes specifically moral beliefs – beliefs about right and wrong, and rights and obligations. Moral beliefs vary from one culture to another. And, as a result, so does moral reasoning.

As noted earlier, Kohlberg's stages of moral development

have been criticised for failing to take account of non-Western forms of moral reasoning. As a result, Kohlberg's system is unlikely to provide valid measurements of moral development in non-Western cultures. Western cultures are often described as individualistic with their emphasis on individual achievement, individual responsibility, and individual freedom. By comparison, many non-Western cultures are described as collectivist because of their emphasis on collective responsibility and on the importance of the group rather than the individual. As a result, people from collectivist cultures are unlikely to reach Kohlberg's Level 3 – postconventional morality – with its emphasis on the *individual's* chosen morality.

A number of researchers see Kohlberg's system as culturally biased. In particular, his postconventional morality is seen to reflect the values of white, male, middle-class Americans (Snarey, 1985). The problems of applying Kohlberg's scheme to non-Western cultures can be seen from Activity 11.

The points made in this section are, to some extent, applicable to all stage theories of moral development.

'West is best'

A number of critics have argued that stage theories of moral development are based on value-judgements. As noted earlier, Gilligan claimed that Kohlberg's scheme reflected male values, so much so that it ignored female versions of morality. Put simply, it assumed that 'male is best'.

A similar argument has been made for culture. Critics argue that stage theories of moral development reflect Western culture and Western values. They are based on the assumption that 'West is best'.

This can be seen clearly from the top level of stage theories. The top level is the 'best'. It is the best morally because it sees the emergence of individual morality. In Piaget's scheme, the individual is autonomous and self-governing when they reach the highest stage of moral development. In Kohlberg's scheme,

Activity 11   Culture and moral reasoning

The Heinz dilemma was presented to an orthodox Hindu in India. What would he do in the following scenario? A man was unable to raise the money for a drug which might save his dying wife's life. Should he steal the drug? Hindu dharma (religious morality) prohibits stealing under any circumstances.

Here is an extract from the interview.

Interviewer:	But his wife is going to die!
Respondent:	There is no way within Hindu dharma to steal even if a man is going to die.
Interviewer:	But doesn't Hindu dharma prescribe that you try to save a person's life?
Respondent:	Yes. And for that you can sacrifice your blood or sell yourself, but you cannot steal.
Interviewer:	Why doesn't Hindu dharma permit stealing?
Respondent:	If he steals it is a sin, so what virtue is there in saving a life? Hindu dharma keeps a man from sinning.

The researcher, Shweder, asked Kohlberg to classify these responses. Kohlberg placed the man at Level 2 – conventional reasoning – based on the view that his reasoning reflected the conventions – the religious dharma – of his social group.

Shweder rejects this placement arguing that this extract and the rest of the interview represents complex reasoning based on ideas of human and spiritual dignity. In view of this, he placed the man at Level 3 – postconventional reasoning – arguing that his morality overrode society's norms and beliefs.

Adapted from Shweder, 1991

Question

How does this research illustrate the problems of defining, describing and measuring moral development in different cultures?

the individual develops their own personal morality when they reach the highest level. In both schemes, this reflects the value Western culture places on individuality (Snarey, 1985).

The top is not only best morally, it is best cognitively. It represents the most sophisticated thinking, the highest-level reasoning. For example, Piaget's Stage 3 – moral relativism – requires the ability to think abstractly and demands more

sophisticated reasoning than Stage 2, the stage of moral realism. Again, these judgements can be seen as a reflection of Western values, in particular the high value placed on abstract thought.

In view of the above comments, a number of researchers argue that the whole idea of moral development needs re-thinking, particularly at the highest level of postconventional morality (Berry et al., 1992).

Summary

1 Piaget produced a stage theory of moral development. There is considerable evidence to support his view that moral reasoning becomes more complex and elaborate as children grow older. However, he appears to have underestimated young children's ability to reason about moral issues.

2 Kohlberg produced the most influential theory of moral development. There is some evidence to support his view that moral understanding develops in stages, that these stages are in a fixed sequence, and that they are universal.

3 Kohlberg's methodology has been criticised – for example, the moral dilemmas he presented may not reflect children's experience. He has also been criticised for culture bias and gender bias.

4 Eisenberg's theory of prosocial reasoning focused on the role of empathy and compassion, factors that were largely missing from Piaget's and Kohlberg's theories.

5 There are important cultural differences in prosocial reasoning, a point Eisenberg herself recognised.

6 Gilligan claims that Kohlberg's system is based on a male justice orientation. As such, it is biased in favour of males. She claims there is a distinctive female view of morality – the care orientation – which focuses on care and responsibility for others.

7 The evidence for Gilligan's views is inconclusive. Some studies provide evidence of gender differences in moral reasoning, others do not.

8 Theories of moral development have been criticised for a) failing to take account of non-Western forms of reasoning and b) what some see as their assumption that Western forms of moral reasoning are superior.

References

Baddeley, A.D. (1976). *The psychology of memory*. New York: Basic Books.

Baillargeon, R. & DeVos, J. (1991). Object permanence in young infants: Further evidence. *Child Development, 62*, 1227-1246.

Barron, A.M. & Foot, H.C. (1991). Peer tutoring and teacher training. *Educational Research, 33*, 174-185.

Bee, H. (2000). The developing child. (9th ed.). Needham Heights, MA: Allyn & Bacon.

Bennett, N. & Dunne, E. (1992). *Managing classroom groups*. Hemel Hempstead: Simon & Schuster.

Berry, J.W., Poortinga, Y.H., Segall, M.H. & Dasen, P.R. (1992). *Cross-cultural psychology: Research and applications*. Cambridge: Cambridge University Press.

Best, D. (1993). Inducing children to generate mnemonic organisational strategies: An examination of long term retention and materials. *Developmental Psychology, 29*, 324-336.

Biesheuvel, S. (1974). The nature of intelligence: Some practical implications of its measurement. In J. W. Berry & P.R. Dasen (Eds.), *Culture and cognition*. London: Methuen.

Binet, A. & Simon, T. (1905). Methodes nouvelles pour le diagnostic du niveau intellectuel des anormaux. *L'Annee Psychologique, 11*, 245-336.

Bisilliat, J., Laya, D., Pierre, E. & Pidoux, C. (1967). La notion de lakkal dans la culture Djerma-Songhai. *Psychopathologie Africaine*, 3, 207-264.

Blaye, A., Kight, P., Joiner, R. & Sheldon, S. (1991). Collaboration as a facilitator of planning and problem solving on a computer based task. *British Journal of Educational Psychology, 61*, 471-473.

Blurton-Jones, N. & Konner, M.J. (1976). !Kung knowledge of animal behavior. In B. Lee & I. DeVore (Eds.), *Kalahari hunter-gatherers*. Cambridge, M.A.: Harvard University Press.

Boehnke, K., Silbereisen, R.K., Eisenberg, N., Reykowski, J. & Palmonari, A. (1989). Developmental pattern of prosocial motivation: A cross-national study. *Journal of Cross-Cultural Psychology, 20*, 219-243.

Borke, H. (1975). Piaget's mountains revisited: Changes in the egocentric landscape. *Developmental Psychology, 11*, 241-243.

Bouchard, T.J. Jr. (1995). Longitudinal studies of personality and intelligence: A behaviour genetic and evolutionary psychology perspective. In D.H. Saklofske & Z. Seidner, (Eds.), *International handbook of personality and intelligence*. New York: Plenum.

Bouchard, T.J. Jr. & McGue, M. (1981). Familial studies of intelligence: A review. *Science, 212*, 1055-1059.

Bower, T.G.R. (1982). *Development in infancy* (2nd ed.). San Francisco: W.H. Freeman.

Bradley, R.H. & Caldwell, B.M. (1976). The relation of infants' home environments to mental test performance at fifty-four months: A follow-up study. *Child Development, 47*, 1172-1174.

Brainerd, C.J. (1978). Neo-Piagetian training experiments revisited: Is there any support for the cognitive-developmental stage hypothesis? *Cognition, 2*, 349-370.

Brainerd, C.J. (1983). Modifiability of cognitive development. In S. Meadows (Ed.), *Development of thinking*. London: Methuen.

Bremner, J.G. (1998). From perception to action: The early development of knowledge. In F. Simion & G. Butterworth (Eds.), *The development of sensory, motor and cognitive capacities in early infancy*. Hove: Psychology Press.

Broman, S.H., Nichols, P.L. & Kennedy, W.A. (1975). *Preschool IQ: Prenatal and early developmental correlates*. Hillsdale, NJ: Erlbaum.

Bruner, J.S. (1966). On cognitive growth. In J.S. Bruner, R.R. Olver & P.M. Greenfield (Eds.), *Studies in cognitive growth*. New York: Wiley.

Bruner, J.S. (1990). *Acts of meaning*. Cambridge, MA: Harvard

University Press.

Bryant, P.E. & Trabasso, T. (1971). Transitive inferences and memory in young children. *Nature, 232,* 456-458.

Buckhalt, J.A., Mahoney, F.J. & Parris, S.G. (1976): Efficiency of self-generated elaborations by EMR and nonretarded children. *American Journal of Mental Deficiency, 81,* 93-96.

Bukatko, D. & Daehler, M.W. (2001). *Child development* (4th ed.). Boston: Houghton Mifflin.

Burman, E. (1994). *Deconstructing developmental psychology.* London: Routledge.

Cameron, C.A., Xu, F. & Fu, G. (1999). Chinese and Canadian children's concept of lying and their moral judgement: Similarities and differences. Paper presented at the biennial meeting of the *Society for Research in Child Development,* Albuquerque.

Case, R.S. (1985). *Intellectual development: A systematic reinterpretation.* New York: Academic Press.

Chorney, M.J., Seese, K., Owen, M.J., Daniels, J., McGuffin, P., Thompson, L.A., Detterman, D.K., Benbow, C.P., Lubinski, D., Eley, T.C. & Plomin, R. (1998). A quantitative trait locus (QTL) associated with cognitive ability in children. *Psychological Science, 9,* 159-166.

Colby, A., Kohlberg, L., Gibbs, J. & Liebermann, M. (1983). A longitudinal study of moral development. *Monographs of the Society for Research in Child Development, 48,* (1-2), no. 200.

Cole, M. & Cole, S.R. (2001). *The development of children* (4th ed.). New York: Worth.

Costanzo, P.R., Coie, J.D., Grument, J. & Farnill, D. (1973). A reexamination of the effects of intent and consequences on children's moral judgement. *Child Development, 57,* 362-374.

Cowan, P.A. (1978). Piaget with feeling: *Cognitive, social and emotional dimensions.* New York: Holt, Rinehart & Winston.

Cowie, H., Smith, P.K., Boulton, M. & Laver, R. (1994). *Cooperation in the multi-ethnic classroom.* London: David Fulton.

Damon, W. (1977). *The social world of the child.* San Francisco: Jossey-Bass.

Danner, F.W. & Day, M.C. (1977). Eliciting formal operations. *Child Development, 48,* 1600-1606.

Deci, E.L., Driver, R.E., Hotchkiss, L., Robbins, R.J. & Wilson, I.M. (1993). The relation of mothers' controlling vocalisations to children's intrinsic motivation. *Journal of Experimental Child Psychology, 55,* 151-162.

Dempster, F.N. (1981). Memory span: Sources of individual and developmental differences. *Psychological Bulletin, 89,* 63-100.

Dodge, K.A. (1991). Emotion and social information processing. In J. Garbner & K.A. Dodge (Eds.), *The development of emotion regulation and dysregulation.* Cambridge: Cambridge University Press.

Doise, W. & Mugny, G. (1984). *The social development of the intellect.* Oxford: Pergamon.

Donaldson, M. (1978). *Children's minds.* London: Fontana.

Duncan, G.J. (1993). Economic deprivation and childhood development. Paper presented at the biennial meetings of the *Society for Research in Child Development,* New Orleans.

Dunn, J. & Plomin, R. (1990). *Separate lives: Why siblings are so different.* New York: Basic Books.

Eisenberg, N. (1983). Children's differentiations among potential recipients of aid. *Child Development, 54,* 594-602.

Eisenberg, N. (1987). The relation of altruism and other moral behaviors to moral cognition: Methodological and conceptual issues. In N. Eisenberg (Ed.), *Contemporary topics in developmental psychology.* New York: Wiley.

Eisenberg, N. & Fabes, R.A. (1998). Prosocial behavior. In W. Damon (Ed.), Handbook of child psychology: Vol 3. *Social, emotional, and personality development* (5th ed.). New York: Wiley.

Eisenberg, N., Hertz-Lazarowitz, R. & Fuchs, I. (1990). Prosocial moral judgment in Israeli kibbutz and city children: A longitudinal study. *Merrill-Palmer Quarterly, 36,* 273-285.

Eisenberg, N. & Lennon, R. (1983). Sex differences in empathy and related capacities. *Psychological Bulletin, 94,* 100-131.

Eisenberg, J., Lennon, R. & Roth, K. (1983). Prosocial development: A longitudinal study. *Developmental Psychology, 19,* 846-855.

Elardo, R. & Bradley, R.H. (1981). The Home Observation for Measurement of the Environment (HOME) scale: A review of research. *Developmental Review, 1,* 113-145.

Elardo, R., Bradley, R.H. & Caldwell, B.M. (1975). The relation of infants' home environments to mental test performance from six to thirty-six months: A longitudinal analysis. *Child Development, 46,* 71-76.

Eyferth, K., Drandt, U. & Wolfgang, H. (1960). *Farbige kinder in Deutschland.* Munich: Juventa.

Eysenck, H.J. (1973). The inequality of man. London: Temple-Smith.

Flynn, J.R. (1987). Massive IQ gains in 14 nations: What IQ tests really measure. *Psychological Bulletin, 101,* 271-291.

Flynn, J.R. (1999). Searching for justice: The discovery of IQ gains over time. *American Psychologist, 54,* 5-20.

Foot, H.C. & Barron, A.M. (1990). Friendship and task management in children's peer tutoring. *Educational Studies, 16,* 237-250.

Frawley, W. (1998). *Vygotsky and cognitive science: Language and the unification of the social and computational mind.* Cambridge, MA: Harvard University Press.

Galton, F. (1869). *Hereditary genius: An inquiry into its laws and consequences.* London: Macmillan.

Garber, H.L. (1988). *The Milwaukee Project: Preventing mental retardation in children at risk.* Washington DC: American Association of Mental Retardation.

Gardner, H. (1976). *The quest for mind.* London: Quartet.

Gardner, H. (1993). *Frames of mind.* London: Harper-Collins.

Gelman, R. (1978). Counting in the pre-schooler: What does and does not develop. In R.S. Seigler (Ed.), *Children's thinking: What develops?* Hillsdale, NJ: Erlbaum.

Gilligan, C. (1982). *In a different voice.* Cambridge, MA: Harvard University Press.

Gilligan, C. & Attanucci, J. (1988). Two moral orientations: Gender differences and similarities. *Merill-Palmer Quarterly, 34,* 223-237.

Ginsberg, H.P. (1981). Piaget and education: The contributions and limits of genetic epistemology. In K. Richardson & S. Sheldon (Eds.), *Cognitive development to adolescence.* Milton Keynes: Open University Press.

Gleitman, H., Fridlund, A.J. & Reisberg, D. (1999). *Psychology* (5th ed.). New York: W.W. Norton.

Glick, J. (1975). Cognitive development in cross-cultural perspective. In F.G. Horowitz (Ed.), *Review of child development research, vol. 4.* Chicago: University of Chicago Press.

Goodnow, J.J. (1990). The socialisation of cognition: What's involved? In J.W. Stigler et al. (Eds.), *Cultural psychology: Essays on comparative human development.* Cambridge: Cambridge University Press.

Gordon, H. (1923). *Mental and scholastic tests among retarded children* (Educational Pamphlet No. 44). London: Board of Education.

Gould, S.J. (1981). *The mismeasure of man.* Harmondsworth: Penguin.

Greenfield, P.M. & Lave, J. (1982). Cognitive aspects of informal education. In D.A. Wagner & H.W. Stevenson (Eds.), *Cultural perspectives on child development.* San Francisco: W.H. Freeman.

Hearnshaw, L.S. (1979). *Cyril Burt,* psychologist. London: Hodder & Stoughton.

Heather, N. (1976). *Radical perspectives in psychology.* London: Methuen.

Hedegaard, M. (1996). The zone of proximal development as basis for instruction. In H. Daniels (Ed.), *An introduction to Vygotsky.* London: Routledge.

Herrnstein, R.J. & Murray, C. (1994). *The bell curve: Intelligence and class structure in American life.* New York: Free Press.

Holstein, C.B. (1976). Irreversible, step-wise sequence in the development of moral judgement: A longitudinal study of males and females. *Child Development, 47,* 51-61.

Horgan, J. (1993). Eugenics revisisted. *Scientific American,* June, 92-100.

Horn, J.M. (1983). The Texas Adoption Project: Adopted children and their intellectual resemblance to biological and adoptive parents. *Child Development, 54*, 266-275.

Howe, M.J.A. (1997). *IQ in question: The truth about intelligence.* London: Sage.

Howe, M.J..A. (1998). Can IQ change? *The Psychologist, 11*, 69-72.

Inhelder, B., Sinclair, H. & Bovet, M. (1974). *Learning and the development of cognition.* Cambridge, MA: Harvard University Press.

Jahoda, G. (1983). European 'lag' in the development of an economic concept: A study in Zimbabwe. *British Journal of Developmental Psychology, 23*, 105-113.

Jensen, A.R. (1969). How much can we boost IQ and scholastic achievement? *Harvard Educational Review, 39*, 1-123.

Jensen, A.R. (1980). *Bias in mental testing.* New York: Free Press.

Jensen, A.R. (1998). *The g factor.* Westport, CT: Praeger.

Juel-Nielson, N. (1965). Individual and environment: A psychiatric and psychological investigation of monozygous twins raised apart. *Acta Psychiatrica et Neurologica Scandinavica*, Supplement 183.

Kagan, J. (1984) *The nature of the child.* New York: Basic Books.

Kail, R. (1990). *The development of memory in children.* (3rd ed.). New York: W.H. Freeman.

Kail, R. (1991). Processing time declines exponentially during childhood and adolescence. *Developmental Psychology, 27*, 259-266.

Kamin, L.J. (1974). *The science and politics of IQ.* Potomac, MD: Lawrence Erlbaum.

Kamin, L.J. (1981). *The intelligence controversy: H.J. Eysenck vs. Leon Kamin.* New York: Wiley.

Karniol, R. (1978). Children's use of intention cues in evaluating behaviour. *Psychological Bulletin, 85*, 76-85.

Keats, D.M. (1985). Strategies in formal operational thinking: Malaysia and Australia. In I. Reyes Lagunes & Y.H. Poortinga (Eds.), *From a different perspective: Studies of behaviour across cultures.* Lisse, Netherlands: Swets & Zeitlinger.

Keeney, T.J., Cannizzo, S.D. & Flavell, J.H. (1967). Spontaneous and induced verbal rehearsal in a recall task. *Child Development, 38*, 935-966.

Klahr, D. (1982). Nonmonotone assessment of monotone development: An information processing analysis. In S. Strauss (Ed.), *U-shaped behavioural growth.* New York: Academic Press.

Klineberg, O. (1971). Race and IQ. *Courier, 24*, No 10.

Kohlberg, L. (1969). Stage and sequence: The cognitive developmental approach to socialisation. In D.A. Goslin (Ed.), *Handbook of socialisation theory and research.* Chicago: Rand McNally.

Kohlberg, L. & Elfenbein, D. (1975). The development of moral judgements concerning capital punishment. *American Journal of Orthopsychiatry, 54*, 614-640.

Kohlberg, L. & Kramer, R. (1969). Continuities and discontinuities in childhood moral development. *Human Development, 12*, 93-120.

Kohlberg, L. Levine, C. & Hewer, A. (1983). *Moral stages: A current formulation and a response to critics.* Basel: Karger.

Kreutzer, M.A., Leonard, S.C. & Flavell, J.H. (1975). An interview study of children's knowledge about memory. *Monographs for the Society for Research in Child Development, 41*, (1, serial no. 159).

Labov, W. (1973). The logic of nonstandard English. In N. Keddie (Ed.), *Tinker, tailor … the myth of cultural deprivation.* Harmondsworth: Penguin.

Leach, P. (1977). *Baby and child.* London: Michael Joseph.

Leutwyler, K. (1996). Paying attention: The controversy over ADHD and the drug Ritalin is obscuring a real look at the disorder and its underpinnings. *Scientific American, 272*, 12-13.

LeVine, R.A. (1970). Cross-cultural study in child psychology. In P. Mussen (Ed.), *Carmichael's manual of child psyhcology* (3rd ed.). New York: Wiley.

Lewontin, R.C. (1976). Race and intelligence. In N.J. Block & G. Dworkin (Eds.), *The IQ controversy.* New York: Pantheon.

Luria, A.R. (1971). Towards the problem of the historical nature of psychological processes. *International Journal of Psychology, 6*, 259-272.

Mackintosh, N.J. (2000). *IQ and human intelligence.* Oxford: Oxford University Press.

McNally, D.W. (1974). *Piaget, education and teaching.* Sydney: New Educational Press.

Meltzoff, A.N. & Moore, M.K. (1994). Imitation, memory, and the respresentation of persons. *Infant Behavior and Development, 17*, 83-99.

Miller, P.H. (1983). *Theories of developmental psychology.* San Francisco: W.H. Freeman.

Moss, E. (1992). The socioaffective context of joint cognitive activity. In L.T. Winegar & J. Valsiner (Eds.), *Children's development within social context, Vol 2: Research and methodology.* Hillsdale, NJ: Erlbaum.

Neisser, U., Boodoo, G., Bouchard, T.J. Jr., Boykin, A.W., Brody, N., Ceci, S.J., Halpern, D.F., Loehlin, J.C., Perloff, R., Sternberg, R.J. & Urbina, S. (1996). Intelligence: Knowns and unknowns. *American Psychologist, 51*, 77-101.

Newman, H.H., Freeman, F.N. & Holtzinger, K.J. (1937). *Twins: A study in heredity and environment.* Chicago: University of Chicago Press.

Newson, J. (1979). The growth of shared understandings between infant and caregiver. In M. Bullowa (ed.), *Before speech: The beginning of interpersonal communication.* Cambridge: Cambridge University Press.

Noelting, G. (1980). The development of proportional reasoning and the ratio concept. *Educational Studies in Mathematics, 11*, 217-253.

Piaget, J. (1923). *The language and thought of the child.* New York: Harcourt Brace, 1926.

Piaget, J. (1926). *The language and thought of the child.* London: Routledge and Kegan Paul.

Piaget, J. (1932). *The moral judgement of the child.* London: Kegan Paul.

Piaget, J. (1933). Social evolution and the new education. *Education Tomorrow, 4*, 3-25.

Piaget, J. (1936). *The origins of intelligence in children.* London: Routledge & Kegan Paul, 1952.

Piaget, J. (1937). *The construction of reality in the child.* New York: Basic Books, 1954.

Piaget, J. (1952). *The child's conception of number.* London: Routledge and Kegan Paul.

Piaget, J. (1958). *The growth of logical thinking from childhood to adolescence.* New York: Basic Books.

Piaget, J. (1959). *The early growth of logic in the child.* New York: Norton, 1964.

Piaget, J. (1972). Intellectual evolution from adolescence to adulthood. *Human Development, 15*, 1-12.

Piaget, J. (1983). Piaget's theory. In P.H. Mussen (Ed.), Handbook of child psychology (4th ed.), *Vol. 1: History, theory and methods.* New York: Wiley.

Piaget, J. & Inhelder, B. (1941). *Le developpement des quantites chez l'enfant.* Neuchatel: Delachaux et Niestle.

Piaget, J. & Inhelder, B. (1951). *La genese de l'idee de hasard chez l'enfant.* Paris: Presses Universitaires de France.

Piaget, J. & Inhelder, B. (1956). *The child's conception of space.* London: Routledge & Kegan Paul.

Piaget, J. & Inhelder, B. (1966). *The psychology of the child.* London: Routledge & Kegan Paul.

Piaget, J. & Inhelder, B. (1968). *Memory and intelligence.* London: Routledge & Kegan Paul, 1973.

Plomin, R. (1990). The role of inheritance in behaviour. *Science, 248*, 183-188.

Plomin, R. & DeFries, J.C. (1985). *Origins of individual differences in infancy: The Colorado Adoption Project.* Orlando, FL: Academic Press.

Plomin, R., Fulker, D.W., Corley, R. & DeFries, J.C. (1997). Nature, nurture and cognitive development from 1-16 years: A parent-offspring adoption study. *Psychological Science, 8*, 442-447.

Plomin, R., Leohlin, J.C. & DeFries, J.C. (1985). Genetic and environmental components of 'environmental' influences. *Developmental Psychology, 21*, 391-402.

Porteus, S.D. (1937). *Intelligence and environment.* New York: Macmillan.

Price-Williams, D.R., Gordon, W. & Ramirez III, M. (1969). Skill and conservation: A study of pottery making children. *Developmental Psychology, 1*, 769.

Quay, L.C. (1971). Language, dialect, reinforcement, and the intelligence test performance of Negro children. *Child Development, 42*, 5-15.

Raven, J.C. (1962). *Coloured progressive matrices.* London: H.K. Lewis and Co.

Reed, T.E. (1969). Caucasian genes in American Negroes. Science, 165, 762-768.

Rogers, C. (1982). *The social psychology of schooling.* London: Routledge & Kegan.

Rogoff, B. (1990). *Apprenticeship in thinking: Cognitive development in a social context.* New York: Oxford University Press.

Rose, S. & Blank, M. (1974). The potency of context in children's cognition: An illustration through conservation. *Child Development, 54*, 499-502.

Rose, S., Kamin, L.J. & Lewontin, R.C.(1984). *Not in our genes.* Harmondsworth: Penguin.

Rosenthal, R. & Jacobson, L. (1968). *Pygmalion in the classroom: Teacher expectation and pupils' intellectual development.* New York: Holt, Rinehart & Winston.

Rutter, M., Maughan, B., Mortimore, P. & Ouston, J. (1979). *Fifteen thousand hours: Secondary schools and their effects on children.* London: Open Books.

Salomon, G. & Globerson, T. (1989). When groups do not function the way they ought to. *International Journal of Educational Research, 13*, 89-99.

Sameroff, A.J., Siefer, R., Baldwin, A. & Baldwin, C. (1993). Stability of intelligence from pre-school to adolescence: The influence of social and family risk factors. *Child Development, 64*, 80-97.

Samuel, J. & Bryant, P. (1984). Asking only one question in the conservation experiment. *Journal of Child Psychology and Psychiatry, 25*, 315-318.

Sayers, J. (1986). *Sexual contradictions: Psychology, psychoanalysis and feminism.* London: Tavistock.

Scarr, S. (1992). Developmental theories for the 1990s: Development and individual differences. *Child Development, 63*, 1-19.

Scarr, S. & Kidd, K.K. (1983). Developmental behaviour genetics. In M.M. Haith & J.J. Campos (Eds.), *Handbook of child psychology, vol 2: Infancy and developmental psychobiology.* New York: Wiley.

Scarr, S. & Weinberg, R.A. (1976). IQ test performances of black children adopted by white families. *American Psychologist, 31*, 726-739.

Schneider, W. & Bjorklund, D.F. (1992). Expertise, aptitude, and strategic remembering. *Child Development, 63*, 461-473.

Segall, M.H., Dasen, P.R., Berry, J.W. & Poortinga, Y.H. (1990). *Human behavior in global perspective: An introduction to cross-cultural psychology.* Boston: Allyn & Bacon.

Seitz, V. (1990). Intervention programmes for impoverished children: A comparison of educational and family support models. *Annals of Child Development, 7*, 73 -103

Shaw, R. & Bransford, J. (1977). Introduction: Psychological approaches to the problems of knowledge. In R. Shaw & J. Bransford (Eds.), *Perceiving, acting, and knowing: Toward an ecological psychology.* Hillsdale, NJ: Erlbaum.

Shayer, M., Kuchemann, D.E. & Wylam, H. (1976). The distribution of Piagetian stages of thinking in British middle and secondary school children. *British Journal of Educational Psychology, 48*, 62-70.

Shields, J. (1962). *Monozygotic twins brought up apart and brought up together.* London: Oxford University Press.

Shotter, J. (1976). The growth of self determination in social exchanges. *Education for Teaching,* May.

Shuey, A. (1966). *The testing of Negro intelligence.* New York: Social Science Press.

Shweder, R.A. (1991). *Thinking through cultures: Expeditions in cultural psychology.* Cambridge MA: Harvard University Press.

Siegal, M. (1991). *Knowing children: Experiments in conversation and cognition.* Hillsdale, NJ: Erlbaum.

Slavin, R.E. (1987). Developmental and motivational perspectives on cooperative learning: A reconciliation. *Child Development, 58*, 1161-1167.

Smith, P.K., Cowie, H. & Blades, M. (1998). *Understanding children's development* (3rd ed.). Oxford: Blackwell.

Snarey, J.R. (1985). Cross-cultural universality of social-moral development: A critical review of Kohlbergian research. *Psychological Bulletin, 97*, 202-232.

Stack, C. (1986). The culture of gender: Men and women of colour. *Journal of Women in Culture and Society, 11*, 322-323.

Steele, C.M. (1997). A threat in the air: How stereotypes shape intellectual identity and performance. *American Psychologist, 52*, 613-629.

Sternberg, R.J. (1985). *Beyond IQ: A triarchic theory of human intelligence.* New York: Cambridge University Press.

Sternberg, R.J. & Suben, J.G. (1986). The socialization of intelligence. In M. Perlmutter (Ed.), *Perspectives on intellectual development: The Minnesota symposia on child psychology.* Hillsdale, NJ: Erlbaum.

Sutherland, P. (1992). *Cognitive development today: Piaget and his critics.* London: Paul Chapman Publishing.

Taylor, P., Richardson, J., Yeo, A., Marsh, I., Trobe, K. & Pilkington, A. (1995). *Sociology in Focus.* Ormskirk: Causeway.

Thomas, E.M. (1969). *The harmless people.* Harmondsworth: Penguin.

Tietjen, A.M. (1986). Prosocial moral reasoning among children and adults in a Papua New Guinea society. *Developmental Psychology, 22*, 861-868.

Tong, R. (1992). *Feminist thought: A comprehensive introduction.* London: Routledge.

Turiel, E. (1983). *The development of social knowledge: Morality and convention.* Cambridge: Cambridge University Press.

Vygotsky, L.S. (1934). *Thought and language.* Cambridge, MA: MIT Press 1962.

Vygotsky, L.S. (1966). Development of the higher mental functions. *In Psychological research in the USSR.* Moscow: Progress Publishers.

Walker, L.J. (1984). Sex differences in the development of moral reasoning: A critical review. *Child Development, 55*, 677-691.

Walker, L.J. (1989). A longitudinal study of moral reasoning. *Child Development, 60*, 157-160.

Walker, L.J. (1995). Sexism in Kohlberg's moral psychology? In W.M. Kurtines & J. Gewirtz (Eds.), *Moral development: An introduction.* Needham Heights, MA: Allyn & Bacon.

Walker, L.J., de Vries, B. & Trevethan, S.D. (1987). Moral stages and moral orientations in real life and hypothetical dilemmas. *Child Development, 58*, 842-858.

Weinberg, R.A. (1989). Intelligence and IQ: Landmark issues and great debates. *American Psychologist, 44*, 98-104.

Wertsch, J.V., McNamee, G.D., McLane, J.B. & Budwig, N.A. (1980). The adult-child dyad as a problem solving system. *Child Development, 51*, 1215-1221.

Williams, W.M. (1998). Are we raising smarter children today? School- and home-related influences on IQ. In U. Neisser (Ed.), *The rising curve: Long-term changes in IQ and related measures.* Washington, DC: American Psychological Association.

Williams, W.M. & Ceci, S.J. (1997). Are Americans becoming more or less alike? Trends in race, class, and ability differences in intelligence. *American Psychologist, 52*, 1226-1235.

Wober, M. (1974). Towards an understanding of the Kiganda concept of intelligence. In J.W. Berry & P. Dasen (Eds.), *Culture and cognition: Readings in cross-cultural psychology.* London: Methuen.

Wood, D.J., Bruner, J.S. & Ross, G. (1976). The role of tutoring in problem solving. *Journal of Child Psychology and Psychiatry, 17*, 89-100.

Wood, D.J., Wood, H.A. & Middleton, D.J. (1978). An experimental evaluation of four face-to-face teaching strategies. *International Journal of Behavioural Development, 1*, 131-147.

Zigler, E. & Styfco, S.J. (1993). Using research and theory to justify and inform Head Start expansion. *Social Policy Report, Society for Research in Child Development, 7*, 1-21.

► Introduction

This chapter looks at the development of identity – the characteristics of the person, both as an individual and as a member of their gender. The chapter looks firstly at theories of the development of individual personality, then at theories of the development of gender identity, and finally at research into the changes brought about through adolescence.

The main theories considered here see personality development, gender development and adolescence in a social context, that is, as taking place in interaction with other people. However, reference will be made to some other theories to complete the picture.

Chapter summary

- Unit 1 looks at theories of the development of personality.
- Unit 2 looks at theories of the development of gender identity and gender roles.

- Unit 3 looks at research into social development in adolescence, relationships with parents and peers, and cultural differences in adolescent behaviour.

Unit 1 Personality development

KEY ISSUES

1 What are the main theories explaining how personality develops?

2 What are the strengths and weaknesses of these theories?

This unit looks in detail at two main theories of personality development. First, the *psychodynamic approach*, looking principally at the theory of Sigmund Freud. Second, the *social learning theory approach*. The unit begins with a brief glance at some traditional approaches to understanding personality.

1.1 Personality traits and types

Personality can be defined as 'those relatively stable and enduring aspects of the individual which distinguish (them) from other people and, at the same time, form the basis of our predictions concerning (their) future behaviour' (Wright et al., 1970).

The four humours For many centuries, the prevailing view was that there were four main personality types. This idea emerged from classical Greek and Roman medicine, which stated that our bodies are governed by four liquids or humours – blood, yellow bile, black bile and phlegm. Each personality type had a preponderance or excess of one of these four humours.

The *sanguine* type had a preponderance of blood, which made them energetic and forceful; the *choleric* type had a preponderance of yellow bile, which made them prone to

anger; the *melancholic* type had a preponderance of black bile, which made them depressive; and the *phlegmatic* type had a preponderance of phlegm, which made them unexcitable and sluggish.

Hans Eysenck In 1947, Hans Eysenck proposed the existence of two principal personality traits – dimensions of personality that we all share to some extent. The two traits are:

- extraversion versus introversion
- neuroticism versus stability.

Extraverts are active, outgoing and sociable, while *introverts* are introspective and withdrawn. *Neurotics* are anxious and tense.

Eysenck designed psychological tests to measure people's scores on these traits. In Eysenck's view, everyone comes somewhere on the extraversion-introversion scale, although most of us are somewhere between extreme extravert and extreme introvert. Similarly, everyone scores somewhere on the neuroticism-stability scale, but most of us are neither extremely neurotic nor extremely stable.

Measuring two traits like this produces four main personality types: stable-extravert; neurotic-extravert; neurotic-introvert and stable-introvert. As Eysenck (1965) pointed out, this coincides exactly with the sanguine, choleric, melancholic and phlegmatic personality types.

Eysenck (1965) claimed our personalities were the result of the excitability and level of activity of our nervous system, and that this level is innate. To a large extent, then, we are each born with our basic personality.

The Big Five Many psychologists have thought of personality as variations on a set of basic traits or dimensions. Until recently,

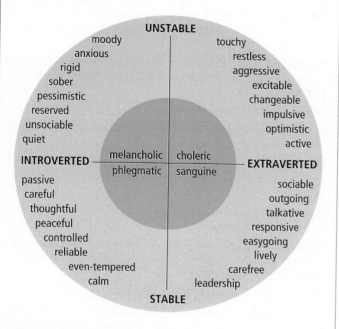

Figure 1 Eysenck's personality types

UNSTABLE

moody
anxious
rigid
sober
pessimistic
reserved
unsociable
quiet

touchy
restless
aggressive
excitable
changeable
impulsive
optimistic
active

INTROVERTED — melancholic | choleric — **EXTRAVERTED**
phlegmatic | sanguine

passive
careful
thoughtful
peaceful
controlled
reliable
even-tempered
calm

sociable
outgoing
talkative
responsive
easygoing
lively
carefree
leadership

STABLE

From Eysenck, 1965

there has been little agreement on what these traits or dimensions are. However, over the past ten years or so, there has been general agreement that adult personality can be described as a variation on five dimensions. These dimensions are often called the Big Five (Bee, 2000). They are:

- **Openness/Intellect:** how artistic, imaginative, insightful and original a person is, and how wide their range of interests is.
- **Conscientiousness:** how efficient, organised, reliable, responsible and thorough they are.
- **Extraversion:** how active, assertive, energetic, enthusiastic, outgoing and talkative they are.
- **Agreeableness:** how affectionate, generous, kind, forgiving, sympathetic and trusting they are.
- **Neuroticism:** how anxious, self-pitying, tense, touchy, worrying and unstable they are.

The initials of these traits spell OCEAN, an easy way to remember them.

The Big Five is simply a description of what are seen as the five basic dimensions of personality. Like Eysenck's classification, it fails to explain how personality develops from infancy to childhood to adolescence to adulthood. For developmental approaches, we need to turn to psychodynamic and social learning theories.

1.2 Psychodynamic theories

The term *psychodynamic* refers to a group of theories of personal development. Each of these theories has its own unique features, but they all share certain key characteristics.

- First, they see the human mind (or *psyche*) as active and dynamic.
- Second, they see the mind as complex, and most of them believe some parts of the mind operate unconsciously.
- Third, they are interested in mental disorders, particularly

neuroses, and see the cause of neurosis to be some kind of mental conflict. (Neuroses is a term used by many psychodynamic theorists to refer to a range of disorders including anxiety disorders, phobias and depression.)
- Fourth, they study processes of individual development from childhood to adolescence or to adulthood.

The most important and influential psychodynamic theory is *psychoanalysis*, founded by Sigmund Freud. The other psychodynamic theories were established by followers of Freud who disagreed with some or other aspects of psychoanalysis and broke away to set up their own approaches.

Freud and psychoanalysis

Sigmund Freud (1856-1939) launched psychoanalysis in Vienna in the 1890s. Psychoanalysis was concerned primarily with understanding and treating mental disorders. However, as the theory developed it began to encompass the whole range of human experience, from dreams and sexuality, to religion, art, literature and society. It also provided a powerful theory of the development of personality.

In psychoanalytic theory, an individual's personality is influenced by three main things.

- First, the relative power of the parts of their mind or psyche.
- Second, their experiences of pleasure and frustration as they develop through childhood.
- Third, the defences their conscious minds employ to cope with psychological threats.

The structure of the psyche

Freud (1923) distinguished three parts to the mind or psyche. The Id ('das es', literally, 'the it'); the Ego, ('das Ich' or 'the I'); and the Superego ('das überich' or 'the above-I').

The Id is innate and unconscious, and contains the biological drives that motivate us. The most important of these drives is Eros, the life drive (Freud, 1920). Eros motivates us to seek pleasure, sensual enjoyment and sex. The driving force of Eros is the *libido* (Latin for lust). The Id has no understanding of the outside world, of reality, or what is socially acceptable or even possible. It is concerned only with instant gratification or satisfaction of its irrational and selfish drives and desires. This urge for gratification is the *primary process* or *pleasure principle*. However, because the Id has no link with reality, it has no way of satisfying its desires, except through fantasy, which does not bring complete satisfaction. As a result, the Id suffers frustrations it cannot resolve.

The Ego begins to split off from the Id in the first few months, and is fully formed round about the age of 2 years. The Ego is conscious and is aware of the outside world. It operates on the *secondary process* or the *reality principle*. The Ego's job is to negotiate a working compromise between the desires of the Id and the restrictions imposed by reality. This means the Ego must regulate the demands of the Id, defer its incessant clamouring for instant gratification, and direct its desires into realistic and socially acceptable channels. In the case of totally unrealistic or unacceptable desires, the Ego tries to block them altogether. The conscious Ego is only a fraction of the total psyche. Most of the psyche is unconscious.

The Superego develops around the age of 5 years. It is the internalised moral voice of the parents. It consists of two parts.

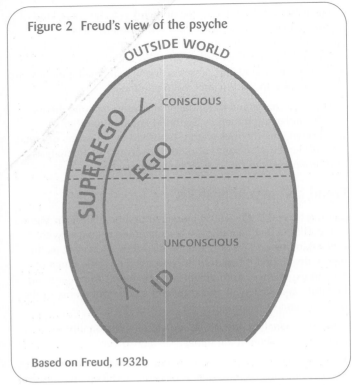

Figure 2 Freud's view of the psyche

Based on Freud, 1932b

First, the *Ego ideal*, the image of what the person would like to be. This part of the Superego rewards the person if they match up to their Ego ideal. Second, the *conscience*, or what the person feels they ought to be. The conscience punishes the Ego for deviating from the moral path. The Superego is partly conscious and partly unconscious, so the Ego is aware of some of its ideals and rules, but not all of them.

The relationship between the three parts of the psyche is tense and even hostile. The Id's drives demand instant gratification. They are opposed by the Superego which seeks to punish the immorality of those desires. The Ego struggles to keep some semblance of order, striving to find a way of satisfying at least some of the Id's desires, while keeping within the bounds of social acceptability and without provoking too much punishment from the Superego.

Personality types According to psychoanalytic theory, the individual struggles with conflicting motivations – the drives of the Id, the rationality of the Ego, and the moral commandments of the Superego. Freud sees the human being as a zone of conflict between drives, reason and morality.

In 1931, Freud distinguished between three basic personality types (which he called 'libidinal' types), each of which is dominated by one part of the psyche.

The erotic type has a psyche dominated by the Id. Love, sex and pleasure are uppermost on their minds.

The narcissistic type has a dominant Ego and is motivated to 'look after Number One'. Their Superego is likely to be weak and there is little check on their selfishness. They may even be prone to criminality.

The obsessional type has a dominant Superego. They are governed by fear of being punished by the conscience.

Various hybrids of the above three types can exist too. The erotic-obsessive-narcissistic type would be the perfectly adjusted human personality (Freud, 1931a).

Key terms

Psychodynamic theories *A family of approaches to psychology, including psychoanalysis and a number of related offshoots.*

Psychoanalysis *An approach in psychology founded by Sigmund Freud. The most influential of the psychodynamic theories.*

Psyche *The inner being or mind.*

Id *The unconscious part of the psyche. The location for the innate drives that motivate us.*

Eros *The life drive, leading to the pursuit of pleasure, sensual gratification and sex. One of the two main innate drives rooted in the Id.*

Libido *The engine that drives Eros (and the stages of child development, see below).*

Primary process/pleasure principle *The principle on which the Id works, namely the pursuit of pleasure, and gratification of innate drives and desires.*

Ego *The conscious part of the psyche.*

Secondary process/reality principle *The principle on which the Ego works to cope with the demands of reality and find acceptable ways for the Id to satisfy its desires.*

Superego *The moral part of the mind, consisting of the Ego ideal and the conscience.*

Ego ideal *One part of the Superego. This contains an idealised image of the self that the Ego would like to be.*

Conscience *The internalised voice of the parents. This punishes the Ego if the person strays from the moral path.*

Erotic type *A personality type where the Id is dominant.*

Narcissistic type *A personality type where the Ego is dominant.*

Obsessional type *A personality type where the Superego is dominant.*

Stages of child development

From 1905, Freud began to map out a sequence of stages in child development. These stages are often known as *psychosexual stages*.

In Freud's theory, the driving force in child development is the *libido*. As childhood progresses, the libido focuses its erotic energy on different parts of the infant's body. Freud thought of the libido as the energy of sensual pleasure flowing through the body, which could become focused on any part of the body that received regular pleasurable stimulation.

Each of us has our own personal body map of *erogenous* or *erotogenic* (sexually exciting) zones, depending on our personal bodily experience. But Freud was interested in the erotogenic zones we all share. These are the mouth, the anus, and the genitals. Freud suggested the child's libido invests a high proportion of its energy in each of these parts of the body in turn. This gives rise to the sequence of stages of psychosexual development. These stages are:

- **The oral stage** (birth to 18 months approx.) – the libido is focused around the mouth

- **The anal stage** (18 months to 3 years approx.) – the libido is focused around the anus
- **The phallic stage** (3 to 5 years approx.) – the libido is focused around the genitals for immature self-stimulatory pleasures
- **The latency period** (5 to 11 years approx.) – the child's libido is engaged in social and intellectual pursuits rather than being focused on the body
- **The genital stage** (beginning with puberty) – the libido invests in genital pleasure again, this time for mature sexual pleasures.

The ages associated with each stage are very approximate. Each child works to their own timetable, and there can be considerable overlap between stages. However, the order of the stages is fixed.

If the child does not receive the right amount of pleasure or gratification at any stage, the libido may remain *fixated* there. If the child received too little gratification, the libido waits around for the pleasure it missed. If the child received too much gratification, the libido's motivation to move on is much reduced. Fixations give rise to distinct adult personality types.

The oral stage At birth, the umbilical cord is cut, and for the first time the infant can feel hunger. A baby can do nothing except bawl when hungry, and someone feeds them. This is pleasurable because it stops the discomfort of hunger, and soon the stimulation of the mouth in feeding becomes pleasurable in itself. The libido invests its energy around the mouth. The main libidinal pleasures of the oral stage are sucking (on the nipple or bottle), and later, as teething begins, biting.

If the child becomes fixated on the pleasures of sucking, they can develop an *oral dependent personality*. Oral dependants are symbolically sucking the rest of their lives. If their fixation was due to excessive gratification, they are likely to become *gratified* oral dependants – reliant on others and cheerfully gullible ('suckers' who 'will swallow anything'). If their fixation was due to insufficient gratification, they may become *frustrated* oral dependants – greedy, addictive (for example, to smoking), envious and impatient. If the child becomes fixated on the pleasures of biting, they are likely to develop an *oral sadistic personality*, becoming cynical, sarcastic, and prone to using 'biting' wit.

Evidence for the existence of the oral dependant types (gratified and frustrated) is quite strong (Kline & Storey, 1977). In a study conducted by Goldman-Eisler (1948), 115 participants were asked to complete self-rating character questionnaires. Analysing their responses, Goldman-Eisler found evidence for two distinct oral types: *oral optimists* who were extravert, nurturant, sociable and ambitious, and *oral pessimists* who were passive, aloof, withdrawn and verbally aggressive. The mothers of 100 of these participants confirmed that oral optimists had been weaned after 5 months, while oral pessimists had been weaned before 5 months. This suggests a link between gratification or frustration during suckling, and oral optimistic or pessimistic characters later in life. Goldman-Eisler interpreted this as support for psychoanalytic theory.

The signs of oral fixation are all fairly obviously linked to the mouth. This is because society accepts oral pleasures so we do not have to hide or disguise our fixations. We accept the role of the mouth as an erotic organ in kissing (and oral sex), and eating and drinking are pleasures we engage in publicly. All of us have some degree of oral fixation, and we can express our orality quite openly and directly.

The anal stage As the Ego develops, the child develops a sense of mastery over their own body, and finds they can control the action of their bowels. The physical pleasure of retaining and expelling faeces makes the anus the next main focus for libidinal investment.

Freud (1908) explored the effect of fixation during the anal stage. Fixation on the pleasure of retaining faeces (or anxiety about expulsion) can lead to the development of the *anal retentive* personality type. This type is characterised by the 'anal triad' – being obsessively clean and orderly, miserly, and obstinate. Anal retentives have a horror of mess or anything that reminds them of faeces. Fixation on the pleasures of expulsion can lead to the extravagant, messy, manic and creative *anal expulsive* personality type.

Fisher and Greenberg (1977, 1996) found evidence to confirm the existence of the 'anal triad' of orderliness, parsimony (miserliness) and obstinacy. Rosenwald (1972) found that people who scored high for anal retentiveness were very reluctant to put their hands into a brown substance resembling excrement. This suggests that anal retentives do have anxieties about faeces.

During the anal phase, the child comes under pressure from the parents over potty training. The child has to choose whether to submit to parental authority and win parental approval, or whether to resist authority and insist on making their own decisions over their bodily functions. From this choice, the child's attitude to authority is established. Some children grow up to be compliant. Others become rebellious, and prone to give those that harass them 'an invitation to a caress of the anal zone to express defiance' (Freud 1908) – in other words, to tell them to 'kiss my arse'.

Society does not approve of anal pleasures. We may eat in company, but we defecate alone, and anal sex is distinctly unmentionable. As a result, the signs of anal fixation are *sublimated*, that is, they express themselves indirectly.

One indirect expression of anal fixation is in attitudes to money. The anal retentive is miserly, hoarding money just as they used to retain their faeces. The anal expulsive is lavish, throwing their money around just as they wanted to do with their faeces when they were children (see Activity 1).

The phallic stage As the child gets a little older, increased physical coordination enables them to stimulate their genitalia. Regular pleasant stimulation encourages the libido to invest much of its energy here, and the phallic stage begins. For the boy, his penis is the centre of phallic pleasure, for the girl it is her clitoris. For the first time, children become strongly aware of sexual differences between boys and girls.

Fixation at the phallic stage leads to the development of the *phallically fixated* personality type. This type is symbolically masturbating for the rest of their lives. They are likely to be hysterical, exhibitionist, self-obsessed and narcissistic (in love with themselves). They are often uncomfortable with the opposite sex, and present an exaggerated display of masculinity or femininity.

In Freud's view, gendering (becoming masculine or feminine) only takes place at the phallic stage, and none of us is ever 100% masculine or 100% feminine. Phallically fixated individuals fear ambiguities in gender, and often feel insecure in

Key terms

Psychosexual stages *The main stages of child development – oral, anal, phallic, latency period, and genital stages.*

Erotogenic zone *Principal zones of the body in which the libido invests its energy. Also known as erogenous zones.*

Fixation *If the child receives too much or too little gratification at any psychosexual stage, libidinal energy may remain invested there, leading to fixation.*

Oral stage *The first stage, where the libido focuses its energy on the mouth.*

Oral dependent *Personality type arising from oral fixation on the pleasures of sucking.*

Oral sadistic *Personality type arising from oral fixation on the pleasures of biting.*

Anal stage *The second stage, where the libido focuses its energy on the anus.*

Anal retentive *Personality type arising from anal fixation on the pleasures of retaining faeces.*

Anal expulsive *Personality type arising from anal fixation on the pleasures of expelling faeces.*

Phallic stage *The third stage, where the libido focuses its energy on the genitals (penis and clitoris) for self-stimulatory pleasures.*

Phallically fixated *Personality type arising from phallic fixation on the pleasures of self-stimulation.*

Latency period *When the libido is less invested in erotic pleasures of the body, and more concerned with social, physical and intellectual engagement with the outside world.*

Genital stage *Mature sexuality, where the libido focuses its energy on the genitals (penis and vagina) for pleasures of intercourse.*

Sublimation *The process whereby libidinous impulses are expressed indirectly in a socially acceptable form.*

---

their own gender identity. As a result, they put on exaggerated displays of being 'all man' or 'all woman'.

The phallically fixated male is likely to be ultra-macho, putting on an aggressive display of masculinity. He may use accessories to exaggerate his machismo – sporting extensive tattoos, driving a fast car or dragging a rottweiler around with him on a chain. The primary audience for this performance is the phallically fixated performer himself. The secondary audience is other men, as he seeks to impress on them that he is more manly than they are. Despite appearances, the desire to impress and attract women comes a poor third.

The phallically fixated female may be an ostentatiously sexually voracious *femme fatale*. Again, her sexual display is firstly to make herself feel good, and secondly to impress and threaten other women. The desire to attract men again comes a poor third.

The latency period During this period, the libido is less engrossed in parts of the body and more concerned with friendships and learning. Fixations cannot happen here.

The genital stage At puberty, the individual enters mature sexuality. Again, the libido invests much of its energy on the genitals (penis again in the case of the male, vagina in the case of the female), but the aim now is for sexual relations with another. The genital stage lasts the rest of the individual's life.

For most people, most of their libidinal energy comes through to the genital stage, but everyone leaves a considerable amount behind in earlier fixations. Everyone's personality is influenced by their fixations. The oral, anal and phallic types outlined above are 'pure' character types. Every combination of fixations and personality characteristics is possible.

Defences

The third factor that affects the development of personality is the use of *Ego defences*. The defences develop during the latency period and are used by the Ego to fend off anxiety. The main source of anxiety lies in unacceptable desires arising from the Id. These desires can be libidinal, or can be aggressive. Other sources of anxiety are memories of upsetting or traumatic experiences that the Ego does not want to remember, or conflict between the Superego and the Ego.

Initially, Freud (1895, 1915) saw repression or motivated forgetting as the main Ego defence. Later he outlined the existence of other defences too (Freud, 1926). Some of the most important defences are:

- **Repression** The Ego deliberately tries to forget a traumatic experience or unacceptable desire, and pushes it down into the unconscious.
- **Denial** The Ego refuses to accept unpleasant reality. For example, the terminally ill patient who just will not accept that they are dying.
- **Rationalisation** The Ego constructs a plausible but false cover story for what it does. For example, the parent who hits their child out of anger, but claims they acted out of proper parental concern for the child rather than anger.
- **Reaction formation** The Ego conceals a motivation or desire that threatens it by turning it into its opposite. For example, the closet gay who is afraid of his homoerotic desires may hide them by becoming ferociously homophobic (hostile to gays).
- **Projection** The Ego attributes its own unacceptable desires to others. For example, the thug who is always getting into fights, but insists that he is merely defending himself against everyone else's hostility to him.
- **Displacement** The Ego takes out its feeling on some substitute object. For example, anger at one's partner, that may cause a lot of damage to the relationship if expressed directly, is taken out on the dog. Phobias (irrational fears) are a kind of displacement.
- **Intellectualisation** The Ego acknowledges what it is doing, but reduces anxiety by stripping it of any emotional content. For example, surgeons know they are cutting into other people's bodies, but see their action as a medical necessity, not an act of violence.

Evidence for Ego defences Research evidence lends support to the existence of these defences. To give two examples:

Sears (1936) looked at projection in people who gave high

Activity 1 Dirty money

Item A Freud's view

'A common usage in speech calls a person who keeps too careful a hold on his money "filzig" (filthy). Wherever archaic modes of thought have predominated or persist – in the ancient civilisations, in myths, fairy tales and superstitions, in unconscious thinking, in dreams and in neuroses – money is brought into the most intimate relationship with dirt. We know that the gold which the devil gives his paramours (illicit lovers) turns into excrement after his departure ... and everyone is familiar with the figure of the Dukatenscheisser ...'

(Dukatenscheisser is a term used in German for a wealthy person who wastes money. Ducats are a kind of gold or silver coin, and the Dukatenscheisser is literally 'a shitter of ducats'.)

Adapted from Freud, 1908

Item B Rolling in it

Questions

1 Look at Items A and B. What evidence do these provide for Freud's claim that money becomes a sublimated substitute for excrement?

2 With reference to Items A and B, suggest why miserliness and stinginess are seen as indications of anal fixation.

---

scores for obstinacy on a psychological test. He found that people who lacked insight into their own obstinacy were more likely to accuse others of being obstinate. People with the same level of obstinacy but who were aware of it were less likely to project the trait onto others. Sears found the same effect with people who were stingy or bashful.

Brewin and Andrews (1998) found that between 20% and 60% of clients undergoing therapy because they had been abused as children said that there were periods in their lives when they had not been able to remember the abuse. In some cases, this amnesia lasted for years. This provides evidence for the existence of repression.

The value of Ego defences Freud saw these defences as unsuccessful and unhealthy on the whole. Repression, for example, does not make unacceptable desires or traumatic memories go away, it merely hides them in the unconscious from where they haunt the Ego, causing anxiety and neurotic

symptoms. Projection can lead to paranoia and poison relations with others, displacement can lead to unfair treatment of others, and the example of reaction formation given above is a recipe for violence.

One defence Freud did see in a positive light was *sublimation*. Here, impulses are transformed into something socially acceptable. For example, sexual and aggressive desires may be expressed in art or sport. In fact, Freud (1930) saw the existence of civilisation itself as due to the sublimation of sexual and aggressive impulses into other, more productive, channels.

His daughter, Anna Freud (1936), took a more positive view of Ego defences. In her view, the aim of psychoanalysis should not be to help the patient get rid of their defences, but to help them use them positively and effectively, protecting the Ego from anxiety without causing trouble with other people.

Ego defences and personality Evidence suggests that Ego defences can and do become part of the individual's personality.

Klein (1951) found that people differ in how they see the world, and distinguished between 'sharpeners' who focus on details, and 'levellers' who like to overlook details and focus on the overall impression. Levellers are more likely to stress uniformity, homogeneity and agreement, while sharpeners stress differences and disagreements. Klein found that levellers were more likely to use denial as a defence than sharpeners.

Myers (2000) cites evidence for a 'repressive coping style' – people who have a high need to be socially accepted show low levels of anxiety, are slow to report negative memories, and are good at forgetting information when instructed to do so. Myers and Brewin (1994) found that female repressors were more likely to have had negative relationships with their fathers.

Overall, there is evidence that orally-fixated people tend to try to change reality with their defences, and favour projection and denial. Anally-fixated people favour controlling defences like intellectualisation, while phallically-fixated people are more prone to using repression (Pervin, 1970).

Evaluation of psychoanalysis

Contributions of psychoanalysis Psychoanalytic theory has made some enduring contributions to psychology. These include the following.

- First, that the mind is complex and that some mental activity is unconscious.
- Second, that children mature through a series of stages.
- Third, that childhood experiences (including relationships with parents) have a lasting effect on later life.
- Fourth, that human beings are motivated by drives (especially the erotic drive), and are neither prisoners of their genes nor simply the products of social conditioning.

Psychodynamic criticisms of psychoanalysis Many later psychodynamic theorists considered Freud's theory to be rather unbalanced. Some, including his daughter Anna Freud, thought he placed too much emphasis on the unconscious, and not enough on the conscious Ego. Some felt he overestimated the importance of childhood experience, and underestimated later experience. Some thought he failed to attach enough importance to other relationships in the child's life. Many felt he overemphasised the role of sexuality in human motivation. Later psychodynamic theories tried to rectify these alleged failings in Freud's theory (see below).

Activity 2   Homophobia

Item A   Experimental evidence

A sample of heterosexual men were given a questionnaire on homophobia (hostility to male gays) to assess their attitudes towards homosexuality. From this sample, 64 participants were selected for the next stage in the research – 35 homophobes, and 29 non-homophobes.

The participants were then shown videos of male homosexual, lesbian and heterosexual erotica. A penile plethysmograph (a ring that fits around the penis) was used to measure the level of sexual arousal of each participant while watching the three types of erotic video.

No differences were found in levels of arousal between the two groups of participants watching the heterosexual and lesbian sex scenes. Levels of arousal watching the male homosexual scenes were as follows:

Percentage aroused by male gay sex scenes

Homophobic group	80%
Non-homophobic group	33%

Adapted from Adams et al., 1996

Question

Read Items A and B. Discuss the psychological motivation for homophobia in terms of Freud's ideas of phallic fixation and the Ego defence of reaction formation.

Item B   Homosexuality in the world of 'rap'

A Los Angeles gang – the macho world of gangsta rap

In the world of 'rap' and 'homeboys', some men indulge in homosexual practices while denying they are gay, and insisting on maintaining an aggressively heterosexual and homophobic image.

The 'homie-sexuals' and 'homo-thugs' are in-the-closet gay homeboys who worship a rap culture that shuns homosexuality. They would not dream of coming out and believe that all gay men should remain in the closet. 'I'm not a faggot – I just mess around with other brothers' is their mantra.

For the homo-thugs, manhood – in its most macho sense – is crucial. They don't believe in openly embracing their (homo) sexuality. Instead, they believe in going out en masse and 'beating the shit' out of openly gay men or 'sissies'.

Adapted from *The Guardian Guide*, 25.8.01

Eysenck's critique Beginning in the 1950s, Hans Eysenck fought a sustained campaign against psychoanalysis. In his *Decline and Fall of the Freudian Empire*, Eysenck (1985) claimed that psychoanalysis was unscientific, ineffective as a therapy, and had encouraged sexual permissiveness and immorality.

The effectiveness of psychoanalytic therapy is discussed in Chapter 36, and Eysenck's opinions about morality may say more about him than about psychoanalysis. However, the accusation that psychoanalysis is unscientific needs to be considered.

Psychoanalysis as a science Science is supposed to deal in observable evidence, but psychoanalysis deals in metaphysical (non-observable) concepts like Ego and Id which cannot be shown to even exist.

According to the philosopher Karl Popper (1934), a theory is only scientific if it makes predictions or hypotheses which can be tested by observation or experiment, and which can be disproved if incorrect. Popper believed that psychoanalysis does not present clear hypotheses for testing, but, because its theory is so complex, it can always come up with an answer for everything. For example, psychoanalysis may predict that children who experience harsh potty training will grow up to be anally retentive. But if they don't, that is not taken as evidence that the prediction is wrong, it is explained away as due to reaction formation. For Popper, this is unscientific.

Supporters of psychoanalysis present a number of defences. Some point out that many sciences refer to invisible and unprovable entities, for example, nuclear physics talks of subatomic particles that no one will ever see. Others argue that many sciences, for example, geology and astronomy, do not lend themselves to experimental testing – 'indeed, experimentation with the heavenly bodies is particularly difficult' (Freud, 1932a).

Some claim that many elements of Freudian theory do present testable hypotheses and are supported by research. Kline (1984) and Fisher and Greenberg (1996) cite evidence for unconscious processing, oral and anal personality types, Ego defences and other Freudian ideas.

Analyst Adam Phillips (in Bragg, 1998), by contrast, accepts that psychoanalysis is not a science, but argues that there are many kinds of truth, not all of which are scientific. In his view, psychoanalysis has a high truth value, even if it is not scientific.

In an interesting twist, modern evolutionary psychology has lent some support to psychoanalytic theory. Badcock (1995) claims that the oral and anal stages do exist, and make sense in terms of survival. In his view, each child is in rivalry with its siblings, and struggles with them to get the best treatment from the mother. The child that suckles most enthusiastically will get the most nourishment. Moreover, suckling releases a hormone in the mother's body that reduces her chances of becoming pregnant, so the baby that suckles longest fends off competition from a younger sibling the longest. Once weaned, the mother checks how well the child is eating by checking its faeces. Badcock argues that the child that controls its bowel movements most effectively will be able to manipulate the mother into giving them more food. In Badcock's view, it pays the child to be oral when suckling, and anal once weaned. He claims other features of psychoanalytic theory can be shown to serve similar survival functions.

Freud's case studies Freud's work has been further criticised on methodological grounds. He studied the childhood recollections of a small sample of white, middle-class Viennese women who were suffering from neuroses, and from this he generated a whole theory of human nature. Neither the reliance on recollection nor the nature of the sample inspire much confidence in Freud's conclusions.

Since the 1980s, Freud has come under more personal attack. His integrity as a scientist has been challenged, he has been accused of dishonesty in the reporting of his case studies, and his whole theory has been condemned as a complete fabrication built on a foundation of lies (Masson 1984; Crews 1993; Webster 1995).

On their own, Freud's case studies do not provide a strong foundation for psychoanalysis. However, many other analysts have written up many more case studies over the years, providing psychoanalysis with a wider and more varied sample, and more controlled evidence from childhood experience. In addition, Freud drew on other sources of evidence to support his theories, including myths, cultural customs and jokes (Sachs, 1991). Freud saw literature as a rich repository of psychological insight, and was as interested in testing his theories with reference to the works of Shakespeare and Goethe as he was in his clinical findings. Psychoanalysis remains influential in literary criticism.

Freud is one of the great pioneers, and provided what some see as the richest and most fruitful theory in psychology. According to Kline (1988), psychoanalysis deserves its popularity because it addresses what really matters in human life – something which much laboratory-based experimental psychology conspicuously fails to do. Psychoanalysis provided a whole vocabulary by which the 20th century understood itself, and, maddening though it may be to its more vitriolic critics, it still will not lie down. 'The climate of our culture remains … resolutely Freudian' (Bresnick, 1998).

A psychosocial approach – Erik Erikson

An important psychodynamic alternative to Freud's psychoanalytic theory was proposed by Erik Erikson (1902-1995). Erikson believed that Freud's theory attached too much importance to the unconscious and sexuality, and too little importance to developments after adolescence. He did not reject Freud's ideas, but tried to balance them with a stronger focus on the conscious Ego, social relationships, and developments throughout life.

Erikson believed that personality emerges through a series of stages in which the individual faces crises or challenges involving their own abilities and relationships with others. He called these stages *psychosocial*. The way the individual resolves the crises presented by each psychosocial stage will contribute to their overall personality development.

Erikson (1950) proposed eight stages in all, four during childhood and four from adolescence to old age. This unit looks at the psychosocial stages of childhood. The later stages are discussed later in this chapter and in the next one.

Stage 1 Early infancy (first year of life). During this stage, the infant's key social relationship is with their caregiver or 'maternal person'. The crisis the infant faces is whether they can trust the caregiver to satisfy their needs. The infant who is fed and comforted by the caregiver is likely to grow up to be a trusting and hopeful personality. The infant who is not satisfied may grow up to be mistrustful and lacking in hope.

Stage 2 Later infancy (ages 1-3 years approx.). In this stage, the important relationships are with the parents. The crisis the child faces is whether or not they can develop autonomy (self-sufficiency). The child who resolves this crisis successfully masters the challenges of feeding, walking and control of their bowels, and develops self-confidence, pride, self-esteem and a sense of will-power. The child who fails to master these challenges is prone to self-doubt and shame, and may lack will-power.

Stage 3 Early childhood (ages 3-5 years approx.). In this stage, the significant relationships are with the family. The crisis the child faces is whether or not they can develop a sense of purpose or initiative in their actions. The child who resolves this crisis successfully can explore and show independence, planning and daring, and grows up to be independent, questioning and responsible. The child who fails to resolve the crisis is likely to grow up lacking independence and purpose, and prone to guilt if they even desire independence.

Stage 4 Middle childhood (ages 5-11 years approx.). In this stage, relationships with school friends, teachers and neighbours become significant. The crisis the child faces here is whether or not they can master tasks. The child who resolves this crisis develops a sense of industry and competence in their abilities. The child who does not resolve this crisis successfully is likely to grow up with a sense of inferiority and inadequacy.

Evaluation

Erikson's theory ties in well with other theories and research into child development. His account of the first stage fits in closely with the work of Mary Ainsworth et al. (1978) on attachment, in which she distinguishes secure and insecure attachment types.

Erikson's sequence of psychosocial stages are also broadly consistent with Freud's psychosexual stages. The crises faced by the child at each of Erikson's stages echo the experiences of the child in the oral, anal and phallic stages and latency period in Freud's theory.

Like Freud, Erikson (1959) believed that therapy could straighten out problems resulting from failures to resolve crises encountered during childhood development.

However, whereas Freud's theory suggests that the individual personality is largely fixed by adolescence, Erikson proposes the existence of four more stages after the onset of adolescence, which suggests that later life developments are important too.

Although Erikson's theory seems persuasive, there is little direct evidence to support it, and he does not explain how the child moves from one stage to the next.

1.3 Social learning theory

Social learning theory emerged in the USA in the 1930s as learning theorists tried to investigate and evaluate aspects of psychoanalytic theory. Over the years, social learning theorists have conducted a large amount of research on children and their relationship to the environment. Social learning theory focuses on observable behaviour and the process of learning. It does not discuss parts of the psyche or stages of development. Two of the leading social learning theorists are Albert Bandura and Walter Mischel.

Albert Bandura and observational learning

Bandura's principal contribution was the idea of *observational learning*. One main form of observational learning is *imitation*, where an individual learns a new behaviour by observing the actions of another – the *model*. The classic study of imitation was conducted by Bandura et al. (1961). They found that children who had seen an adult attacking a 'Bobo doll' (a five foot high punch-bag toy) were more aggressive to the doll than those who had seen the adult quietly playing with other toys. (See pp 316-317 for a more detailed outline of this research.)

The other main form of observational learning is *identification*, where the learner adopts a whole social role from another – the *role model*. Bandura explains the acquisition of gender roles in terms of the child's identification with the same-sex parent.

Reinforcement Observational learning does not need to be reinforced – children can learn new behaviours simply by observing and imitating others. However, new behaviour patterns are most rapidly acquired if reinforcement is applied. For example, if the learner receives a reward for imitating the model, that is likely to encourage the learning of new behaviour. If the learner is punished, that may discourage them from imitating the model.

In addition, Bandura found that learning is affected if the model is rewarded or punished for their behaviour. If the learner sees the model being rewarded for their actions, they are more likely to imitate those actions. This is known as *vicarious reinforcement* – the reinforcement is indirect since the reward is not delivered directly to the learner. On the other hand, if the model is punished for their behaviour, the learner is less likely to imitate that behaviour. Bandura and Rosenthal (1966) found that people learned a negative emotional reaction to a stimulus if they saw someone else receiving an electric shock when that stimulus was presented.

Factors affecting observational learning

Bandura identified five main factors influencing observational learning.

Availability For observational learning to occur, the child must be able to see the model exhibiting the behaviour – either directly from real life, or through the media.

Attention The learner must pay attention to the model and what the model is doing. Attention will be greater if the model is distinctive, powerful, similar to the learner (eg, same sex), and has high status or prestige. Attention will also be greater if the behaviour of the model has usefulness or functional value to the learner.

Retention Observational learning can only occur if the learner can clearly observe, understand and remember the behaviour of the model. The more communicable the behaviour is, the more likely it is to be learned. The child is more likely to remember the behaviour if they can name it.

Motor reproduction Learning is only possible if the learner has the motor skills to reproduce the observed behaviour – that is, to do it themselves. Learned behaviour may not be reproduced immediately. Bandura distinguished between *acquisition* (learning) of a behaviour and *performance* of that behaviour. Some behaviours may be learned but not exhibited for some time. Bandura called this *latent learning*.

Motivation Observational learning is affected by the motivation of the learner. Reinforcement may play a role here.

Social cognitive theory

Bandura believes that the individual plays an active part in their learning experiences. They are not simply shaped by their environment – by the models that present themselves and the rewards and punishments that others provide. They consider and evaluate what they observe, they select what to imitate, they weigh the consequences of adopting this or that behaviour. By 1986, Bandura was calling his approach *social cognitive theory*. This reflected his growing interest in the active role played by the individual in their learning.

Reciprocal determinism According to Bandura, individuals do not merely respond to their environment, their behaviour changes the environment they are responding to. To some extent, then, people engineer the experiences they have. Behaviour and the environment influence each other. Bandura (1973) called this *reciprocal determinism*.

The self and learning Bandura sees the self as central to learning. The individual does not simply learn in response to outside influence such as models and rewards and punishments from others. The self plays an important part in directing learning.

Bandura (1971) suggested that the individual develops a self-concept, a picture of themselves. This allows a person to keep an eye on their behaviour and experiences and to judge and evaluate themselves. Bandura calls this process *self-monitoring*. As a result, *self-reinforcement* or *intrinsic reinforcement* is possible – the individual is able to reward and punish themselves. In Bandura's (1971) words, 'There is no more devastating punishment than self-contempt'. Self-reinforcement is an internal process. For example, a child may take pride and gain pleasure from learning to solve a problem, even when nobody else is present.

People develop a sense of their own abilities and an awareness of the degree to which they can control the factors that influence their lives. Bandura (1986) refers to this as *self-efficacy*. An important part of self-monitoring is judging one's abilities and capacities to learn new behaviours. People with high self-efficacy are confident about learning new behaviours.

Self-efficacy affects motivation. People with high self-efficacy will tend to seize opportunities and rise to challenges. Those with low self-efficacy tend to lower their horizons, avoid opportunities and shrink from challenges.

Evaluation

Social learning theory provides an explanation for how new behaviours are learned. However, it has little to say about personality as such, or about the development of personality.

More recent versions of social learning theory focus on cognitive processes but critics argue that social learning theory has little to say about cognitive development (Grusec, 1992). Bandura tends to see the basic processes of observational learning as the same for all age groups. In this respect, his theory is not developmental.

In his defence, Bandura (1986) did recognise changes in the way people process information as they mature and experience new situations. However, this is a long way from the widespread reorganisation of knowledge and thought proposed by developmental psychologists such as Piaget (Durkin, 1995).

Social learning theory focuses on behaviour which can be directly observed and measured. As a result, it can be tested in laboratory situations. Supporters of social learning theory see this as one of its main strengths. However, laboratory settings are a long way from everyday situations. Whether the findings of laboratory studies reflect behaviours outside the laboratory is questionable. Bandura's Bobo doll experiments have been criticised as artificial. As a result, critics have argued that there are problems generalising from his findings to the wider society. (See p 317 for an evaluation of the Bobo doll studies.)

Walter Mischel and situationism

Bandura largely ignored personality. Walter Mischel (1968) went further – he rejected the idea that personality exists. He based his view on the observation that the same person behaves differently in different situations. If personality is seen as a collection of traits or characteristics which influence a person's response to a range of situations, then similar responses would be expected. If, as Mischel claims, people's responses vary widely depending on the situation, personality, as defined above, does not exist. For example, if a person is honest in one situation and dishonest in another, if they are caring in one situation and uncaring in another, if they are sociable in one situation and unsociable in another, then this suggests that their behaviour is directed by the situation rather than their personality.

For Mischel, people learn to respond to each situation more or less independently of any other situation. Human behaviour

---

Key terms

Observational learning *Learning by watching another's behaviour.*

Imitation/modelling *A form of observational learning where specific behaviours are imitated.*

Model *The person being learned from in imitation learning.*

Identification *A form of observational learning where a particular role or identity is learned.*

Role model *The person being learned from in identification.*

Vicarious reinforcement *When the model receives reinforcement which encourages or discourages the learner to imitate the model.*

Latent learning *When the learner acquires a new behaviour, but does not exhibit it until a later time.*

Reciprocal determinism *Where the individual and the environment influence each other.*

Self-monitoring *The individual observes and evaluates their own behaviour.*

Self-reinforcement/intrinsic reinforcement *The individual rewards or punishes themselves.*

Self-efficacy *A person's judgement of their own capabilities.*

Activity 3   Observational learning

Item A   Learning to wheely

Item B   Vicarious reinforcement

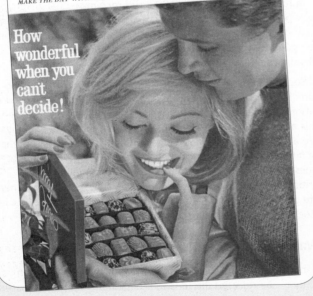

Questions

1 Look at Item A.

a) How does the small girl learn to do a wheely?

b) What effect will receiving praise from the older girl have on the smaller girl's behaviour? Explain your answer.

c) What will be the likely effect on the smaller girl's behaviour to see the older girl receiving praise? Explain your answer.

2 Look at Item B. Use the idea of vicarious reinforcement to explain how the advert is designed to encourage the viewer to buy the product.

---

is therefore governed by stimuli and reinforcement provided by the situation, not by personality traits. For example, one study showed that personality tests were very poor predictors of the behaviour of American Peace Corps volunteers in Nigeria (Mischel, 1965).

In Mischel's view, there is little consistency in any individual's behaviour in different circumstances. He examined a number of studies which attempted to predict people's behaviour on the basis of their personality scores. Mischel (1968) found that correlations of consistency of behaviour in different situations averaged just below 0.3. This is a very weak relationship.

An early study providing support for Mischel's view was

conducted by Hartshorne and May in 1928. They set 11,000 children aged between 8 and 16 behavioural tests of honesty, altruism and self-control in different situations (including home, school, church and sports events). They found most children showed little consistency in their answers – the average correlation between a child's answers was 0.23, indicating a low consistency in behaviour. This suggests that the child who would give an old lady her purse back if she dropped it, would also quite happily pinch sweets from the corner shop if the opportunity arose.

For Mischel (1968), this is evidence that 'the concept of personality traits as broad response dispositions is ... untenable'.

In his view, our behaviour is governed by the reinforcements we receive in each situation. As a result, we learn to behave differently in different situations. Mischel calls his approach *situationism*.

The consistency paradox We believe that people are consistent in their actions, and generally find little evidence to the contrary. Mischel calls this the *consistency paradox* (Mischel & Peake, 1982). In his view, this belief is false. He explains it as follows.

We generally only know other people from a narrow range of situations (for example, at college and on the bus to and from college), and get used to their behaviour in those situations. Since behaviour is governed by the situation, if circumstances remain the same, people's behaviour in those situations is likely to be consistent. From this we wrongly assume that the consistency in their behaviour is due to enduring personality traits. Only if we encounter them in different situations are we likely to see how wide their range of behaviours can be. So, for example, we may find Suzanne the kindest of people at school, but if we saw her at home we'd realise what a horror she is to her little sister!

Cognitive factors Mischel (1973) developed his theory to take cognitive factors into account. He conducted an experiment in which he placed sweets in front of children, and measured how long it took the children to give in to temptation. He found that the resistance of the children was influenced by the way they saw the sweets. If the experimenter described the sweets as 'brown logs', the children resisted well. But if the experimenter drew attention to the tastiness of the sweets, the children caved in and ate them. This suggests that it is not so much the situation itself, but the way the person perceives or evaluates the situation that matters.

This actually allows Mischel to sneak in some person variables through the back door. These take the form of personal cognitive factors like expectations and values which can lead individuals to interpret situations in particular ways. This may give their behaviour some consistency across situations.

Allowing some role to person variables was confirmed by Bowers (1973) who, in a review of 11 studies, found person variables accounting for 13% of the variance (range) in people's behaviour, situation variables accounting for 10%, and 21% due to an interaction between them. The other 56% of the variance in behaviour was put down to random 'error'.

Evaluation

Recent support for situationism comes from Judith Rich Harris (1999) who points out that children 'compartmentalise' their world, and hold a 'separate mental account' for each relationship. Children's behaviour is likely to be influenced by their parents at home, but by their peers outside of the home. As a result, their behaviour shows little consistency across situations – something which the children are neither aware of nor worried about.

Situationism relies on correlations of consistency of behaviour, which Mischel finds to be low (around 0.3). This is supported by Hartshorne and May's correlation of 0.23. However, this has been challenged. Rushton et al. (1981) rejigged Hartshorne and May's figures and found consistency

Key terms

Situationism *An explanation of human behaviour in terms of the situation, not personality. Situationism stresses the inconsistency of an individual's actions in different situations.*

Consistency paradox *The belief that people are consistent in different situations when, according to situationist theorists, they are not.*

correlations of 0.72, which are much higher. Epstein (1979) asked college students to keep diaries of what they did in various situations, what happened to them, and how they felt. Correlations of consistency between one day and the next were low (around 0.3). However, when the sample period was extended from two days to longer periods, for example two 14 day periods, correlations of consistency rose to around 0.8. This suggests people are more consistent than situationism claims.

Most researchers now accept that both personality and situation affect behaviour. In some circumstances situation may be more important – for example, nearly everyone stops at a red light – in others, personality may be more important – for example, in a romantic relationship.

Neither Bandura nor Mischel provide a developmental theory – the processes of learning they describe are essentially the same for all age groups. Nor have they much to say about personality. Bandura largely ignores it. Mischel actually rejects the idea of personality as a collection of traits or characteristics which produce similar or consistent behaviour in a range of situations.

Summary

1   Traditional approaches to personality focus on traits or personality types. These approaches do not explain how personality develops.

2   Freud's psychoanalytic theory states that the individual personality is shaped by three main factors: 1) the relative strength of the Ego, Superego and Id; 2) experience of gratification and frustration during the stages of child development; 3) the use of Ego defences.

3   Erikson's psychosocial approach sees the development of personality in terms of how the individual faces a series of crises and challenges throughout their life.

4   Social learning theory stresses the learning of behaviour rather than stages of child development.

5   Bandura explains child development in terms of observational learning and reinforcement.

6   Mischel's situationism challenges the notion that people develop consistent personalities, and sees behaviour as dependent on the situation.

Unit 2 Gender development

2.1 Sex and gender

Sex

Sex matters. The first question everyone asks when a baby is born is 'Is it a boy or a girl?' In all cultures, the sex of the child is one of the most important facts about them – often *the* most important fact.

In some cultures, the sex of the child may largely determine their life experience. Education, opportunities, legal status and civil rights may differ significantly for the sexes, with females usually getting the worst deal. In other cultures, including our own, the differences in the ways males and females are treated may be less drastic but still significant. Boys and girls are likely to be dressed differently, given different toys, and expected to act and even think differently. This may affect their later lives in important ways.

The *sex* of the child, male or female, is a biological matter, determined by the chromosomes. Females inherit an X chromosome from each parent; males inherit an X chromosome from their mother, and a Y from their father. The female genetic make-up or *genotype* is XX; the male is XY.

Gender

Gender refers to the behaviours, attitudes, beliefs and sense of identity that society deems appropriate to each sex. Those behaviours deemed appropriate to the female sex are defined as *feminine*. Those deemed appropriate to the male sex are *masculine*.

To begin with, infants act in much the same way regardless of their sex (Sanson et al., 1985). As childhood progresses, however, their behaviour starts to diverge. In general, girls start to behave in more feminine ways, boys in more masculine ways.

The child's sense of self as masculine or feminine is called *gender identity*. If the child's behaviours, attitudes and beliefs correspond to those deemed appropriate by society for a person of their sex, then they are said to be conforming to the appropriate *gender role*.

In brief, sex is a biological fact; gender is a social fact (Moghaddam, 1998). However, the terminology is not rigid. Some researchers use the terms sex and gender interchangeably – for example, it is not uncommon to see the term 'sex role' for gender role.

The main question addressed in this unit is how the child becomes gendered – how they acquire their gender identity, and how they come to adopt their gender role. There is a nature-nurture debate here. Some theories suggest gender is a result of being biologically male or female – it is rooted in the genes and the action of hormones. Others claim that gender is culturally or socially constructed, and that each child is taught the 'appropriate' gender role through upbringing and socialisation.

Key terms

Sex *The biological identity of an individual as either female or male.*

Genotype *The genetic make-up of an individual. Females have XX chromosomes; males have XY.*

Gender *The behaviours, attitudes, beliefs and sense of self that society deems appropriate to each sex.*

Feminine *The gender deemed appropriate for females.*

Masculine *The gender deemed appropriate for males.*

Gender identity *An individual's sense of self as being of one gender or the other.*

Gender role *The prescribed set of behaviours, attitudes and beliefs an individual of each sex is supposed to conform to.*

2.2 The nature-nurture debate

In trying to decide how far gender is rooted in biology, and how far it is the result of socialisation, psychologists have followed various avenues of research.

- One avenue is to look at psychological and behavioural differences between the sexes and to see if these have a biological or social basis.
- A second avenue is to see whether *transgendering* – people who do not conform to the gender role or identity deemed appropriate for their sex – has biological or social roots.
- A third avenue is to examine cases of *sex reassignment*. Infants who are born *intersexed* – neither wholly male nor wholly female – can be treated with surgery and hormones to become one sex or the other. On rare occasions, an infant who has suffered damage to the genitals can be raised as a member of the opposite sex. How successful sex reassignment is may provide evidence for how far gender identity is biological or social in origin.
- Finally, cross-cultural research can reveal how universal gender roles are. The more universal they are, the more likely they are to have a biological basis.

Psychological differences between males and females

This section begins with a brief summary of some of the reported psychological differences between males and females. It considers arguments that these differences are biologically based. It then provides a critique of these arguments.

Plenty of studies have reported differences between males and females. For example, research into cognitive abilities indicates that females are better at verbal skills (Halpern, 1992), while males are better at visuo-spatial skills (Masters & Sanders, 1993) and mathematics (Benbow & Lubinski, 1993). These differences may have a biological basis. Moir (1993) claims that male and female brains are different. Males are said to have a dominant right hemisphere, giving them better visuo-spatial and mathematical abilities, while females have a dominant left hemisphere, giving them superior communication and verbal skills. Brain scanning studies conducted by Sally and Bennett Shaywitz indicate that females use both hemispheres for linguistic processing, while males tend to use only the left hemisphere (Kohn, 1995).

Research into behavioural differences suggests that boys are more assertive and physically aggressive in their play than girls (Maccoby & Jacklin, 1974). Again, this may have a biological basis. Young et al. (1964) injected pregnant female monkeys with testosterone, and found that female offspring born to these monkeys were likely to be more aggressive. Since the human male foetus produces testosterone at around six weeks, while the female produces oestrogen, this suggests that the aggressiveness of the male is governed by male hormones and is therefore biological in origin (Money & Erhardt, 1972).

Recent studies found that the level of male hormone bathing the human foetus in the womb correlates with the degree of eye contact the infant gives. Those with the lowest levels of male hormone (mostly girls) gave more eye contact at 12 months than those with the highest levels (mostly males). This may provide the basis for females having greater interest in other people and superior communication skills (Irwin, 2002).

Evaluation

The case for biologically-based sex differences seems strong at first sight. However, there are reasons why these findings should be treated with caution.

- First, studies that find no sex differences are often not published, so the studies that do find differences attract an undeserved amount of attention (Durkin, 1995).
- Second, much evidence is simply contradictory. For example, some studies have shown that boys are not better at maths (eg, Hyde et al., 1990).
- Third, differences found between sexes are often small compared to differences in performance within each sex (Anderson, 1987).
- Fourth, researchers may be unconsciously biased. There is evidence that female researchers are more likely to find women better at verbal skills (Hyde & Lynn, 1988), while male researchers are more likely to find women more conformist than men (Eagly & Carli, 1981). This suggests that researchers can themselves be influenced by sex stereotyping.
- Fifth, if psychological sex differences do exist, they may be the result of socialisation rather than biology. For example, Eccles and Jacobs (1986) suggest that the *belief* that maths is a boys' subject may result in boys performing better at maths. Even differences in brain activity may result from different upbringings and experience rather than being genetically based.
- Finally, the issue of psychological sex differences is a political football, bedevilled by ideology and vested interests. Eagly (1995) suggests feminist psychologists display *beta bias*, wanting to downplay differences as part of their commitment to equal opportunities and equal pay. Equally,

researchers with leanings towards evolutionary psychology may display *alpha bias*, looking for significant differences to confirm their belief that males and females have evolved to play different roles.

Overall, research into psychological differences between the sexes does not settle the nature-nurture debate.

Key terms

Beta bias *A bias that downplays differences between the sexes.*

Alpha bias *A bias that exaggerates differences between the sexes.*

Transgendered people

Most cultures, including our own, assume that there is a clear relationship between sex and gender. It is assumed that biological females will tend to behave in feminine ways (adopting a feminine gender role), regard themselves as feminine (develop a feminine gender identity), and, from puberty, will be heterosexually attracted to males. Similarly, it is assumed that males will adopt a masculine gender role, develop a masculine gender identity, and be heterosexually attracted to females.

In reality, however, things are not so simple. Many individuals do not fit the accepted pattern.

Some people, despite being clearly male or female biologically, may not conform to the gender role, gender identity or sexual orientation deemed appropriate for their sex. Such people can be regarded as *transgendered*. Transgendering may take several forms.

- Some people can be *psychologically androgynous*, that is, they show psychological characteristics of both sexes (Bem, 1974). This can provide greater flexibility in coping with life's demands, and may well be an advantage over being rigidly masculine or feminine.
- Some are *transvestite* and like to wear the clothing of the other sex. During the 20th century, female transvestitism has become acceptable, even normal – few people now bat an eyelid if a woman dresses in a suit and tie. Male transvestitism remains socially taboo (despite the best efforts of Eddie Izzard).
- Some are *transsexual*, with a gender identity at variance with their sexual genotype. Some transsexuals develop a conviction that they are psychologically members of the opposite sex during childhood, others at puberty.
- Some are *bisexual* (sexually attracted to members of both sexes) or *homosexual* (sexually attracted to members of their own sex). Some bisexuals and homosexuals retain the gender identity and/or gender role deemed appropriate to their biological sex, others may not.

Research into the possible biological basis of transgendering has been inconclusive. Transsexuality does not run in families, which suggests it is not genetic. However, there may be some biological influence. A structure in the hypothalamus (called the BTSc) is known to be different for males and females. Evidence suggests that male transsexuals (biologically male, but with a female gender identity) have a female type BTSc, while female transsexuals have a male type. However, this only becomes apparent at puberty and may not be the cause of transsexuality (Phillips, 2001).

Homosexuality Studies into homosexuality have been contentious in the extreme. In the early 1990s, research was published in the USA suggesting that homosexuality had biological roots. Simon LeVay in 1991 claimed to have found a structure in the hypothalamus (the INAH-3) that was smaller in male homosexuals than in heterosexuals, and in 1993 Dean Hamer published findings that sexual orientation was influenced by the gene Xq28. Hamer's work was widely seen as the discovery of a 'gay gene' (Burr, 1996).

The evidence is far from conclusive. For example, LeVay's and Hamer's work has not been confirmed, and concordance rates for homosexuality among monozygotic twins are only around 50%, lower than would be expected if homosexuality was genetic (Phillips, 2001).

The issue is highly political. In the USA, it is illegal to discriminate against any group over innate differences (like sex or race), and the search for a biological basis for homosexuality is in part motivated to give homosexuals the same protection against discrimination (LeVay, 1996). However, while the biologising of homosexuality may have progressive results in the USA, it may be a dangerous tactic elsewhere. For example, the Nazis in 1930s Germany reacted to 'evidence' that homosexuals were biologically different by branding them incurably abnormal and sending them to concentration camps where thousands died.

Many gay activists reject LeVay's and Hamer's work, seeing it as reviving Victorian psychiatric ideas that homosexuals are biological deviants (Rosario, 1998). They insist instead that bisexuality and homosexuality are lifestyle choices or preferences (eg, Garber, 1996).

Psychological explanations Psychologists have proposed alternative explanations for homosexuality. Freud (1905) suggested that one way male homosexuality can arise is if a boy identifies with his mother rather than his father. However, he believed different people can become homosexual for different reasons, and that homosexuals could not all be lumped together in one category.

Daryl Bem's 'exotic becomes erotic' theory suggests that people find the sex they are less familiar with the more exotic, and hence more desirable at puberty. Since most children prefer to play with members of their own sex in childhood, this makes the opposite sex exotic and attractive at puberty. However, those children who prefer the company of the opposite sex find their own sex exotic and hence desirable at puberty (Phillips, 2001). This idea receives support from Roberts et al. (1987) who found that boys who played with girls or played in a feminine way were more likely to become homosexual or bisexual. They found evidence that this was likely to happen to boys who had been separated from their parents due to illness or hospitalisation.

Hormonal explanations There is evidence that hormones may play a role. Female foetuses that were bathed in high levels of male hormones in the womb may develop tomboyish characteristics in childhood (Hines & Kaufman, 1994), and lesbian tendencies at adolescence (Phillips, 2001). Male homosexuality may owe something to the foetus being subject to a rapid ebb and flow of testosterone while in the womb (Cohen, 2001).

Gender as a performance Other approaches reject the whole idea of homosexuality as a fixed identity, whether biologically determined or acquired through socialisation. Judith Butler (1990), for example, sees gender as a performance – behaviour which can conform to gender roles (hence reinforcing and reifying them – making them 'real'), or which can challenge them and create new possibilities. Categories like masculine, feminine, heterosexual and homosexual may be more fluid than we suspect, perhaps so fluid as to be more or less meaningless.

Treating the transgendered Traditionally, transgendered people were seen as psychologically abnormal. Homosexuality was regarded as a psychiatric disorder up until 1973, but just as the DSM III dropped homosexuality from its classification system, so *gender identity disorder* (GID) was first included. GID is identified as persistent discomfort about one's assigned sex. It can arise if the family is unhappy about the sex of their child, causing confusion in the mind of the child as to their own gender (Phillips, 2001). Most children simply grow out of it, but some are given treatment, which can involve incarceration in mental institutions, which can be a harrowing experience for a young person (Scholinski, 1998).

The fact that 85% of children diagnosed with GID are boys, suggests that the diagnosis is reflecting a social bias that masculinity in females is acceptable, whereas effeminacy in males is not. From childhood onwards, the 'sissy' is punished more than the 'tomboy'. Providing treatment for GID may be just another form of sexual engineering, much as the 'treatment' of homosexuality was in the past. Indeed, treating children for GID may merely be a hidden form of attempting to 'treat' possible homosexuality.

The study of transgendered people does not settle the nature-nurture debate. Different theorists and researchers take very different views. Some explain it in terms of biology or genetics, others in terms of socialisation and childhood experience, others insist it is a lifestyle choice. Most see gendered or transgendered identities as fixed, but some even challenge this. So far, the issue remains inconclusive.

Sexual reassignment

It is estimated that up to 1%-2% of infants are difficult to classify as biologically male or female (Fausto-Sterling, 1999). Some may be genetically female (XX) or male (XY), but have experienced high doses of opposite-sex hormones as a foetus, leading to the development of sex organs at odds with their genes. *Congenital adrenal hyperplasia* (a girl born with enlarged clitoris and a sealed vagina) and *androgen insensitivity syndrome* (a boy born with apparently female genitals) are examples of this. Some are *hermaphrodite* – they have the reproduction organs of both sexes. Some are genetically XXY, born with a penis, and developing breasts at puberty (*Klinefelter syndrome*). Individuals who are biologically neither wholly male nor wholly female are termed *intersexed*.

The incidence of intersexuality may have increased in the USA since the 1940s and 50s due to the use of synthetic hormones similar to *androgens* (male hormones) to reduce the chance of miscarriage. This led to some female infants being born with masculinised genitals (Durkin, 1995).

Since the 1930s, intersexed infants have been treated with surgery and hormones in an attempt to make them biologically male or female, and raised accordingly. One pioneer of this approach, John Money, was so convinced of the success of this treatment that he concluded that any intersexed baby could be raised as either sex (Money & Erhardt, 1972).

Money proceeded to develop his *theory of neutrality*, claiming that all children, whether intersexed or not, can be raised successfully to assume whatever gender role and identity is assigned to them, provided they have the appropriate sex organs (which may be natural or artificially constructed). A genetic boy with female sex organs and raised as a girl will become a girl, and vice versa. Gender lies entirely in upbringing, not in the genotype.

'John'/'Joan' The opportunity for Money to put his theory to the test came when a Canadian family had their infant twin boys circumcised for medical reasons in 1966. Due to an accident, the penis of one boy ('John') was severely damaged during the operation. In 1967 Money surgically reconstituted 'John' (then aged 17 months) as a girl, and the child was raised as 'Joan'. Money reported that 'Joan' was tomboyish as a child, but otherwise adjusted well to being a girl, confirming his theory that gender is social, not genetic (Money & Erhardt, 1972).

However, following the case up some years later, Milton Diamond (1982) found that 'Joan' had been unhappy as an adolescent girl, masculine in appearance and behaviour, and uncertain of 'her' gender. When, aged 14, 'she' was finally told the truth of 'her' sex change, 'she' adopted a male name and proceeded to live as a man. Later, he had surgery to build a penis, married a woman and adopted her children (Diamond & Sigurdson, 1997).

Diamond (1982) accepts that intersexed individuals may have flexible gender identities and that reassignment through surgery and upbringing works for them, but the outcome of the 'John'/'Joan' case confirms his view that in non-intersexed individuals, gender has a biological basis, and cannot be changed with surgery and upbringing. However, in a more recently reported case, a male ('Jim') who was subjected to female hormones in the womb, was reconstituted as a female ('Jenny') at 7 months. 'Jenny' grew up to be bisexual in orientation, but quite convinced of her female gender identity (Phillips, 2001).

It may be that Money was right after all that gender is due to upbringing, not genotype, but that gender identity becomes fixed and unalterable sometime before 17 months. However, the number of cases where a non-intersexed infant has been reassigned to the opposite sex is small, and it is difficult to draw any firm conclusions.

Recently, intersex organisations have been established in several countries, the first being the Intersex Society of North American (ISNA), founded by Cheryl Chase in 1993. They oppose the surgical 'normalisation' of intersexed infants on the grounds that it is not being done for the child's benefit, but for the parents'. Intersex organisations celebrate intersexuality as a third sex, and believe that intersexed infants should be left alone until they are old enough to decide which sex they want to be.

Cross-cultural evidence

If gender is biologically based, then gender roles should be uniform across the globe. On the other hand, if gender is socially constructed, then marked divergences between different cultures would be expected.

Margaret Mead (1935) studied tribal peoples in New Guinea, and found substantial differences in gender roles between three tribes there. Among the Arapesh, both sexes were gentle and 'feminine'; among the Mundugumor, both were aggressive, competitive and 'masculine'; while among the Tchambuli, the females were sexually assertive, while the men were vain, insecure, and prone to self-adornment and gossip. Mead's study was hugely influential and has been cited as convincing evidence that gender is cultural, and owes nothing to biology or genes.

However, no other study has produced anything like such startling results. Some of Mead's other work has been branded as sloppy and based on hearsay rather than real research (Freeman, 1996). This calls her integrity as a social scientist into question.

Cross-cultural research into psychological differences between the sexes suggests that the level of economic development of a society is a crucial factor. Gender differences are small in many hunter-gathering societies like the Inuit (Eskimo) and Australian Aborigines, but more pronounced in agricultural societies (van Leeuwen, 1978). Women are more likely to be expected to be compliant and docile in herding societies which suggests that females lose status in those societies where the economic activities of males (herding the animals) is paramount. In terms of cognitive abilities, male superiority in visuo-spatial tasks is found in settled agricultural (and urban) societies, but not among hunter-gatherers (Berry et al., 1992). However, these differences do not rule out the possibility of a biological basis for sex differences in cognition. It could be that innate biological differences are 'brought out' in certain environments, and not others.

Aggression among young males is higher than females in most societies, regardless of whether the society actually encourages male aggression or not. Since females have nurturing responsibility for infants in virtually all cultures, one suggestion is that males adopt aggression as a *gender marker* to distinguish themselves from females (Segall et al., 1990). However, male hormones like testosterone may have some influence.

In conclusion, the available cross-cultural evidence does not enable firm resolution of the nature-nurture debate over gender. The likelihood is that both biology and socialisation have some contribution to make, interacting with each other in highly complex ways to produce gender roles and gender identities.

Key terms

Transgendered *People who do not conform to the gender role or gender identity deemed appropriate to their sex.*

Intersexed *Individuals who are biologically neither wholly male nor wholly female.*

2.3 Theories of gender acquisition: Evolutionary psychology

Darwin Evolutionary theory dates back to the work of Charles Darwin (1809-1882) who suggested that species evolve through the processes of natural selection and sexual selection (Darwin, 1859; 1871). In *natural selection*, individuals with adaptive features or behaviours are more likely to survive, have the opportunity to mate, and pass those features on to the next generation. In *sexual selection*, individuals with features that attract the opposite sex are more likely to mate, and pass their features on to the next generation. As a result, features that are *adaptive* and *attractive* will tend to flourish.

Social Darwinism In the hands of Social Darwinists like Herbert Spencer (1820-1903) and Sir Francis Galton (1822-1911), Darwinian theory changed into a bloody struggle for survival in which the strongest and most cunning flourish and the rest are pushed to the wall. In their view, human beings evolved during the stone age, and we are still basically adapted for stone age life. Moreover, pressures of survival meant that the sexes evolved differently – man as the hunter, woman as the home-maker.

As men used their aggression and intelligence to compete with each other in war and hunting, so women used their beauty and domestic skills to compete with each other for the attention of the best hunter. The hunter looks for the most attractive and docile women to mother his children, the woman looks for the best provider to father hers.

Social Darwinists believed that humanity 'progressed', with different racial and social groups reaching different levels of evolution. For Spencer and Galton, the ruling classes of the white race are the most highly evolved, its men courageous and intelligent, its women beautiful and well-tempered. Galton proposed a politics of selective breeding of the human species – *eugenics* – to keep the 'superior' strains of humanity pure and limit the breeding of 'inferior' groups (see pp 509-510 and 762-763).

Social Darwinism was controversial for its sexism, racism and *biological determinism* – explaining human nature entirely in terms of biology and inheritance, and underestimating the role of learning and culture. However, it exercised considerable influence on Western thinking in the late 19th and early 20th centuries. The Nazis drew heavily on Social Darwinism, which was one of the reasons for its unpopularity after the 1940s.

Sociobiology Evolutionary ideas re-emerged in *sociobiology*, launched by E.O. Wilson (1975). Again it was argued that human beings are basically adapted for life in the stone age and that males and females have evolved differently – man for hunting, woman for home-making (Wilson 1975; Barash 1982).

A new contribution was the idea of the 'selfish gene' (Dawkins, 1976). This suggests that the key to explaining the behaviour of the members of any species, including our own, is the survival of their genetic line. The behaviour of any individual is ultimately selfish – to further the survival chances of that individual's gene.

Evolutionary psychology

Emerging in the 1980s and 90s, evolutionary psychology is a more subtle approach. However, it follows sociobiology in explaining gender differences largely in terms of *reproductive strategies*. Assuming that the goal of most behaviour is to maximise the survival chances of the individual's genetic line, evolutionary psychology explains many differences between males and females in terms of *parental investment theory* (Trivers 1972; Wilson 1978).

Males can produce millions of sperm, can potentially father vast numbers of offspring throughout their adult lives, and their biological responsibility for the development of the offspring in the womb ends once their sperm has fertilised the female's egg. As a result, an effective reproductive strategy for the male is simply to impregnate as many females as possible, thus ensuring his genes flourish in the next generation. In terms of parental investment theory, male investment of time and effort in their offspring can be minimal.

Females, however, can produce only a limited number of eggs and a small number of offspring between puberty and the menopause. Moreover, they have to carry each infant for nine months in the womb. And they have to expend considerable biological resources – in terms of energy and nutrients – on the infant before it is even born. As a result, the best reproductive strategy for the female is to catch her man and keep him, so he will help provide for these precious children she has worked so hard to bear.

Evolutionary psychology sees important differences in male and female behaviour. The male is attracted to the physical appearance of the female, looks being a guide to how healthy she is as a child bearer (Buss, 1987). He is motivated to engage in sexual *promiscuity* or 'short-term mating' (Buss & Schmitt, 1993). The female however, is attracted to the abilities and resources – skills and wealth – of the man, as an indicator of how good a provider he will be (Buss, 1987). She is motivated to settle down with one mate, making home for him and looking after him (Rossi, 1977).

The male's great fear is that the children he is raising are not his own, so he will naturally seek to control his mate's sexual behaviour, to prevent her having sex with anyone else. The female's great fear is that her mate will abandon her for another female. As a result, male and female jealousy is different. Men are most jealous if their partner has sex with another man; women are most jealous if their partner falls in love with another woman (Buss et al., 1992).

From these basic ideas, evolutionary psychologists can develop explanations for almost any human behaviour. For example, they claim that man the hunter is naturally aggressive, sexually dominant, promiscuous, and has good visuo-spatial skills – useful for hunting. Woman the home-maker is domestic, submissive, nurturant, coy and *monogamous* (having a single mate), with better social and verbal skills – useful for keeping the group together, keeping her man, and raising the children. Everything is neatly explained. Gender roles are clearly based on biology and genetics and result from different evolutionary pressures on the sexes (Miller, 1999). (For a more detailed outline of evolutionary psychology and gender roles, see pp 289-290 and 640-645.)

Evaluation Evolutionary psychology promises much. It combines psychology and biology within an evolutionary framework. In principle, this is an excellent idea. In practice, it has been strongly criticised.

- First, it has been accused of biological reductionism and biological determinism – of reducing the complexity of human behaviour to genes and suggesting that it is largely determined by genes (Gould, 1981).
- In the process, evolutionary psychology leaves little space for human reason and free will (Malik, 2000).
- By claiming that gender roles are essentially rooted in biology, evolutionary psychology attaches little importance to culture. It tends to ignore cultural differences in gender

roles which indicate that they are far more flexible than biology would permit. For example, David Schmitt found that male promiscuity is higher in Protestant cultures than Catholic, Buddhist or Muslim ones. He also found variations in female promiscuity – women being more likely to engage in short-term mating as their economic and political power increases, or if there is a shortage of men (Crerar & Leake, 2001).

- Evolutionary psychology has been accused of sexism. Women are relegated to a subservient role. Since this role is rooted in biology, there is little they can do about it.

Darwinian feminism Perhaps the most effective critics of evolutionary psychology are Darwinian feminists like Anne Fausto-Sterling, Patricia Gowaty and Sarah Blaffer Hrdy. They claim that evolutionary psychology has serious flaws, in terms of its factual accuracy and its understanding of Darwinian evolution.

Hrdy (1981) argues that, from a Darwinian viewpoint, monogamy is a bad strategy for females. Since it restricts them to one mate, any genetic flaw he has will affect all her offspring and reduce the chances of her genes passing to future generations. It makes better sense for her to establish a bond with a good provider, and then mate secretly with several males so that her offspring have different fathers. Hrdy and Gowaty provide evidence that females do exactly this in various species – apparently sexually passive and monogamous, they are secretly active and promiscuous (Arden, 1996).

In humans, evidence for female promiscuity is provided by research by Robin Baker and Mark Bellis. They found that women's sexual behaviour actually favoured impregnation by their illicit lovers over their regular partners. Women are more likely to have sex with lovers when fertile and more likely to achieve orgasm with them – which assists fertilisation (Baker, 1996). This suggests that both sexes are designed for promiscuity, which undermines the traditional view of sex and gender presented by evolutionary psychologists.

Fausto-Sterling et al. (1997) point out that natural selection requires variation between individuals in their genetic make-up and behaviours. The picture of standardised gender roles presented by many evolutionary psychologists therefore shows a misunderstanding of Darwinian theory. Natalie Angier (1999) also emphasises variety – in who finds whom attractive, and in mating habits and reproductive strategies. For example, she suggests many males will realise that, since they do not know when a woman is ovulating, any attempt to spread their genes by multiple short-term mating will be a decidedly hit and miss affair. Such men may discover long-term monogamy works better to ensure that their genes flourish.

Both evolutionary psychology and Darwinian feminism are evolutionary theories. Neither provide a psychological account of gender acquisition. Both see the purpose of sex as reproduction. Both see gender as biologically based and arising from evolutionary pressure on reproductive strategies. The traditional view presented by evolutionary psychologists suggests a single strategy for each sex which results in a standard male and a standard female gender role. Darwinian feminism argues that reproductive strategies vary widely within each sex rather than between the sexes. This results in a variety of gender roles.

Finally, some of the criticisms of evolutionary psychology

outlined at the start of this evaluation on page 303 also apply to Darwinian feminism.

Key terms

Adaptive *Physical or behavioural features that improve survival chances.*

Eugenics *A political movement seeking to 'improve' human stock by selective breeding and forced sterilisation of the 'unfit'.*

Biological reductionism *Explaining human nature entirely in terms of biology and ignoring social and cultural factors.*

Biological determinism *Assuming that behaviour is shaped by biological factors.*

Promiscuity *Taking a large number of sexual partners.*

Monogamy *Maintaining a relationship with one long-term sexual partner.*

2.4 Theories of gender acquisition: Psychoanalytic theory

Sigmund Freud

Freud's psychoanalytic theory, emerging in the 1890s, proposed a more psychological view of sexuality and gender. In Freud's view, humans have sex more for pleasure than for reproduction. Human sexual behaviour and gender need to be explained psychologically, not biologically. Evolutionary explanations of gender in terms of different reproductive strategies will not suffice.

Freud doubted that gender had any significant innate basis. In his view, infants are effectively nongendered at birth, but during the phallic phase of development (around 4 or 5 years old) they undergo the *oedipus complex*, and from this experience they construct their gender as masculine or feminine.

The oedipus complex is an emotional tangle involving the child and their parents. Oedipus was a character from Greek mythology who inadvertently killed his father and married his mother. Freud suggested that every little boy harbours unconscious desires to do the same to his own parents.

The boy's tale Freud first outlined the oedipus complex as boys experience it (Freud 1905; 1909; 1924). According to Freud, the boy's primary love object is the one who feeds and nurtures him – the mother. During the phallic stage, the boy's erotic drive or libido invests even more strongly in the mother. He becomes possessive of her and wants to be the centre of her life. This brings him into rivalry with the father, leading to feelings of hostility to the father. The boy feels guilty about these feelings, and afraid that the father will retaliate and punish him by castration. (The boy fears for his genitals because at the phallic stage libidinal energy is focused on the genitals, and it is his libido that has got him into this mess.)

Usually, the boy resolves this terrifying ordeal by renouncing his desire for his mother, and identifying with his father – effectively making a deal with himself that if he grows up to be like dad, then one day he will marry a woman like mum. This leads to the boy developing a strong masculine gender identity (to be like his father) and a strong Superego or conscience

Activity 4 Evolution and gender

Item A | The traditional view

A picture from 1916 entitled, 'Should I Let Him Go Any Further?'

Women are selective, choosy, even fussy, in their choice of sexual partners, men are indiscriminate. Women tend to favour monogamy, men are naturally promiscuous. Women are 'coy', men are 'ardent'.

To bowl over reluctant females, peacocks evolved fancy tails, lions grew magnificent manes and men acquired wealth and status. As Aristotle Onassis put it: 'If women did not exist, all the money in the world would have no meaning.'

Adapted from McKie, 2002

Item B | More recent evidence

Female chimpanzees, baboons and Barbary macaques mate with many males over a short period of time. Female prairie dogs, sand lizards and field crickets will do the same. Promiscuous females often produce larger and healthier litters.

Many human societies provide evidence of similar mating patterns. For example, the Bari people of South America believe that several men can share in a child's parentage and will then help in its upbringing. A woman has sex with many different men in order to maximise the number who can share parenthood and provide for her child. There is nothing particularly coy about her behaviour.

Adapted from McKie, 2002

Item C | Predatory female

Sharon Stone played a predatory manipulator of men in the hit 1992 thriller Basic Instinct.

Item D | Lone mother

Michelle Pfeiffer with her baby. 'I really wanted a child but I didn't want some guy around to drive me nuts.'

Questions

1 What support does Item A provide for the traditional view of gender presented by evolutionary psychologists?

2 What support do Items B, C and D provide for the Darwinian feminists?

(telling him I must not desire mum, I must not hate dad). At adolescence, when he enters the mature genital phase, his libido commits him to heterosexuality.

A less common resolution is to avoid rivalry with the father by becoming more like the mother. This leads to a feminised gender identity and can lead to homosexuality.

The girl's tale Later, Freud (1925; 1931b; 1932c) outlined the female version of the oedipus complex. This is more complicated. The girl's primary love object is also the mother (the one who feeds and nurtures her), but then her libido starts to invest in the father as well. On top of that, her desires towards her father are complicated. She is possessive and wants to be the centre of his life, but she also wants to be like him and have what he has – ie, masculinity. In Freud's view, girls envy the privileges society grants to the male. This is the origin of Freud's notorious idea of female penis envy – not the sexist insult it is usually taken to be, but a recognition that girls resent the social demotion to 'second class citizens' they experience through not having a penis. Freud suggested that girls blame their mothers for making them female and denying them the privileges of their brothers, and this leads to feelings of guilt and fear of the loss of the mother's love.

Unlike the boy's oedipal experience, which is terrifying and threatening and needs to be firmly resolved, the girl's oedipus complex is confusing and depressing, and usually remains largely unresolved. As a result, the female gender identity is more complicated than the male. Typically, she identifies with her mother and is 'feminine', without giving up a desire and ability to take on masculine traits. She does not firmly renounce any desires, so her Superego is less rigid – see Carol Gilligan, pp 527-529 for evidence that females are less rigid in their moral thinking. Having two love objects – mother and father – she is capable of erotic involvement with both sexes later in life.

Just to complicate things even further, Freud suggests that the female has two sex organs, the clitoris and the vagina. She explores the pleasures of her clitoris during the phallic phase, but only discovers the pleasures of vaginal sex as a young adult. Clitoral sex is masturbatory and 'active', whereas vaginal sex is penetrative and 'passive'. As a result, female sexual pleasures are more varied than those of the male.

Freudian theory sees gender as constructed by the individual, not as innate or as the result of socialisation. Although Freud identified 'classic' masculine and feminine identities, he recognised that the presence of siblings – brothers and sisters – can complicate matters, and that each individual has a different experience and arrives at their own version of masculinity or femininity.

After Freud

Melanie Klein One of the most important psychoanalytic theorists of gender after Freud was Melanie Klein. Klein (1928; 1932) was one of the founders of *object relations theory*. In her view, the centre of a child's psychic life is not their libido, but their relationship with their mother. Klein suggested that the child becomes an individual through a series of stages of separation from the mother, of which physical birth is the first step. The child's deepest fear is to be reabsorbed into the mother's body. During the oedipal crisis the child seeks the 'flight to the father' as a liberation from this threat of reabsorbtion.

The point is that boys can make this escape, identify with the father and become masculine. Girls however, cannot fully escape the mother. They cannot identify with the father, because they are female, and remain enmeshed psychologically with the mother, hence feminine.

Psychoanalytic feminism Klein's ideas had a big effect on feminist psychoanalytic theory in the USA.

Dorothy Dinnerstein (1977) suggests that both sexes fear the power of the mother and the danger of reabsorbtion. Once boys have escaped the mother, they fear being drawn back into her power, and grow up with a fear of female power and a desire to control women. Girls, unable to fully escape, grow up feeling mentally dominated by the mother, and look for male partner to take control and free her from this domination. Hence both sexes are complicit in male domination of women in society.

Nancy Choderow (1978) suggests the boy has the easy job. He identifies with the father and breaks completely from the mother – independent from her as a person, and opposite to her in gender. Identity is achieved through separation, but the price paid is that males become self-contained and fear intimacy as a threat to their identity as male. The girl, however, has the much harder job of becoming independent as a person, since she remains the same sex and gender as the mother. Many girls fail to separate fully from the mother and achieve complete individuality. They grow up with a fear of separation and a tendency to over-relate and be dependent on others.

Dinnerstein and Choderow both suggest that the cause of this unhappy state of affairs is that mothers play the prime role in parenting. In their view, if co-parenting were more widespread, with men taking an equal role in raising the children, then the mother would not be the centre of the child's fears. As a result, children would grow up differently, gender roles would change, males would be less afraid of female power and better at intimacy, and females would be more confident in their own power and more independent.

Evaluation

The standard criticism of psychoanalytic approaches can be summarised by the following question – Where is the evidence? For example, critics have argued that the oedipus complex lacks hard evidence from laboratory studies and from other research methods which produce quantitative data. However, 'softer' evidence can be found. For example, Western literature is full of oedipal themes – from Shakespeare's *Hamlet* (circa 1601), Gothic texts like Ann Radcliffe's *Mysteries of Udolpho* (1794), Jane Austen's novels, Bram Stoker's *Dracula* (1897), D.H. Lawrence's *Sons and Lovers* (1913) to modern novels like Thomas Harris's *The Silence of the Lambs* (1989).

The following studies have been used to criticise psychoanalytic approaches. First, children raised by their mothers in lone-parent families and by lesbian couples show no difference in gender identity and gender roles than those raised by heterosexual couples (Golombok et al., 1997). Psychoanalytic theory implies that there would be differences. Second, there is evidence of gender identity in infants well before the phallic stage. For example, infant boys usually prefer 'masculine' toys and girls 'feminine' toys (O'Brien et al., 1983). This suggests that the learning of gender identities and roles may be well underway before the oedipal complex is supposed to be experienced.

Key terms

Penis envy *Freud's controversial idea that girls envy the advantages the boy enjoys through having a penis and being male.*

Object relations theory *A neo-Freudian theory that the key to child development is not the libido but the child's relationship with others (especially the mother).*

Co-parenting *Where both parents share equally in the raising of the children.*

2.5 Theories of gender acquisition: Social learning theory

Like Freud, social learning theory rejects the idea that gender has a genetic basis. However, unlike Freud, social learning theory sees the acquisition of gender as a direct result of learning. It is a relatively straightforward process compared to Freud's picture of children working out their gender identity in an emotional minefield.

In terms of social learning theory, children learn gender roles from the many models around them. These models include parents, peers, teachers and media figures. They provide illustration after illustration for *observational learning* – learning behaviours by observing and imitating the actions of others. Observational learning does not require *reinforcement* – children learn new behaviours simply by observing and imitating others. However, new behaviours are acquired more rapidly if they are reinforced.

Albert Bandura, one of the founders of social learning theory, believed that social learning could be seen most clearly from the learning of gender roles. In all cultures parents present children with direct examples of gender role behaviour. They also reinforce appropriate gender role behaviour in their children with rewards and punishments. Parents *socialise* their children, preparing them for their adult roles by providing them with gender-appropriate toys. For example, in many societies girls are given dolls and cooking equipment in preparation for the maternal and domestic aspects of their adult gender role (Bandura & Walters, 1963).

Reinforcement

To what degree are children reinforced for appropriate gender role behaviour?

Parental reinforcement Considerable research has been conducted into the way parents reinforce their children for gender-appropriate behaviours. Beverley Fagot (1978) studied children aged 20-24 months in the USA. She found that parents encouraged girls to dress up, dance and play with dolls, and rewarded them for signs of dependency and domesticity – eg, following mum around and helping her clean. By comparison, boys were rewarded for playing with blocks and trucks, and for active, physical play. Girls were sometimes criticised for running, jumping and climbing, while boys were discouraged from seeking help and playing with dolls. There is evidence of reinforcement for gender-appropriate behaviour being given to children as young as 18 months (Caldera et al., 1989). Research indicates that children were more likely to acquire rigid gender roles if their mothers had traditional attitudes towards gender and encouraged gender-typed play (Fagot et al., 1986; 1992).

However, the evidence is not clear-cut. Maccoby and Jacklin (1974) examined a range of studies of parental behaviour. They found little evidence that boys and girls were reinforced for gender-specific roles. They found no evidence that boys were rewarded for competitive or independent behaviour – in fact, there were some indications that boys were more likely to be punished for aggression. Maccoby and Jacklin concluded that there was 'a remarkable degree of uniformity in the socialisation of the two sexes'.

Most of the studies surveyed by Maccoby and Jacklin looked at the behaviour of mothers. The behaviour of fathers reveals a somewhat different picture. In one study, preschool children were presented with gender-typed toys and instructed to play with them in the appropriate way – for example, boys were asked to play with dolls in a 'maternal' way. Their parents were unaware of these instructions. Mothers were happy to see their children playing with either same-gender or opposite-gender toys. Fathers, however, did not approve of opposite-gender play. They ridiculed this violation of gender roles, particularly when it was a son behaving in a 'girlish' way (Langlois & Downs, 1980).

This finding has been supported by a number of studies. For example, Siegal (1987) found that fathers were more likely to reinforce gender-appropriate behaviours, especially in their sons. This led to boys adopting gender-specific behaviours earlier and more rigidly than girls.

Despite this evidence, there is little indication that reinforcement by fathers has a significant effect on the learning of gender roles. In fatherless families, boys and girls still emerge with gender-appropriate behaviours. The absence of a father appears to make little difference to boys' gender role development and none to girls' (Stevenson & Black, 1988).

Peer groups These are groups made up of people of similar age and social status – for example, children's friendship groups. There is evidence of considerable pressure in many peer groups to conform to the norms of the group. Judith Rich Harris (1999) argues that peer groups are the most important influence on the child, considerably outweighing the influence of parents. There is evidence that peer groups reinforce gender roles. For example, Langlois and Downs (1980) found that boys strongly disapprove of other boys playing with opposite-gender toys. Such disapproval is found even if the boys' mothers were tolerant of this kind of behaviour.

Modelling

As noted earlier, observational learning based on models can occur without reinforcement. Maybe too much importance has been placed on reinforcement and not enough on modelling as such. Research indicates that children pay more attention to a model if a) the model is the same gender as themselves and b) is behaving in gender-appropriate ways (Bussey & Bandura, 1984). And this selective attention can influence behaviour. In

Activity 5   Psychoanalytic theory and gender

Item A   Jimmy at 4 years old

'When I grow up,' says Jimmy at the dinner table, 'I'm gonna marry Mama'. 'Jimmy's nuts,' says 8-year-old Jane, 'You can't marry Mama and anyway, what would happen to Daddy?'

'He'll be old,' replies Jimmy, 'And he'll be dead.'

Then, awed by the enormity of his words, he adds hastily, 'But he might not be dead, and maybe I'll marry Marcia instead.'

Adapted from Fraiberg, 1959

Item B   Jenny at 4 years old

Jenny: You know, Mommy, when you die I am going marry Daddy.

Mother: I don't think so.

Jenny: I am too.

Mother: You can't. It's against the laws of God and man.

Jenny (close to tears): But I want to.

Mother (comforting her): You'll have your own husband when you grow up.

Jenny: No I won't. I want Daddy. I don't like you, Mommy.

Adapted from Cole & Cole, 2001

Item C   Rambo

This poster shows Sylvester Stallone as Rambo in the 1982 film First Blood. The Rambo films were popular in the 1980s, especially with young males.

Item D   The 'New Man'

The sensitive, nurturant 'New Man' was a popular image of masculinity in the 1980s and early 1990s.

Questions

1   Look at Items A and B. What evidence do they provide for Freud's theory of the oedipus complex in boys and girls?

2   Look at Item C. How might Rambo provide a model for young males trying to establish their gender identity?

3   Why would American psychoanalytic feminists like Dinnerstein and Choderow approve of the image in Item D?

one study, 8 to 9-year-old children watched adult men and women choose between gender-neutral activities – ie, activities not associated with either gender, for example, selecting an apple or a pear. The children tended to follow the choices of adults of the same gender as themselves – if most women chose an apple, most girls did the same (Perry & Bussey, 1979).

However, this is not always the case. A review of over 80 studies of same-gender imitation found that it occurred in only 18 of the studies (Barkley et al., 1977).

Parents as models Parents are an obvious source for observational learning of gender roles. Social learning theorists often point to same-sex parents as the main gender models for children. Girls tend to join their mothers for traditional gender-typed activities such as cooking and shopping, while boys are likely to wash the car and go fishing with their fathers (Lytton & Romney, 1991).

How important are parents as gender role models? Evidence from 'nonconventional families' suggests that they are not very important. A survey of studies of boys from fatherless families indicates there is little difference in their gender role development than from boys who grew up with their fathers (Stevenson & Black, 1988). Similarly, children reared in gay or lesbian families show hardly any difference in gender role development than children of heterosexual parents (Patterson, 1992).

Media models The media, particularly television and advertisements, provides another source of gender models which children may imitate. Research indicates that gender images on TV are highly stereotyped. Typically, men are shown in more dominant and higher status roles, while women tend to be depicted in subordinate roles as secretaries, shop assistants, waitresses, child-minders, nurses and housewives (Durkin, 1985).

In TV adverts, men provide authoritative voices, and are pictured at work, in cars, engaged in sport, or as receivers of services. Women are more often presented in domestic or romantic settings, or as users of products. Men tend to be depicted as active, aggressive, independent problem-solvers, while women are more likely to be presented as dependent, emotional sex objects in need of help in practical matters (Golombok & Fivush, 1994).

Children spend an enormous amount of time watching TV. Does this mean that the images of gender portrayed on television shape their gender identities and gender roles? The short answer is nobody really knows. Some studies have found that the more television children watch, the more likely they are to have traditional attitudes to gender roles (eg, Levy, 1989). However, the correlations are weak and they do not establish a causal link. It may be that children with traditional gender role beliefs like to watch more television.

Other studies have found little or no relationship between the amount of television watched and children's attitudes towards gender roles (eg, Meyer, 1980). And one study found that the more TV children watched, the less likely they were to have traditional attitudes to gender roles (Cheles-Miller, 1975).

Evaluation

Strengths Social learning theory attempts to provide a social account of the acquisition of gender. This focus has its strengths. Gender identities and gender roles change over time and they vary from culture to culture. This suggests that they are learned in a social environment – it is difficult to think of an alternative explanation for these historical and cultural differences.

Weaknesses Critics have argued that social learning theory fails to explain how and why gender roles change over time and vary from culture to culture. Why, for example, are many young girls in modern Western societies attracted to the idea of 'girl power'? Where did this idea come from in the first place?

The supporting evidence for social learning theory is not strong. First, the role of reinforcement in the acquisition of gender roles is not clearly demonstrated. In fact, it seems children pick up gender roles almost regardless of rewards. Second, the evidence for modelling as a basis for gender role acquisition is inconclusive. In addition, it remains unclear whether children adopt their gender roles from models, or whether they choose models on the basis of an already existing gender identity.

Social learning theory has little to say about the actual development of children's gender identity and gender roles. Children's attitudes towards gender and their gender roles appear to change quite significantly as they grow older. Social learning theory fails to provide an explanation for these changes (Stangor & Ruble, 1987).

Social learning theory has been criticised for presenting an oversimplified view of learning. Reinforcement tends to picture the child being manufactured and shaped by the powers that be. Similarly, observational learning has been criticised as oversimplified with the child portrayed as merely imitating same-sex models. In both cases, little is said about the child's view of the situation, about their selection and interpretation of models, about their acceptance or rejection of reinforcement (Schaffer, 1996). Duck (1990) suggests that the relationship between children and media role models is quite complex. Rather than children simply being influenced by what they see, the suggestion is that they actively seek out media figures who reflect their own sense of identity and model themselves on them.

Social learning theory rejects any biological basis for gender, yet biology may have an important role. For example, if boys play more physically energetic games, this may be a result of their motor development rather than social pressure towards adopting a masculine gender role (Scarr, 1992).

Social learning theory tends to describe rather than explain. It fails to give the level of explanation that a theory should provide. For example, it does not explain why rewards work (if indeed they do), how children perceive rewards, why gender roles exist in the forms that they do, how gender roles change, and why society values masculinity and femininity differently (Bem, 1993). Social learning theory is therefore a fairly weak theory of gender acquisition.

2.6 Theories of gender acquisition: Cognitive-developmental theory

Social learning theory has been criticised for largely ignoring a) what the child thinks and b) how gender roles develop. Cognitive-developmental theory, as its name suggests, addresses these two issues.

Cognitive-developmental theory was pioneered in the 1960s by Lawrence Kohlberg. According to Kohlberg (1966), 'The child's sex role concepts are the result of the child's active structuring of his own experiences; they are not passive products of social training'. Cognitive-developmental theory focuses on the child's developing understanding of gender. This is seen to be linked to the child's general cognitive development.

Kohlberg suggests that as children's cognitive frameworks develop they engage in an active search for information about gender. This includes a search for appropriate models from whom to glean information and gain reinforcement, but the emphasis is on the child actively selecting models rather than passively imitating whoever happens to be there.

Stages of gender development

Kohlberg identifies three stages in the acquisition of gender.

Stage 1 Gender labelling This begins around the age of 2½ – 3 years. The child develops a basic sense of gender identity. They can label themselves and others as male or female. At this stage, the child is not clear whether gender is fixed, or whether it changes over time or in different situations. Thompson (1975) confirmed that 2-year-olds can place themselves in the correct category when presented with pictures of male and female children, and by 2½ – 3 can identify the gender of others using cues like hair and clothing. However, they remain unsure of the permanence of gender (Slaby & Frey, 1975).

Stage 2 Gender stability Beginning around 3½ – 4½ years, the child realises that gender is permanent and irreversible – that it is constant over time. Slaby and Frey (1975) found that children at this stage know that they were the same sex as babies, and will be the same sex as adults. However, they are not so sure if gender is constant in different situations.

Children at this stage are still using physical cues – hair and clothing – to identify gender. This means that children can become confused over the gender of an individual if they are cross-dressed. If they see a man dressed in a skirt, they may be unsure if he is still a man (Emmerich et al., 1977).

Stage 3 Gender constancy This begins around 4½ – 7 years. Here the child is sure that gender is constant in different situations, and remains the same even if a person dresses or adopts a hairstyle associated with the opposite gender. With gender constancy, the child is now motivated to adopt the appropriate gender identity and gender role. They start looking for models, and their thoughts and actions become fully gendered.

Cognitive development and gender development Kohlberg was strongly influenced by Piaget's stages of cognitive development (See Chapter 28, Unit 1). He argued that gender identities and gender roles are only possible when children have reached the necessary stage in their cognitive development – when they have developed the mental structures required to *understand* gender. For example, gender constancy becomes possible when the child develops the skills of *conservation* (see p496).

Children must *understand* that gender is constant. Only when

Activity 6   Learning gender roles

Item A   Helping dad

Item B   Beth and Adam

A 6-month-old baby was given to a succession of adults to hold. In some cases the baby was dressed in pink and called 'Beth'; in other cases the baby was dressed in blue and called 'Adam'. Three toys – a train (male gender-typed toy), a doll (female) and a fish (neutral) were available to the adults to give to the baby. Adults of both genders smiled more at 'Beth', and gave 'her' a doll to play with. There was no difference in the likelihood of giving either 'Beth' or 'Adam' a train or toy fish.

Adapted from Will et al., 1976

Item C   Boys and girls come out to play

A similar experiment involved babies of both sexes, sometimes dressed and named appropriately for their sex, sometimes not. The researchers found that babies perceived as 'boys' were given more stimulation and were more likely to be given a hammer to play with, while those perceived as 'girls' received less stimulation and were more likely to be given a doll. The actual sex of the baby was irrelevant to the behaviour of the adults.

Adapted from Smith & Lloyd, 1978

Item D   Television come to Notel

In a Canadian town without access to television ('Notel'), less gender stereotyped attitudes were recorded among children than at two other towns – 'Unitel', which had one television channel, and 'Multitel', which had several. When 'Notel' finally obtained television, researchers noticed an increase in gender stereotyped attitudes among children.

Adapted from Williams, 1986

Questions

1   How might a social learning theorist interpret the behaviour pictured in Item A?

2   Read Items B and C. What support do these studies provide for the idea that adults socialise infants into gender roles?

3   What evidence does Item D provide for the theory that television gives stereotyped images of gender roles, and these images affect the views of children?

they *think* in this way will they consistently behave in gender-appropriate ways. Once children are fully aware of the *concept* of gender, they will relate a range of relevant information to the concept – particular clothes, hairstyles, mannerisms and behaviours that are gender-appropriate. At this stage, models become important – children select gender-appropriate behaviours from the range of available models. This is an active process directed by an understanding of gender constancy. From this point of view, children don't merely imitate models simply because they are rewarded by others for doing so. They imitate models because they consider it appropriate – it makes sense – and this provides its own rewards. In this respect, children socialise themselves.

Kohlberg (1966) rejects social learning theory's view of the sequence that leads to gender acquisition. For social learning theory, the sequence is: 1) I want rewards, 2) I get rewards when I do girl-like things, 3) therefore I want to be a girl, 4) I am a girl. In Kohlberg's view the sequence is: 1) I realise I am a girl, 2) therefore I want to do girl-like things, 3) doing girl-like things is intrinsically rewarding.

Evaluation

Kohlberg focused on two issues largely ignored by social learning theory – 1) the cognitive and 2) the developmental aspects of gender identity and gender roles. These are the main strengths of his theory.

There is evidence to support the idea of stages of gender development. A number of studies have indicated a link between the various stages and gender-typed behaviour. In a study of 2 and 3-year-olds, those with the most developed gender identity were most likely to play with gender-typed toys (Weinraub et al., 1984). A study of gender constancy looked at the response of 4 to 6-year-old children to TV ads in which toys were presented as suitable for either boys or girls. Children with high gender constancy were more likely to pick up these gender messages. For example, if they saw an opposite-gender child playing with a toy, they avoided playing with that toy (Ruble et al., 1981). A further study indicated that same-gender imitation – imitating models of the same gender as themselves – begins after children have acquired gender constancy (Frey & Ruble, 1992).

However, not all the evidence supports Kohlberg. Social learning theorists point out that children show preferences for gender-typed toys and models before gender constancy is acquired (Bussey & Bandura, 1984; 1992).

Despite its strengths, cognitive-developmental theory, like social learning theory, leaves a lot unexplained. Its focus is narrow. By concentrating on the stages of development of children's understanding of gender, little or no account is taken of the role of biology, emotion, motivation, social environment and culture, and no explanation is provided as to why society values masculinity and femininity differently (Bem, 1993).

2.7 Theories of gender acquisition: Gender schema theory

Gender schema theory, also known as gender schematic processing theory, was established by Carol Martin and Charles Halverson (1981; 1987).

Gender schema theory agrees with Kohlberg's cognitive-developmental theory that the key to gender acquisition is the child's understanding of gender. It sees the child as playing an active role in searching for information about gender, and processing that information. However, gender schema theory sees this process beginning at a much earlier age than Kohlberg suggests.

According to gender schema theory, cognitive influence on gender behaviour begins when the child first discovers his or her gender, not when the child acquires full gender constancy. In other words, children do not need to have achieved a full understanding that gender is constant over time and across situations before gender starts to influence their preferences and behaviour.

Once basic gender identity is established, the child starts to look to the environment for information to support and develop their understanding of gender. From around three years old, they begin to develop *gender schemas*. A gender schema is a mental representation of gender, of the characteristics of each gender and of gender-appropriate behaviour. According to Carter and Levy (1988), the establishment of gender schemas is a better predictor of a child's gender-typed cognitions and behaviour than the acquisition of full gender constancy.

Development of gender schemas

Evidence that gender schemas are being developed from an early stage is provided by Fagot and Leinbach (1993) who found that infants as young as 9-12 months react differently to male and female faces. By the age of 2-3 years, children notice sex differences, know their own gender and can label pictures of boys and girls consistently and accurately. Maccoby (1988) suggests that the establishment of basic gender categories is simple – a person is either male or female. It is also important – it acts as an organising principle for new information. Once gender schemas start to be formed (from around 3 years), children begin showing preferences for same-gender company and gendered activities (Martin & Little, 1990).

Fagot et al. (1986) point out that gender role behaviour changes as gender schemas change. Infants of 26 months are largely unable to identify the sex of adults and children from photos, but at 36 months, they can do this. Once they can identify gender from appearance, they start to show a marked preference to play with their own gender. Girls who can identify people's gender from photographs show lower levels of overt aggression, suggesting that once children can recognise gender, they start to conform to gender roles.

However, 2 to 3-year-olds who can identify people's gender from photographs do not show any strong preference for gender-typed toys. This suggests that there is more to gendered behaviour than simple recognition of gender differences and identification of gender identity.

By age 4-6 years, children have developed a complex concept of their own gender, and by 8-10 years, they have a sophisticated understanding of the opposite gender (Martin et al., 1990).

Information processing

Gender schema theory draws on information processing theory to account for how gender schemas develop. It predicts that if a

Activity 7 Cognitive development and gender

Item A Cross-dressing

Item B Gender constancy

Researchers measured the gender constancy of a sample of 2 to 5-year-olds. They found some children had higher gender constancy than others – a greater awareness that gender does not change in different situations or with different clothes and hairstyles. The children were shown a split-screen film with a male on one side and a female on the other. Each model performed a variety of actions, some appropriate to their gender, some more appropriate to the other gender. The researchers found that, regardless of what the models were doing, the boys with higher gender constancy showed a strong preference to watch the male model, while the girls with higher gender constancy showed some preference to watch the female model.

Adapted from Slaby & Frey, 1975

Item C Gender-appropriate behaviour

There is evidence that even quite young children have definite ideas as to what is appropriate for males and females. Take the following assertions by children aged 2½ to 3½ years:

- 'Boys hit people.'
- 'Girls talk a lot.'
- 'Girls give kisses.'
- 'Girls often need help.'
- 'Boys play with cars.'

Adapted from Schaffer, 1996

Questions

1 According to Kohlberg, what would children at Stages 1 and 2 make of Item A?

2 What evidence does Item B provide for the view that children seek same-sex models after they have acquired gender constancy?

3 How can Item C be used to criticise Kohlberg's three stage model?

---

child is presented with an object, they ask themselves if it is relevant to them. For example, 'Dolls are for girls; I am a girl; therefore the doll is relevant to me'. As a result, a girl will pay attention to, play with and remember the doll, while a boy, deciding the doll is irrelevant to him, will pay it less attention.

This may help explain why gender roles and gender stereotypes are so resilient and resistant to change. Children accept information that is consistent with their schemas, and reject information that is inconsistent. Hence children will misinterpret, distort or simply forget if they see adults behaving in counter-stereotypical ways. Seeing a woman with a toy train, and a man quietly sewing, children's recollections are likely to swap the activities round so that the woman and man fit their stereotypes (Carter & Levy, 1988).

In one study, 3-year-olds were presented with a number of gender-neutral items – eg, a burglar alarm, a number puzzle and a shoe stretcher. The children were told that some objects were boys' toys, some were girls', and some were for both genders. As gender schema theory predicts, the children paid more attention to the 'same-gender' objects, and were better at remembering them later (Bradbard et al., 1986).

When asked to remember a series of events associated with a particular gender – such as mending a car or doing the laundry – children remember more of the information which fits their own gender identity (Levy & Fivush, 1993). It appears that even memory is gender-biased.

Evaluation

Advantages According to gender schema theory, as soon as children are aware of their gender they begin to build and develop gender schemas and behave in gender appropriate ways. This process does not depend on the acquisition of gender constancy as cognitive-developmental theory argues. As the studies outlined in this section show, there is evidence to support this view.

A further advantage of gender schema theory is its use of information processing theory. For example, it looks at gender schemas and how they select and organise gender-related information, and how memory processes this information (Stangor & Ruble, 1987).

Disadvantages Gender schema theory shares many of its disadvantages with social learning theory and cognitive-developmental theory. It tends to see the child as an individual rather than a member of a social group. It largely ignores culture.

The creation of gender identities and gender roles is a collective activity. The construction of gender knowledge reflects the culture of which the child is a member. Social relationships and cultural beliefs provide the guidelines for gender differences. These differences are not simply constructed in the child's mind, no matter what their information processing capacities (Whyte, 1998).

Where do gender identities and gender roles come from? Why do they change? Why do they vary from society to society? Gender schema theory, like social learning theory and cognitive-developmental theory, cannot answer these questions without widening its focus to include the wider society, social change and cultural differences (Bem, 1993).

Gender acquisition – conclusion

A broad agreement appears to be emerging that social learning, cognitive processes and cognitive development are all important factors in the acquisition of gender identity and gender roles. For example, Bussey and Bandura (1984)

Key term

Gender schema *A mental representation of gender, of the characteristics of each gender and of gender-appropriate behaviour.*

developed social learning theory in the 1980s to take account of cognitive factors. Their new approach is known as *social cognitive theory* (see p543). It argues that children guide their actions according to whether or not they will bring rewards. Anticipation of future rewards is seen to direct and motivate the development of gender roles.

Stangor and Ruble (1989) updated cognitive-developmental theory, calling their new approach *self-socialisation theory*. They argue that gender schemas and gender constancy serve different purposes. In their view, gender schemas organise information, cognition and understandings, while gender constancy provides the motivation for gender role development and gendered behaviour.

These more recent theories attempt to broaden and combine earlier approaches and develop their insights.

Summary

1. Some researchers argue that gender is largely shaped by nature, that it has a biological or genetic basis. Other researchers argue that gender is largely shaped by nurture, that it is socially or culturally constructed.

2. There is evidence to support both points of view. Many researchers now believe that gender is shaped by both nature and nurture.

3. Research into supposed psychological differences between males and females points to the influence of both nature and nurture. The same applies to studies of transgendered people, sexual reassignment and cross-cultural evidence.

4. Evolutionary psychology explains gender differences in terms of reproductive strategies. The ultimate goal of behaviour is to maximise the survival chances of the individual's genes. Males and females employ different strategies for this purpose. Gender differences result from this.

5. Psychoanalytic theory provides a psychological view of gender. According to Freud, children construct their gender as masculine or feminine from their experience of the oedipus complex. Gender is constructed by the individual, it is not innate or imposed by socialisation.

6. Social learning theory sees the acquisition of gender as a direct result of learning. Gender is largely based on observational learning from models, plus reinforcement of gender-appropriate behaviour.

7. Cognitive-developmental theory focuses on how children think about gender and how gender roles develop. The child actively structures their own gender experiences and selects appropriate models. Kohlberg identifies three stages of gender development. Children can only move to the next stage when they have reached the necessary stage in their overall cognitive development.

8. Gender schema theory sees the child as playing an active role in searching for information about gender and processing that information. It sees ideas about gender influencing the child's behaviour when the child discovers his or her gender. This process is seen to begin at a much earlier stage than Kohlberg suggests. Gender schema theory draws on information processing theory to account for how gender schemas develop – it looks at how children select and organise gender-related information.

Activity 8 Barbie

Item A   Barbie

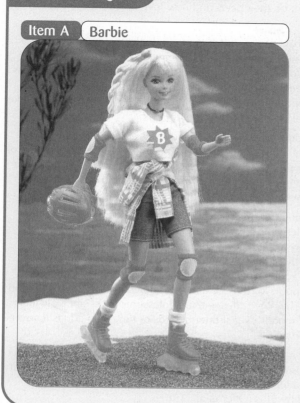

Every girl in America owns an average of eight Barbies. Over 500 million have been sold worldwide. And for Christmas 1995, Barbie was the bestselling girls' toy in the UK. Sun Jewel Barbie, the new fuschia-bikinied and diamond-necklaced model, is the bestselling Barbie ever. Other new models include 'Dance 'n' Twirl', a radio-controlled Barbie who flounces across the dance floor, and a horse and carriage set to take Barbie and Ken (her boyfriend) to the ball.

According to Michelle Norton, PR person for Mattel Toys who created Barbie, 'She's a wonderful role model for little girls. She does everything they want to do and dream of. She's got lovely fashions and a boyfriend. It's a friendship sort of thing.' And it has to be – sex is out as Ken lacks the appropriate parts.

Adapted from the *Observer*, 22.12.1995

Question

Explain the attraction of Barbie from the viewpoint of:

a) social learning theory

b) cognitive-developmental theory

c) gender schema theory.

Unit 3 Adolescence

KEY ISSUES

1 **How do adolescents develop their sense of identity?**

2 **What does research tell us about adolescent relationships with parents and peers?**

3 **How does adolescence differ between cultures?**

3.1 Introduction

Adolescence and puberty

Adolescence is a time of changes. Some of these changes are physical and linked to the onset of *puberty*. Puberty is the beginning of sexual maturity.

In girls, puberty typically begins with breast development, but the most obvious sign is the onset of *menarche* – the first menstruation. In boys, puberty begins with genital growth. Puberty generally occurs earlier in girls than boys. One sign of puberty is a sudden spurt in height, around the age of 12 for girls, and 14 for boys (Katchadourian, 1977).

Evidence suggests that the onset of puberty varies in different historical eras. For example, the average age for menarche seems to have dropped from around 15 in 1840 to 12-13 by the

1970s (Bullough, 1981). It may still be dropping (Lacey, 1998).

Other changes in adolescence are psychological and social. Among these are changes in the individual's sense of identity, and changes in their relationships with parents and peers. This unit looks at the psychological and social changes of adolescence.

Key terms

Puberty *The beginnings of sexual maturity.*

Menarche *The onset of menstruation.*

The creation of adolescence

According to Shaffer (1993), adolescence is a modern Western idea, arising from industrialisation and legislation restricting the employment of children in factories. This legislation separated the world of the child from that of the adult, and produced the uneasy phase of adolescence as the place where these two worlds meet.

Adolescence was extended by the provision of state education. In Britain, school attendance up to the age of 10 was made compulsory in 1880. In 1918, the state took over responsibility for secondary education. Since then the school leaving age was steadily raised, to 16 in 1973.

From the mid-1950s, adolescents were becoming economically more independent from their parents. Youth subcultures developed rapidly – from teddy boys to mods and rockers to hippies, and later to punks and goths. These subcultures identified themselves largely by dress, hairstyles and music, and in some cases by distinct lifestyles, drugs and a defiance of the older generation. By the 1960s, the 'problems' of adolescence and the 'teenage' years were a source of great interest to psychologists – as well as parents, newspaper editors, politicians, clergy and just about everyone else.

The 1960s saw the development of two of the main stereotypes of the adolescent. First, the 'rebellious teenager' who rejected parental discipline and the norms and values of the 'older generation'. The phrase 'generation gap' was coined to reflect this view. Second, the confused and troubled adolescent searching for his or her identity. The phrase 'identity crisis' was coined to reflect this idea.

As the next section shows, the picture of a rebellious teenager struggling with an identity crisis is reflected in psychological theories of adolescence.

3.2   The development of identity in adolescence

The American psychologist G. Stanley Hall (1904) pioneered an interest in adolescence as a time of major psychological change. In Hall's view, adolescence was often a disturbing and stressful time. Since then, most of the work on the development of identity in adolescence has been done by psychologists in the psychodynamic tradition.

Sigmund Freud

For Sigmund Freud (1905), adolescence was when the final stage of psychosexual development – the *genital stage* – took place. After all the excitement of the early stages of development (oral, anal and phallic), the drama of the oedipus complex, and the relative tranquillity of the latency period, the adolescent's libido or sex drive reactivates. The adolescent is motivated to seek sexual gratification from a love object drawn (usually) from peers of the opposite sex. Although Freud's interest was firmly on sexual development, he recognised that adolescents had to detach themselves from the authority of parents, and may become rebellious for a time.

Anna Freud (1968) confirmed the idea of adolescence as a period of major change as the young person tries to rework any sexual conflicts left over from childhood, often leading to emotional instability.

Peter Blos

Blos (1962; 1967) saw adolescence as a period of growing independence and individuality. Following Freud, Blos saw childhood and the oedipus complex as a time of initial *individuation* when the child begins to become a person in their own right. In Blos's view, adolescence is a period of *secondary individuation* when this process is completed.

During this period, the adolescent is likely to be rebellious and emotionally ambivalent towards the parents, with accompanying mood swings. Ambivalence means coexisting but conflicting emotions – for example, a 'love/hate relationship'.

Rejecting emotional closeness with parents creates a sense of loss. Adolescents compensate for this by becoming increasingly dependent on their peers and new love objects for emotional support.

They may also regress to a psychologically immature state of needing substitute parents. This may lead them into hero worship (of rock singers, or sport stars), homoerotic 'crushes' (as in the teenage girl who 'falls in love' with the French mistress), or of subordinating their individuality to some greater cause, like a political or cultural movement.

According to Blos, conflict and crisis are normal and healthy aspects of adolescence. Adolescents must go through a period of crisis in order to separate themselves psychologically from their parents and establish their own identity. And this can result in conflict with their parents.

Evaluation There is plenty of evidence to support Blos's claim that adolescents grow closer to their peers as they gain autonomy from their parents. For example, a study in the USA showed that time spent with parents halved when children became adolescents (Larson & Richards, 1991). And there is some support for Blos's claim that adolescents experience mood swings. There is evidence that adolescents experience a wider range of moods over shorter periods of time than adults (Larson et al., 1996).

However, there is less support for Blos's picture of the conflict and crisis-ridden adolescent. For example, one study found that 80% of adolescents showed no sign of the storm and stress pictured by Blos (Offer et al., 1981).

Key terms

Individuation *The process of separating from the parents to establish an individual identity. This begins in childhood with the oedipus complex.*

Secondary individuation *The completion of the process of individuation during adolescence.*

Erik Erikson

The title of Erikson's book, *Identity, Youth and Crisis* (1968) summarises his view of adolescence. As Erikson puts it, if the adolescent stands back and observes their situation, they would say, 'I ain't what I ought to be, I ain't what I'm gonna be, but I ain't what I was'. The result is confusion and self-doubt – in a nutshell, an *identity crisis*.

Erikson sees adolescence as the fifth stage of psychosocial development. The first four stages occur during childhood (see pp 541-542). According to Erikson, the central task of the adolescent is to forge an identity out of the *role confusion* they experience during their teenage years. He sees the most disturbing aspect of this as their 'inability to settle on an occupational identity' (Erikson, 1959). They are faced with a vast number of occupational roles, along with new sexual roles and religious roles.

The result, according to Erikson, is an identity crisis. Adolescents find themselves asking who they are, and where they are heading in their lives. Often they find such questions difficult to answer. Typically, they gravitate towards a group of peers who can provide them with a sense of identity while they strive to cope with the complexities of leaving childhood behind.

Erikson suggests that adolescents engage in a period of *moratorium*, where they explore different identities and roles without committing themselves to any. Most adolescents will resolve their identity crisis by attaining self integration and achieving a secure personal identity. This enables them to establish intimacy with a member of the opposite sex.

However, some fail to achieve identity, and remain in a state of *identity diffusion*. Erikson identifies four main characteristics of identity diffusion.

- **Fear of intimacy** Afraid that intimacy with another will swamp their attempts to achieve identity, the adolescent may prefer isolation or fantasy affairs with impossible partners.
- **Failure to organise time** Fear of the future may lead to an inability to plan realistically and build for the future.
- **Failure of industry** Anxiety can result in a failure to engage with productive work or study, either by a failure to concentrate, or by obsessive concern with minor details.
- **Formation of negative identity** The adolescent may simply be contrary, and reject the values of others (especially those of parents) without constructing their own set of values.

In Erikson's view, failure to achieve identity can result in social and sexual confusion, which may lead to delinquency or homosexual orientation.

Evaluation Erikson emphasises the importance of crisis in adolescent development. He sees identity as a single goal which the adolescent either achieves or fails to achieve. Failure to achieve identity can lead to delinquency and sexual confusion. Those who successfully make the transition from adolescence to adulthood emerge with a secure personal identity. All of these claims have been challenged.

- First, as noted earlier, adolescence may not be as stressful as Erikson suggests. A review of American research indicates that the typical teenager is 'confident, happy and self-satisfied' (Offer et al., 1988). This is hardly the angst-ridden, confused, self-doubting adolescent pictured by Erikson.
- Second, as outlined in the following section, identity may be more complex than Erikson suggests (Marcia, 1980).
- Third, the suggestion that adolescent identity achievement is largely final is questionable. In today's rapidly changing society, there is evidence of increasing challenges to a stable identity. These challenges include frequent occupational change and change in marital status with the high level of divorce. Such challenges can lead to changes in identity (Smith et al., 1998).
- Fourth, Erikson's claim that failure to achieve identity can lead to delinquency and sexual confusion is questionable. Research into delinquency provides little or no support for this claim (Haralambos & Holborn, 2000). And to suggest, for example, that gay or lesbian lifestyles result from identity diffusion says more about Erikson's values than anything else. He sees identity diffusion and sexual confusion as negative and appears to see non-heterosexual orientations in the same light.

Erikson's methodology has been criticised. He bases his views on individual case studies and his clinical experience of adolescents with psychological problems. In addition, these adolescents are American, male and from the 1960s. Larger

samples, more representative samples, and cross-cultural samples are needed to assess Erikson's claims (Smith et al., 1998).

It is likely that Erikson overestimated the tumult of adolescence because he worked with troubled teenagers in therapy, and because he developed his theory in the 1960s, when the generation gap was clearly evident. In 1960s and 70s America and Europe, conflict between a 'conformist' older generation and a 'rebellious' younger one was often intense, and youth culture celebrated its defiance of established society. Erikson's theory may say more about the 1960s than about adolescence in general.

James Marcia

Marcia (1966; 1980; 1999) developed Erikson's theory in two ways. First, he broadened the idea of identity by suggesting that at any point during adolescence the individual has one out of a possible four *identity statuses*. This compares with Erikson's two alternatives – identity and identity diffusion.

Second, Marcia developed a means for investigating identity statuses. He used semi-structured interviews which included standardised questions. Marcia (1966) interviewed male college students about two areas which Erikson regarded as central to identity formation, 1) their choice of occupation and 2) their political and religious views. He focused on two factors Erikson saw as essential to stable identity formation – *crisis* and *commitment*. Crisis refers to the process of examining alternative beliefs, occupational choices, and future opportunities. Commitment refers to the individual's commitment to a particular set of beliefs and a future occupation.

Marcia (1966; 1999) identified four possible adolescent identity statuses.

- **Identity diffusion status** The adolescent has not started to think seriously about major life issues such as career choices, relationships, or religious and political beliefs, let alone make any commitments in these areas. The diffusion status may be an early stage in the process of identity formation, before the issue of identity has been addressed. Or, it may be a later stage due to failure to reach a commitment after an identity crisis. Remaining in identity diffusion may result in apathy and depression.
- **Moratorium status** An identity crisis. The adolescent experiments with different identities and lifestyles and explores possibilities for the future – occupational choices, a range of political views and religious beliefs. However, no firm commitments are made.

Figure 3   Marcia's identity statuses

	Commitment	
	No	Yes
Crisis No	Identity diffusion	Foreclosure
Yes	Moratorium	Identity achievement

- **Foreclosure status** The adolescent has made a commitment without seriously considering the alternatives and without going through an identity crisis. They do not question the identities imposed by parents and society, and merely conform to external pressure from authority. This makes for an easy adolescence, but the adolescent does not fulfil their potential as an individual. Some may merely delay the identity crisis until later in life. Adolescents in this identity status are committed to a future occupational role and to particular religious and political beliefs.
- **Identity achievement status** The adolescent has worked through their identity crisis, passed through the moratorium status and established their own identity. Firm commitments have been made to occupational goals, political and religious beliefs, and values and ideals. They achieve a stable and coherent sense of themselves and are set up for future life as productive adults.

Marcia suggests that these four identity statuses can be distinguished by level of crisis and level of commitment (see Figure 3). Foreclosure is high commitment without crisis. Moratorium is low commitment with high crisis. Identity diffusion is low commitment without crisis. Identity achievement is high commitment after high crisis.

Marcia (1980) sees the most likely and the healthy route through adolescence as working through identity diffusion to moratorium to identity achievement. Some adolescents may go through a period of foreclosure between identity diffusion and moratorium. Like Erikson, Marcia sees an identity crisis as a necessary stage in order to reach identity achievement. Avoiding crisis by remaining in identity diffusion or foreclosure is not ideal for the reasons outlined above.

Evaluation of Marcia

A number of studies have provided some support for Marcia. For example, a study by Meilman (1979) using Marcia's interview schedule found evidence to support the existence of the four identity statuses. Based on a sample of American males, Meilman found that 12 to 18-year-olds were more likely to be in identity diffusion, while 18 to 24-year-olds were more likely to have reached identity achievement. However, only just over half of the 24-year-olds had reached identity achievement, and moratorium was rare in all age groups.

Marcia's view of the positive effects of identity achievement was confirmed by Coleman and Hendry (1990). They found that identity achievers had high self-esteem and fewer problems with adolescence, while those in identity diffusion had lower self-esteem, poor communication skills, and were more withdrawn.

Like Erikson, Marcia has been criticised for emphasising 'crisis' as the route to achieving identity, when evidence suggests that only a minority of adolescents experience stress during their teens (Siddique & D'Arcy, 1984). However, crisis really refers to challenge. It may, therefore, be misleading to see stress as an indication of crisis.

There is evidence that adolescents do not have a consistent identity status in all areas of their lives. For example, Archer (1982) found that at any one time only 5% of adolescents have the same identity status in their occupational choice and in their political and religious beliefs. This finding suggests that Marcia's picture of identity statuses is oversimplified.

As with Blos and Erikson, Marcia may be generalising from a very untypical generation – adolescents in the 1960s. A study by Waterman and Waterman (1975) compared the identity status of male college students and their fathers. The students tended to have diffusion or moratorium statuses while their fathers were likely to have foreclosure statuses. The fathers had grown up in the 1930s to 1950s when the emphasis was on conformity, on acceptance rather than questioning authority, an emphasis that would encourage a foreclosure identity status. This study suggests that different generations experience adolescence differently.

Key terms

Crisis *The process of exploring alternative identities and examining alternative beliefs, occupational choices and future opportunities.*

Commitment *The individual's commitment to a particular identity, a particular set of beliefs and a future occupation.*

Identity statuses *In Marcia's theory, the various identities that may be adopted during adolescence.*

Identity diffusion status *Failure to think seriously about major life issues and lack of commitment in these areas.*

Moratorium status *An identity crisis. Exploration of possible lifestyles, identities and beliefs. No firm commitments.*

Foreclosure status *Firm commitments without seriously considering the alternatives and without going through an identity crisis.*

Identity achievement status *Establishing a clear and stable identity and making firm commitments after working through an identity crisis.*

Gender, ethnicity and class

Blos, Erikson and Marcia have all been criticised for basing their views of adolescence on white middle-class American males. In doing so, they have largely ignored the possible influences of gender, ethnicity, social class and culture on the experience of adolescence. The influence of culture on adolescence is examined in Section 3.4.

Gender Erikson (1968) claimed that women cannot complete their identity formation until they have married and taken on the social status of their husband. This view of women as a reflection of their male partner has been criticised as old-fashioned and sexist.

Curry (1998) suggests that males may reach identity achievement earlier than females for several reasons. First, the whole course of male individual development since childhood has been about separation from others (see Melanie Klein's work, p553); second, females have less social power; and third, the female gender role is more 'person oriented' than the male's.

Recent studies using Marcia's identity-status interview schedules have found little evidence of differences in identity formation between male and female adolescents. However, there is some evidence that personal relationships may play a more significant part in adolescent identity formation for females (Cole & Cole, 2001).

Ethnicity There is some evidence that ethnic minority adolescents are less likely to have achieved identity formation than majority adolescents. This may be because ethnic identities are threatened by the prejudices and negative stereotypes of the majority culture. In addition, minority group adolescents have to reconcile two identities – a national identity and an identity based on their own ethnic background (Rosenthal, 1987).

Social class There is some evidence that, in terms of religious and political identity, mainly middle-class university students lag behind mainly working-class adolescents who had already joined the workforce (Munro & Adams, 1977). This may reflect the emphasis in universities on questioning and exploring ideas, which might extend the moratorium period.

Storm and stress

Twentieth century psychologists have tended to see adolescence as a stressful, crisis-ridden time. It is pictured as a period of storm and stress, of emotional turbulence and identity crisis.

As noted earlier, much of the evidence for this view was taken from the 1960s, which was hardly a typical decade (see Activity 9, Item A). Despite this, there is some evidence to support the storm and stress view of adolescence. For example, Csikszentmihalyi and Larson (1981) studied 78 adolescents in Chicago, 'bleeping' them periodically on pagers to ask them to report their feelings. The principal finding was that adolescent mood swings were very rapid, much more so than those of adults. In another study, 30-year-olds were asked to look back on their teenage years – they remembered them as a period of turmoil and confusion (MacFarlane, 1964).

However, there is plenty of evidence which contradicts the storm and stress view. As outlined earlier, a number of studies have found that most adolescents appear to be well-adjusted, confident and contented (Offer et al., 1988).

A large-scale study on the Isle of Wight suggests that the 'storm and stress' picture of adolescence has been exaggerated. Conducted by Michael Rutter and his colleagues, a random sample of two hundred 14 to 15-year-olds was drawn from that age group (Rutter et al., 1976). They were given questionnaires and psychiatric interviews and their parents and teachers were interviewed. There was little evidence of severe conflict with parents. However, a minority of adolescents did indicate serious relationship difficulties – for example, 9% of the girls expressed

outright rejection of their father. The emotional turbulence of the storm and stress model was not typical. Only about 20% said they often felt miserable or depressed. Rutter concludes that while 'adolescent turmoil' exists, its importance has probably been overestimated in past research.

Adolescence is a time of social and physical changes for young people. If it is not as stressful as the psychodynamic theorists have assumed, the question is, 'why not?' *Focal theory* provides an answer.

Focal theory

Focal theory, developed by J.C. Coleman (1974, 1980) provides an explanation for how young people cope with the potentially threatening changes of adolescence. The theory is based on interviews with 800 young people about areas of possible anxiety. Coleman (1974) found that for both boys and girls, sexual anxieties worried them most at 11, peer conflicts at 15, and parental conflicts at 17 or 18. Occupational anxieties came later.

It appears that adolescents 'focus' on particular problems at particular times. They 'pace' themselves and go through different adjustments at different times rather than experiencing a major, highly stressful crisis. Overall, Coleman sees adolescence as a period of adjustment, with times of change and times of stability, rather than the period of 'crisis' described by Erikson and Marcia.

Conclusion

Although the storm and stress model of adolescence has been challenged by recent research, not everyone accepts that adolescence is a relatively easy time. Terri Apter (2001) argues that changes in family structures have weakened parental support for many young people who are left at the mercy of a highly pressurised educational system, an increasingly competitive job market, and transient peer groups that do not offer solid or longlasting support. As a result, she argues, eating disorders, alcohol and drug abuse, and suicide are on the increase among socially isolated adolescents and young adults.

It is likely that different generations have very different experiences of adolescence. Conformity to the adult world was much stronger for those who were teenagers in the 1940s, hence the high level of foreclosure among this age group found by Waterman and Waterman (1975). Rebellious youth cultures, often highly politicised, as for example opposition to American military involvement in Vietnam, directed many who reached their teens in the 1960s and 70s. Hence the storm and stress view of adolescence held by Erikson and others writing during that period. And today's adolescents may have a different experience again.

3.3 Relationships in adolescence

Introduction

Research has focused on adolescents' relationship with their parents and with their peers. Researchers in the 1960s and 70s presented the following picture. During adolescence, peers become increasingly important and parents become steadily less important. Adolescents strive for independence and autonomy from their parents. This involves a shift from parent-oriented relationships to peer-oriented relationships.

There is some evidence for this. Larson et al., (1996) found that the amount of time adolescents spend with their parents reduces as the teenage years proceed. Steinberg and Silverberg (1986) argue that as adolescents become more independent from their parents, they become increasingly dependent on their peers.

The prevailing view today is that both parents and peers provide important social and emotional support for adolescents.

Peer relations do increase in importance, especially for leisure and matters of taste and style – for example, clothes and music. But, for important issues to do with future and career, parents remain significant figures in adolescents' relationships.

Researchers in the 1960s and 70s tended to see peer groups taking over from parents – one gained at the expense of the other. Researchers today are more likely to see both as important, but in different ways.

Activity 9   Adolescence

Item A   The 1960s and 70s

The 1960s and early 1970s were years of protest, exploration and change for many young people, particularly in the USA. They challenged the lifestyle and politics of their elders. They adopted alternative lifestyles. Hippies preached 'make love not war' often through a haze of cannabis smoke. Many young people opposed the materialist culture of mainstream society and challenged accepted attitudes on marriage and the role of women.

Thousands of young people took to the streets to oppose America's involvement in the war in Vietnam. Riots exploded in ghettos across the USA as young African Americans protested against racism, poverty and exclusion from mainstream society.

Hippies, USA, 1960s

Anti-Vietnam war demonstration, Washington DC, 1971

Item B   Identity statuses

As part of a survey on adolescents who will be first-time voters in the next election, four teenage girls were asked about their political beliefs.

Amy said she was unsure what she thought. She had read some literature from different parties, and had argued with people of different political persuasions, but had not yet made up her own mind.

Victoria said she was going to vote the same way as her parents, because they understood these things.

Gemma shrugged and said she'd never bothered to think about politics. She went off to read her text messages.

Lisa said she had discussed politics with her family and friends, even having rows with her parents. She had decided that ecological issues were the most important, and would vote for the party with the 'greenest' policies.

Adapted from a student survey

Item C   How do you feel?

A sample of adolescents were asked how far they agreed with a series of statements. The percentages in agreement with some of the statements are given below.

'I feel relaxed under normal circumstances.'	91
'I enjoy life.'	90
'Usually I control myself.'	90
'I feel strong and healthy.'	86
'Most of the time I am happy.'	85

Adapted from Offer et al., 1981

Questions

1   Blos, Erikson and Marcia developed their theories of adolescence in the 1960s.

  a) How can their views be seen as a reflection of young people's experience in 1960s America?

  b) Can their theories be generalised to other times and places?

2   Place each of the girls in Item B in one of Marcia's identity statuses. Give reasons for your placements.

3   What does the evidence in Item C suggest about the 'storm and stress' view of adolescence?

Relations with parents

The fact that parents remain important does not mean that adolescents do not quarrel with them. They do. In a review of a number of studies, Laursen and Collins (1994) found conflict with parents peaking in mid-adolescence, then declining.

Different generations may have different experiences. Rossi and Rossi (1990) looked at parent-child relations in two age groups – those who had been teens in the 1940s and 50s, and those who had been teens in the 1960s and 70s. Both groups showed the lowest ebb of their relations with their parents at 16, but the later generation showed a markedly lower ebb.

Research into the nature of the quarrels reveals they are not random explosions lacking rhyme or reason. Arguments change as adolescence proceeds. In a longitudinal study of 112 adolescents aged 11 to 13, Galambos and Almeida (1992) found that quarrels over chores, appearance and politeness decrease over time, while those over finance increase.

Topics of conflict are not random either. Barber (1994) found parents and adolescents argue over schoolwork, chores, disobedience, social life and friends, the teasing of siblings, and personal hygiene, but avoid conflict over issues like sex, drugs, religion and politics. This suggests that both sides are to some extent managing the situation so as to avoid serious conflict.

Smetana (1988) identified a rather subtle game, with rules relating to conflict with parents. Adolescents are not simply awkward and contrary, they are utilising a sense of fairness and justice. According to Smetana, they feel that certain areas of their life should be under their control – sleeping in late, watching TV to all hours, clothing, hairstyles and friendships. They will vigorously defend their rights in these areas, leading to conflict with intrusive parents. However, they accept parental authority over issues like honesty, mistreatment of younger siblings and cleaning up after parties.

The evidence suggests that, despite rows and conflicts, bonds between adolescents and their parents are not actually weakening in the way earlier researchers suggested (La Freniere, 2000).

Relations with peers

As adolescence proceeds, there is an increase in the amount of time spent with peers, and there is less and less guidance from adults (Brown, 1990). Groups increase in size. Brown (1990) distinguishes the clique from the crowd. A clique is a regular group of tightly-knit friends. It is around the same size as an extended family, and functions as a kind of family. A crowd is a much larger group who share the same reputation, interests and social identity – for example, Liverpool supporters, goths, students, homeboys. Members of crowds may socialise together in clubs or at concerts, but do not necessarily know each other personally.

Dunphy (1963) found that in early adolescence, cliques tend to be single sex. Teenagers meet members of the opposite sex through mixing with the crowd, and eventually mixed-sex cliques can emerge – as in the American television comedy *Friends*. Cliques and crowds are an integral part of heterosexual mixing for most adolescents.

There is evidence that peer groups provide an opportunity for adolescents to develop new identities in a social environment outside the family. This can be seen most clearly in the various youth subcultures that have come and gone since the 1950s – teddy boys, mods, rockers, hippies, skinheads, punks and goths. A study of British hippies, punks and goths showed that group members attached great value to the duration of an individual's involvement with the subculture and the authenticity of their commitment. The 'weekend punk' was scorned – it was important to live the life, not just dress the part (Widdicombe & Wooffitt, 1990).

The attraction of peer groups for adolescents is that they offer equal and reciprocal relationships, in contrast to the unequal authority relationship with parents (Hunter, 1984). Peer groups are usually enjoyable and allow young people to 'be themselves'. Adolescents tend to gravitate towards those of similar backgrounds, interests, and beliefs, as similar people are seen as more supportive and understanding (Youniss & Smollar, 1985). As a result, adolescents do not usually mix with a wide range of others, and cliques tend to be homogeneous in terms of class and race.

Douvan and Adelson (1966) noticed a gender difference in peer groups. Girls tend to prefer closer friendships with same-sex peers than boys. Both sexes want support from friends, but a different kind of support. Girls want to share emotional confidences; boys want allies for when they get in trouble with authority!

Berndt and Keefe (1995) found evidence for peer conformity in disruptive behaviour, the peak age for copying the antisocial behaviour of peers being 15 years. This suggests that adolescents can and do lead one another astray. However, since adolescents choose peers who are similar to themselves, the conformity effect may not be as strong as it appears.

The degree of peer involvement may itself be affected by relationships with parents. In a large study based on self-reports from over 1700 eleven-year-olds, Fuligni and Eccles (1993) found that the children were more likely to seek peer involvement if their parents were seen as authoritarian or uninterested in them. Eleven-year-olds were less peer oriented if they felt their parents were interested in them, involving them in family decisions, and showing concern over what time they came in at night.

Nevertheless, some involvement in peer groups is normal. Palmonari et al. (1989) found that 90% of 16-18 year olds identified themselves as part of a peer group. It has its benefits. Buhrmester (1992) found membership of a peer group is associated with psychological well-being. In a study of 770 Italian adolescents, Kirchler et al. (1991) found membership of a peer group was good for the development of social skills. The same study also found that those who strongly identified with their peer groups also strongly identified with their family.

Conclusion

Peers and parents provide different social worlds, and adolescents participate in both – eating, shopping and doing chores with their parents, spending leisure time with their peers. Brown et al. (1993) conclude that the adolescent moves between two worlds – it is not an either-or situation. Peers do not displace parents, they exist beside them. Durkin (1995) sees the adolescent as inhabiting a number of complex and overlapping worlds, including parents and peers, but also neighbours, teachers and many others.

Key terms

Clique *A small group of personal friends.*

Crowd *In this case, a larger group of young people sharing the same reputation, interests and social identity.*

3.4   Cultural differences

Although the storm and stress model has probably exaggerated the difficulties of adolescence, difficulties do exist. Young people have to cope with the physical changes of puberty and the transition from childhood to adulthood. They have choices to make and an adult identity to form. Are these difficulties an inevitable part of growing up physically and socially in any society? Or are they limited to Western society? Are they generated by Western culture or are they universal – that is, present in all cultures?

Adolescence in non-Western cultures

Margaret Mead's classic study *Coming of Age in Samoa* (1925) is often quoted as evidence that the years of adolescence are experienced very differently in non-Western cultures. Mead described adolescence in 1920s Samoa as 'the age of maximum ease', with little or no evidence of conflict with parents, emotional turmoil or identity crises. She presents a picture of a free and easy society with 'the sunniest and easiest attitudes towards sex', particularly during adolescence.

However, Mead's findings have been questioned by Australian anthropologist Derek Freeman (1983, 1996). He claims her command of the local language was poor, that she was conned by some of the teenage girls she interviewed, and that she saw what she wanted to see. Freeman's research from the 1940s and 1960s presented a very different picture of Samoan society – for example, he reported that girls were expected to be virgins on marriage. In Mead's defence, Freeman's research was conducted after the arrival of Christian missionaries and American military bases, which may well have changed Samoan society.

Leaving aside the debate over Samoa, there is considerable evidence of cultural differences. Some cultures do not even recognise adolescence. For example, among the !Kung of the Kalahari desert in southern Africa, young people are economically self-sufficient by mid-childhood and can marry and reproduce as soon as they reach sexual maturity (Shostak, 1981). Teenage pregnancies are not a problem for the !Kung. Similarly, amongst the Canadian Inuit young people were seen to be adult when they reached puberty – girls usually married before or shortly after puberty and became mothers in their teenage years (Condon, 1987).

Activity 10   Adolescents, parents and peers

Item A   Who matters?

A number of studies conducted in the USA from the 1970s to the 1990s found that adolescents rated core family members, especially parents, as the most important people in their lives. Peers are rated as increasingly important as adolescence progresses but they do not overtake parents.

Relationships with parents and peers should not be seen as completely separate – adolescents and parents usually know a lot of people in common.

Adapted from Durkin, 1995

Item B   Peer groups

Peer groups provide many adolescents with companionship and support – 'You feel needed and secure in who you are'. Conversation in male peer groups tends to revolve around sport, cars and girls in general. Girls' conversation tends to be more intimate and personal – they are more likely to confide in others about their relationships.

Adapted from O'Brien & Bierman, 1988 and Cole & Cole, 2001

Questions

1   How do the findings in Item A cast doubt on the view of adolescence presented by many researchers in the 1960s?

2   Read Item B. Briefly discuss the importance of peer groups to adolescents.

Initiation ceremonies

In many societies an initiation ceremony marks the transition from childhood to adulthood. These ceremonies often have a number of features in common. The young person is separated from society, either alone or with their age-mates. They are instructed by elders in the folklore, history and religion of their society. They take part in a dramatic and intense ritual marking the end of childhood and the beginning of adulthood. Sometimes they are physically changed – boys may be circumcised, and less commonly girls may have their clitoris removed. Both sexes may be cut to produce a pattern of scars. After the ceremony, the young people re-enter society with their new adult status (Delaney, 1995).

Some initiation ceremonies dramatise the transition with a ceremonial 'death' of childhood and 'birth' of adulthood. Boys in some West African societies undergo a spiritual 'death' at puberty. They are isolated in the forest and, when they emerge, they have a new adult name and identity (Gay, 1984).

In the West, childhood and adulthood are separated by years of adolescence. In many non-Western societies, an initiation ceremony can confer adulthood on a child literally overnight.

Broad and narrow socialisation

Arnett (1992) distinguishes between two types of socialisation – broad and narrow. In societies employing *narrow socialisation*, adults closely supervise the young, they have clear and definite expectations of their behaviour, they impose many restrictions on them and draw them rapidly into the adult world at puberty. Such societies may have initiation ceremonies to mark the transition from childhood to adulthood.

According to Arnett, narrow socialisation is typical of small-scale pre-industrial societies. In these societies, conformity is high, social change is limited and gradual, and children tend to adopt the adult roles of their same-sex parent. The difficulties experienced by Western adolescents are largely absent.

Broad socialisation is typical of modern Western industrial societies. These societies are characterised by innovation and change, and a highly specialised division of labour with relatively few children adopting their parents' occupational roles. Broad socialisation is less prescriptive, it encourages self-expression and autonomy rather than conformity. This has its costs as well as benefits. The future is not mapped out, identities are not imposed, and occupational choices are not clear-cut. This can lead to anxiety and self-doubt as adolescents make choices and define their identity.

Conclusion

This unit began with Shaffer's (1993) idea that adolescence is a creation of modern Western society. The cross-cultural evidence presented in this section provides support for this view. It suggests that while puberty is a biological change, adolescence is a culturally created experience.

Summary

1   Psychologists in the 1960s saw adolescence as a period of 'storm and stress', of emotional turbulence, of rebellion, and of identity crisis.

2   According to Peter Blos, conflict and crisis are normal and healthy aspects of adolescence. Adolescents must go through a period of crisis in order to separate themselves psychologically from their parents and establish their own identity. This often results in conflict with their parents.

3   According to Erik Erikson, the central task of the adolescent is to forge an identity out of the role confusion they experience during their teenage years. Adolescence is a time of identity crisis. The adolescent must achieve a stable personal identity for psychological well-being and a productive adult life.

4   According to James Marcia, the most likely and healthy route through adolescence is identity diffusion to moratorium to identity achievement. In the status of identity diffusion, the adolescent has not thought seriously about major life issues nor made commitments. The moratorium status involves an identity crisis in which the adolescent explores possible lifestyles, identities and beliefs without making firm commitments. This is a necessary step to identity achievement. Identity achievement involves a commitment to a set of beliefs and a future occupation. This results in a stable and coherent sense of self.

5   Blos, Erikson and Marcia have been criticised for basing their theories on the experience of adolescence in the 1960s, and on the experience of white middle-class American males. In doing so, they have largely ignored the experience of adolescence in other time periods and cultures. They have also largely ignored the possible influence of gender, ethnicity and social class.

6   Coleman's focal theory argues that adolescents focus on particular problems at particular times. Coleman sees adolescence as a period of adjustment, with times of change and times of stability, rather than a period of crisis.

7   Researchers in the 1960s and 70s saw peers becoming increasingly important and parents correspondingly less important as adolescents strive for independence and autonomy.

8   Today, the prevailing view is that both parents and peers provide important emotional and social support for adolescents. Peers do not displace parents, they exist alongside them.

9   Evidence from other cultures suggests that the experience of adolescence is not universal. In many cultures, children appear to make the transition from childhood to adulthood relatively smoothly and in a relatively short space of time.

10 Historical and cross-cultural evidence suggests that adolescence may be a creation of Western industrial society.

Activity 11   Adolescence across cultures

Item A   Female initiation

At their first menstruation, Arapash girls in New Guinea were given an initiation ceremony to symbolise their transition to adulthood. Margaret Mead describes the ceremony.

Her woven arm and leg bands, her earrings, her old lime gourd and lime spatula are taken from her. Her woven belt is taken off. If these are fairly new they are given away; if they are old they are destroyed. The desire is to cut the girl's connection with her past.

The girl is attended by older women They rub her all over with stinging nettles. They tell her to roll one of the large nettle leaves into a tube and thrust it into her vulva – this will ensure her breasts growing large and strong. The girl eats no food, nor does she drink water. On the third day, she comes out of the hut and stands against a tree while her mother's brother makes the decorative cuts on her shoulders and buttocks. Each day the women rub the girl with nettles. It is well if she fasts for five or six days, but the women watch her anxiously, and if she becomes too weak they put an end to it. Fasting will make her strong, but too much of it might make her die.

Adapted from Mead, 1935

Item B   Male initiation

An Australian Aborigine boy being painted and decorated for his initiation into manhood

A boy from the African Bayaka people about to attend his initiation ceremony

Item C   Child labour

Men and boys in Holmes Mill, Clitheroe, near Preston

Youngsters in an Indian village collecting cow dung to be used as manure

Child labour was common in the West in early industrial society. It is still found in many developing societies. For example, in parts of rural India, children make a vital contribution to the family well-being. They look after cattle, help with sowing crops, weeding and harvesting, they bring in the family's water supply and take food out to workers in the fields.

Adapted from the *New Internationalist*, May 1974

Questions

1   Initiation ceremonies change identities and shape adult roles. With reference to Items A and B, suggest why they are so effective.

2   How can Item C be used to suggest that adolescence is a creation of late industrial society?

References

Adams, H.E., Wright, L.W. & Lohr, B.A. (1996). Is homophobia associated with homosexual arousal? *Journal of Abnormal Psychology, 105*, 440-445.

Ainsworth, M.D.S., Belhar, M.C., Waters, E. & Wall, S. (1978). *Patterns of attachment: A psychological study of the strange situation.* Hillsdale, NJ: Erlbaum.

Anderson, N.S. (1987). Cognition, learning, and memory. In M.A. Baker (Ed.), *Sex differences in human performance.* Chichester: Wiley.

Angier, N. (1999). *Woman: An intimate geography.* London: Virago.

Apter, T. (2001). *The myth of maturity: What teenagers need from parents.* New York: Norton.

Archer, S. (1982). The lower age boundaries of identity development. *Child Development, 53*, 1551-1556.

Arden, R. (1996). *Women, the inside story.* London: Channel 4 television.

Arnett, J. (1992). Reckless behaviour in adolescence: A developmental perspective. *Developmental Review, 12*, 339-373.

Badcock, C. (1995). *PsychoDarwinism.* London: Harper Collins.

Baker, R. (1996). *Sperm wars: Infidelity, sexual conflict and other bedroom battles.* London: Fourth Estate.

Bandura, A. (1971). *Social learning theory.* Morristown, NJ: General Learning Press.

Bandura, A. (1973). *Aggression: A social learning analysis.* Englewood Cliffs, NJ: Prentice Hall.

Bandura, A. (1986). *Social foundations of thought and action: A social cognitive theory.* Englewood Cliffs, NJ: Prentice Hall.

Bandura, A., Ross, D. & Ross, S.A. (1961). Transmission of aggression through imitation of aggressive models. *Journal of Abnormal and Social Psychology, 63*, 575-582.

Bandura, A. & Walters, R.H. (1963). *Social learning and personality development.* New York: Holt.

Bandura, A. & Rosenthal, T.L. (1966). Vicarious classical conditioning as a function of arousal level. *Journal of Personality and Social Psychology, 3*, 54-62.

Barash, D.P. (1982). *Sociobiology and behaviour* (2nd ed.). London: Heinemann.

Barber, B.K. (1994). Cultural, family and personal contexts of parent-adolescent conflict. *Journal of Marriage and the Family, 56*, 375-386.

Barkley, R.A., Ullman, D.G., Otto, L. & Brecht, J.M. (1977). The effects of sex typing and sex appropriateness of modeled behavior on children's imitation. *Child Development, 48*, 721-725.

Bee, H. (2000). *The developing child* (10th ed.). London: Longman.

Bem, S.L. (1974). The measurement of psychological androgny. *Journal of Consulting and Clinical Psychology, 42*, 155-162.

Bem, S.L. (1993). *The lenses of gender: Transforming the debate on sexual inequality.* New Haven, Conn: Yale University Press.

Benbow, C.P. & Lubinski, D. (1993). Consequences of gender differences in mathematical reasoning ability and some biological linkages. In M. Haug, R.E. Whalen, C. Aron & K.L. Olsen (Eds.), *The development of sex differences and similarities in behaviour.* London: Kluwer Academic.

Berndt, T.J. & Keefe, K. (1995). Friends' influence on adolescents' adjustment in school. *Child Development, 66*, 1312-1329.

Berry, J.W., Poortinga, Y.H., Segall, M.H. & Dasen, P.R. (1992). *Cross-cultural psychology: Research and applications.* Cambridge: Cambridge University Press.

Blos, P. (1962). *On adolescence: A psychoanalytic interpretation.* New York: Free Press.

Blos, P. (1967). The second individuation process of adolescence. *Psychoanalytic Study of the Child, 22*, 162-186.

Bowers, K.S. (1973). Situationism in psychology: An analysis and a critique. *Psychological Review, 80*, 307-336.

Bradbard, M.R., Martin, C.L., Endsley, R.C. & Halverson, C.F. (1986). Influence of sex stereotypes on children's exploration and memory: A competence versus performance distinction. *Developmental psychology, 22*, 481-486.

Bragg, M. (1998). *On giants' shoulders.* Radio 4. 4th February.

Bresnick, A. (1998). The originality of listening. *Times Literary Supplement*, 30th October.

Brewin, C.R. & Andrews, B. (1998). Recovered memories of trauma: Phenomenology and cognitive mechanisms. *Clinical Psychology Review, 18*, 949-970.

Brown, B.B. (1990). Peer groups and peer cultures. In S.S. Feldman & G.R. Elliot (Eds.), *At the threshold: The developing adolescent.* Cambridge, MA: Harvard University Press.

Brown, B.B., Mounts, N., Lamborn,S.D. & Steinberg, L. (1993). Parenting practices and peer group affiliation in adolescence. *Child Development, 64*, 467-482.

Bullough, V. (1981). The age of menarche: A misunderstanding. *Science, 213*, 365-366.

Buhrmester, D. (1992). The developmental course of sibling and peer relationships. In F. Boer & J. Dunn (Eds.), *Children's sibling relationships: Developmental and clinical issues.* Hillsdale, NJ: Erlbaum.

Burr, C. (1996). *A separate creation: How biology makes us gay.* New York: Bantam.

Buss, D.M. (1987). Sex differences in human mate selection criteria: An evolutionary perspective. In C. Crawford, M. Smith & D. Krebs (Eds.), *Sociobiology and psychology: Ideas, issues and applications.* Hillsdale, NJ: Erlbaum.

Buss, D.M., Larsen, R., Westen, D. & Semmelroth, J. (1992). Sex differences in jealousy: Evolution, physiology, and psychology. *Psychological Science, 3*, 251-255.

Buss, D.M. & Schmitt, D.P. (1993). Sexual strategies theory: An evolutionary perspective on human mating. *Psychological Review, 100*, 204-232.

Bussey, K. & Bandura, A. (1984). Influence of gender constancy and social power on sex-linked modeling. *Journal of Personality and Social Psychology, 47*, 1292-1302.

Bussey, K. & Bandura, A. (1992). Self regulatory mechanisms governing gender development. *Child Development, 63*, 1236-1250.

Butler, J. (1990). Gender trouble: Feminism and the subversion of identity. London: Routledge.

Caldera, Y.M., Huston, A.C. & O'Brien, M. (1989). Social interactions and play patterns of parents and toddlers with feminine, masculine and neutral toys. *Child Development, 60*, 70-76.

Carter, D.B. & Levy, G.D. (1988). Cognitive aspects of early sex role development: The influence of gender schemas on preschoolers' memories and preferences for sex-typed toys and activities. *Child Development, 59*, 782-792.

Cheles-Miller, P. (1975). Reactions to marital roles in commercials. *Journal of Advertising Research, 15*, 45-49.

Choderow, N. (1978). *The reproduction of mothering.* Berkeley: University of California Press.

Cohen, P. (2001). All hung up about size. *New Scientist, 2290*, 34-35.

Cole, M. & Cole, S.R. (2001). *The development of children* (4th ed.). New York: W.H. Freeman & Co.

Coleman, J.C. (1974). *Relationships in adolescence.* London: Routledge & Kegan Paul.

Coleman, J.C. (1980). *The nature of adolescence.* London: Methuen.

Coleman, J.C. & Hendry, L. (1990). *The nature of adolescence* (2nd ed.). London: Routledge.

Condon, R.G. (1987). *Inuit youth.* New Brunswick, NJ: Rutgers University Press.

Crerar, S. & Leake, J. (2001). Hello, I'm British, fancy some sex? *Sunday Times*, 9th December.

Crews, F. (1993). The unknown Freud. *New York Review of Books*, November.

Csikszentmihalyi, M. & Larson, R. (1981). *Being adolescent: Conflict and growth in the teenage years.* New York: Basic Books.

Curry, C. (1998). Adolescence. In K. Trew & J. Kremer (Eds.), *Gender and psychology*. London: Arnold.

Darwin, C. (1859). *The origin of species by means of natural selection*. London: John Murray.

Darwin, C. (1871). *The descent of man*. London: John Murray.

Dawkins, R. (1976). *The selfish gene*. Oxford: Oxford University Press.

Delaney, C.H. (1995). Rites of passage in adolescence. *Adolescence, 30*, 891-897.

Diamond, M. (1982). Sexual identity, monozygotic twins reared in discordant sex roles and a BBC follow-up. *Archives of Sexual Behaviour, 11*, 181-186.

Diamond, M. & Sigurdson, H.K. (1997). Sex reassignment at birth. *Pediatric and Adolescent Medicine, 151*, 298-304.

Dinnerstein, D. (1977). *The mermaid and the minotaur: Sexual arrangements and human malaise*. New York: Harper Colophon Books.

Douvan, E. & Adelson, J. (1966). *The adolescent experience*. New York: Wiley.

Duck, J.M. (1990). Children's ideals: The role of real-life versus media figures. *Australian Journal of Psychology, 42*, 19-29.

Dunphy, D.C. (1963). The social structure of urban adolescent peer groups. *Sociometry, 26*, 230-246.

Durkin, K. (1985). *Television, sex roles and children: A developmental social psychological account*. Milton Keynes: Open University Press.

Durkin, K. (1995). *Developmental social psychology*. Oxford: Blackwell.

Eagly, A.H. (1995). The science and politics of comparing women and men. *American Psychologist, 50*, 145-158.

Eagly, A.H. & Carli, L.L. (1981). Sex of researchers and sex typed communication as determinants of sex differences in influenceability: A meta-analysis of social influence. *Psychological Bulletin, 90*, 1-20.

Eccles, S. & Jacobs, J.E. (1986). Social forces shape math attitudes and performance. *Signs, 11*, 367-389.

Emmerich, W., Goldman, K.S., Kirsh, B. & Sharabany, R. (1977). Evidence for a transitional phase in the development of gender constancy. *Child Development, 48*, 930-936.

Epstein, S. (1979). The stability of behaviour: Part 1. On predicting most of the people much of the time. *Journal of Personality and Social Psychology, 37*, 1097-1126.

Erikson, E.H. (1950). *Childhood and society*. New York: Norton.

Erikson, E.H. (1959). *Identity and life styles: Selected papers*. New York: International Universities Press.

Erikson, E.H. (1968). *Identity, youth and crisis*. London: Faber and Faber.

Eysenck, H.J. (1947). *Dimensions of personality*. London: Routledge & Kegan Paul.

Eysenck, H.J. (1965). *Fact and fiction in psychology*. Harmondsworth: Penguin.

Eysenck, H.J. (1985). *The decline and fall of the Freudian empire*. Harmondsworth: Penguin.

Fagot, B.I. (1978). The influence of sex of child on parental reactions to toddler children. *Child Development, 49*, 459-465.

Fagot, B.I., Leinbach, M.D. & Hagen, R. (1986). Gender labelling and adoption of sex-typed behaviours. *Developmental Psychology, 22*, 440-443.

Fagot, B.I., Leinbach, M.D. & O'Boyle, c. (1992). Gender labelling, gender stereotyping, and parenting behaviours. *Developmental Psychology, 28*, 225-230.

Fagot, B.I. & Leinbach, M.D. (1993). Gender role development in young children: From discrimination to labelling. *Developmental Review, 13*, 205-224.

Fausto-Sterling, A. (1999). *Sexing the body: Gender politics and the construction of sexuality*. New York: Basic Books.

Fausto-Sterling, A., Gowaty, P.A. & Zuk, M. (1997). Evolutionary psychology and Darwinian feminism. *Feminist Studies, 23*.

Fisher, S. & Greenberg, R. (1977). *Scientific credibility of Freud's theories*. New York: Basic Books.

Fisher, S. & Greenberg, R.P. (1996). *Freud scientifically reappraised: Testing the theories and the therapy*. New York: Wiley.

Fraiberg, S.H. (1959). *The magic years: Understanding and handling the problems of early childhood*. New York: Scribner.

Freeman, D. (1983). *Margaret Mead and Samoa: The making and unmaking of an anthropological myth*. Cambridge, MA: Harvard University Press.

Freeman, D. (1996). *Franz Boaz and the Flower of Heaven: Coming of age in Samoa and the fateful hoaxing of Margaret Mead*. Harmondsworth: Penguin.

Freud, A. (1936). *The ego and mechanisms of defence*. London: Chatto & Windus.

Freud, A. (1968). Adolescence. In A.E.Winder & D.L. Angus (Eds.), *Adolescence, contemporary studies*. New York: American Books.

Freud, S. (1905). Three essays on the theory of sexuality. In A. Richards (Ed.) (1977) *On sexuality*. London: Pelican.

Freud, S. (1908). Character and anal eroticism. In A. Richards (Ed.) (1977) *On sexuality*. London: Pelican.

Freud, S. (1909). Analysis of a phobia in a five-year-old boy. In A. Richards (Ed.) (1977) *Case histories 1*. London: Pelican.

Freud, S. (1915). Repression. In A. Richards (Ed.) (1991) *On metapsychology*. London: Penguin.

Freud, S. (1920). Beyond the pleasure principle. In A. Richards (Ed.) (1991) *On metapsychology*. London: Penguin.

Freud, S. (1923). The ego and the id. In A. Richards (Ed.) (1991) *On metapsychology*. London: Penguin.

Freud, S. (1924). The dissolution of the oedipus complex. In A. Richards (Ed.) (1977) *On sexuality*. London: Pelican.

Freud, S. (1925). Some psychical consequences of the anatomical distinction between the sexes. In A. Richards (Ed.) (1977) *On sexuality*. London: Pelican.

Freud, S. (1926). Inhibitions, symptoms and anxiety. In J. Strachey (Ed.) *Standard edition of the complete psychological works of Sigmund Freud, vol. 20*. London: Hogarth Press.

Freud, S. (1930). Civilisation and its discontents. In A. Dickson (Ed.) *Civilisation, society and religion*. London: Penguin.

Freud, S. (1931a). Libidinal types. In A. Richards (Ed.) (1977) *On sexuality*. London: Pelican.

Freud, S. (1931b). Female sexuality. In A. Richards (Ed.) (1977) *On sexuality*. London: Pelican.

Freud, S. (1932a). Revision of the theory of dreams. In J. Strachey & A. Richards (Eds.) (1964) *New introductory lectures on psychoanalysis*. London: Pelican.

Freud, S. (1932b). The dissection of the psychical personality. In J. Strachey & A. Richards (Eds.) (1964) *New introductory lectures on psychoanalysis*. London: Pelican.

Freud, S. (1932c). Feminity. In J. Strachey & A. Richards (Eds.) (1964) *New introductory lectures on psychoanalysis*. London: Pelican.

Freud, S. & Breuer, J. (1895). Studies on hysteria. In A. Richards (Ed.) (1991) *Studies on hysteria*. London: Penguin.

Frey, K.S. & Ruble, D.N. (1992). Gender constancy and the 'cost' of sex typed behaviour: A test of the conflict hypothesis. *Developmental Psychology, 28*, 714-721.

Fuligni, A.J. & Eccles, J.S. (1993). Perceived parent-child relationships and early adolescents' orientation towards peers. *Developmental Psychology, 29*, 622-632.

Galambos, N.L. & Almeida, D.M. (1992). Does parent-adolescent conflict increase in early adolescence? *Journal of Marriage and the Family, 54*, 737-747.

Garber, M. (1996). Vice-versa: Bisexuality and the eroticism of everyday life. New York: Viking.

Gay, J. (1984). *Red dust on the green leaves: A Kpelle twins' childhood*. Yarmouth, Me: Intercultural Press.

Goldman-Eisler, F. (1948). Breast feeding and character formation. In C. Kluckhohn, H.A. Murray & D.M. Schneider (Eds.), *Personality in nature, society and culture*. New York: Knopf.

Golombok, S. & Fivush, R. (1994). *Gender development*. Cambridge: Cambridge University Press.

Golombok, S., Tasker, F. & Murray, C. (1997). Children raised in fatherless families from infancy: Family relationships and the socioemotional development of children of lesbian and single heterosexual mothers. *Journal of Child Psychology & Psychiatry, 38*, 783-791.

Gould, S.J. (1981). *The mismeasure of man.* Harmondsworth: Penguin.

Grusec, J.E. (1992). Social learning theory and developmental psychology: The legacies of Robert Sears and Albert Bandura. *Developmental Psychology, 28*, 776-786.

Hall, G.S. (1904). *Adolescence: Its psychology and relation to physiology, anthropology, sex, crime, religion and education.* New York: Appleton.

Halpern, D.F. (1992). *Sex differences in cognitive abilities* (2nd ed.). Hillsdale, NJ: Lawrence Erlbaum.

Haralambos, M. & Holborn, M. (2000). *Sociology: Themes and Perspectives* (5th ed.). London: Collins.

Harris, J.R. (1999). How to succeed in childhood. *Wilson Quarterly, 23*, 30-37.

Harris, T. (1989). *The silence of the lambs.* London: Heinemann.

Hartshorne, H. & May, M.A. (1928). *Studies in the nature of character, vol 1: Studies in deceit.* New York: Macmillan.

Hines, M. & Kaufman, F.R. (1994). Androgen and the development of human sex-typical behaviour: Rough and tumble play and the sex of preferred playmates in children with congenital adrenal hyperplasia (CAH). *Child Development, 65*, 1042-1053.

Hrdy, S.B. (1981). *The woman that never evolved.* Cambridge, MA: Harvard University Press.

Hunter, F.T. (1984). Socialising procedures in parent-child and friendship relations during adolescence. *Developmental Psychology, 20*, 1092-1099.

Hyde, J.S. & Linn, M.C. (1988). Gender differences in aggression? A developmental meta-analysis. *Psychological Bulletin, 104*, 53-69.

Hyde, J.S., Fenneman, E. & Lamon, S.J. (1990). Gender differences in mathematics performance: A meta-analysis. *Psychological Bulletin, 107*, 139-155.

Irwin, A. (2002). If we're different it's for the same reason. *Times Higher Education Supplement*, 4th January.

Katchadourian, H.A. (1977). Sexuality. In S.S. Feldman & G.R. Elliot (Eds.), *At the threshold: The developing adolescent.* Cambridge MA: Harvard University Press.

Kirchler, E., Pombeni, M.L & Palmonari, A. (1991). Sweet sixteen ... Adolescents' problems and the peer group as a source of support. *European Journal of Psychology of Education, 6*, 393-410.

Klein, G.S. (1951). The personal world through perception. In R.R. Blake & G.V. Ramsay (Eds.), *Perception: An approach to personality.* New York: Ronald.

Klein, M. (1928). Early stages of the oedipus complex. In *The writing of Melanie Klein, vol 1.* London: Hogarth.

Klein, M. (1932). The psycho-analysis of children. In *The writings of Melanie Klein, vol 2.* London: Hogarth.

Kline, P. (1984). *Psychology and Freudian theory: An introduction.* London: Routledge.

Kline, P. (1988). *Psychology exposed: The emperor's new clothes.* London: Routledge.

Kline, P. & Storey, R. (1977). A factor analytic study of the oral character. *British Journal of Social and Clinical Psychology, 16*, 317-328.

Kohn, M. (1995): In two minds. *Guardian*, 5th August.

Kohlberg, L. (1966). A cognitive-developmental analysis of children's sex-role concepts and attitudes. In E.E. Maccoby (Ed.), *The development of sex differences.* Stanford: Stanford University Press.

Lacey, H. (1998). Too much, too young. *Independent on Sunday*, 18th October.

LaFreniere, P.J. (2000). *Emotional development.* Belmont: Wadsworth.

Langlois, J.H. & Downs, A.C. (1980). Mothers, fathers and peers as socialisation agents of sex-typed play behaviours in young children. *Child Development, 51*, 1237-1247.

Larson, R. & Richards, M. (1991). Daily companionship in late childhood and early adolescence: Changing developmental contexts. *Child Development, 62*, 284-300.

Larson, R., Richards, M., Moneta, G., Holmback, G. & Duckett, E. (1996). Changes in adolescents' daily interactions from ages 10-18: Disengagement and transformation. *Developmental psychology, 32*, 744-754.

Laursen, B. & Collins, W.A. (1994). Interpersonal conflict during adolescence. *Psychological Bulletin, 115*, 277-296.

Lawrence, D.H. (1913). *Sons and lovers.* Duckworth & Co.

LeVay, S. (1996). Queer in the head. *Guardian*, 7th November.

Levy, G.D. (1989). Relations among aspects of children's social environments, gender schematisation, gender role knowledge, and flexibility. *Sex Roles, 21*, 803-824.

Levy, G.D. & Fivush, R. (1993). Scripts and gender: A new approach for examining gender role development. *Developmental Review, 13*, 126-146.

Lytton, H. & Romney, D.M. (1991). Parents' differential socialization of boys and girls: A meta-analysis. *Psychological Bulletin, 109*, 267-296.

Maccoby, E.E. (1988). Gender as a social category. *Developmental Psychology, 24*, 755-765.

Maccoby, E.E. & Jacklin, C.N. (1974), *The psychology of sex differences.* Stanford: Stanford University Press.

McKie, R. (2002). Science recasts Casanova ... as a woman. *The Observer*, 20th January.

Malik, K. (2000). *Man, beast and zombie.* London: Weidenfeld.

Marcia, J.E. (1966). Development and validation of ego identity states. *Journal of Personality and Social Psychology, 3*, 551-558.

Marcia, J.E. (1980). Identity in adolescence. In J. Adelson (Ed.), *Handbook of adolescent psychology.* New York: Wiley.

Marcia, J.E. (1999). Representational thought in ego identity, psychotherapy, and psychosocial developmental theory. In I.E.Sigel (Ed.), *Development of mental representation: Theories and applications.* Mahwah, NJ: Erlbaum.

Martin, C.L. & Halverson, C.F. Jr (1981). A schematic processing model of sex typing and stereotyping in children. *Child Development, 52*, 1119-1134.

Martin, C.L. & Halverson, C.F. (1987). The roles of cognition in sex role acquisition. In D.B. Carter (Ed.) *Current conceptions of sex roles and sex typing: Theory and research.* New York: Praeger.

Martin, C.L. & Little, J.K. (1990). The relation of gender understanding to children's sex-typed preferences and gender stereotypes. *Child Development, 61*, 1427-1439.

Martin, C.L., Wood, C.H. & Little, J.K. (1990). The development of gender stereotype components. *Child Development, 61*, 1891-1904.

Masson, J.M. (1984). *The assault on truth: Freud's suppression of the seduction theory.* New York: Farrar, Straus & Giroux.

Masters, M.S. & Sanders, B. (1993). Is the gender difference in tal rotation disappearing? *Behavior Genetics, 23*, 337-341.

Mead, M. (1925). Coming of age in Samoa: *A psychological study of primitive youth.* New York: American Museum of Natural History, (1973).

Mead, M. (1935). *Sex and temperament in three primitive societies.* New York: Morrow.

Meilman, P.W. (1979). Cross-sectional age changes in ego identity status during adolescence. *Developmental Psychology, 15*, 230-231.

Meyer, B. (1980). The development of girls' sex role attitudes. *Child Development, 51*, 508-514.

Miller, G. (1999). The mating mind: How sexual choice shaped the evolution of the human mind. London: Heinemann.

Mischel, W. (1965). Predicting the success of Peace Corps volunteers in Nigeria. *Journal of Personality and Social Psychology, 1*, 510-517.

Mischel, W. (1968). *Personality and assessment.* New York: Wiley.

Mischel, W. (1973). Toward a cognitive social learning reconceptualisation of personality. *Psychological Review, 80*, 252-283.

Mischel, W. & Peake, P.K. (1982). Beyond déja vu in the search for cross situational consistency. *Psychological Review, 89*, 730-755.

Moghaddam, F.M. (1998). *Social psychology: Exploring universals across cultures.* New York: W.H. Freeman.

Moir, A. (1993). *Brainsex: The real difference between men and women,* London: Michael Joseph.

Money, J. & Erhardt, A.A. (1972). *Man and woman, boy and girl.* Baltimore: Johns Hopkins University Press.

Munro, G. & Adams, G.R. (1977). Ego-identity formation in college students and working youth. *Developmental Psychology, 13*, 523-524.

Myers, L.B. (2000). Deceiving others or deceiving themselves? *The Psychologist, 13*, 400-403.

Myers, L.B. & Brewin, C.R. (1994). Recall of early experience and the repressive coping style. *Journal of Abnormal Psychology, 103*, 288-292.

O'Brien, M., Huston, A.C. & Risley, T.R. (1983). Sex-typed play of toddlers in a day care center. *Journal of Applied Developmental Psychology, 4*, 1-9.

O'Brien, S.F. & Bierman, K.L. (1988). Conceptions and perceived influence of peer groups: Interviews with preadolescents and adolescents. *Child Development, 59*, 1360-1365.

Offer, D., Ostrove, E. & Howard, K.I. (1981). *The adolescent: A psychological self portrait*. New York: Basic Books.

Offer, D., Ostrov, E., Howard, K.I. & Atkinson, R. (1988). *The teenage world: Adolescents' self-image in ten countries*. New York: Plenum Press.

Palmonari, A., Pombeni, M.L. & Kirchler, E. (1989). Peer groups and the evolution of the self system in adolescence. *European Journal of the Psychology of Education, 4*, 3-15.

Patterson, C.J. (1992). Children of lesbian and gay parents. *Child Development, 63*, 1025-1042.

Perry, D.G. & Bussey, K. (1979). The social learning theory of sex differences: Imitation is alive and well. *Journal of Personality and Social Psychology, 37*, 1699-1712.

Pervin, L.A. (1970). *Personality: Theory, assessment and research*. New York: Wiley.

Phillips, H. (2001). Beyond two sexes. *New Scientitst, 2290*, 27-41.

Popper, K. (1934). *The logic of scientific discovery*. London: Hutchinson, 1959.

Roberts, C.W., Green R., Williams, K. & Goodman, M. (1987). Boyhood gender identity development: A statistical contrast of two family groups. *Developmental Psychology, 23*, 544-557.

Rosario, V.A. (Ed.) (1998). *Science and homosexualities*. London: Routledge.

Rosenthal, D.A. (1987). Ethnic identity development in adolescents. In J.S. Phinney & M.J. Rotheram (Eds.), *Children's ethnic socialization: Pluralism and development*. Newbury Park, CA: Sage.

Rossi, A.S. (1977). A biosocial perspective on parenting. *Daedelus, 106*, 1-32.

Rossi, A.S. & Rossi, P.H. (1990). *Of human bonding: Parent-child relations across the life course*. New York: de Gruyter.

Ruble, D.N., Balaban, T. & Cooper, J. (1981). Gender constancy and the effects of sex-typed televised toy commercials. *Child Development, 52*, 667-673.

Rushton, J.P., Jackson, D.N. & Paunonen, S.V. (1981). Personality: Nomothetic or idiographic? A response to Kenrick and Stringfield. *Psychological Review, 88*, 582-589.

Rutter, M., Graham, P., Chadwick, D.F.D. & Yule, W. (1976). Adolescent turmoil: Fact or fiction. *Journal of Child Psychology and Psychiatry, 17*, 35-36.

Sachs, D. (1991). In fairness to Freud: A critical notice of The Foundations of Psychoanalysis by Adolf Grunbaum. In J. Neu (Ed.), *The Cambridge companion to Freud*. Cambridge: Cambridge University Press.

Sanson, A.V., Prior, M. & Oberklaid, F. (1985). Normative data on temperament in Australian infants. *Australian Journal of Psychology, 37*, 185-195.

Scarr, S. (1992). Developmental theories for the 1990s: Developmental and individual differences. *Child Development, 63*, 1-19.

Schaffer, H.R. (1996) *Social development*. Oxford: Blackwell.

Scholinski, D. (1998). The last time I wore a dress. Cited in C. Goodwin, Hidden gender, *Sunday Times*, 4th January.

Sears, R.R. (1936). Experimental studies in projection. 1. Attribution of traits. *Journal of Social Psychology, 7*, 151-163.

Segall, M.H., Dansen, P.R., Berry, J.W. & Poortinga, Y.H. (1990). *Human behaviour in global perspective: An introduction to cross-cultural psychology*. Boston: Allyn & Bacon.

Shaffer, D.R. (1993). *Developmental psychology; Childhood and adolescence*. (3rd ed.). Pacific Grove, GA: Brooks/Cole.

Siddique, C.M. & D'Arcy, C. (1984). Adolescence, stress, and psychological well-being. *Journal of Youth and Adolesccence, 13*, 459-474.

Siegal, M. (1987). Are sons and daughters treated more differently by fathers than by mothers? *Developmental Review, 7*, 183-209.

Shostak, M. (1981). *Nissa: The life and words of a !Kung woman*. Cambridge MA: Harvard University Press.

Slaby, R.G. & Frey, K.S. (1975). Development of gender constancy and selective attention to same sex models. *Child Development, 46*, 849-856.

Smetana, J.G. (1988). Adolescents' and parents' conceptions of parental authority. *Child Development, 59*, 321-335.

Smith, C. & Lloyd, B.B. (1978). Maternal behaviour and perceived sex of infant. *Child Development, 49*, 1263-1265.

Smith, P.K., Cowie, H. & Blades, M. (1998). *Understanding children's development* (3rd ed.). Oxford: Blackwell.

Stangor, C. & Ruble, D.N. (1987). Development of gender role knowledge and gender constancy. In L.S. Liben & M.L. Signorella (Eds.), *Children's gender schemata*. San Francisco: Jossey-Bass.

Stangor, C. & Ruble, D.N. (1989). Different influences of gender schemata and gender contancy on children's information processing and behaviour. *Social Cognition, 7*, 354-372.

Steinberg, L. & Silverberg, S.B. (1986). The vicissitudes of autonomy in early adolescence. *Child Development, 57*, 841-851.

Stevenson, M.R. & Black, K.N. (1988). Paternal absence and sex role development: A meta-analysis. *Child Development, 59*, 793-814.

Stoker, B. (1897). *Dracula*. London: Arrow (1979).

Thompson, S.K. (1975). Gender labels and early sex-role development. *Child Development, 46*, 339-347.

Trivers, R.L. (1972). Parental investment and sexual selection. In B. Campbell (Ed.), *Sexual selection and the descent of man*. Chicago: Aldine.

van Leeuwen, M.S. (1978). A cross-cultural examination of psychological differentiation in males and females. *International Journal of Psychology, 13*, 87-122.

Waterman, C.K. & Waterman, A.S. (1975). Fathers and sons: A study in ego identity across two generations. *Journal of Youth and Adolescence, 4*, 331-338.

Webster, R. (1995). *Why Freud was wrong: Sin, science and psychoanalysis*. London: Harper Collins.

Weinraub, M., Clemens, L.P., Sockloff, A., Ethridge, T., Gracely, E. & Myers, B. (1984). The development of sex role stereotypes in the third year: Relationships to gender labeling, gender identity, sex-typed toy preference and family characteristics. *Child Development, 55*, 1493-1503.

Whyte, J. (1998). Childhood. In K. Trew & J. Kremer (Eds.), *Gender and psychology*. London: Arnold.

Widdicombe, S. & Wooffitt, R. (1990). 'Being' versus 'doing' punk: On achieving authenticity as a member. *Journal of Language and Social Psychology, 9*, 257-277.

Will, J.A., Self, P.A. & Daran, N. (1976). Maternal behaviour and the perceived sex of infant. *American Journal of Orthopsychiatry, 46*, 135-139.

Williams, T.M. (Ed.) (1986). *The impact of television: A national experiment in three communities*. New York: Academic Press.

Wilson, E.O. (1975). *Sociobiology: The new synthesis*. Cambridge, MA: Harvard University Press.

Wilson, E.O. (1978). *On human nature*. Cambridge, MA: Harvard University Press.

Wright, D.S., Taylor, A., Davies, D.R., Sluckin, W., Lee, S.G.M. & Reason, J.T. (1970). *Introducing psychology*. Harmondsworth: Penguin.

Youniss, J. & Smoller, J. (1985). *Adolescent relations with mothers, fathers and friends*. Chicago: University of Chicago Press.

Young, W.C., Goy, R.W. & Phoenix, C.H. (1964). Hormones and sexual behaviour. *Science, 143*, 212-219.

30 Adulthood

> ### Introduction

This chapter looks at growing old through early and middle adulthood to late adulthood and death. It examines the challenges and crises of each stage of adult development and how people cope with them. One of the main themes of the chapter is the increasing diversity of adult life, which no longer fits easily into the neat and tidy stages identified by earlier researchers.

Chapter summary

- **Unit 1 presents a critical analysis of stage theories of early and middle adulthood.**
- **Unit 2 looks at partnerships, divorce and parenthood.**

- **Unit 3 examines theories of late adulthood, cognitive changes in old age, responses to bereavement, and the process of dying.**

Unit 1 Early and middle adulthood

KEY ISSUES

1 **Do people's adult lives move through predictable stages?**

2 **What are the main criticisms of stage theories of lifespan development?**

1.1 Erik Erikson

Erikson (1963) believed that personal development continues throughout an individual's life. Personal identity will therefore be formed, modified and changed during childhood, adolescence, and early, middle and late adulthood.

Erikson identified eight *psychosocial stages* during the lifespan – two in infancy, two in childhood, one in adolescence, and three in adulthood (see pp 541-542 and 562-563). Each stage presents a crisis or challenge. This can be seen as a confrontation between the individual and the demands of their personal and social situations – for example, the demands of parenthood. The way a person deals with each crisis contributes to their overall personality development. A crisis offers both

opportunity and risk – in Erikson's words, 'a turning point for better or worse' (Erikson, 1964).

A person must successfully resolve each crisis in order to be prepared for a) the tasks of each developmental stage and b) the crisis of the following stage. For example, an adolescent must successfully resolve the identity vs role confusion crisis in order to a) successfully deal with the tasks of adolescence, such as career choice and b) resolve the intimacy vs isolation crisis of early adulthood.

Table 1 presents Erikson's stages of adult development and the crisis or challenge associated with each stage.

Early adulthood

According to Erikson the challenge of early adulthood is intimacy versus isolation. *Intimacy* refers to the capacity for closeness and love. It involves the establishment of committed and enduring relationships – close friendships and partnerships.

The danger of this challenge is *isolation* – failure to achieve intimacy, withdrawing from relationships and avoiding commitment. The result is a socially isolated individual with shallow relationships.

The establishment of intimacy often leads to parenthood. Here the importance of intimacy in maintaining relationships can be seen – the stresses of parenthood often place considerable strain on a partnership.

Erikson believed that the establishment of a secure and stable identity was necessary for the achievement of intimacy. A person searching for a satisfactory identity would be too preoccupied and self-absorbed to form close relationships.

Middle adulthood

Erikson sees the crisis of middle adulthood – ages 40-65 – as generativity versus stagnation. Here the challenge is to develop a sense of *generativity*, and conversely to avoid a feeling of *stagnation*.

Table 1	Erikson's stages of adult development

Stage	Crisis
Early adulthood (20-40 years)	Intimacy versus isolation
Middle adulthood (40-65 years)	Generativity versus stagnation
Late adulthood (65 years-death)	Ego integrity versus despair

Generativity is a concern for helping and guiding the next generation – bringing up one's own children and guiding young people in general, for example, teaching them a trade or profession and encouraging their occupational development. Generativity also refers to a concern for producing (generating) something of value to society – being a productive worker, becoming involved in charitable and community projects, or producing something of lasting value such as a book or a work of art.

Those who fail to achieve generativity are faced with stagnation – a feeling of going nowhere, of dissatisfaction with career development or with family life. In Erikson's (1963) words, they often experience a 'pervading sense of stagnation and personal impoverishment (and indulge themselves) as if they were their one and only child'.

Evaluation

Advantages Erikson was one of the first researchers to focus on development after adolescence. His view that development is a lifelong process is now generally accepted. His theory of stages of personality development has provided a springboard and a direction for later researchers.

There is some evidence to support Erikson's stages and developmental crises. For example, people in middle adulthood do seem concerned about generative issues and they report more generative activities (McAdams et al., 1993).

Disadvantages Erikson wrote from the perspective of a white, middle-class Western male in the 1960s. He largely ignored the influence of gender, ethnicity, social class, culture and different time periods on lifespan experience and development. He tended to assume that all human beings experience the same series of crises during their lifespan.

Erikson did admit that women's adult development may well be different from men's. In particular, he saw women's identity to some extent as a reflection of their male partner's identity. As a result, women may not achieve identity until marriage. From today's standpoint, this view is sexist and a reflection of life 50 years ago.

There is some evidence of social class differences in lifespan development. For example, working-class men and women tend to select an occupation, marry and produce children earlier. Middle-class men and women are more likely to go to university and to explore various career options during early adulthood (Neugarten, 1975).

Key terms

Psychosocial stages *Lifespan stages which involve personality development and changes in the individual's social situation. Each stage presents a crisis or challenge.*

Intimacy *The capacity for closeness and love.*

Isolation *Withdrawing from relationships and avoiding commitment.*

Generativity *A concern for helping and guiding the next generation and for producing something of value to society.*

Stagnation *A feeling of going nowhere, of dissatisfaction with career development or family life.*

There is also evidence of the extension of adolescence for members of all social classes, with an adult identity only emerging for many in their late 20s or 30s (Sheehy, 1996) And some of us never 'grow up' – Mick Jagger being a real life example, and Patsy and Eddy from *Absolutely Fabulous* a fictional example.

It is unlikely that the kinds of crises identified by Erikson in 1960s America are reflected in all historical periods and all cultures. Evidence for this point is provided in Activities 1 and 2, and in Unit 3, with reference to late adulthood.

1.2 Daniel Levinson

Levinson (1978, 1986) argues that there are predictable and identifiable periods through which people move during their lives. He claims that 'although each human life is unique, everyone goes through the same basic sequence'. Levinson's 'seasons of man', as the phrase suggests, was initially based on men's lives. On the basis of later research, he claimed it also applied to women's lives.

Levinson (1978) developed his model from a series of in-depth biographical interviews with 40 American men age 35 to 45. They were drawn from four occupational groups – factory workers, business executives, university biology lecturers and novelists. Later, 45 women, also age 35 to 45, were interviewed. They were drawn from three groups – homemakers (housewives), business executives and university lecturers (Levinson, 1996). Participants were asked to review their lives to date, focusing on the turning points, the choices they made and the consequences of those choices.

Eras, phases, transitions and life structures

Eras On the basis of his interview data, Levinson identified four broad *eras* or *seasons*. They are:

- Era of preadulthood (0-22 years)
- Era of early adulthood (17-45 years)
- Era of middle adulthood (40-65 years)
- Era of late adulthood (65 onwards).

Transitions The eras of early and middle adulthood begin and end with a *transition phase*, which lasts about five years. This phase concludes the previous era and prepares the individual for the new era.

Phases Early and middle adulthood are divided into three phases. They are:

- Entry or novice phase – a period of adjustment to the new era
- Mid-era transition phase – when the person becomes increasingly competent at meeting the new challenges
- Culmination phase – a stable phase when the individual confidently manages the demands of the era.

Life structures A *life structure* consists of all the individual's roles and relationships at any point in time. Each era and phase presents new challenges and demands. Individuals respond to these by adapting and changing their life structure. For example, marriage requires a new life structure. It involves a new set of relationships between husband and wife, their in-laws and their friends. It also involves a period of adjustment leading, in many cases, to stability.

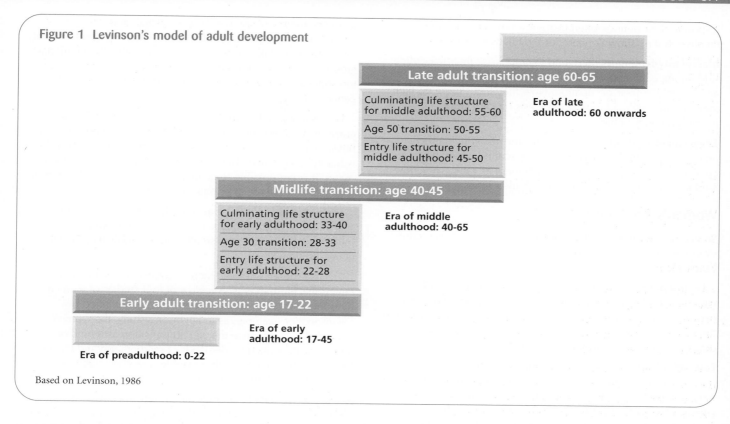

Figure 1 Levinson's model of adult development

Late adult transition: age 60-65

Culminating life structure for middle adulthood: 55-60

Age 50 transition: 50-55

Entry life structure for middle adulthood: 45-50

Era of late adulthood: 60 onwards

Midlife transition: age 40-45

Culminating life structure for early adulthood: 33-40

Age 30 transition: 28-33

Entry life structure for early adulthood: 22-28

Era of middle adulthood: 40-65

Early adult transition: age 17-22

Era of early adulthood: 17-45

Era of preadulthood: 0-22

Based on Levinson, 1986

Era of early adulthood

According to Levinson (1986), early adulthood is the era of 'greatest energy and abundance, contradiction and stress'. This era can bring rewards and deep satisfaction – love, marriage, children and occupational advancement. It can also be a time of worry and stress as important decisions about marriage, children and career have to be made. The following description is based on men's life cycle.

Early adult transition (age 17-22). During this transition phase, most young adults construct a *Dream* – a vision of what they would like to be in the adult world. They may have an image of themselves as a teacher, doctor, sports person or business person, with a partner, a house in the country and holidays abroad. The Dream provides guidance, direction and motivation. The more specific it is, the more likely the individual is to build a life structure which reflects it. According to Levinson (1978), 'If the Dream remains unconnected to his life it may simply die, and with it his sense of aliveness and purpose'.

Entering the adult world (age 22-28). During this phase the main concerns are forming a special relationship – for example, getting married – and career advancement. Many young adults attach themselves to a *mentor* who provides them with career advice and direction. Usually, the mentor is an older, more senior work colleague who encourages, guides and teaches the young adult. This relationship is often close and lasts between 2 and 10 years. However, when it has served its purpose, it can end in resentment – the young adult may find the mentor interfering and the mentor may find his pupil ungrateful.

Age 30 transition (age 28-33). This is a time of self-questioning and re-evaluation. Those who have put all their energies into career advancement and are still single may become concerned about finding a life partner. This phase can be a time of instability for those who are not satisfied with either their relationships or their jobs.

Settling down (age 33-40). Most have succeeded in building a stable and satisfying life structure. They are likely to be anchored in family life and committed to a particular career path. They are developing their occupational skills, advancing their careers, and making important contributions to society.

Era of middle adulthood

Many men see the mid-life transition (age 40-45) as a time of crisis. Thirty-two out of the forty men in Levinson's sample reported experiencing some degree of emotional turbulence. This may be triggered by some or all of the following changes – parents ill or dying, children leaving home, an end to career advancement, an awareness of ageing and physical decline. Most experience self-doubt and confusion as they start to modify the marriage, family and occupational components of their life structure. Some take drastic steps – changing occupations, wives and lifestyles.

Sometimes referred to as a 'mid-life crisis', this is a time for taking stock, for self-assessment, and focusing on the meaning and future of life.

According to Levinson (1978, 1996), people must deal with four developmental tasks during middle adulthood. Each task requires them to reconcile two opposing tendencies within the self. They are:

Young-old Middle age involves seeking new ways of being both young and old – for example, taking up golf to replace more strenuous sports; reassessing being older in a more positive way.

Destruction-creation During middle age, men often look back at their destructive behaviour, for example how they have hurt others or neglected their family as they pursue their career. In response, their outlook often becomes more positive and creative as they show concern for the needs of others.

Masculinity-femininity Men tend to emphasise their masculine side during early adulthood as they attempt to forge ahead aggressively in their occupation. Now they focus more on their feminine side with a growing emphasis on care and understanding for others.

Engagement-separation For men, this means reducing their engagement with the outside world by scaling down their concerns with achieving and advancement at work. They now tend to focus on getting in touch with their inner self.

Women's adulthood

So far, this unit has focused on men's adult years. This section examines Levinson's research in the 1990s on women's adult years.

Levinson (1996) conducted lengthy interviews with 45 women age 35-45 from three groups – housewives, business executives and university lecturers. He found that women follow the same lifespan paths as men but they approach developmental tasks somewhat differently.

Early adulthood During the early adult transition (age 17-22) and entering the adult world (age 22-28), career-oriented women tend to divide their Dream between marriage and career. They tend to define themselves in terms of their relationships with their husband, children and work colleagues. By comparison, men focus more on themselves, they are more individualistic and self-centred, they show less concern for relationships and are less likely to support others. Women find it more difficult than men to find a suitable mentor.

During the age 30 transition (age 28-33), women, like men, re-evaluate their life structure. Those who emphasised marriage and children in earlier phases tended to give more priority to a career and expected their husbands to support them in this area. For some women, this is a time of instability and conflicting aspirations.

The settling down phase for men (age 33-40) is a period of instability for many women. They find the demands of motherhood and career are often in conflict. Only when women reach middle adulthood do they experience the stability that many men find in their 30s.

Middle adulthood Like men, many women experience the midlife transition (age 40-45) as a time of crisis. Whereas the older man can still see himself as attractive, the older woman, due to society's double standard, finds ageing more difficult. Many fear being seen as unattractive and attempt to look younger with various anti-ageing remedies such as skin creams.

For many men, middle adulthood is a time when they reduce their concern with career advancement. A few career-oriented women take similar steps. However, those who have spent their early adulthood taking care of children and working in dead-end, part-time jobs often change direction and attempt to find fulfilment in a career.

Evaluation

The samples Levinson's original sample consisted of 40 American men, age 35 to 45, drawn from four occupational groups – factory workers, business executives, university biology

lecturers and novelists. The sample is small and unrepresentative. The working class is under-represented – only factory workers fall into this category. The other occupational groups are from the top end of the middle class. The sample is too small and unrepresentative to provide a basis for generalisations.

Levinson's female sample is even less representative. It consists of 45 women, age 35 to 45, drawn from housewives, business executives and university lecturers. The working class is barely represented. The occupational groups are untypical. Again, it is not possible to generalise with any confidence from such a small and unrepresentative sample.

Levinson's data for the eras of middle and late adulthood is sparse. Only 15 participants over the age of 45 were interviewed. This is a very small sample – too small to make generalisations from.

Despite these criticisms, there is some evidence to support Levinson's lifespan eras. A review of four studies of women's lives found they broadly followed the eras identified by Levinson. For example, as in Levinson's study, the women appeared to experience the age 30 transition as a time of tension with conflicting demands of motherhood and career. However, the samples in these studies are very small – only 39 women in total (Roberts & Newton, 1987).

Retrospective data Levinson's data is retrospective – his participants looked back over their lives. There are a number of problems with this type of data. First, memories are likely to be selective and at times inaccurate. Second, the participants were looking back over 30 years from the perspective of middle-aged people. They may have seen things somewhat differently in their twenties (Durkin, 1995).

Despite this, there is evidence which partly avoids this problem and provides some support for Levinson's findings. A longitudinal study by Vaillant (1977) followed 94 American men born in the 1920s from their student days over the next 30 years. They were given a lengthy questionnaire every 10 years and interviewed at age 47. In many respects – but not all – their lives fitted Levinson's eras.

A male framework Levinson's eras and phases were constructed from his original sample of men. This framework of lifespan development formed the basis of his later research on women. There may be problems with this. First, women's experience may, to some extent, be 'forced' into a male framework. Second, women's development might appear deficient when measured against a male benchmark. Third, a male framework may result in important aspects of women's experience being overlooked (Durkin, 1995).

The mid-life crisis According to Levinson (1978, 1996), most men and women experience a mid-life crisis – a period of self-doubt and personal upheaval. A number of studies have found little evidence for this. For example, change in middle age was slow and steady for most of the men in Vaillant's (1977) longitudinal study. Research by Lachman and James (1997) indicates that only a minority of their participants experienced 'crisis' and significant changes in their life structure during middle age. It appears that there are wide individual differences in mid-life.

Culture and generation Levinson's sample of men were Americans born in the 1920s. His sample of women were

Americans born in the 1940s. Both samples were drawn from a specific generation and a specific culture. Can Levinson's findings be applied to other time periods and other cultures? There is evidence which suggests they cannot be generalised in this way. Part of this evidence is presented in Activities 1 and 2.

According to Bernice Neugarten (1979), each generation and every culture has a *social clock* – expectations of an appropriate age for starting a job, getting married, having children, buying a house and retiring. For example, a study of Australian students found they expected to get married, have children and become grandparents at a later age than their parents. And they looked forward to a wider range of options and lifestyles in retirement than those of their parents (Peterson, 1996).

The content of the social clock is related to time and culture. For example, the changing role of women will affect their lifespan development. No longer limited to the mother/housewife role, many women now look forward to a career. Research indicates that women on today's social clock who have not begun a career by age 30 suffer from feelings of incompetence and low self-esteem (Helson, 1992).

Recent evidence suggests that future lifespan development will continue to change. 'Jobs for life' are a thing of the past. Adolescence is being extended as increasing numbers of young people take up further and higher education. The high divorce and re-marriage rate is leading to a rapid growth in one-parent

families, serial monogamy and reconstituted families. Increasing numbers of men are starting second families in their 40s, 50s and even 60s. This suggests new challenges, new crises and changing identities. It also suggests that, to some extent, Levinson's lifespan development model is limited to time and place.

Class and ethnicity There were few members of the working class in Levinson's male sample and even fewer in his female sample. Class can make a significant difference to people's lives. Very few of Levinson's blue-collar workers realised their occupational dream. People with working class backgrounds are more likely to have dead-end jobs which offer no occupational advancement and they are more likely to experience early adulthood as a shorter phase than their middle-class counterparts. Considerably more research on class differences is needed in order to assess Levinson's model of lifespan development.

The same applies to ethnic differences. Ethnicity can have a considerable effect on people's lives. For example, the unemployment rate of African Americans, and African Caribbeans in the UK, is double that of the white population.

Summary

1 Erikson argued that personal development continues through eight psychosocial stages during the lifespan.

2 Each stage presents a crisis or challenge. The way an individual deals with each crisis contributes to their overall personal development.

3 Erikson identified three stages of adulthood, each involving a particular challenge.

4 The challenge of early adulthood (age 20-40) is intimacy versus isolation. The challenge of middle adulthood (age 40-65) is generativity versus stagnation.

5 Erikson largely ignored the influence of gender, ethnicity, social class, culture and historical era on lifespan development.

6 Levinson argued that everyone goes through the 'same basic sequence' during their life.

7 He identified four eras or seasons during the lifespan. He divided early and middle adulthood into three phases. In addition, these eras begin and end with a transition phase.

8 Based on his sample of men, Levinson identified the following aspects of early adulthood:

- Early adult transition
- Entering the adult world
- Age 30 transition
- Settling down.

9 Levinson saw the transition to middle adulthood as a mid-life crisis – a time of confusion and emotional turbulence.

10 He believed that most people have to deal with four developmental tasks during middle adulthood, each with two opposing tendencies.

- Young-old
- Destruction-creation
- Masculinity-femininity
- Engagement-separation.

11 Levinson's research indicated that women generally follow the same lifespan development as men but they approach developmental tasks somewhat differently. For example, they tend to divide their Dream between marriage and career.

12 The following criticisms have been made of Levinson's research:

- His samples are small and unrepresentative.
- The data is retrospective.
- His framework is largely based on data from his male sample.
- Other research evidence questions the existence of a mid-life crisis.
- Like Erikson, he tends to ignore the influence of culture, generation, social class and ethnicity on lifespan development.

13 Some researchers argue that stage theories of lifespan development ignore both individual and group differences. They claim that life events are more significant than lifespan stages.

Stage theories Levinson's model, like that of Erikson, is a stage theory. It assumes that people move through predictable stages during their lifespan. It suffers from the problem of all stage theories – lots of people don't fit. In other words, people's lives reveal considerable individual differences. Stage theories also tend to overlook group differences. There is evidence that membership of social class and ethnic groups can make important differences to people's lifespan experience.

Some researchers argue that *life events* are more significant than lifespan stages (eg, Craig, 1992). Life events are particular events that shape people's lives, for example, marriage, parenthood, divorce and the death of a close relative.

Life events, for example, divorce, do not necessarily occur during particular eras, if indeed they occur at all. The next unit looks at some of these life events.

Activity 1   Stuck in adolescence

Item A   Peter and Petra Pan

Patsy and Eddy

Mick Jagger – forever young!

They are a generation of 'half adults' clinging to adolescence because maturity isn't cool. This is the argument put forward by Robert Bly in *The Sibling Society* and Gail Sheehy in *New Passages*. They have become stuck in adolescence.

You see them in Hyde Park: thirty and forty-somethings on rollerblades and skateboards; hanging out at Glastonbury or discussing the merits of Oasis vs Blur at dinner parties. They read *Loaded* and *FHM*, watch *Top of the Pops* and buy their clothes at Gap, Calvin Klein and DKNY – all firms that sell their wares with images of youth. You find them in the more exclusive gyms, such as Chelsea's Harbour Club, struggling to keep the ravages of age at bay.

Their fictional models are Gary and Tony in *Men Behaving Badly* and Eddy and Patsy in *Absolutely Fabulous* – though they are too vain to recognise it. In real life their names are Mick Jagger, Andrew Neil and Richard Branson. Even Tony Blair is not immune from a desire to seem young and hip, as was demonstrated by his presence at the Q and Brits music awards and his shameless acquiescence in being photographed with his Fender Stratocaster electric guitar.

What they share in common is – like Peter Pan – they won't grow up. While childhood is ending earlier, adults are prolonging adolescence into their thirties. Many are not acknowledging their maturity until they hit 40. The seven ages of man have been reduced to three.

Adapted from Beaumont, 1996

Item B   Staying young

Helen Murray, 35, businesswoman
'Being grown-up means being like your parents – responsible about money and having dinner parties. Although I've got a child and a high-powered job, I don't feel grown-up or in control of my life. Being grown-up is not necessarily a positive thing anyway because when you stop growing maybe you begin to stagnate. Besides, I like Pulp and Ash too much!'

Phil Armfield, 40, inventory analyst
'At work I act like a grown-up because I'm trying to project a sensible and mature image, but once I'm out of the building, I can be myself again and say: "Bugger it, I'm going to enjoy myself and worry about it later".'

David Sumpter, 32, software engineer. 'I don't feel any need to "grow up" and settle down and have kids – I can do all that when I'm 45.'

Interviews by Michael Cooke, quoted in Beaumont, 1996

Question

Read Items A and B. What questions do they raise about Erikson's and Levinson's lifespan stages?

Activity 2   History and culture

Item A   Historical change

**CHILDREN AT THEIR
FATHER'S GRAVE**
*Ah yes, around tombs there must gather
the orphan-hearts yet undefiled:
The grave-grass of many a father is
fresher for tears of a child.
The children with infinite yearning have
brought him the garden's best worth,
As though in the dead they were turning
to flowers and freshness of earth.*

At the end of the seventeenth century, the life of the average family man, married for the first time at 27, could be summed up thus: born into a family of five children, he had seen only two or three of them reach the age of 15; he himself had had five children of whom only two or three were alive at his death.

This man, living on average until 52, will have seen about nine people die in his immediate family (not counting uncles, nephews and first cousins), among whom would have been one grandparent (the three others being dead before his birth), both his parents and three of his children.

In the past, in one out of every two cases, the death of young children occurred before that of their father, and half the remaining children saw their father die before they were fully grown. The average age of the children at the death of their first parent was 14.

Today, the 'average' person will be in their 50s when their parents die.

Adapted from Pressat, 1973 and *Social Trends*, 2002

Item B   Life expectancy

Great Britain							Years
	1841	1901	1931	1961	1981	1991	2000
Males							
Life expectancy	41.0	45.7	58.1	67.8	70.9	73.2	75.1
Females							
Life expectancy	43.0	49.6	62.1	73.7	76.8	78.8	80.0

Adapted from *Social Trends*, 2001 and 2002

Item C   Age grades

Amongst many East African peoples, such as the Masai and Nandi, society is divided into age grades. A typical set of grades for males after childhood is junior warriorhood, senior warriorhood, junior elderhood and senior elderhood. Every man is a member of a particular age set and moves from one grade to another with members of his set. Men usually maintain a close and friendly relationship with members of their age set throughout their lives.

Members of a particular age set change their social status all at once as they move together into the next age grade. The transitions from youth to early adulthood to middle age and late adulthood occur in a series of 'jumps'. People make these jumps as members of groups, not as individuals.

Each age grade has particular duties. For example, the warrior grades are responsible for defending the society and the senior grade forms a council of elders in which disputes are settled and decisions affecting the whole society are taken.

Adapted from Beattie, 1964

A Masai warrior

Question

Erikson and Levinson largely ignored history and culture. But these factors can significantly affect lifespan development. Discuss with reference to Items A, B and C.

Unit 2 Family and relationships in adulthood

KEY ISSUES

1 **What effect do partnerships, divorce and parenthood have on those involved?**

2 **How have partnerships, parenthood and the divorce rate changed?**

3 **What effect have these changes had on lifespan development?**

2.1 Introduction

This unit looks at three life events – marriage, parenthood and divorce. Although they are sometimes called life events, they can be seen as processes. Ideally, being a marital partner and a parent are lifelong relationships, and divorce is the end point of what is often a long and painful process.

Over the past 50 years, there have been significant changes in Western society in these areas. Marriage has declined in popularity, and *cohabitation* – living together in a partnership without marriage – has become increasingly common. The divorce rate rocketed from the 1960s to the 1980s, though it has since levelled off. However, it remains high compared to most of the 20th century. Remarriage, as a proportion of all marriages, has grown steadily. The two-parent family is still the norm, but a significant proportion of families are now one-parent or lone-parent families. The term *serial monogamy* has been coined to describe remarriage – a succession of monogamous marriages – and the term *reconstituted families* to describe the recombining of parts of past families on remarriage.

These changes suggest that the lifespan experiences of increasing numbers of people are very different from those described in the lifespan stages identified by researchers in the 1960s.

Some people never marry, and some couples do not have children. Some have long and happy marriages, some are divorced within six months. Some remarry after divorce, some don't. Some remarried couples have children, some don't. This indicates that lifespan experiences can vary considerably.

The evidence presented in this section is based on data produced by the Office for National Statistics and drawn from various issues of *Social Trends*. It indicates that individuals' lifespan experiences can be very different and that these differences may be increasing. As suggested at the close of the previous unit, life events may have as much, if not more, effect on people's lives than lifespan stages.

2.2 Partnerships

Facts and figures

According to Erikson (1963), the crisis or challenge of early adulthood (age 20-40) is intimacy vs isolation. Intimacy refers to the capacity for closeness and love – it involves the establishment of committed and enduring relationships. Marriage is the prime example of such a relationship.

Similarly, Levinson (1978, 1986) sees the era of early adulthood (age 17-40), and particularly the phase 'entering the adult world' (age 22-28), as the time when young adults are concerned with forming a special relationship.

The evidence for marriage supports these claims. However, it indicates that first marriages are taking place later in life. In 1961, the average age at first marriage in England and Wales was 26 for men and 23 for women. By 1999, this had risen to 29 for men and 27 for women. Part of this change may be due to an increase in cohabitation before marriage. In Britain, the proportion of cohabiting non-married women and men doubled between 1986 and 1999. During the last half of the 1990s, around a quarter of men and women cohabited before their first marriage. However, cohabitation does not always lead to marriage. Around two-fifths of cohabiting adults do not intend to marry (*Social Trends*, 2002).

Marriage itself is becoming less popular. In the UK, the number of first marriages peaked in 1971, then decreased by half in 1999. The number of remarriages for one or both partners increased from 1961 to 1991, and has since declined slightly – see Figure 2.

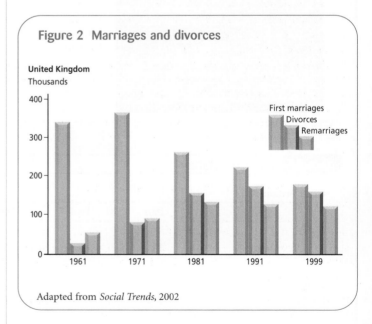

Figure 2 Marriages and divorces

United Kingdom
Thousands

First marriages
Divorces
Remarriages

Adapted from *Social Trends*, 2002

The trend seems to be away from the stages suggested by Erikson and Levinson towards greater individual choice and differences. Increasing numbers of people are cohabiting and remarrying. Just how significant these changes are is difficult to assess. Remarriage suggests that people still have faith in marriage despite previous failure. And, in many respects, the relationship established by cohabitation is the same as that of marriage.

The marital relationship

People have high hopes when they choose to marry.

According to Reibstein and Richards (1992), people in the West expect a lot from their marriage – they expect their partner to be a lover and a friend who satisfies their emotional and sexual needs, and provides companionship and support.

The nature of love In the West, love is now seen as the primary reason for getting married and staying married (Giddens, 1992).

Sternberg (1987) identified three components to love. The emotional component is intimacy or closeness; the psychological/physical component is passion – yearning for union, including sexual union; the cognitive component is commitment.

There are seven possible combinations of these three components.

- commitment alone is empty love
- intimacy alone is liking
- passion alone is infatuation
- commitment plus intimacy gives companionate love
- commitment plus passion give fatuous love
- intimacy plus passion gives romantic love
- all three combined leads to consummate love, the Western ideal (see p298).

Love and marriage Basing the marital relationship on this ideal may be a risky business. The German sociologists Ulrick Beck and Elisabeth Beck-Gernsheim (1995) make the following argument. Traditional societies gave people little choice about their roles in families and marriages. Today, people are largely free from traditional constraints and obligations. In modern industrial society, the individual is increasingly isolated. Close knit communities and extended families have largely broken down. People are turning more and more to their partners for the 'emotional base' and 'security system' that a wider social network and traditional obligations once provided. According to Beck and Beck-Gernsheim (1995), marriage appears to offer 'a sort of refuge in the chilly environment of our affluent, impersonal, uncertain society, stripped of its traditions and scarred by all sorts of risk. Love will become more important than ever and equally impossible'.

Both men and women are increasingly seeking and following careers as individuals in a competitive labour market. This conflicts with the requirements of love, marriage and the family 'where one is expected to sacrifice one's own interests … and invest in a collective project called the family'. Arguments over housework, childcare and whose career should take priority can lead to conflict and resentment which, in turn, can destroy love – the basis of marriage.

Attachment types Not all views of the marital relationship are so pessimistic. The following study indicates that over 50% of marriages are based on a warm and secure relationship.

Hazan and Shaver (1987) claimed that adult romantic relationships reflect their attachment types in infancy. Ainsworth et al. (1978) identified three types of mother-infant attachment – secure, insecure-resistant and insecure-avoidant. Hazen and Shaver's findings indicate that 56% of adult relationships with their partners are secure – trusting, comforting, warm and rewarding. Nineteen per cent are insecure-resistant – anxious and ambivalent about the relationship, wanting a complete merging with their partner, yet fearful of abandonment, and prone to jealousy and emotional turbulence. Twenty-five per cent are insecure-avoidant – independent, unwilling to get too emotionally involved, and prone to affairs or over-work to keep their distance from their partner.

There is some doubt about the claim that early attachments shape later attachments. A lot can happen between attachments in infancy and relationships in later life. And relationships with different partners can vary – you may have an insecure attachment with one partner and a secure attachment with a later partner (Durkin, 1995).

Marital satisfaction Does marriage provide the intimacy and closeness which Erikson and Levinson see as an indication that the challenge of early adulthood has been met successfully? One way of answering this question is to look at surveys of marital satisfaction.

Surveys indicate that many more men than women report being happily married. This finding applies right through to old age (Unger & Crawford, 1992). Possible reasons for this gender difference will be discussed shortly.

Satisfaction varies over time. Some studies have found a steady decline, but more report a U-bend effect, with a fairly rapid drop followed by a gradual rise in satisfaction during middle and late adulthood (Bengtson et al., 1990).

In a series of studies, 168 couples in their first marriage were interviewed during the first three months of marriage and again after one year. The researchers found a decrease in both the quantity and quality of interaction. Intimacy and passion dropped, regardless of whether the couple had had a baby. A shift occurred in shared activities from pleasure and leisure to more practical tasks like trips to the supermarket and housework (Huston & Chorost, 1994).

Marital satisfaction appears to increase with middle age, reflected by a decrease in the divorce rate for this age group. Various explanations have been suggested for this. It may reflect a growth in interpersonal skills and the use of diplomacy to handle difficulties (Perho & Korhonen, 1999). It may indicate the development of companionate love, of increasing dependency and shared experience (Cole, 1984). It may reflect a reduction in idealism about marriage, as the partners increasingly appreciate what they have, rather than pine for what might have been. On the other hand, it may simply be that most unhappy marriages have disintegrated by middle adulthood, so only those who are reasonably happy are left to give their opinions.

A note of caution – surveys asking people to rate their level of satisfaction may be open to various effects which bias the results. For example, reported levels of satisfaction may have more to do with a desire to give a good impression than actual levels. Do husbands report greater satisfaction than wives because they feel it 'reflects on them' if the marriage is unhappy? Do older people report greater satisfaction because it would make a nonsense of their lives to admit they've been together for years and it's still a disaster?

The effects of marriage Young adults who are married are happier and healthier than their unmarried counterparts. They have fewer illnesses and fewer psychological disorders than those who are unmarried (Bee & Boyd, 2002). This may have something to do with marriage. They may have successfully resolved the intimacy vs isolation challenge of early adulthood and reaped the benefits. On the other hand, those who get married may be happier and healthier in the first place.

However, researchers have found little support for this explanation (Waite, 1995).

In terms of happiness, physical and mental health and longevity, married men appear to be the best off and unmarried men the worst. Unmarried women fare considerably better than unmarried men, and are only slightly worse off than married women.

A variety of reasons have been suggested for these differences. Marriage may put greater pressure on women. They usually have the main responsibility for childcare, housework and caring for elderly relatives – plus a husband – and they often have a career as well. Unmarried women seem to handle their single status more successfully than men. They are more likely to have close relations with parents and siblings, to have a female 'support' network in whom they can confide, and to have a successful career (Allen & Pickett, 1987).

The durability of marriage What makes a marriage last? Durkin (1995) lists commitment to marriage as an institution, the ability to accommodate changes in the partner's characteristics over time, good, supportive communications and the ability to resolve conflicts as significant factors. According to Murstein (1976), *homogamy* (similarity between partners in terms of values, interests, education and class) is an important predictor of the success of the marriage. Berk (2001) identifies similarity in family background, marrying after age 20, having 'courted' for at least six months before marriage, delaying pregnancy until after the first year of marriage, having positive relations with the extended family, financial security and coming from maritally stable homes as all predicting more durable and satisfying marriages.

Gottman (1994) identifies three types of relationship which tend to succeed, and two which fail. The successful relationships are:

- Validating, where the partners are supportive and positive and maintain mutual respect even if they disagree
- Volatile, where there are plenty of rows but much affection and fun too
- Avoidant, where conflict is minimised by effectively agreeing to disagree.

The unsuccessful relationships are both hostile.

- Hostile/engaged, where there are rows that can escalate, but little fun or affection
- Hostile/detached, where arguments are kept brief, but there is little positive engagement.

Alternative partnerships

So far, this section has looked at research on heterosexual marriage. It has said little about other types of partnership. Two types will now be briefly examined – homosexual (gay and lesbian) partnerships, and heterosexual cohabitation (unmarried male and female partners who live together).

Lesbian and gay partnerships In the USA, it is estimated that around 70% of lesbians are in committed relationships lasting an average of six years. The figure for gay men is 40%-60% (Bee & Boyd, 2002). In many respects, these partnerships are similar to marriage. Like married couples, gay and lesbian partnerships tend to have a drop in satisfaction during the early months of the relationship. They are more likely to last for the same reasons as marriage, for example, if the partners share

similar backgrounds (Kurdek, 1998).

However, there are two main differences. Lesbian and gay partnerships tend to be more egalitarian. The partners are unlikely to adopt 'male' and 'female' roles, they are more likely to share domestic responsibilities and decision-making (Kurdek, 1998). Lesbians and gays are more likely to see their partner as their only major source of support as they tend to be isolated from their relatives (Hill, 1999).

Lesbian and gay partnerships appear to be steadily increasing in the West. Growing social tolerance means that couples can live openly together, albeit usually in their own communities. This is a further example of the trend towards greater individual choice and differences referred to at the start of this unit.

Cohabitation As noted earlier, cohabitation in the UK doubled between 1986 and 1999. For around 60%, cohabitation was a prelude to marriage. However, 40% did not intend to marry (*Social Trends*, 2002). Growing numbers of people appear to be seeing cohabitation as an alternative to marriage.

Evidence from the USA and Europe indicates that couples who cohabit before marriage are less likely to find marriage satisfying and more likely to divorce (Hall & Zhao, 1995). A number of reasons have been suggested for this. For example, those who cohabit before marriage are less homogamous than those who do not – they are more likely to differ in terms of ethnicity, social class, religion and education (Blackwell & Lichter, 2000).

Figure 3 shows the extent and growth of cohabitation in Britain. It provides further evidence of the increasing diversity of adult lifestyles. Again, it indicates a trend away from the stages suggested by Erikson and Levinson towards greater choice and variety.

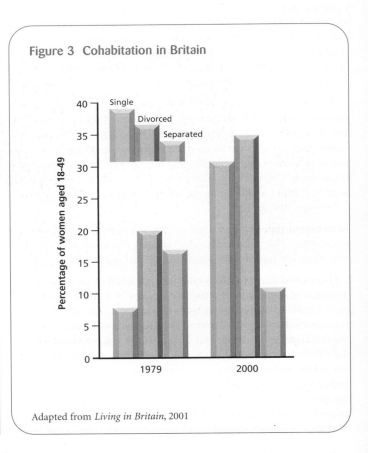

Figure 3 Cohabitation in Britain

Adapted from *Living in Britain*, 2001

Marriage across cultures

The institution of marriage, the reasons for getting married, the rules governing the selection of a partner for marriage and the roles of the married couple vary from culture to culture.

The concept of romantic love is a fairly recent idea developed in the West. It is largely absent in non-Western cultures. The basis for marriage in past Western societies was primarily economic. The idea of romantic love developed amongst the aristocracy in the 18th century and gradually filtered down the social hierarchy (Giddens, 1992).

In the West marriage is usually seen as a union of *individuals* who love each other. In most small-scale non-Western societies, marriage is regarded as a means of uniting two *groups* of people. Marriage involves not only the husband and wife, it also involves their families and kinship groups. In many societies, it is the relatives who exchange gifts on marriage, very little is given to the couple themselves.

Many African societies were traditionally organised on the basis of *lineages* – groups descended from a common ancestor. In some of these societies, women were not allowed to marry a man from their own lineage. A payment of bridewealth was made by the husband to the father of the bride, often in the form of cattle. This was to compensate her lineage for the loss of a working member and for her children who belonged to the husband's lineage. This is sometimes referred to in the proverb, 'The children are where the cattle are not'. Among the Nuer of Sudan, the marriage is not completed until the first child is weaned. Only then does the bride leave her father's home and join her husband in his village (Douglas, 1964).

Comparisons between Western ideas of love and those of Eastern cultures such as China and Japan indicate important differences. The Japanese word for love, 'amae', means to depend on another's benevolence, help, friendship and goodwill. A study of Asian university students indicates that they are less likely than American and European students to see physical attraction, romantic love and passion as a basis for marriage. Instead, they are more likely to stress companionship, similar background, career potential and the likelihood of being a good parent (Dion & Dion, 1993).

Key terms

Marriage *In Western society, the legal union of a man and a woman to live together as a partnership.*

Cohabitation *Living together as a partnership but remaining unmarried.*

Divorce *The legal termination of a marriage.*

Remarriage *A marriage in which one or both partners have formerly been married.*

Lineage *A group descended from a common ancestor. A lineage may own land and property and function as a political unit.*

Activity 3 — Marriage across cultures

Item A — An economic necessity

Inuit women beating fish skin to make into 'fish leather'

In many non-industrial societies, marriage is essential for economic reasons. In traditional Inuit (Eskimo) society, men build igloos and hunt. Women gather edible plants and catch fish. Their skill in sewing animal skins into clothes is indispensable in the Arctic climate. Sewing is a skill that men are never taught, and many of the skills of hunting are kept secret from women.

Adapted from Douglas, 1964

Item B — He was just a bachelor

The anthropologist Claude Lévi-Strauss recalls a pathetic looking bachelor.

'One of the strongest field recollections of this writer was his meeting, among the Bororo of central Brazil, of a man about thirty years old: unclean, ill-fed, sad, and lonesome. When asked if the man was seriously ill, the answer came as a shock: What was wrong with him? – nothing at all, he was just a bachelor, and true enough, in a society where labour is systematically shared between man and woman and where only the married status permits the man to benefit from the fruits of woman's work, including delousing, body painting, and hair-plucking as well as vegetable food and cooked food (since the Bororo woman tills the soil and makes pots), a bachelor is really only half a human being.'

Adapted from Lévi-Strauss, 1956

Question

Compare the reasons for marriage in the West with those in many small-scale societies.

2.3   Divorce and remarriage

Evidence from the previous section suggests that marriage is a good deal, especially for men. It appears to provide people with more benefits than their unmarried counterparts. However, this rosy view of marriage is countered by the divorce rate in Western societies. If present rates continue, around 40% of marriages in Britain and 50% in the USA will end in divorce (*Social Trends*, 2002; Berk, 2001).

In England and Wales, the *divorce rate* – the number of persons divorcing per year per 1000 married people – increased rapidly from 2.1 in 1961, to 6.0 in 1971, to 11.9 in 1981, to 13.5 in 1991 and has since levelled off to 12.8 in 2000 (*Social Trends*, 1993; 2002).

Most divorcees remarry, usually within four years of the divorce. *Remarriages* – a marriage in which one or both partners has formerly been married – as a percentage of all marriages in the UK, have increased from 14% in 1961, to 34% in 1981, to 40% in 2000 (*Social Trends*, 1994; 2002).

Reasons for divorce

According to Daniel Levinson (1978), because 'nature's timing is so bad, we must choose a partner and start a family before we quite know what we are doing or how to do it well'. This view is supported by the fact that the younger the age of marriage, the more likely the couple are to divorce. This suggests that the inexperience and immaturity of youth are factors affecting divorce rates. However, teenage marriages are often linked to other factors associated with higher risks of divorce. They include low income, poor housing, sharing accommodation with relatives and pregnancy before marriage. Age at marriage, therefore, needs to be seen in relation to other risk factors for divorce.

In a longitudinal study, Amato and Rogers (1997) conducted a telephone survey between 1980 and 1992 of 2000 married people in the USA. In common with many other studies, they found that wives reported less satisfaction with their marriage than husbands did. Many wives reported anger, hurt feelings and moodiness, while husbands seemed less than sensitive to their wives' feelings. Among those of the sample who divorced, the commonest reasons given were infidelity, partners wasting money or abusing alcohol or drugs, jealousy, or partners' moods or 'irritating habits'.

Most divorce proceedings are instituted by women (Rice, 1994). This reflects the results of surveys on marital satisfaction outlined in the previous section – they consistently show that wives are less satisfied with marriage than their husbands. This may result from the fact that many women in paid employment also shoulder the main responsibility for housework and childcare.

Research suggests that the way partners deal with marital conflict can affect the risk of divorce. For example, if the wife expresses worries and concerns about the relationship, the husband might respond with anger and resentment and then refuse to talk about the matter. This 'conflict-confronting-conflict-avoiding' pattern is found in many partners who divorce. Another high risk strategy is simply to avoid conflict by leading separate lives. This tends to be found in couples with few interests or friends in common. They simply drift apart (Hetherington et al., 1994).

Remarriages have a high risk of divorce. Various reasons have been suggested for this. Practical concerns, such as financial security and help with raising children, often figure more in remarriage. Such concerns may not provide a firm basis for a lasting relationship. Some people bring to their second marriage the attitudes and behaviours that ended their first. Some, having used divorce to 'solve' the problems of their first marriage, may be more likely to use this 'solution' again. And some might find the stresses of step-family life too difficult to cope with (Bray, 1999).

Reasons for a rising divorce rate

The divorce rate in the UK in 2000 is over six times higher than it was in 1961. Why this rapid rise?

Changes in the law One obvious answer is changes in divorce legislation. It is now much easier to obtain a divorce. For example, the Divorce Reform Act of 1969, which came into effect in 1971, was followed by a rapid rise in the divorce rate. Before this Act, a 'matrimonial offence' had to be proven, and a 'guilty party' had to be found. However, many people who wanted a divorce had not committed adultery, been guilty of cruelty and so on. The 1969 Act defined the grounds for divorce as 'the irretrievable breakdown of the marriage'. It was no longer necessary to prove guilt but simply to show that the marriage was beyond repair.

Changes in the role of women About three-quarters of divorce petitions are from women. The steady growth in female employment during the last 50 years may have increased the pressure on wives by creating a conflict between their domestic and employment roles (Hart, 1976). As noted earlier, there is little evidence of the 'new man' stepping in and sharing the burdens of housework and childcare.

Changing expectations of marriage In many societies, the married couple and their children form an economic unit – for example, the family is the labour force for small-scale farming enterprises. In modern industrial society, people are employed as individuals. Before the widespread movement of women into the labour market, wives were likely to be economically dependent on their husbands. Today, they are less likely to be so.

As a result of these changes, the main reason for marriage is the quality of the relationship. As a result, modern marriages are relatively fragile as they are held together primarily by emotional ties. And if love goes out of the window, there may be little left to hold the couple together (Dennis, 1975).

Changes in social networks A number of researchers argue that the wider social networks of the extended family and community are breaking down (see Beck & Beck-Gernsheim, p336). This means that people rely increasingly on their partners for emotional support. This can lead to emotional overload. There is a greater likelihood of conflict, with marriages breaking under the strain (Leach, 1967).

The effects of divorce

Effects on divorcees In the short-term, divorce is associated with disorientation, stress, depression, low self-esteem and an increase in physical illness and psychological disorders (Chase-Lansdale & Hetherington, 1990).

Long-term effects are less consistent. Some divorcees show

better psychological functioning 5-10 years after separation than when they were married (Wallerstein, 1986). Others are worse off 10 years later. In general, those who remarry appear happier, but those who have a second divorce often experience long-term negative effects (Spanier & Furstenberg, 1987).

There are gender differences in response to divorce. Where there are dependent children, they usually remain with the woman. Men are more likely to experience difficulties living without a partner. Maybe as a result of this, they are more likely to remarry.

Women may experience loneliness and depression, but most prefer being single to an unhappy marriage (Ganong & Coleman, 1994). Some become more self-reliant, taking up educational opportunities and job training, and finding support from family and a network of friends (Hetherington, 1995).

A longitudinal study found that divorced women become more tolerant, independent and non-conformist in the long term, suggesting that for many women, divorce has positive effects (Rockwell et al., 1979).

While men tend to improve their economic position after divorce, the opposite is usually the case for women, especially if they have custody of children. They are faced with an average decrease in household income of 40%-50% (Morgan, 1991). This is particularly likely for working-class women. Remarriage offers one solution and returns most women to their previous financial position. However, women with careers are likely to return to their pre-divorce financial situation even if they do not remarry (Holden & Smock, 1991).

Effects on children Debates over the effects of divorce on children have been raging over the past 50 years. On the one side, there are those who argue that the effects of divorce are wholly negative. They point to research which indicates that the children of divorced couples are typically more aggressive, defiant, negative and depressed, that as adolescents they are more likely to have problems at school, to experiment with drugs and alcohol and commit criminal acts. And as adults, they are more likely to have psychological problems (Bee & Boyd, 2002).

On the other hand, there are those who argue that these effects may result *not* from divorce itself, but from the marital conflict that preceded the divorce. Had the couple stayed together, the effects on the children might have been worse. From this point of view, divorce, in many cases, might be the best course for the children.

Recently published research by Mavis Hetherington (2002) is based on a longitudinal study of 2500 people from childhood, in 1400 families. Conducted in the USA, it includes tens of thousands of hours of videotapes of families at dinner, at play, relaxing and having rows. Hetherington concludes that three out of four children experience little long-term damage from divorce. She admits that 25% of children have serious emotional or social problems which compares with 10% from families that stay together. In her view, the negative effects on children have been exaggerated and we must accept that 'divorce is a reasonable solution to an unhappy, acrimonious, destructive marital relationship' (Hetherington, 2002).

Divorce, remarriage and the lifespan

The increase in divorce and remarriage adds further variety to lifespan experience. Again, it indicates that the diversity of adult experience is greater than indicated by stage theories, such as those of Erikson and Levinson. Divorce and remarriage involve new roles, new identities, new lifestyles and new family arrangements, all of which involve periods of upheaval and adaptation. There are fewer opportunities to construct stable life structures and more periods of transition and crisis (Bee & Boyd, 2002).

2.4 Parenthood

The traditional picture of parenthood in the West is mum, dad and their children living together as a family. Although this remains the experience of most parents and children, it is becoming less common. In recent years there has been a growth in lone parents, stepparents and gay and lesbian parents. This is another example of the increasing diversity of adult lifestyles.

Most adults become parents. In the USA, 90% of women aged 18 to 24 have had a child or expect to have one (Bee & Boyd, 2002). Women with traditional gender identities are more likely to have children. In general, women with high status, well paid occupations are less likely to have children than those in lower level occupations (Berk, 2001).

Effects of becoming a parent

Becoming a parent involves a major shift in role and identity. This shift is not just a private adjustment – becoming a parent is a public matter and changes the relationship between the new parent and society. For example, the state requires parents to take on responsibilities for the health and education of their child.

One immediate effect of parenting is, in many cases, that it matures the parents. Arnett (1998) found new parents reducing their own risk and sensation-seeking behaviour. Some find their new identity as a parent so rewarding that they will maintain an unsatisfactory partnership in order to carry on being a parent (Levinson, 1978).

Despite the celebrations that accompany childbirth, the evidence suggests that satisfaction with the marriage often drops with the birth of the first child (Reibstein & Richards, 1992). Frequently, this is the beginning of the U-bend effect where satisfaction drops and does not improve until middle age when the children have left home. This drop in marital satisfaction may be due in part to lack of sleep and tiredness, in part to arguments over how to raise the children, and to the fact that the parents now have less time to spend with each other (Reichle & Gefke, 1998). However, a decline in marital satisfaction may simply be an effect of married life. It often occurs in the first year of marriage even if the couple have not had a baby (Huston et al., 1986).

Research suggests that there are individual differences in how well couples adjust to parenthood. The following factors are associated with successful adjustment.

- A confiding relationship between the parents
- Good coping strategies and conflict resolution skills
- Support from members of the extended family
  (Berk 2001; Bee & Boyd, 2002)

Rholes et al. (1997) found that people who had anxious or avoidant relations with their own parents were more likely to see parenthood negatively. Women who are dissatisfied with their role as a mother are more likely to reject the child. This can lead to the child becoming difficult and fractious, which increases the woman's dissatisfaction with her role as a mother (Lerner & Galambos, 1985).

Between 10% and 25% of women suffer from postnatal depression. This usually lasts for a few weeks, although in a small number of cases it can last for a year or more. Postnatal depression is more likely to occur if the pregnancy is unplanned, if the mother is anxious, if the father is unsupportive, or if another major life change (like moving house, bereavement or job loss) occurs during pregnancy or soon after. The strongest predictor of postnatal depression is depression during pregnancy (Da Costa et al., 2000).

Parental division of labour

Many women are disappointed with their partner's contribution to childcare and domestic tasks. They often feel they are carrying an unfair burden (Wicki, 1999). There is still a tendency to see childrearing as a female role. Research indicates that gender roles become more traditional on childbirth (Cowan & Cowan, 1987).

There is some evidence of a shift in attitudes towards greater equality during the last 25 years. However, attitudes are one thing, translating them into behaviour is another. Figure 2 indicates a slight move towards the sharing of household tasks. But it also indicates a large gap between how partners think tasks *should be* allocated between them and how they are allocated.

Why is the move to gender equality in the home so slow? This may be partly due to men being unwilling to adopt what some see as a feminine role. It may also be due to men feeling that they are trespassing in female territory. There is evidence that some women find it irritating if their partner 'interferes' in domestic tasks (Lamb et al., 1987).

Parenthood and middle age

Sometime during middle age, most parents will be faced with an 'empty nest', when the children have grown up and left home. Traditionally, this has been seen as a time of crisis for parents, as they reconsider their role in life. It was widely believed that 'empty-nest syndrome' was especially difficult for women as it often coincided with the menopause. It was cited as the cause of widespread mid-life depression among women. However, this seems to be linked to a specific generation – to a generation of women raised to conform to the traditional view that 'being a mother' was the highest status attainable. Many did suffer from empty-nest syndrome (Adelmann et al., 1989).

This does not appear to be true for women of later generations. Recent research suggests that the empty nest is not seen negatively by most parents – mothers or fathers. Most now see it as an opportunity for closer relations with their partner, or new work and study opportunities (Cooper & Gutmann, 1987). Several studies confirm that marital satisfaction increases after the children have left home.

Harris et al. (1986) found that only 1/3 of women report any major transition in their lives when the last of their children left home. Women with jobs or other outside interests saw it as a positive event, those with the most commitment to their role as a mother saw it less positively.

According to Datan (1980), the 'crowded nest' where adult offspring will not leave home is more of a problem. Parents often resent providing for a young adult who demands equality of treatment while doing little to establish equality of domestic responsibility. Moreover, parents resent the loss of their freedom, having an adult 'child' around all the time!

Lone parenthood

In Britain in 2001, 22% of all families with dependent children were headed by lone parents. This is around three times the proportion in 1971. Up until the mid-1980s, most of this

Table 2   Division of household tasks

Great Britain	Actual allocation of tasks						How tasks should be allocated			Percentages
	1983			1991			1991			
	Mainly man	Mainly woman	Shared equally	Mainly man	Mainly woman	Shared equally	Mainly man	Mainly woman	Shared equally	
Household shopping	5	51	44	8	45	47	1	22	76	
Makes evening meal	5	77	17	9	70	20	1	39	58	
Does evening dishes	17	40	40	28	33	37	12	11	76	
Does household cleaning	3	72	24	4	68	27	1	36	62	
Does washing and ironing	1	89	10	3	84	12	0	58	40	
Repairs household equipment	82	6	10	82	6	10	66	1	31	
Organises household money/bills	29	39	32	31	40	28	17	14	66	
Looks after sick children	1	63	35	1	60	39	0	37	60	
Teaches children discipline	10	12	77	9	17	73	8	4	85	

Adapted from *Social Trends*, 1995

increase was accounted for by a rise in the divorce rate. After 1986, the increase was due mainly to a growth in the numbers of never-married lone mothers. Ninety per cent of lone parent families are headed by lone mothers (*Social Trends*, 2002).

Lone parent families tend to have the following characteristics.

- The average age of children is older, with fewer under-fives.
- They are concentrated in inner city areas.
- They are much more likely to live in poverty.
- Lone mothers are less likely to be employed than mothers from two-parent families (Taylor et al., 1995).

Life is difficult for many lone parents. Apart from economic hardship and the absence of support from a partner, they suffer from higher levels of illness than their married counterparts. Research indicates that their children are more likely to perform poorly at school and may be more inclined to anti-social behaviour. However, this may be due to poverty rather than lone parenthood as such (McLoyd, 1998).

Stepparents

Most divorced lone parents remarry and form new two-parent families. Around 6% of all families with dependent children in Britain in 1999 were stepfamilies. Nine out of 10 of these consisted of a couple with at least one child of the female partner from a previous relationship (*Social Trends*, 2002).

Stepfamilies experience a number of difficulties. They lack the boundaries that other families have since the children remain linked to the biological parent outside their new family. Parents have to negotiate with their former spouse over access, holidays, and so on. The authority of stepparents is ineffective before an emotional bond with the stepchildren has been established. This can take time and prove difficult. Largely because of this, the divorce rate for remarried couples with stepchildren is higher than for those without (Bray, 1999).

Gay and lesbian parents

Concerns about children's gender identity and sexual orientation have been the main focus of research on gay and lesbian parenting. Most studies show that children raised by gay and lesbian parents are no different than those raised by heterosexuals (Fitzgerald, 1999). However, most of these studies involve gay or lesbian parents raising their biological children when they were involved with partners of the opposite sex.

A recent study looked at 80 children, conceived by artificial insemination, of lesbian couples and single lesbian mothers. They found no difference in terms of social and cognitive development between these children and those of heterosexual two-parent and lone-parent families (Chan et al., 1998). The evidence suggests that child development depends on child-parent interaction rather than the sexual orientation of the parents.

Conclusion

This unit has focused on partnerships, divorce and parenthood in modern Western societies. In all these areas, there have been significant changes and increasing diversity over the past fifty years. Marriage has declined in popularity and cohabitation has become increasingly common. The divorce rate is significantly higher. Remarriage, as a proportion of all marriages, has grown steadily, and with it the proportion of stepparents. Lone-parent families now make up over one fifth of all families with dependent children. And gay and lesbian couples are now becoming parents.

These changes suggest that the experiences of increasing numbers of people are far more diverse than the lifespan stages identified by researchers in the 1960s.

Summary

1. Most people in Western society marry, but the popularity of marriage is declining.

2. Cohabitation is increasing. Around three-fifths of people now cohabit before marriage.

3. Love is now seen as the primary reason for marriage.

4. Those who are married are healthier and happier than their non-married counterparts. However, men report greater satisfaction with marriage than women.

5. Marital satisfaction appears to follow a U-bend path, with a fairly rapid drop followed by a gradual rise during middle and late adulthood.

6. In many respects, lesbian and gay partnerships are similar to heterosexual partnerships. However, they tend to be more egalitarian.

7. Growing numbers of people appear to regard cohabitation as an alternative to marriage.

8. The reasons for marriage and the roles of the married couple vary across cultures.

9. Divorce has risen steadily in Western society over the part 50 years.

10. The younger the age of marriage, the more likely the couple are to divorce. Most divorce proceedings are instituted by women. Their dissatisfaction may result from combining paid employment with the main responsibility for childcare and housework. Research suggests that the way partners deal with conflict can affect the risk of divorce. Remarriages have a higher divorce rate than first marriages.

11. Reasons for the rising divorce rate include:

- Changes in the law – it is now easier to divorce
- Changes in the role of women – the growth in female employment may result in conflict between their domestic and employment roles
- Changing expectations of marriage – modern marriages are relatively fragile as they are held together primarily by emotional ties
- Changes in social networks – the decline of extended families and close-knit social networks places greater demands on marriage.

12 In the short term, divorce is associated with disorientation, stress and low self-esteem. In the long term, some divorcees show improved psychological functioning, others appear worse off, especially if a remarriage fails. Divorced women appear to fare better than men.

13 Most children appear to experience little long-term damage from divorce. However, around 25% appear to have serious emotional and social problems.

14 Most adults become parents. This involves a major shift in role and identity.

15 Many women are disappointed with their partner's contribution to childcare and domestic tasks. Evidence indicates that they shoulder most of this burden.

16 The empty-nest syndrome appears to be linked to a specific generation. Today, most middle-aged parents see children leaving home as a positive event.

17 The numbers of lone parents and stepparents have increased significantly over the past 50 years.

18 Most studies show that children raised by gay and lesbian parents are no different than those raised by heterosexual parents.

19 Changes in partnerships, divorce and parenthood suggest that the experiences of adults are far more diverse than the lifespan stages identified by researchers in the 1960s.

Unit 3 Late adulthood

KEY ISSUES

1 **What are the main explanations for the changes of late adulthood?**

2 **What cognitive changes take place in old age?**

3 **How do people respond to bereavement?**

Late adulthood is usually seen as the period from age 60 onwards. Life expectancy has steadily risen over the past 100 or so years, from 45 years for men and 49 for women in 1901 in the UK, to 75 and 80 years respectively in 2000 (*Social Trends*, 2002). Those in late adulthood form an increasing proportion of the population.

3.1 Perspectives on late adulthood

Erikson and late adulthood

Late adulthood is Erikson's last stage of lifespan development. It contains the final crisis or challenge – integrity versus despair. To achieve *integrity*, the older person has to come to terms with their life. They must feel satisfied with their achievements and accept their failures and disappointments. A sense of integrity involves feeling whole and complete. With integrity a person can come to terms with death.

A failure to achieve integrity results in *despair*. This is when people look back on life with dissatisfaction. They realise it is too late to turn the clock back, that there is insufficient time to make the changes that will bring integrity. They find it hard to accept that death is near and feel hopeless, bitter and defeated (Erikson, 1950).

Evaluation Erikson's theory is not based on systematic research. There is little evidence to suggest that older adults are more likely to achieve self-acceptance than any other age group. Adults of all ages look back on their lives and reminisce. There is some evidence that older adults are more likely to look back at lost opportunities with sadness and disappointment. And there is also some evidence that people become more reflective and philosophical in old age. However, this does not necessarily mean that integrity versus despair is the critical challenge of late adulthood (Bee & Boyd, 2002).

Disengagement theory

According to Cumming and Henry (1961), old age involves a disengagement from 'normal' social roles, a withdrawal from the community and a retreat into the safe and undemanding world of home and family. Old people become increasingly preoccupied with their inner life, with their own thoughts and memories. As their life space shrinks, they have fewer responsibilities and duties, fewer interactions and fewer social roles. Their individuality increases as they feel less governed by society's regulations. And society makes fewer demands on them.

Disengagement is not passive. Old people actively withdraw and accept the changes of late adulthood. Disengagement theory sees this withdrawal as natural and functional. For Cumming and Henry, this is the best way to age – it has pay-offs all round. Old age is a time to prepare for death and the elderly person achieves peace and tranquillity. And society is already getting along without them, so there is less disruption and distress when they finally die.

Evaluation Although disengagement theory has been influential, it has been strongly criticised on two counts. First, there is considerable evidence which does not support it – many older people do not disengage as the theory states. Second, disengagement is not necessarily 'natural' or 'healthy'.

- Many older people maintain active engagement with the outside world through community organisations, the church and charities (Pratt & Norris, 1994). They place social relationships at the top of their list of priorities for maintaining a high quality of life. Many have a more active social life than during their working life (Ferris & Branston, 1994).

- In the West, most older people are forced to disengage from work roles because of compulsory retirement. This is a cultural rather than a natural requirement. In many non-Western societies, older people have very important roles. Their age and experience bring respect. They are in positions of authority as leaders and judges, making decisions and settling disputes (see Activity 4).

- Disengagement theory is based on the view that withdrawal

is sensible and desirable. Far from disengagement being the healthy option as Cumming and Henry suggest, evidence indicates that those who disengage decline rapidly. Old people in nursing homes fare much better if they take control of their own care (Langer & Rodin, 1976). Personal control and social involvement are important – they result in higher morale and lower levels of depression and other psychological disorders (Bee & Boyd, 2002).

Despite these criticisms, there is evidence that some older people do disengage. The problem with all general theories is a tendency to see the group they are explaining as uniform. The elderly population is not uniform. Their living standards vary and this affects their lifestyles, as does ethnicity, social class, gender and personal choice. For example, after retirement, middle-class people have higher living standards as a result of private and occupational pensions and savings. The options of many working-class people are restricted because of low income (Oppenheim, 1993).

Activity theory

This theory states that older people will only disengage if barriers are erected to prevent them from maintaining a full social life and a range of social roles. One obvious barrier is compulsory retirement. Another barrier is *ageism* – prejudice against older people which sees them as less important and less capable than younger people. This is reflected in derogatory terms such as 'senile', 'crumblies', 'wrinklies', 'geriatrics' and 'old fogies', which hardly encourage older people to engage with the wider society (Norman, 1987).

According to activity theory, the most positive response to old age, physically, psychologically and socially, is active involvement with the wider society and maintaining a range of social roles. Activity theory rejects the view that disengagement is 'natural', sensible and desirable.

Evaluation There is evidence to support activity theory. Older people with active social lives tend to be healthier and happier. This applies even to people with disabilities such as arthritis, for whom social participation can be painful (Zimmer et al., 1995). And there is evidence that older people want greater social involvement. Pressure groups such as Age Concern and Help the Aged in the UK and the American Association of Retired Persons campaign against ageism. In the USA, there are now laws banning discrimination on the basis of age. Older people are using 'grey power' – their spending and voting power – to persuade politicians, retailers and organisations to recognise their special needs and interests. They are increasingly rejecting the stereotypes of old age and emphasising 'youthful' qualities such as fun, curiosity, playfulness and spontaneity, qualities that do not necessarily diminish with age (Featherstone & Hepworth, 1989).

However, as noted in the evaluation of disengagement theory, older people are not a uniform group. There is evidence that some older people prefer the quiet and peaceful life that withdrawal can bring. For example, they might absorb themselves in a hobby and remain perfectly happy (Lee & Markides, 1990).

Socioemotional selectivity theory

This theory assumes that throughout the lifespan people become increasingly selective in their choice of friends and acquaintances (Lang & Carstensen, 1994).

Young people have a wide social network. Some relationships are valuable because they provide information and guidance; others provide support for identity and status – they confirm who the young person is and affirm their worth; and others serve an emotional purpose – the warmth and positive feelings produced by friendships.

As people grow older, they have less need for information and guidance and for confirmation of their identity and worth. As a result, the elderly person's social network becomes smaller. They become more selective, choosing to maintain only those relationships which are emotionally important. They interact mainly with relatives and friends, preferring the company of those with whom they have developed pleasurable and rewarding relationships.

Social interaction does not decline suddenly with old age. According to socioemotional selectivity theory, late adulthood simply continues a lifelong selection process (Berk, 2001).

3.2 Cognitive changes in late adulthood

Late adulthood is often seen as a period of relentless decline in mental faculties. While it is true that the senses lose some of their sharpness – vision starts to decline from around 45, and hearing from 50 or 60, research suggests the effect of age on cognition is complex (Bee & Boyd, 2002). Changes in cognitive functioning do take place, but the picture of ageing as continual, inevitable and irreversible mental decline is simplistic and inaccurate.

Memory

There is evidence that certain memory abilities decline with age.

Short-term memory Experimental evidence indicates a reduction in the capacity of short-term memory in late adulthood. In one experiment participants were shown 7 and 10 digit telephone numbers for a short time on a computer screen. After the numbers disappeared, they were asked to dial them on a push-button telephone. In some of the trials they received the engaged tone and were asked to redial. There was a significant decline with age for recall of the 10 digit numbers, particularly when they had to be redialled (West & Crook, 1990). The results of this experiment are shown in Figure 4.

Figure 4 Age and memory for telephone numbers

7 digits immediately
10 digits immediately
7 digits after busy signal
10 digits after busy signal

Number of digits dialled correctly

Age: 18-35 40-49 50-59 60-69 70-85

Adapted from West & Crook, 1990

Activity 4 Age across cultures

In many small-scale, traditional, non-Western societies old people are powerful, their status is high and their age brings respect and responsibilities. They are a source of wisdom, their knowledge and experience are valued and their advice is sought after. In the words of an old Chinese proverb, 'My father is all-wise but my father's father is even wiser'.

In many societies authority is allocated on the basis of age. As a general rule, the older people become, the greater their say in public life. Amongst East African people, such as the Masai and Nandi, this idea is built into the organisation of the entire society. The society is divided into age grades, for example childhood, junior warriorhood, senior warriorhood, junior elderhood and senior elderhood. People – in this case males – move from one grade to the next, gaining in power and prestige as they grow older. Members of the senior grade form a council of elders in which disputes are settled and major decisions affecting the whole society taken. In some age grade societies the elders communicate with the spirits of the ancestors on whose goodwill the wellbeing of everyone depends.

In Western industrial societies, older people are encouraged to 'look young' and conceal signs of ageing such as grey hair and wrinkles. In other societies, signs of old age are welcomed. For example, among the Venda-speaking people of Southern Africa they indicate approaching contact with the 'real' world of the spirits. In societies where the afterlife is given great significance, the approach of death often enhances rather than reduces a person's status.

Adapted from Beattie, 1964 and Pilcher, 1995

Masai warriors being addressed by a village elder (far left)

A respected older woman speaks at a welcome ceremony for visitors – Irim village, Burkina Faso, Africa

Questions

1   Compare the status of older people in the West with those in small-scale, non-Western societies.

2   Suggest a connection between the worship of ancestors and the position of older people in society.

3   Use the data in this activity to criticise disengagement theory.

Activity 5 Pictures of old age

Item A Powering ahead

Over 60s training for the London Marathon

Item B Negative stereotypes

Negative stereotypes of old people are all around us – in everyday conversation, on television, in advertisements and in our beliefs about the meaning of old age. Old people are often pictured as 'past it', 'has beens' and 'over the hill'.

Sometimes the characterisations of old people are less harsh though still negative. They are like children. They are weak and helpless, they need care and attention, they are forgetful. As such, old people are often seen as a burden both to their families and to society as a whole.

The media often reinforces these stereotypes. Most references to older people in newspapers and TV news picture them as vulnerable and helpless – as victims of crime, as ill-treated by relatives or staff in old people's homes, as living in poverty and unable to fend for themselves, particularly during winter cold spells.

Adapted from Ageism, Help the Aged, 1995

Item C Speaking out

- My husband, a chartered accountant in his fifties, is unemployed. We suspect that age accounts for his inability even to get interviews. Lies and hair-dye are being considered, simply so that he can end his frustration at not being able to use his talents, ability and experience!

- Now I want to experience being old. Why is age thought about as so disreputable, as a kind of disease? What is wrong with white hair and wrinkles and a life lived without stress? Why do people want to be mistaken for their daughter's friends and fiancé?

- Let us reject this idea of old people being a 'burden'. Any number of people on retiring look forward to a change of occupation, to tackling something completely different. Some of these jobs will count as 'gainful' employment, meaning jobs that are paid. Other people will take on voluntary work, not receiving pay and so not 'gainfully' employed, but all the same productively employed in the sense that society benefits from what they do.

Adapted from *New Internationalist*, February 1995

Question

Use Items A, B and C to support activity theory.

Prospective memory Age differences are not the same for all memory tasks. Prospective memory is remembering to do something in the future. Researchers might ask participants to make a phone call every day at the same time for the next two weeks. Experimental evidence indicates that older adults perform prospective memory tasks better than both younger and middle-aged adults. This appears to be due to the use of more effective strategies for remembering. Younger adults tend to rely on rehearsal – repeating to themselves that they have to remember something. Older adults are more likely to use a buzzer in the kitchen or a note prominently displayed to remind them (Loewen et al., 1990). Some laboratory studies suggest that prospective memory declines with age (Einstein et al., 1997). However, older adults often compensate for this by using effective memory strategies.

Everyday memory Memory tasks in the laboratory often take the form of recalling sequences of numbers, letters or words. They can appear artificial and pointless as they often bear little resemblance to everyday life. Do older people do less well on these tasks because they are less motivated, do they have less patience because they are more likely to see the tasks as pointless? If so, the decline in memory with age is more apparent than real. This question can be answered by testing everyday memory.

Everyday memory refers to the recall of events and information from everyday life. These include recalling shopping lists, recipes, newspaper articles, books, movies, birthday parties and conversations. Older adults, particularly after the age of 70, recall events from everyday life less well than younger adults (Brown et al., 1995).

Conclusion Older adults appear to take in information more slowly and find it more difficult to retrieve information from long-term memory. According to some researchers, the decline in memory in old age is due to a decline in the speed of the whole process. Older adults are slower in registering new information, in encoding this information and retrieving it.

Timothy Salthouse (1996) believes this is due to physiological changes in the central nervous system which result in a reduction in the speed with which neurons communicate with each other.

Key terms

Short-term memory *The part of memory that holds limited amounts of information for short periods of time.*

Prospective memory *Memory for doing something in the future.*

Everyday memory *Memory for events and information from everyday life.*

Problem-solving

Laboratory experiments involving problem-solving tasks indicate that problem-solving skills decline in late adulthood. It may be that memory decline makes it more difficult for older adults to keep all the relevant information in mind (Sinnott, 1989).

However, a somewhat different picture emerges from everyday problem-solving. Surveys indicate that older adults are particularly concerned with issues of health. Compared to younger adults, they make faster decisions about whether they are ill and seek medical help sooner. Younger adults are less decisive, they tend to wait and see how a possible health problem develops. Speed and effectiveness in terms of problem-solving appear to be related to the importance attached to the problem, and experience of the problem. This is probably why older people act decisively when faced with a possible health problem (Meyer et al., 1995).

Intelligence

Researchers often distinguish between two types of intelligence – *crystallised intelligence* and *fluid intelligence*. Crystallised intelligence is based on skills and knowledge that people learn as part of growing up. It depends to a large extent on experience and education. For example, it includes vocabulary and the ability to read. Simple tests of crystallised intelligence include the following. What is wallpaper? A rock is hard; a pillow is _____. Crystallised intelligence tests are based on what a person has already learned.

Fluid intelligence is based on abstract reasoning, on how well a person can learn new information and solve new problems. It depends more on information processing skills – the analysis of information and the ability to detect relationships and connections between various pieces of information. Fluid intelligence is measured by the following type of test. What comes next in this series of letters A C F J O?

Research indicates that crystallised intelligence does not decline with age. There is some evidence that it rises with age into late adulthood. This is probably due to the fact that people are constantly adding to their knowledge and skills over the years, at work, at home and during their leisure activities (Horn et al., 1981). Because of this, it can be argued that crystallised tests are biased in favour of older people. Usually, there is no time limit for these tests. If a time limit is placed on the test, older people tend to do less well than younger adults (Stuart-Hamilton, 2000).

However, tests indicate that fluid intelligence declines with age. This decline begins around age 35-40 and continues into late adulthood. It is particularly apparent if a time limit is placed on the test. Without a time limit, the age difference remains but it is reduced (Schaie, 1994).

Cross-sectional and longitudinal studies Researchers have used two methods to examine the relationship between intelligence and age. The *cross-sectional method* tests different age groups at the same point in time. For example, participants in samples 7 years apart in age from 25 to 67 are given the same test. The *longitudinal method* tests the same people at different ages during their lives. For example, the same people are retested 7, 14, 21 and 28 years later.

Werner Schaie (1983) used both methods in what has become known as the Seattle Longitudinal Study. His results are shown in Figure 5. The average IQ score is set at 50 points (the equivalent of the average of 100 used on most tests). The longitudinal data suggests that IQ rises in early adulthood, remains the same in middle adulthood then steadily declines in late adulthood. However, the cross-sectional data indicates an overall decline from around age 30 onwards. And compared to the longitudinal data, IQ scores for middle and late adulthood are significantly lower.

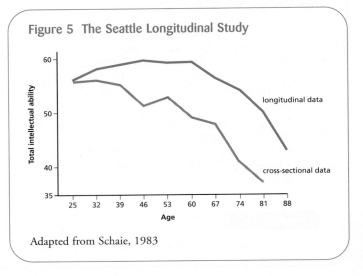

Figure 5 The Seattle Longitudinal Study

Adapted from Schaie, 1983

Why is there a difference between the results of cross-sectional and longitudinal studies? The cross-sectional studies compare different generations. Each generation has different experiences and the further apart the generations, the greater the difference in their experience. There is evidence that this affects IQ scores. As outlined in Chapter 10 (p 268), the Flynn effect shows that in Western societies IQ scores have steadily improved during the 20th century from generation to generation (Flynn, 1999).

Explaining age-related intelligence Some researchers believe that the decline in intelligence in late adulthood can be explained in the same way as the decline in aspects of memory. They claim it is due to physiological changes in the central nervous system, in particular to a decline in the speed with which neurons communicate with each other (Salthouse, 1996).

However, there are other physical aspects of ageing which may reduce IQ scores. Older people are more likely to suffer from arthritis, diabetes, heart problems, respiratory illnesses and rheumatism. Such problems may affect the brain and reduce intellectual performance (Stuart-Hamilton, 2000). There may be even simpler explanations. Older people tend to write more slowly. When speed of writing was controlled for, the age difference on some intelligence tests was halved (Storandt, 1976).

Individual differences Although the evidence indicates that, in general, intelligence declines in late adulthood, there are large individual differences. Research indicates that around 15% of people maintain their intellectual performance throughout their lifespan (Rabbitt, 1980). An interesting and stimulating environment can result in people retaining their mental abilities well into late adulthood. The Seattle Longitudinal Study indicated that declines in intelligence were delayed for people with high educational qualifications and those with stimulating leisure pursuits – reading, travelling and going to concerts, the cinema and the theatre (Schaie, 1996).

Compensation The decline in intelligence in late adulthood is not as depressing as it appears. Older people often develop ways of compensating for this loss. For example, studies have shown that older chess and bridge players can hold their own with younger opponents. In some ways their skills have deteriorated – for example, their memory is not as good as it was. However, they have accumulated a range of strategies over the years which enable them to match younger players (Charness, 1979, 1981).

Key terms

Crystallised intelligence *Intelligence based on learned skills and knowledge.*

Fluid intelligence *Intelligence based on abstract reasoning, on the ability to analyse and detect relationships.*

Cross-sectional method *In terms of age-related intelligence, a method that tests different age groups at the same point in time.*

Longitudinal method *In terms of age-related intelligence, a method that tests the same people at different ages during their lives.*

3.3　Perspectives on bereavement

Late adulthood is a time of bereavement – the death of close friends, relatives and partners. This section looks at responses to bereavement.

Freud's psychoanalytic theory

Freud saw the death of a loved one as an emotional trauma. In order to avoid the grief and pain, the initial response of the Ego is to use defence mechanisms such as denial and repression. However, this is an unhealthy response. If it continues it can lead to physical illness and even to mental disorders. The individual must 'work through' their grief, express their feelings and confront their loss.

Evaluation Freud's theory has been influential with bereavement counsellors who encourage the bereaved person to express their grief and talk to friends about their loss. However, research indicates that avoiding expressions of grief neither prolongs the

experience of grief nor does it necessarily lead to physical and mental problems. One study suggests that avoiding talking about the loss of a loved one reduces both the amount of grief and long-term negative effects (Bonanno et al., 1999).

Bowlby's stages of grief

John Bowlby (1980) argued that the loss of any attachment to a loved one – a parent, a child, or a partner – will result in intense grief. And the closer the attachment, the longer the grief lasts. He claimed that the bereavement process went through a series of four stages.

1   **Numbness** The bereaved person experiences shock followed by disbelief. They feel numb, unable to concentrate, they just 'go through the motions'.

2   **Yearning** This stage involves an awareness of loss and a yearning for the dead person. It is accompanied by a range of intense emotions which may include anger, guilt, anxiety, fear and frustration. Loss of sleep and appetite often occur.

3   **Disorganisation and despair** At this stage, the loss is accepted, but this brings depression and despair. The bereaved person feels exhausted.

4   **Reorganisation** This is a time when the individual regains control. Grief subsides, hope returns, energy increases and sleep patterns are restored.

Catherine Sanders (1989) proposed a similar stage theory of bereavement. It is much the same as Bowlby's except she divided his fourth stage, reorganisation, into two stages – healing and renewal.

Evaluation There are two main criticisms of stage theories of bereavement. First, many bereaved people do not appear to go through these set stages. Second, not everybody has the experiences and feelings contained in these stages. Evidence for these criticisms will now be examined.

Patterns of grieving

Camille Wortman and Roxane Silver (1992) have gathered a large amount of evidence which challenges both Freud's and Bowlby's theories. They identify four distinct patterns of grieving. The percentages in brackets show the proportion of participants in one of their studies who adopted each pattern (Wortman & Silver, 1990).

*   **Normal** Great distress after the loss followed by a fairly rapid recovery (40%)

*   **Chronic** Continuous distress over a period of several years (30%)

*   **Absent** Little distress immediately after the loss or later (26%)

*   **Delayed** Little distress in the first few months but high levels of distress months or years later (4%).

Wortman and Silver argue that the four responses to loss are simply different, they are not 'better' or 'worse'. They reject Freud's view that the 'healthy' response is an expression of grief. They also reject the view of stage theorists, such as Bowlby and Sanders. Wortman and Silver's evidence indicates that the response to loss varies and that people do not go through fixed stages of grief.

3.4   Widowhood

Widowhood refers to the loss of a partner. Five out of six people who experience widowhood are women. This is because women tend to live longer than men, and men tend to have partners younger than themselves. In the UK the life expectancy of men was 75 and women 80 in 2000 (*Social Trends*, 2002). Loss of a partner is usually seen as the most traumatic event in a person's life (Holmes & Rahe, 1967).

Responses to widowhood

In many respects older people cope better than younger people with bereavement. Death in old age is expected and seen as less unfair (Stroebe & Stroebe, 1993). However, sudden and unexpected bereavements can be particularly distressing, leading to extreme shock, confusion and anxiety (Gluhoski & Wortman, 1996).

Wortman and Silver (1990) found that widows who have the most successful and fulfilling marriages experience the most longlasting grief, presumably because they have the most to lose. They also found that widows with the highest level of personal control and self-esteem experienced the greatest difficulties with the loss of their partner. It appears as though their strength came in large part from the relationship itself (Wortman et al., 1993).

In the year following widowhood, the rates of depression for both women and men show a significant rise, though rates of physical illness and death rise only slightly (Stroebe & Stroebe, 1993). Later, the rates of death and mental disorders for widowed people are the same as their married counterparts (Morycz, 1992).

Losing a partner undermines the whole basis of a person's life. It affects their daily routines, their role as a partner, and their sense of personal identity. The surviving partner must construct a new identity as a single person. Many, particularly widows, adjust successfully. They experience widowhood as a time of growth and of independence. They make new friends and develop new skills (Wortman & Silver, 1990).

Gender differences

In general, women adjust more successfully to widowhood than men. Men experience more depression, and are more likely to suffer ill health and death (Stroebe & Stroebe, 1993). Men are more likely to withdraw after the death of their partner and become socially isolated. This may be due to their higher rate of depression. It may also be due to men's greater difficulty in forming close, intimate relationships outside of marriage. As a result, they have less supportive social networks to cushion the loss of their partner (Bennett, 1998).

Many men experience difficulties adjusting because they have relied on their partner's domestic skills – cooking, washing, ironing and housework. They have also tended to rely on their partner for friends and organising their social lives. As a result, men are more likely to remarry than women. Their higher remarriage rate may also reflect the older marriage market – men are relatively scarce and as a result, in greater demand (Durkin, 1995).

Women are less interested in remarriage. Some do not want to play second place to a husband in a traditional marriage, some

are afraid of being widowed again, and some believe it is impossible to replace their late husband (Lopata, 1979). In addition, women have less to gain from remarriage as many have successfully adjusted to their single status. They tend to have strong support networks made up of adult children, other relatives and friends (Field & Minkler, 1988). In general, elderly widows fare as well as married women of their age (McCrae & Costa, 1988).

3.5   The process of dying

This section looks at people's response to their impending death. Are these responses predictable, do they go through a series of stages, or is there no common pattern as death approaches?

Kübler-Ross – stages of dying

Elisabeth Kübler-Ross (1969) identified five stages in response to approaching death.

Denial A refusal to accept that death is imminent, a denial of the seriousness of the illness or the accuracy of the diagnosis.

Anger Resentment and anger are directed towards doctors, nurses, family members or God when the patient realises they may be terminally ill.

Bargaining Attempts are made to bargain with doctors – 'I'll take my medicine, I'll do my exercises' – and with nurses, family members or God, in the hope of living longer.

Depression When denial, anger and bargaining have failed, the person becomes depressed.

Acceptance The final stage in which people accept that they are dying which is often accompanied by a sense of peace.

Evaluation

Kübler-Ross's stages were based on clinical observations of 200 patients, nearly all of whom had cancer. There is no information about how frequently she talked to them, nor how long she observed them. Nor is there any information about their ages though most were apparently young or middle-aged adults.

In terms of age and illness, the sample was unrepresentative. Would the same stages be identified for older patients and for those with other illnesses? Further criticisms of Kübler-Ross are contained in the following section.

A variety of responses

Later research indicates a wide variety of responses to approaching death. Many people do not appear to express the emotions and concerns noted by Kübler-Ross. Nor do they go through the five stages she identified. For example, Edwin Shneidman (1983), from his work with the dying, notes a wide range of responses. These vary from person to person and can appear, disappear, and reappear in any particular order. They include terror, disbelief, complete uncertainty, feelings of injustice and unfairness, fear of pain, fantasies about being suddenly cured and saved from death, and a concern with reputation after death.

A study of 62 women diagnosed with early stages of breast cancer found that rather than going through predictable stages, they responded in different ways (Greer, 1991). Interviews with each of the women three months after diagnosis indicated five main responses.

- **Denial** They deny having cancer and see their treatment as a precaution.
- **Fighting spirit** They see their disease as a challenge and are determined to fight it.
- **Stoic acceptance** They accept the diagnosis but do little or nothing, or they ignore the diagnosis and attempt to carry on as normal.
- **Helplessness/hopelessness** They see themselves as dying with little or no hope of recovery.
- **Anxious preoccupation** They experience persistent anxiety and interpret each ache and pain as a possible recurrence of the disease.

Interestingly the survival rate after 15 years appeared to be related to the response. Only 35% of those whose initial response was either denial or fighting spirit had died compared with 76% of those who had adopted the other three responses (Greer, 1991).

Cultural differences The way people view death will have some affect on their response to approaching death. Views of death are influenced by culture. For example, some Native American cultures see death as part of a natural cycle, which should be approached with calm and composure rather than fought or feared (DeSpendler & Strickland, 1983). Buddhism, a major religion in India, China and Southeast Asia, sees death as a transition to rebirth. To some extent, cultural beliefs about death will influence people's experience of dying.

Summary

1. According to Erikson, the crisis or challenge of late adulthood is integrity versus despair.

2. Disengagement theory states that older people withdraw from the community into the undemanding world of home and family.

3. Activity theory states that older people will only disengage if barriers are erected to prevent them from maintaining a full social life and a range of social roles.

4. Socioemotional selectivity theory assumes that throughout the lifespan people become increasingly selective in their choice of friends and acquaintances.

5. There is evidence that certain memory abilities decline with age. However, older people can compensate for some of this decline by using effective memory strategies.

6. Crystallised intelligence does not decrease with age. It may even increase in some cases. Fluid intelligence appears to decrease with age though there are individual differences – around 15% of people maintain their intellectual performance throughout their life.

7. Psychoanalytic theory states that a person must 'work through' their grief, express their feelings and confront their loss.

8. Bowlby claimed that the bereavement process went through four stages, from numbness to reorganisation.

9. Later research by Wortman and Silver indicated four patterns of grieving. They claim that the response to loss varies and that people do not go through fixed stages of grief.

10. Widowhood undermines the whole basis of a person's life – their daily routine, their roles and identity.

11. In general, women adjust more successfully to widowhood than men.

12. Kübler-Ross identifies five stages in response to approaching death.

13. Later research indicates a wide variety of responses to the approach of death.

References

Adelmann, P.K., Antonucci, T.C., Crohan, S.E. & Coleman, L.M. (1989). Empty nest, cohort, and employment in the well-being of midlife women. *Sex Roles, 20* 173-189.

Ainsworth, M.D.S., Blehar, M.C., Waters, E. & Wall, S. (1978). *Patterns of attachment: A psychological study of the strange situation.* Hillsdale, NJ: Erlbaum.

Allen, K.R. & Pickett, R.S. (1987). Forgotten streams in the family life course: Utilisation of qualitative retrospective interviews in the analysis of lifelong single women's family careers. *Journal of Marriage and the Family, 49,* 517-526.

Amato, P.R. & Rogers, S.J. (1997). A longitudinal study of marital problems and subsequent divorce. *Journal of Marriage and the Family, 59,* 612-624.

Arnett, J. (1998). Risk behaviour and family role transitions during the twenties. *Journal of Youth & Adolescence, 27,* 301-320.

Beattie, J. (1964). *Other cultures: Aims, methods and achievements in social anthropology.* London: Routledge and Kegan Paul.

Beaumont, P. (1996). Thirty-somethings who won't grow up. *The Observer,* 19th May.

Beck, U. & Beck-Gernsheim, E. (1995). *The normal chaos of love.* Cambridge: Polity Press.

Bee, H. & Boyd, D. (2002). *Lifespan development* (3rd ed.). Boston: Allyn & Bacon.

Bengtson, V., Rosenthal, C. & Burton, L. (1990). Families and aging: Diversity and heterogeneity. In R.H. Binstock & L.K. George (Eds.), *Handbook of aging and the social sciences* (3rd ed.). San Diego, CA: Academic Press.

Bennett, M. (1998). Longitudinal changes in mental and physical health among elderly, recently widowed men. *Mortality, 3,* 265-273.

Berk, L.E. (2001). *Development through the lifetime* (2nd ed.). Needham Heights, MA: Allyn & Bacon.

Blackwell, D. & Lichter, D. (2000). Mate selection among married and cohabiting couples. *Journal of Family Issues, 21,* 275-302.

Bonanno, G., Znoj, H., Siddique, H. & Horowitz, M. (1999). Verbal-autonomic dissociation and adaptation to midlife conjugal loss: A follow-up at 25 months. *Cognitive Therapy & Research, 23,* 605-624.

Bowlby, J. (1980). Attachment and loss: Vol. 3. *Loss, sadness, and depression.* New York: Basic Books.

Bray, J.H. (1999). From marriage to remarriage and beyond: Findings from the Developmental Issues in Stepfamilies Research Project. In

E.M. Hetherington (Ed.), *Coping with divorce, single parenting, and remarriage: A risk and resiliency perspective*. Mahwah, NJ: Erlbaum.

Brown, A.S., Jones, E.M. & Davis, T.L. (1995). Age differences in conversational source monitoring. *Psychology and Aging, 10*, 111-122.

Chan, R., Raboy, B. & Patterson, C. (1998). Psychosocial adjustment among children conceived via donor insemination by lesbian and heterosexual mothers. *Child Development, 69*, 443-457.

Charness, N. (1979). Components of skill in bridge. *Canadian Journal of Psychology, 133*, 1-16.

Charness, N. (1981). Ageing and skilled problem-solving. *Journal of Experimental Psychology: General, 110*, 21-38.

Chase-Lansdale, P.L. & Hetherington, E.M. (1990). The impact of divorce on life-span development: Short and long term effects. In P.B. Baltes, D.L. Featherman, & R.M.Lerner (Eds.), *Life-span development and behaviour*. Hillsdale, NJ: Erlbaum.

Cole, C.L. (1984). Marital quality in later life. In W.H. Quinn & G.A. Hughston (Eds.), *Independent aging: Family and social systems perspectives*. Rockville, MD: Aspen.

Cooper, K.L. & Gutmann, D.L. (1987). Gender identity and ego mastery style in middle-aged, pre- and post-empty nest women. *Gerontologist, 27*, 347-352.

Cowan, C.P. & Cowan, P.A. (1987). Men's involvement in parenthood: Identifying the antecedents and understanding the barriers. In P.W. Berman & F.A. Pedersen (Eds.), *Men's transitions to parenthood: Longitudinal studies of early family experience*. Hillsdale, NJ: Erlbaum.

Craig, G.J. (1992). *Human development* (6th ed.). Englewood Cliffs, NJ: Prentice-Hall.

Cumming, E. & Henry, W.E. (1961). *Growing old*. New York: Basic Books.

Da Costa, D., Larouche, J., Dritsa, M. & Brender, W. (2000). Psychosocial correlates of prepartum and postpartum depressed mood. *Journal of Affective Disorders, 59*, 31-40.

Datan, N. (1980). Midas and other midlife crises. In W.H. Norman & T.J. Scaramella (Eds.), *Midlife: Development and clinical issues*. New York: Brunner/Mazel.

Dennis, N. (1975). Relations. In E. Butterworth & D. Weir (Eds.), *The sociology of modern Britain*. Glasgow: Fontana.

DeSpelder, L.A. & Strickland, A.L. (1983). *The last dance: Encountering death and dying*. Palo Alto, CA: Mayfield.

Dion, K.L. & Dion, K.K. (1993). Gender and ethnocultural comparisons in styles of love. *Journal of Social Issues, 49*, 53-69.

Douglas, M. (Ed.) (1964). *Man in society: Patterns of human organisation*. London: Macdonald.

Durkin, K. (1995). *Developmental social psychology: From infancy to old age*. Oxford: Blackwell.

Einstein, G.O., Smith, R.E., McDaniel, M.A. & Shaw, P. (1997). Aging and prospective memory: The influence of increased task demands at encoding and retrieval. *Psychology and Aging, 12*, 479-488.

Erikson, E.H. (1950). *Childhood and society*. New York: Norton.

Erikson, E.H. (1963). *Childhood and society* (2nd ed.). New York: Norton.

Erikson, E.H. (1964). *Insight and responsibility*. New York: Norton.

Featherstone, M. & Hepworth, M. (1989). Ageing and old age. In B. Bytheway et al. (Eds.), *Becoming and being old*. London: Sage.

Ferris, C. & Branston, P. (1993). Quality of life in the elderly: A contribution to its understanding. *Australian Journal of Ageing, 13*, 120-123.

Field, D. & Minkler, M. (1988). Continuity and change in social support between young-old and old-old or very-old age. *Journal of Gerontology, 43*, 100-107.

Flynn, J. (1999). Searching for justice: The discovery of IQ gains over time. *American Psychologist, 54*, 5-20.

Fitzgerald, B. (1999). Children of lesbian and gay parents: A review of the literature. *Marriage & Family Review, 29*, 57-75.

Ganong, L. & Coleman, M. (1994). *Remarried family relationships*. Thousand Oaks, CA: Sage Publications.

Giddens, A. (1992). *The transformation of intimacy: Sexuality, love and eroticism in modern societies*. Cambridge: Polity Press.

Gluhoski, V.L. & Wortman, C.B. (1966). The impact of trauma on

world views. *Journal of Social and Clinical Psychology, 15*, 417-429.

Gottman, J.M. (1994). *Why marriages succeed or fail*. New York: Simon & Schuster.

Greer, S. (1991). Psychological response to cancer and survival. *Psychological Medicine, 21*, 43-49.

Hall, D.R. & Zhao, J.Z. (1995). Cohabitation and divorce in Canada: Testing the selectivity hypothesis. *Journal of Marriage and the Family, 57*, 421-427.

Harris, R.L., Ellicott, A.M. & Holmes, D.S. (1986). The timing of psychosocial transitions and changes in women's lives: An examination of women aged 45 to 60. *Journal of Personality and Social Psychology, 51*, 409-416.

Hart, N. (1976). *When marriage ends*. London: Tavistock.

Hazan, C. & Shaver, P. (1987). Romantic love conceptualised as an attachment process. *Journal of Personality and Social Psychology, 52*, 511-524.

Helson, R. (1992). Women's difficult times and the rewriting of the life story. *Psychology of Women Quarterly, 16*, 331-347.

Hetherington, E.M. (1995, March). *The changing American family and the well-being of children*. Master lecture presented at the biennial meeting of the Society for Research in Child Development, Indianapolis.

Hetherington, E.M. (2002). *For better or worse: Divorce reconsidered*. New York: Harper & Brothers.

Hetherington, E.M., Law, T.C. & O'Connor, T.G. (1994). Divorce: Challenges, changes, and new chances. In F. Walsh (Ed.), *Normal family processes*. New York: Guilford.

Hill, C. (1999). Fusion and conflict in lesbian relationships. *Feminism & Psychology, 9*, 179-185.

Holden, K.C. & Smock, P.J. (1991).The economic costs of marital dissolution: Why do women bear a disproportionate cost? *Annual Review of Sociology, 17*, 51-78.

Holmes, T.H. & Rahe, R.H. (1967). The social readjustment rating scale. *Journal of Psychosomatic Research, 11*, 213-218.

Horn, J.L., Donaldson, G. & Engstrom, R. (1981). Apprehension, memory, and fluid intelligence decline through the "vital years" of adulthood. *Research on Aging, 3*, 33-84.

Huston, T.L. & Chorost, A.F. (1994). Behavioural buffers on the effect of negativity on marital satisfaction: A longitudinal study. *Personal Relationships, 1*, 223-239.

Huston, T.L., McHale, S.M. & Crouter, A.C. (1986). When the honeymoon's over: Changes in the marriage relationship over the first year. In R. Gilmour & S. Duck (Eds.), *The emerging field of personal relationships*. Hillsdale, NJ: Erlbaum.

Kübler-Ross, E. (1969). *On death and dying*. New York: Macmillan.

Kurdek, L. (1998). Relationship outcomes and their predictors: Longitudinal evidence from heterosexual married, gay cohabiting, and lesbian cohabiting couples. *Journal of Marriage & the Family, 60*, 553-568.

Lachman, M.E. & James, J.B. (1997). Charting the course of midlife development: An overview. In M.E. Lachman & J.B. James (Eds.), *Multiple paths of midlife development*. Chicago: University of Chicago Press.

Lamb, M.E., Pleck, J.H. & Levine, J.A. (1987). Effects of increased paternal involvement on mothers and fathers. In C. Lewis & M. O'Brien (Eds.), *Reassessing fatherhood: New observations on fathers and the modern family*. London: Sage.

Lang, F.R. & Carstensen, L.L. (1994). Close emotional relationships in late life: Further support for proactive aging in the social domain, *Psychology and Aging, 9*, 315-324.

Langer, E.J. & Rodin, J. (1976). The effects of choice and enhanced personal responsibility for the aged. *Journal of Personality and Social Psychology, 34*, 191-198.

Leach, E. (1967). *A runaway world?* London: BBC Publications.

Lee, D.J. & Markides, K.S. (1990). Activity and morality among aged persons over an eight-year period. *Journal of Gerontology, 45*, S39-S42.

Lerner, J.V. & Galambos, M.L. (1985). Maternal role satisfaction, mother-child interaction, and child temperament: A process model. *Developmental Psychology, 21*, 1157-1164.

Lévi-Strauss, C. (1956). The family. In H.L. Shapiro (Ed.), *Man, culture and society*. London: Oxford University Press.

Levinson, D.J. (1978). *The seasons of a man's life*. New York: Knopf.

Levinson, D.J. (1986). A conception of adult development. *American Psychologist, 41*, 3-13.

Levinson, D.J. (1996). *The seasons of a woman's life*. New York: Knopf.

Living in Britain: Results from the 2000 General Household Survey (2001). London: The Stationery Office.

Loewen, E.R., Shaw, R.J. & Craik, F.I.M. (1990). Age differences in components of metamemory. *Experimental Aging Research, 16*, 43-48.

Lopata, H.Z. (1979). Widowhood and husband sanctification. In L.A. Bugen (Ed.), *Death and dying: Theory, research, practice*. Dubuque, IA: W.C. Brown.

McAdams, D.P., de St. Aubin, E. & Logan, R.L. (1993). Generativity among young, midlife, and older adults. *Psychology and Aging, 8*, 221-230.

McCrae, R.R. & Costa, P.R., Jr. (1988). Psychological resilience among widowed men and women: A 10-year follow-up of a national sample. *Journal of Social Issues, 44*, 129-142.

McLoyd, V. (1998). Socioeconomic disadvantage and child development. *American Psychologist, 53*, 185-204.

Meyer, B.J.F., Russo, C. & Talbot, A. (1995). Discourse comprehension and problem solving: Decisions about the treatment of breast cancer by women across the life-span. *Psychology and Aging, 10*, 84-103.

Morgan, L.A. (1991). *After marriage ends: Economic consequences for midlife women*. Newbury Park, CA: Sage.

Morycz, R.K. (1992). Widowhood and bereavement in late life. In V.B. Van Hasselt & M. Hersen (Eds.), *Handbook of social development*. New York: Plenum.

Murstein, B.I. (1976). The stimulus-value-role theory of marital choice. In H. Grunebaum & J. Christ (Eds.), *Contemporary marriage: Structures, dynamics and therapy*. Boston: Little, Brown.

Neugarten, B.L. (1975). The future of the young-old. *The Gerontologist, 15*, 4-9.

Neugarten, B.L. (1979). Time, age, and the life cycle. *American Journal of Psychiatry, 136*, 887-894.

Norman, A. (1987). Overcoming an old prejudice. *Community Care*, 29th January.

Oppenheim, C. (1993). *Poverty: The facts* (3rd ed.). London: Child Poverty Action Group.

Perho, H. & Korhonen, M. (1999). Coping in work and marriage at the onset of middle age. *Psykologia, 34*, 115-127.

Peterson, C.C. (1996). The ticking of the social clock: Adults' beliefs about the timing of transition events. *International Journal of Ageing and Human Development, 42*, 189-203.

Pilcher, J. (1995). Growing up and growing older. *Sociology Review*, September

Pratt, M.W. & Norris, J.E. (1994). *The social psychology of aging*. Oxford: Blackwell.

Pressat, R. (1973). *Population*. Harmondsworth: Penguin.

Rabbitt, P.M.A. (1980). A fresh look at reaction times in old age. In D.G. Stein (Ed.), *The psychology of ageing: Problems and perspectives*. London: Elsevier.

Reibstein, J. & Richards, M. (1992). *Sexual arrangements: Marriage and affairs*. London: Heinemann.

Reichle, B. & Gefke, M. (1998). Justice of conjugal divisions of labor – you can't always get what you want. *Social Justice Research, 11*, 271-287.

Rholes, W., Simpson, J., Blakely, B., Lanigan, L. & Allen, D. (1997). Adult attachment styles, the desire to have children, and working models of parenthood. *Journal of Personality, 65*, 357-385.

Rice, J.K. (1994). Reconsidering research on divorce, family life cycle, and the meaning of family. *Psychology of Women Quarterly, 18*, 559-584.

Rockwell, R.C., Elder, G.H. & Ross, D.J. (1979). Psychological patterns in marital timing and divorce. *Social Psychology Quarterly, 42*, 399-404.

Roberts, P. & Newton, P.M. (1987). Levinsonian studies of women's adult development. *Psychology and Aging, 2*, 154-163.

Salthouse, T.A. (1996). General and specific speed mediation of adult age differences in memory. *Journals of Gerontology: Psychological Sciences, 51B*, 30-42.

Sanders, C.M. (1989). *Grief: The mourning after*. New York: Wiley-Interscience.

Schaie, K.W. (1983). The Seattle longitudinal study: A 21-year exploration of psychometric intelligence in adulthood. In K.W. Schaie (Ed.), *Longitudinal studies of adult psychological development*. New York: Guilford Press.

Schaie, K.W. (1994). The course of adult intellectual development. *American Psychologist, 49*, 304-313.

Schaie, K.W. (1996). Intellectual development in adulthood. In J.E. Birren & K.W. Schaie (Eds.), *Handbook of the psychology of aging* (4th ed.). San Diego, CA: Academic Press.

Sheehy, G. (1996). *New passages*. New York: Harper Collins.

Shneidman, E.S. (1983). *Deaths of man*. New York: Jason Aronson.

Sinnott, J.D. (1989). A model for solution of ill-structured problems: Implications for everyday and abstract problem solving. In J.D. Sinnott (Ed.), *Everyday problem solving: Theory and applications*. New York: Praeger.

Social Trends (2002). London: The Stationery Office.

Spanier, G.B. & Furstenberg, F.F., Jr. (1987). Remarriage and reconstituted families. In M.B. Sussman & S.K. Steinmetz (Eds.), *Handbook of marriage and the family*. New York: Plenum.

Sternberg, R.J. (1987). Liking versus loving: A comparative evaluation of theories. *Psychological Bulletin, 102*, 331-345.

Stroebe, M.S. & Stroebe, W. (1993). The mortality of bereavement: A review. In M.S. Stroebe, W. Stroebe & R.O. Hansson (Eds.), *Handbook of bereavement: Theory, research, and intervention*. Cambridge: Cambridge University Press.

Storandt, M. (1976). Speed and coding effects in relation to age and ability level. *Developmental Psychology, 12*, 177-178.

Stuart-Hamilton, I. (2000). Ageing and intelligence. *Psychology Review, 6* (4), 19-21.

Taylor, P., Richardson, R., Yeo, A., Marsh, R., Trobe, K. & Pilkington, A. (1995). *Sociology in focus*. Ormskirk: Causeway.

Unger, R. & Crawford, M. (1992). *Women and gender: A feminist psychology*. New York: McGraw-Hill.

Vaillant, G.E. (1977). *Adaptation to life: How the best and brightest came of age*. Boston: Little, Brown.

Waite, L.J. (1995). *Does marriage matter?* Presidential address to the Population Association of America, Chicago.

Wallerstein, J.S. (1986). Women after divorce: Preliminary report from a ten-year-follow-up. *American Journal of Orthopsychiatry, 56*, 65-77.

West, R.L. & Crook, T.H. (1990). Age differences in everyday memory: Laboratory analogues of telephone number recall. *Psychology and Aging, 5*, 520-529.

Wicki, W. (1999). The impact of family resources and satisfaction with division of labour on coping and worries after the birth of the first child. *International Journal of Behavioural Development, 23*, 431-456.

Wortman, C.B. & Silver, R.C. (1990). Successful mastery of bereavement and widowhood: A life course perspective. In P.B. Baltes & M.M. Baltes (Eds.), *Successful aging: Perspectives from the behavioural sciences*. New York: Cambridge University Press.

Wortman, C.B. & Silver, R.C. (1992). Reconsidering assumptions about coping with loss: An overview of current research. In L. Montada, S. Filipp, & M.J. Lerner (Eds.), *Life crises and experiences of loss in adulthood*. Hillsdale, NJ: Erlbaum.

Wortman, C.B., Silver, R.C. & Kessler, R.C. (1993). The meaning of loss and adjustment to bereavement. In M.S. Stroebe, W.Stroebe & R.O. Hansson (Eds.), *Handbook of bereavement*. Cambridge: Cambridge University Press.

Zimmer, Z., Hickey, T. & Searle, M.S. (1995). Activity participation and well-being among older people with arthritis. *The Gerontologist, 35*, 463-471.

▶ ## Introduction

In 1859, Charles Darwin proposed his theory of evolution by process of natural selection. In 1871, he explicitly stated that human beings had evolved from animals. Ever since then, psychologists have been aware that the study of animal behaviour may throw light on aspects of human behaviour. This study of animal behaviour is known as comparative psychology.

This chapter looks at Darwin's theory of evolution and examines some of its implications for animal behaviour. It also looks at research into learning and intelligence in non-human animals.

Chapter summary

- **Unit 1 introduces the modern theory of evolution and its application to the study of animal behaviour, adaptation and apparent altruism in animals.**

- **Unit 2 considers the concepts of classical and**

operant conditioning and the role which they play in the behaviour of non-human animals.

- **Unit 3 explores social learning and the role of intelligence in non-human animals.**

Unit 1 Evolutionary explanations of animal behaviour

KEY ISSUES

1 **What is evolution and how does it work?**

2 **What is 'altruism' and why does it pose a problem for evolutionary explanations of behaviour?**

3 **What are the principal kinds of apparent altruism identified by evolutionary biologists?**

Key terms

Ontogeny *The growth and development of the individual.*

Phylogeny *Traits or behaviours which are typical in a whole species and which are inherited biologically.*

1.1 Evolution by natural selection

Before we can start to consider in detail the theory of evolution and its relevance for our understanding of behaviour, we need to make a distinction between two terms: *ontogeny* and *phylogeny*. Ontogeny refers to the growth and development of the individual. Examples include a child's intellectual growth and their development of particular skills – for instance, their skills as a gymnast or swimmer. The interaction between the child's own capacities and their environmental experience accounts for this growth and development. Phylogeny on the other hand refers to species-specific traits or behaviour which are inherited biologically. Cats arching their backs when under threat is an example of such behaviour – the response is innate, or biologically inherited, and is found in all members of the species in question. Like many such distinctions, however, the line between ontogeny and phylogeny is frequently blurred in practice, and in most cases we need to take account of both ontogenetic and phylogenetic factors when seeking to explain behaviour. In fact, as we shall see, the relative importance of each is often a matter of controversy which cannot easily be resolved. Some of the reasons for this will become apparent later in the chapter.

The theory of evolution by natural selection, first proposed by Charles Darwin in 1859 with the publication of his book *The Origin of Species*, is one of the best known of all scientific theories. Unfortunately, despite its fame, Darwin's essential insight, and especially its significance for our understanding of behaviour, are frequently misunderstood. The basic idea of natural selection is in fact very simple, however, and has two elements. The first of these is the idea of *heritable variation*. The fact that all species exhibit variations, or differences, between their members is obvious. Only some of these differences, however, can be inherited biologically. If we consider human beings as an example, we can think of many differences between people which clearly cannot be inherited biologically: some people have tattoos and others do not; some people speak only French and others only Swahili; some people prefer Brahms to Louis Armstrong and so on. On the other hand, we can also think of many differences which are inherited biologically – eye colour, height and blood type, to name only three. Each of these three cases provides an example of heritable variation. For instance, eye colour can vary from brown to hazel to blue and so on.

The second element of Darwin's theory is *differential reproductive success*. The idea here is that some heritable variations will be more successful at reproducing themselves than others. This point can best be made by imagining an extreme example. Imagine that there are two individuals, one is predisposed towards celibacy, and the other to heterosexual intercourse. Let us imagine that these predispositions are biologically inherited. Which has the greatest chance of being

Charles Darwin, age 40

reproduced? The answer is obvious – the predisposition to have heterosexual intercourse. In fact, the predisposition to celibacy will not be reproduced at all, and so within a single generation will become extinct. A predisposition to heterosexual intercourse, on the other hand, will obviously reproduce itself handsomely and go on to become very common indeed.

Of course, few variations will be as extreme as this. More usually, a variant will have only a slightly better chance of being reproduced compared to others in the population, and so it will take many generations before the effect of this selective advantage can be seen. Nevertheless, this example illustrates the basic process by which Darwin proposed that evolution works: the differential reproductive success of heritable variations.

Key terms

Heritable variations *Differences amongst members of the same species which are inherited genetically.*

Differential reproductive success *Differences between individuals in a population in the number of surviving offspring they produce.*

The source of variation: genetic mutation

An obvious question raised by the above description of evolution by natural selection is: where do the variations come from? Indeed this was a question voiced by some of Darwin's many critics during the nineteenth century, and for some, the issue of variation was considered to be the major flaw in Darwin's theory. Today, however, we can easily answer this question thanks to our knowledge of genetics. The answer is that variations come about as the result of *genetic mutations*. Essentially, genetic mutations are random copying errors which occur in the DNA of organisms from one generation to the next, which give rise to novel genetic forms. Most frequently, these mutations will be 'deleterious', that is, have a negative effect on

Activity 1   Heritable variations

Item A	'David and Goliath'

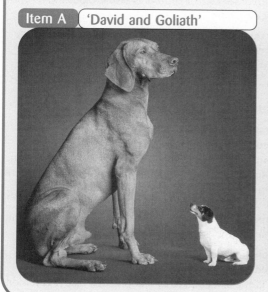

Item B	A manicured poodle

Questions

1   Which of the differences depicted in Items A and B are phylogenetic and which are ontogenetic?

2   Working in pairs, list three differences between you and your partner which are heritable genetically, and three which are not. Note any differences between you which are neither wholly one nor the other, but a combination of both.

the reproductive success of the organism. Once in while, however, a mutation will arise which confers a reproductive advantage on its bearer relative to others in the population. When this happens that individual will, by definition, reproduce more successfully than others, and so will his or her descendants who also possess the mutant gene. In time, the trait in question will 'evolve' to become the dominant form in the population, provided, that is, it is not overtaken by an even more successful variant.

A mistake which was made by some of Darwin's contemporaries, who lacked a knowledge of genetics, was to assume that mutations could not be responsible for evolution because they would become increasingly diluted with each successive generation. For example, a highly successful mutation which conferred a 100% advantage on its bearer would, as a result of dilution by sexual reproduction, only confer a 50% advantage on his or her offspring. This advantage would be further diluted by 50% in the case of their offspring, in whom it would only confer a 25% advantage and so on with each succeeding generation. Thus it was assumed that in only six generations, the original 100% advantage would confer a less than 1% advantage on the descendants who possessed it (Badcock, 1991). If this view were correct, then it would indeed be a damning criticism of Darwin's theory. However, we now know that this is a false view of the mechanism of genetic inheritance.

Thanks ultimately to the pioneering work of Gregor Mendel (1822-84), we now know that the basic units of inheritance – genes – cannot be diluted in the way that Darwin's critics assumed. We now know that rather than half of any one gene being inherited by all of a parent's offspring, half of his or her offspring will inherit the entire gene. In other words, in a sexually reproducing species like human beings, there is a 50% chance that any given parental gene will be inherited by each of its offspring. In those offspring which inherit the gene, therefore, its full advantageous effects will be shown, rather than a diluted effect in all of the originator's descendants.

'Survival of the fittest'

So far, we have been careful to avoid using the phrase 'survival of the fittest' which, in many people's minds, amounts to the same thing as evolution by natural selection as proposed by Darwin. There are a number of reasons for this. For one thing, the phrase 'survival of the fittest' was not coined by Darwin at all, as many people suppose, but by another nineteenth century writer, the political economist and sociologist Herbert Spencer (1820-1903). Furthermore, and partly as result of this legacy, the phrase contains a number of ambiguities.

One of the commonest errors which result from using the term fitness is to confuse its evolutionary meaning with its everyday usage. When, in everyday language, we talk about fitness, we usually mean such things as good health, physical strength and longevity. Whilst such things are no doubt relevant to reproductive success, they do not, in themselves, get us very far in explaining evolution. Let us take physical strength as an example. No matter how physically strong an individual might be in relation to others in the population, this strength will not confer a reproductive advantage upon him unless he is also successful in reproducing. An individual who devoted all their energy to body-building, for example,

but who was not the least interested in having sexual intercourse, would be unlikely to leave any copies of their genes in future generations. Of course, other things being equal (eg, a strong motivation to reproduce) physical strength may well enhance an individual's reproductive success, but in and of itself it is not enough to secure it. As we shall see in later chapters, there are a great many characteristics which might have enhanced our ancestors' reproductive success, but only a few of them have anything to do with everyday definitions of fitness.

The true Darwinian meaning of 'fitness', then, is reproductive success and nothing else. In Darwin's terms, the 'fittest' are the best adapted. They are simply those who have been most successful at reproducing, and 'natural selection' is the term used by Darwin to describe the process by which some individuals enjoy greater reproductive success than others.

Secondly, the phrase 'survival of the fittest', by virtue of its historical association with so-called 'Social Darwinists' like Spencer, carries with it overtones of some rather dubious political ideologies, which hijacked Darwinism for their own purposes. Many writers and politicians of the late nineteenth and early twentieth centuries employed the phrase to suggest that those individuals or even nations which possessed the greatest share of resources somehow deserved to, because they were the 'fittest'. However, not only does this misunderstand the true Darwinian meaning of fitness – that is, the differential reproductive success of heritable variations – it quite inappropriately assumes that the 'fittest' deserve to be the fittest. There is nothing in the Darwinian theory of evolution which leads to any conclusions about who deserves to have what. Such basically ethical and moral questions are really outside the scope of evolutionary theory.

Key terms

Genetic mutation *Random genetic changes which occur between generations, which are the source of variation on which evolution operates.*

Survival of the fittest *A rather misleading term, originating from Herbert Spencer, which is sometimes used to describe the process of natural selection. The term is best avoided in discussions of evolution.*

Natural selection *The process by which the descendants of the most reproductively successful become the most numerous members of a population.*

Group versus individual selection

Another important mistaken belief relating to Darwinian evolution concerns the level at which selection is believed to operate. Although Darwin was himself very clear that evolution acted upon individuals, it became quite common for subsequent biologists to argue that in fact it operated on groups, or even whole species. This error is actually very widespread – one frequently hears people explaining some behaviour or other trait because it enhances the 'survival of the species'.

Group selection Since, as we shall see, the implications of this type of argument are very great indeed, it is important that we establish why *group selection* is a fallacy. Let us take a common example of group selectionist reasoning. Imagine that a species of monkey inhabits an environment where there is insufficient food to support all its members, and that a researcher observes a tendency amongst adult males to kill infants of up to six months old. The group selectionist argument would be as follows. Since there is insufficient food to support the entire population, this infanticidal behaviour (killing of infants) has evolved as a means of controlling the population size and thus ensuring that the species as a whole survives by reducing the number of members to that which can be supported by the available food resources.

Convincing though this example appears, the true Darwinian would not accept this explanation. The most important question would be: are the offspring who are killed genetically related to the male who kills them? If they are, then Darwinian evolution would find the behaviour very difficult to explain. This is because killing one's own offspring has an obviously disastrous effect on one's reproductive success – a gene for killing your children will be about as successful at spreading as a gene for not having any in the first place. If it were found that in the example in question the infants were indeed killed by their own fathers, then it would have to be admitted that Darwinian natural selection could not offer a satisfactory explanation and that group selection might be the solution after all.

Fortunately for Darwinism, the example in question is not hypothetical, but relates to commonly observed behaviour amongst langur monkeys (Hrdy, 1977), as well as other species of monkey, gorillas and African lions (Trivers, 1985). Like many species of primate, langurs are polygynous, that is, live in groups of 10-20 females attached to a single 'dominant' male. Other males live in all-male groups, and on occasion members of these groups attempt to displace a 'dominant' male and take over a 'harem'. Detailed field studies of langur behaviour have revealed that infanticide invariably follows such a take over, and usually involves the new male killing any offspring of less than six months and offspring born within the first six months of his take-over.

There are a number of reasons why a group selectionist explanation – that is, that the behaviour in question evolved as a means of regulating the population size at times of food scarcity, and hence as a benefit to the population as a whole – is implausible. First of all, as Trivers (1985) has pointed out, it does not explain why infanticide only takes place following a take-over of a 'harem' by a new male. Presumably the population would need regulating at other times as well. Secondly, it does not explain why it is only young infants that are killed. Since young infants are vulnerable to death anyway,

consume a smaller share of food resources than more mature animals, and will not themselves reproduce for a considerable time, a far more efficient method of regulating the population would be to kill juvenile and sub-adult females. Thirdly, it does not seem to be able to explain why only the males are involved in population regulation by killing infants. Again, a more reliable method of population regulation would be for adult females simply to cease to reproduce at times of food scarcity. Lastly, the group selectionist explanation cannot account for the fact that females actively resist the attempts made by new dominant males to kill their offspring.

Individual selection Natural selection, however, based upon individual reproductive success as Darwin proposed, seems to offer a far more satisfactory explanation of selective infanticide. First of all, it explains why the males *only* kill offspring who they have not fathered. They are not genetically related to these offspring, and so any effort invested in them either by themselves or by the infants' mothers is, from the males' point of view, wasted. Secondly, in mammals, the act of suckling tends to prevent ovulation in the nursing mother, and so females are usually unable to become pregnant at this time. Thus, by killing the suckling infants of another male, the new male is likely to be able to successfully inseminate the mother more quickly than would otherwise be the case. This point is reinforced by the fact that langur infants are weaned at about eight months, and any infants older than this at the time of the take-over are simply ignored by the new male. They no longer inhibit the mother's ability to conceive, and hence are no longer a threat to the new male's reproductive success. Thirdly, the fact that the new males stop killing newborn infants about six months after the take-over, is explained by the fact that the gestation period of the langur – that is, the time between conception and birth – is about seven months. Thus, any infants born later than six months after the take-over will probably have been fathered by the new male.

It would seem, then, that the Darwinian theory of natural selection, based upon individual reproductive success, can offer a far more plausible explanation of this kind of behaviour. Indeed, it is difficult to see how group selection could explain evolution at all. Of course this is not to deny that traits which evolve by virtue of the advantages they have for individual reproductive success could also have incidental benefits for the group. For example, it is conceivable (although unlikely) that infanticide in langurs, which has evolved as a means of promoting the individual reproductive success of males, does also have the effect of reducing the population size, and hence of benefiting the group as a whole. The crucial point, however, is that this is not why it evolved, and indeed, it would have evolved just the same even if it did not benefit the group as a whole. Put at its simplest: the behaviour evolved because those individual males who were genetically predisposed to carry out infanticide in this way left more copies of their genes than those who were not.

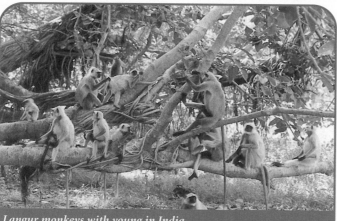
Langur monkeys with young in India

Key terms

Group selection *The view that traits are selected because they benefit the group as a whole.*

Individual selection *The view that traits are selected because they benefit the individual's reproductive success.*

Activity 2   The fallacy of group selection

Item A   Father and son

A lion cub greeting its biological father

African lions live in groups called prides. A pride consists of a number of females, their young and several – usually related – sub-adult males. When young males reach maturity, they are excluded from the pride and band together in search of a pride to take over. When such a takeover is successful, and the existing males of the pride are deposed, the young males proceed to kill any cubs of the males they have displaced. As a consequence, the nursing mothers cease lactating and return to oestrus much more quickly then otherwise would have been the case.

Questions

1   Explain, in terms of individual reproductive success, how infanticidal behaviour in African lions can have evolved.

2   Explain how this behaviour carries different costs and benefits for males and females.

3   Infanticide has sometimes been explained as a means of controlling population size – that is, as something which has evolved because it benefits the *group*. What are the problems with explaining infanticide in this way?

1.2   Biological explanations for apparent altruism

Genes and evolution

As we have seen, evolution is essentially about the tendency of some genes in the population to reproduce more successfully than others. Of course, genes cannot reproduce on their own – they require the organisms in whose cells they reside to do that. Unlike organisms, however, genes are potentially immortal. That is, as long as they are successfully reproduced, they will outlive the individual organisms in which they are 'resident'. Your great-great-great grandmother may no longer be alive, but her genes – at least some of them – are alive and well and living in the cells in your body. What are the implications of this for the evolution of social behaviour?

Genes and relatedness

The reproductive system of mammals (including, of course, human beings) is known as *diploid* – that is, they have two parents and two sets of genes, one inherited from each parent. Genes are located on chromosomes, and in the case of human beings, each chromosome carries in the region of 20,000 genes. In total, most cells in the human body contain two sets of 23

chromosomes (one set from each parent) making a total of 46 chromosomes. The exception to this rule is the sex cells, the sperm and the ovum, which each contain only one set of 23 chromosomes. When these two cells come together in the process of sexual reproduction, the two sets of 23 chromosomes are brought together to form the genetic make-up of a new individual. This genetic make-up is called the *genotype*. The physiology, structure and behaviour which result from this genotype is known as the *phenotype*.

We can see from this brief description of the process of sexual reproduction in mammals that 50% of their genetic material is inherited from each of their parents. Looked at in another way, this means that there is a 50% chance that any of a father's genes, or any of a mother's genes, will be present in each of their offspring.

But if it is possible to calculate the probability that a gene present in a father or mother is also present in one of their offspring, it should also be possible to calculate the probability that other categories of relatives share genes in common. Biologists call this probability of two relatives sharing a gene in common the *degree of relatedness* and it is usually symbolised by the letter *r*. Let us consider the case of siblings. A full sibling is a brother or sister who shares both the same father and the same mother. A half sibling, on the other hand, is a brother or sister who shares either the same father or the same mother, but not both.

First of all, let us calculate the degree of relatedness, or r, for half siblings. Imagine that there are two half-brothers, Fred and Tom, who share the same mother but have different fathers. (Note that Fred and Tom could be from any species which has a diploid reproductive system – from hamsters to human beings!) We begin by calculating the degree of relatedness between one of the half-brothers and his mother. Let us take Fred: he is related to his mother by 50%, so in this case $r = \frac{1}{2}$. Next, we need to calculate the degree of relatedness between Fred's mother and Tom. Since she is also his mother, once again $r = \frac{1}{2}$. To calculate the degree of relatedness between Fred and Tom, we simply multiply together the two values already obtained, so:

$$\frac{1}{2} \times \frac{1}{2} = \frac{1}{4}$$

The degree of relatedness between half siblings is thus $\frac{1}{4}$. In other words, there is a 25% chance that any gene present in an individual will also be present in their half-brother or sister.

Let us now consider the case of full siblings. Imagine that there are two full sisters called Kate and Jane. To begin with, we can proceed in the same way as with half siblings, and calculate the degree of relatedness via the two sisters' mother. Kate is related to her mother by 50% ($r = \frac{1}{2}$) and so is Jane. As in the case of half siblings we simply multiply together these two values to give the degree of relatedness via their mother, so:

$$\frac{1}{4} \times \frac{1}{4} = \frac{1}{2}$$

However, in this case since Kate and Jane are full siblings, they are also related via their shared father. We therefore need to add the degree of relatedness via their father (which will also be $r = \frac{1}{4}$) to the degree of relatedness via their mother, thus:

$$\frac{1}{2} \times \frac{1}{2} = \frac{1}{4}$$

The degree of relatedness between full siblings is thus $\frac{1}{2}$ or, put another way, there is a 50% chance that any gene present in an individual will also be present in their full sibling.

Activity 3   Calculating degrees of relatedness (r)

Item A   Royal Family tree

Item B   The Royal Family

Questions

Using the information given above, calculate the degree of relatedness (r) for the following pairs:

1   Elizabeth II and her sister Princess Margaret.

2   David, Viscount Linley and his aunt, Elizabeth II.

3   Prince William and his first cousin, Peter.

4   Prince Harry and his grandfather, Philip, Duke of Edinburgh.

5   Zara and her great-grandmother, Elizabeth, the Queen Mother.

Genes, evolution and the problem of altruism

It should by now be obvious that if evolution favours the selection of genes which promote their bearer's reproductive success at the expense of others in the population, it will act against those genes which have a negative influence on the reproductive success of their bearers. In particular, we can predict that any gene which promotes the reproductive success of other individuals in the population at the expense of its own bearer will not be selected. Imagine an individual who has a genetic predisposition to cater for his own nutritional needs only after he has ensured that those of all his immediate neighbours have been fully taken care of. It is not difficult to imagine that such an individual would frequently find himself very hungry and, in a situation of scarcity, would in all probability eventually starve to death whilst his neighbours thrived at his expense. It is equally easy to see what would happen to this seemingly admirable gene for placing one's neighbour before oneself – it would perish along with its unfortunate bearers.

Biologists call behaviour which promotes the reproductive success of a recipient at the expense of the actor *altruism*. Thus, if I improve your chances of reproducing and in doing so, reduce my own chances of reproducing, then I am being altruistic. In reproductive terms, you gain and I lose. Notice that altruism is defined in terms of the effects of the behaviour in question. Whilst this is not an issue in the context of nonhuman behaviour, in the case of human beings it does not matter whether an individual intends to be altruistic or not, all that counts from an evolutionary point of view is whether or not the behaviour has that effect.

Key term

Altruism *Any act which benefits the reproductive success of the recipient at the expense of the actor.*

The problem of altruism

As we saw in the previous section, evolutionary theory predicts that altruistic behaviour will not evolve. It has often been suggested that this creates one of the greatest challenges for evolutionary theories of behaviour, for the simple reason that much observed behaviour in both humans and nonhuman animals appears to be self-evidently altruistic. Perhaps for this reason, the so-called 'problem of altruism' (Badcock, 1986) has been the subject of a considerable amount of research by evolutionary biologists and psychologists. This section reviews some of the most significant findings of this research, and shows how apparently altruistic behaviour can be accounted for within an evolutionary theory.

Kin altruism

One of the most obvious forms of *apparent altruism* occurs between relatives. This is as true for animal species as it is for human beings. For example, field studies of Belding's ground squirrels have revealed a surprising form of apparently altruistic behaviour related to the practice of alarm calling (Sherman, 1981). These squirrels, like many species of birds, have been observed giving an alarm call when predators are in close proximity. This call warns other squirrels in the vicinity of the predator's presence, and they are usually able to get away to safety as a result. However, by giving an alarm call, the squirrel conspicuously draws attention to its own presence and hence considerably increases its own risk of being attacked by the predator. The alarm call would thus seem to be a classic example of altruistic behaviour. Sherman's studies have also shown, however, that the beneficiaries of these apparently altruistic calls are overwhelmingly genetic relatives of the very squirrels who raise the alarm (Sherman, 1981).

The question we must answer, therefore, is, why should what appears as altruism be more common amongst individuals who are genetically related than those who are not? To understand the answer to this question, we need to return to our earlier consideration of degrees of genetic relatedness, and to take what Richard Dawkins (1976) calls a 'gene's-eye view' of the situation. Imagine that there is a gene for altruism. Ordinarily, as we have seen, this gene would do very badly in evolutionary terms and fairly quickly die out altogether. Imagine, however, that this gene was not for general indiscriminate altruism, but rather caused its bearers to direct altruism specifically towards their genetic relatives. This is known as *kin altruism*. Whilst the supposedly altruistic individuals might diminish their own personal chances of surviving and reproducing, their behaviour actually increases the chances of their genes surviving and reproducing, by virtue of their presence in genetically related individuals who are the recipients of altruism.

The survival chances of an individual's genes will be improved if his or her kin reproduce. As noted earlier, there is a 50% chance that any gene present in an individual will also be present in their brothers and sisters. Kin altruism therefore makes sense in terms of maintaining the individual's genes in the population. Their genes will have a better chance of surviving if they focus not only on their own well-being, but also on the well-being of their kin.

It can be seen, then, that altruistic behaviour between relatives is, from an evolutionary point of view only *apparent altruism*. It looks like altruism, but once the degrees of relatedness between the various participants is taken into account, we can see that the altruistic individual does not in fact have to pay a price in terms of the ultimate reproductive success of their genes.

This idea is one of the most central in modern evolutionary biology and derives from the pioneering work of a British biologist, W.D. Hamilton, in the 1960s (Hamilton, 1964). Hamilton's theory is usually called the *theory of inclusive fitness*. For our present purposes we need to note that this insight predicts the evolution of kin altruism.

Of course, the chances that an individual's genes will also be present in a relative will depend on the degree of relatedness with that relative. It follows from this, therefore, that the benefit derived from being altruistic towards that relative will decline as the degree of relatedness declines. We can expect, for example, that evolution would favour a lower degree of altruism towards first cousins (where there is only a 12.5% chance that the same genes will be present) than towards full siblings (where there is a 50% chance of the same genes being present). It also follows that this kind of altruism will rarely be at the complete reproductive expense of the altruist – in other words, we should not expect the altruist to die in the process. If I have a choice of saving the life of my brother or my own life, we can expect that evolution would select for saving my own life as there is twice the chance of my genes being present in myself than in my brother.

Evaluation An obvious objection to the idea of kin altruism is that whilst very neat and convincing in theory, it is not difficult to find exceptions to the predictions it makes. You may, for example, feel much closer and more altruistically disposed towards your cousin than your brother; or towards your uncle than your father. Whilst examples of this kind can undoubtedly be found, it is important to emphasise that, as with all evolutionary explanations, we are talking about genetic predispositions towards behaving in particular ways rather than genetic determinants which will invariably produce a certain pattern of behaviour. In the present example, a key issue is how various species actually identify kin. We know, for example, that many species employ a form of phenotypic matching to recognise kin. This means, literally, comparing some physical or behavioural feature of oneself with the same feature in another individual. The more similar the features, the more probable is a

high degree of relatedness. Features compared in phenotypic matching in different species include smell, chemical secretions and coloration. Whilst these methods are usually effective in identifying kin, and yield, on average, significantly higher degrees of altruism towards kin, they are not foolproof and examples can be found of 'mistakes' in most species – ie of identifying and treating non-kin as kin (Trivers, 1985).

Key terms

Apparent altruism *An act which appears to be altruistic but which is shown not to be once the various reproductive costs and benefits are calculated.*

Kin altruism *A form of apparent altruism in which altruistic acts are explained in terms of reproductive benefits to an individual's genetic relatives.*

Activity 4   Kin altruism and kin recognition

Item A   Squirrel rearing experiments

In an attempt to test the basis of kin recognition in ground squirrels, an experiment was conducted by Holmes and Sherman (1982). The researchers wanted to discover whether squirrels identify kin by directly recognising relatedness in some way, or whether they rely instead on some cue of relatedness – in this case, having been reared together. In the experiment, young squirrels were assigned to one of the following four rearing groups:

1 Siblings reared by one mother.
2 Siblings reared by different mothers.
3 Non-siblings reared together by one mother.
4 Non-siblings reared together by different mothers.

Once the animals had matured, different pairings were selected, put together and their behaviour observed. The overwhelming conclusion from this experiment was that squirrels reared together behave towards each other in

Ground squirrels

a much less aggressive way than those reared apart. It does not matter whether the squirrels are actually related genetically, nor whether they are reared by their own genetic mother.

Questions

1 What does this experiment tell us about the kin recognition mechanism in ground squirrels?

2 In view of these findings, would you expect to find ground squirrels reared in non-sibling groups in the wild? Give reasons for your answer.

Reciprocal altruism

So far we have only considered altruistic behaviour directed towards kin. Whilst this is undoubtedly an important category of apparently altruistic behaviour, it is far from being the only category that we need to consider. Ordinary experience tells us that apparently altruistic acts occur every day between completely unrelated individuals. Such acts may be instances of *reciprocal altruism* (Trivers, 1971). Reciprocal altruism refers to situations where the altruist receives a benefit of equal value in return for their initial act of altruism. It is thus another example of apparent altruism as no costs are actually incurred, despite appearances to the contrary.

To understand the logic of how this form of behaviour could evolve, imagine the following hypothetical situation. Like the vast majority of your ancestors, you are a hunter-gatherer, and your survival and that of your family are crucially dependent upon your success as a hunter. However, hunting is an unpredictable business and whilst some of the time you are very successful and manage to kill more than enough food to satisfy the needs of you and your family, at other times you fail to kill anything and as a result you and your family go hungry. What you really need of course is a deep freeze to store your surplus meat until you need it, but unfortunately these will not be invented for another 25,000 years! There is however an alternative. Imagine that you have a neighbour who, like you, sometimes has more than enough to feed him and his family, but at other times does not have enough. Of course, following the 'selfish' theory of behaviour discussed so far, the last thing you should do is to give any of your surplus to your unrelated neighbour, and similarly this is the last thing you should expect him to do for you. Imagine, however, that instead of giving him your surplus for nothing, he agreed that when he has a surplus at some time in the future and you have a shortage, he will repay the favour and give you an equivalent amount of his surplus in return. A moment's reflection will reveal that this course of action will benefit both participants far more than following the straightforwardly selfish policy of keeping your surplus for yourself. It will mean, in short, that instead of having too much food for half of the time and not enough for the other half, both families will have enough food all of the time. We can see therefore that selection will favour the evolution of altruism when the altruistic action is repaid with another of equivalent value – in other words, when an act of altruism is reciprocated, hence the term reciprocal altruism.

A particular problem faced by certain species of fish concerns the tendency for their mouth cavities to become infested with micro-organisms which, if left alone, will decay and ultimately threaten the life of the fish. One such fish is the grouper. Clearly, groupers who can find some means of cleansing their mouth cavities will be at a selective advantage over those who do not, but equally clearly, cleaning one's teeth seems rather a tall order for a fish. However, groupers have succeeded in solving this problem by evolving a remarkable reciprocal relationship with a much smaller species of fish called the cleaner wrasse (pronounced 'rass') (Badcock, 1991). In this relationship, the grouper who requires cleansing simply sits motionless in the water and opens its mouth. The cleaner wrasse then swims in, consumes the various parasites which are troubling the grouper, and swims off again. This is a perfect example of a reciprocal relationship. Both parties gain a benefit which they otherwise would not have – the grouper gets its mouth cavity cleaned out and the wrasse gets a tasty meal.

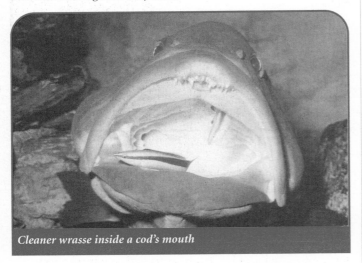

Cleaner wrasse inside a cod's mouth

This example also draws attention to another fundamental feature of reciprocal relationships, however, and that is their vulnerability to exploitation. It is not difficult to see that whilst under the circumstances described, both the grouper and the wrasse enjoy a net benefit from the interaction, each fish is vulnerable to exploitation by the other. Specifically, the grouper has to take a chance on the wrasse eating only the parasites and not taking a meaty chunk out of its cheek, whilst the wrasse has to take the even more obvious risk of being swallowed up by the grouper once it has completed its cleaning task. The problem here, as in all examples of reciprocal altruism, is that both parties may stand to gain more (at least in the short term) by *cheating* – that is, failing to reciprocate – than by sticking to the agreement.

Cheating behaviours It is important to note that whilst cheating in reciprocal interactions might pay, so will the ability to discriminate against cheats. For example, the grouper has evolved to be very choosy about whom it lets into its mouth. Not only are cleaner wrasse very distinctly coloured, but also perform a strange 'head-down' dance unique to them before being accepted by the grouper. Nevertheless, in addition to genuine wrasse, we have also seen the evolution of 'pseudo-cleaner wrasse' which look very similar to the genuine cleaners, and which eat the micro-organisms and even perform the same dance, but also take a chunk out of the unsuspecting grouper's mouth!

It is easy to see that, in the short-run, because they get more food, pseudo-cleaner wrasse should be at an evolutionary advantage over genuine cleaner wrasse. However, their success will inevitably be relatively short-lived. We can predict either that as a result of attack, the population of groupers will decline as the numbers of pseudo-cleaners increases, and hence the success of the pseudo-cleaners will decline accordingly, or a mutation will emerge which enables the grouper to discriminate between genuine and pseudo-cleaners. Either way, we can predict that the success of the pseudo-cleaner will be temporary, albeit perhaps with lethal consequences for the population of groupers. The logic of this argument has led Trivers (1985) to suggest that cheating behaviours and the ability to discriminate against such behaviours have co-evolved, such that there has been an 'evolutionary arms-race' between the two.

Evaluation As with kin altruism, reciprocal altruism is more accurately described as 'apparent' altruism, because in effect – and remember that altruism is defined in terms of effects only – the genes of the individuals concerned enjoy a net reproductive advantage as a result of the behaviour in question. It might thus be considered misleading to refer to it as altruism at all.

The whole idea of reciprocal altruism is also necessarily speculative. Certainly one can find both animal and human examples of apparently reciprocal behaviour, but this is no guarantee that the evolutionary process did indeed select such behaviour. All we can do is to surmise that it did – direct demonstration of such evolutionary processes is almost impossible.

Key terms

Reciprocal altruism *An example of apparent altruism in which the altruist receives a return of equal value to their initial act.*

Cheating behaviour *A failure to reciprocate in a reciprocal relationship.*

Activity 5   Reciprocal altruism

Item A   Vampire bat

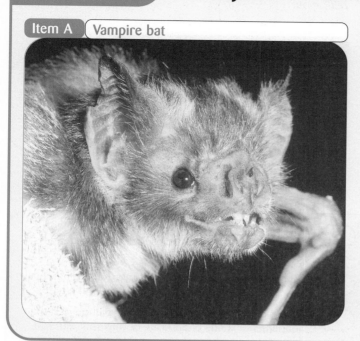

One species in which reciprocal altruism has been observed is the vampire bat – native of Costa Rica. Vampire bats need a regular supply of animal blood to survive. They have been observed regurgitating blood and feeding it to unrelated individuals who have not been successful in finding a host from which to suck blood. In one experiment, Wilkinson put two groups of unrelated vampire bats together to form one large group. He then removed one individual from this group and denied it food. When this individual was returned, it received donations of blood from the others, but predominantly from those with whom it had previously shared a roost.

Adapted from Wilkinson, 1984

Questions

1   Explain why reciprocal relationships such as those found in vampire bats evolve?

2   In this experiment, it was found that reciprocal altrusim was more common between individuals who had associated together for a period of time. Why should this be so?

Induced altruism

Unlike kin or reciprocal altruism, *induced altruism* is the only genuine form of altruism which evolutionary theory predicts (Badcock, 1986). It occurs when one organism successfully exploits another such that the various costs and benefits cannot be explained either in terms of kinship or reciprocity. Unlike kin altruism and reciprocal altruism where both parties gain, induced altruism means that one party gains at the expense of the other. In terms of our definition of altruism, this is the only genuine form of altruism because it gives the beneficiaries a selective advantage at the expense of the victims.

The notion of induced altruism actually covers a great many cases. It may, for example, involve deception such as the entirely non-conscious kind described above in the case of the pseudo-cleaner wrasse. Alternatively, it may involve conscious deception as in the case of a human being who deliberately swindles money out of another by selling him a stolen car. Equally, it could involve no conscious deception at all as, for example, in the case of a man who genuinely forgets to return a book he has borrowed from his colleague. It could also involve quite blatant coercion. An obvious example of this would be the system of income tax which operates in most advanced societies, which requires people who earn more to pay more. In many cases the benefit an individual receives from this taxation varies in inverse proportion with the amount they pay. The altruism of the better off is hardly voluntary, but instead relies on enormous and highly punitive bureaucracies with far-reaching powers to ensure that they 'cooperate'. One can only speculate as to how much tax would be collected if paying it were made voluntary!

Of course one does not need to be aware that one is the victim of induced altruism for it to have taken place. Indeed, it seems likely that the most successful examples of induced altruism (from the point of view of the beneficiaries) will occur when the 'victim' remains unaware and so does not attempt to retaliate. Perhaps the best known example from a non-human species is so-called 'brood-parasitism' amongst cuckoos, who lay their eggs in the nests of neighbouring birds and successfully pass them off as their own, thus saving an enormous amount of parental effort.

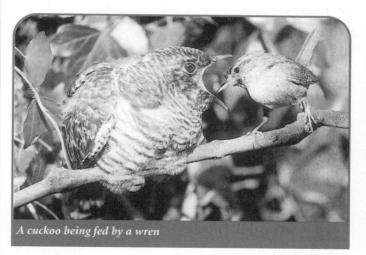

A cuckoo being fed by a wren

Evaluation Although the concept of induced altruism seems to be a logical accompaniment to the two forms of apparent altruism discussed above, it might be argued that it is stretching the point to call such involuntary, and often unknowing, behaviour 'altruism'. Similarly, we might ask whether it is really meaningful to place victims of armed robberies and muggings in the same logical category as taxpayers and people who give Christmas presents without receiving one in return.

More generally, the whole concept of altruism as it is developed by evolutionary biologists has been subject to a number of criticisms. It has been claimed by a number of writers that the notion that human beings are not naturally predisposed towards altruistic behaviour, but will instead tend to pursue their own genetic self-interest, is based upon a particular view of modern capitalist society, rather than on any necessary biological universals (Saglins, 1977). In this respect, capitalist society emphasises individualism and self-interest. As a result, researchers raised in capitalist society will tend to adopt this world view and see evolution as based on individual genetic self-interest. Related to this, it has been alleged by some writers that evolutionary biologists wrongly assume that concepts such as 'altruism', 'aggression' and so on, relate to natural observable categories, whereas in reality, they are theoretical constructs which have emerged at a particular historical moment. This tendency – to attribute concrete reality to abstract theoretical concepts – is known as *reification*.

Key terms

Induced altruism *A form of altruism in which one party gains at the expense of another.*

Reification *Mistakenly assuming that abstract theoretical concepts have a concrete reality.*

Summary

1   Natural selection, as first discovered by Charles Darwin, involves the differential reproduction of heritable variations.

2   The source of heritable variation is now known to be genetic.

3   The idea that traits can evolve solely for the benefit of the group or species is false; evolution acts on individual genes.

5   Relatives share genes in common with predictable frequencies, known as the coefficient of relatedness or *r*.

6   Altruism is any action which promotes the reproductive success of the recipient at the expense of the altruist.

7   Evolutionary theory proposes the evolution of three fundamental kinds of altruism, or apparent altruism: kin altruism, reciprocal altruism and induced altruism.

Unit 2 Classical and operant conditioning

KEY ISSUES

1   **What is classical conditioning, and what are its principal mechanisms?**

2   **What is operant conditioning and what are its principal mechanisms?**

3   **What is the role of classical and operant conditioning in the behaviour of nonhuman animals?**

2.1   Classical (Pavlovian) conditioning

Classical conditioning was the discovery of the Russian physiologist Ivan Pavlov (Pavlov, 1927). The aim of Pavlov's research was to investigate the salivatory responses of dogs. Dogs, like many other species, will salivate spontaneously when food is placed on their tongue. Pavlov noticed, however, that the dogs were not only salivating when presented with food, but also in response to anything that was regularly associated with the presentation of food. Thus, for example, the presence of the experimenter who regularly fed the dogs could produce salivation, even in the absence of food itself.

The starting point of classical conditioning is a natural reflex.

In this case, the dog's tendency to salivate when presented with food is a *natural reflex*. It is something with which the animal is born (that is, genetically determined), and which under normal circumstances will remain with the animal until it dies. Another example would be the tendency to blink when faced with a sudden bright light – this is not something an organism learns, but rather is present from birth.

Acquisition

Pavlov demonstrated the processes involved in classical conditioning in a famous experiment. In this experiment a buzzer is consistently pressed whenever food is presented to the dog. Initially, the sound of the buzzer on its own does not elicit any response from the dog. The sound of the buzzer is repeatedly associated with the presentation of food. Eventually, the dog begins to salivate as a result of the buzzer alone. We can see that the dog has been *conditioned* to respond to an entirely artificial stimulus – in other words, it has learned to salivate at the sound of a buzzer in addition to its natural tendency to salivate in response to food.

Pavlov introduced some terms to describe the processes which occur in this experiment. The *unconditioned stimulus* (UCS) is the natural stimulus which produces the natural reflex – in this case it is the food. The *unconditioned response* (UCR) is the natural reflex response – in this case the salivation which automatically follows the presentation of food. The *neutral* stimulus (NS) is the artificial stimulus prior to its pairing with the UCS – in this case the sound of the buzzer before the experiment. The *conditioned stimulus* (CS) is the sound of the buzzer after it has been paired with the UCS a number of times, and hence is associated with food. The *conditioned response* (CR) refers to the response which is eventually elicited to the CS – in this case the salivation which follows the sound of the buzzer. The conditioned response is behaviourally the same as the unconditioned response, but it is a weaker version of it.

Figure 1 Classical conditioning

Before conditioning

FOOD ⟶ SALIVATION
(unconditioned stimulus)   (unconditioned response)

BUZZER (neutral stimulus)   NO RESPONSE

During conditioning

BUZZER (neutral stimulus) +

FOOD (unconditioned stimulus) ⟶ SALIVATION
                                              (unconditioned response)

After conditioning

BUZZER ⟶ SALIVATION
(conditioned stimulus)   (conditioned response)

Pavlov realised that almost any stimulus could, as a result of conditioning, come to elicit a conditioned response.

Key terms

Natural reflex *Responses which occur naturally in response to stimuli.*

Classical conditioning *The process by which a natural reflex comes to be elicited by an artificial stimulus.*

Unconditioned stimulus *A natural stimulus which produces a natural reflex.*

Unconditioned response *The natural reflex response before it has been conditioned.*

Neutral stimulus *The artificial stimulus before it has been paired with the unconditioned stimulus.*

Conditioned stimulus *The artificial stimulus after it has been paired with a natural stimulus.*

Conditioned response *The response which is elicited by the conditioned stimulus.*

Timing

Experiments have shown that the success of classical conditioning depends very much on the exact timing of the NS and UCS. The most successful effects are found when the NS precedes the UCS and overlaps with it. This is known as *standard* or *forward pairing*. A strong conditioning also occurs when the NS precedes the UCS, but does not overlap with it.

The strength of the conditioning diminishes, however, the longer the interval between the NS and the UCS. In *simultaneous pairing*, where the NS and UCS are delivered at the same time, conditioning tends to be ineffective. This is because the NS is not being used in such a way that it predicts the UCS with which it is being associated. Finally in *backward pairing*, where the UCS precedes the NS, conditioning is again ineffective. This is because, under these conditions, the response does not depend on a relationship being established between the NS and the UCS.

Extinction and spontaneous recovery

As we have seen, one characteristic of natural reflexes is that they are usually permanent. The tendency to salivate when presented with food, or blink in the presence of a bright light, cannot easily be eliminated by a process of learning. Indeed, such natural reflexes would usually only be eliminated as a result of physical damage to the structures concerned or associated neurological damage.

Conditioned responses, on the other hand, are subject to elimination and indeed will usually be eliminated quite rapidly once the pairing of the CS and the UCS ceases. If, for example, a dog is trained to salivate upon the pressing of a buzzer, but the buzzer continues to be pressed without the subsequent presentation of food, the salivation soon diminishes down to nothing. The process by which the CR becomes decoupled from the CS in the absence of the UCS is known as *extinction*.

The process of extinction can be demonstrated experimentally. Once conditioning has been achieved, the experimenter continues to present the CS, but fails to follow it with the UCS. Initially, the animal will continue to display the CR as before, but by the tenth unpaired presentation of the CS, the response will be about half what it was, and by the twentieth unpaired presentation it will have diminished virtually to nothing.

One interesting feature of extinction is that it does not appear to function in the same way as forgetting, where the learned item tends to be lost altogether. Pavlov discovered that an extinct response can, under certain circumstances, return quite suddenly and intact. This is known as *spontaneous recovery*. For example, a CR can become extinct through repeated presentation of the CS. But, if the CS is presented next day the CR may briefly reappear.

It is also significant that once a conditioned response has been achieved and then extinguished, the participant can be re-conditioned much more quickly than initially. This suggests that extinction does not lead to the CR being lost, but rather what Pavlov described as *inhibited*. Some animal behaviourists have suggested that this could be an adaptive mechanism which serves to suppress conditioned responses until they are triggered by some event.

Generalisation and discrimination

Stimulus generalisation Pavlov also discovered a process which he termed *stimulus generalisation*. This occurs when a conditioned subject is presented with a stimulus which is similar, but not identical, to the original CS. For instance, if a dog has been conditioned to salivate to the sound of a particular buzzer, and then a different sounding buzzer is substituted, the dog will still salivate, albeit on a reduced scale. In fact, Pavlov found that as the replacement stimulus becomes more and more unlike to the original, the CS will correspondingly diminish. A very similar sounding buzzer will elicit almost as much saliva as the original, whilst very dissimilar sounding buzzers will elicit much less.

Figure 2 shows this effect. As the results of stimulus generalisation experiments are plotted on a graph, the effect is a bell-shaped curve.

Figure 2 Stimulus generalisation

-1 and +1 are similar to the CS. For example, they may be a buzzer of slightly lower pitch (-1) and a buzzer of slightly higher pitch (+1). As a result, they often produce the same response as the response to the CS. The more dissimilar the stimulus to the CS, the less likely it is to produce the same response (as shown by −5 and 5 on the graph).

The tendency of conditioned stimuli to be generalised to other similar stimuli may have important consequences, particularly in the field of human clinical psychology. For instance, individuals who have developed phobic responses to certain animals may display phobic reactions to similar animals.

In addition to the process of generalisation, Pavlov found that it is possible to condition participants to be extremely discriminating between stimuli. In other words, the natural tendency towards stimulus generalisation can be limited if appropriate discrimination training is carried out. The result is known as *stimulus discrimination*.

Stimulus discrimination In discrimination training, the paired presentations of the CS and the UCS are carried out in the normal way, but on occasion a stimulus similar to the CS is presented, but without the UCS. Thus in a variant of the classic Pavlovian experiment, a dog was conditioned to salivate in response to a black square (the CS). Occasionally, however, a grey square was presented to the dog, but without food (the UCS). Under these circumstances the dog learns to discriminate between the black and grey squares, and only salivates in response to the black square. Although the stimuli are rather similar, the fact that discrimination training has been undertaken means that the animal displays a heightened ability to discriminate between them. Pavlov found that animals were capable of making fine distinctions between stimuli when discrimination training was diligently carried out. However, he also noted that when they are trained to discriminate between

two very similar stimuli (for example, two buzzers of almost indistinguishable pitch) they can develop an experimental neurosis, which can result in failing to learn at all, or in serious cases the animal may show signs of extreme distress.

Higher or second order conditioning

Experiments have shown that it is possible for a second NS to become associated with the first, and then also to elicit the established CS. For instance, if a light is switched on immediately prior to the sounding of a buzzer in the classical Pavlovian salivation experiment, the animal will often learn to salivate in response to the light as well. It is significant, however, that salivation will usually be less than in response to the primary stimulus of the buzzer. This process is known as *higher* or *second order conditioning*.

The significance of classical conditioning in animal behaviour

Classical conditioning is important primarily because it describes and explains the ability of animals to learn certain responses to naturally occurring stimuli. It is tempting to regard classical conditioning as an example of the sort of Darwinian adaptation that was described earlier in this chapter.

An example of learned behaviour in animals is the development of taste aversions. If an animal has the ability to learn that certain foods are likely to produce illness, and hence avoid such foods in the future, then clearly they will be at a selective advantage above those who do not learn this. There is some experimental evidence to support the idea that animals learn taste aversions through classical conditioning. Research by Garcia et al. (1977) involved placing some toxin-laced mutton inside a sheep's hide and then feeding it to wolves and coyotes, who were subsequently ill as a result. After this trial, the animals were allowed to approach some live sheep, but instead of attacking as they normally would, they turned away. This experiment shows how animals can become conditioned to avoid food which makes them ill.

Whilst experiments like this appear to provide impressive evidence in support of the adaptive significance of classical conditioning, there are a number of reasons why we need to be cautious about exaggerating its role in animal behaviour.

First of all, it is important to note that whilst it may be useful for animals to be able to learn in this way, there may be many occasions when it will be more adaptive for the animal to display an instinctive response to a stimulus. For example, an animal who has to learn to flee when approached by a predator will clearly be at a disadvantage over one who does so instinctively. Indeed the result of not doing so may very well be fatal – hardly conducive to successful learning!

Secondly, it appears that some CS/CR relationships are easier to learn than others. In the case of taste aversion, for example, it appears that animals require only one pairing of the taste with the illness to develop a strong aversion. This is quite different from the findings of Pavlov's salivation experiments, where repeated pairings were required to achieve conditioning. In the same way, it seems that in taste aversion pairings the presence of delay between the NS and the UCS does not significantly affect learning. Again this runs counter to the findings of classical conditioning experiments. Finally, it appears that extinction occurs at a much slower rate in the case of taste aversion conditioning.

The possibility that some associations may be more difficult to learn than others, and the fact that this may vary between species, led Seligman (1970) to suggest the concept of *preparedness*. This suggests that animals are more prepared to learn associations which are relevant to their survival (and to their reproductive success) than those which are not. It also suggests that animals may be predisposed *not* to learn associations which may be harmful to their survival and reproductive success. The concept of preparedness therefore rather blurs the distinction which is sometimes made between learned and instinctual behaviour – we see that behaviour is the outcome of a complex interaction between the two.

Key terms

Extinction *The process by which the CR becomes decoupled from the CS in the absence of the UCS.*

Spontaneous recovery *The tendency for extinct responses to return intact quite suddenly.*

Stimulus generalisation *Conditioned responses elicited by stimuli which are similar to the CS.*

Stimulus discrimination *Individuals can learn to discriminate between quite similar stimuli.*

Higher or second order conditioning *The process where a second NS becomes attached to the first and then also elicits the CR.*

Taste aversions *Avoidance of foods with particular tastes – usually indicating that they are harmful.*

Preparedness *The idea that animals are more predisposed to learn associations relevant to their survival and their reproductive success.*

Activity 6 — Classical conditioning

Item A — Fear of sticks

Albert is an elderly man who has recently acquired a two-year-old dog called Rover from a dog rescue home. Albert uses a walking stick, but only when he goes out of the house. The dog is very affectionate to Albert when at home, but whenever he tries to take him out for a walk, the dog becomes very aggressive and on several occasions has bitten Albert. Albert's son, Bob (who does not use a walking stick) has taken Rover out many times without any sign of aggression. Before Rover entered the rescue home, he had regularly been beaten with a stick by his previous owner.

Questions

1 Using the concept of classical conditioning, explain why Rover behaves aggressively whenever Albert tries to take him out.

2 Would you expect Rover's response to being taken out by Albert to last indefinitely? Give reasons for your answer.

3 What advice would you give to Albert on how to eliminate Rover's aggressive behaviour?

2.2 Operant conditioning

The theory of conditioned learning was further developed in the highly influential work of B.F. Skinner and his important concept of *operant conditioning* (Skinner, 1938). Skinner's work was heavily influenced by the work of Edward Thorndike who, in 1898, described his *law of effect*. The law of effect states, in essence, that any behaviour which produces a positive effect in the organism – the solution of a problem, or a state of 'satisfaction', for example – will have a tendency to be retained and repeated on future occasions. The behaviour is then further reinforced by each successful outcome it elicits.

Reinforcement

Thorndike's law of effect was demonstrated in a number of experiments in which he gave animals problems to solve. Thorndike found that once an animal solved a problem – essentially by trial and error – it would then learn to repeat the successful behaviour. In his experiments, Thorndike constructed puzzle boxes in which cats had to operate a latch in order to open the door. Their reward for doing so was a piece of fish placed outside the box. Each time the cat was successful in opening the door, it was placed straight back in the box and the procedure repeated.

Initially the cats behaved in an entirely random way, and only by chance managed to operate the latch and escape. But each time they were returned to the puzzle box, they took less time to escape until eventually they were able to do it almost immediately. In fact, the initial attempt usually took around five minutes, whilst after 10-20 trials it only took around five seconds to escape. Thorndike reasoned, therefore, that it is the *effect* of the successful behaviour – in this case release from the box and a tasty piece of fish – that induces learning. For this reason Thorndike's discovery is called the law of effect.

B.F. Skinner and the 'analysis of behaviour'

In a refinement of Thorndike's experiments with puzzle boxes, B.F. Skinner made use of boxes called Skinner boxes. These were designed to allow controlled experiments on pigeons or rats. In the case of rats, the animal must press a lever to cause the release of a food pellet and in the case of pigeons, the bird must peck a coloured disc to release the food pellet.

According to Skinner's analysis, behaviour (or *operants*) is shaped by its consequences. The consequences of behaviour, for Skinner, fall into three categories: *positive reinforcers*, *negative reinforcers* and *punishers*.

Positive reinforcers involve the presentation of something pleasurable, such as a food pellet. They have the effect of strengthening the behaviours which elicited them. Thus, pigeons who are rewarded with a food pellet for pecking a coloured disc will show an increasing propensity to peck coloured discs.

Negative reinforcers involve the removal of something unpleasant as the result of the behaviour in question. For example, if a rat is given a mild electric shock which is not switched off until a lever is pressed, the rat will show an increasing propensity to press the lever when it is given a shock. In other words, behaviour which produces the removal of the unpleasant stimulus will be strengthened.

Punishers involve the presentation of something disagreeable in response to the behaviour in question. For example, pressing a lever in a Skinner box may result in an electric shock being administered to the animal. As a result, the behaviour in question (pressing the lever) will be weakened.

Behaviour that is not reinforced or punished is likely to become extinct.

Reinforcement and reinforcers

An important consequence of Skinner's reasoning is that whether or not something is a reinforcer or a punisher can only be decided retrospectively. In other words, it is entirely dependent on the response of the organism to the stimulus. Thus, if after several trials, a behaviour is strengthened by a particular consequence, we can say that the consequence in question was a *reinforcer*. This means that we cannot say in advance that something will be a positive or negative reinforcer or a punisher. This is particularly significant in the case of human beings, and can perhaps best be illustrated by the behaviour of children. Very often parents will intend to eliminate bad behaviour in a child by telling it off, for example. However, if the child feels that he or she is lacking attention from the parent, they may experience the telling off as a positive reinforcement – the parent is at last paying attention to them. Under these circumstances, the telling off could have exactly the opposite effect to the one intended: in short, it would encourage the very behaviour it intended to eliminate!

Primary and secondary reinforcers

So far we have concentrated on reinforcers or punishers which are intrinsically pleasurable or painful to the recipient. For example, food pellets act as reinforcers because food is intrinsically pleasurable. These are called *primary reinforcers*. It is also possible, however, for something to become a reinforcer (or punisher) by association with some primary reinforcer. For example, in Pavlov's classic experiment with salivating dogs, the sound of a buzzer can become a reinforcer because of its conditioned association with food. This is called a *secondary reinforcer*. It is not intrinsically pleasurable or painful, but has become so because of its association with a primary reinforcer.

Schedules of reinforcement

So far we have been discussing situations where reinforcement occurs continuously – that is, each time the behaviour in question occurs, it is reinforced. However, research has also been carried out to establish whether various kinds of *partial reinforcement* can also be effective in reinforcing behaviour. This is significant because in real life situations an instance of behaviour may well not lead to the same response on every occasion. Skinner discovered the following schedules of reinforcement:

Continuous reinforcement Every response is rewarded. For example, a pellet of food is released every time a rat presses the lever in a Skinner box.

Fixed interval schedule The first response after a given interval of time is rewarded. For example, rewards may be given at the end of every minute if, at some time during that minute, the response occurs. An example of this is workers who are paid at the end of every week or month.

Variable interval schedule On average the first response after a given interval of time is rewarded, but this time interval may vary.

Fixed ratio schedule Every nth response is rewarded. For example, a pellet of food is released every 10th time a rat presses the lever in a Skinner box.

Variable ratio schedule Every nth response is rewarded on average, but the actual gap between rewarded responses is quite large. For example, a gambler may win, on average, 25% of the games he plays in a year. However, these wins may all occur in a small space of time, followed by a long run of 'bad luck'.

At first sight it might appear that continuous reinforcement, where the reward always follows immediately from every response, would be the most effective way of maintaining conditioned behaviour. However this is not true. In fact Skinner found that maintaining conditioning is most effective with variable ratio schedules. Rats and pigeons in Skinner boxes seem to go on working harder for longer when their actions are rewarded in the most variable way. They will also go on pressing the lever for a long time after the stimulus has been withdrawn (that is, after food pellets have stopped being released). Another way of putting this is to say that extinction is more difficult the more variable and unpredictable the reinforcement has been. In the case of continuous reinforcement, however, the lever pressing stops soon after the reinforcement is withdrawn.

When applying operant conditioning to animal behaviour, the most effective strategy seems to be to establish new behaviours using continuous reinforcement, but then to switch to an irregular and unpredictable schedule of reinforcement such as a variable ratio schedule. This also perhaps explains why people who become compulsive gamblers will continue to gamble, even in the face of only infrequent and irregular wins.

Punishment and negative reinforcement

It is important to make a distinction between punishment and negative reinforcement. Punishment refers to the action of following a given response with an unpleasant or aversive effect. Negative reinforcement refers to a situation where an unpleasant effect is replaced with a more desirable one. For example, rats which have been given mild electric shocks can learn to press a lever which turns off the electricity supply. Pressing the lever effectively replaces an unpleasant effect (the electric shock) with a more pleasant one (the absence of the electric shock). Negative reinforcement is sometimes also known as *avoidance learning*.

Skinner believed that punishment was a much less effective means of changing behaviour than positive or, to a lesser extent, negative reinforcement. This is because punishment can only eliminate a behaviour, not replace it with a new one. However this belief has been challenged. Campbell and Church (1969), for example, argue that punishments can be more effective than reinforcers in changing animal behaviour. However, they also note that there can be serious side-effects of punishment such as anxiety, withdrawal and aggression. In conclusion it seems that punishers are most effective when combined with some kind of reinforcement. For example, if one piece of undesirable behaviour is punished, it will be eliminated most effectively when some other, more desirable, alternative behaviour is positively reinforced.

The role of operant conditioning in animal behaviour

There is no doubt that operant conditioning can be a highly effective way of causing behavioural change in animals. This has been shown experimentally in many species. For example, in one study Boycott managed to train octopuses to avoid crabs (Boycott, 1965). Crabs form a normal part of the octopus's diet, and so we might imagine they have an in-built incentive not to avoid them. However, Boycott showed that by pairing crabs with white squares, and then administering an electric shock to the octopus, they began to avoid crabs when they were paired with white squares and only to approach them when the square

was absent. Similarly, human beings have for many years trained animals to engage in unusual behaviour for entertainment purposes in circuses and zoos.

At the same time, we need to be aware of some of the limitations of operant conditioning as an explanation of learning in non-human animals.

Insight learning The famous Gestalt psychologist Wolfgang Kohler demonstrated that apes can learn by insight (Kohler, 1925). Insight learning is explained in detail in the next unit (see p618). In brief, Kohler demonstrated that apes were capable of finding solutions to problems without going through a process of reinforcement. In one case, Kohler placed an ape in a cage with a number of sticks, and placed a banana outside the cage, beyond the ape's reach. None of the sticks were long enough to reach the banana. Suddenly, Kohler observed the ape joining two of the sticks together to reach the banana. It seems as though the animal just 'saw' the solution to the problem.

Observational learning Albert Bandura (1977) has argued that much learning takes place as a result of observation. That is, the individual observes the success or failure of another individual carrying out a task and imitates their successes. Once again, learning can take place without the need for any reinforcement. Learning by imitation is discussed in the next unit (p617).

Equipotentiality and instinctive drift Basic to Skinner's position is the assumption that any behaviour can be taught using operant conditioning with equal ease. This assumption is known as *equipotentiality*. However, research has shown that some behaviours are in fact much more difficult to acquire than others. In one experiment, Breland and Breland (1961) attempted to train a pig to post a token into a piggy bank in return for a reward. Despite their efforts, the pig seemed unable to acquire this behaviour. Instead it would pick up the token, drop it, root it, pick it up again and drop it again. Breland and Breland argue that the pig was simply reverting to its instinctive behaviour. This suggests that strongly innate behaviour may be very difficult, if not impossible, to alter by operant conditioning. The tendency for behaviour to revert to an innate pattern is called *instinctive drift* by Breland and Breland.

Key terms

Operant conditioning *The process by which desired behaviours are encouraged by systematically rewarding them.*

Positive reinforcers *Desirable rewards which are used to encourage certain behaviours.*

Punishers *Unpleasant effects which are used to discourage undesired behaviours.*

Negative reinforcers *Effects which are used to discourage undesired behaviours and replace them with desired behaviours.*

Primary reinforcers *Effects which are used to reinforce behaviour because of their intrinsically pleasurable consequences.*

Secondary reinforcers *Effects which reinforce behaviour by virtue of their association with some primary reinforcer.*

Partial reinforcement *A situation where the relationship between stimulus and response is not reinforced every time.*

If we think about operant conditioning in terms of evolutionary theory, then the idea of instinctive drift seems quite plausible. It is clear that learning from experience would be of considerable benefit to an organism in some circumstances – in new or rapidly changing environments, for instance. In other cases, however, learning by experience could be very costly – for example, when a mistake results in death or serious injury. In predictable environments with predictable hazards, it would be much more efficient for organisms to possess in-built instinctive responses.

Activity 7   Operant conditioning

Item A   Training a dog

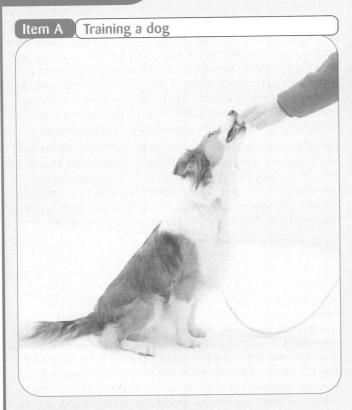

Item B   A feline vandal

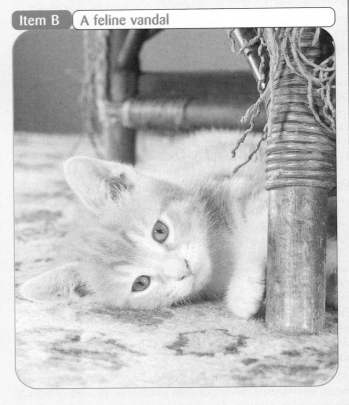

Questions

1   Look at Item A and answer the following questions:

   a) Describe how, using the principles of operant conditioning, you would train a dog to sit when told by a human being to do so.

   b) Would you expect training by this method to lead to permanent obedience in the dog?

   c) What actions do you think might make the dog permanently obedient?

2   Look at Item B and answer the following questions:

   a) Using the principles of operant conditioning, explain how you might advise the kitten's owner to eliminate its scratching behaviour. Identify the role played by punishers and negative reinforcers in your plan.

   b) Are there any difficulties with using an approach based on operant conditioning in a case like this?

Summary

1   Classical conditioning explains how organisms can acquire conditioned responses to stimuli.

2   Evidence suggests that animals are predisposed to acquire some conditioned responses more readily than others.

3   Operant conditioning describes how animals can acquire behaviour through reinforcement and punishment.

4   Schedules of reinforcement can influence the ease with which behaviours are acquired or extinguished.

5   The ease with which behaviours are acquired or extinguished seems to be influenced by evolutionary factors.

Unit 3 Social learning in non-human animals

KEY ISSUES

1 What is social learning?

2 Do nonhuman animals learn socially?

3 What is the nature and extent of intelligence in nonhuman animals?

3.1 The role of social learning in non-human animals

Social learning may be distinguished from other types of learning by the fact that it takes place in the presence of others. For learning to be genuinely social, however, it must occur as a consequence of inputs from the others in whose presence it takes place. Social learning necessarily presumes that animals are capable of memorising new forms of behaviour as a result of observation. It follows from this that we should expect social learning to be more common in social species with good memories. The two principal ways in which social learning in animals occurs are described as *imitation* and *tutoring*.

Imitation

As the name suggests *imitation* is essentially copying. One animal observes another engaging in some behaviour which leads to a benefit, and copies that behaviour. It is interesting that learning by imitation does not require that the learning animal experiences immediate or direct reinforcement of the behaviour in question. Indeed, there may be significant gaps between an animal observing the behaviour in question and actually engaging in it. An example of imitative learning was reported by Herbert and Harsh (1944). They found that cats who were allowed to observe another cat escaping from a puzzle box were themselves able to escape faster than if they had not first made such observations. Interestingly, they also found that the cats learned faster if they observed cats going through the trial and error process of learning how to escape from the puzzle box, than from observing cats already skilled at escaping.

Tutoring

Learning by imitation is essentially a passive process – neither animal takes an active role in teaching the other. In the case of *tutoring* however, as the name suggests, one animal takes the role of an active tutor in relation to the other. This is interesting because whilst in the case of imitation no particular costs are involved, here the tutoring animal must actively devote time and effort to teaching the other. It should come as no surprise, therefore, that this type of learning is most common between those animals who are genetically related to each other.

An example of tutoring is reported by Boesch (1991) who undertook a study of chimpanzees in the Tai National Park in Ivory Coast. Adult chimpanzees are adept at using tools to open nuts. A large rock is used as an anvil, nuts are placed on top of it, and smaller stones are then used to smash the nuts. Boesch found that mothers spend considerable amounts of time demonstrating this skill to their young, and then in correcting their behaviour when they do not perform the task in the right way.

Foraging

Foraging refers to behaviour directed at finding food. There is evidence to suggest that social learning can occur in relation to foraging behaviour. Research undertaken by Galef and Wigmore (1983) supports the view that rats may learn food preferences by imitating other rats. In their study, Galef and Wigmore placed rats in pairs and fed them their usual diets. They then removed one rat from each pair, put it in a separate cage and deprived it of food for 24 hours. These rats were then fed either cinnamon or cocoa flavoured food – but not both. The rats were then put back into the cages with their original companions and left for fifteen minutes. They were then removed again for a further 24 hours. The companion rats – who had only had fifteen minutes to interact with the cocoa or cinnamon fed rats – were then given the option of eating either cinnamon or cocoa flavoured food. The researchers found that these rats then displayed a clear preference for whatever food had been fed to their companion. This experiment would seem to demonstrate that one rat can learn its food preferences from another. When rats come into contact with each other, there is a significant amount of mouth to mouth contact, which probably explains how this kind of social learning is possible.

Another example of possibly learned foraging behaviour relates to the peculiarly British phenomenon of blue tits pecking open the tops of milk bottles left on doorsteps. This behaviour was originally found in isolated parts of Britain. It was first reported in Southampton in 1921, but by 1947 it had spread to most parts of the country. Since this spread was too fast be accounted for by genetic evolution, social learning would appear to be responsible.

However, there are some reservations about this conclusion. First, it is clear that the sort of pecking and tearing behaviour which the blue tits engage in is part of their normal repertoire of foraging behaviour. Blue tits can be routinely observed to peck and tear at the bark of trees. The behaviour may thus be an extension of the bird's instinctual repertoire. Secondly, as Hinde and Fisher (1951) point out, birds who come across open milk bottles would come to associate milk bottles with food. When confronted with an unopened bottle, therefore, they would be inclined to engage in their normal foraging behaviour of tearing and pecking. If this yielded food – which it would – then the behaviour would be reinforced by the process of operant conditioning. Social learning need not play a part at all.

Key terms

Social learning *Any process by which one individual learns from another.*

Imitation *Learning which results from one individual observing and copying the behaviour of another.*

Tutoring *Learning which results from one individual actively demonstrating behaviour to another.*

Activity 8   Social learning in nonhuman animals

Item A   Taking the cream

Item B   Cracking a nut

Questions

1   The behaviour depicted in Item A is often thought to be the result of social learning. However, some researchers have said it might be an example of operant conditioning. How could this debate be settled?

2   Chimpanzees sometimes demonstrate the use of tools to their young. Item B shows two rocks being used as a hammer and an anvil to crack a nut. Devise an experiment to test the hypothesis that this behaviour is an example of social learning.

3.2   Intelligence in nonhuman animals

Whilst there are a number of controversies surrounding the whole concept of intelligence, there is broad agreement that intelligence refers to more than the ability simply to learn by association (classical and operant conditioning). The possession of intelligence is indicated, amongst other things, by the ability to solve complex problems and to acquire and use language. We now turn to a consideration of evidence for intelligence in nonhuman animals.

Insight learning

We have all experienced *insight learning* at some stage. We may have wrestled with a problem for hours, and then all of a sudden, just as we are about to give up, the answer comes upon us in a flash. Some studies would suggest that something similar happens in some animals.

Wolfgang Kohler (1925) conducted a classic series of observations of a captive chimpanzee called Sultan. He placed some bananas in the chimpanzee's cage, but out of his reach. Also in the cage were various objects which could be used to reach the bananas, but none would achieve that result on their own. Kohler found that Sultan made creative use of the tools at his disposal to reach the bananas, such as placing a box under them, standing on it and using a stick to dislodge the fruit. In another experiment, the bananas were placed outside Sultan's cage and he was given two bamboo sticks with which to retrieve them. However, each stick was too short in itself to reach the fruit. The solution? Sultan connected the bamboo sticks together and used the extended stick to retrieve the fruit. When the sticks came apart during the operation, he immediately re-connected them, apparently demonstrating an

awareness that he would not succeed unless he did so. Kohler's point was that this learning was not occurring as a result of trial and error, but as the result of insights into the complex problem with which the animal was faced.

What is less often reported about Kohler's observations, however, was the fact that when Sultan failed to join the two sticks together he was helped to do so by the experimenter. It is also true that Sultan made many 'bad errors', in Kohler's words, such as pushing one stick so far out of the cage that he could not retrieve it. Whether there was insight learning or not, it is at least apparent that the chimpanzee did not display anything like the creativity and insight of a human being faced with similar tasks.

Studies of insight learning in animals are open to a number of methodological criticisms. Insight, by definition, is not open to direct observation. With human beings the problem can be reduced to some extent by the fact that people can give accounts of the experience of having an insight – whether this is Albert Einstein suddenly seeing the truth of the theory of relativity, or a motorist suddenly realising that the reason his car will not start is its lack of petrol. Animals, by contrast, cannot give accounts of any insights they may have and so any conclusion that they have experienced an insight is inevitably based, to some extent, on speculation.

Self-recognition

When babies, or adults who have become sighted in later life, are shown their reflections in a mirror, they respond as though they were looking at a stranger. After a period of self-observation, however, they come to realise that they are seeing a reflection of themselves. The same appears to be true of primates such as chimpanzees and gorillas. In one study,

Gallup (1970) presented chimpanzees with the opportunity to look at themselves in mirrors. Initially, they responded to their reflections with some hostility, as though they were looking at another chimp. Gradually, the chimps became less hostile and began to explore parts of their bodies – especially the anal and genital regions – with the mirrors. The animals were later anaesthetised and some coloured dye was painted onto one of their eyebrows. Once they had come round from the anaesthetic, none showed any interest in the dyed region, until they were again shown their reflections in the mirror. Each of the chimps then started to touch the dyed region with greater frequency than before. This would seem to suggest not only that they were aware of their own appearance in the mirror, but that they had retained an image of their appearance prior to the application of the dye.

Whilst this evidence does suggest some capacity for self-recognition in primates, other researchers have cast some doubt on the validity of Gallup's findings. For one thing, some studies have failed to replicate Gallup's findings. Other researchers (Heyes, 1998) have pointed out that since cognitive ability is impaired in the aftermath of anaesthesia, the behaviour of the chimps at this time cannot be taken to be representative.

Theory of mind

It is often said that human beings possess a *theory of mind*. This means that we are capable of grasping the ideas, perceptions, knowledge, desires and intentions of others. This capacity is of fundamental importance in understanding the nature of human social relations and communication. But can we say that animals possess such a theory of mind?

Animal psychologists have approached this question from two directions. First, they have asked whether animals can correctly attribute knowledge to others. That is, can an animal correctly identify whether another individual possesses some piece of knowledge? Second, they have asked whether animals can employ deception to change the beliefs of another individual to their advantage.

Attribution of knowledge Povinelli et al. (1990) devised an experiment to test whether chimpanzees are able to make accurate judgements about the knowledge possessed by human beings. In this experiment, the chimpanzee is presented with four upturned cups, one of which conceals a piece of food. The only evidence the chimps have as to which cup conceals the food is from two human trainers who point to the cups. One trainer (the knowledgeable one) always sets up the experiment – and hence can be assumed to know which cup conceals the food – whilst the other is always out of the room at this stage. The knowledgeable trainer always points to the correct cup, whilst the other trainer always points to the wrong one. After several hundred trials, the chimpanzees demonstrate a significant preference for the cup indicated by the knowledgeable trainer. But does this demonstrate that chimpanzees possess a theory of mind?

It is always possible that this result could be explained by operant conditioning – the chimpanzee's choice of following the knowledgeable trainer is reinforced by the success of this behaviour. To discount this possibility Povinelli et al. conducted a further experiment using the same animals. In this experiment, a third trainer was introduced such that one trainer placed the food under the cups (again screened from the chimpanzees),

one watched and the third wore a bucket on his head. The chimpanzees tended again to choose the knowledgeable trainer – the one without a bucket on his head, who could hence have known the correct answer – which lends some support to the idea that they possess a theory of mind.

However, caution should be exercised in reaching this conclusion. Even the results of this modified design could still be explained by the development of a simple association between a particular individual (ie the knowledgeable trainer) and a positive outcome. Furthermore, it is important to emphasise that there can be no direct observation of the attribution of knowledge by a chimpanzee. Such a capacity could only be demonstrated definitively if the subject in question were able to give a report of their own experience. Obviously this is not something a chimpanzee can do.

Deception The second approach to this issue relates to the possibility that some animals can actively deceive others. It is argued that such an ability might entail a theory of mind, since it would involve the selective presentation of false information to some other individuals. An experiment to investigate deception was carried out on chimpanzees by Woodruff and Premack (1979). In this study, chimpanzees were allowed to observe a trainer hiding food under one of two containers. A second trainer then entered the room. If the chimpanzee pointed to the correct container, one of the trainers gave it the food (the cooperative trainer), the other trainer kept the food for himself (the competitive trainer). Several of the chimpanzees studied demonstrated the ability, after some time, to discriminate between the cooperative and competitive trainer. When this happened, the chimpanzees showed a tendency to direct the competitive trainer to the 'wrong' container – the container without food – and the cooperative trainer to the 'right' container – the container with food.

Whilst these findings are certainly interesting, it does not necessarily follow that the chimpanzees possess a theory of mind. As with the examples given earlier, it may be equally possible to explain these findings in terms of operant conditioning.

Conclusion

This unit has shown that there is evidence for social learning in nonhuman animals, although the exact nature and extent of this remains uncertain. It does seem, however, that whatever the merits of classical and operant conditioning in accounting for learning in nonhuman animals, these theories do not tell the whole story.

The issue of intelligence in nonhuman animals remains controversial. This seems to result partly from the difficulty in defining precisely what is meant by 'intelligence' and partly from the difficulties in demonstrating the possession of

Key terms

Insight learning *The ability to 'see' the solution to a problem without trial and error or observation.*

Self-recognition *The ability to recognise oneself.*

Theory of mind *The ability to grasp the point of view of others.*

intelligence directly. All we can say is that whilst there are some grounds for believing that nonhuman animals possess intelligence, the research evidence for self-recognition, insight learning and the possession of a theory of mind in animals remains inconclusive.

Summary

1 There is some evidence that some species of nonhuman animals learn socially.

2 Social learning seems to be evident in foraging behaviour in a number of species.

3 Research evidence for self-recognition, insight learning and the possession of a theory of mind in nonhuman animals remains inconclusive.

References

Badcock, C. (1986). *The problem of altruism.* Oxford: Blackwell.

Badcock, C. (1991). *Evolution and individual behavior.* Cambridge, MA: Blackwell.

Bandura, A. (1977). *Social learning theory* (2nd ed.). Englewood Cliffs: Prentice-Hall.

Breland, K. & Breland, M. (1961). The misbehavior of organisms. *American Psychologist, 61,* 681-684.

Boesch, C. (1991). Teaching among wild chimpanzees. *Animal behavior, 41A,* 530-532.

Boycott, B.B. (1965). Learning in the octopus. *Scientific American, 212,* 42-50.

Campbell, B.A. & Church, R.M. (Eds.) (1969). *Punishment and aversive behavior.* New York: Appleton-Century-Crofts.

Darwin. C. (1859). *The origin of species by means of natural selection.* London: John Murray.

Darwin, C. (1871). *The descent of man.* London: John Murray.

Dawkins, R. (1976). *The selfish gene.* Oxford: Oxford University Press.

Galef, B.G. & Wigmore, S.W. (1983). Transfer of information concerning distant foods: A laboratory investigation of the 'information centre' hypothesis. *Animal Behavior, 31,* 748-758.

Gallup, G.G. (1970). *Chimpanzees: Self-recognition.* Science, 167, 86-87.

Garcia, J., Rusiniak, K.W. & Brett, L.P. (1977). Conditioning food-illness in wild animals: Caveant canonici. In H. Davis & H.M.B. Hurwitz (Eds.), *Operant-Pavlovian interactions.* Hillsdale: Lawrence Erlbaum Associates.

Hamilton, W.D. (1964). The genetic evolution of social behaviour, I, II. *Journal of Theoretical Biology, 7,* 1-52.

Herbert, M.J. & Harsh, C.M. (1944). Observational learning by cats. *Journal of Comparative Psychology, 37,* 81-95.

Heyes, C.M. (1998). The theory of mind in nonhuman primates. *Behavioral and Brain Sciences, 21* (1), 103-134.

Hinde, R.A. & Fisher, J. (1951). Further observations on the opening of milk bottles by birds. *British Birds, 44,* 392-396.

Holmes, W.G. & Sherman, P.W. (1982). The ontogeny of kin recognition in two species of ground squirrels. *Animal Behavior, 34,* 38-47.

Hrdy, S.B. (1977). Infanticide as a primate reproductive strategy. *American Scientist, 60,* 40-49.

Kohler, W. (1925). *The mentality of apes.* New York: Harcourt Brace Jovanovich.

Pavlov, I.P. (1927). *Conditioned reflexes.* Oxford: Oxford University Press.

Povinelli, D.J., Nelson, K.E. & Boyson, S.T. (1990). Inferences about guessing and knowing by chimpanzees (Pan troglodytes). *Journal of Comparative Psychology, 104,* 203-210.

Saglins, M. (1977). *The use and abuse of biology.* London: Tavistock.

Seligman, M.E.P. (1970). On the generality of the laws of learning. *Psychological Review, 77,* 406-418.

Sherman, P.W. (1981). Kinship, demography and Belding's ground squirrel nepotism. *Behavioural Ecology and Sociobiology, 8,* 251-259.

Skinner, B.F. (1938). *The behavior of organisms.* New York: Appleton-Century Crofts.

Thorndike, E.L. (1898). Animal intelligence: An experimental study of the associative processes in animals. *Psychological Review Monograph Supplement, 2* (Whole No. 8).

Trivers, R. (1971). The evolution of reciprocal altruism. *Quarterly Review of Biology, 46,* 35-57.

Trivers, R. (1985). *Social evolution.* Menlo Park: Benjamin Cummings.

Wilkinson, G.S. (1984). Reciprocal food sharing in the vampire bat. *Nature, 308,* 181-184.

Woodruff, G. & Premack, G. (1979). Intentional communication in the chimpanzee: The development of deception. *Cognition, 7,* 333-362.

32 Animal cognition

▶ Introduction

This chapter considers several features of animal cognition – how animals receive, process and communicate information. Unit 1 looks at animal navigation and considers research studies of homing behaviour and migration. Unit 2 moves on to examine animal communication and language. It looks at the range of signalling systems employed by non-human animals and explores research studies which have investigated natural language in animals and attempts to teach language to non-human animals. Unit 3 considers memory in non-human animals. It outlines explanations and research studies of memory in non-human animals, and the role of memory in navigation and foraging behaviour.

Chapter summary

- **Unit 1 looks at ways in which animals navigate.**
- **Unit 2 examines ways in which animals communicate.**
- **Unit 3 discussess research on memory in non-human animals.**

Unit 1 Animal navigation

KEY ISSUES

1 **What are the principal mechanisms which are responsible for animal navigation?**
2 **What are the explanations of migration and homing behaviour?**

1.1 Navigation

Many non-human species display impressive navigational skills. These skills underlie both *homing* behaviour – the ability to return to a place of origin – and migration – that is, long distance travel between two locations. Perhaps the simplest form of navigation involves leaving a trail. This method is employed, for example, by the loris (a kind of lemur), which engages in 'urine washing'. This involves the males urinating on their hands and then rubbing this urine into their feet. A scent trail is then left wherever the loris goes, and this enables it to find its way back to its place of origin.

In order to navigate successfully, whether for humans or non-humans, two types of information are required. The first is a knowledge of *where to go*. Human beings would normally use a map to obtain this knowledge. However, this knowledge is of little use without the second kind of information – that is, *how to get there*. Navigation involving both of these elements is known as *true navigation*. Someone with a map, who knows where they need to get to, also needs to know both where they are and in which direction they must travel in order to reach their destination. Human beings can discover their location in a number of ways. Most simply, they can use a landmark. Today, however, modern technology has provided a number of means – from radio direction beacons to global positioning systems (GPS) – which enable us to determine our location. Similarly, modern technology has given us a range of methods to determine in

which direction we must travel to reach our destination – from the simple magnetic compass to the advanced inertial navigation systems used in modern aircraft.

This unit considers the evolved mechanisms by which non-human species are able to discover both where they need to go and how to get there. It begins with a consideration of navigation based on a knowledge of *location*, and by a knowledge of *direction*.

1.2 Navigation by location – piloting

Probably the most straightforward form of navigation involves using physical cues to determine location. The use of various kinds of *landmark* in navigation is called *piloting*. Species vary in the senses which they employ in navigation by piloting. Some use visual cues. Features of the environment are committed to memory, and this allows the animal to locate such things as nests and sources of food in the future. Other species use smell. Salmon, for example, have very well developed olfactory systems which permit them to return to their place of origin on the basis of smell. It is important to note, however, that piloting, either by visual or olfactory cues, is a system based upon memory of previous experience. It does not, therefore, account for an individual's initial migration for which there is no previous experience.

Piloting by visual cues

The ability of certain species to pilot by visual cues has long been accepted by psychologists. A classic experiment carried out by Tinbergen and Kruyt (1938) demonstrated this ability in the digger wasp. Digger wasps leave their burrows in order to forage for food. Tinbergen and Kruyt manipulated the appearance of their burrows by placing a series of pine cones (landmarks) to mark the entrance. After a while, the experimenters moved the cones to a new location. When the foraging wasps returned, they returned not to the true location of their burrow, but to the new location marked by the pine cones. This experiment demonstrated that the wasps employ visual cues to locate their burrows.

Similar effects have been demonstrated in bees. Cartwright and Collet (1983) demonstrated that bees could be trained to find a sucrose (sugar) solution on the basis of visual cues. The solution was always placed a fixed distance and compass bearing from a large cylinder. The researchers found that once the bees had learned to respond to this physical cue, they persistently searched for food in the same place relative to the cylinder. This effect was found whether or not food was actually present, thus demonstrating that it was the physical cue of the cylinder which was responsible for their behaviour.

In other species the evidence is less conclusive. Whilst there may be some evidence that homing pigeons navigate with reference to visual cues, experiments suggest that this is not the complete story. In one experiment, homing pigeons were fitted with lenses which prevented them from seeing landmarks, and then released some eighty miles from their home. In spite of the fact that they could not use visual cues, most either found their way home or at least flew in the correct direction. Explanations for the absence of visual cues in pigeon navigation are discussed later in this unit.

Piloting by olfactory cues or smell

There is evidence that some species navigate by using smell. One of the most studied examples of this is the salmon. Salmon are migratory creatures. This means that, after hatching in a river, they swim downstream to the sea and can travel many thousands of miles away from their place of origin. However, some years later, when the time comes for the salmon to spawn, it returns to the river where it was itself hatched. How does the salmon achieve this extraordinary feat of navigation? The answer appears to be that it does so by smell. One study demonstrated that if the returning salmon's nostrils are blocked, it cannot find its way back to its river of origin (Hasler & Larsen, 1955). Exactly which smell cues the salmon is responding to is not completely understood. One possibility is that they *imprint* on the smells of the river from where they come. This means that, at an early stage of their development, they are receptive to acquiring a sensitivity and attraction towards these particular smells which stay with them as they mature. Another possibility is that they imprint on the *pheromones* – chemical substances

Female salmon returning to spawning grounds in Scotland

secreted and released by their own kin and other members of their population. In all probability, salmon use a combination of both kinds of cue.

In other species, the role played by smell in navigation is less conclusive. Papi (1982) argued that smell is used by homing pigeons, and cites evidence that if their nostrils are blocked, or if their olfactory nerve is cut, they fail to locate their homes as successfully as usual. However, other studies have failed to replicate these findings, and it has been suggested that the discomfort caused by blocking their nostrils or cutting the olfactory nerve may be responsible for the disruption in homing ability (Eysenck, 2000).

Key terms

Piloting *The use of landmarks in navigation.*

Imprinting *The process by which young individuals acquire some behaviour. In the case of navigation by smell, the process by which young acquire a sensitivity to the smell of their environment.*

1.3 Navigation by direction

So far we have considered navigation systems which rely on various kinds of landmark – those which can be seen and those which can be smelt. Such systems rely on memory. We turn now to a consideration of navigation systems which rely on a knowledge of *direction*.

Sun compass

Many experiments have been conducted which seem to demonstrate that pigeons and other birds can navigate by the sun. In one such study, Kramer (1952) trained pigeons to find food by the direction of the sun. He then experimentally altered the apparent position of the sun using a system of mirrors. When he did this, the direction in which the birds travelled changed accordingly.

The ability to navigate by the sun presupposes a sense of time. This is because the position of the sun changes at different times of the day, and so to navigate successfully the bird must compensate for the sun's movement across the sky. Birds – and indeed other animals – are often said to possess an *internal body clock*. This equips the bird with an innate sense of time. Experiments have shown that the internal body clock of birds is regulated by light and dark. In one experiment Schmidt-Koenig (1961) kept a group of pigeons in artificial light conditions, so that their body clocks were altered. When he released the birds into normal daylight, he found that they behaved according to their altered body clock. For example, a bird released at noon, but whose body clock has been altered so that it 'believes' it to be 6am, would fly at an angle of approximately 90° to its normal course. Experiments such as this one suggest that navigation by the sun depends on the bird's ability to make quite elaborate calculations in relation to time and direction.

Whilst the evidence for navigation by the sun is impressive, there is evidence to suggest that pigeons do not rely solely on this method. As pointed out by Keeton (1969), for example, pigeons are still able to find their way home on dull and overcast days when the sun is not visible. Keeton did find, however, that in comparisons between time-clock altered pigeons and normal ones, there was only a significant difference between the two on sunny days. On overcast days, the two sets of pigeons performed equally well. This suggests that there is another method of navigation used by pigeons which is not dependent on the sun.

Magnetic navigation

The earth is like a big magnet. Magnetic force lines originate at each pole, encircle the earth, and return to the opposite pole. Force lines leave each pole at a very steep angle. This angle declines as the line moves towards the equator, where it is horizontal, and becomes gradually steeper again as the line moves towards the other pole. An animal able to detect these variations in angle could, theoretically, use magnetic force as a cue to find its direction.

Experiments have shown that some birds do indeed seem to navigate in this way. Keeton (1969) glued magnets to the heads of a number of pigeons, and released them from several locations with which they were not familiar. The magnets prevented the pigeons from detecting the earth's magnetic field. Keeton found that on overcast days, when they could not navigate by the sun, the magnetised birds were unable to find their way home. Their ability to navigate on sunny days was unimpaired. Without the disruption of magnets, pigeons can find their way home in overcast conditions. This suggests that they use both the earth's magnetic field and the sun to navigate. The importance of magnetic navigation is reinforced by observations by Gould (1982) that pigeons become disoriented in magnetic storms. Similarly, Walcott and Brown (1989) have shown that the navigational abilities of pigeons are impaired in areas of magnetic anomaly (where the magnetic field has abnormal features) such as Jersey Hill in New York.

The physiological basis of the ability to navigate by magnetic compass has also been investigated. Beason (1989) conducted research on the bobolink – a North American migratory bird known to navigate by magnetism. In dissections of these birds, Beason found that a compound called magnetite – a naturally

Activity 1   Navigation by the sun

Item A   Altering time clocks

In an experiment the 'time clocks' of homing pigeons were altered by keeping them in artificial light conditions. The pigeons were kept in conditions which created the impression that the time was in fact six hours later than it was. Under normal circumstances the pigeons flew homewards in an easterly direction as illustrated in the following diagram.

Position of sun in time-altered conditions – that is, 6 hours later.

A pigeon about to land

Item B   A comparison

In another experiment, Keeton (1969) compared the performance of time-clock altered pigeons with those who had not been time-clock altered. He found that, on sunny days, the time-clock altered pigeons could not find their way home, whilst on overcast days the two sets of pigeons performed equally well.

Questions

1   Look at Item A and estimate the number of degrees to their normal course at which the time-altered pigeons flew. Remember that in a 24 hour period the position of the sun alters by 360 degrees.

2   Imagine that the pigeons described in Item A had been time-clock altered by 12 hours. At how many degrees to their normal direction would you then expect them to fly?

3   What does the experiment described in Item B tell you about the methods used by pigeons to navigate?

occurring magnetic substance – was present in their heads. Although this does not conclusively prove that they do indeed navigate by magnetism, it does strongly suggest that this is the case.

Navigation by the stars

Just as there is evidence that some birds navigate by the sun compass, so others appear to make use of the stars. This effect was first identified in research by Sauer and Sauer (1955), who conducted a study of the garden warbler. The garden warbler is a migratory songbird which breeds during the summer in Europe, but migrates to Africa during the winter. When these birds are caged during the migration season, they become restless. Sauer and Sauer demonstrated that when caged warblers are able to see either the night sky or a planetarium, their restless movement becomes directional – that is, instead of moving about arbitrarily, they move towards the direction of their usual migratory destination.

The role of the stars in navigation was demonstrated again in research by Belrose (1958). Belrose released mallards on both clear and overcast nights and made comparisons of their flight paths. He found that whilst the birds all flew in the same direction on clear nights, their flight on overcast nights was disoriented.

Research has also been conducted in order to determine whether the ability to navigate by the stars is learned or innate. One such study, conducted by Emlen (1972), focused on the indigo bunting. The study followed a group of birds reared in a planetarium, where instead of rotating around the north star (Polaris), the stars were made to rotate around another star of the Orion constellation known as Betelgeuse. When the birds were released, they were found to fly in the opposite direction to the one expected. This appears to show that the ability to navigate by the stars is learned and not innate.

It is important to note that whilst these effects have been found in a number of species, there are many species of birds – such as swans – which do not appear to have the ability to navigate in this way.

Key terms

Sun compass *Navigation by the sun's position in the sky.*
Magnetic navigation *Navigation by the earth's magnetic field.*

1.4   Migration

Migration is the mass movement of members of a species from one place to another. Migration can be triggered by a number of things, and these vary between species. In some cases it is triggered by seasonal variations in such things as air temperature, length of days and changes in the weather. In others, it is triggered by environmental factors such as food scarcity.

Migratory species also vary considerably in the distances which they cover. Some species travel many thousands of miles each year – such as the albatross or the salmon – whilst others travel shorter distances – wildebeest, for example, which cross the African plains in search of food and water.

Wildebeest migration, Kenya

Why migrate?

At first sight, migration appears to be a rather costly business. Travel over what can be very long distances clearly involves the expenditure of considerable amounts of energy. Migration can be a hazardous business too. Fisher reports that during only one night in Illinois, 3200 migrating birds died as a result of flying into just seven separate towers (Fisher, 1979).

However, the very fact that so many species seem to have evolved a drive to migrate suggests that the benefits must have outweighed the costs in evolutionary history. The benefits of migration are many. For some species, new locations provide food, water or a new source of mates. For others, they may provide safer weather conditions or an environment free of predators. In general, there are advantages to both locations inhabited by migratory species – one may provide a good source of food, but only be warm enough in the summer. The other may provide a less adequate source of food, but be sufficiently warm to permit survival in winter.

Migration by flight

Migration can be observed in many species of birds. In general, birds migrate in order to spend winter in a warmer climate. Birds often migrate in stages – that is, make a series of short journeys, stopping frequently for food and water. However, some birds – especially those which migrate across oceans – can remain aloft for up to 24 hours at a time. Some birds are known as *soarers*, because they make use of air thermals, much like glider pilots. Storks, for example, fly in this way, utilising the lift generated by warm air rising to aid their flight. Interestingly, storks are usually reluctant to fly across water when they cannot see land on the other side. This may be connected with the fact that thermals are mainly generated over land masses which have been warmed by the sun, and so are unlikely to be found above large expanses of water.

Research suggests that there may be both genetic and learned components in the migratory patterns of birds. In some long-lived species, the pattern is for younger birds to follow the

Geese migrating at night

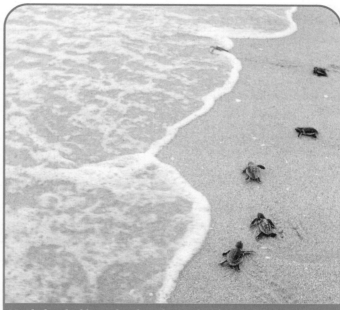

Newly-hatched loggerhead turtles in Florida crawl down to the sea

adults when migrating. However, in others, the drive to migrate and the knowledge of where to migrate to seems to be the product both of genes and experience.

In one study, Perdeck (1958) took a group of mature starlings and a group of newly hatched starlings from their base in Holland to a new location in Switzerland. Whilst the adult birds experienced no difficulty in migrating to their usual location, the young starlings followed a route which was relative to their original hatching location. Therefore, although they did not reach their anticipated destination, they would have done so had they been released from their original location and flown the same distance in the same direction. This demonstrates that whilst adult birds seem to rely on a combination of innate and learned information, the immature birds must rely solely on innate cues.

The role of genes in migratory routes was further investigated by Helbig (1991). Helbig studied two populations of black cap, each of which displayed a different migratory route – one to the south-west and the other to the south-east. Birds from each population were then cross-bred, with the effect that their offspring flew in a direction between that flown by their two parents. This strongly suggests that, for this species anyway, genes play an important part in the direction of migration.

There also appears to be a genetic component in the drive to migrate itself. Biebach (1983) studied a population of robins which had been reared by hand. Within this population, 80% of the birds were migratory whilst the remaining 20% were not. The robins were then cross-bred in the following combinations: migrant/migrant, migrant/non-migrant and non-migrant/non-migrant. The offspring of the migrant/migrant pair were 90% migrants, whilst for the other two pairings, the figure was only 53%. These results suggest that there is a strong genetic component to the drive to migrate, although the less than perfect results suggest that the genetics are complex, and perhaps require environmental interactions to be expressed.

Migration by water

Many aquatic species also migrate. As with birds, aquatic migration can be over many thousands of miles. Underwater

navigation differs from aerial navigation in a number of ways. First of all, migrating birds rely heavily on winds and air currents for their movement. These are obviously absent in the sea. However, aquatic creatures do make use of sea currents as a source of energy for their movement. One example of this is the loggerhead turtle. Female loggerhead turtles lay their eggs on the Florida coast. Once they have hatched, the young turtles enter the Gulf Stream which carries them to the Sargasso Sea – part of the western Atlantic Ocean. The turtles then spend several years there, before returning to their original hatching grounds on the Florida coast.

Another way in which aquatic navigation differs from aerial navigation is in the availability of cues which can be used as an aid to navigation. Navigation by the stars and the sun is inevitably more difficult for creatures which live underwater. Nevertheless, there is evidence that some aquatic creatures do navigate by star and moon light. Captive loggerhead turtles, for example, tend to swim towards light sources. Many aquatic creatures have comparatively poor eyesight, however, which suggests that they do not rely predominantly on visual navigation.

We do know, however, that for many aquatic creatures, smell plays an important part in their migration. The example of the salmon was discussed earlier in this unit. There is considerable evidence that salmon imprint on the smells of their original hatching ground. In one study, two streams flowing into Lake Michigan were artificially scented (Grier & Burk, 1992). Salmon emerging from each stream were then tracked. It was found that in 90% of the cases which were successfully tracked, the salmon returned to the stream from which they initially emerged. This seems to confirm that smell is strongly implicated in the ability of salmon to return to their spawning grounds.

Key term

Migration *Mass movements of members of one species from one place to another.*

Summary

1. Navigation requires a knowledge both of where to go and how to get there.

2. The simplest form of navigation is piloting – using landmarks to determine location.

3. The main methods of piloting rely on sight and smell.

4. The main methods of navigation by direction are by the sun compass, the earth's magnetic force and the stars.

5. Many species migrate – that is, travel from one place to another, often on a seasonal basis – in order to find food, water, mates or a more hospitable climate.

6. Although there are some similarities between aerial and aquatic migration, there are also some important differences.

Unit 2   Animal communication and language

KEY ISSUES

1. **What are the main systems of animal communication?**

2. **Can non-human animals use language?**

2.1   Communication in non-human animals

Before moving on to consider the various systems of communication used by non-human species, it is important to define what is meant by communication. Communication is a two-way process in which *signals* are sent to *receivers*, and receivers exhibit some change as a result. Begging behaviour in the chicks of herring gulls illustrates this. Tinbergen and Perdeck (1950) observed that the chicks signal their desire for food to their parent by pecking a red spot on the parent's bill. In response to this, the parent gives the chick some food. It is this response by the parent bird that demonstrates that communication has taken place.

Considered from an evolutionary point of view, communication systems ought to bestow some adaptive advantage on those who have evolved them. After all, it is difficult to see how such specialised adaptations could come about unless they carried some significant evolutionary advantage. That does not mean, however, that all examples of signalling (either in humans or non-human animals) are

adaptive. Eavesdropping provides an example of non-adaptive signalling.

Eavesdropping Eavesdropping is said to occur when an individual signals to another, but the message is received by a third, unintended, recipient. One of the most obvious examples of eavesdropping occurs when an individual signals danger to other members of the same species (usually kin) and this signal is heard by a predator who uses it to locate and eat the signalling individual.

Deceitful signalling Some signals are designed to deceive. Deceitful signalling is where an individual sends a signal which contains some element of false information in order to gain some advantage. For example, larger and stronger male cricket frogs have lower toned calls than smaller and weaker ones. There is evidence that male cricket frogs lower the tones of their calls when in the presence of male competitors in order to advertise themselves as stronger than in fact they are (Wagner, 1992).

Visual communication

One of the easiest forms of non-human communication to study is visual communication. It is easy to study precisely because it is visual and can therefore be observed. Many examples of visual communication have been documented.

Visual communication is very often involved in courtship behaviour. Many species engage in elaborate visual displays as part of courtship. An example of this is the stickleback. Like many species of fish, the stickleback practises external fertilisation – that is, the female must lay her eggs in a nest where they are then inseminated by the male. When a male stickleback approaches a 'pregnant' female (that is, one carrying unfertilised eggs) he engages in a bizarre form of zig-zagging dance. This dance can, if carried out with sufficient skill, induce the female to lay her eggs in the male's nest, and hence give him the opportunity to fertilise them. In cases where the female remains unimpressed with the male's dance, however, the whole ritual can come to a sudden end and the female leaves the scene (Tinbergen, 1951).

Visual communication is also frequently used as a cue for aggression. Robins, for example, will attack a few red feathers nailed to a post in their territory, and yet will completely ignore an entire stuffed robin which has had its red feathers painted brown (Lack, 1943).

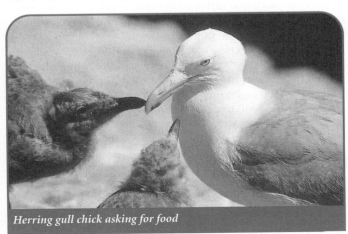
Herring gull chick asking for food

Many examples of visual communication are the product of *ritualisation*. Ritualisation refers to evolved patterns of behaviour which have become stereotypical and exaggerated, and which signify some meaning to the participants involved. A dog, for example, which is behaving aggressively will stand erect, whilst a fearful dog will crouch down. In the case of a crouching dog, for example, the animal is able to indicate submission to the aggressive animal without having to engage in costly and dangerous fighting. Similarly, ritualisation can occur in courtship – an example being the zig-zagging dance of the stickleback mentioned above. One advantage of ritualisation in courtship situations is that because the behaviour is species-specific, individuals are able to avoid the error of mating with members of different species.

Advantages and disadvantages of visual communication

There are many advantages to visual communication. The main advantages are listed below (Grier & Burk, 1992):

- Information is transmitted instantly. Thus, unlike some other forms of communication (such as some examples of chemical communication) the receiver can act upon the information received without delay. This may be particularly important in cases where danger is being signalled.
- Large 'packages' of information can be simultaneously transmitted. For example, an individual's sex, age, status and species can all be readily ascertained visually.
- Visual information is highly directional. The location of the sender can therefore be readily found.
- Some aspects of visual communication are produced only once – and so are economical in the use of energy. Colouration is an example of this. However, it should also be remembered that some visual displays are almost ludicrously costly in terms of effort – the displaying peacock being perhaps the prime example.

The two principal disadvantages of visual communication are as follows:

- Visual communication can only work over quite short distances.
- It also requires good light conditions – it is of little value at night or in poorly lit environments such the deep oceans.

Auditory communication

Many species make use of auditory communication. Auditory communication, like visual communication, is highly flexible. Such communications can vary in pitch, order and volume. Auditory communication can convey many different kinds of information. Male crickets, for example, which make their characteristic sound using their legs, use sounds in a particular sequence to advertise to females that they are of the same species, and hence available for mating.

Many species use auditory communication as a means of alarm calling – that is, drawing attention to the presence of predators. Alarm calling is interesting because, potentially, it might be seen as an example of altruistic behaviour (see Chapter 13). In calling an alarm, the individual also draws attention to itself, potentially making itself more vulnerable to attack. However, Dawkins (1981) has argued that this is mitigated somewhat by the fact that alarm calls of different species often share many acoustic characteristics in common. It is therefore quite difficult to detect the exact (or likely) location of an alarm-calling individual – as Dawkins suggests, they simply indicate 'danger' not 'danger over here'.

Alarm calling is indeed very sophisticated in some species. The vervet monkey is an example of this. Vervets exhibit a system of alarm calling in which the nature of the danger is indicated by the type of call made. Seyfarth and Cheney (1980) made field studies of vervets and found three principal types of alarm call, each eliciting different responses to different kinds of danger. In the first case, a high pitched call indicates the presence of a snake, and results in the monkey rearing up off the ground as soon as possible. Secondly, a loud bark indicates the presence of a leopard – this results in the monkeys climbing up into trees. Finally, a chuckle indicates the presence of an eagle, and results in the monkeys taking cover in bushes or undergrowth. It is easy to see that if these responses were not specialised in this way, the monkeys could face a real risk of attack – there is clearly little point in scurrying into the bushes when faced with a snake, or climbing a tree to escape from an eagle. This specialised alarm calling behaviour in vervet monkeys appears to be learned in infancy. Young vervets often make errors in responding to alarm calls, and these can be fatal in their consequences.

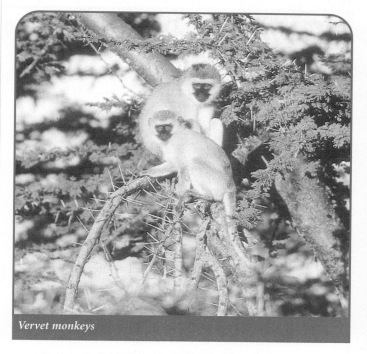

Vervet monkeys

Advantages and disadvantages of auditory communication

There are a number of advantages to auditory communication. These are listed below (Grier & Burk, 1992).

- Auditory communications can occur successfully irrespective of terrain, and can go around obstacles. They also occur successfully in any light conditions.
- Auditory signals, like visual ones, can be transmitted very quickly.
- Auditory signals can be very complex, and hence this form of communication is very flexible. The complex 'song' sequences of some species – such as gibbons, for example – can convey an elaborate array of information on such things as age, sex and rank.

There are, however, also certain disadvantages of auditory communication.

- Sound signals are subject to interference, both from other sounds in the same environment and from the effects of distance.
- Just as one advantage of auditory communication is its ability to transcend obstacles, this also means that there is a risk of sound signals being 'overheard' by predators (see 'eavesdropping', discussed above).

Chemical or olfactory communication

Many species use chemicals to communicate. Communication by this method is often described as *olfactory*. The chemicals concerned are called *pheromones*. Pheromones fall into two categories: *releaser* pheromones and *primer* pheromones. Releaser pheromones have short-lived effects, and usually result in some immediate behavioural change in the receiver. Primer pheromones, on the other hand, have much longer-lived effects and can sometimes result in changes in the receiver's physiology.

A common use of chemical communication is territory marking. This behaviour can easily be observed in dogs, who secrete pheromones in their urine and use this to warn other dogs away from their territory. House mice behave in a similar way (Hurst, 1990).

Chemical communication has also been shown to play a part in incest-avoidance in some species. Looked at from an evolutionary perspective, we should expect incest to be avoided because recessive genes in related individuals are much more likely to be expressed when incestuous matings occur. This increases the likelihood of damaged offspring being produced, and hence has a negative impact on the fitness of the individuals concerned. It has been shown in crickets, for example, that females are able to differentiate between kin and non-kin on the basis of pheromonal cues and, as a result of this discrimination, prefer mating with males to whom they are not related (Simmons, 1990).

In many species, pheromones appear to play a part in the bonds which develop between mothers and their offspring. It is common practice amongst sheep farmers, for example, to cover an orphaned lamb with the fleece of a dead infant, so that the mother of the dead lamb can be persuaded to feed the orphan.

Activity 2 — Deceitful signalling and eavesdropping

Item A — Stotting

Gazelles sometime engage in a form of communication known as 'stotting' which involves bouncing along on all fours. They are often seen stotting in the presence of predators – though not big cats, such as lions, who are able to catch them over short distances. Stotting may indicate that these gazelles are stronger and faster, or it may be an example of deceitful signalling. Whichever, it appears to work. For example, when approached by a pack of African hunting dogs, the stotting gazelles are less likely to be singled out for attack than other members of the herd.

Adapted from Fitzgibbon & Fanshawe, 1988

Item B — Bark beetle

Female bark beetles release a scent when they have found a suitable tree on which to lay their eggs. This scent attracts male beetles to the site. However, there is evidence that this scent also attracts other female beetles – since it indicates the presence of a suitable site for them to lay their eggs.

Questions

1 How might stotting be seen as a deceitful signal?

2 Why do you think that gazelles do not engage in stotting in the presence of their most dangerous predators – such as lions – and yet do so in the presence of less dangerous predators like hunting dogs?

3 What kind of communication (ie visual, auditory, olfactory etc) is being described in each of the items?

4 What term describes the behaviour of the female beetles who receive the signal described in Item B?

Advantages and disadvantages of chemical communication

Grier and Burk (1992) have identified several advantages and disadvantages of this form of communication. The principal advantages are as follows.

- Chemical communication can take place in darkness, through and around obstacles.
- It has a very long range – sharks, for example, can smell blood many miles away.
- This form of communication can be long lasting – as in the case of animals marking their territory.
- Chemical signals are less susceptible to 'eavesdropping' because to receive them usually requires some special adaptation.

The principal disadvantages of this method of communication are:

- Transmission may be slow – this will depend on the size of the molecules concerned.
- Chemical signals may either fade away too quickly – and are susceptible to environmental features such as rain and winds – or sometimes may not fade away quickly enough, making interference with subsequent messages more likely.

Key terms

Communication *A two way process in which signals are sent to receivers, who exhibit some change as a result of receiving the signal.*

Eavesdropping *A situation where an unintended recipient receives a signal of some advantage to itself.*

Deceitful signalling *Sending signals which convey false information as a means of securing some advantage.*

Visual communication *Signals which are seen by the receiver.*

Ritualisation *An evolutionary process whereby patterns of behaviour adopt a symbolic value.*

Auditory communication *Signals which are heard by the receiver.*

Chemical communication *Signals which are detected chemically by the receiver – including smell.*

Pheromones *Chemical substances secreted and released which convey information.*

2.2 Animal language

The question of whether animals either use language naturally, or can be taught to do so, remains controversial. In part, this controversy stems from debates about what, exactly, it means to say that someone, or something, uses language. One of the earliest and most comprehensive attempts to list the characteristics of language was provided by Hockett (1959). Hockett's sixteen characteristics of language are listed in Table 1.

Whilst this list of the characteristics of language is certainly useful, it would probably be a mistake to apply it too rigidly. It is possible to find examples which breach one or more of these conditions, but which are still unquestionably language. Deaf people, for example, do not have 'total feedback' and often

Table 1 — Hockett's characteristics of language

1	**Vocal/auditory** It uses sounds made vocally by one individual and received auditorily by another.
2	**Broadcast/directional** The sound is broadcast, but its direction can be determined by the receiver.
3	**Rapid fading** The sound fades quickly.
4	**Total feedback** The speaker can hear what he or she is saying.
5	**Interchangeability** The same individual can both send and receive messages.
6	**Specialisation** Speech is primarily for communication and not a by-product of anything else.
7	**Semanticity** Language has meaning.
8	**Arbitrariness** Meaning is not intrinsic to words, but becomes assigned – for example different languages use different words to mean the same thing.
9	**Traditional transmission** Language is passed on from one generation to the next.
10	**Learnability** New forms of language can be learned.
11	**Discreteness** Language is made up of small, discrete units which produce meaning when combined.
12	**Duality of patterning** Language becomes organised into meaningful sequences at different levels. For example, phonemes are organised into words, and words are organised into sentences.
13	**Displacement** Speakers can refer to things which are not currently present in space or time.
14	**Openness/productivity** Language can generate new utterances with new meanings.
15	**Prevarication** Language makes it possible to speak of things which are not true and which have not happened – to tell lies.
16	**Reflexiveness** Language can be used by users to talk about themselves.

Adapted from Hockett (1959)

communicate not vocally, but via sign language. Nevertheless, these criteria do provide a comprehensive basis for discussing the question of whether animals can use language.

The honey bee

Honey bees live in colonies which consist of three castes of bee: the queen, sterile workers (female) and drones (males). The role of sterile workers is to collect nectar and bring it back to the hive where it is converted into honey. Worker bees often travel over long distances to find nectar, and work together in a highly cooperative fashion.

The cooperative nectar gathering of the honey bee is facilitated by a complex system of communication, which some have argued resembles a form of language. Honey bees engage in a very complex form of dancing behaviour which conveys information to their colleagues about the location of nectar. Von Frisch (1967) made a study of over 6000 bee dances. For example, von Frisch found that if food is less than 100m away, the bee will perform a comparatively simple dance which involves moving around in a circular motion, changing direction from time to time. If the food is more than 100m away, however, the bee performs a 'wagging' dance – that is instead of moving around in a circle, the bee moves in a figure-of-eight pattern, whilst wagging its abdomen between 3 and 15 times during the central run (see Figure 1). The angle of the central run conveys to the other bees the direction of the nectar source. The distance of the food from the bee is conveyed by the speed at which the bee performs its dance. If the food is further away, it will perform the dance more slowly than if it is nearby. For example, von Frisch found that if the food is 500m away, the bee will complete 6 dance circuits in 15 seconds, whereas if it is 1000m away, it will complete only 2 circuits in the same time.

This form of communication is undoubtedly very complex, but we should exercise caution in considering it language in the sense that human beings use language. For one thing, the communication which goes on is largely visual – although there is some evidence that sound might also play a part. Secondly, bee dancing cannot be described as productive – that is, it cannot generate new meanings in the way that human language can. Thirdly, there is no evidence to suggest that bees can use this language reflexively – ie, to communicate information about themselves.

Vervet monkeys

Communication amongst vervet monkeys was discussed earlier in this unit. To what extent can the signalling system employed in this species be regarded as language use? As noted earlier, vervet monkeys give specific calls to indicate different kinds of danger, and receivers of these signals react accordingly. So a vervet which gives a loud bark is indicating the presence of a leopard, and the receivers of this signal react by climbing into trees.

Undoubtedly this system does have some characteristics of language. It is vocal/ auditory in nature and interchangeable in the sense that individuals can both send and receive messages. It also displays the characteristics of arbitrariness and

Figure 1   Honey bee dances

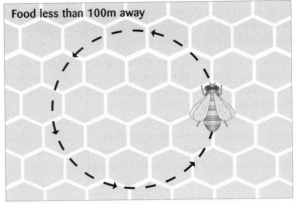

Food less than 100m away

The bee moves in a simple circular movement

Food more than 100m away

direction of food

central run

The bee performs a 'wagging' dance, moving in a figure-of-eight pattern

Activity 3   The honey bee

Item A   Communication of food locations

To investigate the accuracy of the bee's ability to communicate the location of food, von Frisch conducted the following experiment. A group of bees was fed on lavender-scented sugar water placed exactly 750m from the hive. The food was then removed and a series of lavender-scented boards were placed at varying distances from the hive. Observers then watched the boards to see where newly arriving bees landed. They noted that over 60% of the bees observed went to either the board at 700m or 800m – in other words to the two boards nearest the original location of the food.

Adapted from von Frisch, 1967

A honey bee (centre) performing a dance

Questions

1   What do these findings indicate about the ability of bees to communicate the location of food?

2   Based on these findings and what you have read in this unit, should communication in bees be regarded as language? Give reasons for your answer.

semanticity. It is arbitrary because there is no necessary correspondence between a particular sound and the danger to which it refers – the connection seems to be based on convention as in the case of human language. It has semanticity because the sounds have meanings which routinely refer to the same dangers.

This form of language could not be described as displaying productivity, however. For this to be the case, the animals would need to be able to use their language creatively to generate new meanings – as human beings do. Vervet communication appears to be confined to a small number of meanings concerned with specific dangers and appropriate responses to these. Similarly, there is no evidence of reflexivity in vervet communication – monkeys evidently cannot use language to talk about themselves and to describe their own experiences. Furthermore, there is no evidence that vervet monkeys use language in a way which displays what Hockett calls 'duality of patterning' – that is combining units of speech (either individual phonemes or words) into larger units with more complex meanings. A human being can combine words to create long and complex sentences with unique meanings. The vervet monkey, by contrast, shows no evidence of combining sounds in this way – meanings are confined to the primary meanings of the various alarm calls.

2.3   Can non-human animals be taught language?

A considerable amount of research has been carried out over the years to try to ascertain whether or not animals can be taught to use language. At the bottom of this research is a key theoretical debate within the field of linguistics. The American linguist, Noam Chomsky, has argued that human beings are unique in that they possess a biological predisposition to acquire language, and that this is not shared by other species. According to Chomsky (1972), human beings possess an innate *language acquisition device* (LAD) – essentially hard-wiring in the brain – which determines the structure of language. Whilst the actual language which we learn – English, French, Swahili etc – is culturally determined, at a deep level all human languages are dependent on a common deep structure which depends on our possession of this LAD (see pp 476-478).

Thus, for Chomsky, although all human language is learned, our *ability* to learn such a hugely complex system is biologically determined. It follows from Chomsky's view, that it ought to be impossible to teach non-human animals language, since they lack this distinctively human LAD. Most of the recent attempts to teach animals language have, therefore, been in response to Chomsky's claims about the unique linguistic abilities of human beings.

Chimpanzee research

Early research on chimpanzee language acquisition focused on attempts to teach chimps to speak. These were unsuccessful because chimpanzees lack the vocal apparatus which makes speech in human beings possible. Later research has focused instead on the use of signs.

Washoe One of the most famous experiments in teaching language to chimpanzees was carried out by Gardner and Gardner (1969). In this research, the Gardners attempted to teach a young chimpanzee, known as Washoe, American Sign Language (*Ameslan*) – a language used by deaf people which uses hand gestures. Washoe was taught mainly by modelling – that is, was shown the sign and given praise when she copied it, but sometimes her hands were moulded into the correct position if she experienced difficulty in acquiring a particular sign. After ten months of training, at the age of two, the Gardners reported that Washoe had been able to form her first two-word combinations. By the time she had completed her training at about age four, she had learned 132 different words and could produce over 30 different two and three word combinations. This achievement compares poorly with a human being of the same age – the average 4-year-old human knows about 3000 words – but it does appear to demonstrate that chimpanzees have some capacity to learn language.

The significance of the Gardners' research has attracted controversy, however. Much of this centres around the degree to which Washoe was able to use language in a creative manner akin to human beings. Evidence for her ability to do so comes from the fact that she seemed to be able to coin new words. On one occasion, for example, when faced with a picture of a swan, she signed the words for 'water' and 'bird'. But does this necessarily imply that she was using words creatively? According to Terrace (1979) the apparently new word could have arisen from the chance juxtaposition of two words – with no connection between them being made by Washoe. Other examples are more promising however. On another occasion, when a small doll was put in her cup, she made the signs for 'baby in my drink'. This example does tend to support the conclusion that chimpanzees can be taught to use language creatively – albeit at a much lower level than human beings.

The Oklahoma colony One potential weakness of the Gardners' studies of Washoe was that they and their colleagues had themselves to learn *Ameslan* in order to teach Washoe. As a result, they were not especially fluent users of the language. A second possible problem was that Washoe was reared without the company of other chimpanzees. The question of whether chimpanzees will use taught sign language to communicate with each other therefore remained open.

These issues were resolved in a study conducted by Roger Fouts (1972). Fouts established a colony of infant chimpanzees – known as the Oklahoma colony – the members of which were taught to sign by people who had themselves used *Ameslan* since infancy. One of the findings from this study was that the chimpanzees did indeed seem to use sign language when alone to communicate with each other. Fouts also performed an experiment in which one member of the group was shown the location of some food and then returned to the group. Fouts found that the other animals then usually searched in the correct place for the food, suggesting that the original animal had communicated its whereabouts. Whilst this does seem to be evidence for communication of some kind, it does not necessarily follow that the chimpanzees used sign language to communicate this information.

Fouts's study also found evidence for creative language use in chimpanzees. Lucy (one of the chimpanzees) coined the term 'hurt-cry-fruit' to describe a radish – this appears to make sense in view of the hot and bitter taste of this particular vegetable. Similarly, Lucy would sometimes describe a watermelon as 'fruit-drink' or 'candy-drink' – even though she also sometimes used the sign for 'watermelon'. These examples suggest that chimps can use language in a creative and meaningful way – albeit on a far lower scale than mature human beings.

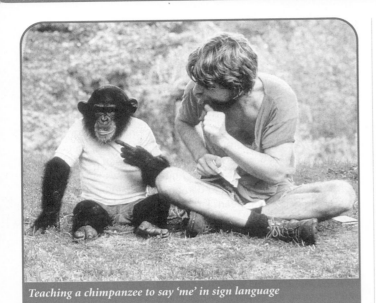
Teaching a chimpanzee to say 'me' in sign language

Nim Chimpsky The view that chimpanzees can use language in a creative way akin to human beings has not passed without criticisms, and it is not surprising that much of this criticism has come from those influenced by the work of Noam Chomsky. Terrace (1979) trained a chimpanzee – rather wittily named *Nim Chimpsky* – to use *Ameslan* as had been done in earlier studies. As with the other studies, Nim Chimpsky acquired a large number of signs and was able to put these together to form simple phrases. However, Terrace argued that this was fundamentally different from the ways in which human beings use language. First, he argued that these abilities could result just from sophisticated trial-and-error learning (along the lines of operant conditioning, discussed in Chapter 31). In his view, the chimps could learn to associate words and things by stimulus-response learning – and whilst this may appear to lead to creative language use, it is in fact fundamentally different from the ways in which human beings use language creatively.

Terrace, following Chomsky, argues that the defining feature of human language use is our ability to form complex grammatical structures – an ability which is regarded as innate. Although he analysed over 19,000 multi-word phrases produced by Nim Chimpsky, he argues that these do not share the grammatical structures which naturally produced human language displays. He shows that the 'mean length of utterance' – the average length, in words, of any combined utterance – of Nim's language was only 1.5 words and, crucially, that this did not increase as the chimp learned more words. Human beings, by contrast, tend to produce much longer utterances, indicating much more complex underlying grammatical structures, and these increase in length and complexity as the individual learns more words.

There is undoubtedly some merit to Terrace's arguments. The real question, however, is whether, like Terrace, we regard chimp language as *qualitatively* different from that produced by human beings, or whether we regard the two as only *quantitatively* different – that is, as being essentially the same in nature, only simpler in the case of chimp language.

Kanzi One recent criticism of earlier chimpanzee language studies has been that they concentrate exclusively on the *production* of language. In contrast researchers such as Savage-Rumbaugh (1986) have focused on *comprehension*. Just as

children learn to understand language before they can produce it, so these researchers have argued that it is much more realistic to concentrate on how chimpanzees come to understand language. This argument has led to a rather different approach to that used by previous researchers. Instead of attempting to teach the chimpanzees sign language, Savage-Rumbaugh and her colleagues used a 'symbol keyboard' – a device in which a symbol on a keyboard produces, via a voice synthesiser, the English word for that symbol when pressed. This method meant that the chimp's trainers could communicate with it directly in English.

In the case of Kanzi, no direct attempt was made to teach him to use language. Kanzi's adopted mother, Matata, was trained in the usual way, and throughout her training she had Kanzi with her. As a result of this exposure, Kanzi spontaneously learned to communicate using the symbol keyboard. Once Matata's training was complete, training was continued with Kanzi, but in this case the training consisted simply of humans communicating with him through the keyboard – no attempt was made to reinforce correct responses, as was usually the case. Not only did Kanzi learn to communicate correctly using the keyboard – he responded correctly 100% of the time to 109 out of 194 test words, and 75% of the time to another 40 words – but he also appeared to have a grasp of syntax and its effect on meaning. He was able to respond accurately to 105 out of 107 'action tasks' (eg 'Kanzi, go get me a coke'), and also to complex requests such as 'get the orange that is in the colony room'.

In a later study, Savage-Rumbaugh et al. (1993) compared the linguistic comprehension of the 9-year-old Kanzi with that of a two and a half-year-old child called Alia. Alia had also been taught to use the symbol keyboard. Both were tested on over 400 novel sentences – which included complex or unusual instructions (such as putting an elastic band around a ball, or fetching a telephone from outside when one was in sight). Savage-Rumbaugh reports that the nine-year-old Kanzi was correct 74% of the time whilst Alia was correct only 65% of the time.

This research suggests that chimpanzees can learn to use language via a symbol keyboard. There is no evidence that chimps who have not had such an opportunity to learn can comprehend language in this way. As a result, it seems

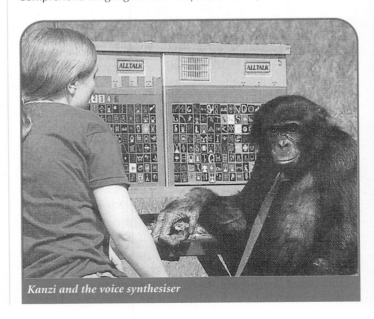
Kanzi and the voice synthesiser

reasonable to conclude that, like human beings, chimpanzees have a period of developmental plasticity during which they are susceptible to acquisition of language if reared in an appropriate environment.

Dolphin research

Research has also been carried out to determine whether dolphins can acquire linguistic competence. Lilly (1965) reported a number of studies which showed that dolphins could, with some success, be taught to mimic human speech. Indeed, anyone who has ever visited a dolphin display at an aquarium has probably heard dolphins singing 'happy birthday' and such like. Lilly showed that dolphins could, via stimulus-response learning, be taught to mimic many human syllables, including counting to ten. It is important to realise, however, that such

mimicry is not the same as linguistic competence.

Further research has confirmed, however, that dolphins can be taught to comprehend human language, albeit at a fairly rudimentary level. Herman et al. (1984) trained two dolphins using different artificial languages. One of these involved a system of gestures and postures adopted by the trainer, and the other a series of computer generated sounds. Herman and his colleagues showed that the dolphins could be taught to understand complex requests – that is, they responded to instructions to fetch objects when the objects in question were not immediately present.

It is important to note, however, that this research merely established the dolphin's ability to respond to linguistic commands. There is no evidence that dolphins can use taught languages to communicate either with human beings or fellow dolphins.

Activity 4 — Teaching language to non-human animals

Item A — Teaching language to gorillas

Koko, a young gorilla, was taught to use American Sign Language. After one year, a second young gorilla, Michael, was introduced. Both gorillas appeared to learn sign language quite easily, and were able to communicate with each other using signs. Koko learned about 400 signs in total. According to Patterson (1978), one indicator that Koko and Michael were really using language in a way similar to human beings, and not just displaying conditioned responses, was that they could show displeasure by using 'swear words'. For example, when displeased with someone, Koko would use the signs 'dirty' and 'toilet', even though she could use these words in their literal sense when indicating either that something is dirty or that a toilet is present.

Adapted from Patterson, 1980

Item B — Teaching language to dolphins

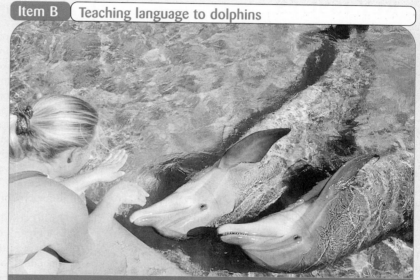

Communicating with dolphins using hand signals

In one study, a dolphin called Akeakami was taught a special form of language in which words were indicated by postures or actions carried out by the trainer at the side of the pool. Akeakami learned a large number of signs and, in one test, responded accurately to every one of 193 new sentences. The researchers considered that the dolphin had a grasp of grammar. This is because it would respond appropriately to four word sentences in which word order is crucial to meaning.

Adapted from Herman, Richards & Wolz (1984)

Questions

1 In what way do the findings described in Item A support the view that gorillas use language simply as a result of stimulus-response conditioning?

2 Consider the experiment described in Item B and explain why a sensitivity to word order might be taken to indicate linguistic abilities similar to human beings.

3 Discuss the ethical implications of attempts to teach non-human animals language.

Summary

1 Communication is a two-way process which involves senders and receivers. It is thought to be evolutionarily adaptive. Two types of communication – eavesdropping and deceitful signalling – can be non-adaptive.

2 Communication can be visual, olfactory or auditory in nature. Each system of communication has both advantages and disadvantages.

3 Many species display complex systems of communication, but there is some debate about whether this should be described as language. Honey bees are capable of communicating complex

information about the location of food sources, and vervet monkeys use an elaborate signalling system to warn of specific dangers.

4 There have been many attempts to teach language to non-human animals. There is no doubt that associations between words and things can be learned by several primate species, who can also learn to use words creatively. There is some doubt, however, about whether this is really akin to the sort of linguistic competence displayed by human beings. The debate is as much theoretical and philosophical as it is empirical.

Unit 3 Memory in non-human animals

KEY ISSUES

1 What is the nature of memory in non-human animals?

2 What is the role played by memory in foraging and food-caching behaviour?

To what extent do non-human animals possess memory? In one sense the answer is obvious: if a species can learn (and as we have seen this is true of most species) they must possess some sort of memory. Equally obvious, however, is the fact that human memory must be much more complex than that found in non-human animals if for no other reason than the language-dependence of much human memory.

Studies of memory in non-human animals have focused on two areas in particular. First has been the role of memory in navigation. Earlier in this chapter we reviewed a number of examples of animal navigation which depend on what can be described as a memory of location. The second area is the role of memory in foraging, and in particular the *food caching* behaviour found especially in many species of bird. Food caching refers to the practice of storing food during times of plenty for retrieval at a later date.

The study of memory in human beings is comparatively straightforward – at least in the sense that it is possible to question people about what they can remember. Since this is not a possibility in the case of non-human animals, it is necessary for researchers to rely on making inferences about memory on the basis of observed natural and experimentally manipulated behaviour.

3.1 Spatial memory

Spatial memory is crucial for navigation. For example, most species need to leave their nesting sites for the purposes of finding food and mates. Memory of some kind would seem to be a precondition of finding their way back after such excursions. Earlier in this chapter we discussed examples of

animal navigation which rely on memory. A particularly well studied example of such memory is in the digger wasp. The female digger wasp makes a burrow in which she lays her eggs. In order to provision her larvae with food, she has to leave the burrow to find insects. Before she embarks on this trip, however, she first makes a reconnaissance flight, during which she seems to commit to memory key features of the landscape around her burrow. In one experiment, Tinbergen (1951) placed a series of pine cones around such a burrow and then, whilst the female wasp was hunting, moved the circle of pine cones 30m away from its original location. Tinbergen then observed that when she returned from her hunting trip, she was unable to find her burrow – even though it was actually very close to the moved pine cones. This suggests that the wasp memorises the spatial arrangement of the environment around her burrow.

This conclusion was confirmed in the next stage of Tinbergen's experiment, which involved replacing the moved circle of pine cones with a circle of stones. At the same time he placed a triangle of pine cones around the actual nest. However, the female wasp still searched for her nest around the circle of stones – and ignored the triangle of pine cones completely. This seems to demonstrate that it is not the pine cones themselves which the wasp has memorised, but their spatial organisation – she was attracted to the circle.

Spatial adaptation

There is evidence to suggest that the kinds of spatial memory possessed by different species are evolutionary adaptations. In general, when a species displays a well developed ability to memorise spatial locations, it seems likely that this ability conferred an evolutionary advantage on its ancestors. This proposition has been examined experimentally.

In one experiment, Gaulin and Fitzgerald (1989) compared the spatial memory of males and females in two species of vole – the meadow vole and the prairie vole. Male and female meadow voles differ in the size of territories they inhabit. The male meadow vole inhabits a territory which is approximately four times the size of that inhabited by the female. Male and female prairie voles, on the other hand, share the same territory. If it is the case that spatial memory is an adaptation, then it can be predicted that male and female meadow voles will differ in their spatial memories, with males having better memories than females, whilst we can expect male and female prairie voles not to differ in this respect.

To test this, Gaulin & Fitzgerald compared males and females of both species in their ability to learn their way around an experimental maze. As predicted, the male meadow vole made significantly fewer errors than the female meadow vole. Again, as predicted, there was very little difference in the performance of the male and female prairie voles.

Key terms

Spatial memory *The ability to remember location.*

Spatial adaptation *The evolution of specific spatial memory abilities which are adaptive in particular environments.*

Foraging *Searching for food.*

Food caching *Hiding and storing food for later consumption.*

3.2   Foraging and food caching

One of the main advantages of the possession of spatial memory in non-human animals is that it permits both foraging (searching for food) and food caching (food storage). Foraging is dependent on memory because the animal must be able to find its way back home. It is also useful to be able to return to a successful foraging site on subsequent occasions. Food caching is very obviously dependent on memory – there is no point in storing food if you cannot remember where it is! Food caching has several advantages. First, if an animal is successful in finding a supply of food greater than it can immediately consume, food caching means that it can be stored for later consumption. Cheetahs, for example, often store large prey high up in trees to prevent less mobile competitors from stealing it. Similarly, where food supplies are seasonal or affected by environmental conditions, food caching is essential if the animal is to have enough to eat at all times. However, food caches are vulnerable to exploitation. Successful food caching requires both that the location is secure and difficult for competitors to find, but also that the caching individual can find the location again when the times comes.

Memory in foraging

Experimental studies have demonstrated the role of memory in foraging in a number of species. In one such study, Menzel (1971) demonstrated the extent of chimpanzees' memory for foraging. A group of chimpanzees were kept in a large enclosure – similar to the habitat in which they would naturally live. The experimenter took a very complex route around the enclosure and, observed by the chimpanzees, hid food in 18 different locations. The chimpanzees were then released to find the food. Instead of recreating the circuitous route taken by the experimenter, the animals took a direct route to the food locations. This suggests that they memorise the food's location, rather than the route taken to reach it. In a refinement of this experiment, half the hidden food items were fruit and half vegetables. When the chimpanzees were released, they went first to the fruit, and then to the vegetables – given the choice,

chimpanzees prefer to eat fruit over vegetables. This shows that they memorise not only location, but salient facts about what is to be found at different locations.

Memory in food caching

Experiments have also been carried out to demonstrate the role played by memory in food caching. Merely to demonstrate that an animal can find a food supply that it has hidden does not demonstrate that memory is involved. This is because the animal may be relying on other cues – such as smell or appearance – to locate the hidden food. For this reason, psychologists have designed experiments in which these possibilities are carefully controlled.

In one experiment, Sherry (1984) demonstrated the role played by memory in the food caching behaviour of the American black capped chickadee. These birds hide seeds and insects in moss or tree bark, and return to retrieve them up to 28 days later. In the experiment, 72 holes were drilled in a number of trees, and each bird was allowed to hide four or five sunflower seeds. The holes were then covered with small material patches, which ensured that sight and smell did not play a part in the bird's ability to retrieve the seeds. The birds were then kept in a cage for 24 hours, after which time they were released back into the experimental site. Sherry found that the birds spent much more time pecking at patches where they had hidden seeds than any other. This strongly suggests that memory is responsible for this food-caching behaviour, as no other cues could be responsible for their ability to locate the food.

A similar experiment was conducted by Jacobs and Liman (1991) with grey squirrels. Each squirrel was released into an experimental area and allowed to bury ten hazelnuts. The squirrels were then removed, and the experimenter also removed their hazelnuts. Further hazelnuts were then randomly buried by other squirrels in the same area. After a period of up to 12 days, the original squirrels were returned, and it was found that they searched in the areas of their original caches. They did so even when they had first to travel past a nut buried by another squirrel. Again, this suggests that the animals had memorised the location of their nut caches.

Grey squirrel burying acorns

Activity 5   Investigating memory in birds

Item A   Natural observation

Clark's nutcracker

Clark's nutcracker – a species of bird – collects thousands of pine seeds during the autumn and buries them in shallow holes for retrieval in winter and early spring. Observation indicates that each bird probably has over 3000 caches in different locations.

Item B   Experimental evidence

A Clark's nutcracker was placed in an aviary with a supply of seeds. It buried some of the seeds in the aviary floor. The bird was then removed along with the seeds it had buried, and the floor of the aviary was swept. Several other birds were introduced, one at a time, and the same procedure followed. A week later, each bird was returned to the aviary on its own. On average, 80% of the time each bird spent searching for food was spent in the locations where it had buried its own seeds.

Adapted from Balda, 1980

Questions

1   What evidence suggests that Clark's nutcrackers rely on memory to locate their food caches?

2   How else might they locate them?

3.3   Cognitive maps

The term *cognitive maps* was introduced by Tolman (1948). The term refers to internal mental representations of spatial relationships in the environment. Research studies of rats, for example, show that they can quickly learn to navigate their way around mazes. Whilst such learning can sometimes be explained in terms of operant conditioning (see pp 613-616), rats also seem able to learn without any obvious reinforcers being present. An early experiment by Maier and Schneirla (1935) appeared to demonstrate the development of cognitive maps in rats. A large and complex maze was constructed, with food located in one portion of the maze, and several blind alleys. The rats were introduced into the maze and allowed to orient themselves. Soon they learned to locate the food box. After a while, one of the blind alleys was opened up to create a short-cut from the start of the maze to the food box. The rats quickly explored the new route, and on subsequent trials made use of the new short-cut to the food. This experiment suggests that the rats possessed an internal map of the maze and, in particular, the location of the food in relation to the start of the maze. It seems unlikely that such a strong finding could have resulted from operant conditioning alone.

There is evidence to suggest that a specific region of the brain – the hippocampus – is responsible for the development of cognitive maps. Experiments, again with rats, show that if the hippocampus is damaged, rats seem unable to learn spatial location. In one study, the performance of normal rats was compared to that of hippocampus-damaged rats (Morris et al., 1982). A solution of powdered milk and water was placed in a tank containing a slightly submerged platform. The milky solution ensured that the rats could not see the platform. Once the normal rats had discovered the location of the platform (initially by random chance), they were quickly able to find it on subsequent occasions and escape from the milky water. The hippocampus-damaged rats, in contrast, were never able to learn the location of the platform.

The involvement of the hippocampus in cognitive mapping has also been demonstrated in other species. The black capped chickadee, for example, which was discussed above, exhibits an enlargement of the hippocampus during autumn – precisely the time when it is engaging in its characteristic food caching behaviour (Smulder et al., 1995). Similarly, the male meadow vole – which, as we saw above, has superior spatial memory to the female – has a significantly larger hippocampus than females of the same species.

Key terms

Cognitive maps *Internal representations of spatial relationships in an animal's environment.*

Hippocampus *An area of the brain which appears to be responsible for the ability to develop cognitive maps and, hence, spatial memory.*

Summary

1   Many species display spatial memory. The extent and nature of spatial memory in a given species seems to be adaptive.

2   Memory seems to be particularly important in foraging and food-caching behaviour. Experiments with food-caching species have demonstrated that they do indeed rely on memory rather than visual or olfactory cues.

3   Spatial memory seems to involve the development of cognitive maps. The ability to develop cognitive maps is dependent on the hippocampus.

References

Balda, R.P. (1980). Recovery of cached seeds by captive Nucifraga caryocatactes. *Zeitschrift fur Tierpsychologie, 52*, 331-346

Beason, R.C. (1989). Magnetic sensitivity and orientation in the bobolink. Paper presented to the *Royal Institute of Navigation Conference.*

Belrose, F.C. (1958). Celestial orientation in wild mallards. *Bird Banding, 29*, 75-90.

Biebach, H. (1983). Genetic determination of partial migration in the European robin *(Erithacus rubecula). Auk, 100*, 601-606.

Cartwright, B.A. & Collet, T.S. (1983). Landmark learning in bees: Experiments and models. *Journal of Comparative Physiology, 151*, 521-543.

Chomsky, N. (1972). *Language and mind* (enlarged edition). New York: Harcourt Brace.

Dawkins, R. (1981). Communication. In D. McFarlane (Ed.). *The Oxford companion to animal behaviour.* Oxford: Oxford University Press.

Emlen, S.T. (1972). The ontogenetic development of orientation capabilities. In S.R. Galler, K.Schmidt-Koenig, G.J. Jacobs & R.E. Bellville (Eds.), *Animal orientation and navigation.* Washington DC: NASA.

Eysenck, M. (2000). *Psychology: A student's handbook.* Hove: Psychology Press.

Fisher, A.C. (1979). Mysteries of bird migration. *National Geographic, 152*, 154-193.

Fitzgibbon, C.D. & Fanshawe, J.H. (1988). 'Stotting' in Thompson's gazelles: An honest signal of condition. *Behavioural Ecology and Sociobiology, 23*, 69-74.

Fouts, R.S. (1972). The use of guidance in teaching sign language to chimpanzees. *Journal of Comparative Physiological Psychology, 80*, 515-522.

Gardner, R.A. & Gardner, B.T. (1969). Teaching sign language to a chimpanzee. *Science, 165*, 664-672.

Gaulin, S.J.C. & Fitzgerald, R.W. (1989). Sexual selection for spatial learning ability. *Animal Behaviour, 37*, 322-331.

Gelder, M., Gath, D. & Mayon, R. (1989). *The Oxford textbook of psychiatry* (2nd ed.). Oxford: Oxford University Press.

Gould, J.L. (1982). The map sense of pigeons. *Nature, 296*, 205-211.

Grier, J.W. & Burk, T. (1992). *Biology of animal behaviour.* Dubuque, IA: WCB Communications.

Hasler, A.D. & Larsen, J.A. (1955). The homing salmon. *Scientific American, 193*, 72-77.

Helbig, A.J. (1991). Inheritance of migratory direction in a bird species: A cross-breeding experiment with SE- and SW-migrating black caps. *Behavioural Ecology and Sociobiology, 28*, 9-12.

Herman, L.M., Richards, D.G. & Wolz, J.P. (1984). Comprehension of sentences by bottlenosed dolphins. *Cognition, 16*, 129-219.

Hockett, C.F. (1959). Animal 'languages' and human language. *Human Biology, 31*, 32-39.

Hurst, J.L. (1990). Urine marking in populations of wild house mice, Mus domesticus. *Animal Behaviour, 40*, 209-222.

Jacobs, L. & Liman, E. (1991). Grey squirrels remember the locations of buried nuts. *Animal Behaviour, 41*, 103-110.

Keeton, W.T. (1969). Orientation by pigeons: Is the sun necessary? *Science, 165*, 922-928.

Kramer, G. (1952). Experiments on bird orientation. *Ibis, 94*, 265-285.

Lack, D. (1943). *The life of the robin.* London: Witherby.

Lilly, J.C. (1965). Vocal mimicry in tursiops: Ability to match

numbers and duration of human vocal bursts. *Science, 147*, 300-301.

Maier, N.R.F. & Schneirla, T.C. (1935). *Principles of animal psychology.* New York: McGraw-Hill.

Menzel, E.W. (1971). Communication about the environment in a group of young chimpanzees. *Folia Primat, 15*, 220-232.

Morris, R.G.M., Garrud, P., Rawlins, J.N.P. & O'Keefe, J. (1982). Place navigation impaired rats with hippocampal lesions. *Nature, 297*, 681-683.

Papi, F. (1982). Olfaction and homing in pigeons: Ten years of experiments. In F.P. Walraff & H.G. Walraff (Eds.), *Avian navigation.* Berlin: Springer-Verlag.

Patterson, F.G. (1980). Conversations with a gorilla. *National Geographic, 154*, 438-465.

Perdeck, A.C. (1958). Two types of orientation in migratory starlings and chaffinches as revealed by displacement experiments. *Ardea, 46*, 1-37.

Savage-Rumbaugh, E.S., Murphy, J., Seveik, R.A., Williams, S., Brakke, K. & Rumbaugh, D.M. (1993). Language comprehension in ape and child. *Monographs of the Society for Research in Child Development, 58*, 3-4.

Sauer, F. & Sauer, E. (1955). Zur Frage der nachtlichen Zugorientierung von Grasmucken. *Rev. Suisse Zool., 62*, 250-259.

Savage-Rumbaugh, E.S. (1986). *Ape language from conditioned response to symbol.* New York: Columbia University Press.

Savage-Rumbaugh, E.S., Murphy, J., Seveik, R.A., Williams, S., Brakke, K. & Rumbaugh, D.M. (1993). Language comprehension in ape and child. *Monographs of the Society for Research in Child Development, 58*, 3-4.

Schmidt-Koenig, K. (1961). Die sonne als Kompass im Heim-Orientierungs-sustem der Brieftauben. *Zeitschrift fur Tierpsychologie, 68*, 221-244.

Seyfarth, R.M. & Cheney, D.L. (1980). The ontogeny of vervet monkey calling: A preliminary report. *Zeitschrift fur Tierpsychologie, 54*, 37-56.

Sherry, D. (1984). Food storage by black-capped chickadees: Memory for the location and contents of caches. *Animal Behaviour, 32*, 937-938.

Simmons, L.W. (1990). Pheromonal cues for the recognition of kin by female crickets, Gryllus bimaculatus. *Animal Behaviour, 40*, 192-195.

Smulder, T.V., Sasoon, A.D. & Devgood, T.J. (1995). Seasonal variation in hippocampal volume in a food storing bird, the black-capped chickadee. *Journal of Neurobiology, 27*, 15-25.

Terrace, H.S. (1979). *Nim.* New York: Knopf.

Tinbergen, N. (1951). *The study of instinct.* Oxford: Clarendon Press.

Tinbergen, N. & Kruyt (1938). Cited in N. Tinbergen (1951). *The study of instinct.* Oxford: Oxford University Press.

Tinbergen, N. & Perdeck, A.C. (1950). On the stimulus situation releasing the begging response in the newly hatched herring gull chick. *Behaviour, 3*, 1-38.

von Friscsh, K. (1967). *The dance language and orientation of bees.* Cambridge, MA: Harvard University Press.

Wagner, W.E., Jr. (1992). Deceptive or honest signalling of fighting ability? A test of alternative hypotheses for the function of changes in call dominant frequency by male cricket frogs. *Animal Behaviour, 44*, 449-462.

Walcott, C. & Brown, A.I. (1989). The disorientation of pigeons at Jersey Hill. Paper presented at the *Royal Institute of Navigation Conference.*

▶ **Introduction**

The focus of this chapter is the application of evolutionary explanations to human behaviour. This approach is known as evolutionary psychology. Evolutionary psychologists are interested in almost all areas of human psychology. This chapter concentrates on three: reproductive behaviour, psychological disorders and the evolution of intelligence.

Chapter summary

- Unit 1 considers the relationship between sexual selection and human reproductive behaviour, and evolutionary explanations for sex differences in parental investment.
- Unit 2 examines evolutionary explanations of human psychological disorders.

- Unit 3 explores the evolution of human intelligence and the relationship between brain size and intelligence.

Unit 1 Human reproductive behaviour

KEY ISSUES

1 How can we explain the evolution of sexual reproduction?

2 What is sexual selection?

3 Is sexual selection a significant force in evolution?

1.1 The problem of sex

The title of this section may seem rather curious. Why should sex be a 'problem'? However, there is a very real sense in which sex, or more specifically sexual reproduction, seems to raise a significant challenge to the Darwinian theory of evolution which was outlined in Chapter 13. To see how, let us briefly remind ourselves of the essence of this theory. Simply put, we can say that evolution will favour those individuals who leave most copies of their genes in future generations. When an individual reproduces sexually, 50% of their genetic material is passed on to each offspring, with the remaining 50% being contributed by the other parent. It is here that the problem arises. Imagine that a given female were to reproduce *asexually* – that is without the need of a male. This process is known as *parthenogenesis*. Under these circumstances, instead of her offspring possessing only 50% of her genetic material, it would instead possess 100%. In other words, it would be a perfect genetic clone of the mother.

It would appear then, that asexual reproduction is a far more efficient way of passing on genes from one generation to another than is reproducing sexually – exactly twice as efficient in fact. Following the logic of the evolutionary argument we can see that were an asexually reproducing mutant to emerge in any population, it ought very quickly to become established as the

dominant form, so much more successful would it be than its sexually reproducing competitors. Why, then, do so many species actually reproduce sexually?

As we might suspect, things are not as straightforward as they first appear. Our knowledge of the evolutionary process should lead us to suspect that for this situation to come about, there must be some important hidden advantages to sexual reproduction which outweigh the considerable costs. And this is precisely what evolutionary biologists have proposed. In the remainder of this section, we shall consider two related explanations for the persistence of sexual reproduction in so many species.

Evolutionary potential

Following the pioneering research of the geneticist R.A. Fisher (1958), it has been argued that one important consequence of sexual reproduction is *recombination*. Recombination is the process by which novel genotypes – new combinations of genes – are produced as a result of sexual reproduction. Two parents might produce four offspring, each of which inherits 50% of their genes from each parent, but (with the exception of identical twins) each will possess a completely unique genotype. This means that sexual reproduction produces considerable diversity, even within the offspring of one set of parents. But why should this be evolutionarily advantageous? After all, if there is an evolutionary successful individual, why break up these successful characteristics by the production of lots of diverse offspring who may not share them?

The answer can be found by considering the effect of environmental change. If an environment remains stable, and a successful organism reproduces asexually, then this may indeed be the most advantageous strategy. If, however, the environment changes, the adaptations which proved successful in the parent may prove to be inadequate to cope with new circumstances faced by the offspring. In this situation, asexual reproduction would become a distinct liability. If, on the other hand, the organism reproduces sexually, then the chances of its offspring possessing novel characteristics which may be able to cope with the altered environment are dramatically increased. Of course, there is no guarantee that these novel characteristics will be beneficial ones, but the point is that there is at least a chance that they will be. This explanation has been supported by evidence which shows that in species which can reproduce both sexually and asexually – for example, liver flukes (parasitic worms) – sexual reproduction is used at times when the offspring are likely to be dispersed to new environments (Daly & Wilson, 1983).

Co-evolution

A related explanation for the persistence of sexual reproduction was put forward by Leigh van Valen (1973). It uses the idea of *co-evolution* – the process by which traits in different organisms evolve in response to each other. The environments of all organisms involve other organisms which are in competition for resources. Once one species makes an evolutionary gain over another, strong evolutionary pressures will exist for the less successful species to respond by evolving some counter-measure. An improvement in the hunting skills of the lion is a big headache for the impala, unless the impala can evolve a corresponding increase in its own running speed. The advantage of sexual reproduction under these circumstances is obvious – increased diversity in offspring greatly increases the chances of such beneficial improvements occurring in subsequent generations.

Biologists have suggested that this explanation has particular relevance in the case of parasites and, particularly, *pathogens* like bacteria and viruses. Pathogens have the advantage that they reproduce very rapidly and can thus evolve novel and more successful variants in short spaces of time. A virus, for example, may reproduce thousands of times during its host's lifetime and as a result evolve more efficient ways of attacking the host's unique biochemistry. If the host were then to reproduce asexually, the virus would possess a considerable headstart over the host's offspring. The offspring would be biochemically identical to its mother, and so equally susceptible to the by now well evolved virus. However, were the host to reproduce sexually, the differences in the offspring's biochemistry may mean that the virus which successfully evolved to attack the mother would not be so successful in the offspring. Sexual reproduction, therefore, may be seen as a weapon in the co-evolution of the virus and host.

Key terms

Asexual reproduction *A mode of reproduction which involves a single parent. Offspring so produced are therefore genetically identical to their parent.*

Sexual reproduction *A mode of reproduction which involves two parents. This produces offspring who are genetically different from their parents.*

Parthenogenesis *The asexual development of an unfertilised ovum into an organism.*

Co-evolution *The process by which traits in separate organisms evolve in response to each other.*

1.2   Sexual selection

The concept of *sexual selection* refers to Darwin's suggestion, made in his book *Descent of man and selection in relation to sex* (first published in 1871) that traits could evolve because they were attractive to members of the opposite sex. We need to distinguish between two forms of sexual selection: *intersexual selection* and *intrasexual selection*. The first, intersexual selection, refers to the effects of choice on the selection of characteristics in the opposite sex. The second, intrasexual selection, refers to competition between members of the same sex for access to mates.

Intersexual selection

How does intersexual selection affect evolution? Take the example of the peacock. Why do peacocks have such large tails? These tails seem to be of no benefit to the peacock. Indeed, the fact that they are so large and heavy that they seriously impede movement would seem to be a distinct evolutionary disadvantage. The solution implied by the idea of intersexual selection, however, is that peacocks have evolved such large tails because peahens prefer them.

On the face of it, this is just as good a reason why a trait should evolve as if it had some obvious physical advantage. After all, evolution is about reproductive success, and what could be more important in securing reproductive success than attractiveness to members of the opposite sex? Peacocks with larger tails will be more attractive to more peahens, will have more mating opportunities and consequently will leave more offspring. Should an individual emerge who has a mutation for an even longer tail, then his reproductive success will be higher, and so the genes for this even longer tail will start to spread – presumably like wildfire.

One could imagine the same effect occurring for practically any trait. Let us take human nose length as an example. Imagine that human females had a tendency to prefer men with longer noses. Males who happened to be blessed with the longest noses would have more mating opportunities than those less generously endowed, and hence genes for long noses would become more numerous in future generations. Over time, we would thus expect to see an increase in the mean nose length of the population. Indeed, we could reasonably expect that after sufficient generations, the average human male would have a very long nose indeed.

Although this might strike you as a rather silly and far-fetched example, it does allow us to raise an interesting and controversial point about the whole concept of sexual selection. At first sight, nose length might appear to be an evolutionarily neutral trait. That is, apart from the possible effects of sexual selection, its length is not going to make much difference to one's reproductive success. However, the process of sexual selection could lead to human noses becoming very long indeed – so long that they became a liability. Imagine a nose of a metre or more in length. First, this is going to impose some considerable limitations on mobility. Second, it is going to put a great strain on the head and neck muscles, probably increasing the risk of injury and disability. Third, there would be a great risk of damage to the protuberance itself – broken noses would probably be commonplace. Fourth, there is the increased risk of inhaling quite large foreign objects. Of course, there may well be many more costs than these, but these examples illustrate the point: sexual selection of this kind could impose very real costs on reproductive success.

Whilst this particular example might seem somewhat frivolous, it is worth remembering that it is a close parallel to what does seem to have happened in the case of the peacock's tail. What we need to consider is whether sexual selection can operate in opposition to natural selection – whether it can cause the selection of traits which, in terms of natural selection, are maladaptive. In order to do this, we shall now consider two alternative views.

Arbitrary drift

This view originates in the work of R.A. Fisher who argued, in the 1930s, that sexual selection makes it quite possible for populations to develop in directions which run contrary to the expectations of natural selection. He suggested that an *arbitrary preference* – a preference which brings no practical benefits – could emerge in the female population. For example, females could prefer mates with longer tails. This might result in the evolution of longer tails despite possible evolutionary costs such as a reduction in mobility and the ability to obtain food. This is essentially because the cost of being unattractive to females would usually be higher than any other costs.

This view suggests that it is indeed possible for traits to emerge purely in response to female preference, even if those traits, in themselves, have nothing to do with adaptation for survival. They can be seen as nothing more than arbitrary fashion accessories, which serve no function other than to attract females.

Good genes

The principal difficulty with Fisher's view would seem to be this: why should females prefer males who possess traits which lower their ability to defend themselves against predators and obtain food? One possible answer might be that a female who bucked the trend by mating with a short-tailed male might benefit in the short run, by virtue of this male's superior ability to defend himself and obtain food. But she would suffer in the long run by producing sons with short tails who would be unlikely to find mates. However, this answer overlooks the effects of individual competition in the evolutionary process. Presumably this mutant female who prefers short tails will also produce daughters. And, because of the benefits of having a mate with a short tail, she is likely to produce more daughters with better survival chances than her long-tail-preferring competitors. If some of these daughters also inherit their mother's preference for short tails, they too will produce more surviving offspring than her competitors. Providing that the increase in reproductive success through the female line outweighs the decrease in reproductive success in the male line, then we could expect a preference for shorter tails to evolve.

Similarly, Fisher's model would seem to assume that at some point females *in general* started to prefer males with longer tails. If we assume, on the contrary, that the population was composed of females who varied in the length of tail they preferred, then it is difficult to see how a preference for longer tails could have become established. The key to this is the recognition that if a trait carries a cost to the male, then it also carries an indirect cost to the female. This occurs both in the form of reduced paternal investment from her mate – he is less able to provide her and her offspring with food and protection – and in reduced survival chances in her sons.

It has thus been argued that when a trait does seem to evolve as a result of sexual selection, it must also carry some – perhaps hidden – benefit for the male and hence, indirectly, for the female as well. It has been suggested by Hamilton and Zuk (1982) that elaborate ornamentation in male birds (such as the case of the peacock's tail) can be seen as evidence that the bird is free of parasites, as the presence of parasites impairs this ornamentation. Therefore, females who prefer males with longer and more elaborate tails would in fact be preferring the parasite-free – and hence more healthy – males. Similarly, Moller (1992) has suggested that such male ornamentation is evidence of symmetry. Symmetrical birds are less likely to have suffered physical stresses or to have poor genetic endowment, and so may be intrinsically better mates. Symmetry is thus a reliable indicator of good health and good genetic endowment.

Intersexual selection in humans

The evidence on human mate preference can be seen largely to support the 'good genes' view of intersexual selection. Whilst the phrase 'beauty lies in the eye of the beholder' might have some literary appeal, it is not born out by the evidence. In the largest study ever conducted of human mating preferences, David Buss surveyed more than 10,000 people drawn from 37 cultures (Buss, 1999). His sample covered all the major religious, racial and ethnic groups. Overwhelmingly, Buss found that, despite superficial cultural differences, a striking number of common patterns exist in human mating preferences around the globe.

Human female mating preferences

Financial resources Perhaps the most striking finding of Buss's research on the mating preferences of human females is the emphasis placed on the financial resources of the male. Buss found that women across all continents, all political systems, all racial and ethnic groups, and all systems of mating placed a greater emphasis than men on the financial resources of a prospective partner. Overall, women judged this to be about twice as important as men. Buss concludes from this that the mating preferences exhibited by modern women reflect the evolutionary adaptations of our ancestral past. Men who held greater resources were better mates because access to these resources improved the female's reproductive success.

Social status A related finding from Buss's research is that women universally value high social status in a mate. Evidence from contemporary hunter-gatherers suggests that ancestral human beings – like their modern counterparts – were very status conscious, and as with modern men, those with the highest status usually command the largest share of resources. American data, for example, show that women place great value on the possession of professional degrees in potential husbands, whilst they overwhelmingly rate lack of education as highly undesirable (Buss, 1999). The finding that women value social status in a potential mate significantly more highly than men again suggests that access to material resources may have been an important determinant of the reproductive success of our ancestors.

Preference for older men Buss found that in all societies surveyed, women preferred men who were older than themselves. Averaged across all the cultures studied, women prefer men who are approximately three and a half years older than themselves (Buss, 1999). Although quite considerable variations exist in the degree of seniority which women prefer in different cultures, women nevertheless exhibit an overwhelming preference for mates older than themselves. This trend, once again, may be related to resources. Older men typically have greater resources than younger men.

Preference for athletic prowess Buss reports that women consistently prefer men who are tall, physically strong and athletic (Buss, 1999). An American study of replies to personal advertisements reveals that advertisements placed by taller men (and which mention the man's height) receive more replies than those placed by shorter men (Lynn & Shurgot, 1984). This preference may again be attributable to characteristics which would have been advantageous in our ancestral environments. Taller, stronger and more athletic men would probably have been more successful hunters than short, weak and cumbersome men.

Preference for healthy and symmetrical males Women consistently rate good health as a highly important determinant of a mate's attractiveness (Buss, 1999). The reasons for this are fairly obvious. Not only are males in poor health less likely to be around to invest in their offspring, but their poor health may indicate a genetic predisposition to illness. Such a predisposition would be evolutionarily harmful if passed on to a female's offspring.

A considerable amount of research now exists to show that both men and women prefer mates who have symmetrical faces and bodies (eg, Grammer & Thornhill, 1994). It has been argued that facial and bodily symmetry indicate a *developmental stability* – that is, a good ability to withstand the effects of genetic and environmental stressors.

Human male mating preferences

Just as human females appear to have remarkably consistent preferences in their choice of mate, so do human males. Whilst men and women seem to share some of their mating preferences – their preference for healthy and symmetrical mates, for example – there are also some notable differences.

Preference for youth Without exception, Buss's data show that in every one of the 37 cultures included in his study, males exhibit a preference for a partners younger than themselves (Buss, 1999). Averaged across the 37 societies, males have a preference for a wife who is two and a half years younger than themselves, although this figure does vary quite considerably between cultures. In general, men rate younger women as more attractive than older women. Once again, the reason for this seems to be related to reproductive success. Whereas males remain able to produce sperm into old age, the fact of the menopause in women means that female fertility declines with age.

Preference for healthy mates As with women, there is ample evidence that human males, cross-culturally, tend to be attracted to women who display indicators of good health. Features such as clear and healthy skin, good hair quality and sound teeth are all judged to be important ingredients of female attractiveness.

Correspondingly, blemishes to the skin, missing or decaying teeth and hair in poor condition are all universally regarded as sexually unappealing. Evidence also suggests that men, like women, have a preference for mates who display symmetry in their faces and bodies. The reasons for this would appear to be the same as for women's preferences (Buss, 1999).

Preference for a particular body shape One feature which seems to vary considerably across cultures and over time is men's preference in relation to female body shape. We only have to look at the portrayal of women in popular art through the centuries to see how these preferences have changed in recent Western history. However, whilst the degree of fat preferred by men seems to be subject to change, there is one thing which remains constant. That is, men's preference for a particular waist-to-hip ratio (WHR). Prior to puberty, both sexes have a similar WHR of between 0.85 to 0.95. After puberty, however, and the associated redistribution of fat in the female, the WHR for women becomes significantly lower than for men. A reproductively healthy female will have a WHR of between 0.67 and 0.80 (Buss, 1999). Women with higher ratios than this exhibit significantly more problems in conceiving, have lower rates of pregnancy and display overall poorer health than those within this range (Singh & Young, 1995). Singh and Young's American research has shown that, regardless of the actual amount of fat a woman has, men universally prefer women with lower WHRs.

Evaluation

Whilst the research on human mate preference does highlight some very interesting similarities and differences in the preferences of males and females, we should be careful not to underestimate the importance of individual and cultural differences. Large scale surveys such as that carried out by David Buss emphasise mean findings across cultures and tend not to focus on differences between or within cultures to the same extent. What we do seem to be able to say, however, is that human mate preferences, like those of other species, are not limitlessly variable and determined entirely by the effects of culture, as some social scientists have in the past assumed. Instead, there does seem to be evidence that evolution has selected the broad parameters in which individual mate preference takes place.

Key terms

Intersexual selection *The process by which traits evolve because they are attractive to mates.*

Intrasexual selection *Evolution resulting from competition between same sex individuals for mates.*

Arbitrary drift *Evolution resulting from mate preferences which do not have any evolutionarily adaptive value.*

Symmetry *Physical equivalence between the two halves of a person's face or body.*

Waist-to-hip ratio (WHR) *The ratio of an individual's waist measurement to their hip measurement.*

Activity 1   Intersexual selection

Item A   Displaying peacock

Item B   Pinocchio

Questions

1   a) How would Fisher's concept of arbitrary drift explain the evolution of peacocks' tails and the possible evolution of very long noses?

    b) What are the main weaknesses of the idea of drift as an evolutionary force?

2   If we discount the possibility that drift alone can explain the evolution of peacocks' tails, how else can their evolution be explained?

Intrasexual selection

Intrasexual selection refers to competition for reproductive success between members of the same sex.

Mating competition

One of the most obvious examples of intrasexual competition is the overt fighting which breaks out between males of many species in the mating season. This is known as *mating competition*. This sort of competition is especially marked in *polygynous* species – that is, species whose mating patterns involve a single dominant male monopolising a 'harem' of several females (mating strategies are discussed later in this chapter). This is because, when the sex ratio is approximately 1:1 (that is, equal numbers of males and females) polygynous arrangements mean that, quite simply, there will not be enough females to go round. Some males will have several females to themselves, whilst others will have none. Under such circumstances, it is not difficult to see why competition between males for females should be so intense.

The concept of mating competition can be applied to human beings. First of all, it is a matter of common observation that human males can often react with violence and aggression in situations where their actual or desired relationship with a female is threatened by another male. In an analysis of research on same-sex homicides involving 'love triangles', Daly and Wilson (1988) show that 92% were male-male homicides. In another study of 'mate guarding tactics' Buss found that men were significantly more likely than women to make threats of violence towards men who made moves on their mates (Buss, 1988).

Women are not exempt from exhibiting mating competition, however. Whilst women are significantly less likely than men to resort to physical violence against other women, they certainly

equal men in their readiness to engage in verbal aggression (Buss, 1999). Women are more likely than men to engage in complex and subtle forms of criticism of their same-sex rivals. Research by Buss and Dedden (1990) shows that women are more likely than men to call their rivals 'fat' and 'ugly', to comment that their rivals' thighs are heavy and generally to make derogatory remarks about the shape and size of their rivals' bodies. It is also significant that the same study found women very quick to make derogatory remarks about their rivals' sexual conduct. Whilst men were fairly indifferent to such remarks in cases where they were only seeking a casual sexual partner, they were much more responsive to allegations of promiscuity in potential long-term mates. All of this suggests that women's verbal aggression is targeted at reducing the attractiveness of their competitors in the eyes of the male.

Post-copulatory competition: sperm competition

A far less obvious form of competition between males occurs only after the act of copulation. There are a number of examples of post-copulatory competition in the animal kingdom, but the principal human example is sperm competition.

Research by Baker (1996) reveals some fascinating facts about the composition of human sperm. The essence of this argument is that sperm from different males can compete with each other inside the female in what Baker describes as a 'war' to fertilise the ovum. Baker argues that human ejaculate contains four different kinds of sperm, all with different functions. First are *blockers*. These are slow, sluggish sperm which, according to Baker, lodge themselves in the cervical channels in an effort to prevent the entry of any rival sperm to the womb. Second are the *killer sperm*. These contain selective spermicidal chemicals which kill the sperm of rival males. Third are the *egg-getters*.

These are described by Baker as 'sleek and athletic', with large heads. It is the job of the egg-getters actually to fertilise the egg. Finally (and somewhat controversially) are the *family-planning sperm*. According to Baker, these sperm function to destroy the male's own egg-getters, at times when it is not in his interests for the female to conceive. They are supposedly produced in greater numbers when the male is stressed.

The fact that human beings – in common with many other species – seem to have evolved this special adaptation, strongly suggests that in our ancestral past human females were less monogamous than we might suppose. If they were indeed predominantly monogamous, then it is difficult to see how such a complex set of arrangements could have been selected.

Key terms

Mating competition *This is the competition which occurs between members of the same sex of a species over access to mating opportunities with members of the opposite sex.*

Post-copulatory competition *Any form of competition between same-sex members of a species which occurs after copulation.*

Sperm competition *Competition which takes place between the sperm of competing males after the female has been inseminated by both or all of them.*

Activity 2   Human intrasexual competition

Item A   The chastity belt

Modelling a chastity belt at Blackpool in 1970. Apparently, sales were 'good'.

Questions

1   Explain how each of the items might be interpreted as an example of intrasexual competition in human males.
2   Can you think of any further examples of intrasexual competition in human males?
3   Can you think of any examples of intrasexual competition in human females?

Item B   The harem

Below is an extract from Montesquieu's *Persian Letters*. In this extract, Usbek, a Persian nobleman visiting France, writes to his chief eunuch (castrated male) who he has left in charge of his harem.

'You are the faithful guardian of the most beautiful women in Persia. I have entrusted to you the most valuable thing that I have in the world; your hands hold the keys of those fateful doors that are opened for me alone...You keep guard both in the silence of the night and the tumult of the day...If the women whom you watch over should want to depart from their duty, you would make them give up such a hope. You are the scourge of vice and the bastion of fidelity.'

From Montesquieu, 1973 (first published in 1721)

Item C   Male reactions to rape

The following extract discusses men's reactions to the rape of their partners.

Reactions to rape provide a particularly revealing window on the psychology of male sexual proprietariness...Men often reject raped women as 'damaged goods', sometimes accusing the victim of having enjoyed or provoked the rape...Even where there is no issue of the illicit copulation having been other than coerced, men still seem to perceive the woman as diminished in value: 'She was mine and now she's been damaged' says one participant in a therapy group for American men whose partners have been raped; 'Something's been taken from me. I feel cheated. She was all mine before and now she's not,' says another.

From Wilson & Daly, 1992

1.3   Sex differences in parental investment

Much of the discussion of reproductive success so far has concentrated upon the reproductive act itself. However, this is only part of the story of how evolution works.

No matter how much effort an individual female puts into choosing genetically 'fit' males, or a male puts into securing numerous mating opportunities, no selection will occur unless the resulting offspring themselves survive, thrive and reproduce. An individual who made all the right choices when selecting a mate, but then acted in ways which prevented their offspring from thriving and reaching maturity would not leave many copies of their genes to future generations. It follows from this observation, therefore, that crucial to an individual's reproductive success will be how their offspring are cared for. This section examines the whole question of *parental investment* and, in particular, considers differences in how human males and females invest in their offspring.

The evolution of maternal investment

In most sexually reproducing species the size of the female gamete – the ovum – is many orders of magnitude larger than the male gamete – the sperm. This inequality in gamete size is known as *anisogamy*. This has important implications for how much each parent has to invest in the reproductive act. Whilst male investment need only last as long as it takes to complete the act of copulation, this is not so for the female who, in many species, must carry the foetus for the whole gestation period. This situation also has implications for the care of offspring after they have been born.

Since the male will have invested very little in the newborn offspring, he will have little to lose should this offspring not survive – after all, he can easily and relatively effortlessly impregnate another female to compensate. From the female point of view, however, after having invested so much in the foetus, the costs of the offspring not surviving would be considerable. It is for this reason, Trivers (1985) suggests, that species with relatively long periods of internal gestation – such as human beings – tend to exhibit predominantly maternal care of offspring.

Anisogamy is closely related to the phenomenon of intrasexual competition – or competition between members of the same sex for mates.

Female choosiness and intrasexual competition

The concept of intrasexual selection was discussed in the previous section. There we saw that competition between males for mates was likely to be particularly intense when the species in question has an equal sex ratio, but practises polygyny. Here we shall consider how sex differences in parental investment will lead to the relative sexual choosiness of females and also promote intrasexual competition.

It should not surprise us to find that where a female invests heavily in her young, she should be particularly discriminating in her choice of mate. After all, there is a direct correlation between the amount of investment given by the female and the cost born by her in the event of bearing the offspring of a male with poor (in evolutionary terms) genetic endowment. We should also expect to see a correlation between the amount of maternal investment required and the degree of choosiness displayed by the female.

Many evolutionary psychologists have argued that human females display a higher level of sexual choosiness than males. In a review of research on the relative willingness of men and women to engage in extramarital sexual encounters, Daly and Wilson report the findings of a survey which showed that 48% of married men interviewed would like to engage in extramarital sex in the future, compared to only 5% of women (Daly & Wilson, 1983). Secondly, the phenomenon of prostitution can be linked to the relative sexual choosiness of women. Prostitution is popularly known as the world's 'oldest profession' with some justification. It has been found to exist in every society which

has been thoroughly studied, and despite the enlightened attitudes which followed the rise of feminism, it shows no sign of diminishing. Estimates of how many men solicit the services of prostitutes vary, but a study by Kinsey et al. in the 1940s suggested that at that time 69% of American men had at some time solicited a prostitute and that for 15% of men this was a regular activity (Kinsey et al., 1948). It is highly significant that prostitution remains almost exclusively a service provided by women for men. It would seem to reflect the fact that men's desire for extramarital casual sex considerably outweighs women's, just as the concept of anisogamy would predict.

The relative sexual choosiness of women may also explain observed differences in the sexual promiscuity of homosexual men and women. In an influential discussion of this subject, Donald Symons suggests that the relative promiscuity of male homosexuals reflects not their homosexuality, but simply the fact that they are men. As Symons has put it: 'Heterosexual men would be as likely as homosexual men to have sex most often with strangers, to participate in anonymous sex orgies in public baths and to stop off in public restrooms for five minutes of fellatio on the way home from work if women were interested in these activities. But women are not interested' (Symons, 1979).

Sexual choosiness in females has implications for male behaviour. Somewhat obviously, the more choosy the females of the species, the more difficult it will be for any individual male to secure matings. This difficulty inevitably increases the degree of competition between males for matings – in other words, the degree of intrasexual competition.

The evolution of paternal investment

So far, this unit has focused on maternal investment. As we have seen, this situation seems to follow from the fact that, physiologically, the female must carry the burden of the initial nurturance of the foetus and so has far more to lose by the failure of an infant to survive than the male. However, this argument would also seem to predict that where the female is not physiologically obliged to invest so heavily in a foetus, she may not be selected to invest so heavily in her offspring. Indeed, there is no reason why, in principle, the sex-role specialisations which we have so far considered should not be reversed. In other words, where females vary more in their reproductive success than males, where there is greater competition between females for males than vice versa, and where males are more choosy than females about their choice of mate, we should also expect to find higher levels of male investment in offspring.

There are indeed a number of species in which this sex-role 'reversal' appears to occur. Perhaps the best known examples of sex role reversal occur in various species of birds. Examples include shorebirds such as the dotterel, and birds such as the emu and lily-trotting jacana (Trivers, 1985). These species of bird are characterised by the fact that the female makes no investment in the young once the eggs have been laid. Once she has laid her eggs, the male broods them until the chicks hatch, and thereafter the young are quickly capable of feeding themselves. As a result of the relatively low investment females have to make, the females of these species are frequently *polyandrous* – that is, they mate with more than one male during a mating season – whereas the males breed only once each season. This is clearly a reversal of the situation in species with high levels of maternal investment. Secondly, females tend to compete with one another for males, and this has led to females being generally larger than males, more active during courtship, more aggressive than males and more brightly coloured – as a means of attracting males through intrasexual selection.

Although there does seem to be evidence for assuming that in human beings it is the mother who has evolved to provide the majority of parental investment, there is also evidence to suggest that paternal investment is a significant factor. First of all, it is clear that meat played a big part in the diet of our early ancestors. Since males would probably have been responsible for hunting, we can assume that offspring who received meat from their fathers would have been at an evolutionary advantage over those who did not. It follows from this that it would be in the evolutionary interests of such males to provision their own offspring with the spoils of their hunting.

Secondly, the fact that human males exhibit such a high level of concern over the sexual activities of their partners, suggests that they have evolved to invest in their offspring. Men demand a high level of confidence of paternity, and this is reflected in such things as sexual jealousy and demands for sexual fidelity in their partner. If males were not selected to invest in their offspring, it is difficult to see why they should be so concerned to ensure that their children are indeed their own.

At the same time, we should expect male parental investment to be more variable than female. This is partly for the reason already mentioned, that confidence of paternity is variable. Whereas there can be no doubt that a particular woman is the mother of a given child, there is always room for doubt in the case of paternity. Overall, we can predict that men with low confidence of paternity will be less likely to invest in their offspring than men with high confidence of paternity. Secondly, the fact remains that men can out-reproduce women by many times. Men will thus face a trade-off between investment in existing offspring and fathering new ones. In cases where males choose to father additional offspring with a different female, we can expect there to be conflict between the mothers of the two sets of offspring over how the father's resources should be split between them. It is perhaps instructive to consider the prevalence of financial conflict in divorce against this background.

Key terms

Anisogamy *Inequality in gamete size.*

Maternal investment *Investment in offspring carried out by the mother.*

Paternal investment *Investment in offspring carried out by the father.*

Activity 3   Sex differences in parental investment

Item A   Always on the look out

Item B   Child support

Questions

1   Item A illustrates sex differences in parental investment in humans. Explain how evolutionary theory predicts the selection of such differences.

2   Item B illustrates the conflicts which can occur between men and women over the provision of resources to their offspring. How does evolutionary theory shed light on such conflicts?

1.4   Reproductive strategies

Evolutionary psychologists and biologists tend to regard patterns of behaviour as *strategies*, which serve the long term reproductive interests of individuals. This section focuses on mating strategies, and reviews mating strategies adopted by human beings.

Types of mating strategy

Mating strategies can be divided into four types:

- **Monogamy** is where a single male is mated to a single female. Monogamy may be lifelong or serial – that is, one monogamous 'pair bond' is replaced with another and so on.
- **Polygyny** is where a single male is simultaneously mated to a number of females. Polygynously-mated males tend to jealously guard their 'harems' of females, since in many species they will be subject to takeover attempts by other, unmated, males.
- **Polyandry** is where a number of males are simultaneously mated to one female. It is rare in mammals, and usually only occurs under quite specific ecological circumstances.
- **Promiscuity** refers to a situation in which there are no stable mating relationships. Males and females meet only to copulate and then the male plays no further part in the rearing of the offspring.

Whilst most species display dominant mating strategies – that is, strategies which most members of the population adopt for most of the time – many adopt different mating strategies at different times and under different circumstances. Indeed, some species, including human beings, at different times display all of the above strategies. Before we move on to look specifically at human mating strategies, we shall first consider the various factors which are related to the adoption of different mating strategies.

Factors associated with mating strategies

Parental investment Mating strategies are closely associated with sex differences in parental investment. In situations where the sustained care of both parents is necessary to ensure the survival of offspring, monogamous mating strategies tend to be adopted. Monogamy is frequently found in birds, for example, where both parents are required to provide sufficient food for infants. Under these circumstances monogamy is simply the best strategy for both the male and female. Although the male could, perhaps, inseminate other females, without his feeding efforts the resulting offspring would be unlikely to survive. In other species, such as most mammals, where male effort is not so crucial for the survival of the young, such effort is most productively directed towards securing additional matings. As a result, such species frequently display polygynous, or in some cases such as chimpanzees, promiscuous mating strategies.

The same logic explains why, in some species, we find polyandrous mating strategies. Although extremely rare in mammals, polyandry is found in some species of birds. In sandpipers, for example, the female often lays two clutches of eggs in each season, with each clutch being incubated by a different male. This situation is possible because there is no real difference in survival rates for infants raised by a single parent instead of two.

Ecological conditions Ecological conditions can explain why some principally monogamous species display occasional polygyny. This has been observed, for example, in a number of migratory songbirds such as finches. In these species, the male arrives at the breeding ground in the spring before the female, and selects a territory on which to build a nest. The quality of territories varies considerably and, importantly, seems to be a major determinant of the number of surviving offspring: the reproductive success of males with good territories is significantly higher than that of males with poor territories. This variation seems to be so great that a curious situation results: a female may enjoy better reproductive success by becoming the second mate of a male with a very good territory, than by having a male with a poorer territory all to herself. The point at which the variation becomes so great that the female is better off opting for polygyny is known as the *polygyny threshold* (Orians, 1969). It may well be that this concept is useful in explaining some of the instances of polygyny in human beings, which is discussed later in this unit.

Sexual dimorphism As has already been noted, an inevitable consequence of polygyny in species with approximately equal numbers of males and females (a 50/50 sex ratio) is competition between males for access to females. In many cases, access to females is ultimately settled by fighting between males, and for this reason there are strong selective pressures towards the evolution of larger and stronger males: the biggest and strongest males win more fights, get access to more females and hence leave more copies of their genes in future generations. For this reason, *sexual dimorphism* – that is, the degree of difference in size between the male and female – is taken as a reliable indicator of the dominant mating strategy of the species: the greater the degree of dimorphism, the more polygynous the species.

There are, however, some exceptions to this. First, there are polygynous species in which male access to females does not depend upon fighting success. For instance in the Weddell's seal, mating takes place in the water, unlike other species of seal, and hence agility may be a more important determinant of reproductive success than size. Accordingly, in this species the male is actually somewhat smaller than the female (Daly & Wilson, 1983). Secondly, there may be a tradeoff between size and agility. Terrestrial monkeys, for example, are usually more dimorphic than arboreal monkeys (those who swing through trees), even though both are polygynous. This would appear to be because although size may help the arboreal varieties to win fights, it makes swinging through the trees more difficult. Evolution thus selects the most advantageous compromise between size and agility (Daly & Wilson, 1983).

Key terms

Mating strategies *The patterns of mating behaviour exhibited by a species. There are four main kinds:*

- *monogamy – a single male is mated to single female;*
- *polygyny – a number of females are mated to a single male;*
- *polyandry – a number of males are mated to a single female;*
- *promiscuity – no stable mating relationships exist.*

Sexual dimorphism *The degree to which the male and female of a species differ physically.*

Activity 4   Predicting mating strategies

Item A   The elephant seal

Relative size of male and female: **MALE** FEMALE

Gestation mode: Internal

Parental investment: Predominantly maternal

Item B   The spotted sandpiper

Relative size of male and female: MALE **FEMALE**

Gestation mode: External

Parental investment: Predominantly paternal

Questions

1 From the information given in items A and B, predict the principal mating strategy (polygyny, monogamy or polyandry) employed by the elephant seal and the spotted sandpiper. Give reasons for your answers.

2 For an imaginary monogamous species, what predictions would you make about the following characteristics:

a) relative size of male and female

b) gestation mode

c) parental investment?

1.5   Human mating strategies

When we come to consider mating strategies in human beings, matters are complicated by the existence of culture. There is no doubt, for example, that human societies display a considerable degree of variation in the ways in which sexual relationships and the relationships between parents and their offspring are organised. To take just one illustration of this, consider the likely reaction of the family and friends of a young British male from a Christian family, who announced that he was planning to live polygynously with several women. Such an announcement would no doubt provoke considerable shock and may very well elicit reactions of alarm, even disgust. Amongst the !Kung of the Kalahari desert, by contrast, such an announcement would be a source of familial pride and social prestige.

In one of the most extensive surveys of human societies, 849 societies were examined and were found to break down in the following way (Murdock, 1967):

Polygynous: 708 (83%)

Monogamous: 137 (16%)

Polyandrous: 4 (<1%)

In view of the foregoing discussions of the evolutionary basis of mating strategies, we should not, perhaps, find these figures surprising. Evolutionary theory would seem to predict that males have more to gain from mating with several partners than do females, which would seem to explain the prevalence of polygyny. Equally, the same argument would predict that males should not, as a rule, be content to share a female with other males as in polyandrous marriages. Indeed, all the evidence suggests that where polyandry in human beings is found, it only occurs as a result of exceptional ecological conditions which effectively preclude other mating strategies. The classic example of human polyandry is found in the Himalayan region where agricultural conditions are such that several men are required to produce enough food to support a single female and her offspring. However, as kinship theory would predict, the men involved in polyandrous marriages are very often brothers. The effect of this is that they will still be related to the wife's children, if only as an uncle.

We do need to interpret figures such as these with caution, however. First of all, even though the majority of human *societies* might be polygynous, it does not follow that the majority of marriages are polygynous. In anthropology the term society is used to refer to social groupings ranging from a few hundred to large scale industrial societies like the United States of America, containing several hundred million people. As it happens, the vast majority of people live in advanced Western societies which are formally monogamous. Even within those societies identified as formally polygynous, it remains the case that the majority of individual marriages will be monogamous. This is because the human species has a 50/50 sex ratio – that is, approximately equal numbers of males and females. It thus follows that only a minority of men could be married polygynously in any human society. Anthropological evidence suggests, as the theory of the polygyny threshold outlined earlier would predict, that those men who are polygynously married tend to be those who hold most resources.

Secondly, the designation of a society as formally monogamous or polygynous may conceal a rather more complex picture of how people actually behave. For example, in most modern industrial societies the dominant pattern of mating is increasingly becoming *serial monogamy* – that is, one monogamous relationship is replaced with another. Furthermore, whilst it is impossible to estimate with any accuracy the degree of marital infidelity which actually takes place, common experience tells us that it is sufficiently common to lead us to regard the notion of monogamy with some suspicion.

Summary

1. Sexual reproduction has evolutionary costs, but these are often outweighed by its advantages.

2. Sexual reproduction results in genetic diversity which may be advantageous, particularly in a changing environment.

3. Sexual selection is the process by which traits are selected through sexual choice. There are two types: intrasexual selection which refers to competition between members of the same sex for mates, and intersexual selection which refers to the evolutionary effects of sexual preferences in either sex.

4. Human males and females both exhibit preferences for mates who display evolutionarily advantageous characteristics.

5. Human beings, like other species, display many examples of intrasexual competition.

6. Mating strategies are associated with sex differences in parental investment, ecological conditions and degree of sexual dimorphism.

7. Human beings display a range of mating strategies, although in the majority of human societies polygyny is practised.

Activity 5   Human polygyny and polyandry

Item A   Sex differences in reproductive benefits of polygyny

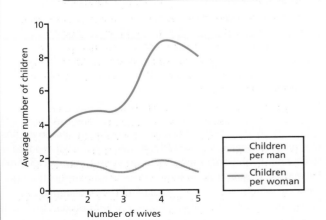

The chart shows the differences in reproductive success for men and women amongst the Temne people of Sierra Leone, in relation to the number of wives a man ever marries.

Adapted from Daly & Wilson, 1983

Item B   Sororal polygyny and cohabitation

Polygynously married men may either cohabit with all their wives in the same dwelling, or alternatively, they may maintain contact with several wives who each live separately. Although there may be economic advantages to having all one's wives under one roof, the scope for conflict between wives is obviously increased. Data suggest, however, that cohabitation amongst wives is much more common when sororal polygyny (that is, when the wives are sisters) is practised. The following table illustrates the correlation between sororal polygyny and cohabitation in a sample of 377 societies in which marriage is usually polygynous:

	Shared dwelling	Separate dwelling
Sororal polygyny	60 societies (81%)	14 societies (19%)
Nonsororal polygyny	96 societies (32%)	207 societies (68%)

Adapted from Daly & Wilson, 1983

Item C   Polygyny, wealth and security

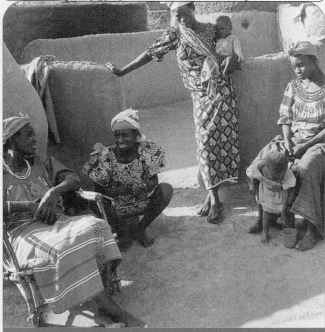

Adama's wives – Zenabou, Bintu, Meryam and Barkissou

Adama is a wealthy man. He lives in a village called Sobtenga in Burkina Faso, a country in northwest Africa. Ten years ago he had two wives.

Zenabou, his first wife, thought polygyny was a good idea. It provided her with a 'sister' to share the burdens of domestic work and childcare. Now she is not so sure. Adama has taken two more wives, the youngest of whom, Bintu, is only 16. He is besotted with Bintu and she clearly enjoys the attention. Despite grumbling, his other wives accept the situation. For marriage is seen primarily as an economic affair and Adama's 12 oxen are proof that he can provide security for his wives and children.

Adapted from Brazier, 1995

Item D   Polyandry

Polyandry among the Nyinba of Nepal. The 12 year old girl on the right is engaged to five brothers, three of whom are pictured here.

The Nyinba people of Nepal practice fraternal polyandry – two or more brothers are married to one wife. They inherited this custom from their Tibetan ancestors who migrated to Nepal centuries ago. They also inherited a love for trading and herding which, together with cultivating the meagre soil, make up the traditional Nyinba economy. Polyandry suits this economy. 'With one or two husbands always on herding or trading trips, one husband will always be at home to care for the wife,' explained Maila Dai, a trader from the village of Bargaau. 'We think polyandry is just like insurance for the wife. If one husband is no good or leaves his wife, there's always another brother.'

Polyandry has been explained as a way of preventing land from being divided up into less profitable units when a family of sons inherits from the previous generation. It also concentrates the wealth of each household by maintaining a large population of working adult males under one roof.

To the Nyinbas, its advantages are obvious. Both men and women talk about the wealth polyandry provides and the way it distinguishes them from their poorer Hindu neighbours. In the words of one mother, 'If my sons partition the land, we will become as poor as the Hindu village of Tey'.

An ideal polyandrous wife is obedient to all her husbands' wishes, never shows sexual favouritism and does nothing to cause conflict between them. She should also have at least one child from each father – otherwise one of the husbands might accuse her of favouritism. (The mother always announces who the father is.)

When asked about jealousy between her husbands, Tsering Zangmo replied, 'But they are brothers. They are never jealous.' However when pressed she giggled and blushed, admitting, 'Well, they only have a very little jealousy. If you like one husband very much, you have to be secret so the others don't know. We make love in the middle of the night, lying naked in sheepskins. We'd never do it just before going to sleep or just before waking up as the others might hear us.'

Adapted from Dunham, 1992

Questions

1   What does item A reveal about the relative reproductive benefits of polygyny to males and females?

2   Read Item B. Why do you think that cohabitation should be so much more common in cases of sororal polygyny than in nonsororal polygyny? You may find it helpful to consider the degrees of genetic relatedness between the adult females and the children in each case.

3   Read Item C. What are the advantages and disadvantages of polygyny for Adama and his wives?

4   Read Item D. What are the advantages and disadvantages of polyandry?

Unit 2 Evolutionary explanations of mental disorders

KEY ISSUES

1 **How can evolutionary theory explain human emotions?**

2 **What are the adaptive functions of anxiety?**

3 **Can evolutionary theory account for depression, schizophrenia and obsessive compulsive disorder?**

Introduction

At first sight, the proposal that evolutionary theory might be able to explain mental disorders in human beings may seem a little far-fetched. We are, after all, accustomed to think about mental disorders as pathological – that is as something harmful, abnormal and undesirable. However, it is important to remember that natural selection does not merely promote behaviour which is 'desirable' in the common sense of the word. As we have emphasised, it promotes behaviour which has a positive consequence for ultimate reproductive success. And, it is quite possible that something which has a positive consequence for ultimate reproductive success may well be undesirable in the ordinary, human, sense of the word. Indeed, as we saw in the last unit, evolution may well have favoured an approach to sexual behaviour in human beings which most of us would regard as morally undesirable!

This unit considers the role of evolutionary explanation in the understanding of a range of mental disorders in human beings.

2.1 The emotions

As Darwin himself recognised, it seems likely that the emotions played an important part in human evolution. It is useful to think of emotions as a kind of defence mechanism, which serves to protect the individual from the most damaging effects of his or her social and physical environment. Take the example of fear. We have all experienced fear at some time: fear of heights, fear of taking an examination, fear of a vicious dog, or fear of a violent person, perhaps. Fear makes us more cautious, more inclined to avoid whatever is causing it and quicker to react when confronted with it. It is not difficult to see how the emotion of fear might have evolved. A person who is afraid of lions will be more likely to take steps to avoid contact with lions than one who is not – and hence, will be less likely to be eaten!

Similarly, take the emotion of anger. Like fear, we have all experienced anger at some time in our life – anger at the theft of a treasured possession, or at a partner's infidelity, or on discovering that we have been the victim of a deception. Just as fear might have evolved to protect us from genuine danger, so we can see how anger might have evolved as a warning to others: interfere with my reproductive success at your peril! Individuals who display anger at the selfish behaviour of others may be more successful than those who do not at discouraging such behaviour, and hence at discouraging threats to their own reproductive success.

As Nesse and Williams (1995) put it: 'an emotion is like a computer program that adjusts many aspects of the machine to cope effectively in a particular kind of situation'. This analogy is a useful one. Computer programs are designed to cope effectively with completely novel inputs. The sentence I have just written is almost certainly unique, for example, but the word-processing program I am using has no difficulty in recognising the keyboard inputs and translating them into text on the screen. In the same way, when human beings are confronted with completely novel situations, the emotions have no difficulty in directing an appropriate response.

As with all evolutionary explanations of human behaviour, it is important to remember that the vast bulk of human adaptations emerged in environments very different to those in which human beings now live. These ancestral environments are called the *environment of evolutionary adaptedness* (or EAA). We should always be aware, therefore, of the possibility that what seems to us to be maladaptive behaviour in the modern environment may have had a perfectly explicable adaptive function when manifested in our EAA. This point is particularly important in the context of mental disorders.

2.2 Anxiety

Anxiety can be described as a general feeling of dread or apprehensiveness. We all feel anxiety at some time, but occasionally people experience levels of anxiety which are so out of proportion with any actual threat, that they are described as having an anxiety disorder. Indeed, Nesse and Williams (1995) report that 15% of the US population has suffered from a clinical anxiety disorder. Many more people seem to exist in a more or less permanent, if sub-clinical, state of anxiety.

The positive functions of anxiety are not too difficult to see. When faced with a threat, anxiety provokes changes in our thinking, our behaviour and our physiological responses. The sudden appearance of a tiger on the scene, for example, provokes a rapid increase in heart rate, glucose and adrenaline levels, which all contribute to a swift 'fight or flight' reaction. However, there does not, at first sight, seem to be a clear reason why we suffer so *much* anxiety – and often over things we can't change anyway.

As noted above, the answer might lie partly in the simple but important fact that natural selection does not operate to produce optimum happiness, but only optimum reproductive success. Thus whilst an excessive amount of anxiety might not make much sense to us from the point of view of our own happiness, it may be more explicable from the point of view of our ultimate reproductive success. Nesse and Williams (1995) introduce what they call the 'smoke-detector principle' to illustrate this point. If we have a smoke-detector which is too insensitive, we run the risk that we will not be alerted to the presence of a fire and as a result will die. If, on the other hand, we have a smoke detector which is excessively sensitive and which gives frequent false alarms, we may suffer a considerable amount of inconvenience in responding to these false alarms, but at least we will not die in a fire. In other words, the costs, in terms of reproductive success, of responding to many false alarms are considerably lower than of not being alerted to a fire at all.

In the same way, although there are real costs in terms of an excessive propensity to anxiety, the costs of an insensitivity to threatening situations may be even higher. Interestingly, the psychiatrist Isaac Marks has coined a term to describe people who are insufficiently prone to anxiety: *hypophobics* (Marks, 1987). Whilst we might be tempted to regard hypophobia as highly desirable state, such people tend to suffer all kinds of personal catastrophes, from being sacked to suffering serious injuries and death as a consequence of their lack of anxiety about things which can cause serious harm.

Key terms

Environment of evolutionary adaptedness (EAA) *The environment in which a trait evolved and in which it was adaptive.*

Hypophobia *A condition in which sufferers experience excessively low levels of anxiety in the face of danger.*

2.3 Depression

Types of depression: unipolar and bipolar

There are two principal types of depression: *unipolar (or major) depression* and *bipolar depression* (sometimes known as manic-depression). The first, unipolar depression, refers to a state of pathological sadness, which can last for significant periods of time and can, in some cases, induce the sufferer to commit suicide or other acts of self-harm. According to DSM-IV (the Diagnostic and Statistical Manual of the American Psychiatric Association) a diagnosis of unipolar depression should be made when five or more of the following symptoms are present every day or almost every day for a period of at least two weeks: sad, depressed mood; loss of interest and pleasure in usual activities; difficulty in sleeping; changes in activity level; weight loss or gain, loss of energy or tiredness, negative self-concept, self-blame and self-reproach; problems with concentration; recurring thoughts of suicide or death.

People suffering from bipolar depression experience both depression as described above, and periods of mania – that is, excessively elated mood, exuberance and self-confidence. Those in the throes of a manic episode may feel excessively capable, display high energy levels and speak effusively about their own abilities and achievements. They also frequently display a heightened libido (sexual drive) and belief in their own sexual prowess. Eventually, however, the manic episode usually gives way to physical and mental exhaustion, and this is typically followed by a period of depression.

Evolution and depression

On the face of it, it is difficult to see how depression could possibly be seen as in any sense an adaptive trait. People who are depressed achieve less, are less sociable and are more at risk of suicide and self-harm than those who are not. Similarly, depression is often associated with a decline in libido, which

would appear to have an obviously negative effect on reproductive success. At the same time, depression seems to be a universal feature of human life – it appears to be found in almost all human societies. If depression is so widespread, then it may not be as maladaptive as it seems.

One possible answer to this question is known as the *rank theory of depression* (Stevens & Price, 1996). To understand what this theory is proposing, we need to consider some possible consequences of human conflict. Evolutionary theory predicts that conflict will exist between individuals over a whole variety of fitness-relevant issues: access to food, access to mates, and child-rearing, to list just three. Although we can predict that natural selection will favour the evolution of strong motivations to win in situations of conflict, it also seems likely that it will favour a strategy of surrender under certain circumstances. Specifically, it will pay an individual to surrender when continuing to fight would incur greater costs than 'cutting one's losses' and giving up. If you are in a physical fight with someone much stronger than you, it is clearly better to stop fighting whilst you are still alive than to continue until you are maimed or killed!

This observation has led to the proposal that depression might be a psychological response to potential defeat in situations of conflict (Stevens & Price, 1996). Rather than continue in a potentially damaging conflict, the onset of depression could be a psychological mechanism which leads the individual to retreat from the conflict. The corresponding loss of self-confidence, loss of energy and belief in one's ability to succeed serve to ensure that the individual does not return to the arena of conflict. In this way, depression could be seen as a form of self-preserving behaviour in situations of social conflict.

Of course, if depression leads to suicide, then it would appear to exceed any adaptive value it may have. However, it is important to remember that in the EAA, the lack of technology would have made it rather difficult to commit suicide. So it could be argued that although suicide and self-harm may sometimes result from depression in the modern world, this would have been less likely at the time when the response evolved.

Just as rank theory explains depression in terms of yielding in situations of conflict, so it may be able to explain manic episodes too. It seems at least plausible to suggest that whilst depression corresponds to the losing position in a conflict, mania might correspond to the winning position. The displays of excessive self-confidence, energy and strength may be successful in heading off potential challenges from others (Stevens & Price, 1996). It should of course also be noted that mania does not seem to pose such a problem from the point of view of evolutionary theory. Unlike the symptoms of depression, the symptoms of mania – high levels of energy, self-confidence and libido, for example – may make a positive contribution to reproductive success.

Postnatal depression

According to Badcock (2000) between 50% and 70% of mothers experience some mild feelings of depression accompanied with weeping within a few days of giving birth. In a much smaller percentage of women this reaction is much more pronounced and can produce a serious depressive illness. In the past, psychologists tended to view all examples of postnatal depression as pathological. However, Badcock (2000) has pointed put that postnatal depression – particularly the much more common mild form – may have an adaptive value. We have already seen that the degree of parental investment required from men and women is very different, and that women have to invest significantly more than men in reproduction. This applies not only to the gestation period, but also to the early nurturing of the baby. It follows from this that to invest in a baby who has a poor chance of making it to adulthood would represent a serious waste of reproductive resources. If instead of doing this, women had some way of assessing the likelihood that an offspring would reach maturity, they would be much less likely to waste resources on unviable (from an evolutionary point of view) offspring. Badcock suggests that this is why postnatal depression may have evolved. He points out that mothers who experience postnatal depression usually report feelings of indifference to their babies. If this produces mild neglect – as in the EAA it almost certainly would have done – then postnatal depression could perhaps be seen as a 'testing' process, whereby mothers assess whether it is worth their while investing any more in their baby than they already have done. In other words, if the baby survives this brief period of maternal neglect, this is a good and reliable indication that they are strong enough to stand a fair chance of making it to sexual maturity.

Key terms

Unipolar depression *A disorder in which a person experiences periods of pathological sadness.*

Bipolar depression *A disorder in which a person experiences periods of pathological sadness followed by periods of elation or 'mania'.*

Rank theory of depression *An evolutionary theory which regards depression as an evolved response to potentially harmful conflict. The idea is that it is better to yield to one's opponent and give up the fight, than to fight to the death.*

Postnatal depression *A depressive illness experienced by some women following childbirth.*

2.4   Schizophrenia

Schizophrenia is a serious psychological disorder which affects about 1% of the British population. According to DSM-IV, the criteria for a diagnosis of schizophrenia are characterised by the following symptoms:

- Hallucinations – for example hearing voices that don't exist.
- Delusions – ideas that are clearly untrue, such as the belief that you are Elvis Presley.
- Control of thoughts – for example, thoughts are being inserted into a person's mind.
- Catatonic behaviour – abnormal movements ranging from wild flailing of limbs to a complete lack of activity.
- Negative symptoms – a lack or reduction of behaviours, for example, a lack of emotion, motivation and interest. These symptoms usually result in social withdrawal and a lowering of social performance.

Schizophrenics frequently suffer serious social problems, such as relationship difficulties, loss of employment or problems with the law. As with other mental disorders, there is no obvious reason why a gene (or set of genes) predisposing people towards schizophrenia might have evolved. There are two broad approaches to the problem, although no agreement exists at present amongst evolutionary psychologists.

The first approach is to consider the possibility that genes predisposing an individual to schizophrenia might also be responsible for other, more obviously adaptive, traits. Although there seems to be a genetic element to the development of schizophrenia, there is not a simple correlation between the possession of gene *x* and the development of this disorder. However, many individuals appear to have a genetic predisposition to schizophrenia (see pp 683-684). This has led some researchers to speculate that the same genetic pre-disposition might produce some other adaptive trait. For example, Nesse and Williams (1995) suggest that a tendency to be suspicious of the motivations of others could be very useful in evolutionary terms, but only becomes maladaptive when it becomes exaggerated with the development of paranoid schizophrenia. Similarly, they suggest that the high levels of creativity and achievement often found in the relatives of schizophrenics could provide support for the idea that its genetic basis has beneficial as well as harmful effects.

A second approach is to try to find an adaptive value for schizophrenic symptoms themselves. Once again, it is important to focus on the value which such symptoms may have had in our EAA. One attempt to provide such an explanation is made by Stevens and Price (1996), and relates to the concept of *optimal group size*. According to Stevens and Price, all social species have an optimal group size – that is where the group is neither too small or too large to be effective. Benefits to an increase in group size include the possibility of cooperative hunting, reciprocal trading of food and childcare, and defence against predators. However, if a group becomes too large, the costs may start to outweigh the benefits. For example, where the group is nomadic, the logistics of moving a large group from one territory to another may outweigh the benefits of size. Similarly, the larger the group, the greater the potential for internal competition for resources and the emergence of 'free riders' – that is, individuals who fail to reciprocate.

In response to this, Stevens and Price suggest that the symptoms of schizophrenia – such as bizarre beliefs, hallucinations, delusions of grandeur etc – may have had the effect of splitting up groups. As an individual with such symptoms emerged, it is possible both that their behaviour becomes incompatible with remaining a member of the original group, and is also likely to induce others to follow them in forming a new group.

Whilst it seems that Stevens and Price have identified an interesting parallel between the characteristics of group leaders and schizophrenics, which may well be applicable to the personalities of certain contemporary religious and political revolutionaries, their analysis should be treated with some caution. The main reason for this is that it seems to rest on a fundamentally group selectionist assumption about the need for groups to regulate their own sizes. In contrast to this, we know that a trait will only evolve if it is actually beneficial in terms of the reproductive success of the individual who possesses it, whether this be through their own reproductive effort or that of their relatives. To say that something has evolved because it benefits the group to which the individual belongs is, as we have seen, a flawed interpretation of evolutionary theory.

Key terms

Schizophrenia *A serious psychological disorder, characterised by such symptoms as hallucinations, delusions, belief in control of thoughts, catatonic behaviour and negative symptoms.*

Genetic predisposition *A situation where an individual's genetic make-up increases their likelihood of developing some trait.*

2.5 Obsessive-compulsive disorder (OCD)

Obsessive-compulsive disorder is a condition in which the sufferer feels compelled to carry out certain, often pointless, actions repeatedly. Common examples of this disorder include compulsive hand-washing – in which the individual is driven to wash their hands again and again, even though there is no rational evidence of their being dirty – obsessive rituals – such as the need to keep checking that one has switched off the cooker – and obsessive thinking, such as the need to continue running over in one's mind an unpleasant event. It is estimated that between one and one and a half million people in the UK suffer from this condition. OCD can be very debilitating, and in severe cases people's lives can be ruined by their compulsive need to carry out certain actions or to repeat cycles of thought. Not only do obsessions sometimes make ordinary social interaction impossible – when, for example, the sufferer believes that other people represent a source of potentially fatal contamination – but the time needed to carry out the obsession can severely limit the time available for normal activities.

As with other mental disorders, the evolutionary value of OCD seems at first sight to be elusive. However, if it is looked at in the context of our EAA, some aspects of the condition may not be too difficult to explain. If we take first the case of checking behaviours which are often characteristic of sufferers of OCD, then it seems clear that individuals who did invest emotional energy in frequently checking their possessions would be less likely to be the victims of theft and deception than those who did not. As we saw in the

discussion of reciprocal altruism (see pp 607-608), a major threat to the establishment of successful reciprocal relationships (and all the benefits which these bestow) is the emergence of cheating – both gross cheating (that is, total non-reciprocation) and subtle cheating (that is, returning less than is received). Clearly a major prerequisite for the avoidance of falling victim to cheats would be the ability – and motivation – to be aware of what one possesses and to take steps to ensure that it is not stolen. In this way, a general disposition towards careful and frequent checking may have been highly adaptive.

Similarly, compulsive cleaning and washing behaviours, which are also common amongst sufferers of OCD, may have performed a valuable function in our EAA. It does not seem unreasonable to assume that, in the EAA, those individuals who kept themselves clean and avoided anything which might 'contaminate' them might have a definite advantage over those who paid insufficient attention to these matters.

In both cases, it is clear that those who suffer from OCD display these tendencies to an exaggerated, and dysfunctional, degree. Nevertheless, it has been suggested by Stevens and Price (1996) that a basic tendency towards such obsessional and compulsive behaviour might have carried with it a significant evolutionary advantage, which would have been absent in those who were not predisposed to such behaviour.

2.6 Evaluation of evolutionary explanations of mental disorders

Whilst evolutionary psychologists have offered some intriguing explanations for the evolution of mental disorders, it is important to remember that these accounts remain very speculative. As with most evolutionary thinking, no clear criteria for proving an explanation exist, and so they can at best be regarded as suggestive.

Nevertheless, it is also clear, as Nesse and Williams (1995) suggest, that just as normal healthy functioning needs to be understood within the context of natural selection, so does illness and pathology. It is also true that by taking an evolutionary approach to the functioning of the body and the mind, we may be forced to reconsider where we draw the line between health and illness – both physical and mental. Such an approach may have long term implications both for how people with psychological disorders are treated, and for how they are viewed by society as a whole.

Summary

1. Evolutionary psychology suggests that human emotions have an evolutionary history in the same way as any other adaptation.

2. Anxiety may have evolved as a mechanism for enhancing preparedness.

3. There may be circumstances under which the symptoms of depression, schizophrenia and obsessive compulsive disorder could confer an adaptive advantage.

Activity 6   Evolutionary explanations of mental disorders

Item A   Depression

Three months ago Mr K, a 35 year old solicitor, experienced the breakup of his marriage of nine years. Before this, he described himself as happy and successful. Since the breakup he has been experiencing great difficulty sleeping and describes himself as 'sad most of the time' and 'worthless and a fraud'. For the last month he has been unable to face going to work and frequently finds himself sobbing for no apparent reason. He has experienced a loss of appetite and libido, and has started to think increasingly about committing suicide and other acts of self-harm.

Item B   Obsessive complusive disorder

Mrs J is a 38 year old housewife with two children of school age. She has always regarded herself as 'house proud', and until recently had lived a normal and fulfilled life. About a year ago, she began to notice that she was spending more and more time cleaning her house, and experiencing heightened levels of anxiety over the possibility that germs might be present. At times, this anxiety was impossible to bear, and by the time she sought help she was regularly getting up during the night to perform her increasingly elaborate cleaning routines before the rest of her family woke up. Her concerns over germs had become so extreme that she began to insist that her family and visitors to the house wear plastic bags over their shoes. She was no longer able to leave the house without experiencing panic attacks at the prospect of coming into contact with germs.

Questions

1   Explain how the two mental disorders in Items A and B might be accounted for by evolutionary theory.

2   What are the difficulties in applying evolutionary theory to mental disorders?

Unit 3   Evolution of intelligence

KEY ISSUES

1   **What is the nature of human intelligence?**

2   **What is the relationship between brain size and intelligence?**

3   **How can we explain the evolution of human intelligence?**

Introduction

The possession of intelligence has generally been regarded as the defining feature of human beings in relation to other species. It is our high level of intelligence that makes us the most complex species behaviourally, because it is intelligence which removes our behaviour from simple genetic causation. Intelligence makes a species 'adaptable' – it enables us to apply abstract knowledge to novel situations and problems. This unit considers the nature of human intelligence, why it evolved and the relationship between brain size and intelligence. Three theories of the evolution of intelligence are examined: *ecological theory*, *social theory* and *sexual selection theory*.

3.1   The nature of intelligence

What is intelligence? This question has provoked a great deal of controversy amongst psychologists, not least because of its implications for how differences in intelligence between people should be measured and conceptualised. This section is less concerned with individual differences in intelligence than with the more general question of what intelligence is, and how human beings as a whole differ from other species in their possession of intelligence.

One of the earliest attempts to define intelligence describes it as 'the faculty of adapting oneself to circumstances' (Binet & Simon, 1915). A similar definition was provided by Weschler (1944), who said it was 'the capacity to understand the world and the resourcefulness to cope with its challenges'. What seems central to both of these definitions is the idea that intelligence equips us with the capacity to respond to unique problems which neither direct experience nor our genetic endowment has equipped us for. We can see this ability clearly if we think about such artificial problems as crossword puzzles. By definition the clues for a crossword puzzle are novel. Yet, by the application of certain very general rules which the seasoned crossword solver learns, a number of possible answers to each problem can be compared until the most likely one is reached.

Intelligence also makes possible thinking, reasoning and planning. When faced with a problem, we do not need to engage in a potentially costly trial and error process, but instead can compare a number of hypothetical scenarios before deciding on which course of action to pursue. These processes can be very complex and involved. At its simplest, the planning process may involve simply comparing the likely tastes of two alternative dishes from a menu when deciding what to have for lunch. At its most complex, it can involve thinking through the likely consequences of a course of action years ahead, and under a variety of different circumstances. Examples of this sort of application of intelligence include politicians developing long term strategies, or companies developing business plans for the next ten years.

Psychologists have debated the degree to which intelligence should be regarded as a general 'all-purpose' problem-solving ability, and how far it should be seen as a collection of discrete 'domain-specific' abilities, relating to particular tasks and needs (such as mate selection, negotiating reciprocal relationships, dealing with kin etc). Although this debate is by no means settled, evolutionary psychologists have tended to emphasise the latter view of intelligence as the most helpful in understanding intelligence in an evolutionary context.

Finally, there remains a considerable, and at times heated, debate about the relative input of genes and environment in the development of intelligence. Although this debate has important implications for how we understand differences in intelligence between individuals and groups, it is of less importance in attempting to understand the evolution of human intelligence. As with most things, evolutionary psychologists generally believe that intelligence results from an interaction between genes and environment. It is worth commenting, however, that the evolutionary view of intelligence suggests that significant differences between individuals and groups would be unlikely to persist since the significantly more intelligent would presumably out-reproduce the less intelligent and eventually become dominant.

3.2 Brain size and intelligence

An issue which has fascinated biologists for more than a century has been the relationship between brain size and intelligence. Is there a simple correlation between brain size and intelligence? Whilst this might seem plausible, the idea can be dismissed fairly quickly. If this were the case, then we should expect human beings to have the largest brains of all mammals. In fact they do not: elephants, for example, which are not noted for their superior intelligence, have brains about four times the size of the human brain.

There is, however, a general relationship between brain size and body size. Relative to body size, the human brain is considerably larger than the brains of our nearest relatives, the primates – primates include monkeys, apes and humans. In terms of this comparison, we should expect the average human brain to weigh some 460 grams. In fact, the figure is nearly 1300 grams (Jerison, 1973).

Actually, quite a lot is known about the brain sizes of our hominid ancestors from the fossil record. We know, for instance, that the Australopithecines had brains of a size broadly consistent with the brain:body size ratio of other primates, whereas homo sapiens have brains of about three times the size of those expected in a primate of equivalent size. Before moving on to consider various explanations for why our ancestors underwent such a dramatic relative increase in brain size, it is important to note that this increase must have carried considerable costs in evolutionary terms. For one thing, an increase in brain size means that a greater proportion of the individual's energy is required to sustain it. For example, whilst a chimpanzee's brain requires about 8% of its total energy to sustain it, the figure for human beings is nearer 22%. This means that larger brains require good and reliable nutrition and it seems no accident that the large expansion in human brain size about two million years ago coincided with the introduction of significant amounts of meat into the diet of our ancestors.

It is also significant that the larger than expected human brain increases the risk of complications during childbirth. As Badcock (2000) points out, the longest axis of the foetus's head only just fits the widest axis of the human female's birth canal. This means that the baby's head must rotate during birth from a sideways position to a backward facing position as it emerges. Thus, unlike other primates where the baby is born facing front, and so mothers can easily reach down to clear the airway or to clear the umbilical cord from around the infant's neck, human mothers are unable to do very much at all at this crucial stage of the birth process.

As a further consequence of the difficulty of giving birth to a large brained infant, three-quarters of human brain growth must take place after birth. The result of this is that human infants are born unusually immature, requiring a much longer and more intense period of parental investment than other primates.

We can conclude from this, therefore, that given the costs of brain enlargement, there must also have been some significant benefits to outweigh these costs. It is to explanations of these benefits that we now turn.

3.3 Ecological theory

It seems clear that one of the selection pressures which produced the increase in intelligence amongst primates was its benefits for successful food gathering. Increases in intelligence would have carried with them improvements both in memory and spatial ability. If we take memory first, it is not difficult to see that individuals with good memories might benefit in food gathering terms by being able to remember where they have successfully foraged in the past. Similarly, those who possess a good cognitive map of a terrain (that is, have well developed spatial abilities) would be more likely both to find food sources in the first place and to be able to return to them in the future. Field studies of primates show that many species have quite remarkable skills in these respects. Boesch and Boesch (1984), for example, have shown that chimpanzees 'remember' the locations of round stones which they use for opening nuts.

But how far can ecological theory account for the distinctively human growth in intelligence? In its favour, the association between the emergence of hunting and the growth in intelligence would seem to lend support to the idea that more intelligent individuals were more successful hunters than were less intelligent individuals. After all, successful hunting requires forethought and planning, a degree of cunning and in the case of group hunting, the ability to coordinate the actions of a number of individuals. Yet there are many other species – lions for example – which have evolved highly successful hunting techniques but without the development of human-style intelligence. In view of this it seems unlikely that the benefits of hunting would, in themselves, be sufficient to account for the emergence of distinctively human levels of intelligence.

3.4 Social theory

As we saw in the discussion of altruism (see pp 606-610), any attempt to understand social behaviour requires that we take into account the behaviour of other members of the same species – or *conspecifics*. This can be seen most clearly in the case of reciprocal altruism. Any reciprocal relationship is vulnerable to cheating. Robert Trivers (1985) made an important distinction between *gross cheating* and *subtle cheating*. Gross cheating involves total non-reciprocation, and subtle cheating involves only partial non-reciprocation. Trivers makes the point that once an individual in a population evolves the ability and motivation to cheat, they and their descendants will be at a considerable selective advantage over the rest of the population. However, this situation will also set up selection pressures for the evolution of *counter-measures* – that is, the selection of individuals who can discriminate between cheats and non-cheats. Once such ability emerges, those who possess it will start to out-reproduce the cheats, until the original cheating strategy becomes a major liability to its bearers.

Trivers goes on to point out that this cycle will continue, selecting for ever more subtle forms of cheating and subsequently ever more subtle forms of detection. Indeed, Trivers describes this process as an 'arms race', since it mimics the processes by which conflicting nations engage in the acquisition of ever more sophisticated and deadly weapons.

But what has this process to do with the evolution of intelligence? Several writers, most notably Trivers himself, have suggested that the evolution of complex psychological mechanisms for the successful exploitation and counter-exploitation of reciprocal relationships carried with it the huge growth in intelligence which is characteristic of human beings. Memory is one example of this. Quite clearly human intelligence is dependent on the possession of a good memory – and in particular, one which is sensitive to considerable detail. It is suggested that human memory may have evolved largely in response to the need to remember how other individuals have behaved in previous exchanges.

Evidence for this view is provided by some influential research by Cosmides and Tooby (1992). They examined how well people performed in a series of tests of logical reasoning ability know as the Wason selection tasks (Wason, 1983). Consider the following example:

The following four cards have a letter on one side and a number on the other.

$$\boxed{D} \quad \boxed{F} \quad \boxed{3} \quad \boxed{7}$$

The following proposition is made. If a card has the letter D on one side it must also have the number 3 on the other. How many cards must you turn over in order to demonstrate that this rule has not been violated?

The logically correct answer is two: the card showing the letter D, to show that it does have a 3 on the other side, and the card showing the number 7 to show that it does not have a D on the other side. No matter what is on the other side of the remaining cards, the rule is not violated.

Cosmides and Tooby show that people in general do very badly in this experiment, with only between 4% and 10% getting it right.

Now consider another example. The following four cards contain information about four people sitting in a bar. On one side is their age, and on the other is the drink they are drinking:

The following proposition is made. If a person is drinking beer, they must be over 18 years of age. Once again, how many cards must you turn over to determine whether this rule has been violated? The answer is two: 'drinking beer' – to show that person is over 18 – and '16 years' to show that they are not drinking beer.

Notice that the logical structure of the two cases is exactly the same. However, Cosmides and Tooby show that in the second case, the proportion getting it right is around 75%. What this seems to suggest, is that we are much better at performing mental tasks which have a content relevant to social exchange and the enforcement of social rules. The first example is an abstract logical problem with no obvious relevance to social costs and benefits. The second, however, relates much more obviously to the question of whether a social rule is followed or violated – just the sort of issue which Trivers suggests we have evolved to be very sensitive about.

This evidence provides powerful support for the view that human intelligence evolved as a consequence of its benefits for successfully managing social exchanges. However, it is important to notice that it does not explain why it was that human beings, and not other species of primates, evolved such high levels of intelligence.

3.5 Sexual selection theory

In his influential book *The Red Queen*, Matt Ridley suggests that the process of sexual selection lies at the heart of the explanation of human intelligence (Ridley, 1993). The process of sexual selection was discussed earlier in this chapter (see pp 639-643). Essentially the idea is this. Individuals who are most successful in attracting mates will leave more copies of their genes to future generations than those who are less successful in this respect. Ridley's argument is that ancestral humans who were more intelligent were generally more successful at attracting mates than their less intelligent counterparts.

There are a number of strands to this idea. First, those who are more intelligent will generally be better at manipulating others in close personal relationships. They will be better both at outwitting sexual competitors and presenting themselves in a way that is attractive to members of the opposite sex. Second, intelligence may well have become an attractive trait because more intelligent individuals would generally have had better hunting and foraging skills. A female who favoured such successful male hunters would have benefited from more frequent supplies of meat, and hence her offspring would have had a better chance of survival. Similarly, 'intelligent genes' passed on to her sons would also have benefited her ultimate reproductive success, since presumably her sons would, like their father, be more attractive to females than the offspring of less successful males.

Of course, this explanation is compatible with the social theory outlined above. Indeed, it seems likely that an explanation of the evolution of human intelligence requires some combination of the three theories outlined in this section.

Activity 7   The evolution of human intelligence

Item A   Letters and numbers

The following is a test of the proposition: 'If a card has the letter J on one side, it must also have the number 7 on the other'.

| J | P | 7 | 9 |

How many cards must be turned over to test the proposition, and which ones are they?

Questions

1   Get eight pieces of card, and make copies of the two sets of cards in Items A and B. Find ten people, and ask five to complete the task in Item A, and five to complete the task in item B. Which item produces more correct responses? (The correct answers are as follows: Item A = J and 9, Item B = Drinking Wine and 12 years old).

2   Are these the results you expected?

3   Provide an evolutionary explanation for the results you obtained.

Item B   Drinking age

The following cards give information about people drinking in a bar. On one side is the drink being consumed, and the other is the person's age. We need to test the following proposition 'If a person is drinking wine, they must be over 18 years old'.

| Drinking Wine | Drinking Lemonade | 30 years old | 12 years old |

How many cards do you need to turn over to test the proposition and which ones are they?

Both items adapted from Cosmides & Tooby, 1992

Summary

1   One of the defining features of human beings is their relatively high intelligence.

2   The comparatively large brains of human beings carry evolutionary costs as well as benefits. In view of this the benefits probably outweigh the costs.

3   Ecological theory states that an increase in brain size leads to improvements in food gathering. As a result, there was selection for higher intelligence.

4   Social theory states that an increase in brain size was due to the evolution of complex psychological mechanisms for the exploitation of reciprocal relationships. These mechanisms make an important contribution to successful adaptation.

5   Sexual selection theory states that more intelligent individuals were more successful at attracting mates and passing their genes on to future generations.

6   All three theories probably contribute to an understanding of the evolution of human intelligence.

References

Badcock, C. (2000). *Evolutionary psychology*. Cambridge: Polity.

Baker, R. (1996). *Sperm wars*. London: Fourth Estate.

Binet, A. & Simon, T.H. (1915). *Method of measuring the development of the intelligence of young children*. Chicago: Chicago Medical Book Company.

Boesch, C. & Boesch, H. (1984). Mental map in chimpanzees: An analysis of hammer transports for nut cracking. *Primates, 25*, 160-170.

Brazier, C. (1995). African village. *New Internationalist*, June, 1995.

Buss, D.M. (1988). From vigilance to violence: Tactics of mate retention. *Ethology and Sociobiology, 9*, 291-397.

Buss, D.M. (1999). *Evolutionary psychology: The new science of mind*. Needham Heights: Allyn & Bacon.

Buss, D.M. & Dedden, L.A. (1990). Derogation of competitors. *Journal of Social and Personal Relationships, 7*, 395-422.

Cosmides, L. & Tooby, J. (1992). Cognitive adaptations for social exchange. In J. Barkow, L. Cosmides & J. Tooby (Eds.), *The adapted mind*. New York: Oxford University Press.

Daly, M. & Wilson, M. (1983). *Sex evolution and behavior* (2nd ed.). Boston: Willard Grant.

Daly, M. & Wilson, M. (1988). *Homicide*. Hawthorne NY: Aldine.

Dunham, C. (1992). Brotherly love. *Observer Magazine*, 18.10.1992.

Fisher, R.A. (1958). *The genetical theory of natural selection* (2nd revised edition). New York: Dover Press.

Grammer, K. & Thornhill, R. (1994). Human facial attractiveness and sexual selection: The roles of averageness and symmetry. *Journal of Comparative Psychology, 108*, 233-242.

Hamilton, W.D. & Zuk, M. (1982). Heritable true fitness and bright birds: A role for parasites? *Science, 218*, 384-387.

Jerison, H. (1973). *Evolution of brain and intelligence*. New York: Academic Press.

Kinsey, A.C., Pomeroy, W.B. & Martin, C.E. (1948). *Sexual behavior in the human male*. Philadelphia: Saunders.

Lynn, M. & Shurgot, B.A. (1984). Responses to lonely hearts advertisements: Effects of physical attractiveness, physique and coloration. *Personality and Social Psychology Bulletin, 10*, 349-357.

Marks, I. (1987). *Fears, phobias and rituals: Panic, anxiety and their disorders.* New York: Oxford University Press.

Moller, A.P. (1992). Female preference for symmetrical male sexual ornaments. *Nature, 357*, 238-240.

Montesquieu, C. (1973). *Persian letters.* London: Penguin. (First published 1721).

Murdock, G.P. (1967). *Ethnographic atlas.* Pittsburgh: University of Pittsburgh Press.

Nesse, R.M. & Williams, G.C. (1995). *Evolution and healing.* London: Wiedenfeld & Nicolson.

Orians, G.H. (1969). On the evolution of mating systems in birds and mammals. *American Naturalist, 103*, 589-603.

Ridley, M. (1993). *The red queen.* London: Penguin.

Singh, D. & Young, R.K. (1995). Body weight, waist-to-hip ratio, breasts and hips: Role in judgements of female attractiveness and desirability for relationships. *Ethology & Sociobiology, 16*, 483-507.

Stevens, A. & Price, J. (1996). *Evolutionary psychiatry.* London: Routledge.

Symons, D. (1979). *The evolution of human sexuality.* New York: Oxford University Press.

Trivers, R. (1985). *Social evolution.* Menlo Park: Benjamin Cummings.

van Valen, L. (1973). A new evolutionary law. *Evolutionary Theory, 1*, 1-30.

Wason, P. (1983). Realism and rationality in the selection task. In J. Evans (Ed.), *Thinking and reasoning: Psychological approaches.* London: Routledge & Kegan Paul.

Weschler, D. (1944). *The measurement of adult intelligence.* Baltimore: Williams & Wilkins.

Wilson, M. & Daly, M. (1992). The man who mistook his wife for a chattel. In J. Barkow, L. Cosmides & J. Tooby (Eds.), *The adapted mind.* New York: Oxford University Press.

Introduction

This chapter examines the way psychological disorders are classified. Classifying disorders seems a reasonable way of proceeding if they are to be studied and treated. After all, the classification of physical illnesses has proved invaluable for their study and treatment by medical researchers and doctors. However, as this chapter shows, things are not as simple as this in the case of psychological disorders.

Chapter summary

- Unit 1 critically examines the classification of psychological disorders.
- Unit 2 looks at dissociative identity disorder and asks to what extent this disorder is created by those who treat it.

- Unit 3 considers culture-bound syndromes. It asks whether these disorders are unique to particular cultures or local versions of disorders found in all societies.

Unit 1 Classification systems

KEY ISSUES

1 What are the main classification systems for psychological disorders?
2 How reliable and valid are they?
3 What are the alternatives to these systems?

1.1 Classification

Everything is unique. No two things are exactly the same. However, if people viewed the world in this way, it is difficult to see how they could make sense of their surroundings and live a normal, ordered life. For example, every chair is unique – in some way every chair differs from every other chair. However, when we see a chair as an object for sitting on, we ignore these differences. In doing so, we have *classified* a large number of unique objects, given them a name – chairs – and identified their common use and characteristics.

Classification involves grouping together things with common properties or shared characteristics, assigning them to a category, and ignoring the differences between them. A *classification system* is a comprehensive list of categories which form a particular subject area. For example, in 1735 the Swedish naturalist Linnaeus developed a classification system for plants and animals. It is still in use today. The Linnaean system provided a means of identifying and differentiating plants and animals.

1.2 Classifying psychological disorders

The first modern classification system for psychological disorders was developed by Emil Kraepelin in 1883. He began

by collecting thousands of case studies of people in mental hospitals. He found that certain psychological problems appeared to have a number of features in common. On this basis, he placed them into different categories, so identifying them as separate disorders.

Kraepelin's classification system was based on a *medical model*. He believed that mental disorders had an organic or physical cause. He saw them as 'mental illnesses', similar in many respects to medical diseases. He observed that certain symptoms tended to appear as a group, to cluster together. These clusters of symptoms were classified as separate and distinct mental illnesses. Kraepelin's classification system formed the basis for today's classification systems of psychological disorders.

Current classification systems

Today's classification systems place psychological problems into categories on the basis of their shared characteristics. They aim to provide a comprehensive list of psychological disorders, a description of the characteristics or symptoms of each disorder, and guidelines for assigning people to particular disorders. This provides clinicians – those who treat mental disorders – with a framework for *diagnosis*. In this sense, diagnosis means identifying the disorder. If a client's symptoms match those listed for a particular disorder in the classification system, then the client will, in all probability, be diagnosed as having that disorder.

Why classification? The following reasons have been given for the importance of classifying psychological disorders.

- Without a reliable and valid classification system, it would not be possible to correctly identify disorders.
- Effective diagnosis is only possible when disorders are classified in terms of their symptoms.

- A correct diagnosis means that clinicians can apply what is known about the disorder to the person they are trying to help.
- A disorder must be classified correctly in order to discover its causes, its likely course or development, and the best way of treating it.
- Without a classification system, clinicians and researchers could not communicate about the disorders they examine. A common language and an agreed method of naming and identifying disorders are essential. A classification system provides this.

Not all researchers agree with the above points. Their views will be examined later.

A medical model

Today, there are two main classificatory systems, ICD-10 and DSM-IV. They are used worldwide for the classification and diagnosis of mental disorders. Both systems are largely based on a medical model. This model assumes that psychological problems are mental health problems – they are problems with health.

The categories in modern classification systems are known as *diagnostic categories* because they form the basis for diagnosing disorders. The characteristics of the disorders listed are often referred to as *symptoms*. The same terminology is used in medicine.

In terms of a medical model, people with mental disorders are 'ill' – their 'symptoms' need identifying in order to 'diagnose' their 'illness' and they require 'treatment' in order to 'cure' their 'illness'.

Psychiatrists – those who traditionally treat psychological disorders – are doctors. They are trained in medicine. They tend to see psychological problems as similar to physical illnesses. In many ways they operate like medical doctors – they diagnose and treat 'health problems'.

This approach is reflected in current classification systems which list mental disorders and identify and distinguish them in terms of their symptoms. One of the main aims of these systems is to improve the quality of diagnosis.

Not all psychologists agree with this approach. Their views will be discussed later.

Key terms

Classification *Grouping together things with common characteristics and assigning them to a particular category.*

Classification system *A comprehensive list of categories which form a particular subject area.*

Diagnosis *In terms of psychological disorders, identifying a particular disorder by matching its symptoms with a particular category.*

Symptoms *In terms of psychological disorders, the behaviours which are seen as evidence of a particular disorder.*

Diagnostic category *A category of mental disorder which serves as a basis for diagnosis by listing the symptoms of the disorder.*

Medical model *An approach which assumes that psychological problems are similar to physical illnesses – they are problems with health.*

1.3   ICD-10 and DSM-IV

The tenth and most recent edition of the World Health Organisation's *International Classification of Diseases* (ICD-10) was published in 1992. It classifies both physical and mental disorders. The American Psychiatric Association's classification, *Diagnostic and Statistical Manual of Mental Disorders* (DSM-IV) is now in its fourth edition, published in 1994. These are the two major classification systems of psychological disorders.

Each system provides *diagnostic criteria* for disorders. These are guidelines for diagnosis. ICD-10's diagnostic criteria for 'severe depressive episode' are given in Table 1. DSM-IV's criteria for 'major depressive episode' are given in Table 2. Despite the differences in name, these are the same disorder.

As can be seen from Tables 1 and 2, ICD-10 and DSM-IV criteria for serious depression share a number of similarities.

- Particular symptoms must be present for a diagnosis.
- A certain number of other symptoms must also be present.
- The symptoms must usually be present for at least 2 weeks.
- There is a considerable overlap of symptoms listed by the two classification systems.

However, there are important differences between the two classification systems. Where ICD-10 is limited to categories and symptoms, DSM-IV includes other considerations for making a diagnosis – see B to E, Table 2.

Multiaxial classification DSM-IV is a multiaxial classification system. It has five axes or dimensions. When a diagnosis is made, the individual is rated in terms of each axis.

- **Axes I and II** are a list of mental disorders and their symptoms. These axes form the basis for diagnosis.

Table 1   ICD-10 Diagnostic criteria for severe depressive episode

For severe depressive episode, all three of the 'typical' symptoms should be present, plus at least four other symptoms, some of which should be of severe intensity. The depressive episode should usually last at least 2 weeks, but if the symptoms are particularly severe and of very rapid onset, it may be justified to make this diagnosis after less than 2 weeks.

Typical symptoms

In typical depressive episodes the individual usually suffers from:

1) depressed mood
2) loss of interest and enjoyment
3) reduced energy.

Other common symptoms are

a) reduced concentration and attention
b) reduced self-esteem and self-confidence
c) ideas of guilt and unworthiness
d) bleak and pessimistic views of the future
e) ideas or acts of self-harm or suicide
f) disturbed sleep
g) diminished appetite.

Table 2 — DSM-IV Diagnostic criteria for major depressive episode

A. Five (or more) of the following symptoms have been present during the same 2-week period and represent a change from previous functioning; at least one of the symptoms is either 1) depressed mood or 2) loss of interest or pleasure.

1. depressed mood most of the day, nearly every day
2. markedly diminished interest or pleasure in all, or almost all, activities most of the day, nearly every day
3. significant weight loss when not dieting or weight gain (eg, a change of more than 5% of body weight in a month), or decrease or increase in appetite nearly every day
4. insomnia or hypersomnia (excessive sleep) nearly every day
5. psychomotor agitation or retardation nearly every day
6. fatigue or loss of energy nearly every day
7. feelings of worthlessness or excessive or inappropriate guilt nearly every day
8. diminished ability to think or concentrate, or indecisiveness, nearly every day
9. recurrent thoughts of death (not just fear of dying), recurrent suicidal thoughts or a suicide attempt or a specific plan for committing suicide.

B. The symptoms do not meet criteria for a mixed episode (a combination of depression and anxiety).

C. The symptoms cause clinically significant distress or impairment in social, occupational, or other important areas of functioning.

D. The symptoms are not due to the effects of a substance (eg, a drug of abuse, a medication) or a general medical condition (eg, hypothyroidism, a disease which affects the adrenal glands).

E. The symptoms are not better accounted for by bereavement.

- **Axis III** concerns 'general medical conditions'. The disorder may be a result of a physical illness such as an infectious disease. A person's medical condition may have important implications for treatment. For example, if they have certain heart conditions and they have been diagnosed with depression, then some antidepressant drugs would worsen their heart condition.
- **Axis IV** lists various 'psychosocial and environmental problems' which may contribute to or result from the disorder. They include bereavement, problems at work, unemployment, financial problems, separation and divorce, and sexual or physical abuse. These problems must be taken into account when making a diagnosis. For example, DSM-IV states that major depressive episode should not be diagnosed if 'the symptoms are not better accounted for by bereavement'.
- **Axis V** assesses how well a person is functioning in various areas of their life, for example at work, during their leisure time, and in terms of their social relationships. People are rated on a scale of 1 to 100, from being in danger of seriously hurting themselves and others to superior functioning on a wide range of activities. This assessment provides an indication of the need for treatment.

Major categories

Both DSM-IV and ICD-10 divide mental disorders into major

Table 3 — DSM-IV Major categories

1. **Disorders usually first diagnosed in infancy, childhood, or adolescence** Includes hyperactivity, childhood anxieties, speech disorders, mental retardation and eating disorders.

2. **Delirium, dementia, amnestic and other cognitive disorders** Covers disorders in which cognition (thinking) is impaired. Includes delirium in which attention wanders and thoughts are incoherent, and dementia in which mental capacities, particularly memory, deteriorate.

3. **Substance-related disorders** The inability to function normally in everyday situations as a result of using substances such as alcohol, barbiturates, amphetamines, cocaine and marihuana.

4. **Schizophrenia and other psychotic disorders** A group of related disorders characterised by loss of contact with reality, marked disturbances of thought and perception, and bizarre behaviour. Delusions and/or hallucinations almost always occur.

5. **Mood disorders** Disturbances of normal mood – extreme depression, abnormal elation, or alternating between depression and elation.

6. **Anxiety disorders** Includes disorders where anxiety is the main symptom – generalised anxiety disorder or panic disorders – and phobias – intense fear of an object or situation.

7. **Somatoform disorders** Disorders in which the symptoms are physical – severe or prolonged pain, paralysis, blindness – but there appears to be no organic/physical cause.

8. **Factitious disorder** Physical or psychological symptoms which are intentionally produced or feigned for no obvious reason other than to assume the role of a sick person.

9. **Dissociative disorders** A sudden change in consciousness which affects memory and identity. For example, a person who forgets their entire past, and adopts a new identity in new surroundings.

10. **Sexual and gender identity disorders** Includes sexual pleasure from exhibitionism, voyeurism, sadism and masochism. Gender identity disorders include dissatisfaction with biological sex and identification with the opposite sex.

11. **Eating disorders** Anorexia nervosa and bulimia nervosa.

12. **Sleep disorders** Too much or too little sleep, disturbed sleep, inability to sleep at conventional times.

13. **Impulse control disorders** Inappropriate behaviour which the individual appears to have no control over – episodes of extremely violent behaviour; stealing repeatedly for no apparent reason; compulsive gambling.

14. **Adjustment disorders** Emotional or behavioural disturbances in response to a major life stressor.

15. **Personality disorders** A longstanding maladaptive pattern of inner experience and behaviour. For example, people with paranoid personality disorder are extremely distrustful and suspicious, avoiding close relationships.

16. **Mental retardation** Intellectual functioning which is significantly below average.

17. **Other conditions that may be a focus of clinical attention** These conditions are not seen as mental disorders, but they may require treatment. They include problems with relationships such as marital conflict and parent/child problems.

categories which are then subdivided into specific disorders – see Tables 3 and 4. For example, under the general category of *Schizophrenia and other related disorders*, DSM-IV divides schizophrenia into five subtypes.

DSM-IV has 16 major categories of mental disorder, ICD-10 has 11.

DSM-IV and ICD-10 – a comparison

Table 1 and Table 2 provide a comparison of the diagnostic criteria for depression given by DSM-IV and ICD-10. As noted earlier, there are many similarities – in particular, a considerable overlap of symptoms.

One of the main differences is the additional considerations for diagnosis given in DSM-IV's multiaxial classification. For example, DSM-IV's diagnostic criteria for major depressive episode includes: 'The symptoms cause clinically significant distress or impairment in social, occupational or other important areas of functioning', drawn from Axis IV. According to Comer (1998), a diagnosis based on a multiaxial classification system is 'expected to be more informative and more carefully considered'.

Tables 3 and 4 provide a comparison of the major categories of mental disorder used by the two classification systems. Considerable efforts have been made over the years to remove inconsistencies between the two systems and bring them closer together. In the latest editions – ICD-10 published in 1992 and DSM-IV published in 1994 – many of the categories are essentially the same.

The main difference between the two systems is the number of major categories – DSM-IV has 16, ICD-10 has 11. However, the actual disorders listed are very similar – they are simply placed within different major categories. For example, DSM-IV has separate major categories for anxiety disorders, somatoform disorders, dissociative disorders and adjustment disorders, while ICD-10 combines these disorders in a single category – neurotic, stress related and somatoform disorders.

Table 4	ICD-10 Major categories

1   **Organic mental disorders** Personality and behavioural disorders due to brain disease, damage and dysfunction – includes dementias such as Alzheimer's disease.

2   **Mental and behavioural disorders due to psychoactive substance use** Substances include alcohol, cannabis, cocaine and hallucinogens.

3   **Schizophrenia, schizotypal and delusional disorders** Includes all sub-types of schizophrenia, as well as schizotypal disorder.

4   **Mood (affective) disorders** Includes depressive episode and other forms of 'depression'.

5   **Neurotic, stress-related and somatoform disorders** Anxiety disorders including generalised anxiety disorder, panic disorder and phobias, adjustment disorders, dissociative disorders and somatoform disorders.

6   **Behavioural syndromes associated with physiological disturbances and physical factors** Includes eating disorders, and non-organic sleep disorders (eg, sleep-walking, night terrors).

7   **Disorders of adult personality and behaviour** Includes personality disorders, habit and impulse disorders (eg compulsive gambling), gender and identity disorders (eg transsexualism), and disorders of sexual preference (eg, voyeurism and paedophilia).

8   **Mental retardation** Learning disabilities, subdivided into mild, moderate, severe or profound 'mental retardation'.

9   **Disorders of psychological development** Specific disorders of the development of speech, language, disorders of the learning of reading, spelling, arithmetic and conditions such as autism.

10   **Behavioural and emotional disorders with onset usually occurring in childhood and adolescence** Includes conduct disorders and disorders of attention.

11   **Unspecified mental disorder** Mental disorder not otherwise specified.

1.4	Reliability

There are two main ways of assessing a classification system. First, is it reliable? Second, is it valid? This section looks at reliability.

A diagnostic classification system is reliable if it leads to the same diagnosis of the same person by two or more clinicians. Put simply, it is reliable if it produces the same results. For example, DSM-IV diagnostic criteria for depression are reliable if two or more clinicians diagnose the same person with major depressive episode.

How reliable are classification systems of psychological disorders? Early versions of DSM were not particularly reliable. For example, in the early 1960s, four experienced clinicians each interviewed 153 people recently admitted to a mental hospital. They based their diagnoses on DSM-I (the first edition of DSM). Only 54% of the diagnoses were the same (Beck et al.,1962).

When very broad categories of disorders were investigated – major categories such as depression and anxiety – agreement on diagnosis was between 54% and 84% (Zigler & Phillips, 1961). However, diagnoses are usually more specific – they differentiate, for example, between different types of depression and anxiety. When the reliability of these more precise classifications was examined, it was very low – agreement on diagnosis was between 32% and 57% (Kendell, 1975).

A reliable classification system is clear and precise. The boundaries between the different categories are clearly marked. New editions of ICD and DSM seek to improve reliability by removing vague descriptions of categories and blurred boundaries between categories. Despite this, studies have rarely found more than 70% agreement on diagnosis between clinicians (DiNardo et al., 1993).

Further aspects of diagnosis

There are many reasons other than the classification system that can lead to disagreement over diagnosis. In other words, there's a lot more to diagnosis than the reliability of the classification system. Further factors which affect diagnosis include the following.

The clinician Research indicates that the attitudes and characteristics of clinicians can affect the reliability of their diagnoses. Differences in age, personality, training, theoretical approach, social class, ethnicity, nationality and gender can all affect judgements on which diagnoses are based.

The client Individuals assessed by clinicians also vary widely in their personal and social characteristics. This may influence the diagnosis they receive. In addition, an individual's behaviour may change from one day to another. For example, a clinician might assess a client who is experiencing an alcoholic delirium. A few days later, when the delirium has lifted, the same client may be assessed by another clinician. A different diagnosis would not be surprising.

The assessment procedure Clinicians use a variety of procedures to provide information on which to base a diagnosis. Most use some form of clinical interview in order to obtain information about a person's past and present behaviour, attitudes and emotions. Some interviews are structured – the questions are pre-set. Other interviews are unstructured – they are free-flowing with few, if any pre-set questions. Sometimes, people are given specialised interviews, such as the Anxiety Disorder Interview Schedule, which tests for specific disorders.

Clinicians use a variety of assessment procedures which produce different amounts and types of data. Clearly, this variation in assessment procedures will produce different amounts and types of information. This will reduce the reliability of diagnosis.

Key terms

Reliability *A reliable classification system produces the same diagnosis when two or more clinicians examine the same person.*

Validity *A valid classification system produces correct diagnoses.*

1.5 Validity

Validity and reliability

A classification system might be reliable but produce the wrong diagnosis. In other words, different clinicians using the same system give the same diagnosis, but that diagnosis is incorrect.

A valid classification system leads to correct diagnosis. Clearly, validity and reliability are closely linked. If a classification system is unreliable and this results in five clinicians giving five different diagnoses of the same person, then, at best, only one of those diagnoses is correct. In this case, a lack of reliability produces a lack of validity.

As outlined in the previous section, research indicates that disagreements about diagnosis may result from unreliable classification systems. Consider the following study. A team of clinicians were asked to re-examine the records of 131 patients in a mental hospital in New York (Lipton & Simon, 1985). They interviewed many of the patients and diagnosed their disorder. Of the 89 patients who originally received a diagnosis of schizophrenia, only 16 were now given the same diagnosis. Only 15 patients had originally been given a diagnosis of mood disorder, now 50 received this diagnosis. Clearly, many of these diagnoses are invalid. Where there is a disagreement between the original and the later diagnosis, one must be incorrect.

Sane in insane places

Let us assume that all the patients in the mental hospital above actually had a psychological disorder. If so, the diagnosis of 'disorder' was correct, but the actual disorder specified was often incorrect. Now, consider the possibility that people *without* a disorder could be diagnosed as psychologically disordered. Clearly, this diagnosis would be invalid. The following study indicates how this might happen.

In a famous experiment entitled 'On being sane in insane places', David Rosenhan (1973) sent eight 'normal' people to twelve different mental hospitals claiming they had been hearing voices saying, 'empty', 'thud' and 'hollow'. All were admitted and seven diagnosed as having schizophrenia. After admission, the 'pseudopatients' behaved normally and reported they no

longer heard voices. Their stay in hospital ranged from 7-52 days during which time they were prescribed a total of 2100 pills. They were eventually discharged with the diagnosis 'schizophrenia in remission'.

This study can be seen as evidence that the classification system on which these diagnoses were based was not valid – it did not result in an accurate diagnosis. According to DSM-IV, auditory hallucinations – hearing voices that do not exist – are a symptom of schizophrenia. However, this conclusion has been criticised. The 'pseudopatients' insisted on being admitted to mental hospitals and persuaded the staff they were hearing voices. All the study shows is that the 'pseudopatients' were good actors – they convinced the staff that their symptoms were real (Spitzer, 1975).

Even if this criticism is accepted, there are still concerns about validity. What about shamans – religious healers in small-scale, non-Western societies – who often claim to hear voices? What about people who hear voices as a normal part of their religious experience? Should these people be diagnosed as having a psychological disorder?

The non-existence of disorders

For a classification system to be valid, the disorders it lists must be 'real'. They must exist in the 'real world', rather than being figments of the clinician's imagination. It is possible to argue that some so-called disorders are not psychological disorders or indeed any kind of 'disorder' at all.

A classic example which illustrates this point is 'drapetomania'. Dr Samuel Cartwright was appointed by the Louisiana Medical Association to investigate the 'strange' behaviour of African-American slaves. In his report, published in 1851, he claimed to have discovered a 'disease' which he called 'drapetomania'. This was a 'mania to seek freedom', an obsessive desire of some slaves to escape from their masters (Zimbardo et al., 1995). From today's perspective, this would be seen as reasonable behaviour and in no way indicative of a mental disorder.

Until 1973, the DSM listed homosexuality as a mental disorder. Thousands of gays were 'treated' in order to 'cure' their 'illness'. DSM-III, published in 1973, no longer classified homosexuality as a disorder. With each new edition of DSM, the American Psychiatric Association (APA) deletes old disorders and adds new ones. Even the powers that be, in this case the APA, accept that some disorders are invalid. In other words, they are not really disorders at all.

The myth of mental illness

Classification systems such as DSM and ICD are largely based on a medical model. Although the term 'mental illness' has been replaced by mental disorder, such disorders are still seen as mental health problems. Some researchers regard this view as invalid.

In 1961, a groundbreaking book entitled *The Myth of Mental Illness* was published. Written by an American psychiatrist, Thomas Szasz, it argued that only a small number of psychological problems could be seen as illnesses, that is, as physiological conditions with physical symptoms. These include alcoholic poisoning and Alzheimer's disease which destroys neurons in the brain. Most psychological problems lack the central characteristics of an illness – they are primarily non-physiological conditions where the 'symptoms' are an individual's feelings, beliefs and perceptions.

Szasz recognised the existence of psychological problems. However, the unhappiness, confusion, anxiety and fear that characterise many psychological disorders have nothing to do with mental 'illness' or 'disease'. Instead, they are 'problems of living'. For example, they are problems of relationships with partners, families, friends and work colleagues. Problems of living have a social rather than a physiological cause. They are problems to be solved rather than diseases to be cured.

According to Szasz, most so-called mental illnesses are a myth, in other words they don't exist. Classification systems which are based on the medical model are therefore based on a false premise – they are invalid.

Symptoms, cause, course and treatment

Classification systems are sometimes said to be valid if each disorder they identify has:

- the same symptoms
- the same causes
- the same course or development.

In addition, the classification should indicate which treatments will be effective for each disorder. Thus, a valid classification system should group together people with the same symptoms, so identifying a disorder with the same cause and course, which responds to the same treatment.

As noted earlier, the same individual can be given different diagnoses by different clinicians. This may reflect a lack of validity of classification systems. For example, DSM-IV lists five subtypes of schizophrenia. Many people diagnosed as schizophrenic don't fit neatly into a particular subtype. In addition, identifying their disorder as a particular subtype gives little indication of its cause, how it might develop, or what treatment might be effective (Davison & Neale, 1998).

Cluster analysis – a statistical technique for assigning people to groups according to particular characteristics – indicates that the majority of psychiatric patients would not be assigned to any recognisable diagnostic category in the standard classification systems (Everitt et al., 1971). Statistical techniques have also highlighted the extensive overlap in symptoms between those diagnosed with schizophrenia and those diagnosed as having other disorders (Bentall, 1990).

As the following chapter indicates, there is often little agreement about the causes of various psychological disorders. For example, in the case of schizophrenia, Richard Bentall remarked that almost every factor known to influence human behaviour has been suggested as a cause of schizophrenia (Bentall et al., 1988).

The diagnostic categories listed in classification systems appear to have limited use in indicating effective treatment. Responses to medication for those diagnosed as schizophrenic or having a bipolar disorder (depression) are variable. For example, drugs such as chlorpromazine (known as neuroleptics or antipsychotics) are often thought of as specific treatments for schizophrenia. But not all people with this diagnosis appear to benefit significantly, while some people with a diagnosis of bipolar disorder (traditionally thought of as unrelated to schizophrenia) do benefit (Crowe et al., 1986). The effectiveness of lithium, a drug traditionally used with people diagnosed as

suffering from bipolar disorder, is similarly variable. In one study, people were randomly assigned to either a neuroleptic, lithium, both or neither. It was found that drug response was related to specific problems but not to diagnoses of disorders: delusions and hallucinations responded to the neuroleptic and mood swings responded to lithium, whatever the diagnosis (Moncrieff, 1997).

The central issue in diagnosis remains one of classification – the idea that particular psychological problems cluster together, that they can be classified as the same disorder with the same cause, course, and response to treatment. On the basis of the evidence outlined above, many researchers see diagnostic classifications as invalid.

Culture, ethnicity, gender and class

The two main classification systems, DSM-IV and ICD-10, have been developed primarily by white, middle-class, Western males. Does this mean, as some researchers claim, that the behaviours seen as symptoms of mental disorders are defined as such because they differ from what is normal in white, male, middle-class, Western culture? If so, DSM-IV and ICD-10 can be seen as ethnocentric, racist, sexist, and biased against the lower classes. And, if this is the case, then they cannot be valid since, in many cases, they will fail to give correct diagnoses. To some extent, diagnoses will reflect the prejudices and biases of those who constructed the classification systems.

To some extent the norms and values of certain groups in society differ from white, male, middle-class, Western culture. This may put members of these groups at greater risk of being diagnosed as mentally disordered. Diagnostic categories can be seen as invalid if the normal, accepted behaviour of members of particular groups results in a greater likelihood of them being diagnosed with a mental disorder.

Minority groups In the United Kingdom, African Caribbeans are at least 3 times and up to 5 times more likely to be diagnosed as schizophrenic than the general population (Nazroo, 1997).

One of the symptoms of schizophrenia is delusions of persecution. A delusion is a belief which is untrue but experienced as true. A person with delusions of persecution feels that people are out to get them, that they are being harassed and ill-treated. They are often angry, argumentative and highly suspicious of others.

Racism is widespread in British society. At least partly as a result of this, African Caribbeans are more likely to have discipline problems at school, to be stopped and searched and arrested by the police, to be the victims of racial attacks, to be unemployed, to be employed in low-skill, low-paid jobs, and to experience a range of other disadvantages. In view of this, it may well be reasonable for African Caribbeans to see themselves as persecuted. In other words, this perception may be accurate rather than delusional. And it may be a widely held view within the group. Surveys have indicated that African Caribbeans are keenly aware of racism, that many perceive the mainstream society as hostile and often view whites with suspicion (Haralambos & Holborn, 2000).

In view of this, there may be a greater likelihood of African Caribbeans being diagnosed as schizophrenic because aspects of their normal behaviour appear to fit the symptom of delusions of persecution.

Gender Classification systems can be seen as lacking validity if diagnostic categories reflect stereotypes of particular groups. This may result in incorrect diagnoses if people are seen to have a particular disorder on the basis of their group stereotype.

Certain personality disorders are diagnosed more frequently in females, others in males. It has been argued that these gender differences result from the fact that the symptoms, and the way they are described in classification systems, mirror traditional gender stereotypes.

Consider the following symptoms of two types of personality disorder.

- **Antisocial personality disorder** Aggressive, impulsive, deceitful, irresponsible, unreliable, insincere, manipulative, disregard for others, lacking shame or remorse.
- **Histrionic personality disorder** Theatrical, over-dramatic, vain, over-concern about appearance, extravagant, self-indulgent, exaggerated emotions (such as crying uncontrollably), need for reassurance and constant approval.

Men are more likely to be diagnosed with antisocial personality disorder, women with histrionic personality disorder. One reason suggested for this gender imbalance is that the diagnostic criteria of these disorders reflect traditional stereotypes of men and women (Kaplan, 1983).

This view has been supported by a number of studies. One study asked clinicians to diagnose fictitious case studies of antisocial personality disorder and histrionic personality disorder. In some versions of each case, the person was identified as male, in others as female. Everything else remained the same. Men were over twice as likely to be diagnosed as having antisocial personality disorder and women over twice as likely to be diagnosed as having histrionic personality disorder (Ford & Widiger, 1989). (See Activity 1, Item C.)

If the descriptions of symptoms in diagnostic categories reflect gender stereotypes, then those categories may lack validity. As a result, they may result in misdiagnosis.

This section has examined two examples of possible sources of bias in classification systems – ethnic and gender bias. The issue of cultural bias is examined in Unit 3.

1.6 Problems with classifying people

Labelling

When people are diagnosed with a psychological disorder, the diagnosis has a tendency to become a *label*. In this sense, the label identifies the person as 'mentally ill', as a schizophrenic, an alcoholic, and so on. A label focuses on one aspect of a person while ignoring others. There is a tendency for people to interpret the person's behaviour in terms of the label.

This can be seen from the way Rosenhan's pseudopatients were treated after being diagnosed as schizophrenic. Case notes were taken on a 39-year-old male pseudopatient's relationships with his family and friends. His relationships were 'normal', they showed no indication of psychological disorder. However, once he was diagnosed as schizophrenic, the facts were 'unintentionally distorted' by the staff to fit with their view of schizophrenic behaviour. Now his relationship became 'unstable' and 'ambivalent' (marked by opposing feelings such as love and hate). He had a good relationship with his wife. Now the relationship was 'punctuated with angry outbursts' (Rosenhan, 1973).

Self-fulfilling prophecy Labels have a tendency to stick – they are difficult to get rid of. They can lead to a *self-fulfilling prophecy*. People may tend to see themselves in terms of the label and act accordingly, particularly when others interpret their behaviour in terms of the label. In this way, the prophecy can fulfil itself and the person labelled as 'mentally ill' may behave in this way. This, in turn, may lead to feelings of inadequacy and self-doubt (Comer, 1998).

Stigma A stigma is a mark of shame and disgrace. It implies that people are morally inferior. The label 'mental illness' carries a stigma in many people's eyes. It can lead to social rejection and discrimination in the labour market – people may have difficulty getting a job or promotion to a more responsible position.

Social control

Labelling people as 'mentally ill' can keep them in their place and prevent them from threatening the powerful (Szasz, 1989). Labelled in this way, their words have little significance, they are not taken seriously. They can be defined as a danger to the community and incarcerated in mental hospitals. The idea of mental illness can therefore be seen as a means of social control. The following examples illustrate this argument.

In the 1950s and 60s, Soviet dissidents – those who opposed government policy in the Soviet Union – were sometimes diagnosed as mentally ill and confined to mental institutions. In this way, their voices were silenced, their ideas discredited, and their threat to the state ended. And, their fate was a deterrent to those who shared their views (see p132).

As outlined earlier, Dr Samuel Cartwright claimed to have discovered a mental illness called drapetomania which affected African Americans. This 'mania' was an obsessive desire for freedom which drove slaves to attempt to escape from their masters. According to Cartwright, any slave who tried to run away more than twice was insane (Comer, 1998).

This served to justify slavery and maintain the power of slave-owners. It also served to justify the harsh treatment of slaves which kept them in their place.

Key terms

Labelling *Labelling theory states that when someone is labelled as a certain type of person, there is a tendency for them to act accordingly and for others to interpret their behaviour in terms of the label.*

Self-fulfilling prophecy *A prophecy that fulfils itself. For example, when a person is labelled they tend to act and see themselves in terms of the label.*

Stigma *A mark of shame and disgrace.*

Social control *Social mechanisms which control people's behaviour.*

1.7 Alternatives to categorical classification and diagnosis

The dimensional approach

DSM and ICD are categorical classification systems. They consist of categories of mental disorders. People are assessed in terms of these diagnostic categories and judged to have a disorder or not. This is a 'yes-no' approach, they've got it or they haven't, they are either 'abnormal' or 'normal'. In some cases, classification systems recognise degrees of a disorder. For example, ICD-10 offers the choice of 'mild', 'moderate' or 'severe' for mood disorders such as depression. However, these alternatives are not provided for most diagnostic categories.

Some researchers reject this clear distinction between 'normality' and 'abnormality'. Instead, they see a continuum with no obvious dividing line. For example, everybody feels anxious or suspicious from time to time, some more than others. Few will ever experience extremes of anxiety such as a series of panic attacks; few will experience paranoia, a state of extreme suspiciousness. From this point of view, psychological disorders can be seen as nothing more than a serious form of normal experiences. They are one end of a continuum.

This view forms the basis of the *dimensional approach*. Categories such as anxiety and depression are retained but people's experiences are described in terms of the degree of anxiety they are suffering or the extent of depression they are feeling. Thus, a person's problems are assessed in terms of the degree to which they have various experiences and concerns.

The phenomenological approach

Many researchers have argued that the problems of diagnosis can be overcome by focusing on specific experiences and behaviours. In Britain, in particular, considerable progress has recently been achieved in understanding specific psychological mechanisms that can lead to unusual beliefs, hallucinations and difficulties in communication (Bentall, 1990).

This is different from a symptom-diagnosis approach. A diagnostic approach is based on a medical model – on the assumption that the problems that are observed cluster together and are, in fact, the 'symptoms' of an underlying illness. The *phenomenological approach* makes no such assumptions, and is not based on a medical model. It does not assume that hearing voices, for example, is a 'symptom' of 'schizophrenia' or some other disorder, but merely sets out to understand the phenomenon of hearing voices.

The psychological formulations approach

In order to understand and explain people's experiences, clinical psychologists have developed an approach known as *psychological formulations* (Hawton et al., 1989; Persons, 1989).

Psychological formulations attempt to explain why people are experiencing difficulties. They usually consist of a list of problems and possible psychological reasons for these. The problem list is a description of the person's actual experiences. Examples include: low mood and lack of motivation, hearing voices, problems functioning at work, paranoia (Persons et al., 1995).

Clients develop their own formulations as the following quotation illustrates. 'The questions people put to me made me reflect on the voices I heard, which I had never really thought about. I was surprised to discover a pattern – whenever I think negatively, I find myself hearing a negative voice' (Romme & Escher, 1993).

Clinical psychologists attempt to develop, in collaboration with the client, ideas about what might have led to the development of these problems. For this reason, formulations are very individual – tailored for each person and relevant to their specific problems.

Typically, a formulation will examine what events have happened in a person's life, and how they have interpreted and reacted to these. Formulations tend to change as the psychologists and their clients learn more about the problems.

Formulations are designed to be 'best guesses' about the problems, and these guesses are tested out over time (Brewin, 1996; Kinderman & Lobban, 2000). The process of developing a formulation is collaborative. Psychologist and client work together to develop a picture of the problems, an explanation of what has caused them, and suggestions for what might help.

Summary

1   The two main classification systems for psychological disorders are ICD and DSM. Both provide diagnostic categories. Both are largely based on a medical model.

2   There is considerable overlap between the two systems. The main difference is the addition in DSM of further dimensions or axes in terms of which the individual is rated.

3   Despite an increase in the reliability of ICD and DSM, studies have rarely found more than 70% agreement on diagnosis between clinicians.

4   There are other sources of unreliability apart from the classification system. These include the clinician, the client and the assessment procedure.

5   A classification system which is reliable is not necessarily valid – it does not necessarily produce a correct diagnosis.

6   Classification systems which lack reliability also lack validity. If different clinicians diagnose different disorders for the same person, then at best only one diagnosis is correct.

7   Diagnostic categories lack validity if people without a disorder are diagnosed as having a disorder. Rosenhan's experiments using pseudopatients indicate that this is possible.

8   For a classification system to be valid the disorders it lists must be 'real'. New editions of DSM and ICD omit disorders which were included in previous editions – an admission that they are not really disorders. Homosexuality provides an example of this.

9   According to Szasz, most psychological problems are not 'mental illnesses'. Instead, they are 'problems of living'. From this viewpoint, classification systems based on a medical model are invalid.

10 Classifications are said to be valid if each disorder they identify has the same symptoms, cause, course, and responds to the same treatment. On this basis, existing classifications lack validity.

11 There is evidence of cultural, ethnic, gender and class bias in classification systems. In this respect, they lack validity.

12 Classifying people as mentally disordered can have harmful effects. It may result in labelling, a self-fulfilling prophecy and stigma.

13 Labelling people as mentally disordered can operate as a means of social control which keeps people in their place, and protects the position and justifies the actions of the powerful.

14 There are various alternatives to categorical classification and diagnosis. These include the dimensional approach, the phenomenological approach and the psychological formulations approach.

Activity 1   Classification and diagnosis

Item A   All shapes, all sizes, all dogs

Item B   Oppositional defiant disorder

DSM-IV gives the following diagnostic criteria for oppositional defiant disorder.

A pattern of negativistic, hostile, and defiant behaviour lasting at least 6 months, during which four (or more) of the following are present:

1) often loses temper
2) often argues with adults
3) often actively defies or refuses to comply with adults' requests or rules
4) often deliberately annoys people
5) often blames others for his or her mistakes or misbehaviour
6) is often touchy or easily annoyed by others
7) is often angry and resentful
8) is often spiteful or vindictive.

Item C   Gender bias

Clinicians were given fictitious case histories for diagnosis. One case described a person with antisocial personality disorder, the other case described a person with histrionic personality disorder. In some versions of each case the person was described as male, in other versions as female. Apart from this, everything else was identical. The results are shown in the bar chart.

Diagnoses of personality disorders

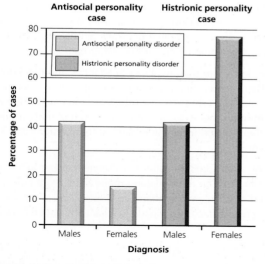

Antisocial personality case   **Histrionic personality case**

Legend:
- Antisocial personality disorder
- Histrionic personality disorder

Y-axis: Percentage of cases (0–80)
X-axis: Diagnosis — Males, Females, Males, Females

Adapted from Ford & Widiger, 1989

Item D   Changing roles

Women are now moving into boxing, something unheard of a generation ago. In 1995, there were 150 women in Britain fighting competitively, almost double the number in 1990. According to Persi Dixon of the Women's International Boxing Feberation, 'In a time when gender roles are changing so much, there is no blueprint of what men's and women's roles are'.

Adapted from Haralambos, 1996

Item E   The Trail of Tears

In the 19th century, medical experts in the USA announced that the forcible removal of Native Americans on to reservations would save them from 'madness'. Living in a 'free society' would drive such 'primitive' peoples 'insane'. Confining them to reservations would protect their mental health. Coincidentally, it would open up vast areas of land for white settlement.

In 1838, the Cherokee Indians were rounded up by the US army, often at bayonet point, and removed from their homeland in Georgia. They were forced to march 800 miles west to a reservation in Oklahoma. During the journey, known as the Trail of Tears, 4000 of the 20 000 marchers died. The medical officer, who had supervised this removal, proudly announced he had not seen a single case of insanity.

Adapted from Comer, 1998 and Josephy, 1994

Questions

1 Briefly explain the idea of classification with reference to Item A.

2 What questions does Item B raise about the validity of diagnostic categories?

3 a) What evidence of gender bias does Item C contain?

   b) How does this question the validity of diagnostic categories?

   c) How might the changing roles of women, referred to in Item D, affect gender bias?

4 How does Item E illustrate the argument that the idea of mental illness can be used to justify the actions of the powerful?

Unit 2 Dissociative identity disorder (multiple personality disorder)

KEY ISSUES

1 What is dissociative identity disorder?
2 To what extent is it caused by those who treat it?

2.1 Introduction

The previous unit looked at the effect of culture on the creation of psychological disorders. To some extent, as culture changes, so does the identification and classification of psychological disorders. Homosexuality provides an example of this. Until 1973, it was listed by DSM as a mental disorder. Western culture is now more likely to see it as an alternative sexual orientation. Largely as a result of this, it was dropped from DSM.

This unit looks at *dissociative identity disorder*. It was accepted as a mental disorder by the American Psychiatric Association in 1980 when it appeared in DSM-III (it was then called multiple personality disorder). This unit examines the argument that dissociative personality disorder is, to some extent, a cultural creation – people believe it exists because of their culture. For example, they have seen it portrayed in films and read about it in books.

Like everybody else, psychologists and psychiatrists are influenced by culture. This is a major factor in the identification of a disorder and its classification. Once a disorder is officially classified, those who diagnose and treat disorders keep a look out for its symptoms. In the case of dissociative identity disorder, some researchers argue that in the process of looking for symptoms, therapists to some extent actually create those symptoms. They then go on to diagnose the disorder. In this sense, the therapists are part of the cause of the disorder.

This view is examined later in the unit. First, what is dissociative identity disorder and what is the standard explanation for it?

2.2 A case study

Consider the following case. For several months, Eve White, a 25-year-old married woman, was treated for 'severe and blinding headaches'. She also complained of 'blackouts' following the headaches. During interviews, she mentioned emotional difficulties which she discussed with the therapist. Her symptoms were commonplace and her emotional problems familiar – marital conflicts and personal frustrations.

Eve was a serious, sober, demure and restrained person. Then, suddenly, during one interview, a 'new' Eve appeared. In the words of her therapist, 'this could only be another woman'. This is how he described her.

'Instead of that retiring and gently conventional figure, there was in the newcomer a childishly daredevil air, an erotically mischievous glance, a face marvellously free from the habitual signs of care, seriousness, and underlying distress, so long familiar in her predecessor. This new and apparently carefree girl spoke casually of Eve White and her problems, always using *she* or *her* in every reference, always respecting the strict bounds of a separate identity. When asked her own name she immediately replied "Oh, I'm Eve Black".'

Over the next 14 months, around 100 hours of interviews were conducted. During the course of therapy, Eve White learned of Eve Black's existence but had no awareness of her presence, her thoughts or her actions. However, Eve Black was aware of the other's thoughts and actions. Despite this, Eve Black's feelings were her own. For example, she regarded Eve White's distress about her failing marriage as silly. And she had little sympathy or compassion for her 'other half'.

Several months into therapy, Eve's headaches and blackouts returned. Then, to her therapist's amazement, a third 'identity' appeared. Eve's eyes shut sleepily during an interview. After a couple of minutes, her eyes opened. She stared blankly around the room, then looked in bewilderment at the therapist and said, 'Who are you?'

The person who asked this question was neither Eve White or Eve Black. She was 'far more mature, more vivid, more boldly capable, and more interesting than Eve White'. And she 'lacks Eve Black's obvious faults and inadequacies'. She called herself Jane.

As time went by, Jane appeared more often and 'stayed out' for longer periods. She took over many of Eve's tasks at home in an effort to relieve and help her (Thigpen & Cleckley, 1954).

The above account is a summary of one of the most fully documented cases of dissociative identity disorder.

2.3 Characteristics of dissociative identity disorder

According to DSM-IV, a person must have at least two separate but coexisting identities or 'alters' in order to be diagnosed with dissociative identity disorder (DID). The average number of identities is 15 for women and 8 for men, though there have been cases of over 100 identities. Often these identities emerge in groups of 2 or 3 at a time. This happened in the case of Eve White who had 22 identities over a 20 year period, before she finally achieved a single, stable identity (Sizemore & Huber, 1988).

When coexisting identities emerge, the switch from one to another is usually instantaneous. Each identity has its own personality, behaviour patterns, memories and relationships. In some cases, an individual can have both male and female identities. And one study showed that changes in handedness (from left-handed to right-handed or vice-versa) occurred in 37% of cases (Putnam et al., 1986).

A diagnosis of DID requires the existence of different identities to be longlasting and disrupting, ie causing considerable disruption to a person's life. A shortlived additional identity, resulting for example, from the effects of a drug, is insufficient for a diagnosis of DID.

Usually, one identity appears more often than the others. Often the identities have no awareness of each other. In some cases each identity is aware of the rest, in other cases only some identities are aware of the rest. Gaps in memory are common – they result from one identity having no awareness of the other identities, and therefore no memory of the thoughts, feelings and actions of those identities.

2.4 The posttraumatic model

In recent years there have been two competing explanations of DID. The first, known as the *posttraumatic model*, developed from psychodynamic theory. It will now be examined.

A case study Consider the following case study. Sybil had 17 identities, some of whom had been with her since the age of three. Her therapist slowly uncovered a horrific tale of trauma and abuse. Sybil was sexually and physically abused by her mother, Hattie. She would often insert objects into her daughter's vagina – buttonhooks, knives, small bottles. Hattie told her, 'You might as well get used to it. That's what men will do to you when you grow up'. Sometimes, Hattie injected water into her daughter's rectum. Sometimes, she would say, 'I'll show you what it's like to be deaf and blind' and lock Sybil in a trunk for hours, blindfold her, and taunt her. Sometimes, Hattie suffocated her until she became unconscious. Hattie enjoyed playing the piano. Sometimes, she would tie Sybil to the kitchen table to listen to her performance. Sometimes, Hattie would give Sybil laxatives and prevent her from using the toilet. This catalogue of abuse continued throughout Sybil's childhood.

Slowly but surely, with her therapist's help, Sybil, now aged 22, recounted these events and expressed her hatred and disgust for her mother. Gradually, her multiple identities faded until a single integrated identity remained (Schreiber, 1973).

The theory The case of Sybil provided the basis for the posttraumatic model of DID. This model developed in the 1980s

and has now become the dominant explanation for the disorder, particularly in the USA. One of its main supporters, David Gleaves, states that DID is 'a posttraumatic condition resulting from overwhelming childhood experiences, usually severe child abuse' (Gleaves, 1996). Posttraumatic means after a trauma; a trauma is an extremely painful and disturbing emotional experience.

DID allows the individual to dissociate – cut themselves off – from these experiences by adopting alternative identities. By escaping into another identity, a person is able to avoid painful memories of childhood trauma. As the above case study indicates, Sybil had a range of identities she could adopt in order to remove herself from her identity as an abused child and from the horrific memories associated with this. Her therapist concluded that Sybil 'sought rescue from without until, finally recognising that this rescue would be denied, she resorted to finding rescue from within. Being a multiple personality was the ultimate rescue' (Schreiber, 1973). DID can therefore be seen as a creative survival strategy in which 'imagination is used to protect against and compensate for experience which has to be denied because it is too terrible to bear and because there is no one there to help the child to bear it' (Mollon, 1996).

The evidence A number of researchers claim to have discovered a strong link between childhood trauma and DID. For example, a study of 355 people diagnosed with DID states that 86% reported histories of sexual abuse and 82% reported physical abuse (Schultz et al., 1989). According to David Gleaves, 'Patients have been found to almost invariably report some form of childhood trauma, most commonly physical abuse, sexual abuse, or both'.

However, as the next section indicates, the link between childhood trauma and DID has been disputed.

Key terms

Trauma *An extremely painful and disturbing emotional experience.*

Posttraumatic condition *A condition that arises after, and as a result of, a trauma.*

2.5 The sociocognitive model

This model begins with the idea that an individual's thoughts and beliefs develop from interaction with others in a social context. This interaction is both direct – person to person – or more indirect via the mass media – books, magazines, films and TV. The *sociocognitive model* argues that DID develops in part from:

- Interactions with therapists – in particular, therapists influence their clients' creation of multiple identities.
- Media portrayals of DID – for example, books and films about DID which inform both the public and professionals about its existence and its symptoms.
- Sociocultural expectations, in particular ideas about multiple identities, seen in phrases like Jekyll and Hyde – from Robert Louis Stevenson's novel *The Strange Case of Dr Jekyll and Mr Hyde* (1886).

The sociocognitive model states that people diagnosed with

DID adopt and enact social roles in terms of their hopes and aspirations and the demands of the various social contexts in which they find themselves. In cases of DID, social roles and personal identities tend to merge to the point where they become virtually indistinguishable. Multiple roles then become multiple identities (Lilienfeld et al., 1999).

Iatrogenesis

Iatrogenesis means caused by medical treatment or examination. The sociocognitive model states that iatrogenesis plays an important part in the cause and maintenance of dissociative identity disorder. In terms of DID, the sociocognitive model states that to some extent DID is created or manufactured by the therapists who diagnose and treat the disorder. This view will now be examined.

The DID 'epidemic'

There were 79 reported cases of DID up to 1970. This number had grown to around 6000 by 1986 and by the turn of the 20th century to tens of thousands (Acocella, 1998). There was a dramatic increase shortly after the publication of the bestselling book *Sybil* (Schreiber, 1973) and the television film of the same name in 1976. Both were based on the case of Sybil outlined above. This increase became an 'epidemic' after 1980 when DID was accepted as a mental disorder by the American Psychiatric Association and appeared in DSM-III (it was then called multiple personality disorder).

There was growing public and professional awareness of DID. The disorder entered mainstream culture. The book and the film about Sybil had been preceded by a book about Eve (Thigpen & Cleckley, 1957) and a film starring Joanne Woodwood entitled *The Three Faces of Eve* (1957). Society was prepared for the onset of DID, as were the professionals, especially when the disorder was officially recognised in 1980.

The multiple identity 'epidemic'

According to Thigpen and Cleckley (1984), there appears to be two competitions going on. First, between some people who have been diagnosed with DID to see who can have the greatest number of identities or alters. Second, between certain therapists to see who can have the greatest number of DID cases. Both the increase in the number of DID cases and the increase in the number of identities parallels the growing public and professional awareness of the disorder. According to the sociocognitive model, these increases are partly due to 'the more your expect, the more you look; the more you look, the more you create, and then, of course, the more you find'. Some researchers have noted that the number of identities tends to increase over the course of treatment. This can be seen in the case of Eve White outlined earlier, when Jane suddenly appeared.

Treatment and the manufacture of DID

It is estimated that 80% of DID patients have no knowledge of their alternative identities before they begin treatment (Putnam, 1989). Are these identities present when treatment begins, and then skilfully revealed by trained therapists? Or, are they a creation of the therapist who, in the process of creating them, literally manufactures the disorder? According to the sociocognitive model, this, to some extent, is exactly what happens. Therapists ask leading and suggestive questions. They unintentionally cue and prompt their clients in a search for what they expect to find (Spanos, 1994).

One therapist who used hypnosis stated that his most frequent hypnotic instruction to a DID patient was 'Everybody listen' (Kluft, 1993). Another therapist used a technique known as the 'bulletin board' which gives DID patients 'a place where personalities can "post" messages to each other' (Putnam, 1989). A third therapist recommended giving names to alternative identities since 'giving an alter a name may "crystallise" it and make it more distinct' (Ross, 1997). According to the sociocognitive model, these techniques may lead to the *manufacture* rather than the *discovery* of multiple identities. Thus, Spanos (1994) states, 'Therapists routinely encourage patients to construe themselves as having multiple identities, provide them with information about how to convincingly enact the role of "multiple personality patient", and provide official legitimisation for the different identities that patients enact'.

In view of the fact that the majority of patients are unaware of alternative identities before treatment, there is a real possibility that identities are being manufactured in the course of treatment. Take the case of Sybil. Her treatment with her psychiatrist Dr Wilbur involved 2354 office sessions plus frequent contacts outside office hours. Their relationship lasted over 20 years. During that time Dr Wilbur painstakingly helped Sybil to reveal her 17 identities, and Sybil's life largely centred on her therapy. Although this is an exceptional case, it does indicate the scope for the creation of multiple identities (Mair, 1999).

Cultural cues

The sociocognitive model states that the experiences and behaviours of people diagnosed with DID are influenced by culture (Lilienfeld et al., 1999). In particular, there are sufficient cues and templates within culture which can provide models for anybody to act out the behaviours associated with DID. In other words, these behaviours are familiar to many members of the general population.

The ease of acting out these behaviours can be seen from laboratory studies. In one experiment, participants were asked to play the role of an accused murderer who claimed to be innocent. They were provided with various suggestions and prompts for their role-play. For example, the experimenter said, 'I think there might be another part of you that I haven't talked to'. Eighty per cent of the participants simulated an alternate identity, often giving this identity a name and a different personality from their own (Spanos et al., 1985). Studies like this show how easy it is for people to act out behaviours typical of DID. Culture provides ready-made guidelines for their role-play.

Many of the people diagnosed with DID see a therapist for some other disorder and at first show no sign of DID. In view of:

* first, the ease with which the symptoms of DID can be acted out;
* second, the assumption by the therapist that these clients probably have some kind of disorder;
* and third, the widespread awareness of DID amongst therapists;

then it is possible that DID can be manufactured during therapy (Lilienfeld et al., 1999).

Child abuse and DID

Sybil is the classic case of the link between child abuse and DID. Researchers such as Greaves (1980) and Coons (1980) who support the posttraumatic model relied heavily on the book *Sybil* and repeatedly drew on it to support their claims (Mair, 1999). If there is a powerful link between DID and child abuse, then this may call into question the arguments advanced by the sociocognitive model. In other words, it is child abuse rather than iatrogenesis which primarily accounts for DID.

A number of doubts have been raised about the claimed link between the traumas of child abuse and DID.

- First, there is no evidence that child abuse is more common amongst DID patients than among psychiatric patients in general.
- Second, if there is a correlation, then this does not prove that child abuse causes DID. For example, both might be caused by an unknown third factor.
- Third, the posttraumatic model is extremely influential. Since the 1980s it has been the dominant theory claiming to explain DID. This may lead therapists to look for child abuse – to seek it out – and encourage them to diagnose DID if they find it.
- Fourth, in seeking evidence for child abuse, there is the possibility that therapists might create it by implanting false memories in their clients. In the presence of a professional, when seeking help and advice from an expert, clients are often vulnerable, impressionable and open to suggestion.

False memories Is the child abuse which many therapists claim is linked to DID genuine? The short answer is we don't know. There is considerable evidence that false memories, especially of early childhood, can be fabricated (Schacter, 1995). One way of dealing with this problem is to look for independent corroborating evidence, that is evidence from sources other than the client which supports his or her claims. In most DID cases where a link with child abuse is claimed, there is no independent evidence to confirm memories of child abuse. Some researchers claim to have produced independent evidence in a few cases, but these claims are disputed.

There is evidence which suggests that at least some of the memories of abuse are false. It is estimated that 25% of those diagnosed with DID in the USA report memories of satanic abuse. Despite many years of intensive investigation, the police have found hardly any evidence of these satanic cults whose activities are supposed to involve multiple murders, cannibalism, human sacrifice, bestiality, gang rape and torture (Lilienfeld et al., 1999).

Why did the posttraumatic model with its emphasis on child abuse become the dominant explanation for DID? This may reflect the influence of *Sybil* – a bestselling book and a popular film. Before this media exposure of DID, there was little support for the link between childhood trauma and DID. It may also reflect the growing concern, even panic, about child abuse which developed during the 1970s and 80s. Since the 1980s, the abuse reported by DID patients to therapists has become increasingly severe. It is tempting to suggest that the greater the concern about child abuse in the wider society, the greater the severity of the abuse expected by therapists, which, in turn, is reflected in the reports given by DID patients (Mair, 1999).

Conclusion

In rare cases, DID may be feigned. Individuals may fake the disorder to gain attention or to avoid blame for a crime or a misdeed. The sociocognitive model states that most cases of DID are real – the disorder does exist. There may be no sign of DID when a client enters therapy but when they leave the disorder often exists. At first, DID symptoms may be a figment of the therapist's imagination. Later, those symptoms can become real – they are experienced by the client and enacted in the client's behaviour.

The sociocognitive model therefore argues that a large part of DID originates and is maintained by iatrogenesis. In other words, it is at least partly caused by the very people who are supposed to treat the disorder – the therapists. And the reason they help to manufacture DID, and why their clients so readily respond to the diagnosis and create the appropriate behaviours, is to be found in the wider culture. Western culture, particularly the culture of the USA over the past 25 years, provides the cues, templates, beliefs, assumptions and concerns which help to generate DID and reliably reproduce it in therapy sessions.

And, if this view is correct, it can be applied, to some extent, to all psychological disorder.

Summary

1. Dissociative identity disorder was officially identified as a disorder by the American Psychiatric Association in 1980.

2. In order to be diagnosed with DID, a person must have two or more separate, but coexisting identities.

3. The posttraumatic model provides the standard explanation for DID. It sees the creation of multiple identities as a survival strategy to escape from the horrific memories of childhood trauma.

4. The sociocognitive model states that in part DID is produced by iatrogenesis – it is created or manufactured by the therapists who diagnose and treat the disorder.

5. Reported cases of DID accelerated rapidly from the 1980s onwards, when it was classified as a disorder in DSM-III.

6. Public and professional awareness of DID developed as a result of media portrayal of the disorder.

7. There are sufficient cues and templates in culture to provide models for acting out the symptoms of DID. These, along with leading and suggestive questions from therapists, may help to create the disorder during therapy sessions.

8. The link between child abuse and DID has been questioned. There is a possibility that this link is created during therapy as a result of false memories unintentionally implanted in clients by their therapists.

Activity 2   Dissociative identity disorder

Item A   Media exposure

Poster for the film The Three Faces of Eve, 1957

Still from the 1976 film Sybil, showing Sally Field as Sybil

JIM CARREY

RENÉE ZELLWEGER

Me, Myself & Irene

Charley Baileygates is a mild-mannered, polite and helpful policeman. His other identity, Hank, is aggressive, foul-mouthed and selfish.

Item B   Times are changing

When I was a graduate studying psychology in the 1970s, I was taught that multiple personality was a rare, almost unheard of disorder. I went through graduate school, internship, psychoanalytic training, and 15 years of clinical practice in Boston without ever meeting a patient who exhibited symptoms of multiple personality. I was never assigned, and never read, any book or article on the subject. And I never knew or heard of anyone who had such a patient in treatment.

A decade later, there has been an explosion in reported cases of dissociative identity disorder. First-year social-work students are routinely assigned several new cases for treatment. There are innumerable seminars, training programmes and weekend workshops that teach clinicians how to recognise and treat dissociative identity disorder.
Adapted from Turkle, 1998

Item C   A place for every identity

One therapist uses a technique known as 'inner board meetings' to identify multiple identities. He describes this method as follows.

'The patient relaxes with a brief hypnotic induction, and the host personality walks into the boardroom. The patient is instructed that there will be one chair for every personality in the system … Often there are empty chairs because some alters are not ready to enter therapy. The empty chairs provide useful information, and those present can be asked what they know about the missing people.'
Adapted from Ross, 1997

Questions

1   With some reference to Item A, suggest reasons for the changing awareness of and concern for DID outlined in Item B.

2   How can Item C be used to argue that iatrogenesis is a factor in the cause of DID?

Unit 3 Culture-bound syndromes

KEY ISSUES

1 **What are culture-bound syndromes?**
2 **Are they local expressions of universal disorders?**
3 **Are they distinct disorders found only in certain cultures?**

3.1 Culture and psychological disorders

Culture is the learned, shared behaviour of members of society. It includes norms – accepted and expected ways of behaving; beliefs – explanations for what happens, statements about what is true and real; and values – views of what is good, worthwhile and worth striving for.

Culture guides and directs behaviour. It places pressure on members of society to conform to certain norms, hold particular beliefs and strive to realise certain values. These pressures and the kinds of behaviour they encourage may contribute to, or even be the main cause of, certain psychological disorders. For example, a number of researchers have argued that eating disorders in the West – anorexia nervosa and bulimia nervosa – are related to Western values about the ideal female figure.

Culture varies from society to society. In other words, norms, beliefs, values and ways of behaving vary from one society to the next. It is possible that psychological disorders vary in the same way. To some extent, each culture may generate its own distinct disorders.

Consider the following behaviour which is found amongst the Inuit (Eskimo) in Greenland, Alaska and the Canadian Arctic. Known as *pibloqtoq* or *Arctic hysteria*, it involves a period of extreme excitement lasting up to 30 minutes. Often the individual has an uncontrollable urge to tear off their clothes and run through the snow crying and screaming. They may break furniture, shout obscenities, and perform various other irrational or dangerous acts for no apparent reason. This is frequently followed by convulsive seizures and a coma lasting up to 12 hours. Usually, the individual has no memory of these events.

Pibloqtoq seems to be a disorder which is found only amongst the Inuit. It appears to be generated by Inuit culture and limited to that culture. The Inuit recognise it as a 'disorder' or 'illness'. Western classification systems define it as a *culture-bound syndrome* (CBS).

3.2 Culture-bound syndromes – definition

Culture-bound syndromes (CBSs) are psychological disorders which are limited to certain cultures. A syndrome is a collection of behaviours or characteristics. DSM-IV defines CBSs as 'recurrent, locality-specific patterns of aberrant behavior and troubling experience that may or may not be linked to a particular DSM-IV diagnostic category'. In other words, CBSs are patterns of behaviour which occur only in a specific locality or region. This behaviour departs from local norms, from expected and accepted standards of behaviour, and is experienced as troubling. It may be a local expression of a disorder listed in DSM or it may not.

DSM continues, 'Many of these patterns are indigenously considered to be "illnesses", or at least afflictions, and most have local names.' In other words, CBSs are considered by the local people (the indigenous people) to be 'illnesses', or at least seen to inflict bodily and/or mental suffering. They have a local name which indicates they are recognised as patterns of behaviour that occur from time to time.

According to ICD-10, CBSs do not fit neatly into the two main classification systems. They are disorders which were first identified in a particular culture or area and continue to be associated with that culture or area. ICD-10 recognises the possibility that CBSs may be local variations of universal disorders. In other words, they may be local cultural expressions of the standard disorders listed in ICD-10 and DSM-IV. As such, so-called CBSs may not be limited to particular cultures or areas.

In practice, CBSs are disorders which were first identified in non-Western societies, which seem strange to Western eyes, and which are difficult to classify in terms of Western diagnostic and classification systems. This can be seen from the following examples of CBSs.

- **Ghost sickness** Found amongst certain Native American peoples, *ghost sickness* involves an extreme preoccupation with death and those who have died. It is often associated with nightmares, hallucinations, fear, anxiety, confusion, and feelings of suffocation.
- **Koro** Found in South East Asia and China, *koro* is an intense fear that the penis is retracting into the body and once fully retracted, will cause death. Attempts to prevent this sometimes result in severe physical damage. A female version of koro is occasionally found in a belief that the vulva and/or nipples are retracting.

3.3 The relationship between culture and psychological disorders

There are three main views of the relationship between culture and psychological disorders (Berry et al., 1992).

Absolute The absolutist view states that the same psychological disorders occur in all cultures, they have the same origins or causes and the same symptoms or expressions. Given this, culture has no influence on any aspect of mental disorder. As a result, there are no such things as CBSs.

Universal The universalistic view states that the same psychological disorders are present in all cultures. However, the causes and expressions of these disorders are affected by culture. This suggests that Western classification and diagnostic systems are applicable to all societies once clinicians are able to interpret the way psychological disorders are expressed in different cultures. So-called CBSs are therefore variations on standard universal disorders.

Culturally relative This position states that at least some psychological disorders are present in only one or some cultures. These culture-bound syndromes are not simply variations of disorders present in all societies. As such, they are not covered by Western classification and diagnostic systems. Conversely, at least some of the disorders listed in DSM-IV and ICD-10 are culture-bound – they are not found in all cultures.

These three approaches will now be examined in more detail.

The absolutist position

There is little evidence to support the absolutist position. Even if CBSs such as pibloqtoq, ghost sickness and koro are variations of universal disorders, the way they are expressed clearly owes much to the local culture.

The absolutist position would appear to find strongest support from disorders which are related to basic biological functions which are common to all human beings. These include organic psychological disorders such as Alzheimer's disease and dementia, and disorders due to psychoactive substances such as alcohol, cocaine and hallucinogens.

However, even here, there is evidence of the importance of culture. The way psychoactive substances are experienced can be influenced by culture. For example, peyote, a powerful hallucinogenic drug, is an important element in the Native American Church, a Native American version of Christianity. In this context, it heightens sensitivity, provides self-knowledge and encourages self-evaluation. For members of the church, the experience is spiritual. However, for white Americans, peyote often produces disturbing and disconcerting visions, extreme mood states and the removal of normal inhibitions (Slotkin, 1965).

This example shows clearly that the effect of peyote is strongly influenced by culture. Its use produces very different experiences in Native Americans and white Americans. This questions the absolutist view that disorders due to psychoactive substances have the same causes and expressions in all cultures.

The universalistic position

This view argues that since all aspects of behaviour are influenced by culture, then the same applies to psychological disorders. However, this does not mean that psychological disorders are culture-specific – limited to one or more cultures. It simply means that their prevalence rates (the extent of the disorder in the population) and their expression (the way they are expressed in behaviour) are influenced by culture. The disorders themselves are universal – present in all cultures.

From a universalistic position, CBSs are variations on universal disorders – they are not culture-bound. This view will now be examined using the example of *amok*, a so-called CBS. Next, the claim that the disorders listed in Western classification systems are universal will be examined by looking at depression in various cultures.

Amok Usually found in males, amok occurs in Malaysia and to a lesser extent in Indonesia and Thailand. This so-called culture-bound syndrome begins with a period of brooding and social withdrawal, followed by an outburst of wild, violent and aggressive behaviour with attempts to injure or even kill others. Following this outburst, the individual sometimes falls asleep or into a stupor for several days and awakes with no apparent memory of their behaviour.

From a universalistic position, amok is *not* a culture-bound disorder if:

- First, it is shown to be a cultural variation of a universal disorder.
- Second, and following from this, it can be found in a variety of cultures across the world.

Yap (1974) argues that it is possible to classify many so-called culture-bound syndromes in terms of Western diagnostic categories. He claims that amok is a cultural expression of the Western disorder *rage reaction*.

There is evidence of behaviour similar to amok outside the cultural area where it more commonly occurs. It has been reported from non-Western societies in Africa, Siberia and the West Indies. In the West, the behaviour of mass murderers who go on shooting sprees for no apparent reason has been likened to amok. In North America, cases include the Calgary Mall Sniper, the Madman in the Tower and the Memorial Day Man (Arboleda-Florez, 1979). In England, in 1987, Michael Ryan walked through the village of Hungerford dressed in a combat jacket. He shot dead 15 people including his mother, and finally shot himself. There appeared to be no reason for his actions (Burton-Bradley, 1987).

If these cases are indeed instances of amok, then they provide strong support for the universalist view that CBSs are simply local versions of disorders that occur in all societies. If the universalists are correct in terms of CBSs, then it follows that the disorders listed in Western classification systems will also occur in all societies. This view will now be examined using the example of depression.

Depression This is a common psychological disorder frequently diagnosed in Western societies. There is considerable evidence that something like depression occurs in every society but its prevalence, expression and recognition are strongly influenced by culture. If this is the case, it would support the universalist position.

First, people from different cultures describe depression in different ways. For example, Chinese people often refer to 'exhaustion of their nerves' and their hearts being 'squeezed and weighed down'. Nigerians sometimes complain that 'ants keep creeping in parts of my brain' (Kleinman & Good, 1985). Hopi Indians in the USA do not have a word for depression in their own language. However, they use the word 'heartbrokenness' to describe the condition of Hopis diagnosed with depression (Manson et al., 1985). From a universalist position these examples merely illustrate different ways of describing the same disorder.

Second, the actual experience of depression appears to vary from culture to culture. In the West, people suffering from depression emphasise inner feeling states such as extreme sadness, helplessness, hopelessness and low self-esteem. In many other cultures, depression is primarily expressed and experienced in somatic (bodily) terms such as fatigue, loss of appetite, backache, headaches. However, from a universalist position, this does not mean that depression does not exist in many cultures, it simply means it is experienced and expressed in different ways.

Third, depression may be unrecognised or denied in certain cultures. For example, depression, as such, is largely unheard of in many Asian societies. This may reflect cultural values which state that public admission of emotional problems is shameful and brings dishonour to the individual and their family. However, expressing depression in terms of somatic symptoms such as fatigue and headaches does not bring shame or carry a stigma (Uba, 1994). Again, from a universalist position, depression exists in all cultures, it is simply viewed and expressed differently.

Fourth, the prevalence rate of depression appears to vary from culture to culture. This has been explained in terms of the variations in social relationships and beliefs between societies. For example, it has been suggested that the extended family structure (often found in Asia) provides the individual with considerable emotional, social and practical support and this tends to prevent the development of depressive symptoms. By comparison, the Western nuclear family is small and isolated and therefore less able to provide this type of support. However, the possibility that culture affects the prevalence rates of depression does not change the universalist position. The extent of depression may vary but the disorder is still found in every society.

Evaluation According to the universalist position:

- So-called CBSs, such as amok, are variations on universal disorders.
- Western diagnostic categories, such as depression, are applicable worldwide.
- The disorders listed in DSM-IV and ICD-10 are universal – they occur in all societies.

Unlike the absolutists, the universalists readily accept that culture is an important component of psychological disorder. They recognise that in different cultures, disorders are described and viewed differently, experienced and expressed differently, may be unrecognised or denied and have different prevalence rates and causes. However, like the absolutists, they claim that the same mental disorders are present in all cultures.

But are they? Is it possible to cut through all these cultural differences and identify the same thing? Are culture-bound syndromes simply standard disorders in exotic clothing? Are the various 'versions' of amok really examples of the same disorder? Can Western psychiatrists accurately interpret the variety of cultural meanings and expressions of depression and correctly diagnose the disorder? Might this variety of meanings and expressions represent different disorders or no disorders at all? Despite these cautions most researchers are universalists – they believe there is a 'common core' of symptoms for every major disorder which allows these disorders to be identified in every culture (Berry et al., 1992).

The culturally relativist position

This position argues that at least some disorders are culture-bound, that they are limited to particular cultures or culture areas. In other words CBSs are just that – culture-bound syndromes.

Cultural relativists also question the universalist view that the disorders listed in DSM and ICD are universal. As outlined earlier, universalists see depression as a universal disorder which, to some extent, is expressed differently in different cultures. However, cultural relativists argue that this variety of expression may indicate specific culture-bound disorders, or it may indicate no disorders at all.

It follows from this that the disorders listed in Western

classification systems may themselves be culture-bound – they may be limited to Western culture. Take the example of eating disorders. Available evidence suggests that anorexia and bulimia are primarily Western disorders. They are often seen as developing from cultural ideals of the female figure common in Western societies. When eating disorders occur in non-Western societies, they are usually found in sections of the population most exposed to Western culture (DiNicola, 1990). It is possible that other disorders listed in DSM and ICD are primarily Western disorders, and therefore largely culture-bound.

Amok reconsidered In the previous section, amok was examined from a universalist viewpoint. It was seen as a variation of a universal disorder. It was claimed that cases could be found worldwide. The idea of amok as a culture-bound syndrome was rejected. This section examines amok from a culturally relativist position and argues that it should be seen as a CBS.

Amok has a long history in Malaysia. It was first described there by European travellers in the 16th century. Some researchers argue that it is generated by Malay culture which condemns aggression and confrontation. In certain situations these stringent rules are broken, for example when an individual is insulted and feels his self-esteem is threatened. This can lead to amok – an explosion of anger (Carr, 1978).

Amok also occurs in Indonesia, which has a similar culture to Malaysia. There the incidence of amok was as high amongst immigrant Chinese as it was in the local population. People of Chinese origin in Indonesia have absorbed much of the local culture. Similarly, there have been cases of amok reported from Chinese living in close proximity with Malays (Kline, 1963). There have been no reports of amok in other Chinese populations, either in China itself or in other parts of the world (Kon, 1994).

Amok is difficult to classify. The examples of violent outbursts in the rest of the world may not be cases of amok. Even if they are accepted as amok, these examples are extremely rare compared with Malaysia and its neighbouring countries. A number of researchers therefore conclude that amok is a culture-bound syndrome (Kon, 1994).

Evaluation The culturally relativist position has a number of points to recommend it.

- First, it starts from the idea that culture generates psychological disorders. Many psychologists would agree with this assumption.
- Second, and following from this, if cultures vary from society to society, then psychological disorders may vary from society to society.
- And third, if this is the case, then CBSs may well exist.

There is evidence to support both the cultural relativist and the universalist position. However, despite the arguments of the cultural relativists, most researchers take the universalist position. But, the vast majority of these researchers are Western or Western trained. Given this, firm conclusions about the relationship between culture and psychological disorders must await 'further research from points of view which are less clearly rooted in a single (Western) cultural tradition' (Berry et al., 1992).

3.4 Conclusion – a critical view

The 1994 edition of DSM listed so-called culture-bound

syndromes in an appendix. The authors lumped together a number of apparently strange and disparate disorders from around the world and placed this motley collection under the heading of culture-bound syndromes. This is hardly a classification, since CBSs are not grouped in terms of major disorders. They are simply listed as disorders that 'may or may not be linked to a particular DSM-IV diagnostic category'. It appears that the authors didn't know what to do with CBSs so they tidied them away in an appendix – or, as some might argue, 'brushed them under the carpet'.

CBSs are non-Western disorders which seem strange, peculiar, alien, exotic, and often unclassifiable, to Western observers. There is a tendency to see Western mental disorders as the 'real thing' – as 'proper' disorders. As a result, non-Western disorders 'are not admitted into the mainstream of psychiatric illness' (Fernando, 1991). Instead, they are relegated to a catch-all category and labelled 'culture-bound syndromes'.

The idea of culture-bound syndromes has been seen as *ethnocentric* – as seeing and judging other cultures in terms of the standards and beliefs of the observer's culture. It is possible that at least some Western disorders are culture-bound. If this is the case, then DSM and ICD are culture-bound classifications and at least some of their diagnostic categories are limited to Western culture. As a result, they are not universally applicable.

Western psychiatry dominates the world and Western classification systems are often taken as 'the bible'. The disorders they list are seen 'as standard and those in other cultures as anomalies' (Fernando, 1991). As a result, disorders which do not fit Western diagnostic categories tend to be seen as exotic oddities to be dumped in appendices and defined as culture-bound syndromes.

Summary

1 The absolutist position states that the same psychological disorders occur in all cultures. They have the same causes and symptoms. Culture has no influence on disorders, therefore there are no such things as CBSs.

2 The universalist position states that the same psychological disorders occur in all cultures. However, the causes and expressions of these disorders are influenced by culture. CBSs are therefore variations of universal disorders.

3 The culturally relativist position states that at least some disorders are culture-bound, that they are limited to particular cultures or culture areas.

4 There is little evidence to support the absolutist position. However, there is evidence to support both the universalist and culturally relativist positions.

5 Western classification and diagnostic systems have been criticised as ethnocentric.

Activity 3   Culture-bound syndromes

Item A   A case of amok?

On Friday 1 June 2001, Crown Prince Dipendra of Nepal attended a family dinner in the royal palace. This was a regular Friday night event. The prince appeared calm and relaxed as he served drinks to guests and family members. Before dinner was served, Dipendra went to his room and returned dressed in his military uniform and carrying two automatic rifles. He shot his mother, then his father, at point blank range, then sprayed the room with bullets killing eight other people including his brother and sister. Dipendra then shot himself and died three days later.

Dipendra was 30 years old and unmarried. He was in love with a young woman from an aristocratic family and wanted to marry her. However, his mother opposed the match and wanted him to marry a woman from a higher ranking family who supported her political views.

Friends described Dipendra as amiable, charming, restrained and intelligent. There was no indication of any violent or homicidal tendencies. Dipendra's behaviour appeared to be completely out of character.

Adapted from *The Observer*, 3.6.2001; *The Sunday Telegraph*, 3.6.2001; *The Times*, 6.6.2001

Prince Dipendra (right)

Item B   Dhat

Dhat has sometimes been seen as a culture-bound syndrome found mainly in India. It is based on the traditional Hindu belief that a loss of semen can result in physical and mental disabilities. The disorder is characterised by extreme anxiety about the release of semen. This is accompanied by feelings of weakness and exhaustion.

Similar beliefs were found in the West during Victorian times. A disorder known as *spermatorrhoea* with symptoms like those of dhat was described in the 1840s. These symptoms included anxiety, depression and various physical ailments. Semen was seen as 'the purest of the body humours'. In 1840, the *Lancet*, a British medical journal, carried an editorial listing a range of physical and mental disabilities that could result from undue semen loss.

Adapted from Singh, 1992.

Questions

1   a) To what extent can Item A be seen as a case of amok?

   b) If Item A is indeed a case of amok, can the disorder be seen as culture-bound? (Nepal is in the Himalayas, north of India.)

2   Can dhat be seen as a culture-bound disorder?

3   To some extent, as culture changes so do psychological disorders.

   a) Briefly discuss with reference to Item B.

   b) What does this suggest about the disorders listed in DSM-IV and ICD-10?

References

Acocella, J. (1998, April 6). The politics of hysteria. *New Yorker*, 64-79.

American Psychiatric Association (1994). *Diagnostic and statistical manual of mental disorders* (4th ed.). Washington, DC: Author.

Arboleda-Florez, J. (1979). Amok. In R.C. Simons & C. Hughes (Eds.), *The culture-bound syndromes: Folk illness of psychiatric and anthropological interest*. Dordrecht: Reidel.

Beck, A.T., Ward, C.H., Mendelson, M., Mock, J.E. & Erbaugh, J. (1962). Reliability of psychiatric diagnosis. 2: A study of consistency of clinical judgments and ratings. *American Journal of Psychiatry, 119*, 351-357.

Bentall, R.P. (Ed.). (1990). *Reconstructing schizophrenia*. London: Routledge.

Bentall, R.P., Jackson, H.F. & Pilgrim, D. (1988). Abandoning the concept of schizophrenia: Some implications of validity arguments for psychological research into psychotic phenomena. *British Journal of Clinical Psychology, 27*, 303-324.

Berry, J.W., Poortinga, Y.H., Segall, M.H. & Dasen, P.R. (1992). *Cross cultural psychology: Research and applications*. Cambridge: Cambridge University Press.

Brewin, C.R. (1996). Theoretical foundations of cognitive-behavior therapy for anxiety and depression. *Annual Review of Psychology, 47*, 33-57.

Burton-Bradley, B.G. (1987). The Hungerford Massacre and its aftermath. *British Journal of Psychiatry, 151*, 866.

Carr, J.E. (1978). Ethnobehaviorism and the culture-bound syndromes: The case of amok. *Culture, Medicine and Psychiatry, 2*, 269-293.

Comer, R.J. (1998). *Abnormal psychology* (3rd ed.). New York: W.H. Freeman.

Coons, P.M. (1980). Multiple personality: Diagnostic considerations. *Journal of Clinical Psychiatry, 41*, 330-336.

Crowe, T.J., MacMillan, J.F., Johnson, A.I. & Johnson, E.C. (1986). The Northwick Park study of first episodes of schizophrenia: II. A controlled trial of prophylactic neuroleptic treatment. *British Journal of Psychiatry, 148*, 120-127.

Davison, G.C. & Neale, J.M. (1998). *Abnormal psychology* (7th ed.). New York: John Wiley & Sons.

DiNardo, P.A., O'Brien, G.T., Barlow, D.H., Waddell, M.T. & Blanchard, E.B. (1993). Reliability of the DSM-III-R anxiety disorders categories using the Anxiety Disorders Interview Schedule-Revised (ADIS-R). *Archives of General Psychiatry, 50*, 251-256.

DiNicola, V.F. (1990). Anorexia multiforme: Self-starvation in historical and cultural context. II: Anorexia nervosa as a culture reactive syndrome. *Transcultural Psychiatric Research Review, 27*, 245-286.

Everitt, B.S., Gourlay, A.J. & Kendell, R.E. (1971). An attempt at validation of traditional psychiatric syndromes by cluster analysis. *British Journal of Psychiatry, 119*, 399-412.

Fernando, S. (1991). *Mental health, race and culture*. London Macmillan/Mind.

Ford, M.R. & Widiger, T.A. (1989). Sex bias in the diagnosis of histrionic and antisocial personality disorders. *Journal of Consulting and Clinical Psychology, 57*, 301-305.

Gleaves, D.H. (1996).The sociocognitive model of dissociative identity disorder: A reexamination of the evidence. *Psychological Bulletin, 120*, 42-59.

Greaves, G.B. (1980). Multiple personality 165 years after Mary Reynolds. *Journal of Nervous and Mental Disease, 168*, 577-596.

Haralambos, M. (Ed.) (1996). *Sociology: A New Approach*. Ormskirk: Causeway.

Haralambos, M. & Holborn, M. (2000). *Sociology: Themes and perspectives* (5th ed.). London: Harper Collins.

Hawton, K., Salkovskis, P.M., Kirk, J. & Clark, D.M. (1989). *Cognitive behaviour therapy for psychiatric problems: A practical guide*. Oxford: Oxford University Press.

Josephy, A.M. (1994). *500 nations: An illustrated history of North American Indians*. New York: Alfred A. Knopf.

Kaplan, M. (1983). A woman's view of DSM-III. *American Psychologist, 38*, 786-792.

Kendell, R.E. (1975). *The role of diagnosis in psychiatry*. Oxford: Blackwell.

Kinderman, P. & Lobban, F. (2000). Evolving formulations. *Behavioural and Cognitive Psychotherapy, 28*, 307-310.

Kleinman, A. & Good, B. (1985). *Culture and depression: Studies in the anthropology and cross-cultural psychiatry of affective disorder*. Berkeley: University of California Press.

Kline, N.S. (1963). Psychiatry in Indonesia. *American Journal of Psychiatry, 119*, 809-815.

Kluft, R.P. (1993). Multiple personality disorders. In D. Spiegel (Ed.), *Dissociative disorders: A clinical review*. Lutherville, MD: Sidran Press.

Kon, Y. (1994). Amok. *British Journal of Psychiatry, 165*, 658-689.

Lilienfeld, S.O., Lynn, S.J., Kirsch, I., Chaves, J.F., Sarbin, T.R. & Ganaway, G.K. (1999). Dissociative identity disorder and the sociocognitive model: Recalling the lessons of the past. *Psychological Bulletin, 125*, 507-523.

Lipton, A.A. & Simon, F.S. (1985). Psychiatric diagnosis in a state hospital: Manhattan State revisited. *Hospital and Community Psychiatry, 36*, 368-373.

Mair, K. (1999). Development of a dogma: Multiple personality and child abuse. *The Psychologist, 12*, 76-80.

Manson, S.M., Shore, J.H., & Bloom, J.D. (1985). The depressive experience in American Indian communities: A challenge for psychiatric theory and diagnosis. In A. Kleinman & B. Good (Eds.) *Culture and depression: Studies in the anthropology and cross-cultural psychiatry of affect and disorder*. Berkley: University of California Press.

Mollon, P. (1996). *Multiple selves, multiple voices: Working with trauma, violation and dissociation*. Chichester: Wiley.

Moncrieff, J. (1997). Lithium: Evidence reconsidered. *British Journal of Psychiatry, 171*, 113-119.

Nazroo, J.Y. (1997). *Ethnicity and mental health: Findings from a national community study*. London: Policy Studies Institute.

Persons, J.B. (1989). *Cognitive therapy in practice: A case formulation approach (Vol. 41)*. London: W. Norton & Company.

Persons, J. B., Mooney, K.A. & Padesky, C.A. (1995). Interrater reliability of cognitive behavioral case formulations. *Cognitive Therapy and Research, 19,* 21-34.

Putnam, F.W. (1989). *Diagnosis and treatment of multiple personality disorder.* New York: Guilford Press.

Putnam, F.W., Guroff, J.J., Silberman, E.K., Barban, L. & Post, R.M. (1986). The clinical phenomenology of multiple personality disorder: Review of 100 recent cases. *Journal of Clinical Psychiatry, 47,* 285-293.

Romme, M. & Escher, S. (1993). *Accepting voices.* London: MIND.

Rosenhan, D. (1973). On being sane in insane places. *Science, 179,* 250-258.

Ross, C.A. (1997). *Dissociative identity disorder: Diagnosis, clinical features, and treatment of multiple personality.* New York: Wiley.

Schacter, D.L. (Ed.). (1995). *Memory distortion: How minds, brains, and societies reconstruct the past.* Cambridge, MA: Harvard University Press.

Schreiber, F.R. (1973). *Sybil.* New York: Warner.

Schultz, R., Braun, G.G. & Kluft, R.P. (1989). Multiple personality disorder: Phenomenology of selected variables in comparison to major depression. *Dissociation, 2,* 45-51.

Singh, S.P. (1992). Is dhat culture-bound? *British Journal of Psychiatry, 160,* 280-281.

Sizemore, C.C. & Huber, R.J. (1988). The twenty-two faces of Eve. *Individual Psychology: A Journal of Adlerian Theory, Research and Practice, 44,* 53-62.

Slotkin, J.S. (1965). The peyote way. In W.A. Lessa & E.Z. Vogt (Eds.), *Reader in comparative religion: An anthropological approach* (2nd ed.). New York: Harper & Row.

Spanos, N.P. (1994). Multiple identity enactments and multiple personality disorder. A sociocognitive perspective. *Psychological Bulletin, 116,* 143-165.

Spanos, N.P., Weeks, J.R. & Bertrand, L.D. (1985). Multiple personality: A social psychological perspective. *Journal of Abnormal Psychology, 94,* 362-376.

Spitzer, R.L. (1975). On pseudoscience in science, logic in remission and psychiatric diagnosis: A critique of Rosenhan's 'On being sane in insane places'. *Journal of Abnormal Psychology, 84,* 442-452.

Szasz, T. (1961). *The myth of mental illness: Foundations of a theory of personal conduct.* New York: Harper & Row.

Szasz, T. (1989). *Law, liberty, and psychiatry: An inquiry into the social uses of mental health practices.* Syracuse, NY: Syracuse University Press.

Thigpen, C.H. & Cleckley, H.M. (1954). A case of multiple personility. *Journal of Abnormal and Social Psychology, 32,* 135-151.

Thigpen, C.H. & Cleckley, H.M. (1957). *The three faces of Eve.* New York: McGraw-Hill.

Thigpen, C.H. & Cleckley, H.M. (1984). On the incidence of multiple personality disorder: A brief communication. *International Journal of Clinical and Experimental Hypnosis, 32,* 63-66.

Turkle, S. (1998, 19 March). Laying out the moods. *London Review of Books,* 3-6.

Uba, L. (1994). *Asian Americans: Personality patterns, identity, and mental health.* New York: Guilford Press.

World Health Organization (1992). *The ICD-10 Classification of mental and behavioural disorders: Clinical descriptions and diagnostic guidelines.* Geneva: Author.

Yap, P.M. (1974). *Comparative psychiatry.* Toronto: University of Toronto Press.

Zigler, E. & Phillips, L. (1961). Psychiatric diagnosis and symptomatology. *Journal of Abnormal Psychology, 63,* 69-75.

Zimbardo, P., McDermott, M., Jansz, J. & Metall, N. (1995). *Psychology: A European text.* London: Harper Collins.

35 Psychopathology

▶ **Introduction**

Psychopathology is the study of psychological or mental disorders. This chapter looks at three psychological disorders – schizophrenia, depression and phobias. The diagnostic criteria or symptoms of each disorder are examined. This is followed by an outline and evaluation of the various explanations suggested for each disorder. These explanations are drawn from various perspectives in psychology including biopsychology or biological psychology, behaviourism, psychodynamic approaches and cognitive psychology.

Chapter summary

- Unit 1 looks at the diagnostic criteria and explanations for schizophrenia.
- Unit 2 looks at the diagnostic criteria and

- explanations for depression.
- Unit 3 looks at the diagnostic criteria and explanations for phobias.

Unit 1 Schizophrenia

KEY ISSUES

1. What is 'schizophrenia'?
2. What are the symptoms of schizophrenia?
3. What are the main types of schizophrenia?
4. What are the causes of schizophrenia?

1.1 What is schizophrenia?

The most important question to ask about schizophrenia is 'what is it?' The answer is not simple. A large number of textbooks on psychology, psychiatry and medicine respond to this question by *describing* 'schizophrenia'. Many therefore read: 'Schizophrenia is … a serious mental illness … characterised by … a loss of contact with reality … hallucinations and delusions …'. But describing something does not mean that it exists. For example, children's encyclopaedias describe a 'unicorn' as being a 'horse-like animal with a single golden horn in the centre of its forehead'. However, this does not mean that unicorns exist.

The problems of psychiatric diagnosis were discussed in Chapter 16. The term 'schizophrenia' may well be one of those rather vague 'diagnoses' referring to a loose collection of problems, roughly equated with 'madness' or 'insanity'. This unit should therefore be read with care, bearing in mind that many psychologists question whether there is such a 'thing' as 'schizophrenia', and that 'it' has a single identity, course and cause. Everybody agrees that the people who experience hallucinations, delusions, confused and disorganised thought processes, a loss of contact with reality, and all of the other behaviours that are grouped together and described as 'schizophrenia', have serious problems. However, that agreement does not mean that everyone agrees that there is a single 'disorder' – schizophrenia – that causes these varied and disparate problems.

1.2 History

In 1898, the German psychiatrist Emil Kraepelin first described what he believed was a cluster of related problems. He called this cluster *dementia praecox*, which means mental deterioration at an early age. In 1908, a Swiss psychiatrist Eugen Bleuler changed the name to schizophrenia, a Greek term meaning 'split mind'. This is why many people think that schizophrenia involves a splitting of the personality like a Jekyll and Hyde character. However, the problems that are called schizophrenia are not really personality problems at all. The split or fragmentation refers to a loss of contact with reality, or to a lack of association between thoughts and emotions, or to a loss of logical connectedness between ideas. Schizophrenia is the disorder that most of us equate with madness – the ultimate mental breakdown.

About 1% of the population are affected by the problems that lead to a diagnosis of schizophrenia. This is a huge public health problem. People usually receive a diagnosis of schizophrenia in their late teens to early twenties in males and the late twenties to forties in females (Johnstone, 1991). The United Kingdom spends about £1.7 billion per year treating 'schizophrenia', which is more than is spent on treating cancer (National Foundation for Brain Research, 1992). Donald Klein (1980) said that if depression is the common cold of psychological disorder, schizophrenia is its cancer.

1.3 The symptoms of schizophrenia

People who have been given a diagnosis of schizophrenia vary widely in their experiences. Many find their thoughts frighteningly disorganised and disturbed. Because there is such a widespread distribution of symptoms, some researchers have suggested that schizophrenia is not a single disorder but a group of separate disorders bundled together under the same name. If this is true, it might explain the wide variety of causes for schizophrenia that have been put forward.

The two major classificatory systems for psychological disorders are DSM-IV (American Psychiatric Association, 1994) and ICD-10 (World Health Organisation, 1992). Both systems provide a similar list of symptoms for schizophrenia and similar guidelines for diagnosis.

DSM-IV divides the symptoms of schizophrenia into the following groups.

- **Control of thoughts**
  Thought insertion – thoughts are being inserted into their mind.
  Thought withdrawal – their thoughts are being taken away from them.
  Thought broadcasting – their thoughts are being broadcast to everyone else, for example through a TV set.
- **Delusions of control** Delusions are ideas which are clearly untrue, but which are experienced as true. Delusions of control means that the individuals believe they are being controlled by others.
- **Hallucinatory voices** An hallucination is a sensory experience that doesn't actually exist but is very real to the individual. In this case the sense is hearing – the individual hears voices which do not exist.
- **Other persistent delusions** These include things that are impossible, for example communicating with aliens from another world, and beliefs which are inappropriate to the individual's culture, for example being able to control the weather.
- **Other persistent hallucinations** Hallucinations involving senses other than hearing, for example, regular sightings of Elvis Presley.
- **Breaks in train of thought** This results in moving rapidly from one topic to another for no apparent reason. Speech is incoherent, disconnected and makes little or no sense.
- **Catatonic behaviour** This refers to motor abnormalities – abnormal movements. These range from a complete lack of activity, to adopting bizarre postures, to wild flailing of the limbs.
- **'Negative' symptoms** These refer to a lack or reduction of behaviours, usually resulting in social withdrawal and a lowering of social performance. Examples include apathy – a general lack of motivation and interest; poverty of speech – communicating little to others; flat affect – a general lack of emotion; inappropriate affect – expressions of emotion which are not appropriate to the situation, for example laughing at bad news.
- **Change in personal behaviour** A significant and consistent change in some aspects of personal behaviour – for example, aimlessness, idleness, a self-absorbed attitude.

Diagnostic guidelines DSM-IV states that a diagnosis of schizophrenia can be made if a) one of the first four symptoms is clearly present or b) two of the other five symptoms are clearly present. In each case the symptoms must be present for at least one month.

Evaluation As noted earlier, many researchers question whether the varied and very different symptoms of schizophrenia listed by DSM-IV and ICD-10 represent a single disorder. In addition, they see it as highly unlikely, in view of this variety of symptoms, that the disorder has a single course and a single cause.

Key terms

Delusions *Ideas which are clearly untrue, but are experienced as true.*

Hallucinations *Sensory experiences that don't actually exist, for example hearing voices.*

Catatonic behaviour *Abnormal motor movement ranging from inactivity to wild flailing of the limbs.*

Negative symptoms *A lack or reduction of behaviours, for example a lack of motivation and interest.*

1.4 Subtypes of schizophrenia

Both DSM-IV and ICD-10 identify a number of subtypes of schizophrenia. They are distinguished by their symptoms. DSM-IV lists the following five subtypes.

Paranoid schizophrenia The main features are delusions, particularly delusions of persecution (believing that people are plotting against them and persecuting them); and hallucinations, particularly auditory hallucinations (hearing voices). Paranoid schizophrenics are usually agitated, angry, argumentative and highly suspicious of others.

Disorganised schizophrenia Once called *hebephrenic schizophrenia* which means 'silly mind'. Symptoms include giggling, pulling faces and flat or inappropriate affect. Disorganised speech is common, as is disorganised behaviour such as not washing, or brushing teeth.

Catatonic schizophrenia Some people in this category spend long periods immobile, in catatonic stupors. Others exhibit catatonic excitement with wild, uncontrolled motor movements. And others alternate between these two extremes.

Undifferentiated schizophrenia People who don't fit into any of the above types. Often their symptoms are drawn from all of the above.

Residual schizophrenia The symptoms are reduced in number and intensity but signs of the disorder are still present. Those in this category are not completely 'cured' but are no longer diagnosed as a 'fully active' schizophrenic.

Evaluation The classification of subtypes has been criticised for its lack of precision. Many people with schizophrenia don't fit neatly into one or another subtype. For example, people with all forms of schizophrenia may have delusions. The creation of the undifferentiated type for these 'misfits' reveals the lack of precision in the classification system. In addition, categorising people into one or other subtype provides little indication of the causes of their disorder, how it might develop, or what treatment might be effective (Davison & Neale, 1998). As a result of this, researchers have developed alternative classifications.

1.5 Alternative classifications of subtypes

Positive and negative symptoms

Researchers often distinguish between two types of symptoms – *positive symptoms* and *negative symptoms*. Positive symptoms are strange and bizarre additions to normal behaviour. They include delusions, hallucinations and disorganised speech. They can be seen as a distortion of normal functions. Negative symptoms refer to a lack of something, an absence of normal behaviour. They include a general lack of emotion, a loss of interest and energy and a withdrawal from social relationships.

Positive symptoms

Delusions More than three-quarters of people diagnosed as schizophrenic suffer from delusions (Butler & Braff, 1991). These are persistent ideas which are clearly untrue but are experienced as true. There are seven main types of delusion experienced by people who have been given a diagnosis of schizophrenia (see Table 1).

Table 1	Types of delusion
Delusions of persecution	People are plotting against them.
Delusions of control	a) Thought broadcasting – their thoughts are being broadcast to everybody else, for example, through a TV set. b) Thought insertion – thoughts are being inserted into their mind. c) Thought withdrawal – their thoughts are being taken away from them.
Delusions of reference	Events refer directly to them when in fact they don't.
Delusions of sin and guilt	They have committed an unforgivable sin, such as having murdered their children.
Hypochondriacal delusions	They have a serious illness when they have not. This differs from hypochondria in that many of the illnesses they identify are not medically recognised. For example, they may believe that their brain is full of mould.
Nihilistic delusions	Either they have ceased to exist or the rest of the world has ceased to exist.
Delusions of grandeur	They are a famous person such as Joan of Arc or Jesus Christ.

Hallucinations An hallucination is a sensory experience which doesn't actually exist but is very real for the person concerned. Around three-quarters of people diagnosed as schizophrenic experience hallucinations. Most hallucinations are auditory (eg voices in the head) but they can involve any of the five senses.

Disorganised speech The speech of a person diagnosed as schizophrenic is often extremely hard to follow. They may produce something known as a 'word salad'. The words seem to be jumbled up and make no sense to the listener. Sometimes a word may be chosen for its rhyme rather than its meaning. Take the following example. *I came to the hospital to play, gay, way, lay, day, bray, donkey, monkey* (Snyder, 1974).

Negative symptoms

Negative symptoms refer to a lack of, or reduction in, behaviour. This makes it difficult to take part in normal, everyday activities. Negative symptoms include the following.

Poverty of speech This refers to a reduction in the amount of speech – saying little and communicating little – or simply communicating little as in vague and repetitive speech.

Flat affect This is a general lack of emotion, reflected in an expressionless face and a flat and monotonous voice.

Apathy A general loss of motivation and interest. People with this symptom often feel drained and lacking in energy.

Social withdrawal Some people diagnosed as schizophrenic withdraw into their own world, distancing themselves from other people.

Other symptoms

Some symptoms do not fit neatly into the positive-negative classification. They include:

Catatonia This refers to motor abnormalities. *Catatonic excitement* involves wild flailings of the limbs and random energetic movements. At the other end of the scale, *catatonic rigidity* is a complete lack of activity, where unusual postures, such as standing on one leg, are maintained for long periods of time. Catatonia appears less common now than it once was.

Inappropriate affect This refers to emotional expressions which are inappropriate to the situation and out of context. For example, a person may laugh when they hear bad news, such as the death of a close relative. Or they may exhibit rapid changes in mood for no apparent reason. For example, during a loving conversation with his wife, a man diagnosed as schizophrenic suddenly started shouting obscenities at her.

Disorganised symptoms

In recent years a third cluster of symptoms – *disorganised symptoms* – have been added to positive and negative symptoms. Disorganised symptoms include bizarre or erratic behaviour, rambling speech and inappropriate affect (Andreasen et al., 1995).

Diagnosis A diagnosis of schizophrenia requires two or more symptoms from one or more of the three categories – positive, negative and/or disorganised. These symptoms must be clearly present for at least one month.

Evaluation There is no general agreement about which symptoms should be included in each of the three categories. This can result in diagnosis being unreliable (Barlow & Durand, 1999).

However, factor analysis does provide some support for the existence of the three subtypes. Factor analysis is a statistical technique which identifies associations or links between things. It suggests that the three types of symptoms – positive, negative and disorganised – do tend to occur together and form identifiable clusters.

Type 1 and Type 2 schizophrenia

This classification system uses positive and negative symptoms to categorise subtypes of schizophrenia. *Type 1 schizophrenia* consists mainly of positive symptoms – delusions, hallucinations and disorganised speech. *Type 2 schizophrenia* consists mainly of negative symptoms – poverty of speech, flat affect and apathy.

Researchers who support this classification claim it has three main advantages. First, the two types appear to have different causes. Evidence concerning this is examined in later sections. Second, the course of the disorder for Type 1 and Type 2 is often different. And third, each type appears to respond differently to different treatment.

Despite these claims, there are problems. Many individuals diagnosed as schizophrenic do not fit neatly into these subtypes.

Many, if not most, reveal a mixture of positive and negative symptoms (Andreasen et al., 1990).

Key terms

Positive symptoms *Strange and bizarre additions to normal behaviour, for example delusions.*

Negative symptoms *A lack or reduction of normal behaviours, for example poverty of speech.*

Disorganised symptoms *Include bizarre behaviour, rambling speech and inappropriate affect.*

Type 1 schizophrenia *Consists mainly of positive symptoms.*

Type 2 schizophrenia *Consists mainly of negative symptoms.*

Activity 1   Subtypes and symptoms

Item A   Unusual postures

This photograph was taken in 1896. The patients have been holding these positions for long periods of time.

Item B   Delusions

I felt as if I was being put on a heavenly trial for misdeeds that I had done and was being held accountable by God. Other times I felt as if I was being pursued by the government for acts of disloyalty. I felt that the government agencies had planted transmitters and receivers in my apartment so that I could hear what they were saying and they could hear what I was saying. I also felt as if the government had bugged my clothing, so that whenever I went outside my apartment I felt like I was being followed and watched 24 hours a day.

Quoted in Comer, 1998

Item C   Strange conversation

Doctor: How do you feel today?
Patient: Fine.
Doctor: When did you come here?
Patient: 1416, you remember doctor (silly giggle).
Doctor: Do you know why you are here?
Patient: Well, in 1951, I changed into two men. President Truman was judge at my trial. I was convicted and hung (silly giggle). My brother and I were given back our normal bodies five years ago. I am a policewoman. I keep a dictaphone concealed on my person.

Adapted from Carson & Butcher, 1992

Item D   Short of words

I may be thinking quite clearly and telling someone something and suddenly I get stuck. What happens is that I suddenly stick on a word or an idea in my head and I just can't move past it. It seems to fill my mind and there's no room for anything else. This might go on for a while and suddenly it's over.

Quoted in Comer, 1998

Questions

1   a) Which of the DSM subtypes of schizophrenia do Items A, B and C fit? Give reasons for your answers.

    b) Item C is difficult to categorise. What criticism of the DSM classification system does this suggest?

2   Categorise the symptoms in Items A to D as positive or negative symptoms. Give reasons for your answers.

1.6 Causes of schizophrenia

Richard Bentall remarked that almost all variables known to influence human behaviour have been suggested as possible causes of schizophrenia (Bentall et al., 1988). Few researchers believe there is a single cause of schizophrenia. Most see the cause as a complex interaction between variables.

As noted in Section 1.1, many psychologists question whether it is possible to identify a single disorder from the large array of symptoms which are collectively called schizophrenia. This makes the search for causes even more problematic. If schizophrenia is indeed a catch-all name for a number of distinct disorders, then there is little point in searching for the causes of 'schizophrenia'. If these distinct disorders exist, then there will probably be different causes for each disorder. It is important to bear these points in mind when considering the 'causes' of schizophrenia outlined in the following sections.

1.7 Biological explanations

This section examines evidence which indicates that, to some degree, schizophrenia is genetically inherited. It also examines aspects of the brain, in particular abnormalities in neurotransmitter activity and brain structure, which may be associated with the onset and development of schizophrenia.

However, these factors, in themselves, do not appear to directly cause schizophrenia. Instead, they are seen to predispose individuals, to make them more vulnerable to the disorder. Other factors need to be present before this predisposition is expressed in schizophrenia.

Genetic factors

There is strong evidence to suggest that a predisposition to develop the problems that lead to a diagnosis of schizophrenia is in some way genetically inherited. The evidence for this will now be examined.

Relatives A large body of evidence indicates that people who have relatives diagnosed as schizophrenic have a greater risk of developing the disorder themselves – and the closer the biological relationship, the greater the risk. Figure 1 summarises the results of some 40 studies of schizophrenia (Gottesman, 1991). It shows the risk of developing the disorder in terms of a person's relationship to someone diagnosed as schizophrenic. Thus, if a person has an identical twin who has schizophrenia, they themselves have a 48% chance of developing the disorder. If they are a grandchild of a schizophrenic, they have a 5% chance of developing the disorder.

These findings do not necessarily mean that schizophrenia has a genetic basis. Related people often share similar environments and, in general, the closer the relationship, the more similar the environment. Environmental influences may therefore lead to the disorder. However, as the following sections indicate, there is evidence to support the genetic argument.

Twin studies Figure 1 shows that if one identical twin suffers from schizophrenia, then the other twin has a 48% chance of developing the disorder. The figure for fraternal twins is 17%. This evidence lends some support to the view that there is a genetic basis for schizophrenia since identical twins share 100% of their genes whereas fraternal twins share around 50%. But it

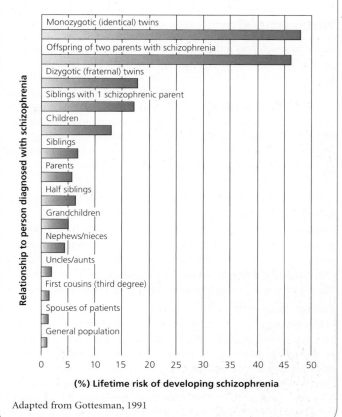

Figure 1 Schizophrenia and relationships

(%) Lifetime risk of developing schizophrenia

Adapted from Gottesman, 1991

doesn't explain, for example, why 52% of identical twins do not develop their twins' disorder. In view of this, genes alone cannot account for schizophrenia.

Do genes in fact have any influence? Most twins grow up in a shared environment. Might the above figures reflect environmental influences? In order to answer this, Gottesman and Shields (1972) studied identical twins who had been reared apart and were therefore likely to grow up in different environments. They found that in 7 out of 12 cases, both twins suffered from schizophrenia. Even this does not necessarily indicate a genetic basis for the disorder. Twins, particularly identical twins, share a similar prenatal environment in the womb. For example, if one twin is exposed to a virus, then the other twin is likely to be exposed to the same virus. And this may account for them both developing schizophrenia, as the viral hypothesis, discussed below, would suggest (Davis & Phelps, 1995).

Adoption studies These studies compare adults diagnosed as schizophrenic, who have been adopted as infants, with their biological parents and their adoptive parents. Because they were reared apart from their biological parents, similarities with those parents would indicate genetic influences. On the other hand, similarities with their adoptive parents would indicate environmental influences.

A large scale study conducted in Copenhagen, Denmark, based on a sample of 5,500 adults adopted in early childhood, found 33 members of the sample diagnosed as schizophrenic. 14% of their biological relatives were diagnosed as schizophrenic by the researchers, compared to only 2.7% of their adoptive relatives (Kety, 1988). These and similar findings from other studies suggest that genetic factors do play a part in the development of schizophrenia.

Which gene/s?

Once research had indicated that schizophrenia may have a genetic basis, the search began for the particular gene or cluster of genes responsible. The investigation has, as yet, proved inconclusive. Gurling et al. (1989) identified an unusual area on chromosome 5 in schizophrenics and concluded that a gene or cluster of genes in this area may predispose people to develop the disorder. Further research failed to confirm this finding (Kendler & Diehl, 1993). Other studies claim to have identified genetic abnormalities associated with schizophrenia on chromosomes 6, 9, 10, 11, 18 and 19 (Comer, 1998).

This type of research is still in its infancy. The technology to identify specific genes remains unreliable. It is difficult to pinpoint particular genes – chromosome 5 holds over 1,000 genes which may be responsible for schizophrenia. And since there are several types of schizophrenia, then each type may be influenced by different genes. This might make sense of the variety of genes apparently associated with the disorder.

Linkage studies Rather than trying to pinpoint a gene for schizophrenia, an alternative method is to identify a characteristic that appears to be inherited and is shared by many or most schizophrenics. The next step is to assume that a gene or genes influencing schizophrenia is nearby, ie assume a genetic linkage. Researchers may have found such a linkage. Move your finger in front of your face and follow it with your eyes. You can probably do this with one long smooth movement of your eyes. Many people with a diagnosis of schizophrenia can't do this, their eyes dart about. This is called an abnormality in smooth pursuit eye tracking. We know that many genes are linked, ie they are inherited as clusters. The gene which causes this abnormality may well be linked to one or more genes which predispose people to the problems that lead to a diagnosis of schizophrenia (Levy et al., 1993).

Evaluation Taken together, studies of the genetic aspects of the causes of schizophrenia provide considerable evidence that inherited factors play a role in the development of the disorder. However, it is difficult to conclude how important such factors are. Opinions remain divided. Some argue that the role of inherited characteristics has been over-emphasised (Torrey, 1992). Others suggest that schizophrenia is probably *only* genetic in origin (McGuffin et al., 1995).

The evidence is suggestive rather than conclusive. Researchers have yet to conclusively identify a single gene or cluster of genes responsible for schizophrenia. There seem to be as many published papers reporting a failure to find specific genetic abnormalities associated with schizophrenia as there are claiming to have found them. In addition, it is not clear *how* genetic factors contribute to the onset and development of schizophrenia.

Brain chemistry – the dopamine hypothesis

Dopamine is a neurotransmitter. It is one of the chemicals in the brain which cause neurons to fire. The original *dopamine hypothesis* stated that schizophrenia results from an excess of dopamine. This causes the neurons that use dopamine to fire too often and transmit too many messages. This 'message overload' may produce many of the symptoms of schizophrenia.

The evidence for this version of the dopamine hypothesis includes the following.

Amphetamines increase the amounts of dopamine. Large doses of amphetamine given to people with no history of psychological disorder often produce behaviour which is very similar to paranoid schizophrenia. Small doses given to people already suffering from schizophrenia tend to worsen their symptoms. Further evidence which points to the connection between dopamine and schizophrenia comes from antipsychotic drugs used to treat the disorder. They work by blocking dopamine receptors, so preventing dopamine-receiving neurons from firing. In addition, L-Dopa, which is used to treat Parkinson's disease (caused by a lack of dopamine), can produce schizophrenic symptoms in individuals with no history of the disorder.

At first, it was thought that schizophrenia resulted simply from an excess of dopamine. However, a number of studies failed to find evidence to support this. A second version of the dopamine hypothesis was then developed. Rather than an excess of dopamine, it was claimed that people with a diagnosis schizophrenia had an excess of dopamine receptors. More receptors leads to more firing and an overproduction of messages. Again, there is evidence to support this view – some autopsies have found an unusually large number of dopamine receptors in the brains of schizophrenics (Owen et al., 1987). But again, the evidence is inconclusive. Other studies have failed to reveal an excess of dopamine receptors (Farde et al., 1997).

There are further problems with the dopamine hypothesis. First, antipsychotic drugs which block dopamine receptors do not appear to help a significant number of people with a diagnosis of schizophrenia. They appear much more effective in cases of Type 1 schizophrenia than in Type 2. Second, these drugs block dopamine receptors fairly quickly, yet even when they are effective the symptoms can take weeks or even months to subside.

A further challenge to the dopamine hypothesis comes from the development of new types of drugs such as clozapine which are known as *atypical antipsychotic drugs*. These drugs block fewer dopamine receptors than traditional antipsychotics. However, they block many receptors for the neurotransmitter serotonin. They appear particularly effective in reducing the symptoms of Type 2 schizophrenics. Recent research suggests that schizophrenia may result from the interaction of serotonin and dopamine rather than dopamine alone (Kapur & Remington, 1996).

The evidence for a relationship between neurotransmitters and schizophrenia is conflicting and inconclusive. As Davison and Neale (1998) conclude, 'Schizophrenia is a disorder with widespread symptoms covering perception, cognition, motor activity and social behaviour. It is unlikely that a single neurotransmitter, such as dopamine, could account for them all.'

Structural brain abnormalities

Ever since schizophrenia was first identified, researchers have tried to discover some form of brain abnormality which might cause the disorder. Modern scanning techniques have accelerated this search. There are three main ways of scanning the brain – Positron Emission Tomography (PET) which images brain functions and Computerised Axial Tomography (CAT) and Magnetic Resonance Imaging (MRI) which picture brain structure.

PET scans have shown a tendency towards abnormally low activity in the frontal lobe of the brain in Type 2 schizophrenics, who show mainly negative symptoms (Andreasen et al., 1990). Those who display mostly positive symptoms – Type 1 – tend to have abnormalities of the limbic system and temporal lobes of the brain. Bogerts (1993) sees this as evidence that there are two distinct types of schizophrenia which are caused by different brain abnormalities.

Enlarged ventricles CAT scans have shown that the ventricles in the brain of schizophrenic patients tend to be larger than normal. Ventricles are chambers within the brain which are filled with cerebro-spinal fluid. In itself, this enlargement might not be a problem. However, it may indicate that nearby parts of the brain have not developed fully or have atrophied – wasted away. There is evidence to support this idea. Some studies indicate that schizophrenics tend to have smaller frontal lobes, smaller amounts of cortical grey matter, and a reduced blood flow in their brains (Comer, 1998). The apparent link between schizophrenia and brain abnormalities has led to a search for the cause of those abnormalities.

The viral hypothesis

At the beginning of this unit, we noted that Kraepelin described schizophrenia as mental deterioration at an early age. MRI scans support Kraepelin's idea that the brain has deteriorated. They point to the possibility that brain damage, at or before the time of birth, could be a factor in the development of schizophrenia. The main development of the brain occurs between the fourth and sixth months of pregnancy (the second trimester). If the brain of a person diagnosed as schizophrenic hasn't developed properly, this may indicate that something occurred during the second trimester to retard development. Bogerts (1993) found that the brains of people diagnosed as schizophrenic in his study showed no evidence of tissue repair. This only happens after the foetus has been growing for 6 months which also suggests that their brains, if they have been damaged, were damaged before this time.

What might cause such damage to occur? Torrey and Peterson (1973) put forward the *viral hypothesis*. They discovered that schizophrenics are more likely to have been born in the late winter/early spring months and so came to the conclusion that in the second trimester of pregnancy, their mothers would have been more likely to catch a viral infection such as influenza. They suggested that this virus could cause irreversible damage to the baby's growing brain which might, later in adolescence, manifest itself as schizophrenia.

A number of studies provide support for the viral hypothesis. Research in the Netherlands found a higher rate of schizophrenia among people born during influenza epidemics (Takei et al., 1995). A study of the Helsinki flu epidemic of 1957 indicated that children whose mothers were exposed to influenza during the second trimester were more likely to develop schizophrenia (Mednick et al., 1988). Other studies, however, have questioned the viral hypothesis. For example, other researchers have examined the Helsinki data and found no relationship between influenza during pregnancy and schizophrenia in later life (Crow, 1994).

Conclusion The evidence suggests that biochemical, brain structure and viral factors are significant in the development of schizophrenia. However, many people with these abnormalities do not develop the disorder. As noted earlier, most researchers regard these factors as predispositions rather than direct causes.

The diathesis-stress model

Most researchers believe there is a biological and genetic basis for schizophrenia. However, they agree that these factors should only be seen as a predisposition to the disorder. They make people more vulnerable to schizophrenia but do not automatically result in the disorder. Biological and genetic factors do not operate in a vacuum, they operate in an environment. The environment includes culture, social relationships in general, and family relationships in particular. Environmental factors can encourage or discourage the translation of a predisposition for schizophrenia into the disorder itself.

This argument forms the basis of the *diathesis-stress model*. Diathesis means predisposition. Stress refers to environmental stress, for example traumatic events such as the death of a close relative or disturbing social situations such as a dysfunctional or maladapted family. The diathesis-stress model explains psychological disorders as an interaction between a predisposition to the disorder and environmental stress. Both are necessary for the disorder to develop.

Support for the diathesis-stress model comes from an important ongoing study in Finland (Tienari et al., 1994). The researchers found 171 women diagnosed as schizophrenic who had a child that was adopted before the age of 4. The adoptive families were interviewed and given a series of tests. On this basis, they were judged to be 'healthy', 'mildly disturbed' or 'severely disturbed'. None of the adopted children raised in 'healthy' families developed schizophrenia. However, 9% raised in 'mildly disturbed' families and 11% in 'severely disturbed' families developed the disorder. This suggests that a well-adjusted family environment protects children who may be predisposed to schizophrenia, whereas a disturbed family environment may encourage this predisposition to express itself in the disorder. Results from this study are examined in more detail in Activity 2.

Key terms

Linkage studies *Studies based on the fact that genes tend to be linked and inherited as clusters.*

Dopamine hypothesis *There are various versions of this hypothesis. The original version states that schizophrenia results from an excess of dopamine.*

Viral hypothesis *States that brain damage associated with schizophrenia is caused by a viral infection of the foetus between the fourth and sixth months of pregnancy.*

Predisposition *Something about an individual which increases the likelihood that they will behave in a certain way. In terms of psychological disorders, it makes them more vulnerable to the disorder, more likely to develop the disorder.*

Diathesis-stress model *Assumes that certain factors predispose individuals to schizophrenia. However, the disorder only develops when the predisposition is combined with environmental stress.*

Activity 2 The diathesis-stress model

Item A The model

Adapted from Zubin & Spring, 1977

Item B Application of the model

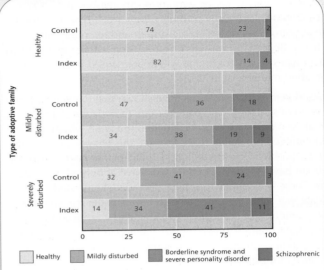

Index group – adopted children of mothers diagnosed as schizophrenic.

Control group – adopted children of mothers with no psychological disorder.

Adapted from Tienari et al., 1990

Questions

1   Using the diagram in Item A, briefly outline the diathesis-stress model.

2   What support does Item B provide for the model?

1.8 Social and psychological explanations

Social class

Over 50 studies conducted in North America and Europe have found that people in the lowest social class have higher rates of schizophrenia than people in higher social classes. Two main theories have been put forward to explain this.

Social selection theory This theory assumes that people with schizophrenia drift down the social ladder into the lowest social class. As a result of their disorder, they may lose their jobs or be limited to low-skill, low-paid employment.

Sociogenic theory This theory states that it is the experience of being a member of the lowest class that explains the higher rate of schizophrenia. Being at the bottom of society can be humiliating and degrading. Unemployment and low status jobs bring little respect, poverty carries a stigma. Low income, poor housing, inadequate schools and high crime rates make life stressful. These experiences may make the development of schizophrenia more likely.

There is evidence which gives some support to both these theories. A study conducted in England and Wales found that male schizophrenics tended to have jobs which were lower in status and pay than those of their fathers. In other words, they were likely to move out of the class into which they were born and down the social ladder (Goldberg & Morrison, 1963). This supports the social selection theory. A study from the USA found that fathers of schizophrenics were more likely to be from the lowest social class. In other words, those who developed

schizophrenia tended to remain in the class in which they were born. This provides some support for the sociogenic theory (Turner & Wagonfeld, 1967).

Family systems theory

Can family life influence the onset of schizophrenia and/or affect a person's chances of recovering from the disorder? Judging from Tienari's study of adoptive families in Finland outlined earlier, the answer is 'yes'. Family systems theorists argue that schizophrenia results, at least in part, from a *dysfunctional family* – a family that does not function properly and, as a result, causes harm to its members.

The schizophrenogenic mother This term was coined to describe a mother who is domineering and insensitive. She is both overprotective and rejecting. Her actions are often contradictory – she can be verbally accepting yet behaviourally rejecting, eg she says 'yes' but her actions say 'no'. This sets up lines of faulty communication between her and her child. This can lead to the onset of schizophrenia in the child (Fromm-Reichman, 1948). Interesting though this theory is, later studies have found little evidence of the schizophrenogenic mother and the effect she is supposed to have (Davison & Neale, 1998).

The double-bind hypothesis One aspect of the above theory has been developed – the idea of contradictory communication which Bateson et al. (1956) called *double-bind communication*. In some families parents communicate with their child in this way. For example, the mother says she wants a hug and then pulls away from the child when he tries to hug her. The child is placed in a double-bind, no-win situation and cannot avoid displeasing its parents. As a result, the child may get confused and suspicious and this may contribute to the onset of schizophrenia.

A number of retrospective studies – studies which look back over people's lives – have provided support for the double-bind hypothesis. However, systematic investigations have failed to find evidence to support it (Comer, 1998).

Expressed emotion Some researchers have looked at how family interaction affects the development of schizophrenia rather than its onset. Brown et al. (1966) examined the progress of schizophrenics discharged from hospital and returned to their families. The researchers used the idea of *expressed emotion* (EE). Families were classified as high or low EE families. High EE families expressed considerable emotion – higher levels of concern for, or hostility towards, the patient. 58% of the patients returned to high EE families relapsed – their symptoms reappeared – compared to only 10% of those returning to low EE families. A number of later studies have produced similar findings.

Evaluation Although many researchers believe that dysfunctional families contribute to the onset or development of schizophrenia, the opposite may be true. The presence of a person diagnosed as schizophrenic may produce a dysfunctional family – he or she may create the family problems which researchers observe. There is probably some truth in both these views as the following study indicates. Recently discharged people who had been given a diagnosis of schizophrenia were observed in family situations. Before they were discharged, their families had been classified as high in expressed emotion. Critical comments by family members increased the expression of schizophrenic symptoms. The symptoms expressed by the patients increased the number of critical comments (Rosenfarb et al., 1995).

Psychodynamic theory

According to Freud, schizophrenia involves a *regression* (going back) to the oral stage. This is the first stage of psychosexual development when the infant is completely self-indulgent, concerned only with the satisfaction of its own needs. This regression results from a conflict between a person's need to gratify their impulses and their experiences of the 'real world'. If they find the world harsh and uncaring – for example, if their parents withhold love and nurturance – there is a tendency to regress to the oral stage. This can lead to the self-indulgent symptoms of schizophrenia such as delusions of grandeur – seeing themselves as famous people like Jesus Christ or Elvis Presley.

However, the individual is still living in the 'real world' and attempts to cope with this by re-establishing contact with 'normal' reality. This can result in further schizophrenic symptoms, for example auditory hallucinations such as hearing voices. This can make their situation appear real and reasonable, especially if the voices appear to come from an ultimate authority such as God.

Freudian ideas have been largely bypassed by today's theories of schizophrenia. This is partly because they are difficult to operationalise – put in a form which can be measured and tested – and partly because they have simply gone out of fashion.

Cognitive approaches

Cognitive approaches examine how people think, how they process information. Researchers have focused on two factors

which appear to be related to some of the experiences and behaviours of people diagnosed as schizophrenic. First, *cognitive deficits* which are impairments in thought processes such as perception, memory and attention. The word deficit means that something is missing or lacking. Second, *cognitive biases* which affect the way people see and interpret the world. Cognitive biases are present when people notice, pay attention to, or remember certain types of information better than others.

Cognitive deficits

There is evidence that people diagnosed as schizophrenic have difficulties in processing various types of information, for example visual and auditory information. Research indicates that their attentional skills may be deficient – they often appear easily distracted.

A number of researchers have suggested that difficulties in understanding other people's behaviour might explain some of the experiences of those diagnosed as schizophrenic. Social behaviour depends, in part, on using other people's actions as clues for understanding what they might be thinking. Some people who have been diagnosed as schizophrenic appear to have difficulties with this skill.

Cognitive deficits, such as those outlined above, have been suggested as possible explanations for a range of behaviours associated with schizophrenia. These include reduced levels of emotional expression, disorganised speech and delusions.

The above findings have been used to support three main conclusions.
- First, deficits in information processing can leave people vulnerable to many of the behaviours typically seen as symptoms of schizophrenia.
- Second, when people with such vulnerabilities experience stressful events, these deficits make it harder to cope.
- Third, the resulting emotional pressure can lead to increased cognitive deficits which, in turn, can lead to further deficits.

Evaluation There are a number of problems with using the idea of cognitive deficits to explain the behaviour of those defined as schizophrenic.
- Cognitive approaches do not explain the causes of cognitive deficits – where they come from in the first place. To provide explanations, cognitive researchers turn to other approaches. For example, they might turn to biological approaches and explain cognitive deficits in terms of abnormalities in neurotransmitter activity or brain damage.
- Cognitive deficits are usually identified by tests designed to

measure cognitive skills. Based on the results of these tests, few differences have been found between people with a diagnosis of schizophrenia and people with a diagnosis of bipolar disorder (manic depression). This suggests that a) there are problems with broad diagnostic categories such as schizophrenia and b) that cognitive deficits do not fully explain the behaviour of those diagnosed as schizophrenic.

- As a result of these problems, many clinical psychologists, especially in Britain, have begun to investigate the psychological processes involved in particular experiences. Rather than trying to explain 'schizophrenia', they study specific behaviours such as auditory hallucinations – hearing voices. In doing so, they focus on the idea of cognitive biases.

Cognitive biases

As noted earlier, cognitive biases refer to selective attention (when people notice or remember certain types of information more than others), and particular interpretations and views of the world. The idea of cognitive biases has been used to explain some of the behaviours which have been traditionally regarded as 'symptoms' of 'schizophrenia'.

Delusions The most common delusion that people diagnosed as schizophrenic report is that others are trying to harm or kill them – delusions of persecution. Research suggests that these delusions are associated with specific biases in reasoning about and explaining social situations. Many people who experience feelings of persecution have a general tendency to assume that other people cause the things that go wrong with their lives.

Auditory hallucinations There is evidence that auditory hallucinations – hearing voices where none exist – are related to cognitive biases. To some extent, people see themselves in terms of their social networks – their networks of social relationships. Some people tend to see themselves as powerless compared to other, more powerful, individuals in their social network. This bias can lead them to see themselves as worthless, useless and incompetent.

Most people experience an 'inner voice' when thinking in words – for example, when deciding what to do, or when struggling with a problem. There is evidence that some people who experience auditory hallucinations mistake their inner speech for speech from an external source. Those who see themselves as powerless sometimes hear 'voices' saying 'He's useless', 'He's worthless'. The status and power gap they see between themselves and others in their social network is mirrored in the relationship they have with the 'voice'. The bigger the gap, the more powerful the 'voice' and the more control it has.

Evaluation The idea of cognitive biases has provided useful insights which have added to the understanding of behaviours which have traditionally been seen as 'symptoms' of 'schizophrenia'. However, the cognitive approach as such does not provide an explanation of the origin of such biases. Some researchers believe that cognitive biases develop from childhood experiences. These can affect the way people interpret information and react to events in later life. For example, highly distressing or traumatic experiences such as sexual abuse and physical assault can lead to a cognitive bias which sees the world as a dangerous and threatening place. And this, in turn, may lead to feelings of persecution.

Key terms

Cognitive deficits *A lack of certain cognitive skills. Impairments in thought processes such as perception, memory and attention.*

Cognitive biases *Particular ways of seeing and interpreting the world.*

Selective attention *Noticing or remembering certain types of information better than others.*

Culture

Culture is the learned, shared behaviour of members of a society. It varies from society to society and changes over time within the same society. As with all psychological disorders, the idea of culture leads to two important questions about schizophrenia. First, is the disorder universal – does it occur in all societies, in all times and all places? Second, what effect does culture have on the onset and development of the disorder?

Universality According to the World Health Organisation (WHO, 1979), schizophrenia is universal – it is found in every culture. WHO researchers examined 1202 patients in psychiatric centres in North and South America, Europe, Africa and Asia. They diagnosed 77.5% of the patients as schizophrenic. There are two main problems with this research. First, the researchers were trained in Western psychology and used Western diagnostic techniques. They were therefore looking at people from different cultures through Western eyes and through the lens of Western psychology. This may result in a misinterpretation and misdiagnosis of non-Western behaviour (Berry et al., 1992).

Second, the people they diagnosed as schizophrenic were not a representative sample of the world's cultures. They belonged to societies which had been strongly influenced by Western culture and were following Western patterns of industrialisation and urbanisation. Research from small-scale, traditional non-Western rural societies indicates that paranoid schizophrenia is rarely found there (Murphy, 1982). In view of this and similar research findings, it would be premature to see schizophrenia as universal.

Cultural effects There is evidence to suggest that culture can affect the onset and development of schizophrenia, its diagnosis and its extent. For example, the Irish Republic has four times the hospitalisation for schizophrenia than England. Murphy (1982) argues that this difference can be partly explained by various aspects of Irish culture. In particular, the verbal agility and wit of the Irish 'increases the complexity and reduces the clarity of information to which people are exposed' which often results in 'double-speak' and 'double-think' (Murphy, 1982).

Culture can also affect the diagnosis and therefore the rates of schizophrenia. One study showed that hospital psychiatrists in New York diagnosed 61.5% of their patients as schizophrenic compared to 33.9% in London. However, members of the same research team using the same diagnostic techniques reduced this difference to 29.2% and 35.1% respectively (Leff, 1982). If professional psychiatrists cannot agree on a diagnosis of schizophrenia, any conclusions about the causes of the disorder and the effects of culture must, at best, be tentative.

Summary

1. Many psychologists question whether the varied problems diagnosed as schizophrenia form part of a single disorder with a single course and cause.

2. DSM-IV identifies five subtypes of schizophrenia with a wide range of differing symptoms.

3. Biological explanations state that a predisposition for schizophrenia is genetically inherited. This is based on evidence from studies of the relatives of those diagnosed as schizophrenic. There is also evidence that schizophrenia is associated with abnormalities in neurotransmitter activity and brain structure.

4. The diathesis-stress model explains psychological disorders as an interaction between a predisposition for the disorder and environmental stress. Both are seen as necessary for the disorder to develop.

5. There appears to be a link between social class and schizophrenia – people in the lowest social class are more likely to be diagnosed as schizophrenic.

6. Family systems theory states that schizophrenia results, at least in part, from dysfunctional families.

7. According to psychodynamic theory, schizophrenia results from regression caused by a conflict between a person's need to gratify their impulses and their experiences of the 'real world'.

8. Cognitive approaches explain some of the behaviours traditionally seen as symptoms of schizophrenia in terms of cognitive deficits and cognitive biases.

9. Whether schizophrenia is universal – present in all cultures – is debatable. However, evidence suggests that culture can affect the onset, development, diagnosis and extent of the disorder.

Activity 3 — Diagnosing and explaining schizophrenia

Item A — Identical quads

The Gernain sisters age 4

The Genain sisters were identical quadruplets born in the USA in 1930. Several members of their family had a history of psychological problems. The sisters grew up in a troubled family. For example, their mother reported that her husband had made several attempts to choke her. Each sister was treated very differently by her parents. For example, Nora was their favourite – she was always first to be burped and fed. Each of the sisters developed schizophrenia but in each case the disorder differed in terms of symptoms, severity, duration and outcome.

Adapted from Sarason & Sarason, 1996

Item B — The double bind

A young man who had largely recovered from an acute schizophrenic episode was visited in hospital by his mother. Because he was glad to see her, he put his arm around her. At this, she stiffened. He withdrew the arm and she asked, 'Don't you love me anymore?' He then blushed and she said, 'Dear, you must not be so easily embarrassed and afraid of your feelings'. The patient was only able to stay with her a few minutes longer and after she had gone, he assaulted an aide.

Adapted from Bateson et al., 1956

Item C — Mixed messages

Item D — Jane's dreamworld

Jane has been diagnosed as schizophrenic. She is in a perpetual reverie, her own little dreamworld, which consists of a game of tennis. It is a mixed doubles; she is the ball. Jane sits motionless and silent and eats only when fed. The adults in the family are in a state of conflict, her father and his mother being ranged against her mother and her mother's father. The two halves of the family communicate only through Jane; she is the go-between. The strain eventually becomes too much for her and she escapes into her dreamworld. However, as her 'dream' shows, even in this world she cannot escape from the clutches of her family.

Adapted from Haralambos & Holborn, 2000

Item E   Shamans

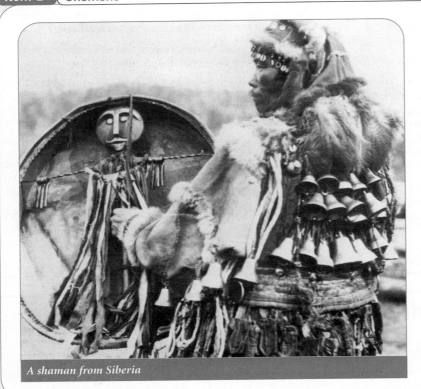

A shaman from Siberia

Shamans are religious healers who communicate with the 'spirit world'. They were found in many small-scale, traditional societies in North America and Siberia. Scratching-Woman was a shaman in the nomadic, reindeer-herding Chukchee tribe of Siberia. Scratching-Woman beat his drum incessantly as the spirits entered him. One of the spirits gave short snorts. It was the fawn of a wild reindeer whose mother had been killed by a wolf. The fawn had become Scratching-Woman's assistant. Another spirit entered the shaman with a dismal howl. It was the wolf who had killed the fawn's mother. When Scratching-Woman wanted revenge on one of his enemies, he transformed himself into this wolf, taking care beforehand to turn his enemy into a reindeer. Then, of course, he was quite certain of victory.

Adapted from Bogoras, 1965

Questions

1   What does Item A reveal about the limitations of a single explanation for schizophrenia?

2   With reference to Item B, explain what Bateson means by the 'double-bind'. How does the cartoon in Item C illustrate this?

3   How can Jane's behaviour in Item D be explained in terms of her family relationships?

4   Some researchers argue that the 'visions' of shamans are the same as the hallucinations of schizophrenics. Others disagree. With reference to Item E, briefly discuss the problems of identifying schizophrenia in different cultures.

Unit 2 Depression

KEY ISSUES

1   **What are the main types of depression?**

2   **What are the major symptoms of depression?**

3   **What are the main explanations for depression?**

2.1   What is depression?

Most of us feel sad from time to time. Sometimes we feel we have no energy, that the world is cold and unrewarding, that we are incompetent or even worthless, that the future holds little or nothing for us. Usually, these experiences are temporary and relatively mild. But for some people they are severe, long-lasting and occur together. When this happens, psychiatrists describe their condition as *depression*.

Depression has been called the 'common cold' of psychiatry – it is the most common psychological problem that people face (Seligman, 1973). In Britain, in 1998, nine million people sought help from their general practitioners for depression (British Psychological Society, 2000). It is estimated that around five per cent of adults aged 18 to 74 will experience serious depression.

DSM-IV identifies three main types of depression. *Unipolar disorder*, or *major depressive episode*, is the most common and most severe form of depression. It is the focus of this unit. *Dysthymic disorder* is not as intense but it spans a longer period of time. *Bipolar disorder*, or *manic depressive disorder*, is a condition where episodes of depression alternate with periods of relative normality and periods of mania – extreme elation accompanied by overactivity, chaotic moods and irritability.

2.2 Symptoms of major depressive episode

DSM-IV refers to unipolar disorder as *major depressive episode*. DSM-IV diagnostic criteria for major depressive episode are given on page 661.

Comer (1998) divides the symptoms of major depressive episode into emotional, motivational, behavioural, cognitive and physical symptoms. Emotionally, the depressed individual is intensely unhappy, feels empty and finds little or no pleasure in anything. Motivational symptoms include a lack of drive, determination and initiative. Behaviourally, there is a marked slowdown of activity or, alternatively, behaviour can be agitated. Cognitive symptoms include negative views of self – as undesirable and inadequate – and of the future – as bleak and unwelcoming. Physical symptoms can include disturbed sleep, constipation, headaches, lack of sex drive, changes in appetite, disruption of the menstrual cycle and constant tiredness.

ICD-10 divides depressive episodes into mild, moderate and severe. ICD-10 diagnostic criteria for *severe depressive episode* are listed on page 660.

Key terms

Unipolar disorder or major depressive episode *The most common and most severe form of depression.*

Dysthymic disorder *A milder, but usually longer-lasting form of depression.*

Bipolar disorder or manic depressive disorder *Episodes of depression alternating with periods of normality and mania.*

Activity 4 Symptoms of depression

Item A Beatrice

For several years, Beatrice had been irritable, but then for a six-month period, her irritability bordered on the irrational. She screamed in anger or sobbed in despair at every dirty dish left on the coffee table or on the bedroom floor. Each day the need to plan the dinner menu provoked agonising indecision. She had her whole family walking on eggs. She thought they would be better off if she were dead.

Beatrice could not cope with her job. As a branch manager of a large chain store, she had many decisions to make. Unable to make them herself, she would ask employees who were much less competent for advice, but then she could not decide whose advice to take. Each morning before going to work, she complained of nausea. Some days she was too upset to go to work. She stopped seeing her friends. She spent most of her time at home either yelling or crying.

Beatrice's husband loved her, but he did not understand what was wrong. He thought that she would improve if he made her life easier by taking over more housework, cooking, and childcare. His attempt to help only made Beatrice feel more guilty and worthless.

Adapted from Comer, 1998

Questions

1 Match Beatrice's behaviour with the DSM-IV diagnostic criteria for major depressive episode listed on p661.

2 On the basis of this, would you diagnose her behaviour as a major depressive episode? Give reasons for your answer.

2.3 Biological explanations

Genetic influences

The medical model sees psychological problems as illnesses with physical causes. Genes are often singled out as one of the causes of depression. From this viewpoint, people with a particular genetic makeup are seen to have a predisposition to depression.

Family studies There appears to be a tendency for depression to run in families. This suggests a possible genetic component. The closer the genetic relationship, the more likely people are to share a diagnosis of depression. First degree relatives – brothers, sisters, sons, daughters, fathers and mothers – share 50% of their genes. First degree relatives of people diagnosed with depression are two to three times more likely to receive a similar diagnosis than first degree relatives of those who have not received a diagnosis of depression (Oruc et al., 1998).

Twin studies Monozygotic (MZ) twins or identical twins share 100% of their genes. Dizygotic (DZ) twins, also known as fraternal or non-identical twins, share around 50% of their genes.

If genes are a factor in depression, then we would expect a higher proportion of identical twins to share the disorder. A number of studies have supported this. For example, a study based on nearly 200 pairs of twins found that when an MZ twin was diagnosed with unipolar disorder, there was a 46% chance that the other twin would receive a similar diagnosis. The figure for DZ twins was 20% (McGuffin et al., 1996).

Adoption studies Most twins and first degree relatives share the same environment for part of their lives. It is therefore difficult to separate genetic and environmental influences. This problem is partly solved by adoption studies. These studies compare people who have been adopted at an early age with their biological and adoptive relatives. Since they were raised apart from their biological relatives, similarities with those relatives would indicate genetic influences. Most studies of adoptees diagnosed with depression show that their biological relatives are more likely than their adoptive relatives to have a similar diagnosis – 20% of their biological relatives compared with 5-10% of their adoptive relatives, which is the rate for the general population (Harrington et al., 1993).

Linkage studies These studies attempt to identify sequences of genes that appear to be inherited along with a predisposition to develop depression. A study of the Amish community in Pennsylvania found that four extended families had a high likelihood of developing depression. From 81 people studied, 14 were diagnosed as having bipolar disorder. This disorder appeared to be linked with a specific genetic marker on chromosome 11 (Egeland et al., 1987). However, later research, both within the Amish community and in other populations, failed to replicate this finding (Kelsoe et al., 1989).

Biochemistry

People do not inherit depression as such. Nor do they directly inherit a tendency for depression or a risk of depression. What they inherit are genes, and genes make proteins. Both neurotransmitters and neurotransmitter receptors are proteins. Genetic differences could therefore present themselves as differences in biochemistry and thus influence depression.

Neurotransmitters Antidepressant drugs are often effective in reducing the symptoms of unipolar disorder. One group of antidepressant drugs increases the levels of the neurotransmitters serotonin and noradrenaline. This finding formed the basis of one of the main biochemical theories of depression. Put simply, unipolar disorder is, at least in part, caused by low levels of serotonin and noradrenaline. However, exactly how the levels of these neurotransmitters affect depression is not clear. For example, one theory states that low levels of *both* neurotransmitters can lead to depression, another theory states that low levels of *either* neurotransmitter can lead to depression. Yet another theory states that it is the balance between these neurotransmitters and their relationship to other neurotransmitters that contributes to depression (Barlow & Durand, 1999). Further research is needed in order to discover the exact biochemical mechanisms of depression.

Hormones People suffering from unipolar disorder often have high levels of the hormone cortisol. Cortisol is known as the 'stress hormone' because it is produced in times of stress. The high levels of cortisol are not surprising as many depressive episodes are preceded by stressful events. Given this, the levels of cortisol may be a result rather than a cause of depression – they are produced as a response to stress rather than causing the disorder.

The release of hormones is regulated by neurotransmitters. Recent research indicates that the relationship between hormones and neurotransmitters needs to be examined in order to understand the contribution of both to depression (Ladd et al., 1996). Research into this relationship is still in its infancy.

Evaluation

The evidence examined in this section indicates that biological factors influence depression. However, quite how and why they influence depression is far from clear. Although genes appear to be involved, the role of genetic factors in depression is enormously complex. We do not know which genes are involved for which people. And we do not know what these genes do or how they are inherited.

Similarly, we know very little about the way in which neurotransmitters like serotonin actually work. More to the point, we do not know that biochemical changes cause depression. It seems equally likely, perhaps more likely, that depression causes biochemistry to alter. Developing depression changes emotions, thoughts, behaviour, facial expression, posture, speech rate, and so on. Why should it not also alter biochemistry?

In fact, there is experimental evidence of this. It is possible to induce depression-like states in dogs, by teaching them that there is nothing that they can do to avoid electric shocks (and yes, such research does have its ethical problems). These depression-like states are accompanied by a reduction in noradrenaline and serotonin levels (Miller et al., 1977). Clearly, there is nothing genetic or biochemical that is wrong with the dogs. Their biochemistry changes as they learn they cannot escape pain (see pp 693-694 for further details of this research).

Even if biological factors are seen as a cause of depression, this does not rule out the many psychological and social theories which will now be considered. Many researchers support the diathesis-stress model (see p685), seeing biological factors as predisposing certain people to depression. However, for these predispositions to be translated into the disorder requires environmental factors.

2.4   Psychodynamic views

Psychodynamic theories usually start from the assumption that depression is related to some kind of loss experienced in early childhood. Freud, who developed the first psychodynamic theory of depression, was struck by the similarity between depression and the response to the death of a loved one. Both often involve extreme sadness, loss of appetite, disturbed sleep and withdrawal from social life. For most people who experience the loss of a loved one, this phase is temporary. But for some, things get worse and they develop depression.

Freud believed that these people were either under or over-gratified during their infant years – they received either too little or too much love from their parents. Both experience loss. Those who received too little love feel unworthy and as a result have low self-esteem. Those who received too much love find the experience so pleasurable, they want it to last for the rest of their lives. But the kind of love and nurturance they received as infants is not forthcoming as they grow older. As a result, both desperately seek to compensate for their loss – either for the love they never had or for the love they can never find again. Both become overly dependent on others for love and affection and the self-worth and self-esteem they bring. Why do people who have experienced loss in early childhood become depressed in later life as a result of the loss of a loved one? Their adult loss brings back the loss they experienced in childhood, amplifying their feelings of being unwanted and unworthy. They regress (go back) to the oral stage of infancy when the original loss occurred. In this respect, depression has been interpreted as an appeal for love and security (Blatt, 1974).

Freud also noted that depression often involves guilt and self-criticism. Again, this is seen to be related to loss during early childhood. For example, feelings of anger and hostility result if the child's needs for love and affection are not met. However, these feelings are repressed as the child is afraid of cutting itself off from those it depends on. Anger and hostility are turned inwards, the child blames itself for the loss which leads to guilt and self-criticism. The loss of a loved one in adult life brings back these childhood experiences. Added to this, the adult may unconsciously blame the loved one for dying or deserting them and feel anger as a result. And again, this anger may be turned inwards leading to the guilt and self-blame that often accompany depression.

Many people become depressed without losing a loved one. Freud accepted this but argued the loss can be *imagined* or *symbolic*. For example, some people may believe their parents only love them if they do well. Thus, if they fail an examination, fail to get to university, or fail to get a good job, they may feel they have lost their parents' love. They therefore experience losing a loved one, an *experience* which may be imagined (they haven't) or symbolic (the loved one isn't dead but the loss feels as though they've died).

The above outline is only a brief and partial account of Freud's theory. However, it indicates some of the ideas which have influenced later theories. Research has generally supported the view that loss in early life makes people more vulnerable to depression. For example, Crook and Eliot (1980) found that depressed adults are more likely than nondepressed adults to have lost a parent before the age of five. Extensive research by Bowlby (1969) indicated that separation from the primary caregiver – usually the mother – during a child's early years can lead to an inability to form close personal relationships. This may result in emotional problems which trigger depression in later life.

Evaluation One of the problems with Freud's theory is the difficulty of testing his ideas. It is difficult, if not impossible, to disprove a theory which is largely based on the workings of the unconscious mind. Although certain aspects of Freud's theory have been rejected by later theorists, there is evidence that childhood loss is related to depression. However, not all studies support this finding (Parker, 1992). And although some studies indicate that depressed people direct anger and hostility towards themselves, other studies do not (Klerman, 1984).

2.5 Behavioural views

From a behavioural perspective, depression results from a lack of positive reinforcement (rewards) and/or an excess of unpleasant experiences (punishments). This often involves a life change. For example, unemployment and retirement can lead to a loss of positive reinforcement – a loss of rewarding social relationships and reduced status and income. They can also lead to unpleasant experiences such as the shame and stigma of unemployment or, in the case of retirement, being treated in terms of the negative stereotypes of old age.

Research by Lewinsohn et al. (1979), showed that depressed people receive fewer positive reinforcements and are likely to have more unpleasant experiences than nondepressed people. The researchers found that a lack of social reinforcement – the approval and companionship of others – was particularly important.

Depression, at least in the early stages, may bring a secondary gain of sympathy and support from friends and relations. However, the depressed person's behaviour may then cause a lack of social reinforcement. Family and friends may grow tired of their negative attitudes and moods and start to avoid them. In one study, participants stated that they felt worse than usual after a short phone conversation with a depressed person (Coyne, 1976). A reduction in social reinforcement in response to depression can, therefore, worsen the disorder.

Evaluation Much of the evidence to support the behavioural position is based on self-report studies in which people report on their experiences of depression. Self-reports can be biased and inaccurate, especially if those involved are still depressed. Also, it is not always clear from these studies whether a lack of positive reinforcement preceded the depressive episode and contributed to its cause, or resulted from it and contributed to its maintenance, or both.

2.6 Cognitive theories

Cognitive theories state that people become depressed because of the way they think about themselves and their situation.

Learned helplessness

Seligman's (1975) theory of *learned helplessness* combines ideas from behavioural and cognitive approaches. It states that people become depressed when they think they have no control over their lives and that they themselves are responsible for their helplessness.

Seligman's theory developed from a series of experiments with dogs. The dogs were divided into two groups. On the first day of

Figure 2 A shuttle box

the experiment, one group rested. The other group were strapped down and given electric shocks at random intervals. There was no way of escaping the shocks. On the second day both groups were placed in a shuttle box – see Figure 1. This box was divided into two compartments. Shocks were given in one compartment and the dogs could avoid them by jumping over a barrier into the second compartment. The experimenters dimmed the lights as a warning before the shocks were given.

The first group of dogs – those who had rested on the previous day – quickly learned to avoid the shocks by jumping into the second compartment. The second group – those who had been given inescapable shocks – did not. They lay down and whined, passively accepting the painful shocks. Seligman argued that these dogs had *learned to be helpless*. Their experience from the previous day had taught them there was no escape from the shocks. Even though the situation was different – they were no longer strapped down – they still behaved as though they had no control over their situation.

From this and similar experiments, Seligman observed that the effects of learned helplessness in animals were similar to the symptoms of depression in humans. For example, animals trained to be helpless passively accepted their situation – they ate little, they showed little or no interest in sex or social life generally. Studies of learned helplessness in rats indicate lower levels of the neurotransmitters serotonin and noradrenaline. Again, this mirrors findings in depressed humans. However, given the differences between animals and humans, we can't simply jump to the conclusion that learned helplessness is central to depression in human beings.

Seligman's experiments with animals led to a series of laboratory experiments with humans in an attempt to discover whether people trained to be helpless would act accordingly and display symptoms of depression. In one experiment (Hiroto, 1974), participants were exposed to a loud, unpleasant noise which they couldn't turn off. They were then placed in front of a 'finger shuttle box', a box with a handle on top. Moving the handle from one side to the other would turn the noise off. Most participants, however, simply sat and passively accepted the noise. But a second group of participants, who had not received helplessness training – they had not been exposed to the initial noise which couldn't be turned off – soon learned to move the handle and cut off the noise. This, and similar experiments, indicated that participants trained in helplessness displayed some of the symptoms of depression – passively accepting their situation and withdrawing from social contact in the laboratory. However, not all helplessness experiments supported these findings. In some cases, they produced the opposite results – helplessness training appeared to improve the performance of participants in laboratory tasks (Wortman & Brehm, 1975). This led to a revision of Seligman's theory with the addition of the idea of *attributions*.

Attributions An attribution is an explanation of why something happens. People use attributions in everyday life – they attribute reasons or causes to their own behaviour and the behaviour of others. In terms of the revised theory, helplessness and depression result from the type of attributions people make – the explanations they give for their own behaviour and situation. Seligman et al. (1979) found that depressed people tend to attribute their lack of control and negative experiences to three types of causes which are all related to the way they see themselves.

Internal causes – coming from within oneself rather than the external environment – 'I am inadequate'.

Stable causes – an enduring trait rather than one which changes with the situation – 'I will always be inadequate'.

Global causes – those that affect every aspect of life – 'I am inadequate at everything'.

Consider Colin who has major depressive disorder. If Colin fails his driving test he will attribute his failure to the fact that he has no common sense (internal), that he has never had any common sense so he will probably fail next time (stable) and, to make matters worse, his lack of common sense is all pervading so he will probably blow the house up when he changes the plug on the hairdryer (global).

According to Seligman, this type of attribution leads to a feeling of helplessness. This in turn may contribute to depression since the attribution states that there is nothing that can be done to change the situation. A large number of studies have supported this view. One study looked at students who did badly in their psychology examination. Two days after the exam, students who attributed their failure to internal, stable and global causes continued to be mildly depressed. However, students who made different attributions – it was a particularly difficult exam; I wasn't feeling well on the day – had recovered (Metalsky et al., 1987).

Despite support for the revised version of the learned helplessness theory, there are still unanswered questions. First, where does this type of attribution come from? Second, does it precede or follow depression? In other words, is it a cause or result of depression? Some researchers argue that a depressive attributional style develops from childhood experiences and therefore predisposes certain people to depression. Sexual abuse in childhood, overprotective parents and harsh discipline have all been linked to the development of this type of attribution (Rose et al., 1994).

Most researchers claim that a depressive attributional style precedes depression but, on its own, it is not sufficient to cause depression. It may be accompanied by negative and severely stressful events (Abramson et al., 1989).

Evaluation The theory of learned helplessness has produced a plausible explanation of the relationship between helplessness, attributional style and depression. And a large body of research has produced evidence to support the theory. However, there are a number of problems. First, evidence from animal studies cannot be generalised to humans, though it can provide important leads. Second, much of the evidence for humans comes from laboratory experiments in which the participants are often college students. This raises two problems – the artificiality of the laboratory situation and the unrepresentativeness of college students. In terms of the example of psychology students discussed above, we must be cautious of generalising from mildly depressed students to people with serious depression. Third, much of the evidence for a depressive attributional style comes from answers to the Attributional Style Questionnaire (see Activity 5, Item D). Some research suggests that this questionnaire forces people into this type of thinking and does not reflect their everyday thinking (Anderson et al., 1994).

Beck's cognitive theory of depression

Viewing the world One of the key principles of modern psychology is the idea that we actively construct our view of the world. To a large degree we see what we believe is there.

Most psychologists believe that complex human processes such as emotions are controlled by *cognitive schemas* (Anderson, 2000). These are mental constructions of the world – mental representations of objects, people, events and situations. People do not appraise each event afresh, as something new. Instead, what they see and what they hear is categorised, shaped and understood in the light of cognitive schemas.

This idea led to one of the most influential theories of depression – Beck's (1967) cognitive model.

Negative thinking Beck's *cognitive theory of depression* suggests that people who become depressed tend to think differently about themselves and the world around them. Their beliefs, attitudes and thought processes make them more vulnerable to depression. In particular, they have a depressive way of viewing and representing the world.

Beck argues that cognitive schemas about the self develop as a result of childhood experiences (Beck, 1967; Beck et al., 1979). For instance, a child might be brought up to believe that only perfect behaviour is acceptable. Anything less means they are worthless and that people are unlikely to love them. When these schemas are triggered by stressful events, they can lead to particular ways of processing information and looking at the world. This can result in *negative automatic thoughts* – thoughts which automatically spring to mind picturing a negative view of self. For example, 'I'm no good', 'I'm so disappointed with myself'.

Seeing the self in negative terms can lead to *errors in thinking*. For example:

- **Arbitrary inference** – drawing conclusions without evidence. If a taxi driver doesn't talk to me, this means he thinks I'm a nobody.
- **Selective abstraction** – forming conclusions from an isolated detail while ignoring contradictory evidence. Your boss praises your work and suggests a number of changes. This means, 'He is dissatisfied with my work'.
- **Overgeneralisation** – drawing a conclusion from a particular event and applying it generally. A leaky tap means, 'I'm a poor husband'.

Negative thoughts and errors in thinking can produce a *negative cognitive triad* – negative views of 1) the self, 2) the world and 3) the future. For example, I am worthless, the world is a miserable place, the future is hopeless. This conclusion allows no space for positive thoughts.

Evaluation There is plenty of evidence to support Beck's theory. Research indicates that compared to nondepressed people, depressed individuals have more negative thoughts about themselves, the world, and the future. In addition, they are more likely to make the kind of errors in thinking that Beck identified. The key question, however, is whether negative thinking precedes and contributes to the onset of depression or whether it results from depression and contributes to its maintenance. According to Davison and Neale (1998), 'the relationship in all likelihood works both ways; depression can make thinking more negative, and negative thinking can probably cause and certainly worsen depression'.

Longitudinal studies – studies of a group of people over time – are needed to investigate this question. The ongoing Temple-Wisconsin study of cognitive vulnerability to depression provides some preliminary answers. First year university students who were not depressed were assessed every few months. Results for the first 2 years suggest that negative thinking predisposes people to depression. Seventeen per cent of high-risk participants (those with high scores for negative thinking) compared to one per cent of low-risk participants (those with low scores) went on to experience a major depressive episode (discussed in Barlow & Durand, 1999).

Key terms

Learned helplessness *A feeling of helplessness which is learned and leads to passive acception of the situation.*

Negative automatic thoughts *Thoughts which automatically spring to mind and present a negative view of self.*

Negative cognitive triad *Negative views of the self, the world and the future.*

2.7 Social origins of depression

Cognitive theories of depression recognise the role of social factors – for example, childhood experiences and stressful events. There is considerable evidence to support this view. A study by Brown and Harris (1978) entitled *The social origins of depression* was based on interviews with women living in the inner London borough of Camberwell. Some of the women were receiving psychiatric treatment and some were selected randomly from the general population. The researchers found a clear link between depression and stressful life events such as job loss and divorce. In the case of women diagnosed with depression, stressful life events had occurred four times more frequently in the six months before the interview.

Brown and Harris also found a number of social *vulnerability factors* that appeared to increase the impact of stressful life events and increase the likelihood of depression. Vulnerability factors for the women in their study included:

- Lack of a strong, supportive social network which allows people to confide in each other.
- Having three or more children under age fourteen at home.
- The loss of their own mother before the age of eleven.
- Being a member of the working class rather than the middle class.

Brown and Harris argued that a combination of stressful life events and vulnerability factors often leads to depression. They suggested that vulnerability factors lower people's self-esteem and reduce their psychological coping resources.

Evaluation Depression doesn't develop in a vacuum – it develops within a social framework. This observation is one of the strengths of Brown and Harris's research. It points to the importance of social relationships rather than focusing entirely on the individual.

In general, Brown and Harris's findings have been supported by further research. For example, Costello (1982) found that depressed women were less likely to have close friends they could confide in. In other words, they were less likely to have a supportive social network.

However, there is more to depression than stressful life events and vulnerability factors. For example, many divorced women with dependent children, living on low incomes in rundown inner-city areas, do not become depressed.

Culture and depression Studies of the relationship between culture and depression examine the impact of social factors in a wider framework. As with all psychological disorders, the concept of culture raises a number of important questions. Is depression universal – is it found in all cultures? If it is, to what extent, if at all, are the prevalence, causes and expressions of depression affected by different cultures? Or is depression limited to particular cultures? These questions are examined in detail in the unit on culture in the previous chapter (see pp 674-675).

2.8   Women, men and depression

Two and a half times more women than men were treated for depression in England and Wales from 1994 to 1998 (*Social Trends*, 2001). These rates are similar for the USA and other Western societies. The following explanations have been put forward for this difference.

The figures One argument states that the actual rate of depression is the same for both sexes. However, the treatment rate differs because men find it less acceptable to admit to symptoms of depression and to seek treatment. This is questionable. Interviews with men and women with similar levels of depression showed that they were equally likely to a) label themselves as depressed and b) seek treatment (Amenson & Lewinsohn, 1981). However, it is possible that much male depression remains undiagnosed because it is expressed in alcohol abuse and aggression rather than the standard symptoms.

Biological factors Some researchers have suggested that fluctuations in hormonal levels associated with the menstrual cycle, childbirth, the menopause and taking oral contraceptives may affect brain chemistry in women and result in higher levels of depression (Leutwyler, 1997). Researchers generally agree that these factors are unlikely to explain the large gender difference in depression. Most see social factors as more important (Cochrane, 1995).

The housewife role The American sociologist Jessie Bernard (1976) writes, 'In truth, being a housewife makes women sick'. Compared with unmarried women, wives are more likely to suffer from depression, other psychological disorders and physical ill-health. Marriage can be seen as a safety-net for men (in that suicide rates for married men are lower than for single men), but a cage for women (in that suicide rates for married women are higher than for single women). A number of studies indicate that married women employed outside the home fare far better than full-time housewives. According to Oakley (1974), full-time housewives have low-status, unpaid, monotonous, dead-end jobs, they are often socially isolated, they are economically dependent on men, with little power or control over their lives.

Women as carers Women are still primarily responsible for childcare and for the care of sick and elderly relatives (Taylor et

al., 1995). Women's care role involves them in the problems of others which may increase their levels of stress and make them more vulnerable to depression (Shumaker & Hill, 1991).

Stress is often associated with lack of control, unpredictability and a lack of social support. Caring for pre-school and school age children may have these characteristics. A child-carer is less likely to have the ability to control aspects of her day – the needs of the kids come first – and is often isolated from other adults.

Disadvantage Compared to men, women are more likely to have low-status, low-skill and low-paid jobs. They are more likely to be dependent on state benefits and to live in poverty. Ninety-eight per cent of lone-parent families are headed by women – they make up over a quarter of all families with dependent children in Britain. Compared with two-parent families, lone-parent families are more likely to depend on state benefits, to live in substandard housing and to have health problems (*Social Trends*, 2001). Research indicates that poverty and social disadvantage increase stress levels which may well make women more vulnerable to depression.

Conclusion No one factor explains the difference in rates of depression between women and men. Recent explanations focus on women's position in society – in the home and in the workplace, as wives, mothers and carers – and the disadvantages that often result from their position – lack of income, status, power and control.

2.9   The diathesis-stress model

The previous section concluded that no one factor accounts for gender differences in depression. Many researchers believe that no one theory can provide an adequate explanation for depression. They argue for an integration of biological, psychological and social theories. The diathesis-stress model provides an example of this approach.

As outlined earlier (see p685), the diathesis-stress model sees psychological disorders as an interaction between a predisposition (the diathesis) to the disorder and stressors (the stress) in the environment. The stressors are seen to trigger the predisposition and from this interaction, the disorder develops. In terms of depression, predispositions include biological factors, loss in childhood, learned helplessness, negative thinking and social circumstances. These factors are seen to put people at risk, to make them more vulnerable to depression.

Stressful events which have been linked to depression include the death of a loved one, the loss of a job, and marital breakup. For example, data from the USA indicates that the depression rate of people who are separated or divorced is three times the rate for married people (Weissman et al., 1991).

In this way, the diathesis-stress model combines ideas and data from different theories of and approaches to depression.

Summary

1. There are three main types of depression – unipolar disorder or major depressive episode, disthymic disorder and bipolar or manic depressive disorder.

2. Biological explanations state that a) people with a particular genetic makeup have a predisposition to depression and b) abnormal levels of neurotransmitters and hormones are involved in the onset and maintenance of depression.

3. Psychodynamic theories argue that certain childhood experiences, usually some kind of loss, make people more vulnerable to depression.

4. From a behavioural perspective, depression results from a lack of positive reinforcement.

5. Cognitive theories argue that the way people think can contribute to the onset and maintenance of depression. Seligman's learned helplessness theory points to a depressive attributional style. Aaron Beck points to negative cognitive schemas, cognitive errors and negative thinking.

6. There is evidence that social factors, such as a lack of close friendships, can make people more vulnerable to depression.

7. In Western societies, women are twice as likely as men to be diagnosed as depressive. Recent explanations focus on women's position in society, particularly their lack of power and control over their lives.

8. Many researchers argue that no one theory can account for depression. They argue for an integration of biological, psychological and social theories.

Activity 5   Explaining depression

Item A   The Tennyson family tree

The English poet Alfred Tennyson

ELIZABETH
b.1776
Recurrent bouts
of depression

MARY
b.1777
'Ferocious pessimism'
constant quarrelling
and gloominess

CHARLES (D'EYNCOURT)
1784-1861
'Inherited his father's instability
and fretfulness'; spendthrift
tendencies; expansive, grandiose
activities and interests

ELIZABETH FYTCHE
1781-1865
'Easy going' and
'sweet tempered'

=

GEORGE CLAYTON TENNYSON
1778-1831
Vacillating moods 'between
frenzy and lethargy' spendthrift,
alcoholic, 'fits', insanity

GEORGE
Died in
Infancy.
1806

CHARLES
1808-1879
Addicted to laudanum;
'complete nervous
break-down'; had to
be segregated from
outside world;
extreme mood swings
and 'recurrent fits of
psychopathic depression'

MARY
1810-1884
Of a wild sort
of countenance;
obsessed with
spiritualism

EDWARD
1813-1890
Confined in insane
asylum for almost
60 years; severe
melancholia;
death from
manic exhaustion

SEPTIMUS
1815-1866
'Suffered from
nervous depression';
frequent treatments
for melancholia;
'the most morbid
of all the Tennysons'

CECILIA
1817-1909
'Mental
disturbance
and
depression';
eccentric

FREDERICK
1807-1898
Irritability; eccentric;
violent temper and
volatile; obsessed
with spiritualism

ALFRED
1809-1892
Recurrent depression...
required treatment;
trances possibly
epileptic but not
thought so by physician;
possibly transient
hypomanic episodes;
'dwelling in an
element of gloom'

EMILY
1811-1889

ARTHUR
1814-1899
'Suffered much
from depression';
one year in
Crichton
Institution for
the insane

MATILDA
1816-1913
'Some mental
derangement'
occasionally attributed
to childhood
accident; religious
obsessions; 'did not
entirely escape the
black-bloodedness
of the Tennysons'

HORATIO
1819-1899
'Strange personality
was legendary';
rather unused to
this planet';
perceived himself
as vulnerable to
the 'weakness of
the Tennysonian
temperament'

Adapted from *Scientific American*, February 1995

Item B — Ellen

Ellen saw herself as her boss's favourite – her sense of self-worth depended on this. She became depressed when her boss hired another female assistant who she saw as more able, attractive and likeable than herself. This threatened her imagined status with her boss. As a child, Ellen was the apple of her father's eye. However, when she was five, another child was born. Her reaction was to try harder and harder to obtain praise and reassurance from her father. It worked. When her 'rival' appeared in the office she redoubled her efforts but, in her eyes, the boss failed to recognise this. She eventually became depressed, overwhelmed by her workload.

Adapted from Bemporad & Vasile, 1990

Item C — Mr Downing

Mr Downing has been unemployed for several years. Dependent on state benefits, he can't afford leisure activities and spends most of his time stuck in the house.

'We don't go out, we don't go anywhere, we can't even afford to go to the pictures once a month. Imagine spending a year where the best thing you can look forward to is the housework. You go mad, your brain starts to turn purple. The kids are running round, screaming their heads off, you tend to get ratty, the more often you lose your temper, it has an effect on you. I think it does have an effect on your health both physically and psychologically. It depresses you looking at what other people have and what you can't have.'

Adapted from Cohen et al., 1992

Item D — The Attributional Style Questionnaire

Try to vividly imagine yourself in the situation that follows. If such a situation happened to you, what would you feel had caused it? Events may have many causes, but we want you to pick only one – the *major* cause – if this event happened to *you*. Please write this cause in the blank provided. Next we ask you some questions about this cause. Circle one number after each question.

Situation: You meet a friend who acts in a hostile manner toward you.

1 Write down the one major cause

_____

2 Is this cause due to something about you or to something about other people or circumstances?

Totally due to other
people or   1 2 3 4 5 6 7   Totally due
circumstances   to me

3 In the future, will this cause again be present?

Will never again   Will always
be present   1 2 3 4 5 6 7   be present

4 Is the cause something that influences just this situation, or does it also influence other areas of your life?

Influences just   Influences all
this particular   1 2 3 4 5 6 7   situations in
situation   my life

Adapted from Peterson & Seligman, 1987

Item E — Negative thinking

I can't bear it. I can't stand the humiliating fact that I'm the only woman in the world who can't take care of her family, take her place as a real wife and mother, and be respected in her community. When I speak to my young son Billy, I know I can't let him down, but I feel so ill-equipped to take care of him; that's what frightens me. I don't know what to do or where to turn; the whole thing is too overwhelming … I must be a laughing stock. It's more than I can do to go out and meet people and have the fact pointed up to me so clearly.

From Fieve, 1975

Item F — Treatment rates for depression

England & Wales	Rates per 1000 patients	
	Males	Females
Deprived industrial areas	34	77
Industrial areas	27	71
Prosperous areas	22	57
Suburbia	21	55

Adapted from *Social Trends*, 2001

Questions

1   Item A shows part of the family tree of the English poet Alfred Tennyson. What support does it provide for the claim that depression has a genetic basis?

2   How might a psychodynamic theorist explain Ellen's depression in Item B?

3   Explain Mr Downing's state of mind in Item C using a) behavioural theory and b) a social origins approach.

4   Much of the evidence for the role of attributions in learned helplessness comes from the Attributional Style Questionnaire. Item D is taken from this questionnaire. Critics have argued it forces people into this style of thinking and does not reflect their everyday thinking. Briefly discuss with reference to Item D.

5   a) Identify features of Beck's cognitive triad in Item E.

b) Explain how Item E illustrates negative thinking.

6   Suggest reasons for the variation in treatment rates for different areas shown in Item F.

Unit 3 Phobias

KEY ISSUES

1   **What are the main types of phobia?**

2   **What are the major symptoms of phobias?**

3   **What are the main explanations for phobias?**

3.1   Types of phobia

Phobias form part of a group of disorders known as *anxiety disorders*. A phobia is an irrational and persistent fear of an object, activity or situation which creates an overwhelming urge to avoid it. The distress produced by phobias is so intense that it interferes with people's ability to function normally. It is estimated that around 14% of people in Western society develop a phobia at some time in their lives, with women being twice as likely as men to experience the disorder (Comer, 1998).

Specific phobias

As their name suggests, *specific phobias* involve fear of specific objects or situations. There are probably as many specific phobias as there are objects and situations. Among the more common are arachnophobia (fear of spiders), claustrophobia (fear of enclosed spaces), aerophobia (fear of flying) and acrophobia (fear of heights). The following is an example of tonitrophobia (fear of thunderstorms).

'At the end of March each year, I start getting agitated because summer is coming and that means thunderstorms. I have been afraid since my early twenties, but the last three years have been the worst. I have such a heartbeat that for hours after a storm my whole left side is painful. I say I will stay in the room, but when it comes I am a jelly, reduced to nothing. I have a little cupboard and I go there, I press my eyes so hard I can't see for about an hour, and if I sit in the cupboard over an hour, my husband has to straighten me up.' (Melville, 1977)

This account illustrates some of the physical and psychological aspects of the anxiety associated with phobias. These include sweating, rapid heart beat, avoidance behaviour and, occasionally, a feeling that breathing is difficult.

The DSM-IV criteria for specific phobias are outlined in Table 2.

Table 2   DSM-IV criteria for specific phobias

1   A marked and persistent fear that is excessive or unreasonable, cued by the presence or anticipation of a specific object or situation (eg, flying, heights, animals, receiving an injection, seeing blood).

2   Exposure to the phobic stimulus almost invariably provokes an immediate anxiety response, which may take the form of a panic attack.

3   The person recognises that the fear is excessive or unreasonable.

4   The phobic situation is avoided or else is endured with intense anxiety or distress.

5   The avoidance, anxious anticipation, or distress in the feared situation interferes significantly with the person's normal routine, or there is marked distress about having the phobia.

Social phobias

Social phobics fear humiliation in public places. Some fear eating in restaurants or using public lavatories, others fear meeting strangers or public speaking. They are afraid that someone will see them expressing their fear – by blushing, a trembling hand or a quavering voice – and think badly of them. As a result, they try to avoid certain social activities and situations. Consider the case of Edith:

'Edith is afraid of writing her name in public. She can't use cheques or credit cards to shop or to eat in a restaurant. She no longer can play golf because she can't sign the golf register. She can't sign any papers that require approval of a notary public, and she can't vote because she can't sign the voting register.' (Zimbardo, 1992).

This account illustrates the main characteristics of all phobias 1) a fear which most people would regard as irrational and unreasonable, 2) an avoidance of fear-producing situations, 3) an impairment of the ability to lead a normal life.

Agoraphobia

This is a fear of public places – of shopping malls, crowded streets, travelling on public transport. Consider the case of Leo:

'One ordinary day, while tending to some chore, taking a walk, driving to work – in other words, just going about his usual business – Leo Green was suddenly struck by a wave of awful terror. His heart started pounding, he trembled, he perspired profusely, and he had difficulty catching his breath. He became convinced that something terrible was happening to him – maybe he was going crazy, maybe he was having a heart attack, maybe he was about to die. As the attacks became more frequent, he began to avoid situations where he had experienced an attack, then others where he might find it particularly difficult to cope with one by escaping and getting help. He started by making minor adjustments in his habits – going to a supermarket at midnight, for example, rather than on the way home from work when the store tended to be crowded. Gradually, Leo Green got to the point where he couldn't venture outside his immediate neighbourhood, couldn't leave the house without his wife, or sometimes couldn't leave at all. What started out as an inconvenience turned into a nightmare. Like a creature in a horror movie, fear expanded until it covered the entire screen of his life.' (Sarason & Sarason, 1996)

At first sight, *agoraphobia* appears to be another social phobia. However, in most cases it begins with a series of panic attacks. A panic attack is a feeling of intense fear with physiological symptoms such as rapid breathing, increased heart rate, sweaty palms and dizziness. The sufferer has a feeling of impending doom and often fears dying, going mad or losing control. As a result, they are afraid of having a panic attack in a place where they don't feel safe and where there may be nobody around to help them. Where social phobics are afraid of others watching them, agoraphobics are fearful for themselves. Safety, rather than embarrassment, is their main concern. In extreme cases, agoraphobics are unable to leave home for years on end.

DSM IV classifies cases of agoraphobia which are linked to panic attacks as a type of panic disorder – *panic disorder with agoraphobia*.

Activity 6   Identifying phobias

Item A   Arachnophobia

'Seeing a spider makes me rigid with fear, hot trembling and dizzy. I have occasionally vomited and once fainted in order to escape from the situation. These symptoms last three or four days after seeing a spider. Realistic pictures can cause the same effect, especially if I inadvertently place my hand on one.'

Adapted from Melville, 1977

Item B   Fluid consumption

'The minute I entered a restaurant it was a complete nightmare. I would sit down and feel the sweat pouring off me. Then my heart would start racing and I'd go redder and redder. It's something about eating in front of people – I'm convinced they're watching and judging me.' Alice also had trouble travelling on the tube and would react suddenly with hot flushes, sweating and palpitation. 'I only had to cough and it would trigger all my symptoms – I was convinced the whole train was looking at me. After that the blushing and sweating would start.'

Adapted from *The Independent on Sunday*, 14.1.1996

Questions

1   What type of phobia do Items A and B represent? Give a reason for your answer.

2   What details of Items A and B show that these are phobias rather than 'normal' fears?

3.2   Explaining phobias

Biological explanations

Genetic factors Phobias tend to run in families which suggests a genetic component. The prevalence rate for both specific and social phobias is higher in first degree relatives than more distant relatives and the general population. For example, one study showed that 64% of people with a blood and injection phobia have a first degree relative who shares the same disorder. The prevalence rate for the general population is 3-4% (Ost, 1992).

It is possible to interpret the results of such studies in a number of ways. They may indicate 1) genetic influence; 2) environmental influence – for example children may model their phobias on those of their parents. Research indicates that relatives are likely to share the *same* phobia (Barlow & Durand, 1999); or 3) a mixture of genetic and environmental influences.

Autonomic nervous system Research indicates that the autonomic nervous system (ANS) is more easily aroused in some individuals than in others. This makes them more sensitive to environmental stimuli. Since the ANS is involved in fear – an important aspect of phobias – the arousal level of the ANS may make some more vulnerable to phobias than others. There is some evidence that ANS arousal levels may be genetically based (Lacey, 1967).

Biological preparedness From an evolutionary perspective, many aspects of behaviour are influenced by genes which have become established in human populations because of their survival value. Seligman's (1971) *preparedness theory* suggests that humans have a genetically based tendency to respond quickly to danger, often without thinking. Many of the more common phobias are based on things which may have threatened human survival, particularly in the distant past. These include phobias of snakes, spiders, heights and darkness. Those who feared such dangers were more likely to survive and pass their genes on to future generations. In terms of preparedness theory, we are genetically 'prepared' or predisposed to fear things which have threatened human survival for hundreds of thousands of years.

An experiment by Ohman et al. (1975) may provide support for this view. One group of participants were conditioned to fear snakes and spiders by pairing slides of them with an electric shock. A second group were conditioned to fear houses and flowers. After a short shock-free period, the second group lost their fear of houses and flowers. However, the first group retained their fear of snakes and spiders for much longer. This can be seen as supporting preparedness theory – it's difficult to see how fear of flowers would help the survival of the species!

However, the results of this experiment, and preparedness in general, may have nothing to do with genes. Snakes, spiders, heights and darkness can be dangerous and therefore merit a healthy respect and even fear. This may be simply learned as part of culture. If so, it is culture rather than biology which explains the 'popularity' of many phobias.

Evaluation Biological theories are at best suggestive rather than conclusive. They suggest why some people are predisposed to phobias and why some phobias are more common than others. However, the evidence used to support biological theories can often be used to support alternative environmental explanations.

Psychodynamic explanations

Psychodynamic theorists see phobias as a result of the conflict between the Id and the Ego. According to Freud, the Id is a part of the mind which has unacceptable impulses (usually aggressive or sexual). The fear that these impulses might be expressed in behaviour causes anxiety. In response to this anxiety, the impulses are *repressed* – they are pushed into the unconscious by the Ego, by means of various defence mechanisms. However, they remain in the unconscious and are often *displaced* – the anxiety produced by the feared Id impulses is transferred to an object or situation which becomes the focus for a phobia. The phobia, in some way, represents the source of the original anxiety. For example, a woman's fear of snakes may represent her fear of male genitalia. By avoiding the phobic object or situation, the person avoids having to face up to and deal with the repressed conflict.

In 1909, Freud published a case study on phobia. His client was a boy called Little Hans. Little Hans was five years old when he developed a fear of horses after seeing a horse that was pulling a bus fall over and kick its feet in the air. He was terrified and thought that the horse was dead. Freud concluded that the boy was battling with an unresolved Oedipus complex. According to Freud, all little boys have this complex which involves wanting to possess their mother. They see their father as a rival for their mother's love and want to kill him. Freud believed that Little Hans was unconsciously terrified that his father would discover his desires and castrate him. He argued that the boy's Ego had displaced this repressed fear of his father onto horses and that Hans feared horses because he associated them with his father. Freud said that the boy was afraid of the black around horses' mouths and the blinkers at the side of their eyes because they were like his father's moustache and eyeglasses. He went on to say that Little Hans wished that his father would fall down dead, like the horse, so that he could have his mother for himself.

Cognitive explanations

Cognitive theorists argue that the way people think about, judge and appraise situations, affects the likelihood of a fearful response.

People with phobias tend to focus on negative aspects of situations. Having experienced a negative event, this negative focus means they are more likely to believe it will recur in the future.

DiNardo et al. (1988) studied people who had a traumatic experience with dogs. Some developed a phobia for dogs, others did not. Those who developed a phobia were more likely to believe they would have a similar negative experience in the future.

Phobias can be maintained or made worse by the way people think about their situation. A high level of anxiety may lead to *catastrophising* – imagining the worst possible outcome of every situation whilst ignoring the possibility of positive outcomes. Consider the following example of thoughts running through the head of someone with a social phobia who is about to give a speech to a large group of people.

'What if I forget what I am going to say? I will look foolish in front of all these people. Then I will get even more nervous and start to perspire and my voice will shake and I'll look even sillier. Whenever people will see me from now on they will remember me as the foolish person who tried to give a speech. (Zimbardo et al. 1995)

In this example, the person feeds on their own fear, so reinforcing their phobia.

Evaluation Cognitive explanations have the advantage of showing why certain people may be more prone to develop phobias and how those phobias may be maintained or made worse. Particular thought patterns predispose them to the disorder, then serve to maintain it.

Behavioural explanations

Behavioural explanations assume that phobias are learned. People are seen to learn their fears of certain objects or situations and then to avoid the things they fear.

Classical conditioning In the following experiment, Watson & Rayner (1920) attempted to condition a baby boy called Little Albert to develop a phobia of white rats. For several weeks, Albert happily played with a white rat, showing no fear. One day, while he was playing with the rat, the experimenters struck a steel bar with a hammer close to Albert's head. Albert was very frightened by the noise. This was repeated each time he reached for the rat. Albert then developed an intense fear of white rats, whether the steel bar was hit in the presence of the rat, or not.

This experiment illustrates the view that phobias are acquired through classical conditioning. In terms of the above example, the unconditioned stimulus (the loud noise) produced the unconditioned response (fear). The conditioned stimulus (the white rat) then becomes associated with the unconditioned stimulus (the loud noise) which produces the conditioned response (fear of the rat).

Operant conditioning This refers to learning to behave in certain ways because the behaviour is reinforced. In terms of phobias, *avoidance* of the phobic object or situation is reinforced by the reduction of anxiety. In the case of Little Albert, his avoidance behaviour is obvious. As soon as he was shown the rat, 'he began to crawl away so rapidly that he was caught with difficulty before he reached the end of the mattress' (Watson, 1930).

Avoidance maintains the fear and preserves the phobia. Frequent contact with a phobic object may reveal that it is harmless, which will lead to the extinction of the fear and the removal of the phobia. However, people with phobias go to great lengths to avoid the object of their fears, often planning ahead and putting up with all manner of inconvenience.

Mowrer's two-factor model combines classical and operant conditioning to explain how phobias are acquired and maintained. According to this model, phobias are acquired through classical conditioning, but thereafter they are maintained through operant conditioning. The relief from anxiety that people get when they avoid the thing they are afraid of is seen as a negative reinforcer (Mowrer, 1939).

Evaluation There is evidence to support behavioural views that phobias are learned and that classical and operant conditioning can be important processes involved in the development of phobias. However, there is also evidence that not all phobias develop in this way.

*   First, many people have frightening experiences and do not develop phobias about them. As outlined in the previous section, DiNardo et al's (1988) study of people who had a traumatic experience with dogs showed that some developed a phobia of dogs and others did not.
*   Second, many people have phobias which are *not* preceded

by frightening experiences. For example, people with phobias of snakes, flying and heights often report they cannot recall any previous frightening experience with the things they now fear (Ost, 1987).

*   Third, there is evidence that some people develop phobias simply by *modelling*. This refers to learning behaviour by observing and imitating the behaviour of others. For example, a mother is with her child and sees a spider running along the floor. She screams with fright, which in turn, frightens the child so much that it cries. The child comes to associate the spider with fear and develops a phobia of spiders.

    However, modelling does not appear to be a major cause of phobias. Few people with phobias report they developed their fear by observing others with a similar phobia. And many people observe others with a phobia but do not develop a similar phobia themselves (Comer, 1998).

*   Fourth, behavioural theory fails to explain why some objects or situations are more likely than others to form the basis for phobias. Why, for example, are people more likely to fear snakes, heights and dogs rather than lambs and trees, or more to the point, gas appliances and electrical outlets which can be extremely dangerous (Marks, 1969)?

Key terms

Preparedness theory *States that humans have an inborn predisposition to respond quickly to danger.*

Repression *The prevention of Id impulses from entering conscious awareness.*

Displacement *With reference to phobias, the transference of Id impulses to an object or situation which becomes the focus for a phobia*

Catastrophising *Imagining the worst possible outcome of every situation.*

Classical conditioning *A form of learning based on an association between two stimuli.*

Operant conditioning *A form of learning based on reinforcement.*

Modelling *Learning by observing and imitating the behaviour of others.*

Summary

1 There are two main types of phobia. Specific phobias involve fear of particular objects or situations. Social phobias involve fear of humiliation in public places.

2 Phobias tend to run in families which suggests a genetic component. Alternatively, this may indicate an environmental influence (children learn phobias from their parents), or both.

3 Preparedness theory states that humans are genetically disposed to respond rapidly to danger. Many common phobias (eg, of snakes, heights, darkness) are based on things which may have threatened human survival in the past.

4 Psychodynamic theory sees phobias resulting from the displacement of repressed impulses to an object or situation which becomes a focus for a phobia.

5 Cognitive theory states that people with phobias tend to focus on negative aspects of situations. The way people typically think, eg, catastrophising, affects the likelihood of a fearful response.

6 Behaviourists argue that phobias are learned by classical conditioning and reinforced by operant conditioning.

Activity 7   Learning to fear

Item A   Running water

When she was seven, Ann went for a picnic to the woods with her aunt and mother. After eating, she wandered off by herself. As she was climbing over some large rocks, her foot became wedged and the more she tried to escape, the more tightly she got stuck. Her screams for help went unanswered and she became increasingly frightened. As she struggled to get free, Ann heard the sound of a nearby waterfall. Eventually, she was found by her aunt but, from then on, she was terrified of running water. She had to be held down to take a bath and when travelling by train, the windows had to be covered to prevent her seeing rivers and streams.

Adapted from Bagby, 1922

Questions

1   Use the idea of classical conditioning to explain Ann's phobia in Item A.

2   Use the idea of modelling to explain the increase of ornithophobia described in Item B.

Item B   Birds

Alfred Hitchcock's film *The Birds*, about birds attacking people, led to an increase in ornithophobia – fear of birds – in the 1960s.

References

Abramson, L.Y., Metalsky, G.I. & Alloy, L.B. (1989). Hopelessness depression: A theory-based subtype of depression. *Psychological Review, 96*, 358-372.

Amenson, C. & Lewinsohn, P. (1981). An investigation into the observed sex difference in prevalence of unipolar depression. *Journal of Abnormal Psychology, 90*, 1-13.

American Psychiatric Association (1994). *Diagnostic and statistical manual of mental disorders* (4th ed.). Washington, DC: Author.

Anderson, C.A., Miller, R.S., Riger, A.L., Dill, J.C. & Sedikedes, C. (1994). Behavioral and characterological attributional styles as predictors of depression and loneliness: Review, refinement, and test. *Journal of Personality and Social Psychology, 66*, 549-558.

Anderson, J.R. (2000). *Cognitive psychology and its implications* (5th ed.). New York: Worth.

Andreasen, N.C., Arndt, S., Alliger, R., Miller, D. & Flaum, M. (1995). Symptoms of schizophrenia: Methods, meanings, and mechanisms. *Archives of General Psychiatry, 52*, 341-351.

Andreasen, N.C., Flaum, M., Swayze, V.W., Tyrrell, G. & Arndt, S. (1990). Positive and negative symptoms in schizophrenia: A critical reappraisal. *Archives of General Psychiatry, 47*, 615-621.

Bagby, E. (1922). The etiology of phobias. *Journal of Abnormal Psychology, 17*, 16-18.

Barlow, D.H. & Durand, V.M. (1999). *Abnormal psychology: An integrative approach* (2nd ed.). Pacific Grove, CA: Brooks/Cole.

Bateson, G., Jackson, D., Haley, J. & Weakland, J. (1956). Toward a theory of schizophrenia. *Behavioural Science, 1*, 215-264.

Beck, A.T. (1967). *Depression: Clinical, experimental and theoretical aspects*. New York: Harper Row.

Beck, A.T., Rush, A.J., Shaw, B. & Emery, G. (1979). *Cognitive therapy of depression*. New York: Guilford.

Bemporad, J.R. & Vasile, R.G. (1990). Psychotherapy. In A.S. Bellack & M. Hersen (Eds.), *Comparative treatments of adult disorders*. New York: Wiley.

Bentall, R.P., Jackson, H.F. & Pilgrim, D. (1988). Abandoning the concept of schizophrenia: Some implications of validity arguments for psychological research into psychotic phenomena. *British Journal of Clinical Psychology, 27*, 303-324.

Bernard, J. (1976). *The future of marriage*. Harmondsworth: Penguin.

Berry, J.W. Poortinga, Y.H., Segall, M.H. & Dasen, P.R. (1992). *Cross-cultural psychology: Research and applications*. Cambridge: Cambridge University Press.

Blatt, S.J. (1974). Levels of object representation in anaclitic and introjective depression. *Psychoanalytic Study of the Child, 29*, 107-159.

Bogerts, B. (1993). Recent advances in the neuropathology of schizophrenia. *Schizophrenia Bulletin, 19*, 431-445.

Bogoras, W. (1965). Shamanistic performance in the inner room. In W.A. Lessa & E.Z. Vogt (Eds.), *Reader in comparative religion: An anthropological approach* (2nd ed.). New York: Harper & Row.

Bowlby, J. (1969). *Attachment and loss, Vol.1: Attachment*. London: Hogarth.

Bowlby, J. (1973). *Attachment and loss, Vol.2: Separation*. London: Hogarth.

British Psychological Society Division of Clinical Psychology. (2000). *Understanding mental illness and psychotic experiences: A report by the British Psychological Society Division of Clinical Psychology*. Leicester: British Psychological Society.

Brown, G.W., Bone, M., Dalison, B. & Wing, J.K. (1966). *Schizophrenia and social care*. London: Oxford Univerity Press.

Brown, G.W. & Harris, T.O. (1978). *Social origins of depression: A study of psychiatric disorder in women*. London: Tavistock.

Butler, R.W. & Braff, D.L. (1991). Delusions: A review and integration. *Schizophrenia Bulletin, 17*, 633-647.

Carson, R.C. & Butcher, J.M. (1992). *Abnormal psychology and modern life*. Glenview, IL: Scott, Foresman & Co.

Cochran, R. (1995). Women and depression. *Psychological Review, 2*, 20-24.

Cohen, R., Coxall, J., Craig, G. & Sadiq-Sangster, A. (1992). *Hardship Britain: Being poor in the 1990s*. London: CPAG.

Comer, R.J. (1998). *Abnormal psychology* (3rd ed.). New York: W.H. Freeman.

Costello, C.G. (1982). Social factors associated with depression: A retrospective community study. *Psychological Medicine, 12*, 329-339.

Coyne, J.C. (1976). Depression and the response of others. *Journal of Abnormal Psychology, 82*, 186-193.

Crook, T. & Eliot, J. (1980). Parental death during childhood and adult depression: A critical review of the literature. *Psychological Bulletin, 87*, 252-259.

Crow, T.J. (1994). Prenatal exposure to influenza as a cause of schizophrenia. *British Journal of Psychiatry, 164*, 588-592.

Davis, J.O. & Phelps, J.A. (1995). Twins with schizophrenia: Genes or germs? *Schizophrenic Bulletin, 21*, 13-18.

Davison, G.C. & Neale, J.M. (1998). *Abnormal psychology* (7th ed.). New York: John Wiley & Sons.

DiNardo, P.A., Guzy, L.T., Jenkins, J.A., Bak, R.M., Tomasi, S.F. & Copland, M. (1988). Etiology and maintenance of dog fears. *Behaviour Research and Therapy, 26*, 241-244.

Egeland, J.A., Gerhard, D.S., Pauls, D.L., Sussex, J.N. et al. (1987). Bipolar affective disorders linked to DNA markers on chromosome 11. *Nature, 325*, 783-787.

Farde, L., Gustavsson, J.P. & Jonsson, E. (1997). D2 dopamine receptors and personality traits. *Nature, 385*, 590.

Fieve, R.R. (1975). *Moodswing*. New York: Morrow.

Fromm-Reichmann, F. (1948). Notes on the development of treatment of schizophrenia by psychoanalytic psychotherapy. *Psychiatry, 11*, 263-273.

Goldberg, E.M. & Morrison, S.L. (1963). Schizophrenia and social class. *British Journal of Psychiatry, 109*, 785-802.

Gottesman, I.I. (1991). *Schizophrenia genesis*. New York: W.H. Freeman.

Gottesman, I.I. & Sheilds, J. (1972). *Schizophrenia and genetics: A twin study vantage point*. New York: Academic Press.

Gurling, H.M., Sherrington, R.P., Brynjolfsson, J., Read, T., et al. (1989). Recent and future molecular genetic research into schizophrenia. *Schizophrenic Bulletin, 15*, 373-382.

Haralambos, M. & Holborn, M. (2000). *Sociology: Themes and perspectives* (5th ed.). London: Harper Collins.

Harrington, R.C. Fudge, H., Rutter, M.L., Bredenkamp, D., Groothues, C. & Pridham, J. (1993). Child and adult depression: A test of continuities with data from a family study. *British Journal of Psychiatry, 162*, 627-633.

Hiroto, D.S. (1974). Locus of control and learned helplessness. *Journal of Experimental Psychology, 102*, 187-193.

Kapur, S. & Remington, G. (1996). Serotonin-dopamine interaction and its relevance to schizophrenia. *American Journal of Psychiatry, 153*, 466-476.

Kelsoe, J.R., Ginns, E.I., Egeland, J.A., Gerhard, D.S. et al. (1989). Re-evaluation of the linkage relationship between chromosome 11p loci and the gene for biopolar affective disorder in the Old Order Amish. *Nature, 342*, 237-243.

Kendler, K.S. & Diehl, S.R. (1993). The genetics of schizophrenia: A current, genetic-epidemiologic perspective. *Schizophrenic Bulletin, 19*, 261-285.

Kety, S.S. (1988). Schizophrenic illness in the families of schizophrenic adoptees: Findings from the Danish national sample. *Schizophrenic Bulletin, 14*, 217-222.

Klein, D.F. (Ed.) (1980). *Diagnosis and drug treatment of psychiatric disorders: Adults and children* (2nd ed.). Baltimore: Williams & Wilkins.

Klerman, G.L. (1984). History and development of modern concepts of affective illness. In R.M. Post & J.C. Ballenger (Eds.), *Neurobiology of affective disorders*. Baltimore: Williams & Wilkins.

Johnstone, E.C. (Ed.) (1991). Disabilities and circumstances of schizophrenic patients: A follow-up study. *British Journal of Psychiatry, 159*, supplement 13.

Lacey, J.I. (1967). Somatic response patterning and stress: Some revisions of activation theory. In M.H. Appley & R. Trumball (Eds.), *Psychological stress*. New York: McGraw-Hill.

Ladd, C.O., Owens, M.J. & Nemeroff, C.B. (1996). Persistent changes in corticotropin-releasing factor neuronal systems induced by maternal deprivation. *Endocrinology, 137*, 1212-1218.

Leff, J.P. (1982). *Psychiatry around the globe: A transcultural view*. New York: Marcei Dekker.

Leutwyler, K. (1997). Depression's double standard. *Scientific American, 7*, 53-54.

Levy, D.L. Holzman, P.S., Matthysse, S. & Mendell, N.R. (1993). Eye tracking dysfunction and schizophrenia: A critical perspective. *Schizophrenia Bulletin, 19*, 461-536.

Lewinsohn, P.M., Youngren, M.A. & Grosscup, S.J. (1979). Reinforcement and depression. In R.A. Depue (Ed.), *The psychobiology of the depressive disorders*. New York: Academic Press.

Marks, I.M. (1969). *Fears and phobias*. New York: Academic Press.

McGuffin, P., Katz, R., Watkins, S. & Rutherford, J. (1996). A hospital-based twin register of the heritability of DSM-IV unipolar depression. *Archives of General Psychiatry, 53*, 129-136.

McGuffin, P., Owen, M.J. & Farmer, A. (1995). *Genetic basis of schizophrenia. Lancet, 346*, 678-682.

Mednick, S.A., Machon, R., Hottunen, M.O. & Bonnett, D. (1988). Fetal viral infection and adult schizophrenia. *Archives of General Psychiatry, 45*, 189-192.

Melville, J. (1977). *Phobics and obsessions*. New York: Penguin Books.

Metalsky, G.I., Halberstadt, L.J. & Abramson, L.Y. (1987). Vulnerability and invulnerability to depressive mood reactions: Toward a more powerful test of the diathesis-stress and causal mediation components of the reformulated theory of depression. *Journal of Personality and Social Psychology, 52*, 386-393.

Miller, W.R., Rosellini, R.A. & Seligman, M.E.P. (1977). Learned helplessness and depression. In J.D. Maser & M.E.P. Seligman (Eds.), *Psychopathology: Experimental models*. San Francisco: W.H. Freeman.

Mowrer, O.H. (1939). A stimulus-response analysis of anxiety and its role as a reinforcing agent. *Psychological Review, 46*, 553-566.

Murphy, H.B.M. (1982). *Comparative psychiatry: The international and intercultural distribution of mental illness*. Berlin: Springer.

National Foundation for Brain Research. (1992). *The cost of disorders of the brain*. Washington DC: Author.

Oakley, A. (1974). *Housewife*. London: Allen Lane.

Ohman, A., Erixon, G. & Lofberg, I. (1975). Phobias and preparedness: Phobic versus neutral pictures as continued stimuli for human autonomic responses. *Journal of Abnormal Psychology, 84*, 41-45.

Oruc, L., Ceric, I. & Loga, S. (1998). Genetics of mood disorders: An overview. Part one. *Medical Archives, 52*, 107-112.

Ost, L-G. (1987). Age of onset in different phobias. *Journal of Abnormal Psychology, 96*, 223-229.

Ost, L-G. (1992). Blood and injection phobia: Background and cognitive, physiological, and behavioral correlates. *Journal of Abnormal Psychology, 101*, 68-74.

Owen, F., Cross, A.J., Crow, T.J. & Poulter, M. (1978). Increased dopamine receptor sensitivity in schizophrenia. *Lancet, 2*, 223-226.

Parker, G. (1992). Early environment. In E.S. Paykel (Ed.), *Handbook of affective disorders*. New York: Guilford.

Peterson, C. & Seligman, M.E.P. (1987). Explanatory style and illness. Special illness: personality and physical health. *Journal of Personality, 55*, 237-265.

Rose, D.T., Abramson, L.Y., Hodulik, C.J., Helberstadt, L. & Gaye, L. (1994). Heterogeneity of cognitive style among depressed inpatients. *Journal of Abnormal Psychology, 103*, 419-429.

Rosenfarb, I.S., Goldstein, M.J., Mintz, J. & Nuechterlein, K.H. (1995). Expressed emotion and subclinical psychopathology observable within the transactions between schizophrenic patients and their family members. *Journal of Abnormal Psychology, 104*, 259-267.

Sarason, I.G. & Sarason, B.R. (1996). *Abnormal psychology* (8th ed.). Upper Saddle River, NJ: Prentice-Hall.

Seligman, M.E.P. (1971). Phobias and preparedness. *Behavior Therapy, 2*, 307-320.

Seligman, M.E.P. (1973). Fall into helplessness. *Psychology Today, 7*, 43-48.

Seligman, M.E.P. (1975). *Helplessness*. San Francisco: W.H. Freeman.

Seligman, M.E.P., Abramson, L.V., Semmel, A. & Von Beyer, C. (1979). Depressive attributional style. *Journal of Abnormal Psychology, 88*, 242-247.

Shumaker, S.A. & Hill, D.R. (1991). Gender differences in social support and physical health. *Health Psychology, 10*, 102-111.

Social Trends. (2001). London: The Stationery Office.

Snyder, M. (1974). Self-monitoring of expressive behaviour. *Journal of Personality and Social Psychology, 30*, 526-537.

Takei, N., van Os, J. & Murray, R.M. (1995). Maternal exposure to influenza and risk of schizophrenia: A 22 year study from the Netherlands. *Journal of Psychiatric Research, 29*, 435-445.

Taylor, P., Richardson, J., Yeo, A., Marsh, I., et al. (1995). *Sociology in Focus*. Ormskirk: Causeway.

Tienari, P., Lahti, I., Sorri, A., Naarala, M., Moring, J., Kaleva, M., Wahlberg, K.E. & Wynne, L.C. (1990). Adopted-away offspring of schizophrenics and controls: The Finnish adoptive family study of schizophrenia. In L. Robins & M. Rutter (Eds.), *Straight and devious pathways from childhood to adulthood*. New York: Cambridge University Press.

Tienari, P., Wynne, L.C., Moring,J., Lahti, I., Naarala, M., Sorri, A., Wahlberg, K.E., saarento, O., Seitamaa, M. & Kaleva, M. (1994). The Finnish adoptive family study of schizophrenia: Implications for family research. *British Journal of Psychiatry Supplement, 23*, 20-26.

Torrey, E.F. (1992). Are we overestimating the genetic contribution to schizophrenia? *Schizophrenic Bulletin, 18*, 159-170.

Torrey, E.F. & Peterson, M.R. (1973). Slow and latent viruses in schizophrenia. *Lancet, 819*, 22-24.

Turner, R.J. & Wagonfeld, M.O. (1967). Occupational mobility and schizophrenia. *American Sociological Review, 32*, 104-113.

Watson, J.B. (1930). *Behaviorism* (rev. ed.). Chicago: University of Chicago Press.

Watson, J.B. & Rayner, R. (1920). Conditioned emotional reactions. *Journal of Experimental Psychology, 3*, 1-14.

Weissman, M.M., Bruce, M.L., Leaf, P.J., Florio, L.P. & Holzer, C. (1991). Affective disorders. In L.N. Robins & D.A. Regier (Eds.), *Psychiatric disorders of America: The epidemiologic catchment area study*. New York: Free Press.

World Health Organisation (1979). *Schizophrenia: An international follow-up study*. New York: John Wiley.

World Health Organisation (1992). *The ICD-10 Classification of mental and behavioural disorders: Clinical descriptions and diagnostic guidelines*. Geneva: Author.

Wortman, C.B. & Brehm, J.W. (1975). Responses to uncontrollable outcomes: An integration of the reactance theory and the learned helplessness model. In L. Berkowitz (Ed.), *Advances in social psychology*. New York: Academic Press.

Zimbardo, P.G. (1992). *Psychology and life*. (13th ed.). New York: Harper Collins.

Zimbardo, P.G., McDermott, M., Jansz, J. & Metaal, N. (1995). *Psychology: A European text*. London: Harper Collins.

Zubin, J. & Spring, B. (1977). Vulnerability: A new view of schizophrenia. *Journal of Abnormal Psychology, 86*, 103-126.

36 Treating mental disorders

▶ **Introduction**

This chapter looks at various methods of treating psychological disorders. It examines the ideas and assumptions on which each method is based, details the treatment each provides, and assesses the effectiveness of that treatment.

Chapter summary

- **Unit 1 looks at biological therapies.**
- **Unit 2 looks at behavioural therapies.**
- **Unit 3 looks at cognitive behaviour therapies.**
- **Unit 4 looks at psychodynamic therapies.**

Unit 1 Biological therapies

KEY ISSUES
1 **What are the main biological therapies?**
2 **What are their advantages and disadvantages?**

1.1 Introduction

Psychological research shows clearly that chemicals can affect our mood and behaviour. These chemicals may be produced within the body – for example, adrenaline, testosterone, oestrogen – or taken into the body – for example, alcohol, caffeine, nicotine, heroin. It is entirely logical to suggest that since such substances influence us, then, in certain cases, they can be used to benefit us.

Many people take in chemicals which affect their body and lead to changes in their mood and behaviour. Some smoke cigarettes, drink alcohol or take street drugs. Some buy 'energy drinks' that affect their mood and motivation either through the 'sugar rush' or because the drinks contain high levels of caffeine.

It isn't surprising, therefore, that people have tried to improve mental well-being and treat psychological problems through biological or physical treatments – treatments which affect the body and, in turn, the mind. Indeed, some psychologists have strongly advocated the use of psychotropic (mind-altering) drugs. Timothy Leary was a professor of psychology at Harvard University in the USA in the 1960s. He experimented with LSD, a powerful hallucinogenic drug. He believed that LSD 'opens the mind' and coined the phrase 'Turn on, tune in, drop out'. Leary spent a number of years in prison for drug possession and was widely criticised for his views, though he was strongly supported by a number of young people. His last wish was to have his ashes scattered in space. In 1997, a year after his death, his ashes, along with those of Gene Roddenberry the creator of *Star Trek*, were sent into orbit around the earth.

1.2 The medical model

Most people in the UK who seek help for psychological problems do so through their General Practitioner. They will then either be treated by their GP, referred to a psychiatrist, or, very occasionally, to a clinical psychologist. Psychiatry is the branch of medicine that specialises in mental disorders, whereas clinical psychology is a branch of psychology. The vast majority of people with psychological problems therefore receive either no help, or only *medical* help (British Psychological Society, 2000).

Biological therapy or treatment is also known as somatic (meaning related to the body) or physical treatment. It is largely based on a medical model which sees psychological disorders as 'illnesses' which require treatment by doctors. It uses the medical language of patient, symptoms, diagnosis, illness, medication, treatment and cure. Most physical treatment for mental disorders is through medication – psychiatric drugs account for about a quarter of the medication prescribed on the National Health Service in the UK.

As Chapter 16 outlined, the medical model classifies psychological disorders in terms of diagnostic categories. Disorders are identified in terms of their symptoms. Similarly, types of medication tend to be classified as treatments for these symptoms and the disorders or 'illnesses' they represent. Thus, a number of drugs seen as suitable for the treatment of depression are known as *anti-depressants*.

1.3 Drug treatment

Drug treatment or *chemotherapy* (treatment using chemicals) is based on the idea that psychological disorders are due, at least in part, to an imbalance of chemicals in the body. For example, there may be too much or too little of particular neurotransmitter chemicals in the nervous system. Drug treatment often aims to redress this imbalance and restore equilibrium – that is, return neurotransmitter chemicals to their 'normal' level. Since these biochemicals affect mood and behaviour, restoring equilibrium should result in 'normal' mood and behaviour.

Antidepressants

According to one influential biological theory, depression is due to low levels of the neurotransmitter serotonin and/or noradrenaline. Antidepressant drugs are believed to increase the levels of one or both of these neurotransmitters. This section looks at the three main types of antidepressants.

MAOIs Monoamine-oxidase inhibitors (MAOIs) inhibit or block the oxidising enzymes that break down serotonin and noradrenaline. This results in higher levels of these neurotransmitters.

MAOIs were the first antidepressants to become widely available. As with most psychiatric drugs, they were discovered by trial and error. When a MAOI was tested as an anti-TB drug, it was found to induce euphoria – a feeling of wellbeing.

MAOIs are effective antidepressants. Research indicates that around half of mildly to severely depressed people who have taken MAOIs are helped by them (Thase & Rush, 1995). Their main disadvantage is that they are seriously toxic (poisonous) if taken with certain foods – for example, some cheeses and Marmite. They also have a range of unpleasant side-effects including blurred vision, dry mouth, dizziness, nausea, urinary retention and heart problems.

Tricyclics Like MAOIs, tricyclics block the oxidising enzymes that break down serotonin and noradrenaline. Tricyclics have two main advantages over MAOIs. Research indicates that they are more effective. Between 60% and 65% of those who take tricyclics are helped by them compared with around 50% who take MAOIs (Keller et al., 1995). In addition, tricyclics are less dangerous than MAOIs, and they do not require food restrictions. However, like MAOIs, they have a number of negative side-effects. These include heart problems, tiredness, anxiety, dry mouth and gastric disorders.

SSRIs Selective serotonin-reuptake inhibitors (SSRIs) work in a similar way to the other types of antidepressants. However, they are more selective – they only prevent the break down of serotonin. As a result, they have an effect on mood but avoid some of the side-effects of the other antidepressant drugs.

Under the trade name Prozac, this drug was aggressively marketed from the 1980s onwards. Hailed as the 'wonder drug', the 'happy pill' and the 'magic bullet', Prozac is effective, but no more than the tricyclics (Tollefson et al., 1995). Sales of Prozac rocketed and millions have taken the drug worldwide. This was partly due to aggressive marketing and partly to the belief that it has fewer negative side-effects than other antidepressants. More recently, this belief has been questioned. There is evidence that Prozac can produce insomnia, low sexual desire, anxiety and gastrointestinal problems. In addition, there have been reports that it may lead to suicidal and aggressive thoughts and impulsive behaviour (Barlow & Durand, 1999).

Evaluation There is no doubt that antidepressant medication helps a significant number of people. Even if this provides only temporary relief from the symptoms of depression, it is still important. Short-term relief can prevent suicide and reduce the pain and anguish suffered by individuals and their families.

Between 40% and 50% of people do not respond to antidepressant drugs. However, there are other therapies which appear equally effective, for example cognitive behaviour therapy. Such therapies avoid the negative side-effects that drugs can produce.

Would a combination of therapies prove even more effective? Research suggests that combining antidepressant medication with a non-drug therapy is at best only slightly more effective than either treatment alone (Karp & Frank, 1995).

Anxiolytics

Drugs which reduce anxiety are known as *anxiolytics*. They are also known as *antianxiety drugs* or *minor tranquillisers*. The main anxiolytics in use today are a class of drugs called benzodiazepines. They are sold under trade names such as Valium, Librium and Xanax.

Benzodiazepines are the most prescribed drugs in the world. They are used to treat a variety of anxiety disorders, though they are rarely used for phobias. Benzodiazepines increase the activity of the neurotransmitter GABA which reduces bodily arousal. This leads to muscle relaxation, a release of tension and a general calming effect.

When they were first introduced in the 1960s, benzodiazepines seemed to be just what the doctor ordered. They appeared to reduce anxiety without making people too tired and to reduce tension, so providing a good night's sleep. Nor did they seem to be particularly toxic, even in large doses. However, as time went on, some serious problems became apparent.

- Benzodiazepines do not usually 'cure' anxiety disorders. When the medication stops, anxiety often returns, as strong as ever (Ballenger, 1995).
- The drugs are highly addictive both psychologically and physically. They produce serious withdrawal symptoms after long-term usage. As a result, there is general agreement that they should be used for only a week or two at the most (Barlow & Durand, 1999).
- Benzodiazepines can produce a number of harmful side effects – drowsiness, lack of concentration and coordination, impaired memory, depression and aggression (Elsesser et al., 1996).
- Benzodiazepines can exaggerate or amplify the harmful effects of other drugs. For example, combined with alcohol, they can slow respiration to a dangerous level (Ballenger, 1995).

Evaluation Benzodiazepines are effective in bringing short-term relief from the symptoms of anxiety. This appears to be the limit of their effectiveness, in view of the problems associated with their long-term use. Benzodiazepines don't 'cure' anxiety disorders – usually the symptoms return once the medication stops.

Some psychologists see their use as counter-productive. They can be seen as a means of avoiding the real problem. Reliance on benzodiazepines means that a person's fears are never addressed and overcome (Fyer et al., 1987).

Antipsychotic drugs

Antipsychotic drugs are used to treat psychotic disorders. These disorders are characterised by a loss of contact with reality – they often involve hallucinations and delusions. The most common psychotic disorder is schizophrenia.

Antipsychotic drugs are also called *neuroleptics* or *major tranquillisers*. They were first developed in the 1940s and are now the preferred medical treatment for psychotic disorders. In the 1990s, a new class of 'atypical' neuroleptics came into use.

According to one influential biological theory, schizophrenia is due, at least in part, to an excess of the neurotransmitter dopamine. Neuroleptics reduce the level of dopamine. Atypical neuroleptics affect the production of both dopamine and serotonin.

Neuroleptic drugs are used in the acute phase of schizophrenia – when psychotic experiences are most intense or distressing. Afterwards, they can be used either intermittently, when the person feels unwell, distressed or under stress, or when the person has partly or totally recovered in order to try to prevent further episodes (Herz et al., 1991).

Neuroleptics are not perfect treatments. They are not 'cures' even though they may eliminate some symptoms and make psychotic experiences less intense and distressing. They do not help everyone, and rarely remove problems completely. According to one estimate, the more traditional neuroleptics help 65% of those treated, while atypical neuroleptics help 85% (Elsesser et al., 1996).

As with all drugs, neuroleptics can have negative side-effects. Between 20% and 40% of those treated with more traditional neuroleptics experience muscle tremors and rigidity – they shake and shuffle their feet (Strange, 1992). Other side-effects include *dystonia* – muscle contractions which produce uncontrollable movements of the face, neck, tongue and back, and *akathisia* – restlessness, agitation, and discomfort of the limbs which causes individuals to constantly fidget and pace up and down (Comer, 1998). Although many of these side-effects are not found with atypical neuroleptics, these drugs have their own problems. For example, one per cent of those using one of the atypical neuroleptics suffer from a life-threatening drop in white-blood cells (Alvir et al., 1995).

Largely because of the side-effects produced by neuroleptics, around 50% stop taking these drugs after one year and up to 75% after two years (Davison & Neale, 1998).

Evaluation Despite negative side-effects, and despite the fact that neuroleptics rarely provide a cure, these drugs are often regarded as the single most effective treatment for psychotic disorders. According to Comer (1998), they have 'revolutionised' the treatment of schizophrenia. According to Davison and Neale (1998), they are 'an indispensable part of treatment for schizophrenia and will undoubtedly continue to be the primary intervention until something better is discovered. They are surely preferable to the straitjackets formerly used to restrain patients.'

Ritalin

Ritalin is a stimulant, similar to the street drug speed. It is often used to treat attention-deficit/hyperactivity disorder (ADHD). Children who appear to have difficulty concentrating and are seen as disruptive and difficult to control are increasingly diagnosed as having ADHD and treated with Ritalin or similar drugs. During the first half of the 1990s, the numbers diagnosed with ADHD in the USA more than doubled to over two million. It is estimated that between 10 and 12 per cent of all American boys, and a smaller but growing number of girls, may take Ritalin (Leutwyler, 1996).

Both the diagnosis of ADHD and its treatment with drugs are controversial. According to many psychiatrists, the disorder exists, the diagnosis is usually correct and the treatment is effective. In most cases, drug treatment appears to aid concentration, enabling children to focus on tasks. It has a quieting effect, bringing a significant reduction in disruptive and aggressive behaviour. Its negative side effects – sleep disturbance, headache and stomach-ache – don't appear too serious (Comer, 1998).

However, there is growing opposition to the diagnosis and treatment of ADHD. Some researchers question its very existence – does the behaviour used to diagnose ADHD indicate a 'real illness' which requires 'medication'? And, even if the disorder does exist, have cases been developing as rapidly as the statistics indicate, or has it simply been 'overdiagnosed'? A diagnosis of ADHD can be a convenient label to justify the use of drugs to damp down exuberant and active children who parents and teachers find difficult to control (Wheatley, 1996). And the use of drugs such as Ritalin can, according to Arnold and Jensen (1992) in a highly respected psychiatry textbook, produce a 'zombie effect'.

Evaluation The use of drug treatment, particularly with children, raises important ethical questions. Should powerful, mind-altering and addictive drugs such as Ritalin be prescribed? If, as some argue, ADHD is not a 'real' disorder, but simply a label attached to behaviour which parents and teachers see as a problem, then the answer is 'no' (Baldwin, 2001). But, if the disorder does exist, then some argue that, at least in extreme cases, it is unethical to withhold effective medication (National Institute for Clinical Excellence, 2000).

Drug treatment – conclusion

Drug treatment, or chemotherapy, is based on the medical model. Drugs are 'prescribed' as 'medication'. They are used to 'treat' the 'patient' in order to alleviate their 'symptoms' or 'cure' their disorder. The assumption is that psychological disorders have a biological basis. Their treatment, therefore, involves changes in biology – in particular, changes in the body's biochemistry. This is what drugs do.

Drugs often provide effective treatment for at least some of the symptoms of psychological disorders. But these symptoms often reappear after the course of treatment ends. In other words, some drug treatments have a high relapse rate. This suggests two important possibilities. First, drugs treat the symptoms or effects of a disorder rather than the disorder itself. In other words, the causes of disorders are left untouched. Second, the presumed biological causes of disorders may simply be symptoms. For example, rather than high levels of dopamine causing schizophrenia, the reverse may be true – schizophrenia causes high levels of dopamine. If these possibilities are correct, then drug treatment cannot 'cure' disorders, it can only alleviate or reduce their symptoms.

This does not mean that drugs are ineffective. Treating symptoms can allow people to live with a disorder, it can make their lives more bearable and, in extreme cases, it can prevent suicide. And drug treatment can be combined with other forms of therapy. For example, people with severe depression may lack the will to take part in demanding and intensive psychological therapy. Taking pills requires little effort, it can be effective, at least in the short term, and this may motivate people to seek alternative treatment.

Finally, all drugs have negative side-effects for a significant number of people who take them. At times, the side-effects can be experienced as more distressing than the disorder itself.

Key terms

Chemotherapy *Treating disorders using chemicals; drug treatment.*

Antidepressants *Drugs used to treat depression.*

Anxiolytics *Drugs used to treat anxiety disorders. Also known as antianxiety drugs or minor tranquillisers.*

Antipsychotic drugs *Drugs used to treat psychotic disorders, particularly schizophrenia. Also known as neuroleptics or major tranquillisers.*

Ritalin *A stimulant often used to treat attention-deficit/hyperactivity disorder (ADHD).*

Activity 1   Drug treatment

Item A   ADHD and drug treatment

Over the last few years, parents, teachers and health authorities have become increasingly aware of attention-deficit/hyperactivity disorder (ADHD) and more and more children are receiving treatment. But are we guilty of drugging children to control their behaviour instead of finding out what is making them unhappy, out of step with their families, and in trouble at school?

Neuroscientist Professor Steven Rose describes it as the 'medicalisation' of social difficulties and is critical of what he calls a wave of 'syndromitis' which sees behaviour as biological and capable of being dealt with by drugs.

Some ADHD experts argue that if the symptoms of the disorder are severe, then they probably have a biological cause – a deficiency in the neurotransmitters which control a child's ability to cope with the information and stimuli coming into his or her brain. They say that when the brains of ADHD children are scanned, using sophisticated new techniques, quite abnormal patterns can be observed.

But Steven Rose argues that this is putting the cart before the horse. 'I wouldn't be surprised if there was evidence of differences in brain functions in these kids,' he says. 'But if you or I were very unhappy, anxious or distressed and had our brains scanned while we were in this state, our patterns would show up differently too.'

Adapted from Wheatley, 1996

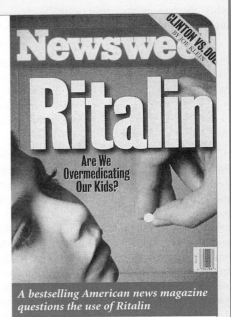

A bestselling American news magazine questions the use of Ritalin

Item B   Antipsychotic medication

Here are a variety of views on antipsychotic medication given by users of the mental health services in the UK.

Antipsychotic medication – for

'Without major tranquillisers myself and my family feel I may not have survived, as hyperactivity and starvation led to rapid weight loss as well as psychological symptoms.'

'The drug blocks out most of the damaging voices and delusions and keeps my mood stable.'

'Injections seem to dampen down the voices. They decrease the voices, but not altogether.'

'Medication is a necessary evil as I have very little to fall back on otherwise. The medication stops psychotic symptoms, or has in the past.'

Antipsychotic medication – against

'They do not cure the causes of conditions, they have the side-effects of making you unnaturally doped, enormously fat.'

'The dosages depressed me and made me feel my motivation, ideas and whole autonomy were being removed.'

'With major tranquillisers, I feel as if I'm in a trance. I don't feel like myself.'

Anonymous personal accounts

Adapted from Cobb, 1993

Item C Benzodiazepines

In 1999 in the UK, 17 million prescriptions were written for benzodiazepines. These minor tranquillisers or antianxiety drugs, with trade names such as Librium, Valium and Temazepam, are prescribed for various anxiety conditions. According to the 'antibenzos' campaign, tens of thousands of people have become addicted to these drugs since the 1950s and hundreds have died as a result. The campaigners believe that, for over 20 years, pharmaceutical companies deliberately withheld information about the more dangerous side-effects of benzodiazepines.

In 1994 the Department of Health issued guidelines on prevention of benzodiazepine dependence, yet many GPs are ignoring the advice. There is widespread failure to adhere to the 1988 Committee of Safety of Medicines guidelines to prescribe them for no more than four weeks.

Adapted from *The Observer*, 5.11.2000

Rohypnol, one of the many brand-name drugs containing benzodiazepine

Questions

1 What does Item A indicate about the possible dangers and limitations of drug treatment?

2 In view of Item B, why should those who receive drug treatment be made fully aware of

   a) possible side-effects and

   b) alternative treatment?

3 Read Item C.

   a) Drug companies are in business to make a profit. Suggest possible dangers of this objective.

   b) Why might GPs fail to follow guidelines for treatment?

1.4 Psychosurgery

Psychosurgery is the most extreme form of physical intervention in psychiatry. Also known as neurosurgery, it is the use of brain surgery to cure or alleviate psychological disorders. Psychosurgery can be seen as the most extreme consequence of the medical model – the brain is disturbed, part of the brain is defective, so cut it out!

Modern psychosurgery was introduced in 1935 by the Portuguese neuropsychiatrist Egas Moniz, who saw it as a cure for schizophrenia. The technique involved cutting the connections between the prefrontal lobes and the rest of the brain – an operation known as a *prefrontal lobotomy*. Moniz believed that many mental disorders resulted from 'fixed thoughts' which interfered with the rest of the brain. Cut off – literally – such thoughts at source and the problem was solved.

For the next 25 years psychosurgery was widely accepted and practised. In the USA, Moniz's procedures were enthusiastically developed by Walter Freeman and James Watts (Freeman & Watts, 1942). Their technique involved inserting a needle through the eye socket and rotating it to destroy brain tissue. According to one estimate, some 40,000 people in the USA were subjected to this type of psychosurgery (Kalinowsky, 1975).

By the 1950s, there was a growing realisation that such crude and imprecise surgery not only failed to 'cure' the patients, it seriously damaged their brains. And, in some cases, it killed them. Psychosurgery left thousands like zombies – apathetic, withdrawn, listless, indifferent, subdued, unresponsive and emotionally flat. Other side-effects included brain seizures, partial paralysis, huge weight gain, impaired memory and intellectual abilities, loss of motor coordination and, in up to 6% of cases, death (Valenstein, 1986).

Despite this catalogue of horrors, one of the main reasons for the decline of psychosurgery was the increasing availability of drug treatment. By comparison, psychosurgery was an expensive, complicated, and cruel method of treatment (Comer, 1998). By 1960, the number of prefrontal lobotomies was greatly reduced.

Today, psychosurgery is rare. It is used only as a last resort when other treatments have been unsuccessful. Surgical techniques have improved and growing knowledge of the brain has led to more precise and selective intervention. In recent years, psychosurgery has occasionally been used for severe cases of obsessive-compulsive disorder, when other treatments have failed. A review of 33 patients who received surgery for this disorder indicated that about 30% improved considerably (Jenike et al., 1991).

Evaluation Despite the advances in psychosurgery, and its very limited use as a last resort, many clinicians believe that the destruction of brain tissue is unethical. The process cannot be reversed and it is highly likely to have negative side-effects. In the UK, psychosurgery is strictly controlled by the Mental Health Act. The British Psychological Society has gone further and called for all psychosurgery to be banned (BPS, 1999).

1.5 Electroconvulsive therapy (ECT)

Electroconvulsive therapy (ECT) was originally developed in the 1930s as a treatment for schizophrenia by two Italian psychiatrists, Ugo Cerletti and Lucio Bini. It was applied to a range of disorders, but it soon became clear that its effectiveness was limited to the treatment of depression.

ECT involves passing an electrical current of 70 to 130 volts through the brain. This causes a brain seizure which produces convulsions lasting up to two minutes. Treatment usually covers 6 to 10 sessions, with 2 to 3 days between each session.

In the past, ECT was a frightening and even barbaric form of treatment. Contortions were often severe, with limbs flailing. Bruising was common, and sometimes bones were fractured. And the patient was usually awake. In more recent times, patients have been given a short-acting anaesthetic and a muscle-relaxant drug which reduces contortions to mild tremors. They awake after about ten minutes, unaware of the treatment. Even so, an ECT session can be a frightening experience.

The use of ECT has declined considerably from the 1970s onwards. However, Lucy Johnstone (1996) has estimated that around 20,000 people receive ECT each year in the UK. Today, it is used to treat severely depressed people who have failed to respond to other forms of treatment. According to one estimate,

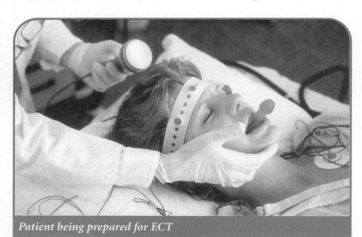

Patient being prepared for ECT

50% – 70% of those receiving ECT benefit from the treatment. However, because the relapse rate (the return of the disorder) is up to 60%, ECT needs to be followed by further drug treatment or psychotherapy (Fernandez et al., 1995).

Evaluation – advantages Supporters of ECT argue that it often works where other treatments have failed. They claim that its negative side-effects, such as memory loss and confusion, are short-lived. In many cases, the side-effects are less severe than those of drug treatment. And ECT can save lives – severe depression can lead to suicide (Taylor & Carroll, 1987).

Evaluation – disadvantages ECT is still controversial. Nobody knows how it works. It has been described as 'about as scientific as kicking a television set because it is not working' (Heather, 1976). Some continue to see it as barbaric (Johnstone, 1996), and some see it as ineffective (Breggin, 1996). ECT has a high incidence of relapse – the depression often returns. The side-effects may be more serious than its supporters claim. There is evidence of permanent memory loss, which can be very distressing, and of personality change (Taylor & Carroll, 1987). The British Psychological Society has called for ECT to be used only with the consent of the person involved, and then only in the most extreme cases (BPS, 1999).

Key terms

Psychosurgery *The use of brain surgery in an attempt to cure or alleviate psychological disorders.*

Prefrontal lobotomy *Cutting the connections between the prefrontal lobes and the rest of the brain.*

Electroconvulsive therapy (ECT) *Passing an electrical current through the brain with the aim of alleviating severe depression.*

Summary

1. Biological therapies are based on the medical model.

2. Drug treatment aims to treat psychological disorders by changing the body's biochemistry.

3. Antidepressant drugs appear to help a significant number of people though they can have negative side-effects.

4. Axiolytics are generally effective in alleviating the symptoms of most anxiety disorders. However, they are highly addictive and have a number of harmful side-effects.

5. Antipsychotic drugs are the preferred medical treatment for schizophrenia. They may eliminate some symptoms and alleviate others. However, they can have serious side-effects.

6. Ritalin is used to treat attention-deficit/hyperactivity disorder (ADHD). Its use is controversial, particularly as some researchers question the existence of ADHD.

7. Drug treatment has been criticised for treating the symptoms of disorders and leaving their causes untouched.

8. Psychosurgery is rarely used today. It is usually undertaken as a last resort when other treatments have failed.

9. Electroconvulsive therapy (ECT) aims to treat severe depression by passing an electric current through the brain. It is normally used when other treatments have been unsuccessful.

Unit 2 Behavioural therapies

KEY ISSUES

1 **What are the main behavioural therapies?**
2 **How effective are they?**

Behavioural therapies are based on the ideas of classical and operant conditioning. Treatment based on classical conditioning is usually known as *behaviour therapy*. Treatment based on operant conditioning is usually known as *behaviour modification*.

Behavioural therapies aim to change specific *behaviours*. They assume that both 'normal' and 'abnormal' behaviours are *learned*. It follows from this that new 'adaptive' and 'desirable' behaviours can be learned, and existing 'maladaptive' and 'undesirable' behaviours can be unlearned or extinguished.

2.1 Behaviour therapy – classical conditioning

Behaviour therapy is often used to treat phobias. It assumes that 1) phobias are learned by classical conditioning and 2) they can be unlearned by a similar process. The previous chapter outlined how Little Albert was conditioned to fear a white rat by pairing the rat with a frightening noise – a steel bar struck with a hammer beside his head. Albert then developed an intense fear of white rats whether the frightening noise was heard in the presence of the rat or not (see pp 701-702). In terms of behaviour therapy, Albert's phobia can be removed by *counterconditioning* – learning a new response to the feared stimulus. This is the principle behind *systematic desensitisation*.

Systematic desensitisation

This approach was developed by a South African psychiatrist, Joseph Wolpe (1958). It takes clients through the following steps.

- Step 1 – clients are taught muscle relaxation techniques.
- Step 2 – with the help of a therapist, clients construct a *fear hierarchy* – a list of feared objects or situations ranked from the least to the most feared. For example, a person with arachnophobia – fear of spiders – might imagine a spider in various situations from a picture in a book (least feared) to crawling over their hand (most feared).
- Step 3 – in the presence of a therapist, clients then confront each item in the hierarchy while they are in a state of deep relaxation. They start with the least feared item and move on once they feel relaxed and unafraid in its presence. This confrontation may be imagined or actual (eg, the spider actually crawls over their hand). The process continues until they reach the top of the hierarchy and feel relaxed in the presence of all the items. If systematic desensitisation works, clients have been counterconditioned – they have learned a new response to a stimulus. In this case, they feel relaxed rather than terrified in the presence of a spider.

Evaluation Systematic desensitisation is the main treatment for phobias. It is very effective and is generally considered to be better than other therapies. One survey found that 75% of people with specific phobias improved with systematic desensitisation therapy (McGrath et al., 1990). It has also proved helpful in the treatment of sexual dysfunctions, posttraumatic stress disorder and asthma attacks (Emmelkamp, 1994).

Flooding

This approach directly exposes clients to the objects or situations they fear. It hits them hard. For example, someone with a fear of heights is taken to the top of a tower block and encouraged to stay there. In theory, 'flooding' the client – exposing them repeatedly to the feared stimulus – will allow them to see that there is no basis for their fear. If the therapy works, this leads to the extinction of the fear.

Flooding is an extreme form of therapy. Clients find it very frightening and discomforting. Because of this many therapists only use it as a last resort, when other treatments have failed. Despite this, it can be helpful. People with specific phobias can lose their fear after only three sessions of flooding (Marks, 1987).

Implosion therapy

This is a variation of flooding. Rather than physically facing the feared stimulus, clients are asked to imagine it. With the help of a therapist, the client is asked to create and experience a feared situation. Sometimes therapists attempt to heighten this experience and increase the level of anxiety. This can be seen from the following example. A woman has a phobic fear of snakes. Her therapist asks her to imagine the following scene.

'Close your eyes again. Picture the snake out in front of you, now make yourself pick it up. Reach down, pick it up, put it in your lap, feel it wiggling around in your lap, leave your hand on it, put your hand out and feel it wiggling around. Kind of explore its body with your fingers and hand. You don't like to do it, make yourself do it. Make yourself do it. Really grab onto the snake. Squeeze it a little bit, feel it. Feel it kind of start to wind around your hand. Let it. Leave your hand there, feel it touching your hand and winding around it, curling around your wrist' (Hogan, 1968).

Implosion therapy aims to show clients that their fears are groundless. After several sessions of facing their worst fears, some realise this – their fears disappear ('implode') or are reduced in intensity (Gelder et al., 1989).

Aversion therapy

Like the behaviour therapies examined so far, *aversion therapy* is based on the idea of classical conditioning. However, in one respect it has the opposite aim – to produce rather than reduce anxiety.

Aversion therapy attempts to remove 'unwanted' or 'maladaptive' behaviours by linking them to unpleasant or painful experiences. For example, cigarettes have been laced with a chemical that makes people violently sick. Similarly, people have been given a 'medication' that reacts with alcohol to induce nausea. In the past, attempts were made to 'cure' homosexuality by pairing photographs of naked men with painful electric shocks. In theory, these unpleasant experiences would be associated with the 'unwanted' behaviour and remove it.

Aversion therapy has been used to treat alcoholism, overeating, smoking, self-mutilation, and a range of so-called 'sexual deviance'. In general it has a bad name – bad for those who are on the receiving end, bad because it doesn't appear to work very well and bad because its morality is questionable. Research indicates that its effects are at best slight and short-lived (Smith et al., 1991). Many therapists reject aversion therapy on ethical grounds. It inflicts considerable discomfort and sometimes pain on the client. In an extreme case, people with alcoholism were injected with a drug that paralysed their bodies while they tasted alcoholic drinks (Sanderson et al., 1963).

An alternative to direct physical discomfort is provided by *covert sensitisation*. This involves asking people to imagine unpleasant or frightening scenes in association with the behaviour they seek to remove – for example, to imagine vomiting and drinking alcohol (see Item C, Activity 2). However, this version of aversion therapy appears as ineffective as its more physical counterpart.

One of the main ethical attacks on aversion therapy resulted from its use to 'cure' homosexuality. Critics have seen it as a punishment for behaviour regarded as immoral by a prejudiced society. Gay activists have accused behaviour therapists of maintaining homophobia by 'treating' homosexuals (Silverstein, 1972).

Key terms

Behaviour therapy *Therapy based on the ideas of classical conditioning.*

Behaviour modification *Therapy based on the ideas of operant conditioning.*

Counterconditioning *Unlearning an existing response to a stimulus and replacing it with a new learned response.*

Systematic desensitisation *A treatment which aims to countercondition phobic fears. Feared objects and situations are ranked in a hierarchy. The client confronts each from the least to the most feared while deeply relaxed, moving on only when the fear is extinguished.*

Flooding *A treatment which aims to remove phobias by directly exposing clients to the objects or situations they fear.*

Implosion therapy *A treatment which aims to remove phobias by asking clients to imagine they are directly facing the objects and situations they fear.*

Aversion therapy *A treatment which aims to remove 'maladaptive' behaviours by directly linking them to unpleasant experiences such as electric shocks and nausea.*

Covert sensitisation *A type of aversion therapy which links 'maladaptive' behaviours to imagined unpleasant or frightening scenes.*

2.2 Behaviour modification – operant conditioning

In terms of operant conditioning, behaviours are learned and maintained as a result of reinforcement. This applies to so-called 'normal' and 'abnormal', 'adaptive' and 'maladaptive' behaviours. For example, the temporary sense of well-being produced by drugs has a reinforcing effect which increases the likelihood of further drug taking. The temper tantrums of a child or the bizarre behaviour of someone with schizophrenia may be reinforced by the attention they receive.

Therapies based on the principles of operant conditioning aim to bring about specific changes in behaviour. This is known as *behaviour modification*. It involves rewarding 'appropriate' behaviour, and withholding rewards for 'inappropriate' behaviour. This approach usually works best with children, or in institutions such as mental hospitals, schools and prisons. Children can be observed and supervised by parents and teachers working with therapists. As a result, their behaviour can be consistently and systematically reinforced. In mental hospitals and prisons, inmates are overseen and supervised by staff which again provides the opportunity for systematic reinforcement.

Childhood problems that have been treated with some success by operant conditioning therapies include bed-wetting, nail-biting, tantrums, hyperactivity, disruptive behaviour and learning difficulties (Kazdin, 1994).

The token economy

Token economies illustrate the application of operant conditioning principles to adults in institutional settings. They were introduced into mental hospitals in the USA in the 1960s. Tokens, such as plastic discs, are given as rewards for 'desirable' behaviour. The tokens can then be exchanged for privileges. In theory, tokens reinforce 'appropriate' behaviour.

Ayllon and Azrin (1968) introduced a token economy in a women's ward in a mental hospital. The patients were consistently rewarded with tokens for taking care of themselves – for washing, brushing their hair, cleaning their teeth, dressing themselves and making their beds. The tokens could be exchanged for privileges such as watching a movie, listening to records, extra food and renting a private room. 'Desirable' behaviours increased significantly with the token economy. However, when it was withdrawn, there was a marked decrease in these behaviours (see Activity 2, Item E).

People in long-stay mental hospitals tend to become institutionalised. They become passive, apathetic and withdrawn, or their behaviour becomes increasingly bizarre. In both cases, behaviour becomes increasingly removed from 'normal' everyday activity. One of the most successful token economies was applied to patients diagnosed as schizophrenic in a long-stay hospital. Some were mute and totally withdrawn. Others repeatedly screamed, buried their faces in food, smeared faeces on the walls, and assaulted staff and other inmates (Paul & Lentz, 1977).

A token economy was introduced to one group of patients and their behaviour compared to patients whose treatment was unchanged. The self-care and social skills of the token economy group improved significantly and many of their symptoms were reduced. At the start of the programme, 90% of the patients in both groups were receiving antipsychotic drugs. Four and a half years later only 11% of the token economy group received drugs compared with 100% of the other group. Over 10% of the token economy group were released into the community for 'independent living', but none of the other group.

Evaluation Token economies were popular in the 1960s and 70s. They are less so today for the following reasons.

- The effects they appear to produce may not be primarily due to token economies. Patients may be responding to increased attention, a planned system of activity, and improved monitoring, rather than a desire for tokens. In the above study, the token economy group was moved to a new mental health centre where they were kept busy by the staff for 85% of their time, compared with only 5% for the other group. Gordon Paul, one of the researchers, saw the token economy as playing a 'secondary role' in their improvement (Davison & Neale, 1998).

- Token economies may not really change behaviour – people may simply mimic or fake 'desirable' behaviour in order to get tokens. Take the case of John, a middle-aged man who had the delusion that he was the United States government. He did not respond to his name. When a token economy was introduced into his hospital, he eventually used his name to obtain tokens. However, in his words:

> 'We're tired of it. Every damn time we want a cigarette, we have to go through their bullshit. "What's your name? … Who wants the cigarette? … Where is the government?" Today, we were desperate for a smoke and went to Simpson, the damn nurse, and she made us do her bidding. "Tell me your name if you want a cigarette. What's your name?" Of course, we said, "John". We needed the cigarettes. If we told her the truth, no cigarettes. But we don't have time for this nonsense. We've got business to do, international business, laws to change, people to recruit. And these people keep playing their games' (Comer, 1998).

- Token economies raise ethical issues. Is it ethical to withhold 'privileges' such as watching TV because a severely disordered person does not do what a nurse thinks is desirable? Are people's human rights threatened when staff can control their access to food and their freedom of movement? Some researchers believe that token economies can violate basic human rights (Emmelkamp, 1994).

Despite these criticisms of token economies, they can have beneficial effects. According to Ronald Comer (1998), 'They were among the first hospital treatments that actually helped change schizophrenic symptoms, got chronic patients moving again, and enabled some to be released from the hospital'.

Key term

Token economy *A procedure for behaviour modification based on rewarding 'appropriate' behaviour with tokens which can be exchanged for privileges.*

Summary

1. Behavioural therapies are based on the assumption that all behaviours are learned.

2. It follows that 'undesirable' and 'inappropriate' behaviours can be unlearned.

3. Behaviour therapy based on classical conditioning is often used to treat phobias. It assumes that phobias are learned by classical conditioning and unlearned in the same way by a process known as counterconditioning.

4. Systematic desensitisation is the main treatment for phobias. It is effective, bringing improvement to around 75% of people treated for specific phobias.

5. Aversion therapy, which aims to extinguish 'maladaptive' behaviours by linking them with unpleasant experiences, is largely ineffective. It has been criticised on ethical grounds.

6. In terms of operant conditioning, behaviours are learned as a result of reinforcement.

7. Therapies based on operant conditioning aim to treat disorders by systematically reinforcing 'appropriate' and 'desirable' behaviours.

8. This approach can be seen in token economies which reward 'appropriate' behaviours with tokens which can be exchanged for privileges.

9. Token economies have been criticised as follows.

   - The effects they appear to produce may be primarily due to increased attention rather than the rewards which tokens bring.

   - They may not really change behaviour. People may simply mimic or fake 'appropriate' behaviour to obtain tokens.

   - They may violate basic human rights.

   However, there is evidence that token economies can have beneficial effects.

Activity 2   Behavioural therapies

Item A   A fear of flying hierarchy

Read from the bottom up.

■ The plane starts down the runway, and the motors get louder as the plane increases speed and suddenly lifts off.

■ The plane encounters turbulence.

■ The plane has taken off from the airport and banks as it changes direction. I am aware of the 'tilt'.

■ The plane is descending to the runway for a landing. I feel the speed and see the ground getting closer.

■ I am looking out the window and suddenly the plane enters clouds and I cannot see out the window.

■ I notice the seat-belt signs light up, so I fasten my seat belt and I notice the sound of the motors starting.

■ I am now inside the plane. I move in from the aisle and sit down in my assigned seat.

■ I walk down the ramp leading to the plane and enter the door of the plane.

■ I hear my flight number announced, and I proceed to the security checkpoint with my hand luggage.

■ I am entering the terminal. I am carrying my bags and tickets.

■ I am driving to the airport for my flight. I am aware of every plane I see.

■ It is ten days before the trip, and I receive the tickets in the mail.

■ I have called the travel agent and told him of my plans.

■ A trip has been planned, and I have decided 'out loud' to travel by plane.

Adapted from Comer, 1998

Item B   A fear of rats

Twenty-one people with an extreme fear of rats were asked by a therapist to imagine various scenes in which they were touched by rats, clawed by rats, had their fingers nibbled by rats, and had other close encounters with rats. After this, 20 of the participants were able to open a rat's cage and 14 could actually pick a rat up. A control group of 22 people with similar fears were asked to relax and to imagine neutral, non-fearful scenes. Later, only 3 of them were able to open the cage and 7 refused to even enter the room.

Adapted from Hogan & Kirchner, 1967

Item C — Covert sensitisation

'I'd like you to vividly imagine you are sitting in a pub tasting an alcoholic drink. See yourself tasting it, capture the exact taste, colour and consistency. Use all of your senses. After you've tasted the drink, you notice that there is something small and white floating in the glass – it stands out. You bend closer to examine it more carefully, your nose is right over the glass now and the smell fills your nostrils as you remember exactly what the drink tastes like. Now you can see what's in the glass. There are several maggots floating on the surface. As you watch, revolted, one manages to get a grip on the glass and, undulating, creeps up the glass. There are even more of the repulsive creatures in the glass than you first thought. You realise that you have swallowed some of them and you're very aware of the taste in your mouth. You feel very sick and wish you'd never reached for the glass and had the drink at all.'

Adapted from Clarke & Saunders, 1988

Item E — With and without tokens

Patients in a mental hospital received tokens for taking care of themselves (eg, brushing their hair and cleaning their teeth) and doing various chores (eg, making their beds). The token economy was withdrawn after 20 days and restarted after a further 20 days. The effects of this on the patients' behaviour are shown in the chart.

Adapted from Ayllon & Azrin, 1965

Item D — A token economy

A token economy was introduced in a class where the children were behaving badly and making little progress in their studies. Good behaviour and academic progress were rewarded with tokens which could be exchanged for privileges like watching a movie and extra break time. Accuracy in reading tests increased from 40% to 85%, and disruptive behaviour decreased from 50% to 5%.

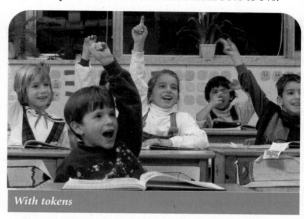

With tokens

Adapted from Ayllon & Roberts, 1974

Item F — Faking it

Behaviour modification techniques have been used to encourage anorexics to eat. However, there is a danger that they will 'eat their way out of hospital', tricking the staff that their eating behaviour has returned to normal. In such cases, they resume self-starvation once they have 'escaped'.

Adapted from Bruch, 1978

Questions

1 a) How might Item A be used to reduce fears of flying?

   b) Construct a fear of heights hierarchy with six items.

2 With reference to Item B,

   a) What is implosion therapy?

   b) How does it work?

3 How is the imagined behaviour described in Item C supposed to prevent 'undesirable' behaviour?

4 With reference to Item D, explain how token economies work.

5 What does the chart in Item E suggest about the strengths and weaknesses of token economies?

6 Behaviour modification techniques may not 'really' change behaviour. Explain with reference to Item F.

Unit 3 Cognitive behaviour therapy

KEY ISSUES

1 **What is cognitive behaviour therapy?**
2 **How effective is it?**

3.1 Key elements of cognitive behaviour therapy

Cognitive behaviour therapy (CBT) is a very popular form of psychological therapy. It is straightforward, practical, and has proved successful in treating a wide range of problems.

The main assumption behind CBT is that psychological difficulties depend on how people think or interpret events (cognitions), how people respond to these events (behaviours), and how this makes them feel (emotions) (Beck et al., 1979). The key elements of CBT can be summarised as follows.

- It focuses on influence of thoughts, beliefs and thinking patterns in each problem area.
- It deals with the *here-and-now*, although it also considers the influence of past events.
- It is *problem-orientated* and *structured*. It is a step-by-step approach which aims to identify and solve problems.
- Therapy is a *collaborative* effort between patient and therapist – they work together.
- A *good relationship* between therapist and client is a necessary component of therapy.
- The therapist adopts an *active* and *directive* role throughout therapy. The patient is also active, carrying out *homework* assignments and other tasks.
- The therapist uses *questions* to guide the client to identify their thoughts and problems and to generate alternative solutions.
- The therapy is *open* and *explicit*. This involves giving a rationale for each step and seeking regular feedback from the client.
- The therapy is based on an *educational* model with the patient learning skills and a method to deal with problems during and after therapy.

Common steps taken in CBT

1 **Explaining the ideas behind and purpose of CBT** People are given a straightforward explanation of what CBT is, and how it might help them.

2 **Specifying and listing problems** People are asked to produce a list of the difficulties and problems they are experiencing. They are usually asked for a list of their goals for the therapy – to help both the therapist and client ensure they are moving in the right direction.

3 **Identifying feelings-thoughts-behaviours for each problem** This is the key to CBT, because it is these links that are at the heart of the therapy. Examples are given in Table 1.

4 **Identifying negative automatic thoughts** These are thoughts which automatically spring to mind and present a negative view of self. For example, a person who is depressed might think, 'I'm no good', 'I'm so disappointed with myself'; a

| Table 1 | Feelings-thoughts-behaviours | | |

Problems	Emotions	Cognitions	Behaviours
Relationship with spouse	Anger	He shouldn't criticise me.	Cynicism, arguing
	Anxiety	What if he leaves me?	Unassertiveness, approval seeking
Work difficulty	Sadness	I'm not smart enough.	Social withdrawal
	Frustration	I'll never get this right.	Procrastination, non-completion of tasks

person who is anxious and fearful might think, 'I'm never in control', 'I always feel helpless'. Clients are taught to recognise negative automatic thoughts and to generate alternative thoughts.

5 **Familiarising clients with the concept of distortions or thinking errors** Negative automatic thoughts are linked to *errors in thinking*. For example, they can lead to overgeneralisation – drawing a conclusion from a particular event and applying it generally. For instance, being made redundant means, 'I'm no good' – a poor worker, husband, father, and so on. Therapists explain the idea of errors in thinking and attempt to identify and change such thinking patterns in the client.

6 **Generation of alternative thoughts and/or responses** The therapist helps the individual consider other explanations or interpretations of the self, events and situation. For example:

- 'Is there any other way you could look at this situation?'
- 'What is the evidence to support each alternative view?'
- 'How might someone else (eg, a good friend) think or react?'
- 'How might you have seen it before you became depressed?'
- 'What would you say to someone else with this problem?'

Sometimes this search is assisted by setting up a behavioural experiment or practical test.

- 'Can you think of any way you could find out if you are correct about this?'
- 'Could you and I devise any test for this or a way of researching it further?'

7 **Addressing maladaptive underlying schemas** Many therapists attempt to change not only 'surface level' negative automatic thoughts, but also 'maladaptive underlying schemas' – sets of dysfunctional beliefs that give rise to the negative thoughts.

Schemas are mental constructions which are used to understand and interpret the world. For example, a person may believe in fate. This means that, to some extent, what happens to them is beyond their control, it is due to fate. Carried to its extreme, fatalism can be maladaptive and self-destructive. It states, for example, that there is nothing a person can do to get out of their situation of depression, despair, anxiety or fear. Therapists attempt to identify such maladaptive schemas, and, together with the client, modify or change them.

8   **Behavioural techniques** Most therapists do not only use cognitive techniques. They also use behavioural techniques, as the name cognitive *behaviour* therapy suggests.

These techniques differ in some respects from those of behavioural therapy, examined in the previous unit. They are seen as assisting in the process of helping a person learn new ways of thinking about and reacting to a problem. They are not intended to change specific behaviours, but rather to change the focus and direction of behaviour in general – for example, to adopt positive and practical courses of action to solve problems.

Key terms

Negative automatic thoughts *Thoughts which automatically spring to mind and present a negative view of self.*

Errors in thinking *Drawing conclusions which are contradicted by the available evidence.*

Maladaptive underlying schemas *Views of the world which are maladaptive or dysfunctional for the individual. They underlie and give rise to negative thoughts.*

3.2   CBT in practice

This section looks at a specific example of CBT – Aaron Beck's cognitive behaviour therapy for depression (Beck et al., 1979; Beck, 1997). The therapy is divided into four main phases.

Phase 1 This phase is designed to encourage the client to become more active. Depressed people often do very little and tend to become socially withdrawn. Clients are encouraged to draw up an activity schedule and stick to it. This should lead to an increase in confidence and an improvement in mood. Table 2 shows an example of a partially completed weekly schedule of hourly activities prepared by a therapist and client.

Phase 2 In this phase, therapist and client work together to identify and invalidate negative automatic thoughts. The client's 'homework' is to learn to recognise these thoughts and to write them down. Client and therapist then investigate whether there is any justification for negative automatic thoughts. More often than not, they decide that these thoughts are groundless – they have no basis in reality. For example, if the client frequently concludes, 'I'm useless', there are often plenty of examples from their behaviour which contradict this assessment of self.

Table 3 provides an example of a discussion between a therapist and a client. The client was convinced that her grades weren't good enough to get into the university of her choice. This fear was groundless.

Phase 3 In this phase, the therapist shows the client how negative automatic thoughts can lead to errors in thinking and vice versa. The student in Table 3 was using a thought process known as dichotomous or all-or-nothing thinking. Only a grade A was good enough, anything below was 'terrible'. Therapists help clients to identify and correct various errors in thinking.

Table 2   An activity schedule

	Monday	Tuesday	Wednesday	Thursday	Fr
9-10		Go to grocery store	Go to museum	Get ready to go out	
10-11		Go to grocery store	Go to museum	Drive to doctor's appointment	
11-12	Doctor's appointment	Call friend	Go to museum	Doctor's appointment	
12-1	Lunch	Lunch	Lunch at museum		
1-2	Drive home	Clean front room	Drive home		
2-3	Read novel	Clean front room	Washing		
3-4	Clean bedroom	Read novel	Washing		
4-5	Watch TV	Watch TV	Watch TV		
5-6	Fix dinner	Fix dinner	Fix dinner		
6-7	Eat with family	Eat with family	Eat with family		
7-8	Clean kitchen	Clean kitchen	Clean kitchen		
8-12	Watch TV, read novel, sleep	Call sister, watch TV, read novel, sleep	Work on rug, read novel, sleep		

Adapted from Beck et al., 1979

Table 3   Negative thoughts

Therapist:	Why do you think you won't be able to get into the university of your choice?
Client:	Because my grades were really not so hot.
Therapist:	Well, what was your grade average?
Client:	Well, pretty good up until the last semester in high school.
Therapist:	What was your grade average in general?
Client:	A's and B's.
Therapist:	Well, how many of each?
Client:	Well, I guess, almost all of my grades were A's but I got terrible grades my last semester.
Therapist:	What were your grades then?
Client:	I got two A's and two B's.
Therapist:	Since your grade average would seem to me to come out to almost all A's, why do you think you won't be able to get into the university?
Client:	Because of competition being so tough.
Therapist:	Have you found out what the average grades are for admissions to the college?
Client:	Well, somebody told me that a B+ average would suffice.
Therapist:	Isn't your average better than that?
Client:	I guess so.

Adapted from Beck et al., 1979

This shows the client that in many cases there is no justification for their negative thoughts and the depressed mood which accompanies those thoughts.

Phase 4 This phase is concerned with identifying and doing something about the maladaptive or dysfunctional schemas which are seen to underlie negative thoughts. According to Beck, these ways of viewing the world have predisposed individuals to depression in the first place. Table 4 provides an example of a maladaptive 'happiness schema' and how the therapist tries to deal with it. This discussion shows how CBT combines thoughts, emotions and behaviours. The client is asked to test her thoughts about happiness by doing something active.

Table 4	A maladaptive schema
Therapist:	On what do you base this belief that you can't be happy without a man?
Client:	I was really depressed for a year and a half when I didn't have a man.
Therapist:	Is there another reason why you were depressed?
Client:	As we discussed, I was looking at everything in a distorted way. But I still don't know if I could be happy if no one was interested in me.
Therapist:	I don't know either. Is there a way we could find out?
Client:	Well, as an experiment, I could not go out on dates for a while and see how I feel.
Therapist:	I think that's a good idea. Although it has its flaws, the experimental method is still the best way currently available to discover the facts. You're fortunate in being able to run this type of experiment. Now, for the first time in your adult life you aren't attached to a man. If you find you can be happy without a man, this will greatly strengthen you and also make your future relationships all the better.

Adapted from Beck et al., 1979

3.3   Evaluation

CBT is becoming increasingly popular for the following reasons.

- It works.
- Research indicates that the thinking behind CBT is correct

(see pp 716-717). For example, people do change their cognitions with CBT and this appears to be the main reason for its success (Hollon et al., 1996).

- It is a positive therapy which encourages people to develop their personal skills to promote new ways of thinking and behaving.
- It is a democratic therapy which shows respect for the client, offers them choice, allows them to collaborate with the therapist, and gives them the opportunity to shape their own future. It is popular with clients who want to develop a greater sense of control (Beck et al., 1979; Scott, 1992).

Is CBT as good as this evaluation suggests? The short answer is probably 'no'. It is not a panacea – a 'cure-all' – as the evidence outlined below indicates. Do changes in cognition solve problems *or* are they a result or a consequence of solving problems? In the case of depression, changes in cognition are found after successful drug treatment – people have a more positive outlook. It is likely that any therapy that works results in changes in cognition (Davison & Neale, 1998).

Despite these reservations, CBT has proved an effective treatment for a number of disorders.

Depression CBT is a well-established treatment for depression. Research indicates that 50% to 60% of those treated with CBT for depression show no recurrence of depressive symptoms (Comer, 1998). Relapse rates (a return of the disorder) are lower after CBT than after treatment with antidepressant drugs (Freeman & Reinecke, 1995).

Anxiety CBT has been used successfully to treat panic disorder and general anxiety disorder. One survey indicated that 85% of people treated with CBT for panic disorder remained free from it for two years or more (Ost & Westling, 1995).

Hallucinations and delusions The use of CBT for hallucinations is relatively new. Research indicates that even if the frequency of hallucinations remains the same, CBT can reduce the distress they cause and increase the control people feel they have over them (Haddock et al., 1998) (see Activity 3, Item B).

CBT also appears to reduce the number and severity of delusions. One survey reported a 25% reduction in 'symptom severity' produced mainly by changes in delusions. Interestingly, two studies found that people continued to improve even after therapy ended (Sensky et al., 2000).

Summary

1   According to CBT, psychological disorders result from cognitions (how people think about events), behaviours (how people respond to events), and emotions (how this makes them feel).

2   CBT focuses on the here-and-now. It is a step-by-step, problem-orientated approach based on collaboration between therapist and client. It is an open, explicit, educational procedure in which the client takes active steps to improve their situation.

3   Clients learn to identify negative thoughts and errors in thinking. They learn to generate alternative thoughts. They also learn to recognise and change maladaptive schemas.

4   CBT also involves a behavioural element. Clients learn to change the focus and direction of their behaviour.

5   Beck's cognitive behaviour therapy for depression has four phases.
- Encouraging the client to become more active
- Identifying and invalidating negative automatic thoughts
- Recognising and correcting errors in thinking
- Identifying and replacing maladaptive underlying schemas.

6   CBT has successfully treated a number of disorders including depression and anxiety disorders. It has also helped people cope with hallucinations and delusions.

Activity 3 Cognitive behaviour therapy

Item A Is CBT new?

In a poem written in 1411, Thomas Hoccleve (1386-1437), a pupil of Chaucer, offers advice to people who are 'destitut of joye and good hope'. Hoccleve says that his depression was helped by talking about his problems to a companion ('Now, gode sone, telle on thi grevaunce') which are discussed in the light of a collection of negative thoughts concerning the present and future. Hoccleve is given two pieces of advice, to keep busy and to seek company. His companion then used rational arguments. Hoccleve was advised that negative thoughts can cause problems ('be war of thoght, for it is perillous'). Following this, Hoccleve's depressive thoughts were exposed to challenge one by one. Hoccleve was reminded that he was not short of money – he could always afford 'mete & drinke & clooth' – and he was talented – he could write a 'goodly tale or two'. We can only assume that Hoccleve felt this therapy was successful, because he repeated the advice to his employer, the Prince of Wales, the future King Henry V.

Henry V

Adapted from Kinderman, 1994

Item B Talking about voices

Starting therapy with Paul – the clinical psychologist – was terrifying. I sat, avoiding eye contact, even avoiding looking up from the ground. Often I shook and often jumped at any unexpected sound. I was terrified. But it soon became clear that Paul was not interested in my psychiatric label. And it was also clear he was prepared to address the issue of my voices without belittling them or treating them as weird.

The first session the voices were shouting and it was hard to concentrate. Paul recognised this and actually asked me what was going on with the voices. I didn't feel at all 'loony'. Paul made me feel that I was of some importance. Paul spoke – I needed him to speak and put me at my ease. Previously, I had seen a psychotherapist who waited for me to speak and often would not reply even when I had braved to utter a word.

The collaborative relationship I have with Paul gives me confidence that my ideas, as well as his, are important. I get to say what I want to work on – I have some power in this relationship. Paul gives me feedback and some idea of his reaction and tells me what areas he might like us to cover. He does this whilst giving me a lot of power and I feel that I am in control.

Talking about the 'voices thing' became open and normal. It has not been shied away from. We have discussed where the voices come from, the effect they have on me, how the voices feed on my present feelings and how I can, hopefully, partially control them.

We have discussed coping strategies, some successful, some not so, and some just plain silly (humming whilst they are speaking: I could only think of Dionne Warwick songs!). One long-term strategy – challenging the voices – has proved to be the hardest but the most successful. As soon as a voice pops into my head, I try to test out, with previous evidence, what the voice is saying. The voices often come up and interrupt sessions. We don't just ignore them, we deal with them. It now seems to me that the voices always feed off negative images I have about myself. I can think about the voices being a by-product of my own self-image.

Val – personal account, British Psychological Society, 2000

Questions

1 Identify aspects of CBT in Item A.

2 Judging from Val's statement in Item B, why did she find CBT helpful?

Unit 4 Psychodynamic therapy

KEY ISSUES

1 What is psychodynamic therapy?

2 How effective is it?

4.1 Introduction

Psychodynamic therapy has developed from Freud's psychoanalysis. Today's psychodynamic therapists see themselves as part of a tradition deriving from Freud. There are various psychodynamic theories, from Freud's psychoanalysis to Melanie Klein's object relations theory. Therapies reflect these differences. For example, Freud's psychoanalysis focuses on the resolution of psychosexual conflicts. Therapies based on object relations theory emphasise the importance of emotional bonds. They attempt to deal with the inner conflict which results from a disruption of those bonds, particularly the mother-child bond during the child's early years.

Despite these differences, psychodynamic therapies have a number of factors in common. They assume that human beings have a number of defence mechanisms which serve to
1) prevent awareness of inner conflicts and traumatic memories,

and 2) suppress impulses and desires which are seen as socially unacceptable.

Mental pain can result from memories of traumatic experiences. Traumas (from the Greek meaning 'wound') may include experiences we all share, like the first realisation in childhood that we are not the centre of our mother's life. For some people, they may also include extremely painful experiences such as child abuse.

Inner conflicts can result from a desire to express our sexual and aggressive impulses and the demands of society which seek to keep these impulses under control.

In Freud's theory, *repression* is the most important defence mechanism. It pushes inner conflicts, traumatic memories and forbidden impulses out of conscious awareness and buries them in the unconscious. However, this does not make them go away. Repression can lead to a range of psychological disorders which Freud called *neuroses* – anxiety disorders, panic attacks, hysteria, phobias, and obsessive and compulsive behaviour.

Insight The aim of psychodynamic therapy is to bring repressed material into conscious awareness. Only then can it be dealt with, resolved and settled. This awareness, known as *insight*, is the key to psychodynamic therapy. Once a person gains insight into their hidden anxieties and conflicts, and also into the defences they have used to repress them, then they are well on the way to solving their problems.

Gaining insight takes time. People usually have one or more 50 minute sessions a week, often for several years. Therapists guide discussions so that clients discover their underlying problems for themselves. A number of techniques are used to develop insight. These techniques will now be examined.

4.2   Techniques to develop insight

Free association

During therapy sessions, clients are often asked to freely associate, that is to say whatever comes into their mind and give free rein to their thoughts and feelings. They are asked to carry on talking even if what they say seems irrelevant, unimportant, idiotic, unacceptable, or rude.

Clients must not censor what they say. They must disregard the social conventions which direct conversation. In this sense, free association is free from the normal constraints which govern social interaction. However, in another sense, it is not free. Psychodynamic therapists assume that unconscious mechanisms direct free association. In this way, free association is seen to reflect unconscious conflicts, hidden desires, repressed traumas – material which is too painful, too shocking, or too threatening to bring directly into consciousness.

Clients are encouraged to lead the discussion. Therapists intervene to probe associations and ask clients to develop particular points.

Table 5 contains an instruction to a client to freely associate. Table 6 is an example of free association. It shows how a woman from New York reveals inner conflicts and threatening impulses.

Table 5   A directive for free association

In ordinary conversation, you usually try to keep a connecting thread running through your remarks, excluding any intrusive ideas or side issues so as not to wander too far from the point, and rightly so. But in this case you must talk differently. As you talk, various thoughts will occur to you which you like to ignore because of certain criticisms and objections. You will be tempted to think, 'That is irrelevant or unimportant or nonsensical', and to avoid saying it. Do not give in to such criticism. Report such thoughts in spite of your wish not to do so. Later, the reason for this will become clear.

Adapted from Ford & Urban, 1963

Table 6   Free association

Client:	So I started walking, and walking, and decided to go behind the museum and walk through Central Park. So I walked and went through a back field and felt very excited and wonderful. I saw a park bench next to a clump of bushes and sat down. There was a rustle behind me and I got frightened. I thought of men concealing themselves in the bushes. I thought of the sex perverts I read about in Central Park. I wondered if there was someone behind me exposing himself. The idea is repulsive, but exciting too. I think of father now and feel excited. I think of an erect penis. This is connected with my father. There is something about this pushing in my mind. I don't know what it is, like on the border of my memory. *(Pause)*
Therapist:	Mm-hmm. *(Pause)* On the border of your memory?
Client:	(The patient breathes rapidly and seems to be under great tension.) As a little girl, I slept with my father. I get a funny feeling. I get a funny feeling over my skin, tingly-like. It's a strange feeling, like a blindness, like not seeing something. My mind blurs and spreads over anything I look at. I've had this feeling off and on since I walked in the park. My mind seems to blank off like I can't think or absorb anything.

Adapted from Wolberg, 1967

Resistance This occurs when free association no longer flows freely. The client seems unwilling or unable to discuss important or difficult areas of their life. There are long pauses. The client changes the subject, appears to forget something, starts cracking jokes or looking out of the window. The rules of free association are broken. Clients stop talking, claiming what they have to say is too shameful, silly, unimportant or painful.

Therapists assume that resistance is due to defence mechanisms keeping painful and threatening thoughts in the unconscious. Yet these are the very thoughts that therapists want to reveal and probe. They sometimes point out resistance to the client in an attempt to overcome it. Most clients find free association difficult and usually take some time before they can give a resistance-free account.

Transference

Psychodynamic therapists from Freud onwards realised that clients tend to develop very intense feelings towards them. Therapists often saw these feelings as a reflection of the client's relationships to important figures in their childhood, particularly their parents. In other words, clients *transferred* feelings from these figures to the therapist. For example, if they hated their father, this hatred might be transferred towards the therapist.

Clients come to rely on the therapist just as they relied on their parents. As a result, they tend to reenact childhood relationships and the emotions which accompanied them.

Psychodynamic therapy uses transference as part of the therapeutic process. The therapist tries to explain transference to the client with the aim of revealing hidden conflicts and repressed memories. This can be seen from Table 7 which illustrates how a discussion on transference aids the recall of painful memories.

Table 7   Transference

Client:	I get so excited by what is happening here. I feel I'm being held back by needing to be nice. I'd like to blast loose sometimes, but I don't dare.
Therapist:	Because you fear my reaction?
Client:	The worst thing would be that you wouldn't like me. You wouldn't speak to me friendly; you wouldn't smile; you'd feel you can't treat me and discharge me from treatment. But I know this isn't so, I know it.
Therapist:	Where do you think these attitudes come from?
Client:	When I was nine years old, I read a lot about great men in history. I'd quote them and be dramatic. I'd want a sword at my side; I'd dress like an Indian. Mother would scold me. Don't frown, don't talk so much. Sit on your hands, over and over again. I did all kinds of things. I was a naughty child. She told me I'd be hurt. Then at fourteen I fell off a horse and broke my back. I had to be in bed. Mother told me on the day I went riding not to, that I'd get hurt because the ground was frozen. I was a stubborn, self-willed child. Then I went against her will and suffered an accident that changed my life, a fractured back. Her attitude was, 'I told you so'. I was put in a cast and kept in bed for months.

Adapted from Wolberg, 1967

Interpretation

The therapist is constantly interpreting what the client says and does. The client's free association, resistance and transference are analysed and interpreted, and related to his or her present problems. These *interpretations* are presented to the client when the therapist decides the time is right. Ideally, this is when the client is on the verge of making a similar interpretation. If the timing is wrong, the therapist's interpretations will probably be rejected – a process known as *denial*.

However, denial provides further evidence for interpretation. It may indicate that the original interpretation was correct. It may

have been rejected because it was too painful or threatening for the client to accept.

Table 8 provides an example of a therapist's interpretation of transference. The client rather grudgingly accepts this interpretation and the insight it brings.

Table 8   Interpretation

Client:	I don't understand why you're holding back on telling me if this step is the right one for me at this time in my life.
Therapist:	This has come up before. You want my approval before taking some action. What seems to be happening here is that one of the conflicts you have with your wife is trying to get her approval of what you have decided to do, and that conflict is occurring now between us.
Client:	I suppose so. Other people's approval has always been very important to me.

Adapted from Woody & Robertson, 1988

Interpreting dreams According to Freud (1900), 'The interpretation of dreams is the royal road to a knowledge of the unconscious activities of the mind'. He believed that defence mechanisms such as repression are weakened during sleep. As a result, repressed wishes, desires and conflicts are expressed in dreams, albeit in a symbolic and disguised form (see pp 384-385 for an outline of Freud's theory of dreams).

Many psychodynamic therapists try to help clients interpret their dreams, in order to uncover repressed desires and conflicts and so gain insight.

Working through

In session after session, therapist and client go over the same issues, interpreting and reinterpreting with the aim of gaining deeper insight. This process is known as *working through*. Clients are required to face up to sexual tensions and conflicts, traumatic childhood experiences with parents and siblings, and interpretations which often cause pain and anguish.

In order to deal with and resolve internal conflicts, gaining insight must be an emotional as well as an intellectual process. Clients must experience *catharsis*, an emotional reliving of repressed feelings. This leads to a release of emotional tension, a purging of the emotion which accompanies internal conflicts and repressed traumas. This makes it easier for clients to confront their problems and, hopefully, resolve them.

4.3   Evaluation

Psychodynamic therapy has often been criticised as unscientific and unverifiable. The evidence on which it is based comes from case studies of individual clients. These studies rely heavily on the therapist's interpretations, which are open to bias. They are largely based on information acquired retrospectively – adults recalling their early years. Memories of childhood experiences are often partial and selective – and they can be false. There is plenty of evidence that false memories exist, and that they can be implanted by suggestion and leading questions (Loftus, 1993).

Key terms

Repression *A defence mechanism which prevents awareness of forbidden impulses, inner conflicts and traumatic memories.*

Insight *Bringing repressed material into conscious awareness.*

Free association *Saying whatever comes to mind and giving free rein to thoughts and feelings even if this goes against social conventions.*

Resistance *Blocks against free association. As a result, the client is unwilling or unable to say certain things.*

Transference *Redirecting feelings about one person to another person.*

Interpretations *A therapist's analysis and understanding of what a client says and does – in particular, an analysis of a client's repressed feelings, conflicts and memories.*

Denial *A client's rejection of a therapist's interpretations.*

Working through *Going over and over issues and interpretations in order for the client to experience catharsis and gain insight.*

Catharsis *A reliving of repressed feelings and experiences which leads to an emotional release.*

Since many of the processes analysed by therapists occur at an unconscious level, it is difficult, if not impossible, to determine if they exist at all (Nietzel et al., 1994). For example, are internal conflicts real? Does repression actually occur?

Take the case of insight. It is largely based on the interpretations of the therapist. And these interpretations tend to vary depending, among other things, on the theoretical background of the therapist. For example, Freudians tend to base their interpretations on psychosexual conflicts, object relations theorists tend to base them on problems with social relationships in childhood (Marmor, 1987). Which of these interpretations, if any, is correct? And are clients developing insight on the basis of objective data or are they simply accepting the interpretations of their therapist? Some researchers argue that the development of insight is a social conversion process whereby the client is gradually converted to the views and beliefs of their therapist (Bandura, 1969).

But do the above criticisms matter? Surely the most important question is: Does psychodynamic therapy work?

Effectiveness

How can the effectiveness of therapy be measured? One answer is to ask the client. This raises a number of problems. For example, a 'small improvement' for one client might be a 'large improvement' for another. At what point should the client be asked? Ideally, at the end of treatment. However, psychodynamic therapy may take years. In some cases, clients are asked to assess their progress during treatment, in others when the treatment has ended. These two forms of assessment are not directly comparable.

If clients have improved during or after therapy, is this due to the therapy? There are many cases of *spontaneous remission* – improvement without any professional treatment. One way of assessing the effect of therapy is to compare two groups of people diagnosed with the same disorder. The first group receives treatment, the other does not. If the improvement of the treatment group is significantly greater than that of the non-treatment group, then it can be argued that therapy is effective. However, there are still problems. Are we comparing like with like – for example, are the psychological and social characteristics of the two groups similar? For instance, is the severity of the disorder the same for members of each group? Are the social characteristics – ethnicity, class, gender and age – of each group similar? Some or all of these factors may affect the impact of therapy.

A further method of assessment involves comparing different treatments for the same disorder – for example, drug treatment versus psychodynamic therapy. However, this method has many of the same problems as the treatment versus non-treatment group comparison.

In view of these and other methodological problems, it is not surprising that there is little agreement about the effectiveness of psychodynamic therapy. At one extreme, Hans Eysenck (1952) argues that it appears to be less effective than no treatment at all. At the other extreme, a survey of 475 studies concluded that a wide range of therapies, including psychodynamic therapy, were significantly more effective than no treatment at all. The researchers concluded that, 'The average person who receives therapy is better off at the end of it than 80% of persons who do not' (Smith et al., 1980). However, like all effectiveness studies, the two mentioned above have been seriously criticised for methodological weaknesses (Davison & Neale, 1998).

In the absence of any firm conclusions, some researchers have suggested the 'dodo bird' conclusion. The Dodo, in Lewis Carroll's *Alice's Adventures in Wonderland*, organised a race. At the end, it was decided that everybody was a winner and all must have prizes. Some researchers argue the same is probably true about the various psychotherapies (Luborsky et al., 1975).

Summary

1. Psychodynamic theory assumes that human beings have a number of defence mechanisms which serve to a) prevent awareness of inner conflicts and traumatic memories and b) suppress impulses and desires which are seen as socially unacceptable.

2. Psychodynamic therapy aims to bring repressed material into conscious awareness. Only then can it be dealt with and resolved.

3. A number of techniques are used to develop insight.

They include:
- Free association
- Interpretation
- Transference
- Working through

4. Psychodynamic therapy has often been criticised as unscientific and unverifiable.

5. There are various views on the effectiveness of psychodynamic therapy. However, the studies on which these views are based can be criticised on methodological grounds.

Activity 4 Psychodynamic therapy

Item A Transference

David, a 50-year-old business executive, had been in therapy for about a year. He complained about depression and anxiety. He felt weak, incompetent and a failure. After many sessions of free association and dream analysis, his therapist suspected that David's feelings reflected his relationship with his father – a highly critical man who was never satisfied with his son's achievements.

In one session, David (the client) had strong words for his therapist.

Client: I really don't feel like talking today.

Therapist: (*Remains silent for several minutes, then*) Perhaps you'd like to talk about why you don't feel like talking.

Client: There you go again, making demands on me, insisting I do what I just don't feel up to doing. (*Pause*) Do I always have to talk here, when I don't feel like it? (*Voice becomes angry and petulant*) Can't you just get off my back? You don't really give a damn how I feel, do you?

Therapist: I wonder why you feel I don't care.

Client: Because you're always pressuring me to do what I feel I can't do.

Adapted from Davison & Neale, 1998

Item B Interpreting dreams

Freud (1900) stated that 'The interpretation of dreams is the royal road to a knowledge of the unconscious activities of the mind'. He argued that many of the objects and activities in dreams are symbolic – they stand for something else. For example, objects which suggest penetration such as snakes, guns, swords and umbrellas, can symbolise the penis. And objects suggesting receptacles, such as boxes, purses and caves, can symbolise the vagina.

Adapted from Freud, 1900

I HAD A DREAM ABOUT A SNAKE....

Questions

1 Read Item A.

   a) How can it be seen as an example of transference?

   b) How can an analysis of transference be useful for therapy?

2 With some reference to Item B, suggest some of the problems of interpreting dreams.

References

Alvir, J. J., Lieberman, J.A. & Safferman, A.Z. (1995). Do white-cell count spikes predict agranulocytosis in clozapine recipients? *Pychopharmacology Bulletin, 31,* 311-314.

Arnold, L.E. & Jensen, P.S. (1992). Attention-deficit disorder. In H.I. Kaplan & B. Sadock (Eds.), *Comprehensive textbook of psychiatry* (4th ed.). Baltimore: Williams & Wilkins.

Ayllon, T. & Azrin, N.H. (1965). The measurement and reinforcement of behavior of psychotics. *Journal of Experimental Analysis of Behavior, 8,* 357-383.

Ayllon, T. & Azrin, N.H. (1968). *The token economy: A motivational system for therapy and rehabilitation.* New York: Appleton-Century-Crofts.

Ayllon, T. & Roberts, M.D. (1974). Eliminating discipline problems by strengthening academic performance. *Journal of Applied Behavior Analysis, 7,* 71-76.

Baldwin, S. (2001). When 'No' means 'Yes': Informed consent themes with children and teenagers. In C. Newnes, G. Holmes, & C. Dunn (Eds.), *This is madness too: Critical perspectives on mental health.* Ross-on-Wye: PCCS Books.

Ballenger, J.C. (1995). Benzodiazepines. In A.F. Schatzberg & C.B. Nemeroff (Eds.), *The American Psychiatric Press textbook of psychopharmacology.* Washington, DC: American Psychiatric Press.

Bandura, A. (1969). *Principles of behavior modification.* New York: Holt, Rinehart & Winston.

Barlow, D.H. & Durand, V.M. (1999). *Abnormal psychology: An integrative approach* (2nd ed.). Pacific Grove, CA: Brooks/Cole.

Beck, A.T. (1997). Cognitive therapy: Reflections. In J.K. Zeig (Ed.), *The evolution of psychotherapy: The third conference.* New York: Brunner/Mazel.

Beck, A.T., Rush, A.J., Shaw, B.F. & Emery, G. (1979). *Cognitive therapy of depression.* New York: Guilford Press.

Breggin, P. (1996). *Toxic psychiatry.* London: Fontana.

British Psychological Society. (1999). *Comments on the Review of the Mental Health Act 1983.* Leicester: British Psychological Society.

British Psychological Society Division of Clinical Psychology. (2000). *Understanding mental illness and psychotic experiences: A report by the British Psychological Society Division of Clinical Psychology.* Leicester: British Psychological Society.

Bruch, H. (1978). *The golden cage: The enigma of anorexia nervosa.* Cambridge, MA: Harvard University Press.

Clarke, J.C. & Saunders, J.B. (1988). *Alcoholism and problem drinking:*

Theories and treatment. Sydney: Pergamon Press.

Cobb, A. (1993). *Safe and effective? MIND's views on psychiatric drugs, ECT and psychosurgery.* London: MIND Publications.

Comer, R.J. (1998). *Abnormal psychology* (3rd ed.). New York: W.H. Freeman.

Davison, G.C. & Neale, J.M. (1998). *Abnormal psychology* (7th ed.). New York: John Wiley & Sons.

Elsesser, K., Sartory, G. & Maurer, J. (1996). The efficacy of complaints management training in facilitating benzodiazepine withdrawal. *Behavior Research and Therapy, 34,* 149-156.

Emmelkamp, P.M. (1994). Behavior therapy with adults. In A.E. Bergin & S.L. Garfiel (Eds.), *Handbook of psychotherapy and behavior change* (4th ed.). New York: Wiley.

Emmelkamp, P.M.G., Bouman, T.K. & Scholing, A. (1992). *Anxiety disorders: A practitioner's guide.* New York: John Wiley & Sons.

Eysenck, H.J. (1952). The effects of psychotherapy: An evaluation. *Journal of Consulting Psychology, 16,* 319-324.

Fernandez, F., Levy, J., Lachar, B. & Small, G. (1995). The management of depression and anxiety in the elderly. *Journal of Clinical Psychiatry, 56,* 20-29.

Ford, D.H. & Urban, H.B. (1963). *Systems of psychotherapy: A comparative study.* New York: Wiley.

Freeman, A. & Reinecke, M.A. (1995). Cognitive therapy. In A.S. Gurman & S.B. Messer (Eds.), *Essential psychotherapies: Theory and practice.* New York: Guilford.

Freeman, H. & Watts, J.W. (1942). *Psychosurgery.* Springfield IL: Thomas.

Freud, S. (1900). *The interpretation of dreams.* London: Hogarth Press.

Fyer, A., Leibowitz, M., Gorman, J., Compeas, R., Levin, A., Davies, S., Goetz, D. & Klein, D. (1987). Discontinuation of alprazolam treatment in panic patients. *American Journal of Psychiatry, 144,* 303-308.

Gelder, M., Gath, D. & Mayon, R. (1989). *The Oxford textbook of psychiatry* (2nd ed.). Oxford: Oxford University Press.

Haddock, G., Tarrier, N., Spaulding, W., Yusupoff, L., Kinney, C. & McCarthy, E. (1998). Individual cognitive-behavior therapy in the treatment of hallucinations and delusions: A review. *Clinical Psychology Review, 18,* 821-838.

Heather, N. (1976). *Radical perspectives in psychology.* London: Methuen.

Herz, M.I., Glazer, W.M., Mostert, M.A., Sheard, M.A., Szymanski, H.V., Hafez, H., Mirza, M. & Vana, J. (1991). Intermittent vs maintenance medication in schizophrenia. *Two-year results. Archives of General Psychiatry, 48,* 333-339.

Hogan, R.A. (1968). The implosive technique. *Behavior Research and Therapy, 6,* 423-431.

Hogan, R.A. & Kirchner, J.H. (1967). A preliminary report of the extinction of learned fears via a short term implosive therapy. *Journal of Abnormal Psychology, 72,* 106-111.

Hollon, S.D., De Rubeis, R.J. & Evans, M.D. (1996). Cognitive therapy in the treatment and prevention of depression. In P.M.Salkovskis (Ed.), *Frontiers of cognitive therapy.* New York: Guilford.

Jenike, M.A., Baer, L., Ballantine, T., Martuza, R.L. Tynes, S., Giriunas, I., Buttolph, M.L. & Cassem, N.H. (1991). Cingulotomy for refractory obsessive-compulsive disorder: A long-term follow-up of 33 patients. *Archives of General Psychiatry, 48,* 548-555.

Johnstone, L. (1996). Move to outlaw electrotherapy. *The Observer,* 12th December.

Kalinowsky, L. (1975). Psychosurgery. In A. Freedman, H. Kaplan & B. Sadock (Eds.), *Comprehensive textbook of psychiatry.* Baltimore: Williams & Wilkins.

Karp, J.F. & Frank, E. (1995). Combination therapy and the depressed woman. *Depression, 3,* 91-98.

Kazdin, A.E. (1994). Psychotherapy for children and adolescents. In A.E. Bergin & S.L. Garfiel (Eds.), *Handbook of psychotherapy and behavior change* (4th ed.). New York: Wiley.

Keller, M.B., Harrison, W., Fawcett, J.A., Gelenberg, A., Hirschfeld, R.,M., Klein, D., Kocsis, J.H., McCullough, J.P., Rush, A.J., Schatzberg, A. & Thase, M.E. (1995). Treatment of chronic depression with sertraline or imipramine: Preliminary blinded response rates and high rates of under-treatment in the community. *Psychopharmacology Bulletin, 31,* 205-212.

Kinderman, P. (1994). Cognitive-behavioural therapy for depression in the year 1411. *Clinical Psychology and Psychotherapy, 1,* 116-119.

Leutwyler, K. (1996). Paying attention: The controversy over ADHD and the drug Ritalin is obscuring a real look at the disorder and its underpinnings. *Scientific American, 272,* 12-13.

Loftus, E.F. (1993). The reality of repressed memories. *American Psychologist, 48,* 518-537.

Luborsky, L., Singer, B. & Luborsky, L. (1975). Comparative studies of psychotherapies. *Archives of General Psychiatry, 32,* 995-1008.

Marks, I. (1987). *Fears, phobias and rituals.* Oxford: Oxford University Press.

Marmor, J. (1987). The psychotherapeutic process: Common denominators in diverse approaches. In J.K.Zeig (Ed.), *The evolution of psychotherapy.* New York: Brunner/Mazel.

McGarth, T., Tsui, E., Humphries, S. & Yule, W. (1990). Successful treatment of a noise phobia in a nine-year-old girl with systematic desensitization in vivo. *Educational Psychology, 10,* 79-83.

National Institute for Clinical Excellence. (2000). *Guidelines for the use of methylphenidate (ritalin, equasym) with children with ADHD.* London: National Health Service Executive.

Nietzel, M.T., Bernstein, D.A. & Milich, R. (1994). *Introduction to clinical psychology* (4th ed.). Englewood Cliffs, NJ: Prentice Hall.

Ost, L.G. & Westling, B.E. (1995). Applied relaxation vs. cognitive behavior therapy in the treatment of panic disorder. *Behavior Research and Therapy, 33,* 145-158.

Paul, G.L. & Lentz, R. (1977). *Psychosocial treatment of the chronic mental patient.* Cambridge, MA: Harvard University Press.

Sanderson, R.E., Campbell, D. & Laverty, S.G. (1963). An investigation of a new aversive conditioning treatment for alcoholism. *Quarterly Journal on the Studies of Alcoholism, 24,* 261-275.

Scott, J. (1992). Chronic depression: Can cognitive therapy succeed when other treatments fail? *Behavioural Psychotherapy, 20,* 25-34.

Sensky, T., Turkington, D., Kingdon, D., Scott, J.L., Scott, J., Siddle, R., O'Carroll, M. & Barnes, T.R. (2000). A randomized controlled trial of cognitive-behavioral therapy for persistent symptoms in schizophrenia resistant to medication. *Archives of General Psychiatry, 57,* 165-172.

Silverstein, C. (1972). *Behavior modification and the gay community.* Paper presented at the annual convention of the Association for Advancement of Behavior Therapy, New York.

Smith, J., Frawley, P.J., & Polissar, L. (1991). Six- and twelve-month abstinence rates in inpatient alcoholics treated with aversion therapy compared with matched inpatients from a treatment registry. *Alcoholism: Clinical and Experimental Research, 15,* 862-870.

Smith, M.L., Glass, G. & Miller, T. (1980). *The benefits of psychotherapy.* Baltimore: Johns Hopkins University Press.

Strange, P.G. (1992). *Brain biochemistry and brain disorders.* Oxford: Oxford University Press.

Taylor, J.R. & Carroll, J.L. (1987). Current issues in electroconvulsive therapy. *Psychological Reports, 60.*

Thase, M.E. & Rush, A.J. (1995). Treatment-resistant depression. In F.E. Bloom & D.J. Kupter (Eds.), Psychopharmacology: The fourth generation of progress. New York: Raven Press.

Tollefson, G.D., Holman, S.L., Sayler, M.E. & Potvin, J.H. (1995). Fluoxetine, placebo, and tricyclic antidepressants in major depression with and without anxious features. *Journal of Clinical Psychiatry, 13,* 13-22.

Valenstein, E.S. (1986). *Great and desperate cures.* New York: Basic Books.

Wheatley, J. (1996). The attention seekers. *The Times Magazine,* 28th September.

Wolberg, L.R. (1967). *The technique of psychotherapy.* New York: Grune & Stratton.

Wolpe, J. (1958). *Psychotherapy by reciprocal inhibition.* Stanford, CA: Stanford University Press.

Woody, R.H. & Robertson, M. (1988). *Becoming a clinical psychologist.* Madison, CT: International Universities Press.

▶ Introduction

This chapter looks at a number of issues that demand the attention of psychologists, those who study psychology, and those who are on the receiving end of psychology. First, is psychological knowledge value free – is it objective and unbiased? Second, can psychology change the world for the better? Third, do psychologists treat those who participate in their research reasonably and fairly?

Chapter summary

- Unit 1 looks at the issue of gender bias in psychological theory and research.
- Unit 2 looks at the issue of cultural bias in psychological theory and research.
- Unit 3 explores the ethical issues raised by research involving human participants.
- Unit 4 explores the ethical issues raised by research involving non-human animals.

Two promises and two issues

One of the main reasons why psychology has become so important and so widespread in the modern world is because it *promises value-free knowledge about people*. To call knowledge 'value free' is another way of saying that it is objective. When we think of objective, value-free knowledge, we typically think of science. Compared to politicians or company directors, scientists are supposed to study the world as it is and to describe it without vested interests. Applying scientific methods to human beings holds out the promise of giving us *unbiased* information which can be used for the good of all. Rather than having to put up with what are ultimately the 'opinions' of wise people, or the preaching of those who claim to have a direct line to God, or the dubious authority of politicians with their own 'axe to grind', psychology promises to give us the truth, and nothing but the truth, about human nature.

A second enchanting promise follows from this first one. Equipped with objective psychological knowledge, we can change the world for the better. We can change the 'attitudes' that lead to prejudice and oppression; we can improve the condition of the mentally disordered; prevent crime by understanding the motives of the criminal; improve relationships in the workplace and increase productivity; work out the best ways to educate our children and to steer them on a path to becoming productive adults; and we might even improve the performance of our sports stars. The possibilities seem endless, since every personal, social, economic and political problem involves 'psychology' at some level. If those in power – in institutions such as prisons, schools, hospitals, law courts, business corporations, not to mention psychotherapists, counsellors, and social workers – are informed by objective and value-free psychological knowledge, then we can rest assured that everything is for the best. Policy decisions and other decisions about how to act can be made in the light of reliable knowledge. Psychology, in this case, would be doing a good job of promoting human welfare and wellbeing.

Here we have the two main promises that underpin the popularity of psychology as a discipline: the production of value-free knowledge and its application to improve human lives. But acting on these two promises has given rise to two sets of issues that will be dealt with in this chapter. The first set of issues is to do with *bias*, and the second to do with *ethics*.

Bias First, if psychological knowledge turns out to be *biased* – to favour men over women, whites over blacks, the rich over the poor, the able-bodied over the disabled, the heterosexual over the homosexual – then there will be cause for great concern and complaint. The complaint will be all the greater since, in this case, the promise of objectivity will have turned out to be a kind of deception. It is one thing to be given an *opinion* that turns out to be biased, but bias in what are supposed to be *facts* is doubly worrying. On top of being unreliable, it undermines our trust in the expert on whom we depend. Psychology, in this case, could be accused of being a hidden form of political control and a way of defending the 'status quo'. It would be accused of improving the welfare and wellbeing of those in power at the expense of those in relatively subordinate positions. In discussions about the social role of psychology, we see both of these positions put forward – for some, psychology is a means of promoting human wellbeing; for others it is a means of defending the 'status quo'. The debate hinges on whether it is the wellbeing of humanity as a whole that is being helped by psychological knowledge and techniques, or just the wellbeing of the already well off.

Ethics The second set of issues around *ethics* are to do with what price psychologists (and society generally) are prepared to pay in trying to gain this knowledge. Do we have the right to sacrifice animals in psychological experiments in order to gain knowledge? What limits should be put on the way psychologists can treat animals? Also, what ethical guidelines should be followed when using human beings as participants in psychological research? Is it justifiable to mistreat individual human participants in order to benefit society, for instance?

Unit 1 Gender bias in psychological theory and research

KEY ISSUES

1 Is it possible for psychological knowledge to be 'value free'?
2 Is psychology gender biased?
3 What can be done to prevent gender bias?

Key terms

Bias *Falling short of 'objectivity' and 'value neutrality'. The basic definition of bias is a predisposition or prejudice. Bias becomes particularly obvious when it is a 'leaning' towards or against specific groups or individuals.*

Reflexivity *This is a complex concept that has subtly different meanings in different contexts. In this context it means a critical reflection on the ways in which a researcher's own values, and the values of their local community, influence the work they do.*

1.1 Is 'value-free knowledge' an impossible ideal?

Psychologists are becoming increasingly aware that the ideal of producing 'value-free' knowledge is difficult, it not impossible, to reach. In 1985, for example, the president of the American Psychological Association said during her presidential address that:

'Contemporary analysts recognise that, whatever their intentions, scientists are the products of their society and time, and their construction of social reality is shaped by the world view and values of the culture in which they were reared. These belief systems can influence all phases of the research in which scientists engage, from choice of problem to interpretation of results' (Spence, 1985).

The assumptions and values of scientists can influence:

- the questions they ask
- the way they set up their investigations
- the theories they invent
- the conclusions they draw.

This happens, according to Spence, regardless of the positive intentions of scientists to be as objective as possible. It is therefore very important for researchers to critically examine the assumptions and values they bring to their research. If they do not, then they are in danger of thinking of their results as 'objective', when in reality they have been strongly influenced by values. This critical examination of one's assumptions and values and the role they play in influencing one's work is one of the meanings of the word *reflexivity*. This problem of the influence of values and assumptions in shaping scientific knowledge applies to all sciences, and not just psychology. A recent National Academy of Sciences document in the USA, for example, states that scientists should recognise the way in which social biases influence their work 'by trying to identify their own values and the effects those values have on their science' (Harding, 1993).

A further important point made by Spence is that the belief systems and values of scientists are themselves 'shaped by the world view and values of the culture in which they were reared'. This points to the social nature of these values and beliefs and suggests that much of the subject matter studied by psychologists is social in origin, and hence can change with the times and across cultures. This is certainly the case with the question of gender bias in psychology. As more and more women became psychologists from the 1960s and 70s onwards (previously, like most other disciplines, psychology had been very much 'male dominated'), and as Western culture as a whole became more conscious of gender inequalities, so psychologists became more aware that their knowledge had been biased in a 'male' direction.

1.2 The feminist challenge

Gender bias is a clear case in which the values and assumptions of psychologists have come to influence psychological knowledge. The quotation from Spence above stated that 'scientists are the products of their society and time'. If the society and time are mainly sexist, then that sexism is likely to be reflected in psychological research.

Like many institutions, psychology departments and laboratories have been dominated by men until fairly recently. Most psychologists who are women have stories to tell about the difficulties of making a career in a man's world. But the influence of gender on psychology is not just to do with personal stories of difficulty and resistance. In recent years, an active group of psychologists have been working to show the various ways in which psychological knowledge is full of gender bias. Often these psychologists are explicit about their political agenda – they are *feminist* psychologists. The political feel of this is put well by Dale Spender (1982):

'When students come to learn about economics or sociology (or language, literature, education, philosophy …) they are taught about men, and men's view of the world, and this is a lesson in male supremacy' (quoted in Burr, 1998).

Such statements pose a real challenge to the objectivity of psychological knowledge. For most of its existence, feminist psychologists argue, psychology has been about men asking male questions, in male ways, for male purposes. If these male questions and answers do not apply to women, or do not take into account a female perspective, then psychology can be accused of being gender biased.

1.3 An example of alpha bias: 'sex differences' research

The question of identifying gender bias, however, has been complicated by two other related forms of bias. To argue that psychology is biased because it doesn't take account of women, their experience, and their concerns, is to assume that there is a *difference* between men and women. How else could feminists talk about a 'male perspective'? But is there really such a difference, and, if so, what is the nature of the difference? The reason this becomes complicated is because people sometimes exaggerate differences and play down similarities, and sometimes exaggerate similarities and play down differences. The first has been called (by Hare-Mustin and Maracek, 1988) *alpha bias* and the second, which we will look at in the following section, *beta bias*.

The following descriptions of male and female characteristics can be seen as an example of alpha bias – exaggerating 'sex differences'.

'Big boys are made of – independence, aggression, competitiveness, leadership, task orientation, outward orientation, assertiveness …

Big girls are made of – dependence, passivity, fragility, low pain tolerance, non-aggression, non-competitiveness, inner orientation, interpersonal orientation, empathy, sensitivity, nurturance' (Bardwick, cited in Wetherell, 1986).

A lot of psychological research on the subject of 'sex differences', as the quotation above illustrates, argues that there are clear and distinct psychological differences between males and females (eg, Johnson, 1976; de Castillejo, 1973). It is commonly argued that:

- Men are more 'instrumental' and 'agentic' (ie, they like to be actively involved in practical tasks and to define their own agendas)
- Women are more 'expressive' and 'communal' (ie, they like to talk amongst themselves and express how they feel).

Another common claim is that:

- Men are independent, aggressive, competitive, assertive and task-oriented
- Women are dependent, passive, fragile and people-oriented.

At its extreme, such arguments hold that men like to fix cars and put up shelves whilst women prefer to talk about fashion and the latest developments in soap operas. This kind of account is prone to *alpha bias* since it emphasises the differences between males and females, lumping all women into one category and all men into another.

Eleanor Maccoby and Carol Jacklin (1974) wrote a famous

critical review of such research on 'sex differences'. The first obvious critical point is that most of this research was conducted by male researchers. But their main objection was scientific. They argued that these differences had been greatly exaggerated, and in fact the results were inconclusive in all but four areas:

1 Females really do tend to be more verbally skilled than males

2 Males have better visual-spatial ability

3 Boys tend to overtake girls in mathematical ability at around 12 years

4 Boys are typically more physically aggressive.

One of the reasons for this exaggeration is that the experimental studies were poorly designed. However, the implication of this review is that a male bias lurks behind the findings. These predominantly male psychologists, it was suggested, *want* (whether consciously or not) women to be different. Perhaps the bias is also self-serving – it benefits men. In thinking of men and women as psychologically very different, men can continue with their sexist ways as if these were natural. For instance, an instrumental and agentic man should 'naturally' run the company, whereas an expressive and communal woman should 'naturally' run the family! Maccoby and Jacklin were very influential in showing that research that searches for 'sex differences' between men and women is subject to *alpha bias*, since the differences are exaggerated. One way of putting this would be to say that the sex differences exist in the mind of the psychologists (in their belief-systems, values and world views), but not necessarily in the real world.

Key terms

Alpha bias *Exaggerating the differences and understating the similarities between males and females.*

Beta bias *Exaggerating the similarities and understating the differences between males and females.*

Activity 1   Sex differences

Item A   When a mature woman is not a mature person

In 1972, a fascinating study was published (Broverman et al., 1972) which explored the way mental health professionals thought about men and women. The researchers asked a large number of these applied psychologists (both men and women) to describe the qualities of:

1   The mature, healthy, socially competent adult

2   The mature, healthy, socially competent man

3   The mature, healthy, socially competent woman.

The descriptions of the 'mentally healthy man' and the 'mentally healthy adult' were virtually identical. Both were characterised as having instrumental qualities (that is, being able to do things) and some of the more desirable expressive

traits (that is, about their feelings and ways of connecting with the social world). But the description of the 'mentally healthy woman' was quite different. She was characterised as more submissive, more easily influenced, as excitable in minor crises, concerned with her appearance and more likely to have her feelings hurt. She was less independent, less dominant, less aggressive, less objective and less adventurous. These findings showed that mental health professionals equated 'men' with 'adults' – to be a mentally healthy man is to be a mentally healthy adult. But this was not true of their ideas about women – to be a mentally healthy woman was not seen as equivalent to being a mentally healthy adult.

Adapted from Stainton Rogers & Stainton Rogers, 2001

Item C   Gender and culture

The wife most likely to be kissed

The take-charge movie camera

Questions

1   In what ways can Item A be seen as gender biased?

2   Compare Items A and B. What are the similarities between psychologists and people in general in the way they see men and women?

3   With some reference to Item C, suggest where gender bias in psychology comes from.

1.4   An example of beta bias: gendered morality

So far we have concentrated on *alpha bias* wherein differences between males and females are exaggerated and similarities ignored. But gender bias can also take the opposite form – of ignoring real differences between the genders and assuming a male norm. Ignoring such differences is called *beta bias*. And when a male norm is also assumed, we talk of *androcentrism* – literally putting man at the centre of things and marginalising or treating as trivial a female perspective. A good example of beta bias and androcentrism is provided by research into the psychology of moral development. The most prominent psychologist to study moral development in the 20th century was a man called Lawrence Kohlberg. Kohlberg's sad fate is that his work is nowadays more often used to illustrate gender bias than morality.

Kohlberg's stages of moral development

Male moral development There are two broad ways in which Kohlberg was androcentric. First, in conducting his early research into morality, he used only male participants. His idea was that moral reasoning develops much in the way Piaget argued that all kinds of reasoning develops. Namely, as people get older, they become more sophisticated in their reasoning abilities, and pass through what can be thought of as cognitive stages of development. To investigate this idea, he conducted a longitudinal study (a study over time) which began with 72 males aged 10-16 from Chicago. He presented them with stories involving moral dilemmas and studied their responses to see if

there were any patterns in the ways in which they made sense of the dilemmas. Kohlberg identified three levels of moral reasoning from their responses, each one more advanced than the next: first the preconventional level, then the conventional level, and finally the postconventional level. Each level has two stages, producing a developmental sequence of six stages (see p525).

Strictly speaking, Kohlberg should have said that his theory of moral development was a theory about how males engage in moral reasoning, since all the data had come from male participants. Kohlberg was apparently taking it for granted that there were no differences in the moral reasoning of men and women. This is a form of beta bias, since gender differences are minimised and similarities maximised. Kohlberg seems simply not to have considered it important that his theory was based only on males. His androcentrism was so strong that he did not even consider the question of gender. This was typical of the USA in the 1950s. (See pp 524-526 for a detailed outline of Kohlberg's theory of moral development.)

Female moral development Kohlberg's theory was later applied to girls and women. They were presented with the same moral dilemmas, asked the same questions and their responses were coded in the same way. On average, they performed less well than the boys and men. For example, in one study, only 18% of females compared with 28% of males were able to reason at the highest level (Haan et al., 1968). The average female only reached Stage 3 whereas the average male made it to Stage 4. It appeared that girls and women were less morally developed than men.

This is the second way Kohlberg was androcentric. He and

other researchers assumed that his stages of moral development and the methods he devised for measuring moral development were equally applicable to males and females. The assumption is that male morality is the norm. Again this is an example of beta bias, which ignores the possibility of differences between the genders. This can lead to downgrading and undervaluing females – in this case, their morality appears stunted and underdeveloped. However, as the next section argues, this conclusion may simply reflect beta bias. There may be a distinctive female morality and a distinctive female path of moral development.

Gilligan's critique of Kohlberg

According to Carol Gilligan (1982), there are distinctive male and female views of morality. Gilligan interviewed 29 women between the ages of 15 and 33 who were attending couselling sessions about whether or not to abort an unwanted pregnancy. They were therefore facing moral dilemmas of their own. On the basis of these interviews, Gilligan claims that women's moral reasoning was directed by a *care orientation*, rather than the more masculine *justice orientation*.

This distinction can be seen clearly by comparing Kohlberg's Stage 6 with Gilligan's highest stage in the development of the care orientation. For Kohlberg, Stage 6 is the most advanced form of moral thinking. At this stage, people base their reasoning on universal ethical principles which they themselves have chosen – for example, principles of justice such as universal human rights and respect for the dignity of the individual. For Gilligan, this is primarily a *male* way of thinking.

Gilligan found that her female participants tended not think like this. Instead of talking about abstract principles, they discussed the impact that their decision might have on the feelings of real, concrete people such as friends, family and partner. They didn't remove or detach themselves from the situation in order to make an objective decision that might be right irrespective of particular circumstances. Instead, they reasoned in a way that dealt with the specific context at hand.

What annoyed Gilligan is that, judged from Kohlberg's perspective, this makes her female participants out to be inferior moral reasoners. As in Haan et al's study, it typically leaves them at Stage 3, far behind those at Stage 6 who think universally according to abstract principles. Gilligan's response was to turn the tables on Kohlberg: it is not females who are inferior, it is Kohlberg who is androcentric. Gilligan proposed an alternative theory in which two different ways of moral reasoning – the care orientation and the justice orientation – are given equal value and importance. She suggests that those oriented to care put people before principles, those oriented to justice put principles before people. (See pp 527-529 for a detailed outline of Gilligan's theory of moral development.)

Evaluation of the Kohlberg/Gilligan debate about bias

Evaluating Kohlberg's theory Kohlberg's research has been accused of beta bias, that is ignoring real differences between the genders, and of androcentrism, that is putting man at the centre of things. The following evidence has been used to make these accusations.

- Kohlberg's sample was all male.

- He based his theory on findings from this sample.
- The main characters in his moral dilemmas were male.
- He assumed that the methods he developed for measuring moral development were equally applicable to both genders.
- He assumed that the stages of moral development he devised were equally applicable.
- He was blissfully unaware of the possibility of gender differences in moral reasoning.
- Because of the above points, Kohlberg accepts male morality as the standard in terms of which all morality is measured.
- As a result, females tend to get lower scores of moral reasoning – they appear inferior to males.
- Kohlberg therefore undervalues and downgrades female morality.

Evaluating Gilligan's research Gilligan has pointed out the dangers of assuming that there is no difference between males and females, and of assuming that male norms are society's norms. However, has she gone too far in the opposite direction? Is she in danger of drawing too stark a contrast between the moral reasoning of men and women? In other words, can she be accused of alpha bias – of exaggerating the differences and understating the similarities between males and females? A number of critics have accused her of doing just this. Their reasons include the following.

- Gilligan's sample was small – only 29 young women.
- It was unrepresentative – women receiving counselling for an unwanted pregnancy.
- Her study was based on a specifically female moral dilemma.
- It was also based on a real and very personal moral dilemma. Kohlberg's participants were presented with fictional stories of moral dilemmas.
- A number of studies have found no significant gender differences in the use of care or justice orientations (see p528).
- Some feminists have accused Gilligan of undermining the women's movement by confirming sexual stereotypes – by portraying women as caring, nurturant and emotional.

In offering an explanation for gender differences in moral reasoning, Gilligan turns to psychoanalytic theory. This theory puts a lot of importance on the early relationship a child has with their primary caregiver, who is usually the mother. Specifically, Gilligan drew upon Chodorow's (1978) theory. Chodorow argues that little boys have to make an early and clear separation from the mother in order to 'identify' with the father. Little girls, by contrast, can continue to have an emotionally intimate relationship with the mother, since it is with her that they come to 'identify'. This leaves little boys having to deal with the problem of separation, which they typically manage by controlling emotions, becoming more task-centred, learning not to depend on relationships, and so on. In short, by detaching themselves emotionally – exactly what is required to reason in a Stage 6 way. In other words, as a result of this process of separation from the mother, boys end up feeling more detached from other people than girls, and so think in a more detached way about moral questions. Such theories not only depend upon clear differences between males and females, and hence risk alpha bias, but also suggest that such differences run deep into the psyche and are fundamental to personality.

Arguably, the main difference between this and the 'sex

differences' research discussed earlier in Section 1.3, is that in Gilligan's theory the 'essentially female' is valued positively.

1.5 Distinguishing the descriptive level from the explanatory level in psychological theories

At this point, it is useful to separate out two parts of a typical scientific account: the descriptive and the explanatory.

- **Descriptive** The descriptive part claims to do no more than to describe how something is. For example, Section 1.3 reports research which attempts to describe the psychological differences between males and females. Males are described as 'instrumental', 'agentic' and so on, and women are described as 'expressive' and 'communal'. Likewise, in Section 1.4, Kohlberg *describes* the different ways in which people of different ages engage in moral reasoning, whilst Gilligan describes differences between a care orientation and a justice orientation.

- **Explanatory** The explanatory part, on the other hand, aims to explain *why* the world is organised in the way the description says it is. Why are males aggressive and females passive? Why do females typically take a care orientation and males a justice one?

Note that in offering an explanation it is important that the description be accurate. There is no point in giving a great explanation for why males are more aggressive than females if, in fact, they are not! Using this distinction, we can say that Maccoby and Jacklin (1974) identified alpha bias in the *descriptions* offered by sex-differences researchers. When pushed to explain *why* men and women are different, some psychologists have argued that such differences are natural – it is just the way that men and women are. In other words, these qualities are seen as naturally occurring *gendered traits*. Just as women have different bodies than men, so they have different ways of thinking and feeling, and different preferred ways of acting. In this way of thinking, sex leads automatically to gender. In other words, biological sex differences lead to cultural gender differences – to gender norms and gender roles.

Explanations for the naturalness of these supposed 'sex differences' tend to be evolutionary. A typical argument is that dividing up work along gender lines (men doing the hunting, women the domestic work) made good evolutionary sense for the survival of our early ancestors. Therefore, the theory goes, different preferences became hard-wired into men and women through natural selection (for a critical discussion of some of these proposed gender differences see pp 289-290 and 549-551).

It is here that the distinction between descriptive and explanatory parts of scientific work becomes particularly useful. It may be possible to agree on a description that important differences may exist between males and females and yet to disagree on how these differences should be explained or how they came about. We have already seen that one way of accounting for 'sex differences' is by pointing to innate, genetically-grounded differences between men and women. The label 'sex differences' suggests that any psychological or behavioural differences are simply an extension of biological sex – having 'female' chromosomes and a typically 'female' cocktail of hormones leads naturally to typically 'female' behaviour.

Another group of psychologists have favoured 'nurture' style explanations, and they have a tendency to label their research 'gender differences' rather than 'sex differences'. In other words, these two groups may be looking at the same 'differences', but one group thinks of these as biological differences (hence the use of the word sex) and one group thinks of them as learned social differences which take on meaning in the social world (hence the use of the word gender). The label 'gender differences', in other words, suggests learned and culturally influenced ways of being. Researchers in this tradition are more likely to use explanatory concepts such as gender roles, gender norms, gender identity, and so on, since these concepts stress the learned and performed aspects of gender differences (see key terms).

Key terms

Sex differences *Biologically-based differences between males and females.*

Gender differences *Culturally-based differences between males and females. Differences based on learning rather than biology.*

Gender roles *The different roles that males and females are expected to play in a given society – eg, in many societies military roles are restricted to men and child-rearing to women.*

Gender norms *The different norms that males and females are expected to follow – eg, in many societies men are expected to be assertive and forceful and women to be modest and submissive.*

Gender performance *Thinking of gender as organised by norms and roles leads to the idea that gender is something that is performed or 'acted out' rather than something natural.*

Gender identity *How a person thinks of themselves in terms of gender.*

1.6 The politics of the nature/nurture debate and sex and gender

It is no surprise that the so-called nature/nurture debate (discussed fully in Chapter 38) should crop up when studying differences between males and females. It is no surprise that arguments about differences between males and females are not just scientific arguments, they are also political arguments. They are the kind of political arguments that feminists have been having for well over 100 years. Should women:

- have equal rights to men?
- be paid the same for doing the same work?
- be allowed to do the same jobs as men?
- be allowed to go to university?
- have the vote?

Some of the answers to these questions may sound obvious in 21st century Britain, but each of them were battles that had to be fought and won, and some of them have yet to be won – women are still paid less than men for doing the same jobs, and are less likely to get promoted. In fighting these battles, feminists had to overcome not just practical obstacles, but also obstacles of bias. In every case, those in power made arguments to the effect that women should not vote or go to university since they are naturally different from men. This kind of argument has been called *essentialist*, since it holds that the difference in question is natural and inevitable (or 'essential'). An essentialist argument implies that a given difference:

- does exist (descriptive level),
- is natural (explanatory level),
- ought to exist (political/moral level), and
- cannot be changed (political/practical level).

Valerie Walkerdine (1991) tells the story of how when women were first permitted to enter university there was an outcry from the conservative male establishment. They argued that such intellectual activity would lead to the shrivelling up of the ovaries of these young women. They shouldn't be allowed in since it would damage their ability to do what nature really intended – to have babies! This is a classic essentialist argument. It shows how arguments which explain gender differences as natural fit neatly into sexist rhetoric. The moral of this political story is that ideas and knowledge can have very real practical and social consequences.

Of course we now know that such claims are nonsense and that it is a good thing for women to go to university. But the lesson is that arguments that such and such a situation should not be changed since it is 'natural' are often political arguments dressed up as facts. Sadly, psychologists have often found themselves providing the so-called facts, and hence bolstering the status quo. The counter argument, which tends toward nurture rather than nature, holds that situations of gender difference:

- have been set up by people,
- can be changed by people, and that
- some people will not want it changed (especially those who benefit from the arrangement)
- whilst some people will want to see change (especially those who lose from the arrangement).

Here we can again see how explanations of descriptions can have real world consequences. For example, from this 'nurture' perspective it may be agreed that women tend to be more passive than men in some areas of life. But this description is *explained* as the result of women typically finding themselves in passive roles due to the way the social world has been arranged. Change the social world, let the same women go to good universities, obtain powerful jobs, define their own life-styles and, so the argument goes, you will not see the same passivity. In terms of this argument, the differences are gender differences, not sex differences, and they are socially constructed.

Key term

Essentialism *An argument about gender is called essentialist if it claims that differences between males and females are real, natural and unchangeable.*

1.7 What can be done to prevent gender bias?

Interestingly, some feminists have suggested that it is the 'detached' or even 'isolated' quality of boys and men that leads them to value the forms of objectivity and neutrality that have been so central to science. Science itself, from this point of

view, comes to appear as a male area of interest. It is a small step from here to associate science and technology with the domination and even abuse of nature. Carolyn Merchant (1979), for instance, identifies the mastery and control typical of science with masculinity. And it is often the case that 'mother nature' is portrayed as a female whose intimate secrets are to be revealed to the probing male scientist, who is rewarded for his objectivity with knowledge and power. This kind of argument informs many of the proposals made by feminist psychologists to change the nature of psychology in a more 'female' direction (Wilkinson, 1986). Such proposed changes are designed explicitly to prevent male bias in psychology. Much of this work has gone under the label of 'feminist standpoint theory'. Such proposals include the need to:

- Develop an awareness that science can never be completely 'value free' and that objectivity is a myth.
- Illustrate through research the ways in which knowledge is influenced by gender.
- Be explicit about one's own values in research, and encourage research that is value based rather than value free.
- Recognise the importance of cultural and historical *context* to psychological questions.
- Include personal experience – both of participants, and of researchers – as central to research.
- Allow participants to genuinely *participate* in research, rather than being passive objects for observation.
- Foster a sensitivity to power relationships and questions of inequality which influence research (a child typically has less power, for example, than an adult, and this should be taken into account when conducting research with children).
- Adopt 'social constructionist' ways of thinking and researching that alert psychologists to the ways in which our social and psychological worlds are humanly made.
- Use qualitative methods and other 'alternative' techniques which allow context, experience and power into the research, and which don't disguise the values that are involved.

1.8 The personal is political

Feminist psychologists have accused their male colleagues of dressing up political views in the language of science and objectivity. To avoid gender bias, psychologists must reflect upon their personal involvement in their research and also upon the political implications of their research. In other words, it is not enough to claim they are trying to discover 'the truth' about some 'psychological object'. A researcher is always in a complicated relationship with what they are researching, and this must be acknowledged. This leads to some fairly serious self-questioning on the part of feminist researchers. Consider this extract from Wendy Hollway (1984):

'Early modern feminism was telling women like me that we were equal to men because we were the same as them. Certainly this fitted in with my pre-feminist assumptions that men represented all that was interesting, admirable, powerful and desirable. I was attracted to men, partly because I aspired to be like them. I was keen to develop so-called masculine skills … I learned to service my car, how to build houses and wire up electrical circuits.'

Wendy Hollway here emphasises a desire for no differences to exist between herself and men. She therefore tended towards beta bias and had an interest in attacking psychological theories that saw men and women as essentially different. 'Difference' between males and females, from this point of view, is considered a 'bad' thing. One acts in a 'good' way by showing how such difference is really an illusion. Or, if difference does exist, by showing that it need not exist, and that it is possible and desirable to eliminate it. But she goes on to point out that this view became a problem for her:

'Why was this a problem? Surely equality was desirable? To compete with men like this necessitated a negative definition of myself as women … Women were a group I put myself outside of. When I made generalisations about women (almost always derogatory), I did not include myself in the group I was talking about.'

This deep self-questioning is typical of feminist research in psychology, and shows the need to reflect on the way personal feelings can enter into scientific work. The concept or idea of 'women' still existed for Wendy Hollway – she simply didn't include herself as part of the 'typically female'. Was she herself androcentric? A better feminism, in her view, would *not* involve siding with men against the rest of women. This story from Hollway shows how important it is, when tackling gender bias, to reflect on your own personal life and to recognise the extent to which all of us are caught up in the complex webs of gender bias. This is one meaning of the old feminist slogan: the personal is political.

Summary

1 Psychologists are becoming much more aware of the problem of bias in psychology, and that producing completely 'value-free' knowledge is not possible.

2 Bias is a prejudice or predisposition. An unbalanced set of weighing scales is hence 'biased' if it is predisposed to one side rather than the other. Bias is usually *towards* or *against* something or someone.

3 When dealing with gender bias, *alpha bias* involves exaggerating the differences between genders, and *beta bias* involves exaggerating the similarities.

4 Kohlberg's theory of moral development provides an example of beta bias. It ignored the possibility of a distinctly female morality. It resulted in women appearing to be inferior to men in terms of moral reasoning.

5 Gilligan's identification of a distinctive female morality helped to redress this imbalance. However, she may have exaggerated the differences between males and females. Critics have accused her of alpha bias.

6 There are differences between males and females. The main debate lies in the explanation for these differences – are they biologically based (nature) or culturally based (nurture)?

7 Feminist psychologists have tended to reject biologically-based explanations as a) untrue, b) androcentric and c) political.

8 Feminist psychologists have challenged 'androcentrism' in psychology, and taken steps to expose and avoid gender bias. They tend to be 'social constructionist' in their approach and to emphasise: meaning and subjectivity rather than objectivity; involvement and participation rather than neutrality and detachment; and qualitative rather than quantitative methods.

Unit 2 Cultural bias

KEY ISSUES

1 **What is culture and cultural bias?**

2 **Can changes in culture over time lead to changes in psychological knowledge?**

3 **To what extent have psychologists ignored the significance of culture?**

4 **Is the experimental method free from cultural bias?**

Although this situation is changing quite rapidly, the vast majority of psychologists throughout history have been men. It is also true that the vast majority of psychologists are from rich industrialised countries, and most, in fact, are from the USA. In short, most of what we call psychological knowledge is based on findings from research conducted using students from US university campuses.

This raises the question of the extent to which knowledge from one specific culture can be generalised to the rest of the world. Could it be that North Americans act in a way that is typical of North Americans, and not of anybody else? If so, then knowledge based on their actions will be culturally specific – it will be limited to United States' culture. If this knowledge is assumed to apply to everybody, then we might call it culturally biased, particularly when it is recognised that at least three quarters of the world's population live in relative poverty outside of industrialised societies.

2.1 Culture and cultural bias

Defining culture

Culture is the learned shared behaviour of members of society. It is learned rather than inborn or innate. It is shared in the sense that most people in a particular society share a similar culture. Language is an aspect of culture. For example, most people in British society have learned the English language and are able to communicate in terms of it.

Culture includes norms – accepted and expected ways of behaving; beliefs – explanations for what happens, statements about what is true and real; and values – views of what is good, worthwhile and worth striving for.

Some definitions of culture focus on meaning. For example, Rohner (1984) defines culture as an organised system of meanings which provides a shared way of making sense of different aspects of the world. Religion provides an example of an aspect of culture which imposes meaning on a range of events and relationships – birth, puberty, marriage and death are often given particular meanings and significance by religion.

Cultures are not static – they change. Fashions in clothes over the past 100 years provide an example of cultural change. Cultures vary from society to society. For example, fashion norms in one society may be seen as unusual, strange or even bizarre in another society.

Defining subculture

A *subculture* is a 'culture within a culture'. It refers to a group within a larger society whose members have certain norms, values and beliefs which are different from the mainstream culture. For example, it has been argued that ethnic minority groups in the United Kingdom have distinctive subcultures. The term *youth subculture* has been used to describe the behaviour of certain groups of young people. For example, so-called heavy metal subculture is distinguished by a particular style of music, distinctive clothes and hairstyles, a love of powerful motorbikes and the open road, and a dislike of straight, nine-to-five lifestyles.

Cultural bias

Cultures and subcultures are clearly vital aspects of human behaviour. They guide and direct action, they shape perception, they influence thought, they constitute world views. Psychology is the study of human thought and action. But, for most of its history, psychology has largely ignored culture. Only in the last 20 or 30 years have psychologists realised its significance. There is now a recognised subdiscipline called *cultural psychology* or *cross-cultural psychology* which examines psychological questions across cultures. For example, a cross-cultural psychologist would examine attachments between caregiver and child in a range of different cultures.

This ignorance of culture over much of psychology's history is one example of cultural bias. Various forms of cultural bias are outlined below. They are examined in more detail in later sections.

- **Ignoring culture** The term bias suggests a one-sided, distorted view. In this sense ignoring culture can be seen as a biased view, since it leaves out one of the most important constituents of human behaviour.
- **Culture doesn't matter** Many psychologists have assumed that the findings of research conducted in the West are universally applicable – they apply to all societies, no matter what the differences between their cultures. Cross-cultural research clearly shows that this assumption is wrong. Culture does matter.
- **Cultural change doesn't matter** Cultures change over time. Cultural or historical change must be taken into account. Many psychologists have assumed that their findings apply to past, present and future societies. This assumption cannot

be made, it must be tested.
- **Culture and psychology** Psychology is a Western, largely North American creation with a relatively short history. It will inevitably reflect Western culture and cultural changes over the past 150 or so years. Indeed, psychology has often been accused of having a Western cultural bias.
- **Ethnocentrism** This is the most obvious form of cultural bias. It incorporates aspects of the preceding forms of bias. Ethnocentrism means seeing and evaluating other cultures in terms of the norms and values of your own culture. Psychology has often been accused of ethnocentrism – of seeing and judging the world in terms of Western, and more particularly, North American culture. Western psychologists have been accused of seeing the West as the centre of the world and looking out and looking down from this vantage point.

Key terms

Culture *The learned, shared behaviour of members of a society. Culture includes social norms, attitudes, values and beliefs which are generally shared by people in a particular society.*

Subculture *Learned, shared behaviour which is distinctive to certain groups within a society. While sharing many aspects of the mainstream culture, these groups have certain norms, values and beliefs which differ from the culture of society as a whole.*

Ethnocentrism *Judging, evaluating and interpreting other cultures in terms of the standards and beliefs of one's own culture.*

2.2   Historical bias

The fact that cultures change over time offers the possibility of studying cultural bias by looking at *historical changes* in cultures. Cultural bias that shows up through looking at historical changes in a culture is sometimes called *historical bias*. A good example of this is the changing views of homosexuality. Before 1973, homosexuality was identified in the *Diagnostic and Statistical Manual of Mental Disorders* (DSM) as a pathology or illness. Psychological theories were proposed as to its causes and how to 'cure' it, and psychological techniques were developed in an attempt to 'help' homosexuals with their 'problem'. After 1973, it was removed from the DSM and hence no longer considered an 'illness' or 'problem'. Since that date, psychologists have begun turning their attention to identifying the new pathology or problem of 'homophobia' – an irrational prejudice towards homosexuals.

This example shows that as a culture changes, so views on things like sexuality and deviance may also change. British culture has changed a lot in terms of how gay sexuality is viewed. Less than half a century ago, homosexuality was generally considered by the heterosexual majority to be either a sin or illness, and certainly a crime. Today it is more acceptable, with high-profile gay TV personalities such as Julian Clary, Graham Norton, and Josh and Brian of *Big Brother* commanding widespread approval and even adoration. Homophobia (hatred of gay people) still exists, but now it is also likely that homophobic people will be the target of general criticism, particularly amongst the educated public. As the general cultural feeling about homosexuality changes, so do the psychological theories, as reflected in the removal of homosexuality from the DSM. We can draw the following conclusions from this:

- Psychological knowledge is inevitably influenced and biased by the prevailing attitudes, values and beliefs of the mainstream culture.
- As culture changes, so to some extent does psychological knowledge.
- But, at the same time, prevailing attitudes, values and beliefs are influenced by psychological knowledge, which has become an important part of our culture.

As another example of such change, consider the following entry for 'aversion therapy' from the *Encyclopaedia of Psychiatry for General Practitioners*, 1972.

'The aim of this variety of behaviour therapy is to discourage a form of behaviour which is undesired yet repeatedly performed. In the simplest way, punishing a child for misbehaving can be considered "aversion therapy", but by using the experimental findings of psychological learning theory the techniques have been enormously refined. Aversion therapy is most frequently applied in alcoholism and sexual perversions, notably transvestism, fetishism and homosexuality. In one successful method in transvestism the patient repeatedly cross-dresses on an electrified grid, and electric shocks just strong enough to be definitely painful are applied to the feet according to a pre-determined schedule during the cross-dressing. The outcome with sexual deviants also depends upon the severity of the patient's personality disorder, and the extent of his normal sexual interest which one hopes will replace his deviant behaviour.'

Hopefully, the application of this kind of 'treatment' to gay people and cross-dressers is now a thing of the past, since viewing such 'life-style choices' as abnormal and ill is increasingly seen as an ugly prejudice. Times change, and so does psychology.

2.3   Universal etics and local emics

A useful distinction made by cultural psychologists is that between the *etic* and the *emic* (see also pp 301-303). Behaviours which are thought to be universal (to occur worldwide without exception) are called etics, and behaviours which are thought to be specific to one, or perhaps a few cultures, are called emics (Berry, 1989). The goal of most psychology, particularly experimental psychology that aims to be a natural science, is to discover etic, or universal aspects of psychology. To put it crudely, psychologists are usually not interested in how this or that person's mind 'works', but in how the human mind works. Problems of bias occur if psychological knowledge thought to be etic, or universal, is in fact emic, or specific to the place where it was 'discovered'.

Moghaddam (1998) identifies various examples of etics. For instance:

- In all cultures there is a norm whereby people take turns whilst speaking. If a person is addressed, they are expected to respond – if they do not, it is taken that there is something wrong with the interaction.
- It is a universal quality of human beings to evaluate the world in negative and positive terms, and to make these

evaluations central to existence.
- It is also true that inequalities of power and status occur in all societies.

Other behaviours, such as playing tennis, participating in classroom discussions, and driving on the left side of the road, are clearly emic. If we assume in our research that everybody drives on the left or plays tennis, then cultural bias creeps in. Treating an emic as if it was etic in this way is known as an *imposed etic*.

Key terms

Historical bias *A form of cultural bias revealed when looking at the effects on knowledge of changes in culture through time.*

Emic *Behaviours that are specific to one or a few cultures or subcultures.*

Etic *Behaviours that are universal.*

Imposed etic *Assuming that an emic is an etic, that is assuming that a local behaviour is universal.*

Kohlberg, again

Kohlberg claimed that his theory of moral development was universally applicable or etic. Gilligan rejected this claim, arguing that it was gender biased (see pp 527-529). Other research has indicated that Kohlberg's theory has a built in cultural bias. In particular, his third level (Stages 5 and 6) appears to be limited to wealthy, urbanised, Western nations with well-developed bureaucracies and strong economies.

In a review of cross-cultural research which used Kohlberg's theory and techniques, Snarey (1985) found that people from poor rural or village cultures (such as rural Kenya, rural Turkey, New Guinea and Guatemala) never reason at Level 3 (Stages 5 and 6). Again, the conclusion Kohlberg would have drawn from this is that such people are morally inferior since they operate at a lower level of moral development, and at a lower cognitive level.

Instead, it seems much more likely that the theory is culturally biased. It was born in the USA and, like other US exports such as Coca-Cola, McDonalds and Bruce Springsteen, has a typical US feel to it. Level 3 emphasises individual morality and personal responsibility. This reflects the focus on individualism, on individual freedom and responsibility, found in Western cultures, and in particular amongst middle-class, white, urban North Americans. In placing this kind of reasoning at the pinnacle of his stages of moral development, Kohlberg is reflecting the values of this group. He is making a statement of *value* which is hidden by the fact that it is dressed up in the language and procedures of science. To assume that Level 3 moral reasoning is universal, that is found in all cultures, is to impose an emic – to treat what is culturally specific as if it were culturally universal.

See pp 525-526 or further comment on cultural bias in Kohlberg's theory of moral development.

Optimistic bias

Research conducted in the 1950s on how people perceive risks of various sorts eventually led to the conclusion that most people are over-optimistic about the risks they face. This over-optimism came to be called *optimistic bias*, which can be defined as the tendency for people to think they are less likely than their peers to suffer from negative life events such as specific illnesses, prison sentences, mugging, nuclear attack, and so on. Much data gathered in the 1980s, using various methods, supported this conclusion (Weinstein, 1987). This was considered an important finding, since it was reasoned that if people are too optimistic – if, for instance they think that compared to others they are not likely to develop AIDS – then they may be less likely to take necessary precautions. If, to give another example, you are optimistic that you will not suffer any harmful effects from global warming, then it may be that you will not commit yourself to protecting the environment. After a review of the relevant studies, Taylor and Brown (1988) concluded that 95% of people exhibit OB (or optimistic bias).

But is OB really culturally universal (etic), or is this research itself culturally biased (an imposed etic)? Kleinnhesselink and Rosa (1991) point out that most researchers of optimistic bias would predict that there should be no differences across cultures in the extent to which people 'suffer from' OB. This prediction is based on theories such as that of Weinstein (1987) which hold that the reason so many people are optimistically biased is because the human brain is a faulty information processor. Our brains have to deal with so much information that it is normal to 'cut corners'. Optimistic bias is therefore explained as the end result of a kind of information processing short-cut. So, for example, when asked to compare how at risk you are of becoming a drug addict or catching a sexually transmitted disease compared to the 'average' person, you are likely to be swayed by your own personal experience or by comparing yourself not with an 'average' person but with someone you associate with the risk in question. Hence, for Weinstein, ordinary people are under the influence of 'cognitive illusions' which together produce the mistaken impression of being less at risk than the average person. In sum, the reason no cultural differences would be expected is because the OB phenomenon is *explained* as an effect of the way brains *naturally* and *normally* function. All humans have basically the same brain, therefore all should be optimistically biased. In terms of this reasoning, OB is an *etic* phenomenon.

However, broad differences between Western and non-Western cultures have in fact been found in the ways people perceive and act upon risk. This evidence indicates that the Western response to risk is distinct from the non-Western. Kleinnhesselink and Rosa (1991) found that Western societies are more individualistic than non-Western societies, which are typically more collective. This means that when thinking about risks, Westerners tend to think in terms of the individual, whereas non-Westerners tend to think in terms of the group. This leads Westerners to be more prone to OB, since they think that, as individuals, they are able to control the risks they face. This was backed up by Heine and Lehman (1995) who found Canadians (Westerners) to have a higher level of OB than Japanese (non-Westerners). Morrison (1999) even found two tribes in Malawi to be unrealistically *pessimistic* in the face of certain risks – such as the risk of catching malaria. Taken together, these findings suggest that the

original OB work was culturally biased since it is more applicable to Westerners than to non-Westerners (Joffe, 1999). In other words, the early research, through mistakenly assuming OB to be etic, imposed what is in fact an *emic* phenomenon on to all cultures. This provides another example of an imposed etic.

2.4 Bias in experimental method

How come psychologists can even claim to produce 'culture free', 'objective' knowledge? The main reason, the usual story, is that, unlike priests, politicians and wise grandmothers, they tend to use experimental methods.

Changing minds

Consider the following situation. You've been all but rejected at a job interview, but you've been given one last chance to change the interviewing panel's mind. Your wise uncle tells you to wear a suit, be polite and don't be afraid to crack the odd joke. How does he know – common-sense, personal experience? Can you depend on either of these? Don't his suggestions simply reflect his own bias and prejudice? You'd be far better asking a psychologist who has conducted experiments on changing minds. You would obtain objective data on which to base your interview performance. For example, you might learn that 'credible, serious-looking communicators' are most likely to change opinions.

This is why the teaching of scientific methods is such a central part of any training in psychology. It is also why a good experimental method, just like a good set of scales or good dice, should be designed to cut out the possibility of bias.

Just such an experiment on changing minds was attempted by Hovland and Weiss (1951). Their study took place in the USA before nuclear submarines had been invented, during the 'cold war' when North Americans were deeply suspicious of communists from the USSR. In their experiment, they tried to persuade the participants that it was indeed possible to build such a thing as a nuclear submarine. They hypothesised that people would be more likely to change their minds and agree with this possibility if they heard the argument from someone with 'high credibility'. Their independent variable therefore had two conditions to it. A message communicated by a 'low credibility communicator' (a message from Russian communists), and a 'high credibility communicator' (a message from J. Robert Oppenheimer, a prominent and respected American scientist). Having these two conditions means that it is possible to manipulate or vary the independent variable in a controlled way, to see if it has an effect on the dependent variable. In other words, some participants can be exposed to the 'low credibility communicator', and some to the 'high'. The dependent variable in this experiment was measured by scores of opinion change. The hypothesis was that there would be more opinion change in those participants who heard the claim about submarines from Robert Oppenheimer. This is exactly how the results turned out. But even experiments are not immune from cultural bias. How, for example, did the experimenters *know* that Russian communists would be low on credibility and Oppenheimer high on credibility? As Stainton Rogers et al. (1996) put it:

'They (the experimenters) could only have known this because they shared the same common-sense cultural knowledge as the subjects (the participants) of their experiments. The effect is "obvious" because they (the experimenters) "knew" it in advance.'

Key term

Optimistic bias *The tendency for people to think they are less likely than their peers to suffer from negative life events.*

In other words, the experimenters were drawing upon a taken-for-granted cultural assumption held by people in the US during the 1950s. We would not expect this taken-for-granted assumption to apply in many other places (certainly not in the USSR!). Bias is therefore *built in* to the very design of the experiment. Just like your uncle's advice, this seemingly 'objective' finding is ultimately based on 'common-sense' and 'personal experience'. The results emerged because the participants and the experimenters share – or at least are aware of – the same values (communists should not be trusted, but Oppenheimer – the father of the US atomic weapons project – is perfectly trustable and reliable). The phenomenon, in other words, is emic, and only *looks* like it is etic.

Of course it might be argued in defence of the experiment that what matters are not the details of *who* is found credible, but just that *whoever* is found credible in a given place at a given time will be more persuasive. But stripped of its 'details' this seems a fairly banal, trite and insignificant finding since the word 'credible' simply means 'convincing', 'believable', 'reliable'. So to say that those who are credible are persuasive is not to say very much more than stating 'being a bachelor causes men to be unmarried'.

The appearance of science

What we can say is that in a culture that believes in science, knowledge that looks like it is 'scientific' is more convincing than knowledge that doesn't. This is probably why those who want to persuade others to fall in line with their politics or ideology so often use the language of science. Sadly, because science gives the appearance of being value free, it provides the best vehicle for the unnoticed smuggling in of bias and prejudice. Consider the following example of *drapetomania*.

'In the 1800s, Dr Cartwright 'identified' a disease of slaves, *drapetomania* … Much like a cat's unfortunate habit of straying, drapetomania was characterised as an irrestrainable propensity on the part of slaves to run away to escape from slavery. Quite clearly, slavery itself was not seen to be the problem since running away was a mental illness of the slaves themselves! Seen as such, fleeing the plantation was irrational pathology, not a rightful protest. Slaves were insane if they bucked the racist system.' (Howitt & Owusu-Bempah, 1994)

Dr Cartwright had been appointed by the Louisiana Medical Association to investigate the 'strange' behaviour of African-American slaves. His report, published in 1851, was entitled 'The diseases and physical peculiarities of the negro race'. Written in impressive 'scientific' jargon, backed by his medical credentials and an authoritative medical association, it did little more than reflect the prejudices of white American subculture in the southern states. Drapetomania was 'scientific' nonsense.

Similarly, the experimental method has all the trappings of science. It promises objective knowledge. But as the example of the nuclear submarine indicates, experimental data may simply mirror cultural common-sense.

2.5   Evaluation

In recent years much good work has been done to expose the cultural biases in psychology. This should lead to psychologists taking a broader perspective on their research questions, such as always considering whether they are dealing with an emic or an

etic phenomenon. This move is part of a broader trend towards globalisation. In short, with modern transport and communications systems, the world has effectively 'shrunk' in the sense of becoming far more and far more quickly accessible. International collaborations are now far easier to undertake, and this is good for avoiding parochialism and recognising cultural factors.

A recognition of the importance of culture and the removal of cultural bias leads to all sorts of interesting questions. For example:

- What effect does culture have on human psychology?
- To what extent is human behaviour culture specific and to what extent is it universal?

These questions are now being explored as the title of Fathali Moghaddam's (1998) book suggests – *Social psychology: Exploring universals across cultures.*

The significance of cultural psychology can be seen from Unit 3 Culture-bound syndromes in Chapter 34. Only with an awareness of culture would the following questions be asked.

- Do particular cultures generate particular psychological disorders?
- Are psychological disorders universal but simply expressed in different ways in different cultures?

Despite these developments, cultural psychology still has a long way to go. First, it is still in a fairly marginal position – it has not yet entered mainstream psychology. This can be seen from the following example of ethnocentrism.

The 1994 edition of DSM listed so-called culture-bound syndromes in an appendix. The authors lumped together a number of apparently strange and disparate disorders from around the world and placed this motley collection under the heading of culture-bound syndromes. These 'syndromes' are 'not admitted into the mainstream of psychiatric illness' (Fernando, 1991). Instead, they are relegated to a catch-all category and labelled 'culture-bound syndromes'.

Western psychiatry dominates the world and Western classification systems are often taken as 'the bible'. The disorders they list are seen 'as standard and those in other cultures as anomalies' (Fernando, 1991). As a result, disorders which do not fit Western diagnostic categories tend to be seen as exotic oddities to be dumped in appendices and defined as culture-bound syndromes. (See pp 673-676 for a fuller discussion of culture-bound syndromes.)

Second, cultural psychology is still in a relatively underdeveloped state. Theoretical and methodological innovations are needed. Problems include:

- Difficulties in measuring culture and its impact. How, for example, do we know that people's behaviour is directed by culture or by the situation they find themselves in?
- A tendency to treat culture in an over-simplified way. For example, assuming that culture is shared to the same degree by all members of society.
- A tendency to describe cultures with broad brush stokes – for example, this is an 'individualistic culture', this is a 'collectivistic culture'. Such broad generalisations cover up much of the detail and subtlety of culture.

Despite these problems, cultural psychology is here to stay. One form of cultural bias is ignoring culture – assuming that all human beings are essentially the same. Slowly but surely, this form of cultural bias is being eroded.

Summary

1 Being unaware of culture or dismissing it as insignificant can be seen as forms of cultural bias.

2 Most psychological knowledge has been produced from students on US university campuses by white, middle-class US males.

3 The assumption that this knowledge applies to all human beings is an example of cultural bias.

4 Historical bias is a form of cultural bias. It ignores the possibility that knowledge is influenced by changes in culture over time.

5 The distinction between etics and emics is useful when looking at cultural bias. Behaviours which are etic are universal; behaviours which are emic are specific to one or a few cultures or subcultures.

6 The imposed etic assumes that culture-specific behaviour is universal. This is an example of cultural bias.

7 Kohlberg's theory of moral development and Weinstein's research on optimistic bias have been seen as examples of the imposed etic. Critics have argued that their findings are not universal, that they are limited to Western culture.

8 Cultural bias is present in the research process itself. For example, the findings of Hovland and Weiss' experiment on opinion change simply reflected common-sense cultural knowledge.

9 Cultural psychology generates new and interesting questions. It reveals ethnocentrism and exposes cultural bias. It recognises the significance of culture.

Activity 2   Identifying cultural bias

Item A   Traditional Cheyenne culture

The Cheyenne lived on the Great Plains of the USA, west of the Mississippi River and east of the Rocky Mountains. The following account describes part of their traditional way of life which came to an end at the close of the 19th century when they were defeated by the US army and placed on reservations.

The Cheyenne believe that wealth, in the form of horses and weapons, is not to be hoarded by the owner. Instead it is to be given away. Generosity is highly regarded and people who accumulate wealth and keep it for themselves are looked down upon. A person who gives does not expect an equal amount in return. The greatest gift they can receive is prestige and respect for their generous action.

Bravery on the battlefield is one of the main ways a man can achieve high standing. Killing an enemy, however, does not rank as highly as a number of other deeds. Touching or striking an enemy with the hand or a weapon, rescuing a wounded comrade, or charging the enemy alone while the rest of the war party looks on are amongst the highest deeds of bravery. The Cheyenne developed war into a game. Killing large numbers of the enemy is far less important than individual acts of courage which bring great respect from

Cheyenne photographed in 1889

other members of the tribe. The brave deeds of a warrior are recounted at meetings of the warrior societies. They may lead to his appointment to the tribal council and to the position of war chief, which means others will follow him into battle and respect his leadership.

Adapted from Hoebel, 1960

Item B   Lancet editorial

In 1840, the *Lancet*, the journal of the British Medical Association, carried an editorial on the physical and mental harm caused by the loss of semen. Doctors believed that virtuous young men absorbed the spermatic fluid which enriched the blood and vitalised the brain. Sir Isaac Newton was quoted as saying he had never lost a drop of semen.

Adapted from Singh, 1992

Item C   Education, race and culture

Differences in the expectation of classroom interaction between Britain and the West Indies create cultural misunderstanding. In the West Indies, children were not expected to talk or contribute within the classroom as much as in Britain. British teachers see this lack of response as indicating either silent hostility or low intelligence.

Adapted from Howitt & Owusu-Bempah, 1994

Item D   IQ tests and culture

The ability to answer the kinds of questions asked by IQ testers depends heavily on one's past experience. During World War 1, the Army Alpha test asked Polish, Italian and Jewish immigrants to the USA to identify the product manufactured by Smith and Wesson and to give the nicknames of professional baseball teams. For immigrants who could not speak English, the Army Beta test was designed as a 'non-verbal' measure of 'innate intelligence'. That test asked the immigrants to point out what was missing from each of a set of drawings. The set included a drawing of a tennis court with the net missing. The immigrants who could not answer such a question were thereby shown to be genetically inferior to the tennis playing psychologists who devised such tests for adults.

Adapted from Rose et al., 1984

A picture-completion test

Item E   Research methods and literacy

The major research methods of social psychology, the laboratory procedure and survey methods, are not suitable for many parts of the world. This is in part because such methods require participants to be literate, but more importantly because such methods require familiarity with the idea and culture of research. The very research methods of social psychology have local rather than universal applicability. Roughly one billion adults aged 15 years and over in the world are illiterate. About 97% of these are in the developing countries.

Adapted from Moghaddam, 1998

Questions

1   Psychologists study topics such as aggression, relationships and motivation. Judging from Item A, why is culture relevant to such research?

2   How can Item B be seen as an example of historical bias?

3   Read Item C.

   a) Why might some British teachers see the lack of contribution from African-Caribbean children as indicating 'low intelligence' or even 'hostility'?

   b) In what way does the confusion indicate cultural bias in education?

4   a) Identify examples from Item D where something 'local' (emic) is assumed to be 'universal' (etic).

   b) What is the danger of assuming that tests such as these are objective measures of innate intelligence?

5   Read Item E.

   a) Why might psychological research methods be 'local' in their usefulness and not 'universal'?

   b) Do you think that Item E shows that psychology is biased against people who are illiterate?

Unit 3   Ethical issues raised by research involving human participants

KEY ISSUES

1   **What ethical guidelines are applicable to psychologists?**

2   **What is socially sensitive research?**

3   **What special ethical and practical issues are raised by socially sensitive research?**

3.1   Introducing ethics

Ethics is the study of the nature and basis of moral thought, feeling and behaviour. Ethics and morality are to do with what is right and wrong. It is usual for professional groups, such as lawyers, doctors, teachers and scientists, to work according to a *code of ethics*. Codes of ethics are often written down in some form. They are guidelines that help professionals to steer their conduct in a direction that maximises positive outcomes and minimises negative outcomes.

Scientists, including psychologists, often have professional bodies called *ethics committees*. An ethics committee is made up of a group of interested and informed professionals. When a psychologist proposes to do a piece of research, they write a 'research proposal' outlining in detail what is to be done, how, and why. As part of this proposal, it is expected that the researcher will outline any ethical issues that are raised by the research, and how the researcher will deal with these issues. One of the most important jobs of an ethics committee is to scrutinise such proposals and to judge, on the basis of agreed principles, whether or not the proposal can be given 'ethical clearance'. This is, whether or not it is acceptable from an ethical point of view.

There are numerous ethical issues that are raised when undertaking research involving human participants. The most important ones have been dealt with in Chapter 15, Ethics and research. This chapter should be consulted as important background to this unit. There, two classic studies in social psychology were used to illustrate the ethics of research – the Milgram study of obedience and the Zimbardo simulation of prison life. These studies raise various ethical issues because they violate various cherished moral principles. These principles include:

Do not harm other people Both Milgram's and Zimbardo's studies caused a significant amount of psychological suffering to those people who participated.

Respect the autonomy of others Both studies placed participants in situations where their autonomy was not respected. Autonomy refers to an individual's right to freedom of action, their right to make their own decisions. In the Milgram study participants were verbally coerced into continuing with the experiment, and in the Zimbardo study one group of participants were permitted to restrict the autonomy of another.

Do not lie to people or knowingly deceive them The design of both studies involved deception of the participants. Milgram's participants were deceived as to the nature of the experiment, and Zimbardo's were not told that they would be arrested by state police at the start of the study.

Key terms

Ethics *The study of the nature and basis of moral thought, feeling and behaviour.*

Ethics committee *A committee employed to scrutinise research proposals and to judge, on the basis of agreed principles, whether or not the proposal can be given 'ethical clearance'.*

Ethics as steering a difficult course between two obstacles

It would be naive and incorrect to draw the conclusion that people such as Milgram and Zimbardo are simply liars who harmed other people in their research and intruded upon their autonomy. Both Milgram and Zimbardo present arguments that any harm caused to their participants by their experiments is outweighed by the good that comes from what we learn from their findings. This kind of weighing up of the pros and cons is called a cost-benefit analysis.

Ethical decisions are rarely 'cut and dried' issues in which there is one correct answer. It is more accurate to think of the process of reaching ethical decisions as like steering a difficult path between two dangerous obstacles. On one side, we must avoid harming people, on the other side, if we shy too far away from harming people, we will neglect important knowledge that might lead to longer-term harm to more people, or a missed opportunity to provide benefits to humanity.

Balancing the wrongs done to the individual against the benefits offered to society

In this light, it is significant that both Milgram and Zimbardo (and their many supporters) saw themselves as making *ethical* points through the very nature of their research. Both wanted to show the harm that people can do to one another, simply through the influence of sometimes barely noticeable social factors. Zimbardo is explicit that his research question is itself ethical – he describes his research as concerned with the 'banality of evil'. By this he means to correct the illusion that bad deeds are done by bad people. He suggests instead that what we typically have are evil-generating *situations*, not evil *people*. Milgram's point is very similar. Both argue that a small amount of controlled harm and deception was necessary to drum home these broader ethical points about the banality of evil and the power of social situations.

The bottom line for these researchers is that the knowledge we now have about the situational causes of 'evil' is useful to humanity as a whole, and can justify the relatively minor amount of harm done to the participants. How we measure the benefit to society of such studies is less clear. Some would say that they tell us nothing we didn't already know from bitter real-world experience. Bettelheim (cited in Miller, 1986), for instance, was scathing about Milgram's claims to be promoting ethics, calling the study 'vile' and valueless. As a Holocaust survivor he knew first-hand about the evils that otherwise ordinary people can commit.

3.2 The BPS ethical principles

In 1998 the British Psychological Society published the latest version of its *Ethical principles for conducting research with human participants*. These can be thought of as guidelines designed to help researchers to make judgements as they steer a path between ethical obstacles. In brief, these include:

1 **Informed consent** Research participants must explicitly give their consent to take part, and this consent must be based on adequate information – it must be *informed*. They must know what they are letting themselves in for, and must agree to this.

2 **Deception** Sometimes full informed consent is not possible since it would ruin the design of the study. In such situations psychologists use deception. But the BPS guidelines state that 'intentional deception of the participants over the purpose and general nature of the investigation should be avoided whenever possible'. In attempting to avoid deception, researchers should: carefully consider other ways of pursuing their research goals (alternative, non-deceptive procedures may be available); consult with colleagues about the possible impact of deception on participants; and reveal the deception to the participants after the experiment, as part of debriefing.

3 **Debriefing** Once the study is finished participants must be given a full disclosure telling them the aims of the research and how the design met these aims. If distress or other negative emotions are caused, the debriefer must offer reassurance and support.

4 **Protection from harm** Researchers have a responsibility to protect their participants from physical or mental harm

during the study. If undesirable consequences do result from participation, the researcher is obliged to detect and remove these. As part of protection from harm, the guidelines stress the importance of *confidentiality* (this is usually achieved by making sure any information provided by the participant is anonymous and untraceable) and of making it clear that the participant can *withdraw* at any point during the investigation.

Evaluation

Guidelines such as these were drawn up precisely because of debates that resulted from ethically questionable studies such as those conducted by Milgram and Zimbardo. It is very unlikely that either of these two studies would be granted ethical clearance in Britain and North America today. Such guidelines are an indication that it is no longer acceptable for psychologists to 'play god' and cause harm to other individuals in the name of a higher goal (usually 'the good of society') without seriously considering the costs as well as the benefits. They are part of a growing recognition that research participants have rights and must be accorded status and dignity (see the discussion of the terminological shift from 'subjects' to 'participants' on page 219. This must be considered a positive move.

However, psychologists operate within a rapidly changing world, and it is crucial that ethical guidelines and regulations constantly adapt to these changes. Both psychology itself and society's conception of morality are undergoing changes. For instance, as knowledge of the brain increases, psychology is becoming increasingly 'high-tech' (involving brain-scanning technology, for example) and increasingly allied to medicine and biology (the brain is a biological organ that can malfunction). The more this happens, the bigger become the ethical issues. For example:

- Ought we to give drugs to 'hyperactive' children with attention-deficit/hyperactivity disorder? (See pp 708-709 and 758-759).

- Under what conditions should laser surgery of the brain be allowed? (It is increasingly used in cases of extreme anorexia, for instance.)

- Is it ethical to screen young children in order to discover which ones are in danger of becoming psychopaths?

These are big ethical questions, and it is arguable that the current guidelines do not adequately deal with them.

Finally, it is also the case that cultural changes in moral thinking are related to developments in psychology. For example, many psychologists are encouraging us to think of criminal psychopaths as having mental problems rather than as being bad people. If psychologists are increasingly becoming the judges of morality, this raises the question of 'who judges the judges'? Serious thought needs to be applied to the problem of changing morality.

3.3 Socially sensitive research

This section looks at the ethical and practical issues raised by research that is socially sensitive. It begins by examining three definitions.

Research with social consequences Sieber and Stanley (1988)

define socially sensitive research as:

'Studies in which there are potential consequences or implications, either directly for the participants in the research or for the class of individuals represented by the research. For example, a study that examines the relative merits of day care for infants against full-time care by the mother can have broad social implications and thus can be considered socially sensitive. Similarly, studies aimed at examining the relation between gender and mathematical ability also have significant social implications.'

This is a broad definition that includes any research that may have serious social consequences. Most applied work in psychology would come under the heading of 'socially sensitive', since applied research necessarily has social consequences, otherwise it wouldn't be applied. Certainly much of the research discussed in Unit 1, which directly or indirectly involves gender issues, is highly socially sensitive by this definition.

Research on taboo topics A more restricted definition of socially sensitive research is provided by Farberow (1963) who discusses research that deals with 'taboo' topics. Taboo topics are topics that are emotionally charged and difficult to face. A good example is research into child sexual abuse. A characteristic of taboo topics is that they tend to be shrouded in secrecy and difficult to talk about, raising special technical as well as ethical difficulties for the researcher.

This focus on taboo is different to the focus given by Sieber and Stanley with their examples of gender and mathematical ability and the relative merits of different kinds of care for infants. These examples tend to be emotionally charged not because they are taboo but because of their *controversial* nature (see Activity 3). They are controversial because the conclusions reached are likely to lead to social consequences. For instance, if it is argued that boys are better at mathematics than girls then this may have the consequence of lowering the expectations that girls, their teachers and families have of them in this area, and this in turn may become a 'self-fulfilling prophecy'. Taboo topics, by contrast, are not necessarily controversial in this way. In fact, by definition they are often not spoken about at all, and so are rarely even acknowledged sufficiently to allow a 'controversy' to develop. Both, however, are certainly examples of socially sensitive research.

Research which poses a threat to those involved A third definition accommodates both of those above. For Lee (1995), socially sensitive research is: 'research which potentially poses a substantial threat to those who are or have been involved in it'. Note that this accommodates both previous definitions since the threat can be the result of either a taboo, or of the fact that an issue is controversial.

Lee (1995) identifies three broad areas of socially sensitive research.

- **Research which poses an intrusive threat.** This is research that looks at questions and issues that are stressful, and of a private, personal, even possibly sacred, nature. This may include things like research into people's financial situation or their sexual behaviour. Stenner (1993), for instance, studied the feelings of romantic jealousy amongst soon-to-be-married couples. This turned out to be a very sensitive topic since partners revealed information unknown to the other which could potentially upset the marriage. Although these need not be sensitive topics for everyone and for all cultures, for many participants such research is highly sensitive.

- **Research which poses a threat of sanction.** This includes research into illegal or 'deviant' activity. The threat here is that information may be disclosed which might lead to otherwise hidden deviant activity being revealed. Lucia Sell-Trujillo (2001), for instance, studied a social practice common on the Spanish island La Gomera called *relating as conocidos.* A conocidos is an acquaintance that can be called upon to provide a favour, even if that favour is against the law. Such research is sensitive because this way of relating is usually kept mysterious, even to those who engage in it. To reveal what is going on may result in profound changes to people's relationships, and possibly to the local culture.

- **Research which poses a political threat.** Some topics are political in that they mesh or clash with the vested interests and power struggles of various groups, individuals or institutions. Brewer (1990), for instance, studied policing in Northern Ireland, an intensely political question given the long history of violence in that region. But questions of education, race and ethnicity, health and so on can also be, or become, political 'hot potatoes' – a topic that people become hypersensitive towards.

Special technical and ethical issues faced by researchers of socially sensitive topics

Doing socially sensitive research raises special technical as well as ethical difficulties for the researcher. Some of these are listed below, but it is important to note that all of the BPS ethical guidelines listed previously continue to apply to sensitive research.

- Researching sensitive and threatening topics can require a great deal of innovation and imagination on the part of the researcher. For example, it is often simply not possible to ask direct questions and expect direct answers when secrecy is an inherent part of the topic under study. So, in her study of 'relating as conocidos', Sell-Trujillo found it necessary to engage in participant observation, effectively becoming a part of the daily life of the islanders she observed. As part of his study of jealousy amongst couples, Stenner involved his participants in role-playing activities so that they could provide their information in an indirect, less threatening way.

- Trust plays an especially important role in the data collection process. Often in sensitive research the researcher enters into the confidence of the participant, since personal information is disclosed. It is thus important to build a trusting relationship and to ensure confidentiality at all times. This also means treating participants as human beings with equal standing to the researcher, and not as 'objects' to be manipulated.

- The researcher must make themselves aware of the consequences of publishing the sensitive information they acquire. Participants should be made aware of the publishing process and should be given the option to withdraw from the research and withhold their contribution.

- The researcher should also do all they can to block and otherwise prevent any negative repercussions that might follow from the research.

- Researchers should, where possible, be explicit about their own values and how they influence the research being undertaken.

- If researching political issues and issues involving clear power dynamics it is sometimes the researcher who can find themselves in the relatively powerless position. It can be difficult to get research access to people in powerful positions and it is common in such situations for the researcher to be pressured to take a biased viewpoint, or if the conclusions threaten the powerful, to stop the research entirely. This is one of the reasons psychologists usually end up studying people in relatively powerless positions, such as children, institutionalised adults, blue-collar workers, and so on.

Summary

1. Ethics is the study of the nature and basis of moral thought, feeling and behaviour.

2. Psychologists work according to ethical principles such as: the ideal of informed consent; the avoidance or minimisation of deception; the requirement to debrief participants; and the obligation to protect participants from harm.

3. Socially sensitive research includes research which has social consequences, research on 'taboo' topics, and research which poses a significant threat to those involved.

4. Special technical and ethical issues raised by socially sensitive research include: the need for methodological innovation; the importance of trust; the obligation to be aware of the consequences of the research and to make the participants aware of this too; the requirement to block negative repercussions; the need to be explicit about the researchers' own values; and the problem of dealing with powerful figures.

Activity 3   Socially sensitive research

Item A   Bowlby and his 'affectionless psychopaths'

In 1951, John Bowlby made an influential argument, based on studies of children evacuated from cities during World War 2 and of 'delinquent' children. He argued that separation from the mother is highly traumatic for young children and can lead to a failure to establish strong emotional attachments. Children who fail to establish strong attachments to their mother by the age of about three may never be able to form attachments to humans and may become 'affectionless psychopaths' (dangerous people with severe emotional difficulties).

Bowlby campaigned widely to spread the message that mothers should stay at home with their children and develop strong emotional attachments with them. Mothers who do not devote themselves to childcare, he implied, are in danger of turning their children into damaged and dangerous adults. This includes mothers who leave their children with child carers in order to work. Later studies by psychologists such as Clarke and Clarke (1976), Rutter (1982) and Tizzard, (1991) have argued that separation need not be damaging, that children can form many attachments (not just with mother) and that even with early separation, later secure relationships can be formed.

Item C   The feminist response

Free and available childcare has long been a demand of the feminist movement as essential for women's liberation. At the same time, feminists have challenged the assumption that women are responsible for childcare. It is not surprising that psychological theories that appear to confirm women's place in the home, that claim children suffer if they are not in the full-time care of their mothers, and that suggest that children who have personal or behavioural problems in their later lives have been inadequately mothered, have attracted particular criticism.

Adapted from Burman, 1994

Item B   An ideal mum?

April 1955, a time when Bowlby's ideas were popular

Item D   Blaming the mother

'Through the child, the mother was made responsible for violence and social chaos in the world outside the family, a world from which she was more or less excluded.'

Singer, 1992

Questions

1 Read Item A. In what ways was Bowlby's research 'socially sensitive'?

2 Why would Bowlby probably approve of mum in Item B?

3 Read Item C. Why did Bowlby's theory provoke such outrage, particularly from feminists?

4 In what respect does Bowlby's theory make mothers responsible for 'violence and social chaos' (Item D)?

Unit 4 Psychological research and other activity with non-human animals

It is now known that chimpanzee DNA differs from human DNA by only 1.6%. In other words, 98.4% of chimpanzee and human DNA is shared in common. Does this mean that chimpanzees should be given basic rights just as human beings are? Does it mean that we should resist those who tend to treat chimpanzees as if they were objects owned by people and usable by people as they please? Does it mean that we should stop using chimpanzees in our scientific research? If you think the answer to this last question is 'yes' then it is also important to recognise that we only *know* that so much genetic information is shared between chimpanzees and people because scientists have conducted research to find out. This raises one of the important issues to be dealt with in this unit. What justifies research with non-human animals? And, more practically, what guidelines and restrictions do psychologists who work with animals have in place to guide and limit the way animals are treated?

4.1 Laws and guidelines on research with animals

Before examining the debates that have taken place around this question, let us first turn to some of the guidelines that have been imposed upon psychologists who involve animals in their research.

In 1985, the British Psychological Society (BPS) and the Experimental Psychology Society (EPS) jointly published guidelines on the use of animals in psychological research. The drawing up of these guidelines was overseen by a new BPS committee called the Standing Advisory Committee on Standards for Psychological Research and Teaching Involving Animals (SACSPRATIA). Shortly afterwards, an Act of Parliament governing all animal research in the UK was passed – called the Animals (Scientific Procedure) Act of 1986. More recently SACSPRATIA was renewed, improved and, thankfully, renamed the Standing Advisory Committee on the Welfare of Animals in Psychology (SACWAP). SACWAP reviewed the guidelines, and put forward a new Statement of Policy on the Use of Animals in Psychology in 1998. These new guidelines have been approved by both the BPS and the EPS and appear in the current BPS Code of Conduct Booklet. In order to find out what position the British Psychological Society takes on the controversial issue of the welfare of animals in psychology, these two sets of guidelines are the best place to look. First we will examine the 1985 guidelines, then the 1998 guidelines.

Basically, the 1985 guidelines take the form of a checklist of 14 points. Psychologists who work with animals are required to carefully consider these guidelines when preparing any work with animals.

Summary of the 1985 *Guidelines on the use of animals in psychological research*

1 **The law** The United Kingdom has various laws protecting animals that must be complied with, otherwise prosecution may result. The laws are designed to prevent 'pain, suffering, distress or lasting harm' and all researchers working with animals that will suffer must be in possession of a licence from the Home Office. The most significant part of the 1985 legislation was the requirement that before a licence will be given, the Home Office must do a cost-benefit analysis. This is the *costs* of undertaking the research (for example, any pain and suffering inflicted on animals) must be weighed against the likely *benefits* of the research for humanity. UK legislation also stipulates that harmful procedures should be avoided where possible, but where not possible, a local ethical review committee must be convinced of the impossibility of avoidance of harm, pain and distress. If given ethical clearance, it is necessary for any adverse effects on animals to be formally recognised and assessed, and for measures to reduce harm, pain and distress to be implemented wherever possible. These legal requirements apply to all animal research in the UK, and not just to psychological research.

2 **Ethical considerations** A cost-benefit analysis must establish that any suffering or harm caused is justified by the knowledge gained through the procedure. Researchers are also instructed to consider if alternative ways of gaining the knowledge that do not negatively affect animals are possible.

3 **Species** The researcher must carefully consider which species of animal to work with. Some procedures may cause more pain or discomfort to some species than to others, for instance.

4 **Number of animals** Efforts must be made to use the smallest number of animals necessary for effective research. For example, the use of better experimental designs can reduce the number of animals required.

5 **Endangered species** Unless part of a serious effort of conservation, animals from endangered species should be neither collected for research purposes, nor manipulated in experiments.

6 **Animal suppliers** Full records should be kept of where animals have come from and what studies they have been involved in, and those who supply animals must be reputable and accountable.

7 **Caging and social environment** When keeping animals in cages it is necessary to take account of the social behaviour of the species in question. Some species require fewer animals per cage, for instance, and some fare better when kept in the company of their own species.

8 **Fieldwork** Research in the field should be conducted so as to minimise the disturbance of animals in their natural habitats. For instance, even simple observations of wild animals can hinder their breeding. The researcher should be informed about the needs and preferences of different species.

9 **Aggression and predation including infanticide** In studying things like aggression, predation and infanticide amongst animals it is recommended that observations be made of encounters in natural settings rather than, for example, staging aggressive encounters. If staging is necessary, then ways of minimising any pain and injury should be considered, such as separating animals with glass walls, restricting the number of animals involved and keeping the studies as short as possible.

10 **Motivation** Some studies involve depriving animals, for instance, of food. If such studies are strictly necessary, consideration must be taken of the animal's regular patterns of consumption and its metabolic needs. Deprivation may affect some species more than others, and this must be considered when selecting animals.

11 **Aversive stimulation and stressful procedures** Some experiments involve the use of pain and other stressors. The investigator in such cases must have considered alternative ways of conducting their experiments. However, if the use of aversive stimuli is seen as absolutely necessary, then the pain and stress must be kept to the minimum level required. For example, if studying learning in rats by using an electric shock, mild shocks that cause little obvious distress should be used if possible. It is not necessary to use strong shocks in many learning experiments.

12 **Surgical and pharmacological procedures** It is necessary for investigators to acquire a Home Office licence before undertaking surgery on vertebrate animals and before using drugs as part of an experimental procedure. Staff must have had the necessary training and experience, and must be aware of how to use anaesthesia and how to prevent infections that may result from surgery. Investigators using drugs must be experienced and aware of the different pharmacological effects that drugs have on different animals. For instance, a drug that is harmless to one species may be toxic to another.

13 **Anaesthesia, analgesia and euthanasia** In research involving surgery, care must be taken to reduce any pain and suffering by, for instance, using analgesics (eg, pain killers) and anaesthetics where appropriate. The condition of animals must be monitored on a frequent basis. If an animal is found to suffer severe and enduring pain it must be killed (euthanasia).

14 **Independent advice** Investigators conducting research with animals should always consult a qualified second opinion – preferably from a veterinarian, but certainly from someone not involved in the research – whenever any doubts about the wellbeing of an animal arise.

Evaluation of the 1985 guidelines

You will notice that all of these guidelines are to do with the use of animals in psychological *research*. They cover the selection and supply of animals for research, their preparation for use in experiments, their treatment during experiments, their care after experiments, and so on. This focus on research is a little too narrow, since animals are also used for *teaching* purposes (eg, rats may be used for demonstrations of the principles of learning theory). Also, increasingly, psychologists are using animals as *therapy assistants*, because the presence of animals, from fish to cats and dogs, can be very comforting and therapeutic to some people. Another growing field involves doing therapy on psychologically disturbed animals – 'pet therapy', for example. Finally, some psychologists may be involved in the use of animals for commercial purposes (advertising, for instance). All of these activities with animals need to be regulated to ensure that animals are correctly treated.

The 1998 *Statement of policy on the use of animals in psychology*

The following statement, published as part of the BPS code of conduct, ethical principles and guidelines (May 1998), is the most recent proposal on this topic (proposed by SACWAP). The guidelines are broader in scope and begin to accommodate the use of animals in therapy, teaching and commerce as well as in research. In the list from 1-9 below, these guidelines are quoted directly:

1 Members of the Society take differing views about the merits of animal research in psychology. Some are opposed in principle, others believe such research has made a vital contribution to human and animal welfare in the past and will continue to do so. Recognising this absence of consensus, the Society seeks to sustain a constructive discussion between the viewpoints.

2 Recognising that animals are currently used for psychological purposes, such as research, teaching and therapy, the Society seeks to further their welfare.

3 The Society endorses the principles of Replacement, Reduction and Refinement: that animals should only be used when there are no alternatives; that the number of animals used in procedures causing pain or distress should be minimised; and that the severity of such procedures should be minimised.

4 All use of animals in psychology must be consistent with the relevant legislation and its accompanying guidance documents, primarily the Animals (Scientific Procedures) Act (1986). The Society is particularly concerned that in all psychological use of animals, the benefits to be gained should clearly outweigh the costs to the animal(s) involved.

5 The Society has prepared a set of ethical guidelines for the use of animals in psychology, and expects all members to abide by them [note – these are the 1985 guidelines discussed above].

6 Failure to abide by the relevant laws or the Society's ethical guidelines will constitute a breach of the Code of Conduct that applies to all Members including Chartered Psychologists.

7 The Society will not accept for publication in its books and journals primary reports of research using animals in a way that is inconsistent with relevant legislation and the Society's ethical guidelines.

8 This policy will apply to any psychological work involving animals (see 2 above) even when that work has a wider

focus that includes other disciplines.

9 In furtherance of this policy, the Society's Scientific Affairs Board has established a Standing Advisory Committee on the Welfare of Animals in Psychology.

Activity 4 Animal rights and animal wrongs

Item A   Anticipatory drinking

In 1900, Sherrington conducted a series of animal experiments designed to discover which parts of the body are necessary for the expression of emotions to occur. Could a dog still show a fearful or a disgusted response, for example, if its heart and stomach had been surgically disconnected from its brain? To test this Sherrington transected the vagus nerves and the spinal cord of dogs and cats. This operation destroyed the connection between the brain and the heart, lungs, stomach, bowels, spleen, liver and so on. He called these mutilated dogs and cats 'head and shoulder' animals.

In one study, to test whether 'head and shoulder' dogs would still exhibit the 'disgust behaviour' of ordinary dogs he offered them as food the flesh of another, now dead, dog. The 'head and shoulder' dogs refused to eat, thereby showing that the 'disgust behaviour' was still intact despite the fact that the brain had been disconnected from most of the other major bodily organs.

Item B   Harlow's monkeys

In the 1960s Harry Harlow conducted a series of experiments with rhesus monkeys on the topic of attachment. These involved separating infant monkeys from their mothers at birth. In one experiment, eight such infant monkeys were isolated in separate cages. In each cage Harlow placed two artificial 'mothers': one constructed out of soft terry towelling material, and the other constructed out of a bare wire frame. Half of the baby monkeys received milk from a container and teat attached to the soft surrogate mother, and half received milk from the wire surrogate. Harlow found that the monkeys fed by the wire mother would visit 'her' only to feed and would then, especially when deliberately terrified, cling for comfort to the milkless soft surrogate.

The two 'mothers'

In later studies, Harlow exposed the baby monkeys to harsh rejections. In one variation, the soft surrogate was fitted with metal spikes that could be protruded through the towelling, forcing the monkey away. In another, strong jets of air were emitted from the surrogate. But in all cases the monkey would return to the soft surrogate once the 'rejection period' had finished.

Harlow concluded that comfort and security rather than food formed the basis for early mother/infant attachment. However, attachment to the soft surrogate mother was not sufficient for healthy social development. The infant monkeys showed many problems in adulthood. They were either indifferent or abusive to other monkeys, and they had difficulty with mating and parenting.

Questions

1 Why do you think these studies used non-human animals rather than people?

2 Do you think it is morally acceptable to treat animals in these kinds of ways?

3 Do you think that what was learned from these experiments justifies the suffering that the animals were put through?

4 What steps would you take to minimise the suffering of the animals in these experiments?

4.2   Arguments *for* working with non-human animals in psychology

Guideline 1 in the 1998 statement above refers to the continued existence of a heated debate amongst psychologists, and also the general public, on the question of the use of animals by psychologists. We will now explore this debate. As with any debate, there are pros and cons for each position. The following are the pros.

1 **Animal work helps us to further psychological knowledge.** Darwin established that all animals are ultimately evolved from common ancestors, and molecular biologists added to this by discovering that all animals (apart from a few bacteria) are constructed from essentially the same chemical blueprint of DNA. It has therefore become plausible that the study of animal behaviour and physiology can illuminate our understanding of human psychology. Many of the principles of learning theory, for instance, were developed using animals such as dogs, rats and pigeons. And these principles apply to people as well – people can be conditioned just as rats can. Likewise, studies on animals of the brain pathways that are used to process emotional information, such as those related to fear, are likely to be informative about the processing of emotional information in people.

2 **Working with animals makes it easier to tightly control experimental designs, and hence to achieve better**

objectivity in research. Think of how much easier it would be to run a learning experiment with mice than with human beings. Mice are smaller and so require less space. They have a relatively high rate of reproduction, so new mice are relatively easily available. It is estimated that nowadays some 25 million mice are born in scientific laboratories every year! They tend to live in or close to the laboratory and so complicated arrangements do not need to be made before they are on site and available. They can be easily kept in a small, contained space, such as a Skinner box, since that is more or less how they would be kept as pets anyhow. Their behavioural responses can be measured in a relatively unambiguous way. They don't require debriefing as to the reasons for the experiment. For these and several more reasons, non-human animals are typically more controllable and manageable than human animals. Of course this rosy picture of comparatively manageable animals should not fool you into thinking that there are no practical problems that arise in animal work.

3   **Animal work helps in the advance of medical knowledge and is beneficial to humanity.** Although chimpanzees are, genetically speaking, the closest 'relatives' to human beings, animals such as mice are also genetically very similar to us. As a result, we share very similar physiology with other animals. For instance, the internal biochemistry of a mouse is regulated by hormones in much the same way as ours. This means, amongst other things, that mice tend to get the same diseases for the same reasons as we do. As a result, a case can be made that chimpanzees, rats, mice and many other animals provide good 'models' for working out what makes us physically and, by extension, psychologically unwell, and what can be done to put this right. Work with animals is therefore useful in saving or prolonging human life, in increasing health, and in reducing human suffering.

Much of this work has been medical rather than psychological. Animal work in medicine has led to the development of vaccines for many diseases, such as tetanus and whooping cough, and has been vital in the development of procedures such as organ transplantation. But we should expect psychological similarities too. For example, work on learning theory using animals has had an impact on the development of therapies used with people. A strong statement of this kind was made by the British Association for the Advancement of Science in 1990: 'Continued research involving animals is essential for the conquest of many unsolved medical problems, such as cancer, AIDS, other infectious diseases, and genetic, developmental, neurological and psychiatric conditions'.

4   **Animals can be used in experiments where it would be unethical to use humans.** Although humans are very similar in biological terms to many other animals, we do not consider it morally acceptable to test out new scientific and medical procedures and to explore possible causes of pathological conditions using human beings. Many modern medical products and other consumer products have been tested using animals for this reason. In fact, the Medicines Act of 1968 requires by law that all new medicines have been tested on non-human animals before being used by humans.

5   **Animal work can be interesting in its own right.** Studying animal behaviour can be done for its own sake and,

arguably, needs no other justification than that it is interesting. The discipline of ethology, for instance, developed as the study of animals in their natural environments. As numerous popular natural history television programmes illustrate, ethology is something that is of general interest to people, not only to scientists. The same can be said for psychological work that looks into questions such as whether non-human animals can learn merely from observing one another, whether they can learn rudimentary language skills, and so on.

6   **Animal work can help us to know more about how and why animals suffer.** A case could be made that it is only through increasing our scientific knowledge about animals that we can answer questions such as the extent to which different animals are capable of suffering and the exact conditions an animal requires for mental and physical health. Our knowledge of such questions is surprisingly limited. Bateson (1992) argues that for an animal to suffer it must possess receptors that are sensitive to painful stimulation, and brain structures which enable it to be conscious of its suffering experience. On this basis, Bateson suggests, for example, that insects probably do not experience pain.

7   **Animal work can help animals.** Although nobody would claim that 'sacrificing' animals in experiments is helpful for the victims concerned, some work that psychologists do with animals, such as so-called 'pet therapy', is designed to improve the quality of life of the animals treated. Also, ethological research may provide knowledge which helps improve the conditions of animals in captivity – such as in zoos or on farms. Much of the knowledge we need to help conserve rare animals and endangered species comes from ethological studies of animals in their natural environment.

4.3 Arguments *against* working with non-human animals in psychology

1   **It is ethically wrong to attempt to further human welfare at the expense of harm and suffering to animals.** Many people have strong convictions that much work using animals is not justified by the benefits that follow from it. Some, such as the philosopher Peter Singer (1975), liken our modern treatment of animals to the way in which human slaves were treated historically. One day, the argument goes, we will look back with horror at the way we treat animals, just as we now look back in horror at human slavery. Singer sees similarities between our treatment of animals and other forms of oppression, such as racism and sexism. His argument is that animals should have 'rights' just like people. At this point in history they lack such rights. Animals are 'sacrificed' to science, industry and business every minute of every day. The 'good health' and 'progress' of humanity seems possible only at the price of a mountain of animal corpses. This is an ethically problematic position.

2   **The story of 'human progress' is a kind of 'emotional blackmail'.** The killing of animals is typically justified through a kind of 'us or them' argument. Crudely put, the argument states that if the animals don't suffer, then people will. In this way, arguments *against* harming animals in experiments are made to look as if they were really

arguments *for* harming people. The implication is that there are no limits to human 'progress'. In principle, we can prevent human illness and death. This, of course, is ultimately a delusion, since there must always be limits to human progress. But in not accepting limits, the 'human progress' argument can go on forever, and it will always be necessary to 'sacrifice' animals in the never-ending quest of making human life more and more comfortable and tranquillised. So, an important argument against the harmful use of animals in research is an argument based on setting a *limit* to human progress. As put by Tom Regan (1983): 'If abandoning animal research means that there are some things we cannot learn, then so be it'.

3   **It may be possible to develop non-harmful alternatives to using animals in experiments.** As it is relatively easy to conduct research with animals, there is not much pressure to look for alternative ways of answering our scientific and medical questions that do not harm animals. If the use of animals were made more difficult, then other techniques would have to be developed as a replacement. New technologies, such as CAT scans and MRI scans make it possible to 'look' inside living bodies without having to harm them, and these could be developed in some cases as an alternative to harmful procedures. Computer simulations can also be used, since these can be very sophisticated and might provide useful models for situations in which real animals would otherwise be used. Another alternative, in some cases, is to use 'tissue cultures' (isolated sections of animal tissue) rather than whole live animals.

4   **Animal work is of limited value in helping us to further psychological knowledge.** It is a scientific fact that we humans share nearly all our DNA with chimpanzees (98.4% of it is shared). But, given this genetic similarity, it is striking how very different humans and chimpanzees actually are. Chimpanzees have nothing like the sophisticated powers of language that we have. Their use of tools is vastly less complex than ours, and they do not develop sophisticated cultures in the way that we do. If anything, this suggests that even a tiny difference in genetic constitution can lead to enormous differences in the psychological functioning of animals. As a result, it cannot be assumed that the behaviour, thoughts and feelings of chimpanzees, let alone mice, makes a good model for that of humans. Chimpanzees, if they can be described as getting 'depressed' at all, are unlikely to get depressed for the same reasons and in the same ways as humans. From this perspective, experiments on animals tell us little about human psychology.

5   **Ethological fieldwork can be harmful.** Even ethological fieldwork on animals may cause disruption to the animals being studied, even though they are not directly harmed. For example, repeated handling through capture – often needed so animals can be tagged for identification – can produce distress in animals and increase their energy expenditure.

Evaluation of the debate

Guidelines for animal research drawn up by bodies such as the British Psychological Society reflect the ongoing debate. For example, the 1998 BPS guidelines show greater concern for animal welfare than those of 1985. This reflects the growing opinion against using animals in laboratory studies. Despite this,

many animal rights activists reject such guidelines, seeing them as condoning animal research.

Most people, however, are pleased to see that animal research is being more tightly regulated. Compared to the recent past, the following positive changes have been made to ensure professional responsibility in dealings with non-human animals:

* If research using animals is claimed to be beneficial to humanity then that has to be *explicitly shown* as part of a cost-benefit analysis.
* If such research is shown to benefit humanity in concrete ways then this still needs to be weighed against any suffering caused to animals, and these costs have to be explicitly evaluated.
* Non-harmful alternative ways of answering the questions set in the research need to have been carefully considered.
* The design of experiments must be carefully thought through with an eye to minimising the number of animals that need to be used (eg, by employing more powerful statistical techniques).
* Scientific publications of research using animals are increasingly required to be explicit about the ethical issues that were involved.
* Any suffering caused must be kept to a minimum.
* Careful and informed decisions need to be made about the species of animal to be used.
* The conditions animals are kept in must meet high standards.
* The animals need to have come from legally recognised and accountable sources.
* There are tight controls over what can be done with animals after they have served in psychological studies.
* Animal care staff must be educated about the principles of animal psychology.
* If and when animals need to be killed, this must be done using humane and approved techniques to minimise suffering.
* If and when animals are used as part of psychology teaching, it is strongly suggested that ethical issues are discussed with students, and students should be encouraged to form their own views on ethical questions.

However, this issue is one that is changing fast. It must be recognised as being part of a broader cultural and historical change taking place in the UK and elsewhere towards giving more consideration to animals and to the environment. Just as psychologists are now more likely to refer to those they work with as 'participants' rather than 'subjects', so the hope is that we will stop talking about doing research *on* animals and start working *with* animals. It is also important that this be a change in attitude and practice and not a mere switching of words.

Psychologists must not be complacent about having to change their views in the face of these broader shifts. In fact, to conclude, this chapter as a whole tells the story of how this broader shift has affected all areas of psychology. Psychologists, some enthusiastically and some reluctantly, are moving towards a far more reflexive and thoughtful relationship to their subject matter. This relationship increasingly involves taking account of the biases that influence our work, and of the ethical consideration we owe to those, both human and non-human, we work with. In short, psychology is becoming an integrated part of society.

Summary

1 Research with animals in psychology raises many ethical issues. This research is regulated by ethical guidelines produced by bodies such as the British Psychological Society (BPS).

2 The 1998 BPS guidelines extended those of 1985 and began to accommodate the use of animals in teaching and therapy as well as in research.

3 Arguments *for* working with non-human animals include:

- Animal work helps us to further psychological knowledge.

- Working with animals makes it easier to tightly control experimental designs, and hence to achieve greater objectivity in research.

- Animal work helps in the advance of medical knowledge and is beneficial to humanity.

- Animals can be used in experiments where it would be unethical to use humans.

- Animal work can help us to know more about how and why animals suffer.

- Animal work can help animals.

4 Arguments *against* working with non-human animals include:

- It is ethically wrong to attempt to further human welfare at the expense of harm and suffering to animals.

- The story of 'human progress' is a kind of 'emotional blackmail' - it is used to justify the killing of animals.

- It may be possible to develop non-harmful alternatives to using animals in experiments.

- Animal work is of limited value in helping us to further psychological knowledge.

- Even ethological fieldwork on animals may cause disruption to the animals being studied.

References

Bateson, P. (1992). Do animals feel pain? *New Scientist, 134*, 30-33.

Bem, S.L. (1974). The measurement of psychological androgyny. *Journal of Consulting and Clinical Psychology, 42*, 155-162.

Berry, J. (1989). Imposed etics derived emics: The operationalisation of a compelling idea. *International Journal of Psychology, 24*, 721-735.

Bowlby, J. (1951). *Maternal care and mental health.* Geneva: World Health Organisation.

Broverman, I.K., Vogal, S.R., Broverman, D.M., Clarkson, F.E. & Rosenkrantz, P.S. (1972). Sex-role stereotypes: A current appraisal. *Journal of Social Issues, 28*, 59-78.

Brewer, J.D. (1990). Sensitivity as a problem in field research: A study of routine policing in Northern Ireland. *American Behavioral Scientist, 33*, 578-593.

British Psychological Society. (1998). *Code of conduct, ethical principles and guidelines.* Leicester: BPS.

Burman, E. (1994). *Deconstructing developmental psychology.* London: Routledge.

Burr, V. (1998). *Gender and social psychology.* London: Routledge.

Chodorow, N. (1978). *The reproduction of mothering.* Berkeley: University of California Press.

Clarke, A.M. & Clarke, A.D. (1976). *Early experience: Myth and evidence.* London: Open Books.

de Castillejo, I. (1973). *Knowing women: A feminine psychology.* London: Hodder and Stoughton.

Farberow, N.L. (1963). *Taboo topics.* New York: Atherton Press.

Fernando, S. (1991). *Mental health, race and culture.* London Macmillan/Mind.

Gilligan, C. (1982). *In a different voice: Psychological theory and women's development.* Cambridge, MA: Harvard University Press.

Haan, N., Smith, B. & Block, J. (1968). Moral reasoning of young adults. *Journal of Personality and Social Psychology, 10*, 183-201.

Harding, S. (Ed.) (1993). *The racial economy of science.* Bloomington and Indianapolis: Indiana University Press.

Hare-Mustin, R.T. & Maracek, J. (1988). The meaning of difference: Gender theory, postmodernism and psychology. *American Psychologist, 43*, 455-464.

Heine, S.J. & Lehman, D.R. (1995). The cultural construction of self-enhancement: An examination of group-serving biases. *Journal of Personality and Social Psychology, 72*, 1268-1283.

Hoebel, E.A. (1960). *The Cheyennes.* New York: Holt, Reinhart & Winston.

Hollway, W. (1984). Gender difference and the production of subjectivity. In J. Henriques, W. Hollway, C. Urwin, C. Venn & V. Walkderdine (Eds.), *Changing the subject: Psychology, social regulation and subjectivity.* London: Methuen.

Hovland, C.I. & Weiss, W. (1951). The influence of source credibility on communicative effectiveness. *Public Opinion Quarterly, 15*, 635-650.

Howitt, D. & Owusu-Bempah, J. (1994). *The racism of psychology: Time for change.* Hemel Hempstead: Harvester Wheatsheaf.

Johnson, R.A. (1976). *She: Understanding feminine psychology.* New York: Harper and Row.

Joffe, H. (1999). *Risk and the other.* Cambridge: Cambridge University Press.

Kleinnhesselink, R.R. & Rosa, E.A. (1991). Cognitive representations of risk perceptions: A comparative study of Japan and the United States. *Journal of Cross-Cultural Psychology, 22*, 11-28.

Lee, R.M. (1995). *Doing research on socially sensitive topics.* London: Sage.

Maccoby, E. & Jacklin, C. (1974). *The psychology of sex differences.* Stanford, CA: Stanford University Press.

Merchant, C. (1979). *The death of nature.* London: Wildwood House.

Miller, A.G. (1986). *The obedience experiments: A case study of controversy in social science.* New York: Praeger.

Moghaddam, F.M. (1998). *Social psychology: Exploring universals across cultures.* New York: Freeman & Co.

Regan, T. (1983). *The case for animal rights.* Berkeley: University of California Press.

Rohner, R. (1984). Toward a conception of culture for cross-cultural psychology. *Journal of Cross-Cultural Psychology, 15*, 111-138.

Rose, S., Kamin, L.J. & Lewontin, R.C. (1984). *Not in our genes: Biology, ideology and human nature.* Harmondsworth: Penguin.

Rutter, M. (1982). *Maternal deprivation reassessed.* Harmondsworth: Penguin.

Sell-Trujillio, L. (2001). *Relating as Conocidos: Observing a social practice in an island context.* Unpublished Ph.D. Thesis: London School of Economics and Political Science.

Sieber, J.E. & Stanley, B. (1988). Ethical and professional dimensions of socially sensitive research. *American Psychologist, 43*, 49-55.

Singer, E. (1992). *Child-care and the psychology of development.* London: Routledge.

Singer, P. (1975). *Practical ethics.* Cambridge: Cambridge University Press.

Singh, S.P. (1992). Is dhat culture-bound? *British Journal of Psychiatry, 160*, 280-281.

Snarey, J.R. (1985). Cross-cultural universality of social-moral development: A critical review of Kohlbergian work. *Psychological Bulletin, 97*, 202-232.

Spence, J.T. (1985). Achievement American style. *American Psychologist, 40*, 1285-1295.

Spender, D. (1982). *Invisible women.* London. Routledge.

Stainton Rogers, W. & Stainton Rogers, R. (2001). *The psychology of gender and sexuality.* Buckingham: Open University Press.

Stainton Rogers, R., Stenner, P., Gleeson, K. & Stainton Rogers, W. (1996). *Social psychology: A critical agenda.* Cambridge: Polity Press.

Stenner, P. (1993). Discoursing jealousy. In E. Burman & I. Parker (Eds.), *Discourse analytical research: Readings and repertoires of texts in action.* London: Routledge.

Taylor, S.E. & Brown, J.D. (1988). Illusion and well-being: A social psychological perspective on mental health. *Psychological Bulletin, 103*, 193-210.

Tizzard, B. (1991). Employed mothers and the care of young mothers. In A. Phoenix, A. Woollett and E. Lloyd (Eds.), *Motherhood: Meanings, practices and ideologies.* London: Sage.

Walkerdine, V. (1991). *Schoolgirl fictions.* London: Verso.

Weinstein, N.D. (1987). Unrealistic optimism about susceptibility to health problems: Conclusions from a community wide sample. *Journal of Behavioural Medicine, 10*, 481-495.

Wetherell, M. (1986). Linguistic repertoires and literary criticism: New directions for a social psychology of gender. In S. Wilkinson, (Ed.), *Feminist social psychology.* Milton Keynes: Open University Press.

Wilkinson, S. (1986), (Ed). *Feminist social psychology.* Milton Keynes: Open University Press.

► Introduction

This chapter looks at some of the broader conceptual debates within psychology. Rather than dealing with specific studies, or particular methods, it introduces some of the more philosophical and political arguments that rage or murmur within psychology. Are our activities guided by choice and free will, or are they determined by forces beyond our control? Can human activity be reduced to biology, or is there a specific and irreducible 'psychological' level of analysis? Are we creatures of nature, or products of culture? Is psychology a natural science, or should it belong in the humanities?

Chapter summary

- Unit 1 discusses the free will versus determinism debate.
- Unit 2 addresses the problem of reductionism.

- Unit 3 examines the nature-nurture debate.
- Unit 4 looks at the debate as to whether or not psychology is a science.

Unit 1 The free will versus determinism debate

KEY ISSUES

1 What are determinism and free will?

2 What different positions have psychologists taken on the free will/determinism debate?

3 What role does 'accountability' play in discussions of free will?

Do we have 'choice' in how we act, or are we 'driven' by forces outside of our control? Is our behaviour directed by our genes, giving us little say in the matter? Are we programmed by our culture, by our schooling and training, to behave in particular ways? Or do we define our own destinies for ourselves and act accordingly? Do we behave like an orchestra – programmed by the genetic code of a musical score and conducted by the rhythmic hands of hormones? Or are we like a jazz quartet that improvises according to the feeling and demands of the situation? These are questions of determinism and free will.

1.1 Defining determinism and free will

Determinism What exactly is determinism? The *Concise Oxford Dictionary* defines determinism as:

'the doctrine that all events, including human actions, are determined by causes regarded as external to the will'. Note that *by definition,* determinism is opposed to the idea of free will. Causes 'external to the will' may be either external to the

individual (eg, an action may be a response to stimulation from the environment) or internal (eg, an action caused by a hormone secreted into the blood). What matters is that the causes are *external to the will* of an individual.

Free will An act of free will is an act that is independent of external or internal causes, and so is not coerced or forced. If the will is free, it is not directed or constrained. In other words, it is autonomous, it has the freedom to act independently.

1.2 The importance of the idea of 'choice'

In the background of this debate is the following question: how much weight, if any, should be given to the idea that people can *choose* what they do?

Strict determinism holds that we have no choice, since our actions are determined by forces outside of our will. This position developed from the discoveries of the natural sciences, like physics, chemistry and biology, that nature appears to be governed by physical laws and that we, being also made of physical matter, should be no exception. It was the successes of these sciences that provided the basis for thinking that what people do is determined by causes. The determinism/free will debate can be seen as an *extension* of a way of thinking that works well in one place (in describing the actions of chemicals, or the movements of the planets, for instance) to another place (describing the actions of people). Is this extension workable? Can it be applied to human action? To psychology?

To argue that determinism is not applicable to human action is to argue that people are *different* in some fundamental way from other objects and animals in the world. Arguments for such differences include the following:

- Humans live in a world mediated and constructed by language and meaning.
- We operate according to judgements of right and wrong (normative judgements).
- We have legal and political systems and institutions that assume a concept of free will.
- Unlike other objects and animals, we are interested in interpreting and studying the world and ourselves.

For some, these differences mean that it is illegitimate to use strictly deterministic arguments in psychology. The extension of natural science perspectives to cover human action can be seen as a kind of colonisation. When Europeans colonised the Americas they extended European culture to that continent. But there were already Native Americans living there before it was 'discovered'. Likewise, scientific thought moved from its home territory of physical objects and started to colonise human action. But there were already ways of thinking about human action in place before scientific psychology was 'discovered'. To continue the parallel, just as there was violent conflict between European colonisers and Native Americans, so the deterministic position encountered conflicts with other cherished ways of thinking. The free will/determinism debate arises in this zone of confrontation.

1.3   The Cartesian settlement

Historically, this kind of confrontation has been going on for many centuries. In fact, one of the roles played by philosophers in the last 500 years has been to provide ways of thinking that allow a kind of truce or settlement to be made between scientific and normative (moral, ethical, religious, political) ways of thinking. The most famous of these settlements is that invented by the 17th century French philosopher René Descartes. Descartes gave his name to *Cartesian dualism* (see Chapter 39). This dualism has been enormously influential in the development of psychology. Cartesian dualism is basically a clear distinction between mind and body. This provided a way of arguing that humans are fundamentally different from other objects and animals. Descartes developed a tradition that argues that God gave us free will, and that it is this that distinguishes humans from objects and mere animals. Although much criticised, this is a clever solution. It allows us to think of human beings as uniquely placed somewhere between the natural world (governed deterministically by causes) and the supernatural world (in which God has absolute free will). In this way of thinking, the 'mind' has free will, the 'body' is determined, and human beings are a combination of mind and body. This allowed a 'settlement' because deterministic science could continue dealing with objects (including the human body), but thought or 'mind' was exempt from scientific study.

For many scientists, the dualistic settlement is problematic for several reasons.

- It leads us to give up asking questions. We simply have to accept that humans have free will and that this makes us different from animals.
- It polarises the issue into extremes. Complete determinism is thought to reign in the physical world. Complete free will is thought to reign in the mental world.
- The 'mind-body' polarisation is compounded by the fact that, for Descartes, this dualism was also heavily *value*

laden. Freedom is the highest value. To be determined is to be servile: the human body is the dumb slave of the free mind.

- More importantly for psychologists, such a view more or less excludes the scientific study of psychology. For this reason, some of the founding fathers of the major perspectives on scientific psychology held strong views about the determined nature of human thought, feeling and action. We will now briefly consider some of these views.

Key term

Cartesian dualism *A fundamental distinction made by Descartes between mind and body.*

1.4   Some classic responses from psychologists to the free will/determinism debate

William James and 'soft determinism'

James was one of the founding fathers of psychology. As such, it was necessary for him to directly confront the question of the extent to which deterministic thinking can be extended to psychological questions. In his classic book *Principles of Psychology* (1890) he explicitly recognised the existence of a conflict between a deterministic 'natural science' view of the world and other more 'common-sense' views which assume the existence of choice. James' 'settlement' of this problem was subtly different to that of Descartes. James was a pragmatist and so offered a pragmatic or practical solution. Basically, he argued that psychology, if it is to be a natural science, must think deterministically and approach its subject matter as if it were like any other object in the world. However, practically speaking, this need not mean that we abandon the notion of free will or other 'non-scientific' ways of thinking. James argued that, just as there are many types of tools for different jobs, so there are many kinds of explanation that are useful in many different contexts. This means that deterministic explanations need not colonise every other type of explanation.

In another strand of argument, James looked scientifically at what we mean by 'will'. For him, the most essential example of something like a 'will' in operation is the phenomenon of *attention*. You, reader, for example, can voluntarily *pay attention* to what I am now writing about James. When you pay attention, your consciousness is dragged away from other things that may occupy you (such as the colour of your wallpaper or what you will be eating tonight) and focused upon a particular object of attention. Of course your attention may already be drifting away, but you can, by an effort of will, drag it back to the argument at hand! What is the cause of you paying attention? On one level, the cause is that you voluntarily chose to do it. Your 'will' was hence a cause of your attending behaviour. James saw one of the jobs of psychology as being able to explain this kind of phenomenon. He cleverly introduced a new concept – *soft determinism* – to get at the kind of situation where our behaviour is caused by our own 'will'. He suggested that there must be a mechanism or system in the brain that is capable of generating such effects of the will. This enables him to draw a distinction between actions that are caused by this hypothetical system or mechanism, and actions that are not caused by it (reflex behaviour, for instance). Actions caused by this mechanism could be described as 'freely willed'. They are 'determined' by this mechanism, but as this explanation includes the will, James called it soft determinism. Less pragmatically inclined thinkers may consider this a case of 'having your cake and eating it'.

A psychodynamic view: psychic determinism

Freud was particularly unhappy with dualistic arguments about the origins of free will. He thought they were merely expressions of ignorance and arrogance. He did not buy the argument that human beings are sufficiently different from other objects and animals to invalidate the application of deterministic science to them. For him, this is wishful thinking. Scientific progress will inevitably overcome such bias, he thought. Consider the following quotation from Freud (1915).

'In the course of centuries the naive self-love of men has had to submit to two major blows at the hands of science. The first was when they learnt that our earth was not at the centre of the universe but only a tiny fragment of a cosmic system of scarcely imaginable vastness … The second blow fell when biological research destroyed man's supposedly privileged place in creation and proved his descent from the animal kingdom and his ineradicable animal nature. This revaluation has been accomplished in our own days by Darwin, Wallace and their predecessors, though not without the most violent contemporary opposition. But human megalomania will have suffered its third and most wounding blow from the psychological research of the present time which seeks to prove to the ego that it is not even master in its own house, but must content itself with scanty information of what is going on unconsciously in its mind.'

The above quotation from Freud is very relevant to the question of determinism and free will. If you read it carefully, you will see that Freud is setting up a kind of battle between two opponents.

- On the one hand, there is science. Science, in this story, is good, brave and speaks the truth.
- On the other hand, there is human megalomania and naive self-love.

Megalomania (the delusion of thinking of yourself as all-powerful) and naive (simple-minded) self-love are bad things. But fortunately, science is winning this battle, since it has hit human megalomania with wounding blows. Question: What is the most wounding thing for self-love and megalomania? Answer: To be forced to face up to the fact that you are not all powerful and that you ought not to love yourself quite so much.

In the story told by Freud, science has done this by making us see:

- that our little planet is not the centre of the universe, but merely one planet amongst others orbiting one sun amongst others (the Copernican revolution)
- that we are not special among God's creations, but merely one form among others that evolution has taken over its long history (the Darwinian revolution)
- that we are not rational beings who choose our own destinies, but irrational beings driven by animal passions that we are rarely even aware of (the Freudian revolution).

For Freud, we *like to think* that we have free will, just as we like to think that we are the centre of the universe and that we

are not animals. It flatters us to think this, but it is not true. Free will, for Freud, is largely a myth. Even something as seemingly 'accidental' as a slip of the tongue (such as calling your partner 'dad' by mistake) is determined by the unconscious according to psychodynamic theory. For example, Freud argued that many criminals are driven by unconscious forces into situations where they are likely to get themselves caught. In this way, he argued that many criminals unconsciously *want* to get caught because they *want* to be punished (usually for emotional 'crimes' they imagine they committed when they were children).

The psychodynamic position is sometimes called *psychic determinism* since it is unconscious 'psychic' forces that are seen to drive us. Of course, if you present this idea to a convicted criminal, they will most likely see it as completely untrue, and believe that they were just unfortunate to get caught, and that it was the last thing they wanted. As Freud insisted, we *like to think* we are not determined.

However, although Freud saw our mental processes as largely governed by unconscious psychic forces, the whole point of psychoanalysis is to increase insight and to increase conscious control of these psychic forces. Freud's theory can therefore be seen as another kind of soft determinism.

A behaviourist view: environmental determinism

The behaviourist B.F. Skinner's view of determinism was in many ways very similar to that of Freud. He even wrote a book called *Beyond Freedom and Dignity* (1971) to attack what he saw as the 'myth' of free will (he thought of free will as an 'explanatory fiction'). Like Freud, he argued that we flatter ourselves into thinking we are what he called 'autonomous man'. Someone who is autonomous is completely independent and able to freely will their own actions (they are 'master in their own house' to borrow Freud's expression). For Skinner, we only think we are free and autonomous because we are ignorant of the true causes of our behaviour. However, whilst Freud thought the true causes of behaviour are to be found in the unconscious, Skinner thought they are to found in the *environment*. We act as we do because our actions have been shaped in the past by *reinforcers*. We are simply repeating what has been rewarded and avoiding what has been punished. Skinner hence advocated an *environmental determinism* that is distinct from Freud's psychic determinism. As Skinner (1971) puts it:

'Man's struggle for freedom is not due to a will to be free, but to certain behavioural processes characteristic of the human organism, the chief effect of which is the avoidance of, or escape from, so-called "aversive" features of the environment.'

Humanistic psychology – in defence of free will

Humanistic psychologists such as Abraham Maslow and Carl Rogers provide the best example of an approach to psychology based on the idea that people have free will. Whilst they recognise that people can be pushed and pulled by 'causes', they also believe that this is not *necessarily* the case. If we develop into fully authentic and self-actualised individuals, then we take control of our lives and become the active and responsible agents of our own actions.

The philosophical movement of existentialism was very influential to humanist psychologists. Philosophers such as Heidegger and Sartre argued that to be *authentic* we have to take charge of our own lives and live them according to our own designs. For them, it is all too easy to slip back into being inauthentic by letting others determine our lives, or by telling ourselves that we are determined by biology, the stars, god, or some other excuse. To live a life determined by external forces is to live a 'tranquilised' life and not to fulfil one's truly human potential. For such reasons, humanists think of approaches such as psychodynamics and behaviourism as dangerously pessimistic. They are dangerous because they trap us into thinking of ourselves as passively determined by forces over which we have no control. Humanistic psychologists see determinism as undermining human dignity. They see one of their tasks as encouraging people to become more active, and to

develop their powers as agents able to exercise free will (see Chapter 21 for more examples of this).

Key terms

Soft determinism *Actions which have the 'will' as one of their causes.*

Psychic determinism *The doctrine that our lives are dictated by unconscious psychic forces.*

Environmental determinism *The doctrine that our behaviour is dictated by factors in our surroundings.*

Activity 1 — Free will and determinism

Item A — Psychodynamic theory

Sigmund Freud saw the unconscious mind or Id as the largest part of the psyche. He believed that human beings are primarily motivated by innate or inborn drives. These drives take the form of impulses and desires which are rooted in the Id. There are two main drives – 1) the life drive, which involves an appetite for sensual and sexual pleasure, and 2) the aggressive drive, which gives rise to feelings of aggression towards the self and others. These drives underlie all human behaviour.

Item B — Behaviourism

B.F. Skinner believed that all behaviour is learned through a process of conditioning. Operant conditioning is a form of learning based on reinforcement. Positive reinforcement encourages behaviours by means of rewards. Negative reinforcement encourages behaviours by the removal of unpleasant events when those behaviours occur. Human beings are shaped by the conditioning they receive. They respond to reinforcement and act accordingly.

Item C — Humanistic psychology

Humanistic psychologists like Abraham Maslow and Carl Rogers believe that human beings have the potential to take control of their own lives. In particular, they have the potential for self-actualisation – to find fulfilment, to achieve happiness, to discover meaning in life, to develop self-understanding and to create a sense of self-worth. This potential exists in every individual – its discovery, development and growth rest primarily with the individual. Each person is ultimately responsible for creating himself or herself – for seeking and achieving self-actualisation.

Item D — Perspectives in pictures

Questions

1 Read Item A. Why is Freud often accused of 'psychic determinism'?

2 Like Freud, Skinner is often accused of adopting a deterministic perspective. Suggest why, with some reference to Item B.

3 Read Item C. Why are humanistic psychologists often seen as emphasising people's capacity for choice and free will?

4 Match each picture in Item D with one of the three perspectives outlined in Items A, B and C. Give brief reasons for your choices.

1.5 The central role of accountability in arguments for free will

I stated earlier that the free will/determinism debate arises in a zone of confrontation between natural science and other ways of thinking. Over what kinds of issues did these conflicts arise? As you might expect, one of the main sources of conflict was and is over questions of *morality* or right and wrong. Questions of right and wrong are part of a broader set of questions around *accountability*. For instance, if we do something wrong, we are typically called to account for our action if we are caught. That is, we are asked to provide an explanation, or an excuse, or some other justification. In short, we are usually accountable to others for how we act. Accountability is not just to do with bad things, however. The flip side is that we are praised and sometimes celebrated when we do something good.

Strict determinists, however, think that we have no choice in things like the friends we choose, the moods we get into, or the crimes we may think about committing. Such an extreme position raises an obvious problem when it comes to accountability. Namely, in our ordinary, everyday thinking, we tend to assume that people can make their own decisions about things. If we want to listen to the radio, and nothing is stopping us, we will go ahead and listen. More than this, we ordinarily put a great deal of *value* on our freedom to choose. To have choice taken away is a bad thing – which is why we think of imprisonment as a punishment and slavery as immoral. To give another example, some of us like to think that what separates us from animals is our capacity to choose what we do. A person can choose not to kill an antelope, or to kill it in a humane way. A lion cannot. Arguably, if we have no choice in what we do, we shouldn't be *blamed* when we do something wrong, and we shouldn't be *praised* when we do something right. That is, we cannot be held *accountable* for our actions.

Imagine these two situations.

- In the first situation, a tree branch falls on your head after being snapped by a strong gust of wind. In this situation it makes no sense to *blame* that branch or that wind for the pain that results.

- In the second situation, the same branch hits you on the head, but this time you know that it had been thrown by a long-standing enemy. Unlike the first situation, you suspect that this pain has been caused *deliberately* – your enemy *intended* to hurt you. In other words, he or she threw the stick for a reason.

In situations like this second example, where people deliberately do things that we consider bad, questions of accountability are usual. We tend to respond by *blaming* or by getting into moral and ethical debates (such as about the extent to which we might also be to blame for upsetting our enemy in the first place). The first situation, by contrast, deals simply with physical *causes*, and not reasons. If we accept the cause (a gust of wind dislodges a weakly connected branch), we do not apply moral judgements of blame, praise or responsibility. And we do not imagine that the wind or the branch acted for a 'reason' – these were simply physical causes.

Extreme determinist positions hold that all of human behaviour fits into something like the first situation. They believe that talk of 'blame' and 'morality' is out of date and pre-scientific, and that we should replace such terms with accurate and objective scientific descriptions. Extreme free-will positions hold that a clear distinction should be made between these two situations, and that human action fits into the second. Accountability, they argue, is a necessary and essential part of this second situation.

Key term

Accountability *Processes whereby people are held accountable to others for their actions, and consequently blamed or praised.*

The 'natural world' and the 'social world'

Some argue for the need to separate out two very different 'worlds' as follows:

- One is the world of natural objects connected by natural forces such as gravity. In this natural world things happen as a result of causes. Everything that happens is *determined* by a prior cause – the pain was caused by the impact of the stick on your head; the strength of the impact was caused by the velocity obtained by a given mass of stick under the force of gravity; the fall of the stick was caused by the action of the wind, and so on. It is usually the job of the natural sciences to establish these causes.

- The other is the world of human actions connected by human rules, laws and moral norms – the social world. In this world things happen as a result of *reasons*. Everything that happens in that world takes on *meaning* in relation to these reasons, and can be judged as good, bad or indifferent – my enemy threw a stick at me because, having never forgiven me for insulting him, he wants to hurt me, and so on. *Language* is central to the social world.

Of course no one would claim that *everything* in this second 'human' or 'social world' is done for a reason. A person might throw a stick for their dog that hits a passer-by *accidentally*, for example. Or they might have been forced at gun-point to throw the stick. And sometimes we behave unreasonably and unthinkingly due to physical causes, as when we are blind drunk or on the point of physical exhaustion. But such things are usually taken as *exceptions* to the rule that *usually* we are responsible and accountable for our actions – hence we apologise for our bad behaviour, and offer as an excuse that we were drunk, implying that this is not how we always behave. Most of us assume that people have some degree of free will and that this is of crucial importance to the survival of any social community.

The fact is that, rightly or wrongly, we do hold each other to be morally responsible and otherwise accountable, in that we do blame and praise each other all the time. Deterministic thinking clashes with this ordinary way of thinking. But determinism also clashes with legal thinking, the law being a formalisation of common-sense accountability. For example, the British legal system, like many other legal systems, is based upon the idea that responsible adults can choose to obey the law. Of course it is possible that somebody can be judged to have 'diminished responsibility' (they might be 'criminally insane', for example) but such cases are precisely exceptions that prove the rule that most people are considered to have free will. For this reason, many people argue that it is important to hold onto the idea that people do have some degree of free will, and that this is a very important part of being a responsible human. In fact, as I write, there is a debate going on between psychologists, teachers and politicians about whether or not we should blame school bullies for bullying children. The 'no blame' approach which gained popularity in the 1990s is now being criticised by psychologists and politicians who believe that to reduce bullying it is necessary to be clear to the bully that they are to blame for the problem. The 'no blame' approach, by contrast, sees bullying behaviour itself as something caused by other factors, and so rather than taking the side of the bullied against the bully, it sees both as part of a broader problem.

Activity 2 — The defence of Daniel Sickles

In USA in the late 1850s, Daniel Sickles killed the lover of his wife. When he went to trial in 1859 he was found not guilty of murder. This is what his lawyer said in his defence.

'He would have been false to the instincts of humanity if that rage of jealousy had not taken possession of him. When once it has entered within his breast, he has yielded to an instinct which the Almighty has implanted in every animal or creature that crawls the earth. "Jealousy is a rage of man" and although all the arguments that my learned opponents can bring, or that can be suggested, that a man must be cool and collected when he finds before him in full view, the adulterer of his wife, yet jealousy will be the rage of that man, he will not spare in the day of vengeance.'

Adapted from Stearns, 1989

Questions

1. According to the lawyer's defence, did Daniel Sickles have 'free will' in this case, or was he determined by forces beyond his control?

2. What does the defence lawyer present as the true cause of Daniel Sickles' actions?

3. Why do you think the 'learned opponents' of the lawyer tried to suggest that a person must be 'cool and collected' in such situations?

4. Who is being blamed in this defence?

1.6 Free will and biology

Nowadays psychologists do not get so excited about the free will/determinism debate. It seems clear that the human organism is extremely complex and is made up of multiple interconnected systems working at different levels of determination. For instance, some of our behaviours are purely reflex – as when we automatically blink at a puff of air directed at our eye-ball. But we can also blink voluntarily, and this is a very different activity, involving more complex biological structures in the brain. Between reflex and voluntary actions we have habit. Habitual actions are actions that have been learned so well that they become 'second nature'. An experienced typist, for instance, does not have to exercise their 'will' before hitting each key in typing a letter. However, if a mistake is made, then the typist may have to pay conscious attention to what they are doing. Cognitive neuroscientists nowadays talk of different levels of information processing.

- Reflex processing is fully automatic
- Habit may involve both fully or partially automatic processing
- Deliberate action, on the other hand, involves fully conscious or 'executive' control.

From this perspective there is no need to make an absolute decision about whether we are 'free' or 'determined'. In a sense, this represents an escape from a pseudo-debate. The debate was false because it wrongly assumed that the relationship between any two events must either be absolutely determinate or else capricious (unpredictable). However, even the natural sciences are full of examples of relationships between events that cannot be specified in a determinate way – it is extremely difficult and sometimes impossible to accurately predict the weather, for instance. In fact, since the development of thermodynamics, physicists have recognised that pure determinism is only possible in a closed system, for example in the laboratory where variables can be controlled, and that fully deterministic explanations are the exception rather than the rule.

The work of Silvan Tomkins (1962) is important on this point. He argued that instead of thinking in either/or terms (either we are completely determined or completely free), we should talk of *degrees of freedom*. This is a phrase borrowed from Gibbs (a mathematical physicist) who used it to explain the behaviour of complex systems. In comparing two systems (two computers for instance), it is often the case that one is more complex than another. A definition of a more complex system is a system *able to do more*. A system able to do more is, in an important sense, more free. The system in question might be a biological system – a human being for instance. Comparing two 65-year-old men, it may be that one of them, being healthy, is able to do considerably more than the other who is very ill. The healthy man has more *degrees of freedom* than the unhealthy man. If we compare a plant with a human being, it is clear that the human being is able to do considerably more than the plant – although there are many things the plant can do that the human cannot! The human organism is, in Gibbs' information theory terms, more *complex*, having more degrees of freedom. Complexity can thus be defined as the number of independently variable states of a given system. Complexity can thus range from:

- Complete redundancy (where no change or variability is possible), to
- Complete randomness (where any change is possible).

Tomkins thus argues for a continuum of degrees of freedom. This is much more sensible than taking the classical view, wherein there are only two possible states: complete freedom or complete determinacy. Both of these extremes would make life unviable.

Importantly, in assessing the freedom of a complex organism like a person it is also necessary to take into account the complexity of the environment. Freedom would then be defined as a joint function of the complexity of the system (the organism) and the complexity of the environment. There is no point in being an organism capable of doing many, many things if the nature of your environment does not allow you to do these things. The implication of this perspective is that a person becomes freer in two ways:

- First, through an increase in the number of things the person wants to do, and
- Second, through an increase in the person's capacities to satisfy these wants.

This is how Tomkins (1962) sums up the problem of free will and determinism:

'Man is neither as free as he feels nor as bound as he fears. There are some aspects of himself, as of his environment, which he may easily transform, some aspects which he may transform only with difficulty and others which he can never transform. He is driven by motives which vary from those with minimal freedom, such as the need for air, to those with maximal freedom, such as the wish for excitement.'

Key term

Complexity or degrees of freedom *The number of independently variable states of a given system.*

Summary

1. Determinism is 'the doctrine that all events, including human actions, are determined by causes regarded as external to the will'. Note that by definition determinism is opposed to the idea of free will.

2. An act of free will is an act that is independent of external or internal causes, and so is not coerced or forced.

3. The idea of determinism assumes that human beings, like the subject matter of the natural sciences, are governed by physical laws.

4. A 'dualism' between mind and body was proposed by Descartes wherein body is causally determined, and the mind is not.

5. William James proposed 'soft determinism' as a solution to the free will/determinism debate. He saw the 'will' as a cause of some behaviours.

6. Freud's psychodynamic view states that humans are primarily irrational beings, driven by impulses and desires rooted in the unconscious. Freud has been accused of 'psychic determinism'.

7. B.F. Skinner saw human behaviour as shaped by conditioning. Free will is a myth. Humans respond to reinforcers in the environment. Skinner has been accused of 'environmental determinism'.

8. Humanistic psychologists claim that human beings have the potential to exercise free will.

9. 'Accountability' is central to debates on free will, since to be accountable (answerable and judgeable) to others for our actions supposes that we are responsible and can choose what we do. Part of accountability is offering reasons for our actions, and reasons, unlike causes, imply choice.

10. Increasingly, the free will/determinism debate is seen as a pseudo-debate. Rather than seeing human action as resulting from either free will or determinism, researchers argue that there are degrees of freedom. Often human action falls between the two extremes of free will and determinism.

Unit 2 Reductionism

KEY ISSUES

1. **What is reductionism?**
2. **How does the mind/brain problem relate to reductionism?**
3. **Are organisms reducible to their genes?**

2.1　Defining reductionism

Reductionism and determinism are closely linked, and where you find one, you typically find the other. Reductionism is the attempt to explain complex wholes (these might be societies, organisms, or molecules) in terms of the units out of which these wholes are made up. Hence a society can be reduced to individual people. A reductionist would then try and explain societies (a complex whole) in terms of the actions of individuals (the units that make up societies). But can we also take a person as a complex whole that can be explained in terms of the units that make that person up? Of course. Each person, for example, can be reduced to organs, and each organ to cells. Cells can be reduced to organelles, which can be reduced to molecules, to atoms, to protons, neutrons and electrons, perhaps to quarks, and there, at the quantum level, for now, we stop. Note that an implication of this way of thinking is an implied hierarchical ranking of the sciences. The basic, most fundamental science would be physics, then chemistry, then biology and only then, at the much 'softer' end, would you find psychology and, even softer, sociology. This is summed up by a controversial statement by Francis Crick, who said: 'there is only one science – physics; everything else is social work'. The dream here is to find one single explanatory language at the micro-physical level that can explain everything – a so-called 'Grand Theory of Everything'.

Reductionism is very controversial. For some, such as Lewis Wolpert (an embryologist from University College London) it is the defining feature of science. For others, such as Steven Rose (a biologist from the Open University) it is better thought of as the defining feature of pseudoscience or bad science. To unpack this controversy it is useful to separate out three different kinds of reductionism (from Rose, 1997).

1   **Methodological reductionism** This involves the practical analysis (breaking down) of a complex system into its component parts. The experimental method, for instance, involves breaking a complex system down into variables so that one or more of these can be manipulated in a controlled way to see the effect that this has on other clearly measurable variables. For this to work, the variables need to be removed from the context in which they function so that they can be accurately measured and manipulated. In a sense, science functions by caging little pieces of a reality that would otherwise be too complicated to get a handle on.

2   **Philosophical reductionism** This is the attempt to find a 'Grand Theory of Everything'. This grand theory will be like a single language that can be used to talk about everything in the universe. Currently, the different sciences speak very different languages. Cellular biologists, for instance, tend to use the language of molecules and do not attend to the basic chemistry involved, nor to the underlying micro-physics. They hence do not typically 'speak' chemistry or physics. Philosophical reductionists, however, wish to see a single language that can be used for everything.

3   **Ideological reductionism** This is when reductionism serves political purposes. For instance, during the 1950s and 1960s in the USSR, people who dared to speak out against communism were often certified as mentally ill and locked up in mental hospitals. To do this is to explain a political action (speaking out) as if it were merely the symptom of a disease (a mental illness). Something complex and social is reduced to the psychological and biological level in a way that is very convenient for those in political power.

Breaking wholes into parts and using parts to explain wholes

All three forms of reductionism involve the breaking of wholes into parts. But reductionism does not just involve breaking something down into smaller and smaller components. It involves *explaining* a complex whole in terms of something more simple and known. It is one thing to know that the brain is composed of neurons that communicate using electrical impulses and chemical transmitter substances. These are

Key terms

Reductionism *The attempt to explain complex wholes in terms of the units of which these wholes are made up.*

Methodological reductionism *The kind of practical reductionism undertaken in experiments.*

Philosophical reductionism *The philosophical quest for a Grand Theory of Everything.*

Ideological reductionism *Reducing political issues to supposedly non-political questions.*

statements of fact, and we could not know these facts without this *methodologically reductionist* process of breaking wholes into parts. However, it is another thing to use this information to explain something more complex – for example, to explain a psychological state such as 'being happy' in terms of communications between neurons. To give another example, it is one thing to know that organisms reproduce themselves through genes that contain strings of DNA. It is another thing to explain a given complex behaviour, such as a person jumping with joy at winning the lottery, in terms of DNA (a 'gene for joyful jumping'). It is the second *explanatory* move in these two examples that can be called *reductionist*. Note, both of these examples of reductionism are also examples of determinism. The first holds that the state of happiness is *determined* by neurons, the second that it is *determined* by genes.

The form of reductionist explanations

Reductionist explanations therefore always have the same form. They always say 'such and such a complex thing *is only* such and such a simple thing'. Hence the reductionist argues that happiness *is only* neural firing and neural firing *is only* the expression of genes. This form is clearly visible in the following reductionist statement from Francis Crick, an eminent molecular biologist.

'You, your joys and your sorrows, your memories and your ambitions, your sense of personality and free will, are in fact no more than the behaviour of a vast assembly of nerve cells and their associated molecules' (Crick, 1994).

Here, Crick identifies a group of complex things which all happen to be 'psychological' (personality, memory, emotions, ambitions, free will) and claims that these *are only* the behaviour of neurons. His statement fits perfectly with the form that we identified above as reductionist. It is clearly also a deterministic statement, in that there is no place for free will. In fact free will is itself caused by the material fact of 'a vast assembly of nerve cells'. This demonstrates the close connection between reductionism and determinism. In fact, Crick's is a further type of determinism to be added to the list developed in Unit 1:

*   It is not *psychic* determinism (as in Freud), where the complexities of thought, feeling and behaviour are reduced to unconscious drives (ie, explained as unconscious drives).
*   It is not *environmental* determinism (as in Skinner), where these complexities are reduced to environmental reinforcers.
*   It is instead a form of *biological* determinism, where these complexities are reduced to biological processes (here, those taking place in the physical brain).

The problem with statements such as that made by Crick, is that they ignore the many other factors that play an important role in things like memory, emotions, personality, ambitions and free will. Our emotions, for example, do indeed depend upon brain activity, but they do not depend *only* on this. To make a simple analogy, our ability to walk certainly does depend upon having legs that work. But this does not mean that our legs are the *cause* of our walking, let alone the *only* cause of our walking.

Neuroscientists, who study the brain, are often very critical of the kind of reductionist statement made by Crick. Susan Greenfield, for instance, points out that the brain itself *changes* as a result of experience. This phenomenon of brain 'plasticity' shows that, to some extent, the way Crick's 'vast assembly of nerve cells' actually works is itself 'caused by', in the sense of 'shaped by', the experiences that a person has had through their life, and especially during childhood. This suggests that psychological experiences determine the brain as much as the brain determines psychological experiences. One cannot be *reduced* to the other.

One final example: a car engine cannot work without a spark plug, but the functioning of the engine cannot be *reduced to* (and explained in terms of) the action of a spark plug.

Activity 3   Attention-deficit/hyperactivity disorder

Item A   ADHD as a biological brain dysfunction

Many children throughout the world are currently being prescribed powerful and addictive amphetamine-based drugs such as methylphenidate (MPH) for a condition known as ADHD (attention-deficit/hyperactivity disorder). This condition – which used to be called simply 'hyperactivity' – is a label given by medical personnel, teachers and parents in response to certain kinds of undesirable behaviour on the part of the child. For example, children who are disruptive in the classroom, who do not pay attention to what they are told, who misbehave and who generally appear 'hyped-up', are likely now to be considered to have ADHD. Many psychologists argue that such behaviour is caused by a biological brain dysfunction. This is a view shared by many major multi-national drugs companies, who produce MPH based drugs (such as Ritalin and Equasym) to treat this new condition. This has given rise to a major debate, summarised in Items B and C.

Ritalin, the main drug prescribed for ADHD

Item B   A critical position

Professor Steve Baldwin is very critical of the use of drugs to treat ADHD. He argues that:

1   There is no good evidence showing that ADHD is a biological brain dysfunction – a criticism accepted by the federal government of the USA in an inquiry reported in 1998.

2   There is therefore no good reason to drug children and teenagers diagnosed with ADHD, especially given that there are known harmful effects of these drugs, including addiction.

3   The drug companies make enormous amounts of money selling their drugs, and these companies wield a good deal of political power, given that they donate millions of dollars to political organisations such as the United States Congress.

4   The drug companies also wield power over academic researchers, since they supply a good deal of the funding necessary for scientific research.

5   In view of the above, drugging children and teenagers with amphetamines should be seen not as a medical act based on science, but as an act of social control, based on expediency, economics and politics.

Adapted from Baldwin, 2000

Item C   A moderate position

Dr Paul Cooper takes a moderate position somewhere between what he sees as the extremes of the 'brain dysfunction' view and the critical view. The relevant parts of his argument are that:

1   ADHD is not *just* a biological condition, since it also has social and psychological aspects to it.

2   It is true that no definitive causal relationship has been found between particular abnormalities of the brain and ADHD. However, certain brain regions (the striatal region and the frontal lobes) have been 'implicated' (they *may* play *some* role in ADHD).

3   But then psychologists are hardly ever able to provide *definitive* evidence of a clear causal link between the things they study, so the ADHD/brain abnormality link is no exception.

4   So even though we have no conclusive findings, we do have a theory, and this points us in the direction of a partly biological cause.

5   We can therefore act on the basis of the *theory*, and whatever facts we do have. It is up to clinical professionals to exercise their judgement given that there are no hard facts to tell them what to do.

6   There is some evidence that using drugs on children and teenagers does reduce their problematic behaviour, so this is an argument for continuing the practice.

7   A major advantage of diagnosing children with ADHD is that we don't have to *blame* the child or hold them responsible for their deviant behaviour, and likewise we don't have to accuse the parents of being bad parents, since *if* it is a genuine disorder, it is not their fault.

Adapted from Cooper, 2000

2.2 The mind-brain problem as an example of reductionism

Crick's work (discussed above) provides a good point of entry into the so-called 'mind-brain' problem. Basically, the problem is whether or not it is reasonable to *explain* the phenomenon of 'mind' (ie, our thoughts, feelings, consciousness, memory and so on) in terms of the physical brain.

Eliminative materialism If qualities of the mind can be explained by pointing to observable processes going on in the physical brain, then we have a reductionist explanation. Crick is one person who believes this, Armstrong is another. Armstrong (1968) argues that: 'The mind is nothing but the brain … We can give a complete account of man in purely physio-chemical terms'. The logical conclusion of such a position is that we should stop using terms like 'feelings', 'consciousness' and so on, and start using descriptions of the bits of the brain that are at work instead. Instead of 'I am feeling afraid' we might say 'the amygdala of my brain is being stimulated'. The argument that we should replace so-called 'old fashioned', 'mentalistic' terms with high-tech scientific descriptions is known as *eliminative materialism*.

Functionalism The traditional counter-argument to eliminative materialism is a position known as *functionalism*. This is the solution offered by many cognitive psychologists (Gardner, 1985). Functionalism, as the name suggests, places importance on what a psychological process *does*. This can be contrasted with the materialist position that looks at what something is physically *made of*. Functionalists argue that what a psychological function, like memory or consciousness, is *made of* is largely irrelevant. To make this argument they typically use a computer analogy. A large mainframe computer and a small personal computer may have very little in common in terms of what they are made of. However, in performing the same computation what they *do* is the same. They can hence be said to be *functionally equivalent*. Likewise, a plastic pace-maker is made out of very different stuff to a heart, but in acting as a pump, it is functionally equivalent. This enables cognitive psychologists to argue that, in principle, psychological functions could be done using silicon rather than biological tissue. From this perspective it is no good reducing 'mind' to the physical substance of 'brain', since this misses the functional nature of both.

Emergent interaction theory This perspective has evolved from numerous sources, including the work of Sperry (1987). Mental states are viewed as *emergent properties* of brain states. That is, brain states give rise to mental states, but mental states are not reducible to the brain, and take on a relatively autonomous form. Once mental states have emerged from brain processes, they can *act back* on the brain. Mind and brain are hence thought of as entities that *interact*: thinking in a particular way can change the state of one's brain, for instance. Try deliberately thinking about a humiliating episode in your life. Remembering this may well bring back feelings of humiliation to you. Presumably, this means that your deliberate act of memory brought about a change in your brain. This perspective is antagonistic to reductionism.

2.3 Another example: genetic reductionism

'We are at the dawn of a genetic age. The Human Genome Project, the largest biological research enterprise in history, promises to have our entire genetic structure mapped by 2001. Our media report new scientific claims of genes associated with diseases, conditions, behaviours or personality traits so regularly that it seems that we are being provided with a gene-of-the-week. Scientists have identified or claimed genes for cystic fibrosis, Huntington's disease, Fragile X syndrome, breast cancer, Alzheimer's disease, colon cancer, bipolar illness, obesity, homosexuality, alcoholism, 'novelty seeking', shyness, bed wetting – the list gets longer weekly. James Watson, co-discoverer of the double helix structure of DNA and founding father of the Human Genome Project, has declared, "We used to think our fate was in the stars. Now we know, in large part, it is in our genes"' (Conrad & Gabe, 1999).

This quotation nicely conveys the current atmosphere around genetic research. The Human Genome Project, we are led to believe, will help to solve many of the health problems of humanity. It will also explain complex psychological and social issues such as homosexuality, bipolar depression, shyness and 'novelty seeking'. In with the package, as the statement from James Watson makes clear, is a commitment to a determinist position: 'our fate … is in our genes'. Unlike his former colleague Francis Crick, Watson at least adds the phrase 'in large part' to his statement about determinism. This is important, because it means that he avoids making the reductionist statement that our fate *is only* in our genes. In fact, this would be a nonsensical statement since one of the most interesting aspects of modern genetics is that molecular biologists can now manipulate the nature of organisms by manipulating their genetic makeup (as in 'genetically modified tomatoes' that have the benefit of an added fish gene). It is also within our powers to modify human beings through manipulations at the genetic level. This certainly does indicate that genes play a powerful role in creating and organising the structure of life-forms. But it equally well shows that, now, genes are coming to depend on us as much as we depend on them. Unless one is prepared to argue that scientists are genetically determined to manipulate genes, one must concede that the Human Genome Project seriously undermines the argument that our fate is determined by genes. Some of these issues are discussed further in Unit 3.

Evaluation of reductionism

Reductionism typically fails because it oversimplifies and so neglects the complexity of what is being 'explained'. It is based upon a dream of simplicity: human societies can be explained by the psychology of individuals, the psychology of individuals can be explained by examining the functioning of the brain, the functioning of the brain can be explained by what is coded at the genetic level, genetics can be explained in terms of chemical reactions, chemical reactions can be explained through the laws of physics. The reality being discovered by scientists is very different from this dream. As we move down to a level we hope to be more simple, we discover unexpected complexities which themselves give rise to more things that need to be explained, not less. Hence brain scientists such as Greenfield (2000) have found great difficulties with the quest to directly map a single psychological function onto a single area of the brain:

'Any one function depends on the contributions of many brain areas, yet any one brain area will participate in any number of diverse functions. For example, the visual system uses at least thirty different areas of the brain, while any single region, such as the prefrontal cortex, which lies behind the forehead, has been associated with functions as diverse as depression, memory, and personality itself.'

The same story is repeated at the genetic level, where genes are found to work together and with other parts of the body in complex and unpredictable ways, making it impossible to specify a single gene for any single activity such as 'doing the washing up'. The more our media become dominated by stories and images about powerful new technologies such as brain scanners and gene therapies, the more we will have to be on our guard against the seductive simplicities of reductionism. Even Lewis Wolpert, cited earlier as a believer in the power of reductionism, has recently toned down his views:

'My confidence in reductionism, which I claim is at the heart of all good science, was however a bit undermined when I learned that thousands of our genes code for different … molecules on the cell surface that receive signals from other cells, and further thousands are involved in getting the messages to the cells' DNA. What are they all doing and how will we ever find out?' (Wolpert, 1997).

To finish this unit, a very sensible evaluation of the debate on reductionism is provided by Steven Rose (1997):

'The triumph of the reductionist methodology of experimental science since its birth in the 17th century has been to extract simplicity from complexity. It has worked brilliantly in dealing with the problems set by physics and by chemistry, even biochemistry, the chemistry of living systems. However, many of the phenomena science wishes to explain, from the dynamics of weather and ecosystems to the history of life itself, from the orchestrated metabolism of a single cell to development of the fertilised egg into the fully formed adult and the workings of the human brain, seem irreducibly complex. Isolating single variables can only confuse. New methods are required.'

Summary

1 Reductionism is an attempt to explain wholes in terms of the parts which make them up. It is an attempt to explain something complex entirely in terms of something simple.

2 Rose (1997) distinguishes *methodological, philosophical* and *ideological* forms of reductionism.

3 The mind-brain problem is the problem of whether what we call the 'mind' can be reduced to physical brain processes.

4 *Eliminative materialists* claim that mind can be reduced to brain, *functionalists* argue that what something does is more important than what it is made of, and *emergent interaction theorists* hold that mind is an emergent property of brain and that both can interact.

5 Genetic reductionists hold that human behaviour can be explained by genes.

6 Both eliminative materialist and genetic reductionist positions are problematic given the *complexity* that is being discovered at both the neural and the genetic levels. Isolating single variables fails to provide adequate explanations. It appears that only by looking at the interaction between variables can adequate explanations be developed.

Unit 3 Nature and nurture

KEY ISSUES

1 **What is the historical background to the nature-nurture debate?**

2 **Is intelligence genetically determined?**

3 **Why is it important to move beyond the nature-nurture debate?**

The nature-nurture debate is concerned with how much of human behaviour is influenced by nature (by the structure and functioning of our bodies, especially the coordination of this by genes) and how much by nurture (learning, socialisation and experience). As with the determinism/free will debate, historically this debate has been deeply polarised and heavily political. It is thus very important to avoid the artificial separation of 'nature' and 'nurture' that often occurs in this debate. In fact, parts of this unit can be taken as examples of reductionism. Those who stress nature tend to reduce complex psychological phenomena and action to biology and, more specifically, genetics. Those who stress nurture tend to reduce them to the social environment. The nature-nurture debate crops up in many areas of psychology, but usually in those that have a *developmental* aspect to them. Typical areas include:

- intelligence (see pp 509-521)
- gender development (see pp 546-560)
- the development of psychological disorders (see Chapter 35) the acquisition of language (see pp 474-479)
- perceptual development (see pp 453-460).

Today, most psychologists accept that the concepts of 'nature' and 'nurture' cannot be meaningfully separated, and the *interactions* between organism and experience are where the action is.

3.1 Some historical background to the debate

Empiricism and nativism

The nature-nurture debate goes back a long way. Before the beginnings of modern psychology there was a philosophical debate between the *empiricists* and the *nativists*.

Empiricists believed that the human infant is born with no knowledge or skills. They used the metaphor of the *tabula rasa* or 'blank slate'. The idea is that knowledge and skills must be 'written on' the child by the hand of experience. The infant learns what it learns through instruction from others and through its own direct experiences. John Locke (1632-1704) was an empiricist. Without nurture, he implied, we are nothing.

Nativists (such as Jean-Jacques Rousseau 1712-1778), on the other hand, argue that we are born with most of the qualities we will display as an adult. Socialisation may interfere with the unfolding of our natural qualities (by helping or hindering), but basically our character and predispositions are innate. Nativist educators thought of themselves as like gardeners: the flower is already contained as a potential in the planted seed, and the gardener's job is to make sure the conditions are right for it to grow.

Inside and outside

One way of thinking about this split is in terms of a distinction between what is inside the organism and what is outside. Empiricists place greater importance on what is outside the organism – the environment. Development is then a matter of forces from the outside shaping what is inside, much as a potter may shape wet clay into any form they choose. The outside is active, the inside passive. Nativists place greater importance on what is inside the organism. What is inside will, outside conditions being favourable, unfold according to its own natural programme. This polarisation between empiricists and nativists was still clearly in evidence during early 20th century psychology.

- A modern form of empiricism (the nurture position) was advanced by Watson in the form of *behaviourism*. For him, and later for Skinner, organisms from mice to monkeys to men and women were almost infinitely open to the influence of the environment. In Watson's words:

    'Give me a dozen healthy infants, well-formed, and my own specialised world to bring them up in and I'll guarantee to take any one at random and train him to become any type of specialist I might select – a doctor, lawyer, merchant-chief and, yes, even beggar-man and thief, regardless of his talents, penchants, abilities, vocations and race of his ancestors' (Watson, 1925).

- An extreme form of nativism (the nature position) was advanced by William McDougall (1908) who tried to explain social behaviour by invoking a long list of 'instincts' such as 'the gregarious instinct', 'the instinct of acquisition', 'the instinct of self-abasement', and so on. In McDougall's words:

    'The human mind has certain innate or inherited tendencies which are the essential springs or motive powers of all thought and action, whether individual or collective, and are the bases from which the character and will of individuals and of nations are gradually developed' (McDougall, 1908).

Nature and nurture in conflict

There is an important early dimension to the nature-nurture debate that is missed in the above summary. Namely, in the early days of scientific psychology there was a belief in the profound antagonism between 'nature' and 'nurture'. One of the early roles assigned to psychology was to manage the 'evolution' of society to ensure that it developed in positive and productive directions. Part of this involved studying and managing the *socialisation* of its youngest members. According to Danziger (1978), the concept of socialisation originated in the late 1930s. It was used to mean the process by which an individual is transformed into a person. As a concept, it developed out of the earlier concepts of moralisation (transforming an amoral infant into a moral citizen) and civilisation. Basically, the idea is that human beings start out amoral, uncivilised and unsocialised. In short, they begin with base animality – raw 'nature'. The trick, it was thought, was to transform this raw material into socialised, civilised and moralised humanity. That is, nurturing was to take place in spite of nature. From this perspective, education is less like gardening (the *romantic nativist* metaphor) and more like animal training (the *classical nativist* metaphor). If nature is a wild animal, then nurture is the process of breaking and taming that animal. The two terms (nature and nurture) were thus often set against one another. This is nowhere more apparent than in psychodynamic theory. Consider the following summary of Freudian ideas.

'The unconscious mind is the part of the mind that stands nearest to the crude instincts as they are inborn in us, and before they have been subjected to the refining influences of education. It is commonly not realised how extensive is the work performed by these influences, nor how violent is the internal conflict they provoke before they finally achieve their aim. Without them, the individual would probably remain a selfish, impulsive, aggressive, dirty, immodest, cruel, egocentric and conceited animal, inconsiderate of the needs of others, and unmindful of the complicated social and ethical standards that go to make a civilised society' (Jones, 1928).

The strong negative feelings about 'nature' ring out loud and clear in this quotation from Ernest Jones, one of the most respected Freudians. In our 'natural' form, we are bestial – dirty, aggressive, crude and cruel. Thank heavens for nurture! Through the 'extensive work' of nurture (particularly the 'refining influences of education') in combating this unpleasantness, we become civilised citizens. Such ideas form a simple formula: all things bad are equated with nature and all things good with nurture. As indicated above, this form of nativism is classical rather than romantic. It goes back to classical philosophers such as Thomas Hobbes (1588-1679), who thought of nature as anti-social, rather than romantics like Jean-Jacques Rousseau, who saw in nature an ideal way of being.

Key terms

Empiricists Those (following Locke) who believe that experience is all important and that nature is effectively a blank slate.

Romantic nativists Those (following Rousseau) who hold that nature unfolds according to its own inherent process and should be encouraged by nurture.

Classical nativists Those (following Hobbes) who stress that nature is a powerful force with its own tendencies, but that these tendencies are bad and should be suppressed by nurture.

3.2   The politics of eugenics

The above story of an antagonism between nature and nurture shows just how ideological the debate was (and continues to be). It is 'ideological' because it involves vested interests, emotional investments and political views as well as science. This situation was compounded in the late 19th and early 20th centuries by another directly political issue. This led to 'nativist' (nature) arguments getting a very bad name. The issue is called *eugenics*. Francis Galton, one of the most important and celebrated early British psychologists, defined eugenics (which he helped to invent) as follows:

'Eugenics is the science of improving stock, which is by no means confined to judicious mating, but which, especially in the case of man, takes cognisance of all influences that tend in however remote a degree to give the more suitable races or strains of blood a better chance of prevailing speedily over the less suitable than they otherwise would have had' (Galton, 1883, cited in Rose, 1985).

Galton was Charles Darwin's cousin. He was obsessed with the idea of hereditary genius and with the idea that some races and classes were superior to others. He draws the concept of 'stock' from animal husbandry. Some animals are from good 'stock', some from bad. He extended this to humans, arguing that some humans are from good stock (they are stronger, more intelligent, more civilised, etc), some from bad stock. In this story, then, nature is not simply a bad thing (as in classical nativism). There can be good natures and bad natures, and these are inherited from generation to generation. Groups identified as having 'bad natures' included the poor, the disabled, and those from non-white races. The eugenics movement argued for the application of a kind of animal husbandry to humans. The more suitable races or 'strains of blood' should be encouraged to breed, the less suitable should be discouraged. To this end, it was deemed necessary to study the 'hereditary faculties of different men, and of the great differences in different families and races'. Once this knowledge had been attained, then 'inefficient' strains could be eliminated or reduced. Galton considered this task to be a moral duty. He asked whether 'it might not be our duty to do so by such efforts as may be

reasonable, thus exerting ourselves to further the ends of evolution more rapidly and with less distress than if events were left to their own course'.

As part of the eugenics movement, many thousands of poor, handicapped and otherwise disadvantaged people were sterilised to prevent them from reproducing. There was a profound sense of anxiety on the part of the ruling elite that the 'less suitable races and strains' were swamping the 'more suitable' and that this would destroy civilisation as we know it. The belief was that social and medical progress was beginning to change the natural course of evolution. Left to nature, the story goes, evolution would cause the strongest and best to survive and the weakest to die. But with good sanitation and improved medicine, these supposedly mentally and physically weak people were allowed to survive and began reproducing at a rapid rate. There was a good deal of talk about the probable 'decay' of the 'race' unless urgent steps were taken. As well as the practice of eugenics, the psychology of 'individual differences' was invented by Galton to help in the effort to purify the human stock. It was Galton, in the work cited above, who coined the phrase *nature-nurture*.

The following quotation from William Guy (1873) speaks volumes about where this early concern for nature versus nurture came from.

'What man possessed of sense, curiosity or fancy, could gaze unmoved on this mixed mass of poverty, destitution and crime which makes up the lower stratum of our artificial society? ... What part of all this misery is the result of personal defects and vices – of sloth, unthrift, incapacity; how much of what may be called ineptitude in the State! How is it possible to resist the inquiry whether when more than three centuries ago, our ancestors established a poor law, they ought not rather to have given us a good police force' (cited in Rose, 1985).

In the above quotation the terms of the debate are clearly political. Are poverty, destitution and crime the result of the way in which the State is organised? This would be a 'nurture' position (good teaching, good examples and good management can produce good people). Or are they the result of personal defects and vices? In this context, this would be the 'nature' position (in which case no amount of 'socialisation' can help, and force is needed). As Rose (1985) argues, this kind of political question was very much at the forefront during the development of early psychology. In fact, early psychology developed to address these kinds of 'real world' problems. The answer given by the nativists was that, for the most part, poor, sick and downtrodden people are in that state because they are biologically inferior.

The ideas and practices of eugenics were taken to the extreme by the Nazis in their attempt to murder as many 'non-Aryans' as was possible, again under the dubious pretext that 'bad blood' was swamping 'good blood'. What now seems obvious is that these 'nature' based explanations are pseudo-scientific ways of furthering very unpleasant political agendas. The discipline of psychology has yet to fully live down this bad-smelling 'skeleton' in its 'closet', and many still refuse to acknowledge it.

3.3   The nature of intelligence

One of the key questions studied by those who developed Galton's psychology of 'individual differences' was the nature of

Activity 4   Eugenics

Item A   Eugenics in pictures

A poster from the 1930s illustrating the eugenics movement's view of the future.

This 1930s poster says, 'We peasants are clearing out the muck'. It shows a German peasant shovelling away Communists and Jews.

Item B   Cleansing the population

In the USA, during the first half of the 20th century, compulsory sterilisation programmes were enacted to prevent those with genetically-based diseases from reproducing. Doctors instructed patients with such disorders to undergo sterilisation or to have a pregnancy terminated. 'Public health genetics' was the order of the day.

In Sweden, a law legalising sterilisation was passed in 1934. Although it did not allow people to be sterilised against their will, many were pressured into taking this step. In the words of one Swedish doctor, 'We dreamed we could improve human body and soul'. Between 1935 and 1975, nearly 63,000 people, almost all of them women, were sterilised in Sweden.

In Nazi Germany, human genetics was known as 'race hygiene'. The implications of this chilling phrase are clearly seen when translated into action. It is estimated that some 350,000 people were forcibly sterilised for genetically-based 'defects' in Nazi Germany from 1934 to 1939. It was assumed that the only way to improve society was to breed from the finest genes and eradicate the worst. The Nazis' 'final solution' was the slaughter of over six million Jews, Gypsies, gays, and people seen as having physical disabilities and psychological disorders.

Adapted from Muller-Hill, 1994

Question

In what ways can the thinking behind the eugenics movement be seen as:

a) determinist

b) reductionist

c) nativist?

intelligence. The study of intelligence was a central part of Galton's research program into the 'hereditary faculties of different men, and of the great differences in different families and races'. As you might expect from the above, there was a built-in prejudice towards assuming that intelligence is innate or biologically determined. It was thought of as the kind of thing that the 'superior stock' has plenty of and the 'inferior stock' lacks. Given this context, it is no wonder that the nature-nurture debate on intelligence has been highly controversial! (See pp 509-510 for further discussion of Galton and intelligence.)

The early intelligence testing movement in America and the UK was built upon the following assumptions:

1 That intelligence is a 'thing' (that it has stable qualities).

2 That, being a thing, it can be measured (hence the development of IQ tests).

3 That individuals have different 'amounts' of intelligence (hence each person can be given an IQ score, with 100 being the average).

4 That these differences between people in intelligence are the result of genetic differences.

5 Therefore intelligence is hereditary.

Heritability

One of the key features of work in this field has been to put a figure on the heritability of intelligence. Biological determinists tend to put the heritability of intelligence at about 80%. But what does heritability mean?

The heritability of a trait (such as intelligence) refers to the proportion of the *variability* of that trait in a population that results from heredity or genetic variance. If the heritability of a trait is 100%, this means that all of the variation shown in a given population with regard to this trait is genetic in origin. But, even for physical traits like height, heritability does not reach 100%. Variations in height between members of a population will be influenced, to some extent, by environmental factors such as diet.

In studying the heritability of intelligence and other traits, psychologists have sought resemblances between people who are genetically related. The logic for this is that if a trait is heritable, then people who share more genes should resemble each other more with regard to that trait than those who have less in common genetically. The ideal participants in such studies are identical or monozygotic twins, since these share all of their genes. Of course the problem here is that people who are related may also share similar environments, thus spoiling the comparison. To overcome this, psychologists have used studies comparing adopted children with those reared in their biological families. Two questions are typical here.

1 How similar (with regards to a given trait) are identical twins who were separated at birth? If they turn out to be very similar despite different environments of upbringing, this suggests genetic influence on the trait.

2 Are identical twins more alike than non-identical (fraternal or dizygotic) twins despite sharing the same environment? If they are, then this indicates the importance of genetic factors.

The hereditary figure for intelligence of 80% was arrived at on the basis of numerous studies based on the outline above. However, the quality and reliability of these studies, particularly the early ones, has been seriously called into doubt (Rose et al., 1984). First, there are numerous methodological problems in many of the studies. It is very difficult, for instance, to ensure that there are no similarities between the 'environments' of parents that adopt and natural parents, especially given the tendency for adoption agencies to match environments. Very often questions of the similarity of environments was inadequately assessed and poorly reported. Further, as Rose et al. (1984) state, 'inadequate sample sizes, biased subjective judgements, selective adoption, failure to separate so-called "separated twins", unrepresentative samples of adoptees, and

gratuitous and untested assumptions about similarity of environments are all standard characteristics in the literature of IQ genetics'.

The Burt scandal

Worse follows. A belief in the findings of bad research may reflect the politics and ideology of the believer. Rose et al. (1984) suggest that it suited those who wanted to defend their positions of power to believe in the genetic basis of intelligence because this provided a natural justification for inequalities in society and for their own comfort. Should we help the poor and down-trodden? No, since they are in that position due to their biology. Most of them naturally lack intelligence, and those that don't will be clever enough to help themselves. Should we forsake some of our own wealth and power in the name of greater equality? No, since we have these things due to our greater intelligence, and these good things would be wasted on lesser mortals.

The problem of ideology is well illustrated by the so-called Sir Cyril Burt scandal. Burt was knighted for his contributions to society. Those contributions were that he was held to have proven that intelligence is almost completely genetic. He was praised for his outstanding studies and for producing the most conclusive and solid evidence available. Yet, until the mid-1970s, nobody had checked carefully what he had actually done in his research. When this was done (first by Leo Kamin, then by Oliver Gillie, then by Clarke and Clarke – two of Burt's former students – and finally by Leslie Hearnshaw, a former admirer) it appeared that Burt had faked his data, invented two mysterious assistants who supposedly did the work (of whom no traces have been found) and fabricated figures. In short, the findings were fraudulent. The fact that these findings found their way into 'nearly every psychological textbook' (Mackintosh, 1980) shows just how much psychologists, and society more generally, wanted to believe what Burt had to say.

Sadly, this kind of thinking has not gone away. In 1994, Herrnstein and Murray published a book called *The Bell Curve: Intelligence and Class Structure in American Life* in which it was argued that traits like intelligence are largely genetic and largely responsible for social success. This was combined with anxieties about the US national intelligence level being reduced by low IQ genes on account of the high proportion of low IQ single mothers and low income mothers who are supposedly encouraged to reproduce due to subsidies from the US government. The arguments are strikingly similar to those of the eugenicists, although instead of 'bad blood' swamping the 'good' we have 'maladapted genes' swamping the 'gene pool'. Another similarity is the biased use of largely poor quality research and the dressing up of politics in the language of science.

The nurture reaction

At times, it is very difficult to sort the science from the ideology, especially when an issue becomes 'socially sensitive'. Once 'nature' explanations became associated with a conservative political agenda, then it became politically 'progressive' to advocate a nurture position. To be against social inequality became associated with holding the view that differences between people, particularly in intelligence, are to do with the relative advantages of upbringing and education. This resulted in numerous education programmes that were designed to enrich the environment of disadvantaged children in order to increase their intelligence and skills – for example, the *Head Start* programmes begun in the 1960s in the USA.

There is no doubt that the nurture position too can be overstated – to the extent that genetics is ignored completely. And, there is no doubt that value judgements, politics and ideology strongly influence many researchers' commitment to a nurture position. However, there is considerable evidence, based on methodologically sound research, that nurture has a major influence on IQ. Part of this evidence is outlined on pages 509-521.

How to become a world-class violinist ...

Another area where 'nurture' is currently being emphasised where 'nature' had been before, concerns the acquisition of expert performance. Traditionally, people talked of 'gifted' musicians and sports people, implying a genetic basis to expert performance. However, Ericsson and Charness (1999) show that the main factor that distinguishes top level professional violinists from less successful violinists is the amount of practice they have put in. By the age of 20, top professionals had practised for more than 10,000 hours, whilst by the same age, the less successful violinists had only practised for 5,000 hours. Such predictive differences in amount of practice are detectable as

early as age 4-6 for top level professionals (who put in about 4 concentrated hours a day). To reach the top, about 10 solid years of your life must be dedicated solely to practice! The same message was repeated in a recent Channel 4 documentary looking into why the Germans have a far better record of winning penalty shoot-outs in top level football matches than the English. Basically, the Germans practice a good deal, whilst the English, encouraged by a long line of managers, prefer to think that such things are decided by the hand of fate.

Piaget – an interactionist view

In many ways, the nature-nurture debate on intelligence was superseded back in the 1920s by the work of Jean Piaget. Piaget had been employed designing intelligence tests, but was soon intrigued by the errors that children made. This led him to question the value of IQ as a measure of the child's intellectual capacity, and to focus instead on the process of intellectual development in the child.

In Piaget's view, children's mental structures interact with their environment and, as a result of this interaction, children proceed through stages of cognitive development. Piaget's theory is called an *interactionist theory* as nature and nurture are seen to interact – to work on each other – as the child's intellect develops. (See pp 491-500 for further discussion of Piaget.)

Activity 5   Thinking about nature and nurture

Item A   Romans then and now

Imagine that we could take 1000 fertilised human eggs from Roman women of AD 80 and transplant them into 1000 modern women of Rome AD 1980. Further imagine that we did the same in reverse, and took ova from modern Roman women and transplanted them into Ancient Romans. What would be the result? First, for many reasons, not all of the fertilised ova, in either context, would be carried to term. Of those that were born live, not all the babies would survive to reach 20. However, those that made it to 20 living in AD 2001 would be Italians, speaking Italian and participating in 21st century Italian culture. Likewise, those living in AD 101 would all be Romans, speaking Latin and participating in the culture of the second century. Both groups would be to all intents and purposes indistinguishable from their non-transplanted peers. To believe otherwise would be to assume that genes carry cultural information or that there have been psychologically significant genetic changes in human beings over that time. Only on the wildest fringes of sociobiology are such ideas held.

Adapted from Stainton Rogers et al., 1995

Item B   Males and females

In most texts on child development, the reader learns that it is the way a child is reared that matters most in the formation of gender identity. We learn of Margaret Mead's observations in various cultures that led her to conclude that the environment was all-important, and we read about studies showing that genetic males who are misjudged at birth to be females, and subsequently reared as females, grow up to identify with that gender identity rather than the one coded by their genes. Missing from these descriptions, however, is the growing evidence that biology matters a great deal in the formation of a person's gender role. Sigmundson and Diamond (1999) show that genetic males who were thought to be females and who were reared as females (dresses, long hair, etc) often failed to acquire a female gender identity. They rebelled against it, refused to wear dresses, refused to urinate sitting down. Some became depressed, even attempting suicide. Once their gender was surgically and/or hormonally corrected to match their gender identity, they usually made immediate adaptations.

Adapted from Ceci & Williams, 1999

Item C   Gender and drink

Babycham, a bubbly champagne-like drink, was invented in the 1950s. At last, women could go to the pub and ask for a drink which was not seen as a man's drink. 'I'd love a Babycham' said pretty women on countless posters and commercials and millions of women lapped it up. In its heyday it sold a million bottles a week and any man who bought one ran the risk of having his manhood questioned.

The stigma attached to women in pubs, especially women drinking 'men's drinks' has largely

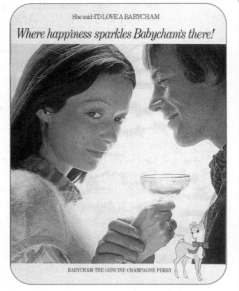

She said: I'D LOVE A BABYCHAM

Where happiness sparkles Babycham's there!

BABYCHAM-THE GENUINE CHAMPAGNE PERRY

Early 1970s

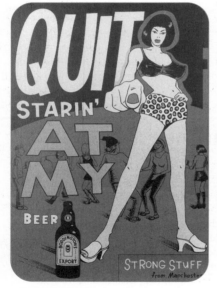

Early 1990s

disappeared. Women now drink beer – and in pint glasses. Babycham's sales have slumped. In the 1990s a TV advertising campaign attempted to sell Babycham to men. It had little success.

Boddingtons hope for more success with their new superhero, Tankard Girl. She is mean and moody and heads the advertising campaign launched in 1995 for Boddingtons Export.

Adapted from Haralambos, 1996

Item D   Brain plasticity

One exciting area of research in neuroscience is the study of brain plasticity, where physical changes can be seen in the degree and extent of connections between neurons in certain brain regions, as a result of injury, or more commonly, simple everyday experience. As the brain becomes more sophisticated, it appears to exploit instinct less and less and instead uses increasingly the results of individual experience, of learning. Hence individuality, I would argue, becomes more evident: the balance starts to tip correspondingly away from nature toward nurture – the effects of the environment. It is in this personalisation of the brain, crafted over the long years of childhood and continuing to evolve throughout life, that a unique pattern of connections between brain cells creates what might best be called a 'mind'.

Adapted from Greenfield, 2000

Questions

1   What does Item A tell us about the importance of nurture?

2   According to Ceci and Williams (1999), more recent views on gender identity often suggest that 'biology is irrelevant'. What evidence in Item B indicates that this may not be so?

3   Would you explain the changes illustrated in Item C in terms of nature or nurture? Give reasons for your answer.

4   Read Item D. What is 'brain plasticity'? Why is this relevant for the nature-nurture debate?

3.4   Beyond nature versus nurture

In various ways, the polarised distinction between nature and nurture is misleading. Psychologists are increasingly moving away from an 'either/or' way of thinking, as the following quotation indicates.

'Nearly all responsible researchers agree that human traits are jointly determined by both nature and nurture … The battle today seems more over the specific genetic and environmental mechanisms than over whether genes or environments matter' (Ceci & Williams, 1999).

The classic debate relied upon an over-simplified separation of nature and nurture. This returns us to the questions of reductionism and determinism. The problem is when people

attempt to reduce a complex behaviour or trait down to something supposedly simple like a single gene or particular type of environment. Nobody denies, for instance, that genes play a profound role in the expression and maintenance of certain traits. What is controversial is when we are led to believe that aspects of human personality and behaviour can be *reduced* to traits that have a linear, one to one relationship with genes.

In *Lifelines*, the biologist Steven Rose (1997) has made a powerful criticism of the idea that the way we are and the things we do can be mapped on to a cocktail of 'genes for' specific and independent traits. He calls this false idea *neurogenetic determinism* since the claim is that genes directly determine brain states that in turn directly determine behaviour. The route from even simple physical phenotypical expressions (such as having blue or brown eyes) to an underlying genetic situation is surprisingly complicated and non-linear. Rose says that instead of talking of a 'gene for blue eyes' we should say 'one or more genes *in whose absence* the metabolic pathway that leads to pigmented eyes terminates at the blue-eye stage'. When dealing with complex psychological questions, the route becomes infinitely more tortuous, non-linear and non-deterministic. The take-home message is not to deny the power of genes, but to recognise that genetic influence is often so highly mediated and indirect that it can be impossible to describe.

The problem, to return to the beginning of this unit, is that it is simply not possible to make the clear separation between the 'inside' and the 'outside' that the nature-nurture debate requires. The following list of seven points illustrates the problem with making this separation.

1   At any point in its life, an organism is the unique result of a developmental history that is the consequence of interaction between internal and external factors.

This means that there is no way of knowing in advance, simply from looking at the DNA, what an organism will be like, except in the most general of terms. At every moment the inner state of the organism is contingent on what is available environmentally. It is not a question of 'first' there is nature and 'second' there is nurture 'added to' this.

2   The 'inside' and the 'outside' can never be clearly specified.

The 'environment' of a cell nucleus is the cell cytoplasm; that of a cell is typically a cluster of other cells; that of an organ is the organ system in which it functions; that of an individual person may be their family, town, culture, society, country and so on. In other words, although the debate began with a distinction between 'social environment' and 'hereditary biology' it is now clear that one aspect of biology (cell cytoplasm) can be the environment that nurtures another aspect of biology (the cell nucleus). This means that 'nature' can 'nurture' and that one 'environment' plays the role of the inside or nature to another. This makes a problem of both terms in the debate.

3   'External factors' (the 'environment') are in fact partly a result of the organism itself or those that preceded it.

Organisms, especially humans, produce and consume the conditions of their own lives. The environment is not the brute external world, but the ecological niche within which an organism functions. Birds build nests, badgers dig holes, people build societies. What is environmentally relevant for one animal is effectively non-existent for another. For geneticists, this question of the organism helping to create the environment that in turn shapes it, comes under the heading of so-called 'gene-environment correlations'. Three kinds of gene-environment correlations are:

- **Passive** For example, children inherit the environment created by their predecessors without having to do anything active about it. If their predecessors are bookish and scholarly, they will inherit a good library, which may well (but not necessarily) influence their development, and so on.
- **Reactive** Infants who are phenotypically happy and fun-loving (which may well involve a genetic contribution) tend to provoke positive reactions from carers. At first inadvertently, but later deliberately, these children therefore 'shape' the nature of their own environment by provoking

particular reactions from others (the same carers presented with a grumpy infant may respond less enthusiastically).
- **Active** People, from a young age, try to build the kind of environment for themselves that best suits their characteristics. Joyful people seek situations in which they can find joy, for instance (called *niche picking*). Bookish intellectuals surround themselves with more and more books (called *niche building*). It would be incorrect here to say that 'genes' are selecting their own 'environments' (since genes are not agents that can 'select' in this way), but to the extent that these traits are influenced by genes, we can talk of phenotypes constructing their environments.

4   An implication of the previous point is that it can never be said that a group of individuals (children in a family, say) *share the same environment*.

Each individual can respond differently to the same situation, and similarly to different situations depending upon their own unique circumstances. This distinction between 'shared' and 'non-shared' environments used by geneticists is hence deeply problematic and only ever a matter of degree.

5   It is not the case that 'genes' and 'environment' are the only factors contributing to development.

Another very significant factor is *developmental noise* (Lewontin, 1993). Such 'noise' is the result of random events that always interrupt and influence the way a genotype develops phenotypically. For instance, all symmetrical organisms, from fruit flies to humans, develop slight asymmetries despite the genes being identical on the left and right. So, your left hand fingerprints are distinguishable from your right, just as a fruit fly will have different numbers of sensory bristles on one side than the other. These universal developments are the result of chance. Random noise has played a decisive role in evolution too. It is unlikely that wings developed in order to fly, since they would have started small, and small wings are no good for flying. More likely, says Lewontin, that 'wings' originally developed for another purpose (as heat-regulatory devices), and then accidentally became useful for flying.

6   The last example suggests that, as well as organisms creating environments, there is a sense in which environments create organisms.

As soon as large, flat, heat-regulatory devices created the accidental possibility of flight, then simultaneously we see created a new 'air-borne' environment where none previously existed (since flying was previously not a problem to be solved). This environment then sets the conditions for later adaptations to develop in, shaping the mutation of new, better designed flying animals. The 'outside' and the 'inside' have been mutually shaping one another for billions of years.

7   As a result of many of the above points, heritability estimates are of very limited scientific value since they are highly situationally specific.

That is, as put by Ceci and Williams (1999), 'they are descriptions of the relative contributions of genes and environments to the expression of a trait in a specific group, place, and time. Such estimates tell us nothing about the relative contributions if the group, place, or time is changed.'

Summary

1   Nativism and empiricism represent an early philosophical form of the nature-nurture debate.

2   The nature-nurture debate centres on the question of the relative importance of what is inside or what is outside an organism.

3   In the early days of scientific psychology, nature and nurture were pitted against one another, since nature was often perceived as requiring domination by nurture.

4   Eugenics is the 'science of improving stock'. It is an embarrassing example of a politically and scientifically corrupt use of the argument for innate qualities.

5   One of the main sites of controversy has been the nature-nurture debate over intelligence.

6   It is important to move beyond the nature-nurture debate and to recognise that the distinction between inside and outside that it rests upon is problematic.

7   Today most researchers believe that human traits are shaped by both nature and nurture.

Unit 4 Psychology as a science

KEY ISSUES

1   **What do the origins of scientific psychology tell us about its status as a science?**

2   **What is the nature of science?**

3   **Why have the scientific credentials of psychology been criticised so often?**

4   **Is psychology a natural science or social science?**

4.1   The origins of scientific psychology

In one sense, psychology began the moment people started thinking systematically about their own patterns of behaviour, their own feelings and foibles, their own nature. Certainly the ancient Greek Aristotle could be considered a psychologist in this sense. Perhaps, so too could thinkers like Spinoza who, in the 17th century, put forward a comprehensive theory of the emotions, or novelists such as George Eliot and Fyodor Dostoevsky, who were careful observers of human thinking, feeling and behaviour. But professional psychologists tend to think of their discipline as beginning relatively recently. It was only about 120 years ago, for example, when psychologists such as Wundt set up the first proper psychology laboratories and began systematically to do experiments. The birth of modern psychology, according to this story, happened when people began using scientific methods to study psychological questions in an organised way. First we humans invented science. Then we extended our invention so that we too became its objects.

According to the traditional histories, then, modern psychology was born at the moment that proper scientific methods and theories were applied to the understanding of people. Some even date the origin quite precisely: 1879, since it was in 1879 that Wilhelm Wundt set up his laboratory in Leipzig, Germany. Debates about psychology and science are therefore debates about modern scientific psychology. Why should the extension of scientific thought and practice to the study of human beings have taken so long to begin? Why should

it be so controversial? A good place to look to understand the debate about the science status of psychology is to these early origins of scientific psychology, since it was then that the issues could be seen most clearly.

The exclusion of psychology from the Cartesian settlement

One reason why scientific psychology took so long, compared to many other sciences, to develop was because of the 17th century Cartesian settlement discussed in Unit 1 of this chapter. Descartes' dualism between mind and body ensured that everything that fell under the category 'body' could be studied scientifically. 'Mind', by contrast, could *not* be studied scientifically. To begin with, for Descartes, 'mind' did not exist in time and space and therefore could not become the 'object' of study. Secondly, mind itself is the subject that does the scientific studying, and so it can not become an object for itself. So in the Cartesian settlement, which was hugely influential, mind was excluded from science. Descartes held to a view that became enormously popular in modern science – bodies of all kinds were basically machines. They are explainable by purely scientific means and can, in principle, be taken apart to see how they work. In short, bodies were completely up for grabs for science, whilst mind was completely out of bounds. It is responsible for the higher things in life: morality, religion, truth (which also pleased the religious powers that be in Descartes' day).

The exclusion of psychology from the Kantian settlement

Any philosophical settlement of controversial issues has a limited shelf-life. Descartes' worked for a while, but holes began to appear in it. By the late 18th century, a new way of making sense of the relationships between science and other domains of existence was necessary. This time the settlement was provided by a German philosopher, Immanuel Kant (1724-1804). For Kant, Newtonian physics provided the best model of science, since it was fully mathematical. In Kant's view, for a subject to become a proper science, it must be amenable to the application of mathematics. 'Mental life', Kant argued, was not amenable to mathematics, and so psychology could not become a science.

So in that case, why did scientific psychology ever get going?

Basically, Kant defied would-be psychologists to apply mathematical measurements to mental processes. Ernst Weber rose to this challenge in 1834 by claiming that sensations could be measured indirectly. He noticed, amongst other things, that if you present two noises or two light flashes to people in a sequence whereby the two signals get increasingly close together, there comes a point when the perceiver can only detect one noise or light, even though there are, in physical reality, two. This threshold is called the point of 'just noticeable difference'. In this way, Weber was able to get a mathematical measure of the relationship between the objective stimulus, and the subjectively felt sensation. Fechner took over this project and formulated this relationship as a law: the Weber-Fechner law. This holds that: 'Equal absolute increments of sensation correspond to equal relative increments of the stimulus'.

Nobody was particularly interested in the actual content of this law which founded psycho-physics (indeed, it quickly became apparent that the law did not hold up very well), but what was of interest was that Kant had been proved wrong. No matter how small the gain to knowledge, it had been shown that mental processes could be subjected to 'mathematisation'. This was the baton that was picked up by Wilhelm Wundt, who extended Weber and Fechner's work and, more importantly, set up a laboratory in which to do so. It is important to realise that when Wundt started experimental psychology he did not believe that the precision methods of the natural sciences could be applied to all aspects of human psychology. The scientific status was won, but at the cost of a highly restricted set of psychological questions. Indeed, he restricted 'scientific' experimental psychology to very simple psychological processes involving psychological reactions to basic stimuli. His main method, *systematic introspection*, required research participants to be very well trained. Not anybody could be a participant, because not everyone could be relied upon to be able to make sensitive discriminations in what they feel in response to various stimuli. He argued against applying these methods to the more complex psychological processes of thought and memory, and criticised some of his followers for doing so. In other words, Wundt would have been critical about the scientific nature of much of modern psychology.

The other 'founding father', William James, was far more inclusive about what he considered valid subject matter for psychology. He included things like the 'stream of consciousness', for instance. But James too can be counted amongst those critical of the scientific credentials of psychology. Toward the end of his life he gave up psychology in preference for philosophy. He referred to his own classic work *The Principles of Psychology* (1890) as a 'loathsome, distended, tumefied, dropsical mass', and believed that it showed only that there was no such thing as a *science* of psychology.

Despite these modest and somewhat critical beginnings, psychology nevertheless took off rapidly as a science. To explain this we can point to four broad factors that contributed to the development of psychology as a science:

1   Chapter 21 Perspectives outlines how Darwin's work laid the foundation for a scientific psychology by erasing the distinction between human and animal and opening the door to thinking about 'the mind' and human behaviour as no different in kind than any other aspect of nature. This was one major breakthrough that allowed the development of scientific psychology. If the human mind is just another part of nature, then like other parts of nature it can be studied scientifically.

2   Another factor was the development of scientific *methods* (such as those of Fechner and Weber). It is one thing having the *idea* that psychology ought to be a science. It is another thing to develop methods that actually allow things considered 'psychological' to be studied in a scientific way. Wundt was able to set up his laboratory in 1879 because he had simple methods such as systematic introspection.

3   A third major factor was a growing social need (particularly in the USA and Northern Europe, where scientific psychology began) for solutions to human problems such as crime, mental illness, education and poverty. The end of the 19th century was a time when schools, hospitals, mental asylums and other institutions were being built on a vast scale. There was a growing need to invent specialists with technical knowledge of how to deal with human problems. What could be done with children who refused to go to school; who are too clever for the rest of their classmates, or not clever enough? Questions such as these became important – for example, in the USA more than one public high school a day was built between 1890 and 1920 (Danziger, 1994). Just as the natural sciences gave rise to technologies for engineering the physical world into a more functional order, so psychology promised to provide technologies for 'humaneering' the modern social world – with all its new 'human' problems – into an efficiently working system.

4   A fourth major factor in this development was the fact that science was fast becoming the only respectable way of gaining 'proper' knowledge. The scientific method was proving to be very powerful in other disciplines, and scientific knowledge was increasingly seen as the way to replace irrational and superstitious beliefs with 'true facts'. If psychology as a discipline was to be taken seriously, and to be given a serious role in society, it had to be scientific.

So, in summary, psychology became a science because:

- Darwin's theory of evolution made it conceptually possible
- The development of methods made it technically possible
- The social and political situation made it practically necessary
- The pro-science cultural climate made it socially desirable.

4.2   The nature of science

It is a mistake to think of science as a single and simple thing. There are hundreds of sciences, each with slightly different characteristics suited to their different subject matters. Each has its own peculiar methods and language. Historically, it seems that as soon as a general characteristic of science is identified which would enable us to say 'THIS is science', some new scientific discovery, new theory, or new method comes along which changes the definition. If anything, science is all about continual change and flexibility. However, generally speaking, and with this warning in mind, we can identify seven broad characteristics of science:

1   **Science has empirical aspects.** As well as *thinking* about the nature of the world, scientists tend to use techniques that attempt to bring the scientist *in contact* with the world. This *empirical* (meaning 'experience-based') aspect of science is usually contrasted with other ways of gaining knowledge through reason, logic and argument (these are sometimes called 'rationalist'). For the empirically minded, no amount of argument and reason is a substitute for actually *looking* (or touching, or any other *sensory experience* for that matter) at how things are.

2   **Science involves methods.** This 'sensory experience' of nature tends not to be direct. To be empirical, scientists tend to use empirical *methods*. In a sense, methods, techniques and other scientific instruments *mediate* between the scientist and the world under study (think of how a telescope or microscope mediates or 'goes between' the observer and the observed, for example, or how a thermometer allows heat to be quantified and measured). Methods allow aspects of the world that would otherwise be invisible and untouchable to 'show up' to the scientist.

3   **Science involves being methodical.** These empirical methods should be rigorous and, as the word implies, *methodical*. The techniques used in contacting the aspect of the world under study, for example, should be followable in a clear, step-by-step fashion such that another person could reasonably repeat or *replicate* the study. The circumstances of the study should be controllable and carefully *controlled* so that the scientist can be reasonably sure that they are studying one thing and not another. Measurements and distinctions must be *precise*.

4   **Science aspires to be objective.** The observations made about the world should be as *objective* as possible. That is, the scientific observer should try to keep their preconceptions, prejudices and biases about what they are seeing to a minimum. Although absolute objectivity may be impossible, an effort is made to see the world as it is, and not just as we expect it to be or wish it to be.

5   **Scientific procedures should ideally be repeatable.** The results of observations should be checked out by other equally objective scientists, and published results, being public knowledge, should also be checked out. In this way, claims to knowledge are scrutinised very carefully so that false claims are, hopefully, weeded out. The scientific knowledge that remains, given points 1-5, should be reliably *repeatable*.

6   **Science involves theory.** Being empirical does not mean that there is no place for thinking in science. In fact *theory* plays a key role in most sciences (although at different times in history, theory has played a greater or lesser role in science). Theories are usually informed guesses about how the things the scientist is interested in *work*. In this sense science often has two sides to it. A *descriptive* side, where an aspect of the world is observed and described as accurately and objectively as possible. And an *explanatory* side, where the scientist tries to find out not just how things are, but also how they work. Hence Darwin's theory of natural selection

is an *explanation* for the observations that had been described by himself and previous naturalists. Various facts were widely known in Darwin's time, for example that plants and animals once alive were now extinct; that animals could be bred to improve the stock; that many slightly different varieties of plant and animals existed. These *descriptions* were *explained* in Darwin's theory by the mechanism of natural selection.

7   **Science allows predictions to be made.** Where you have a theory, you can make *predictions* about what else you are likely to find, and how things will work under different conditions. Darwin's theory for example, predicted that there must be some physical mechanism which produces variations in organisms of each new generation which can then be 'naturally selected'. It was not until the 1920s that the concept of the 'gene' provided support for this prediction. So theories stimulate further empirical work to test them, and on the basis of what is discovered during the tests or experiments, new theories can be generated, and so on in a *cycle* which, hopefully, leads to more and better knowledge.

4.3 | But does psychology fit the bill as a science?

There is no doubt that psychologists, over the last hundred years, have adopted an empirical approach, used scientific methods in controlled conditions, developed and tested theories which have been checked out in public by other scientists, and so on. But even today there are many that would challenge psychology's status as a proper natural science. Many of these are 'outsiders' to the discipline. Many biologists, physicists and chemists have accused psychologists of failing to generate reliable, objective knowledge of real social value. Philosophers such as Gilbert Ryle and Ludwig Wittgenstein have been fairly scathing about the scientific pretensions of psychology, claiming that psychologists are struggling to study what is in effect an illusion of language. Politically informed critics have condemned the tendency of psychologists to treat as matters of fact what are in fact matters of politics and ethics. Even medical doctors have joined in the attack. Back in 1941, for instance, Dr Kenyon wrote a diatribe against psychology called *The Myth of Mind* in which he concludes that 'the so-called science of psychology as it exists today is a mass of contradictory theories. To call it a science in such circumstances is absurd … While science is a discipline of general and impersonal facts, psychology remains a collection of personal and antagonistic theories. In psychology there does not appear to be anything on which psychologists are generally agreed, and there are consequently no generally accepted laws to give it even the semblance of a science.'

However, increasingly, psychologists from within the discipline have begun getting 'critical' about their science status. Let us look at some of the common 'external' and 'internal' criticisms.

Some common criticisms of the science status of psychology

The story in Section 4.1 told of how psychology overcame certain obstacles and achieved institutional recognition as a science. However, we also saw that the founding fathers were actually very critical about the developments that followed their lead. These developments were quite rapid and quite diverse. In part, these developments were the result of an increasing social and practical need for something like psychology. This is one source of common criticism of psychology as a discipline:

1 **Psychology is torn between being an applied, practitioner craft and being a pure science.** A discipline can be practically useful without being properly scientific. Teaching, for instance, is a useful discipline, but not a science. Historians of psychology (Rose, 1985; Danziger, 1994) have conclusively shown that the rapid development of early psychology, particularly in the USA, was a direct result of its perceived practical usefulness, and only secondarily of its pure credentials as a science. In 1927, Jastrow (cited in Danziger, 1994), who was very much part of these developments, put it like this:

   'It is the outstanding feature of our reconstructed psychology that it realised and accepted the obligation to apply to education, to social relations, to practical affairs, to the control of human behaviour generally, normal and abnormal, desirable and undesirable, the conclusions arising from the scientific study of the mental side of man.'

   This criticism is that these 'conclusions' were not forthcoming, and yet psychology was popular in its applied form anyway. This is fine, but it should not pretend to be a science.

2 **Psychology treats what are really political questions as if they were scientific, and this makes it pseudoscientific.** Another common criticism (see Malson, 1998; Morss, 1996) follows from the above point. To the extent that psychology is to do with 'the control of human behaviour generally, normal and abnormal, desirable and undesirable' it is to do with politics. This makes psychology a kind of 'soft' police force. It tries to shape people into thinking, feeling and acting as society dictates they should (see Chapter 37 Issues, and the earlier section on eugenics). This is a world away from the kind of science that Wundt and James had in mind, yet it came to dominate psychology shortly after their deaths. It is as if the founding fathers had done the work of persuading the intellectual society that psychology *could* be a science, but once that had been done, the floodgates were opened and *any* kind of work on thoughts, feelings or behaviour could be undertaken under the banner of scientific psychology. Psychology, from the position of this criticism, is not science, it is politics.

3 **Psychology lacks a clearly defined object of study.** One of the defining features of the natural sciences is that they have a very clear idea about *what* they are studying, *how* and *why*. The quotation from Kenyon above is scathing about the lack of agreement amongst psychologists, and there are still plenty of critics today who would agree with him. As put by Staats (1991) 'psychology has so many unrelated elements of knowledge with so much mutual discreditation, inconsistency, redundancy, and controversy that abstracting general meaning is a great problem'. This is brought out clearly in Chapter 39 Perspectives where it can be seen that each of the main 'perspectives' in the discipline works with a different sense of what psychology is actually *about*. This basic disagreement over the essential subject matter does not help the cause of scientific psychology. In Kuhn's (1962)

terms, this means that psychology is not a mature science since it lacks a 'paradigm' – an agreed and exemplary model of what a science is all about. Consider the following list of examples:

- What Freud thought of as 'the psychological' (mostly unconscious processes), for example, bears almost no resemblance to Wundt's subject matter (consciousness).
- The behaviourist revolution in US psychology was really a change in definition as to *what counts as psychological*. In other words, for Watson, Skinner and the like, the new subject matter of psychology was *behaviour*. For radical behaviourists, Freud's unconscious and Wundt's conciousness do not exist! They believed that Freudians and Wundtians were not only studying a product of their imagination, but also using methods that fell short of scientific standards.
- The 'psychological' for humanists is something different again – the 'whole' person, including emotions and subjectivity. They believe that other psychologists had artificially divided the psychological up into portions, and were hence studying only the dead product of their own dissections.
- For psychologists in the 'psychometric' tradition, started by Francis Galton, the proper subject matter is different again. They study 'individual differences' by administering tests and questionnaires to large numbers of people.
- For cognitive psychologists, to give a final example, the 'psychological' that should be studied by psychologists is essentially 'information processing'. How are stimuli from the environment 'processed' in the brain and transformed in the process?

4 **In the absence of a clearly defined object of study, psychologists have defined their practice reactively (in reaction to other psychologists).** That is to say, psychologists of different camps have defended and justified what they do in large part by arguing that it is better than what *other psychologists* have done. For instance, behaviourism carved itself out, in part, as being not *introspectionism* (introspectionism largely ignored behaviour). Cognitivism carved itself out, in part, as being *not behaviourism* (behaviourism largely ignored the mind). Humanism too, carved itself out as not experimental psychology (experimental psychology ignores the 'whole person'). In this sense, the eyes of these psychologists are more on each other than on their subject matter, which has a tendency to disappear in the controversy.

5 **Through being over-keen to be accepted as scientific, psychologists have ended up providing a distorted account of their subject matter.** This criticism sometimes goes under the label of *scientism*. Unlike proper science, scientism is the copying or 'aping' of science. This accusation is most often levelled at behaviourist approaches, but it has also been applied more broadly as an attack on all forms of experimentation in psychology (Harré & Secord, 1978). The gist of the critique is that human psychology is an enormously complex thing, but that psychological explanations have typically provided crude simplifications, in part so that their work could be called scientific. Now, a *good* simplification is good science, since it is the discovery of simplicity in what previously looked complicated. A scientific explanation showing that the morning star and the evening star are both manifestations of the planet Venus is a useful simplification.

But to seriously contend that everything important about human learning can be modelled on the learning of a rat risks *reductionism* – a crude simplification. There are various aspects of such distortion, according to the critics:

- First, a mechanistic model (that people are machines) is imposed upon us, when, according to some critics, we are not machines, nor do we behave like machines.

- Second, things such as 'personality' and 'attitude' that only make sense in context are stripped of context and treated as 'variables' in an experimental or psychometric design. This translation distorts that actual nature of things like personality.

- Third, human behaviour generally, when studied in an experimental context, is stripped from its broader context. If that broader context is what makes the behaviour meaningful, then this transformation is meaningless.

- Fourth, the normative (ethics, values, morality) and subjective aspects of human beings, which some hold to be of great importance in defining our nature, are basically removed from standard experimental designs and people are treated as if they were determined by causes, not reasons (see Unit 1 above). Through the application of such scientism, people are devalued and even debased.

6 **There is very little agreement amongst psychologists as to what counts as a 'fact' in their discipline.** In part, this is because much of human action is meaningful action which is done for reasons and purposes. When dealing with 'meaning', one inevitably comes up against the problem of the possible existence of many interpretations of any given act. Is a waving hand: a salute? a goodbye? a hello? a bid at an auction? a vote? a cry for help? The point is that any action can be any or none of these depending upon the specific context and the meanings that are laid upon it in that context. For Gergen (1980) two of the implications of this for the science of social psychology are:

- Virtually any experimental result developed as support for a given theory may be used as support for virtually any alternative theory. Since participants' actions are open to a variety of interpretations, they can be used to fit a variety of theories.

- Psychological theory provides abstractions for which there are no unambiguous particulars or instances. Take the concept of unconscious drives. It is not possible to state with certainty that a particular action is an example of an unconscious drive.

7 **Psychology's concepts are in a conceptual muddle.** This critique has come from influential philosophers such as Ludwig Wittgenstein, Gilbert Ryle and John Austin who influenced the development of 'ordinary language philosophy'. The basic argument is that just because words like 'forgetting', 'mind', 'attitude', 'understanding' and 'emotion' exist in ordinary language does not mean that they exist as real, tangible things in reality. Psychologists have taken 'psychological' words from ordinary language, and treated them as if they were measurable mental properties that have a causal influence on other measurable mental properties. According to critics, this is why psychologists have such trouble reaching agreement – their basic terms are not sufficiently clear.

4.4 Views of science

As noted earlier, there are many different views of science. Each view will, to some extent, give different answers to the questions: Is psychology a science? Can psychology become a science? This section looks at two of the most influential views of science.

Thomas Kuhn – 'normal science'

In *The Structure of Scientific Revolutions*, Thomas Kuhn (1962) argues that 'normal science' – the way science is usually conducted – bears little relationship to standard views of the scientific method. According to Kuhn, science operates within a *paradigm* – a theoretical framework which states how the world operates. An example is Einstein's paradigm in physics. A paradigm not only presents an explanation of how something works, it also states what questions scientists should ask and the methods they should use to answer them.

Most of the time, scientists in a particular discipline operate within a single paradigm. For example, until the 16th century, Western astronomy was based on the *theory of terracentricity* – the idea that planets and the sun move round the earth. It is possible to support this idea with observations and measurements. And it is possible to ignore or explain away contradictory evidence which might challenge it.

According to Kuhn, most scientists are committed to the existing paradigm. There is no major change within a scientific discipline until one paradigm is replaced by another. Kuhn calls this process a *scientific revolution* – it is sudden and revolutionary because a whole way of thinking about the world is swept away within a relatively short space of time. Scientific revolutions occur when evidence accumulates which cannot be explained in terms of the existing paradigm. This happened with the Copernican revolution in astronomy in the 16th century. Copernicus stated that the sun, not the earth was the centre of the universe and that the planets orbited the sun. This view of the universe appeared to make sense of observations that could not be explained in terms of the previous paradigm.

Kuhn's views question the belief that science is objective. He presents a picture of scientists working in their own communities, deeply committed to their shared paradigm which they do their best to defend. Switches from one paradigm to another are strongly resisted, often in the face of conflicting evidence.

Where does psychology stand in terms of Kuhn's view of science? First, psychology is in a pre-scientific or pre-paradigmatic stage. So far, it has failed to develop a single, dominant paradigm. Instead, psychology consists of a range of competing perspectives – psychodynamic, behaviourist, evolutionary, humanist and so on. As such, psychology cannot be seen as a science in Kuhn's terms.

Second, psychology has often been criticised for lacking objectivity. As such, critics argue, it cannot be seen as a scientific discipline. However, in this respect, Kuhn would see psychology as little different from the so-called 'hard sciences' such as physics and chemistry. Kuhn sees commitment to a paradigm in the hard sciences as based as much on values and beliefs as on objective knowledge.

Karl Popper – falsification

In *The Logic of Scientific Discovery*, Karl Popper (1959) argues that the distinguishing characteristic of science is the development of theories which can be tested against evidence and be capable of falsification. In other words, scientific theories are constructed in such a way that they can be shown to be untrue.

Theories that survive falsification tests are not necessarily true. They have simply not been falsified. The following oft-quoted example illustrates this point. 'All swans are white' is a scientific statement because it can be falsified. But, however many times it is confirmed by observation, it cannot be accepted as true because the very next swan might be black, red, blue or yellow. In this respect, there are no absolute truths in science.

Popper has little time for many of the claims made by social scientists that their work is scientific. He is particularly scathing of psychodynamic theory which he sees as impossible to falsify. Concepts like the Id, Ego and Superego and processes such as repression cannot be directly observed and measured. According to Popper, psychodynamic theory fails to produce testable hypotheses which can be falsified. As a result, it is not scientific.

However, Popper believes that theories of human behaviour which are open to the possibility of falsification can be developed. He argues that social scientists, like natural scientists, should start with a statement or hypothesis that can be tested. This hypothesis should be very precise and should state exactly what will happen in particular circumstances. Researchers should constantly try to find evidence which disproves or falsifies their predictions. In Popper's view, the experimental method provides the precision and control required to test hypotheses. The possibility of doing this in psychology is examined in the following section.

Key terms

Paradigm *A dominant theoretical framework in a scientific discipline.*

Normal science *Working within the confines of a paradigm without seriously questioning or challenging that paradigm.*

Scientific revolution *The replacement of one paradigm with another.*

Falsification *Proving that a statement or hypothesis is untrue or false.*

4.5 Laboratory experiments

At first sight, the laboratory experiment in psychology appears to offer the control and precision which Popper sees as essential for testing scientific statements. It provides a controlled environment in which variables can be isolated and manipulated, observed and measured. It allows experiments to be replicated – repeated under the same conditions. It provides a reliable setting to test and falsify hypotheses.

Since their discipline began, psychologists have expended considerable time and effort refining the methodology of laboratory experiments. They have developed a battery of techniques in the hope of ensuring that the results of experiments are reliable and valid. These techniques are examined in detail in on pp 231-235 and pp 251-259.

The human factor

Despite this outpouring of effort, reflected in large and detailed books on research methods, critics argue that laboratory experiments in psychology can never attain the objectivity and rigour of experiments in the natural sciences. This is because experiments in psychology involve human beings – participants and experimenters.

The natural scientist investigates the behaviour of matter and assumes that matter always reacts predictably to external stimuli. Matter has no intentions, purposes, motives or meanings which direct its behaviour. Human beings do. Human beings don't simply *react* to stimuli presented to them in the laboratory. They give meanings to those stimuli and *act* in terms of those meanings. The laboratory situation is a social situation. The actions of both participants and experimenters reflect this.

Some psychologists argue that the laboratory experiment is not appropriate for the study of human beings. Since every aspect of the experiment will be given meanings by the participants, it is not possible to say with any certainty what is directing the participants' actions. Specific examples of this problem are outlined on pp 234-235 and pp 263-266. They will be briefly summarised here.

Demand characteristics These are cues or clues in an experiment that convey the researcher's hypothesis to the participant. For example, participants try to make sense of experiments and give meaning to the tasks they perform. They may try to guess what the experiment is about and how the researcher expects them to behave. They may act in terms of these expectations and try to please the researcher (Orne, 1962). If they do this, they are responding to demand characteristics rather than to the independent variable.

Evaluation apprehension Some participants may experience *evaluation apprehension* – they may be worried about how they appear to the researcher and what the researcher might think about them. For example, they may try to look good and behave in ways which are socially acceptable. This is known as the *social desirability effect*.

Laboratory experiments are designed to measure responses to independent variables. If participants are concerned about how they appear to the researcher, then this might affect their response to the independent variable.

Investigator effects This refers to the ways in which researchers influence the behaviour of participants. For example, a smile, a frown, or a questioning look from the experimenter might encourage participants to behave in particular ways. The same applies to the characteristics of the experimenter – whether they are male or female, black or white, attractive or unattractive, cheerful or solemn, and so on. All these factors may affect the participants' behaviour.

Researchers sometimes expect and hope that experiments will produce certain results. These hopes and expectations may influence participants. For example, a smile when their behaviour matches the expected findings may encourage participants to continue to behave in that way (Rosenthal, 1966).

Artificiality Both the laboratory setting and the tasks participants are asked to perform can appear artificial and unrealistic. In a laboratory experiment, participants are removed from their everyday settings. They are directed by an experimenter, often in the company of complete strangers. For many people, this is a brand new experience far removed from their everyday lives. It can appear artificial and 'unreal'.

Sometimes the tasks participants are asked to perform appear meaningless. For example, learning nonsense syllables in memory experiments may make little sense to participants. However, not all experimental tasks are as artificial as this. Some experiments attempt to simulate life outside the laboratory – for example, experiments on eyewitness testimony which show participants a film of an accident or a robbery. But even this is a long way from the real thing.

Ecological validity This refers to the extent to which the findings of an experiment can be generalised to settings outside the laboratory. Critics argue that participants are unlikely to behave normally and naturally in a laboratory because of the artificiality of the setting and the tasks. As a result, it is unlikely that their behaviour in the laboratory will reflect their behaviour in other settings. If this is the case, then laboratory experiments will tend to have low ecological validity – it is unlikely that their findings will apply to other settings.

Some researchers argue that the laboratory experiment in psychology falls short of the standards required by the scientific method. And, if there are problems with laboratory experiments, these problems are magnified with other research methods – field experiments, naturalistic and participant observation, questionnaire surveys and interviews. The control and precision offered by these methods is considerably less than that provided by laboratory experiments.

4.6 Evaluation: In defence of scientific psychology

First, it is all too easy to find examples of poor science in psychology and to thereby dismiss the whole discipline. Such criticism is much easier than the difficult task of actually doing good scientific psychological work.

Related to this is a second point. We should not think of the 'psychology and science debate' as an 'all or nothing' issue. *Some* aspects of human behaviour might be amenable to scientific study, others not so easily. Early scientific psychology, for example, emerged from other scientific disciplines such as physiology. There is no question that the scientific method is usefully applied to working out how, for example, the visual system works, and it is a short step from there to begin asking questions about the psychology of perception – How is visual information organised in the brain? How do physical stimuli relate to felt sensations and perceptions? Psychologists who work on topics such as these act and think very much like natural scientists.

However, it is a much bigger leap to apply scientific methods to larger and less well understood aspects of psychology. It is no surprise, therefore, that *social psychologists* regularly debate the 'science issue'. Social psychologists deal with questions such as leadership, attitude formation, prejudice and so on, which are

comparatively:

- Closer to common sense
- Closer to the social sciences
- More difficult to define objectively
- More subject to distortion through decontextualisation
- More directly linked to immediate political concerns.

This does not mean that social psychology is a problem for psychology. It is, however, a challenge. More positively, it is a space where psychology comes into potentially productive dialogue with sociology, history, anthropology and so on. The point is that when assessing the 'science question' it must be recognised that psychology as a discipline extends all the way from the study of visual perception to the study of social groups. Consider this textbook, for example. It covers a wide range of topics including the instinctive behaviour of animals, the structure of the brain, the sense of self, the formation of personal relationships and the formation of cultures! Scientific techniques and thinking can be more easily applied to some of these topics than to others.

The challenge all psychologists face is to work out ways of doing science that acknowledge the full complexity of the subject matter. This leads to a final issue.

4.7 What kind of science? The natural sciences and the social sciences

Some psychologists, however, take a different path. They argue that psychology should not be a natural science. Usually, these challenges make the argument that human thoughts, feelings and actions are not the kinds of things that can be studied objectively. In studying a 'state of mind' or an 'attitude', for example, one is studying a 'point of view'. How, the critics argue, can something so 'subjective' be studied 'objectively' as if it were an 'object'?

Further, it is argued that human thoughts, feelings and actions are not predictable in the way that physical processes (such as the moon orbiting the earth) are predictable. Human behaviour, as many of the chapters of this book illustrate, changes in many respects over time (through history) and across cultures. This is largely because people learn what to do from other people, and styles of life are passed down from generation to generation in the form of tradition. In this respect we should not think of human behaviour as something natural which is governed by discoverable natural laws. Instead, many of the patterns we observe in human life – getting married in church, driving on the left, speaking English, watching football, going to pubs, etc – are the result of socialisation into a given culture. Such behaviour often follows regular patterns not because it is determined by natural causes, but because it is organised by social rules and norms, and backed up by social, not natural laws.

This gives us a way of understanding how to divide up which aspects of psychology can be scientific in the natural sense, and which not. Crudely speaking, we can make a distinction between the study of things that have been made up or constructed by people, and the study of things that have not been made up or constructed by people. Some things depend upon us for their existence, other things do not. A chair has been made by people, but the wood out of which it is made (unless it has been genetically engineered) has not. Although this distinction has its own problems, historically it has allowed a difference to be drawn between two very distinct sets of disciplines:

- **The natural sciences** – such as biology, physics, chemistry, geology and so on (which study what seems not to have been made by people) and
- **The social sciences** – such as sociology, anthropology, economics, and politics (which study what seems to have been made by people).

Psychology is very much a 'hybrid' which combines both of these. This is because the subject matter of 'the psychological' is composed of parts that are natural, parts which are humanly made, and parts which are difficult to assign to either category. On the one hand, some of our behaviour, such as reflex actions like knee jerks and pupil dilations, is clearly 'natural' and determined by clearly definable causes. We did not 'make' our own bodies in the way that we make chairs and computers. On the other hand, some of our behaviour is 'made up' by people. Being a traffic warden and giving parking tickets to illegally parked cars is a 'socially constructed' thing to do. Such practices are not 'determined by causes', they are 'performed for reasons'. We would expect all people at all times (unless there is something wrong with them) to respond to a light hammer tap on the knee with an involuntary upward movement of the lower leg. We would not expect all people at all times to go around sticking parking tickets on cars. People are partly constructed by people, and partly not. Let us explore this distinction further.

Dilthey and Vico

In 19th century Germany, when psychology was emerging as a modern science, this ambiguous or hybrid status could be clearly seen. The German philosopher Wilhelm Dilthey, however, who coined the distinction between sciences of nature and sciences of human historical productions, argued that psychology is a social science and not a natural science. For Dilthey, a natural science strives to explain nature by objectively describing the lawful causal relations out of which the natural world is built. A social science, by contrast, aims to understand some human event or construction by recreating its meaning for the actors involved, and their reasons for acting.

The natural sciences 'explain', the social sciences 'understand'. A similar distinction had been made in 1725 by the Neapolitan Gianbattista Vico. Vico argued that we stand far more chance of understanding the humanly made world than the natural one, since it is easier for people to understand what people have themselves created. The causes of natural things, by contrast, must necessarily be far more difficult to establish, since we didn't cause them ourselves.

Wundt and Windelband

Wilhelm Wundt, often seen as the 'founding father' of modern psychology, proposed that psychology should be split in two. Some aspects of this 'hybrid' psychology can be studied as a natural science (as discussed above), but the most important bits should be part of the social sciences – Wundt called this aspect of psychology *Volkerpsychologie* or 'folk-psychology'. Another German philosopher, Wilhelm Windelband, argued for a reworking of Wilhelm Dilthey's natural science/social distinction into a distinction between:

- **Nomothetic knowledge** which strives to find universal laws of reality that apply in all times and places, and
- **Idiographic knowledge** which strives to 'bring to life' the specific details of a unique event or occurrence.

One of his main reasons for this influential 'reworking' was that psychology did not fit neatly into either the natural science category, or the humanities category. With his new distinction Windelband was able to argue that psychology, despite its 'human' subject matter (which would make it a social science) may *approach* that subject matter *nomothetically* (ie, like a typical natural science). In other words, Windelband's emphasis is not on whether a part of the world is natural or humanly made, but on whether it is to be approached with the aim of discovering universal laws or bringing unique events to meaningful life. This distinction between the natural and the social sciences is still very much alive and well in current debates, such as those about qualitative methodology.

Summary

1. Before psychology could develop as a scientific discipline it had to break through the philosophical settlements made by Descartes and by Kant, both of which excluded the possibility of a scientific psychology.

2. Wundt was able to break through these settlements since he built on the work of Weber and Fechner which provided basic ways of making psychological questions accessible to mathematical analysis.

3. The following factors contributed to the development of psychology as a science – the Darwinian revolution; the development of methods; the social need for an applied discipline of social control; and the widespread value accorded to science.

4. Natural science is an *empirical* endeavour which employs scientific methods in *controlled* conditions which permit *replication*. Scientists try to be as *objective* as possible in their observations, which can be *checked out* by other scientists. Science also involves the development of *theories* which make sense of existing observations and predict new observations which can be *tested* through the same scientific process.

5. There have been long historical debates as to whether psychology is a science. Critics claim that psychology is torn between being applied and being pure; that it treats political questions as if they were scientific, thereby risking accusations of pseudoscience; that it lacks a clearly defined object of study; that it has defined its scientific identity reactively; that it has been scientistic; that there is little agreement over 'facts'; and that its main concepts are muddled.

6. Psychology is situated somewhere in between the natural sciences and the social sciences, and this is the source of a good deal of controversy over its science status.

References

Armstrong, D.M. (1968). *A materialist theory of the mind*. New York: Humanities Press.

Baldwin, S. (2000). How should ADHD be treated? *The Psychologist, 13*, 598-599.

Ceci, S.J. & Williams, W.M. (Eds.) (1999). *The nature-nurture debate: The essential readings*. Oxford: Blackwell.

Conrad, P. & Gabe, J. (1999). *Sociological perspectives on the new genetics*. Oxford: Blackwell.

Cooper, P. (2000). How should ADHD be treated? *The Psychologist, 13*, 599-600.

Crick, F. (1994). *The astonishing hypothesis: The scientific search for the soul*. New York: Scribners.

Danziger, C. (1994). *Constructing the subject: Historical origins of psychological research*. Cambridge: Cambridge University Press.

Danziger, K. (1978). *Socialization*. Harmondsworth: Penguin.

Ericsson, K.A. & Charness, N. (1999). Expert performance: Its structure and acquisition. In S.J. Ceci & W.M. Williams (Eds.), *The nature-nurture debate: The essential readings*. Oxford: Blackwell.

Freud, S. (1915/1975). *Introductory lectures on psychoanalysis*. Harmondsworth: Penguin.

Gardener, H. (1985). *The mind's new science: A history of the cognitive revolution*. New York: Basic Books.

Gergen, K.J. (1980). Toward intellectual audacity in social psychology. In R. Gilmour & S. Duck (Eds.), *The development of social psychology*. London: Academic Press.

Greenfield, S.A. (2000). *The private life of the brain*. London: Penguin.

Haralambos, M. (Ed.) (1996). *Sociology: A new approach* (3rd ed.). Ormskirk: Causeway.

Harré, R. & Secord, P.F. (1978). *The explanation of social behaviour*. Oxford: Blackwell.

Herrnstein, C. & Murray, R.J. (1994). *The bell-curve: Intelligence and class structure in American life*. New York: Free Press.

James, W. (1890). *Principles of psychology*. New York: Henry Holt.

Jones, E. (1928). *Psycho-analysis*. London: Ernest Benn.

Kuhn, T.S. (1962). *The structure of scientific revolutions*. Chicago: University of Chicago Press

Kenyon, F. (1941). *The myth of the mind*. London: Watts & Co.

Lewontin, R.C. (1993). *The doctrine of DNA: Biology as ideology*. Harmondsworth: Penguin.

Mackintosh, N.J. (1980). Book review of *Cyril Burt: Psychologist* by J.S. Hearnshaw, *British Journal of Psychology, 71*, 174-175.

Malson, H. (1998). *The thin woman*. London: Routledge.

McDougal, W. (1908). *Social psychology*. London: Methuen and Co.

Morss, J.R. (1996). *Growing critical*. London: Routledge.

Muller-Hill, B. (1994). Lessons from the dark and distant past. In A. Clarke (Ed.), *Genetic counselling: Practice and principles*. London: Routledge.

Orne, M.T. (1962). On the social psychology of the psychology experiment: With particular reference to demand characteristics and their implications. *American Psychologist, 17*, 776-783.

Popper, K. (1959). *The logic of scientific discovery*. London: Hutchinson.

Rose, N. (1985). *The psychological complex*. London: Routledge.

Rose, S. (1997). *Lifelines: Biology, freedom and determinism*. Harmondsworth: Penguin.

Rose, S., Kamin, L.J. & Lewontin, R.C. (1984). *Not in our genes: Biology, ideology and human nature*. Harmondsworth: Penguin.

Rosenthal, R. (1966). Covert communication in the psychological experiment. *Psychological Bulletin, 67*, 356-367.

Skinner, B.F. (1991). *Beyond freedom and dignity*. Harmondsworth: Penguin. (First published in 1971).

Sperry, R.W. (1987). Consciousness and causality. In R.L. Gregory (Ed.), *The Oxford companion to the mind*. Oxford: Oxford University Press.

Staats, A.W. (1991). *Psychology's crisis of disunity: Philosophy and method for a unified science*. New York: Praeger.

Stainton Rogers, R., Stenner, P., Gleeson, K. & Stainton Rogers, W. (1995). *Social psychology: A critical agenda*. Cambridge: Polity.

Stearns, P. (1989). *Jealousy: The evolution of an emotion in American history*. New York: New York University Press.

Tomkins, S. (1962). *Affect, imagery, consciousness*. Vol. 1. London: Tavistock.

Watson, J. (1925). *Behaviourism*. New York: Norton.

Wolpert, L. (1997). Reduced science. *The Independent on Sunday*, 1st June.

▶ Introduction

This chapter begins with a simple truth. Things can appear differently depending upon how we *approach* them. The following poem written by Kipling illustrates this point.

> Six wise men of India
> An elephant did find
> And carefully they felt its shape
> (For all of them were blind).
>
> The first he felt towards the tusk,
> 'It does to me appear,
> This marvel of an elephant
> Is very like a spear'.
>
> The second sensed the creature's side
> Extended flat and tall,
> 'Ahah!' he cried and did conclude,
> 'This animal's a wall'.
>
> The third had reached towards a leg
> And said, 'It's clear to me
> What we should all have instead
> This creature's like a tree'.
>
> The fourth had come upon the trunk
> Which he did seize and shake,
> Quoth he, 'This so-called elephant
> Is really just a snake'.
>
> The fifth had felt the creature's ear
> And fingers o'er it ran,
> 'I have the answer, never fear,
> The creature's like a fan!'
>
> The sixth had come upon the tail
> As blindly he did grope,
> 'Let my conviction now prevail
> This creature's like a rope'.
>
> And so these men of missing sight
> Each argued loud and long
> Though each was partly in the right
> They all were in the wrong.

Each of the wise men approached the elephant differently and emerged with a different picture of what the elephant was like. This chapter looks at approaches in psychology. It shows how each approach gives a different picture of what human beings are like.

Chapter summary

- Unit 1 deals with the evolutionary approach.
- Unit 2 deals with the biopsychological approach.
- Unit 3 deals with the psychodynamic approach.
- Unit 4 deals with the behaviourist approach.
- Unit 5 deals with the cognitive approach.
- Unit 6 deals with the humanistic approach.
- Unit 7 deals with the social constructionist approach.

The guiding metaphors of each approach

The six wise men of India made sense of something unfamiliar and complex by comparing it with something familiar and less complex. They used a process we can call *seeing as*. The elephant was seen as a spear, a wall, a tree, a snake, a fan and a rope.

Psychological approaches use this process of *seeing as*. Each approach sees human beings in a particular way. The aim of science is to check if the world is really like we think it is. Usually, an attempt is made to systematically represent *seeing as* in the form of a *model*. Each psychological approach presents a model of human behaviour. If this simplified model behaves like the real thing, then we assume that our way of *seeing as* is a good model – that it actually does represent the real thing.

Models can be seen as metaphors. A metaphor states that one thing is another thing that it resembles. Metaphors are often used to point to the essence of what is being described. For example, a human being *is* a biological machine; a human being *is* an information processor; a human being *is* a free spirit.

In this chapter, the phrase *guiding metaphor* will be used to refer to the main model used by each psychological approach. The characteristic guiding metaphors for each approach are as follows.

- **The evolutionary approach** views human and animal behaviour and cognition *as if* these were adaptive solutions to problems of survival which have emerged over a long history of evolution. The human being is seen as an integrated cluster of adaptive functions.

- **The biopsychological approach** views psychological processes *as if* they are produced by biological structures and processes. The human being, in short, is seen as a complex biological machine.

- **The psychodynamic approach** views human thought, feeling and behaviour *as if* these were the end result of internal dynamic processes involving conflicts between different parts of our psyche. The human being is seen as the site of a 'psycho-drama' of largely unconscious internal dynamic conflicts.

- **The behaviourist approach** views human and animal behaviour *as if* it were a response to, or elicited by, events in the environment. The human being is seen as the sum of their personal history of conditioning.

- **The cognitive approach** views human thought, feeling and action *as if* these were the end result of a complex and largely unconscious job of *information processing*. The human being is seen as a computer that manipulates and processes incoming information, yielding an output that is useful to the organism.

- **The humanistic approach** views people *as if* they were unique individuals capable of defining their own lives and achieving authenticity and self-actualisation. The human being is seen as an ethical actor with free will.

- **The social constructionist approach** views human beings *as if* they were producers of languages, activities and cultures which in turn produce them. The human being is seen as the product of, and contributor to, an ongoing social conversation.

This chapter outlines each approach and sets it in historical context. The key concepts used are explained and then illustrated by looking at how each approach would go about studying the topic of emotion. The typical methods used by each approach are discussed, as well as the main strengths and weaknesses of the approaches.

Unit 1 The evolutionary approach

KEY ISSUES

1 **What role did Darwin's theory of evolution play in the development of psychology?**

2 **How do emotions appear from an evolutionary perspective?**

3 **What are the key methods used in the evolutionary approach?**

Modern biology was unified by the theory of evolution developed by Charles Darwin (1809-1882). Darwin's *theory of evolution by natural selection* provided the conceptual ground needed for the discipline of psychology to develop half way through the 19th century. It is important and useful to know *why* this is so.

1.1 Historical background: How did evolutionary biology help make the discipline of psychology possible?

Darwin helped to change the dominant metaphors and models used in the Western world to make sense of *what people are* and of their *place in the world*. The following story is a brief and simplified account of the dominant pre-Darwinian metaphors and models. It provides a useful point of contrast which makes it clear how the biological guiding metaphor represents a *change* in our way of *seeing as*.

Before Darwin: the story of the 'Great Chain of Being'

The Great Chain of Being A particularly important and influential way of viewing *people* and their *place* in the world was constructed in Ancient Greece by the philosopher Aristotle (384-322 BC). Translated into English, this is the concept of the *Great Chain of Being*. This influential story was picked up by Medieval Christians as a central aspect of their picture of the person. Basically, all life forms are seen as being links in an enormous chain. This chain is like a ladder that leads from the most lowly weeds and leeches right up to God. The closer to God a creature is, the more of God's spiritual perfection it contains. Humankind, in this view, is nature's crowning perfection: the most Godlike creature of God's creations. Beyond humans, however, there are angels, and beyond angels, God Himself. What is important is that humans are defined in relation to their *place* in this chain. Humans represent a mid-way point between the *bodily matter* of beasts and the eternal and *non-bodily spirit* of the divine. Our *psyche* (which is the Greek word for 'soul'), in terms of this image, is a little piece of divine and eternal spirit which is temporarily housed in a mortal body of flesh.

Dualism This story is one of the origins of *dualism*: the division of the person into two separate substances – body and soul, or matter and thought. Note also that this dualism is not neutral, but *value-laden*. Typically, the body (at the bottom of the chain) comes to stand for all that is bad, and the soul (at the top of the chain) for all that is good. The 17th century philosopher and scientist René Descartes (1596-1650) made this dualism central to modern philosophy and science. He called the two substances *extension* (anything which exists or 'extends' in time and space) and *thought* (which does not extend in time or space). His dualism was similarly value-laden. Extension was seen as *passive* and thought was seen as *active*. Human bodies (forms of extension) were seen as complicated clockwork machines that are passive unless moved by some other force. This force could be external, as in response to an outside stimulus, or internal as a result of control by the active human soul (a form of thought). For Descartes, the difference between humans and animals is that animals lack a soul, and are therefore simply passive machines responding to external forces.

From our perspective, an important implication of this dualism is the idea that it is possible to study extension *scientifically*. Thought, however, cannot be studied scientifically since it is thought that actively does the scientific thinking. This dualism is the reason why, for most of human history, a science of *psychology* (literally, the science of the soul or psyche) was not considered possible (although various people critical of the dominant tradition made attempts). Natural science – whether chemistry, biology, physics, geology or whatever – has traditionally dealt with objects or bodies (forms of extension) and the forces that produce and direct them. A science of the soul, however, would be a contradiction in terms since the soul is that part of the human that is not physical and hence not passively determined by external forces. Psychology as a possible discipline was hence excluded from scientific study, implicitly by Descartes and, later, explicitly by another hugely influential philosopher, Immanuel Kant (1724-1804). The experts on the soul were philosophers and theologians, and only they had the right to speak of it and define it. (See p504 for further discussion of dualism.)

Key term

Dualism *Dividing things into two aspects – for example, 'the mind' and 'the body'.*

The Darwinian revolution

To summarise the above pre-psychological *guiding metaphor* or picture of the person:

1   Humans are made up of two separate parts – the body and the soul.

2   Humans are different from other animals and so cannot be directly compared with non-human animals.

3   What makes humans different from other animals (the soul or psyche) cannot be studied scientifically since, not being an object (extensive), it is not objective and not subject to the laws of nature.

Charles Darwin helped make a significant change to this way of *seeing as*, and in so doing, helped to create a new picture. The image of humans presented in this new picture made it possible to develop a science of the psyche. In this sense, Darwin and his followers made modern psychology possible by changing our view of *who and what we are*. He did this by proposing a new mechanism to explain the evolution of the species. Others before him had proposed theories of evolution. Lamarck (1744-1829), for example, argued that the Great Chain of Being results from the fact that each organism has an innate drive to perfect itself, and that each adaptation that makes an organism more perfect can be passed down to its offspring. Also Herbert Spencer (1820-1903), a follower of Lamarck, coined the phrase 'survival of the fittest' in 1852. What Darwin contributed when he published *The Origin of the Species* in 1859 was the *mechanism* that explains how evolution is possible: *natural selection*.

Natural selection almost defines itself. Basically the theory assumes that there is a state of competition for scarce resources, where many creatures struggle against one another for essentials such as food and shelter. Those organisms that are well adapted to their surroundings will do well and will go on to reproduce (they are *naturally selected*). Those who are poorly adapted, feeble or weak will die off before reproducing (they are *de-selected*). An important aspect of Darwinism is that the variations between organisms (those things that make them more or less adapted and so more or less likely to be selected) are *random and arbitrary*. There is nothing inherently 'perfect' about the long neck of a giraffe, but in an environment where a long neck makes for a full belly, the owner of the long neck will survive, reproduce and, as we know since Mendel (1822-1884) discovered genes, pass on their long neck genes.

Materialism In proposing a mechanism to explain evolution, Darwin effectively erased the dividing line between humans and other animals. After Darwin, we think of ourselves as being descended from primates. Likewise, the mind/body dualism was profoundly challenged. Darwin began thinking of the human mind not as a bit of eternal and divine spirit, but as a complicated form of biological adaptation. In other words, Darwin replaced dualism with a single 'substance'. He referred to his position as *materialist*, and he was well aware that this was a provocative and even dangerous position to adopt, not least because of its atheism. In his notebooks from the late 1830s, he discusses how to present his views to the public in a less threatening way:

> 'To avoid stating how far, I believe, in materialism, say only that emotions, instincts, degrees of talent, which are hereditary are so because brain of child resembles parent stock' (Darwin's *M Notebooks*, Gruber & Barrett, 1980).

Darwin was not the first to think in this materialist way. Indeed, his father and his grandfather shared similar beliefs. However, in proposing natural selection as an explanatory mechanism, he was able to put together a powerful, and difficult to dismiss, model. Informed by this new *way of seeing*, the mind came to be treated as another natural object. Once *naturalised* in this way, there was no reason why the mind should not be treated scientifically just like any other *material* form. In other words:

1   The dualism of body and soul is challenged and the soul reduced to the body.

2   The distinction between human and animal is erased.

3   The 'soul', having been *naturalised*, came to be seen as something which could be studied scientifically.

Darwin thereby helped to change profoundly the way human beings see themselves. Note that this is not just a matter of new scientific findings. Darwin also provoked a reorganisation of the meaning of life and of our place within it. His notebooks show that he was deeply interested in *psychological* questions (such as the difference between sanity and insanity, the nature and nurture of selfishness and pride) and in *metaphysical* questions (such as the nature of free will, the problem of evil and the pre-existence of the 'soul'). As you might expect, he answers both psychological and metaphysical questions by turning to biology. (See pp 600-603 for further discussion of Darwin.)

In a sense, once a new *guiding metaphor* has been accepted by a scientist, then that scientist is faced with a new task: everything that has been understood according to the 'old' way of seeing must be *reinterpreted* and viewed 'afresh' according to the new. This is a kind of *revolution*, but a revolution in ideas: a conceptual revolution.

Activity 1   From dualism to materalism

Item A   A cartoon from *Punch*

MAN·IS·BVT·A·WORM·

Item B   Two primates

Darwin is pictured in both these 19th century cartoons. Item A illustrates the path of evolution ending with humans. Darwin appears with a bald head and a white beard. Item B shows two primates with ape-like bodies. The one on the left has Darwin's head.

Questions

1   How do these cartoons illustrate a new guiding metaphor?

2   How do they suggest it is now possible to study human beings scientifically?

1.2   Genes and behaviour

Darwin's theory of natural selection was given a tremendous boost by the 20th century confirmation of Mendel's discovery of *genes* as the means by which inherited information is transmitted and modified. The gene is thus the *unit of inheritance*. It is essentially a strand of DNA (short for

deoxyribonucleic acid) made out of a sequence of nucleotides. A given gene can be thought of as a kind of code. When the code is 'read' by the body, a particular function results, such as the making of a polypeptide chain by stringing together amino acids. Genes are codes, then, in the sense that they contain information which can be used as a kind of blueprint for the construction of the various features and organs of the body. Taken together, all of the genes of a given organism are called its 'genome'. The genome is a kind of coded instruction manual for how to build that organism. Genes are passed from parents to their offspring as part of a *chromosome*.

The excitement over the evolutionary approach is even greater in the 21st century because very soon scientists believe they will be able to map the whole of the human genome. Added to this is the conviction on the part of some evolutionary psychologists that genes do not just explain the building of the material body as such, but they also can be used to explain forms of *behaviour*. This is an important distinction. It is one thing to say that blue eyes are inherited by way of genes. It is quite another to say that washing the dishes, running a marathon or seducing a would-be lover are genetically inherited.

Part of the excitement about the possibility of explaining behaviour genetically arose as a result of studies in the early to mid 20th century by people such as Lorenz and Tinbergen, who showed that, for example, the attachment behaviour of geese, or the territorial fighting of sticklebacks is a kind of genetically coded programme. Once set in motion by the appropriate trigger (a fish-sized red object is enough to make a male stickleback attack), this programme will automatically 'unfold', giving rise to typical patterns or sequences of behaviour. The basic story, again, is that forms of behaviour that are adaptive (such as territorial fighting behaviour that increases the possibility of survival and reproduction) will be naturally selected.

Dawkins (1976) coined the famous term 'the selfish gene' to convey the idea that organisms, including humans, are predisposed to behave in ways that increase their chances of producing offspring. We are naturally in competition, not just with other organisms, but especially with other humans.

This idea, as you might imagine, becomes much more controversial when applied to more complex human behaviour. Consider the following quotation which suggests, firstly, that there are clear differences between men and women in terms of hygiene and tidiness, and secondly that these differences are genetic.

'Many studies have shown that there is a marked difference in how well men and women register and remember details, and to a man dust on a shelf or a scum ring around a bath are just that – details. Even if he does notice them, he may simply not accord them the importance a woman does. To her dirt is offensive, to him it is part of the natural world. From very early childhood males have a greater tolerance for, and even liking for, dirt. What a man perceives as "clean" a woman might find dirty, and what he finds merely "dirty" she might find utterly disgusting. His sense of smell is different too; the stale socks and sweaty shirt don't bother him because they are among the pheromone-related smells that women are acutely aware of but men simply do not detect.' (Moir & Moir, 1998)

The evolutionary approach has developed considerably in the last 20 or so years. Evolutionary explanations have been proposed for pretty well every psychological question, such as why men and women often have different desires; how the structure of the brain evolved; how people function in crowds; what causes mental illnesses, and so on. To illustrate, we will now turn to the role of the evolutionary approach in dealing with just one specific psychological issue: the nature of emotion.

1.3   The evolutionary approach to emotion

Darwin's contribution

In line with the above discussion, we must look at how an 'old' way of seeing emotion becomes translated into an evolutionary way of seeing. Before Darwin, it was *philosophers* who had the most to say about emotions. Discussions of emotion often had a central place in debates about *ethics* (such as how to live a good life). Aristotle, Spinoza, Descartes, Hume and most other major philosophers saw emotions as central to questions of ethics. Also, when Darwin was alive, *Romanticism* was a powerful force in art, poetry and literature. The romantics made the expression of emotion central to their view of the good, the true and the beautiful.

Darwin's contribution to our way of seeing emotion was completely different. Rather than discussing emotions in connection with lofty issues like ethics and beauty, he made us look at human expressions of emotions next to animal expressions. In his book *The Expression of the Emotions in Man and Animals* (1872), he argued that human emotions are proof of our having evolved from 'lower' animals. Why do we uncover our teeth when in a furious rage? Why does our hair bristle when we are terrified? Darwin's answer was that such reactions hark back to an earlier stage of evolution when we would have actually fought using our canine teeth and when we would have been covered in thick hair. These responses were *adaptive* in that previous context – raising our fur when scared would make us look bigger and more threatening to a predator or opponent. Nowadays, much like our appendix, they serve no real purpose, except as lingering signs to an alert biologist which prove 'that man once existed in a much lower and animal-like condition' (Darwin, 1872).

It is now thought that Darwin overplayed the argument that emotions are 'throwbacks' that now serve no real purpose. Emotions, if anything, are *more fully developed* in humans than in other animals, and serve many complex motivational and communicative functions. However, in Darwin's defence it should be said that this was not his only argument, and that in discussing shame and blushing he argues the opposite: that this is a particularly *human* emotional expression, and that it requires sufficient *intellect* to blush.

Perhaps the decisive contribution Darwin made was the form or style of his explanation: *functionalism*. A functional explanation always looks for a function. Hence Darwin asks after the function of uncovering the teeth when angry, or the function of bristling hair. Once a plausible function has been found – scaring predators or preparing the canine teeth so that they can be plunged into the flesh of an enemy – then we have a 'first stab' at a biological explanation. This might not be the right answer, but it is a *possible* answer. If you have followed so far, you should have been drawn into viewing emotions as biological things. You are beginning to speak 'Darwinese'.

Jealousy and paternity confidence

Evolutionary psychologists have become more confident, and apply functionalist arguments not just to emotional expressions, but to the feelings themselves. Consider Daly et al's (1982) evolutionary explanation for male jealousy. For them, the fact that it is more difficult for males to be confident that a baby is 'theirs' (what they call *paternity confidence*) has led, through evolution, to the development of a particularly male form of sexual jealousy: 'the dogged inclination of men to possess and control women, and the use or threat of violence to achieve sexual exclusivity and control'.

This theory basically supplies male jealousy with a function: enhancing paternity confidence. Male jealousy, they argue, gives men the natural aggressive motivation necessary for guarding against their partner having sex with someone else, and thus conceiving a baby from another man. Women, unlike men, can be confident that they are the mothers of their children. According to this evolutionary logic, women therefore get jealous less about sex and more about the possibility of a romantic *commitment* between their partner and someone else (Buss et al., 1992). Female jealousy, in this second theory, is serving another function: enhancing partnership commitment.

Essentially, the evolutionary argument is that we don't need to learn to get jealous of sexual rivals because our relationship to rivals and partners has been fixed during the long evolution of our species. Our genetic ancestors, the story goes, who were jealous were better able to protect their reproductive 'interests' and so more likely to survive and reproduce. Their type of biology was naturally selected.

Universal faces?

Paul Ekman (1982) has argued that a basic group of emotions, including fear, disgust, happiness, sadness, surprise and anger are 'hard-wired' into human biology – that is genetically encoded as a result of evolution. His evidence for this is that these emotions are universally recognised. He claims that if you take any normal and healthy person from any part of the world and show them a picture of a person expressing one of these emotions – for example, smiling in happiness or with eyebrows raised in surprise – then they will be able to recognise the emotion being expressed. Why? Because, he argues, these facial expressions are a kind of natural language that does not need to be learned, since it is innate. A newly born baby, for instance, does not need to learn how to cry and how to express their distress at the trauma of birth.

Ekman and his colleagues tested this theory by choosing a culture – the Fore people of New Guinea – that, at the time of the study, was relatively isolated from the West and from Western media images. If these people associate the same emotions with the same facial expressions that we in the West do, then this would provide good evidence that we are not dealing with something that is learned or culturally transmitted. Ekman showed a group of Fore people images of the facial expressions we associate with six basic emotions and asked them, through a translator, to match the faces to little stories. Would they, for example, match the image of the smiling female face to the little story 'Her friends have come and she is happy'? The results showed that indeed the Fore people do recognise the same emotional expressions as us except that they were less likely to distinguish between fear and surprise. (See pp 409-410 for further discussion of Ekman's theory.)

Evolving emotional brains

The evolution of emotions has been linked to the evolution of the brain. MacLean (1949) saw the human brain as having three main levels – 1) the hindbrain which controls basic bodily

functions including patterns of movement, 2) the limbic system which controls emotion and 3) the forebrain which deals with higher cognitive functions.

The hindbrain evolved with reptiles. The limbic system developed with the earliest mammals. Unlike reptiles, mammals need maternal care-giving, they need to form infant attachments. For MacLean, emotions are made possible by the limbic system. The final region, distinctive to higher mammals, is the neocortex in the forebrain. Human frontal lobes, for instance, are much bigger than those of lower mammals. Frontal lobes have multiple connections with the limbic system, and so are likely to play an emotional role too.

This argument suggests that the biology of the brain concerned with emotions is adaptive. It evolved as a result of natural selection. (See pp 401-410 for further discussion of the brain and emotion.)

Key terms

Functionalism *The idea that things can be explained by the functions they perform.*

Paternity confidence *The degree of certainty a male has that his offspring are his own.*

1.4 Methods used in the evolutionary approach

The comparative method

The evolutionary approach relies heavily on the comparative method. It makes comparisons between species, between cultures, and between behaviour patterns today and in the past.

Comparison between species This involves making careful comparisons between different species in order to identify shared and distinct evolutionary adaptations. For example, Darwin used this method when searching for similar emotional expressions amongst humans and non-human animals. MacLean used this method when comparing reptilian and mammalian brains.

When similarities are found between human and non-human animals, it is often assumed that these traits have a long evolutionary history. Their presence in humans suggests that they are genetically based. This, in turn, suggests that humans are genetically predisposed to behave in certain ways.

Comparison between cultures This involves comparing different cultures, particularly comparisons between cultures which have had no contact with each other. Paul Ekman used this method when he compared the isolated Fore people of New Guinea with people in the West. Both identified the same emotions with the same facial expressions. This is seen to indicate a biological basis for recognising emotion. It suggests that this ability evolved because it had an adaptive function.

Comparison between past and present Evolutionary psychologists assume that a large part of human behaviour today owes its origin to evolutionary adaptations in the distant past. For example, it is often assumed that our early ancestors were regularly threatened by predators. Faced with this threat, aggression was selected for and those who could ward off predators were more likely to reproduce. This provides the basis for aggression in modern human behaviour.

Other methods

Evolutionary psychologists have used a range of research methods from laboratory studies to questionnaires. This can be seen from Buss et al's (1992) study of male and female jealousy. This study was conducted to see if the kind of jealousy predicted by evolutionary theory was present in today's men and women. Male and female students were asked to imagine a) their partner was having sex with another person (sexual infidelity) and b) their partner was forming a strong emotional attachment to another person (emotional infidelity). On the basis of questionnaires, blood pressure measurements and skin-conductivity tests, the results were as predicted by evolutionary theory – men rated sexual infidelity as more distressing, women rated emotional infidelity as more distressing.

1.5   Evaluation of the evolutionary approach

Strengths

- The evolutionary approach is grounded in natural science and claims to provide us with a greater understanding of the nature of human beings. Specifically, it shows that our minds and our bodies have been constructed through a long evolutionary history.
- It allows us to see and understand the connections and

differences between human beings and other animals.
- Adding an evolutionary dimension provides a fuller understanding of human behaviour both in the past and in the present.

Weaknesses

- Evolutionary psychology begins with a very big assumption – that the biological purpose of all organisms is to reproduce their genes as often and as successfully as possible. This assumption provides the starting point for explaining all sorts of behaviour – for example, male and female jealousy about their partner, kinship patterns and helping behaviour. Such explanations are based largely on speculation.
- The functional explanations produced by evolutionary psychologists are at best 'likely stories' or 'educated guesses'. Theories like those of Buss and Daly about male sexual jealousy are extremely controversial and usually considered to be little more than speculation.
- There is little or no direct evidence to support evolutionary explanations of human behaviour. For example, specific biological structures – individual genes or groups of genes – have yet to be discovered for the supposed genetically-based behaviour patterns of human beings.
- Evolutionary explanations of complex human behaviour are often trite, banal and unsatisfactory. Think of the rich variety of the thousands of religions created by human beings. How can evolutionary theory explain this rich diversity other than by saying that the ability to devise belief systems which make sense of the world is adaptive?

Summary

1. The evolutionary approach is fundamental to the development of psychology as a discipline.

2. Darwinian biological theory led to a big change in the guiding metaphors used in our pictures of the person.

3. A key aspect of this change was that dualism was undermined by materialism, and the distinction between non-human animals and humans was blurred.

4. The discovery of the gene as the unit of inheritance is fundamental to the evolutionary approach.

5. Evolutionary explanations typically involve providing functional explanations.

6. The evolutionary approach relies heavily on the comparative method. This involves comparisons between species, between cultures, and between past and present behaviour.

7. The evolutionary approach shows that the human mind and body have been formed by evolutionary processes.

8. Many explanations provided by the evolutionary approach have little direct evidence to support them.

Activity 2 — Team games

Item A — Lacrosse

Native Americans of the Choctaw tribe playing lacrosse in the 19th century

Item B — Soccer

Lens vs Arsenal in the Champions League

Question

How might evolutionary psychologists explain team games?

Unit 2 — The biopsychological approach

KEY ISSUES

1. **What is the biopsychological approach?**
2. **What biological structures are involved in the experience and expression of emotions?**
3. **What are the main methods of the biopsychological approach?**

2.1 Biopsychology

The concept of evolution now provides the unifying framework for all biology. However, within that broad framework, we can separate out the biopsychological approach. This approach is sometimes called the biological/medical approach.

The scope of biopsychology can be seen from Table 1 which lists the contents of a standard undergraduate textbook, *Biopsychology* by John P.J. Pinel (1997).

The biology of stress Biopsychologists are interested in the relationship between biology and psychology. They focus on the biological basis of behaviour. This focus can be seen clearly from a biopsychological approach to stress. The response to stress involves a range of biochemical and physiological changes. These include the release of various neurochemicals –

Table 1 — Contents of *Biopsychology*

1	Biopsychology as a neuroscience
2	Evolution, genetics, and experience: Asking the right questions about the biology of behaviour
3	The anatomy of the nervous system
4	Neural conduction and synaptic transmission
5	What biopsychologists do: The research methods of biopsychology
6	Human brain damage and animal models
7	The visual system: From eye to cortex
8	Mechanisms of perception
9	The sensorimotor system
10	The biopsychology of eating and drinking
11	Hormones and sex
12	Sleep, dreaming, and circadian rhythms
13	Drug addiction and reward circuits in the brain
14	Memory and amnesia
15	Neuroplasticity: Development, learning, and recovery from brain damage
16	Lateralisation, language, and the split brain
17	Biopsychology of emotion, stress, and mental illness

changes. These include the release of various neurochemicals – neurotransmitters and hormones – and physiological changes such as an increase in the heart rate and an increase in muscle tone. Biopsychologists examine these biological changes and their relationship to other aspects of stress-related behaviour – for example, the relationship between the way a stressor is perceived and the biology of the stress response.

The brain and behaviour Biopsychologists are particularly interested in the brain – how it works, what the different parts of the brain do – their functions – and how these parts are connected. Chapter 22 Brain and behaviour examines this approach. It looks at the various areas of the brain and examines their functions. For example, it examines the extent to which functions such as memory and visual perception are located within specific brain areas. It also considers the relationship between different parts of the brain – for example, memory is composed of several processes, and various parts of the brain are involved in remembering.

Biology and psychological disorders Biopsychologists have had a major influence on the explanation and treatment of psychological disorders. A flavour of their approach is provided by John Pinel's approach to schizophrenia and depression in his *Biopsychology*.

When looking at the causal factors of these disorders he singles out two – genes and biochemicals. Studies indicate that if people have relatives diagnosed with schizophrenia or depression, then they have a greater risk of developing the disorders themselves. This suggests the possibility of genetic predisposition. For example, Pinel states that a series of studies have 'established schizophrenia's genetic basis'.

Pinel then considers the 'neural mechanisms' of schizophrenia and depression. In particular, he looks at neurotransmitters such as dopamine and serotonin. He outlines research which suggests that an excess or depletion of certain neurotransmitters is associated with both disorders.

Finally, Pinel looks at the drugs that have been used to treat schizophrenia and depression. In particular, he examines their effects on neurotransmitters – whether they release or inhibit particular neurotransmitters and the effect that this has on the expression, or 'symptoms', of the disorders.

The biological/medical model Biopsychology is sometimes referred to as the biological/medical model, particularly with reference to psychological disorders. This is because it is the dominant model when it comes to the diagnosis and treatment of disorders.

Psychiatrists, the main group who treat psychological disorders, are trained in medicine. They tend to use the medical language of patient, symptoms, diagnosis, illness, treatment and cure. And the most common treatments today for a range of psychological disorders are drugs which alter the body's biochemistry.

2.2 Biopsychology and emotion

This section takes a brief and partial look at the biopsychological approach to the emotions. It illustrates the types of questions it asks and the types of evidence it uses. A more detailed account of biopsychological theories of emotion is given in Chapter 24.

- **The ANS** The autonomic nervous system (ANS) controls internal organs such as the heart, liver, stomach, sweat glands and blood vessels. According to the James-Lange theory of emotions, when we experience different emotions like anger, fear and happiness, we are literally feeling the sensations that come from the responses of the ANS. For example, the brain registers behaviours such as a pounding heart and interprets this as fear. In William James' (1894) words, 'We feel sorry because we cry, angry because we strike, afraid because we tremble'.

- **The thalamus** The Cannon-Bard theory states that an area of the brain known as the thalamus is the main centre for emotions. Normally, the thalamus is inhibited or restrained by the cerebral cortex. When emotionally significant stimuli reach the cortex – for example, fear resulting from the threat of injury – this restraint is removed. The thalamus then sends signals to the rest of the body – to the ANS and the muscles – that initiate appropriate emotional behaviours such as fight or flight.

- **The Papez loop** Named after the anatomist James Papez, the Papez loop consists of a number of brain structures forming an integrated loop (see Figure 1). There is evidence that the Papez loop is involved with the control of emotional behaviours. For example, damage to or electrical stimulation of the loop can give rise to emotional states, particularly aggression (LeDoux, 1993).

Figure 1   The Papez loop

cingulate gyrus

fornix

septum

hypothalamus

amygdala

hippocampus

- **The amygdala** In recent years, a part of the Papez loop – the amygdala – has been singled out as particularly involved with emotion. LeDoux (1998) refers to the amygdala as the brain's 'emotional computer'. Damage to and electrical stimulation of the amygdala in monkeys, and damage to the amygdala in humans, can affect the control of emotions, especially fear.

- **Neurochemicals** Neurotransmitters such as dopamine and serotonin and hormones such as cortisol and adrenaline have been linked to emotions. For example, drugs such as Ecstasy and Prozac affect serotonin levels which, in turn, can influence our moods. Similarly, the release of hormones such as adrenaline can lead to arousal of the ANS which again can affect our moods.

- **Hemispheric asymmetry** It has been suggested that in right-handers, the right hemisphere of the brain deals with the processing of emotional information more than the left hemisphere (Oatley & Jenkins, 1996). Right-handed people

recognise pictures of emotional expressions better when they are presented to the left eye (from which information is processed by the right hemisphere) than to the right eye (from which information is processed by the left hemisphere). Try this yourself in Activity 3.

Activity 3   Emotions and the brain

Item A   Face A

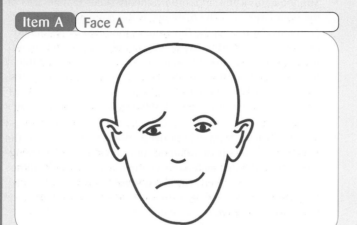

Look at the nose on the left-hand side – Face A. Does this face seem more happy than sad or more sad than happy?

Now look at the nose of the right-hand side – Face B. Does this face seem more happy than sad or more sad than happy?

If you are right-handed, you are likely to see Face B as happier. If you are left-handed, you are likely to see Face A as happier.

Adapted from Oatley & Jenkins, 1996

Item B   Face B

Questions

1   Did the results come out as predicted?

2   Try this activity with both right and left-handed people.

3   What support, if any, do the results provide for the link between hemispheric asymmetry and emotion?

2.3   Methods used in the biopsychological approach

The biopsychological approach involves the study of biological structures and their functions. This is reflected in the research methods used by this approach. Items 1-5 on the following list are some of the main methods used to study the role of brain processes in emotion. Items 5 and 6 are typically used by biopsychologists in the study of psychological disorders.

1   **Anatomy** At its crudest, this involves simply opening up the body and identifying the structures. Anatomy has become increasingly sophisticated, however. LeDoux's work on the amygdala involved using chemical tracers to identify neural pathways in the brain. A small amount of tracer is injected into the brain area of interest. This is absorbed by local neurons, transported down their axons, and passed on to another region of the brain. The tracer makes this transport visible. Thus LeDoux was able to show that fear-relevant information from the auditory thalamus is passed on to the lateral amygdala for further processing.

2   **Lesions** A lesion is an injury. In studying how the brain

works, valuable information can be obtained by studying the effects that lesions have on people and animals. The lesion technique assumes that any skill that can be performed before the injury, but not afterwards, is the function of the brain area damaged. (This, however, is not always the case – see p 351.)

3   **Stimulation** Tiny electrodes can be inserted into the brain (usually of animals) to see what effects mild electric current has on specific regions. This can indicate the function of particular brain areas. For example, electrical stimulation of the lateral hypothalamus is a powerful reward – a rat will press a lever until it is exhausted in order to receive pleasurable bursts of stimulation.

4   **Visualisation of brain activity** There are now several technologies that allow us to 'see' brain activity more or less as it happens. These allow us to answer questions like *where* is the brain most active when a person is experiencing joy? The EEG (electroencephalogram) measures electrical activity. For example, Davidson et al. (1990) found an increase in left frontal cortex activation during happiness and right frontal cortex activation during disgust. PET scans (Positron Emission Tomography) provide pictures of the brain based on amount of blood flow – the idea being that higher blood

flow equals greater brain cell activity. fMRI scans (functional Magnetic Resonance Imagery) provide pictures of the brain by using what is effectively a large and powerful magnet.

5 **Chemical manipulation** Since brain activity involves chemical changes, brain functions can be influenced and investigated by using drugs which increase or decrease chemical activity. As noted earlier, certain drugs can affect particular neurotransmitter levels.

6 **Twin and adoption studies** These studies are used to assess possible genetic contribution to behaviour. For example, if particular behaviours of identical twins (who share the same genes) are more similar than those of non-identical twins (who share only 50% of their genes) then this may indicate a genetic influence on those behaviours. Similarly, if the behaviour of adopted children reflects that of their biological rather than their adopted parents, then this may indicate a genetic influence.

2.4 Evaluation of the biopsychological approach

Strengths

- The biopsychological approach is grounded in natural science and is very strong at dealing with organic processes.
- Biopsychology has identified important links between

biology and behaviour. As noted earlier, there are biological aspects of emotion and psychological disorders.

- In recent years, rapid advances in biochemistry and genetics have increased our understanding of these links.

Weaknesses

- Critics have accused biopsychologists of seeing human beings as little more than biological machines. There is a tendency to ignore or downplay the social and cultural side of human existence.
- As a result, biopsychologists have sometimes been accused of reductionism – reducing behaviour to biological factors. Complex mental and emotional processes are unlikely to be caused solely by genes, neurotransmitters and hormones.
- Biopsychology's 'prescription' for treating psychological disorders tends to see people as machines that can be 'fixed' when they 'go wrong'. For example, depression is not simply a biological dysfunction – it is also about real problems with living in the social world.
- Treatments for disorders may confuse cause and effect. Often it is not clear whether biochemical imbalances result from rather than cause psychological disorders. Prescribed drugs may therefore be treating the symptoms of the disorder rather than its cause.

Summary

1 Biopsychology looks at the biological basis of behaviour.

2 Biopsychologists are particularly interested in the brain and the functions it performs.

3 Biopsychology has had a major influence on the explanation and treatment of psychological disorders.

4 Many of the methods used by biopsychologists are concerned with observing and measuring organic processes.

5 Biopsychology has identified important links between biology and behaviour.

6 Critics have accused biopsychology of reductionism – of reducing behaviour to biological factors, of seeing human beings as biological machines.

Activity 4   A new psychological disorder

Item A   Homophobia

It's 2010, ten years into the new millennium. A new psychological disorder has been discovered. It is called homophobia. This disorder involves a prejudice, and sometimes discrimination, against gay people. Those who suffer from homophobia sometimes attack gay people and often avoid them at all costs.

Item B   A homophobe

Questions

1 How might a biopsychologist discover the causes of homophobia?

2 What treatment might they suggest for this new disorder?

Unit 3 The psychodynamic approach

KEY ISSUES

1 **What are the key concepts used in the psychodynamic approach?**

2 **How does it explain emotion?**

3 **What are the main methods used in psychodynamics?**

3.1 Introduction and key concepts

Sigmund Freud (1856-1939) was the pioneer of the psychodynamic approach – he founded *psychoanalysis*. Psychoanalysis is both a theory and a therapy designed to explain and treat the *neuroses*. Neuroses are forms of mental disorder involving emotional over-reaction and inappropriate behaviour. They are distinguished from the *psychoses* because, unlike the psychotic, the neurotic has insight into what they are doing. Psychoanalysis is also a general theory of personality and its development.

The psychodynamic approach is broader than Freud, however. It includes the so-called *neo-Freudians* who developed as well as challenged Freud's psychoanalysis, but who still emphasised the *dynamic* or motivational nature of the psyche – all psychodynamic theories share the idea that unconscious forces determine thoughts, feelings and actions.

Brief historical background

After training as a neurologist, Freud went on to study hysteria. His book (with Breuer) *Studies on Hysteria* (1895) outlined the broad psychoanalytical approach to neurotic conditions. This approach states that neurotic feelings and behaviour (symptoms) result from long forgotten emotional experiences. These symptoms are also *symbolically related* to the forgotten experiences. For instance, the partial blindness of a hysteric (a symptom) may result from having seen something very upsetting as a child (the cause). Or an inability to speak (a symptom) may result from having been forbidden to tell a terrible secret (the cause). The emotional event is forgotten, but it still has a strong influence, since it results in a hysterical symptom. For Freud, the memory of the upsetting event still exists, but it is *unconscious*.

The concept of the unconscious is fundamental to psychodynamics. The *cathartic method* is designed to help the patient to remember the unconscious event, and thereby to raise it to consciousness. Once conscious, the idea is that the neurotic symptoms no longer fulfil any function, and so disappear.

In later works, such as *The Interpretation of Dreams* (1900) and *Three Essays on the Theory of Sexuality* (1905), Freud argued that the emotional events that cause neuroses are usually sexual in nature. But more than this, the events may never have happened in reality – instead they could be *fantasised* during childhood. This was part of Freud's general theory of psychosexual development, which held that children are sexual beings with infantile sexual desires.

Freud's theory of psychosexual development

For Freud, early childhood experiences have a powerful influence on adult personality. He outlined five developmental stages, each of which has its own way of channelling what Freud thought of as the sexual energy of *libido*.

- **Oral stage** From birth to around one and a half, libido pleasure is centred on the mouth and its activities, such as sucking, feeding and crying. Infants explore the world using their mouths, putting new objects into it.

- **Anal stage** From the end of the oral stage to around 3 or 4 years, the dominant site of pleasure becomes the anus. This is related to toilet training, where the child must learn to control its impulses, and comes to derive pleasure from retaining and expelling faeces.

- **Phallic stage** From the end of the anal stage to around 5 years, the dominant site of pleasure becomes the genitals. Children acquire a fascination with their own genitals and those of others. They also become sexually interested in their opposite sex parent, which leads to the Oedipus complex – the same-sex parent is viewed as a rival for the desired opposite-sex parent. For Freud, these complexes are resolved by identification with the same sex-parent – they are too strong to beat as rivals, so better join them and become like them.

- **Latency stage** After the resolution of the Oedipus complex, there is a period of 'latency' where there is no dominant site of sexual pleasure.

- **Genital stage** This is the stage of 'adult' sexuality, which begins at puberty. The genitals are again the dominant site of libido pleasure, but now they are capable of functioning in a fully sexual way. (See Chapter 29, pp 535-541).

This theory could be called an 'obstacle race' theory, since at each stage there are obstacles or conflicts that must be overcome in order to proceed to the next stage. At the anal stage, the obstacle is the fact that the child's parents insist that it be toilet trained. In order to become more 'civilised', or at least 'house trained', the child must control its impulses which had free rein in the oral stage. At the phallic stage, the obstacle faced, from the child's point of view at least, is the same-sex parent who stands in the way of the pleasure the child imagines it can get with the opposite-sex parent. At each stage, it is also possible that either under-stimulation (eg, too little oral satisfaction) or over-stimulation (eg, too much genital satisfaction) might occur.

What happens if these obstacles are not overcome? Freud argued that it is possible to get *fixated* or stuck at any of these stages, and that adult personalities express the point at which they got stuck. In this context, Freudians talk of *oral* and *anal* personalities. A Freudian might call you oral if you talk a lot and eat and drink a lot, and might call you *anal* if you are particularly mean and stubborn.

The Id, Ego and Superego

Freud was a creative thinker who continued to develop his ideas as he matured. He made an important set of revisions to his theory in *The Ego and the Id* (1923). He argued that personality is made up of three components that exist in dynamic tension, as if in a never-ending wrestling match.

- **The Id** (Id means simply 'it') is unconscious. It 'contains' primitive drives and emotions and works according to the *pleasure principle*. It is concerned only with self-gratification.
- **The Superego** 'contains' ideals and moral values and strives to avoid disdain and to acquire esteem. It is 'thanks' to the Superego that we feel guilt, shame and pride, because the Superego is concerned with doing right.
- **The Ego** is mostly conscious. It tries to steer a path between the extremes of the Id and of the Superego, so that the total person can manage to live in reality. If we were all Id, there would be social chaos since everyone would be 'out for themselves'. If we were all Superego, we would lose touch with our vital needs and life would lose its meaning. The Ego therefore works according to the *reality principle*. It recognises both the need for some constraints in order to live in a civilised way, and the need to satisfy basic drives and express basic emotions.

The defence mechanisms

Freud invited us to think of our conscious life, and of our Ego in particular, as if they were the very tip of an iceberg, the vast majority of which exists below the surface of consciousness. Our conscious sense of who we are as a whole (the Ego) *depends upon* this vast amount of unconscious material. Freud borrowed the concept of the Id from Georg Groddeck (1923) who, in his *Book of the It*, said 'what we call our ego behaves essentially passively in life … we are "lived" by unknown and uncontrollable forces … Man is lived by the it.'

Following Groddeck, Freud believed that we delude ourselves, largely through self-love or vanity, into thinking that we are the rational centres of our universe – that we live according to our choices and decisions, and have the power to determine our own lives. In truth our Egos are fragile and cannot bear too much reality. Reality must be carefully filtered to make it 'acceptable' *before* we become conscious of it, just as what appears on children's TV has been carefully censored to ensure that young minds are not corrupted. As early as *Studies on Hysteria* (1895), Freud argues that the Ego uses *defence mechanisms* to protect itself from the anxiety that is generated by unwelcome ideas. Defence mechanisms are unconscious. The main ones are:

- **Repression** This is forgetting in the sense of repelling and avoiding an unwelcome idea or event. Recall the earlier point that hysterical neurotics may 'forget' an unpleasant emotional scene and that this leads to the formation of a symptom which is symbolically related to that scene. The scene has therefore been *repressed*. It is as if the emotional scene had been submerged beneath the surface, but ripples (the symptom) can still be seen. This submersion into unconsciousness *defends* the Ego from the anxiety of having to think about it.
- **Regression** If each person *progresses*, or goes forward through the five psychosexual stages, then *regression* is to go backwards. Under very stressful circumstances, an adult might regress to the oral activity of sucking their thumb and perhaps even screaming for mummy. This is defensive

because the situation does not have to be registered and dealt with in a more adult way, and so unpleasant realities can be avoided.

- **Reaction formation** A person can unconsciously defend against a thought, feeling or action that generates too much anxiety simply by thinking, feeling or doing the opposite. An example of this is to respond to someone you really hate as if you loved them.
- **Projection** Attributing to someone else the thoughts and feelings that are in fact your own: 'You hate me' instead of 'I hate you', for instance.
- **Denial** Flatly refusing to accept something that is true: 'I do not hate you'.
- **Sublimation** Refining something unacceptable so that it passes as acceptable. For example, an architect may sublimate basic sexual urges into building a phallic tower.
- **Rationalisation** Putting an intellectual gloss on something that is really motivated by emotions or drives. For example, leading a promiscuous lifestyle and claiming that it's being done for scientific research purposes.
- **Splitting** Dividing the Ego in two, like Jekyll and Hyde, so that one part of the self can always blame the other for what it doesn't like.

Relationship to the biological approach: Civilisation and its discontents

Freud saw himself as following in Darwin's footsteps. He accepted evolutionary theory and was convinced of the basic animal nature of the human being. In large part, the Id can be understood as representing this basic animal nature – it is governed by 'instincts' or 'drives' such as libido. The Ego and Superego are higher-order systems that emerged out of the more basic Id system – just as humans emerged from ape-like ancestors, or mammals emerged out of reptiles, when viewed from an evolutionary perspective.

Freud added another interesting new dimension to Darwin's picture. He posed the following question: given that humans are animals driven by the same instinctive forces for survival as other animals, how is it that we are able to live together in civilised social communities? His answer was that we pay a heavy price for our civilisation.

The price we pay for civilisation is that we have learned to renounce our animal desires and drives. The Ego and the Superego are adaptations that permit our survival – they fulfil *functions*. The Superego functions to hold the lusty and animal-like Id in check for the good of society, and the function of the Ego is to balance the two for the ultimate good of both. Freud's point is that the effect of this psychodynamic situation is that the animal nature of our being is pushed into the *unconscious*. In short, we are animals, but to live together, we have to be unaware of this fact, and believe ourselves to be something different!

However, the price we pay for repressing our animal drives and desires is neurosis. Freud argues that we need to find some way of expressing these drives and desires without disrupting society. His solution is expressing them in art and literature.

The neo-Freudians

Freud's ideas have been developed and challenged by his

Key terms

The unconscious *The place of thoughts, feelings and desires which are not usually recalled to consciousness but which continue to influence our lives.*

Libido *A drive composed of basic sexual energy.*

followers who are often referred to as neo-Freudians. They include:

- Anna Freud, who developed her father's notion of Ego defence mechanisms.
- Carl Jung, who emphasised the *collective* nature of the unconscious, and criticised Freud's preoccupation with sexuality, founding what he called *analytical psychology*.
- Melanie Klein, who was influential in developing the *object relations* school of psychoanalysis which emphasised very early infant relationships (and influenced the work of Bowlby).
- Wilhelm Reich, who developed controversial therapies based around sexuality.
- Alfred Adler, who stressed the importance of feelings of inferiority and superiority to Ego development, as implied in the famous concept of an 'inferiority complex'.
- Erik Erikson, who proposed a model of development that continued throughout the life span (rather than ending at puberty) and that stressed the influence of the social world on development.

3.2   The psychodynamic approach to emotion

One way in which Freud conceptualised the emotions was as a by-product of the internal 'debates' going on between Id, Ego and Superego. For instance, he talked of Ego as feeling *pride* after resisting a temptation that would be objectionable to Superego. But most of what we call emotions were seen by Freud as originally primitive *drives* which are 'discharged' from the Id. These become altered and modified as they take part in the dynamic internal debate between Ego and Superego, becoming 'attached' to certain ideas, images or memories in the process. Emotions are never taken at 'face value' but are seen as clues to these underlying dynamics. The defence mechanisms are important here.

In discussing jealousy, for example, Freud (1922) identifies three kinds: *normal* (or competitive) jealousy; *projected* jealousy and *delusional* jealousy.

Normal jealousy For Freud, some amount of jealousy is normal – it is 'one of the earliest impulses of infantile affectivity'. In fact, if a person feels *no* jealousy, Freud takes this as a sign that it must have been repressed, and is therefore playing a significant unconscious role.

Projected jealousy Projection is a defence mechanism. For Freud, people who have committed an infidelity, or who have wished to, can repress this and project the desire onto their partner, who they then become jealous of. Instead of 'I wish to be (or am) unfaithful', what comes to consciousness is 'you wish to be (or are) unfaithful'.

Delusional jealousy Delusional jealousy is a stronger form of projected jealousy. According to Freud, it occurs when the actual or wished-for infidelity is of a homosexual nature: 'As an

attempt at defence against an excessively strong homosexual impulse, it would be paraphrased by the formula: *I certainly do not love him, she loves him*'.

Note that when discussing emotions, such as jealousy, Freud works with a division between a drive and passion-centred Id (which will naturally have an amount of 'normal' jealousy) and a set of normative and often moral social rules (internalised by the Superego). Those rules might be simplified as saying: 'don't be unfaithful if you are married', or 'be heterosexual, not homosexual'. Emotions are re-shaped, twisted and contorted in the 'battle' between basic drives and desires and social requirements and expectations. As the social requirement to be heterosexual was particularly strong in Freud's day, so any homosexual desires had to be especially strongly repressed, leading to a severe form of 'delusional' jealousy.

3.3   Methods used in the psychodynamic approach

Many present-day researchers use a range of conventional statistical methods to test psychodynamic theories. However, the classic psychodynamic methods are *clinical* techniques designed to be of therapeutic value rather than of pure scientific value. It is important to recognise that psychodynamic approaches are pulled in these two, often different, directions – to discover neutral facts and to solve people's personal problems. The main classic techniques are:

- **The cathartic method** This was used in Freud's early work and chiefly involved *hypnosis* in order to bring repressed material into consciousness. The idea was that people could recall things under hypnosis that would be repressed when fully conscious.
- **Free association** Freud later abandoned hypnosis in preference to other techniques like *free association*. Here, the patient is encouraged to give voice to any and all thoughts which enter their mind when undergoing therapy. For example, if a person associates their sister with the word jealousy, this may indicate a possible unconscious connection related to sibling rivalry (see p720).
- **Dream interpretation** Freud claimed to be able to discover psychoanalytically useful information by interpreting patients' dreams. Dreams provide clues to psychodynamic processes, hence a person jealous of his sister who dreams that he is his sister may be interpreted as wishing to take the place of his sister (see pp 384-386).

3.4   Evaluation of the psychodynamic approach

Strengths

- The psychodynamic approach provides a fascinating theory that has been applied to everything from individual therapy to film criticism to an account of civilisation.
- Although the psychodynamic approach is no longer very popular within psychology, its ideas continue to influence the discipline.
- It remains influential outside psychology, for example in literacy criticism.

Weaknesses

- It is very difficult to translate psychodynamic concepts into a set of simple, testable statements. Concepts like the Id, Ego and Superego and processes such as repression cannot be directly observed and measured.
- As a result, critics argue that psychodynamic theory fails to provide the 'hard facts' needed to test hypotheses. Without observable and measurable data, many have rejected the approach as unscientific.
- Some critics claim that the individual therapy offered by the psychodynamic approach does not work. This claim is debatable. Many who have undergone therapy have nothing but praise for the way it has helped with their problems.

Summary

1. The psychodynamic approach is based on Freud's work and has been developed by the neo-Freudians.

2. Freud's theory of psychosexual development includes four main stages: oral, anal, phallic and genital, plus a stage of latency.

3. Freud divided the mind into three parts: the Id (source of the 'animal' drives), the Ego (which tries to deal with reality), and the Superego (which includes the voice of conscience).

4. The Ego defends itself using 'defence mechanisms' such as repression, regression, reaction-formation, sublimation, denial, rationalisation and splitting.

5. Freud saw himself as developing and adding to the biological approach.

6. Emotions are viewed as the product of the complex dynamics taking place between Id, Ego and Superego, but in their pure form they are drives.

7. Three key methods associated with the psychodynamic approach are the cathartic method, free association and dream interpretation.

Activity 5   An obsessional neurotic

Item A   The diagnosis

Freud had a patient whom he diagnosed as an obsessional neurotic. The man was afraid to go out for fear of killing everyone he met. He spent all his time preparing an alibi in case he was accused of murder.

During psychoanalysis, Freud told him that he did not want to kill everyone but someone, that what he called an alibi was really a 'defence'. The man told Freud that when he was seven, he had wished his father dead. His father had recently died from a painful illness.

Adapted from Appignanesi & Zarate, 1992

Questions

1 In terms of psychodynamic theory:

a) Who was the 'someone' that the man wanted to kill?

b) Why did he want to kill him?

2 Why did Freud call the alibi a 'defence'?

3 Suggest how Freud might have 'treated' the man's disorder.

Unit 4   The behaviourist approach

KEY ISSUES

1   **What did Thorndike, Watson, Pavlov and Skinner contribute to the behaviourist approach?**

2   **How are emotions studied from a behaviourist perspective?**

3   **What are the main methods used by behaviourists?**

4.1   Introduction and key concepts

Thorndike's 'law of effect'

During the first few years of the 20th century, Edward Thorndike (1874-1949) was busy conducting experiments trying to discover how cats and dogs learn about their environment. By putting them in 'puzzle-boxes' involving different tasks – for example, how to escape from the box and how to get food – Thorndike could get a simple measure of animal intelligence by timing how long they take to solve the puzzle.

At first, Thorndike wanted to know if animals could learn such tasks simply by watching other animals (imitation). He quickly found that they couldn't, and so proposed that learning occurs by a more simple 'trial and error' mechanism – the animal randomly tries a variety of behaviours. If these are rewarded, then they are repeated. If they are punished, then they are avoided. He proposed an explanation for this based on the strength of what he called *stimulus-response associations*. If a stimulus (say a lever) has led in the past to the appearance of food (the reward) when pressed (the response), then the stimulus (lever) response (press) association will have been strengthened. This makes it more likely that the animal will press the lever again next time it sees it. Thorndike called this the *law of effect*. Thorndike's law was to become central to behaviourism.

The founder of behaviourism: J. B. Watson

J. B. Watson (1878-1958) coined the term behaviourism ('behaviorism' is the US spelling) in a provocative manifesto entitled *Psychology as the behaviorist views it* (1913). He was unhappy with what he saw as the amateur and unscientific nature of early 20th century psychology. He wanted to abandon:

1   Concern with the nature of consciousness (which he saw as continuing a now defunct mind-body problem).

2   Use of introspection (eg, studying one's own or another's thoughts and feelings as they arise in consciousness).

3   An overly human-centred perspective (which had been made popular by the introspective study of consciousness).

4   Commitment to the idea that human behaviour is determined by innate or 'inherited' factors.

In this way, he argued that psychology could 'shape up' and become a proper science by concentrating on what was directly observable: behaviour. Any careful observer can see when a behaviour occurs (eg, a person quickly removing their hand

from a hot object) but cannot see when a conscious experience occurs (such as the feeling of pain, which can only be experienced by the one feeling it). Psychology should limit itself to what is directly observable. We can directly observe and measure two events in the above example as follows:

Event A: The *stimulus* – the hot object, of which we can ask objective things like 'how hot is it?'

Event B: The *response* – the removal of the hand, of which we can ask objective things like 'how fast did it move?'

If we strip away any reference to unobservable internal thoughts and feelings, behaviour can be seen as an observable response to an observable stimulus. The behaviourist can then start asking some new and interesting questions – for example, can we predict and control behaviour by manipulating relationships between stimuli and responses?

Pavlov's dogs and classical conditioning

Behaviourism was given a major boost by the researches of the Russian physiologist Ivan Pavlov (1849-1936). Pavlov's work on *conditioning* became one of the bases of behaviourist theory. Pavlov noticed that dogs salivate when they anticipate food. This can be prompted by the smell of the food but also, as any dog owner knows, by other related stimuli such as the sight of the food bowl or the tone of voice of the feeder. Pavlov reasoned that stimuli such as the dog bowl or a tone of voice acquire the function of making the dog salivate because they have been associated with the food. *Learning*, in other words, is acquired by *association*, and this process is called *classical conditioning*. Some technical terms can help to clarify this situation.

- The food is an *unconditioned stimulus* or UCS (since the dog does not need to learn to want it and learn to salivate in its presence).
- The salivation prompted by food is an *unconditioned response* or UCR (since salivation-to-food occurs without learning).
- The dog bowl is a *conditioned stimulus* or CS (since the bowl must be associated with food before it can stimulate salivation – ie, the bowl-food link must be learned).
- The salivation prompted by the dog bowl is a *conditioned response* or CR (since salivation to bowls must be learned).

Pavlov then did experiments to show that repeatedly pairing the sound of a bell (a *conditioned stimulus*) with the presentation of dog food (the *unconditioned stimulus*) leads to conditioning. That is, the dog quickly learns to salivate to the sound of a bell alone. He went on to examine the circumstances under which this learning would occur, how long it would last, and what circumstances would lead to its disappearance (or *extinction*). In other words, he began to answer the question of how behaviour can be predicted and controlled. (See pp 610-612 for a more detailed outline of Pavlov's experiments.)

B. F. Skinner and the development of operant conditioning

The type of conditioning Pavlov discovered is called *classical conditioning.* B.F. Skinner (1904-1990) drew on Thorndike's work for his theory of *operant conditioning. Operant* behaviour is behaviour that *operates* upon some aspect of the environment to produce consequences. In Skinner's studies, for instance, a pigeon may peck at a light, or a rat may press a lever in order to get food. Such behaviours are operant because they produce consequences – they get food for the animal. The rat or pigeon has *learned* to do this because the light-pecking or lever-pressing behaviour has been *reinforced. Reinforcement* is a key term in operant conditioning, and it comes in two forms: reward (getting something good like food or drink or some other pleasure) and punishment (getting something bad like an electric shock or some other pain). The behaviour of our rat is *shaped* by the way it is reinforced, since behaviours that are rewarded are repeated, and those that are punished tend to be avoided.

Note that in classical conditioning the learned behaviour (the *conditioned response*) is typically a 'reflex' response (such as salivating or blinking) that has come to be associated with a 'substitute' stimulus (a bell which has come to act as substitute for the food). In other words, the association between food and the salivation does not need to be learned, since such reflexes are automatic. During the conditioning, the bell takes the place of the food as the elicitor of the reflex. The story is different in operant conditioning, because an operant behaviour like pushing a lever is not an *automatic response* like salivating when in the presence of desired food, shivering when cold, or blinking when startled, which are responses to classical conditioning.

Skinner shared with Watson an emphasis on the importance of the *environment* in determining behaviour. The environment 'prods' and 'lashes' the organism, shaping its behaviour as it does so. This process is difficult to observe in the 'wild' of a natural environment, however. So, like Thorndike, Skinner began to study the influence of reinforcement in the controlled environment of a laboratory where the 'prods' and 'lashes' could be deliberately controlled. Skinner could then vary the *schedule of reinforcement* used (if one out of ten lever presses are consistently rewarded, for instance, this is termed a *fixed ratio reinforcement*). In this way, it can be shown that different schedules produce different speeds of learning and different rates of extinction – occasional random reinforcement, for instance, keeps an otherwise unrewarded animal responding the longest. (See pp 613-616 for a more detailed outline of operant conditioning.)

4.2   The behaviourist approach to emotion

Emotion, what emotion?

The most important thing to note about behaviourist accounts of emotion is that, strictly speaking, they are only interested in emotion in so far as it is *behaviour.* This excludes any consideration of emotional *feelings* and *subjective experiences.* This led one key behaviourist (Duffy, 1941) to argue that the concept of emotion should be abandoned altogether. She argued that there is no difference in kind between responses we call 'emotional', and those we call 'unemotional', and hence the concept has no scientific use. Skinner held a similar position, arguing that we use concepts like 'pride' and 'frustration' as a pre-scientific shorthand (an 'explanatory fiction'), since we don't understand what is really going on (which is, of course, the shaping of behaviour by reinforcement).

Key terms

Unconditioned stimulus (UCS) *An aspect of the environment that naturally generates a response.*

Unconditioned response (UCR) *The natural response to a UCS.*

Conditioned stimulus (CS) *An aspect of the environment that generates a response due to a learned association.*

Conditioned response (CR) *the learned response to a CS.*

Operant behaviour *Behaviour that operates on the environment to produce consequences.*

Little Albert, fear conditioning and neurosis

Watson was slightly less strict. He argued for the existence of three primary emotions – fear, rage and love. His most famous 'experiment' was in fact a study of fear conditioning (this experiment is now regarded as highly unethical). Little Albert, an 11-month-old boy, was given a white rat to play with by Watson and his assistant Rayner (1920). He liked the rat, and played happily with it. Watson and Rayner knew that Albert was scared of loud noises – he cried, for example, if a metal bar was struck with a hammer behind his head. Translated into Pavlovian terminology, we can see that the loud noise is an unconditioned stimulus and the crying an unconditioned response.

In the next phase, they banged the bar each time Albert was given the rat. After several such pairings, Albert was again presented with the rat, but this time with no noise. He cried in distress simply at the sight of the rat, indicating that fear conditioning had occurred – the rat had become a conditioned stimulus. Note that this is *classical conditioning.* The fear response to the loud bang is an automatic or reflex association. Watson and Rayner demonstrated that such fear responses can be transferred or carried over to other stimuli (the rat), thus making a contribution to our understanding of 'irrational' fears (as in many phobias). This is a contribution to understanding the *neuroses* that Freud was also interested in – neurosis is *defined* in terms of persistent emotional over-reactions. Pavlov too was able to generate neurotic behaviour in experimental animals, and to remove it. Little Albert's conditioned fear was not removed, since his mother, quite understandably, withdrew him from the study. (See p223 for further details of this experiment.)

Aggression and depression

Aggression and depression both have strong emotional components and have both been studied from a behaviourist perspective. Dollard et al. (1939) drew upon Hull's idea of *drive* to develop their *frustration aggression hypothesis* (see pp 312-313). The theory holds that when environmental conditions prevent access to an expected positive reinforcer, the organism becomes 'frustrated' and a drive is produced which finds its 'outlet' in aggressive behaviour.

The first version of Seligman's (1971) *learned helplessness* theory of depression was also based on behaviourist principles – animals placed in a environment where punishments are unavoidable develop depression-like behaviour patterns. Liddel's (1954) work was an important forerunner to this. He spent 26 years studying chronic emotional disorder in sheep and goats, which he and his team managed to induce by:

'subjecting the animal day after day to a rigid and unvarying pattern of 10 second signals, always followed by shock and separated by equal intervals of time ... The experimental neurosis ... was truly chronic and strikingly affected not only the animal's behaviour in the laboratory but its mode of living in the barn and pasture 24 hours a day for the remainder of its life.'

4.3 Methods used in the behaviourist approach

Behaviourists argue strongly for the use of carefully designed, laboratory-based experimental methods. The aim is to produce a simplified and controllable environment in comparison to the complex, largely uncontrollable environment outside of the laboratory. All key terms in a theory must be *operationally defined* – explicitly defined in a form which can be measured. For instance, 'frustration' alone is a vague and ambiguous term. Ten different scientists might have ten different understandings of what it means. An *operational definition*, by contrast, supplies a shared and objective definition based on observable behaviour. Hence Dollard et al. (1939) operationally define frustration as when environmental conditions prevent access to an expected positive reinforcer. Some specific methods include:

- **The Skinner box** This is a box inside which an animal is kept. The box usually contains a lever or a light that can be pressed or pecked (depending upon the animal used), and a means for presenting the reinforcement (eg, a place where food pellets can be inserted and accessed by the animal). Outside the box there is a device for measuring and recording the animal's responses.

- **Aversion therapy** This is a technique, based on classical conditioning, used in an attempt to eliminate unwanted behaviour. An alcoholic, for example, might be treated by pairing the consumption of alcohol with the ingestion of a noxious chemical that causes sickness and nausea. The aim is to condition the patient to associate alcohol consumption with nausea, thus punishing the behaviour (see pp 711-712).

- **Programmed learning** This is an approach to education based on operant conditioning. The material to be learned is designed in such a way that the pupil is almost always right, and able to do the task. The tasks are arranged so that they very gradually get more difficult, but the pupil does not experience this difficulty and so is not frustrated, and so continues to learn.

- **Behaviour modification** Skinner proposed that behaviour can be modified by carefully arranging the environment so that 'wanted' behaviours are rewarded, and unwanted behaviours are ignored (to punish them directly would be to draw unwanted attention to them). In *token economies* for instance, desired behaviour is rewarded by the giving of a token which can be 'cashed in' for food or some other pleasurable reinforcer. (See pp 712-713 for further information on token economies.)

4.4 Evaluation of the behaviourist approach

Strengths

- Behaviourists claim that their approach is scientific. It emphasises the need to define concepts precisely and in a form which can be measured. As far as possible, behaviourists deal only with objectively observable events.
- Behaviourists claim support for their theories from a vast range of experimental data.
- There is evidence that some psychological disorders – for example phobias – benefit from treatment based on behaviourist ideas (see p711).

Weaknesses

- Critics argue that behaviourism fails to deal with the complexity of human psychology. It provides a narrow and simplistic view of behaviour and ignores the hidden and personal aspects of human life.
- Behaviourists have been accused of reductionism – of reducing all human behaviour to learning by association and reinforcement.
- The ethics of token economies have been questioned. Are people's human rights threatened when staff in institutions can control their access to food and freedom of movement?
- There are two main criticisms of aversion therapy. First, it doesn't work very well. Second, it is ethically unsound – it inflicts discomfort and sometimes pain.

Summary

1. Thorndike's law of effect is based on what he called stimulus-response associations. It became central to behaviourism.

2. Behaviourists argue that, to be properly scientific, psychology should concentrate on behaviour and not on unobservable things like thoughts and feelings.

3. Pavlov's work on classical conditioning became one of the bases of behaviourist theory. Classical conditioning involves a 'reflex' response.

4. B. F. Skinner developed the idea of operant conditioning based on reinforcement and punishment. Operant conditioning does not involve 'reflex' or automatic responses.

5. Since the feelings involved in emotions are unobservable, behaviourists argue that emotions should be studied as behaviour.

6. The behaviourist approach stresses:
   - Precise, operationally defined definitions
   - Rigorous laboratory experiments
   - Objective observation of actual behaviour.

7. The Skinner box, aversion therapy, programmed learning and behaviour modification are methods or techniques that have emerged from a behaviourist approach.

8. Critics have argued that behaviourism presents a narrow and simplified view of human psychology, that it is reductionist, and that it is sometimes ethically unsound.

Activity 6   Behaviourism in action

Item A   A token economy

Questions

1   Explain how a token economy is based on operant conditioning.

2   What ethical issues are raised by token economies?

Unit 5 The cognitive approach

KEY ISSUES

1   **What are the key concepts used in the cognitive approach?**

2   **How are emotions studied from a cognitive perspective?**

3   **What are the main methods used in the cognitive approach?**

5.1   Introduction and key concepts

Cybernetics and the concept of feedback

If you are reading this book to help you get an A-level, then this implies that an event in the future is causing your present behaviour. This poses a problem for scientific determinism, since causes should come *before* effects, not after them – you are responding to a stimulus that has not yet happened! How can we think about this?

In the 1940s, Norbert Weiner (1948) founded the science of cybernetics, which is the study of communication and control systems in organisms, machines and organisations. Cyberneticists study the flow of information in systems, and are particularly interested in *goal directed activity* – ie, activity done for a *purpose*. A key concept they use is *feedback*. Feedback is the process whereby information about the output of a system is returned or 'fed-back' to the input, so that the behaviour of the system can be influenced. A thermostat is a simple example. As the temperature goes above a chosen setting, the heater is turned down. When the temperature falls below that setting, the

heater is turned up. In this way, a constant temperature is maintained. The output of the system (the heat of the room) is fed-back as information. This fed-back information is then used to modify the output (eg, the heat will be turned down if the room is 'too hot'). Here we have a simple way of designing a goal-directed system – ie, a system with the goal of maintaining a set temperature. As Richards (1996) points out, the relevance of this to psychology was enormous: 'purposive behaviour was no longer mysterious'. The implication of this will become clear once we have examined a second key concept: *information*.

The concept of information

At around the same time as the birth of cybernetics, Claude Shannon (1948) developed *information theory*, which allowed the concept of information – central to cybernetics and then cognitive psychology – to be accurately measured. Once information could be measured, it became possible to ask questions like: 'How much information can this channel carry?', 'How fast can information be transmitted from this source to that target?' and 'How much information can be stored here?'. Also in the 1940s, the first computers were built. The concept of information was 'cutting edge' to say the least. It was not long before the above questions were asked not only of artificial information processing machines like computers, but also of the human mind. To give just three classic examples of early cognitive psychology:

- In George Miller's hands (1956), for instance, human memory becomes a device for *storing and retrieving information*. He was able to show that STM (short-term memory) has an *information capacity* of roughly seven bits of information.

- With the work of Colin Cherry (1953), *attention* becomes the means by which the cognitive system shifts its focus between the different *sources of information* that are available.

- For Noam Chomsky (1965), the complexities of language-use are made possible by a biological information processing gadget called LAD (the Language Acquisition Device).

In short, the cognitive approach views the mind *as if* it were a complex information processor. A mechanism can be called 'cognitive' in so far as it processes information, and there are several ways of processing information, including:

1 Reception (the taking-in of information)

2 Transmission (the sending-out of information)

3 Storage (the holding of information)

4 Modification (changing the nature of information)

5 Co-assembly (joining information together).

The human mind, from a cognitive perspective, includes various types of cognitive mechanism (other chapters in this book deal with these more fully). The list usually includes: memory mechanisms; perceptual mechanisms; attention mechanisms; mechanisms for language; mechanisms for thinking; and some sort of 'central' mechanism for generating consciousness. Each mechanism is cognitive in that it processes information in the above ways, receiving it, transmitting it, storing it, modifying it and co-assembling it with other information. Further, each mechanism interacts with the other mechanisms in complex ways. For example, *remembered information* (eg, the memory of the sound of a purring cat) is likely to have been:

- processed by the *perceptual mechanisms* (eg, hearing and feeling cats purr)
- under the influence of *attentional mechanisms* (eg, the cat is attended to and not the mat it sits on)
- shaped by *language mechanisms* (eg, knowing the words 'cat' and 'purr' and their relation to other words in a language)
- and by the *thought mechanisms* (eg, working out that a purring cat is a happy cat)
- and finally modified into conscious form by the *consciousness-generating mechanism* (eg, being consciously aware of our memory that cats purr).

Plans and the structure of behaviour

The above heading is the title given to a book by Miller, Galanter and Pribram. If Watson's *Psychology as the behaviourist views it* (1913) was the manifesto of the behaviourist approach, then *Plans and the Structure of Behaviour* (1960) is the manifesto of the cognitive approach (Richards, 1996). This book combines the notions of *feedback* and *information* in a new concept: the TOTE unit. TOTE means 'test-operate-test-exit'. It is a simple feedback loop that permits behaviour to be structured (meaningfully organised) according to a cognitive plan (a goal). For example, in hammering a nail, you might:

T: test the situation by seeing if the nail is straight

O: operate by hitting the nail with the hammer

T: test the situation by seeing if the nail is hammered in far enough

E: exit (ie, end the task) if it is in far enough (return to a second O if it is not).

A TOTE unit like this can be thought of as a basic 'plan', but the idea is that such plans are 'nested' inside wider plans – for example, 'plans for building cupboards' are contained within 'plans for generating a practical and pleasant living space'. It is a small step from here to begin thinking of such plans as if they were *computer programs*. The actions of the organism can then be seen as programs that are run-through in order to reach goals. If those goals are flexible and 'learned' then they may be considered part of the organism's *software*. But if they are 'built in' to the basic evolutionary design of the information processing mechanisms, then they may be considered as *hardware*. Although the concept of TOTE never caught on, the basic idea of *action being structured by programmed goals which function as feedback loops* became deeply influential.

Key terms

Feedback *The process whereby information about the output of a system is returned or 'fed-back' to the input, so that the behaviour of the system can be influenced.*

Cybernetics *The study of communication and control systems in organisms, machines and organisations.*

TOTE *'Test-operate-test-exit' – a basic feedback plan discussed by Miller et al. (1960).*

Significant forerunners to the cognitive approach

Although the cognitive approach proper began in the late 1940s with the developments outlined above (feedback, information, and the computer analogy), there are several psychologists who developed 'cognitive' ideas before this time, and who can therefore be considered forerunners. These include:

- **Jean Piaget** (eg, 1929). Piaget's developmental psychology was cognitive in that he proposed a stage model of the development of the child's intellect. His notion of schemas is particularly cognitive, since a schema is a mental representation that acts as a kind of program to guide sequences of action (much like Miller et al's TOTE concept). In fact, the notion of schemas dates back at least to Kant (1781).

- **Frederic Bartlett** (eg, 1932). Bartlett's work on memory was also based upon the 'cognitive' idea of schemas. For him, new memories are made sense of against the background of already existing structures of knowledge (schemas). New information is therefore processed in a way that is influenced by old, or already stored, information.

- **Edward Tolman** (eg, 1948). Although he worked within the behaviourist tradition, Tolman argued that animals learn with the help of *cognitive maps* that, like schemas, are mental representations of the learning situation. These maps permit animals to have an expectancy about the consequences of their actions, and hence basic feedback loops are possible.

- **Kurt Lewin** (eg, 1936). Lewin's influential brand of social psychology was based on a German approach called *Gestalt psychology*. This approach stresses the ways in which people's thinking and perception lend form and order to the world, much as when we look up on a clear night and see ordered forms such as 'the plough' and 'Orion's belt' rather than random clusters of stars. Gestalt had a strong cognitive 'flavour' in its emphasis on the ordering of information in knowledge.

The cognitive approach to emotion

Labelling theory

The most famous experiment on the nature of emotion from a cognitive perspective was conducted by Stanley Schachter (a student of Kurt Lewin) and Jerome Singer (1962). This experiment is described in Chapter 24, pp 404-405. For our purposes here, the most significant aspect of the study is the idea that a 'cognitive label' is decisive in producing an emotional state. This idea became extremely influential despite the less than conclusive findings of the study. Emotion, from this perspective, has two components. First there is bodily arousal, produced by the autonomic nervous system. This 'hot' bodily component, according to Schachter and Singer, is fairly crude and undifferentiated, and feels much the same in anger, fear, elation or any other emotion. Then there is an act of cognitive labelling, which is fast, subtle and cool and which 'makes sense' of the situation. It labels the arousal as a particular emotion. The combination of bodily arousal and mental sense-making gives rise to clearly differentiated emotional states. Cognition therefore becomes central to emotion in this theory, since without it we have relatively 'blind' and indistinct states of arousal.

Interruption theory

Mandler (1984) developed Schachter's theory that 'emotional experience is constructed out of autonomic arousal and evaluative cognitions' and gave it an even more cognitive twist. Recall that the cognitive approach tends to view behaviour as organised by plans. Sequences of actions (such as hammering nails) are viewed as goal-directed or purposive. Mandler argued that when organised sequences of actions (or thoughts) are *interrupted*, this generates bodily arousal. This bodily arousal provokes cognitive 'meaning analysis', which 'makes sense' of the arousal *and* the interruption that caused it, thereby constructing the experience of an emotion. As well as explaining what Schachter's theory left mysterious (ie, what causes the arousal in real life), Mandler's theory also provides an information processing role for the ANS arousal. That is, the arousal caused by the interruption serves as a signal to the organism that 'something is going on, something needs to be done'. The arousal itself, in other words, is just more information to be processed.

Appraisal theory

Lazarus's appraisal theory (1991) takes a cognitive approach to its extreme, since for him cognitive appraisal is the single most important factor in *initiating* emotions, in *determining their intensity and duration* and in *differentiating* different emotions. In dealing with how people cognitively 'make sense' in relation to emotions, Lazarus made a distinction between *primary* and *secondary* appraisal. Primary appraisal searches for information about whether an event has relevance for personal wellbeing: 'does this situation affect me personally?' If it does, then we are 'set up' to be emotional. Secondary appraisal scans the situation for information about what to do, how to cope, who is

responsible, and so on. Hence 'anger' can be defined as a primary appraisal of something as *bad* for our wellbeing and a secondary appraisal that this was *caused* by someone else. If we 'cope' by dwelling on this secondary appraisal, we will prolong the intensity and duration of the anger. If our secondary appraisal discovers that we are to blame, then we may feel guilt instead of anger, according to this theory. (See p406 for further discussion of appraisal theory.)

Methods used in the cognitive approach

- **Emphasis on controlled experiments** The cognitive approach shares with behaviourism a strong concern to conduct reliable, laboratory-based experiments. Unlike behaviourists who just focus upon observable behaviour, cognitivists use experiments to try and find out what goes on 'inside the head' of the participants.

- **Experiments designed to reveal internal information-processing** In the Schachter and Singer (1962) study, for instance, the idea is that people injected with adrenaline, who have been misinformed about the effects it will have on them, begin trying to 'make sense' of their situation. This 'making sense' is unobservable cognitive (information processing) activity, and it goes on 'inside the heads' of the participants. This would be unacceptable to a behaviourist. However, a cognitivist would argue that this cognitive activity, in the right circumstances, causes a person to have an emotion, and to behave differently as a result. If we want to explain behaviour, it is therefore crucially important to know how people 'make sense' of their situation.

- **Use of computers in experiments** Nowadays, most cognitive experiments involve getting participants to respond to stimuli presented on computer screen, but the aim is the same – to gain access to what goes on in the mind between the arrival of a stimulus, and the emitting of a response.

Evaluation of the cognitive approach

Strengths

- The cognitive approach addresses *some* of the complexities of the inner world, such as the unconscious information processing underlying our perception of the world around us.

- Its theories are based on what many consider to be scientifically respectable experiments – controlled laboratory-based experiments which produce 'hard' quantifiable data.

Weaknesses

- There is a tendency to picture the individual as an information processing machine, a bit like Mr Spock from *Star Trek*.

- Critics argue that the cognitive approach tends to overestimate the role of rational, logical thought processes.

- There is a tendency to detach the individual from their social context – from the situation they are in and the interaction in which they are involved.

Summary

1. The cognitive approach sees the individual as a kind of computer.

2. Three concepts are essential to the development of the cognitive approach – feedback, information, and purposeful planning. These concepts became scientifically important in the late 1940s, alongside the development of computer technology.

3. Something can be considered 'cognitive' if it involves the processing of information.

4. The cognitive approach views the human mind as containing various information processing mechanisms for functions like memory, perception, attention, language, thinking and consciousness.

5. Piaget, Bartlett, Tolman and Lewin can be considered significant forerunners to the cognitive approach.

6. Three good examples of the cognitive approach to emotions are labelling theory (Schachter and Singer), interruption theory (Mandler), and appraisal theory (Lazarus).

7. Cognitivists prefer to use reliable and objective experimental methods, which permit them to guess at the way the mind is processing information.

Activity 7   Making sense of falling

Questions

1. How might a cognitivist explain the emotions expressed in the two cartoons?

2. What makes this a 'cognitive' explanation?

Unit 6 The humanistic approach

KEY ISSUES

1. **What are the key concepts in the humanistic approach?**

2. **How are emotions thought about from a humanistic perspective?**

3. **What are some of the methods used by humanistic psychologists?**

6.1   Introduction and key concepts

Humanism as the 'third force'

The humanistic approach to psychology emerged at roughly the same time as the cognitive approach – it had its roots in the 1940s and grew healthy and strong in the 1950s and 60s. The two key figures were Carl Rogers (1902-1987) (considered the founder of humanistic psychology) and Abraham Maslow (1908-1970), both of whom worked in the USA. In the UK, R.D. Laing (1927-1989) was a prominent humanistic figure. The humanistic approach is notable for being open to more *philosophical* influences, such as *existentialism* – a philosophy which states that we must define our lives for ourselves. Maslow called the humanistic approach the *third force* in psychology. He saw the first two forces as being psychoanalysis and behaviourism (cognitivism was not yet well established enough to be considered a 'force').

- **The first force** Psychoanalysis concentrates on the dynamics going on 'privately' inside the mind.

- **The second force** Behaviourism concentrates on what is going on 'publicly' in observable behaviour.

- **The third force** Humanism, for Maslow, ought to try and combine the two into a unified 'complete picture' of the whole person, private and public.

The idea of the 'whole person'

Humanistic psychologists argue that both psychodynamic and behavioural psychologists treat human beings as if they were objects. Both psychodynamic and behavioural approaches do indeed view human behaviour as determined by causes which, unless we are psychologists, we are unlikely to be aware of. Behaviourists, for example, see no difference in principle between a laboratory rat and a person – both are biological organisms determined by forces in the environment. For humanistic psychologists, this is to ignore what is special and most dignified about human beings – the possibility that we can define our own agendas, take an active role in steering our own destinies, and determine our own ways of living.

The problem with other forms of psychology, from a humanistic perspective, is that if you *treat* people as objects, then they may well *become* like objects. Humanists, by contrast, see the job of psychology as encouraging people not to become like objects but instead to develop their full potential as human beings. This means that psychologists should treat their clients and participants as 'whole human beings', rather than objects. Humanistic psychologists often object to calling those who take part in studies 'subjects', since this implies that they are powerless pawns in a psychologist's game. They prefer words like 'participants' and 'clients', and they prefer to emphasise mutual respect, cooperation and empathy. Two key concepts related to this idea of the 'whole person' are 'self-actualisation' and 'unconditional positive regard':

- **Self-actualisation** is a phrase coined by Maslow to describe what he saw as the highest level of human potential – the peak of human development. At a low level of human development we are determined by basic needs such as food and warmth. But as we 'grow' psychologically, we find our needs change and we become concerned with things like safety, and then love. Once we have 'secured' these, we can grow beyond them and become concerned with things like self-esteem. At the highest stage, self-actualisation, a person realises their full potential, they achieve fulfilment, and fully develop all aspects of themselves. (See pp 400-401 for further discussion of Maslow.)
- **Unconditional positive regard** is a phrase coined by Rogers as part of his Client Centred Therapy. Whatever a client thinks or says should be viewed positively and this positive reinforcement should not depend upon what the client does, but should be unconditional. This is because for Rogers, many mental health problems stem from the fact that people's actual sense of themselves (their 'self concept') does not match up to what they would like (their 'ideal self'). The therapy should therefore provide a positive space wherein the client can develop (ideally towards self-actualisation).

6.2 The humanistic approach to emotion

From a humanistic approach, emotions are first of all conscious feelings experienced by a given individual. There are two implications of this that we will deal with in turn. First, emotions must be approached via an 'inward route'. Second, emotions must be considered in relation to their 'significance'.

The 'inward route'

Humanists argue that emotions should not be approached from the *outside* as if they were objects that could be looked at. Instead they should be approached from the *inside*. That is, we should ask people, and ourselves, to describe emotions as they or we consciously experience them. As Barrell and Richards (1982) say of jealousy:

'We cannot look outside ourselves and find jealousy located in the world, except insofar as its expression in the behaviour of others is concerned. The feeling itself can only be found within us. Because factors contributing to jealousy lie inside us, they must be discovered via an inward route.'

'Signification'

Signification is the process by which one thing indicates – acts as a sign of – another thing. In the old saying 'red sky at night, shepherd's delight', for instance, a red sunset is taken as *signifying* good weather in the morning. The red sky, we might say, has become *significant*. But notice that the red sky is not significant *by itself*. It becomes significant only because it indicates something else – tomorrow's weather. But more than this, it becomes significant only because it indicates something else *to someone* – in this case, to a shepherd. To another person, who spends little time outdoors, the red sky might be meaningless. To another, it might signify as something 'beautiful'. And so on. For humanistic psychologists it is important to look at the signification of emotions – if someone is jealous, we need to ask what this means *for them* as a unique individual. This is a big difference from behaviourist and biological approaches, which try very hard to *remove* signification from emotions.

Key terms

Existentialism *A philosophy which holds that we must define our lives for ourselves.*

Self-actualisation *The peak of human potential.*

Signification *The process by which one thing indicates another thing.*

6.3 Methods used in the humanistic approach

Humanistic psychologists prefer methods which address the 'whole person' and which allow access to the ways in which emotions and the situations which give rise to them signify for a given person. Hence there is a preference for qualitative rather than quantitative methods – for methods such as in-depth interviews that encourage self-disclosure and allow access to the personal experience and subjectivity of participants.

This approach has also given rise to numerous therapy techniques such as:

- **Role playing** Participants or clients play the role of, for example, significant others in their lives.
- **Psychodrama** Several participants or clients act out scenes of emotional significance.

- **Group therapy** A form of therapy where clients form a group and share experiences and reflect upon their interactions.

6.4 Evaluation of the humanistic approach

Strengths

- The humanistic approach takes an optimistic view of human nature, seeing people as essentially good. It speaks up for the more noble aspects of human existence, insisting on the value of 'truly human' qualities such as free will, autonomy and self-definition.
- This is reflected in humanistic therapy. For example, Carl Rogers' *client-centred therapy* emphasises unconditional positive regard and encourages clients to discover themselves and search for their own, individual meanings for life.

Weaknesses

- The humanistic approach is characterised by a good deal of theoretical reflection and by continual critique of the dangers of other approaches. Despite the large amount of theorising, the pay-off in terms of useful psychological explanations has been fairly small.
- Some critics have seen the humanistic approach as a collection of recipes for living containing advice for getting the best out of life, rather than an approach which explains human behaviour.

Summary

1. Carl Rogers and Abraham Maslow are two of the key figures in the humanistic approach.

2. Humanistic psychologists think of their approach as a 'third force' in psychology, which is concerned with the person as a whole human being, not as an object.

3. Self-actualisation and unconditional positive regard are two important concepts which express the humanistic interest in developing self-potential.

4. Humanists approach emotions via an 'inward route' – ie, from the point of view of the person experiencing the emotion.

5. Emotions and other psychological topics need to be understood in terms of their signification. Signification is the process whereby one thing indicates another thing.

6. Qualitative methods are usually preferred in the humanistic approach.

7. Humanistic therapy methods include role play, psychodrama and group therapy.

Unit 7 The social constructionist approach

KEY ISSUES

1. **What are the key concepts in the social constructionist approach?**

2. **How are emotions thought about from a social constructionist perspective?**

3. **What are some of the methods used by social constructionist psychologists?**

7.1 Introduction and key concepts

'Socially constructed' means 'made by people' – with the word 'social' emphasising *many* people rather than one person. This approach therefore asks to what extent our psychological realities are socially constructed. In comparison to all of the other approaches, social constructionist psychologists draw inspiration from the *social* sciences, and especially sociology. In fact, it was two sociologists, Berger and Luckmann, who wrote the first explicitly social constructionist book: *The Social Construction of Reality* (1968). They identified three 'moments' to the social construction process:

- **Internalisation** Where, through socialisation, the *significations* (see above) of the social world become part of the private world of the individual. This is summed up in the statement: *social reality constructs the person.*

- **Externalisation** Where, through acting in the social world, individuals contribute to the building of that world and to generating the significations that make it meaningful. This is summed up in the statement: *the person constructs social reality.*

- **Objectification** Where the externalised products of people (the socially constructed world) come to have a separate reality from those who made them, just as a book or a film can take on a 'life of their own' once created. Sometimes we forget that we created the social world at all, and treat it as though it were natural or even supernatural (this extreme form of objectification is called *reification*).

Social constructionist psychologists, such as Rom Harré, John Shotter and Ken Gergen, tend to be very critical of the idea of making psychology a *natural* (as opposed to a social) science, since they argue that most of what is important in human psychology is socially constructed. This argument involves extending the humanistic argument about the importance of signification or *meaning*. The humanistic argument is that events take on meaning to the extent that they *signify* something to an individual. I can only insult you if you interpret what I say as an insult, for instance. This depends upon your 'frame of reference', which can be thought of as a *personal signifying system*.

Social constructionists extend this and argue that *culture* supplies the signification systems that are then 'internalised' by individuals. Hence culture shapes the meanings that are given to events. For example, moving one's head from side to side means 'no' in the UK and in most European countries, but in Bulgaria it means 'yes'. Social constructionists stress both *cultural* and *historical* differences in the meaning of things. The meanings of issues such as madness, crime, gender and sexuality have changed dramatically over the years (historical variation), and are very different in different cultures (cultural variation). In this sense, people in different places and different times live in very different *realities*. Consider the following activity.

Activity 8   Social constructions

Item A   The social construction of cattle

Cows bask on a busy street in New Delhi.

The consequence of being categorised as a bullock in Britain may well be to be fattened up and rapidly slaughtered, whereas a heifer will be allowed a longer life of milk production. But in Spain a bullock may have a different fate in the bullring. In Hindu India, the cow is sacred. Sometimes garlands are placed around the necks of cows to honour them, water is poured at their feet, and oil rubbed on their foreheads. They are permitted to go practically anywhere and eat anything. The cow is a symbol of goodness and fruitfulness providing people with milk and cheese. Not eating beef is a sign of gratitude and respect.

Adapted from Stainton Rogers et al., 1996 and Keene, 1997

Item B   Childhood as a social construction

Childhood is socially constructed. This is clear from historical and cross-cultural studies which show that childhood is constructed very differently in different times and places. Even within a single society at a single point in time, childhood means different things to different social groups.

Item C   Little adults

In medieval Europe, the idea of childhood did not exist. This does not mean that children were neglected. It means that in medieval society there was no awareness of childhood as a separate state. That is why, as soon as the child could live without the constant care of their mother, they belonged to adult society – they became little adults.

Today, many psychologists devote themselves to the problems of childhood. Their findings are transmitted to parents by way of a mass of popular literature. This preoccupation was unknown in the Middle Ages.

Adapted from Aries, 1973

Item D   Childhood in pictures

Questions

1   How does Item A show that cattle are socially constructed?

2   Look at Items B, C and D. In what ways can childhood be seen as a social construction?

7.2   The social constructionist approach to emotions

Social constructionists tend *not* to ask questions like 'What is jealousy?' or 'What is anger?' Instead they ask questions like 'In what different ways do people *construct* the meaning of jealousy?' and 'Do people of different cultures get angry at the same things?' Stenner and Stainton Rogers (1998), for example, found numerous distinct ways of constructing the meaning of jealousy amongst a sample of 47 participants from the UK. These included:

- Jealousy as a vehicle by which one partner exploits and controls another
- Jealousy as the painful result of betrayal
- Jealousy as a sign of personal insecurity and inadequacy
- Jealousy as a natural loss of control that comes from being too much in love
- Jealousy as a sign of psychological weakness and immaturity
- Jealousy as a result of wounded pride.

It seems likely that the way jealousy is constructed influences how people act in relation to it. For example, those who construct it as the painful result of betrayal are likely to support and comfort the jealous person, whilst those who construct it as a means of exploitative control are likely to criticise and undermine the jealous person. Likewise, constructing it as the result of wounded pride suggests that the jealous person simply needs time to withdraw and 'lick their wounds'. How we construct reality has an effect on how we act.

Historical variations

Using Stenner and Stainton Rogers' data, Beryl Curt (1994) has argued that there have been some broad historical changes in the way jealousy is constructed in the UK and USA.

- *Jealousy as natural* is the oldest construction (according to *Deuteronomy*, 4:24, even God professes himself to be jealous). In the 19th century, it was common for men to literally get away with murder if the victim was their wife and the motive was 'justifiable' because the jealousy was 'natural'.
- In the 1920s and 30s, the construction of *jealousy as a psychological problem* gained popularity (alongside the growth of psychology).
- In the 1960s *jealousy as a vehicle of exploitation* became widespread (alongside the growth of the 'flower power' and 'consciousness raising').

Nowadays, as the above study found, each of these constructions exists alongside the others, providing us with a repertoire of constructions to draw upon in making sense of jealousy. However, it is not difficult to find cultures where different constructions are at play. Consider the following extract from Hupka (1981).

Cultural variations

'On her return trip from the local watering well, a married woman is asked for a cup of water by a male resident of the village. Her husband, resting on the porch of their dwelling, observes. Subsequently, they approach the husband and the three of them enjoy a lively and friendly conversation into the late evening hours. Eventually, the husband puts out the lamp, and the guest has sexual intercourse with the wife. The next morning the husband leaves the house early in order to catch a fish for breakfast. Upon his return, he finds his wife having sex again with the guest. The husband becomes violently enraged and mortally stabs the guest.'

- If this story were told to an Ammassalik Inuit, it would seem perfectly normal, since, in this culture, the 'putting out the lamp' ceremony is a well understood invitation to a male guest to have sex with the wife of his male host. *Without* this ceremony, however, violent jealousy may be expected – hence the murder on return from the fishing trip.
- A member of the Native American Pawnee tribe, by contrast,

would consider the story unbelievable, since in traditional Pawnee culture it was unacceptable for any man to dare to ask a married woman for water.

- Finally, for the Toda of Southern India the story would also seem strange, since it would be considered perfectly normal for the guest to have sex again with the wife, and no cause for jealousy.

The above points illustrate the social constructionist view that *culture* provides the frameworks within which individuals 'make sense' of the world and their emotions.

7.3 Methods used in the social constructionist approach

The research task in most social constructionist psychology is to get a clear *understanding* of the different constructions in play. Like humanists, social constructionists tend to reject the application of 'natural science' methods (such as the laboratory experiment) in favour of more qualitative techniques. As they deal with signification and meaning, social constructionists focus on the contexts in which meanings occur. Meanings are constructed in particular contexts *and* particular contexts influence the way meanings are constructed. Social constructionists often looks at the following types of data.

- Transcribed interviews with individuals (standard interview) or groups (focus groups)
- Naturally occurring conversations between people
- Articles in magazines and newspapers
- Cultural products such as films, novels and TV programmes.

They then *interpret* this data, organising it into themes or trying to work out the function of particular statements.

7.4 Evaluation of the social constructionist approach

Strengths

- Social constructionism attempts to view the world through the eyes of those who construct it.
- If social constructs direct action, this view is essential. Without it, it would not be possible to understand human action.

Weaknesses

- Social constructionists seek to *understand* rather than *explain*. They attempt to interpret the 'social realities' which people construct and live in, rather than explaining where those 'social realities' came from.
- Understanding tends to replace the causal explanations of the natural sciences. If, as is argued, our worlds are more socially constructed than natural, then psychology should not model itself on the natural sciences. This moves psychology closer to literature and history than to physics and biology, leaving us with many *interpretations* and little possibility for sorting out the true from the false.

Summary

1. Social constructionists argue that much of psychology should be a social and not a natural science.

2. Social reality is seen to be constructed in three 'moments': internalisation, externalisation and objectification.

3. Culture is seen as a powerful force which shapes our views of reality.

4. Social constructionists stress the importance of cultural and historical differences in the way psychological issues, such as madness, crime and sexuality, are constructed.

5. Emotions are approached as things that are constructed differently by different people at different times. The aim of much social constructionist research is to identify the different constructions that exist.

6. Social constructionists tend to prefer qualitative methods that help in the interpretation of social constructs.

Chapter conclusion: the fable of the bloated frog

We began this chapter with a poem from Kipling, showing how the world shows up differently to us, depending on how we approach it. This is the final verse of the poem.

> And so these men of missing sight
> Each argued loud and long
> Though each was partly in the right
> They all were in the wrong.

As Kipling might have predicted, advocates of each approach in psychology have 'argued loud and long'. Though each is doubtless partly right, could it be that all are wrong? One problem is that we often expect science to tell us how the world *really is*, not merely how it *can be seen*. Yet if we have learned one thing about the way that science progresses, it is that the world often turns out to be more complex than previous scientists had thought. More than this, we often find in the history of science, and certainly in the history of psychology, a typical mistake. This is the mistake of taking a *way of seeing* which 'works' perfectly well in one place, and stretching it too far by trying to make it apply in every place. That is, just because something works in a *local* context does not mean it will work *globally*.

The distinction between the local and the global is used frequently in discussions of science. *Global* in this scientific sense means more than the simple geographical image of the *globe* or 'planet earth'. A global explanation is one that applies *everywhere*, a local explanation applies only in one, two or a few instances. The wise man holding the elephant's tail is quite sensible to model this as a rope. This model, in other words, works well (but not too well) as a local explanation of the tail, but is stretched too far when generalised as a global explanation for the *whole* elephant. Lest we become too elephant-centred in our examples, let's move on to frogs.

> A frog once saw a bull,
> and thought him beautiful.
> Though an egg was rather bigger
> than she was, she liked his figure,
> and saw his size
> with envious eyes.
>
> To grow as big as he, she held
> her breath, and stretched her lungs, and swelled.
> She said, 'My sister, watch me swell:
> I'm big enough? I'm doing well?'
> 'You're not.' 'You're nowhere near: too small.'
> The wretched creature did her worst,
> breathed in once more – and burst.

La Fontaine's fable *The frog who wished to make herself as big as the bull* serves as a useful warning about the difficulties of moving from the relatively local to the relatively global. If you try and stretch a model to cover everything, unless it is particularly complex and sophisticated, that model will collapse. The fable warns us that each of the seven approaches outlined in this chapter is good at answering some questions and poor at answering others. Each approach can be stretched too far, but luckily, it usually happens that another approach has developed to deal with exactly what the rest ignore. Each approach is truly a *way of seeing as*. It is important to be aware that there are always other ways of seeing, and that each way of seeing has its necessary limitations.

References

Appignanesi, R. & Zarate, O. (1992). *Freud for beginners*. Cambridge: Icon Books.

Aries, P. (1973). *Centuries of childhood*. Harmondsworth: Penguin.

Bartlett, F.C. (1932). *Remembering*. Cambridge: Cambridge University Press.

Barrell, J.J. & Richards, A.C. (1982). Overcoming jealousy: An experimental analysis of common factors. *The Personnel and Guidance Journal, 61*, 40-47.

Berger, P. & Luckmann, T. (1968). *The social construction of reality*. Harmondsworth: Penguin.

Buss, D.M., Larsen, R.J., Westen, D. & Semmelroth, J. (1992). Sex differences in jealousy: Questioning the "fitness" of the model. *Psychological Science, 7*, 367-372.

Cannon, W.B. (1927). The James-Lange theory of emotion: A critical examination and an alternative theory. *American Journal of Psychology, 39*, 106-124.

Cherry, E.C. (1953). Some experiments on the recognition of speech, with one and with two ears. *Journal of the Acoustical Society of America, 25,* 975-979.

Chomsky, N. (1965). *Aspects of a theory of syntax.* Cambridge, MA: MIT Press.

Curt, B.C. (1994). *Textuality and tectonics: Troubling social and psychological science.* Buckingham: Open University Press.

Daly, M., Wilson, M. & Weghorst, S.G. (1982). Male sexual jealousy. *Ethology and Sociobiology, 3,* 11-27.

Darwin, C. (1872). *The expression of emotions in man and animals.* London: Murray.

Davidson, R.J., Ekman, P., Saron, C.D., Senulis, J.A. & Friesen, W.G. (1990). Approach-withdrawal and cerebral asymmetry: Emotional expression and brain physiology. *Journal of Personality and Social Psychology, 58,* 330-341.

Dawkins, R. (1976). *The selfish gene.* Oxford: Oxford University Press.

Dollard, J., Doob, L., Miller, N., Mowrer, O.H. & Sears, R.R. (1939). *Frustration and aggression.* New Haven: Yale University Press.

Duffy, E. (1941). An explanation of emotional phenomena without the use of the concept 'emotion'. *Journal of General Psychology, 25,* 283-293.

Ekman, P. (1982). *Emotion in the human face.* New York: Cambridge University Press.

Freud, S. (1922). Some neurotic mechanisms in jealousy, paranoia and homosexuality. In J. Strachey (Ed.), *Standard edition of the complete works of Freud.* London: Hogarth Press.

Groddeck, G. (1923/1976). *The book of the it.* New York: International Universities Press.

Gruber, H. & Barrett, P.H. (1980). *Darwin on man: A psychological study of scientific creativity.* Chicago: University of Chicago Press.

Hupka, R. (1981). Cultural determinants of jealousy. *Alternative Lifestyles, 4,* 310-357.

James, W. (1894). What is emotion? *Mind, IX,* 188-204.

Keene, M. (1997). *Examining four religions.* London: HarperCollins

Lazarus, R.S. (1991). *Emotion and adaptation.* Oxford: Oxford University Press.

LeDoux, J.E. (1993). Emotional memory systems in the brain. *Behavioural Brain Research, 58,* 69-79.

LeDoux, J.E. (1998). *The emotional brain.* New York: Phoenix.

Lewin. K. (1936). *A dynamic theory of personality: Selected papers.* New York: McGraw-Hill.

Liddel, H. (1954). *Conditioning and the emotions.* London: Vision Press.

MacLean, P. (1949-1970). The limbic brain in relation to the psychoses. In P. Black (Ed.), *Physiological correlates of emotion.* New York: Academic Press.

Mandler, G. (1984). *Mind and body: Psychology of emotion and stress.* London: W.W. Norton.

Miller, G.A. (1956). The magic number seven plus or minus two: Some limits on our capacity for processing information. *Psychological Review, 63,* 81-97.

Miller, G.A., Galanter, E. & Pribram, K.H. (1960). *Plans and the structure of behaviour.* New York: Rinehart & Winston.

Moir, A. & Moir, B. (1998). *Why men don't iron: The real science of gender studies.* London: HarperCollins.

Oatley, K. & Jenkins, J.M. (1996). *Understanding emotions.* Oxford: Blackwell.

Piaget, J. (1929). *The child's perception of the world.* New York: Harcourt and Brace.

Pinel, J.P.J. (1997). *Biopsychology* (3rd ed.). Boston: Allyn and Bacon.

Richards, G. (1996). *Putting psychology in its place.* London: Routledge.

Schachter, S. & Singer, J. (1962). Cognitive, social and physiological determinants of emotional state. *Psychological Review, 69,* 378-399.

Seligman, M. (1971). Phobias and preparedness. *Behaviour Therapy, 2,* 307-320.

Shannon, C.E. (1948). A mathematical theory of communication. *Bell System Technical Journal, 27,* 379-423 and 623-656, July and October.

Skinner, B.F. (1991). *Beyond freedom and dignity.* Harmondsworth: Penguin.

Stainton Rogers, R., Stenner, P., Gleeson, K. & Stainton Rogers, W. (1996). *Social psychology: A critical agenda.* Cambridge: Polity Press.

Stenner, P. & Stainton Rogers, R. (1998). Jealousy as a manifold of divergent understandings: A Q methodological investigation. *The European Journal of Social Psychology, 28,* 71-94.

Tolman, E. (1948). Cognitive maps in rats and men. *Psychological Review, 55,* 189-208.

Watson, J. B. (1913). Psychology as the behaviorist views it. *Psychological Review, 20,* 158-177.

Watson, J. B. & Rayner, R. (1920). Conditioned emotional reactions. *Journal of Experimental Psychology, 3,* 1-14.

Weiner, N. (1948/1999). *Cybernetics: Or control and communication in the animal and the machine.* Cambridge, MA: MIT Press.

Author index

Subject index